Readings in Sociology

Warren Kidd • Mark Kirby • Francine Koubel

John Barter • Tanya Hope • Alison Kirton

Nick Madry • Paul Manning • Karen Triggs

Heinemann Educational Publishers
Halley Court, Jordan Hill, Oxford OX2 8EJ
a division of Reed Educational & Professional Publishing Ltd

OXFORD   MELBOURNE   AUCKLAND
JOHANNESBURG   BLANTYRE   GABORONE
IBADAN   PORTSMOUTH (NH)   USA   CHICAGO

Heinemann is a registered trademark of
Reed Educational & Professional Publishing Ltd

Text © Warren Kidd, Mark Kirby, Francine Koubel, John Barter, Tanya Hope,
Alison Kirton, Nick Madry, Paul Manning, Karen Triggs, 1998

First published 1998

02 01 00 99 98 10 9 8 7 6 5 4 3 2 1

British Library Cataloguing in Publication Data
A catalogue record for this book is available from the British Library

ISBN 0 435 467069

Designed by Wendi Watson
Cover design by Sarah Garbett
Typeset by Wyvern 21 Ltd
Printed in Great Britain at The Bath Press

Dedication

In September 1997 we lost Lina Patel, an excellent Sociology and Humanities teacher, committed to the struggle for social justice through education. The authors dedicate this book to her memory.

Acknowledgements

The publishers would like to thank the following for permission to reproduce copyright material: Addison Wesley Longman for *Poverty and Wealth: Citizenship deprivation and privilege* by John Scott, 1994, on pp. 455–9, and *Conflicts About Class* by David Lee and Bryan Turner (eds), 1996, on pp. 114–18. Reprinted by permission of Addison Wesley Longman Ltd.; Jeffrey C. Alexander for his 'Introduction' to *Neofunctionalism* (ed. J. Alexander), 1985, on pp. 46–9; Phillip Allan for 'The Classless Society?' by Geoff Payne, in *General Studies Review*, 1:1, November 1991, on pp. 120–3; Ashgate Publishing Limited for *Sex, Gender and Society* by Ann Oakley, 1972, on pp. 151–2, 'Feminism and Antiracism: an exploration of the political possibilities' by Caroline Knowles and Sharmila Mercer, in A. Cambridge and S. Feutchwang (eds), *Anti-racist strategies*, Avebury (Wildewood), 1990, on pp. 195–9; The Association for the Teaching of the Social Sciences (ATSS) for 'Class Today: Fashions at Odds with Facts' by John Westergaard, in *Social Science Teacher*, 25:2, 1996, on pp. 134–8; Blackwell Publishers for *From Post-Industrial To Post-Modern Society* by K. Kumar, 1995, on pp. 280–4; *Free Markets and Food Riots* by J. Walton and D. Seddon, 1994, on pp. 390–5; *Thinking Sociologically* by Zygmunt Bauman, 1990, on pp. 18–20, *Theorizing Patriarchy* by Sylvia Walby, 1990, on pp. 63–7; Marion Boyars Publishers Ltd for *Limits to Medicine - Medical Nemesis: The Expropriation of Health* by Ivan Illich, published by Marion Boyars Publishers, 1976, on pp. 409–11; Lynette Burrows for extracts from her article in *The Sunday Telegraph* 27/10/96, on p. 496; Cambridge University Press for 'Idle Thieving Bastards? Scholarly Representations of the "Underclass"' by Paul Bagguley and Kirk Mann, in *Work, Employment and Society*, 1992, 6:1, © BSA Publications, published by Cambridge University Press, reproduced with permission on pp. 129–33, *Selected Writings* by Emile Durkheim (ed. A. Giddens), 1972, on pp. 330–2; *Realist Social Theory: the morphogenetic approach* by Margaret Archer, 1995, on pp 81–5; 'The "Chicago School" of American sociology, symbolic interactionalism, and race relations theory' by Barbara Lal, in J. Rex and D. Mason (eds), *Theories of Race and Ethnic Relations*, 1988, on pp. 178–81; Carfax Publishing Limited (PO Box 25, Abingdon, Oxon OX14 3UE) for 'They employ cleaners to do that: habitus in the primary classroom' by Diane Reay, *British Journal of Sociology of Education*, 16:3, 1995, on pp. 258–60, 'The number of ethnic minority students in British higher education: some grounds for optimism' by Tariq Modood, in *Oxford Review of Education*, 19:2, 1993, on pp. 245–9; City Journal for 'Cities or Urbanisation?' by David Harvey, *City*, 1:2, Jan 1996, on pp. 515–17; Constable Publishers for 'The myth of the drug taker in the mass media' by Jock Young, in J. Young and S. Cohen, *The Manufacture of the News*, 1973, on pp. 469–72; Eichborn Verlag for 'Modernity and the state: East, West' by Claus Offa, in *Die Kontroverse. Weizsäckers Parteienkritik in der Diskussion*, © Eichborn GmbH & Co Verlag KG, Frankfurt am Main, 1992, on pp. 534–7; Faber & Faber for *The Sacred Canopy: Elements of a Sociological Theory of Religion* by Paul L. Berger, 1967, on pp. 572–5; Lewis S. Feuer for *Toward the Critique of Hegel's Philosophy of Right* by Karl Marx and Freidrich Engels , in L.S. Feuer (ed) *Basic Writings on Politics and Philosophy*, 1984, on pp. 566–7; Anthony Giddens for *The New Rules of the Sociological Method* by Anthony Giddens, 1976, on pp. 75–7; The Guardian for the extracts from an article by Yasmin Alighai-Brown, © The Guardian, 11/8/93, on p. 175; HarperCollins Publishers Ltd for *The Language of the Genes* by Steve Jones, 1994, on pp. 153–5; HMSO for *Inequalities in Health - The Black Report* by P. Townsend and N. Davidson, 1982, on pp. 412–15. Crown copyright is reproduced with the permission of the Controller of Her Majesty's Stationery Office; Hodder & Stoughton Educational / Edward Arnold for 'Culture, Communications and Political Economy' by Peter Golding and Graham Murdock, in J. Curran and M. Gurevitch (eds), *Mass Media and Society*, 1991, on pp. 324–5; I.B. Tauris for *Disasters, relief and the media* by Jonathan Benthall, 1993, on pp. 492–4; The Independent on Sunday for the diagrams on p. 174, *Independent on Sunday* 7/7/91; Lawrence & Wishart for *Capital: A Critique of Political Economy*, vol. III by Karl Marx, 1984, on p. 109; 'The Eighteenth Brumaire of Louis Bonaparte' by Karl Marx, in *Marx and Engels, Selected Works*, vol.11; 1851-1853, 1979, on pp. 108–9; 'Americanism and Fordism' in *Selections from the Prison Notebooks* by Antonio Gramsci, 1971, on pp. 276–9, *The German Ideology* by Marx and Engels, 1970, on pp. 468–9, 'Manifesto of the Communist Party', in *Marx and*

(Acknowledgements continue on page vi)

Contents

1 Introduction   **1**

Reading sociology   1
How to use this book   1
Authors' acknowledgements   3

2 What is sociology?   **4**

2.1 The spirit of change: the origins of sociology   6
2.2 Comte's image of sociology   10
2.3 Durkheim's image of sociology   12
2.4 Sociology as humanism   14
2.5 How to 'think sociologically'   18
2.6 The problems of 'theory'   21
2.7 Defending sociology from its critics   24
2.8 Malestream sociology   27
Further reading   30

3 Sociological theory   **31**

3.1 Marxism: a basic outline   33
3.2 Weber and the role of ideas in history   38
3.3 Durkheim and the abnormal division of labour   42
3.4 The emergence of neo-functionalism   46
3.5 Power/knowledge   50
3.6 Against post-modernism   54
3.7 Structuration theory   59
3.8 Sylvia Walby and the theory of patriarchy   63
Further reading   68

4 Research methods   **69**

4.1 Positivism or positivisms?   71
4.2 Giddens' new rules of the sociological method   75
4.3 Realism and social science   78
4.4 The problems of merging structure and action   81
4.5 Ethnomethodology   85
4.6 The ethnographic approach   89
4.7 The variety of sampling techniques   93
4.8 Official statistics   99
Further reading   104

5 Stratification: class   **105**

5.1 Karl Marx on class   108
5.2 Max Weber: class, status and power   110
5.3 Conflicts about class   114
5.4 A classless society?   120
5.5 Who rules Britain?   123
5.6 Representations of the 'underclass'   128
5.7 Class today: fashions at odds with facts   134
5.8 'Fractured identities': social class and post-modernity   139
Further reading   144
Coursework suggestions   144

6 Stratification: sex and gender   **145**

6.1 What is a woman?   147
6.2 Sex, gender and society   151
6.3 The battle of the sexes   153
6.4 A feminist social science   156
6.5 Feminism in action   158
6.6 New developments in gender relations   161
6.7 Men, masculinity and feminism   165
6.8 Sex and gender: a contemporary view   167
Further reading   169
Coursework suggestions   170

7 Stratification: 'race' and ethnicity   **171**

7.1 Racism in the UK   173
7.2 Early twentieth-century migration to Britain   176
7.3 The 'Chicago School', symbolic interactionism and 'race'   178
7.4 Colonial immigrants and status   182
7.5 Marxism, ideology and migrant labour   185
7.6 Ethnicity and intelligence   189
7.7 Post-modern racial identities   191
7.8 Feminism – a black and white issue   195
Further reading   200
Coursework suggestions   200

8 Family   201

8.1	Marxist views of the development of modern family structures	203
8.2	Functionalist views on the roles of the family	206
8.3	The growth of the symmetrical family	208
8.4	Feminist views on the symmetrical family and the role of the housewife	211
8.5	The importance of familiar ideology – is the family in crisis?	214
8.6	Theories of abuse in the family	217
8.7	The relationship between family and definitions of gender and sexuality	223
8.8	The post-modern family?	227
	Further reading	*231*
	Coursework suggestions	*231*

9 Education and training   232

9.1	Compensatory education	235
9.2	How schools produce an amenable and fragmented labour force	237
9.3	New schools for new times?	241
9.4	Access to higher education	245
9.5	Power and discourse in primary classrooms	249
9.6	Schooling and sexualities	252
9.7	Acting powerfully: habitus in the primary classroom	257
9.8	De-constructing black educational under-achievement	261
	Further reading	*266*
	Coursework suggestions	*266*

10 Work, organizations and leisure   267

10.1	The political economy of the world's capitalisms	270
10.2	Americanism and Fordism	276
10.3	Fordism and Post-Fordism	280
10.4	From societies to flows	285
10.5	Capitalism, patriarchy and gender inequalities	289
10.6	The labour process and the politics of production	294
10.7	The McDonaldization of society	298
10.8	The Devil makes work	303
	Further reading	*307*
	Coursework suggestions	*307*

11 Culture and identity   308

11.1	Relativism and culture	311
11.2	Television, ethnicity and cultural change	312
11.3	Gender and the look of love	314
11.4	Popular culture as the culture of the subordinate	316
11.5	Youth subcultures and retro styles	318
11.6	Cultures of consumption	319
11.7	Baudrillard and post-modern culture	321
11.8	The political economy of popular culture	323
	Further reading	*326*
	Coursework suggestions	*326*

12 Deviance   327

12.1	The functions of crime and punishment	329
12.2	Common sense, criminology and 'sceptical' sociology	332
12.3	A new criminology?	337
12.4	Moral panics, 'mugging' and social control	342
12.5	New left realism	348
12.6	Women, crime and the 'malestream criticism'	352
12.7	Visions of social control	356
12.8	Crime, policing and the 'risk society'	360
	Further reading	*364*
	Coursework suggestions	*364*

13 World development   365

13.1	The new international division of labour	368
13.2	Aid: rhetoric and reality	372
13.3	The effect of the debt crisis	376
13.4	Poverty and world hunger	379
13.5	Development and the environment	382
13.6	The end of the Third World	386
13.7	The IMF, structural adjustment and food riots	390
13.8	Globalization in question	396
	Further reading	*401*
	Coursework suggestions	*401*

14 Health   402

14.1	Paradigms of knowledge: magic, religion and science	404
14.2	Talcott Parsons, functionalism and the sick role	406
14.3	Iatrogenesis and medical nemesis	408

14.4 Explanations of class inequalities in health 412
14.5 Women's movements for health throughout the world 415
14.6 'Race', ideology and health research 420
14.7 Disease and disorder 423
14.8 Feminism and the sociology of the body 426
Further reading 429
Coursework suggestions 430

15 Wealth, welfare and poverty **431**

15.1 From Poor Law to Beveridge 433
15.2 Care in the community 437
15.3 Welfare regimes 441
15.4 Women and welfare states 444
15.5 Poverty and racism 448
15.6 Power, privilege and income inequality 452
15.7 Poverty and wealth 455
15.8 The class analysis of poverty 460
Further reading 465
Coursework suggestions 465

16 The mass media **466**

16.1 Traditional Marxism and dominant ideology 468
16.2 Deviancy amplification and the media 469
16.3 The effects of the media 473
16.4 How and why do women 'read' magazines? 477
16.5 War reporting 482
16.6 Investigating media bias 487
16.7 The reporting of 'disasters' in the media 491
16.8 Patriarchal ideology and femininity in the media 495
Further reading 499
Coursework suggestions 499

17 Community, locality and nation **500**

17.1 Gemeinschaft and Gesellschaft 502
17.2 Cornerville: an early ethnographic study 503
17.3 Postwar romanticism 506
17.4 Postwar conflict theory 508
17.5 Community as cultural symbolism rather than structure 511

17.6 A critique of 'communitarian utopianism' 515
17.7 The Californian School 518
17.8 National identity: in the mind of the beholder 524
Further reading 528
Coursework suggestions 528

18 Power and politics **529**

18.1 The power élite 531
18.2 The state in 'modernity' 534
18.3 A new world order? 538
18.4 Knowledge and power in the post-modern condition 541
18.5 Power, discipline and discourse 545
18.6 The end of the political? 548
18.7 The reinvention of politics in a 'risk society' 551
18.8 Beyond left and right 555
Further reading 558
Coursework suggestions 559

19 Religion and belief systems **560**

19.1 An introduction to theories of religion 561
19.2 Marxist interpretations of the role of religion in society 566
19.3 Durkheimian interpretations of the role of religion in society 568
19.4 Religion, ideology and utopia 570
19.5 Religion, world-building and reality 572
19.6 An overview of the secularization debate 575
19.7 Moving the sociology of religion forward: the body and religion 582
19.8 Foucault, sexuality and religious discourse 587
Further reading 591
Coursework suggestions 591

Exploring themes in sociology **592**

Author index **593**

Subject index **596**

Engels, Selected Works in One Volume, 1968, on pp. 33–7, *Forever England: Reflections on Masculinity and Empire* by Jonathan Rutherford, 1997, on pp. 165–7, *The origin of the family, private property and the state* by Freidrich Engels, 1946, on pp. 203–5; Macmillan Press Ltd. for 'Capitalism, Patriarchy and Job Segregation by Sex' by Heidi Hartmann, in A. Giddens and D. Held (eds), *Classes, Power and Conflict*, 1982, on pp. 289–93, *The Devil Makes Work* by J. Clarke and C. Critcher, 1985, on pp. 304–6, *Policing the Crisis: Mugging, the state and law and order* by Stuart Hall, Chas Critcher, Tony Jefferson et al, 1978, on pp. 342–8, *Women and Crime* by Frances Heidensohn, 1996 (2nd ed), on pp. 352–5, *The Golden Bough Vol. 1: the magic art*, by J.G. Frazer, 1936, on pp 404–6, *What Makes Women Sick: gender and the political economy of health* by L. Doyal, on pp. 416–19, 'Community Care' by Alan Walker, in M. McCarthy (ed) *The New Politics of Welfare*, 1989, on pp. 437–40, *Welfare and the State* by Lois Bryson, 1992, on pp. 444–8, *Understanding Poverty* by Pete Alcock, 1993, on pp. 449–51, *Women's Worlds* by R. Ballaster et al., 1991, on pp. 477–81, *The Division of Labour in Society* by Emile Durkheim, 1984, on pp. 42–5, *Positivism in Social Theory and Research* by Christopher Bryant, 1985, on pp. 71–4, *New Philosophies of Social Science* by William Outhwaite, 1987, on pp. 78–80, *Race and Racism in Britain* by John Solomos, 1993, on pp. 176–7, *The family in question: changing households and familiar ideologies* by D. Gittins, 1993 (2nd ed.), on pp. 214–17, *Gender, Family and Society* by Faith Robertson Elliot, 1996, on pp. 218–22; Macmillan Educational Australia for *Social Research* by Sotirios Sarantakos, 1993, on pp. 93–9; Manchester University Press for *War and the Media: propaganda and persuasion* by Phillip M. Taylor, 1992, Manchester University Press, Manchester, UK, on pp. 482–6, *The postmodern condition: a report on knowledge* by Jean-Francois Lyotard, 1984, Manchester University Press, Manchester, UK, on pp. 541–4, *Religion and Ideology* by Robert Bocock and Kenneth Thompson (eds), 1985, Manchester University Press, Manchester, UK, on pp. 562–5; Professor Robert Miles, Professor of Sociology at the University of Glasgow, for *Racism and Migrant Labour* by Robert Miles, 1982, on pp. 185–8; The New Statesman for 'The SDP and the new political class' by R. Samuel, in *New Society*, 22 April 1982, © New Statesman 1982, on p. 54, 'Education cannot compensate for society' by Basil Bernstein, in *New Society*, 26 February1970, on pp. 235–7, *In Defence of Sociology: Essays. Interpretations and Rejoinders* by Anthony Giddens, April 7 1995, © New Statesman 1995, on pp. 24–7; The New York Times for the extract from the article by D. Halberstam, 21 February 1991. Copyright © 1991 by The New York Times Company. Reprinted by Permission on p. 484; The Office for National Statistics for the table from *Family Expenditure Survey 1988*, Office for National Statistics, © Crown copyright 1988, on p. 325; Open University Press for *Common Culture* by Paul Willis, 1990, on pp. 318–19, 'Making black people sick: "race", ideology and health research' by Waqar Ahmad, in *Race and Health in Contemporary Britain* by Waqar Ahmad, 1993, on pp. 420–2, *The Company She Keeps* by Valerie Hey, 1997, on pp. 89–92, *The Making of Men: Masculinities, Sexualities and Schooling* by Mairtin Mac An Ghaill, 1994, on pp. 252–6; Oxford University Press for *Policing the Risk Society* by Richard V. Ericson and Kevin D. Haggerty, 1997, reprinted by permission of Oxford University Press on pp. 360–3, *Race, Community and Conflict: A study of Sparkbrook* by John Rex and Robert Moore, 1974, reprinted by permission of Oxford University Press on pp. 508–11, *The Power Elite* by C. Wright Mills. Copyright © 1956 by C. Wright Mills. Renewed 1984 by Yaraslave Mills. Used by permission of Oxford University Press, Inc. on pp. 531–3, *Max Weber: Essays in Sociology*, edited by H. H. Gerth & C. Wright Mills. Translation copyright 1946, 1958 by H.H. Gerth and C. Wright Mills. Used by permission of Oxford University Press, Inc. on pp. 110–13; Penguin Books Ltd for 'Introduction' by Stanley Cohen, in *Images of Deviance*, edited by Stanley Cohen (Penguin Books, 1971) copyright © Penguin Books Ltd, 1971. Reproduced by permission of Penguin Books Ltd on pp. 332–6, *A Fate Worse Than Debt* by Susan George (Penguin Books, 1988) copyright © Susan George, 1988. Reproduced by permission of Penguin Books Ltd on pp. 376–9, *The End of the Third World: Newly Industrializing Countries and the Decline of an Ideology* by Nigel Harris (Penguin Books, 1987) copyright © Nigel Harris, 1986. Reproduced by permission of Penguin Books Ltd on pp. 386–9, *Poverty and the planet: a question of survival* by Ben Jackson, World Development Movement (Penguin Books 1990, Revised edition 1994) copyright © World Development Movement, 1990, 1994. Reproduced by permission of Penguin Books Ltd on pp. 379–82, *The History of Sexuality vol.1: An Introduction* by Michel Foucault, translated by Robert Hurley (Allen Lane 1979, first published as *La volonté de savoir* 1976) copyright © Éditions Gallimard, 1976. Translation copyright © Randomj House, Inc., 1978. Reproduced by permission of Penguin Books Ltd on pp. 587–90, *Invitation to Sociology: A Humanistic Perspective* by Peter L. Berger (Penguin Books, 1966) copyright © Peter L. Berger, 1963. Reproduced by permission of Penguin Books Ltd on pp. 14–17, *Prophecy and Progress: The Sociology of Industrial and Post-Industrial Society* by Krishan Kumar (Penguin Books, 1978) copyright © Krishan Kumar, 1978, 1986. Reproduced by permission of Penguin Books Ltd on pp. 6–9, *Housewife* by Ann Oakley (Allen Lane, 1974) copyright © Ann Oakley, 1974. Reproduced by permission of Penguin Books Ltd on pp. 211–13, 'The means of correct training' by Michel Foucault, from *Discipline and Punish* , by Michel Foucault (Penguin Books, 1984) copyright © Michel Foucault, 1975. Reproduced by permission of Penguin Books Ltd on pp. 545–7; Pine Forge Press for *The McDonaldization of Society* by George Ritzer, 1993, pages 4–13, copyright © by Pine Forge Press. Reprinted by permission of Pine Forge Press on pp. 298–303; Pluto Press, London, for *What is to be done about law and order? Crisis in the nineties* by John Lea and Jock Young, 1993, on pp. 348–51, *Aid: Rhetoric and Reality* by Teresa Hayter and Catherine Watson, 1985, on pp. 372–5; The Policy Studies Institute for 'Culture and Identity' by Tariq Modood, in Tariq Modood et al (eds) *Diversity and Disadvantage: Ethnic Minorities in Britain*, 1997, on pp. 191–5; Polity Press for *Visions of Social Control: Crime, Punishment and Classification* by Stanley Cohen, 1985, on pp. 356–9, *Jean Baudrillard: from Marxism to Postmodernism and Beyond* by Douglas Kellner, 1989, on pp. 321–3, *The Sociology of Health and Illness* by Sarah Nettleton, on pp. 426–9, *The Three Worlds of Welfare Capitalism* by Gøsta Esping-Andersen, 1990, on pp. 441–3, *Who Gets What?* by John Westergaard, 1995, on pp. 452–4, 'The Reinvention of Politics: Towards a theory of reflective modernization' by Ulrich Beck, in U. Beck, A. Giddens, S. Lash, *Reflexive modernization: politics, traditions and aesthetics in the modern social order*, 1994, on pp. 551–4, *Beyond Left and Right: The Future of Radical Politics* by Anthony Giddens, 1994, on pp. 555–8, *Against Postmodernism* by Alex T. Callinicos, on pp. 54–8, *The Constitution of Society* by Anthony Giddens, 1984, on pp. 59-62, *Who Rules Britain?* by John Scott, 1991, on pp. 124–8, *Fractured Identities: Changing Patterns of Inequality* by Harriet Bradley, 1996, on pp. 139–42, *Family connections: an introduction to family studies* by David Morgan, 1996, on pp. 223–7; Prentice Hall Europe for *Modern Social Theory: from Parsons to Habermas* by Ian Craib, 1984, on pp. 21–4, *Family and the state of theory*, D. Cheale, 1991, on pp. 228–30, *Power/Knowledge: Selected Interviews and Other Writings* by Michel Foucault, edited by Colin Garden, © Harvester Press Ltd, 1972, 1977, on pp. 50–3; Prentice-Hall, Inc. for *Studies in Ethnomethodology* by Harold Garfinkel, © 1967. Reprinted by permission of Prentice-Hall, Inc., Upper Saddle River, NJ, on pp. 85–8 ; Random House for the extracts from *Travels in Hyper-Reality* by Umberto Eco, Jonathan Cape, on pp. 489, 490; *The State We're In* by Will Hutton, Jonathan Cape 1996, on pp. 270–5, *The Way We Live Now*, Richard Hoggart, Chatto & Windus 1996, on pp. 311–12, *The Second Sex* by Simone de Beauvoir, Jonathan Cape 1997, on pp. 228–30; Robert Speller & Sons for *A General View of Positivism* by Auguste Comte, 1957, on pp. 10–11; Rogers, Coleridge and White for 'Single, white, fertile' by Joan Smith, in *Different for girls*, 1997, on pp. 495–8; Routledge for *Working Class Community: Some general notions raised by a series of studies in northern England* by Brian Jackson, Routledge and Kegan Paul 1972, on pp. 506–8, *The Symmetrical Family* by M. Young and P. Wilmott, Routledge and Kegan Paul 1975, on pp. 208–10, *Whose Welfare?* by Tony Cole, 1986, on pp. 433–6, *Official Statistics* by Martin Slattery, 1986, on pp. 100–3, *Television, Ethnicity and Social Change* by Marie Gillespie, 1995, on pp. 313–14, *Reading the Popular* by John Fisk, 1989, on pp. 316–17, *Cultures of Consumption: masculinities and social space in late twentieth century Britain* by Frank Mort, 1996, on pp. 319–21, *The New Criminology: for a social theory of deviance* by Ian Taylor, Paul Walton and Jock Young, 1972, on pp. 337–41, 'Development and the Environment: Managing the Contradictions?' by Michael Redclift, in L. Sklair (ed), *Capitalism and Development*, 1994, on pp. 383-5, 'Globalisation and the Future of the Nation-State' by Paul Hirst and Grahame Thompson, in *Economy and Society*, 24:3, 1995, on pp. 396–400, 'Parsons' contribution to medical sociology' by Bryan S. Turner, in *Talcott Parsons on Economy and Society* by R.J. Holton and B.J. Turner, 1986, on pp. 407–8, *Seeing and Believing: the influence of television* by Greg Philo, 1990, on pp. 473–6, 'Whose illusion? Whose reality? Some problems of theory and method in mass media research' by John Eldridge, in *Getting the Message* by J. Eldridge, Glasgow University Media Group, 1993, on pp. 487–91, *The symbolic construction of community* by Anthony Cohen, 1995, on pp. 511–14, *Community and Association* by Ferdinand Tönnies, 1974, on pp. 502–3, 'Forget Baudrillard: interview with Sylvere Lotringer' by Jean Baudrillard, in M. Gane (ed) *Baudrillard Live: Selected interviews*, 1993, on pp. 548–51, *The Elementary Forms of the Religious Life* by Emile Durkheim, on pp. 568–9, *Ideology and Utopia: An Introduction to the Sociology of Knowledge* by Karl Mannheim,1936, on pp. 570–1, *The Sociology of Religion: Theoretical and Comparative Perspectives* by Malcolm B. Hamilton, 1995, on pp. 575–81, *An Introduction to Sociology: Feminist Perspectives* by Pamela Abbott and Claire Wallace, 1997 (2nd ed.), on pp. 27–30, *Suicide: A Study in Sociology* by Emile Durkheim, 1952, on pp. 12–14, *The Protestant Ethic and the Spirit of Capitalism* by Max Weber, 1992, on pp. 34–41, *Breaking Out Again: Feminist Ontology and Epistemology* by Liz Stanley and Sue Wise, 1993 (2nd ed.), on pp. 156–7, 'Third Wave Feminism and Black Women's Activism' by Pragna Patel, in Heidi Safia Mirza (ed), *Black British Feminism: A Reader*, 1997, on pp. 158–60, *Gender Transformations* by Sylvia Walby, 1997, on pp. 161–4, *Colonial Immigrants in a British City: A Class Analysis* by John Rex and Sally Tomlinson, 1979, on pp. 182–5, 'Black women in education: a collective movement for social change' by Heidi Safia Mirza, in *Black British Feminism: A Reader*, 1997, on pp. 262–5, *Specialisation and Choice in Urban Education: The City Technology Experiment* by G. Whitty, T. Edwards and S. Gerwitz, 1993, on pp. 241–4, *Schooling in Capitalist America: Educational reform and the contradictions of economic life* by Samuel Bowles and Herbert Gintis, 1976, on pp. 238–40; Rowohlt for the extract from DIE NEUE INTERNATIONALE ARBEITSTEILUNG Copyright © 1977 by Rowohlt Tashenbuch Verlag GmbH, Reinbek bie Hamburg. English translation copyright © Cambridge University Press, 1980, on pp. 368–71; Sage Publications Ltd for *'Race' in Britain Today* by Richard Skellington, copyright © Richard Skellington 1996, reprinted by permission of Sage Publications Ltd on pp. 173–5, *Economies of Signs and Space* by S. Lash and J. Urry, copyright © S. Lash and J. Urry 1994, reprinted by permission of Sage Publications Ltd on pp. 285–8, *Religion and Social Theory* by Bryan S. Turner, copyright © Bryan S. Turner 1991 (2nd ed.), reprinted by permission of Sage Publications Ltd on pp. 582–6; The Tessa Sayle Agency for 'A brief history of gender' by Ann Oakley, in Ann Oakley and Juliet Mitchell (eds), *Whose afraid of feminism? Seeing through the backlash*, 1997, on p. 168; Simon & Schuster for the extract reprinted on pp. 189–90 with the permission of The Free Press, a Division of Simon & Schuster from THE BELL CURVE: Intelligence and Class Structure in American Life by Richard J. Herrnstein and Charles Murray. Copyright © 1994 by Richard J. Herrnstein and Charles Murray, for the extract reprinted on pp. 206–7 with the permission of The Free Press, a Division of Simon & Schuster from THE END OF HISTORY AND THE LAST MAN by Francis Fukuyama. Copyright © 1992 by Francis Fukuyama, and for the extract reprinted on pp. 206–7 with the permission of The Free Press, a Division of Simon & Schuster from FAMILY SOCIALIZATION AND INTERACTION PROCESS by Talcott Parsons and Robert F. Bales. Copyright © 1955 by The Free Press; copyright renewed 1983 by Robert F. Bales and Helen W. Parsons; The Times Educational Supplement for 'Gay Pupils' by M. Lilley, in *Times Educational Supplement*, 5 April 1985, © Times Supplements Limited, 1998, on p. 253; Trentham Books for *Changing Classroom Cultures: Anti-racism, politics and schools* by Debbie Epstein, 1993, on pp. 249–51; Professor Bryan S. Turner for *The Body and Society* by B. J. Turner, on pp. 423–5; University of California Press for 'Los Angeles 1965-1992: From crisis-generated restructuring to restructuring-generated crisis' by Edward Soja, in Scott and Soja, *The City: Los Angeles and Urban Theory at the End of the Twentieth Century*, copyright © 1996 The Regents of the University of California, on pp. 518–24; University of Chicago Press for *Street Corner Society: The Social Structure of an Italian Slum* by William Foote Whyte, 1981, on pp. 503–5; Verso for *The Politics of Production* by Michael Burawoy, 1985, on pp. 294–7, 'The Class Analysis of Poverty' by Erik Olin Wright, in *Interrogating Inequality*, 1994, on pp. 460–4, *Imagined Communities* by Benedict Anderson, 1983, on pp. 525–7; The Women's Press for 'Here's Looking at You, Kid' by Suzanne Moore, from *The female gaze: women as viewers of popular* culture, edited by L. Gammon and M. Marshment, on pp. 315–6.

The publishers have made every effort to contact copyright holders. However, if any material has been incorrectly acknowledged, the publishers would be pleased to correct this at the earliest opportunity.

Introduction

Reading sociology

Over the past five years or so the world of sociology has become a rapidly expanding market – offering you, the reader, a whole variety of 'introductory' texts aimed at a number of different levels of understanding and study, from the interested lay-reader, A level and undergraduate students to post-graduates. That this simple observation is true can be tested by visiting any good-sized academic bookshop and browsing through the sociology or social sciences section. Why then is there a need for another sociology text? What makes this book different from others already on the market?

Although the world of sociology offers many choices to the interested reader – whatever his or her intentions for reading are it is not a common nor a familiar world for those taking their first steps in it. A more detailed analysis of the sociology section in a bookshop would reveal a potentially confusing and daunting array of titles – the majority of which seem to be 'introducing' this, or offering 'neo-' and 'post-' that. And – since it is true to say that a book can not be judged by its cover – a brief reading of such books may simply confirm to the worried reader what he or she expected in the very first place: a world full of jargon, theories and complex arguments. So, where should one start in this world? How can one discover an answer to the question: *what is sociology?*

The authors of this volume believe that an answer to the question, *what is sociology?* can be seen to lie in reading (in an accessible fashion) the work of actual sociologists themselves: those employed by universities and research groups to theorize and study the social world in which we find ourselves. We hope that this volume offers an invitation to 'read sociology' – to see for yourself what sociologists have to say.

This work developed from the A level text *Sociology in Perspective*, published in 1997 – a text which all the authors of this volume contributed to. This text, *Readings in Sociology*, is not an exclusive companion volume to *Sociology in Perspective*, although it can be used like this. It has been designed as a general companion to all good sociology textbooks – for both A level and undergraduate students alike.

The authors of this text share a belief that there is something of tremendous value in reading sociology in the original. However, we also all recognize that reading the works of sociologists can, at times, be confusing, daunting and a far from easy process. It is at this point that we hope this book can help – to guide you, the reader, through the world of sociology by offering help in understanding the ideas expressed by sociologists: help in the form of comments, suggestions, explanations and questions to test your understanding.

How to use this book

This is not a general textbook to be used for the day-to-day note-taking required of you when studying sociology. Rather, it is a book that can be used for more in-depth and contemporary knowledge at various points in a sociology course: to read around the subject.

Structure and order

When putting together a book of this nature, a number of decisions are both made by, and forced upon, the writers. Originally, we intended to follow the chapter order of *Sociology in Perspective* and provide eight readings for each section of the syllabus: two 'founding' readings, two 'classic' post-World-War-II readings and four up-to-date readings – all eight to cover contemporary issues and concerns and to represent, fairly, most dominate theoretical perspectives.

This rigid structure, although important in the initial stages for organizing the book as a whole, did not always prove realistic in practice. Some chapters have 'written themselves', becoming more contemporary than others. Some – because of their contemporary nature and the current concerns and preoccupations of sociology itself – deal with some theories and not others, etc. As a whole, however, we hope that *Readings in Sociology* provides the reader with a wealth of information covering all perspectives, from the founders themselves, through early structural functionalism as envisaged by Parsons, through the Marxist and neo-Marxist revivals in the 1970s, the popularity of micro sociological perspectives such as symbolic interactionalism in the late 1970s, the expansion of feminist-orientated sociology and up to and including the spread in popularity of post-structuralism, neo-functionalist ideas, the New Right, post-modernism and contemporary responses against post-modernity.

The chapters themselves each deal with a specific topic area – deviance, health, world development, etc. although it is crucial to note here that the nature of sociology is such that although teachers, examiners and textbook writers carve up sociological knowledge into these distinctive areas, sociologists themselves, more often than not, do not recognize these distinctions and often work across more than one field of inquiry. Given this, it is extremely important for you to be able to demonstrate an awareness of the holistic nature of sociology as a discipline – to see the links between the topics. For example, issues of culture and identity are often linked to the media, whereas an important issue in media sociology is the representation of crime in the media which links to the deviance chapter. Equally, ill-health could be seen as a form of deviance – which shows that there are links between the sociologies of health and deviance, and so on. On reading this book, it may well be that you find other readings by the same author or different readings in different chapters which share a common theoretical perspective.

The order of the chapters

After this brief introduction, *Readings in Sociology* is divided into a further eighteen chapters – mirroring sectional divisions within the major A level sociology syllabuses. To aid readers in their journey through this book we have tried to arrange the chapters in a logical order.

Firstly, we deal with a sample of readings that answer the vital question 'what is sociology'? This chapter is followed by a chapter on sociological theory and a separate chapter on research methods. We have separated sociological theories (chapter 3) from sociological research methods (chapter 4) since, although they are frequently tested together, this afforded us more time and space to give attention to these – the core of all sociology. Equally, the topic of stratification has been divided into three chapters – class (chapter 5), sex and gender (chapter 6) and 'race' and ethnicity (chapter 7) again, to give more attention to these areas.

We recommend that, whatever else – i.e. in whatever order you wish to investigate the readings in this book – you nonetheless read chapters 2, 3 and 4 *first* – and in this order. This should then give you a basic grounding in sociology before you attempt the topics which are based upon sociological theories and methods.

The readings

The actual readings themselves have been chosen on a number of criteria: accessibility, their contemporary or classic status, importance to contemporary debates, interest, and finally their lack of availability elsewhere (unless they are such a classic reading that we simply had to include it).

References

Details are given for each of the readings provided at the start of each section within each chapter. The details for references provided within the various readings themselves are provided after the extract in question – and reflect the information given by the original source.

Bibliographical references listed after the readings are presented as follows:

Oakley, A. (1972) *Sex, Gender and Society*, London: Temple Smith.

Within the extract, a reference to this book would be shown like this: Oakley (1972). If a reading has references to two or more publications by the same author in the same year then these are referred to as *a* and *b*, etc. – e.g. (1972a) and (1972b).

Making primary sources accessible

In order to assist with your understanding of the various readings collected within *Readings in Sociology* we have endeavoured to provide five levels of help:

- a chapter summary section at the start of each chapter – to enable the reader to see at a glance the content of the chapter in question
- an introduction to each chapter detailing the importance of the readings chosen and attempting to draw links between them
- editorial comments for each reading, based on ideas and issues explained in more depth in the introduction to the chapter
- definitions of key terms, as they appear in the text of the readings, to aid understanding of the difficult language sometimes used by sociologists
- questions which you can use to test your understanding of the readings.

We hope that these features help you to make the most of your time spent reading this book.

Questions and questioning

Each section in each chapter contains questions based on the reading. Some of these questions are comprehension questions, others are stimulus questions. The former require you to pick out ideas from the reading, the latter require you to reflect upon the reading using sociological knowledge from elsewhere.

Coursework suggestions

Some students of sociology – whether at Advanced or undergraduate level – will find themselves, at some point, undertaking a piece of sociological research. Chapters 5–19 of *Readings in Sociology* offer some suggestions for research at the end of the chapter. (It was not felt appropriate for chapters 1–4 to provide coursework suggestions since these chapters provide a framework for the other chapters anyway.)

If you do undertake a piece of original sociological research as part of your sociology course, it is important that you work closely with your tutor – informing him or her of all decisions you make at every stage.

To help you in the initial stages of choosing a project we offer some suggestions. You can use them as they are, or adapt them to your own requirements. All the suggestions offered here reflect ideas contained within the readings themselves.

Using the indexes

Given the interrelated or holistic nature of sociology as a subject, many ideas, themes and issues raised in the readings in one chapter of *Readings in Sociology* relate to ideas in other chapters. To help you to investigate these connections fully we have provided an *author index* and a *subject index* at the back of the book.

Reading around the subject

You will find a table on page 592 that is designed to help you explore the different themes between the readings in this volume. While not an exhaustive list, it should help you to begin to see and explore the connections between the chapters.

Taking sociological investigation further

We hope that this book will inspire you to take your reading of sociology further still. It may well be the case that you wish to read more from one of the books from which we have taken a reading, or, alternatively, you may wish to read more from a particular author. If this is the case, we hope that the *further reading* section at the end of each chapter and the various bibliographical references will help you in this goal. It is very important that as a student of sociology you are able to find the time to read around the subject – something that we hope this book allows you to do.

Equally, if you have enjoyed the challenge of reading sociological ideas and feel that you understand more about both the subject, and society itself, then we will be satisfied to think that our time writing this book has been well spent. We wish you luck, and hope that you enjoy *Readings in Sociology*.

Authors' acknowledgements

The creation of a book such as this involves many more people than simply those who have their names on the front cover. Although the nine members of this writing team take responsibility for this work, we could not do so without the continued help, support and contributions made by various other people – in particular those involved in the publication and production of this volume at Heinemann Educational such as Jane Tyler, Alistair Christie and Robert Bircher, all of whom helped at different stages in the production process with different skills and expertise. In particular we would like to thank Sue Walton who agreed to our proposals and who has supported us in the writing of this book from the very beginning.

Finally, to conclude, an acknowledgement must be made of the support, encouragement and patience shown to us by our friends, families, colleagues and especially our students – towards whom this book is aimed.

Warren Kidd
Mark Kirby
Francine Koubel
John Barter
Tanya Hope
Alison Kirton
Nick Madry
Paul Manning
Karen Triggs

What is sociology?

Chapter summary

Reading 2.1 **The spirit of change: the origins of sociology** *page 6*
Krishan Kumar describes the original aim of sociology as a way of thinking about industrial society. Kumar describes the social, cultural and historical factors that lead to the emergence of the 'sociological spirit'.

Reading 2.2 **Comte's image of sociology** *page 10*
Auguste Comte describes the nature of early so-called 'scientific' sociology – known as 'positivism'.

Reading 2.3 **Durkheim's image of sociology** *page 12*
In Durkheim's key work *Suicide*, he sets out his image of a 'scientific sociology' – and the value that such a subject has for human knowledge.

Reading 2.4 **Sociology as humanism** *page 14*
For Peter L. Berger sociology is a 'humanistic perspective': in other words, it can be used to explain human life, and in doing so, the observations made by sociologists can contribute towards the increase of tolerance and freedom in society.

Reading 2.5 **How to 'think sociologically'** *page 18*
Zygmunt Bauman offers a definition of sociology, and in doing so, puts forward arguments why we should embrace and value it as a way of thinking.

Reading 2.6 **The problems of 'theory'** *page 21*
What characterizes sociology for many is its emphasis upon abstract systems of thought – or theory. Ian Craib discusses the shortcomings of theory.

Reading 2.7 **Defending sociology from its critics** *page 24*
Despite its increased popularity sociology still has its critics. Anthony Giddens asks why this is the case and, in doing so, defends the subject itself.

Reading 2.8 **Malestream sociology** *page 27*
For many feminists, traditional sociology has been concerned with the role of men in society, while ignoring the realities of life for women – a criticism made by Abbott and Wallace.

Introduction: Reading sociology

For many potential students, parents and members of the public, 'sociology' is an obscure subject, often seen to be full of jargon – something unfamiliar and detached from the realms of daily life and common-sense thought. A more extreme idea of the consequences of a sociological education, often cited by members of the New Right, is that the subject of sociology is damaging to social order: it teaches young people to be openly critical of authority. Others still, see sociology as only of use to those interested in a career in the welfare/caring professions.

When approaching sociology for the first time – at whatever level of study, for what ever reasons – it is important to be able to separate the rhetoric from the reality, to attempt to see through the politics and value-judgements of those who often have never actually read any sociology at all. To understand the nature of sociological insights, we must first ask ourselves the question: *what is sociology?*

The question *what is sociology?* is one not often deemed necessary to be asked of our other social science colleagues such as historians and geographers. Due to the National Curriculum we are all, more or less, familiar with the aims of these subjects. A major problem, though, for sociologists when faced with this question of definition is that simple definitions such as it is *the study of society* do not seem to do the subject justice, and more complex or sophisticated definitions may be guilty of the problems of jargon which causes so many in society to be wary of the subject in the first place. Having said this, the popularity of sociology continues. It offers for many within the education system a fresh start in post-compulsory education. It offers fresh insights and new ways of thinking about the world around us.

In short, the question *what is sociology?* may be best answered by the observation that there is no single set of cosily agreed knowledges that constitute a single 'sociology', but rather there are many sociologies – and that the study of sociology involves the manipulation of many varied viewpoints on the nature of social life.

Following on from the 'what' of sociology is the 'why'? Or, in other words, the next question academics, teachers and students of sociology are frequently asked is: *what is the value of sociology?* How can thinking about society in the ways offered by sociology benefit both the individual and the wider social group? Finally, to understand the nature of sociological inquiry in the world around us, we also need to understand the 'how': *how do people do sociology?* What methods of information gathering do sociologists employ in their work?

The readings in this chapter address these three questions, as in many senses does the spirit of the whole book. The authors of this book feel that one can best understand what sociology is by taking as a starting point the reading of actual pieces of sociology in the original.

This chapter starts by setting the historical scene for the development of the way of thinking about society which we today know as 'sociology'. In **reading 2.1** Kumar (1978) describes the origins of sociology at the time of the 'founders'. Kumar notes that with industrialization in Europe in the nineteenth century social life was seen to be a thing of new and exciting possibilities – a new age was seen to have dawned, one where, through their reason and rationality, humans could truly understand the dynamics of social life. This spirit, this desire to use human reason to lead to understanding and mastery of life, can be seen as a reflection of Enlightenment thought upon the origins of sociology. For the founders, sociology was 'futureology': the industrial society of our present was only at its very early stages of development at the birth of sociology. The aim of this new 'science of society' was to predict the future direction that 'progress' would take.

Readings 2.2 and **2.3** by Auguste Comte (1957) and Emile Durkheim (1952) respectively, illustrate this confidence the founders had for the ability of sociology to understand society. Comte argues that sociology or, in his terms the 'Positive Philosophy of Society', represented a new and better science than all before it. He argues that there exists a 'hierarchy of the human sciences' with sociology having mastery over all others in the search for truth. In keeping with this image of the sociologist – as someone who adopts a scientific approach to the study of social life and social living – Durkheim argues that sociology can be used to understand 'social facts' into even the most personal and intimate reaches of our lives.

Readings 2.4 and **2.5** by Peter L. Berger (1963) and Zygmunt Bauman (1990) respectively offer answers to the question 'why is sociology valuable?' They both argue that sociological insights are needed in order for contemporary society to move towards tolerance and freedom. As Berger suggests, unlike the 'puppets of society', those familiar with sociology, those able to think critically about the world around them, are able to see beyond and behind the day-to-day running of social life. Sociology thus is able to teach us to go beyond the common-sense, to make the familiar unfamiliar, to 'de-bunk' or pull-apart matters of daily routine to see what lies beneath. For Bauman, sociology allows us to understand society as a web of mutual interdependencies and in doing so, to understand where we are in society all the better. Increased understanding is in turn seen to lead to greater self-awareness and therefore the widening of opportunities for freedom.

Reading 2.6 by Ian Craib (1984) discusses the nature of sociological thought in a very different light to the images of sociology held by both Berger and Bauman. Craib notes that although the ability to theorize is central to sociology, the creation of vast amounts of theory often leads the outside observer to think that much sociology is pointless. Yet although Craib feels that much theorizing is a 'trap' which many sociologists fall into, he also recognizes that theory is important – provided it is done correctly – since it does enable us to dig beneath the surface of society by giving us frameworks within which discussion can take place.

In keeping with a theme explored by many of the authors in this chapter, Anthony Giddens (1996), in **reading 2.7**, takes issue with the critics of sociology. He argues that despite many changes in society around us, the importance of sociology hasn't declined, but rather, sociology needs to continue its search for understanding.

This chapter concludes with a powerful critique of much sociology based upon the observations of the 'founding *fathers*': the idea, that from a feminist perspective, sociology has been for too long concerned with the day-to-day realities of men in society, at the expense of making women 'invisible' in the sociological field of inquiry. In **reading 2.8**, Abbott and Wallace (1997) suggest that sociology has value – but only when it drops its 'malestream' (male-orientated) character.

The issues of what is sociology, how do sociologists study society and what is the value of sociological insights, are explored further in the remaining sections of this book. We hope that the reader – interested to find out more about sociology, for whatever reason – will enjoy what can perhaps best be described as a journey through a history (albeit an unavoidably disjointed one) of sociological thought, from founding and classic works, through to contemporary sociological concerns.

Reading 2.1
The spirit of change: the origins of sociology

Krishan Kumar (from) *Prophecy and Progress: The sociology of industrial and post-industrial society* (1978) Harmondsworth: Penguin. pp. 13–17 and 20–5.

Editorial comments

For Kumar, sociology – as conceived by the founders – is essentially an expression of various nineteenth-century ideas, or 'ideologies' of 'progress': the belief that, due to the rise of science, humans could understand and master the forces of nature and the forces of society.

The ideologues of progress

WHEN SOCIOLOGY ARRIVED in Europe early in the nineteenth century, it marked the culmination of a strand of thinking about man and society that was increasingly directed towards the future. Strictly speaking, western social thought had felt the pull of the future ever since, in the fifth century, St Augustine produced his grand work of synthesis, *The City of God*. In this Christian apologia he fused the Greek and Hebraic traditions into a philosophy of history, a theory of development, that looked forward to the end of secular history, and a movement from life in the earthly to life in the heavenly city. Such eschatological preoccupations continued to affect thought and action throughout the subsequent centuries. But the backward-looking spell of the memory of the world of classical antiquity remained, to bewitch thinkers into a sense that the great, **golden age** of man was really in the past, by comparison with which present times were mean and secondhand. This spell was decisively broken only towards the end of the seventeenth century. It came in the victory of the 'Moderns' over the 'Ancients', following a long-drawn-out literary controversy, and the conviction thereafter that modern philosophy and modern science were not only the equal of that of the ancient world, but immeasurably more pregnant with great and far-reaching developments for mankind.

With this victory, as J. B. Bury was the first to point out a long while ago, the idea of progress became firmly established in the European mind. Mankind could now be seen as advancing, slowly perhaps but inevitably and indefinitely, in a desirable direction. In a sense it was illogical to try to determine the happy end-point of this progression; but the attraction to do so proved irresistible. However dimly perceived, the future was seen in terms of the triumph of some existing quality or principle deemed to be of supreme worth, or as constitutive of man's or society's very nature. It might be reason, science, or liberty. But whatever it was, the principle whose fulfilment was predicted and sometimes promoted cast its light back on to the present and the past. The end, the future, became the vantage point, from which to view the present and past states of mankind; since it was only

at the end of man's development that the principle would be seen in its clearest and fullest expression. No doubt, contrariwise, discerning that future would depend on the most fundamental analysis of present trends. But, just as in human biology our interest and the focus of our investigations is on the developed organism and not intrinsically, for themselves, on the materials and processes that produce it, so in social biology, or sociology, the thing that has to be kept in mind, the informing principle of our inquiry, must be the social forms that were in the making, and whose future outlines could only roughly be seen. The chronological line – past, present, and future – was barren as well as deceptive. Only the perspective of the future revealed what was important in the past, and linked it to our lives in the present. The future was the guiding thread. Pascal said it, in the *Pensées*, in a spirit of irony; but what he said would have been taken as a solemn statement of intent by the ideologues of progress: 'The present is never an end, the past and the present are our means. Only the future is our end. Thus we never live; but we hope to live …'

The eighteenth century produced numerous, more extended and developed, statements of this sort. Two were especially important to the versions offered by the later sociological tradition: those of Turgot and Condorcet. To these thinkers were later linked two others, also French, and key figures in the establishment of the 'new science' of society: Henri, Comte de Saint-Simon, who was the first to analyse systematically the new industrial society that was emerging, and to suggest a plan for its organization; and Auguste Comte, who gave the new science its name, 'sociology', and laid down an elaborate programme for it to follow which has had a profound influence both in Europe and America. These four – 'the prophets of Paris', their biographer Frank Manuel (1965) has called them – were linked by more than the ordinary bonds of intellectual influence. They were disciples and friends, strong bonds even when the friendships turned to bitter enmity. Condorcet was the self-confessed disciple and devoted admirer of Turgot, and in many respects his own work was a fulfilment and a development of the unpublished sketches of the latter. Saint-Simon's work reveals a close reading of Condorcet's writings, down to the existence of a manuscript in which Condorcet's *Progress of the Human Mind* was analysed under explicit headings – 'ideas to be adopted', 'ideas to be rejected'. Comte was for some years Saint-Simon's secretary and his acknowledged pupil, though he later broke sharply with his former master; he, too, wrote of Condorcet as *'mon prédecesseur immédiat'*.

There was therefore an exceptionally strong line linking the eighteenth-century *philosophes* of progress and the nineteenth-century fathers of sociology. And what gave the group its distinctiveness was its fascination with movement and change, its profound impression that human life had experienced a vast and varied succession of different modes of thinking and behaving in the course of history. That succession was of course continuing – such was the discoverable law of social development – and these men felt themselves witnesses to yet another momentous mutation, one which was lifting human life to a newer and higher plane, and whose basic principle and promise could be discerned by all unprejudiced thinkers. Such men could not but be struck by the conviction that the contemporary equals the merely temporary. The tribulations of their private and public lives amounting, in Condorcet's case, to his condemnation to death by the Jacobins – could be borne on the missionary belief that these were but the travails of the new order. As Manual says,

they were intoxicated with the future: they looked into what was about to be and they found it good. The past was a mere prologue and the present a spiritual and moral, even a physical, burden which at times was well nigh unendurable. They would destroy the present as fast as possible in order to usher in the longed-for future, to hasten the end.
(Manuel, 1965)

... The triumphant success of **Newtonian physics** dazzled the eighteenth-century philosophers. They hoped to discover in human society a principle of order, of equilibrium, equivalent to the operations of gravity in Newton's mechanical universe. Montesquieu's great masterpiece of the mid-century Enlightenment, *The Spirit of the Laws*, was conceived basically in mechanistic terms; the good polity was subject to technical breakdown because of a failure to operate in accordance with its true character. The genius legislator, by fathoming the spirit of a nation's laws, could effect a restoration, and set the machine working once more so that it might continue its regular motions ...

It was in the course of the French Revolution that the word 'revolution' acquired its modern meaning, its modern associations of novelty and fundamental change. It was only then that 'revolution' ceased to be a phenomenon of the natural or divine order, made by non-human, elemental forces, and became part of a man-made conscious purpose to create a new order based on reason and freedom. No matter that this particular attempt failed to make and secure the new world. Henceforward the idea of fundamental transformation, of the whole restructuring of human society, became deeply lodged in the European mind and, by a later export, in the consciousness of the rest of the world.

Nor was it necessary that this transformation should be brought about by violence, in the manner of the French attempt. The lesson drawn from the course of the French Revolution – particularly by those thinkers whom we are considering – was that revolutionary violence was at most an expedient, necessary perhaps in the conditions of particular societies, to hasten on the changes already being effected by more fundamental, long-term social and intellectual forces. The new society matures in the womb of the old, as Marx was later to put it; 'force is the midwife to the old society pregnant with the new'. Against which Lenin later pencilled in the laconic comment, 'Some births are difficult, others are easy.' Political revolution was to become an obsession for some of the self-styled disciplines of the early sociologists. But for the masters themselves it was always a secondary matter. The revolution that absorbed them, that they saw working itself out before their eyes, that they sought to analyse and promote with all their strength: this revolution had altogether grander dimensions. It was nothing less than the coming into being of an entirely new order of society, one based on reason and science, whose realization would necessarily have as a consequence the fullest extension of human freedom.

It is an irony not uncommon in history, that one of the most powerful and influential statements of this view should have been written by a man fleeing from the agents of that very French Revolution that did so much to further this conception. In 1793 the Marquis de Condorcet, one of the earliest and most enthusiastic supporters of the Revolution, and a fervent disciple of Turgot, was in hiding in Paris, condemned to death by the Jacobins for his former Girondist stance. In the shadow of the guillotine he composed the *Esquisse d'un tableau historique des progrès de l'espirit humain (Sketch for a Historical Picture of the Progress of the Human Mind)*. Condorcet has been described as 'the last of the *philosophes*', and his *Esquisse* as a 'dramatic paean, a passionate affirmation of rationalist faith, the climactic expression of the eighteenth-century quest for reason in history'. In it he synthesized and bodied out the ideas of Turgot and of the other eighteenth-century ideologists of progress, giving however to those ideas a form and an utterance vastly bolder and more appealing than any of his predecessors. The *Esquisse* was the form in which the eighteenth-century idea of progress was generally assimilated by western thought. It was a consciously written manifesto, which was necessarily referred to both by those who affirmed allegiance to its message – such as Saint-Simon and Comte – and by those who denounced it. Malthus' pessimistic *Essay on Population* appeared as a formal refutation of Condorcet's ideas. The influential conservative school of de Maistre made the tenets of the *Esquisse* the main target of their war on the ideology of the eighteenth-century Enlightenment; de Bonald anathematized it as the 'Apocalypse of the new Gospel'.

Much of what Condorcet had to say expressed in a terser, more self-evident way, Turgot's idea of the inherent capacity of man for change and progress, and thus of his history as the progressive realization of that capacity. Man had so far progressed through nine stages; the tenth, of which the French Revolution was the herald, lay in the future. But in a number of ways Condorcet significantly modified the tenor of Turgot's thought, and introduced elements which were to feature centrally in the sociological schemes of Saint-Simon and Comte.

Condorcet radically **securalized** the philosophy of history that he inherited from Turgot. What Turgot offered was still a **theodicy** – one, it is true, couched in concrete, historical terms, but still penetrated by the idea that behind the laws of history there lay a transcendental sanction, corresponding to the unique, divinely-ordained quality of human history as opposed to natural history. Providence was still the guiding force of history, as it had been for St Augustine. Condorcet, atheist and passionate secularist, not only took God out of the story, he injected his account with a violent anti-religious bias. The laws of human history were seen as the products of that history itself, the results of the activities of men and not of God. Progress was an autonomous human creation, not the expression of the divine purpose working itself out on earth.

With this ejection of a residual theology, Condorcet could begin the process of reuniting the worlds of man and of nature, so impressively pulled apart by Turgot. He could do so because he kept the basic idea that the laws of human society were not the laws of a static system, like the laws of equilibrium, but dynamic, temporal and historical. The fact of progress, and of its necessary continuation into the future, could be demonstrated from the facts of history with the same degree of probability, and with the same lack of any absolute certainty, that Hume had shown characterized the laws of nature. The idea of progress and the methods of science could be reconciled. The phenomena of the human and of the physical worlds were all on the same plane, all susceptible to observation and explanation by the same method. 'They are equally susceptible of being calculated,' wrote Condorcet, 'and all that is necessary, to reduce the whole of nature to laws similar to those which Newton discovered with the aid of the calculus, is to have a sufficient number of observations and a mathematics that is complex enough.'

Peace having been made with the methodology of the future, it was possible to ask what this new science of history could deliver with regard to the society of the future. And here Condorcet made claims strikingly similar to those soon to be advanced by Auguste Comte, the designator if not the founder of sociology, the new science of society. History, thought Condorcet, was 'a science to foresee the progression of the human species', a science of social prediction which could be a source of great power. For by foreknowledge it was possible to 'tame the future' (Comte's '*prevoir pour pouvoir*'). The careful study of history revealed the central developmental tendencies of the evolution of society, and by the extrapolation of these we were in a position to see something of the future stages of that evolution. 'These observations on what man has been and what he is today will later lead to the means of assuring and accelerating the new progressions which human nature still permits him to hope for.'

'A science to foresee the progression of the human species' – one hardly dared hope to find so apt and complete a description of the intellectual enterprise later embarked upon by the pioneers of sociology. For here is Comte's pronouncement of the aim of the new science sociology:

> The aim of every science is foresight [prévoyance]. For the laws established by observation of phenomena are generally employed to foresee their succession. All men, however little advanced, make true predictions, which are always based on the same principle, the knowledge of the future from the past ... The foresight of the astronomer who predicts with complete precision the state of the solar system many years in advance is absolutely the same in kind as that of the savage who predicts the next sunrise. The only difference lies in the extent of their knowledge. Manifestly, then, it is quite in accordance with the nature of the human mind that observation of the past should unveil the future in politics, as it does in astronomy, physics, chemistry, and physiology. The determination of the future must even be regarded as the direct aim of political science, as in the case of the other positive sciences. Indeed, it is clear that knowledge of what social system the elite of mankind is called to by the progress of civilization – knowledge forming the true practical object of positive science – involves

a general determination of the next social future as it results from the past.
(Comte, 1822)

The overriding commitment to the prediction of future states of society was one element in Condorcet's legacy to nineteenth-century sociology. The other was equally influential, in touching on an aspect of the idea of progress that haunted the minds and affected the actions of many a nineteenth-century thinker. If the progress of mankind was inevitable, stretching in a continuous chain from man's infancy to the furthest point of his development, what then should be the role of the individual at any given stage? In a strict sense there should really be nothing for him to do but acknowledge the inevitability of change, welcome it when it came, and commit himself to the direction of its currents as they pulled him along. But few were willing to rest on this position, for the good reason that very few thinkers, and none of the important ideologists of progress, held to a view of progress as mechanical as this sketch implied. They were none of them mindless Panglossians, accepting all the features of any given society, at any stage, as the necessary germs of the next stage. They realized that there were distortions, lags, retardations, powerful counter progressive forces, at all stages in the progress of man. While none of these could ultimately halt that necessary progress, they could put mankind to much suffering in the process of trying to do so.

There was therefore a special merit, argued Condorcet – and others after him – in promoting the tide of progress, easing the birth-pangs of the new society. Indeed on a rational understanding of history it became the duty of every enlightened being to throw his energies into shaping and developing the forces of progress. Especially was this true at this point in time when, as indicated by the French Revolution, mankind was on the verge of a passage to an order of society marked by the highest utilization of its capacity for reason and freedom.

And who were in the vanguard of the advance of reason? To whom should one most be looking, as the prime agency of the transition to the new order? Condorcet's answer was again pregnant with consequences for the whole, more systematic discussion of just this issue in nineteenth-century sociology. It was the scientists who, as a group, carried the seeds of the future within them. Science was the fullest embodiment of the principles and tendencies of the European Enlightenment. It represented the distillation, as it were, in its purest form of the **rationalist philosophy** with which the Enlightenment had fought the superstitious and unregenerate forces of Church and State. Therefore the new society, whose whole informing principle was to be rationality, should be guided and shaped by the men of science.

References

Comte, A. (1822) appendix to *Systeme de Politique Positive*, Paris.

Manuel, F. E. (1965) *The Prophets of Paris*, New York: Harper Torchbooks.

Key terms

The following key terms appear in the text above. They have been defined below to aid with the reading of this item.

golden age the belief that the past was better than the present and that in the present something important has been lost

Newtonian physics the developments in the scientific study of the physical universe made by Newton, usually associated with the study of mechanical forces and of gravity in particular

secularized lacking in religious beliefs; the decline of religion

theodicy religious discussions concerning the existence and nature of good and evil

rationalist philosophy the belief that 'reality' can be best understood through the intellect rather than through the use of sensory experience

Questions

1 In your own words, describe the sort of society in Europe that gave 'birth' to sociology as a new subject.

2 Explain how the idea of 'progress' was important for the founders of sociology.

3 From reading about the time that the founders lived, evaluate the fact that much sociology has been built upon their observations. Should we reject their ideas because of the fact that they lived so long ago?

Reading 2.2 **Comte's image of sociology**

Auguste Comte (from) *A General View of Positivism* (1957) New York: Robert Speller & Sons, pp. 1–7.

Editorial comments

In this description of 'positivism', Comte suggests that sociology is not just a scientific basis to understand society – but that it should also be used as a basis to reform social life. Comte argued that sociology would replace religion as the principle organizational basis for an industrial society. In this extract he lays out these intentions.

A general view of positivism

POSITIVISM CONSISTS ESSENTIALLY of a Philosophy and a Polity. These can never be dissevered; the former being the basis, and the latter the end of one comprehensive system, in which our intellectual faculties and our social sympathies are brought into close correlation with each other. For, in the first place, the science of Society, besides being more important than any other, supplies the only logical and scientific link by which all our varied observations of phenomena can be bought into one consistent whole. Of this science it is even more true than of any of the preceding sciences, that its real character cannot be understood without explaining its exact relation in all general features with the art corresponding to it. Now here we find a coincidence which is assuredly not fortuitous. At the very time when the theory of society is being laid down, an immense sphere is opened for the application of that theory; the direction, namely, of the social regeneration of Western Europe. For, if we take another point of view, and look at the great crisis of modern history, as its character is displayed in the natural course of events, it becomes every day more evident how hopeless is the task of reconstructing political institutions without the previous remodelling of opinion and of life. To form then a satisfactory synthesis of all human conceptions is the most urgent of our social wants: and it is needed equally for the sake of Order and of Progress. During the gradual accomplishment of this great philosophical work, a new moral power will arise spontaneously throughout the West, which, as its influence increases, will lay down a definite basis for the reorganization of society. It will offer a general system of education for the adoption of all civilized nations, and by this means will supply in every department of public and private life fixed principles of judgement and of conduct. Thus the intellectual movement and the social crisis will be brought continually into close connection with each other. Both will combine to prepare the advanced portion of humanity for the acceptance of a true spiritual power, a power more coherent, as well as more progressive, than the noble but premature attempt of mediaeval Catholicism.

The primary object, then, of Positivism is two-fold: to generalize our scientific conceptions, and to systematize the art of social life. These are but two aspects of one and the same problem. ... I shall first explain the general spirit of the new philosophy. I shall then show its necessary connection with the whole course of that vast revolution which is now about to terminate under its guidance in social reconstruction.

This will lead us naturally to another question. The regenerating doctrine cannot do its work without adherents; in what quarter should we hope to find them? Now, with individual exceptions of great value, we cannot expect the adhesion of any of the upper classes in society. They are all more or less under the influence of baseless metaphysical theories, and of aristocratic self-seeking. They are absorbed in blind political agitation and in disputes for the possession of the useless remnants of the old theological and military system. Their action only tends to prolong the revolutionary state indefinitely, and can never result in true social renovation.

Whether we regard its intellectual character or its social objects, it is certain that Positivism must look elsewhere for support. It will find a welcome in those classes only whose good sense has been left unimpaired by our vicious system of education, and whose generous sympathies are allowed to develop themselves freely. It is among women, therefore, and among the working classes that the heartiest supporters of the new doctrine will be found. It is intended, indeed, ultimately for all classes of society. But it will never gain much real influence over the higher ranks till it is forced upon their notice by these powerful patrons. When the work of spiritual reorganization is completed, it is on them that its maintenance will principally depend; and so too, their combined aid is necessary for its commencement. Having but little influence in political government, they are the more likely to appreciate the need of a moral government, the special object of which it will be to protect them against the oppressive action of the temporal power.

... I shall explain the mode in which philosophers and working men will co-operate. Both have been prepared for this coalition by the general course which modern history has taken, and it offers now the only hope we have of really decisive action. We shall find that the efforts of Positivism to regulate and develop the natural tendencies of the people, make it, even from the intellectual point of view, more coherent and complete.

But there is another and a more unexpected source from which Positivism will obtain support; and not till then will its true character and the full extent of its constructive power be appreciated. I shall show ... how eminently calculated is the Positive doctrine to raise and regulate the social condition of women. It is from the feminine aspect only that human life, whether individually or collectively considered, can really be comprehended as a whole. For the only basis on which a system really embracing all the requirements of life can be formed, is the subordination of intellect to social feeling: a subordination which we find directly represented in the womanly type of character, whether regarded in its personal or social relations.

Although these questions cannot be treated fully in the present work, I hope to convince my readers that Positivism is more in accordance with the spontaneous tendencies of the people and of women than Catholicism, and is therefore better qualified to institute a spiritual power. It should be observed that the ground on which the support of both these classes is obtained is, that Positivism is the only system which can supersede the various subversive schemes that are growing each day more dangerous to all the relations of domestic and social life. Yet the tendency of the doctrine is to elevate the character of both of these classes; and it gives a most energetic sanction to all their legitimate aspirations.

Thus it is that a philosophy originating in speculations of the most abstract character, is found applicable not merely to every department of practical life, but also to the sphere of our moral nature. But to complete the proof of its universality I have still to speak of another very essential feature. I shall show, in spite of prejudices which exist very naturally on this point, that Positivism is eminently calculated to call the Imaginative faculties into exercise. It is by these faculties that the unity of human nature is most distinctly represented: they are themselves intellectual, but their field lies principally in our moral nature, and the result of their operation is to influence the active powers. The subject of women ... will lead me by a natural transition to speak ... of the Aesthetic aspects of Positivism. I shall attempt to show that the new doctrine by the very fact of embracing the whole range of human relations in the spirit of reality, discloses the true theory of Art, which has hitherto been so great a deficiency in our speculative conceptions. The principle of the theory is that, in co-ordinating the pri-

mary functions of humanity, Positivism places the Idealities of the poet midway between the Ideas of the philosopher and the Realities of the statesman. We see from this theory how it is that the poetical power of Positivism cannot be manifested at present. We must wait until moral and mental regeneration has advanced far enough to awaken the sympathies which naturally belong to it, and on which Art in its renewed state must depend for the future. The first mental and social shock once passed, Poetry will at last take her proper rank. She will lead Humanity onward towards a future which is now no longer vague and visionary, while at the same time she enables us to pay due honour to all phases of the past. The great object which Positivism sets before us individually and socially, is the endeavour to become more perfect. The highest importance is attached therefore to the imaginative faculties, because in every sphere with which they deal they stimulate the sense of perfection. Limited as my explanations in this work must be, I shall be able to show that Positivism, while opening out a new and wide field for art, supplies in the same spontaneous way new means of expression.

I shall thus have sketched with some detail the true character of the regenerating doctrine. All its principal aspects will have been considered. Beginning with its philosophical basis, I pass by natural transitions to its political purpose, thence to its action upon the people, its influence with women, and lastly, to its aesthetic power. In concluding this work, which is but the introduction to a larger treatise, I have only to speak of the conception which unites all these various aspects. As summed up in the positivist motto, *Love, Order, Progress*, they lead us to the conception of Humanity, which implicitly involves and gives new force to each of them. Rightly interpreting this conception, we view Positivism at last as a complete and consistent whole. The subject will naturally lead us to speak in general terms of the future progress of social regeneration, as far as the history of the past enables us to foresee it. The movement originates in France, and is limited at first to the great family of Western nations. I shall show that it will afterwards extend, in accordance with definite laws, to the rest of the white race, and finally to the other two great races of man.

Questions

1 What does Comte mean when he describes positivism as both a philosophy and a polity?

2 What do you think it means when Comte says that the aim of positivism is to 'systematize the art of social life'?

3 Comte recommends that any society should be organized using sociological knowledge. Evaluate this idea from a feminist viewpoint.

4 To what extent can Comte – reflecting attitudes of the time – be accused of racism?

5 What do you think Comte means by what he calls the 'positivistic motto': 'love, order, progress'?

Reading 2.3 **Durkheim's image of sociology**

Emile Durkheim (from) *Suicide: a study in sociology* (1952) London: Routledge & Kegan Paul, pp. 35–9.

Editorial comments

Durkheim's study of suicide was an attempt to demonstrate to his wider academic peers the value of sociology in understanding the nature of social life and human behaviour. Like Comte before him, Durkheim believed that sociology was a science – and that as such it could explain 'social facts'. Taking suicide as an example of what is, on the surface, the most personal and individual of all social acts, Durkheim claims instead, that wider social forces are responsible for rates and patterns of suicide in different societies.

Suicide

SOCIOLOGY HAS BEEN in vogue for some time. Today this word, little known and almost discredited a decade ago, is in common use. Representatives of the new science are increasing in number and there is something like a public feeling favourable to it. Much is expected of it. It must be confessed, however, that results up to the present time are not really proportionate to the number of publications nor the interest which they arouse. The progress of a science is proven by the progress toward solution of the problems it treats. It is said to be advancing when laws hitherto are unknown are discovered, or when at least new facts are acquired modifying the formulation of these problems even though not furnishing a final solution. Unfortunately, there is good reason why sociology does not appear in this light, and this is because the problems it proposes are not usually clear-cut. It is still in the stage of **system-building** and philosophical synthesis. Instead of attempting to cast light on a limited portion of the social field, it prefers brilliant generalities reflecting all sorts of questions to definite treatment of any one. Such a method may indeed momentarily satisfy public curiosity by offering it so-called illumination on all sorts of subjects, but it can achieve nothing objective. Brief studies and hasty intuitions are not enough for the discovery of the laws of so complex a reality. And, above all, such large and abrupt **generalizations** are not capable of any sort of proof. All that is accomplished is the occasional citation of some favourable examples illustrative of the **hypothesis** considered, but an illustration is not a proof. Besides, when so many various matters are dealt with, none is competently treated and only casual sources can be employed, with no means to make a critical estimate of them. Works of pure sociology are accordingly of little use to whoever insists on treating only definite questions, for most of them belong to no particular branch of research and in addition lack really authoritative documentation.

Believers in the future of the science must, of course, be anxious to put an end to this stage of affairs. If it should continue, sociology would soon relapse into its old discredit and only the enemies of reason could rejoice at this. The human mind would suffer a grievous setback if this segment of reality which alone has so far denied or defied it should escape it even temporarily. There is nothing necessarily discouraging in the incompleteness of the results thus far obtained. They should arouse new efforts, not surrender. A science so recent cannot be criticized for errors and probings if it sees to it that their recurrence is avoided. Sociology should, then, renounce none of its aims; but, on the other hand, if it is to satisfy the hopes placed on it, must try to become more than a new sort of philosophical literature. Instead of contenting himself with metaphysical reflection on social themes, the sociologist must take as the object of his research groups of facts clearly circumscribed, capable of ready definition, with definite limits, and adhere strictly to them. Such auxiliary subjects as history, ethnography and statistics are indispensable. The only danger is that their findings may never really be related to the subject he seeks to embrace; for, carefully as he may delimit this subject, it is so rich and varied that it contains inexhaustible and unsuspected tributary fields. But this is not conclusive. If he proceeds accordingly, even though his factual resources are incomplete and his formulae too narrow, he will have nevertheless performed a useful task for future continuation. Conceptions with some objective foundation are not restricted to the personality of their author. They have an impersonal quality which others may take up and pursue; they are transmissible. This makes possible some continuity in scientific labour – continuity upon which progress depends.

It is in this spirit that the work here presented has been conceived. Suicide has been chosen as its subject, among the various subjects that we have had occasion to study in our teaching career, because few are more accurately to be defined and because it seemed to us particularly timely; its limits have even required study in a preliminary work. On the other hand, by such concentration, real laws are discoverable which demonstrate the possibility of sociology better than any dialectical argument. The ones we hope to have demonstrated will appear. Of course we must have made more than one error, must have overextended the facts observed in our inductions. But at least each proposition carries its proofs with it and we have tried to make them as numerous as possible. Most of all, we have striven in each case to separate the argument and interpretation from the facts interpreted. Thus the reader can judge what is relevant in our explanations without being confused.

Moreover, by thus restricting the research, one is by no means deprived of broad views and general insights. On the contrary, we think we have established a certain number of propositions concerning marriage, widowhood, family life, religious society, etc., which, if we are not mistaken, are more instructive than the common theories of moralists as to the nature of these conditions or institutions. There will even emerge from our study some suggestions concerning the causes of the general contemporary maladjustment being undergone by European societies and concerning remedies which may relieve it. One must not believe that a general condition can only be explained with the aid of generalities. It may appertain to specific causes which can only be determined if carefully studied through no less definite manifestations expressive of them. Suicide as it exists today is precisely one of the forms through which the collective affection from which we suffer is transmitted; thus it will aid us to understand this.

Finally, in the course of this work, but in a concrete and specific form, will appear the chief methodological problems elsewhere stated and examined by using

greater detail. Indeed, among these questions there is one to which the following work makes a contribution too important for us to fail to call it immediately to the attention of the reader.

Sociological method as we practice it rests wholly on the basic principle that social facts must be studied as things, that is, as realities external to the individual. There is no principle for which we have received more criticism; but none is more fundamental. Indubitably for sociology to be possible, it must above all have an object all its own. It must take cognizance of a reality which is not in the domain of other sciences. But if no reality exists outside of individual consciousness, it wholly lacks any material of its own. In that case, the only possible subject of observation is the mental states of the individual, since nothing else exists. That, however, is the field of psychology. From this point of view the essence of marriage, for example, or the family, or religion, consists of individual needs to which these institutions supposedly correspond: paternal affection, filial love, sexual desire, the so-called religious instinct, etc. These institutions themselves, with their varied and complex historical forms, become negligible and of little significance. Being superficial, contingent expressions of the general characteristics of the nature of the individual, they are but one of its aspects and call for no special investigation. Of course, it may occasionally be interesting to see how these eternal sentiments of humanity have been outwardly manifested at different times in history; but as all such manifestations are imperfect, not much importance may be attached to them. Indeed, in certain respects, they are better disregarded to permit more attention to the original source whence flows all their meaning and which they imperfectly reflect. On the pretext of giving the science a more solid foundation by establishing it upon the psychological constitution of the individual, it is thus robbed of the only object proper to it. *It is not realized that there can be no sociology unless societies exist, and that societies cannot exist if there are only individuals.* Moreover, this view is not the least of the causes which maintain the taste for vague generalities in sociology. How can it be important to define the concrete forms of social life, if they are thought to have only a borrowed existence?

But it seems hardly possible to us that there will not emerge, on the contrary, from every page of this book, so to speak, the impression that the individual is dominated by a moral reality greater than himself: namely, collective reality. When each people is seen to have its own suicide-rate, more constant than that of general mortality, that its growth is in accordance with a coefficient of acceleration characteristic of each society; when it appears that the variations through which it passes at different times of the day, month, year, merely reflect the rhythm of social life; and that marriage, divorce, the family, religious society, the army, etc., affect it in accordance with definite laws, some of which may even be numerically expressed – these states and institutions will no longer be regarded simply as characterless, ineffective, ideological arrangements. Rather they will be felt to be real, living, active forces which, because of the way they determine the individual, prove their independence of him; which, if the individual enters as an element in the combination whence these forces ensue, at least control him once they are formed. Thus it will appear more clearly why sociology can and must be objective, since it deals with realities as definite and substantial as those of the psychologist or the biologist.

Key terms

The following key terms appear in the text above. They have been defined below to aid with the reading of this item.

system-building creating knowledge and ideas about the world in an organized fashion

generalizations using a small section of the population (a sample) to make wider, more general statements about society as a whole

hypothesis a proposition to test by further research; usually in the form of a prediction of a future event

Questions

1 In your own words, identify Durkheim's main aims from his study of suicide.

2 What does Durkheim say about the value of sociology as a means of understanding society?

3 According to Durkheim what should be the relationship between the sociologist and his or her object of study?

4 What, according to Durkheim, is the relationship between the individual and the wider society?

5 To what extent does Durkheim have a 'scientific' notion of what sociology is?

Reading 2.4 **Sociology as humanism**

Peter L. Berger (from) *Invitation to Sociology: a humanistic perspective* (1963) Harmondsworth: Penguin, pp. 186–99.

Editorial comments

For Berger sociology is a 'humanism' – by this he means that it can be used to improve the human condition: that it is of great value to encourage humans to use their consciousness to question themselves and their creation (society) because by questioning we can start the process of changing society to better suit our needs.

Sociology as a humanistic discipline

SOCIOLOGY, FROM THE beginning, understood itself as a science. Very early in our argument we discussed some methodological consequences of this self-understanding. In these final remarks, we are not concerned with **methodology** but rather with the human implications of having an academic discipline such as sociology. We have tried to depict in previous chapters the way in which sociological perspective helps to illuminate man's social existence. In the last digression we briefly asked what the ethical implications of such perspective may be. We now conclude by looking once more at sociology as one discipline among many in that particular corner of the social carnival that we call scholarship.

One very important thing that many sociologists can learn from their fellow scientists in the natural sciences is a certain sense of play with regard to their discipline. Natural scientists, on the whole, have with age acquired a degree of sophistication about their methods that allows them to see the latter as relative and limited in scope. Social scientists still tend to take their discipline with grim humourlessness, invoking terms such as '**empirical**', 'data', '**validity**' or even 'facets' as a voodoo magician might his most cherished hobgoblins. As the social sciences move from their enthusiastic puberty to a mellower maturity, a similar degree of detachment from one's own game may be expected and, indeed, can already be found. One can then understand sociology as one game among many, significantly but hardly the last word about human life, and one can afford not only tolerance but even an interest in other people's epistemological entertainments. …

Sociology will be especially well advised not to fixate itself in an attitude of humourless scientism that is blind and deaf to the buffoonery of the social spectacle. If sociology does that, it may find that it has acquired a foolproof methodology, only to lose the world of phenomena that it originally set out to explore – a fate as sad as that of the magician who has finally found the formula that will release the mighty *jinn* from the bottle, but cannot recollect what it was that he wanted to ask of the *jinn* in the first place. However, while eschewing scientism, the sociologist will be able to discover human values that are endemic to scientific procedures in both the social and the natural sciences. Such values are humility before the immense richness of the world one is investigating, an effacement of self in the search for understanding, honesty and precision in method, respect for findings honestly arrived at, patience and a willingness to be proven wrong and to revise one's theories, and, last but not least, the community of other individuals sharing these values.

The scientific procedures used by the sociologist imply some specific values that are peculiar to this discipline. One such value is the careful attention to matters that other scholars might consider pedestrian and unworthy of the dignity of being objects of scientific investigation – something one might almost call a democratic focus of interest in the sociological approach. Everything that human beings are or do, no matter how common-place, can become significant for sociological research. Another such peculiar value is inherent in the sociologist's necessity to listen to others without volunteering his own views. The art of listening, quietly and with full attention, is something that any sociologist must acquire if he is to engage in empirical studies. While one should not exaggerate the importance of what is often nothing more than a research technique, there is a human significance at least potentially present in such conduct, especially in our nervous and garrulous age in which almost nobody finds the time to listen with concentration. Finally, there is a peculiar human value in the sociologist's responsibility for evaluating his findings, as far as he is psychologically able, without regard to his own prejudices, likes or dislikes, hopes or fears. This responsibility, of course, the sociologist shares with other scientists. But it is especially difficult to exercise in a discipline that touches so closely on the human passions. It is evident that this goal is not always achieved, but in the very effort lies a moral significance not to be taken lightly. This becomes particularly appealing when one compares the sociologist's concern for listening to the world, without immediately shouting back his own formulations of normative disciplines, such as theology or jurisprudence, where one meets with the constant compulsion to squeeze reality into the narrow frame of one's value judgments. Sociology appears by comparison as standing in an apostolic succession from the **Cartesian** quest for 'clear and distinct perception'.

In addition to these human values that are inherent in the scientific enterprise of sociology itself, the discipline has other traits that assign it to the immediate vicinity of the humanities if they do not, indeed, indicate that it belongs fully with them. ... Just because the social is such a crucial dimension of man's existence, sociology comes time and again on the fundamental question of what it means to be a man and what it means to be a man in a particular situation. This question may often be obscured by the paraphernalia of scientific research and by the bloodless vocabulary that sociology has developed in its desire to legitimate its own scientific status. But sociology's data are cut so close from the living marrow of human life that this question comes through again and again, at least for those sociologists who are sensitive to the human significance of what they are doing. Such sensitivity, as we have argued, is not just an adiaphoron [a non-essential attribute] that a sociologist may possess in addition to his properly professional qualifications (such as a good ear in music or a knowing palate for food), but has direct bearing upon sociological perception itself.

Such an understanding of the humanistic place of sociology implies an openness of mind and a catholicity of vision. It should be readily conceded that such a posture may be acquired at the cost of rigorously closed logic in the task of sociological system-building. ... Such a system is neat, even aesthetically pleasing. Its logic is one-dimensional and closed within itself. That this sort of intellectual edifice is inviting to many orderly minds is demonstrated by the appeal that positivism in all its forms has had since its inception. The appeal of Marxism and Freudianism has very similar roots. To conduct a sociological argument and then to veer off from its seemingly compelling sociologistic conclusion must give the appearance of being inconsequential and less than rigorous in one's thinking. ... All this can readily be admitted – and yet followed by the contention that the inconsequence is due not to the perversity of the observer's reasoning but to the paradoxical many-sidedness of life itself, that same life he is committed to observe. Such openness to the immense richness of human life makes the leaden consequences of sociologism impossible to sustain and forces the sociologist to permit 'holes' in the closed walls of his theoretical scheme, openings through which other possible horizons can be perceived. ...

The notion of humanism has been closely connected with that of intellectual liberation since the **Renaissance**. Enough has been said in preceding pages to serve as a substantiation of the claim that sociology stands rightfully in this tradition. In conclusion, however, we may ask in what way the sociological enterprise in America (itself now constituting a social institution and a professional sub-culture) can lend itself to this humanistic mission. ...

If the sociologist can be considered a **Machiavellian** figure, then his talents can be employed in both humanly nefarious and humanly liberating enterprises. If a somewhat colourful metaphor may be allowed here, one can think of the sociologist as a *condottiere* of social perception. Some *condottieri* fight for the oppressors of men, others for their liberators. Especially if one looks around beyond the frontiers of America as well as within them, one can find enough grounds to believe that there is a place in today's world for the latter type of *condottiere*. And the very detachment of sociological Machiavellianism is a not inconsiderable contribution in situations where men are torn by conflicting fanaticisms that have one important thing in common – their ideological befuddlement about the nature of society. To be motivated by human needs rather than by grandiose political programmes, to commit oneself selectively and economically rather than to consecrate oneself to a totalitarian faith, to be compassionate and sceptical at the same time, to seek to understand without bias – all these are existential possibilities of the sociological enterprise that can hardly be over-rated in many situations in the contemporary world. In this way, sociology can attain to the dignity of political relevance as well, not because it has a particular political ideology of its own to offer, but just because it has not. Especially to those who have become disillusioned with the more fervent political eschatologies of our era, sociology can be of assistance in pointing to possibilities of political engagement that do not demand the sacrifice of one's soul and of one's sense of humour. ...

The fact remains that if sociology has a humanistic character, that character will have to manifest itself within the academic milieu, if only for statistical reasons. We would contend that, despite the uncomplimentary remarks just made, this is a realistic possibility. The university is much like the church in its susceptibility to seduction by the powerful of this world. But university people, like churchmen, develop a guilt complex after the seduction has been accomplished. The old Western tradition of the university as a place of freedom and of truth, a tradition fought for with blood as well as ink, has a way of reasserting its claims before an uneasy conscience. It is within this persistent academic tradition that the humanistic impulse in sociology can find its living space in our contemporary situation.

It is obvious that a difference exists in the problems faced in this regard in a graduate school concerned with the training of a new generation of sociologists and in an undergraduate situation. In the former case, the problem is relatively easy. Naturally the writer would feel that the conception of sociology developed here should find its place in the 'formation' of future sociologists. The implications of what has been said about the humanistic dimension of sociology for graduate curricula in the discipline are obvious. This is not the place to develop them. Suffice it to say that humanistic literary waxing at the expense of technological professionalism is the course that we envisage in this connection. Evidently one's conception of sociology as a discipline will decide one's views as to how sociologists should be educated. But whatever this conception may be, it will be relevant to only a limited number of students. Not everyone, blessedly, can become a full-fledged sociologist. The one who does, if our argument is accepted, will have to pay the price of disenchantment and find his way in a world that lives on myth. We have said enough to indicate how we believe this to be possible.

The problem is obviously a different one in an undergraduate college. If a sociologist teaches in such a situation (most sociologists do), very few of his students will go on to graduate schools to study his particular field. It is even probable that very few of the sociology majors will, going on instead to social work, journalism, business administration, or any number of other occupations in which a 'sociological background' has been deemed useful. A sociologist teaching in many an average college, looking over his classes of young men and women desperately intent on social mobility, seeing them fight their way upward through the credit system and argue over grades with pertinacity, understanding that they could not care less if he read the phone directory to them in class as long as three credit hours could be added to the ledger at the end of the semester – such a sociologist will have to wonder sooner or later what sort of vocation it is that he is exercising. Even a sociologist teaching in a more genteel setting, providing intellectual pastime to those whose status is a foregone conclusion and whose education is the privilege rather than the instrumentality of such status, may well come to question what point there is to sociology, of all fields, in this situation. Of course, in state universities as well as in Ivy League colleges there are always the few students who really care, really understand, and one can always teach with only those in mind. This, however, is frustrating in the long run, especially if one has some doubts about the pedagogic usefulness of what one is teaching. And that is precisely the question that a morally sensitive sociologist ought to ask himself in an undergraduate situation.

The problem of teaching students who come to college because they need a degree to be hired by the corporation of their choice or because this is what is expected of them in a certain social position is shared by the sociologist with all his colleagues in other fields. We cannot pursue it here. There is, however, a particular problem for the sociologist that is directly related to the debunking, disenchanting character of sociology that we discussed before. It may well be asked with what right he peddles such dangerous intellectual merchandise among young minds that, more likely than not, will misunderstand and misapply the perspective he seeks to communicate. It is one thing to dispense the sociological poison to such graduate students as have already committed themselves to full-time addiction and who, in the course of intensive study, can be led to understand the therapeutic possibilities present in that poison. It is another thing to sprinkle it liberally among those who have no chance or inclination to proceed to that point of deeper understanding. What right does any man have to shake the taken-for-granted beliefs of others? Why educate young people to see the precariousness of things they had assumed to be absolutely solid? Why introduce them to the subtle erosion of critical thought? Why, in sum, not leave them alone? ...

We maintain that the teaching of sociology is justified insofar as a liberal education is assumed to have a more than etymological connection with intellectual liberation. Where this assumption does not exist, where education is understood in purely technical or professional terms, let sociology be eliminated from the curriculum. It will only interfere with the smooth operation of the latter, provided, of course, that sociology has not also been emasculated in accordance with the educational ethos prevailing in such situations. Where, however, the assumption still holds, sociology is justified by the belief that it is better to be conscious than unconscious and that consciousness is a condition of freedom. To attain a greater measure of awareness, and with it of freedom, entails a certain amount of suffering and even risk. An educational process that would avoid this becomes simple technical training and ceases to have any relationship to the civilizing of the mind. We contend that it is part of a civilized mind in our age to have come in touch with the peculiarly modern, peculiarly timely form of critical thought that we call sociology. Even those who do not find in this intellectual pursuit their own particular demon, as Weber put it, will by this contact have become a little less stolid in their prejudices, a little more careful in their own commitments and a little more sceptical about the commitments of others – and perhaps a little more compassionate in their journeys through society.

Let us return once more to the image of the puppet theatre that our argument conjured up before. We see the puppets dancing on their miniature stage, moving up and down as the strings pull them around, following the prescribed course of their various little parts. We learn to understand the logic of this theatre and we find ourselves in its motions. We locate ourselves in society and thus recognize our own position as we hang from its subtle strings. For a moment we see ourselves as puppets indeed. But then we grasp a decisive difference between the puppet theatre and our own drama. Unlike the puppets, we have the possibility of stopping in our movements, looking up and perceiving the machinery by which we have been moved. In this act lies the first step towards freedom. And in this same act we find the conclusive justification of sociology as a humanistic discipline.

Key terms

The following key terms appear in the text above. They have been defined below to aid with the reading of this item.

methodology the study of obtaining data through the use of research

empirical based upon research

validity a 'true' picture of what has been researched/tested

Cartesian philosophy based upon an up-date of the ideas of Descartes, who is considered to have provided no adequate explanation of how the mind and the body were in union

Renaissance the period in history after the Middle Ages where the ideas of Ancient Rome and Ancient Greece were returned to by European scholars, artists and scientists

Machiavellian based upon the ideas of philosopher Machiavelli who argued that the ends always justified the means; in popular usage it refers to someone who is scheming

Questions

1 According to Berger what is the value of sociology?

2 Evaluate the idea that members of society are like 'puppets'.

3 Evaluate Berger's recommendation that sociology can aid political decision-making.

4 Why and how might sociological knowledge contribute to greater freedom, according to Berger?

Reading 2.5 **How to 'think sociologically'**

Zygmunt Bauman (from) *Thinking Sociologically* (1990) Oxford: Basil Blackwell, pp. 1–10.

Editorial comments

In this extract Bauman attempts to both define sociology and to explain how sociology differs from other subjects, and from the 'common-sense' thought used in everyday life. Bauman also outlines what he thinks the point, and value, of sociology is.

Sociology – what for?

ONE CAN CONCEIVE of sociology in a number of ways. The simplest way is to think of a long line of library shelves, tightly packed with books. All books have the word 'sociology' in their titles, or in subtitles, or in their list of contents (this is why the librarian put them on these shelves in the first place). The books carry the names of their authors, who describe themselves as sociologists (that is, are classified as sociologists in their official titles of teachers or researchers). Thinking of these books and their authors, one thinks of a body of knowledge accumulated over the long years during which sociology has been practised and taught. And so one thinks of sociology as a sort of binding tradition – a certain volume of information all newcomers to the field, whether they want to become practising sociologists or merely to avail themselves of whatever sociology may offer, must first consume, digest, appropriate. Or, better still, one thinks of sociology in a way that includes the constant influx of newcomers (new books are always being added to the shelves, after all): one things of it as of a continuing activity – a going concern, a constant testing of the received lore of wisdom against new experience, a constant adding to the accumulated knowledge and changing of it in the process. ...

... the first thing we find out when looking at the library shelves filled with sociology books is that they are surrounded by other shelves, all bearing names different from that of 'sociology'. In most university or college libraries one would probably discover that the closest neighbours are the shelves carrying the labels 'history', 'political science', 'law', 'social policy', 'economics'. The librarians who arranged such shelves close to each other probably had the readers' comfort and convenience in mind. They assumed (or so we may guess) that the readers browsing through sociology shelves would occasionally reach for a book placed on, say, history or political science shelves; and that this may happen more often than searching the contents of, say, physics or mechanical engineering shelves. In other words, the librarians assumed that the subject-matter of sociology is somewhat nearer to that of the bodies of knowledge for which names like 'political science' or 'economics'

stand; perhaps also that the difference between sociology books and the books placed in their immediate vicinity is somehow less pronounced, clear-cut and uncontentious than the differences between sociology and, say, chemistry or medicine.

Whether these thoughts crossed their minds or not, the librarians did the right thing. The bodies of knowledge they made into neighbours have got much in common. They are all concerned with the *human-made* world: with the parts of the world, or the aspect of the world, that bears an imprint of human activity, which would not exist at all but for the actions of human beings. History, law, economics, political science, sociology all discuss human actions and their consequences. This much they share, and for this reason they truly belong together. If, however, all these bodies of knowledge explore the same territory, what, if anything, sets them apart? What is 'that difference which makes the difference' – the one that justifies the division and separate names? On what basis do we insist that, all the similarities and sharing of grounds and interests notwithstanding, history is not sociology, and neither is political science?

Off-hand, we are all prompted to give a simple answer to those questions: divisions between bodies of knowledge must reflect the divisions in the world they investigate. It is the human actions, or the aspects of the human actions, which differ from each other, and the divisions between bodies of knowledge merely take cognizance of this fact. Thus, we will be tempted to say, history is about the actions which took place in the past and are no more, while sociology concentrates on the current ones, or on such general qualities of actions as do not change with time; anthropology tells us of human actions in societies spatially remote and different from our own, while sociology focuses its attention on actions that take place in our society (whatever that may mean), or such aspects of action which do not vary from one society to another. In the cases of some other close relatives of sociology, the 'obvious' answer will be somewhat less obvious – but one can still try: and so political science mostly discusses such actions as pertain to power and the government; economics deals with the actions related to the use of resources as well as production and distribution of goods; law is interested in the norms that regulate human behaviour and in the way such norms are articulated, made obligatory and enforced. ... We can see by now that were we to continue in a similar way, we would be bound to conclude that sociology is a sort of residual discipline, feeding on what other disciplines left unattended. The more the other disciplines took under their own microscopes, the less remained for sociologists to talk about; as if 'out there', in the human world, there was a limited number of facts waiting to be split, and picked up, depending on their intrinsic character, by specialistic branches of investigation.

The trouble with such an 'obvious' answer to our question is that, like most other beliefs which appear to us self-evident and obviously true, it remains obvious only as long as we refrain from looking closely at all the assumptions one must tacitly make to accept it. So let us try to trace back the stages by which we came to see our answer obvious.

Where did we get the idea that human actions divide into a certain number of distinct types in the first place? From the fact that they have been classified in such a way and that each file in this classification has been given a separate name (so that we know when to speak of politics, when of economics, and when of legal matters – and what to find where); and from the fact that there are groups of credible experts, knowledgeable and trustworthy people, who claim exclusive rights to study, to give an informed opinion, to guide or advise some types of actions rather than others. But let us pursue our inquiry one step further: how do we know at all what the human world is 'by itself', that is, before it has been split into economics, politics or social policy, and independently of such a split? Most certainly, we have not learned it from our own life experience. One does not live now in politics, then in economics; one does not move from sociology to anthropology when travelling from England to South America, or from history to sociology when one grows a year older. If we can separate such domains in our experience, if we can tell that this action here and now belongs to politics while another has an economic character, it is only because we have been taught to make such distinctions beforehand. What we really know, therefore, is not the world itself, but what we are doing with the world; we are putting into practice, so to speak, our *image* of the world, a model put neatly together from the building blocks we got from the language and our training. ...

As a first and tentative summation, we may say that what sets sociology apart and gives it its distinctive character is the habit of viewing human actions as *elements of wider figurations:* that is, of a non-random assembly of actors locked together in a web of *mutual dependency* (dependency being a state in which the probability that the action will be undertaken and the chance of its success change in relation to what other actors are, or do, or may do). Sociologists would ask what consequences this being locked together would have for the possible and the actual behaviour of human actors. Such interests shape the object of sociological inquiry: figurations, webs of mutual dependence, reciprocal conditioning of action and expansion or confinement of actors' freedom are the most prominent preoccupations of sociology. Single actors, like you and me, come into the view of sociological study in their capacity as units, members or partners in a network of interdependence. The central question of sociology, one could say, is: in what sense does it matter that in whatever they do or may do people are dependent on other people; in what sense does it matter that they live always (and cannot but live) in the company of, in communication with, in an exchange with, in competition with, in cooperation with other human beings? It is this kind of question (and not a separate collection of people or events selected for the purpose of study, nor some set of human actions neglected by other lines of investigation) that constitutes the particular area of sociological discussion and defines sociology as a relatively autonomous branch of human and social sciences. Sociology, we may conclude, is first and foremost a *way of thinking* about the human world; In principle one can also think about the same world in different ways.

Among these other ways from which the sociological way of thinking is set apart, a special place is occupied by so-called *common sense*. Perhaps more than other branches of scholarship, sociology finds its relation with common sense (that rich yet disorganized, non-systematic, often inarticulate and ineffable knowledge we use to conduct our daily business of life) fraught with problems decisive for its standing and practice.

Indeed, few sciences are concerned with spelling out their relationship to common sense; most do not even notice that common sense exists, let alone that it presents a problem. Most sciences settle for defining themselves in terms of boundaries that separate them from or bridges that connect them with other sciences – respectable, systematic lines of inquiry like themselves. They do not feel they share enough ground with common sense to bother with drawing boundaries or building bridges. Their indifference is, one must admit, well justified. Common sense has next to nothing to say of the matters of which physics, or chemistry, or astronomy, or geology speak (and whatever it has to say on such matters comes courtesy of those sciences themselves, in so far as they manage to make their recondite findings graspable and intelligible for lay people). The subjects dealt with by physics or astronomy hardly ever appear within the sight of ordinary men and women: inside, so to speak, yours and my daily experience. And so we, the non-experts, the ordinary people, cannot form opinions about such matters unless aided – indeed, instructed – by the scientists. The objects explored by sciences like the ones we have mentioned appear only under very special circumstances, to which lay people have no access: on the screen of a multi-million-dollar accelerator, in the lens of a gigantic telescope, at the bottom of a thousand-feet deep shaft. Only the scientists can see them and experiment with them; these objects and events are a monopolistic possession of the given branch of science (or even of its selected practitioners), a property not shared with anybody who is not a member of the profession. Being the sole owners of the experience which provides the raw material for their study, the scientists are in full control over the way the material is processed, analysed, interpreted. Products of such processing would have to withstand the critical scrutiny of other scientists – but their scrutiny only. They will not have to compete with public opinion, common sense or any other form in which non-specialist views may appear, for the sample reason that there is no public opinion and no commonsensical point of view in the matters they study and pronounce upon.

With sociology it is quite different. In sociological study there are no equivalents of giant accelerators or radiotelescopes. All experience which provides raw material for sociological findings – the stuff of which sociological knowledge is made – is the experience of ordinary people in ordinary, daily life; an experience accessible in principle, though not always in practice, to everybody; and experience that, before it came under the magnifying glass of a sociologist, had already been lived by someone else – a non-sociologist, a person not trained in the use of sociological language and seeing things from a sociological point of view. All of us live in the company of other people, after all, and interact with each other. All of us have learned only too well that what we get depends on what other people do. All of us have gone more than once through the agonizing experience of a communication breakdown with friends and strangers. Anything sociology talks about was already there in our lives. And it must have been, otherwise we should be unable to conduct our business of life. To live in the company of other people, we need a lot of knowledge; and common sense is the name of that knowledge.

Deeply immersed in our daily routines, though, we hardly ever pause to think about the meaning of what we have gone through; even less often have we the opportunity to compare our private experience with the fate of others, to see the *social* in the *individual*, the *general* in the *particular*; this is precisely what sociologists can do for us. We would expect them to show us how our individual *biographies* intertwine with the *history* we share with fellow human beings. And yet whether or not the sociologists get that far, they have no other point to start from than the daily experience of life they share with you and me – from that raw knowledge that saturates the daily life of each one of us. For this reason alone the sociologists, however hard they might have tried to follow the example of the physicists and the biologists and stand aside from the object of their study (that is, look at your and my life experience as an object 'out there', as a detached and impartial observer would do), cannot break off completely from their insider's knowledge of the experience they try to comprehend. However hard they might try, sociologists are bound to remain on both sides of the experience they strive to interpret, inside and outside at the same time. (Note how often the sociologists use the personal pronoun 'we' when they report their findings and formulate their general propositions. That 'we' stands for an 'object' that includes those who study and those whom they study. Can you imagine a physicist using 'we' of themselves and the molecules? Or astronomers using 'we' to generalize about themselves and the stars?)

Questions

1 According to Bauman, how can we start to think about the subject of sociology?

2 What does Bauman say about the relationships between the various knowledges produced by the social sciences?

3 According to Bauman, what is the relationship between sociology and common-sense thought?

4 What consequences might 'doing sociology' have for power relationships in society?

5 Why do you think that some in authority might try to discredit the practice of sociology?

Reading 2.6 **The problems of 'theory'**

Ian Craib (from) *Modern Social Theory: From Parsons to Habermas* (1984) London: Harvester Wheatsheaf, pp. 3–13.

Editorial comments

Craib raises for discussion an important problem in contemporary sociology: the subject relies upon theory to gain insights into the world around us, but this very same theory can obscure the subject for those new to trying to understand it. Thus, sociological theory often does not liberate thought, but constrains it. For Craib, theory is important – but it is also responsible for many of the problems of contemporary social thought.

What's wrong with theory and why we still need it

THE VERY WORD 'theory' sometimes seems to scare people, and not without good reason. Much modern social theory is either unintelligible, or banal, or pointless. The reader does not feel she is learning anything new or anything at all; there is certainly no excitement. Even for the specialist sociology student or teacher, it requires a lot of hard work with the minimal result of simply being informed. Few people feel at home with theory or use it in a productive way.

At the same time theory increases and proliferates: it might sometimes seem that this is the result of a highly developed society allowing people to earn sizeable incomes from playing complicated games, but it would not happen if there were not real problems which force people to turn to theory. Self-indulgence is not the only reason for the existence of theory. Indeed, the problems that force people to theory do not belong solely to sociological research; they are problems we all face in our everyday lives, problems of making sense of what happens to us and the people around us, the problems involved in making moral and political choices.

So, somewhere there are real reasons leading people to produce theoretical work, and there must also be reasons why the result is so often unhelpful. The journey between the problems and the results is undertaken on sociological theory courses as well as in producing theory and it has the same pitfalls. It is not made any easier by the fact that in teaching theory we start with the result. The nature of sociology is not such that we can move directly from the more practical and informative studies of the social world to social theory. Social theory is by definition *general*, it claims some relevance to all the separate areas studied by sociologists. We can not move directly from, say, a study of workers' attitudes to a theory since any worthwhile theory must deal with much more than workers' attitudes. We have to bring the two together, use our studies of the real world as the raw material of theory and use our theory to help us understand the results of our studies of the real world.

But when we learn theory, we must start with theory and that makes life difficult.

Other things make it difficult as well. Ours is not a culture that accepts easily theory in its more elaborate, worked out form. Most of us learn, almost unconsciously, to distrust it, or we become convinced that it is beyond us. *Social* theory generates its own special prejudices. Most of us know little about the natural sciences, but we will nonetheless accept that theoretical physics is a 'good thing': it seems to have useful practical results and even if we know in advance that we can't understand it, those few clever souls who can ought to be encouraged. On the other hand, social theory appears to have no practical results. Worse, it takes something we know about already in intimate detail – our own social life – and makes of it unintelligible nonsense.

If this were not enough, the teaching and learning of social theory itself operates within, and helps to create, a peculiar mystique which in turn creates a disturbing environment in which to study. The teacher of theory who, for example, is concerned only or primarily with theory, tends to receive from her colleagues a grudging respect combined with a barely veiled hostility. In departments where it is the researcher into the real world who attracts money and reputation, the theorist is a luxury, an amusement and a nuisance. On balance she is lower rather than higher in the unofficial order. Many people who see themselves primarily as theorists react to this by building a protective arrogance, returning two-fold any scorn they might receive. They refuse to compromise their concerns and indeed retreat perhaps even further into the obscure and the difficult. The process frequently starts amongst postgraduate students and it serves to make the necessary gap between teacher and student much wider than it need be at all levels. Amongst students themselves, because theory is so obviously difficult, the theorist takes on an aura that puts her apart from others; she is seen as somehow brighter, better, more able. I have no doubt that many students (and teachers) deliberately deploy this advantage, half-consciously seeking more obscure ways of expressing themselves, adopting the latest translations from Europe before anybody else, puffing out their theoretical feathers.

All these problems are there before we even start the journey. My guess is that most people start it because they have no choice, it comprises a compulsory course at some stage in their student career and they grit their teeth and get on with it. What can be done about it? It is no use pretending that theory can be made easy, but it can be made easier.

Theoretical thinking

The first step is to look again at the way we approach the subject. Because we start with the result, it is too easy for students and teachers to imagine that the whole process is a matter of learning what various theorists have said, of learning *theories*. Of course, it is that, but in one sense it is the least important aspect. It is possible, in fact quite easy, once you get used to long words, to know what Talcott Parsons has to say and to reproduce it in acceptable form in essays and exam papers. And apart from the purpose of passing exams, it is quite useless. Theory is only a help if we can learn from it, and we can only learn from it if we can use it.

Another way of putting this is that it is less a matter of learning theory than of learning to *think theoretically*. It can be likened to learning a new language in a particularly difficult way, not by gradually building up vocabulary and learning the various grammatical rules, but by listening to the language being spoken, in all its complexity, its slang, dialects etc. It is only just an exaggeration to liken it to being carried off to a very different society, a tribal village in New Guinea, say, where much of what happens is unfamiliar, and having to learn the language there by listening to people speak it.

Such a process can be made easier if we have some insight into the purposes of the inhabitants, and I said earlier that the problems which lead people to theory are problems we all face in our everyday lives. I think the truth is that we all think theoretically but in a way of which we are not often aware. What we are not used to is thinking theoretically in a systematic manner, with all the various constraints and rigours that that involves; when we do see such thinking, it is, at first, foreign to us.

What, then, are the problems in response to which we all think theoretically without realizing it? Most of us are affected in some way by events of which we have no control and the causes of which are not immediately obvious. Some of these are unexpected, some happen at first in a slow and less noticeable way. A member of the family might be made unemployed, for example, or fail to gain an expected place at university or college; some product or service might suddenly become unavailable because of a strike, or because of government or local authority economies; over a long period an income – wage, social security benefit, unemployment pay, pension, student grant or whatever – might buy less and less. We can do things to alleviate the effects of all of these, but they happen whether we as individuals like it or not, and it is by no means clear why they happen. There are similar, more intimate events in our personal lives: the slow changes in the relationship between parents and children or between lovers, which no-one wills but which nonetheless happen. I might suddenly find a friend has turned hostile for no obvious reason. On an even more personal level, I might fall in love at the most inconvenient and unexpected time, or find myself in the grip of some other violent emotion which comes from nowhere and seems to dominate my life. ...

Theory is an attempt to explain our everyday experience of the world, our 'closest' experience, in terms of something which is not so close – whether it be the other peoples' actions, our past experience, our repressed emotions or whatever. Sometimes, and this is perhaps the most difficult, the explanation is in terms of something of which we do not and cannot have any direct experience at all and it is at this level that theory really tells us something new about the world. ...

Social theory is employed for the same purposes: to explain and understand experience on the basis of other experiences and general ideas about the world. Given this, it's possible to look at some difference between everyday theoretical thinking and social theory. The first is that social theory attempts to be much more systematic about both experience and ideas. In sociology the real systematization of experience often takes place in the supposed absence of theory and there is considerable debate about whether this is possible or desirable. I suspect that it would now be generally recognized that some simple 'objectivity' or completely 'unbiased' organization of facts is not possible, but in any case the steady and systematic attempt to gather knowledge about peoples' experience can in itself produce knowledge which is at first sight strange. ... General ideas on the other hand are systematized through subjecting them to rules of logic – the ideas in a theory should follow from each other, not contradict each other, at the very least they should have clearly defined relationships to each other. It is important to realize that there is no conclusive end to this process on either level: we can always discover more about our world and organize it in different ways, according to different principles. ...

I said earlier that social theory can only be made easier, not easy. For example, it is not possible to trace the theories examined in this book back to everyday problems; the problems had already been subjected to many centuries of philosophical thought and developments in knowledge before the theories arose. Nevertheless they can be seen as asking sensible questions about the world (even if the answers aren't always sensible). Perhaps the best way to learn 'theoretical thinking' is not just by reading and understanding theory but by asking the theory questions and speculating on the answers. That is the way in which the book will proceed: What questions does the theory ask? What questions can we ask the theory? It should be (to begin with) above all an imaginative game. Having some idea of what Parsons says, can we, for example, explain the election of Ronald Reagan and Margaret Thatcher in Parsonian terms; or can we use Parsons to understand the increasing divorce rates or changes in the level and nature of crime. The first step is always to speculate, to try to *invent* an answer. The rigour of logic and facts will follow on all too quickly. The pay-off is that if we can do it well, if we can use our theory to find out about the world, then our range of effective action increases, we become more free.

All this could be read as an apologia for theory, a justification of its obscurities and difficulties. I nonetheless meant what I said at the very beginning – that much modern theory is unintelligible, banal or pointless. In the process of theoretical thinking, a number of things can go wrong.

Theoretical traps

The first trap lies prior to theory proper and there have been times when sociologists have seemed especially prone to falling into it. This is the trap of only collecting facts, of becoming absorbed in technical debates about methodology and statistical correlation. The real function of theory has to do with the interpretation of whatever facts we might be able to discover and agree on, and indeed it will become apparent that in some cases we need a theory to tell us what the facts are. The first truly theoretical trap is what I shall call the *'crossword puzzle trap'*.

One of the most influential books in sociology in the last twenty years has, paradoxically, not been a work of sociology at all but a study of the history of the natural sciences: Thomas Kuhn's *Structure of Scientific Revolutions*. Kuhn makes a distinction between what he calls 'revolutionary' and 'normal' science, and it is the latter which is important for my present point. Normal science is routine science. The scientist is in possession of accepted theoretical knowledge, routine experimental procedures and the instruments necessary to carry them out. These

(together with other elements) comprise what Kuhn calls a '**paradigm**'. Her scientific activity consists of trying to manipulate certain features of the natural world, suitably isolated in experimental situations, to fit the paradigm. In the same way as a crossword puzzle provides a frame and a set of clues, so the paradigm gives us a general framework and indications of what the world should be like, and the scientist sets about filling in the squares in detail. Now I think there are a number of reasons why the social scientist should not employ theory in this way, however productive it might be for the natural sciences, and that is a matter of debate. The complexity of the subject matter of social science, the impossibility of isolating significant aspects of the social world in order to carry out experiments, the fact that human activity is self-conscious and reflective, all combine to make such puzzle-solving activity damaging, what some people call '**reductionist**': it reduces the complexity of the real world to a set of theoretical concepts.

For example, we do not learn much about my reaction to impotence by sticking the label of '**patriarchy**' on it; we need to show not only how the nature of patriarchy conditions and determines both my impotence and my reaction to it, but also the way that these processes interact with others (for example, a changing labour market which gives greater opportunity for women to embark on full time careers) in order to understand the full complexity of the situation. Otherwise something is lost. We need then, to take account of all the various links ('mediations') between what the theory tells us and the experience or event we are trying to understand.

The second trap I shall call the *'brain-teaser trap'*. I mentioned earlier that in systematizing our ideas about the world, a number of second-order problems arise, not directly connected with explaining something. I gave as an example what we mean by 'explanation'. Many such problems are very important and without doubt a number will arise in the course of this book. But many might be unsolvable, or bear little relation to what we are trying to do; they are nonetheless fascinating problems and I know from my own experience that a great deal of pleasure can be derived from tackling them – the same sort of pleasure that can be derived from the 'brain teasers' sometimes found in the 'quality' Sunday papers. I think it is a 'permissible' activity as long as it is recognized for what it is; it is when it is mistaken for the theoretical enterprise as a whole that theory seems to be (and is) irrelevant.

A good example is the debate imported into social theory from British analytic philosophy, about whether or not a person's reasons for their actions are to be considered as causes of their actions. There is a crucial issue here to do with the very nature and possibility of a social science, but the terms of the debate are so limited in their scope and exclude so many dimensions of human action that it seems to me that the real problem disappears. Indeed I think it is possible to establish elegant solutions on either side, none of which are much concrete help to social analysis and none of which are conclusive.

Thirdly, there is the *'logic trap'*. This might sound odd since I've already suggested that a central aspect of theoretical thinking is the attempt to achieve logical coherence between different parts of a theory. My point is that it is possible to take this to an absurd extreme ... a theory might be demolished on logical grounds that if taken to the extreme would mean that no theory at all was possible. The main point here is that whilst a theory must strive for internal coherence, for logical order, the world itself is often illogical or logical in a different way to theory, which must be capable of allowing for this difference. There are a

number of examples of supposedly theoretical arguments which are really competitions in logic that have long left behind any concern with explaining or understanding the social world.

Finally, there is the *'description trap'* ... an explanation tells us something we didn't know and couldn't discover simply by looking; a description tells us only what we can discover by looking. A great deal of modern theory seems to me to describe something, often something we know very well, in abstract theoretical terms, and then pretend that it is an explanation. It is perhaps this which contributes most to the bad name of theory: endless pages of long words which, when we translate them, tell us the obvious. Talcott Parsons is particularly vulnerable on this point.

So, I have tried to show why theory is necessary and some of the traps into which it can fall. However social theory is frightening for another reason: there is so much of it and so many different types.

Key terms

The following key terms appear in the text above. They have been defined below to aid with the reading of this item.

paradigm a world view

reductionist an idea, theory or explanation which reduces the complex nature of social life to a simple factor – usually seen as a criticism of an idea

patriarchy a male-dominated system of society

Questions

1 Identify the problems of sociological theory from the point of view of those new to the subject of sociology.

2 How is it possible for 'everyday thinking' to also be theoretical?

3 How does sociological theory differ from 'everyday theory'?

4 What four 'traps' in sociological theory does Craib identify? Explain these in your own words.

5 What do you think the value of theory is for sociology?

Reading 2.7 **Defending sociology from its critics**

Anthony Giddens (from) *In Defence of Sociology: Essays, interpretations and rejoinders* (1996) Cambridge: Polity, pp. 1–7. [This article first appeared as 'In Defence of Sociology' in the *New Statesman*, April 7 1995.]

Editorial comments

Giddens answers the critics of sociology in this piece – aimed more at a popular audience than a specialized sociology audience. He identifies the main worries people have about sociology and then goes on to defend the subject by illustrating its importance and possible futures.

In defence of sociology

THERE'S SOMETHING ABOUT sociology that raises hackles other academic subjects fail to reach. Economics may be the dismal science, full of obscure terms few can understand and seemingly irrelevant to the practical tasks of day-to-day life. Yet sociology is often indicted on all counts – diffuse and lacking a coherent subject-matter, as well as being jargon-ridden. What do you get when you cross a sociologist

with a member of the Mafia? An offer you can't understand.

What is it with sociology? Why is it so irritating to so many? Some sociologists might answer: ignorance; others: fear. Why fear? Well, because they like to think of their subject as a dangerous and discomfiting one. Sociology, they are prone to say, tends to subvert: it challenges our assumptions about ourselves as individuals and about the wider social contexts in which we live. It has a direct connection with political radicalism. In the 1960s, the discipline seemed to many to live up to this firebrand reputation.

In truth, however, even in the 1960s and early 1970s sociology wasn't intrinsically associated with the left, let alone with revolutionaries. It came in for a great deal of criticism from Marxists of various persuasions who, far from regarding the subject as subversive, saw it as the very epitome of the bourgeois order they found so distasteful.

In some aspects and situations of its development sociology has in fact a long history of being bound up with the political right. Max Weber, commonly regarded as one of its classical founders, inclined more to the right than to the left and was savagely critical of the self-proclaimed revolutionaries of his time. Vilfredo Pareto and Robert Michels both flirted with Italian fascism towards the end of their lives. Most sociologists have probably been liberals by temperament and political inclination: this was true of Emile Durkheim and in later generations of R. K. Merton, Talcott Parsons, Erving Goffman and Ralf Dahrendorf among many other prominent sociological thinkers.

Sociology has currently been going through a hard time in the very country where it has long been most well developed, the US. A prominent American sociologist, Irving Louis Horowitz, recently published a book entitled *The Decomposition of Sociology*, a work which he reports was 'more a matter of pain rather than pride to have felt the need to write'. The discipline, he argues, has gone sour. Three sociology departments, including a distinguished one, at Washington University, St Louis – where Horowitz himself once worked – have recently been closed down. Yale University houses the oldest sociology department in the United States: its resources have just been cut by almost half.

Undergraduate student numbers in sociology in the US have fallen substantially over the two decades since the 1970s – from a record high of 36,000 students in 1973 to below 15,000 in 1994. According to Horowitz, however, the travails of sociology aren't just expressed in declining student appeal. They are to do with the parlous intellectual state of the discipline. Sociology, he says, might not in the past have been linked to an overall political standpoint, but since the 1960s it has increasingly become so. The subject has become the home of the discontented, a gathering of groups with special agenda, from the proponents of gay rights to liberation theology. Sociology is decomposing because it has come to be just what its critics always saw it as, a pseudo-science; and because there has been an outflow of respectable, empirically-oriented social scientists into other, more narrowly defined areas – such as urban planning,

demography, criminology or jurisprudence. The deterioration of sociology doesn't imply the disintegration of social research, which is still flourishing in many domains; but much of such research has degenerated into pure empiricism, no longer guided by worthwhile theoretical perspectives. What has disappeared is the capacity of sociology to provide a unifying centre for the diverse branches of social research.

Shutting down of the sociology departments at Washington University and elsewhere has provoked a heated debate in the US – to which Horowitz's is one among a variety of contributions. William Julius Wilson, well-known for his writings on the urban poor, has argued that sociology has become too detached from issues on the public agenda and should focus its concerns on matters of practical policy. After all, as he says, there's hardly a dearth of social problems for sociologists to study, with the cities falling into ruin, division between white and black as rigid as they ever were and violent crime a commonplace.

Is sociology in the doldrums? And if so, is this in some sense a peculiarly American phenomenon or something that applies worldwide? Or was sociology perhaps always the rag-tail affair its critics have long proclaimed it to be?

Let's deal first of all with the old chestnut that sociology doesn't have a proper field of investigation. The truth of the matter is that the field of study of sociology, as understood by the bulk of its practitioners, is no more, but no less, clearly defined than that of any other academic area. Consider, for example, history. That discipline has an obvious subject-matter, it would seem – the past. But the past embraces everything! No clear or bounded field of study here, and history is every bit as driven by methodological disputes about its true nature as sociology has ever been.

Sociology is a generalizing discipline that concerns itself above all with modernity – with the character and dynamics of modern or industrialized societies. It shares many of its methodological strategies – and problems – not only with history but with the whole gamut of the social sciences. The more empirical issues it deals with are very real. Of all the social sciences, sociology bears most directly on the issues that concern us in our everyday lives – the development of modern urbanism, crime and punishment, gender, the family, religion, social and economic power.

Given that sociological research and thinking are more or less indispensable in contemporary society, it is difficult to make sense of the criticism that it is unenlightening – that it is common sense wrapped up in somewhat unattractive jargon. Although specific pieces of research could always be questioned, no one could argue that there is no point in carrying out, say, comparative studies of the incidence of divorce in different countries. Sociologists engage in all sorts of research which, once one has some awareness of them, would prove interesting, and be thought important, by most reasonably neutral observers.

There is, however, another, more subtle reason why sociology may appear quite often to proclaim what is obvious to common sense. This is that social research doesn't, and can't, remain separate from the social world it describes. Social research forms so much a part of our consciousness today that we take it for granted. All of us depend upon such research for what we regard *as* common sense – as 'what everyone knows'. Everyone knows, for example, that divorce rates are high in today's society; yet such 'obvious knowledge', of course, depends upon regular social research, whether it happens to be carried out by government researchers or academic sociologists.

It is therefore to some degree the fate of sociology to be taken as less original and less central to our social existence than actually it is. Not only empirical research but sociological theorizing and sociological concepts can become so much part of our everyday repertoire as to appear as 'just common sense'. Many people, for instance, now ask whether a leader has charisma, discuss moral panics or talk of someone's social status – all notions that originated in sociological discourse.

These considerations, obviously, don't help with the issue of whether sociology as an academic discipline is in a state of sorry decline or even dissolution since its heyday in the 1960s, if that period was indeed its apogee. Things *have* changed in sociology over the past thirty years, but not all for the worse. For one thing, the centre of power has shifted, but it does so no longer. Especially so far as sociological theorizing is concerned, the centre of gravity has shifted elsewhere, particularly to Europe. The major sociological thinkers now are over here rather than over there, authors like Pierre Bourdieu, Niklas Luhmann or Ulrich Beck.

Sociology in the US appears to have become over-professionalized, with research groups concentrating on their own patch, having little knowledge of, or interest in, anyone else's. Everyone in American sociology has a 'field' and whatever the sociologist's specialty happens to be effectively defines that identity. Quantophrenia is rife in American sociology departments. For many if you can't count it, it doesn't count; the result, to say the least, can be a certain lack of creativity.

There's a good deal of justification for William Julius Wilson's advice to sociologists to engage in research immediately relevant to public policy issues and to participate forcefully in the wide debates their work may arouse. After all, many questions raised in the political arena are sociological – questions to do, for instance, with welfare, crime or the family. Sociological work is relevant, not just to their formulation as particular types of policy question, but to grasping the likely consequences of whatever policies might be initiated in relation to them.

Reconnecting sociology to a public policy-making agenda wouldn't address the other issues raised about the so-called decline of sociology. What of the disaggregation of sociology, of which Horowitz makes so much? Is it a discipline without a common conceptual core, in danger of breaking up into unconnected specialties? And have the most innovative authors moved elsewhere? Most important of all, perhaps, has it lost its cutting edge?

If one compares sociology to economics, it has to be conceded that sociology is much more internally diverse. In economics there exists a variety of different schools of thought and theoretical approaches, but the neo-classical view tends to dominate almost everywhere and forms the basic stuff of virtually all introductory texts. Sociology isn't to the same degree in the thrall of a single conceptual system. However, this surely should be seen more as a strength than a weakness. I don't believe such diversity has produced complete disarray, but instead gives voice to the pluralism that must exist when one studies something as complex and controversial as human social behaviour and institutions.

Is there any evidence that talented scholars who might once have been attracted to working in sociology have now migrated elsewhere? There's no doubt that in the 1960s some were drawn into sociology because they saw it, if not offering a route to revolution, as trendy and new; and it doesn't have that reputation any longer. But most such individuals probably weren't interested in a career within the confines of the academy. More relevant are factors that have affected the academic world as a whole, not sociology in particular. Many talented people who might once have gone into academic life probably won't do so today, because academic salaries have fallen sharply in relative terms over the last two decades and working conditions have deteriorated.

Yet a good cause could actually be made for saying that British sociology is doing better than in previous generations. Compare, for instance, the fortunes of sociology in Britain over recent years with those of anthropology. In the early postwar period, this country boasted anthropologists of worldwide reputation; no crop of comparably distinguished sociological authors was to be found at that time.

Now things are more or less reversed. There are few, if any, anthropologists of the current generation who can match the achievements of the preceding one. British sociology, however, can offer a clutch of individuals with a worldwide reputation, such as John Goldthorpe, Steven Lukes, Stuart Hall, Michèle

Barrett, Ray Pahl, Janet Wolff and Michael Mann.

Moreover, in sheer statistical terms, sociology is not in decline in this country in the way it has been in the US. A-level sociology is extremely popular and flourishing rather than shrinking. University admissions in sociology are, at worst, stable in relation to other subjects.

Everything in the sociological garden isn't rosy – although was it ever? Funding for social research has dropped off sharply since the early 1970s; there isn't the scale of empirical work there once was. But it would be difficult to argue that sociology is off the pace intellectually, especially if one broadens the angle again and moves back to a more international perspective. Most of the debates that grab the intellectual headlines today, across the social sciences, and even the humanities, carry a strong sociological input. Sociological authors have pioneered discussions of post-modernism, the post-industrial or information society, globalization, the transformation of everyday life, gender and sexuality, the changing nature of work and the family, the 'underclass' and ethnicity.

You might still ask: what do all these changes add up to? Here there is a lot of sociological work to be done. Some of that work has to be investigatory or empirical, but some must be theoretical. More than any other intellectual endeavour, sociological reflection is central to grasping the social forces remaking our lives today. Social life has become episodic, fragmentary and dogged with new uncertainties, which it must be the business of creative sociological thought to help us understand. William Julius Wilson's argument is certainly important: sociologists should focus their attention on the practical and policy-making implications of the changes currently transforming social life. Yet sociology would indeed become dreary, and quite possibly disaggregated, if it didn't also concern itself with the big issues.

Sociology should rehone its cutting edge, as neo-liberalism disappears into the distance along with orthodox socialism. Some questions to which we need new answers have a perennial quality, while others are dramatically new. Tackling both of these, as in previous times, calls for a healthy dose of what C. Wright Mills famously called the sociological imagination. Sociologists, don't despair! You still have a world to win, or at least interpret.

Questions

1 Identify the criticisms made about sociology within the extract.

2 What does Giddens say about the current situation for sociology?

3 Why might some people fear sociology?

4 What possible futures does Giddens identify for sociology?

Reading 2.8 **Malestream sociology**

Pamela Abbott and Claire Wallace (from) *An Introduction to Sociology: Feminist perspectives* (1997) 2nd edn, London: Routledge, pp. 1–6.

Editorial comments

For Abbott and Wallace traditional sociology is seen as 'malestream' – it is male knowledge based upon the male experience in society and controlled by male sociologists in high academic positions. Through a feminist perspective, Abbott and Wallace seek to expose this malestream bias and to give women a voice through sociological investigation.

Feminist critiques of malestream sociology, and the way forward

Setting the agenda

SOCIOLOGY REMAINS A male-dominated discipline, and this has fundamental implications for its theories, methods, research and teaching. Despite some thirty years' criticism of the discipline for its **malestream** orientation and bias, much remains the same. While the majority of students taking the subject are women, a majority of lecturers are male. Women are less often found in the senior posts in the discipline, and women are taught 'malestream' sociology – that is, they are inducted into knowledge that plays a key role in justifying the inferior structural position of (the majority of) women in modern British society. Ann Oakley suggested in 1974 that:

male orientation may so colour the organization of sociology as a discipline that the invisibility of women is a structured male view, rather than a superficial flaw. The male focus, incorporated into the definitions of subject areas, reduces women to a side issue from the start.
(Oakley, 1974)

However, there has been some progress. Sociologists can no longer afford to ignore women and gender divisions, and there is discussion about the changes needed for the malestream bias to be overcome. There has been a steady flow of books published by women writing from feminist perspectives in sociology, and most academic social science publishers have a Feminist, Gender or Women's Studies list. However, much sociological research continues to focus on men and boys and to ignore women and girls or to incorporate women but without modifying the theories that justified their subordinate status. There is still a tendency, albeit a declining one, to generalize from male samples to the whole population, for textbooks to 'add women on' as an appendix – an extra topic or chapter – rather than fully incorporating research findings on women in each substantive area, and for feminist perspectives to be seen as an addendum deserving at most one or two lectures or something that can safely be left for women to teach as an option course. The very success of this textbook indicates that there has been a demand for an alternative perspective. It is now the case that in Britain and the USA few courses in sociology could be designed without at least some recognition of feminist perspectives, while journal articles and research designs are routinely required by their reviewers to problematize gender, or to include a gender perspective. Indeed, in the Anglo–American cultures feminist perspectives are more developed and more influential in sociology than in most other social science disciplines. Sociology nevertheless remains a male-dominated discipline, and in many other parts of the world a gender perspective is marginalized, missing or (as in the former Communist countries) treated with outright hostility.

Within Western sociology we can identify a number of malestream responses/defences to feminist sociology – at one extreme ghettoization, and at the other, colonization and theft.

By ghettoization we mean the marginalization of feminist sociology as something the female lecturers can do or that can be taught on Women's Studies courses. While gender divisions may be accepted as important, gender is added on as another variable along with class and race; the serious challenge posed by feminists to malestream theories is ignored or distanced. In the main, men do not teach on these courses – possibly because they are not seen as prestigious or likely to lead to promotion.

At the other extreme we find colonization and theft

– the development of male studies and the argument that men need to study men in a way analogous to the way in which women have argued the need to study women. Seidler (1994), for example, has argued that issues of gender and masculinity are now central to social theory. Dianne Richardson and Victoria Robinson (1994) suggest that the development of male studies may actually enable men to avoid taking seriously the key issues about masculinity that feminists have highlighted. They point out that men's studies is mainly concerned with masculine subjectivity rather than with research that would provide a greater understanding of how men gain, maintain and use power to subordinate women. Indeed, men's studies is conceived as concerned with liberating men. As Jalna Hanmer has suggested,

To conceive of the study of men to be about liberating men is to have little interest in any area of social analysis that seriously critiques men as men, as part of the problem, not just to women and each other but to society and our continuation as a species.
(Hanmer, 1990)

The other move has been to rename Women's Studies or to develop new courses entitled 'Gender Studies'. Indeed, some publishers have changed the name of their list from Women's Studies to Gender Studies (Richardson and Robinson, 1994). Similarly some courses have been retitled Gender Studies rather than Women's Studies. In some (many) cases this has not changed the content of courses – the concern has been to recognize that feminist research and theorizing are not just on women and for women but must include an analysis of women in relationship to men, and that if women are to be liberated men must change. However, in others the change involves the notion that it is as important to study men as women, and fails to recognize the ways in which malestream disciplines, including sociology, have been implicated in the subordination of women. As Richardson and Robinson point out, the move towards gender studies 'represents a de-radicalization of women's studies, taking the heat off patriarchy' (1994). The danger is that the key insights and challenges to malestream sociology made by feminists will be diluted. The key issue for feminists is not that gender divides – that differences between men and women need to be taken seriously – but that the subordination and exploitation of women (albeit recognizing differences and divisions *between* women) need to be explained and overcome. In other words, an awareness needs to be maintained that the subjectivity of women has to be understood in a structural relationship with men – a relationship of subordination and exploitation.

The feminist challenge to malestream sociology is

one that requires a radical rethinking of the content and methodology of the whole enterprise, one that recognizes the need to see society from the position of women as well as from the standpoint of men – to see the world as fundamentally gendered. Indeed, it is the feminist challenge to sociology that has been instrumental in triggering the now almost taken-for-granted understanding that there is a variety of standpoints – gendered, racialized, disabled, sexualized, aged – that need to be recognized; we need not only to deconstruct 'human' into men and women, but also to deconstruct these categories themselves.

Thus many of the criticisms we have made above apply as much, if not more, to questions of ethnicity. Sociology is a discipline that has been and is dominated by white males who are middle-class by destination if not by origin. Women have come into the discipline and challenged the blinkered view of malestream sociology, but they too have tended to be white. Racialized women have criticized many white feminist sociologists for their one-sided view; racialized people are even more under-represented in the discipline than white women. Acutely aware of this, we have attempted to incorporate material on racialization and ethnic divisions and to explore theories which have tried to analyse these processes. Other forms of diversity have also emerged as important – differences based upon age, upon disability, upon sexuality. These other forms of social division – of oppression and disadvantage – have emerged partly as a result of the space created by a feminist politics. ...

As soon as we take the feminist criticisms of malestream sociology seriously we realize that we need to ask new, different questions and that in order to answer them we need to develop new tools, new concepts and new theories. This is because malestream sociology has in the main seen women's roles as natural and therefore not investigated or problematized them; sociology's tools, concepts and theories have been developed to investigate the public world of men and are inadequate for investigating the world that women inhabit and the relationships between men and women. Questions such as 'Why don't men care for children?', 'Why do men and not women have leisure?', become key issues to be researched and theorized in malestream research, and the methods used in malestream research are seen to be inadequate for investigating women's lives.

Britain is increasingly integrated into Europe and more European material is becoming available. We have therefore tried to include comparative material where possible, including some comparison between Eastern and Western Europe. Although some issues – such as women's oppression within the family – are as important in other parts of the world as in Britain,

they are often treated differently. Hence, although domestic violence is usually a consequence of women failing to fulfil their wifely duties, just what these wifely duties are can vary considerably throughout the world. In some countries women may be attacked because their families failed to supply them with the full dowry, whereas in other countries women are attacked for failing to cook or clean or manage the housekeeping budget adequately. Many of the issues are the same. In Eastern Europe women were not liberated by their entry into the working world, although Western feminists had seen this as the road to independence. However, in order to understand why women are disadvantaged in the work force under both Communism and capitalism we need to use feminist perspectives.

The sociological imagination

Sociology is about understanding the relationship between our own experiences and the social structures we inhabit. However, in the 1960s and 1970s women began to express the feeling that sociology did not relate to their experiences, because it examined the world only from the perspective of men. Indeed, existing theories and explanations could be challenged, they argued, if the perspective of women was also taken into account. The realization of this failure of sociology to speak to the experiences of women, and its consequent failure to theorize comprehensively, led feminists to examine more closely why this was the case – why sociology, despite its claims to neutrality, had a malestream bias. Dorothy Smith (1979) argued that this was because women's concerns and experiences were not seen as authentic, but subjective, while men's were seen as the basis for the production of true knowledge. Consequently, sociological knowledge portrayed women as men saw them, not as they saw themselves. Sociology also played a key role in maintaining women's subordinate and exploited position. While sociology claimed to put forward a detached and impartial view of reality, in fact it put forward a view from the perspective of men.

It has been argued that women are relegated by political theory, by sociology and within other disciplines to a more 'natural' role, one tied to their biology and to nature, while men are seen as more part of the cultural life of society – cultured man/natural woman. French feminists have argued that women constitute the 'Other' against which culture, society, men and so on are constructed. Thus women are gendered but men are not. Men are seen as part of universal rationality – those who analyse and understand the world from a scientific perspective – and women are the ones who need explaining or 'bringing in'. Arguments for the special perspective and understanding of women often reinforce this point of view. Women are seen as subject to a special perspective which is rooted in the unique experiences of their bodies, of motherhood and menstruation, which are different from that of men. Some feminists have therefore argued that differences between men and women are rooted in the biological differences of bodily development, while others argue that differences between men and women are a cultural construction.

We would prefer to argue that gendering is a process whereby jobs, activities and people are 'sexualized' just as they can become 'racialized'; biological differences are used *post hoc* to justify subordination and exploitation and are not the *basis* of the original differentiation. This is not a fixed process but is culturally and socially variable, so that to be understood it needs to be subjected to sociological analysis.

References

Hanmer, J. (1990) 'Men, power and the exploitation of women', in Hearn, J. and Morgan, D. (eds) *Men, Masculinities and Social Theory*, London: Unwin Hyman.

Oakley, A. (1974) *The Sociology of Housework*, London: Martin Robertson.

Richardson, D. and Robertson, V. (1994) 'Theorising Women's Studies, Gender Studies and masculinity: the politics of naming', *European Journal of Women's Studies, 1*, pp. 11–27.

Seidler, V. J. (1994) *Unreasonable Men*, London: Routledge.

Smith, D. E. (1979) 'A peculiar eclipse: women's exclusion from men's culture', *Women's Studies International Quarterly, 1*, pp. 281–95.

Key term

The following key term appears in the text above. It has been defined below to aid with the reading of this item.

malestream the belief held by some feminists that sociology ignores women

Questions

1 According to Abbott and Wallace what are the key problems with traditional sociological thought?

2 What do Abbott and Wallace mean by the 'ghettoization' and 'marginalization' of feminist sociology?

3 Why do you think malestream bias might have occurred in sociology?

4 Suggest ways of getting over the problems of malestream bias.

Further reading

The following texts may represent a useful starting point for further investigation of the ideas contained within this chapter.

For a good summary of the origins of sociology and its classical inheritance, see the introductory chapter of:

Worsley, P. (1987) *The New Introducing Sociology*, 3rd edn, Harmondsworth: Penguin.

For an accessible introduction to many major concerns of sociology written by one of today's important sociological thinkers, see:

Giddens, A. (1986) *Sociology: a brief but critical introduction*, 2nd edn, London: Macmillan.

Equally, for the reader interested in social theorizing from classical to modern thinkers, see:

Giddens, A. (1995) *Politics, Sociology and Social Theory*, Cambridge: Polity.

3

Sociological theory

Chapter summary

Reading 3.1 **Marxism: a basic outline** *page 33*
The Manifesto of the Communist Party was purposely written to reach a large audience. It contains the basic viewpoint of Marxism, suggesting capitalism is characterized by class conflict which is also the key motor of historical change.

Reading 3.2 **Weber and the role of ideas in history** *page 38*
Max Weber's book *The Protestant Ethic and the Spirit of Capitalism* outlined in detail his view that ideas can cause change as well as material factors, leaving this work to also stand as an implicit critique of the Marxist theory of history

Reading 3.3 **Durkheim and the abnormal division of labour** *page 42*
Emile Durkheim's first book, *The Division of Labour in Society*, emphasizes his desire to understand the social consequences of economic change, and in particular the impact on social solidarity of the growth of individualism. The work also contains a clear critique by Durkheim of the individualistic free-market ideas which form the basis of the contemporary New Right.

Reading 3.4 **The emergence of neo-functionalism** *page 46*
A very recent trend in sociology has been a revival of interest in the work of Talcott Parsons and an attempt to reformulate functionalism in the light of the criticisms of the original version. One of the leading advocates of this neo-functionalism is Jeffrey Alexander.

Reading 3.5 **Power/knowledge** *page 50*
Michel Foucault presents his distinctive view on the way knowledge and claims to the truth are really all examples of a power struggle which is omnipresent, that is, always present and never able to be solved. His views echo the earlier philosophy of Nietzsche. This section comprises his answers in an interview.

Reading 3.6 **Against post-modernism** *page 54*
Alex Callinicos is one of the most consistent opponents of the trend in sociology known as post-modernism. Here he argues that the emergence of post-modernism reflects the growth of overconsumptionism among the rich, and the transition from Marxism to liberalism of the generation that grew up in the upheavals of the 1960s.

Reading 3.7 **Structuration theory** *page 59*
At the basis of Anthony Giddens' general theory of structuration, which is a complex attempt to overcome the structure/action duality which has been at the heart of sociology, is his argument that social structures need to be seen as enabling and not simply constraining. In order to do this he offers a somewhat unorthodox view of what constitutes social structures.

Reading 3.8 **Sylvia Walby and the theory of patriarchy** *page 63*
Patriarchy is the central concept in feminist sociology and Sylvia Walby has worked on producing a detailed outline of the working of this concept and the way it interacts with other structures such as capitalism.

Introduction: Reading sociological theory

You cannot have sociology without sociological theory, since it provides the key concepts and models which allow us to make sense of the massive number of facts about society which can be collected. Theory is even involved in the collection of these facts, since in order to decide which facts to collect, that is, which questions to ask, you need to think about society or the particular aspect of society you are studying. This

is really all theory is, though the large-scale overarching notions of how society operates, which are characteristic of classical sociology, is sometimes known as 'grand theory'. Whichever brand of theory, anyone who thinks about the nature of society is theorizing and as a result you cannot do sociology without doing some sociological theory. You could compare your view of what makes society work with the views presented below and become a theorist yourself.

Sociological theory has come a long way since the time when sociology seemed to consist merely of a debate between functionalism and Marxism, with a side irritant of interactionism. Despite this, the key themes evident in those debates are still being considered today and sociological theory still, therefore, reaches back to the classics of Marx, Durkheim and Weber.

For this reason, this chapter starts with selections from the key works of each of these thinkers. In *The Manifesto of the Communist Party*, Marx and Engels (1848) (**reading 3.1**) scripted a document purposely intended to convey their view of the world to a larger audience, and with the aim of helping build an international communist movement. It summarises the key themes and concepts which later Marxist theory has built upon, notably class analysis, class conflict and the materialist conception of history.

In *The Protestant Ethic and the Spirit of Capitalism*, Max Weber (1905) (**reading 3.2**) considered the role of ideas in historical transformation, in this case, religious ideas. His work serves as a critique of the Marxist materialist conception of history, and is one of the most important examples of the influence on sociology of philosophical idealism (the belief that the ideas people hold are the most important basis of their actions). As a comment on the sociology of religion, the work is still debated today, but its significance as a counterblast to materialism (the belief that basic material needs are the key motivating basis of human action) goes wider than that, asking us to consider the relative importance of material facts and ideas on human action and the course of history.

In *The Division of Labour in Society*, Emile Durkheim (1897) (**reading 3.3**) sought to outline the consequences for society of a change in economic production techniques. The book (his first) reflects Durkheim's fear that society may be in danger of falling apart and outlines his belief that intervention by the state may be necessary to avoid this. It therefore reflects Durkheim's critique of free-market theories, and since these form the cornerstone of contemporary New Right thinking, his work has great contemporary relevance.

The rest of the chapter seeks to show examples of more recent developments in sociological thinking, which, however, can nonetheless be traced back to the debates that motivated the founders of the subject.

The demise of Parsonian functionalism occurred in the 1970s, though it is still the subject of exam questions today. In the meantime, the critique of functionalism offered by the varieties of conflict theory, ended its dominance in sociological theory. However in the 1990s, we have seen the emergence of neo-functionalism, building on suggested weaknesses within conflict theory itself and trying to rescue what is seen as still valuable in the original functionalist theory. It is however a distinctive and more sophisticated brand of thinking, which nonetheless reflects the seeming re-emergence of concern with Parsons' (1937, 1951) work. Jeffrey Alexander (1985) is a leading exponent of neo-functionalism and here (**reading 3.4**) he provides an outline of some of its key beliefs.

The 1980s were dominated to some extent by varieties of Marxism, notably the structural Marxism of Louis Althusser (1966, 1968, 1971) and the somewhat different Marxism of Antonio Gramsci (1971, 1977). It is the collapse of the former approach that has led to the emergence and growing dominance of views associated with post-structuralism, and it is an interpretation of the latter that has provided much impetus for the growth of post-modernism. Together these ideas dominated sociology in the early 1990s. One of the most influential thinkers associated with this broad current of thinking is the French social thinker, Michel Foucault (1967, 1970, 1980). Central to his work is the conception of power/knowledge which questions whether it is ever possible to arrive at the truth, or whether claims to the truth are simply power struggles. In this extract (**reading 3.5**) from an interview with Foucault, he talks about the problems in the notion of science as a search for the truth, the view that emerged as a result of the set of ideas that developed in the period known as the Enlightenment – which occurred broadly in the seventeenth and eighteenth centuries, and was characterized by a belief in reason and the rejection of traditional authority, both political and religious – a movement that inspired sociology, and the rejection of which is a central tenet of post-modernist approaches to sociology.

The next reading is from a writer critical of the post-modern approach. Callinicos (1989) (**reading 3.6**) is a Marxist who argues that post-modernism is an internally contradictory set of ideas whose emergence reflects the growth of affluent groups in the Thatcher and Reagan periods in the 1980s and their concern to justify their over-indulgence in 'the good things in life' while allowing them to ignore the problems caused by consumerism and late capitalism. Another alternative to post-modernism is offered by Rob Stones (1996) who argues that the post-modern notion that we cannot arrive at any truths offers a very defeatist agenda for sociology, but he also rejects as complacent some critiques of post-modernism. He argues that we can move forward in sociology as long as we deal with the philosophical problems raised by post-structuralism and post-modernism and also recognize the validity of the notion of reflexivity in sociological thinking. He advocates the development of a 'past-modern' sociology.

Reflexivity is about the recognition that as human beings, we think about and monitor our own actions and this makes us different from other research subjects, most notably the research subjects of the natural sciences. Reflexivity owes its existence to the influence of action-orientated sociology derived ultimately from Weber. Its growth reflects the demise of more structurally-orientated sociology (classically: Marxism and functionalism) and its emergence has reopened the perennial sociological debate about the relative importance of social structures and social action in the make-up of society. Recent theoretical developments have often sought to try to theorize the links between these two approaches to try to overcome this problem. One of the most influential is the development of structuration theory by Anthony Giddens (1984). This extract (**reading 3.7**), taken from his book *The Constitution of Society*, concerns his argument about the enabling, as well as constraining, power of social structures.

The 1980s and 1990s have also seen the emergence of a distinctively feminist sociology, arising originally from the rise of the women's liberation movement in the 1970s. A key concept utilized by feminist sociologists is that of patriarchy and in this extract (**reading 3.8**), Sylvia Walby (1990) considers some of the issues involved in fleshing out this concept to provide a general theory of the way society operates, and how power structures exist which reinforce gender inequalities.

As stated, it is hoped that the selection of readings in this chapter offers a picture of some of the more recent influences on the contemporary development of sociological theory – meaning you do not have to rely solely on theories from the 1940s and 1950s anymore.

Since any kind of sociology at all must at some stage involve thinking about the nature of society, sociological theory underlies all other work in sociology, and so the readings in this chapter point towards developments and arguments that feature in other chapters in this book. This is as it should be since, as already mentioned, sociological theory underlies all sociology.

References

Althusser, L. with Balibar, E. (1966) *For Marx*, London: Allen Lane.

Althusser, L. (1968) *Reading Capital*, London: New Left Books.

Althusser, L. (1971) *Lenin and Philosophy and Other Essays*, London: New Left Books.

Foucault, M. (1967) *Madness and Civilization*, London: Tavistock.

Foucault, M. (1970) *The Order of Things*, London: Tavistock.

Foucault, M. (1980) *Power/Knowledge: Selected interviews and other writings 1972–1977*, Brighton: Harvester.

Gramsci, A. (1971) *Selections from the Prison Notebooks* (edited by Q. Hoare) London: Lawrence & Wishart.

Gramsci, A. (1977) *Selections from Political Writings, 1910–1920* (edited by Q. Hoare) London: Lawrence & Wishart.

Parsons, T. (1937) *The Structure of Social Action*, Glencoe: Free Press.

Parsons, T. (1951) *The Social System*, London: Routledge & Kegan Paul.

Stones, R. (1996) *Sociological Reasoning: Towards a postmodern sociology*, Basingstoke: Macmillan.

Reading 3.1 **Marxism: a basic outline**

Karl Marx and Friedrich Engels (from) 'The Manifesto of the Communist Party', in K. Marx and F. Engels, *Selected Works in One Volume* (1968, originally published in 1848) London: Lawrence & Wishart, pp. 35–44.

Editorial comments

This is rightfully the first document that people look to in order to understand the Marxist view of society. It was originally drawn up as a manifesto for the Communist League, an international association of workers, following a congress held in London in November 1847. The first section outlines the way that history can be understood on the basis of a materialist analysis centred on class struggle and, as such, contains an outline of key Marxist concepts.

Manifesto of the Communist Party

Bourgeois and proletarians

THE HISTORY OF all hitherto existing society is the history of **class struggles**.

Freeman and slave, patrician and plebeian, lord and serf, guild-master and journeyman, in a word, oppressor and oppressed, stood in constant opposition to one another, carried on an uninterrupted, now hidden, now open fight, a fight that each time ended, either in a revolutionary re-constitution of society at large, or in the common ruin of the contending classes.

In the earlier epochs of history, we find almost everywhere a complicated arrangement of society into various orders, a manifold gradation of social rank. In ancient Rome we have patricians, knights, plebeians, slaves; in the Middle Ages, feudal lords, vassals, guild-masters, journeymen, apprentices, serfs; in almost all of these classes, again, subordinate gradations.

The modern bourgeois society that has sprouted from the ruins of **feudal society** has not done away with class antagonisms. It has but established new classes, new conditions of oppression, new forms of struggle in place of the old ones.

Our epoch, the epoch of the bourgeoisie, possesses, however, this distinctive feature: it has simplified the **class** antagonisms. Society as a whole is more and more splitting up into two great hostile camps, into two great classes directly facing each other: Bourgeoisie and Proletariat. ...

The feudal system of industry, under which industrial production was monopolized by closed guilds, now no longer sufficed for the growing wants of the new markets. The manufacturing system took its place. The guild-masters were pushed on one side by the manufacturing middle class; division of labour between the different corporate guilds vanished in the face of division of labour in each single workshop.

Meantime the markets kept ever growing, the demand ever rising. Even manufacture no longer sufficed. Thereupon, steam and machinery revolutionized industrial production. The place of manufacture was taken by the giant, Modern Industry, the place of the industrial middle class, by industrial millionaires, the leaders of whole industrial armies, the modern bourgeois.

Modern industry has established the world-market, for which the discovery of America paved the way. This market has given an immense development to commerce, to navigation, to communication by land. This development has, in its turn, reacted on the extension of industry; and in proportion as industry, commerce, navigation, railways extended, in the same proportion the bourgeoisie developed, increased its capital, and pushed into the background every class handed down from the Middle Ages.

We see, therefore, how the modern bourgeoisie is itself the product of a long course of development, of a series of revolutions in the modes of production of exchange.

Each step in the development of the bourgeoisie was accompanied by a corresponding political advance of that class ... the bourgeoisie has at last, since the establishment of Modern Industry and of the world-market, conquered for itself, in the modern representative State, exclusive political sway. The executive of the modern State is but a committee for managing the common affairs of the whole bourgeoisie.

The bourgeoisie, historically, has played a most revolutionary part.

The bourgeoisie, wherever it has got the upper hand, has put an end to all feudal, patriarchal, idyllic relations. It has pitilessly torn asunder the motley feudal ties that bound man to his 'natural superiors,' and has left remaining no other nexus between man and man than naked self-interest, than callous 'cash payment'. It has drowned the most heavenly ecstasies of religious fervour, of chivalrous enthusiasm of philistine sentimentalism, in the icy water of egotistical calculation. It has resolved personal worth into exchange value, and in place of the numberless indefeasible chartered freedoms, has set up that single, unconscionable freedom – Free Trade. In one word, for exploitation, veiled by religious and political illusions, it has substituted naked, shameless, direct, brutal exploitation.

The bourgeoisie has stripped of its halo every occupation hitherto honoured and looked up to with reverent awe. It has converted the physician, the lawyer, the priest, the poet, the man of science, into its paid wage-labourers.

The bourgeoisie has torn away from the family its sentimental veil, and has reduced the family relation to a mere money relation. ...

The bourgeoisie cannot exist without constantly revolutionizing the instruments of production, and thereby the relations of production, and with them the whole relations of society. Conservation of the old modes of production in unaltered form, was, on the contrary, the first condition of existence for all earlier industrial classes. Constant revolutionizing of production, uninterrupted disturbance of all social conditions, everlasting uncertainty and agitation distinguish the bourgeois epoch from all earlier ones. All fixed, fast-frozen relations, with their train of ancient and venerable prejudices and opinions, are swept away, all new-formed ones become antiquated before they can ossify. All that is solid melts into air, all that is holy is profaned, and man is at last compelled to face with sober senses, his real conditions of life, and his relations with his kind.

The need of a constantly expanding market for its products chases the bourgeoisie over the whole surface of the globe. It must nestle everywhere, settle everywhere, establish connections everywhere.

The bourgeoisie has through its exploitation of the world-market given a cosmopolitan character to production and consumption in every country. To the great chagrin of Reactionists, it has drawn from under the feet of industry the national ground on which it stood. All old-established national industries have been destroyed or are daily being destroyed. They are dislodged by new industries, whose introduction becomes a life and death question for all civilized nations, by industries that no longer work up indigenous raw material, but raw material drawn from the remotest zones; industries whose products are consumed, not only at home, but in every quarter of the globe. In place of the old wants, satisfied by the productions of the country, we find new wants, requiring for their satisfaction the products of distant lands and climes. In place of the old local and national seclusion and self-sufficiency, we have intercourse in every direction, universal inter-dependence of nations. And as in material, so also in intellectual production. The intellectual creations of individual nations become common property. National one-sidedness and narrow-mindedness become more and more impossible, and from the numerous national and local literatures, there arises a world literature.

The bourgeoisie, by the rapid improvement of all instruments of production, by the immensely facilitated means of communication, draws all, even the most barbarian, nations into civilization. The cheap prices of its commodities are the heavy artillery with which it batters down all Chinese walls, with which it forces the barbarians' intensely obstinate hatred of foreigners to capitulate. It compels all nations, on pain of extinction, to adopt the bourgeois mode of production; it compels them to introduce what it calls civilization into their midst, i.e., to become bourgeois themselves. In one word, it creates a world after its own image. ...

The bourgeoisie, during its rule of scarce one hundred years, has created more massive and more colossal productive forces than have all preceding generations together. Subjection of Nature's forces to man, machinery, application of chemistry to industry and agriculture, steam-navigation, railways, electric telegraphs, clearing of whole continents for cultivation, canalization of rivers, whole populations conjured out of the ground – what earlier century had even a presentiment that such productive forces slumbered in the lap of social labour?

We see then: the means of production and of exchange, on whose foundation the bourgeoisie built itself up, were generated in feudal society. At a certain stage in the development of these means of production and of exchange, the conditions under which feudal society produced and exchanged, the feudal organization of agriculture and manufacturing industry, in one word, the feudal relations of property became no longer compatible with the already developed productive forces; they became so many fetters. They had to be burst asunder; they were burst asunder.

Into their place stepped free competition, accompanied by a social and political constitution adapted to it, and by the economical and political sway of the bourgeois class.

A similar movement is going on before our own eyes. Modern bourgeois society with its relations of production, of exchange and of property, a society that has conjured up such gigantic means of production and of exchange, is like the sorcerer, who is no longer able to control the powers of the nether world whom he has called up by his spells. For many a decade past the history of industry and commerce is but the history of the revolt of modern productive forces against modern conditions of production, against the property relations that are the conditions for the existence of the bourgeoisie and of its rule. It is enough to mention the commercial crises that by their periodical return put on its trial, each time more threateningly, the existence of the entire bourgeois society. In these crises a great part not only of the existing products, but also of the previously created productive forces, are periodically destroyed. In these crises there breaks out an epidemic that, in all earlier epochs, would have seemed an absurdity – the epidemic of over-production. Society suddenly finds itself put back into a stage of momentary barbarism; it appears as if a famine, a universal war of devastation had cut off the supply of every means of subsistence; industry and commerce seem to be destroyed; and why? Because there is too much civilization, too much means of subsistence, too much industry, too much commerce. The productive forces at the disposal of society no longer tend to further the development of the conditions of bourgeois property; on the contrary, they have become too powerful for these conditions, by which they are fettered, and so soon as they overcome these fetters, they bring disorder into the whole of bourgeois society, endanger the existence of bourgeois property. The conditions of bourgeois society are too narrow to comprise the wealth created by them. And how does the bourgeoisie get over these crises? On the one hand by enforced destruction of a mass of productive forces; on the other, by the conquest of new markets, and by the more thorough exploitation of the old ones. That is to say, by paving the way for more extensive and more destructive crises, and by diminishing the means whereby crises are prevented.

The weapons with which the bourgeoisie felled feudalism to the ground are now turned against the bourgeoisie itself.

But not only has the bourgeoisie forged the weapons that bring death to itself; it has also called into existence the men who are to wield those weapons – the modern working class – the proletarians.

In proportion as the bourgeoisie, i.e., capital, is

developed, in the same proportion is the proletariat, the modern working class, developed – a class of labourers, who live only so long as they find work, and who find work only so long as their labour increases capital. These labourers, who must sell themselves piecemeal, are a commodity, like every other article of commerce, and are consequently exposed to all the vicissitudes of competition, to all the fluctuations of the market.

Owing to the extensive use of machinery and to division of labour, the work of the proletarians has lost all individual character, and, consequently, all charm for the workman. He becomes an appendage of the machine, and it is only the most simple, most monotonous, and most easily acquired knack, that is required of him. Hence, the cost of production of a workman is restricted, almost entirely, to the means of subsistence that he requires for his maintenance, and for the propagation of his race. But the price of a commodity, and therefore also of labour, is equal to its cost of production. In proportion, therefore, as the repulsiveness of the work increases, the wage decreases. Nay more, in proportion as the use of machinery and division of labour increases, in the same proportion the burden of toil also increases, whether by prolongation of the working hours, by increase of the work extracted in a given time or by increased speed of the machinery, etc.

Modern industry has converted the little workshop of the patriarchal master into the great factory of the industrial capitalist. Masses of labourers, crowded into the factory, are organized like soldiers. As privates of the industrial army they are placed under the command of a perfect hierarchy of officers and sergeants. Not only are they slaves of the bourgeois class, and of the bourgeois State; they are daily and hourly enslaved by the machine, by the overlooker, and, above all, by the individual bourgeois manufacturer himself. The more openly this despotism proclaims gain to be its end and aim, the more petty, the more hateful and the more embittering it is.

The less the skill and exertion of strength implied in manual labour, in other words, the more modern industry becomes developed, the more is the labour of men superseded by that of women. Differences of age and sex have no longer any distinctive social validity for the working class. All are instruments of labour, more or less expensive to use, according to their age and sex. ...

But with the development of industry the proletariat not only increases in number; it becomes concentrated in greater masses, its strength grows, and it feels that strength more. The various interests and conditions of life within the ranks of the proletariat are more and more equalized, in proportion as machinery obliterates all distinctions of labour, and nearly everywhere

reduces wages to the same low level. The growing competition among the bourgeois, and the resulting commercial crises, make the wages of the workers ever more fluctuating. The unceasing improvement of machinery, ever more rapidly developing, makes their livelihood more and more precarious; the collisions between individual workmen and individual bourgeois take more and more the character of collisions between two classes. Thereupon the workers begin to form combinations (Trades' Unions) against the bourgeois; they club together in order to keep up the rate of wages; they found permanent associations in order to make provision beforehand for these occasional revolts. Here and there the contest breaks out into riots.

Now and then the workers are victorious, but only for a time. The real fruit of their battles lies, not in the immediate result, but in the ever-expanding union of the workers. This union is helped on by the improved means of communication that are created by modern industry and that place the workers of different localities in contact with one another. It was just this contact that was needed to centralize the numerous local struggles, all of the same character, into one national struggle between classes. But every class struggle is a political struggle. And that union, to attain which the burghers of the Middle Ages, with their miserable highways, required centuries, the modern proletarians, thanks to railways, achieve in a few years.

This organization of the proletarians into a class, and consequently into a political party, is continually being upset again by the competition between the workers themselves. But it ever rises up again, stronger, firmer, mightier. It compels legislative recognition of particular interests of the workers, by taking advantage of the divisions among the bourgeoisie itself. Thus the ten-hours' bill in England was carried.

Altogether collisions between the classes of the old society further, in many ways, the course of development of the proletariat. The bourgeoisie finds itself involved in a constant battle. At first with the aristocracy; later on, with those portions of the bourgeoisie itself, whose interests have become antagonistic to the progress of industry; at all times, with the bourgeoisie of foreign countries. In all these battles it sees itself compelled to appeal to the proletariat, to ask for its help, and thus, to drag it into the political arena. The bourgeoisie itself, therefore, supplies the proletariat with its own elements of political and general education, in other words, it furnishes the proletariat with weapons for fighting the bourgeoisie.

Further, as we have already seen, entire sections of the ruling classes are, by the advance of industry, precipitated into the proletariat, or are at least threatened in their conditions of existence. These also supply the proletariat with fresh elements of enlightenment and progress.

Finally, in times when the class struggle nears the decisive hour, the process of dissolution going on within the ruling class, in fact within the whole range of old society, assumes such a violent, glaring character, that a small section of the ruling class cuts itself adrift, and joins the revolutionary class, the class that holds the future in its hands. Just as, therefore, at an earlier period, a section of the nobility went over to the bourgeoisie, so now a portion of the bourgeoisie goes over to the proletariat, and in particular, a portion of the bourgeois ideologists, who have raised themselves to the level of comprehending theoretically the historical movement as a whole.

Of all the classes that stand face to face with the bourgeoisie today, the proletariat alone is a really revolutionary class. The other classes decay and finally disappear in the face of Modern Industry; the proletariat is its special and essential product.

The lower middle class, the small manufacturer, the shopkeeper, the artisan, the peasant, all these fight against the bourgeoisie, to save from extinction their existence as fractions of the middle class. They are therefore not revolutionary, but conservative. Nay more, they are reactionary, for they try to roll back the wheel of history. If by chance they are revolutionary, they are so only in view of their impending transfer into the proletariat, they thus defend not their present, but their future interests, they desert their own standpoint to place themselves at that of the proletariat.

The 'dangerous class', the social scum, that passively rotting mass thrown off by the lowest layers of old society, may, here and there, be swept into the movement by a proletarian revolution, its conditions of life, however, prepare it far more for the part of a bribed tool of reactionary intrigue.

In the conditions of the proletariat, those of old society at large are already virtually swamped. The proletarian is without property; his relation to his wife and children has no longer anything in common with the bourgeois family-relations; modern, industrial labour, modern subjection to capital, the same in England as in France, in America as in Germany, has stripped him of every trace of national character. Law, morality, religion, are to him so many bourgeois prejudices, behind which lurk in ambush just as many bourgeois interests.

Key terms

The following key terms appear in the text above. They have been defined below to aid with the reading of this item.

class struggle the notion that in all existing societies production involves the exploitation of one group by another and this creates antagonistic classes who will struggle with each other over the surplus produced in the economic process

feudal society the economic and political system of the Middle Ages which existed before capitalism and was based on a ruling aristocracy, whose rule was based on ownership of the land and the mass of the population (serfs or peasants) who were required to provide free labour on the lord's land

class the key Marxist concept about which so much has been written that it is impossible to summarize it in a few lines, but all agree that it is a social relationship based on a particular relationship to work, production and the economic sphere

Questions

1 According to Marx and Engels, what is the distinctive feature of the 'epoch of the bourgeoisie'?

2 Explain in your own words why Marx and Engels consider the bourgeoisie to have played a revolutionary role in history.

3 Using material from the reading above and elsewhere, explain why Marx and Engels describe the modern state as 'but a committee for managing the common affairs of the whole bourgeoisie'.

4 Suggest three examples of the way the bourgeoisie has 'given a cosmopolitan character to production and consumption in every country'.

5 Explain and assess the statement that: 'Differences of age and sex have no longer any distinctive social validity for the working class'.

Reading 3.2 **Weber and the role of ideas in history**

Max Weber (from) *The Protestant Ethic and the Spirit of Capitalism* (1992, originally published in 1905) London: Routledge, pp. 13–14 and 16–27.

Editorial comments

As part of his comparative studies of religion, Weber considered some of the reasons why the leading lights in European society were Protestants. His investigation into the social effects of particular beliefs and ideas is a classic example of the idealist notion in sociology that ideas can have an important impact on social behaviour and social change. In this extract from the introduction of the book, Weber outlines the main themes of his work.

The Protestant ethic and the spirit of capitalism

A PRODUCT OF modern European civilization, studying any problem of universal history, is bound to ask himself to what combination of circumstances the fact should be attributed that in Western civilization, and in Western civilization only, cultural phenomena have appeared which (as we like to think) lie in a line of development having *universal* significance and value.

Only in the West does science exist at a stage of development which we recognize today as valid. Empirical knowledge, reflection on problems of the cosmos and of life, philosophical and theological wisdom of the most profound sort, are not confined to it, though in the case of the last the full development of a systematic theology must be credited to Christianity under the influence of Hellenism, since there were only fragments in Islam and in a few Indian sects. In short, knowledge and observation of great refinement have existed elsewhere, above all in India, China, Babylonia, Egypt. But in Babylonia and elsewhere astronomy lacked – which makes its development all the more astounding – the mathematical foundation which it first received from the Greeks. The Indian geometry had no **rational** proof; that was another product of the Greek intellect, also the creator of mechanics and physics. The Indian natural sciences, though well developed in observation, lacked the method of experiment, which was, apart from beginnings in antiquity, essentially a product of the **Renaissance**, as was the modern laboratory. Hence medicine, especially in India, though highly developed in empirical technique, lacked a biological and particularly a biochemical foundation. A rational chemistry has been absent from all areas of culture except the West.

The highly developed historical scholarship of China did not have the method of Thucydides. Machiavelli, it is true, had predecessors in India; but all Indian political thought was lacking in a systematic method comparable to that of Aristotle, and, indeed, in the possession of rational concepts. Not all the anticipations in India (School of Mimamsa), nor the extensive codification especially in the Near East, nor all the Indian and other books of law, had the strictly systematic forms of thought, so essential to a rational jurisprudence, of the Roman law and of the Western law under its influence. A structure like the canon law is known only to the West. ...

Organization of political and social groups in feudal classes has been common. But even the feudal state of *rex et regnum* in the Western sense has only been known to our culture. Even more are parliaments of periodically elected representatives, with government by demagogues and party leaders as ministers responsible to the parliaments, peculiar to us, although there have, of course, been parties, in the sense of organizations for exerting influence and gaining control of political power, all over the world. In fact, the State itself, in the sense of a political association with a rational, written constitution, rationally ordained law, and an administration bound to rational rules or laws, administered by trained officials, is known, in this combination of characteristics, only in the Occident, despite all other approaches to it.

And the same is true of the most fateful force in our modern life, capitalism. The impulse to acquisition, pursuit of gain, of money, of the greatest possible amount of money, has in itself nothing to do with capitalism. This impulse exists and has existed among waiters, physicians, coachmen, artists, prostitutes, dishonest officials, soldiers, nobles, crusaders, gamblers, and beggars. One may say that it has been common to all sorts and conditions of men at all times and in all countries of the earth, wherever the objective possibility of it is or has been given. It should be taught in the kindergarten of cultural history that this naïve idea of capitalism must be given up once and for all. Unlimited greed for gain is not in the least identical with capitalism, and is still less its spirit. Capitalism *may* even be identical with the restraint, or at least a rational tempering, of this irrational impulse. But capitalism is identical with the pursuit of profit, and forever *renewed* profit, by means of continuous, rational, capitalistic enterprise. For it must be so: in a wholly capitalistic order of society, an individual capitalistic enterprise which did not take advantage of its opportunities for profit-making would be doomed to extinction.

Let us now define our terms somewhat more carefully than is generally done. We will define a capitalistic economic action as one which rests on the expectation of profit by the utilization of opportunities for exchange, that is on (formally) peaceful chances of profit. Acquisition by force (formally and actually) follows its own particular laws, and it is not expedient, however little one can forbid this, to place it in the same category with action which is, in the last analysis, oriented to profits from exchange. Where capitalistic acquisition is rationally pursued, the corresponding action is adjusted to calculations in terms of capital. This means that the action is adapted to a systematic utilization of goods or personal services as means of acquisition in such a way that, at the close of a business period, the balance of the enterprise in money assets (or, in the case of a continuous enterprise, the periodically estimated money value of assets) exceeds the capital, i.e. the estimated value of the material means ... of production used for acquisition in exchange.

For the purpose of this conception all that matters is that an actual adaptation of economic action to a comparison of money income with money expenses takes place, no matter how primitive the form. Now in this sense capitalism and capitalistic enterprises, even with a considerable rationalization of capitalistic calculation, have existed in all civilized countries of the earth, so far as economic documents permit us to judge. In China, India, Babylon, Egypt, Mediterranean antiquity, and the Middle Ages, as well as in modern times. These were not merely isolated ventures, but economic enterprises which were entirely dependent on the continual renewal of capitalistic undertakings, and even continuous operations. However, trade especially was for a long time not continuous like our own, but consisted essentially in a series of individual undertakings. Only gradually did the activities of even the large merchants acquire an inner cohesion (with branch organizations, etc.). In any case, the capitalistic enterprise and the capitalistic entrepreneur, not only as occasional but as regular entrepreneurs, are very old and were very widespread.

Now, however, the Occident has developed capitalism both to a quantitative extent, and (carrying this quantitative development) in types, forms, and directions which have never existed elsewhere. All over the world there have been merchants, wholesale and retail, local and engaged in foreign trade. Loans of all kinds have been made, and there have been banks with the most various functions, at least comparable to ours of, say, the sixteenth century. Sea loans, *commenda*, and transactions and associations similar to the *Kommanditgesellschaft*, have all been widespread, even as continuous businesses. Whenever money finances of public bodies have existed, money-lenders have appeared, as in Babylon, Hellas, India, China, Rome. They have financed wars and piracy, contracts and building operations of all sorts. In overseas policy they have functioned as colonial entrepreneurs, as planters with slaves, or directly or indirectly forced labour, and have farmed domains, offices, and, above all, taxes. They have financed party leaders in elections and *condottieri* in civil wars. And, finally, they have been speculators in chances for pecuniary gain of all kinds. This kind of entrepreneur, the capitalistic adventurer, has existed everywhere. With the exception of trade and credit and banking transactions, their activities were predominantly of an irrational and speculative character, or directed to acquisition by force, above all the acquisition of booty, whether directly in war or in the form of continuous fiscal booty by exploitation of subjects.

The capitalism of promoters, large-scale speculators, concession hunters, and much modern financial capitalism even in peace time, but, above all, the capitalism especially concerned with exploiting wars, bears this stamp even in modern Western countries, and some, but only some, parts of large-scale international trade are closely related to it, today as always.

But in modern times the Occident has developed, in addition to this, a very different form of capitalism which has appeared nowhere else: the rational capitalistic organization of (formally) free labour. Only suggestions of it are found elsewhere. Even the organization of unfree labour reached a considerable degree of rationality only on plantations and to a very limited extent in the *Ergasteria* of antiquity. In the manors, manorial workshops, and domestic industries on estates with serf labour it was probably somewhat less developed. Even real domestic industries with free labour have definitely been proved to have existed in only a few isolated cases outside the Occident. The frequent use of day labourers led in a very few cases – especially State monopolies, which are, however, very different from modern industrial organization – to manufacturing organizations, but never to a rational organization of apprenticeship to the handicrafts like that of our Middle Ages.

Rational industrial organization, attuned to a regular market, and neither to political nor irrationally speculative opportunities for profit, is not, however, the only peculiarity of Western capitalism. The modern rational organization of the capitalistic enterprise would not have been possible without two other important factors in its development: the separation of business from the household, which completely dominates modern economic life, and closely connected with it, rational book-keeping. A spatial separation of places of work from those of residence exists elsewhere, as in the Oriental bazaar and in the *ergasteria* of other cultures. The developments of capitalistic associations with their own accounts is also found in the Far East, the Near East, and in antiquity. But compared to the modern independence of business enterprises, those are only small beginnings. The reason for this was particularly that the indispensable requisites for this independence, our rational business book-keeping, and our legal separation of corporate from personal property, were entirely lacking, or had only begun to develop. The tendency everywhere else was for acquisitive enterprises to arise as parts of a royal or manorial *household* (of the *oikos*), which is, as Rodbertus has perceived, with all its superficial similarity, a fundamentally different, even opposite, development.

However, all these peculiarities of Western capitalism have derived their significance in the last analysis only from their association with the capitalistic organization of labour. Even what is generally called commercialization, the development of negotiable securities and the rationalization of speculation, the exchanges, etc., is connected with it. For without the rational capitalistic organization of labour, all this, so far as it was possible at all, would have nothing like the same significance, above all for the social structure and all the specific problems of the modern Occident connected with it. Exact calculation – the basis of everything else – is only possible on a basis of free labour.

And just as, or rather because, the world has known no rational organization of labour outside the modern Occident, it has known no rational socialism. Of course, there has been civic ceremony, a civic food-supply policy, mercentalism and welfare policies of princes, rationing, regulation of economic life, protectionism, and *laissez-faire* theories (as in China). The world has also known socialistic and communistic experiments of various sorts: family, religious, or military communism, State socialism (in Egypt), monopolistic cartels, and consumers' organizations. But although there have everywhere been civic market privileges, companies, guilds, and all sorts of legal differences between town and country, the concept of the citizen has not existed outside the Occident, and that of the bourgeoisie outside the modern Occident. Similarly, the proletariat as a class could not exist, because there was no rational organization of free labour under regular discipline. Class struggles between creditor and debtor classes; landowners and the landless, serfs, or tenants; trading interests and consumers or landlords, have existed everywhere in various combinations. But even the Western mediaeval struggles between putters-out and their workers exist everywhere only in beginnings. The modern conflict of the large-scale industrial entrepreneur and free-wage labourers was entirely lacking. And thus there could be no such problems as those of socialism.

Hence in a universal history of culture the central problem for us is not, in the last analysis, even from a purely economic view-point, the development of capitalistic activity as such, differing in different cultures only in form: the adventurer type, or capitalism in trade, war, politics, or administration as sources of gain. It is rather the origin of this sober bourgeois capitalism with its rational organization of free labour. Or in terms of cultural history, the problem is that of the origin of the Western bourgeois class and of its peculiarities, a problem which is certainly closely connected with that of the origin of the capitalistic organization of labour, but is not quite the same thing. For the bourgeois as a class existed prior to the development of the peculiar modern form of capitalism, though, it is true, only in the Western hemisphere.

Now the peculiar modern Western form of capitalism has been, at first sight, strongly influenced by the development of technical possibilities. Its rationality is today essentially dependent on the calculability of the most important technical factors. But this means fundamentally that it is dependent on the peculiarities of modern science, especially the natural sciences based on mathematics and exact and rational experiment. On the other hand, the development of these sciences and of the technique resting upon them now received important stimulation from these capitalistic interests in its practical economic application. It is true that the origin of Western science cannot be attributed to such interests. Calculation, even with decimals, and algebra have been carried on in India, where the decimal system was invented. But it was only made use of by developing capitalism in the West, while in India it led to no modern arithmetic or book-keeping. Neither was the origin of mathematics and mechanics determined by capitalistic interests. But the *technical* utilization of scientific knowledge, so important for the living conditions of the mass of people, was certainly encouraged by economic considerations, which were extremely favourable to it in the Occident. But this encouragement was derived from the peculiarities of the social structure of the Occident. We must hence ask, from *what* parts of that structure was it derived, since not all of them have been of equal importance?

Among those of undoubted importance are the rational structures of law and of administration. For modern rational capitalism has need, not only of the technical means of production, but of a calculable legal system and of administration in terms of formal rules. Without it adventurous and speculative trading capitalism and all sorts of politically determined capitalisms are possible, but no rational enterprise under individual initiative, with fixed capital and certainty of calculations. Such a legal system and such administration have been available for economic activity in a comparative state of legal and formalistic perfection only in the Occident. We must hence inquire where that law came from. Among other circumstances, capitalistic interests have in turn undoubtedly also helped, but by no means alone nor even principally, to prepare the way for the predominance in law and administration of a class of jurists specially trained in rational law. But these interests did not themselves create that law. Quite different forces were at work in this development. And why did not the capitalistic interests do the same in China or India? Why did not the scientific, the artistic, the political, or the economic development there enter upon that path of rationalization which is peculiar to the Occident?

For in all the above cases it is a question of the specific and peculiar rationalism of Western culture. Now by this term very different things may be understood, as the following discussion will repeatedly show. There is, for example, rationalization of mystical contemplation, that is of an attitude which, viewed from other departments of life, is specifically irrational, just as much as there are rationalizations of economic life, of technique, of scientific research, of military training, of law and administration. Furthermore, each one of these fields may be rationalized in terms of very different ultimate values and ends, and what is rational from one point of view may well be irrational from another. Hence rationalizations of the most varied character have existed in various departments of life and all areas of culture. To characterize their differences form the view-point of cultural history it is necessary to know what departments are rationalized, and in what direction. It is hence our first concern to work out and to explain genetically the special peculiarity of Occidental rationalism, and within this field that of the modern Occidental form. Every such attempt at explanation must, recognizing the fundamental importance of the economic factor, above all take account of the economic conditions. But at the same time the opposite correlation must not be left out of consideration. For though the development of economic rationalism is partly dependent on rational technique and law, it is at the same time determined by the ability and disposition of men to adopt certain types of practical rational conduct. When these types have been obstructed by spiritual obstacles, the development of rational economic conduct has also met serious inner resistance. The magical and religious forces, and the ethical ideas of duty based upon them, have in the past always been among the most important formative influences on conduct.

Key terms

The following key terms appear in the text above. They have been defined below to aid with the reading of this item.

rational behaviour based on a clear understanding of a problem and calculating the costs and income involved in business transactions

Renaissance a period in Western European history famed for the emergence of certain ideas which influenced modern thinking

Questions

1 What does Weber identify as 'the most fateful force in modern life'?

2 Explain in your own words the distinction Weber makes between a capitalist and a capitalistic adventurer.

3 In what ways does the definition of capitalism provided by Weber differ from that provided by Marxist writers?

4 Provide three examples of what Weber entitles the process of rationalization and explain how he sees these as unique to Western Europe.

5 To what extent do you agree with the assertion that 'the magical and religious forces, and the ethical ideas of duty based upon them, have in the past always been among the most important formative influences on conduct'?

Reading 3.3 **Durkheim and the abnormal division of labour**

Emile Durkheim (from) *The Division of Labour in Society* (1984, originally published in 1897) London: Macmillan, pp. 310–22.

Editorial comments

Emile Durkheim's first book is mainly quoted for his theory of the transition from organic to mechanical solidarity, and the possibility of social consensus in the era of individualism. However, in the second half of the book, Durkheim elaborates upon some of the problems he identified as the abnormal division of labour. It is here that his famous concept of 'Anomie' was first raised. This extract is taken from the chapter where he considers another abnormal form, the forced division of labour.

The forced division of labour

THE INSTITUTION OF classes or castes constitutes one organization of the **division of labour**, one that is closely regulated. Yet it is often a source of dissension. Since the lower classes are not, or no longer are, satisfied with the role that has fallen to them by custom or law, they aspire to functions that are prohibited to them and seek to dispossess those who exercise them. Hence civil wars, which arise from the way in which labour is shared out.

No similar phenomenon is to be observed within the organism. Doubtless in moments of crisis its different elements war with one another, feeding at the expense of one another. But a cell or an organ never attempts to usurp any role other than that which is rightfully its own. The reason for this being the case is that each anatomical element proceeds mechanically towards its goal. Its constitution and place in the organism determine its vocation; its task is a consequence of its nature. It can perform it badly, but it cannot assume that of another, unless the latter abandons it, as happens in the rare cases of substitution about which we have spoken. The same does not hold good for societies. Here the chance factor is greater. There is a larger gap between the hereditary tendencies of the individual and the social function he will fulfil. Hereditary tendencies do not signify with such direct necessity any set function. The field is open to trial and error and discussion, as well as being open to the free play of a host of causes that may make the individual nature deviate from its normal path, thus creating a pathological state. Since the organization is more flexible, it is also more delicate and amenable to change. We are certainly not predestined from birth to any particular form of employment, but we nevertheless possess tastes and aptitudes that limit our choice. If no account is taken of them, if they are constantly frustrated in our daily occupation, we suffer, and seek the means of bringing that suffering to an end. There is no solution other than to change the established order and create a new one. For the division of labour to engender solidarity, it is thus not sufficient for everyone to have his task: it must also be agreeable to him.

This condition is not realized in the instance we are examining. Indeed, if the institution of class or caste sometimes gives rise to miserable squabbling instead of producing solidarity, it is because the distribution of social functions on which it rests does not correspond, or rather no longer corresponds, to the distribution of natural abilities. For, whatever may have been asserted, it is not solely the spirit of imitation that makes the lower classes end up by having ambitions for the upper-class life. To tell the truth, imitation of itself cannot even explain anything, for it supposes something other than itself. Imitation is only possible between creatures who already resemble one another, and according also to the degree of resemblance. It does not occur between different species or varieties. The same is true for moral contagion as is true for physical contagion: it only manifests itself in fields favourable to it. For needs to spread from one class to another, the differences originally separating these classes must have disappeared or grown less. As a result of the changes that have occurred in society, one group must have become capable of carrying out functions that were originally beyond its capacity, at the same time as another group was losing its original superiority. When the plebeians began to dispute with the patricians the honour of performing religious and administrative functions, it was not merely to imitate them but it was because they [the plebeians] had become more intelligent, more wealthy and more numerous, and their tastes and ambitions had in consequence been modified. Through these transformations the congruence in a whole sector of society was broken between the aptitudes of individuals and the kind of activity allocated to them. Constraint alone, more or less violent, more or less direct, henceforth binds them to these functions. In consequence only an imperfect, troubled form of **solidarity** can exist. ...

The forced division of labour is thus a second morbid

type that we can distinguish. But we must not mistake the meaning of the term. What causes constraint is not any kind of regulation, since on the contrary the division of labour, as we have just seen, cannot do without this. Even when functions are allocated in accordance with set rules, the distribution is not necessarily the result of constraint. ... Constraint begins only when regulation, no longer corresponding to the true state of affairs and consequently without any moral foundation, is only maintained by force.

Conversely, we may therefore state that the division of labour only produces solidarity if it is spontaneous, and to the degree that it *is* spontaneous. But spontaneity must mean not simply the absence of any deliberate, formal type of violence, but of anything that may hamper, even indirectly, the free unfolding of the social force each individual contains within himself. It not only supposes that individuals are not consigned forcibly to performing certain determined functions, but also that no obstacle whatsoever prevents them from occupying within the ranks of society a position commensurate to their abilities. In short, labour only divides up spontaneously if society is constituted in such a way that social inequalities express precisely natural inequalities. ...

We have just seen that any external inequality compromises organic solidarity. This effect is not very harmful to lower societies, where solidarity is above all ensured by a community of beliefs and sentiments. Indeed, however strained may be the ties deriving from the division of labour, as it is not they that bind the individual most strongly to society, social cohesion is not threatened. The dissatisfaction arising from thwarted aspirations is not sufficient to turn those who suffer from it against the social order that is its cause, for they continue to adhere to it. ... Such inequalities are not only even found to be tolerable, but also natural.

This is exactly the opposite to what occurs when organic solidarity becomes predominant, for then everything that causes it to weaken touches the social bond in its most vital spot. Firstly, since in these conditions specialized activities are exercised almost continuously, they cannot be disturbed without some suffering occurring at every moment. Then, as the collective consciousness grows weaker, the contestation that arises cannot be so completely neutralized. The sentiments held in common no longer possess the same strength, so as to keep the individual, in spite of everything, bound to the group. Subversive tendencies, lacking in future any countervailing force, emerge more readily. Losing increasingly the transcendency that placed it, as it were, above human interests, the social organization no longer has the same power to resist. Yet at the same time it is more strongly under attack. As the work of wholly human

hands, it can no longer so effectively oppose human demands. At the very moment when the flood tide grows more violent, the dyke that contained it is breached. Thus the situation becomes much more dangerous. This is why in organized societies it is indispensable for the division of labour to attain more nearly that ideal of spontaneity we have just defined. If societies attempt – and they should attempt – to eliminate external inequalities as much as possible, it is not only because the undertaking is a noble one, but because in solving this problem their very existence is at stake. For they cannot continue to be sustained unless all their constituent parts are solidly linked, and solidarity is only possible on this condition. Thus we may predict that this matter of doing justice will become still more absolute as the organised type of society develops. However considerable the progress already realized in this domain may be, it probably gives only a very slight idea of what will be accomplished later.

Equality in the external conditions of the struggle is not only needed to secure each individual to his function, but also to link these functions with one another.

Indeed, contractual relationships necessarily develop with the division of labour, since the latter is not possible without exchange, of which contract is the legal form. In other words, one of the important varieties of organic solidarity is what might be termed contractual solidarity. It is undoubtedly incorrect to believe that all social relationships can be reduced to a contract, all the more so because a contract assumes the existence of something other than itself. However, there are special ties that originate in the will of individuals. There is a *consensus* of a certain kind that is expressed in contracts and that, in the higher species, represents an important factor in the general *consensus*. Thus it is necessary in higher societies for contractual solidarity to be shielded so far as possible from anything that might disturb it. For if, in less advanced societies, it can remain unstable without much difficulty arising, for the reasons we have stated, in a position where it is one of the pre-eminent forms of social solidarity it cannot come under threat without the unity of the body social being threatened at the same time. The conflicts that arise from contracts therefore assume greater seriousness the more importance the contract itself assumes in general life. What is more, whilst there exist primitive societies that do not even intervene to resolve these conflicts, the law of contract in civilized peoples becomes ever more voluminous. This law's sole purpose is to ensure the regular co-operation of functions that enter into relationships in this way.

But in order to achieve this result, it is not enough for the public authority to ensure that undertakings entered into are kept. It must also, at least in roughly the average number of cases, see that they are spontaneously kept. If contracts were observed only by force or the fear of force, contractual solidarity would be in an extremely parlous state. A wholly external order would ill conceal a state of contestation too general to be contained indefinitely. Yet it may be argued that for this danger not to be feared, it is enough that contracts should be freely agreed. This may be true, but the difficulty is not resolved by this, for what constitutes free consent? Verbal or written acquiescence is not sufficient proof of it – it is possible to acquiesce only under duress. All constraint must therefore be absent. But where does constraint begin? It does not consist only in the direct use of violence, for indirect violence suppresses freedom equally effectively. If the undertakings that I have forced from someone by threatening him with death is morally and legally null and void, how could it be valid if, in order to obtain it, I have profited from a situation that, it is true, I had not caused, but that put someone else in a situation where he had either to give way to me or die?

In any given society, every object of exchange has, at any moment, a fixed value that might be called its social value. It represents the amount of useful work intrinsic to it. By this must be understood not the total labour that it may have cost, but the part of that effort capable of producing socially useful effects, that is, effects that correspond to normal needs. Although such a quantum cannot be calculated mathematically, it is none the less real. The principal conditions as a function of which it varies can even be grasped without difficulty. These are, especially, the sum total of effort needed for the production of the object, the intensity of the needs that it satisfies, and finally the extent of the satisfaction that it affords. Moreover, in fact it is around this level that the average value fluctuates. It only diverges from it under the influence of abnormal factors. In that case the public consciousness generally more or less perceives this deviation. That consciousness finds unfair any exchange where the price of the article bears no relationship to the effort expended and the services it renders.

Having enunciated this definition, we assert that the contract is not fully agreed to unless the services exchanged are equivalent in social value. In these conditions each person will receive the object that he desires and hand over what he gives in return – what both are worth. This equilibrium of wants that the contract proclaims and embodies therefore happens and is maintained of its own accord, since it is only a consequence and a different form of the very equilibrium of things. It is truly spontaneous. It is occasionally the case that we desire to receive more for the product that we are surrendering than it is worth.

Our ambitious are boundless and are consequently only moderated when they are mutually held in check by one another. But this constraint, which prevents us from satisfying freely even our most inordinate wants, cannot be confused with that which removes from us the means of obtaining a just reward for our labour. The first type of constraint does not exist for the healthy person. The second type alone merits that appellation; it alone changes consent. But it does not exist in the cases we have just cited. If, on the contrary, the values exchanged do not produce an equilibrium when balanced against one another, they could only do so if some external force were thrown into the scales. There is injury done to both sides. ...

Every form of superiority has repercussions on the way in which contracts are arrived at. If therefore it does not depend upon the person of individuals and their services to society, it invalidates the moral conditions of the exchange. If one class in society is obliged, in order to live, to secure the acceptance by others of its services while another class can do without them, because of the resources already at its disposal, resources that, however, are not necessarily the result of some social superiority, the latter group can lord it over the former. In other words, there can be no rich and poor by birth without their being unjust contracts. This was the more true when the social condition was itself hereditary and the law sanctioned all kinds of inequalities.

Nevertheless, such injustices are only strongly felt as long as contractual relationships are little developed, and the **collective consciousness** is strong. Because of the rarity of contracts, less opportunities occur for injustices to arise, and the common beliefs particularly neutralize their effects. Society does not suffer, because it is not endangered. But, as labour becomes more divided up and social doctrine weakens, these injustices become more unbearable, because the circumstances that give rise to them recur more frequently, and also because the sentiments they arouse can no longer be tempered so completely by countervailing ones. To this the history of contract bears witness, for it tends increasingly to declare invalid those agreements where the contracting parties are too unequally placed.

Originally any contract, concluded in due form, had the force of obligation, no matter how it had been obtained. Consent was not the prime factor in it. A consensus of wills was not sufficient to bind, and the bonds formed did not result directly from this consensus. For the contract to exist a necessary and sufficient condition was that certain ceremonies should have been carried out, certain words pronounced, and the nature of the undertakings entered into was determined not by the intentions of the parties, but by the formulas employed. The consensual contract only appears at a comparatively recent date. It is a first step along the path of justice, yet for a long time the consent that was sufficient to validate agreements could be very imperfect in nature, that is, extorted by force or fraud. ...

Yet, apart from the fact that it is incorrect to say that any form of regulation is the product of constraint, it so happens that liberty itself is the product of regulation. Far from being a type of antagonist to social action, it is the resultant. It is so little a property inherent in the state of nature that it is, on the contrary, a conquest by society over nature. Men are naturally unequal in physical strength; they are placed in external conditions that give unequal advantages. Domestic life itself, with the property inheritance that it implies and the inequalities that flow from this, is, of all forms of social life, the one that most narrowly depends upon natural causes. We have just seen that all these inequalities are the very negation of liberty. In the final analysis what constitutes liberty is the subordination of external to social forces, for it is only on this condition that the latter can develop freely. Yet such a subordination is rather an utter reversal of the natural order. Thus it can only be realized progressively, as man raises himself above things so as to regulate them as he wishes, stripping them of their fortuitous, absurd and amoral character, that is, to the extent that he becomes a social being. For he cannot escape from nature save by creating another world in which he dominates it. That world is society.

The task of the most advanced societies may therefore be said to be a mission for justice. That in fact they feel the need to tread this path as we have already demonstrated, and this is proved also by everyday experience. Just as the ideal of lower societies was to create or maintain a common life as intense as possible, in which the individual was engulfed, ours is to inject an even greater equity into our social relationships, in order to ensure the free deployment of all those forces that are socially useful. However, when we consider that for centuries men have contented themselves with a justice that is much less than perfect, we may begin to ask whether such aspirations are not perhaps ascribable to impatient acts that lack any reason, whether they do not represent a deviation from the normal state rather than an anticipation of the normal state to come – whether, in brief, the way to cure the ill whose existence they lay bare is to satisfy these aspirations or to combat them. The propositions established in the preceding books allow us to answer with precision this question that preoccupies us. There are no better justified needs than these trends, for they are a necessary consequence of the changes that have taken place in the structure of societies. Because the segmentary type is vanishing and the organized type developing, because organic solidarity is gradually substituting itself for the solidarity that arises from similarities, it is indispensable that external conditions should be evened out. The harmony between functions, and consequently in existence, is at this price. Just as ancient peoples had above all need of a common faith to live by, we have need of justice. We can rest assured that this need will become ever more pressing if, as everything leads us to foresee, the conditions that dominate social evolution remain unchanged.

Key terms

The following key terms appear in the text above. They have been defined below to aid with the reading of this item.

division of labour the dividing up of tasks and the development of specialized occupations which enable work to be undertaken utilizing specialist skills

solidarity feeling of belonging and togetherness based on a shared moral code, consisting of a system of norms and values

collective consciousness the set of norms and values which act as a guide to behaviour in society and influence the behaviour of individuals in that society

Questions

1 What does Durkheim argue does not occur within biological organisms, but is an important feature of society?

2 Why might social inequalities not precisely express natural inequalities?

3 On what basis does Durkheim argue that it is incorrect to believe that all social relationships can be reduced to a contract?

4 What precedes organic solidarity and how are the two forms of solidarity different?

5 Provide three examples of what Durkheim means by 'constraint'.

Reading 3.4 **The emergence of neo-functionalism**

Jeffrey Alexander (from) 'Introduction', in J. Alexander (ed.) *Neofunctionalism* (1985) London: Sage, pp. 7–16.

Editorial comments

Many sociology textbooks still rely on a ritualized battle between functionalism and conflict theory. This battle was however finished by the 1960s, ending in the demise of classical functionalism. However, as Alexander makes clear in this extract, by the mid-1980s there was a resurgence of interest in the sociology of Talcott Parsons, leading to the growth of neo-functionalism. Jeffrey Alexander is a leading advocate of this approach and in this extract he makes clear how this approach both grows out of, but also differs from, the functionalism which 'crashed in the 1960s'.

Neo-functionalism

IT IS HISTORY that Parsonian sociology, né 'functionalism,' crashed in the 1960s. The king fell; and for a long time it looked as if he would share Humpty Dumpty's fate; that is, nobody would be able to put him back together again. It has now become clear that this is not the case. The Parsonian legacy – if not Parsons' original theory – has begun to be reconstructed. We are witnessing today the emergence of neofunctionalism, not functionalism exactly, but a family relation.

'Functionalism' was never a particularly good word for Parsons' sociological theory. Its use was more the upshot of intuition and tradition than of theoretical logic. The term evidently emerged from the study group that L. J. Henderson conducted at Harvard in the 1930s. A physiologist deeply affected by biological functionalism and by Pareto, Henderson introduced Parsons, Homans, Merton, and other fledgling theorists at Harvard to Canon's powerful use of **homeostasis** in *The Wisdom of the Body*; he also evangelized for Pareto's general theory, in which systems and equilibrium concepts played prominent roles. Holmans moved from here to the functionalist anthropology of Radcliffe-Brown. Parsons went on to Durkheim and Weber. He began using the term in the late 1930s, implying by it a vague notion of system and 'interdependent parts,' and he made it a central and elaborate feature of his Presidential Address to the ASA in 1945. Yet if we look at references to functionalism among the younger group of Harvard-trained theorists in the 1930s and 1940s – Homans, Parsons, Merton, Barber, and Davis among others – we see quite a bewildering variety of epistemological, ideological, empirical, and theoretical connotations.

Even as 'functionalism' emerged as a major theoretical movement in the late 1940s, however, its ability for precise denotation was fiercely contested. Merton (1967) was regarded as one of its principal exponents; but in the late 1940s, he set out to strip the term of its ideological implications, its status as an abstract model, and its substantive empirical commitments. He sought to reduce it, via the anthropology of Radcliffe-Brown, to a kind of supermethod. To be functionalist, Merton held, was quite simply to explain causes by effects. But although this response to critics was enormously successful in a diplomatic sense, it was not, it seems to me, particularly helpful theoretically. It had much more to do with the anthropologists' critique of nineteenth-century **evolutionary theory** than with the actual practice of sociological functionalism in the twentieth century. It did not, in fact, actually describe what the foremost practitioners of functionalism, Merton himself very much included, actually did.

Merton's students, themselves key figures in the first functionalist heyday, provide further evidence for the ambiguity of the term. Coser, Goulder (1960) and Goode (1960) developed a distinctively 'left functionalism,' to use Gouldner's term. They stressed the theory's accessibility to critical and materialist thought and claimed that functionalism was a crucial element for explaining disintegration and social conflict. By the mid-1960s, Parsons – the arch 'integrationist' of the tradition – himself denied the functionalist designation, suggesting that his **cybernetic emphasis** and interchange model made such a static label obsolete. Henceforth, his collaborators and students would refer to their work as 'action theory.'

Despite such contradictory usage and internal dissent, however, 'functionalism' seems to be a name that has stuck. I want to take the bull by the horns and suggest that the term indicates nothing so precise as a set of concepts, a method, a mode, or an ideology. It indicates, rather, a tradition. Qua tradition, certain distinctive characteristics can, indeed, be adduced fairly from the efforts that have been conducted and criticized in their names. Traditions, of course, are accessible only through interpretation. What follows indicates my own sense of the future direction of this tradition as much as a discovery of its past.

(1) Although not providing a model in an explanatory sense, functionalism does provide a general picture of the interrelation of social parts, a model in a more descriptive sense. Functionalism models society as an intelligible system. It views society as composed of elements whose interaction forms a pattern that can be clearly differentiated from some surrounding environment. These parts are **symbiotically** connected to one another and interact without a priori direction from a governing force. This understanding of system and/or 'totality' must, as Althusser (1970) has forcefully argued, be sharply distinguished from the Hegelian, Marxist one. The Hegelian system resembles the functionalist, but it posits an 'expressive totality' in which all of a society's or culture's parts are seen as representing variations on some 'really' determining, fundamental system. Functionalism suggests, by contrast, open-ended and pluralistic rather than monocausal determinism.

(2) Functionalism concentrates on action as much as on structure. Its conception of action, moreover, focuses as much on expressive activity and the ends of action as on practicality and means. In particular, functionalism is concerned with the degree to which ends succeed in regulating and stipulating means. It seems quite mistaken, in this regard, to equate functionalism with the sociologism of Durkheim or the **quasi-utilitarianism** of Radcliffe-Brown.

(3) Functionalism is concerned with integration as a possibility and with deviance and processes of social control as facts. Equilibrium is taken as a reference point for functionalism systems analysis, though not for participants in actual social systems as such. It is used in several different ways, as a homeostatic, self-correcting equilibrium, as a moving equilibrium to describe developmental structures of growth and change, and as a partial equilibrium model of the type that Keynes used to describe the systemic strains in a capitalist economy.

(4) Functionalism posits the distinctions between personality, culture, and society as vital to social structure, and the tensions produced by their interpenetration as a continuous source of change and control. In addition to 'social' or institutional analysis, then, functionalism focuses on a relatively autonomous culture and on the centrality of socialization.

(5) Functionalism implies a recognition of differentiation as a major mode of social change – whether cultural, social, or psychological – and of the **individuation** and institutional strains that this historical process creates.

(6) Functionalism implies the commitment to the independence of conceptualization and theorizing from other levels of sociological analysis. Each of these six theses can certainly be identified with other lines of work in the social sciences. No other tradition, however, can be identified with all of them.

It is true, of course, that these are certainly not the only, or even the principal, characteristics of functionalism that are lodged in the public mind or social science. ... Parsons' functionalism gave sociologists a lot to choose from. Depending on their intellectual and historical circumstances, they took their choice.

Beginning in the early 1960s, historical and intellectual developments allowed the negative elements in this complex picture increasingly to dominate the collective consciousness of the discipline. By the mid 1970s they had crystallized into a conventional wisdom that froze the functionalist image in time. This was doubly unfortunate, for it was precisely at this time that the most sophisticated interpretations of Parsons' theorizing had begun to change dramatically.

This changing understanding has unfolded over the last 10 years. It has taken place for several reasons. One must look first, ironically, to the very success of the 'vulgate'. The critical vulgarization of Parsons succeeded in undermining his overwhelming authority. Once this hegemony had been destroyed, parts of his theoretical system could much more easily be appropriated in creative ways. One was no longer viewed as a 'Parsonian' if one incorporated significant insights from Parsons' work, despite the best efforts of recalcitrant 'anti-Parsonian warriors' to make the anachronistic and polemical label stick. Second, the ideological climate had noticeably cooled. A younger generation of theorists emerged who did not experience the political need to attack the liberalism for which Parsons stood. In the present neoconservative climate, indeed, it is hard to remember how Parsons' social-democratic reformism could have inspired such political hatred and venality. Third, European social theory has begun to grow once again. Without the earlier, exaggerated American attachment to Parsons, these Europeans, especially Germans, have been able to appropriate Parsons in surprisingly positive ways. Fourth, functionalist theory was, quite simply, a very sophisticated theoretical scheme. Parsons had a genial intelligence matched by few of his peers, or ours. That is the necessary, if not the sufficient, reason why the functionalist tradition still has the makings of a successful sociological theory.

What has been emerging from this reconsideration is less a theory than a broad intellectual tendency. I call it neofunctionalist in conscious similitude to neo-Marxism. First, like neo-Marxism, this development has involved a determined critique of some of the basic tenets of the original theory. Second, like neo-Marxism, it has sought to incorporate elements of purportedly antagonistic theoretical traditions. Third, like neo-Marxism, this neofunctionalist tendency is manifest in a variety of often competing developments rather than in a single coherent form. Let me consider each of these parallels in turn.

Neo-Marxism began in the 1950s as a movement of critical reflection on what came to be called orthodox Marxism; it began, that is, as an interpretative genre. What happened was that a series of self-consciously revisionist interpretations 'discovered' – in reality, produced – a different Marx. Neo-Marxist interpretation emphasized a radically different periodization of Marx's work, highlighting the significance of the early over the later writings. It found in Marx a very different epistemological framework, emphasizing idealism rather than materialism or Kantianism. It located new, significant intellectual precursors like Hegel, rather than thinkers like Saint-Simon and Ricardo. It claimed for Marx strikingly different ideological affinities, arguing for a democratic and humanistic Marx rather than a Leninist, authoritarian one.

Over the last decade a similar process of reinterpretation has ensued within, or on behalf of, the functionalist tradition. The ideological rereading has perhaps been the most dramatic. The argument for a non-conservative functionalism, a more conflict-oriented and critical reading, was begun by leftist theorists like Atkinson (1972) in the early 1970s, who claimed that Parsons' theory was not fundamentally different from Marx's or even from that of Marcuse, which embodied the theory of New Left. Other critical theorists, like Taylor (1979) and Gintis (1969), who identified even more closely with Marxism, began also to stress the parallels between Parsons and Marx and the critical side of the functionalist approach. The latest development of this influential movement within critical theory is the interpretation that Habermas has developed in the *Theory of Communicative Action* (1984), which finds significant liberating elements in Parsons' thought even while it scores his conservatism. Rocher's (1975) early interpretation, for example, stressed that Parsons' theory could rise above its American bias despite Parsons' own personal commitments to it. Menzies (1976) documented some socialist implications in Parson' stratification theory. In an extraordinarily revealing reversal of his earlier position, Gouldner (1980) described Parsonian sociology as contributing to a liberal theory of civil society that could provide a democratic and humanistic alternative to orthodox Marxism. My own work on Parsons' ideology (Alexander, 1978) has tried to bring out its critical potential, though I have pointed to the much more quiescent view of modern life that develops in his later work.

Most of these theorists have revised the epistemological understanding of Parsons as well, viewing him as much less idealistic than the earlier, established position had claimed. Taylor sees functionalism as giving significant weight to economic and political, not just cultural, factors; and Habermas goes to the extent of criticizing Parsons for an anti-normative explanation of political and economic spheres. ...

Finally, most of these new interpretations of the meaning of Parsons' work have generated new periodizations. The thrust has been to argue against the orthodox position that Parsons' work necessarily improved with age. Habermas and Menzies, for example, praise his earlier writing but see in the later work a systems bias that involves serious reification. Adriaansens (1980) attacks the middle-period work, especially *The Social System*, as a fundamental deviation from the synthetic thrust of the early and later work, a view that is shared by Sciulli and Gerstein (1985). Although I have argued for the analytical superiority of Parsons' later work (Alexander, 1983), I have also suggested that his essays of the late 1930s and 1940s, because they are more empirically concrete, more group-oriented, and more critical, provide a significant corrective to his later work on social change.

Neo-Marxist interpretation gradually paved the way for social scientific explanation that moved in the same direction. New substantive theory and new empirical work were produced by the older generation of scholars like Hobsbawm and Genovese – who sought to salvage the Marxian legacy – and eventually by a younger generation attracted to neo-Marxism for intellectual and political reasons. Once again, within functionalism the situation has been much the same. In the course of the turbulent period of the 1960s, an older generation of functionalists initiated subtle but often far-reaching changes in 'orthodox' theory. Suggesting new twists on traditional ideas and incorporating what had usually been taken to be antagonistic theories, these sociologists drew upon Tocqueville, Weber, Marx, and Habermas in their efforts to attain new levels of empirical specificity, a fuller appreciation for power and conflict, and more probing kinds of ideological critiques. Following in their wake, theorists in the younger generation have taken up a variety of neofunctionalist paths. This recent movement, moreover, has not been confined to the United States. The extraordinarily revival of Parsonianism in Germany has, in fact, been a reconstruction of Parsons' legacy in a neofunctionalist vein, providing new substantive theories and empirical explorations of diverse scope and outstanding quality. ...

Neofunctionalism, then, responds sharply to the ideological and epistemological attacks that were levelled at the orthodox tradition. The two other major substantive challenges to functionalism have emerged from conflict and interactionist approaches. If anything, neofunctionalist theorists have been even more concerned with responding to these. ...

What is truly important about these contributions,

however, is not that they have 'taken account' of contemporary theoretical developments. It is that they have done so from the point of view of a common tradition; it is this common tradition that allows the 'whole' of each contribution to be more than the mere sum of its parts. The lessons of 20 years of theoretical debate become articulated in a functionalist way. The idea of a system with interrelated and relatively autonomous parts, the tension between ends and means, the reference to equilibrium, the distinction between personality, culture, and society, the sensitivity to differentiation as a master trend, and a commitment to independent theorizing. ... In the quest for scientific accumulation, the coherence that this kind of coordinated revision provides is a definite advantage. But there are more substantive advantages as well. Within a neofunctionalist framework, materialist reference is never separated from culture or personality systems; contingency is related to systemic process; ideological criticism of society occurs within a multifaceted understanding of social differentiation; and thinking about conflict is intertwined with theories of integration and societal solidarity. ...

No one knows where such developments will lead, whether a neofunctionalist school actually will emerge, or whether, instead, neofunctionalism will shape contemporary sociology in less conspicuous ways. In the past, Parsons' controversial reputation meant that even some of the participants in this revival were loathe to acknowledge his influence. The movement to reappropriate Parsons in a neofunctionalist way is gaining momentum. Whether it is simply old wine in new bottles, or a new brew, is something history will decide.

References

Adriaansens, H. P. M. (1980) *Talcott Parsons and the Conceptual Dilemma*, London: Routledge & Kegan Paul.

Alexander, J. C. (1978) 'Formal and substantive voluntarism in the work of Talcott Parsons: A theoretical and ideological reinterpretation', *American Sociological Review, 43.*

Alexander, J. C. (1983) 'The modern reconstruction of classic thought: Talcott Parsons', in J. C. Alexander, *Theoretical Logic in Sociology*, vol. 4, Berkeley: University of California Press.

Althusser, L. (1970) 'Marxism is not a historicism', in Althusser, L. and Balibar, E. (eds) *Reading Capital,* London: New Left Books.

Atkinson, D. (1972) *Orthodox Consensus and Radical Alternation*, New York: Basic Books.

Gintis, H. (1969) *Alienation and Power* (doctoral dissertation) Harvard: Harvard University.

Goode, W. J. (1960) 'A theory of role strain', *American Sociological Review, 25.*

Gouldner, A. (1960) 'The norm of reciprocity', *American Sociological Review, 25.*

Gouldner, A. (1980) *The Two Marxisms*, New York: Seabury.

Habermas, J. (1984) *Theory of Communicative Action*, vol. 1, Boston: Beacon.

Menzies, K. (1976) *Talcott Parsons and the Social Image of Man*, London: Routledge & Kegan Paul.

Merton, R. K. (1967) 'Manifest and latent functions', in Merton, R. K. (ed.) *On Theoretical Sociology*, New York: Free Press.

Rocher, G. (1975) *Talcott Parsons and American Sociology*, New York: Barnes & Noble.

Sciulli, D. and Gerstein, D. R. (1985) 'Social Theory and Talcott Parsons in the 1980s', *Annual Review of Sociology, 11*

Taylor, J. G. (1979) *From Modernization to Modes of Production*, London: Humanities Press.

Key terms

The following key terms appear in the text above. They have been defined below to aid with the reading of this item.

homeostasis a term derived from biology describing a process which helps maintain a system in a stable state in relation to a changing external environment

evolutionary theory the general name for a set of early theories influenced by biology which suggested that societies changed slowly by adapting to the environment in which they grew up and to changes in this environment

cybernetic emphasis the central element of Parsons' later thinking, which suggested that societies are governed by sets of networks that exist in a hierarchical relationship. This led him to emphasize the importance of cultural values and the state, as regulating mechanisms of society

symbiotically relating to a close relationship between two interdependent variables

utilitarianism a philosophical theory based on the notion that humans seek to maximize happiness or satisfaction and that this is the key motivation to their behaviour

individuation a process by which individual human beings come to be seen as having some autonomy in social action, which may be seen as atomization

Questions

1 Explain in your own words the parallels Alexander sees between the emergence of neo-Marxism and the emergence of neo-functionalism.

2 Why does Alexander feel that functionalism was never a very good description of Parsons' contribution to sociology?

3 Suggest how the work of Habermas draws upon the early work of Talcott Parsons.

4 To what extent do you agree that neofunctionalism is simply 'old wine in new bottles'?

5 How convincing is the argument that 'functionalism concentrates on action as much as on structure'?

Reading 3.5 **Power/knowledge**

Michel Foucault (from) *The Foucault Reader* (1984), edited by P. Rabinow, Harmondsworth, Penguin, pp. 67–75.

Editorial comments

This extract contains Foucault's lengthy written answer to a question asked in an interview with him about the role of the intellectual. As such, it relates to the wider question of the possibility of – and the role of – the human sciences. The belief in reason, as the basis for societal reforms, placed intellectuals in a key role. However, Foucault follows in a long tradition of those sceptical of this notion, from Nietzsche's (1969, orig. pub. 1887) *Genealogy of Morals* through to Heidegger (1961, orig. pub. 1953). What these thinkers share is a belief that reason cannot be the hope of society, since it is often the justification given by people anxious to gain power. The truth is a strong claim to power, hence the power/knowledge link. This view sees the dark side of rationality, as exemplified by the Holocaust and the atomic bombs used on Hiroshima and Nagasaki, and does not therefore see any hope in the search for overall truth. Foucault argues instead that local struggles without overarching theoretical justifications should be the basis of action.

References

Heidegger, M. (1961) *An Introduction to Metaphysics*, New York: Anchor Books.

Nietzsche, F. (1969) *Genealogy of Morals and Ecce Homo*, New York: Random House.

Truth and power

Q: The work you do, these preoccupations of yours, the results you arrive at, what use can one finally make of all this in everyday political struggles? You have spoken previously of local struggles as the specific site of confrontation with power, outside and beyond all such global, general instances as parties or classes. What does this imply about the role of intellectuals? If one isn't an 'organic' intellectual acting as the spokesman for a global organization, if one doesn't purport to function as the bringer, the master of truth, what position is the intellectual to assume?

M F: For a long period, the 'left' intellectual spoke and was acknowledged the right of speaking in the capacity of master of truth and justice. He was heard, or purported to make himself heard, as the spokesman of the universal. To be an intellectual meant something like being the consciousness/conscience of us all. I think we have here an idea transposed from Marxism, from a faded Marxism indeed. Just as the proletariat, by the necessity of its historical situation, is the bearer of the universal (but its immediate, unreflected bearer, barely conscious of itself as such), so the intellectual, through his moral, theoretical, and political choice, aspires to be the bearer of this university in its conscious, elaborated form. The intellectual is thus taken as the clear, individual figure of a universality whose obscure, collective form is embodied in the proletariat.

Some years have now passed since the intellectual was called upon to play this role. A new mode of the 'connection between theory and practice' has been established. Intellectuals have become used to working, not in the modality of the 'universal', the 'exemplary', the 'just-and-true-for-all', but within specific sectors, at the precise points where their own conditions of life or work situate them (housing, the hospital, the asylum, the laboratory, the university, family, and sexual relations). This has undoubtedly given them a much more immediate and concrete awareness of struggles. And they have met here with problems which are specific, 'nonuniversal,' and often different from those of the proletariat or the masses. And yet I believe intellectuals have actually been drawn closer to the proletariat and the masses, for two reasons. Firstly, because it has been a question of real, material, everyday struggles, and secondly because they have often been confronted, albeit in a different form, by the same adversary as the proletariat, namely, the multi-national corporations, the judicial and police apparatuses, the property speculators, etc. This is what I would call the **specific intellectual** as opposed to the 'universal' intellectual.

This new configuration has a further political significance. It makes it possible, if not to integrate, at least to rearticulate categories which were previously kept separate. The intellectual *par excellence* used to be the writer: as a universal consciousness, a free subject, he was counterposed to those intellectuals who were merely *competent instances* in the service of the state or capital – technicians, magistrates, teachers. Since the time when each individual's specific activity began to serve as the basis for politicization, the threshold of *writing*, as the sacralizing mark of the intellectual, has disappeared. And it has become possible to develop lateral connections across different forms of knowledge and from one focus of politicization to another. Magistrates and psychiatrists, doctors and social workers, laboratory technicians and sociologists have become able to participate, both within their own fields and through mutual exchange and support, in a global process of politicization of intellectuals. This process explains how, even as the writer tends to disappear as a figurehead, the university and the academic emerge, if not as principal elements, at least as 'exchangers', privileged points of intersection. If the universities and education have become politically ultrasensitive areas, this is no doubt the reason why. And what is called the crisis of the universities should not be interpreted as a loss of power, but on the contrary as a multiplication and reinforcement of their power effects as centres in a polymorphous ensemble of intellectuals who virtually all pass through and relate themselves to the academic system. The whole relentless theorization of writing which we saw in the 1960s was doubtless only a swansong. Through it, the writer was fighting for the preservation of his political privilege; but the fact that it was precisely a matter of theory, that he needed scientific credentials, founded in linguistics, seminology, psychoanalysis, that this theory took its references from the direction of Saussure or Chomsky, etc., and that it gave rise to such mediocre literary products, all this proves that the activity of the writer was no longer at the focus of things.

It seems to me that this figure of the 'specific' intellectual has emerged since the Second World War. Perhaps it was the atomic scientist (in a word, or rather a name: Oppenheimer) who acted as the point of transition between the universal and the specific intellectual. It's because he had a direct and localized relation to scientific knowledge and institutions that the atomic scientist could make his intervention; but, since the nuclear threat affected the whole human race and the fate of the world, his **discourse** could at the same time be the discourse of the universal. Under the rubric of this protest, which concerned the entire world, the atomic expert brought into play his specific position in the order of knowledge. And for the first time, I think, the intellectual was hounded by political powers, no longer on account of a general discourse which he conducted, but because of the knowledge at his disposal: it was at this level that he constituted a political threat. I am speaking here only of Western intellectuals. What happened in the Soviet Union is analogous with this on a number of points, but different on many others. There is certainly a whole study that needs to be made of scientific dissidence in the West and the socialist countries since 1945.

It is possible to suppose that the 'universal' intellectual, as he functioned in the nineteenth and early twentieth centuries, was in fact derived from a quite specific historical figure: the man of justice, the man of law, who counterposes to power, despotism, and the abuses and arrogance of wealth the universality of justice and the equity of an ideal law. The great political struggles of the eighteenth century were fought over law, right, the constitution, the just in reason and law, that which can and must apply universally. What we call today 'the intellectual' (I mean the intellectual in the political, not the sociological sense of the word; in other words, the person who utilizes his knowledge, his competence, and his relation to truth in the field of political struggles) was, I think, an offspring of the jurist, or at any rate of the man who invoked the universality of a just law, if necessary against the legal professions themselves (Voltaire, in France, is the prototype of such intellectuals). The 'universal' intellectual derives from the jurist or notable, and finds his fullest manifestation in the writer, the bearer of values and significations in which all can recognize themselves. The 'specific' intellectual derives from quite another figure, not the jurist or notable, but the savant or expert. I said just now that it's with the atomic scientists that this latter figure comes to the forefront. In fact, it was preparing in the wings for some time before, and was even present on at least a corner of the stage from about the end of the nineteenth century. No doubt it's with Darwin or, rather, with the post-Darwinian evolutionists that this figure begins to appear clearly. The stormy relationships between evolutionism and the socialists, as well as the highly ambiguous effects of **evolutionism** (on sociology, criminology, psychiatry, and eugenics, for example), marks the important political struggles in the name of a 'local' scientific truth – however important the latter may be. Historically, Darwin represents this point of inflection in the history of the Western intellectual. (Zola is very significant from this point of view: he is the type of the 'universal' intellectual, bearer of law and militant in equity, but he ballasts his discourse with a whole invocation of nosology and evolutionism, which he believes to be scientific, grasps very poorly in any case, and whose political effects on his own discourse are very equivocal). If one were to study this closely, one would have to follow how the physicists, at the turn of the century, re-entered the field of political debate. The debates between the theorists of socialism and the theorists of relativity are of capital importance in this history.

At all events, biology and physics were to be a privileged degree the zones of formation of this new personage, the specific intellectual. The extension of technico-scientific structures in the economic and strategic domain was what gave him his real importance. The figure in which the functions and prestige of this new intellectual are concentrated is no longer that of the 'writer of genius', but that of the 'absolute savant'; no longer he who bears the values of all, opposes the unjust sovereign or his ministers, and makes his cry resound even beyond the grave. It is, rather, he who, along with a handful of others, has at his disposal, whether in the service of the state or against it, powers which can either benefit or irrevocably destroy life. He is no longer the rhapsodist of the eternal, but the strategist of life and death. Meanwhile we are at present experiencing the disappearance of the figure of the 'great writer'.

Now let's come back to more precise details. We accept, alongside the development of technico-scientific structures in contemporary society, the importance gained by the specific intellectual in recent decades, as well as the acceleration of this process since around 1960. Now the specific intellectual encounters certain obstacles and faces certain dangers. The danger of remaining at the level of conjectural struggles, pressing demands restricted to particular sectors. The risk of letting himself be manipulated by the political parties or trade union apparatuses which control these local struggles. Above all, the risk of being unable to develop these struggles for lack of a global strategy or outside support; the risk, too, of not being followed, or only by very limited groups. In France we can see at the moment an example of this. The struggle around the prisons, the penal system, and the police-judicial system, because it has developed 'in solitary', among social workers and ex-prisoners, has tended increasingly to separate itself from the forces which would have enabled it to grow. It has allowed itself to be penetrated by a whole naïve, archaic ideology which makes the criminal at once into the innocent victim and the pure rebel – society's scapegoat – and the young wolf of future generations. This return to anarchist themes of the late nineteenth century was possible only because of a failure of integration of current strategies. And the result has been a deep split between this campaign with its monotonous, lyrical little chant, heard only among a few small groups, and the masses who have good reason not to accept it

as valid potential currency, but who also – thanks to the studiously cultivated fear of criminals – tolerate the maintenance, or rather the reinforcement, of the judicial and police apparatuses.

It seems to me that we are now at a point where the function of the specific intellectual needs to be reconsidered. Reconsidered but not abandoned, despite the nostalgia of some for the great 'universal' intellectuals and the desire for a new philosophy, a new world-view. Suffice it to consider the important results which have been achieved in psychiatry: they prove that these local, specific struggles haven't been a mistake and haven't led to a dead end. One may even say that the role of the specific intellectual must become more and more important in proportion to the political responsibilities which he is obliged willy-nilly to accept, as a nuclear scientist, computer expert, pharmacologist, etc. It would be a dangerous error to discount him politically in his specific relation to a local form of power, either on the grounds that this is a specialist matter which doesn't concern the masses (which is doubly wrong: they are already aware of it, and in any case implicated in it), or that the specific intellectual serves the interests of state or capital (which is true, but at the same time shows the strategic position he occupies), or, again, on the grounds that he propagates a scientific ideology (which isn't always true, and is anyway certainly a secondary matter compared with the fundamental point: the effects proper to true discourses).

The important thing here, I believe, is that truth isn't outside power, or lacking in power: contrary to a myth whose history and functions would repay further study, truth isn't the reward of free spirits, the child of protracted solitude, nor the privilege of those who have succeeded in liberating themselves. Truth is a thing of this world: it is produced only by virtue of multiple forms of constraint. And it induces regular effects of power. Each society has its regime of truth, its 'general politics' of truth: that is, the types of discourse which it accepts and makes function as true; the mechanisms and instances which enable one to distinguish true and false statements, the means by which each is sanctioned; the techniques and procedures accorded value in the acquisition of truth; the status of those who are charged with saying what counts as true.

In societies like ours, the 'political economy' of truth is characterized by five important traits. 'Truth' is centered on the form of scientific discourse and the institutions which produce it; it is subject to constant economic and political incitement (the demand for truth, as much for economic production as for political power); it is the object, under diverse forms, of immense diffusion and consumption (circulating through apparatuses of education and information whose extent is relatively broad in the social body, notwithstanding certain strict limitations); it is produced and transmitted under the control, dominant if not exclusive, of a few great political and economic apparatuses (university, army, writing, media); lastly, it is the issue of a whole political debate and social confrontation ('ideological' struggles).

It seems to me that what must now be taken into account in the intellectual is not the 'bearer of universal values'. Rather, it's the person occupying a specific position – but whose specificity is linked, in a society like ours, to the general functioning of an apparatus of truth. In other words, the intellectual has a threefold specificity: that of his class position (whether as petty-bourgeois in the service of capitalism or 'organic' intellectual of the proletariat); that of his conditions of life and work, linked to his condition as an intellectual (his field of research, his place in a laboratory, the political and economic demands to which he submits or against which he rebels, in the university, the hospital, etc.); lastly, the specificity of the politics of truth in our societies. And it's with this last factor that his position can take on a general significance and that his local, specific struggle can have effects and implications which are not simply professional or sectional. The intellectual can operate and struggle at the general level of that regime of truth which is so essential to the structure and functioning of our society. There is a battle 'for truth,' or at least 'around truth' – it being understood once again that by truth I do not mean 'the ensemble of truths which are to be discovered and accepted', but rather 'the ensemble of rules according to which the true and the false are separated and specific effects of power attached to the true', it being understood also that it's a matter not of a battle 'on behalf' of the truth, but of a battle about the status of truth and the economic and political role it plays. It is necessary to think of the political problems of intellectuals not in terms of 'science' and 'ideology,' but in terms of

'truth' and 'power'. And thus the question of the professionalization of intellectuals and the division between intellectual and manual labour can be envisaged in a new way.

All this must seem very confused and uncertain. Uncertain indeed, and what I am saying here is above all to be taken as a hypothesis. In order for it to be a little less confused, however, I would like to put forward a few 'propositions' – not firm assertions, but simply suggestions to be further tested and evaluated.

'Truth' is to be understood as a system of ordered procedures for the production, regulation, distribution, circulation, and operation of statements.

'Truth' is linked in a circular relation with systems of power which produce and sustain it, and to effects of power which it induces and which extends it. A 'regime' of truth.

This regime is not merely ideological or superstructural; it was a condition of the formation and development of capitalism. And it's this same regime which, subject to certain modifications, operates in the socialist countries (I leave open here the question of China, about which I know little).

The essential political problem for the intellectual is not to criticize the ideological contents supposedly linked to science, or to ensure that his own scientific practice is accompanied by a correct ideology, but that of ascertaining the possibility of constituting a new politics of truth. The problem is not changing people's consciousnesses – or what's in their heads – but the political, economic, institutional regime of the production of truth.

It's not a matter of emancipating truth from every system of power (which would be a chimera, for truth is already power), but of detaching the power of truth from the forms of hegemony, social, economic, and cultural, within which it operates at the present time.

The political question, to sum up, is not error, illusion, alienated consciousness, or ideology; it is truth itself. Hence the importance of Nietzsche.

Key terms

The following key terms appear in the text above. They have been defined below to aid with the reading of this item.

'specific' intellectual the idea of someone who produces ideas related to a specific limited goal, as opposed to the universal intellectual who seeks ideas and answers covering the whole of society

discourse a set of ideas which together produce a distinctive way of looking at and thinking about the world, and which are not amenable to criticism from another discourse which itself has its own ideas and assumptions

evolutionism the doctrine that things change slowly and gradually, sometimes implying an almost automatic change outside the control of humanity

Questions

1 Explain in your own words the distinction drawn by Foucault between the 'specific' intellectual and the 'universal' intellectual.

2 When, according to Foucault, did the 'specific' intellectual emerge?

3 What obstacles and dangers does the 'specific' intellectual face?

4 How far do you agree with the view that we should think of intellectuals 'not in terms of "science" and "ideology" but in terms of "truth" and "power"'?

5 Assess the arguments for and against the statement that 'truth isn't outside power'.

Reading 3.6 **Against post-modernism**

Alex Callinicos (from) *Against Postmodernism* (1989) Cambridge: Polity, pp. 162–5 and 167–71.

Editorial comments

Callinicos writes that he wrote this book to challenge what he calls the 'strange mixture of cultural and political pessimism and light-minded playfulness' which he found irritating as it swept over more and more theoretical debates in the 1980s.

His argument in this extract is that it is possible to locate a material basis for the rise of these ideas in the opportunities for 'overconsumptionism' in the Reagan-Thatcher era, which attracted many of the 1968 generation of radicals who, by then, were thoroughly disillusioned, including François Lyotard (1984), an ex-member of the Trotskyist group Socialisme ou Barbarie. He recognizes that in its attack on universal theories, post-modernists have mainly attacked Marxism, and as a Marxist he offers his own material analysis and critique of this trend.

Reference

Lyotard, F. (1984) *The Postmodern Condition*, Manchester: Manchester University Press.

The children of Marx and Coca Cola

WE BEGAN WITH Lyotard, so let us finish with him (in more senses than one). He writes: 'Eclecticism is the degree zero of contemporary general culture: one listens to reggae, watches a western, eats McDonald's food for lunch and local cuisine for dinner, wears Paris perfume in Tokyo and "retro" clothes in Hong Kong; knowledge is a matter for TV games' (Lyotard, 1984). It all depends, of course, on who 'one' is. This is more than an *ad hominem* remark, though it is a bit rich that Lyotard should ignore the majority of the population even in the advanced economies to whom such delights as French scent and Far Eastern travel are denied. To whom then is this particular combination of experiences available? What political subject does the idea of a postmodern epoch help constitute?

There is an obvious answer to this question. One of the most important social developments in the advanced economies during the present century has been the growth of the **'new middle class'** of upper-level white-collar workers. John Goldthorpe writes: 'While in the early twentieth century, professional, administrative and managerial employees accounted for only 5–10 per cent of the active population in even the most economically advanced nations, by the present time they quite generally account in Western societies for 20–25 per cent' (Goldthorpe, 1982). The new middle class, conceived as wage-earners occupying what Erik Olin Wright called 'contradictory class locations' between labour and capital and performing primarily managerial and supervisory tasks, is in all likelihood a considerably smaller group that these figures reflect – perhaps 12 per cent of the British working population (Wright, 1978). Nevertheless, both because of the social power its members exercise, and because of the cultural influence it exerts on other white-collar workers who aspire to promotion into its ranks, the new middle class is a force to be reckoned with in every major Western society.

Raphael Samuel has painted an evocative portrait of this salaried middle class, which, unlike the traditional petty bourgeoisie of small capitalists and independent professionals,

> distinguishes itself more by its spending than its saving. The Sunday colour supplements give it both a fantasy life and asset of cultural cues. Much of its claim to culture rests on the conspicuous display of good taste, whether in the form of kitchenware, 'continental' food, or weekend sailing and cottages. New forms of sociability, like parties and 'affairs' have broken down the sexual apartheid which kept men and women in rigidly separate spheres.
>
> Class hardly enters into the new middle class conception of themselves. Many of them work in an institutional world of fine gradations but no clear lines of antagonism.
>
> The new middle class have a different emotional economy than [sic] that of their pre-war predecessors. They go in for instant rather than deferred gratification, making a positive virtue of their expenditure, and treating the self-indulgent as an ostentatious display of good taste. Sensual pleasures, so far from being outlawed, are the very field on which social claims are established and sexual identities confirmed. Food, in particular, a postwar bourgeois passion, ... has emerged as a crucial marker of class.
> *(Samuel, 1982)*

It is not hard to think of the economic conditions of such practices – thus saving becomes much less important when social position comes to depend less on accumulated capital than on skill in negotiating a managerial hierarchy, and when credit is readily available to expand consumption. It is also tempting to see Postmodernism as somehow the cultural expression of the rise of the new middle class. This would, I think, be a mistake. For one thing the new middle class is less a coherent collectivity than a heterogeneous collection of strata, occupying the same contradictory position within the relations of production, but disarticulated by varying power-bases; for example, one important source of differentiation within the new middle class is likely to be employed in the public or private sector – a university lecturer, for examples, does not always experience an identity of interest with a City bond-dealer. For another thing, inasmuch as the term 'Postmodernism' has any genuine cultural referents – these data from the 1960s or later, whereas the new middle class has been around a lot longer. This suggests the need for an analysis which, like Anderson's genealogy of Modernism – seeks to isolate the historical conjuncture in which all the talk about a postmodern era began.

Two developments seem to me decisive. The first is what Mike Davis described as 'the emergence of a new, embryonic regime of accumulation that might be called **overconsumptionism'**, by which he means 'an increasing political subsidization of a sub-bourgeois, *mass* layer of managers, professionals, new entrepreneurs and rentiers'. Davis argues that American capitalism experienced in the 1970s and 1980s both the crisis of the old **Fordist regime of accumulation** based on the articulation of semi-automatic mass production and working-class consumption and a redistribution of wealth and income in favour, not simply of capital, but of an increasingly assertive new middle class. The tax and welfare cuts pushed through by the first Reagan administration meant that low-income families lost at least $23 billion in income and federal benefits, while high-income families gained more than $35 billion. 'The old charmed circle of the poor getting poorer as the rich get richer is being superseded by the trend of poorer poor and richer rich, as the proliferation of low-wage jobs simultaneously enlarges an affluent market of non-producers and bosses.' The result is a 'split-level economy', involving 'as *Business Week* notes, a more sharply bifurcated consumer market structure, ... with the masses of the working poor huddled around their K-Marts and Taiwanese imports at one end, while at the other there is a (relatively) "vast market for luxury products and services, from travel and designer clothes, to posh restaurants, home computers and fancy sports cars"' (Davis, 1986).

Although Davis's argument is somewhat weakened by his reliance on the regulation school's inadequate crisis theory, there seems to me little doubt that he is referring here to a phenomenon of general significance. The Reagan-Thatcher era saw, not the abandonment of Keynesianism, but an important reorientation of fiscal policy, one of whose main features was a redistribution from poor to rich – the British government's social security 'reforms' and drastic cuts in the taxation of those in higher-income brackets, both implemented in the spring of 1988, followed the pattern set by Reaganomics. Other developments promoted the expansion of upper-income consumption – for example, the heady growth of the financial sector thanks first to the boom in Third World lending in the 1970s and then to the bull market of the mid-1980s. The 1980s were after all the decade when the term 'Yuppie' became part of common parlance. ...

The 'pathological prosperity' (in Davis's words) which characterized the Western economies' recovery from the 1974–5 and 1979–82 recessions thus involved a certain reorientation of consumption towards the new middle class, a social layer whose conditions of existence tend to encourage high expenditure. But there is something else that needs to be taken into account to make sense of the peculiar mood of the 1980s – the political fallout from 1968. 1968 was the year when a combination of crises – the May–June events in France, the student and ghetto revolts in the US, and the Prague Spring in Czechoslovakia – seemed to augur the breakup of the prevailing order both East and West. In the ensuing radicalization a generation of young Western intellectuals were won to militant political activity, often in one of the far left organizations, usually Maoist or Trotskyist in allegiance, which mushroomed at the end of the 1960s. Ten years on, the millennial expectations of imminent revolution that flourished in 1968 had been dashed. The status quo proved to be more solidly based than it had seemed. Where change took place, perhaps most notably with the collapse of the Southern European dictatorships, the beneficiary was, at best, social democracy rather than revolutionary socialism. The far left disintegrated throughout Europe at the end of the 1970s. In France, where hopes had been raised highest, the fall was most precipitous. The **nouveaux philosophes** helped to convert the Parisian intelligentsia – largely *marxisant* since the Popular Front and the Resistance – to liberalism. The parliamentary left won office in 1981 for the first time since the Fourth Republic amid an intellectual scene characterized by the complete rout of Marxism. ...

Twenty years after, in 1988, with Western capitalism seemingly restabilized under the leadership of the New Right, the retreat of the generation of 1968 from the revolutionary beliefs of their youth had gone even further. As Chris Harman remarked '[i]f the fashion in 1968 was to drop out and to drop acid, now, apparently, it is to drop in and drop socialist policies' (Harman, 1988). The observations of the twentieth anniversary of 1968 were remarkable chiefly for the disillusioned retrospects of former student leaders. *Marxism Today*, which had made a marketing strategy out of the progressive abandonment of anything resembling socialist principle, was especially strident in its renunciation of revolutionary hopes which it had never shared. ...

Fundamentally, attempts ... to explain away 1968 run aground on the fact of its sheer scale. The May–June events in France, after all, embraced not just student barricades in the Latin Quarter and the occupation of the Sorbonne, but the greatest general strike in European history. They were simply the most dramatic episode in what Harman in his magisterial history of the period calls a 'three-fold crisis – of American hegemony in Vietnam, of authoritarian forms of rule in the face of a massively enlarged working class, and of Stalinism in Czechoslovakia' – a crisis which produced a *generalized* upturn of class struggle throughout Western capitalism which continued into, and was initially exacerbated by the onset of world recession after the 1973 oil crisis (Harman, 1988). This upturn – the greatest Western Europe had seen since the aftermath of the Russian Revolution – comprised, alongside May–June 1968 in France, the Italian 'May in slow motion' which began in the autumn of 1969; the wave of strikes against the 1970–4 Heath government in Britain, which culminated in Heath's overthrow by the miners; the Portuguese Revolution of 1974–5; and the bitter industrial conflicts which accompanied the death agonies of the Franco regime in Spain during 1975 and 1976. While industrial militancy never achieved anything like this pitch in the US, the interaction of the antiwar movement, the black ghetto risings, and the student revolt helped produce at the end of the 1960s the worst American domestic political crisis perhaps since the Civil War. And there were echoes elsewhere – the *cordobazo* in Argentina, an explosion of worker and student militancy in Australia, the Quebec general strike of 1972.

The failure of these struggles to make any long-term inroads into the power of capital was a contingent one, reflecting not the immanent logic of the system but the dominance of the Western working-class movement by organizations and ideologies which, whether stemming from the social democratic or the Stalinist traditions, were pledged to achieving partial reforms within a framework of class collaboration. The intervention of the French Communist Party to end the general strike of May–June 1968 was repeated on numerous occasions elsewhere, from the Social Contract struck by the British Trade Union Congress with the Labour government of 1974–9 to the 1977 Moncloa pact through which the Spanish Communist and Socialist Parties pledged their support to Franco's heirs. Class compromises of this kind allowed Western capital to weather the great recessions of the mid-1970s and early 1980s and indeed to use them to restructure and to rationalize. As the working class of the advanced countries moved from the offensive to the defensive, the far left found itself isolated, no longer swimming with the stream; in these less favourable circumstances, many organizations collapsed, their activities succumbing to a 'crisis of militancy' provoked by the fact that their labours had not been met with the easy success they had expected.

The political odyssey of the 1968 generation is, in my view, crucial to the widespread acceptance of the idea of a postmodern epoch in the 1980s. This was the decade when those radicalized in the 1960s and early 1970s began to enter middle age. Usually they did so with all hope of socialist revolution gone – indeed, often having ceased to believe in the desirability of any such revolution. Most of them had by then come to occupy some sort of professional, managerial or administrative position, to have become members of the new middle class, at a time when the overconsumptionist dynamic of Western capitalism offered this class rising living standards – a benefit often denied the rest of the workforce: hourly real wages in the US fell by 8.7 per cent between 1973 and 1986 (Business Week, 27 April 1987). This conjuncture – the prosperity of the Western new middle class combined with the political disillusionment of many of its most articulate members – provides the context to the proliferating talk of postmodernism. Let me, before continuing, make one point clear. I do not claim that, say, Foucault's philosophy or Rushdie's fiction is in any very direct sense to be derived from the economic and political developments discussed above. I am rather concerned to explain here the *acceptance* by quite large numbers of people of certain ideas.

The main themes of postmodernism become intelligible, I believe, against the background of the historical conjuncture of the late 1970s and the 1980s. For example, a principal feature of poststructuralism is its **Aestheticism**, inherited from Nietzsche and reinforced by the attempts of Derrida, Foucault *et al.* to articulate the philosophical implications of Modernism. Richard Shusterman notes the emergence of 'an intriguing and increasingly salient current in contemporary Anglo-American moral philosophy (and culture) toward the aestheticization of the ethical. The idea here ... is that aesthetic considerations are or should be crucial and ultimately perhaps be paramount in determining how we choose to lead or shape our lives and how we assess what a good life is' (Shusterman, 1988). The main example he gives is that of Rorty, whose prominence in the 1980s reflected his role in translating poststructuralist themes into an analytical idiom. Perhaps the most interesting instance of this tendency is provided in the Nietzschean notion of an 'aesthetics of existence' developed by Foucault in his last books. What is striking about the philosophical drift towards Aestheticism is how well it accords with the cultural mood of the 1980s. It has become a truism to say that this was a decade obsessed with style. Theorists of post-Fordism were right to note a certain differentiation of markets and the proliferation of designer brands crucial to whose appeal was the suggestion that, in buying, say, Levi 501s one was gaining access to a certain lifestyle, although they greatly exaggerated the scale of these developments. In various aspects of life one could detect a similar association of certain kinds of consumption with forming oneself into a particular kind of person; among the most important was a narcissistic obsession with the body, both male and female, less as an object of desire than – when disciplined by diet and exercise into a certain shape – as an index of youth, health, energy, mobility. This stylization of existence (to borrow Foucault's phrase) is surely best understood against the background, not of New Times, but of good times for the new middle class, a class which found itself in the 1980s with more money in its pocket and easier access to credit, without the pressure to save to which the old petty bourgeoisie was subject.

A further striking feature of talk about post-modernism is its apocalyptic tone, which is perhaps most strident in the writings of Baudrillard and his followers, such as Arthur Kroker. Now there is quite a strong sense in which an expectation of imminent disaster has been an endemic feature of Western culture for much of this century, and certainly since Auschwitz and Hiroshima. But I think something more involved here that this 'routinized apocalypse', as Frank Kermode (1988) calls it. For what has been the experience of the generation of 1968? They lived through a period, in the late 1960s and early 1970s, when great historical transformations seemed on the agenda, and when many believed that the immediate future was finely balanced between Utopia and distopia, between socialist advance and reactionary tyranny (a belief which events like the Chilean coup of September 1973 did nothing to undermine). The hope of revolution has gone, but it has not generally been replaced, I think, by positive belief in the virtues of capitalist democracy. Apart from anything else, even for those who mistakenly believe that capitalism has overcome its economic contradictions, there are so many other potential catastrophes hovering on the horizon – nuclear war, and ecological collapse, for example. For those holding such views, it is plausible to believe that we are entering a phase of development to which classical Marxism, with its orientation on class struggle, is irrelevant, but which by no means fulfils the promises of liberalism.

The success enjoyed by Lyotard and Baudrillard, quite out of proportion with any slight intellectual merit their work might have, thus becomes comprehensible. Both were strongly identified with 1968. Baudrillard, for example, says: 'My work really started with the movements of the 1960s' (Baudrillard, 1988). Both offer lengthy philosophical commentaries on the present – unlike Derrida, who has concentrated on the deconstruction of theoretical texts, or Foucault, whose main preoccupation was with the genealogy of modernity. Both have followed a trajectory since the late 1960s and early 1970s which has taken away from an explicitly political stance – on the spontaneist, anti-Lennist wing of the post-war 1968 far left (with which Deleuze and Guattari have been much more enduringly identified) – towards the adoption of what amounts as an aesthetic pose based on the refusal to seek either to comprehend or to transform existing social reality. What could be more reassuring for a generation, drawn first towards and then away from Marxism by the political ups and downs of the past two decades, than to be told – in a style decked out with the apparent profundity and genuine obscurity of the sub-Modernist rhetoric cultivated by '68 thought – that there is nothing that they can do to change the world? 'Resistance' is reduced to the knowing consumption of cultural products – perhaps the 'Postmodern' works of art whose authors have often sought to embody in them this kind of thinking, but if not any old soap opera will do just as well, since, as Susan Sontag has often emphasized, Aestheticism involves 'an attitude which is neutral with respect to content' (Sontag, 1983). The kind of ironic distance from the world which was so important a feature of the great works of Modernism has become routinized, even trivialized, as it becomes a way of negotiating a still unreconciled reality which one no longer believes can be changed.

As I have argued elsewhere:

> The discourse of postmodernism is best seen as the product of a socially mobile intelligentsia in a climate dominated by the retreat of the Western labour movement and the 'overconsumptionist' dynamic of capitalism in the Reagan-Thatcher era. From this perspective the term 'postmodern' would seem to be a floating signifier by means of which this intelligentsia has sought to articulate its political disillusionment and its aspiration to a consumption-oriented lifestyle. The difficulties involved in identifying a referent for this term are therefore beside the point, since talk about postmodernism turns out to be less about the world than the expression of a particular generation's sense of an ending.
> *(Callinicos, 1990)*

... Postmodernism must be understood largely as a response to failure of the great upturn of 1968–76 to fulfil the revolutionary hopes it raised. During this upturn themes which had been marginalized for half a century enjoyed a brief revival – not simply the idea of socialist revolution, conceived as a democratic irruption from below rather than the imposition of change from above, whether by a social democratic administration or a Stalinist party, but also the avant-garde project of overcoming the separation of art and life.

These aspirations have once again been largely side-lined. But to believe that this will permanently remain the case supposes that there will be no more explosions in the advanced countries comparable to 1980s' pathological prosperity suggests otherwise. World capitalism has not escaped from the period of crises which began in the early 1970s, nor has it somehow magically abolished the working class: on the contrary, the 1980s were marked by the rise of new labour movements based on proletariats created by recent industrialization – *Solidarność* in Poland, the Workers' Party in Brazil, the Congress of South African Trade Unions, the new South Korean labour movement. The project of 'radicalized Enlightenment' first outlined by Marx, for whom the contradictions of modernity could be resolved only by socialist revolution, still awaits realization.

References

Baudrillard, J. (1988) 'Lost in the hyper market', *City Limits*, 8 December.

Callinicos, A. (1990) 'Reactionary Postmodernism?', in Boyne, R. and Rattansi, A. (eds) *Postmodernism and Social Theory*, London: Macmillan.

Davis, M. (1986) *Prisoners of the American Dream*, London: Verso.

Goldthorpe, J. (1982) 'On the service class, its forma-tion and future', in Giddens, A. and Mackenzie, G. (eds) *Social Class and the Division of Labour*, Cambridge: Cambridge University Press.

Harman, C. (1988) *The Fire Last Time*, London: Bookmarks.

Kermode, F. (1988) *History and Value*, Oxford: Blackwell.

Lyotard, F. (1984) *The Postmodern Condition*, Manchester: Manchester University Press.

Samuel, R. (1982) 'The SDP and the new political class', *New Society*, 22 April.

Shusterman, R. (1988) 'Postmodernist aesthetics: a new moral philosophy', *TCS 5*.

Sontag, S. (1983) 'Notes on Camp', in *A Susan Sontag Reader*, Harmondsworth: Penguin.

Wright, E. O. (1978) *Class, Crisis and the State*, London, Verso.

Key terms

The following key terms appear in the text above. They have been defined below to aid with the reading of this item.

new middle class a group identified by a number of sociologists comprising professional and managerial workers, and growing as a proportion of the work-force.

overconsumptionism the way in which tax and wel-fare cuts have meant that the poor get poorer, while those in the new middle class enjoy a hefty rise in living standards

Fordist regime of accumulation a model of an econ-omy and society based on Henry Ford's mass pro-duction techniques – involving production line assembly with a detailed division of labour to allow mass production, together with the use of advertising to ensure the continuance of mass consumption (nec-essary to sustain mass production at profitable levels)

nouveaux philosophes a group of French predomi-nantly right-wing thinkers

aestheticism a belief that thinkers should be judged in terms of their beauty or style rather than more func-tional scientific criteria

Questions

1 Explain in your own words the two crucial devel-opments Callinicos argues are behind the rise of post-modernism.

2 What does Callinicos argue post-modernism reduces the idea of 'resistance' to?

3 Using material from the reading and elsewhere, out-line what is meant by the crisis in the Fordist model of accumulation.

4 Suggest examples of how cultural tastes have changed in recent years.

5 How far do you agree with the statement that the success enjoyed by Lyotard and Baudrillard is 'quite out of proportion with any slight intellectual merit their work might have'?

Reading 3.7 **Structuration theory**

Anthony Giddens (from) *The Constitution of Society* (1984) Cambridge: Polity, pp. 169–79.

Editorial comments

The division between structural and social action approaches in sociology is a long-standing one, but it is also a division that more contemporary writers have begun to question. Anthony Giddens is a leading example of this trend, and his theory of structuration focuses instead on social practices where structures are both the result and the basis of social actions. Giddens argues that we need to consider social structures not simply as constraining or limiting our action, as in classical approaches, most notably in the work of Emile Durkheim, but instead as also enabling human action to take place and therefore enabling societies to exist. While not without its critics, Giddens' attempted synthesis is a powerful one, and in this extract he explains his thinking, while also answering some of his critics.

Structure and constraint: Durkheim and others

MOST FORMS OF structural sociology, from Durkheim onwards, have been inspired by the idea that structural properties of society form constraining influences over action. In contrast to this view, structuration theory is based on the proposition that structure is always both enabling and constraining, in virtue of the inherent relation between structure and agency (and agency and power). All well and good, a critic may say – and some indeed have said – but does not this conception in fact sacrifice anything akin to structural 'constraint' in Durkheim's sense? Does not speaking of structure as both constraining and enabling pay only lip service to the former? For in structuration theory 'structure' is defined as rules and resources. It is perhaps easy to see how structure in this sense is implicated in the generation of action but not so apparent where constraint enters in. For there seems to be no way in which the 'externality' of social phenomena to individual activity is sustained. Such a notion must be defended, it might be suggested, whatever the flaws in the writings of those mainly responsible for advocating it. Thus Carlstein remarks:

> A major drawback in Gidden's paradigm is that the enabling aspects of structure are not sufficiently balanced by constraining ones. There are too few principles of limitation, and by this I do not simply mean the moral-legal-normative social constraints emphasized by Durkheim and Parsons, i.e. structures of legitimation. I am referring to basic constraints of mediation and resource limitation rooted in certain biotic-cum-physical realities of existence. Surely, structure must also imply limits to variation and to contingency in social systems (socio-environmental systems). Of course there is room for variation and human creativity. History has proven over and over again how the application of ideas and inventions in all realms of practice alters the received structure. But the latter is heavily biased towards the past, and imposes hard screening on things that are produced and reproduced. …
> *(Carlstein, 1981)*

I shall argue here, however, that the theory of structuration in no way minimizes the significance of the constraining aspects of structure. But 'constraint' as discussed in structural sociology tends to have several senses (Durkheim's terminology, for what it is worth, actually oscillated between the terms '*contrainte*' and '*coercion*'); and 'constraint' cannot be taken as a uniquely defining quality of 'structure'.

In structuration theory structure has always to be conceived of as a property of social systems, 'carried' in reproduced practices embedded in time and space. Social systems are organized hierarchically and laterally within societal totalities, the institutions of which form 'articulated ensembles'. If this point is ignored, the notion of 'structure' in the theory of structuration appears more idiosyncratic than it really is. One of the circumstances which Durkheim usually associates with constraint (also hinted at in the quotation from Carlstein) depends upon the observation that the *longue durée* of institutions both pre-exists and outlasts the lives of individuals born into a particular society. This is not only wholly compatible with structuration theory but is also inherent in its very formulation – although the 'socialization' of the individual into society should be understood as involving mutual time process, connecting the 'life-cycles' of both infant and parental figures. In his earlier writings Durkheim heavily emphasized the constraining elements of socialization, but later he in fact came to see more and more clearly that socialization fuses constraint and enablement. This is easily demonstrated in the instance of learning a first language. No one 'chooses' his or her native language, although learning to speak it involves definite elements of compliance. Since any language constrains thought (and action) in the sense that it presumes a range of framed, rule-governed properties, the process of language learning sets certain limits to cognition and activity. But by the very same token the learning of a language greatly expands the cognitive and practical capacities of the individual.

A second context in which Durkheim tends to speak of constraint also offers no logical difficulties for structuration theory. However, we have to be careful to avoid some of the dilemmas to which Durkheim's own analyses at this point give rise. Societal totalities, Durkheim points out, not only pre-exist and post-date the lives of the individuals who reproduce them in their activities; they also stretch across space and time away from any particular agent considered singly. In this sense the structural properties of social systems are certainly exterior to the activities of 'the individual'. In structuration theory the essentials of this point can be put as follows. Human societies, or social systems, would plainly not exist without human agency. But it is not the case that actors create social systems: they reproduce or transform them, remaking what is already made in the continuity of *praxis*. The span of **time-space distanciation** is relevant here. In general (although certainly not universally) it is true that the greater the time-space distanciation of social systems – the more their institutions bite into time and space – the more resistant they are to manipulation or change by any individual agent. This meaning of constraint is also coupled to enablement. Time-space distanciation closes off some possibilities of human experience at the same time as it opens up others.

Durkheim's own formulations of this issue, however, is wanting, because it is couched in the terminology of what has come to be called by so many writers 'emergent properties'. Thus Durkheim remarks:

> The hardness of bronze lies neither in the copper, nor in the tin, nor in the lead which have been used to form it, which are all soft and malleable bodies. The hardness arises from the mixing of them. The liquidity of water, its sustaining and other properties, are not in the two gases of which it is composed, but in the complex substance which they form by coming together. Let us apply this principle to sociology. If, as is granted to us, this synthesis sui generis, which constitutes every society, gives rise to new phenomena, different from those which occur in consciousnesses in isolation, one is forced to admit that these specific facts reside in the society itself that produces them and not in its parts – namely its members. In this sense therefore they lie outside the consciousness of individuals as such, in the same way as the distinctive features of life lie outside the chemical substances that make up a living organism.
> (Durkheim, 1982)

I have quoted this passage at some length just because it is so well-known and has been referred to so often as a particularly persuasive formulation. Social systems do have structural properties that cannot be described in terms of concepts referring to the consciousness of agents. But human actors, as recognizable 'competent agents', do not exist in separation from one another as copper, tin and lead do. They do not come together *ex nihilo* to form a new entity by their fusion or association. Durkheim here confuses a hypothetical conception of individuals in a state of nature (untainted by association with others) and real processes of social reproduction.

A third circumstance in which 'constraint' appears in Durkheim's writings is in juxtaposition to the scope of action of the agent. Durkheim gives the following among other examples:

> When I perform my duties as brother, husband, or citizen, and carry out the commitments I have entered into, I fulfil obligations which are defined in law and custom which are external to myself and my actions. Even if they conform to my own sentiments and I feel their reality within me, that reality does not cease to be objective, for it is not I who have prescribed those duties.
> (Durkheim, 1982)

The point here is that 'social facts' have properties that confront each single individual as 'objective' features which limit that individual's scope of action. They are not just external but also externally defined, incorporated in what others do or in what they consider right and proper to do.

There is surely something correct about this claim, but Durkheim was prevented from spelling it out satisfactorily because of ambiguities about the motion of externality. In linking externality and constraint, especially in his earlier writings, he wanted to reinforce a naturalistic conception of social science. In other words, he wanted to find support for the idea that there are discernible aspects of social life governed by forces akin to those operative in the material world. Of course, 'society' is manifestly not external to individual actors in exactly the same sense as the surrounding environment is external to them. The parallel thus turns out to be at best a loose one, and a concern with it rests uneasily in Durkheim's later work alongside a recognition that the 'facticity' of the social world is in certain basic respects a very different phenomenon from the 'giveness' of nature.

Durkheim concentrated mostly upon social constraints in his various discussions of the nature of sociology. However, as Carlstein quite rightly points out – and as I have accentuated earlier, drawing upon the time-geography of which he himself is an expositor – fundamental constraints upon action are associated with the causal influences of the body and the material world. I have already indicated that these are regarded as of essential importance in structuration theory. Capability and coupling constraints, within definite material settings, do indeed 'screen' (as he puts it) the possible forms of activity in which human beings engage. But these phenomena are also at the same time enabling features of action. Moreover, as I have pointed out, there are major shortcomings in the usual formulations of time-geography.

The above aspects of constraint/enablement are not the same as, and are not to be reduced to, the operations of power in social life. Durkheim's sociology, in fact, may be seen as irremediably flawed in respect of the absence of a conception of power distinguished from the generalized constraining properties of 'social facts'. Consider one final celebrated passage from Durkheim. Constraint, he says, is

> intrinsically a characteristic of [social] facts ... the proof of this is that it asserts itself as soon as I try to resist. If I attempt to violate the rules of law, they react against me so as to forestall my action, if there is still time. Alternatively, they annul it or make my action conform to the norm if it is already accomplished but capable of being reversed; or they cause me to pay the penalty for it if it is irreparable. ... In other cases the constraint is less violent; nevertheless, it does not cease to exist. If I do not conform to ordinary conventions, if in my mode of dress I pay no heed to what is customary in my country and in my social class, the laughter I provoke, the social distance at which I am kept, produce, although in a more mitigated form, the same results as any real penalty.
>
> (Durkheim, 1982)

Constraint here refers to the structuration of social systems as forms of asymmetrical power, in conjunction with which a range of normative sanctions may be deployed against those whose conduct is condemned, or disapproved of, by others. As Durkheim's statement indicates, the constraints generated by different types of resource may range from naked physical coercion to much more subtle ways of producing compliance. But it does no good at all to collapse this meaning of constraint into the others. Moreover, as I have strongly underlined, power is never merely a constraint but is at the very origin of the capabilities of agents to bring about intended outcomes of action.

Each of the various forms of constraint are thus also, in varying ways, forms of enablement. They serve to open up certain possibilities of action at the same time as they restrict or deny others. It is important to emphasize this point because it shows that those, (including Durkheim and many others) who have hoped to find a distinctive identity for 'sociology' in the identification of structural constraint are embarked on a vain enterprise. Explicitly or otherwise, such authors have tended to see in structural constraint a source of causation more or less equivalent to the operation of impersonal causal forces in nature. The range of 'free action' which agents have is restricted, as it were, by external forces that set strict limits to what they can achieve. The more that structural constraint is associated with a natural science model, paradoxically, the freer the agent appears – within whatever scope for individual action is left by the operation of constraint. The structural properties of social systems, in other words, are like the walls of a room from which an individual cannot escape but inside which he or she is able to move around at whim. Structuration theory replaces this view with one which holds that structure is implicated in that very 'freedom of action' which is treated as a residual and unexplicated category in the various forms of 'structural sociology'.

Three senses of 'constraint'

Let me first of all consider the meaning of constraint in respect of material constraint and constraint associated with sanctions, then move to structural constraint. What is constraint when we speak of the constraining aspects of the body and its location in contexts of the material world? It evidently refers here to limits which the physical capacities of the human body, plus relevant features of the physical environment, place upon the feasible options open to agents. The indivisibility of the body, finitude of the life span and 'packing' difficulties in time-space are all examples of such limits. ... We are so used to treating these as enabling qualities that it is necessary to make something of a conceptual switch to stress that they are constraining also. Of course, these constraints are not wholly 'given', once and for all: the invention of electronic communication, for example, has altered the pre-existing relation between presence and the sensory media of the body. Alone among the categories mentioned above, constraint in this sense does not derive from the impact which the activities or social ties of actors have upon those of other actors. Physical capability and coupling constraints are limits to the feasible social lives that people can lead. ...

Turning to power as a source of constraint, again it needs to be stressed that power is the means of getting things done, very definitely enablement as well as constraint. The constraining aspects of power are experienced as *sanctions* of various kinds, ranging from the direct application of force or violence, or the threat of such application, to the mild expression of disapproval. Sanctions only very rarely take the shape of compulsion which those who experience them are wholly incapable of resisting, and even this can happen only for a brief moment, as when one person is physically rendered helpless by another or others. All other sanctions, no matter how oppressive and comprehensive they may be, demand some kind of acquiescence from those subject to them – which is the reason for the more or less universal purview of the dialectic of control. This is familiar enough ground. Even the threat of death carries no weight unless it is the case that the individual so threatened in some way values life. To say that an individual 'had no choice but to act in such and such a way', in a situation of this sort evidently means 'Given his/her desire not to die, the only alternative open was to act in the way he or she did.' Of course, where the threat offered by a sanction is not as lethal, compliance may depend more on mechanisms of conscience than on fear of any sanction – something, in fact, upon which Durkheim laid considerable emphasis in talking of 'moral sanctions'. In the case of sanctions there are obviously major asymmetries in the constraint/enablement relation. One person's constraint is another's enabling. However, as critiques of **zero-sum theories of power** have shown, such asymmetries by no means exhaust the scope of the concept of power. ...

What, then, of structural constraint? Once constraint deriving from sanctions is separated off, Durkheim's other points collapse into one if scrutinized at all closely. To say that society pre-exists the lives of each of its individual members at any given moment is only to identify a source of constraint in so far as its pre-existence in some way limits possibilities open to them. To emphasize that individuals are contextually situated within social relations of greater or lesser span is similarly only to identify a source of constraint if it is shown how this limits their capabilities. In each case constraint stems from the 'objective' existence of structural properties that the individual agent is unable to change. As with the constraining qualities of sanctions, it is best described as *placing limits upon the range of options open to an actor, or plurality of actors, in a given circumstance or type of circumstance.*

Take the example given by Durkheim, that of the enactment of contractual obligations, or one particular type of contract, the labour contract. Contract, of course, involves strongly defined legal sanctions, but let us conceptually filter them out. The contractual relations of modern industry face the individual with a set of circumstances which limit available options of action. Marx says that workers 'must sell themselves' – or, more accurately, their labour power – to employers. The 'must' in the phrase expresses a constraint which derives from the institutional order of modern capitalist enterprise that the worker faces. There is only one course of action open to the worker who has been rendered propertyless – to sell his or her labour power to the capitalist. That is to say, there is only one feasible option, given that the worker has the motivation to wish to survive. The 'option' in ques-

tion could be treated as a single one or as a multiple set of possibilities. That is to say, a worker may have a choice of more than one job opening in the labour market. Marx's point, however, is that these options effectively are of a single type. In respect of the rewards they offer to the worker, and of other features of the worker–employer relationship, all wage labour is effectively the same – and supposedly becomes even more so with the further development of capitalism.

All structural properties of social systems have a similar 'objectivity' *vis-à-vis* the individual agent. How far these are constraining qualities varies according to the context and nature of any given sequence of action or strip of interaction. In other words, the feasible options open to agents may be greater than in the case of the labour contract example. Let me reaffirm once more the theorem that all structural properties of social systems are enabling as well as constraining. The conditions of the capitalist labour contract may heavily favour employers as workers are dependent upon the resources that employers provide. Both sides derive their livelihood from the capital/wage-labour relation, heavily asymmetrical though it may be.

This analysis does not invalidate the sorts of claim that social scientists or historians make when they talk of 'social forces' without reference to agents' reasons or intentions. ...

Why is it that some social forces have an apparently 'inevitable' look to them? It is because in such instances there are few options open to the actors in question, given that they behave rationally – 'rationality' in this case meaning effectively aligning motives with the end-result of whatever conduct is involved. That is to say, the actors have 'good reasons' for what they do, reasons which the structural sociologist is likely to assume implicitly rather than explicitly attributing to those actors. Since such good reasons involve a choice from very limited feasible alternatives, their conduct may appear to be driven by some implacable force similar to a physical force. There are many social forces that actors, in a meaningful sense of that phrase, are 'unable to resist'. That is to say, they cannot do anything about them. But 'cannot' here means that they are unable to do anything other than conform to whatever the trends in question are, given the motives or goals which underlie their action.

I take it as one of the main implications of the foregoing points that there is no such entity as a distinctive type of 'structural explanation' in the social sciences; all explanations will involve at least implicit reference both to the purposive, reasoning behaviour of agents and to its intersection with constraining and enabling features of the social and material contexts of that behaviour.

References

Carlstein, T. (1981) 'The sociology of structuration in time and space: A time-geographic assessment of Giddens' theory', in *Swedish Geographical Yearbook*, Lund: Lund University Press.

Durkheim, E. (1982) *The Rules of the Sociological Method*, London: Macmillan (orig. pub. 1895).

Key terms

The following key terms appear in the text above. They have been defined below to aid with the reading of this item.

time-space distanciation the way in which advances in transport and communication have meant that social relations become stretched across time and space

zero-sum theories of power theories that suggest that there is only a fixed amount of power and therefore any gain in power by some will be matched by a loss of power by others

Questions

1 Explain in your own words Giddens' critique of structural sociology.

2 Explain why Giddens feels that various forms of constraint are also 'forms of enablement [which] serve to open up certain possibilities of action' (page 61, column one).

3 Giddens is critical of Durkheim's use of naturalistic analogies. Explain why this is, and what implications this has for the pursuit of sociology.

4 Suggest three examples of situations where structures enable action as well as constraining it.

5 Evaluate the criticism of structuration theory – acknowledged by Giddens – that his theory is in danger of 'sacrificing anything akin to structural constraint'.

Reading 3.8 **Sylvia Walby and the theory of patriarchy**

Sylvia Walby (from) *Theorizing Patriarchy* (1990) Oxford: Blackwell, pp. 173–79 and 200–1.

Editorial comments

Patriarchy, meaning male rule or control, is the key concept which has emerged in the feminist tradition in sociology. In recent years there have been several attempts to develop this term beyond a descriptive account of gender oppression, to try to analyse the mechanisms by which it works. Walby's work is perhaps the best known of these, attempting as it does to arrive at an explanation of gender oppression that links together the concepts of patriarchy, capitalism and racism. In this extract she outlines her argument that the nature of patriarchy has changed over time, moving from a private patriarchy to a public patriarchy.

From private to public patriarchy

Progress or regress?

PATRIARCHY IS NOT a historical constant. Modifications in gender relations over the last century or so have been interpreted variously as progress, regress and involving no overall change. Liberals typically define them as progress, Marxists as regress followed by stasis, and radical feminists as embracing no significant change. There are, of course, exceptions to these correlations of position within a perspective, but nonetheless they are common.

Liberal feminists have usually painted a picture of progress composed of the winning of the vote, entry into education, growth of the number of women in top jobs and the increase in the number of women in public life. Women have won rights and entered jobs and posts previously barred to them. Such advances accumulate and provide the basis of the next reform.

Marxists have typically argued that the development of capitalism led to a worsening of the position of women, with the separation of the home from paid work, but with little change in degree of inequality since then. Capitalism is considered to need the conventional family form, so there is little prospect of further major alteration in gender relations until there have been major changes in capitalism.

Radical feminists have generally concluded that for every victory won by women there has been a patriarchal backlash in another area. Patriarchy is a dynamic system in which men usually give up an activity only when they no longer wish to undertake it. If women do win a victory, then patriarchal forces will regroup and regain control over them in a different way (see, for instance, Millett's (1977) account of the development of new forms of control over women via sexuality after the winning of **political citizenship**).

International and multicultural perspectives on gender are divided in similar ways on the issue of progress or regress. The traditional view that modernization and Westernization have been progressive for women has been challenged both by those who have argued that these developments have been regressive, leading to the greater exploitation of women's labour by the capitalist West, and those who maintain that cultures are necessarily incomparable. The traditional position tended towards a white Western **ethnocentricity** which highlighted the disadvantages, but not the advantages of, non-British cultures for women. However, to declare cultures necessarily incomparable would mean that we could never talk of degrees of oppression nor even discuss the effects of imperialism.

In order to deal positively with these issues I think it is important to differentiate between degrees and forms of patriarchy. Degrees of patriarchy refers to the intensity of oppression on a specified dimension, for instance the size of the wages gap between men and women. Forms of patriarchy refers to the overall type of patriarchy, as defined by the specific relations between the different patriarchal structures. It is important not to conflate these two dimensions.

British feminists have won significant reforms which ameliorate a number of the features of patriarchy, but some have eventually resulted in a different form of patriarchy. Further, different ethnic groups may have different forms of patriarchy, without it being appropriate to suggest that one is better for women than another. Recent British history has seen a change in both the degree and form of patriarchy. There have been reductions in some specific aspects of patriarchy, but progressive reforms have been met with patriarchal counter-attack, often on new rather than the same issues. Private patriarchy has given way to public patriarchy.

Distinguishing forms of patriarchy

The conceptual distinction between different aspects of patriarchy has a long history in the analysis of gender relations. Most previous attempts to utilize the differentiation of the private and public have been narrowly restricted to one aspect of patriarchy. A classic early account is that of Rosaldo (1974), who argues that women's subordination is due to their confinement to the private sphere. She states that men's work is always more highly valued than is that of women. She suggests that women's subordination is a universal phenomenon, although it varies in degree, and that it is to be explained by the universal fact that women are confined to the private sphere of the family because they bear and rear children.

Women's subordination in the private sphere may be ameliorated when they are able to combine together, rather than be separated from each other. Rosaldo proposes that women's status would be lowest in those societies where there is the clearest split between the public and the private and where women are isolated from one another.

Other accounts have focused upon the spatial and historical variability in the private–public division. Boserup (1970) provides an empirically rich account of the different forms of sexual divisions of labour, especially in agriculture, on a world basis. She suggests that there are two main forms of sexual division in agricultural societies. In the first, found in most of Africa, women do most of the farming; the men have a restricted range of jobs, perhaps land clearing and hunting. In the second, found in places of plough agriculture such as Asia, men do most of the field labour. This can be further differentiated into those forms where the woman is in seclusion and veiled and those where the woman does perform some domestic labour. (There is another variant in which both sexes do a lot of agricultural labour.) Finally there are complex systems in which these different patterns are overlaid, though separated by class, caste or ethnicity. In the latter the wives of the ruling men are domesticated, while lower categories of women engage in public labour. Indeed the possibility of the first group of women to be domesticated may be predicated upon the exploitation of the labour of a subordinated group of women and men. The two groups of women are differentiated by class, caste or ethnicity. Colonial Europeans disrupted these patterns creating further complex systems of sexual division of labour.

As Beneria and Sen (1986) note, Boserup's account is undertheorized, especially in her use of modernization theory, rather than specifying the capitalist forces at work. However, I think it is also underformulated regarding gender relations. Boserup provides empirical support for an argument that there are major patterns in the sexual division of labour, but does not provide us with any theoretical understanding of this. ...

Guillaumin (1981) makes a distinction between the collective and private appropriation of women, the latter being a restrictive expression of the former. Patriarchal appropriation includes not only that of women's labour, but all aspects of women from their sexuality to psychological care. Juteau and Laurin (1986) develop this conception, pointing out that even if certain categories of women, such as nuns, escape private appropriation, they are, like all women, subject to collective appropriation. These materialist feminists provide a critical insight by making a distinction between different forms of appropriation simultaneously with recognizing that together they form one system of appropriation. The distinction between collective and private forms catches some important differences in the ways the appropriation is performed. This enables a comparison between the position of women in the form of patriarchy to which they are subject, without any necessary implications for the degree of patriarchy. However, the way the distinction is used places certain limitations on its heuristic utility for capturing historical change. This is because the focus is either on specific institutions or the whole. Rather it is better to have distinctions which relate to the different interconnection between the elements of patriarchy, and their relative significance in different eras.

The notion that there are two major historical forms of patriarchy is discussed in the work of Dworkin (1983) and Carol Brown (1981). Dworkin differentiates patriarchal control over women according to the regulation of their sexuality and reproductive capacity. In the first, the farming mode, the relationship involves being kept and exploited for life; in the second, the brothel mode, women ostensibly have more freedom since they are not possessed for life, but they lose support from men when their sexual and reproductive periods are over. This emphasizes the sexual dimension in the differentiation of the two forms of patriarchy. It is related to Dworkin's overall theory, which places sexuality centrally in relation to gender, even to the extent of conflating the two. Thus it is consistent with her theory of gender relations for her typology of forms of patriarchy to use sexuality as the key dimension. Evidence to support Dworkin's claim includes the movement in the main locus of control over women's sexuality from the private to the public sphere. As women are increasingly able to leave husbands and to engage in non-marital sexual relations, then public forms of control (e.g., via pornography) become more and more important. However, following my argument that sexuality is but one site of patriarchal relations, Dworkin's typology of patriarchal forms is limited because of this restriction and her failure to justify its exclusive focus.

Similarly, Brown is concerned only with a restricted area of patriarchy in her theory, that is, labour, and hence has a typology based upon this. As discussed in the chapter on household production, Brown's work produces powerful insights into the changing relationship of children to mothers and fathers, but is limited by this restriction to labour. It is powerful as an account insofar as the relationship between paid work and domestic work is the key to differences in women's position. Indeed today, with the changing form of the family, the labour market is an especially significant base of patriarchy.

Hernes (1984) also makes a distinction between private and public forms of patriarchy. Her explanation is specific to an analysis of the state, in particular the Norwegian state, though it applies, to a lesser degree, to all the Western industrialized nations that have developed a welfare state. She argues that women have reduced their dependence upon their husbands (private patriarchy), but increased their dependence upon the welfare state both as employees of the state and as clients receiving state services (public patriarchy).

I think that the distinction between private and public types of patriarchy does grasp important differences in form, but the accounts of Dworkin, Brown and Hernes are limited by their restriction to specific arenas, sexuality, labour and the state. We need one which takes into account the full range of patriarchal relations.

I would suggest that the different forms are dependent upon the interaction of six key patriarchal structures. These are the patriarchal mode of production; patriarchal relations in paid work; patriarchal relations in the state; male violence; patriarchal relations in sexuality; and patriarchal relations in cultural institutions including religions, media, education. In different times and places some of the structures are more important than others. The elimination of any one does not lead to the demise of the system as a whole. Logically there could be many forms, since I have identified six structures within patriarchy and two other major systems with which it has been in articulation. I am going to suggest that in recent Western history there have been two major forms, one of which can usefully be subdivided into two. The purpose of doing this is to demonstrate that patriarchy is not an ahistoric, universalistic concept. Further, I am arguing that the different aspects of gender inequality are sufficiently interrelated to be understood in terms of a system of patriarchy.

Critics who argue that the concept of patriarchy cannot deal with historical change have been shown to be wrong. It is sometimes argued that unless a theory of a social system comprehends a theory of the motor of change then it does not constitute a social system. However, I would argue that it is not necessary for a social system to have an inbuilt dynamic of change in order to be conceptualized as a social system. Indeed such a suggestion is an unwarranted a priori assumption. It is predicated on evolutionary notions of society. Patriarchy changes but it does not have an intrinsic evolutionary mechanism. This does not mean that it cannot be a social system. However, the understanding of change in patriarchal relations is an important question which should not be reduced to historical accident.

Private and public patriarchy

I am distinguishing between two forms of patriarchy:

private and public. They differ on a variety of levels: firstly, in terms of the relations between the structures and, secondly, in the institutional form of each structure. Further, they are differentiated by the main form of patriarchal strategy: exclusionary in private patriarchy and segregationist in public patriarchy. Private patriarchy is based upon household production, with a patriarch controlling women individually and directly in the relatively private sphere of the home. Public patriarchy is based on structures other than the household, although this may still be a significant patriarchal site. Rather, institutions conventionally regarded as part of the public domain are central in the maintenance of patriarchy.

In private patriarchy it is a man in his position as husband or father who is the direct oppressor and beneficiary, individually and directly, of the subordination of women. This does not mean that household production is the sole patriarchal structure. Indeed it is importantly maintained by the active exclusion of women from public arenas by other structures. The exclusion of women from these other spheres could not be perpetuated without patriarchal activity at these levels.

Public patriarchy is a form in which women have access to both public and private arenas. They are not barred from the public arenas, but are nonetheless subordinated within them. The expropriation of women is performed more collectively than by individual patriarchs. The household may remain a site of patriarchal oppression, but it is no longer the main place where women are present.

In each type of patriarchy the six structures are present, but the relationship between them, and their relative significance, is different. For instance, I am not arguing that in private patriarchy the only significant site is that of the household. In the different forms there are different relations between the structures to maintain the system of patriarchy.

In the private system of patriarchy the exploitation of women in the household is maintained by their non-admission to the public sphere. In a sense the term 'private' for this form of patriarchy might be misleading, in that it is the exclusion from the public which is the central causal mechanism. Patriarchal relations outside the household are crucial in shaping patriarchal relations within it. However, the effect is to make women's experience of patriarchy privatized, and the immediate beneficiaries are also located there.

In the public form of patriarchy the exploitations of women takes place at all levels, but women are not formally excluded from any. In each institution women are disadvantaged.

The second aspect of the difference between private and public patriarchy is in the institutional form of each of the structures. This is a movement from an

individual to a more collective form of appropriation of women. There has also been a shift in patriarchal strategy from exclusionary to segregationist and subordinating.

I have traced the movement from private to public patriarchy within each of the six patriarchal structures. Within paid work there was a shift from an exclusionary strategy to a segregationist one, which was a movement from attempting to exclude women from paid work to accepting their presence but confining them to jobs which were segregated from and graded lower than those of men. In the household there was a reduction in the confinement of women to this sphere over a lifetime and a shift in the main locus of control over reproduction. The major cultural institutions ceased to exclude women, while subordinating women within them. Sexual controls over women significantly shifted from the specific control of a husband to that of a broader public arena; women were no longer excluded from sexual relations to the same extent, but subordinated within them. Women's exclusion from the state was replaced by their subordination within it. ...

Conclusion

Patriarchy comes in more than one form; each form can be found to different degrees. British history over the last century or so has seen a shift to a more intensive form of private patriarchy and then a dramatic reversal of this with a move towards public patriarchy. This latter shift was a result of the successes of first-wave feminism against the background of an expanding capitalist economy. It took its forms in different ethnic groups. The British form of public patriarchy involves the market as well as the state, while there is a different sub-type of public patriarchy in Eastern Europe in which the state plays a more central part in comparison with the market.

The major historical changes are different for gender relations from those of capitalist class relations. Gender and class have independent historical dynamics, although of course they do have effects upon each other. The rise of capitalism transformed class relations, changing the very classes which constituted society. This historical shift did not have such dramatic effects upon gender relations: men remained the dominant gender; all six patriarchal structures continued across this period; only a minor shift in the relative significance of public and private sites of patriarchy occurred. The trajectory towards an intensified private form of patriarchy, which can be identified as far back as the seventeenth century, accelerated.

Gender relations are not static, and a developed concept of patriarchy is the best way of theorizing the changes. The idea of patriarchy does not necessarily give rise to fixed, ahistoric analysis.

Women are not passive victims of oppressive structures. They have struggled to change both their immediate circumstances and the wider social structures. First-wave feminism is a much more important historical force than is usually considered. This major feminist push changed the course of history. However, it did not lead to an elimination of all the forms of inequality between men and women which it sought to eradicate. In some ways early feminists won their goals, and their successes were considerable. However, in response, patriarchy changed in form, incorporating some of the hard-won changes into new traps for women.

The form of patriarchy in contemporary Britain is public rather than private. Women are no longer restricted to the domestic hearth, but have the whole society in which to roam and be exploited.

References

Beneria, L. and Sen, G. (1986) 'Accumulation reproduction and women's role in economic development: Boserup revisited', in Leacock, E. and Safa, H. I. (eds) *Women's Work: Development and the division of labour by gender*, South Hadley: South End Press.

Boserup, E. (1970) *Women's Role in Economic Development*, London: Allen & Unwin.

Brown, C. (1981) 'Mothers, fathers and children: from private to public patriarchy', in Sargent, L. (ed.) *Women and Revolution: The unhappy marriage of Marxism and feminism*, London: Pluto Press.

Dworkin, A. (1983) *Right Wing Women: The politics of domesticated females*, London: Women's Press.

Guillaumin, C. (1981) 'The practice and power of belief in nature, part 1: the appropriation of women', *Feminist Issues 1*.

Hernes, H. M. (1984) 'Women and the welfare state: the transition from private to public dependence', in Holter, H. (ed.) *Patriarchy in a Welfare Society*, Oslo: Universitetsforlaget.

Juteau, D. and Laurin, N. (1986) 'Nuns in the labour force: a neglected contribution', *Feminist Issues*, Fall.

Millett, K. (1977) *Sexual Politics*, London: Virago.

Rosaldo, M. Z. (1974) 'Woman, culture and society: a theoretical overview', in Rosaldo, M. Z. and Lamphere, L. (eds) *Woman, Culture and Society*, Stanford: Stanford University Press.

Key terms

The following key terms appear in the text above. They have been defined below to aid with the reading of this item.

liberal feminists liberal feminism mainly seeks to achieve equality through legal changes

Marxists (feminists) Marxist feminism seeks to achieve equality through involvement in Marxist revolutions linking the fight against patriarchy to the fight against capitalism

radical feminists radical feminism sees the main division in society as that between men and women – an oppressive relationship which women can only escape by living separately from men

political citizenship the possession of political rights, notably the right to vote (won by women in the UK following the Suffragette campaign in 1918 and finally on an equal footing with men in 1928)

ethnocentricity viewing the world from the perspective of your own particular society, notably by using your own particular experiences as a standard of normality; this often ends up with others being seen as inferior

Questions

1 Explain in your own words the ways in which the degree and form of patriarchy can differ, according to Walby.

2 What does Walby mean by the distinction she makes between 'exclusionary strategies' of patriarchy and 'segregationist strategies' of patriarchy?

3 Walby argues that 'British history over the last century or so has seen a shift to a more intense form of private patriarchy and then a dramatic reversal of this with a move towards public patriarchy' (page 66, column two). Explain in your own words what she means by this and identify the key mechanism she sees as responsible for the latter shift.

4 Suggest three examples of oppression women face under private patriarchy and three examples of oppression women face under public patriarchy.

5 How far do you find the distinction between public and private patriarchy a convincing one?

Further reading

The following texts may represent a useful starting point for further investigation of the ideas contained within this chapter.

Primary texts

Gerth, H. and Mills, C. W. (eds) (1948) *From Max Weber, Essays in Sociology*, London: Routledge and Kegan Paul.

Giddens, A. (ed.) (1988) *Emile Durkheim: Selected writings*, Cambridge: Cambridge University Press.

Marx, K. and Engels, F. (1968) *Selected Works in One Volume*, London: Lawrence & Wishart.

Pearce, F. (1989) *The Radical Durkheim*, London: Unwin Hyman.

Stones, R. (1996) *Sociological Reasoning: Towards a past-modern sociology*, Basingstoke: Macmillan.

Secondary texts

Bottomore, T. and Nisbet, R. (1979) *A History of Sociological Analysis*, London: Heinemann.

Cuff, E. C., Sharrock, W.W. and Francis, D. W. (1990) *Perspectives in Sociology*, 3rd edn, London: Routledge.

Jones, P. (1993) *Studying Society: Sociological theories and research practices*, London: Collins Educational.

4

Research methods

Chapter summary

Reading 4.1 **Positivism or positivisms?** *page 71*
Christopher Bryant outlines the key basic beliefs of positivism and points to the many varieties of positivism, leading to the conclusion that we need to understand that there are many positivisms rather than the monolithic approach as represented in certain textbooks.

Reading 4.2 **Giddens' new rules of the sociological method** *page 75*
Anthony Giddens responds to *The Rules of the Sociological Method*, written by Emile Durkheim, explaining where and how he disagrees with Durkheim and injecting a more social action, informed approach to methodology.

Reading 4.3 **Realism and social science** *page 78*
William Outhwaite outlines the basis of one of the most recent methodological approaches to emerge in sociology – namely realism. He points to some of the key implications of this approach and contrasts it with the older positivist and phenomenological approaches.

Reading 4.4 **The problems of merging structure and action** *page 81*
Margaret Archer has been a consistent critic of the attempt (seen most famously in Anthony Giddens' work) to merge together consideration of social structures and social action. She outlines the problems in this and also considers some of the methodological implications which flow from her critique, based on a realist approach to sociology.

Reading 4.5 **Ethnomethodology** *page 85*
While ethnomethodology developed into a whole theoretical approach in sociology, it first came to prominence with the series of breaching experiments promoted by Harold Garfinkel as a way of exploring the methodology by which people make sense of the world. This reading outlines some of the purposes of these experiments.

Reading 4.6 **The ethnographic approach** *page 89*
Drawing ultimately on the insights of anthropology and with participant observation as one of its most notable methods, the whole ethnographic approach is concerned with achieving a detailed and valid picture of reality. Here, Valerie Hey discusses some of the issues involved in utilizing this method.

Reading 4.7 **The variety of sampling techniques** *page 93*
While probably not the most exciting subject in the world, this issue is probably one of the most important when considering the methodological value of any sociological study. Here, Sotirios Sarantakos discusses and evaluates a whole variety of sampling techniques.

Reading 4.8 **Official statistics** *page 99*
Martin Slattery outlines some of the main sources of official statistics that are of use to sociologists, along with some points about the way to interpret with care the figures they present.

Introduction: Reading sociological methodology

One of the key things that distinguishes science from common sense is the careful application of a rigorous methodology designed to ensure we can tell truths from falsehoods. It is on this basis that sociology was seen as a science. However, the philosophical issues surrounding whether we can use the scientific method, as first applied to rocks and plants – and indeed whether there is such a thing as truth, and whether we can gain access to it – remain important methodological issues which we need to confront before we rush out into the world with clipboards and questionnaires. The term methodology refers to the whole framework of beliefs which underlies social research and can be distinguished from method, which simply refers to the particular technique that is used (e.g. questionnaires, interviews, observation, etc.). Before conducting research, we need to think about the tools of the trade.

The first selection of readings in this chapter comprise recent statements on this issue. Firstly, in **reading 4.1**, Christopher Bryant (1985) points to the inadequacy of most treatments of the approach known as positivism. He points to the variety of approaches that exist and which share that name, and furthermore discusses some of the key principles that lie behind this approach in sociology.

One of the classical sociologists who was associated with developing the methodological implications of positivism was Emile Durkheim (1938, orig. pub. 1895) in his *Rules of the Sociological Method*. Anthony Giddens (1976) (**reading 4.2**) who has been more influenced by the social action/phenomenological arguments in sociology wrote his *New Rules of the Sociological Method* as a dialogue with the principles outlined by Durkheim, and he ends up with very different conclusions.

More recently we have seen the emergence of a third distinctive approach in sociology – that known as realism. This is associated primarily with structuralist approaches, but with a rejection of positivistic notions of evidence and empirical evidence in particular. In **reading 4.3**, William Outhwaite (1987) outlines some of the key implications of a realist approach for the social sciences, and in **reading 4.4**, Margaret Archer (1995) – one of the key contemporary exponents of the realist approach – argues that the attempt, most notably by Anthony Giddens (1984), to combine and conflate social structural and social action analysis is a mistake and that instead we need to recognize these as linked but analytically separate levels of analysis which require distinct methodological approaches.

One very distinctive approach which developed in sociology in the 1960s and 1970s was that of ethnomethodology. While this is also quite properly a theoretical approach in sociology, its name should alert us to the fact that it is also concerned with a methodology of studying the methodology of humans in the creation of society. In **reading 4.5**, Harold Garfinkel (1984) outlines some of the methodologies he used to identify the way people make sense of social situations.

The word 'ethnos' has also been more recently attached to the growth in interest in ethnography as a methodology for sociology. This approach, which ultimately developed from the anthropological studies of less developed societies, has been adapted by those with an interest in understanding how individuals and social groups interpret and create the world around them. In **reading 4.6**, Valerie Hey (1997) outlines how she used an ethnographic approach in her recent study of girls' friendships inside London schools.

One issue that does arise with ethnographic research is the extent to which such studies can be seen to have a bearing on the rest of society, leading to discussion of the whole question of representativeness; and this brings us to the issue of sampling, an area that does not often grab the headlines but is nonetheless important if we are to claim that we can make statements about the whole of society. The selection from Sarantakos (1993) (**reading 4.7**) runs through the wide variety of sampling techniques and discusses some of the issues that arise in relation to them.

Finally, it is important to remember the large volume of material of interest to sociologists which arises from official government surveys – material known as official statistics. In **reading 4.8** – an extract from his book on the subject – Martin Slattery (1986) reflects on the important questions sociologists need to ask when confronted with official statistics. He also considers the wide variety of official statistics that are available for use by sociologists.

The study of methodology is important for the quite simple reason that we seek to explain the world and we must therefore ensure that the process of studying and researching does not itself introduce any distortions it is possible to avoid and therefore to present an inaccurate picture of reality. As easy as it is to outline this as an aim, it is extremely difficult to achieve in practice, which is why the study of methodology is so fundamental to all aspects of sociology.

References

Durkheim, E. (1938, orig. pub. 1895) *The Rules of the Sociological Method*, Glencoe: Free Press.

Giddens, A. (1984) *The Constitution of Society*, Cambridge: Polity.

Reading 4.1 **Positivism or positivisms?**

Christopher Bryant, *Positivism in Social Theory and Research* (1985) London: Macmillan, pp. 1–10.

Editorial comments

The term positivism has been central to theoretical debates over methodology in sociology. However, for too long it has been considered a monolithic (meaning only one form of) brand of social thinking. In this reading, Christopher Bryant outlines some of the key points of positivism and draws attention to the many varieties of social thought that have been labelled positivist.

Positivism or positivisms?

THE TERMS 'POSITIVISM' and 'sociology' are both commonly supposed to have originated with Comte, and in particular his *Cours de philosophie positive* (6 vols. 1830–42). Although true of the second, this is misleading with respect to the first term insofar as Comte wrote not about 'positivism' (even if his supporters quickly did) but about 'the positive philosophy' and 'the positive method', and Saint-Simon before him had also advocated a positive philosophy. The correct identification of the origins of the term is, however, but a minor issue, given that to originate a term is not to secure a monopoly on its subsequent usage; both positivism and sociology have long since ceased to be the preserve of Comte and his followers. Indeed positivism in philosophy has come to be associated with **epistemologies** which make experience the foundation of all knowledge, and also with their complementary ontologies which propose a division between objects which are accessible to observation (about which knowledge is therefore possible) and objects which are not (and about which there can therefore be no knowledge); and positivism in sociology has come to be associated with the very idea of a social *science* and the quest to make sociology scientific. Inevitably both the philosophical and sociological debates about positivism have proved complicated in that what counts as foundation and as experience, and what counts as science, are themselves highly contentious matters. In the last two decades in sociology, 'positivist' and 'neo-positivist' have become so much pejorative terms that self-avowed positivists are hard to come by. Even so, critics detect positivists everywhere, though disconcertingly few of them seem to have taken exception to the inclusion of sociology among the 'social sciences', whether in the categorization of intellectual pursuits or in the social organization of academic disciplines into faculties. ...

I want first to consider the most systematically developed of general definitions, or formulations, of positivism, that presented by the philosopher, Kolakowski, and extended by the sociologist, Giddens (Kolakowski, 1996; Giddens, 1974). I shall argue that general formulations such as this are of value in that they point up certain central issues, but that this value is strictly limited in that they are so insensitive to much of what the debate about positivism in sociology has been about in different intellectual and cultural contexts. I shall then introduce the three main contexts. By proceeding in this way, I hope to supply the qualifications without which, as MacIntyre (1979) has noted, the term 'positivism' is not very informative.

In his 'overall view', Kolakowski presents positivism as 'a collection of rules and evaluative criteria for referring to human knowledge', and 'as a normative attitude, regulating how we use such terms as "knowledge", "science", "cognition" and "information"' (1966). There are four main rules (K1–K4) and they indicate what counts as knowledge and what may reasonably be asked.

K1   *The rule of phenomenalism*
This states that 'We are entitled to record only that which is actually manifested in experience'. It admits **phenomena** to knowledge but not **noumena**, existence but not essence. Kolakowski stresses that 'positivists do not object to inquiry into the immediately invisible causes of any observed phenomenon, they object only to any accounting for it in terms of occult entities that are by definition inaccessible to human knowledge'. Positivism, then, leaves no place for metaphysics. This rule is the one most often attributed to positivism. ...

The application of the rule of phenomenalism to sociology presents certain difficulties, three of which are important enough to introduce now. First, the idea that we can know reality only on the basis of experience may be thought to provide a warrant for empiricism and induction. ... Nevertheless, from Comte onwards, many 'positivist' sociologists have insisted that theories are indispensable in the identification of significant experience and the selection of objects for observation. Of course it can be argued that it is still a failing of these sociologists that they acknowledge the indispensability of theory only in the selection of facts whose constitution is an atheoretical given. Even so, this stricture cannot properly be levelled at Weber, the celebrant of **value relevance**, and yet Weber remains, in the judgement of some, a positivist.

Second, the emphasis on experience would seem to necessitate a neutral observation language for the recording of experience, i.e. a language which adds nothing to experience. Be this as it may, there have been few explicit proponents of a neutral observation language among leading sociologists during the last hundred years. ...

Although there are few notable claimants for a neutral observation language in sociology, it is regrettably evident that most empirical social researchers have paid little attention to internal connections between concepts, hypotheses, objects of inquiry and empirical findings. They have learnt from Popper – a self-avowed critical rationalist but a positivist to his German critics – the idea of testing theories against facts which are independent of them, without asking in what sense, if any, facts which are defined in the same term as theories are also independent of them.

Third, as Kolakowski himself notes, it is difficult to be sure just what is in principle accessible to observation, and what is not. This issue has been revived in the discussion of the new 'realism' which, in its construction of explanations, has recourse to hidden structures and mechanisms of a kind which Comte would supposedly have dismissed as metaphysical (cf. Keat and Urry, 1975).

K2   *The rule of nominalism*
The rule of nominalism follows from the first rule and is often merged with it. It states 'that we may not assume that any insight formulated in general terms can have any real referents other than individual facts'. 'According to nominalism', Kolakowski continues, 'every abstract science is a method of abridging the recording of experience and gives us no extra, independent knowledge in the sense that, via its abstractions, it opens access to empirically inaccessible domains of reality'. Thus the general entities of **metaphysics** are dismissed as fictions 'for they illegitimately ascribed existence to things that have no existence such as names or words'. ...

The translation of this rule to sociology poses a special problem. Does the rule of nominalism demand that social facts be in some way reducible to individual facts? ... Much of the confusion derives from a failure to separate two distinctions – the particular and the universal, and the individual and the social – for social facts can be treated as particulars, as both Rickert and Weber demonstrated in their discussions of historical individuals.

K3   *The rule that refuses to call value judgements and normative statements knowledge*
According to the rule of phenomenalism, 'we are obliged to reject the assumption of values as characteristics of the world for they are not discoverable in the same way as the only kind of knowledge worthy of the name' (Kolakowski, 1996). In addition, the rule of nominalism renders untenable 'the assumption that beyond the visible world there exists a domain of values "in themselves", with which our evaluations are correlated in some mysterious way'. In sociology, however, the issue has not been whether values are objects in the world, but rather whether evaluations can be justified scientifically or rationally. For this Giddens' version of the rule, viz 'judgements of value have no empirical content of a sort which renders them accessible to any tests of the "validity" in the light of experience', is more appropriate (1974).

The French tradition from Saint-Simon to Durkheim tried to find some law of history which governed the variations in values and norms to be found in societies of different social types, in the belief that such a law would allow moral and political choice and decision making to proceed on a scientific basis. In other words, it sought a unity of scientific knowledge and political evaluation. If, on the other hand, there are no such laws, but science is still synonymous with knowledge or rational discourse, then moral and political judgements can only reflect arbitrary choices. In this connection Weber's position is interesting. It is arguable whether he equates knowledge with science – the German *'Wissenschaft'* is not identical in meaning to the English 'science' – but he certainly does describe the forces which generate basic values as demonic. Such a view has exposed him to Habermas's change of arbitrary decisions, of unargued commitments. In America the Kantian dualism attributed to Weber has been used by some sociologists to justify the plying of their technical skills for hire. These sociologists are then accused, not of arbitrary subscription to particular values, but of amoralism, of unconcern for value commitments altogether, in the name of value freedom and in the belief that visible commitments would sully their greatest asset, their reputation for objectivity. The Durkeimian, the Weberian, and this particular American position have all been labelled positivist, and yet they are very different. The first looks forward to the eventual scientific determination of political choices, the second laments the depolitization which follows from the misrepresentation of ineliminably political issues as matters that can be resolved by science, and the third promotes a science which warms to the prospect of money whilst shifting uncomfortably at the very mention of politics.

K4 Belief in the essential unity of the scientific method

Kolkowski's fourth tenet is also full of difficulties. Some positivists have argued that the unity of science stems from a single fundamental law from which all other laws are ultimately derived (Saint-Simon's candidate was the law of gravity) or from certain evolutionary processes common to nature and society (*vide* Spencer on differentiation). Kolakowski, however, does clearly refer to the unity of scientific *method*. Even so, there remain grave difficulties in that among 'positivist' intellectual formations from Comte onwards one repeatedly encounters the twin claims that all the sciences possess certain principles and practices in common and that each science must elaborate principles and practices of its own in response to the particular character of its objects of inquiry. As this covers most possibilities, it is imperative that the idea of the unity of scientific method be given a specific meaning or otherwise it becomes the kind of notion that one can accept or reject without it making any difference either way. From Comte to Popper, however, no version of the unity of scientific method has ever won universal assent. In any case there are now philosophers of science who dispute the idea of unity of method even in natural science, as Feyerabend, with his sorties *Against Method* (1975), vividly testifies.

Giddens discusses the particular problems of positivism in sociology, as distinct from the general problem of positivism in philosophy, in connection with 'the assertion that the concepts and methods employed in the natural sciences can be applied to form a "science of man", or a natural science of sociology' (1974). His account of positivism in sociology is thus most directly related to Kolakowski's fourth rule, belief in the unity of scientific method, although it also has connections with the other three. According to Giddens, 'the "positivistic attitude" in sociology may be said to comprise three connected suppositions' (G1–G3).

G1 The methodological supposition that the procedures of natural science may be directly adapted to sociology

This assumes that 'phenomena of human subjectivity, of volition and will, do not offer any particular barriers to the treatment of social conduct as an object on a par with objects in the natural world' (Giddens, 1974). Such a supposition, however, only invites the awkward question 'How much adaptation is necessary before adaptation can no longer be deemed "direct"?' For example, does Weber's attempt to combine interpretive understanding and causal analysis constitute a direct or an indirect adaptation: is it positivist or is it not? It is also worth noting that few sociologists since Comte and Spencer have actually known much about the procedures of the natural sciences. Instead, those who have sought to be scientific have attended either to what they suppose to be the procedures of the natural sciences, or to what philosophers from the Vienna Circle to Popper, Kuhn and even Feyerabend have given them to understand are the procedures of science, or to what leading figures in statistics, from Pearson to Blalock, have put forward as acceptable empirical social research analogues to the controlled experiment of natural science. In consequence there has never been much consistency as to what it is that sociology is supposed to adapt or adopt.

G2 The analytical supposition that the end-result of sociological investigations can be formulated as 'laws' or 'law-like' generalizations of the same kind as those established by natural scientists

Here the inclusion of 'law-like generalizations' is evidence of ambiguity as to what counts as a law. One such ambiguity arises with the dual suggestion that natural laws are universal (i.e. not bound by time and space) and that they obtain with a natural necessity, whereas social laws are bound by historical period and culture and do not obtain with a natural necessity. ... This view dismisses the false unity of scientific method proposed by positivism, but keeps faith with the idea of unity itself, which is then called 'naturalism'. The favoured candidate of this anti-positivist naturalism is currently 'realism', but in principle other alternatives are possible.

G3 The practical assumption that sociology has a technical character

This assumes that sociological knowledge is purely 'instrumental' in form and that sociological research acquires findings which 'do not carry any logically given implications for practical policy or for the pursuit of values' (Giddens, 1974). The trouble here is that the French tradition of positivism did seek findings which carry logically given implications for practical policy. Also, although concern for the correct use of reliable research instruments can lead to a sociology which restricts itself to only such objects of inquiry as its 'hard-science' techniques allow it to pursue – indeed this is often said to have happened with the development of empirical social research in America – in the French tradition, at least, there was no special interest in research instrumentation but rather a commitment to the comparative and other macro methods. Thus, whilst positivist sociology can refer to a narrow preoccupation with scientifically attested research techniques (instrumental positivism) the French tradition of positivism shows that it can also refer to broad theory of social development. ...

Inspection of the attempts made by Kolakowski and Giddens to articulate overall views of positivism confirms their limited value. Although they provide general orientations and highlight certain central issues, overviews of this kind cannot do justice to important variations in the characterization of positivism in sociology at different times and places, as Giddens himself recognizes (1977). At the very least, then, overviews need to be complemented by analyses of these different characterizations. It is not possible to attend to all of them but ... I shall discuss those that have crystallized in three different intellectual and cultural contexts. All three are complex, however, and the remarks which follow anticipate only a few of the more distinctive features of each. The first is the French tradition of positivism from Saint-Simon to Durkheim. I shall begin with it because it was the first so to call itself. Three of the twelve tenets I shall later attribute to it deserve immediate note, viz that all knowledge is relative, that choices as to moral and political action and policy are now, or will in the future be, resolvable in terms of doing that which is consistent with the laws of history and society, and that society is a reality *sui generis*. This last tenet provides an important point of contrast with the prevailing individualism of Spencer and other British social scientists. The second discussion is of developments in German and Austrian social theory and research before 1933 and after 1945. In particular I shall argue that there are continuities between the *Methodenstreit* and the *Werturteilsstreit* of the era before the First World War and the *Positivismusstreit* of the 1960s in that the following issues recur: the constitution of the object worlds of the natural and cultural sciences; the relationship of the knowing subject to the object world; the status of the referents of general concepts and other products of abstraction; the status of the connections posited between objects; the unity, or otherwise, of science; and the purposes of knowledge and the relations between theory and practice. Inevitably, Weber figures prominently in this discussion but it also affords opportunities to consider the Vienna Circle and Popper. The third development discussed is that of empirical social research in America from the 1930s to the present. Empirical social research had its origins in Europe but it rose to pre-eminence only in America where it may be said to have constituted an 'instrumental positivism'. Three of its five main characteristics merit summary statement here, viz the preoccupation with the refinement of statistical techniques and research instrumentation, the endorsement of an individualistic conception of society and the commitment to a version of the idea of value-freedom which is very different from Weber's though it has often been proffered in his name. All three of these characteristics distinguish it from the French tradition.

References

Comte, A. (1830–42) *Cours de Philosophie Positive*, Paris: Bachelier.

Feyerabend, P. (1975) *Against Method*, London: New Left Books.

Giddens, A. (1974) *Positivism and Sociology*, London: Heinemann.

Giddens, A. (1977) *Studies in Social and Political Theory*, London: Hutchinson.

Keat, R. and Urry, J. (1975) *Social Theory as Science*, London: Routledge & Kegan Paul.

Kolakowski, L. (1996) *Positivist Philosophy: From Hume to the Vienna Circle*, Harmondsworth: Penguin.

MacIntyre, A. (1979) 'Positivism', in Mitchell, G. D. (ed.) *A New Dictionary of Sociology*, London: Routledge & Kegan Paul.

Key terms

The following key terms appear in the text above. They have been defined below to aid with the reading of this item.

epistemologies theories of knowledge that consider the extent to which we can arrive at true knowledge of the world – and on what basis

phenomena/noumena the distinction between that which is immediately observable (phenomena) and that which is not (noumema). Critics of positivism state that it concentrates solely on the former and that this ignores the point that things which are not observable can and do exist

value relevance Weber's argument that your interests would determine your choice of research topic but that this should not mean you would allow your values to intrude into the actual way you researched the issue

metaphysics philosophical speculation about the world which is not amenable to scientific investigation and therefore, for some, cannot count as knowledge

Questions

1 Explain what Bryant means by naturalism and identify what he calls the favoured contemporary version of anti-positivistic naturalism in sociology.

2 Outline in your own words the three component parts of positivism in sociology.

3 Drawing on material in the reading and from elsewhere, outline in detail the three versions of positivism that Bryant identifies.

4 Explain what is meant by instrumental positivism.

5 To what extent do you agree that sociology should restrict itself to the study of objects that are accessible to observation?

Reading 4.2 **Giddens' new rules of sociological method**

Anthony Giddens (from) *The New Rules of the Sociological Method* (1976) London: Hutchinson, pp. 155 and 157–62.

Editorial comments

Giddens' book echoes the title of Durkheim's much earlier book, seen as a key basis of positivism or, more recently, realism. Here, Giddens examines the key legacy of the interpretative tradition in sociology and uses this to develop his own thoughts on sociological methodology. These hinge ultimately on his view that society and nature are very different entities and therefore any attempt to arrive at a social science modelled on the natural sciences will fail.

Some new rules of sociological method

THE SCHOOLS OF 'interpretative sociology' have made some essential contributions to the clarification of the logic and method of the social sciences. In summary form, these are the following: the social world, unlike the world of nature, has to be grasped as a skilled accomplishment of active human subjects; the constitution of this world as 'meaningful', 'accountable' or 'intelligible' depends upon language, regarded however not simply as a system of signs or symbols but as a medium of practical activity; the social scientist of necessity draws upon the same sorts of skills as those whose conduct he seeks to analyse in order to describe it; generating descriptions of social conduct depends upon the hermeneutic task of penetrating the frame of meaning which lay actors themselves draw upon in constituting and reconstituting the social world. ...

Orthodox functionalism, as represented most prominently by Durkheim and latterly by Parsons, does embody an attempt to draw theoretical connections between intentional action and institutional analysis, via the theorem that the moral values upon which social solidarity rests also appear as motivating elements in personality. This view, I have tried to show, serves only to replace the notion of action with the thesis that the properties of social and personality systems have to be examined in conjunction with one another: the member of society does not figure here as a skilled, creative agent, capable of **reflexively** monitoring his behaviour (and in principle capable of doing so in the light of anything he may believe he can learn from Parsons' theories!). Moreover, the Parsonian starting-point in the so-called 'Hobbesian problem of order' has the consequence that Parsons' theoretical scheme is no more able adequately to cope with asymmetries of power and divisions of interest in society then are the various traditions of 'interpretative sociology' that I have discussed. I have therefore set out an alternative view, that certainly is capable of more detailed development, but whose outlines should be clear. The production of society is brought about by the active constituting skills of its members, but draws upon resources, and depends upon conditions, of which they are unaware or which they perceive only dimly. Three aspects of the production of interaction can be distinguished: those of the constitution of meaning, morality and relations of power. The means whereby these are brought into being can also be regarded as modalities of the reproduction of structures: the idea of the **duality of structure** is a central one here, since structures appear both as condition and consequence of the production of interaction. All organizations or collectivities 'consist of' systems, their existence depends upon modes of *structuration* whereby they are reproduced. The reproduction of structures of domination, one must emphasize, expresses asymmetries in the forms of meaning and morality that are made to 'count' in interaction, thus tying them in to divisions of interest that serve to orient struggles over divergent interpretations of frames of meaning and moral norms.

The production of interaction as 'meaningful', I have proposed, can usefully be analysed as depending upon 'mutual knowledge' which is drawn upon by participants as interpretative schemes to make sense of what each other says and does. Mutual knowledge is not corrigible to the sociological observer, who must draw upon it just as lay actors do in order to generate descriptions of their conduct; in so far as such 'knowledge' however, can be represented as 'commonsense', as a series of factual beliefs, it is in principle open to confirmation or otherwise in the light of social scientific analysis. Recent developments in the philosophy of natural science, I have argued, are relevant to elucidating the logical status of claims to knowledge made in the social sciences. But their relevance is limited by features of the latter which have no immediate parallel in the natural sciences; and in any case such developments themselves have to be subjected to critical scrutiny. Kuhn's use of the term 'paradigm' shares important elements in common with other versions of the notion of what I have called 'frame of meaning', and as Kuhn applies it to analysing the history of science also raises similar difficulties to these other versions. Thus Kuhn exaggerates the internal unity of 'paradigms', as Winch does 'forms of life', and consequently does not acknowledge that the problem of the mediation of different frames of meaning has to be treated as the *starting point* of analysis. When conjoined to an insistence upon a distinction of sense and reference, this allows us to grasp the significance of the hermeneutic recognition of the authenticity of meaning-frames without slipping into a relativism which forecloses the possibility of any rational evaluation of them. The mediation of paradigms or widely discrepant theoretical schemes in science is a hermeneutic matter like that involved in the contracts between other types of meaning-frames. But sociology, unlike natural science, deals with a pre-interpreted world, where the creation and reproduction of meaning-frames is a very condition of that which it seeks to analyse, namely human social conduct: this is, to repeat, why there is a **double hermeneutic** in the social sciences that poses as a specific difficulty what Schutz, following Weber calls the 'postulate of adequacy'. I have suggested that Schutz' formulation of this, based upon the thesis that the technical concepts of social science have to be in some way capable of being reduced to lay notions of everyday action, will not do. It has in fact to be reversed: rather than, in some sense, the concepts of sociology having to be open to rendition in terms of lay concepts, it is the case that the observing social scientist has to be able first to grasp those lay concepts, i.e. penetrate hermeneutically the form of life whose features he wishes to analyse or explain.

The relation between technical vocabularies of social science and lay concepts, however, is a shifting one: just as social scientists adopt everyday terms – 'meaning', 'motive', 'power', etc. – and use them in specialized senses, so lay actors tend to take over the concepts and theories of the social sciences and embody them as constitutive elements in the rationalization of their own conduct. The significance of this is recognized only marginally in orthodox sociology, in the guise of 'self-fulfilling' or 'self-negating' prophecies, which are regarded simply as nuisances that inhabit accurate prediction. But although causal generalizations in the social sciences in some aspects may resemble natural scientific laws, they are in an essential way distinct from the latter because they depend upon reproduced alignments of unintended consequences; in so far as they are announced as generalizations, and are picked up as such by those to whose conduct they apply, their form is altered. This once more reunites us with the theme of reflexivity, central to this study, and leads inevitably to a whole range of further issues, concerning the tasks of social

science as critical theory. I shall pursue these issues in another work. But it is important to stress that social science stands in a relation of tension to its 'subject-matter' – as a potential instrument of the expansion of *rational autonomy of action*, but equally as a potential *instrument of domination*.

In conclusion, and in summary form, here are some new 'rules of sociological method'. The latter phrase is only intended ironically. I do not claim that the presuppositions that follow are 'rules' in the sense in which I have suggested that term is most appropriately used in the social sciences. Rather, they are a skeletal statement of some of the themes of the study as a whole, and are merely designed to exemplify its differences form the famous sociological manifesto that Durkheim issued some eighty years ago. This statement does not in and of itself constitute a 'programme' for sociological research, although I regard it as an integral part of such a programme. The sub-classification provided below works roughly as follows. Section A concerns the 'subject-matter of sociology': the production and reproduction of society; Section B, the boundaries of agency, and the modes in which processes of production and reproduction may be examined; Section C, the modes in which social life is 'observed' and characterizations of social activity established; Section D, the formulation of concepts within the meaning-frames of social science as meta-languages.

A

ONE: *Sociology is not concerned with a 'pre-given' universe of objects, but with one which is constituted or produced by the active doings of subjects.* Human beings transform nature socially, and by 'humanizing' it they transform themselves; but they do not, of course, produce the natural world, which is constituted as an object-world independently of their existence. If in transforming that world they create history, and thence live *in* history, they do so because the production and reproduction of society is not 'biologically programmed', as it is among the lower animals. (Theories men develop may, through their technological applications, affect nature, but they cannot come to constitute features *of* the natural world as they do in the case of the social world.)

TWO: *The production and reproduction of society thus has to be treated as a skilled performance on the part of its members*, not as merely a mechanical series of processes. To emphasize this, however, is definitely not to say that actors are wholly aware of what these skills are, or just how they manage to exercise them; or that the forms of social life are adequately understood as the intended outcomes of action.

B

ONE: *The realm of human agency is bounded. Men produce society, but they do so as historically located actors, and not under conditions of their own choosing.* There is an unstable margin, however, between conduct that can be analysed as intentional action, and behaviour that has to be analysed **nomologically** as a set of 'occurrences'. In respect of sociology, the crucial task of nomological analysis is to be found in the explanation of the properties of structures.

TWO: *Structures must not be conceptualized as simply placing constraints upon human agency, but as enabling.* This is what I call the *duality of structure*. Structures can always in principle be examined in terms of their *structuration* as a series of reproduced practices. To enquire into the structuration of social practices is to seek to explain how it comes about that structures are constituted through action, and reciprocally how action is constituted structurally.

THREE: *Processes of structuration involve an interplay of meanings, norms and power.* These three concepts are analytically equivalent as the 'primitive' terms of social science, and *are logically implicated both in the notion of intentional action and that of structure*: every cognitive and moral order is at the same time a system of power, involving a 'horizon of legitimacy'.

C

ONE: *The sociological observer cannot make social life available as a 'phenomenon' for observation independently of drawing upon his knowledge of it as a resource whereby he constitutes it as a 'topic for investigation'.* In *this* respect, his position is no different from that of any other member of society; 'mutual knowledge' is not a series of corrigible items, but represents the interpretative schemes which both sociologists and laymen use, and must use, to 'make sense' of social activity, i.e. to generate 'recognizable' characterizations of it.

TWO: *Immmersion in a form of life is the necessary and only means whereby an observer is able to generate such characterizations.* 'Immersion' here – say, in relation to an alien culture – does not, however, mean 'becoming a full member' of the community, and cannot mean this. To 'get to know' an alien form of life is to know how to find one's way about in it, to *be able* to participate in it as an ensemble of practices. But for the sociological observer this is a mode of generating descriptions which have to be mediated, i.e., transformed into categories of social-scientific discourse.

D

ONE: *Sociological concepts thus obey what I call a double hermeneutic*: (1) Any generalized theoretical scheme in the natural or social sciences is in a certain sense a form of life in itself, the concepts of which have to be mastered as a mode of practical activity generating specific types of descriptions. That this is already a hermeneutic task is clearly demonstrated in the 'newer philosophy of science' of Kuhn and others. (2) Sociology, however, deals with a universe which is already constituted within frames of meaning by social actors themselves, and reinterprets these within its own theoretical schemes, mediating ordinary and technical language. This double hermeneutic is of considerable complexity, since the connection is not merely a one-way one (as Schutz seems to suggest); there is a continual 'slippage' of the concepts constructed in sociology, whereby these are appropriated by those whose conduct they were originally coined to analyse, and hence tend to become integral features of that conduct (thereby in fact potentially compromising their original usage within the technical vocabulary of social science).

TWO. In sum, the primary tasks of sociological analysis are the following: (1) The hermeneutic explication and mediation of divergent forms of life within descriptive metalanguages of social science; (2) Explication of the production and reproduction of society as the accomplished outcome of human agency.

Key terms

The following key terms appear in the text above. They have been defined below to aid with the reading of this item.

reflexivity the idea that human behaviour is based on self-awareness and of how our behaviour will elicit reactions – the possible outlines of which we reflect upon before acting

duality of structure Giddens' argument that structures should not be seen as merely constraining action but also of enabling it to take place

structuration the way that structures of society are reproduced or modified through social interaction, leading to a view of the creation and dynamism of society, based on human action or social practice

double hermeneutic the argument that sociology involves understanding at two levels, namely an understanding of the world created by human actors and secondly an understanding of the concepts developed by sociologists to explain these actions

nomological analysis this is concerned with trying to

find law-like explanations and is more at use in structure-type explanations. It can be contrasted with idiographic explanations, which seek to consider the unique nature of experience or an individual and can thus be seen more at use in social-action-type explanations

Questions

1 What, according to Giddens, are the essential contributions of interpretative sociology to the method and logic of the social sciences?

2 Explain what is meant by the 'Hobbesian problem of order'.

3 Suggest three examples of how human beings act reflexively.

4 In what ways does the work of Thomas Kuhn contribute to the argument developed by Giddens in this extract?

5 To what extent do you agree with the argument that 'sociology is not concerned with a pre-given universe of objects'?

Reading 4.3 **Realism and social science**

William Outhwaite (from) *New Philosophies of Social Science* (1987) London: Macmillan, pp. 51–3 and 58–60.

Editorial comments

As the title of Outhwaite's book suggests, realism is a new philosophy of science that has arisen in recent years to challenge both positivism and phenomenology as the overarching philosophies of methodology in sociology. In this reading, Outhwaite considers some of the implications for sociology and social science of a realist approach.

Realism and social science

THE LOGICAL POSITIVIST thesis of unified science made strong claims for the unity of the laws of science or of the language of science, based on a physicalist reductionism. The contemporary debates focus instead around the weaker claim of a methodological unity of science, in the sense that the methods of the natural sciences can, in general, be applied to the social sciences or; as Bhaskar puts it, 'that it is possible to give an account of science under which the proper and more-or-less specific methods of both the natural sciences and social sciences can fall'. **Naturalism** in this sense 'does not deny that there are significant differences in these methods grounded in real differences in their subject matters and in the relationships in which their sciences stand to them' (Bhaskar, 1979). What it claims is that a realist interpretation can meaningfully be given to social scientific knowledge.

Bhaskar starts from the question: 'What properties do societies possess that might make them possible objects of knowledge for us?' He argues, 'that societies are irreducible to people', 'that social forms are a necessary condition for any intentional act, that their *pre-existence* establishes their *autonomy* as possible objects of scientific investigation and that their *causal power* establishes their reality'. This in turn entails a 'transformational model of social activity': Society is both the ever-present *condition* (material cause) and the continually reproduced *outcome* of human agency.'

> The conception I am proposing is that people, in their conscious activity, for the most part unconsciously reproduce (and occasionally transform) the structures governing their substantive activities of production. Thus people do not marry to reproduce the nuclear family or to work to sustain the capitalist economy. Yet it is nevertheless the unintended consequence (and inexorable result) of, as it is also a necessary condition for, their activity.
> (Bhaskar, 1979)

This in turn entails a relational conception of the subject matter of the social sciences, in which the practices of agents take place within a set of structurally (and hence relationally) defined positions. Where these relations are part of the definition of the relata, as in buyer/seller; they will be termed internal relations; where they are contingent (e.g. shopper/traffic warden), they are external relations.

This abstract model of social reality, which of course displays strong similarities with other contemporary specifications of the relation between action and structure, is clearly compatible with wide variations in the degree to which particular actions are structured. It does not take the expertise of a labour lawyer to notice that the contractual obligations of an academic are very different from those of the majority of workers. A more interesting, and less determinate area of controversy arises between those who stress the essentially voluntary character of all human actions and those who emphasize structural constraints (which may of course be enabling as well as constraining in a narrow sense). There are powerful currents in textual interpretation, for example, which would analyse this book as the more or less automatic product of a set of theoretical and ideological structures, plus a residual category of authorial desire and a few other material conditions. ...

What does emerge, I think, from this discussion, is that we must look more closely at the relations between social structures and the activities they govern. Roy Bhaskar suggests three '**ontological** limitations on a possible naturalism':

(1) Social structures, unlike natural structures, do not exist independently of the activities they govern;
(2) Social structures, unlike natural structures, do not exist independently of the agents' conceptions of what they are doing in their activity;
(3) Social structures, unlike natural structures, may be only relatively enduring (so that the tendencies they ground may not be universal in the sense of space-time invariant).
(Bhaskar, 1979)

... Realist philosophies of science abandon a number of positivist assumptions about scientific theorizing. The most important of these are probably the **theory–observation distinction** and the **covering-law model of explanation**, which are replaced, respectively, by the idea of a complex network of relatively 'theoretical' and relatively 'observational' statements and by the idea of explanation as the attempt to represent the generative mechanisms which bring about the *explanandum*. A corollary of the latter principle is that explanation is not identified with prediction, the latter being possible, strictly speaking, only where the system is closed by natural or experimental means. For practical purposes in the social sciences we can forget about closures, so that any predictions we make will be necessarily tentative and will not provide decisive tests of our theories.

If, then, the criteria of theory-choice in the social sciences are purely explanatory, how are we to judge explanations? It will be remembered that the realist model of explanation involves three basic steps, the postulation of a possible mechanism, the attempt to collect evidence for or against its existence, and the elimination of possible alternatives. We shall therefore feel we have a good explanation if

1 the postulated mechanism is capable of explaining the phenomena
2 we have good reason to believe in its existence
3 we cannot think of any equally good alternatives.

So far so good, but this abstract model does not help in the characteristic situation in the social sciences in which we are expected to choose between several alternative theories and their associated mechanisms and where the object of inquiry is complex and over-determined. Any guidelines will be necessarily vague, but I think that the following principles are not entirely trivial. First, we should not be afraid of theoretical abstraction, since 'observational' statements have no special privilege in this framework. Entities are not to be multiplied unnecessarily, but nor are they to be excluded for being unobservable. Second, the realist emphasis on the **stratification of reality** should make us aware of the need to fit particular explanations within a wider context. This does not mean that the social totality needs to be invoked to explain the most microscopic social event, but it does mean, for example, that micro-economic theories should connect up with propositions about economic systems and their reproduction, and are inadequate to the extent that they do not. In other words, and this may be counted as a third principle, *a priori* considerations of this kind have a part to play in the evaluation of social theories. I have already discussed some apparently *a priori* constraints on social theories of the relation between agency and social structure, although it emerged that the precise form of their interrelations was a matter for empirical determination in each case.

I do not think one can go far beyond these very general principles. Where two or more theories score equally well according to all these criteria, there seem to be no general grounds for rational preference. Simplicity is an obvious candidate, but a preference for simplicity in all cases cannot be justified once one abandons conventionalist positions for which it is pretty well the only available criterion. There is however something of importance behind discussions of simplicity: namely, the idea that choices thus governed maximize the speed of scientific advance by making theories more easily testable. I do not here want to go into the question whether the choice in all cases of the simpler theory *does* in fact have these beneficial consequences, but merely to uphold the underlying principle, that theories should be adopted which on the whole maximize the chances of further intertheoretical debate within the sciences concerned. In other words, we should adopt, other things being equal, theories which are open in this way, rather than, say, reductionist theories, which close off discussion within one level even if they promise to reopen it at another.

The slogan, then, is 'keep them talking'. Once again, it might be thought that this *desideratum* would be best satisfied by conventionalist metatheories. This however seems not to be the case if we recall that the 'talking' necessarily includes the rational critique of existing theories, and it is precisely conventionalism which tends to block off theoretical criticism with its doctrine of the arbitrariness of 'definitional questions'. Once again, it needs to be stressed that the most powerful reason for adopting a realist metatheory is to acquire a framework for the rational discussion of ontological questions.

This principle of dialogue-preservation may be relevant to theory-choice in a further way. It has been suggested by Mary Hesse and others, that in those cases, particularly frequent in the social sciences, in which there are no clear scientific grounds for the choice between two or more theories, it may be legitimate to choose on grounds of general social values (Hesse, 1980). And among such values, the maximization of serious discussion might well be argued to have a special place, for the Habermasian reason that it may be a condition for consensus on central issues of truth and justice.

The realist emphasis on the legitimacy and importance of theoretical argument should not be understood to imply the depreciation of empirical research. What it does suggest, I think, is that such research cannot achieve useful results in the absence of theo-

retical reflection on the structuration of empirical data and a rejection of empiricism, understood as an exclusive focus on social phenomena which are empirically observable and measurable. As Bhaskar puts it,

> the conceptual aspect of the subject matter of the social sciences circumscribes the possibility of measurement. … For meanings cannot be measured, only understood. Hypotheses about them must be expressed in language, and confirmed in dialogue. Language here stands to the conceptual aspect of social science as geometry stands to physics. And precision in meaning now assumes the place of accuracy in measurement as the a posteriori arbiter of theory. It should be stressed that in both cases theories may continue to be justified and validly used to explain, even though *significant* measurement of the phenomena of which they treat has become impossible.
> *(Bhaskar, 1979)*

The upshot, I think, is that a realist strategy for the social sciences needs to engage in a detailed way with the conceptions of interpretation which have been worked out within the frameworks of **hermeneutics** and **critical theory**.

References

Bhaskar, R. (1979) *The Possibility of Naturalism*, Brighton: Harvester.

Hesse, M. (1980) *Revolutions and Reconstructions in the Philosophy of Science*, Brighton: Harvester.

Key terms

The following key terms appear in the text above. They have been defined below to aid with the reading of this item.

naturalism the belief that there is some basis for a methodological unity of the sciences in which the methods of the natural sciences can, in general, be applied to the social sciences

ontological relating to theories about the nature of existence and, more particularly, about the nature of fundamental existence

theory-observation distinction a key element of positivism is that observations and theories are quite distinct. This is a view that realists reject

covering-law model of explanation the belief that the central aim of all science, including social science, is the pursuit of general or covering laws of explanation. This idea is associated with positivism but is rejected by realists

stratification of reality realists believe that society is composed of a number of layers and that therefore observation of surface phenomena is insufficient to

give a full explanation – there is a need to understand the underlying generative mechanisms

hermeneutics the belief that there is an important distinction to be made between nature and the mind or spirit – and the belief that the stress needed to be on understanding of subjective interpretation, through textual and other interpretation, which is seen as very different from our approach to understanding nature

critical theory a brand of thinking very critical of positivism – most notably associated today with the work of Jürgen Habermas

Questions

1 Explain in your own words what is meant by a 'transformational model of social activity'.

2 Suggest two examples of the way we reproduce society through our actions, apart from those mentioned in the extract.

3 What are the key criteria realists use to decide if an explanation is a good explanation?

4 What problem remains in choosing between theories, and how does Outhwaite suggest we resolve this?

5 To what extent do you agree with the assertion that social scientific predictions can only be tentative?

Reading 4.4 **The problems of merging structure and action**

Margaret Archer (from) *Realist Social Theory: the morphogenetic approach* (1995) Cambridge: Cambridge University Press, pp. 101–7 and 115–17.

Editorial comments

Margaret Archer has been a consistent critic of theories such as Giddens' (1984) structuration theory, which seek to conflate structure-type and action-type explanations in sociology through the use of the concept of social practice. She argues that they are methodologically not reducible to one another and that such attempts merely cause confusion. Her alternative view, based on a realist view, is also outlined in this reading.

Reference

Giddens, A. (1984) *The Constitution of Society*, Cambridge: Polity.

The problems of structure and agency

The deficiencies of central conflation: structure and agency as methodologically areducible

TO TREAT 'STRUCTURE' and 'agency' as inseparable is central to the notion of 'duality'. This method of transcending dualism then produces an ontology of 'social practices' which are held to be the ultimate constituents of social reality. There is a decentring of the subject here because human beings only become people, as opposed to organisms, through drawing upon structural properties to generate social practices. There is an equivalent demotion of structure, which only becomes real, as opposed to virtual when instantiated by agency. These ontological assumptions have direct implications for practical social theorizing, for they enjoin that social theory should concern itself exclusively with 'social practices'. These alone are the subject matter of the social sciences. If this is the case then its corollary is central **conflation**, for the implication is that neither 'structure' nor 'agency' have independent or autonomous or anterior features, but only those properties which are manifested in and reproduced or transformed through 'social practices'.

Now, the view defended throughout this book is that conflation is always an error in social theory. The deficiencies of its 'upwards' and 'downwards' versions were those of **epiphenomenalism**; that structure and agency respectively were deprived of relative autonomy and could thus be reduced to one or the other. Central conflation instead deprives *both* elements of their relative autonomy, not through *reducing* one to the other, but by *compacting* the two together inseparably. Yet this very compression is what advocates of structuration theory consider to be its strength – a method of conceptualizing social life where there is no divorce, rupture or disjunction between the minutiae of everyday activities and the structures which are necessarily reproduced or transformed in the practices of everyday living. We do not intend to reproduce the English language each time we generate a grammatically correct sentence in it, but this is the inexorable consequence of our so doing. Enter the knowledgeable actor and exit the cultural dope; enter structure as a medium of action and exit structural properties as constraints upon it: these are the attractions of central conflation, the bonuses accrued by abandoning traditional dualisms and transcending them through the notion of 'duality'.

For the critics of central conflation, the central question is whether 'duality' merely throws a blanket over the two constituents, 'structure' and 'agency' which only serves to prevent us from examining what is going on beneath it. Twelve years ago I referred to this approach as 'sinking rather than linking the differences between structure and agency' (Archer, 1982). In similar vein, Smith and Turner criticized it as a vicious circle where 'agency presupposed structure and structure presupposes agency' (Smith and Turner, 1986). More recently, Thompson comments that the problem of structure and agency has not so much been 'resolved as dissolved' in structuration theory (Thompson, 1989). In other words, **elision** is hailed as a virtue by advocates of central conflation, whereas the compression of structure and agency into 'social practices' is condemned as a vice by its critics because it entails the repression of properties which are distinct to each and distinguishable from one another.

At the end of the day, the fundamental argument between the Elisionists and their opponents (at both the ontological and methodological levels) is about the stratified nature of social reality. Whilst the Elisionist does not deny the stratification of the world, basically only three strata figure in their theorizing – the natural, the biological and the social. These three alone are credited with independent properties and therefore it is only the interplay between these (relatively) autonomous entities which can permissibly figure in Elisionist theorizing. The crucial difference is that those opposed to elisionism delineate at least two additional strata, with their own distinctive emergent and irreducible properties – personal psychology (mind as emergent from body) and socio-cultural structures (structure as emergent from social relations). For the latter, therefore, 'the social' is not one and indivisible but made up of heterogeneous constituents. Because of this, examination of their interplay is central to any adequate form of social theorizing (since the relative autonomy of each stratum means that its properties are capable of independent variation, combination and above all, influence).

The debate is thus about whether an adequate theory of social reality can be cast in homogeneous terms, that is referring only to 'social practices', or whether it must deal with heterogeneous elements because of its stratified nature. Cohen (1990) is perfectly clear that the former is the position adopted by Elisionists and upholds an unstratified view of social reality: 'Giddens lays the foundations of structuration theory at the intersection between theories of action and theories of collectivities, arguing as he proceeds that the division between these theoretical domains obscures the fact that collectivities and action do not comprise heterogeneous constituents of social life'.

Effectively, this debate invokes one which has a long history, namely the traditional dispute about the relations between the two disciplines of psychology and sociology, one which found the Individualists and the Holists on opposite sides. The point at issue is not about the boundaries between these disciplines, which in academia are largely artificial, but whether the two do and should possess separate and identifiable bodies of concepts *because* they refer to heterogeneous entities (individual and society: agency and structure: subjectivity and objectivity). As an issue it is quite distinct from admitting that frequently 'Psychologists, dealing in principle with individuals, have not been able to abstract from the societal environment, nor sociologists, dealing in principle with social wholes, from individual motivations, purposes, beliefs and attitudes'. Certainly, this correct observation points to a legitimate area of study, 'social psychology', whose claims to existence represent a difficulty for Holistic downwards conflationists and Individualist upwards conflationists alike. Obviously the Methodological Individualist in search of 'rock bottom explanations' seeks to make individual dispositions the terminus of their explanations and thus *does* wish to abstract from the social environment. In consequence, 'social psychology' is limited in scope and by principle to the study of how 'other people' (and purely as people, never as incumbents of positions or as parties in structured relationships) serve to affect individual dispositions, attitudes, opinions etc. What is vaunted as the principled explanation of individualistic theorizing is

psychology itself – hence the attempt to isolate 'primordial' dispositions, prior to their expression in any social context, as the ultimate bedrock of any acceptable account. The methodological Holist takes the opposite point of view, with the individual seen in Durkheim's famous phrase as 'indeterminate material' upon which social forces and factors imprint themselves. Again 'social psychology' is reduced in scope to the study of circumstances in which societal socialization fails and the consequences of the resulting 'deviance' for the social whole – with the implication that appropriate (re)socialization can always mould the individual 'material' appropriately. What is vaunted as the principled explanation of holistic theorizing is 'sociology' alone – hence the injunction to explain one social fact only by another.

The Elisionist, of course, differs from each of these stances. While they both, for entirely different reasons grounded in their divergent ontologies, sought to *minimize* the brief of 'social psychology', the central conflationist seeks to *maximize* it. Individual dispositions cannot be abstracted from their social environment, whose structural properties must be drawn upon for their expression yet such properties depend upon individual intentionality for their instantiation. (The intention need not be *to* instantiate, as in the English language example, but individuals have to intend something when deciding to speak, for this to be the result.) In short, because 'social practices' are the central concern of the Elisionist and because these are an inseparable compound of structure and agency, central conflationists are not dealing with heterogeneous constituents of social life, but with one homogeneous though Janus-faced entity which is how 'social practices' are conceptualized. It follows from this that the entirety of their theorizing could very properly be called 'social psychology', since their weakly stratified ontology of the world as a whole only acknowledges that autonomous properties pertain to 'biology' and 'nature', which would require their own concepts and propositions, but denies heterogeneity to anything 'in between' them. Homogeneous 'social practices' take up all this terrain and can thus be conceptualized in the same way which is at once 'social' and 'psychological'.

It follows that those who defend the existence of a more robustly stratified social world will agree in repudiating the psychological reductionism of the Methodological Individualist and rejecting the sociological reductionism of the Methodological Holist, but they cannot conclude from this that there is nothing but 'social psychology', as conceived of by the central conflationist. They cannot concur because their stratified view of social reality means they acknowledge emergent properties at different 'levels' within it, which must be conceptualized in their own terms

– ones which are neither reducible to one another nor, because of their relative autonomy (and hence capacity for independent variation) such that they can be compacted together and treated as a homogeneous entity.

Thus, on the one hand, 'social psychology' can tell us nothing about individual characteristics such as perception, consciousness and cognition nor about the psychology of personal proclivities and antipathies. Although it may add a great deal about their exercise and even modification in social settings, these autonomous individual properties have to be granted *before* we can talk of their exercise or modification, and, as features emergent from the biological stratum, they themselves constrain (and enable) what *can* be socially expressed and modified. On the other hand the properties and powers of structures themselves, such as electoral systems, banking or capitalism, are not explained by 'social psychology' (let alone psychologism) since they form its very context. 'Social psychology' may again add a great deal to our understanding of their maintenance or modification but what is maintained and how it is transformed means that these structural properties have *first* to be granted *before* analysing their stability or change, since they themselves distribute interests in change and are differentially malleable to it. ...

We have just seen how the Elisionists' stand-point confronts considerable opposition. To vindicate themselves against their opponents, they have to demonstrate two things in order to defend construing the social as a homogeneous entity, i.e. such that 'structure' and 'agency' do not comprise heterogeneous constituents with relatively autonomous properties:

1   How structures can be rendered in terms of 'social practices', without any remainder save their material element. In other words can structures be adequately conceptualized as *nothing but* part of the parcel that is 'social practices'?
2   How agents can be construed in terms of 'social practices', without any remainder, save their biological element. In other words can people be adequately conceptualized as *nothing but* the other part of the parcel which makes up 'social practices'?

Let us examine these two points in turn.

Structure and the ontology of praxis

The Elisionist defence requires a complete reconceptualization of 'structure', in conformity with the ontology of praxis, and therefore one which breaks with both traditional and contemporary alternatives. Thus, the definition of social structure which is generic to Methodological Individualism, namely, 'patterns of aggregate behaviour that are stable over time', is jettisoned, primarily for its explicit atomism, secondarily for its assumption that nothing but a process of

aggregation is involved in structuration, thirdly for making the visible pattern reproduced synonymous with 'structure' and finally for the presumption that to be a structure *is to be* relatively enduring. Next, the definition most closely associated with Methodological Holism, namely, 'lawlike regularities that govern the behaviour of social facts', is dismissed firstly, for the explicit reification of structure by its severance from action, secondly, for the assumption that regularities are lawlike in producing ineluctable consequences, thirdly, for holding that these operate in steam-roller fashion immune from human intervention, and lastly, for assuming that structures endure and unfold over the heads of actors like mechanical and naturalistic forces (Porpora, 1989).

Finally, social structure which is conceived of by Methodological Realists as 'systems of human relations among social positions' is rejected primarily because structures refer to actual forms of social organization, that is, to real entities with their own powers, tendencies and potentials, secondly, because the social relations upon which they depend are held to have independent causal properties rather than being mere abstractions from our repetitive and routinized behaviour, and, most importantly, because these relations which constitute structures pre-date occupants of positions within them, thus constraining or enabling agency. In short, realists, who would also disassociate themselves from the definitions endorsed by Individualists and Holists, see social *structure as quintessentially relational* but none the less real because of its emergent properties which affect the agents who act within it and thus cannot be reduced to their activities. Because the Elisionist seeks to conceptualize structure (and culture) in terms of 'social practices', this relational conception is not acceptable since relations themselves are credited with properties distinct from practices, potentials irreducible to practices, powers influential of praxis and are pre-existent to practitioners. Instead, the Elisionist needs a concept of structure which is implicated *in* social practices and not one like the relational, where structures cannot be compressed into practices and exert their own, relatively autonomous, influence over them.

Hence, Giddens deliberately advances a non-relational conception of structure, redefined as 'rules and resources' which are implicated in social practices and have no existence independent of them. Thus he writes, 'by the term structure I do not refer ... to the descriptive analysis of relations of interaction which "compose" organizations or collectivities, but to the system of generative rules and resources' (Giddens, 1976). Conceived of as 'rules and resources', several more refinements are needed before structural properties can become co-extensive with social practices, without remainder, that is, without their possessing any existence or influence autonomous from, or anterior to, or influential of social practices. For obviously, to concede any of the last three points would leave structure with a surplus of features which lie beyond practices, yet which influence them – thus rendering the ontology of praxis both inconsistent and incomplete.

Firstly, then, the re-definition shifts the referents of 'structure' away, from identifiable forms of social organization (the division of labour, educational systems, political parties …) and links them instead to underlying organizing principles, which generate what they do only because agents draw upon them in particular ways in the course of the social practices in which they engage. Thus, what others had taken to be real entities constitutive of structure (e.g. an educational system), become here, not structures themselves but only the 'visible pattern' produced by agency manipulating 'rules and resources' in ways which perpetuate this patterning. Secondly, when it is objected that even here things like educational systems still figure in Elisionist theory, it is quickly countered that this visible pattern has no independent existence or influence but is only an abstraction from the repertoire of repetitive or routinized practices surrounding education. Institutions themselves are thus reconstrued as 'regularized practices', whose very regularity (i.e. endurance) depends upon agency invoking the same structural principles in the same way because praxis has become routinized. …

Analysis of institutions like schools and universities universally shows that certain groups or classes of individuals have restricted opportunities for entry, yet how can these forms of discrimination be construed in terms of 'rules' since they actually traduce the rights of the agents concerned? Thus, 'what is at issue is the fact that the restrictions on opportunities operate differentially, unevenly affecting various groups of individuals whose categorization depends upon certain assumptions about social structure; and it is this differential operation or effect which cannot be grasped by the analysis of rules alone' (Thompson, 1989). Indeed it cannot, which is why Emergentists stress the need to acknowledge the prior structuring of groups, that is the differential distribution of life chances among them as independent structural features which affect how anyone goes on or gets on educationally. Yet Elisionists have the avowed intention of avoiding any notion of structure as pre-constituted which means that reproduced relations between classes, sexes or ethnic groups 'cannot be admitted to the definition of structure. To do so would be to contradict the idea that structures only exist in their instantiation, since to talk of reproduced relations implies structures of social relationships which endure (exist) over time' (Layder, 1981).

Were the Elisionist to counter that it was the 'resources' element which was at play in accounting for differential restrictions on things like educational opportunities, two difficulties would be encountered. On the one hand resources are held only to be 'material existents' which acquire significance solely in conjunction with rules. Therefore rules would have to be adduced governing the uses of financial and cultural capital in educational situations. Yet even if there were such a rule as 'buy the best you can' there would still remain the same intractable problem that the prior distribution of these resources itself differentially constrains who can buy what, that is, in which educational practices they actually can engage. On the other hand, the Elisionists' remaining way out is to conceptualize such educational restrictions as the unintended consequences of social practices. Thus, Giddens himself gives the example of a poverty cycle where maternal deprivation – poor schooling – low paid employment – maternal deprivation operate as a homeostatic loop coordinated and controlled exclusively through the unintended consequences of day-to-day social activity. What this does not explain is why some groups enter the loop in the first place, for it is not *their* practices which set their life chances, determine the definition of instruction, the linkages between educational and occupational opportunity etc. Nor can any of their practices extricate them from the loop without overcoming stringent constraints whose differential distribution again begs the question of why and how they *are* differentially distributed in society. Any attempt to dispose of these questions by simply invoking the unacknowledged conditions of action, which is part of the Elisionist equation of social structure with practical knowledge, finds itself in the same cul de sac. Victims of educational discrimination are not victimized by their lack of 'discursive penetration' of the situation in which they find themselves. We could endow them with all the findings of educational sociology without changing the fact that their situation places objective limitations on the resources at their disposal and the rules they are *able* to follow. To know that public schools convey educational advantages which inner city comprehensives do not is only useful to those with the means to turn their knowledge into practice.

Thus, when 'structural properties' are defined as 'rules and resources' in order to construe them as co-extensive with 'social practices' there is always a remainder which cannot be accommodated. The ontology of praxis constantly comes up against an interface with another level of social reality whose features cannot be construed as practices themselves, their unacknowledged conditions or unintended consequences. Structure asserts a stubborn relative autonomy from social practices because of its prior and independent influence which shapes the practice of different groups in different ways. Structural features which mould our practices are clearly indispensable for explaining them, yet if they cannot themselves be assimilated to the category of practices then our explanations are made

up of these two heterogeneous elements – structures and practices. This remainder, those aspects of structure which 'rules and resources' do not encompass, are properties emergent from social relations which constitute a distinct stratum of social reality.

References

Archer, M. S. (1982) 'Morphogenesis versus structuration', *British Journal of Sociology, 33.*

Cohen, I. R. (1990) 'Structuration theory and social order', in Clark, J. et al (eds) *Anthony Giddens: Consensus and Controversy*, Basingstoke: Macmillan.

Giddens, A. (1976) *New Rules of Sociological Method*, London: Hutchinson.

Layder, D. (1981) *Structure, Interaction and Social Theory*, London: Routledge & Kegan Paul.

Porpora, D. V. (1989) 'Four concepts of social structure', *Journal for the Study of Social Behaviour, 19.*

Smith, J. W. and Turner, B. S. (1986) 'Constructing social theory and constituting society', *Theory, Culture and Society, 3.*

Thompson, J. B. (1989) 'The theory of structuration', in Held, D. and Thompson, J. B. (eds) *Social Theory in Modern Societies: Anthony Giddens and his critics*, Cambridge: Cambridge University Press.

Key terms

The following key terms appear in the text above. They have been defined below to aid with the reading of this item.

conflation reducing structure and action to one level

epiphenomenalism theories that treat some elements of society as having no causal power themselves, merely changing due to changes in some more fundamental element of society

elision Margaret Archer uses this word to describe the attempt to merge together consideration of social structures and social action by using the single term, social practices – something she strongly opposes

Questions

1 Why does Archer argue that treating structure and action as inseparable leads to the decentring of the subject?

2 Identify and name the strata into which society is divided, according to the opponents of elisionism.

3 How do the meanings of the term 'social structure' differ in the accounts given by Archer and by Giddens?

4 How convincing do you find Archer's argument that it is not possible to merge together consideration of social structures and social actions? Give reasons for your answer.

Reading 4.5
Ethnomethodology

Harold Garfinkel (from) *Studies in Ethnomethodology* (1967) New Jersey: Prentice-Hall Inc., pp. 36–8, 44–50 and 75.

Editorial comments

Garfinkel rejected the notion that people are 'cultural dopes', that is, that societal norms and values are unproblematically programmed into them through the process of socialization. This led him to reject the

then predominant functionalism and instead to concentrate on how people actively construct the common sense that is seen as the basis of society. In order to demonstrate the importance of this 'background' to social interaction, he devised experiments where these conventions would be breached and when the results were considered it was found that a range of emotions from bewilderment to anger had indeed been produced. This also pointed to the way people tried to make sense out of seemingly nonsensical situations. This reading outlines his rationale and some descriptions of the experiments he conducted.

Studies in ethnomethodology

Making commonplace scenes visible

IN ACCOUNTING FOR the stable features of everyday activities sociologists commonly select familial settings

such as familial households or work places and ask for the variables that contribute to their stable features. Just as commonly, one set of considerations are unexamined: the socially standardized and standardizing, 'seen but unnoticed', expected, background features of everyday scenes. The member of the society uses **background expectancies** as a scheme of interpretation. With their use actual appearances are for him recognizable and intelligible as the appearances-of-familiar-events. Demonstrably he is responsive to this background, while at the same time he is at a loss to tell us specifically of what the expectancies consist. When we ask him about them he has little or nothing to say.

For these background expectancies to come into view one must either be a stranger to the 'life as usual' character of everyday scenes, or become estranged from them. As Alfred Schutz pointed out, a 'special motive' is required to make them problematic. In the sociologists' case this 'special motive' consists in the programmatic task of treating a societal member's practical circumstances, which include from the member's point of view the morally necessary character of many of its background features, as matters of theoretic interest. The seen but unnoticed backgrounds of everyday activities are made visible and are described from a perspective in which persons live out the lives they do, have the children they do, feel the feelings, think the thoughts, enter the relationships they do, all in order to permit the sociologist to solve his theoretical problems.

Almost alone among sociological theorists, the late Alfred Schultz, in a series of classical studies of the constitutive phenomenology of the world of everyday life, described many of these seen but unnoticed background expectancies. He called them the 'attitude of daily life'. He referred to their scenic attributions as the 'world known in common and taken for granted'. Schutz's fundamental work makes it possible to pursue further the tasks of clarifying their nature and operation, of relating them to the processes of concerted actions, and assigning them their place in an empirically imaginable society.

The studies reported in this paper attempt to detect some expectancies that lend commonplace scenes their familiar, life-as-usual character, and to relate these to the stable social structures of everyday activities. Procedurally it is my preference to start with familiar scenes and ask what can be done to make trouble. The operations that one would have to perform in order to multiply the senseless features of perceived environments; to produce and sustain bewilderment, consternation, and confusion; to produce the socially structured affects of anxiety, shame, guilt, and indignation; and to produce disorganized interaction should tell us something about how the structures of everyday activities are ordinarily and routinely produced and maintained. ...

Background understandings and 'adequate' recognition of commonplace events

What kinds of expectancies make up a 'seen but unnoticed' background of common understandings, and how are they related to persons' recognition of stable courses of interpersonal transactions? Some information can be obtained if we first ask how a person will look at an ordinary and familiar scene and what will he see in it if we require of him that he do no more than look at it as something that for him it 'obviously' and 'really' is not.

Undergraduate students were assigned the task of spending from fifteen minutes to an hour in their homes viewing its activities while assuming that they were boarders in the household. They were instructed not to act out the assumptions. Thirty-three students reported their experiences.

In their written reports students "behaviourized" the household scenes. Here is an excerpt from one account to illustrate my meaning.

> A short, stout man entered the house, kissed me on the cheek and asked, 'How was school?' I answered politely. He walked into the kitchen, kissed the younger of the two women, and said hello to the other. The younger woman asked me, 'What do you want for dinner, honey?' I answered, 'Nothing.' She shrugged her shoulders and said no more. The older woman shuffled around the kitchen muttering. The man washed his hands, sat down at the table and picked up the paper. He read until the two women had finished putting the food on the table. The three sat down. They exchanged idle chatter about the day's events. The older woman said something in a foreign language which made the others laugh.

Persons, relationships, and activities were described without respect for their history, for the place of the scene in a set of developing life circumstances, or for the scenes as texture of relevant events for the parties themselves. References to motives, propriety, subjectivity generally, and the socially standardized character of the events were omitted. Descriptions might be thought of as those of a keyhole observer who puts aside much of what he knows in common with subjects about the scenes he is looking at, as if the writer had witnessed the scenes under a mild amnesia for his common sense knowledge of social structures.

Students were surprised to see the ways in which members' treatments of each other were personal. The business of one was treated as the business of the others. A person being criticized was unable to stand on dignity and was prevented by the others from taking offence. One student reported her surprise at how freely she had the run of the house. Displays of conduct and feeling occurred without apparent concern for the management of impressions. Table manners were bad, and family members showed each other little politeness. An early casualty in the scene was the family news of the day which turned into trivial talk.

Students reported that this way of looking was difficult to sustain. Familiar objects – persons obviously, but furniture and room arrangements as well – resisted students' efforts to think of themselves as strangers. Many became uncomfortably aware of how habitual movements were being made; of *how* one was handling the silverware, or *how* one opened the door or greeted another member. Many reported that the attitude was difficult to sustain because with it quarrelling, bickering, and hostile motivations became discomfortingly visible. Frequently an account that recited newly visible troubles was accompanied by the student's assertion that his account of family problems was not a 'true' picture; the family was *really* a very happy one. Several students reported a mildly oppressive feeling of 'conforming to a part'. Several students attempted to formulate the 'real me' as activities governed by rules of conduct but gave it up as a bad job. They found it more convincing to think of themselves in 'usual' circumstances as 'being one's real self'. Nevertheless one student was intrigued with how deliberately and successfully he could predict the other's responses to his actions. He was not troubled by this feeling.

Many accounts reported a variation on the theme: 'I was glad when the hour was up and I could return to the real me.'

Students were convinced that the view from the boarder's attitude was not their real home environment. The boarder's attitude produced appearances which they discounted as interesting incongruities of little and misleading practical import. How had the familiar ways of looking at their home environments been altered? How did their looking differ from usual?

Several contrasts to the 'usual' and 'required' way of looking are detectable from their accounts. (1) In looking at their homes as boarders they replaced the mutually recognized texture of events with a rule of interpretation which required that this mutual texture be *temporarily* disregarded. (2) The mutually recognized texture was brought under the jurisdiction of the new attitude as a definition of the essential structures of this texture. (3) This was done by engaging in interaction with others with an attitude whose nature and purpose only the user knew about, that remained undisclosed, that could be either adopted or put aside at a time of the user's own choosing, and was a matter of wilful election. (4) The attitude as an intention was sustained as a matter of personal and willed compliance with an explicit and single rule, (5) in which, like a game, the goal of the intention was identical with looking at things under the aus-

pices of the single rule itself. (6) Above all, looking was not bound by any necessity for gearing one's interests within the attitude to the actions of others. These were the matters that students found strange.

When students used these background expectancies not only as ways of looking at familial scenes but as grounds for acting in them, the scenes exploded with the bewilderment and anger of family members.

In another procedure students were asked to spend from fifteen minutes to an hour in their homes imagining that they were boarders and acting out this assumption. They were instructed to conduct themselves in a circumspect and polite fashion. They were to avoid getting personal, to use formal address, to speak only when spoken to.

In nine of forty-nine cases students either refused to do the assignment (five cases) or the try was 'unsuccessful' (four cases). Four of the 'no try' students said they were afraid to do it; a fifth said she preferred to avoid the risk of exciting her mother who had a heart condition. In two of the 'unsuccessful' cases the family treated it as a joke from the beginning and refused despite the continuing actions of the student to change. A third family took the view that something undisclosed was the matter, but what it might be was of no concern to them. In the fourth family the father and mother remarked that the daughter was being 'extra nice' and undoubtedly wanted something that she would shortly reveal.

In the remaining four-fifths of the cases family members were stupefied. They vigorously sought to make the strange actions intelligible and to restore the situation to normal appearances. Reports were filled with accounts of astonishment, bewilderment, shock, anxiety, embarrassment, and anger, and with charges by various family members that the student was mean, inconsiderate, selfish, nasty, or impolite. Family members demanded explanations: What's the matter? What's gotten into you? Did you get fired? Are you sick? What are you being so superior about? Why are you mad? Are you out of your mind or are you just stupid? One student acutely embarrassed his mother in front of her friends by asking if she minded if he had a snack from the refrigerator. 'Mind if you have a little snack? You've been eating little snacks around here for years without asking me. What's gotten into you?' One mother, infuriated when her daughter spoke to her only when she was spoken to, began to shriek in angry denunciation of the daughter for her disrespect and insubordination and refused to be calmed by the student's sister. A father berated his daughter for being insufficiently concerned for the welfare of others and of acting like a spoiled child.

Occasionally family members would first treat the student's action as a cue for a joint comedy routine which was soon replaced by irritation and exasperated anger at the student for not knowing when enough was enough. Family members mocked the 'politeness' of the students – 'Certainly Mr. Herzberg!' – or charged the student with acting like a wise-guy and generally reproved the 'politeness' with sarcasm.

Explanations were sought in previous, understandable motives of the student: the student was 'working too hard' in school; the student was 'ill'; there had been 'another fight' with a fiancée. When offered explanations by family members went unacknowledged, there followed withdrawal by the offended member, attempted isolation of the culprit, retaliation, and denunciation. 'Don't bother with him, he's in one of his moods again'; 'Pay no attention but just wait until he asks me for something'; 'You're cutting me, okay I'll cut you and then some'; 'Why must you always create friction in our family harmony?' Many accounts reported versions of the following confrontation. A father followed his son into the bedroom. 'Your Mother is right. You don't look well and you're not talking sense. You had better get another job that doesn't require such late hours.' To this the student replied that he appreciated the consideration, but that he felt fine and only wanted a little privacy. The father responded in a high rage, 'I don't want any more of *that* and of *you* and if you can't treat your mother decently you'd better move out!'

There were no cases in which the situation was not restorable upon the student's explanation. Nevertheless, for the most part family members were not amused and only rarely did they find the experience instructive as the student argued that it was supposed to have been. After hearing the explanation a sister replied coldly on behalf of a family of four, 'Please, no more of these experiments. We're not rats, you know.' Occasionally an explanation was accepted but still it added offence. In several cases students reported that the explanations left them, their families, or both wondering how much of what the student had said was 'in character' and how much the student 'really meant'.

Students found the assignment difficult to complete. But in contrast with on-lookers' accounts students were likely to report that difficulties consisted in not being treated as if they were in the role that they were attempting to play, and of being confronted with situations but not knowing how a boarder would respond.

There were several entirely unexpected findings. (1) Although many students reported extensive rehearsals in imagination, very few mentioned anticipatory fears or embarrassment. (2) On the other hand, although unanticipated and nasty developments frequently occurred, in only one case did a student report serious regrets. (3) Very few students reported heartfelt relief when the hour was over. They were much more likely to report partial relief. They frequently reported that in response to the anger of others they became angry in return and slipped easily into subjectively recognizable feelings and actions.

In contrast to the reports of the on-looking 'boarders' very few reports 'behaviourized' the scene.

Background understandings and social effects

Despite the interest in social effects that prevails in the social sciences, and despite the extensive concern that clinical psychiatry pays them, surprisingly little has been written on the socially structured conditions for their production. The role that a background of common understandings plays in their production, control, and recognition is, however, almost *terra incognita*. This lack of attention from experimental investigators is all the more remarkable if one considers that it is precisely this relationship that persons are concerned with in their common sense portrayals of how to conduct one's daily affairs so as to solicit enthusiasm and friendliness or avoid anxiety, guilt, shame, or boredom. The relationship between the common understandings and social effects may be illustrated by thinking of the acting out student-boarders' procedure as one that involved the production of bewilderment and anger by treating an important state of affairs as something that it 'obviously', 'naturally', and 'really', is not. ...

Concluding remarks

I have been arguing that a concern for the nature, production, and recognition of reasonable, realistic, and analysable actions is not the monopoly of philosophers and professional sociologists. Members of a society are concerned as a matter of course and necessarily with these matters both as features and for the socially managed production of their everyday affairs. The study of common sense knowledge and common sense activities consists of treating as problematic phenomena the actual methods whereby members of a society, doing sociology, lay or professional, make the social structures of everyday activities observable. The 'rediscovery' of common sense is possible perhaps because professional sociologists, like members, have had too much to do with common sense knowledge of social structures as both a topic and a resource for their inquiries and not enough to do with it only and exclusively as sociology's programmatic topic.

Key term

The following key term appears in the text above. It has been defined below to aid with the reading of this item.

background expectancies the socially constructed expectations about behaviour on which social life is founded, but which are rarely seen as the subject of investigation

Questions

1 How does Garfinkel seek to outline the content of background expectancies?

2 Why does Garfinkel believe that a study of common sense activities is useful for sociology?

3 Identify the elements of a situation which are omitted in ethnomethodological analysis.

4 Suggest three situations, other than those mentioned in the reading, that might be amenable to ethnomethodological analysis.

5 To what extent does the demonstration of background expectancies in common-sense situations mean that these are important factors in all social situations?

Reading 4.6 **The ethnographic approach**

Valerie Hey (from) *The Company She Keeps* (1997) Buckingham: Open University Press, pp. 45–52.

Editorial comments

In this reading, Valerie Hey discusses some of the methodological issues surrounding her study of girls' friendships and the way these are affected by class, gender, sexuality and race. Her study consisted of participant observations conducted at two schools, but also with a wider ethnographic framework which sought to avoid girls disappearing when translated into male-dominated theories of youth culture. Here she discusses some of the problems she faced.

Learning your place

Ethnographic practices and cultural lessons: accessing the borderlands

RESEARCH IS INVARIABLY accomplished by an uneven struggle about the messy complexities of life. Apart from having to overcome (or work around) official suspicion I also was confronted by unofficial opposition. No wonder Martyn Hammersley once remarked that 'Research was like a voyage of discovery where you spend most of your time out at sea'.

In electing to study girls and their cultures I was already committed to assessing precisely those spaces designed to keep intruders out. Other researchers have noted the material impenetrability of girls' social networks:

> Boys flock; girls seldom get together in groups above four whereas for boys a group of four is almost useless. Boys are dependent on masculine solidarity within a relatively large group. In boys' groups the emphasis is on masculine unity; in girls' cliques the purpose is to shut out other girls.
> *(Henry, 1966)*

Certainly there were few scripts available for conducting an empirical sociological investigation into girls and their friendship. Mandy Llewellyn (1980) captured the challenge precisely when she wrote:

> Once I had entered the field I encountered a mass of problems and dilemmas, some of them generally related to this style of research, others more specifically concerned the focus of my study. These latter involved the difficulties of gaining some sort of purchase on the privatized, fairly excluding spheres inhabited by adolescent girls.

This section traces the complications associated with researching across the public and the private domain. It specifically focused upon how girls' relationships are, as McRobbie and Garber pointed out, 'well insulated' so that they can 'effectively exclude not only other "undesirable" girls but also boys, adults, teachers and researchers' (1980).

One incident condensed for me what is at stake for girls in making themselves available for adult scrutiny in such conditions.

Desperately seeking Sandra?

It is assumed I think, that even if women researchers know girls are 'excluding', sharing a gender provides grounds for rapport. Indeed, feminist researchers warn against the exploitative potential of female/female

field relations. My own initial encounter demonstrated the opposite – the fragility of rapport between researcher and researched. As a new girl in the field and as a new girl at school I made mistakes. I cite one instance which taught me a great deal about how girls exercise power through the veto of exclusion as well as the structured antagonism arising from class relations.

At Eastford School I was originally sponsored by the head of the English department. She suggested to me that I might like to initiate my study through shadowing Sandra, a white working-class girl in her fourth year. I was told that Sandra was 'interesting'. I approached Sandra and explained my study and asked if I might 'go around' with her and her friends the next day to get to know her. She seemed keen, and appeared to have consented and I smugly congratulated myself on the success of our affinity. I arranged to meet her the following day, and went to collect her from the classroom. I was met by Sandra behaving as if I was a known social outlaw. 'It's that woman!' she yelled, running to the back of the classroom, seeking protection from her teacher. I retreated mortified by embarrassment, and muttered something incoherent to the bemused teacher and her class and disappeared into the sanctuary of the girls' toilets – one of the few private places in the school.

I had not attended to the gaps between what is said and what is meant. I had not been sufficiently **self-reflexive**, forgetting both my adultness and my class status. Sandra educated me. Clues about how Sandra might have framed my intentions were abundant, but I had missed them. Earlier, in our first conversation I asked her how she spent her spare time. She told me that she went 'wally watching' (that is, looking at the local middle-class culture vultures) at the local arts centre. Anyone who has this view about the voyeuristic pleasures of social observation of the other has clearly worked out the costs of being positioned as the object of the (sociological) gaze.

This particular incident not only sensitized me to the particular salience of class antagonism at Eastford but it promoted my recognition of the imperatives of divisions and difference as the prevailing terms through which girl subjects also learned their place. It was here in the field, in 'among the women' that schooling's denial and mystification of power and differences emerged to forcefully invest girls' cultures. Marginalizing the discourses of power merely intensified the social and psychological investments girls had in securing, through their friendship, places for themselves which *did* at some level acknowledge the lived significance which the school so furiously displaced and denied.

Engagingly therefore, girls' discourse of difference operated most powerfully in precisely those spaces into which I had been confined: the backstage of classrooms; the periphery of schools; the playing fields; the local off-site amenities; the cemetery; the local cafe; the shops; the canteen, and the school yard. It was outside of, or 'underneath' surveillance that the girls could best pursue their social task of discovering who they were inside their same-sex relationships.

Becoming marginalized placed me in precisely those same locales as the girls I was studying. Furthermore, as I have intimated, the margins of both schools were highly generative spaces dense with important sources of counter-information and counter-identifications. It was in many ways precisely the place to be. Recognition was one thing, access, as the Sandra incident reveals, another. Negotiating with the girls demanded methodological creativity, and most of all the capacity to secure and sustain their trust.

Field relations: trading in femininity – talking to the girls

Surviving marginalization at the same time as researching it emphasized the reliance one has upon those who are being studied. This research therefore was only made possible through the sponsorship of key individuals, most notably that offered by Saskia, Carol and Suzy (at Eastford) and Jude (at Crossfield). These alliances were further embedded by my participation in the public spaces of the school as well as private (girls' locker room) cultures.

In the course of the fieldworks I played rounders; went on cross-country runs; attended registration/pastoral time; stood around on fields at playtime; ate in the cafeteria; sat in on swathes of lessons; occasionally visited the staffroom; went to school plays and end of term demob ceremonies and leavers' assemblies. Rushing around covering the official as well as the more illicit of girls' activities demanded, at 35, a certain stamina as well as a willing suspension of disbelief on the part of both the girls and myself. It was required not only by the demands of participant observation but also as a test of my commitment to the girls. I did draw the line occasionally (and so did the girls) but mostly I boldly went where the girls in my study boldly went, even if this meant bunking or going behind the bike sheds (so they could have a smoke). Interestingly and significantly the trial of my acceptability as a researcher (that is, that I would not tell the teachers) replicated the social tests of girls' friendships.

My fieldwork effectively involved a series of complex trade-offs. In the course of the study, the girls and I developed an implicit microeconomy of exchange and barter. The girls provided access to their social lives in return for certain tangible goods: my attention; advice; sweet money; access to a warm room; or absence from lessons. These small trades are endemic in most field relations but because they smack of the marketplace there is very little reference to them and like a lot of the 'housework' of research, these details seldom surface in research reports or theses.

In the course of my time in the schools I got to know about 50 girls reasonably well, 20 of these girls very well and three sufficiently well to have been invited to their homes and to have invited them to mine. One girl even sent me a note during a lesson. Others kept up communication after I left the schools, updating me on their present situations. Yet other girls sent me notes which they had stored away; others offered me diaries to read, I offered mine in return.

I only managed my study through the immense tolerance of the girls who accommodated me during lunch hours, free time at breaks, morning tutor times and who invited me home when they had been sent off the premises as a result of the no-cover action. There were girls (like Carol) who took me in hand and showed me the ropes, who let me tag along with them on their jaunts to the local prom and recreation ground. Neither I, nor my stomach, will ever forget our many visits to the Pond Cafe safe refuge for so many of Eastford's working-class school refuseniks. However, willingness to indulge researchers is frequently constituted from the conditions of subjects' relative powerlessness.

A similar concern surfaces in this study. The girls' general toleration of a nosy intruder (Sandra notwithstanding) signified a potentially exploitative situation. Such conditions are an implacable fact of researching on those less powerful than oneself. Looking back at my practice and accounting for my decisions, the issue as I see it of breaking the pretence that one can somehow (singlehandedly) dissolve the contradictions (of being a feminist working on girls' relative powerlessness) has meant my acceptance that research relations are necessarily made in, and constituted by these conditions of difference.

Despite seeking to establish non-exploitative field relations, I was never able to evade the facts that as a white woman with a middle-class education not only was I generally more powerful than most of the girls but my agenda was in part to appropriate parts of their lives for my own use. This is not to represent girls as powerless – in this I endorse Beverley Skeggs (1994) who also argues that girls' actions are about contesting power within terms which recognizes the force of social divisions.

Taking up this position is much more uncomfortable than assuming the orthodox cosier fantasy of imagining that our feminism secures for us the privilege of 'becoming one of the girls' through wishing away the differences between us and them. What is required is not only more reflexivity (about who 'we' are) but also a more finessed sense of how these power rela-

tions (including those of research) shift and are contested by their subjects/objects in the everyday.

In terms of my own practice I tried to be as clear about what I was up to as I felt was appropriate. But at all times during the research the girls knew that I was a researcher and that I was observing their interactions (even though rumours circulated that I was variously a social worker, headteacher, probation officer, police officer or someone's mum).

The debate about ethics is one of the most engaged and detailed within feminist methodology; there is a vast literature. Inevitably issues of ethics become intensely focused when one is researching across the boundaries between the public and the private. As Johnson eloquently puts it, 'To render such accounts public is immediately to activate all the relations of power we traced … especially where the practice crosses the major cultural differences'.

I too, am acutely aware of this dilemma, since insisting on moving the cultural backstage (of girls and schooling) to the front stage (particularly at this time when the mainstream research gaze is mesmerized by the government's agenda), opens up not only a proverbial can of worms for the dominant but also, as I have hinted, for feminism(s). My stance certainly (re)activated as well as captured/disrupted the dominant forms of power and their circulation since what was discovered was not, as other researchers imagine, 'collective images of a non-subordinated sense of self' (Ribbens and Edwards 1995) but precisely the conditions of contradiction and oppression (as well as their refusal) within which girls and ourselves live.

The point of my move to uncover the workings of power in the culture was not to search for a return to a buried originary feminine realm beyond the world of oppression but to tease out the ways in which girls (and by analogy women) consent to, as well as resist, the multiple forms of subordinations, as well as to identify and analyse those occurrences when girls subordinate and oppress each other. Girl–girl social relations (as I have hinted) constituted a gendered (and hence collective) cultural code. However this was not easily appropriable, since it was one of the conditions of girls' general cultural subordination that rendered girls' investment in privacy, secrecy and intimacy and each other. Therefore it was only through moving into the same covert realm where girls managed their relations that it became possible to understand how the borderlands worked as *private* feelings, *personal* affiliations and *personal* writings – where 'difference(s)' (if you like) could be traced in how girls (privately) lived their own antagonistic relations with and against each other. I take the view that furthering our understanding of girls means we have to occupy the interstitial spaces of schooling to reflect upon the cultural power activated there. A defining moment in this research dilemma was when I discovered the significance of note-writing.

In/significances: a methodological and ethical note on schoolgirl notes

The significance of girls' notes only impressed itself on me after I had been involved in the research for several months. In so far as teachers noticed girls' extracurricular activities they called girls' notes 'bits of poison' or 'garbage'. Girls referred to them as 'bits of silliness'. As far as I was concerned they were sociologically fascinating because they were important means of transmitting the cultural values of friendship.

It emerged that not only did these writings constitute visible evidence of the extensive emotional labour invested by girls in their friendships, they also comprised a 'pocket ethnography' of girlfriend work. The correspondences materialized particular aspects of girls' interpersonal relationships to confirm that girls produced the private, encoded by feminine forms of power.

A typical note would take the form of a piece of writing addressed to a specific girl. (Ninety per cent of what girls wrote about concerned their own relations with each other – only a few spoke about boyfriends). The note was then passed more or less surreptitiously to the recipient who would then write back. The original author would respond and so on. Other girls would act as postwomen, circulating the document between the correspondents.

In the course of my study I collected over 50 correspondence sequences from Erin and Saskia's group at Eastford School. From Crossfield School I collected about 20 others, predominantly from within Jude's group. I did not see boys engage in this activity. Evidence from other research indicates that boys do different things both in classrooms and within their friendships.

The struggle to take these notes seriously owed something to the difficulties of purloining these 'secret writings'. Girls were experts in these 'invisible' communication activities, and only a few teachers ever noticed them or wilfully intervened to eliminate them. Scrabbling around on the floor after double maths to retrieve the discarded letters was hard to explain to another adult. One of the teachers I spoke with

scooped them up out of her classroom dustbin to offer them to me, saying that they were 'little bits of garbage'. Becoming, as one colleague described it, 'an academic bag-lady' is at odds with the notion of research as a serious scientific endeavour.

Sometimes girls just left them on desks or floors. Towards the end of my year in the schools, I asked my key informants for any they might have retained, not expecting any response. To my surprise they provided me with more examples. Some of the girls had stored them for four years or more.

Equally, converting the 'garbage' into data presents other problems. The raw material persists in being the opposite of what data is supposed to be. Everything about this material conspired to render it unavailable as data. The word data carries sedimented meanings about self-importance and substantiality. And yet they retained for me sociological interest not least because some of these notes took the form of correspondence chains that lasted a week and included over 50 separate exchanges. The girls' notes were intentionally 'marginal'; for example, they were written on the margins of other more official writing. A number were written on the back of rough drafts of schoolwork. They were often difficult (if not impossible) to decipher. If I had not also been attending to the flux of the girls' friendships through observations and interviews I would have had little purchase upon their actual sequence, let alone their importance. That they are important, if fragmentary, moments in the making of schoolgirl selves is explored further.

Race and ethnicity

Since I had decided that the main method of my study was to be participant observation I anticipated that as a white woman I would be far less likely to find acceptance in black and Asian girls' groups. This means that what I have to say about girls' same-sex relations cannot be extended to account for how various groups of black or Asian girls do their friendship work.

My pragmatic methodological choice had important theoretical ramifications in that it meant that I was able to access the workings of how girls constructed forms of white working-class racism. It soon emerged that the racial and racist divisions between girls at Crossfield School were policed through the social pressures exerted within friendship groups.

References

Henry, J. (1966) *Culture Against Man*, London: Tavistock.

Llewellyn, M. (1980) 'Studying girls at school: the implications of confusion', in Deem, R. (ed.) *Schooling for Women's Work*, London: Routledge & Kegan Paul.

McRobbie, A. and Garber, J. (1980) 'Girls and subcultures', in Hall, S. and Jefferson, T. (eds) *Resistance Through Rituals*, London: Hutchinson.

Ribbens, J. and Edwards, R. (1995) 'Introducing qualitative research on women in families and households', *Women's Studies International Forum, 18*.

Skeggs, B. (1994) 'Situating the production of feminist ethnography', in Maynard, M. and Purvis, J. (eds) *Researching Women's Lives from a Feminist Perspective*, London: Taylor and Francis.

Key terms

The following key terms appear in the text above. They have been defined below to aid with the reading of this item.

field relations relations between the researcher and the subjects of the research while actually conducting research in the field

self-reflexive the notion that we regulate our own behaviour in relation to any social situation and our interpretation of it

Questions

1 What does Valerie Hey mean by saying that she was 'not sufficiently self-reflexive'?

2 How does Valerie Hey seek to avoid the problem of marginalization?

3 How does this reading illustrate the problems involved in gaining access in participant observation studies?

4 Apart from black and Asian girls, suggest two other social groups within the school that Hey could not easily have researched.

5 To what extent do you think Hey managed to achieve non-exploitative field relations?

Reading 4.7 **The variety of sampling techniques**

Sotirios Sarantakos (from) *Social Research* (1993) Victoria: Macmillan Education Australia, pp. 126–43.

Editorial comments

Since, with the exception of the census, sociologists do not study the whole population in which they are interested, but instead allow a sample of that population to stand in for the whole population, there is a need to ensure that such samples are selected using procedures that will ensure as far as possible that the sample is representative of the population if this is desired. In this reading, Sarantakos describes the main forms of sampling and some of the issues that arise in relation to their application.

Sampling techniques

THERE ARE BASICALLY two types of sampling, the random or **probability sampling** and the **non-probability sampling**.

Probability sampling

This employs strict probability rules in the selection process: every unit of the population has an equal, calculable, and non-zero probability to be selected in the sample. It allows computation of accuracy of selection, and offers a high degree of representativeness; however, the method is expensive, time-consuming and relatively complicated, since it requires a large sample size, and the units selected are usually widely scattered.

Non-probability sampling

This method is less strict and makes no claim for representativeness. It is generally left up to the researcher or the interviewer to decide which sample units should be chosen, and is employed in explanatory research, observational research, and qualitative research.

Types of probability sampling

The majority of social researchers employ probability sampling for several reasons, but especially due to its high reliability, degree of representativeness and high generalizability of the results. Probability sampling is employed in many forms. The most common types are described below.

Simple and systematic random sampling are two types of sampling widely employed by social researchers either as the only sampling procedure or as part of other types of probability sampling.

Simple random sampling

This type of sampling gives all units of the target population an equal chance to be selected. The sample units are selected by means of the methods described below.

The lottery method

Choosing respondents by the lottery method follows a procedure that can be described in the following steps:

Step 1

This means identifying or constructing a *sampling frame*, that is, a list of the units of the target population. Such frames are, for instance, the electoral role, student records, rating records, etc. and include names and addresses of sample units in alphabetical order and numbered accordingly.

Step 2
Names are substituted by numbered marbles or discs so that each marble or disc corresponds to a name from the sampling frame. All marbles are placed in an urn.

Step 3
Marbles are mixed well and one marble is drawn from the urn. The number of this marble is registered and the corresponding name in the sampling frame is ascertained. This is the first respondent. The marble is returned to the urn or is left out (both methods are legitimate). This process is continued until the required number of respondents is reached. If an already drawn number is selected for a second or third time it is ignored. ...

The method of random numbers
This method is similar to the lottery method, with the exception that urn and marbles are replaced by tables of random numbers, which are available in the form of small books or in the appendix of texts on statistics. ...

Choosing the sample through the method of random numbers is as follows:

Step 1
A sample frame is identified or constructed as in the lottery method.

Step 2
Appropriate tables of random numbers are selected.

Step 3
Numbers are picked from the tables randomly, registered and the corresponding names identified in the sampling frame. ...

The computer method
This is similar to the methods described above. It only differs in the second step, whereby the urn or table of random numbers is replaced by a computer. This method becomes even more significant if the sampling frame is available in the computer. Then the computer can identify not only numbers but also names and addresses of the respondents. The computer can complete the selection of the sample and even provide a print-out containing a list of all respondents. The selection of the respondents through this method is as follows:

Step 1
A sampling frame is identified or constructed.

Step 2
The computer is instructed to print randomly *x* numbers (as many as the sample units), to be selected randomly between the numbers 0 and *n* (*n* being the number of units in the target population).

Step 3
The names that correspond to these numbers are identified. These are the subjects of the study. ...

Systematic sampling
Systematic sampling and simple random sampling differ in that in the latter the selections are independent from each other; in systematic sampling the selection of sample units is dependent on the selection of a previous one.

The population units are specially prepared and the sample selected in a *systematic* way, by means of various techniques, of which the sampling fraction method is very common.

When the *sampling fraction method* (symbolized by *k*) is employed, samples are drawn from a sampling frame on the basis of the sampling fraction that is equal to N/n, where N is the number of units in the target population, and *n* the number of units of the sample. For instance, if the target population is 4800 and the intended sample size 600, the sampling fraction is 8 (i.e. 4800/600=8).

To select a sample through the method of sampling fraction, the following steps are followed:

Step 1
A sample frame is identified or constructed.

Step 2
The sampling fraction *k* is computed (as above, $k=N/n$)

Step 3
A number between 0 and *k* is randomly selected. (In the above example, since *k*=8, the random number would be between 0 and 8).

Step 4
All numbers between 0 and *N* that result from adding *k* to this random number are selected. The process is repeated until *N* is reached. For example, if the random number is 6 and *k* is 8, the numbers are 6, 14 (6 plus 8), 22 (i.e. 14 plus 8), 30 (i.e. 22 plus 8), etc.

Step 5
The names on the sampling frame that correspond to the numbers drawn above are identified.

Step 6

These names correspond to the respondents to be included in the sample.

Stratified random sampling

This is a special form of simple or systematic random sampling, in which the population is divided into a number of strata and a sample is drawn from each stratum. These subsamples make up the final sample of the study.

The division of the population into strata is based on one or more criteria, for example sex, age, economic status, etc. The sample size can be *proportionate* or *disproportionate* to the units of the target population. For instance, the target population (consisting of equal numbers of males and females) may be divided into two strata, for example males and females. Then, if a proportionate stratified sample is drawn, 5 per cent from each group may be taken. If the researcher decides for a disproportionate sample, 5 per cent of males and 10 per cent of females may be taken.

A stratified sample is employed when there is a need to represent all groups of the target population in the sample, and when the researcher has a special interest in certain strata. In this sense, the method is very economical, offers accurate results and a high degree of representativeness, and is very useful.

A stratified sample is drawn in the following way:

Step 1

First the target population is divided into a number of strata according to the number of the significant groups in the population.

Step 2

The sampling frames for each of these groups are identified; if not available, relevant sampling frames must be developed.

Step 3

Employing one of the methods discussed above, a sample is drawn from each group. This can be proportionate or disproportionate to the number of units in the population.

Step 4

The individual samples are merged into one; this constitutes the sample for the study. ...

Cluster sampling

Characteristic of this sampling method is that firstly groups of elements (clusters) are selected (e.g. schools, classes, etc.) and then individual elements are selected from these clusters. To choose the clusters and the respondents from the clusters one of the methods discussed above can be employed.

Cluster sampling is a popular sampling method and is employed primarily:

- when no sampling frame is available for all units of the target population;
- when economic considerations are also significant; and
- when cluster criteria are significant for the study.

Caution: Cluster sampling is biased by the fact that the respondents come from a specialized population group (dictated by the choice of clusters) and may not, for that reason, represent the whole spectrum of the population. ...

Multi-stage sampling

In this method, a sequence of samples is drawn from already selected samples but only the last sample of subjects is studied. In all other aspects the multi-stage sampling is similar to the simple or systematic sampling.

The main advantage of this sampling procedure is that it allows the establishment of a sample that is directly related to the research object. With every additional drawing, the sample becomes more specific and more relevant to the research question, and the results are expected to become equally relevant and more representative.

The methods of choosing a sample through the multi-stage sampling method proceeds as follows:

Step 1

A sampling frame for the target population is identified.

Step 2

A large probability sample is chosen; the units of this sample are usually referred to as *primary selection units*. A sample from the primary selection units is then chosen.

Step 3

The procedure is repeated until the target sample size is reached.

Step 4

The last drawing constitutes the sample of the study. ...

Area sampling

Area sampling is a multi-stage sampling applied in geographical areas. In this case, the sample of the study is the final-stage sample drawn in a series of samples taken from geographical areas where each stage refers progressively to smaller and more concrete areas, for example state, region, city, suburb, street, household. In addition, this method is a form of cluster sampling related to areas as clusters.

This procedure shows how widespread the respondents are geographically in the context of Australia, or the chosen state. Such a method guarantees that a high representation of respondents from as many geographical areas as possible will appear in the study. ...

Multi-phase sampling

The process of unit selection in a multi-phase sampling procedure is the same as in multi-stage sampling. Firstly, the primary selection units are chosen. Then a sample is drawn from these units and so on. However, in a multi-phase sampling procedure each sample is adequately studied before another sample is drawn from it. Consequently, while in multi-stage sampling only the final sample is studied, in multi-phase sampling all samples are researched. This offers an advantage over other methods, because the information gathered at each phase helps the researcher to choose a more relevant and more representative sample. ...

Panel studies

Longitudinal research is characterized by the fact that it employs a sampling procedure in which the respondents of the original sample are studied on more than one occasion. In general, the sample contains the same respondents, who are then interviewed, for instance every year for a period of 5 years, or before and after the occurrence of certain significant events. This form of longitudinal research is known as *panel studies*.

Longitudinal studies appear also in another form as *trend studies*. In this form, the research is repeated several times as above, but different samples are studied at each stage of the project.

Longitudinal research is employed when the investigator is interested in changes or just continuity over time, that is, recognition and examination of patterns. In this sense, the method provides many advantages over other forms of sampling, which do not consider the time factor, related to comparisons over time as well as to precision and economy. It is, however, affected by a number of problems that must be kept in mind. Writers suggest that the following problems must be kept in mind when using panel studies; they are related to:

* convincing respondents to take part in the study
* motivating respondents to fill in relevant questions accurately, especially those of a personal and sensitive nature
* maintaining the same structure and same criteria at each stage
* avoiding or minimizing drop outs
* mortality, migration, and change of residence

* preparation of data
* panel conditioning, whereby respondents become gradually interested in the research study, learn more about it and can, in this way, cause distortions in the research findings.

Nevertheless, this is a very useful method, and is widely used by social scientists all over the world in the context of industry, household studies, service industries, sociological and psychological studies. ...

Spatial sampling

This is a method of sampling people temporarily congregated in a space. A typical example of how this method operates would be as follows: A number of interviewers approach the crowd (e.g. in a mass demonstration in the city square) and choose their respondents randomly and in a systematic way, for example, by walking three steps into the crowd and interviewing the person on their right. This process is then repeated until the interviewers have walked through the crowd. The people interviewed in this way constitute the sample of the study. ...

Non-probability sampling

Non-probability sampling procedures do not employ the rules of probability theory, do not claim representativeness, and are usually used for exploration and qualitative analysis. Some of these techniques can, with some adequate 'treatment' be converted into probability methods. The accidental sampling, the purposive sampling, the quota sampling, and the snowball sampling are non-probability sampling techniques; they are presented below.

Accidental sampling

This type of sampling is employed in qualitative research and in other studies where representativeness is not an issue. It is also known as 'incidental sampling', 'chunk sampling', 'grab sampling' and 'haphazard sampling'. When this sampling technique is employed, all units for study that the researcher accidentally comes in contact with during a certain period of time are considered. The investigator might stand at a street corner, in front of a shopping centre, or at a university entrance, and interview a certain number of persons passing by between, say, 11.00 and 12.00 o'clock on certain days of the week.

Such samples are easy to construct and evaluate. Nevertheless, they are not claimed to be representative of the whole population. However, in studies where this sampling procedure is employed, representativeness is not significant. ...

Purposive sampling

In this sampling technique the researchers purposely

choose subjects who, in their opinion, are thought to be relevant to the research topic. In this case, the judgement of the investigator is more important than obtaining a probability sample.

The process of sampling in this case will involve identification of the informants, and arranging times for meeting them. ...

Quota sampling

Quota sampling is a version of stratified sampling with the difference that instead of dividing the population into strata and choosing randomly a number of respondents it works on 'quotas' set by the researcher. In a sense, it is a non-random proportional stratified sampling procedure.

In simple terms, the researcher sets a 'quota' of respondents to be chosen from specific population groups, by defining the basis of choice (e.g. gender, marital status, ethnicity, education, etc.) and by determining its size (e.g. 60 parents of toddlers; 35 policewomen; 66 teachers and so on). The choice of the actual respondents is usually left up to the interviewer.

The way quotas are determined varies, depending on a number of factors related to the nature and type of the research. For instance, the researcher might advise the interviewer to survey 50 female students who will attend the next Monday methodology class and 50 male students who walked out of the student union immediately after 5 p.m. on the last Friday of June; or 100 fathers who attend the local Baby Health Clinic immediately after 9.00 a.m. on the next Monday. The choice is left to the interviewer or left up to chance (as in the last sample).

Another way of determining the quotas is based on more strict procedures. One such method is by choosing respondents according to their proportion in the entire population. For instance, if the study is about attitudes of ethnic and non-ethnic Australians to youth homelessness, and the respondents are to be chosen by means of quota sampling, the investigator may proceed as follows. In the first place, she or he must decide which type of quota will be most suitable for the study. This decisive criterion might be ethnicity. If this is the choice, and if the proportion of ethnic Australians in the community in question is 26 per cent, the quota of the ethnic Australians would be 26 per cent and that of the non-ethnic Australians 74 per cent of the sample. In a sample of 400 respondents the researcher will advise the interviewer to choose (in some way, namely freely or according to a specific criterion) 104 ethnic and 296 non-ethnic Australians.

In another form, quota sampling considers all significant dimensions of the population and ensures that each dimension will be represented in the sample. This is usually referred to as *dimensional sampling* and is used particularly when the sample is small. In such cases, this procedure guarantees that at least one case from each dimension of the universe will be included in the sample.

Quota sampling is quite common in the social sciences because it is less costly than other techniques, does not require sampling frames, is relatively effective, and can be completed in a very short period of time. It is however, limited, especially with respect to representativeness, control of sampling, and field-work requirements. Problems of abuse and bias caused by the interviewer, who may turn to the first available, convenient and least resistant person, are hard to avoid. However, quota sampling normally is not meant to be a random procedure, and should not be expected to provide random data.

The interviewers usually choose respondents who fall into set quotas and criteria, as defined by the researcher. ...

Snowball sampling

In this type of sampling researchers begin the research with the few respondents who are available to them. They subsequently ask these respondents to recommend any other persons who meet the criteria of the research and who might be willing to participate in the project. If and when such respondents are recommended, the investigator approaches them, collects the information required and asks them to recommend other persons who might fit the research design and be willing to be studied. This process is continued until the sample is *saturated*, that is, until no more substantial information is achieved through additional respondents, or until no more respondents are discovered. ...

This method is employed when the lack of sampling frames makes it impossible for the researcher to achieve a probability sample, when the target population is unknown, or when it is difficult to approach the respondents in any other way.

Sampling procedures in qualitative research

It has quite often been argued that qualitative researchers do not use sampling procedures. This is not correct. It is more accurate to say that they employ sampling procedures that correspond to the philosophy of this type of research, and that are less structured, less quantitative, and less strict than the techniques quantitative researchers employ.

Normally, qualitative studies employ a form of non-probability sampling, such as accidental or purposive sampling, as well as snowball sampling and theoretical sampling. Qualitative sampling is biased by the nature of the underlying qualitative framework, which is perceived as an investigative process, not very different from detective work, where 'one makes gradual sense of a social phenomenon, and does it in large part by contrasting, comparing, replicating, cataloguing and classifying the objects of one's study.' Sampling here comes after factors and conditions become clear and directive, and making decisions about sampling before the study has begun is neither proper nor useful.

Nevertheless, qualitative research has no strict agreed-on rules of sampling employed by all researchers. Sampling procedures employed by qualitative researchers are those mentioned above (accidental, purposive, snowball sampling and so on) or a version or combination of quantitative sampling procedures. A type of sampling introduced some time ago in the area of qualitative research and gradually becoming popular is *theoretical sampling*, which will be introduced briefly below.

For some researchers *theoretical* sampling is a new concept. This form of sampling has been very well established in the context of grounded theory, and is characterized by the fact that the collection of data is controlled by the merging theory, in that the researcher has to constantly look for new units and data, and justify the theoretical purpose for which each additional group is included in the study.

The researcher who employs theoretical sampling will continue adding new units to the sample until the study has reached a *saturation* point, that is, until new data are produced through inclusion and analysis of new units.

Irrespective of the type of sampling chosen, several sampling parameters have to be considered before a qualitative study can begin. Although qualitative sampling is a function of the research process itself and is decided on while the research is in progress, depending on the outcome of the study, researchers do have to decide at the onset at least about a number of issues, such as the informants, actors or respondents who will be studied, the setting where research will take place, the events and processes to be considered in the investigation, and the time when research will be conducted. In any case, sampling procedures in qualitative research are inevitably related to a number of issues and choices, and even 'not making a choice' is a choice!

Qualitative researchers have to make a choice at some stage about the *kind of people* they will include in their study, particularly since the number of subjects in these studies is very small. If they intend, for instance, to study the quality of life of unmarried mothers in Broken Hill, they have to decide whom they will include in their study. Given that the number of unmarried mothers is relatively large, a sample selection is inevitable.

Equally inevitable is the choice of *time*. Qualitative researchers will have to decide whether to contact their respondents on working days, on weekends, during the school holidays, in summer or winter, in the afternoons, in the evenings or any other time. Choosing the 'right' time is important and has significant effects on the results.

Apart from this, the qualitative researcher will make a choice about the *kind of event* to be studied, namely whether it will be a routine event, a special event, an unexpected event, or all types of event. In any case making a choice is inevitable.

Finally, a choice regarding the *place* in which the research will be conducted (e.g. the home, the club, the work place, a friend's house, etc.) has to be made.

The sampling procedures employed by qualitative researchers demonstrate a number of characteristics; many writers note that qualitative sampling is directed:

- not towards large numbers of respondents but rather towards *typical* cases
- not towards fixed samples but towards one that will change in size and type or subjects
- not towards statistical or random sampling but towards *suitable* cases, and purposive sampling
- not towards statistical sampling but towards *theoretical sampling*
- towards fewer global settings than quantitative sampling
- not towards a sample that is selected before the study has started, but (often) while the study is in progress
- not towards a strictly defined size but a sample whose number will be expanded while the study is in operation
- not towards representativeness but rather towards *suitability*.

As stated earlier, the range of qualitative research has significantly widened in scope and purpose during the past 10 years, allowing researchers more choice than before. It is interesting, then, to see Miles and Huberman (1984) give qualitative researchers the following advice: 'Just thinking in sampling-frame terms is healthy methodological medicine'.

Non-response

The various types of sampling enable the researcher to identify the respondents who will be included in the study. In most cases the sampling procedures will result in a list of names and addresses to be used at a later stage in order to approach the respondents. In other cases sampling will bring the researcher or the interviewer face-to-face with the respondent.

Despite efforts made by the research personnel to contact the respondents selected by the sampling methods, several subjects will not be contacted. Research experience shows that some respondents will not be at home at the arranged time; others will be unsuitable due to inability to communicate; while others will have moved away, and others will simply refuse to co-operate. A certain number of respondents will remain unavailable even after intensive efforts on the part of the researcher. How will the investigator compensate for this loss of subjects? Can they be ignored? Can equivalent or similar subjects be taken from the same area as a substitute for the unavailable subjects?

There are various answers to these questions. Some theorists suggest that the best way of meeting this problem is prevention. This means that the researcher should test the response rate of his study by means of pilot studies, estimate the expected drop-out rate and take a sample that is larger than the required sample, that is, large enough to compensate for the expected non-response rate. This method, however, causes obvious problems, which cannot be justified methodologically.

Some researchers prefer to ignore the non-respondents and to proceed with the rest of the sample. The underlying justification for this is that the missing units are thought to be similar to those who responded, and the study is not affected by the lost units. This seems to be a popular way of responding to the problem,

especially if the response rate is relatively high, and if the necessary steps for reducing the non-response have been followed, but again not without problems.

The suggestion to ignore the non-respondents has been criticized by many who believe that such a device causes problems and has negative effects on the results. For these theorists, the missing respondents are assumed to be different from those who responded, and for this reason the study consciously excludes an interesting part of the target population. Their view is that non-respondents should not be left out. Some suggest that they have to be substituted, in a form similar to quota sampling, whereby the researcher advises the interviewer to select extra respondents who are similar in certain characteristics to the non-respondents. Other suggest that the substitute respondents should be similar to those who responded after the second or subsequent reminder. In any case, for these researchers substitution seems to be imperative, when all possible methods of approaching the original respondents were fruitless.

Non-response is a research problem, but can be met with some degree of success if the research has been planned accurately and systematically.

Reference

Miles, M. B. and Huberman, A. M. (1984) *Qualitative Data Analysis: a sourcebook of new methods*, Beverley Hills: Sage.

Key terms

The following key terms appear in the text above. They have been defined below to aid with the reading of this item.

probability sampling another name used for random sampling, the technique where every unit in a population has the same chance of being selected as part of the sample

non-probability sampling another name for non-random sampling, the technique where certain selection criteria are drawn up – such as social class or gender – which means that not every unit in the population has an equal chance of being selected. This does not however mean that the sample is any less valid or that its findings will be any less representative

Questions

1 Explain in your own words the difference between probability sampling and non-probability sampling.

2 Suggest two reasons why sociologists might use a panel study.

3 Suggest two reasons why sociologists might use spatial sampling.

Reading 4.8 **Official statistics**

Martin Slattery (from) *Official Statistics* (1986) London: Tavistock, pp. 18–25 and 28–9.

Editorial comments

Secondary data – that is, data that is not collected directly by the person researching a problem – is an important element in much sociological research, and certainly in coursework produced by sociology students. It is clearly useful in terms of the amount of information available and the cost of obtaining it in

terms of both time and money. The most important source of secondary data is official statistics, that is, statistics collected and published by the government to enable decisions to be made about policy and its implementation. Since it is not collected by sociologists, but widely used by them, there are a number of issues that need to be taken into account when using this data. In this extract from his book on the subject, Martin Slattery summarizes the data that is available from official statistics and discusses some of the issues that arise in considering its usage by sociologists.

Official statistics

The history of official statistics

THOUGH THE CENSUS and official departments of statistics are very recent phenomena, the collection of facts and figures by government about its people is as old as the most ancient of civilizations, beyond William the Conqueror's *Domesday Book*, beyond even Herod's survey at the time of the birth of Christ. However such population 'counts' were very limited. They had only two main purposes – the collection of taxes and the conscription of able-bodied men into the king's army. The word statistics itself derives from the Latin *status* or political state and the German *statistik* or *state-istic*, facts and figures for the use of the state. Such 'political' arithmetic however did not become either properly organized or scientific until the scientific revolution in Europe in the seventeenth century and the growth of European nationalism. Every nation state was now determined to gather as many facts as possible about their populations, trade, finance, taxes, and armed forces in the fierce balance of power between such states as Bismark's Germany and Napoleon III's France.

However even by the early twentieth century the official collection and analysis of social statistics was very limited and amateurish. It took two world wars, the pioneering efforts of social surveyors like Charles Booth and Seebohm Rowntree, and the post-war demand by the electorate for the government to provide both economic management and a welfare state to put British **official statistics** on a professional footing. The Government Statistical Service (GSS) was set up in 1941 and expanded thereafter from population statistics to those on economic, social, and psychological issues. Under the leadership of Claus Moser and the patronage of Harold Wilson the GSS became an integral part of the 1960s Labour government's attempt to modernize Britain. It grew to over 500 professional staff and over 6,000 support staff and established an international reputation for its sheer professionalism. However amid the depression of the 1970s and the 'cuts' of the 1980s, the GSS has had both its size and status pruned.

Sources of official statistics

Nevertheless in serving modern government the GSS and its agencies produce such a wealth of facts and figures every year that an 'official guide' has to be published for even academic experts to find their way round the volumes produced. The GSS however is not a giant 'fact-finding factory' as in Canada or the EEC but a relatively decentralized organization made up of the statistics divisions of all the major government departments plus the two main collecting agencies – the Business Statistics Office and the Office of Population Censuses and Surveys (OPCS) – with the Central Statistical Office (CSO) co-ordinating the whole system. The major collection of official statistics is the census. More regular and up-to-date official statistics are collected by:

1 The registration and administrative procedures of a variety of government departments like the Registrar General.
2 Official sample surveys, the most important of which are *multipurpose surveys*. Whilst national statistics offer a static picture of British society, a sort of snapshot, multipurpose surveys offer a continuous picture revealing the general trends and dynamics of social change. The three most important for our purposes are the following.

The Family Expenditure Survey (FES)

This is a fortnightly diary completed by a random sample of 11,000 households outlining their weekly and monthly expenditure patterns. It includes questions on income and such outgoings as food, clothing, drink, heat and light, insurances and credit payments. It began in the 1950s and is a unique source of highly reliable information on household income and expenditure. It is however limited by its **response rate** (70 per cent) and by referring only to households not individuals or families.

The General Household Survey (GHS)

This was started in 1971 by the OPCS as a means to covering gaps in other sources of official statistics, gaps in time, in detail, in testing relationships between social variables and between official surveys. It is not tied to any one single topic and so is very flexible and can be easily adapted to new social trends or official needs. It covers five main subject areas – population, housing, employment, education, and health – and it is based on a stratified sample of 15,000 households selected from the electoral register. It is very reliable and has an exceptional response rate (84 per cent).

The Labour Force Survey (LFS)

This began in 1973 when Britain joined the Common Market. It is a survey on the size and structure of the labour force carried out every two years in collaboration with the member countries of the EEC to aid Community policy-making on such issues as regional development and to provide a basis for distributing the social fund to 'needy' areas. It offers invaluable information on the whole European picture and provides an important basis for comparing and improving British statistics.

A list of the other major official surveys is given below and backed up by about 250 'ad hoc' government surveys; it shows the enormous sweep and depth of detail available to both officials and sociologists, covering everything apparently possible from national readership to working conditions, ethnic groups to contraception.

All this information is regularly published as follows.

General digests

1 The *Monthly Digest of Statistics* – a monthly collection and update of all official statistics ranging from population through to finance and the weather.
2 The *Annual Abstract of Statistics* – probably the most authoritative and most quoted of official publications. It dates back to the mid-nineteenth century and covers just about every aspect of economic, social, and industrial life.
   Its tables cover time-spans of ten years or more, thus highlighting trends and allowing comparison.
3 *Social Trends* – probably the most 'popular' of official publications. It is colourfully illustrated, easy to read, and covers all the main sociological areas as well as providing occasional essays on particular topics: 'The government's bumper annual fact-pack on the state of Britain' was how *The Times* referred to it.
4 *Regional Trends* – similarly readable and illustrated, this publication provides a regional breakdown of the national statistics in *Social Trends*.
5 *Economic Trends* – an 'economic' version of *Social Trends* covering the main economic indicators, statistics and trends in the UK economy. For more detailed economic analysis there is also:
   (a) *British Business* – a collection of statistics and commentary from the Department of Trade and Industry;
   (b) The *UK National Accounts* (the CSO *Blue Book*) and the *UK Balance of Payments* (the CSO *Pink Book*) – sort of national and international balance sheets covering ten years or more;
   (c) The *Economic Progress Report* – a monthly publication by the Treasury providing official analysis and background on government policy and on the current economic situation.

Scotland, Wales, and N. Ireland have similar publications of their own.

Departmental publications

Each government department also collects and publishes its own statistics. Examples include the *Defence Statistics* and the Department of the Environment's statistics on the homeless. For our purposes though these publications are especially useful:

1 *Population Trends* – a quarterly publication of tables and articles by the OPCS on a wide range of demographical and medical issues. It also provides useful series and fact packs for schools.
2 *Criminal Statistics, England and Wales* – produced by the Home Office (Scotland has a separate legal system and set of statistics) and covering an enormous range of criminal activities from gambling to terrorism, as well as the general trends in crime, sentencing, and police prosecution.
3 The *Employment Gazette* – published monthly by the Department of Employment, it provides up-to-date statistics on all forms of employment, unemployment, and economic activity, plus very useful articles on how such statistics are defined and collected.

There is also *Britain – An Official Handbook*, the CSO update magazine *Statistical news*, and most especially for a student's purposes the CSO's little pocket reference card 'The UK in figures' which summarizes the main official facts and figures.

Behind all these official surveys and publications, though, lies the 'Big Daddy' of them all, the *census*.

The census

This is the most authoritative, comprehensive and detailed national survey there is. It is so large, so expensive, and so thorough that even the government can only afford to conduct one every ten years and it takes at least five years fully to digest and analyse. As David Rhind explains:

> The Census of Population is certainly a major decennial event in Britain: the taking of the 1981 Census involved the employment of more than 129,000 people, cost about £45 million and was designed to elicit information from every one of the two million or so households in this country.
> *(Rhind, 1983)*

This enormous official undertaking takes years of planning and as David Rhind (1983) points out, it 'is the most important single source of information about the number and condition of the people' because it is so thorough, detailed, and regular.

Censuses in one form or another can be dated back to the Ancient Egyptians, Greeks, and Romans but modern censuses – in the sense of being detailed and regular – have only occurred in Europe since the nineteenth century.

The first full British census was carried out in 1801

Table 1 Some other major surveys

	frequency	date	sampling frame	sample size	unit of analysis	type of respondent	response rate (%)	location
National Food Survey	continuous from	1940	electoral register	15,000	households	housewife	52	GB
International Passenger Survey	continuous from	1964	international passengers at ports, airports, etc.	260,000	individual traveller	individual traveller	88	GB
New Earnings Survey	annual from	1970	national insurance numbers	170,000	employees	employers	82	GB
Survey of Personal Incomes	annual from	1954/5	inland revenue records	144,000	tax units	local tax offices	95	UK
English House Condition Survey	irregular from	1967	valuation list	9,000	households	household heads	83	E
National Dwelling and Housing Survey	ad hoc	1977/9	valuation list	915,000	households and individuals	one adult in household	85	GB
National Readership Survey	continuous from	1956	electoral register	30,000	individuals	individuals	75	GB
EEC Consumer Attitude Survey	four-monthly from	1974	electoral register	12,000	individuals	household heads	84	GB
National Child Development Survey	ad hoc surveys of cohort	1958	birth records	17,000	individuals in cohort	cohort members and others	87	GB
National Training Survey	ad hoc	1975/6	electoral register	54,000	individuals	working adults	72	GB
Workplace Industrial Relations Survey	three-yearly from	1980	census of employment	2,700	establishments	managers and worker representatives	76	GB
National Travel Survey	regular from	1965	electoral register	15,000	individuals	households heads	85	GB

Source: Hakim (1982)

and every ten years thereafter. But it wasn't until 1841 that detailed information was asked and the 'head of household' made the main respondent. This followed the Civil Registration Act of 1837, the establishment of the office of Registrar General under the commissionship of Dr William Farr. From then on all vital statistics – of births, deaths, marriages, etc. – had to be registered in England and Wales (but not until 1855 in Scotland). The legal basis for the census was established by the 1920 Census Act which made completion of the census form compulsory and allowed Parliament to authorize each census simply by an Order in Council. ...

Comments and criticisms

Inevitably in such a massive operation errors occur. Some people are missed entirely, some double-counted; some characteristics such as age and occupation are wrongly recorded, wrongly coded or wrongly key-punched. In the processing of the 1981 census there were 100,000 keying errors according to the Registrar General's Review. Certain social groups seem especially vulnerable to 'getting lost' – the old, adolescents, and infants (as all their ages are likely to get distorted), and immigrants. Such omissions may well affect the overall picture of these particular groups.

Second, many of the definitions (though pre-tested) may lead to misinformation due to ambiguity or misunderstanding. ...

Third, the British census is much more limited than most other countries' and does not include questions in such topics as religion, income, and race. This may reflect British respect for personal privacy but from a sociological point of view it does mean valuable social information is missed out.

Extensive checks are made by the OPCS to eliminate errors and gaps – for example they undertake a re-run of the census shortly after census day and extensive cross-checks are made with other sources of data like the GHS. The OPCS estimates however that the 1981 population count was only half a per cent below the true figure (only 240,000 people were missed out of 54 million or more), a classic example of the professionalism and reliability of British census data.

The advantages and disadvantages of official statistics

Obviously the main advantage of using official social statistics is simply the great wealth of information available on a very wide range of economic, social, and political issues. Such data is readily available and often the only information produced on many topics. Official statistics allow the examination of trends over time, comparisons between social groups and geographical regions, and 'before and after studies', enabling sociologists to examine the effects for example of legislation like the 1972 Raising of the School Leaving Age or 1971 Divorce Reform Act.

However official statistics do also have their limitations and problems from a sociological point of view:

- They are collected essentially for official, administrative, and political purposes. Often therefore they do not cover areas of particular interest to sociologists (or only in passing) such as income and wealth.
- Official definitions are often non-sociological and would be seriously criticized by sociologists as we shall see later.
- Comparisons between censuses and even official surveys like the GHS are often very difficult because definitions have been changed or no longer 'mean' the same. Moreover due to the time taken to plan and publish official surveys their definitions tend to be out of date in a world that is changing so rapidly.
- Much official data is not published or is inaccessible either because of the cost involved or for political reasons. To avoid embarrassment governments occasionally withhold information or limit its publication (e.g. the *Black Report on Health in Britain* – see Townsend and Davidson, 1980 – was originally published as a mere 260 duplicated copies by the DHSS).

Finally official statistics only provide 'quantitative' data. There are no official statistics on British public opinion or attitudes – though the establishment of the *British Social Attitudes Survey* is a step in that direction.

References

Hakim, C. (1982) *Secondary Analysis in Social Research*, London: Allen & Unwin.

Jowell, R. and Airey, C. (1984) *British Social Attitudes*, Aldershot: Gower.

Rhind, D. (ed.) (1983) *A Census User's Handbook*, London: Methuen.

Townsend, P. and Davidson, N. (1980) *Inequalities in Health*, Harmondsworth: Penguin.

Key terms

The following key terms appear in the text above. They have been defined below to aid with the reading of this item.

official statistics statistics published by the government in a variety of forms

response rate the proportion of questionnaires given out that are filled in and returned, and so included in the findings

Questions

1 Which government survey other than the census has the largest sample size?

2 Which government survey other than the census has the highest response rate?

3 What was studied by Booth and Rowntree and why did this have an impact on the production of official statistics?

4 Slattery suggests that the 1981 census estimate of population was only half a per cent below the true figure. Why was this not true for the 1991 census?

5 Suggest the publication which would be most useful for the study of trends in wage rates?

6 Evaluate the usefulness of official statistics for sociological purposes.

Further reading

The following texts may represent a useful starting point for further investigation of the ideas contained within this chapter.

Primary texts

Durkheim, E. (1938, orig. pub. 1895) *The Rules of the Sociological Method*, Glencoe: Free Press.

Giddens, A. (1976) *The New Rules of the Sociological Method*, London: Hutchinson.

Secondary texts

Chignall, H. (1996) *Theory and Methods*, Lewes: Connect.

McNeill, P. (1990) *Research methods*, 2nd edn, London: Routledge.

May, T. (1993) *Social Research*, Buckingham: Open University Press.

Harvey, L. and MacDonald, M. (1993) *Doing Sociology: a practical introduction*, London: Macmillan.

Williams, L. and Dunsmuir, A. (1991) *How To Do Social Research*, London: Collins Educational.

5

Stratification: class

Chapter summary

Reading 5.1 **Karl Marx on class** *page 108*

In the first of two extracts Marx discusses the proposition that while, in one sense, a class can be said to be formed when a group of people objectively share a common position in relation to the means of production, *vis-à-vis* another class or classes, to the extent that they lack any sense of consciousness of their common class interests, they do not form a class. The second extract – an unfinished fragment – indicates that, whatever the tendency to reduce his view of stratification in capitalist society to a model of two polarized antagonistic classes, Marx fully understood its complexity in terms of the existence of numerous intermediate class fractions.

Reading 5.2 **Max Weber: class, status and power** *page 110*

This reading illustrates how Weber shared Marx's belief that class could be defined in exclusively economic or market terms. However, Weber carefully distinguished class, defined in this way, from other related forms of stratification, each reflecting different types of power. Power in the economic sphere is stratified into classes, in the social sphere into status groups and in the political sphere it is based on parties and interest groups.

Reading 5.3 **Conflicts about class** *page 114*

David Lee and Bryan Turner – in their introduction to *Conflicts About Class: Debating inequality in late industrialism* – summarize the various contributions to the debate about the continuing relevance of the concept of class. They consider the competing claims proposed regarding the death of class analysis and the advent of classlessness.

Reading 5.4 **A classless society?** *page 120*

Geoff Payne's article looks at the related issues of social mobility, equality of opportunity, meritocracy and notions of classlessness and social justice. He summarizes the data from large-scale surveys of social mobility in Britain and considers the different ways in which these have been interpreted by the protagonists in the debate about the extent to which the effects of class origins have become divorced from class destinations.

Reading 5.5 **Who rules Britain?** *page 123*

John Scott discusses the extent to which there exists in the UK a distinctive 'capitalist class' and the processes through which it is able to reproduce itself. He claims that Britain is dominated by a 'business class' that is cemented together through interlocking directorships, family ties, and the public school system.

Reading 5.6 **Representations of the 'underclass'** *page 128*

Paul Bagguley and Kirk Mann look at the debate surrounding the very use of the term 'underclass' and the various ways in which it has been used to portray groups experiencing multiple deprivation in Britain and the USA. They suggest that the term lacks academic precision and its use is often seen as a device to be used to demonize the poor and as such is a reflection of upper-class ideology.

Reading 5.7 **Class today: fashions at odds with facts** *page 134*

John Westergaard summarizes the main theme of his book *Who Gets What?*, in which he challenges the view that class inequality has been eclipsed in contemporary capitalist society. He outlines his belief that class analysis can be informed by elements of both Marxist and Weberian theory, before going on to argue that empirical evidence of a 'hardening' of class inequalities makes claims of classlessness, or the death of class, difficult to square with the 'facts'.

Reading 5.8 **'Fractured identities': social class and post-modernity** *page 139*

Harriet Bradley identifies 'post-modern' strands of thinking which have challenged the primacy of class and which provide a more flexible approach to dealing with the relationship between class and other aspects of inequality. However, she believes that this 'promising new direction' for class analysis, as yet, lacks sufficient empirical backing.

Introduction: Reading the sociology of stratification: class

Social stratification refers to the division of a society into a hierarchy of distinct social groups each having specific life chances and a distinctive style of life. The problem that has confronted sociologists for much of the history of the discipline has been how to classify the social strata and explain the causal mechanisms behind their formation, in a way that meets universal approval, not only among sociologists as an academic community, but also in the subjective perceptions of the people they attempt to describe.

Traditionally sociologists have focused on the social class dimension of stratification, but its pre-eminence has been challenged by 'post-modernist' views that social class has been 'decentred' as a source of identity, being replaced by a whole range of 'fractured identities' revolving around status and consumption, nationality and ethnicity, gender and age as well as a variety of new social movements. This reflects the general shift in emphasis associated with post-modernism in sociology, particularly post-structuralist versions, towards the study of social meanings as they are located within cultures. Post-modernists thus tend to reject 'foundationalist' accounts of society (i.e. the search for underlying structures) and 'totalizing' narratives (i.e. theories that claim to explain the whole of society). Class analysis is an example of a 'totalizing discourse' which post-modernist thinking might reject.

All of the readings in this chapter, to a greater or lesser extent, relate to the issue of whether or not social class in its various guises should be regarded as a useful tool with which to understand society. A key part of the debate concerns how far it is possible to claim that social class exists in an objective structural sense, independently of people's awareness of it, and how far social class is only of significance when it is generally perceived as such in the consciousness of members of society?

Sociologists who adopt a 'class-based' view of stratification, according to which inequality stems from differential command over economic resources, take the view that such differences in economic power signify class relations as objective realities, even if the power is invisible to the wielders or the victims. Karl Marx (1962 and 1969) was well aware of this distinction and, while he emphasized the fact that social class is determined by different positions in the social organization of production – whereby a group of people who objectively share a common position in relation to the means of production could be described as a

'class *in* itself' – consciousness of class was necessary before they could be described as forming a 'class *for* itself'.

The first extract in **reading 5.1** demonstrates the importance attached by Marx to class consciousness as a prerequisite of class action. The second extract clearly illustrates that he understood the complexity resulting from the number of intermediary class locations in capitalist society whereby many groups or individuals were in an ambiguous position, unable to identify their interests with either the bourgeoisie or the proletariat. This was a temporary phenomenon according to Marx, eventually 'polarization' would occur when more and more people would come to identify their interests with one class or the other.

The work of Max Weber can be seen as a debate with Marx. Weber implicitly agreed with Marx's distinction between 'class in itself' and 'class for itself'; however he saw class as only a potential basis for the mobilization of conflicting class interests and believed that in capitalist society, class consciousness resulting in class conflict was by no means inevitable. In **reading 5.2** Weber argues that stratification has three conceptually distinct dimensions, which relate to different spheres of power. As part of his overall theory of power, Weber's analysis of class went beyond the economic dimension by linking it to the facet of status. If class reflects differences in economic power, especially in the market-place, status marks differences in the social sphere of prestige or honour. If social classes are distinguished in terms of their different 'market situation', status groups are distinguished according to different styles of life. According to Weber (1946), 'classes' are stratified according to their relations to the production and acquisition of goods, whereas 'status groups' are stratified according to the principles of their consumption of goods as represented by 'special styles of life'. Status groups, unlike classes, by their very nature tend to have a sense of identity and common purpose. Classes and status groups are potentially competing bases of mobilization and group formation in relation to the distribution of power. Weber saw this as an impediment to the development of radical class consciousness. In Weberian sociology the inevitability of class is denied and may, under certain conditions, take second place to status.

The initial positions set out by Marx and Weber can be seen in contemporary sociological debates about the claimed demise of social class as the primary basis of social identity and action. In **reading 5.3**, Lee and Turner (1996) consider the competing accounts of neo-Marxist (or 'strong') class theory and neo-Weberian ('weak') class theory and their continuing relevance. In light of late-twentieth-century developments, class analysis may have become outmoded, and they summarize the critiques of class by separating them into two types: the 'myths of classlessness'. First are the substantive assertions about the actual distribution of class power and privilege in contemporary society. Second is the rumoured 'death of class' itself – that is, the extent to which there is anything left for class analysis to do. They tend to conclude that capitalist societies are demonstrably not classless and that 'the persistence and stability of class inequality continues to give a clear agenda for sociologists to work at'.

Reading 5.4 approaches the issue of classlessness in relation to the degree of fluidity in the class structure of British society. Geoff Payne (1991) reviews the evidence of data from social mobility surveys and contrasts the differing interpretations of sociologists on the 'left' and those on the 'right'. The former view, which includes Goldthorpe and Marshall, defends class analysis and highlights the persistence of class-related differences in phenomena such as voting behaviour, chances of social mobility, etc., while the latter, which includes Saunders, has tended to subordinate the centrality of 'class effects' concentrating instead on how the class structure changes and individuals and groups compete in it on more or less equal terms. In **reading 5.5**, John Scott (1991) refers to the high degree of social closure in access to élite positions in British society when discussing the class reproduction of the capitalist class. In answering the question: *Who Rules Britain?*, he concludes that there is a distinct 'capitalist class' in British society, which can be said to truly constitute a ruling class (in terms of political domination), due to the fact that its economic dominance is sustained by the operations of the state and because its personnel are disproportionately represented in élite political positions.

Continuing an exploration of the contours of class at the extremes of society, **reading 5.6** questions the extent to which a distinctive group can be said to exist at the bottom of the class hierarchy. The use of the term 'underclass' as an analytical concept seems to be of dubious value and is more likely to result in the further social exclusion of the people in question. Bagguley and Mann (1992) argue that it has become so emotionally and ideologically charged it must be regarded as intellectually bankrupt. Whatever definition is adopted to describe the 'sub-class', the distinctiveness of its deepening poverty and the sheer scale of its effects tend to undermine notions of classlessness.

John Westergaard (1996) also criticizes the fashionable argument of classlessness, claiming that it is very much at odds with the facts. In **reading 5.7**, he argues that such a view has misunderstood the fundamental nature of social class and has ignored hardening class inequalities. Westergaard, adopting a Marxist position, reasserts the salience of class predicated on social divisions arising from a society's economic organization. From this flows differential command over resources, and consequently (drawing on elements of Weberian analysis) he notes the existence of differential access to rewards that are to be seen in fundamental aspects of people's life experiences or 'life chances' in the form of various inequalities. Westergaard is aware of the need for class consciousness if a class in itself is to ever become a class for itself, but also points to the importance of the objective features of class 'in itself' in shaping the character of society and peoples' experiences. Westergaard's main argument is that Britain the 1980s and '90s saw the effects of class increase in their potency, with power being increasingly concentrated at the top.

Discussions in the previous reading concluded that despite claims about the 'classless society', modern Britain is characterized by widening gaps between rich and poor. It is also becoming increasingly apparent that inequalities of class overlap with other inequalities such as those of ethnicity, gender and age. As patterns of stratification have become increasingly complex it is necessary to consider the fact that social class is just one of a number of different aspects of inequality.

In **reading 5.8**, Harriet Bradley (1996) identifies several strands of thinking which have challenged the primacy of class. She states firstly that the changes that have occurred in the class structure mean that the old frameworks for thinking about class are no longer applicable; secondly, other forms of inequality, such as 'race' and gender, are not reducible to class and each needs to be considered in its own right; thirdly, post-modernism has focused attention on the diversity of social experience. It tends to endorse pluralism through its focus on the specific positions of different groups and in its extreme form undermines all notions of collectivities such as class, preferring to talk in terms of atomized individuals.

Bradley does not believe, however, that post-modernists necessarily abandon the study of class, gender and ethnicity altogether, rather they tend to consider them in terms of discourses or social constructs; in other words, with consideration of the ways in which they have come to be defined, by whom and in whose interests. Post-modernism is thus a major challenge to the concept of class, as it proposes that class has been 'decentred' as a source of identity, being replaced by a whole range of 'fractured identities' revolving around status and consumption, nationality and ethnicity, gender and age, as well as a variety of 'new social movements'. While accepting some of the insights provided by post-modernism, Bradley concludes, nevertheless, that class, as either a set of lived economic relationships, or class analysis, as a set of social categories, is not dead – but there must be a recognition of how class relations are shaped by other forms of inequality.

In spite of recent trends to diminish its importance in sociological analysis, 'social class' is likely to remain a crucial explanatory variable. It is clearly true that other forms of inequality such as gender and race are distinct dimensions of inequality and that their subordination cannot be primarily explained by the workings of capitalism as this does not answer the question why certain groups are singled out for segregation under this economic system. It is equally true that the three types of stratification – class, gender and ethnicity – are not mutually exclusive, they co-exist, each type of inequality overlapping and compounding another. However, sociologists who favour the use of class analysis argue that in the public sphere, gender and ethnic inequality operate largely through class inequality. Even if subjective awareness of class inequality *has* diminished, they would point to the continuing objective realities of class. Virtually every variable in society shows a correlation with class, a fact most convincingly demonstrated by the enduring class inequalities in the risks of death. Perhaps it could be said that social class continues to be sociology's 'only independent variable' (Stinchcombe, cited in Wright, 1979).

Reference

Wright, E. O. (1979) *Class, Structure and Income Determination*, New York: Academic Press.

Reading 5.1 **Karl Marx on class**

(1) Karl Marx (from) 'The eighteenth brumaire of Louis Bonaparte', in *Marx and Engels Collected Works*: vol. II; 1851–1853 (1979) London: Lawrence & Wishart. [Abridged from Coser, L. A. and Rosenberg, B. (eds) (1969) *Sociological Theory: a book of readings*, London: Collier Macmillan, pp. 384–5.]

(2) Karl Marx (from) *Capital: a critique of political economy*: vol. III (1984), London: Lawrence & Wishart. [In Bendix, R., and Lipset, S. (eds) (1967) *Class, Status and Power: Social stratification in comparative perspective*, 2nd edn, London: Routledge & Kegan Paul, pp. 5–6.]

Editorial comments

The first of these two short extracts from Karl Marx (1818–83) captures the essence of the constituents of class for Marx: large numbers of people who share similar economic conditions that separate them from other classes can be said to constitute a class, or what Marx referred to elsewhere as 'a class *in* itself'. According to Marx, only when such a class developed consciousness of its class interests (class consciousness) and a desire to further these interests did it become a 'class *for* itself'.

Marx's view of class is often inferred as a dichotomy of classes becoming increasingly polarized into hostile camps. The apparent failure of this prediction is often cited as a weakness of Marxist class theory. However, the second (unfinished) extract shows that Marx was well aware of the true complexity of class in capitalist society and the tendency for there to be internal divisions within the bourgeoisie and the proletariat. As a revolutionary, Marx believed it was necessary to overcome these divisions by promoting class consciousness among all those who own merely their own labour power.

Both readings emphasize the fundamental importance attached by Marxists to positions in the social relations of production as the determinants of class interests.

Are the peasants a class?

THE SMALL PEASANTS form a vast mass, the members of which live in similar conditions, but without entering into manifold relations with one another. Their mode of production isolates them from one another, instead of bringing them into mutual intercourse. The isolation is increased by Frances's bad means of communication and by the poverty of the peasants. Their field of production, the small holding, admits of no division of labour in its cultivation, no application of science and, therefore, no multiplicity of development, no diversity of talents, no wealth of social relationships. Each individual peasant family is almost self-sufficient; it itself directly produces the major part of its consumption and thus acquires its means of life more through exchange with nature than in intercourse with society. The small holding, the peasant and his family; alongside them another small holding, another peasant and another family. A few score of these make up a village, and a few score of villages make up a Department. In this way, the great mass of the French nation is formed by simple addition of **homologous magnitudes**, much as potatoes in a sack form a sackful of potatoes. In so far as millions of families live under economic conditions of existence that divide their mode of life, their interests and their culture from those of the other classes and put them in hostile contrast to the latter, they form a class. In so far as there is merely a local interconnection among these small peasants, and the identity of their interests begets no unity, no national union and no political organization, they do not form a class. They are consequently incapable of enforcing their class interest in their own name, whether through a parliament or through a convention. They cannot represent themselves, they must be represented. Their representative must at the same time appear as their master, as an authority over them, as an unlimited governmental power, that protects them against the other classes and sends them the rain and the sunshine from above. The political influence of the small peasants, therefore finds its final expression in the executive power subordinating society to itself.

A note on classes

THE OWNERS MERELY of labour-power, owners of capital, and landowners, whose respective sources of income are wages, profit, and ground-rent, in other words, wage-labourers, capitalists, and land-owners, constitute the three big classes of modern society based upon the capitalist mode of production.

In England, modern society is indisputably most highly and classically developed in economic structure. Nevertheless, even here the stratification of classes does not appear in its pure form. Middle and intermediate strata even here obliterate lines of demarcation everywhere (although incomparably less in rural districts than in the cities). However, this is immaterial for our analysis. We have seen that the continual tendency and law of development of the capitalist mode of production is more and more to divorce the means of production from labour, and more and more to concentrate the scattered means of production into large groups, thereby transforming labour into wage-labour and the means of production into capital. And to this tendency, on the other hand, corresponds the independent separation of landed property from capital and labour, or the transformation of all landed property into the form of landed property corresponding to the capitalist mode of production.

The first question to be answered is this: What constitutes a class? – and the reply to this follows naturally from the reply to another question, namely: What makes wage-labourers, capitalists, and landlords constitute the three great social classes?

At first glance – the identity of revenues and sources of revenue. There are three great social groups whose members, the individuals forming them, live on wages, profit, and ground-rent respectively, on the realization of their labour-power, their capital, and their landed property.

However, from this standpoint, physicians and officials, e.g., would also constitute two classes, for they belong to two distinct social groups, the members of each of these groups receiving their revenue from one and the same source. The same would also be true of the infinite fragmentation of interest and rank into which the division of social labour splits labourers as well as capitalists and landlords – the latter, e.g., into owners of vineyards, farm owners, owners of forests, mine owners, and owners of fisheries.

[Here the manuscript breaks off]

Key term

The following key term appears in the text above. It has been defined below to aid with the reading of this item.

homologous magnitudes large numbers of people sharing similar characteristics

Questions

1 Explain in your own words what Marx meant by the terms:
   a 'class *in* itself'
   b 'class *for* itself'.

2 Why is the distinction between a 'class *in* itself' and 'class *for* itself' so important in the Marxist theory of class?

3 With reference to the first extract in this reading, would Marx have described the peasants as constituting a 'class *in* itself' or a 'class *for* itself'?

4 Explain in your own words what Marx meant by the phrase 'stratification of classes in their pure form', as used in the second extract.

5 The second extract was unfinished and could be interpreted in a number of ways. It could be seen as evidence of the fact that Marx himself doubted

his theory of class polarization or it could be seen as reiterating his view that ownership or non-ownership of the means of production is the fundamental basis of class membership in capitalist society. Which of these points do *you* think Marx was trying to emphasize in this extract? Give reasons for your answer.

Reading 5.2 **Max Weber: class, status and power**

Max Weber (from) *Essays in Sociology* (1946) translated by H. H. Gerth and C. Wright Mills, Oxford: Oxford University Press. [Abridged from Bendix, R. and Lipset, S. (eds) (1967) *Class, Status and Power: Social stratification in comparative perspective,* 2nd edn, London: Routledge & Kegan Paul, pp. 21–8.]

Editorial comments

In this reading, Weber (1866–1920) appears to agree with Marx that class is an economic phenomenon – class situation pivots on ownership or non-ownership of capital – however, for Weber it will also vary within and between these categories according to 'market situation', reflecting the value of marketable skills. He took issue with the Marxist assumption that radical class consciousness was bound to occur.

Status groups, unlike classes, tend to have a sense of identity and common purpose. Those sharing a similar status position often form communities which display themselves in a specific style of life, and may become highly self contained. As a result, status affiliations can cut across class lines and Weber saw this as an impediment to the development of radical class consciousness.

The extract demonstrates Weber's hierarchical and pluralistic notion of class and class action, the expression of which – though rooted in economic interests – is mediated by the variable links between class, status and parties. In line with Weber's general sociological position, he gives a much greater role to subjectivity and meaning in the relationship between economic interests and class consciousness, seeing the development of class action as a voluntaristic process and, as a result, far from inevitable.

Class, status and power

Determination of class-situation by market-situation

IN OUR TERMINOLOGY, 'classes' are not communities; they merely represent possible, and frequent, bases for communal action. We may speak of a 'class' when (1) a number of people have in common a specific causal component of their life chances, in so far as (2) this component is represented exclusively by economic interests in the possession of goods and opportunities for income, and (3) is represented under the conditions of the commodity or labour markets. [These points refer to 'class situation', which we may express more briefly as the typical chance for a supply of goods, external living conditions, and personal life experiences, in so far as this chance is determined by the amount and kind of power, or lack of such, to dispose of goods or skills for the sake of income in a given economic order. The term 'class' refers to any group of people that is found in the same class situation.] ...

  Class situations are further differentiated: on the one hand, according to the kind of property that is usable for returns; and, on the other hand, according to the kind of services that can be offered in the market. Ownership of domestic buildings, productive establishments; warehouses; stores; agriculturally usable land, large and small holdings – quantitative differences with possibly qualitative consequences; ownership of mines; cattle; men (slaves); disposition over mobile instruments of production, or capital goods of all sorts, especially money or objects that can be exchanged for money easily and at any time; disposition over products of one's own labour or of others' labour differing according to their various distances from consumability; disposition over transferable monopolies of any kind – all these distinctions differentiate the class situations of the propertied just as does the 'meaning' which they can and do give to the utilization of property, especially to property which has money equivalence. Accordingly, the properties, for instance, may belong to the class of **rentiers** or to the class of **entrepreneurs**.

  Those who have no property but who offer services are differentiated just as much according to their kinds of services as according to the way in which they make use of these services, in a continuous or discontinuous relation to a recipient. But always this is the generic connotation of the concept of class: that the kind of chance in the *market* is the decisive moment which presents a common condition for the individual's fate. 'Class situation' is, in this sense, ultimately 'market situation'. The effect of naked possession *per se*, which among cattle breeders gives the non-owning slave or serf into the power of the cattle owner, is only a forerunner of real 'class' formation. However, in the cattle loan and in the naked severity of the law of debts in such communities, for the first time mere 'possession' as such emerges as decisive for the fate of the individual. This is very much in contrast to the agricultural communities based on labour. The creditor–debtor relation becomes the basis of 'class situation' only in those cities where a 'credit market', however primitive, with rates of interest increasing according to the extent of dearth and a factual monopolization of credits, is developed by a **plutocracy**. Therewith 'class struggles' begin.

Those men whose fate is not determined by the chance of using goods or services for themselves on the market, e.g., slaves, are not, however, a 'class' in the technical sense of the term. They are, rather, a 'status group'.

Communal action flowing from class interest

According to our terminology, the factor that creates 'class' is unambiguously economic interest, and indeed, only those interests involved in the existence of the 'market'. Nevertheless, the concept of 'class-interest' is an ambiguous one: even as an empirical concept it is ambiguous as soon as one understands by it something other than the factual direction of interests following with a certain probability from the class situation for a certain 'average' of those people subjected to the class situation. The class situation and other circumstances remaining the same, the direction in which the individual worker, for instance, is likely to pursue his interest may vary widely, according to whether he is constitutionally qualified for the task at hand to a high, to an average, or to a lower degree. In the same way, the direction of interests may vary according to whether or not a communal action of a larger or smaller portion of those commonly affected by the 'class situation', or even an association among them, e.g., a 'trade union', has grown out of the class situation from which the individual may or may not expect promising results. [Communal action refers to that action which is oriented to the feeling of the actors that they belong together. Societal action, on the other hand, is oriented to a rationally motivated adjustment of interests.] The rise of societal or even of communal action from a common class situation is by no means a universal phenomenon.

The class situation may be restricted in its effects to the generation of essentially *similar* reactions, that is to say, within our terminology, of 'mass actions'.

However, it may not have even this result. Furthermore, often merely an **amorphous** communal action emerges. For example, the 'murmuring' of the workers known in ancient oriental ethics: the moral disapproval of the work-master's conduct, which in its practical significance was probably equivalent to an increasingly typical phenomenon of precisely the latest industrial development, namely, the 'slow down' (the deliberate limiting of work effort) of labourers by virtue of tacit agreement. The degree in which 'communal action' and possibly 'societal action' emerges from the 'mass actions' of the members of a class is linked to general cultural conditions, especially to those of an intellectual sort. It is also linked to the extent of the contrasts that have already evolved, and is especially linked to the *transparency* of the connections between the causes and the consequences of the 'class situation'. For however different life chances may be, this fact in itself, according to all experience, by no means gives birth to 'class action'; (communal action by the members of a class). The fact of being conditioned and the results of the class situation must be distinctly recognizable. For only then the contrast of life chances can be felt not as an absolutely given fact to be accepted, but as a resultant from either (1) the given distribution of property, or (2) the structure of the concrete economic order. It is only then that people may react against the class structure not only through acts of an intermittent and irrational protest, but in the form of rational association. There have been 'class situations' of the first category (1), of a specifically naked and transparent sort, in the urban centres of antiquity and during the Middle Ages; especially then, when great fortunes were accumulated by factually monopolized trading in industrial products of these localities or in foodstuffs. Furthermore, under certain circumstances, in the rural economy of the most diverse periods, when agriculture was increasingly exploited in a profit-making manner. The most important historical example of the second category (2) is the class situation of the modern 'proletariat'.

Status honour

In contrast to classes, *status groups* are normally communities. They are, however, often of an amorphous kind. In contrast to the purely economically determined 'class situation' we wish to designate as 'status situation' every typical component of the life fate of men that is determined by a specific, positive or negative, social estimation of honour. This honour may be connected with any quality shared by a plurality, and, of course, it can be knit to a class situation: class distinctions are linked in the most varied ways with status distinctions. Property as such is not always recognized as a status qualification, but in the long run it is, and with extraordinary regularity. In the subsistence economy of the organized neighbourhood, very often the richest man is simply the chieftain. However, this often means only an honourific preference. For example, in the so-called pure modern 'democracy', that is, one devoid of any expressly ordered status privileges for individuals, it may be that only the families coming under approximately the same tax class dance with one another. This example is reported of certain smaller Swiss cities. But status honour need not necessarily be linked with a 'class situation'. On the contrary, it normally stands in sharp opposition to the pretensions of sheer property.

Both propertied and propertyless people can belong to the same status group, and frequently they do with very tangible consequences. This 'equality' of social esteem may, however, in the long run become quite precarious. The 'equality' of status among the American 'gentlemen', for instance, is expressed by the fact that outside the subordination determined by the different functions of 'business', it would be considered strictly repugnant – wherever the old tradition still prevails – if even the richest 'chief' while playing billiards or cards in his club in the evening, would not treat his 'clerk'; as in every sense fully his equal in birthright. It would be repugnant if the American 'chief' would bestow upon his 'clerk' the **condescending 'benevolence'** marking a distinction of 'position', which the German chief can never dissever from his attitude. This is one of the most important reasons why in America the German 'clubby-ness' has never been able to attain the attraction the American clubs have.

Guarantees of status stratification

In content, status honour is normally expressed by the fact that above all else a specific *style of life* can be expected from all those who wish to belong to the circle. Linked with this expectation are restrictions on 'social' intercourse (that is, intercourse which is not subservient to economic or any other of business's 'functional' purposes). These restrictions may confine normal marriages to within the status circle and may lead to complete **endogamous** closure. As soon as there is not a mere individual and socially irrelevant limitation of another style of life, but an agreed-upon communal action of this closing character, the 'status' development is under way.

In its characteristic form, stratification by 'status groups' on the basis of conventional styles of life evolves at the present time in the United States out of the traditional democracy. For example, only the resident of a certain street ('the street') is considered as belonging to 'society', is qualified for social intercourse, and is visited and invited. Above all, this differentiation evolves in such a way as to make for strict submission to the fashion that is dominant at a given time in society. This submission to fashion also exists among men in America to a degree unknown in Germany. Such submission is considered to be an indication of the fact that a given man *pretends* to qualify as a gentleman. This submission decides, at least **prima facie,** that he will be treated as such. And this recognition becomes just as important for his employment chances in 'swank' establishments, and above all, for social intercourse and marriage with 'esteemed' families, as the qualification for duelling among Germans in the Kaiser's day. As for the rest: certain families resident for a long time, and, of course, correspondingly wealthy, e.g., 'F. F. V., i.e. First Families of Virginia', or the actual or alleged descendants of the 'Indian Princess' Pocahontas, of the Pilgrim fathers, or of the Knicker-bockers, the members of almost inaccessible sects and all sorts of circles setting themselves apart by means of any other characteristics and badges ... all these elements **usurp** 'status' honour. The development of status is essentially a question of stratification resting upon **usurpation**. Such usurpation is the normal origin of almost all status honour. But the road from this purely conventional situation to legal privilege, positive or negative, is easily travelled as soon as a certain stratification of the social order has in fact been 'lived in' and has achieved stability by virtue of a stable distribution of economic power.

'Ethnic' segregation and 'caste'

Where the consequences have been realized to their full extent, the status group evolves into a closed 'caste'. Status distinctions are then guaranteed not merely by conventions and laws, but also by *rituals*. This occurs in such a way that every physical contact with a member of any caste that is considered to be 'lower' by the members of a 'higher' caste is considered as making for a ritualistic impurity and to be a stigma which must be expiated by a religious act. Individual castes develop quite distinct cults and gods.

In general, however, the status structure reaches such extreme consequences only where there are underlying differences which are held to be 'ethnic'. The 'caste' is, indeed, the normal form in which ethnic communities usually live side by side in a *societalized* manner. These ethnic communities believe in blood relationship and exclude exogamous marriage and social intercourse. Such a caste situation is part of the phenomenon of '**pariah**' peoples and is found all over the world. These people form communities, acquire specific occupational traditions of handicrafts or of other arts, and cultivate a belief in their ethnic community. They live in a '**diaspora**' strictly segregated from all personal intercourse, except that of an unavoidable sort, and their situation is legally precarious. Yet, by virtue of their economic indispensability, they are tolerated, indeed, frequently privileged, and they live in interspersed political communities. The Jews are the most impressive historical example.

A 'status' segregation grown into a 'caste' differs in its structure from a mere 'ethnic' segregation: the caste structure transforms the horizontal and unconnected coexistences of ethnically segregated groups into a vertical social system of super- and subordination. Correctly formulated: a comprehensive societalization integrates the ethnically divided communities into specific political and communal action. In their consequences they differ precisely in this way: ethnic coexistences condition a mutual repulsion and disdain but allow each ethnic community to consider its own honour as the highest one; the caste structure brings about a social subordination and an acknowledgement of 'more honour' in favour of the privileged caste and status groups. This is due to the fact that in the caste structure ethnic distinctions as such have become 'functional' distinctions within the political societalization (warriors, priests, artisans that are politically important for war and for building, and so on). But even pariah people who are most despised are usually apt to continue cultivating in some manner that which is equally peculiar to ethnic and to status communities: the belief in their own specific 'honour'. This is the case with the Jews. ...

Status privileges

For all practical purposes, stratification by status goes hand in hand with a monopolization of ideal and material goods or opportunities, in a manner we have come to know as typical. Besides the specific status honour, which always rests upon distance and exclusiveness, we find all sorts of material monopolies. Such honorific preferences may consist of the privilege of wearing special costumes, of eating special dishes taboo to others, of carrying arms. ...

The decisive role of a 'style of life' in status 'honour' means that status groups are the specific bearers of all 'conventions'. In whatever way it may be manifest, all 'stylization' of life either originates in status groups or is at least conserved by them. Even if the principles of status conventions differ greatly, they reveal certain typical traits, especially among those strata which are most privileged. Quite generally, among privileged status groups there is a disqualification that operates against the performance of common physical labour. ...

Parties

Whereas the genuine place of 'classes' is within the economic order, the place of 'status groups' is within the social order, that is, within the sphere of the distribution of 'honour'. From within these spheres, classes and status groups influence one another and they influence the legal order and are in turn influenced by it. But 'parties' live in a house of 'power'.

Their action is oriented toward the acquisition of social 'power', that is to say, toward influencing a communal action no matter what its content may be. In principle, parties may exist in a social 'club' as well as in a 'state'. As over against the actions of classes and status groups, for which this is not necessarily the case, the communal actions of 'parties' always mean a societalization. For party actions are always directed toward a goal which is striven for in a planned manner. This goal may be a 'cause' (the party may aim at realizing a program for ideal or material purposes), or the goal may be 'personal' (sinecures, power, and from these, honour for the leader and the followers of the party). Usually the party action aims at all these simultaneously. Parties are, therefore, only possible within communities that are societalized, that is, which have some rational order and a staff of persons available who are ready to enforce it.

Key terms

The following key terms appear in the text above. They have been defined below to aid with the reading of this item.

rentiers people who draw income from rents or investments

entrepreneurs those undertaking business ventures

plutocracy domination of society by a ruling class made up of rich people

amorphous unorganized

condescending 'benevolence' gracious behaviour towards a presumed inferior

endogamous restricting choice of marriage partners to those within the same social group

prima facie at first sight or on the face of it

usurp, usurpation to seize possession of something without necessarily having the right to do so

societalized societalization occurs when an awareness of common class interests develops at the level of society as a whole

diaspora a cultural identity associated with a particular ethnic group that has experienced geographical dispersal and lives a largely segregated existence. Examples include black people in the USA and Jews in Nazi-occupied Europe

pariah a social outcast

sinecures paid positions with no duties attached

Questions

1 Explain in your own words the differences, according to Weber, between class and status as forms of stratification.

2 Briefly explain how Weber's views of *social class* differed from those of Marx.

3 Discuss the relative merits of Marxist and Weberian accounts of stratification, and suggest which is most relevant to an understanding of stratification in contemporary capitalist society.

Reading 5.3 **Conflicts about class**

David Lee and Bryan Turner (eds) (from) *Conflicts About Class: Debating inequality in late industrialism* (1996) Harlow: Longman, pp. 4–11, 13–14, 17 and 19.

Editorial comments

Lee and Turner consider the competing claims proposed regarding the death of class analysis and the advent of 'the classless society'. They conclude that the existence of class divisions and their effects on peoples' lives is an objective reality that can be established on empirical grounds. However, while scarcity of resources and inequalities in their distribution are apparently features of all social organizations, the viability of the concept of class itself, as a means of understanding scarcity and inequality in their contemporary forms, has been questioned. Lee and Turner consider the theoretical and methodological issue of whether class really works as a concept and a tool for sociological research. They make a distinction between 'strong' and 'weak' usage of class in sociology. Marxism is the major example of the former, while Weberian versions of class have been the foremost representatives of the latter. They then briefly outline the various positions that have been adopted by sociologists in the debate over the relative merits of strong and weak conceptions of class.

Conflicts about class

Myths of classlessness

WHAT IS ARGUABLY the oldest 'myth' of classlessness originated in Germany at the end of the nineteenth century when Eduard Bernstein attempted to persuade the Marxist Social Democratic Party to adjust its strategy to the actual conditions, as he saw them, of the time (Bernstein, 1899). Bernstein made claims about improvements (or 'embourgeiosement') in the economic situation of the masses which have become standard to '**revisionism**' and reformism within and without socialist labour movements (cf. for example Crosland, 1956). Bernstein rejected the Marxist argument that **polarization** and **pauperization** were taking place, recognized a significant improvement in the wages of the working class (largely, he thought, because of the technological advances wrought by capitalism), noted a significant increase in the size of the middle class, rejected the argument of increasing economic crisis and suggested that capitalism could be reformed through parliamentary politics rather than by its revolutionary overthrow. Technical change, the growth of the middle class, the growth of income, mobility and political and social differentiation – these themes were picked up by many non-Marxist writers too during the first half of the twentieth century (a useful overview is Goldthorpe *et al.* 1987: Introduction). These sort of arguments seemed especially plausible to scholars in the United States where, compared with Europe, working-class living standards were high, political rhetorics of socialism and class conflict much weaker, and the analysis of ethnic and communal differences more salient than social class.

It was also from the United States that a second highly influential myth of classlessness originated and took hold: the thesis of the separation of ownership and control. The pioneering empirical work of Berle and Means (1932) on US manufacturing companies purportedly demonstrated that the development of **joint stockholding** and the growth of large industrial corporations had marginalized the significance of the old-style capitalist. Control of business was passing to professional managements who increasingly were recruited 'meritocratically' (i.e. according to certificated technical competence), so their authority did not essentially rest on legal ownership of the company. Here too both Marx himself and his followers in the early twentieth century, despite working from a European context and having very different political objectives, had already suggested that ownership interest was being displaced by managers and effective control by finance capital (Hilferding, 1910; Lenin, 1916). By accepting this change, with its implications of **managerial revolution**, they saddled themselves and later generations of Marxists with having to explain how the capitalist class nevertheless remains both cohesive and *capitalist*. By contrast, liberal theorists ever since have found it easy to argue that because capital holding now substantially derived from the savings, insurances and pensions of ordinary workers, capital *ownership* has become largely democratized and the capitalist class is no more (for a recent example see Saunders, 1990).

The implication of these two influential myths is that neither of Marx's celebrated phases of class formation, and the 'predictions' he had made about them, could any longer be sustained: class had ceased to exist both 'in itself' as an objective social cleavage defined by relations of ownership and non-ownership of the means of production and 'for itself' as emergent groupings of economic interest with potential for oppositional 'class consciousness'. As early as 1959 sociologists were being urged to forget about class (Nisbet, 1959). During the years of the **Cold War** such arguments were incorporated, mainly by US sociologists, into a detailed theory of the 'withering away' of class with the clear political implication that capitalism was in no danger of revolutionary upheaval and that it was communism that was likely to change.

Classlessness, citizenship and post-modern capitalism

... Within the past two decades or so, however, the rise of the neo-liberal New Right in Western politics has overlapped with a wider intellectual shift involving renewed claims that by the late twentieth century, capitalism had so fundamentally changed as simply to render the terms of class analysis redundant. ...

No less than four ' new' myths of classlessness have been involved here: in rough order of emergence, those of citizenship, post-industrialism, post-Fordism and post-modernism.

Citizenship

The study of democracy and citizenship has in fact long been a necessary adjunct to the study of class inequality. One of the peculiar features of capitalist society has been the combination of systemic and profound social inequalities (namely the existence of social classes) and a parallel set of institutions relating to democratic participation and citizenship (namely the welfare state). It was T. H. Marshall (1981) who referred to **welfare-capitalism** as 'the hyphenated society' to suggest that welfare and the market were essential if ultimately irreconcilable ingredients of modern capitalism. His analysis established a tradition in post-Second World War sociology that

theoretical class analysis must address fundamental questions relating to democratic processes and citizenship as a form of political membership. And in so far as 'citizenship' (and welfare) reduced the salience of class divisions, it always provided the potential for a myth of classlessness.

A more usual liberal argument these days, however, is that the incompatibility between citizenship and inequality is more apparent than real and that there is a parallel between market-based inequality and the freedoms of the political market place (Holton and Turner, 1989). That is, economic markets provide the best institutional context for the realization of equality of opportunity, but equality of opportunity is perfectly compatible with inequality of outcome (Turner, 1986). The parliamentary system also functions as a type of political market place within which political parties compete for power and influence with similarly unequal political outcomes. Within this liberal framework, freedom of choice as a consumer in the economic arena is a necessary component or support for political individualism within the democratic arena, and their co-existence makes radical class interpretations of inequality redundant.

Post-industrialism

The notion of post-industrialism absorbed something of earlier liberal theories of the meritocratic logic of twentieth-century industrialism. In a post-industrial society theoretical knowledge as such, rather than private capital formation, forms the axial principle of society and is the primary source of social innovation and policy development. The idea is particularly associated with the writings of Daniel Bell (1973) who attempted to describe how this change in the organization of capital society was associated with developments in the economy: the decline of manufacturing as the principal form of economic activity, the growth of the service industry and a corresponding decline in the agricultural sector. This **axial principle** of knowledge gave supremacy to professional and technical occupations which, Bell argued, constituted a New Class. It also gave fresh significance to the role of university intellectuals as the producers of new knowledge. The theory of post-industrial society has given rise to a variety of debates in class analysis with respect to the importance of the new middle class, the role of technicians, the deskilling of the labour force, the creation of a new working class and the productive significance of the intellectual worker.

Post-Fordism

The thesis of '**post-Fordism**' was developed just a few years later (Piore and Sabel, 1984; cf., however, Wood (ed.) 1989). Post-Fordism, it is argued, represents a very different form of capitalism characterizing the world economic system of today which increasingly is highly globalized and deregulated. The new forms of 'disorganised' capitalism do not operate on the basis of full mass employment. Rather there is a high degree of what is called 'flexible specialization' in the use of labour and post-Fordist production systems are highly automated in order to introduce some degree of flexibility into dedicated machinery. ...

Certainly in North America, post-Fordism has disrupted class communities which might form the basis of opposition to the social system. European writers too have embraced the implications of post-Fordism by arguing that these structural changes spelt the end of the working class as an organized, fully employed, coherent social group. For example, in his famous commentary on these developments the former Marxist André Gorz pronounced a farewell to the working class (Gorz, 1982; see also Harvey, 1989).

Post-modernism

With the growth of post-modern theory, the last of the four developments we are considering, it is clear that much of what had gone before, Bell's work in particular, anticipated theoretical developments in the analysis of post-modern culture. For example Bell's emphasis on theoretical knowledge and the role of computerized information in many respects anticipated the account of the post-modern condition presented by writers like J. F. Lyotard (1984) and furthermore Bell's focus on the importance of **hedonism** within a consumer society also laid some of the foundations for later analyses of the **aestheticization of everyday life** in terms of new cultural practices. Although post-modernism as a theory and post-modernity as a condition of society are surrounded by a large measure of theoretical uncertainty and conceptual confusion (Turner, 1990) it may be defined as involving in social and economic terms a society in which social classes are no longer important because the social structure is extraordinarily complex and chronically fragmented along a variety of dimensions including gender, age, ethnicity and culture. It is also a society in which the main locus of social division has shifted from the sphere of social production to that of consumption and culture. Post-modernity thus involves the growing importance of the culture industry such as tourism, the aestheticization of everyday life through new patterns of consumerism, the construction of social identity by individual choice rather than by traditional location, the pluralization of personal identity and the life course, and the disappearance of the structured life span or life project. In economic terms post-modernity means a post-Fordist economy with highly specialized production systems involving multi-skilled workers, a globalization of markets which are also segmented, and a dependence

upon new management techniques to bring about more precise levels of industrial control. Finally, in political terms, there are new ideologies of self-reliance and competitiveness.

Commentators have noted that many of these so-called post-modernist themes contain echoes of the political analysis of the New Right, and this is particularly evident in a reassessment of the significance of the 'citizenship' issue. Among recent influential critiques of class analysis, Clark and Lipset are somewhat unusual in that their case still rests on arguments about the growth of welfare – as well as on familiar liberal claims for working-class emancipation through affluence and education (see Clark, Lipset and Rempel, 1993). The paradox at which post-modernist analyses point, however, is that the processes which have to some extent undermined the reproduction of social classes in the late twentieth century are also the conditions which have largely undermined the forms of social citizenship recognized within the Marshallian framework. The latter emerged under conditions of **Keynesian** economic and political policies: a consensus about the importance of full employment, a commitment to a democratic revolution in the education sphere, the maintenance of the household and a general commitment to social security. It is becoming more usual to argue instead that the supports of 'welfare' citizenship, such as the conventional family and the nation state, appear to be disappearing (Roche, 1992). Welfare regimes lack the capacity adequately to respond to current patterns of internal migration, labour market flexibility or the globalization of various key legal and political authorities. Thus Beck (1992, 1994), working in the German context and Anthony Giddens in Britain (Giddens, 1990) argue that conventional notions of class, citizenship and capitalism appear to be dated, if not obsolete. We need an entirely new vocabulary to describe the fragmented structures, individualistic processes and deregulated social and natural environment of late twentieth-century society.

All these new myths of classlessness, however, and their implications for the conceptual structure of sociology, command little support among many of the academics who have been associated with empirical class analysis. They complain of the tendency of the relevant authors to treat speculative assertions about the direction in which all societies are supposedly heading as if they were securely established fact. They point out that claims of post-Fordism, post-industrialism and the shift from production to '**consumption cleavages**' have generated a great deal of critical research and discussion in rebuttal. A vital part of the defence of traditional forms of class analysis has been that liberal and post-modern myths of classlessness persistently ignore the findings of rigorously conducted research, research which has increasingly employed very sophisticated techniques of data gathering and analysis and which are already sufficient to show the survival of class divisions within the new world order. On this view then, the existence of class divisions and their profound effects on people's lives is an objective finding which sociology can claim to have established. But this brings us to the conceptual issues surrounding the sociology of class.

The death of class metaphors? (i) 'strong' class theories

... A crude division can be made between 'strong' and 'weak' usage of class in sociology. Strong class theories, of which Marxism is by far the major example, can be said to adopt a holistic approach: that is, class is or was in some sense a causal factor in historical change and the overall organization of society and its institutions. It impinges on the lives of individuals even though they themselves may be unaware that their own actions contribute to its continuance. Weak class explanations, by contrast, reject the suggestion that class may be 'more than the sum of its parts' or that classes are independent entities in any sense. Classes are in the first place simply empirically identifiable groupings of individuals who have certain analytically significant situations (such as their possession of property or highly paid skills) in common. Weberian sociologies of class have been the foremost representatives of this form of explanation. They reflect Max Weber's commitment to interpretative methods in sociology, and his view that any link between class membership and other aspects of meaningful or communal action must be regarded not as necessary but contingent. ...

Marx's much quoted treatment of the proletariat as a class 'in itself' (by virtue of its structural location in capitalist production) which becomes a class 'for itself' (by pursuing its supposedly objective class interests) conceals a real gap in his thought. What is the precise causal linkage between the broader changes in society and the consciousness and actions of individuals? Marx's own writings contain contradictory answers. Mostly, as Lockwood argues in a celebrated essay (Lockwood, 1981), Marx glossed over the problem with assumptions mirroring nineteenth-century **utilitarianism**; proletarian revolutionary action is guided by the rational pursuit of objectively identifiable (class) interest (e.g. in overthrowing exploitation). At other times, however, he embraces a mind-as-blank-paper **behaviourism** which depicts people as puppets or what Marx himself calls bearers (*träger*) of the structures they inhabit. Arguably, these contradictory theories of action account for the subsequent division of Marx's followers into 'humanist' and 'structuralist'. ...

The death of class metaphors? (ii) Weak class explanations

It is at this point that we must consider the crucial role which the authority of Max Weber's theoretical ideas about social inequality has played for (non-Marxist) supporters and critics of class analysis alike. In the last fifty years, major phases in the debate have been associated with careful reinterpretation of Weber's incomplete and ultimately somewhat **elliptic** writings. ...

Stratification, for Weber, denoted in the first place the subdivision of individuals and/or households into unequally and hierarchically ordered groupings. So 'class', broadened out from its association with property to include other forms of economic interest including 'ownership' of occupational skills, was simply one form of stratification. Equally important, however, was *status* stratification, which included divisions based on religious or legal rights but also distributional inequalities of esteem, consumption and 'life style'.

Weber's writings enabled more sophisticated liberal sociologists in the USA and elsewhere to accept that some class inequalities, in Weber's sense, would continue to exist, as a result of the operation of the labour market. But many nevertheless proposed that as class recedes in significance 'stratification' becomes centred around divisions of status in the sense of consumption and life style. Status inequality in this sense, however, really implied a metaphor of gradations between points on a continuum, rather than dichotomous fractures (Ossowski, 1963). Several scales of occupational 'status' were devised and in the USA became the principal device through which to measure 'social background' and its effect on life courses, and in particular the social mobility of individuals between positions of different prestige or socio-economic status (cf. Glass (ed.) 1954; Blau and Duncan, 1967). ...

What explanatory mileage, then, does the term 'class', once stripped of its Marxist associations, contain? Clearly, much depends on whether resort to the Weberian explanatory framework avoids falling into the trap of 'explanatory failure'. We noted Holmwood and Stewart's (1983) complaint that, having generally failed to show the link between abstract class concepts and concrete events, social theorists had the habit of appealing to the uniqueness of the circumstances to protect the theory from rejection. But whereas this criticism seemed principally aimed at Marxism and historical class analysis, the polemic by Pahl (1989) directed a somewhat blunter version of the explanatory failure argument at *all* class analysis regardless of pedigree. True, as he was to explain later, his words were intended for a non-sociological audience concerned with urban affairs. His main target was the simplistic way in which urban analysts had linked the existence of urban problems (deprivation, pollution, planing blight and so on) to the rise of protest movements. In doing so they invoked what Pahl calls the '**false mantra**', by which consciousness and action are linked to a determining structure. But the implications for mainstream class analysis were soon recognized. It is possible, moreover, to find passages in neo-Weberian writings which seem to bear out Pahl's argument (see for example Marshall, G. *et al.*, 1988 and Crompton's assessment 1993).

It can in fact be argued that Weberian class explanation is more vulnerable to the opposite criticism, namely, that its very reluctance to conceptualize classes as having independent causal force in themselves results in the smuggling of a series of inadequate metaphors of 'structure' ('stratification', 'closure', 'mobility') by the back door in lieu of a theory explaining the coherence of class positions (Lee, 1994). Much debate, for example, surrounds the issue of what constitutes the boundaries of classes themselves and what provides the common element of the occupations which positional class schema include within class categories – other than the imposed decision of the investigator to adopt this particular grouping. ...

There is no doubt, then, that all forms of class analysis have become very vulnerable to critique at a number of levels: theoretical, philosophical and above all, in the political climate of academia in the 1980s and 1990s, ideological. At the heart of this critique, a kind of Weberian fundamentalism is evident which seems to be seeking to rescue the writings of the master from the structural **apostasy** of existing class analysis in any form. Neo-liberal sociologists in particular have been able to make an impact because the tradition of political theory on which they draw, stemming from work of writers like Popper and Hayek, is heavily committed, like Weber himself, to individualist methodology. But neo-liberalism overlaps with the post-modern philosophical critique of '**grand narratives**' (Lyotard, 1984) which sees Weber as a forerunner of its enthusiasm for irony and relativism. Thus, a fundamental re-reading of Weber is again at the heart of change – as action theorist, individualist, philosopher, and early post-modernist. But is this the time to preside over the death of class analysis *per se* – or not?

References

Beck, U. (1992) *Risk Society: Towards a new modernity*, London: Sage.

Beck, U. (1994) 'The debate on individualisation theory in today's sociology in Germany', *Soziologie, 3* (Journal of the Deutsche Gesellschaft fur Soziologie) pp. 119–201.

Bell, D. (1973) *The Coming of Post-Industrial Society*, New York: Basic Books.

Berle, A. A. and Means, G. C. (1932) *The Modern Corporation and Private Property*, London: Macmillan.

Bernstein, E. (1899) *Die Voraussetzungen des Sozialismus und die Aufgaben der Sozialdemokratie*, Stuttgart: Dietz.

Blau and Duncan (1967) *The American Social Structure*, New York: Wiley.

Clarke, T., Lipset, S. and Rempel, M. (1993) 'The declining political significance of social class', *International Sociology, 8,* (3) pp. 293–316.

Crompton, R. (1993) *Class and Stratification*, Cambridge: Polity.

Crosland, A. (1956) *The Future of Socialism*, London: Jonathon Cape.

Giddens, A. (1990) *The Consequences of Modernity*, Cambridge: Polity.

Glass, D. V. (ed.) (1954) *Social Mobility in Britain*, London: Routledge & Kegan Paul.

Goldthorpe, J. *et al.* (1987) *Social Mobility and Class Structure in Modern Britain*, 2nd edn, Oxford: Clarendon Press.

Gorz, A. (1982) *Farewell to the Working Class*, London: Pluto.

Harvey, D. (1989) *The Condition of Post-Modernity*, Oxford: Blackwell.

Hilferding, R. (1910) *Finance Capital*, London: Routledge & Kegan Paul, 1981.

Holmwood, J. and Stewart, A. (1983) 'The role of contradictions in modern theories of social stratification', *Sociology*, vol. 17, no. 2.

Holton, R. and Turner, B. S. (1989) *Max Weber on Economy and Society*, London: Routledge & Kegan Paul.

Lee, D. (1994) 'Class as a social fact', *Sociology*, vol. 28, no. 2.

Lenin, V. I. (1916) *Imperialism: The highest stage of capitalism*, Moscow: Progress Publishers.

Lockwood, D. (1981) 'The weakest link in the chain: some comments on the Marxist theory of action', *Research in the Sociology of Work, 1*, pp. 435–81.

Lyotard, J.-F. (1984) *The Postmodern Condition: a report on knowledge*, Manchester: Manchester University Press.

Marshall, G. *et al.* (1988) *Social Class in Modern Britain*, London: Hutchinson.

Marshall, T. H. (1981) *The Right to Welfare and Other Essays*, London: Heinemann.

Nisbet, R (1959) 'The decline and fall of social class', *Pacific Sociological Review, 2* (1) pp. 11–17.

Ossowski, S. (1963) *Class Structure in the Social Consciousness*, London: Routledge & Kegan Paul.

Pahl, R. E. (1989) 'Is the emperor naked?', *International Journal of Urban and Regional Research*, December.

Pahl, R. E. (1993) 'Does class analysis without class theory have a promising future?', *Sociology*, vol. 27.

Piore, M. and Sabel, C. (1984) *The Second Industrial Divide: Possibilities for prosperity*, New York: Basic Books.

Roche, M. (1992) *Rethinking Citizenship: Welfare, ideology and change in modern society*, Cambridge: Polity.

Saunders, P. (1990) *A Nation of Home Owners*, London: Unwin.

Turner, B. (1986) *Equality*, London: Tavistock.

Turner, B. (1990) *Theories of Modernity and Post-Modernity*, London: Sage.

Wood, S. (ed.) (1989) *The Transformation of Work*, London: Hutchinson.

Key terms

The following key terms appear in the text above. They have been defined below to aid with the reading of this item.

revisionism the belief among some socialists that a communist transformation of society is best achieved through reform rather than revolution

polarization the tendency for two classes to develop in opposition to each other

pauperization the notion that 'the proletariat' or 'working class' become increasingly impoverished

joint stockholding the system by which company assets are owned by shareholders as opposed to a single individual

managerial revolution the theory that individual owners/managers of capitalist firms have been replaced by professional managers

'Cold War' the period from 1945 until the 1980s, in which world security was characterized by a military 'stand-off' between the USA and the Soviet Union

welfare-capitalism a situation in which state welfare intervenes in the workings of the market

axial principle the key determining factor

post-Fordism the era of capitalism in which production is organized to meet flexible demand and its impact on the nature of social relations generally

hedonism the belief that pleasure is the highest good

aestheticization of everyday life the idea that aspects of everyday life may be perceived as having their own artistic merit

Keynesian relating to the economic theory that influenced British governments from the 1930s to the 1970s, based on the ideas of John Maynard Keynes, who proposed that the economy required state intervention to overcome slumps in demand and mass unemployment

consumption cleavages divisions within a population in terms of their patterns of consumer spending

utilitarianism the philosophy that judges actions on the basis of their ability to produce happiness

behaviourism an approach to the study of human behaviour that seeks to observe responses to external stimuli rather than the subjective element of consciousness

elliptic difficult to understand

false mantra repetition of a political viewpoint, as if it were a sacred text used as a chant or incantation, which is actually untrue

apostasy abandoning faith in a belief

grand narratives large-scale theories that claim to explain the whole of society and its development on the assumption that it is possible to arrive at objective and absolute truth

Questions

1 Distinguish between the concepts of classlessness and the 'death of class'.

2 Briefly explain each of the four 'new myths of classlessness' identified by Lee and Turner.

3 What reasons are mentioned in the reading for some sociologists suggesting that the word 'class' should be jettisoned?

4 Explain the difference between what Lee and Turner refer to as 'strong class theories' and 'weak class theories'.

5 How far do you agree that it is time to preside over the death of class analysis?

Reading 5.4 **A classless society?**

Geoff Payne (from) 'The Classless Society?', in *General Studies Review* (1991) vol. 1, no. 1, Oxford: Phillip Allan, pp. 11–14.

Editorial comments

Geoff Payne's article begins by discussing the contemporary relevance of the concepts of 'classlessness' and 'equality of opportunity' to British political dialogue. He states that it is not difficult to establish that Britain is still a society stratified by social class. However, changes have occurred in British society, both in terms of occupational transition (absolute social mobility) and the relative chances of members of different social class categories to achieve upward mobility (relative social mobility). He then summarizes the data from large-scale surveys of social mobility in Britain and considers the different ways in which these have been interpreted by the protagonists in the debate about the extent to which the effects of class origins have become divorced from class destinations. 'New Right' sociologists argue that we should be celebrating the fact that more people are achieving upward mobility than ever before as a reward for their 'natural' talent. Others argue that net upward mobility has resulted in changes in the shape, but not the openness, of the class structure. Payne finally considers the issue of gender and mobility which he believes can be used to cast doubt on the New Right claim that ability is 'natural'.

The classless society?

WHAT DID JOHN Major mean when, as a new Prime Minister, he talked of Britain as 'a classless society'? At the heart of his vision was his own experience of growing up in humble circumstances, the son of a circus entertainer, and going on to occupy the highest office of state in the land. He was not saying that there are or should be no differences in wealth or income between people. His point was that people should have equal opportunities to compete for positions of influence or financial reward.

A similar yardstick of classlessness was used in the famous Labour Party Political Broadcast in 1987, which portrayed Neil Kinnock as the son of a mining family, who had got on in life and now led a major political party. Here the emphasis was on the social welfare institutions of society, such as the education system and the National Health Service, providing the mechanisms for equalizing opportunity. We therefore see that the twin ideas of classlessness and equality of opportunity are central to British political dialogue. Indeed, they can be traced back for at least half a century in much the same form.

Equality of condition

Mr Major and Mr Kinnock were not claiming that everybody's conditions of wealth and health were the same, only that the chances of doing well should not be restricted to one group in society. In a strict sense, however, we could think of a classless society as one in which everybody lived in completely equal conditions. In practice this is unrealistic. Every human society ever studied has had a form of **hierarchical** structure, with some people having more power, or social honour, or material well-being, than others. The nature of this differentiation is, however, highly variable. While social hierarchy may, at a rather abstract level, be a scientific principle of how societies are organized, it is not much help to us in making sense of the particular forms of hierarchy in our present-day society.

'Class' is one such form of hierarchy. Writers in a Marxist tradition have argued that people's class is determined by their 'relationship to the means of production'. In other words, those who own land, factories, capital, and who employ other people, fall into one class. Those who own nothing that can give rise to production, except their own capacity to labour, and who are employed make up another, much larger class. Within these two broad – and mutually antagonistic – classes there are sub-divisions into smaller classes, such as different grades of managers, professionals, specialist white-collar workers, small businessmen and farmers (peasants). Writers who use this framework might accept that material differences or conflicts between classes have been reduced, but they still see class as an automatic outcome of a society based on capitalism as its economic system.

Measuring classlessness

It is an easy matter to demonstrate that Britain is socially differentiated into groups with different levels of wealth, physical comfort, power and health. However, that is not the point of the present debate about classlessness. Here the focus is on opportunities to move from one group (with its advantages or disadvantages) to another. Sociologists have studied these movements from social origins to current social destinations, referring to them as 'social mobility'.

Using jobs as the basis for classifying people into groups is an established tradition, as in the Census and many other sets of official statistics. A job is strongly associated with a certain level of income and, hence, lifestyle and chances of good housing, health, etc. On average, people in any given occupation have similar levels of educational qualifications, similar friends, even marry people from similar jobs and have similar attitudes on political and social questions. When someone moves from a family background where the main breadwinner works in one particular job to an adult destination working in a different occupation, we can reasonably argue that such a person has been socially mobile.

The only **caveat** that we need to enter is that the two jobs would need to be associated with different levels of living. Occupations are conventionally grouped into broad categories, such as 'skilled manual work', 'professionals and managers', or 'routine white-collar workers'. Government statisticians, market researchers and social scientists use a variety of these categorization schemes, some broad and simple with three or five categories (or 'classes') and some more specific and detailed with, say, 17 'socio-economic groups', to take an example from the Census. When we talk about classlessness, then, we use these categories as points of reference and the categories themselves depend on underlying economic processes which themselves create and destroy types of employment.

Occupational transition

One of the keys to understanding the greater affluence of modern society, the changes experienced by our parents and grandparents this century, and why social mobility occurs is 'occupational transition'. As societies industrialize, fewer people work in agriculture and more work in manufacturing. In a later phase, employment shifts from manufacturing into service industries, such as education, banking, government and leisure, to create what the American sociologist Daniel Bell has called 'post-industrial society'. The nature of work is transformed, with more people doing well-paid white-collar work and fewer doing poorly paid, dirty or dangerous manual work.

This change works in two ways. First, in advanced economies, the manufacture of goods is increasingly mechanized, so requiring fewer workers, while whole industries become uncompetitive as the cheaper labour available in Third World countries encourages the 'export of jobs'. Britain's historical dominance in the production of coal and steel and in heavy engineering, such as shipbuilding, has been declining most of this century. The call for skilled craftsmen and less-skilled labouring is, as a consequence, much less. In traditional heavy industry areas, such as Scotland,

manual work has been reduced by more than one fifth since the First World War, while skilled manual work, which used to be a third of all employment, is now down to about 20% of all jobs.

Conversely, white-collar occupations have expanded. The importance of science and technology has created more and larger organizations designed to provide education, information, research and health. Greater affluence and new technology have made the finance, insurance and banking systems the most rapidly growing sector of employment. Co-ordination and control of the economy and social order has increased. All of these processes create brand-new occupations (systems analyst, traffic warden, management consultant, agronomist are all creations of the last 30 years) and expand the numbers in existing ones, such as teacher, accountant, nurse or secretary.

Social mobility

This occupational transition helps to generate upward social mobility, because there are more professional and managerial posts to fill every year, even in periods of recession. Furthermore, most of these jobs require educational qualifications and intellectual ability. A simple test for access can be whether or not a person has the ability (usually demonstrated by having the formal qualifications) to do the job in question.

In a classless society, with **universal education**, there should be few barriers blocking access to the more desirable occupations, so that a person's background should not determine what job he or she can enter. We would, therefore, expect a lot of movement up and down the occupational hierarchy. If we compare family or origin with current occupational class and think of society as having three classes, recent studies suggest a fairly open society. Over one third of the population moves up at least one class, and about one sixth moves down a class, so that in total about 55% of people experience social mobility.

Studies of social mobility are expensive to conduct because they need large sample surveys to gather data. Three studies which can be directly compared are those carried out by Nuffield College, Oxford, in 1972; the re-analysis of the British General Election Study, 1983; and the Essex University Class Project in 1984. Unfortunately, two of these studies report only on male mobility, so we are restricted to discussing men (Table 1). For simplicity, the table omits movements to and from the intermediate class; it shows only those for service and manual classes, using the 'origin' of the father's occupational class and the 'destination' of the son's current occupational class.

The table elaborates on what we already know about upward mobility. Moves up from manual to service class tend to be higher by the 1980s (25% or 20%, compared with 16%): people born in the service class are more able to retain their position (they also benefit from the creation of new jobs in this class), and fewer of those born in the manual class now remain there – results to be expected from what we know about occupational transition.

Relative and absolute mobility

It should be noticed that more people move up (from manual work to white-collar or professional/managerial work) than move down. This is because modern society is characterized by occupational transition, a process which owes little to the short-term policies of particular governments or political parties. This has led some writers of the Left to distinguish between the change in occupational structure, and the workings of our systems of education, health, recruitment and promotion. In this perspective, the key question is not the 'absolute' number of people obtaining good jobs. Instead, it is how the 'relative' chances of different groups getting good jobs compare and change over time, when we discount the effect of occupational transition. For writers such as Goldthorpe or Marshall and Rose, what matters is not the absolute rate of mobility (e.g. the 55% who experience mobility) but rather the 'relative' chances of obtaining entry to a desirable occupational class, if we hold the numbers in such classes constant (using statistical techniques). A comparison of the chances of, say, a miner's son and a businessman's son of becoming Managing Director of Midland Bank is what really reveals whether we have built a classless society in Britain.

If we compare such chances but still leave in the changes due to occupational transition, we find that in 1984 service-class children are three times more likely to be successful than children of manual workers. This difference had fallen since 1972 (when it was a 3½ to 1 advantage), but is still substantial. If, on the other hand, we use statistical techniques to remove the occupational transition effect from our calculations, we find 'no significant reduction in class inequalities has in fact been achieved' (Goldthorpe, 1987): 'there have been no changes in social fluidity' (Marshall *et al.*, 1988). There is thus a paradox of more people being upwardly mobile, but relative chances, independent of occupational change, remaining the same.

Interpreting mobility

In a recent debate Saunders has accused Goldthorpe and Marshall and Rose of taking an unrealistic measure as the test of classlessness by ignoring the occupational transition effect. Only when origin is completely unrelated to destination, he says, will critics on the Left accept that there is true equality of opportunity. That ignores both overall greater afflu-

Table 1 Absolute male social mobility in three British studies *(% of origin)*

| Mobility | | Study | | |
Origin	Destination	1972	1983	1984
Service class	Service class	58	62	60
Manual class	Service class	16	24	20
Service class	Manual class	19	16	20
Manual class	Manual class	61	53	51

ence, and the reality of social differentiation. Marshall and Rose have replied that writers on the New Right, such as Saunders, ignore the extent of disparities in wealth and social circumstances and wrongly assume that rewards and ability explain patterns of mobility.

It certainly is true that absolute rates of mobility do not, on their own, provide a full answer. Suppose that 70% of today's service class are recruited from origins in other classes: is this high or low, good or bad? If 85% of the population started in the other classes, then 70% is not too bad, but it means that the other classes are not at present achieving their full share (i.e. 85%) of the best occupations. Saunders is stressing that the 70% is quite good, while Marshall and Rose are saying the missing 15% is what really matters.

The figures of 70% and 85% are taken from the Essex survey and refer to male mobility. For a variety of historial reasons, we know less about female mobility. We also know virtually nothing about the mobility of specific groups, such as ethnic minorities or those with obvious disadvantages, such as the physically disabled, or those growing up in areas of high unemployment. The broad patterns of mobility almost certainly hide pockets of disadvantage. To take a single example, women's employment is concentrated in three main sectors: routine, white-collared office work; semi-professional jobs, like nursing, teaching and librarianship: and personal service work, such as hair-dressing, retail sales and cleaning. Their equality of opportunity is restricted, because their destinations are, on average, less advantageous than those of men. (However, women are now entering the professions in increasing numbers.)

This gender difference in mobility brings us to the question of explaining mobility. Saunders has argued that the rewards of achievement drive mobility; without rewards there will be no striving. He has also suggested that mobility calls for individual ability, and that may be genetically inherited. There are two problems with these arguments. First, boys and girls show more or less equal levels of educational qualifications – but do not always enter the same jobs (i.e. classes). Second, if ability is genetic, why has it apparently increased in the 1970s and 1980s, when educational qualification and mobility rates have increased? And, third, if mobility extracts the most able in each generation from the lower classes, from where are the new upwardly mobile children coming?

It seems more plausible to suggest that ability is much more randomly distributed among our population and that social and economic processes hold the key to equality of opportunity. This means looking at education, income and recruitment practices – rather than genes. It might also remind us that Mr Major's father was not just a circus performer, but also an agent and businessman, and that 'classlessness' is too important an issue for the operation of a modern society to be entrusted to the **rhetoric** of the Right or the Left.

References

Goldthorpe, J. H. (1987) *Social Mobility and Class Structure in Modern Britain*, 2nd edn, Oxford: Clarendon.

Marshall, G. *et al.* (1988) *Social Class in Modern Britain*, London: Hutchinson.

Saunders, P. (1990) *Social Class and Stratification*, London: Routledge.

Key terms

The following key terms appear in the text above. They have been defined below to aid with the reading of this item.

hierarchical organization in grades or levels

caveat a cautionary note

universal education free education for all between the ages of 5 and 16

rhetoric the use of language for effect (often in public speech, and often in support of a particular political point of view)

Questions

1 a Explain in your own words the difference between the concepts of 'equality of opportunity' and 'equality of condition'.

  b Is the idea of a classless society best defined in terms of equality of opportunity or equality of condition? Give reasons for your answer.

2 Describe the difference between 'absolute' and 'relative' mobility and the way in which they are measured.

3 Briefly outline the main trends in absolute and relative mobility in postwar Britain.

4 Using the data in the reading, on absolute and relative social mobility in modern Britain, present an argument, either in favour of, or against, the view that Britain has become a more open society.

5 a How far would you agree with the view that the increase in the number of upwardly mobile people in British society is indicative of a meritocracy based on 'natural' ability?

  b To what extent do you believe that Britain has become classless?

Reading 5.5 **Who rules Britain?**

John Scott (from) *Who Rules Britain?* (1991) Cambridge: Polity, pp. 63–72, 90–2, 115 and 17.

Editorial comments

John Scott demonstrates the existence of a 'capitalist business class' within which he identifies four 'ideal type' capitalist economic locations which are defined by property, which functions as power. Scott describes the characteristics of these different types of capitalist, but points out that the significant thing is that the boundaries between them are blurred by the overlap and mobility which exists among them. The vast bulk of capitalist class households are socially and culturally unified in interests and outlook.

Having declared that a capitalist class still exists, Scott turns his attention to the changes in the mechanism by which it is reproduced. He argues that there has been a partial separation of capital reproduction and class reproduction. By this he is referring to the fact that, although the process of capital accumulation is still controlled by the individuals who occupy capitalist class locations, these individuals are less likely than in the past to owe their privileged and advantaged position to inherited access to entrepreneurial capital. Upper-class families have become successful at reproducing themselves not just through the transmission of economic capital but increasingly through cultural capital, which allows them to be more successful than others in the educational 'race'.

Is there still a capitalist class?

DOES BRITAIN STILL have a capitalist class? There may be, in a purely statistical sense, a privileged class at the top of the class hierarchy, but the question is whether this is a capitalist class similar to those that existed in the eighteenth and nineteenth centuries: a privileged class rooted in a position of economic dominance in a capitalist system of production. ...

Capitalist-class households owe their position in the stratification system to the fact that one or more of their members occupies a capitalist economic location. 'But what are the capitalist economic locations in the modern economy? ...

Who are the capitalists?

Capitalist economic locations, I wish to argue, comprise positions within a structure of control over property, positions which are filled through specific patterns of recruitment and remuneration. A capitalist-class household is one whose advantages and life chances derive from the benefits which accrue from property and from involvement in the processes through which it is controlled. Max Weber described these advantages as being rooted in property and the commercial uses to which property is put. ...

Managerialist writers saw the rise of the joint stock company as undermining personal property holdings through share dispersal and through the creation of bureaucratic hierarchies of corporate management. Those who served in the **corporate bureaucracies**, they argued, had replaced the capitalist entrepreneurs as the leading force in the modern economy. Even some writers who continue to be influenced by Marxist theory claim that the 'managers' comprise a '**service class**' which has displaced the capitalist class. It is important to recognize, however, that a decline in personal forms of control does not necessarily spell the decline of the capitalist class itself. Capitalist economic locations can persist alongside subordinate 'service' locations. Central to a capitalist location is the ability to ensure that property is used to one's sectional advantage. Those who merely 'serve' in the corporate bureaucracies are the servants of capital and, hence, of those who benefit from this capital. Those who benefit disproportionately and who are involved in the control over property – on whatever basis – are the occupants of capitalist locations.

This argument does not, of course, apply to all forms of property. Almost everybody has some kind of property – personal effects, consumer goods, cars, and houses – but most of this property is mere 'property for use'. It is consumed directly in order to provide improved living standards and is, in general, a depreciating asset. Cars and clothing, for example, rapidly lose their value. Houses are rather less likely to depreciate, and normally show a long-term appreciation in value. Nevertheless, a person's family home remains merely 'property for use', as its appreciating value cannot usually be realized: a home which is sold must normally be replaced with another if the person is not to become homeless. The bulk of people's everyday property is irrelevant to the occupancy of capitalist economic locations.

Capitalist economic locations are defined by property which functions as capital, that is to say, in relation to various forms of 'property for power': property which gives control over the lives of other people. This kind of property – shares, land, and other commercial assets – is typically an appreciating asset. It has a commercial use, which means that it both grows in value and generates an income. This enhanced value is readily realizable because the assets are marketable. Capitalist economic locations are rooted in particular forms of 'property for power'.

The qualification 'particular forms' is important, as small-scale capital must be distinguished from its large-scale counterpart. Although small-scale capital may sometimes offer high personal rewards, entry to true capitalist locations is neither easy nor frequent from these '**petty bourgeois**' locations. True capitalist locations, the basis of a capitalist class, are to be found only in the sphere of large-scale capital. Giant business enterprises, large landed estates, and massive share portfolios are the foundations of the capitalist class.

Figure 1 sets out a typology of capitalist economic locations, using two dimensions: the *nature* of a person's involvement in units of capital and the *number* of units in which there is an involvement. Participation in the control and rule of units of capital may follow from personal property ownership or from the occupancy of a directorship. The pure cases of involvement through property ownership occur where business activity is direct and unmediated by such legal forms as those of the joint stock company. In such circumstances, capitalist locations rest upon active involvements or passive benefits in personally owned and controlled units of capital. Once business enterprise comes to be organized through the joint stock company, people can achieve positions of power and influence through their occupancy of a directorship. The limiting case of involvement through a directorship is where the director holds no personal shareholding in the enterprise which he or she directs but is a mere occupant of a ruling position in a system of impersonal capital. The question of the number of units of capital in which people are involved is important, as it influences the character of a person's involvement. Those involved in a single unit of capital, for example, can give it their full attention, while those involved in many units must divide their time among them. Single and multiple involvements, therefore, require different mechanisms of action.

Cross-classifying these two dimensions gives the four categories of Figure 1. The *entrepreneurial capitalist* is one whose involvement in business is indistinguishable from the existence of a joint stock company and its system of directorships. The entrepreneurial capitalist exercises direct and immediate control over all aspects of business operations, and the ideal type corresponds to the image of the entrepreneur in classical economics and in classical Marxism. The *rentier capitalist* is one who has personal investments in a number of units of capital through direct-ownership stakes, membership of partnerships and trusts, or shareholdings. The orientation of the rentier capitalist is passive, by contrast to the active involvement of the entrepreneurial capitalist, and the ideal type corresponds to the image of the 'dividend recipient' and 'coupon clipper' in Marxism and **Fabian** theory. The *executive capitalist* is involved exclusively as an office holder in a joint stock company. In the limiting case, the executive capitalist is propertyless and dependent purely on the remuneration of office, corresponding to the managerialist image of the business leader in the modern corporation. The *finance capitalist* is also, in the limiting case, propertyless, but occupies directorships in numerous units of capital. While the executive capitalist is one who plays a full-time bureaucratic role, the finance capitalist spreads his or her involvements by acting as part-time 'outside' or 'non-executive' director. By virtue of involvement in a number of separate units of capital, the ideal type of the finance capitalist corresponds to the image depicted in Marxist theory. ...

The rise of the joint stock company transformed the relationship between individual property holders and the businesses in which their property functioned as capital. The capitalist entrepreneur ceased to be the immediate owner of the undertaking, becoming a shareholder in a company which, in turn, owned the business assets. By adopting the joint stock form, entrepreneurs could draw on the funds of other individuals, who also became shareholders in the company. This led to a differentiation between the active shareholder – the capitalist entrepreneur – and the mass of passive shareholders who provided the capital and received the dividends but who played no active part in running the business. ... Despite the fact that large numbers of shares are held by a myriad of small shareholders, the owner of the majority stake has effective control of the business. Similarly, a large minority holding may be enough to ensure a working control of the company. The entrepreneurial capitalist of the twentieth century is one who holds a majority or a substantial minority of the shares in a company.

But the joint stock company did not simply lead to a differentiation between the entrepreneurial capitalist and the mass of small shareholders. It also transformed the position of the rentier capitalist. They became shareholders with substantial but non-controlling interests in large companies, shareholders whose holdings form parts of diversified portfolios of investments. ... The typical rentier capitalist adopts an 'absentee' stance towards property. The rentier's interest lies merely in the income which the property generates and its impact on his or her wealth. Though passive with respect to the actual operations of the enterprises in which they invest, however, the rentiers are necessarily involved in the management of the property itself. A substantial portfolio of investments and other assets must be carefully stewarded if it is to generate an optimum income – the rentier must pay attention to the spread of investments, their relative yields, and the incidence of taxation. ...

Where controlling holdings are held by financial institutions and corporate interests, rather than by particular individuals and families, property and control over property have become 'depersonalized'. In such a situation of impersonal property, the powers of corporate rule are exercised by boards of directors whose members have, at most, only small shareholdings in the enterprises which they direct. Although their personal shareholdings may be, and often are, extremely valuable in monetary terms, they amount to insignificant fractions of the total capital of the businesses and provide no basis for personal control of an entrepreneurial kind. Rather, the boards of directors function *collectively* as capitalists, their powers of corporate rule being dependent upon the impersonal structure of corporate and institutional shareholding.

The executive capitalist is the director of a single unit of capital, while the finance capitalist is a

No. of involvements	Nature of involvement	
	Property ownership	Directorship
Single	Entrepreneurial capitalist	Executive capitalist
Multiple	Rentier capitalist	Finance capitalist

Figure 1 Capitalist economic locations

'multiple director' sitting on the boards of a number of companies. The executive capitalist is typically a full-time official of an enterprise, occupying a post at the heart of its system of rule. Many of the most important will hold office as 'Chief Executive', 'Managing Director', or, in the United States, 'President', but there is also a wide range of executive titles corresponding to particular business roles. Executive capitalists stand at the heads of the corporate bureaucracies which are filled by those in service locations, and the typical executive capitalist is one who has risen from a service location relatively late in his or her career. For this reason, the executive capitalist location is a relatively insecure basis for membership in the capitalist class. A person who occupies a capitalist location for the whole of their life has a considerably greater chance of enjoying the advantages of a privileged life style and of passing them on to their children. The late entrant to an executive capitalist location may earn a large enough income to enjoy this life style for a period, but only the most highly paid and most financially astute will be able to continue to enjoy them after retirement.

The growth of institutional shareholdings led to the development of a system of 'finance capital', a system of capital mobilization in which industry and finance were fused. Within this system, the fusion of enterprises at board level led to the emergence of an 'inner circle' of company directors who function as finance capitalists. Occupants of these locations have insignificant personal stakes in the enterprises of which they are directors, but they have accumulated large numbers of directorships and represent the interests of the controlling institutions on the boards of the controlled companies. The typical finance capitalist holds non-executive directorships and depends not on high earnings from a particular enterprise but on the accumulation of fees from numerous directorships. While the executive capitalist is centrally involved in the collective rule of a particular unit of capital, the finance capitalists play a part in the coordination and cohesion of numerous separate enterprises. Their interests are not limited to one particular company, but extend to whole industries or to the economy as a whole.

The ideal typical locations defined in Figure 1 are, in Weber's terms, locations among which mobility is both easy and frequent, and particular individuals may occupy a number of locations simultaneously. Rentier capitalists, for example, were well-placed for recruitment to the boards of companies which came under institutional control during the 1930s, and as the shareholding institutions sought to cement their growing links with industrial companies, the rentiers were important recruits to these boards as well. Thus, many finance capitalists were – and are – also rentier capitalists with extensive personal interests in the success of the capitalist system as a whole. Similarly, entrepreneurial capitalists, as their interests in their own companies decline, become attractive recruits to the ranks of the finance capitalists, and may also diversify their holdings to adopt a rentier stance towards the system of property. Many top salaried executives who lack a propertied background are able to achieve entry to the ranks of the finance capitalists. Executive entrants, however, are in an insecure position unless they are able to convert their high incomes into property holdings and enter the ranks of the rentiers. The categories of capitalist economic locations, therefore, overlap considerably in concrete situations. ...

It is very rarely the case today that a particular capitalist-class household owes its life chances exclusively to its members' occupancy of a particular economic location or to involvement in a narrow sector of the economy. The boundaries between rentiers and entrepreneurs, executives and finance capitalists are blurred by the overlap and mobility which exists among the occupants of these locations. For this reason, neither the typology of locations nor the distinction between land ownership and other forms of property ownership should be seen as defining distinct *class segments*. Such economic differentiation as does exist is not generally associated with a parallel social and cultural differentiation into separate groups with divergent interests. While it is possible to recognize some persisting separation of industrial entrepreneurs, 'traditional' landowners, and corporate executives, for example, the vast bulk of capitalist class households are unified in both interests and outlook.

Capitalist economic locations, therefore, comprise those of the rentier, the entrepreneur, the executive, and the finance capitalist. In land, commerce, finance, and industry, large-scale undertakings are controlled and ruled by the occupants of these locations, operating through systems of personal and impersonal possession. The capitalist business class of Britain today consists of those whose family wealth and life chances are generated by the involvement of their members in these capitalist economic locations. ...

Class reproduction and capital reproduction

... I have tried to show that entrepreneurial capitalists have not completely disappeared – far from it – and that rentier capitalists have become an increasingly important force alongside the growth of impersonal institutional capital. But if the capitalist class has not disappeared, it is clear that the structure of the class and the mechanisms through which it is reproduced have altered.

The reality glimpsed by managerialist writers is, in

fact, a partial dissociation of the mechanisms of *class reproduction* from those of *capital reproduction*. Executive and finance capitalist locations are central to the reproduction of capital within the sphere of impersonal possession and those who occupy these locations, together with those in service-class locations, are the 'managers' of institutional capital. But this involvement in the reproduction of capital does not necessarily mean that they simultaneously reproduce a privileged and self-perpetuating capitalist class.

It is possible, in principle, for there to be free and open access to these capitalist and service locations, with all positions held by salaried bureaucrats who subside into middle class obscurity on completion of their business careers. In fact, I have shown, this is not the case. Executive capitalist and, especially, finance capitalist locations are occupied by those from an entrepreneurial or rentier background. ... Rentier capitalists depend upon the system of impersonal possession, but the reproduction of the system of impersonal possession does not necessarily result in the reproduction of the rentiers themselves. The rentier capitalists who monopolize executive and finance capitalist locations depend upon other mechanisms for the reproduction of their rentier locations and class privileges. An important avenue for enquiry is how this class reproduction is to be explained.

The reproduction of a capitalist class involves the reproduction of a structure of intermarried households with similar life chances. The class reproduction of entrepreneurial capitalists in Britain today ... is a direct consequence of their personal ownership and control of capital. Although the system of personal property holding has become more complex in its structure, reliance on direct personal shareholdings for majority or minority control is nothing new. But the ... rentiers of the twentieth century ... depend upon the operation of the system of impersonal possession. To the extent that rentiers are able to participate in corporate rule, as executive and finance capitalists, they have a direct supervisory position in the affairs of the system on which their privileges depend.

By taking on these positions, they are able to ensure that the system continues to advantage them through its operations. Their recruitment to these locations is not a simple matter of merit and talent, but reflects the advantages accorded by the possession of a particular kind of social background. This background of property and privilege allows the link between capital and class reproduction to be sustained. Rentiers are able to monopolize access to these locations through the informal networks of social connections which bind the wealthy together. These social networks, rooted in family and schooling, are important elements in class reproduction. ...

I argued above that there has been a partial separation of the mechanisms of class reproduction from those of capital reproduction. The capitalist class no longer owes its privileges and advantages exclusively to inherited access to entrepreneurial locations. In the system of impersonal capital the recruitment of executive and finance capitalists depends upon the possession of educational credentials and other attributes deemed relevant to the performance of these tasks. The public schools play an important role in the acquisition of educational credentials. Members of the capitalist class can use their wealth to purchase a privileged education for their children, so ensuring that they are well placed in the educational race and stand a much enhanced chance of attending the universities of Oxford and Cambridge. It is the degrees of these universities which are still regarded by those who recruit executives and directors as being most appropriate for a career in business. Wealthy families are able to convert their wealth into the 'cultural assets' of the educational system, which can then be reconverted into enhanced economic opportunities and prospects for wealth accumulation.

But entry to capitalist locations depends not simply on educational credentials; it depends also on other, less formal attributes which are rooted in upper-circle background and public schooling. The success of members of capitalist-class households in entering capitalist locations depends, to a substantial extent on the social assets inherent in attendance at the 'right' school or college and which are manifest in comportment, speech, and dress. The 'old boy network' builds and reinforces these class attributes and provides people with the contacts and connections needed to improve their career prospects. When being considered for appointment or promotion, they find that the majority of those who are involved in the process of selection have themselves been through the same system and have come to accept its features as ensuring the normal and natural attributes of the 'right man' (*sic*) for the job. Miliband recognized that this same process operates in the state élite: 'Those who control and determine selection and promotion ... are likely to carry in their minds a particular image of how a high ranking civil servant or military officer ought to think, speak, behave and react; and that image will be drawn in terms of the class to which they belong.'

Without any need for a consciously intended bias in recruitment, the established 'old boys' sponsor the recruitment through their networks of contacts of each new generation of old boys. The public schools and Oxbridge colleges are the foundations of these networks which interconnect the various upper circles. Membership of the principal London clubs reinforces these connections by providing a venue for informal meetings among the old boys who may meet in other business and political contexts and by providing opportunities for pursuing careers and interests. Useem has argued that club membership is especially important for those at an early stage in their careers. For those who lack multiple directorships or are not yet involved at the centre of the major business organizations, 'participation in the club world doubles the probability of serving on a public board'.

There exists a capitalist class with an *inner circle* of finance capitalists in Britain today, but these people are not the basis of an *upper circle* of status superiors. They are involved to varying degrees, and in varying ways, in the intersecting upper circles which have replaced high society at the top of the status hierarchy. It is in and through the informal social networks which connect these upper circles that class reproduction is ensured.

Key terms

The following key terms appear in the text above. They have been defined below to aid with the reading of this item.

corporate bureaucracies the administrative systems characteristic of large business organizations consisting of salaried employees

service class the managers and administrators of financial corporations who exercise delegated authority

petty bourgeois referring to the self-employed owner of a small business

Fabian referring to a socialist organization known as the Fabian Society, which advocated the justification of socialism on moral grounds

Questions

1 Describe the four capitalist economic locations in Scott's typology and their role in capitalist accumulation. Which category has become the most significant in terms of the organization of the capitalist class?

2 Distinguish between capital reproduction and class reproduction. Explain why the latter has become important.

3 Explain the importance of the public school system to the process of class reproduction.

4 To what extent do you agree with Scott's view that 'the vast bulk of capitalist class households are unified in both interests and outlook'?

5 What are the implications of Scott's findings for the debate about the extent to which British society has become more open and meritocratic?

Reading 5.6 **Representations of the 'underclass'**

Paul Bagguley and Kirk Mann (from) 'Idle, thieving bastards? Scholarly representations of the "underclass"', in *Work, Employment and Society* (1992) vol. 6, no. 1, pp. 113–14, and 117–25.

Editorial comments

Bagguley and Mann explore the origins of the term 'underclass' and, as the title of their article would suggest, they consider the numerous abuses to which it has been put. They note that the meanings imputed to the term can shift from a focus on the problems *faced by* the 'underclass' to the problem *of* the 'underclass'. While the concept was used initially in a 'sympathetic' way, more recently it has been adopted by various neo-conservative thinkers in ways that appear to blame the victims for their own multiple deprivation. Bagguley and Mann believe this has played into the hands of right-wing ideologues who have constructed a classic moral panic around the demonology of illegitimacy, violent crime and idleness.

Bagguley and Mann proceed to look at the question: how do we know this 'underclass' exists? They consider that, certainly in Britain, the empirical evidence does not support the idea of an inter-generational class of people located consistently, over time, at the very bottom of society. They believe that the concept of an underclass is a frequently recurring myth which results in 'lazy' explanations that are unsupported by empirical evidence. Because of this, they believe it is an instrument of ruling-class ideology, serving to obscure the processes that perpetuate social inequality and leading to ineffective social policy.

Idle thieving bastards?
Scholarly representations of
the 'underclass'

Introduction

... ours is becoming in some areas an ugly society, the irresistible consequence of a large minority abandoned to long term unemployment and declining living standards. The underclass, so long prophesized, is now emerging, alienated from the rest of society, bored, threatening and without hope.
(Shirley Williams, addressing the 1985 SDP conference in Torquay)

'It's unemployment that's responsible,' said Robyn. 'Thatcher has created an alienated underclass who take out their resentment in crime and vandalism. You can't really blame them.'
'You'd blame them if you were mugged going home tonight,' said Vic.
(Lodge, 1988)

IT IS RARE for sociological terms to enter journalism, popular fiction and political debate, but the 'underclass' succeeds where others fail. Terms and concepts such as 'marginalized strata', 'excluded groups', 'reserve army of labour', 'the pauper class', 'the residuum' and, most recently, the 'underclass' have all been used to describe a section of society which is believed to exist within but at the base of the working class. Very few of these terms are located within any coherent theory of social divisions, and most are descriptively vague. It might be argued that they are a form of sociological shorthand, a way of referring to a social phenomenon with which we are all very familiar. It is simply a matter of common sense, after all, to acknowledge that the working class has within it, or below it, strata that are particularly poor. That it is a matter of 'common sense' is precisely the problem. Should social scientists be in the business of reproducing 'common sense' ideas, particularly when these are ill defined and contradictory? It is doubtful that these terms mean the same thing to their respective advocates. There is considerable discursive 'leakage' between the respective meanings of each of these terms, with vastly different explanatory, moral and policy implications. In this instance a term such as the 'underclass' can be used by some quite incompatible bed fellows (Field, 1989; Wilson, 1987; Murray, 1984, 1990).

Myrdal, referring to the unemployed, is often credited with the dubious distinction of introducing the term 'the underclass' into social scientific discourse (Myrdal, 1964). In the 1970s the term was introduced into Britain in rather different ways by both Giddens (1973) and Rex (1983) to refer to racial and ethnic divisions. In Britain at the moment it is often

used to refer to the extremely poor sections of society (Dahrendorf, 1987; Saunders, 1990). In the USA the 'underclass' is portrayed as consisting almost entirely of these poor black Americans who live in the ghettos of the deindustrialized Northern cities. In some versions, such as Murray's single parenthood, drug culture, violent crime and unemployment are seen as characteristics and/or causes of the underclass. Here a subtle shift occurs from the problems faced by the 'underclass' to the problem *of* the 'underclass'. Blaming the victim has a long and inglorious history in relation to such ideological imagery (Macnicol, 1987; Mann, 1984). ...

'Over here': American commentators on Britain

In the 1980s with the return of mass unemployment some American commentators suggested that an underclass could emerge in Britain. ...

More recently the US social policy commentator Charles Murray has reaffirmed the view that in Britain the underclass is not necessarily black. Instead (Murray, 1990) he claims:

There are many ways to identify an underclass, I will concentrate on three phenomena that have turned out to be early warning signals in the United States: illegitimacy, violent crime, and drop out from the labour force.

Here we have the key ideological 'pointers' for a classic right-wing **moral panic**; 'early warning signals', and the classic unholy trinity of right-wing **demonology**: 'illegitimacy' (children without the correct sex role models), 'violent crime' (the threat to private property), and 'drop out from the labour force' (and they don't want to work either!). In popular language they are just 'idle thieving bastards'. Murray implies that he finds the sexual activities of the underclass understandable and their dislike of paid work reasonable, given the provision and levels of public welfare. What he feels the British underclass needs is to be adequately socialized. The values of the patriarchal family and the work ethic need to be firmly driven into the psyche of the individual. This can only be achieved by getting rid of the: 'wrong headed policies that seduce people into behaving in ways that seem sensible in the short term but are disastrous in the long term' (Murray, 1990). ...

Perhaps the really dangerous class is not the underclass but those who have propagated the underclass concept. In the last ten years or so academics, politicians and writers have adopted the underclass and during its trans-Atlantic crossing have turned it into something vaguely 'yobbish'. Because it is ill defined and sloppy the underclass can mean whatever the user intends it to mean. Or so it seems. Vandalism, hooliganism, street crime, long term unemployment, joyriders, drug abuse, urban riots, a decline in family values, single mothers and a host of other 'social problems' have been pinned on the British underclass. Their existence is never doubted, and it is often just a case of arguing over whether the causes are social, economic or down to individual pathology. The conversation cited earlier between Robyn and Vic in *Nice Work* could just as easily be between Wilson the liberal and Murray the neo-conservative.

But how do we know this underclass exists? What evidence is there of the underclass being reproduced over the generations? These are the crucial questions, since if there is very little evidence of an inter-generational class of people located consistently at the very bottom of society, it would seem we are not discussing a class over time. Certainly in Britain there is virtually no evidence of an underclass having a constant **constituency** at all. In the 1880s it was the Irish, the casual labourer and the 'pauper' who comprised the 'residuum' (Stedman-Jones, 1984). During the interwar period the long-term unemployed of the depressed areas were condemned as unemployable. Yet during both world wars these sub-groups of the working class were conscripted into the army and the labour market never to re-appear. ... But the advocate of the underclass concept is not deterred by historical evidence. It is claimed things are different now, the causes more profound (welfare benefits are higher and these people have televisions!), and more difficult to address. Alternatively, if the underclass is not here already, it's just around the corner, the warning signs are there for all to see, we must remain vigilant (Field, 1989).

Causality is certainly one of the questions that has to be addressed if any discussion of intra-class divisions is to be credible. Often the claim that there is a substratum beneath the working class proper is linked to the provisions of public welfare. For those on the left it is linked to the decline of the welfare state which has produced the underclass. The 'yuppies' have taken the spoils and left the underclass isolated and poor. The consensus of the 1950s and 60s has gone, and it is now a case of each strata for themselves. The underclass are portrayed as social cripples who have had their crutches knocked away (Field, 1989).

For Marxists there are similarities between the underclass and the idea of a lumpen-proletariat/reserve army of labour. In this view the existence of an underclass is reduced to some key function they serve for capital. They are kept poor but dependent

in order to encourage them to join the labour market when required. They also function to keep the wages of the employed low in order to stave off the tendency of the rate of profit to fall (Ginsberg, 1979; Gough, 1979). Why some groups rather than others should consistently perform these functions tends to be ignored. Since no team sheet appears with the names of the reserves listed what stops them getting into the field of play?

As we have already seen, the right also blames the welfare state. In their view welfare creates dependency by undermining the motivation of the poor to work. The poor are victims of the '**nanny state**' who now need to be weaned off welfare. As Walker (1990) points out, there are powerful echoes of the earlier idea of a 'culture of poverty', in which antisocial behaviour and amoral values serve to pass on a 'cycle of deprivation'. Despite a lack of empirical evidence to support such a claim, and indeed with much that contradicted it, the assertion is made once again. Public welfare activities, it is argued, protect the hide of the poor from the spur of the market.

Instead of working they can live off the dole, and, as time passes, even those who might have escaped by using their entrepreneurial skills come to accept those values. They express their natural abilities, not in legitimate small businesses, but in illegal activities. Drug dealing and street robbery replace small shop keeping. Family life becomes a thing of the past as young men and women abandon marriage in favour of casual sex and single parent benefits. Their offspring then learn the same values and the cycle is underway again. The answer lies in cutting welfare benefits and pressing the suspected members of the underclass into work. ...

The British debate on the 'underclass'

The notion of an emergent 'underclass' in contemporary Britain, consisting largely of the long-term unemployed, has once again attracted the attention of British academics (Dahrendorf, 1987; Pahl, 1988; Saunders, 1990). What puzzles us is why both 'left' and 'right' academics find the concept of an emergent (always emergent, never clearly extant) underclass so attractive when it has been so thoroughly destroyed by social scientific analysis. Most recently in Britain this has been done yet again by Macnicol (1987, 1990) and Gallie (1988).

Dahrendorf has recently attempted to make a strong case for the emergence or existence of an 'underclass' in Britain. It is not clear from Dahrendorf's account whether he thinks there is already an underclass, or if one is in the process of emerging in Britain. He is, however, rather more equivocal about its existence in the United States. His emphasis is on the inter-generational character of deprivation, suggesting that the underclass has been around for some time, and he even gives an estimate of its size – 5 per cent of the British population. However he writes constantly about the emergence in the future of an underclass and the dangers to British society that it poses. This underclass, according to Dahrendorf, cannot be helped by conventional policies to expand the economy, since they lack the motivation to take jobs (Dahrendorf, 1987). He also refers to it as a new class. He characterizes this new class as a group subject to the multiple deprivations of poor education, unemployment, 'incomplete families' and poor housing (Dahrendorf, 1987). The implication being that there is a distinct fraction of the working class, or even a class 'below' the working class, that has distinct political and material interests. However, Dahrendorf is somewhat ambivalent if not self contradictory about the underclass's political potential:

> The underclass is indeed not the source of tomorrow's revolution; it is not a revoluntary force at all.
>
> Whether it grows in size and hardens in separateness, or whether the boundary between it and the rest becomes more penetrable, is critical for the moral hygiene of British society but also for its social and political stability.
> *(Dahrendorf, 1987)*

This concern with the 'morality' and 'culture' of the underclass reveals the concept's wider social scientific brethren – the familiar old theories of the **'culture of poverty'** and 'cycles of deprivation'. Such notions, however, have had a rather undistinguished intellectual career over the past hundred years or so. As Macnicol (1987) argues:

> ... proponents of the underclass concept seem only half aware of its conceptual flaws and completely ignorant of its long and undistinguished pedigree. Indeed it is they who have displayed the greatest present time orientation, with little ability to **defer gratification** until the present debate has been examined.

Dahrendorf's uncritical enthusiasm for the concept and Pahl's (1988) cautious and mildly critical response are somewhat surprising, given that the Department of Health and Social Security and the, then, Social Science Research Council devoted a major research programme to the examination of the inter-generational transmission of deprivation in the 1970s, and found the idea severely lacking in empirical evidence to support it (Brown and Madge, 1982). The research was stimulated, or rather 'ordered', by Sir Keith Joseph's views on the persistence of poverty in the early 1970s. Joseph's central idea was of the inter-generational transmission of poverty through a 'cycle of deprivation', where inadequate child-rearing leads to failure at school, which leads to unemployment and unstable families, which continued the inadequate rearing of children. These core ideas have been the mainstay of sections of undergraduate texts on poverty for years. In that context they are discussed critically in association with notions of the 'culture of poverty' (Jordan, 1974; Lewis, 1969; Townsend, 1979). As Macnicol argues, there is a cycle of rediscovery of the core ideas on both the political right and the political left.

This current cycle of rediscovery is odd given the otherwise widely accepted lack of evidence to support the underclass thesis from a recently completed research programme (Rutter and Madge, 1977); Brown and Madge, 1982). In particular evidence (Rutter and Madge, 1977) showed that children from disadvantaged families did not 'inherit' the disadvantages of their parents on a scale sufficient for this to be an adequate explanation of material deprivation:

> At least half of the children born into a disadvantaged home do not repeat the pattern of disadvantage in the next generation. Over half of all forms of disadvantage arise anew in the next generation. On the one hand, even where continuity is strongest many individuals break out of the cycle, and on the other many people become disadvantaged without having been reared by disadvantaged parents.

> ... The concept of an underclass conflates a number of diverse social processes and obscures a range of fundamentally different social relations. The examples given on the constituents of the underclass begin to reveal this diversity – the long-term unemployed, those in the secondary labour market, single mothers, blacks, young working class people.

This conflation and dissimulation has two consequences. Firstly, it leads to poor social science. It encourages the development of incorrect social explanations – for example the confusion of dependent and independent variables in empirical analyses. The explanations developed are frequently 'lazy' in the sense that they choose selectively from empirical evidence, or worse make claims that are not justified from the available data. Others, such as Dahrendorf, are worse – there is no systematic data at all. For example, the focus on single mothers emphasizes their marital status and long-term dependence on public welfare. It is then assumed that they inculcate their offspring with the idea that welfare dependency carries no stigma or material disadvantage. From this it is claimed that the next generation are less willing or able to escape. Is it simply a peculiar coincidence that so many of those who are thought to constitute the underclass are the historic victims of patriarchal exclusion? What evidence is there that women find social security benefits so attractive that they 'get themselves pregnant'? But even if this were the case, what evidence is there that single mothers teach their children to accept poverty and make no effort to escape it? Frequently supporters of the underclass thesis fail to rigorously test their claims in competition with other explanations against appropriate empirical evidence.

The second consequence is inappropriate policy formulation; for example, inner city initiatives which seek to encourage an 'enterprise culture' as an alternative to the dependency culture implied in theories of the inter-generational transmission of social disadvantage. Irresponsible fathers are seen as a major cause of single motherhood resulting in the rearing of children without the appropriate 'role models', to use Wilson's term. Policies are being introduced in Britain under conditions which may prove to be punitively stigmatizing for single mothers. Implicit in the underclass concept is an idealized male model of lifetime permanent employment. This is very much a post Second World War phenomenon for men, and fails to address not only the labour market situation of women, but also the impact of changes in the patterns and opportunities of women's employment. Women are now much more attached to the labour force, albeit largely in segments such as part-time employment and the service sector where remuneration is literally poor. For the underclass theorists women exist only as mothers, not as participants in the labour market in their own right. Consequently they largely overlook the extensive gender restructuring of paid employment over the postwar period. Women's labour market position does not enter into their explanations.

The underclass: ideology of the upperclass

One never hears of the Wall Street underclass demoralized by their junk bond dependency culture! The divorces, white collar crime, drug taking, drinking, the phenomenal benefits of state welfare dependency (£7 billion in tax relief on mortgage interest alone in 1989), and the casual sex of the middle classes does not of course demoralize them.

It is widely recognized that in the past middle class observers of the poor discussed the impoverished in ways which served to 'blame the victims'. The paupers of the 1830s were feckless idlers who had been cushioned by the allowance systems. Malthus, Smith, Ricardo and Bentham set the agenda by highlighting the problems the poor posed for the economy and society. Fifty years later the poor were discussed in rather different terms. They were now seen as a residuum whose behaviour was conditioned by their genes, their oppressive environment and/or their geographical isolation from the beneficial influences of the middle classes. **Social Darwinism**, positivist social science and the racist language of imperialism were used to call for improvements in the 'race'. By the

1920s and 1930s they became a class of 'unemployables' who had lost the will to work. Confined to the 'depressed areas' of the North, Scotland and South Wales, they were required to undergo the brutal and futile Genuinely Seeking Work Test.

There are two features of these debates about the poor which stand out. First, it is worth noting how easily the criteria for defining this stratum change with wider changes in economic and social conditions. Second, the dominant ideas of the day have been consistently used by the middle classes to facilitate a redefinition of the poor. Classical political economy, utilitarianism, Social Darwinism, eugenics, social psychology and, most recently, sociology, have all been invoked to 'explain' the persistence of poverty. This middle class 'gaze' (Foucault, 1976) is firmly rooted in these wider social and ideological conditions. There appears to be a desperate need for the middle classes to justify their relatively privileged place in society by pointing to the failings of the poor. The history of racism and exclusion along with the dependency promoted by the patriarchal family, all this too is set aside. Once again the snapshot of today if superimposed on to the Victoriana of Social Darwinism to produce a picture which hypocritically focuses on the poor. The underclass is the ideology of the dominant upper and middle classes.

We should clarify what we mean here by ideology. We are not arguing for some spurious **dominant ideology thesis**, where beliefs generated by the upper classes or by the capitalist system are apparently injected into subordinate strata somehow inoculating them against their insubordinate tendencies. We have both argued extensively elsewhere against using such models, especially in relation to the poor and the unemployed (Bagguley, 1991; Mann, 1991) and we broadly concur with Abercrombie *et al*. (1980) on these questions. What kind of ideology, then, is the underclass thesis? We prefer to use a 'critical' concept of ideology most recently associated with authors such as Giddens (1979), Thompson (1990) and Urry (1981). This involves an analysis where one has to demonstrate that beliefs: '... serve, *in particular historical circumstances*, to establish and sustain relations of domination' (Thompson, 1990, our emphasis). Such an understanding of ideology does not necessarily imply a dominant ideology thesis. Following Thompson we would claim that certain dominant groups use such beliefs to help them sustain relations of domination. Hence it is not a functionalist model, it focuses on the intended and unintended consequences of beliefs, not on spurious needs of social systems. In our view the concept of the underclass is a set of ideological beliefs held by certain groups among the upper and middle classes. It helps them sustain certain relations of domination of class, patriarchy and race towards the unemployed, single mothers and blacks through the formulation of state welfare policies.

Of course the working class has its own ideas about 'dossers' and 'scroungers'. It would be misleading to suggest that it was only the middle classes who develop and hold ideological beliefs (Mann, 1991). Moreover, legitimacy for the view that the poor are a stratum at the very base of the working class has been gained in a succession of historical periods by pointing to existing social divisions. The independent labourer was contrasted with the pauper, the labour aristocrat with the residuum, the respectable working class with the 'roughs', the 'affluent worker' with the 'underclass'. Since Mayhew distinguished between the artisans and the labourers of London, observers have been confident that they could see clear demarcation lines within the working class. Today the worker who has a mortgage, a company pension scheme and a car is seen to stand apart from those who exist in the trench of welfare dependency. As with any ideological construct the underclass concept is founded upon some observable partial truths. Some working-class people are indeed much poorer than others, but the underclass concept serves to conceal causal factors rather than reveal them.

The concept of an underclass is a chaotic rather than rational abstraction (Sayer, 1984), and therefore is ideological in its consequences. A rational abstraction would enable the relevant causal processes to be identified and theorized. Chaotic concepts, like the underclass, actually obscure causal processes. The concept of the underclass, whilst in a limited descriptive sense is accurate – there are ecological correlations between unemployment and other social phenomena – obscures the processes that generate these apparent correlations. In our view the underclass concept, because of its inherent theoretical, methodological and empirical flaws, is a demonstrably false set of beliefs. In spite of this certain social and political groups insist in continuing to use it. It obscures the real problems of poverty, and the real state welfare dependency of the wealthy. The underclass is *the* ideology of the upper class.

References

Abercrombie, N. *et al.* (1980) *The Dominant Ideology Thesis*, London: Allen & Unwin.

Bagguley, P. (1991) *From Protest to Acquiescence? Political movements of the unemployed*, London: Macmillan.

Brown, N. and Madge, N. (1982) *Despite the Welfare State*, London: Heinemann.

Dahrendorf, R. (1987) 'The erosion of citizenship and its consequences for us all', *New Statesman*, 12 June, pp. 12–15.

Field, F. (1989) *Losing Out: The emergence of Britain's underclass*, Oxford: Blackwell.

Foucault, M. (1976) *The Birth of the Clinic*, London: Tavistock.

Gallie, D. (1988) 'Employment, unemployment and social stratification', in Gallie, D. (ed.) *Employment in Britain*, Oxford: Blackwell, pp. 465–92.

Giddens, A. (1973) *The Class Structure of the Advanced Societies*, London: Hutchinson.

Giddens, A. (1979) *Central Problems in Social Theory*, London: Macmillan.

Ginsgerg, N. (1979) *Class, Capital and Social Policy*, London: Macmillan.

Gough, I. (1979) *The Political Economy of the Welfare State*, London: Macmillan.

Jordan, B. (1974) *Poor Parents: Social policy and the cycle of deprivation*, London: Routledge.

Lewis, O. (1969) *La Vida*, London: Panther Books.

Lodge, D. (1988) *Nice Work*, Harmondsworth: Penguin.

Macnicol, J. (1987) 'In pursuit of the underclass', *Journal of Social Policy, 16*, pp. 293–318.

Macnicol, J. (1990) 'Nightmare on easy street', *The Times Higher Educational Supplement*, 29 June, p. 15.

Mann, K. (1984) 'Incorporation, exclusion, underclasses and the unemployed', in Harrison, M. L. (ed.) *Corporatism and the Welfare State*, Aldershot: Gower.

Mann, K. (1991) *The Making of an English 'Underclass'?*, Milton Keynes: Open University Press.

Murray, C. (1984) *Losing Ground*, New York: Basic Books.

Murray, C. (1990) *The Emerging British Underclass*, London: Institute of Economic Affairs.

Myrdal, G. (1964) *Challenge to Affluence*, London: Victor Gollancz.

Pahl, R. E. (1988) 'Some remarks on informal work, social polarization and the social structure', *International Journal of Urban and Regional Research, 12*, pp. 247–67.

Rex, J. (1983) *Race Relations in Sociological Theory*, London: Routledge.

Rutter, M. and Madge, N. (1977) *Cycles of Disadvantage: a review of research*, London: Heinemann.

Saunders, P. (1990) *Social Class and Stratification*, London: Routledge.

Sayer, A. (1984) 'Eliminating the yahoo: eugenics, social Darwinism and five Fabians', *History of Political Thought, 8*, pp. 521–44.

Stedman-Jones, G. (1984) *Outcast*, Harmondsworth: Penguin.

Thompson, J. B. (1990) *Studies in the Theory of Ideology*, Oxford: Polity.

Townsend, P. (1979) *Poverty in the UK*, Harmondsworth: Penguin.

Urry, J. (1981) *The Anatomy of Capitalist Societies*, London: Macmillan.

Walker, A. (1990) 'A poor idea of poverty', *The Times Higher Educational Supplement*, 17 August, p. 16.

Wilson, W. J. (1987) *The Truly Disadvantaged: The inner city, the underclass and public policy*, Chicago: University of Chicago Press.

Key terms

The following key terms appear in the text above. They have been defined below to aid with the reading of this item.

moral panic the tendency of the mass media to focus public concern on the behaviour of particular 'deviant' groups leading to a societal reaction that is disproportionate to the 'problem'

demonology the portrayal of certain groups in the population as 'folk devils' and the scapegoats for social problems

constituency membership

'nanny state' an expression popularized by the 'New Right' during the administration of Margaret Thatcher which sought to discredit state intervention by likening adult dependency on state welfare to a child that remains dependent on its nanny for too long

'culture of poverty' a theory that the poor, under certain circumstances, develop a way of life that perpetuates their poverty

defer gratification to put off rewards or enjoyment until later

social Darwinism a theory which sees social inequality as a function of 'natural inequalities' that are justified according to the principle of 'survival of the fittest'

dominant ideology thesis the (largely discredited) idea that the mass of the population have accepted the legitimacy of the existing capitalist order without question

Questions

1 a What do you understand by the terms 'culture of poverty' and 'cycles of deprivation'?

   b How have these concepts been used by some British academics to explain the existence of an 'underclass'?

   c On what basis do Bagguley and Mann reject this approach?

2 a Why do Bagguley and Mann believe that the 'underclass concept' is a myth?

   b How far do you agree with the views of the authors of this article on this point?

3 Explain why you think sociologists either should, or should not, continue to use the term 'underclass'?

Reading 5.7 **Class today: fashions at odds with facts**

John Westergaard (from) 'Class today: fashions at odds with facts', *Social Science Teacher* (1996) vol. 25, no. 2, Spring, pp. 2–5.

Editorial comments

In this reading, Westergaard states his belief in the continuing salience of class analysis to an understanding of the structures of inequality in capitalist society – particularly in the socio-political context of Britain in the 1990s. He begins with a discussion of the reasons why some politicians and academics have argued that class is an outmoded concern. He then outlines his belief that empirical evidence of a 'hardening' of class inequalities makes claims of classlessness and the death of class, difficult to square with the 'facts'. On the question of political mobilization, he suggests that class politics has not been eclipsed, though its expression in voting is currently weak – which may reflect disillusionment in the possibility of change through the traditional vehicle of class politics: the Labour party.

Class today: fashions at odds with facts

FOR THE PAST 15 years or so, it has become commonplace to argue – or merely to assume – that class is an outmoded concern. Commonplace in as much as **media gurus** often read the signs of the new times they see that way. Commonplace in as much as many politicians, too, take class to be a thing of the past.

Politicians of the right and centre do so because they have always been inclined to equate their faith in societal unity with achieved reality. Now many politicians of the **ostensible left** do so as well because they take their own return to electoral favour to depend on support from an allegedly fast-grown, classless 'middle mass' of the population. But the notion that the 1980s and '90s have seen class off the stage has become quite commonplace – though far from universal – also among sociologists and other professional social scientists.

Why some sociologists see class as an outmoded concern

It is not a new notion, of course. There is a great deal in it which echoes the **postulates** of **embourgeoisement** some 30–40 years ago; and it is a notion, now, which comes in various forms. One form, in our own profession, is quite simply to look aside from class, and set other priorities for research and debate; priorities for example, concerning gender and ethnic divisions, assumed to supersede class divisions; priorities concerning matters of personal identity and cultural flux, assumed to have shaken loose from the structural determinacy associated with class; and so on. Another form involves more specific assertion that a spread of high consumption, of personal ownership of homes and company shares, of access to private insurance, has dramatically eroded once pervasive class inequality. A modified version of this latter thesis is perhaps the most common. It exempts from the postulate of mass classlessness a minority 'underclass', who are acknowledged to be poor; whether poor through their own failings or poor through the harshness of a new economic climate. But in this version, still, the underclass is an exception: a minority varyingly – and bafflingly – set at anything between maybe a tenth and a third of the population; yet no more than a minority anyway. The rest – the nine-tenths, or two-thirds, or whatever – are designated 'classless' by virtue of a new affluence, security and consumer empowerment they are supposed to share.

Why it is that assumptions and ideas of this sort have become commonplace is not hard to understand. They fitted with the policy-making mood from the late 1970s onwards, which sought **market liberalization**, yet had to deny risks of increased class division in consequence. More paradoxically, they seemed to fit the dominant electoral trends, which on a superficial interpretation suggested just that decline of class division which policy-leading opinion hoped for. In Britain, just as three Conservative general election victories in the 1950s had triggered ideas of embourgeoisement, so four such victories from 1979 to 1992 did much to revive similar ideas in this new era. The simple inference became, now as then: if class division in

organized politics is fading, then it must be because its roots in socio-economic inequality are crumbling. And wider changes were taken to make that inference plausible. Neither the massive shifts in the world economy from the mid-1970s onwards, nor the collapse of the Soviet empire in the late 1980s, had been generally predicted. That unpredictability, together with various features of these shifts themselves, encouraged postmodernist views that flux prevails where there was once thought to be structure. The notion of class structure became a prime victim of such views.

But it is one thing to explain this change of fashion that denies class structure. It is quite another to test it by reference to logic and fact. The latter is my main concern here. Before I turn to this, however, I must say a little about what I mean by class and class structure.

The meaning of class and class structure

Very summarily, I take class to be a set of social divisions that arise from a society's economic organization; and I see three main aspects to analysis of these divisions. The first concerns the nature and location of power in the society's economic organisation: what is the pattern and purpose of arrangements for command over scarce resources; and who exercises such command? The second aspect is closely linked to the first. If access to command is skew, so will access to rewards be skew: what, then, are the consequent patterns of inequalities in people's life experiences? I say inequalities in the plural because a range of features is involved: inequalities of income and security; of influence, authority and personal autonomy; of opportunity, even of sheer health and physical survival. But the more these various inequalities coincide to mark off the same people from others, and the sharper the inequalities too, the more it makes sense to talk of a 'class structure' manifest in everyday life. The third aspect concerns the very wide set of issues around people's perceptions of their own and others' places and prospects in this class structure, their reactions and responses in cultural, political and ideological terms.

The views of Marx and Weber

Some brief further comments. I draw on both Marx and Weber for this approach to class: on Marx especially for my first emphasis on command over scarce resources; on Weber especially for my next emphasis on the distribution or rewards and **'life chances'**; on both for the point that I place people's perceptions, reactions and responses last in the analytical sequence – though not thereby least in significance. But more like Weber, certainly unlike Marx in his prophetic moods, I postulate no single, simple path for translation of class inequalities of power and life chances into political and ideological class mobilization, let alone into some radical or evolutionary mobilization of the subordinate classes in capitalist societies. Indeed there may be little such mobilization at all. There are a number of industrialized societies in which even moderate working-class organization has long been weak – the USA and Japan most notably – yet where a class structure has long been sharp by reference to skewness of economic command and people's life changes alike. Class 'in itself', to use Marx's terminology, does not necessarily become class 'for itself'.

The view that there has been an increase in the potency of class

But class 'in itself' may be highly potent nonetheless, as a force to shape both societal character and people's life experiences. My main argument will be that the potency of class to those effects has in fact grown over the past fifteen years or so, not diminished. And to show this I should, according to the approach I have just outlined, start with the changing configurations of economic and associated political command. There can indeed be no doubt that power in that sense has become increasingly concentrated 'at the top'. Let me focus on the case of Britain in particular. If the power of private business postwar could be said to have been tempered by welfare state measures, by **Keynesian** prescriptions for macro-economic management, by labour market boom and by the formal representation of trade unions in so-called **corporatist consultation**, then all that has been fragmented since the late 1970s. If enhancement of business power on those scores within any one country has been countered by the further internationalization of market forces, then this has at the same time strengthened the command of capital organised on a worldwide scale, to weaken opportunity for opposing influences organized at best on a national scale. If new mass consumer empowerment is said to offer a thriving alternative counter-weight to command by large corporate business, it has proved important to resist either the still steady trends to capital concentration, or the effects of a much increased inequality of incomes, which has brought any consumer empowerment far more to the few than to the many.

This is the gist of my case under the first heading to my approach. I shall say more about it later, because it points to a consolidation of upper class power and privilege alike, which tells most starkly against all class-eclipse pontification. Meanwhile, I turn to my second heading: class inequalities of life experience. I have already touched on their most obvious manifestation, systematic inequalities of income. And those inequalities have indeed widened dramatically in the 1980s and '90s: in almost all industrial

countries for which there are time-series records; and especially in Britain.

Growing class inequalities since 1979

The trend to income polarization is now well known; but not so its sheer scale and the details of its incidence. Estimates from official survey data for Britain show that, over the years 1979 to 1992, real incomes among the poorest fifth of the population either actually dropped or grew hardly at all; this according to which of two alternative modes of calculation one uses. By contrast, which ever the mode of calculation, real income boomed at the top: by over 50% among the best-off one fifth, by 60% among the top tenth alone. Commentators are prone to shrug off this contrast between extremes with a claim that 'average' affluence grew sizably as well in this period: by some 30% or more; but the point is seriously misleading. The average is an artefact, raised high in large part by the good fortune of the well-to-do and the wealthy. Well over half the population saw gains in real income during the period distinctly below both the artefactual average and the much more evenly spread gains of the earlier postwar growth era. Both by this measure and a number of others, there is less reason to talk about exclusion of a new minority underclass than about majority experience of lagging steadily more behind upper-level prize winnings.

The forces behind this have been two-fold in the main. On the one hand, the tax-benefit system has been regarded to favour upper-level people. An estimate from the Institute of Fiscal Studies thus shows changes on this front, from 1979 to 1989, yielding nearly half the aggregate gains to just the richest 10% of households, only one fifth of the total proceeds to the poorer and poorest 60% altogether. On the other hand, hardening market forces – in part worldwide and abetted, of course, by shifts of public policy at both international and national level – have spread economic insecurity wide, and again tended to polarize incomes in, as well as outside, work. Even among the diminished number of full-time employees, British earnings survey data for the years 1980–90 thus display much the same pattern of widening inequality as do the data on incomes overall; high boom for high level work; near-stagnation at the bottom; mid-level gains below artefactual average gains.

I need to stress that all this represents essentially a growth of class inequalities. It does not arise from shifts of household structure, for example; for the relevant information standardizes for these. Nor does it come from gender inequality per se. For though women continue to be sharply disadvantaged – not least through lower placement generally in the economic structure of class than men – gender inequalities, by themselves, have if anything somewhat narrowed over recent years. Ethnic divisions – which again come to expression in good part as relatively low class placement of their victims – have certainly been sharpened by the new spread of economic insecurity; but as effect rather than cause, in a society like Britain where black and brown people in any case make up only five-to-six percent of the population.

Some myths of class erosion

What of mass empowerment through new ownership, new consumer choice, new opportunities? I must be brief, to leave myself time for other issues. But while ownership of homes has indeed continued to spread, one effect is to multiply divisions between owners of good homes and poor homes, between secure owners and insecure owners. Personal shareholding has widened; but still only to a minority, most of whom in turn have only pocket-sized stakes. Most remarkably, moreover, spread of ownership on these scores has left the overall concentration of property undented. Indeed, that concentration has actually increased. The richest 5% of adults, for example, held 36% of all personally owned marketable wealth in 1981, but 38% at the end of the decade; when the value of dwellings is excluded their share in personal capital ownership rose from 45% to fully 53% over the same period. Access to private pensions, again, has continued to spread; but it remains deeply stratified by reference to its incidence and its terms alike. Class-eclipse theorists have often joined postmodernists in celebrating a new consumerism, which is supposed to have turned consumption into a search for identity rather than a means to make do. But this involves sociological fantasy far more than fact; and facts point to a widening of consumer inequalities of choice, as inequalities of income have widened. As for a new opening of opportunities in life, the evidence from social mobility data so far underlines rather an erosion of opportunities for the many, now, who cannot find paid work or risk losing it. With all this making for more class-divided life experience over the past decade and a half, it is not entirely surprising to find signs that class inequalities in the risks of death, too, may recently have widened.

The existence of an upper class

To my own mind, the oddest feature of all to current class-denying theory is its unconcern with the question of an upper class. Class-denying theory 30–40 years ago did have something to say on this matter. It postulated not only working-class embourgeoisement; but also – however contestably – an erosion of upper-class privilege and power: through redistribution of income and wealth; through state encroachment on property rights and business autonomy; through a benign managerial revolution within private

enterprise. By contrast, present-day postulants of class collapse have had virtually nothing to say about this issue. Yet, in all logic, they should have. For if there is still an upper class, then there is *ipso facto* a class structure, whatever may be its shape below the top.

And if we define an upper class by its possession of concentrated privilege and power – which is what I do – then the presence of an upper class is still more evident in Britain today that 15 years ago. About the concentration of privilege, I need say little more than I have said already. Gains in real income, for example, have been the grander the closer one gets to the top: 60% over 12–13 years for the best-off tenth of the population; but more than 100% over just 9 years (to 1992) for board members of the top 100 companies; more still, over still fewer years, for chief executives of enterprises moved from public to private ownership. And high income is itself a form of power. It is forceful consumer power, for one thing, when for example the richest 5% of the population command as much post-tax income as the entire poorest third. Moreover, personal and family status, influence, know-how and known-whom, also usually go closely with money. Privilege at the top shades into everyday power.

The existence of power élites

But there is command involved also more directly. Peak incomes come mainly from key places in the networks of control and ownership over corporate business. These are networks between company boards, financial power-houses including pension funds, and consultant agencies. Strategic control is exercised largely through corporate holdings and corporate deployment of funds. But there are, of course, people behind these seemingly impersonal operations; and the people in the key places share, within their small circles, in command over capital assets which many times exceed their own personal packages of wealth. That is not new to the 1980s and '90s. But this concentration of economic command has increased: both through the liberalization of market forces in that period, and through public policy associated with it.

One way of describing those shifts in power relationships at the top is to talk of a dismantlement of corporatism. More accurately, however, it is tripartite corporation that has been dismantled. Trade unions have lost their former accreditation to have some say in policy; but in just that process, business accreditation has been enhanced. One sign of this is the proliferation of new agencies for public policy – unelected **quangos** in effect – with a strong business presence at their heads: NHS Trusts, TECs, inner-city development corporations, and so on. Conversely, of course, elected local authorities have lost powers apace. A less visible but all the more potent sign of the new bipartite corporation – new in Britain, that is, though familiar say in Japan – comes in the still closer, if informal, links of common commercial interest forged between governing party politicians and business corporations. These links come to occasional highlight in media-exposed scandals; the Pergau dam affair; the arms-to-Iraq business, on which the Scott report is due soon; the payments-to-MPs issues, which provoked establishment of the Nolan committee. But the most salient point here for analysis of power relationships concerns less the instances of so-called 'sleaze', even of plain illegality or deception, that arise. It concerns rather the *routine* presence of tight links between business and political élites: now more potent than for a long time before, and now celebrated in tone-setting ideology. With that shift of climate, too, has come a set of new prescriptions for policy on matters still in the public sphere: prescriptions for cost-effectiveness by short-term monetary criteria; prescriptions, in short, borrowed from business, and often implemented by a growing cadre of managers and management consultants.

A lot of this has now become familiar. My purpose in rehashing it is not to argue, here, about the virtues and vices of a re-invigorated **business hegemony**. It is more simply to note that hegemony, and to underline its association with a marked further concentration of privilege as well as power at the top of our society. The upper class, whose presence all this denotes, is very tiny in numbers but very rich in resources. Its strengthened presence is itself enough to make a mockery of contentions that class structure has dissolved.

Has there been an eclipse of class politics?

You will remember that I reserved questions concerning cultural formation and political mobilization for consideration in the third and last phase of class analysis; and pressure of space forces me to leave them virtually aside now. What I can say is only that fashionable commentary has been too simplistic in taking electoral trends to signify a definitive eclipse of class politics. Labour – the party which in Britain historically was the institutionalized vehicle of class politics – indeed lost support dramatically around the turn of the 1980s; and if it comes to office in 1996 or '97, it will be as a party whose leaders seem set on disengaging it from class politics. But voters still divide their allegiances as much on a class basis as, in relative terms, they did in the 1960s and '70s. No less importantly, survey after survey during the last ten years shows them to hold views about socioeconomic issues which both remain class-divided on a number of scores and yet show widespread unease over class inequalities and the concentration of privilege and power at the top. If this finds only weak expression in the ways people vote, it may be in good part because disillusionment with politics, politicians and once-accepted means of social change is now also widespread. But all that goes far beyond my compass on this occasion.

| Key terms

The following key terms appear in the text above. They have been defined below to aid with the reading of this item.

media gurus influential media figures who act as opinion leaders

ostensible left those who profess to be politically left-wing

postulates assertions which are not based on any proof

embourgeiosement the theory, first put forward in the 1960s, that increasing affluence would lead the working class to assume 'bourgeois' – or middle-class – characteristics

market liberalization allowing the economy to operate according to the principles of the free market

life chances the relative opportunity to obtain those things generally regarded as desirable in society

Keynesian relating to the economic theory that influenced British governments from the 1930s to the 1970s, based on the ideas of John Maynard Keynes, who proposed that the economy required state intervention to overcome slumps in demand and mass unemployment

corporatist consultation this refers to the nature of economic and political decision-making characteristic of British society from 1945 to 1980, based on consultation between the trade unions, the CBI (Confederation of British Industry) and the state

quangos quasi-autonomous non-governmental organizations

business hegemony the dominance of ideas which accept the legitimacy of 'business values'

Questions

1 Identify three reasons, mentioned by Westergaard, why some sociologists see class as an outmoded concern.

2 Explain in your own words how Westergaard is influenced by aspects of both Marxist and Weberian class analysis.

3 Explain what Westergaard sees as the three main 'aspects' of class analysis.

4 What does Westergaard mean when he claims that we have witnessed 'an increase in the potency of class' in the first two 'phases' of class analysis?

5 How far do you agree with Westergaard's argument that there has been 'an increase in the potency of class'?

6 To what extent do you think the Labour party has disengaged from class politics and, in the light of recent political history, has their decision been vindicated?

Reading 5.8 'Fractured identities': social class and post-modernity

Harriet Bradley (from) *Fractured Identities: Changing patterns of inequality* (1996) Cambridge: Polity, pp. 67–73 and 78–9.

Editorial comments

Bradley suggests that it is necessary to develop new approaches to class, and considers the possibilities offered by three different strands of post-modernist theory. While these have raised some interesting questions about class they have not provided the answers, and Bradley does not subscribe to the post-modernist views which may go too far in dismissing class as a source of identification. The concept of class consciousness in the Marxist sense of a 'class for itself' is problematic, but she believes it is still worth exploring the significance of class identity. However, she does accept that class has become a passive rather than an active identity, by which she means that people may be aware of class but they aren't prepared to do anything much about it. It remains, nevertheless, a potent force for identity among certain politicized working-class communities.

Bradley concludes that the most promising direction for class analysis is for it to adopt the more flexible approaches indicated by post-modernism, through considering how class relates to those forms of inequality that tended to be marginalized by classic theory. In her view, there must be a recognition of how class relations are themselves shaped by other forms of inequality.

Class: beyond Marx?

New directions: post-modern possibilities

Class was not a central concern within original post-modern theory, with its interest in cultural change. However, sociologists concerned to develop a 'sociology of post-modernism' have started to explore the issue of social divisions. As we have seen, post-modernism is a broad church with divergent strands. We can distinguish three tendencies, however:

1 Some theorists attempt to combine a post-modern account of culture with traditional Marxist class theory.
2 Others suggest that post-modern culture is bringing an end to class inequalities.
3 A third group argue that class is still relevant but that it should be conceptualized in terms of consumption more than production.

Jameson (1991) is one of the former, as is Harvey (1989). Both combine an account of post-modern cultural development with analysis of a **globalizing capitalism**. For Jameson the significant features of the new phase of capitalist development are the power of transnational corporations and the development of a co-ordinated world market. Harvey and Jameson display the Marxist concern with the changing nature of the capitalist ruling class and lend support to the arguments of Bottomore and Brym (1989) that capitalist power has been greatly strengthened in recent decades. However, neither has much to say about other class groupings. Harvey seems to assume 'business as usual'; Jameson justifies his vagueness by the idea that we are still in the 'trough' between two capitalist epochs and cannot predict class outcomes:

> The post-modern may well ... be little more than a transitional period between two stages of capitalism, in which the earlier forms of the economic are the process of being restructured on a global scale ... That a new international proletariat (taking forms we cannot yet imagine) will re-emerge from this convulsive upheaval it needs no prophet to predict
> *(Jameson, 1991)*

While this may be true, it is of little help in developing an account of the contemporary class dynamic.

At the opposite extreme Beck (1992) and Crook *et al.* (1992) both suggest that post-modern change is inexorably bringing an end to class and other sorts of inequality. Beck believes that old class communities are breaking down and class ties weakening as a result of what he calls 'a social surge of individualization'. He envisages the future as an 'individualized society of employees'. It should be noted that Beck's account was derived from his study of European societies, primarily West Germany, a society in which working-class affluence was a well-established fact up to the period of German reunification. Beck actually makes an exception of Britain, of which he says:

Class membership is very apparent in everyday life and remains the object of consciousness and identification. It is evident in speech ... in the sharp class divisions between residential areas ... in types of education, in clothing and in everything that can be included under the concept of 'lifestyle'.
(Beck, 1992)

Crook *et al.* (1992) offer a similar account, drawing on the Australasian context; they predict a decline in the social significance of class, gender and ethnicity as society becomes more individualized and the media play more part in influencing people to identify with particular '**symbolically similated communities**' such as various consumer groups. In stark contrast to Jameson, they suggest that the service class has now replaced the capitalist class as the élite; but they see membership of the service class as so fluid 'that the very existence of a class system will have to be called in question'. The future for all forms of stratification they see as 'fluid and apparently chaotic'.

While Beck and Crook *et al.* present these arguments as a general theory of change (a position at odds with some post-modernists' insistence on local narratives), we could alternatively read these as accounts of particular societies where fragmentation and individualization have progressed further than is the case in Britain. But their claims are subject to the criticism that can be aimed at all versions of classlessness: that is, the continuing evidence, both quantitative and qualitative, of substantial economic inequalities within most capitalist societies (Edgell, 1993) and the lack of substantial proof that collective identification is waning. At this stage, the post-modern version of classlessness cannot be seen as more than a vision of a possible future.

These forms of post-modernism offer two scenarios: one in which nothing very much has changed and one in which everything is changing. An intermediate position affirms the reality of capitalist inequality but offers a new reading of its nature. In this view consumption rather than production becomes the key aspect of class formation. Lyon (1994) states 'if post-modernity means anything, it means the consumer society' and speaks of the new world of 'rock videos' theme parks and shopping malls'. Some post-modernists see class communities dissolving in the face of consumerized life-styles. Others suggest that consumption-based cleavages based for example on housing tenure, are replacing classes (Saunders, 1984). The most sophisticated approach links consumption to other aspects of class formation and reproduction.

Zygmunt Bauman, in one of the most powerful accounts of a 'post-modern society', argues that its key feature is that capital has emancipated itself to a considerable extent from labour, an idea also put forward by some Marxists, such as Sivanandan (1990). The core relation between capital and the other social classes has changed; capital now engages labour in the role of consumers rather than producers (Bauman, 1992). As a result of these developments, a key new social group has come into being which Bauman here calls the 'new poor' (another version of the underclass, etc.). This group, characterized by unemployment, dependency and poverty, is not to be seen as part of the labour reserve but as *permanently displaced*. However, because of people's increasing dependency on the market, the social unrest which one might expect to develop in such circumstances does not manifest itself; seduced by the glamour of the new consumerism, most people conform. Capital, Bauman believes, has made use of the 'pleasure principle' to win the battle for control of production, thereby greatly reinforcing its position of social dominance. He argues, as has Dahrendorf (1987), that the state may be forced to take repressive measures to keep the losers, 'the new poor', in order; increasing policing and surveillance, the loss of citizen rights. Seduction and repression become the twin axes of class domination.

Bauman's account clearly owes much to Marxism in its stress on an all-powerful capitalist class and a manipulated working class. Others have used the consumption scenario in a less pessimistic way. Turner (1988) suggests that the expansion of mass culture and consumerism, accompanied by the interweaving of 'high' and 'popular' cultural styles that typifies post-modern culture, may erode traditional status hierarchies, bringing a cultural democratization even if economic inequalities endure. Others draw on the influential work of Bourdieu (1986) on taste and status distinctions to explore the role of consumption as an aspect of class. They discern groups sharing a common 'habitus' or life-world with a distinctive set of practices, attitudes and tastes which individuals use to shape their perception of social space. For example, Savage *et al.* (1992) use this framework to distinguish a number of different consumer groupings within the 'new middle classes'. Managers and bureaucrats share an old-fashioned, middle-of-the road pattern of consumption, which can be distinguished from that of public-sector professionals, who favour more intellectual pursuits, and a high-minded health-conscious lifestyle, such as that often satirized by reference to the *Guardian* reader. (The former group, we can assume, would chose *The Times* or *Telegraph*). The trend-setting group, however, are the upwardly mobile 'yuppie' young private-sector professionals who exemplify the post-modern spirit with its mix of high and low culture (opera *and* rap music, visits to the theatre *and* to theme parks) and its pursuit of expensive pleasure of all kinds.

Consumption patterns, then, can be seen either as equalizing or divisive; but whichever view is held, it is suggested that consumption is becoming more important in people's self-identification. Such consumption groups can be seen as recent manifestations of status, as described by Weber. Turner (1988) argues that in contemporary capitalist societies status is more politically and socially crucial than class (a view quite in line with Weber's discussion of status groups), while stressing that it is necessary to analyse contemporary societies in terms of both status *and* class.

The stress on consumption as an aspect of class is to be welcomed in line with my argument that versions of class limited to occupation are too narrow. But there is a danger of going too far in the other direction and ignoring production altogether. There is as yet little empirical *proof* of the assertion that consumption and consumption identities are more important to people than employment and work identities. This remains to be explored.

Post-modern thinking about class raises some interesting questions, but so far the answers are sketchy. There is a need for careful empirical exploration to justify the claims that are being made. Such research might centre on the issue of identity, since this is crucial to the ideas of the non-Marxist post-modernists.

Class, identity and action

Traditional class theory raised this issue in terms of class consciousness, which has long been a contentious concept. Marx argued that consciousness rises directly from social being: that is, that material experiences, such as that of exploitation, are the basis of class identification. But Marx also claimed that those who control the means of production also control the production of ideas in society. From this derives the notion of the dominant ideology by which the capitalists legitimate their own social domination and which produces a 'false consciousness' in the proletariat that blocks an awareness of their true class

situation. The idea of false consciousness has been considered crude by later Marxists, who have employed the alternative notion of a 'contradictory' consciousness, where elements from people's direct experience combine with ideas drawn from media and other vehicles of dominant thinking, to produce an often inconsistent package of ideas about society (Mann, 1970).

Weberians reject these ideas, arguing that there is no necessary one-way causal link between material experience, consciousness and action. Consciousness can be influenced by a whole range of factors, not just material conditions. For Weberians, class consciousness has to be approached through empirical research into people's ideas and images of class. However, such research is difficult to conduct and its findings are often hard to interpret. For example, twenty years after Goldthorpe et al. (1969) had surveyed Luton workers and concluded that their attitudes to work were instrumental, individualistic and economistic, Devine revisited the affluent workers' community and found that a more **ethnographic** approach revealed a more complex mix of attitudes (1992).

Marshall et al. (1988) also argue that working-class culture displays both collectivist and individualistic, instrumental and solidaristic values, and has always done so. Their national survey of class in Britain in the 1980s suggests that people show a clear awareness of class inequalities and of their own class positions. The British Social Attitude surveys of recent years have also demonstrated a consistent sense of class among respondents. However, sometimes these findings are influenced by the questions that are asked, for example if people are presented with a list of fixed choices of class positions to select from. Scase argues that sociologists often have to work very hard to get their informants to formulate a class identification and offer them 'considerable assistance' (Scase, 1992). Where a more open-ended approach is employed the results are likely to be more ambiguous and complex. Lash (1984) interviewed working people in America and found that they came up with a bewildering variety of images of class. A small survey of working people carried out in the early 1990s in the north-east of England, a region where traditional class loyalties and ties are believed still to be stronger than in southern England, found that a majority of respondents did not identify themselves as belonging to any particular class (Bradley, 1994).

Post-modernists approach this question using the concept of identity rather than consciousness, the latter term being associated with discredited **'grand narratives'**. They suggest that class as traditionally defined is no longer a potent source of identity. As the old stable communities based around class and occupation break up, 'collective sources of member-ship' which promoted social identification are displaced (Mercer, 1990). Complexities surrounding changing patterns of work, the changing gender com-position of employment and the rise in unemployment add to the confusion around class. It is suggested that consumer identities may be replacing class identities, especially in view of the importance of media and fashion in most people's lives (Featherstone, 1991).

As Parmar (1990) puts it, 'identities are not fixed but always in a state of flux'. Post-modernists stress that identities are not determined by a single aspect of 'social being' such as class but are made up of a multitude of elements. In such a view, individuals are perpetually adapting their identities in line with per-sonal choice. Crook *et al.* (1992) explore this possi-bility through their idea of 'symbolic communities': numerous foci for belonging and identification are pro-vided by the experience of modern living, especially through the media. Some of these may provide an enduring source of social identification (lesbianism or gayness, for example). Others are relatively transient. They suggest that some such simulated symbolic communities' might develop around worthy causes such as peace or the environment: 'they also form on such diverse unifying themes as soccer, feminism, *Neighbours*, retirement, sociology, Placido Domingo, being gay, socialism, monarchism, *Star Trek* and astrology' (Crook *et al.*, 1992).

These arguments are persuasive in stressing the complexity of processes of social identification. However, the accounts may go too far in dismissing class as a source of identification. It was suggested [previously] that class is now a passive rather than an active identity. We could go further and say that at the moment class identities are submerged identi-ties, pushed out of sight by others which jostle more urgently for public attention. Moreover, people are often reluctant to talk in class terms in a society in which classlessness, though not attained, is seen as the desired ideal. Class becomes a stigmatized or spoiled identity, rather than one which people acknowledge with pride (Bradley, 1994). ...

Yet elements of working-class identification still emerge within communities or through industrial strug-gles. One example is the Miners' Wives Support Groups which evolved during the coal dispute of 1984–5. Suspicious of feminism which they saw as a middle-class movement, the miners' wives nevertheless built a campaign on a specific identification of class and gen-der interests, reflected in their campaign anthem:

> United by the struggle, united by the past
> Here we go, here we go, we're the women of the
> working class!

Class meanings are not yet extinct; and they are more easily judged to be so by people in comfortable positions. Mark Hudson describes tellingly the shock of a middle-class encounter with a traditional work-ing-class community:

> If you had wondered if terms like 'middle class' and 'working class' still had any meaning, or if such a thing as 'working-class culture' could still be said to exist, you were immediately disabused of your illu-sions. The moment you arrived in East Durham, you were *in it* – up to your neck. In East Durham, it often seemed that there *was* nothing else. And ... if it made you feel uneasy, if you couldn't wait to get away from it, that meant you were middle class.
> *(Hudson, 1994)*

Summary and conclusions

... Post-modernism promises a more flexible approach, which could move the analysis of class to a broader framework and deal with its relation to other aspects of inequality. I have argued here that the promise has not yet been fulfilled. Some post-modern accounts of class reinvent older ideas of **embourgeoisment** and classlessness or alternatively reassert the centrality of the changing labour/capital relationship in a global con-text. Others have focused on consumption as increas-ingly central to economic relationships. This promising new direction as yet lacks sufficient empirical backing. There is a tendency simply to *assume* that class aware-ness is vanishing. Research needs to be done to ascer-tain exactly how class meanings and identities relate to other aspects of social identification.

It has proved very difficult to conduct credible soci-ological research into class without using some kind of occupational-based schema to categorize individu-als in the study. Such schemes enable sociologists to study factors such as mobility using sophisticated sta-tistical techniques. It is unlikely that such impressive research tools will be abandoned, but there is need for redefinition of categories to include the excluded sections of the population. It is worth endorsing Marshall's proposal (1988), that study of class should take a more qualitative turn, which could better uncover class meanings.

The final message of this chapter is that neither class, as a set of lived economic relationships, nor class analysis, as a set of social categories, is dead. But there must be recognition of how class relations are shaped by other forms of inequality. As Jonathan Rutherford argues:

> Class is still a conceptual necessity for understand-ing the dynamics of society, but the restructuring of its processes and the decline of old class identi-ties and cultures has coincided with a proliferation and dispersal of other political and social antago-nisms.
> *(Rutherford, 1990)*

References

Bauman, Z. (1992) *Intimations of Postmodernity*, London: Routledge.

Beck, U. (1992) *Risk Society*, London: Sage.

Bottomore, T. and Brym, R. (eds) (1989) *The Capitalist Class*, Hemel Hempstead: Harvester Wheatsheaf.

Bourdieu, P. (1986) *Distinction: a social critique of the judgement of taste*, London: Routledge & Kegan Paul.

Bradley, H. (1994) 'Class and class consciousness in a northern conurbation', in Blackburn, R. (ed.) *Social Inequality in a Changing World*, papers presented to Cambridge Social Stratification Seminar, September 1993, pp. 151–68.

Crook *et al.* (1992) *Postmodernization*, London: Sage.

Dahrendorf, R. (1987) 'The erosion of citizenship and its consequences for us all', *New Statesman*, 12 June, pp. 12–15.

Devine, F. (1992) *Affluent Workers Revisited*, Edinburgh: Edinburgh University Press.

Edgell, S. (1993) *Class*, London: Routledge.

Featherstone, M. (1991) *Consumer Culture and Postmodernism*, London: Sage.

Goldthorpe, J. *et al.* (1969) *The Affluent Worker in the Class Structure*, Cambridge: Cambridge University Press.

Harvey, D. (1989) *The Condition of Post Modernity*, Oxford: Blackwell.

Hudson, M. (1994) *Coming Back Brocken*, London: Jonathon Cape.

Jameson, F. (1991) *Postmodernism or, the Cultural Logic of Late Capitalism*, London: Verso.

Lash, S. (1984) *The Militant Worker: Class and radicalism in France and America*, London: Heinemann.

Lyon, D. (1994) *Postmodernity*, Milton Keynes: Open University Press.

Mann, M. (1970) 'The social cohesion of liberal democracy', *American Sociological Review*, 35, pp. 423–39.

Marshall, G. *et al.* (1988) *Social Class in Modern Britain*, London: Hutchinson.

Mercer, K. (1990) 'Welcome to the jungle: identity and diversity in postmodern politics', in Rutherford, J. (ed.) *Identity*, London: Lawrence & Wishart, pp. 43–71.

Parmar, P. (1990) 'Black feminism, the politics of articulation', in Rutherford, J. (ed.) *Identity*, London: Lawrence & Wishart, pp. 101–26.

Rutherford, J. (ed.) (1990) *Identity*, London: Lawrence & Wishart.

Saunders, P. (1984) 'Beyond housing classes: the sociological significance of private property rights in means of consumption', *International Journal of Urban and Regional Research*, 8 (2), pp. 202–27.

Savage, M. *et al.* (1992) *Property, Bureaucracy and Culture: Middle-class formation in contemporary Britain*, London: Routledge.

Scase, R. (1992) *Class*, Buckingham: Open University Press.

Sivanandan, A. (1990) 'All that melts into air is solid: the hokum of New Times', *Race and Class*, 31, pp. 1–31.

Turner, B. (1988) *Status*, Milton Keynes: Open University Press.

Key terms

The following key terms appear in the text above. They have been defined below to aid with the reading of this item.

globalizing capitalism the increasing tendency for capitalist transnational organizations to operate across the whole globe – both in terms of setting up production facilities and developing markets for their products – with little national loyalty to the country in which they originate.

symbolically simulated communities 'communities' of people who participate in a shared system of values about the symbolic significance of particular patterns of consumption. The shared references to items of consumption allow people to recognize themselves and others through such symbols – however, because consumption emphasizes individuality, it does not result in a 'real' community

ethnographic relating to ethnography – the study of small-scale communities in their naturalistic setting, observing life in as unobtrusive a way as possible

grand narratives large-scale theories that claim to explain the whole of society and its development on the assumption that it is possible to arrive at objective and absolute truth

embourgeiosement the theory, first put forward in the 1960s, that increasing affluence would lead the working class to assume 'bourgeois' – or middle-class – characteristics

Questions

1 At the beginning of the reading Bradley discusses three different 'tendencies' in post-modernist theorizing of class. Identify and describe each one in your own words.

2 Why do some post-modernist thinkers believe that consumption patterns tend to have an equalizing effect while others see them as divisive?

3 How far does Bradley agree with post-modern theories concerning the significance of class as a source of identity?

4 Do you think class is becoming more, or less, significant than other dimensions of stratification? Give reasons for your answer.

Further reading

The following texts may represent a useful starting point for further investigation of the ideas contained in this chapter.

For books covering the subject of social class in an accessible and concise way, see:

Adonis, A. and Pollard, S. (1997) *A Class Act*, London: Hamish Hamilton.

Edgell, S. (1993) *Class*, London: Routledge.

Saunders, P. (1990) *Social Class and Stratification*, London: Routledge.

For more detailed and comprehensive introductory texts, see:

Crompton, R. (1993) *Class and Stratification: an introduction to current debates*, Cambridge: Polity.

Devine, F. (1997) *Social Class in America and Britain*, Edinburgh: Edinburgh University Press.

Hamilton, M. and Hirszowitz, M. (1993) *Class and Inequality*, Hemel Hempstead: Harvester Wheatsheaf.

Scase, R. (1992) *Class*, Milton Keynes: Open University.

Scott, J. (1996) *Stratification and Power*, Cambridge: Polity.

For an up to date neo-Marxist view of social class, see:

Wright, E. O. (1997) *Class Counts*, Cambridge: Cambridge University Press.

For some examples of recent research on class in Britain, see:

Abercrombie, N. and Warde, A. (eds) (1994) *Stratification and Social Inequality: Studies in British society*, Lancaster: Framework Press.

Coursework suggestions

1 Images of class

A research project that would combine stratification with the mass media and culture and identity topic areas would be to carry out an investigation into the representation of social class in the mass media. This could take the form of a semiological analysis of contemporary media output in an attempt to assess the extent to which images of social class are consciously represented in contemporary cultural iconography. It might be interesting to consider ways in which such imagery has changed in the last 40 years. It might be possible to tie this research in with an attempt to ascertain whether or not class is still central as a source of identification for people; the part played by the media; and to what extent there is cultural consensus in the recognition of the imagery of class. For an example of semiological analysis of a television programme, see: Fiske, J and Hartley, J (1979) *Reading Television*. See also Kirby *et al.*, *Sociology in Perspective*, chapter 10, pp. 390–408 and chapter 15, pp. 611–12, for further information on how to develop such an approach.

2 Social class, 'depthlessness' and youth culture

In a related area of study, there has been increasing sociological discussion about the extent to which contemporary youth culture has become classless and, as some would argue, lacking in meaning or purpose. You could attempt to devise a way of testing this view by considering the various ways in which it might be possible to 'read' contemporary youth culture. It could also involve surveying the views of young people themselves on the issue of the alleged depthlessness and classlessness of contemporary popular youth culture. See chapter 11 of this book and Kirby *et al.*, *Sociology in Perspective*, chapter 10, pp. 394–7 and 408–12, for some further ideas on this.

3 How do sociological classifications of social class rate with the public?

A new system of classifying social class in Britain was unveiled in December 1997 by the ESRC (the Economic and Social Research Council). The ESRC Report was commissioned in 1995 by the Office for National Statistics and was edited by Professor David Rose of Essex University. The new scheme, which contains eight classes, is meant to improve on the Registrar General's classification, which dates from 1911. This was featured in *The Times* newspaper on Monday, 15 December 1997. (See also Rose, D. (1995) *A Report on Phase 1 on the ESRC Review of Social Classifications*, Swindon, ESRC.) Carry out a survey of the public to gauge their reaction to the new scheme and perhaps compare it with their views on other classifications in order to assess its usefulness. You could carry out a similar project to look at the best way to incorporate women into such classificatory schemes – see Kirby *et al.*, *Sociology in Perspective*, chapter 4, pp. 121–4, for some examples of classificatory schemes and pp. 153–5, for ideas on women and class theory.

4 Social class in sociology degree courses

Carry out a survey of the sociology departments at British universities, in order to find out the relative importance attached to social class in contemporary degree courses. This could take the form of some quantitative data on the number of courses and amount of time devoted to the sociology of 'class'. This could be combined with qualitative responses from academic staff regarding the salience of class in contemporary sociology.

6

Stratification: sex and gender

Chapter summary

Reading 6.1 **What is a woman?** *page 147*
These extracts are taken from French feminist philosopher Simone de Beauvoir's *The Second Sex*. She argues that many of the life-chance differences and accompanying inequalities between men and women are a product of socialization rather than determined by 'natural' or biological differences.

Reading 6.2 **Sex, gender and society** *page 151*
These extracts from feminist sociologist Ann Oakley's 1972 book *Sex, Gender and Society* argue, after Simone de Beauvoir, that 'nurture' and not 'nature' ordains unequal social and economic roles for men and women. Pointing out that gender roles vary from society to society, Oakley suggests that what may seem fixed and immutable – that women's principal social and economic role is that of wife and mother – is merely a question of belief.

Reading 6.3 **The battle of the sexes** *page 153*
Steve Jones, a professor of genetics, describes some of the recent findings of genetics research into sex and evolution, in this extract from his book *The Language of the Genes*. He argues that sex and sexual behaviour are to an extent determined by genetic and evolutionary necessity. Put another way, men and women have evolved different forms of sexual – and, therefore, social – behaviour in order that human genes may mingle in reproduction and aid the evolutionary process.

Reading 6.4 **A feminist social science** *page 156*
Feminist social scientists Liz Stanley and Sue Wise are highly critical of 'malestream' sociological research methods and methodologies that exclude or marginalize women. In this extract they argue that an 'androcentric' or 'male-focused' sociology entrenches women's oppression, even as it claims to uncover new 'truths' about women's lives. Stanley and Wise suggest that feminist sociologists must build a new version of social science in which research reflects women's lived experiences and demystifies the process by which women's oppression occurs.

Reading 6.5 **Feminism in action** *page 158*
This extract from an article by black feminist campaigner Pragna Patel illustrates the feminist insistence that social theory and social practice should emerge together. Her piece describes some of the campaigns through which her organization, Southall Black Sisters, has pressed for changes to the law and challenged commonly-held perceptions about men's and women's behaviours.

Reading 6.6 **New developments in gender relations** *page 161*
This extract is taken from feminist sociologist Sylvia Walby's recent book, *Gender Transformations*. Walby points out that whilst there have been recent notable changes, and often improvements, in women's lives and life-chances, women are still subject to discrimination and oppression. She concludes that there has been a shift of emphasis within the patriarchal system, from private to public forms of patriarchy.

Reading 6.7 **Men, masculinity and feminism** *page 165*
Sociologist Johnathan Rutherford considers what some have labelled the contemporary crisis of masculinity, outlining the effects of recent social and economic changes on traditional male roles and status and the subsequent 'anti-feminist' reactions that have emerged from some men.

Reading 6.8 **Sex and gender: a contemporary view** *page 167*
Feminist sociologist Ann Oakley describes very recent sociological work on 'sex' and 'gender'. She shows that 'sex', like 'gender', is culturally constructed and must be a site for sociological investigation, too.

Introduction: Reading the sociology of stratification: sex and gender

The sociology of sex and gender addresses the observable differences between men's and women's life-patterns. It asks 'how' and 'why' men and women have access to, and make, different life choices.

Each attempt to answer these 'how' and 'why' questions is framed by a particular analytical perspective. The set of readings that make up this chapter are, in the main, written from a feminist perspective. This is because feminists have done most of the work that has shaped the sociology of sex and gender's current existence.

In fact, a body of work on sex and gender that consciously claims an existence apart from other stratification theories has emerged only fairly recently, although social theorists have always researched and/or speculated upon sex and gender differences. For example, we can look towards the work of genetic and evolutionary theorists and sociobiologists who tend to conclude that life-choice and life-pattern differences between men and women are determined by genetic or biological necessity. They argue that cultural practices reflect this necessity. However, sociologists, and feminist sociologists in particular, have argued that ideas like these are simply a reflection of men's desire to justify the generally more powerful social and economic positions that they hold. They argue that genetic, evolutionary and sociobiological theorists are asking research questions that will tend to uphold traditional views on appropriate social roles when their findings emerge. They have also argued that some male theorists have changed and shaped their data to fit their existing prejudices about sex and gender differences. As feminist sociologists have taken issue with the work of these theorists, genetic, evolutionary and sociobiological ideas have become the accepted province of sociology, dealt with in what is broadly known as the 'nature/nurture' debate.

French feminist philosopher Simone de Beauvoir (1972, originally published in 1953) prefigured this debate in *The Second Sex* (**reading 6.1**). She famously stated: 'One is not born, but rather becomes, a woman.' She meant that the socialization process was primarily responsible for the apparent differences between men's and women's lives, creating strong men who engaged in paid work and acted as the protectors of weak women who bore children at home. This state of affairs mitigated against the attainment of equality and liberty for women, said de Beauvoir, and as such must be overturned. In the extracts from *The Second Sex* reproduced here, de Beauvoir asks 'What is a Woman?', examining mid-century cultural prejudices and the accompanying biological determinist arguments that said women's natural place was in the home.

British feminist sociologist Ann Oakley (1972) takes up de Beauvoir's themes in her book *Sex, Gender and Society* (**reading 6.2**). She argues that although all societies ascribe gender roles to biologically determined 'sex', those roles vary from culture to culture. In her view, this proves that the social and economic roles played by men and women are the product of a society's beliefs about what is correct male and female behaviour rather than laid down by 'nature'. In her view, a comparison of male and female anatomy tends to affirm the similarity of the two sexes as humans rather than underpin their differences. Differentiation between the sexes has occurred in modern societies, she argues, as a result of men's collective desire to stay 'on top'. Claims that women's lives are determined by their potential to bear a child do not hold water, she points out, when most women spend less than 3 per cent of their lives actively engaged in the childbearing process.

Both Simone de Beauvoir and Ann Oakley take issue with the Western cultural tradition that emphasizes men's social and economic domination over women, pitting their evidence that 'femininity' is a matter of socialization, not birth, against the evidence held up by natural scientists researching genetics and evolution, and by sociobiologists. Their attempt to discredit biological determinism is ongoing, with other feminist sociologists and anthropologists taking up and developing their arguments. But whilst feminist and other sociologists have exposed the evident flaws in 'nature's' corner of the ring, biological determinism lingers on, albeit that its exponents are ostensibly more cautious in their conclusions.

Professor of genetics Steve Jones (1994) writes in the introduction to his book *The Language of Genes* (**reading 6.3**):

> In its early days, human genetics suffered greatly from its high opinion of itself. It failed to understand its own limits. Knowledge has brought humility to genetics as to other sciences …

The extract from Jones' book included here steers clear of claims that genetic imperatives *unquestionably* produce gendered cultural practices. But the work in genetics that Jones describes clearly links sex, sexual behaviour and gender to the demands of human genes.

Some feminist social scientists have suggested that the practice of 'science' itself is detrimental to women's interests and is therefore lacking in objectivity. They emphasize its 'male' preoccupations and its tendency to justify men's power relative to women. Liz Stanley and Sue Wise (1993) argue in *Breaking Out Again* that science – in this case social science – can be 'truly scientific' but sexist research methods and methodologies must be eradicated first. In **reading 6.4** – a short extract from their book – they speak of a 'feminist social science' which will help liberate women from oppression.

Contemporary feminist social science research, investigating the inequalities between men and women, is careful to address women's differing life experiences as they are affected by 'race', class, age, sexuality or other factors. Such considerations have risen directly from debate within the feminist movement, as groups of feminist activists have shown that their life experiences, and hence their concerns, differ from those of other women. In **reading 6.5** – an extract from her article 'Third wave feminism and black women's activism' – feminist campaigner Pragna Patel (1997), of London's Southall Black Sisters, discusses the possibilities and difficulties of organizing feminist campaigns that recognize women's differing experiences, perspectives and needs. The reading also serves as an example of the feminist idea that social theory about women's oppression should emerge alongside social practices to end oppression – like the campaigning activities that Patel mentions.

Feminist ideas and campaigns have unquestionably played a part in transforming gender relations in Britain and other Western nations. In **reading 6.6** – taken from her book *Gender Transformations* – feminist sociologist Sylvia Walby (1997) assesses the quantifiable changes that have occurred. She does not foresee an end to patriarchy, however. Rather she updates her earlier work *Theorising Patriarchy* (1990) to conclude that there have been changes in the form rather than in the fact of inequalities between women and men.

Some men have argued, in the face of the transformed gender relations described by Walby, that to coin a popular phrase, 'feminism has gone too far'. Sociologist Johnathan Rutherford (1997) – in **reading 6.7** – rounds up their claims, alongside a short assessment of men's changing social and economic fortunes. In this extract from *Forever England: Reflections on race,* *masculinity and empire* he argues that: 'Men may be doing badly, but women are still worse off.' Anti-feminists David Thomas (1993) and Neil Lyndon (1992) disagree, however, whilst US poet Robert Bly (1991) exhorts men to 'reclaim' their injured masculinities.

The ideas of Thomas, Lyndon and Bly have been attractive to some because they are premised on a simplistic and traditional understanding of 'sex' and its relationship to 'gender'. In **reading 6.8**, feminist sociologist Ann Oakley (1997) debunks that traditional understanding, in an extract from her essay 'A brief history of gender'. Oakley shows how the idea of 'sex' as fixed – based on male and female genital and other characteristics – is a false premise. She argues that 'sex' is as much a construction of history and society as she showed 'gender' to be in her earlier work. She suggests that there is no necessary correlation between 'sex' and 'gender' and that the currently-existing distinction between them serves to legitimize theoretical work from natural scientists on 'sex', whilst 'gender' is left to sociology. 'Sex', she argues, is properly the preserve of sociology too.

Recent work in the sociology of 'sex' and 'gender', like Oakley's, illustrates the nature of the broader discipline. Sociology exists to examine established truths and traditions. Such an examination may allow those truths and traditions to be challenged. This process has occurred as feminist sociologists have proved wrong some previous assumptions about men's and women's behaviours, life-choices and life-patterns. These sociologists, and others whose work is influenced by their ideas, have begun to create a new sociology which represents the lives of women and men in contemporary society more clearly.

References

Bly, R. (1991) *Iron John*, Shaftesbury: Element Books.

Lyndon, N. (1992) *No More Sex War: The failures of feminism,* London: Sinclair-Stevenson.

Thomas, D. (1993) *Not Guilty: In defence of the modern man*, London: Weidenfield & Nicolson.

Walby, S. (1990) *Theorising Patriarchy*, Oxford: Blackwell.

Reading 6.1 **What is a woman?**

Simone de Beauvoir (from) *The Second Sex* (1997, originally published in 1953) London: Vintage, pp. 13–16, 18–21, 29 and 295.

Editorial comments

French feminist philosopher Simone de Beauvoir's book *The Second Sex* is widely held to be a classic of feminist literature. Her work has proved a starting point for many later feminist sociologists as it asks important 'how' and 'why' questions about women's social and economic status.

De Beauvoir argues that men have historically put themselves at the centre of the social world whilst women have been relegated to its margins. Her contention is that social systems and received wisdom tend to aid men in maintaining their powerful social positions. Women's historic role has been to prove to men, through their subordinate existence, just how powerful and important they are. De Beauvoir terms women 'the Other' to men's dominant status as 'the One'.

De Beauvoir's investigations into the emergence of women's constrained life-chances and subordinate status enable her to suggest that women's lives need not necessarily be so. If women are 'made' and not 'born' what is to stop them re-making themselves differently?

Note: You may find Simone de Beauvoir's style of writing difficult to understand at first. Read carefully and slowly, looking up terms that you don't understand. Some terms are defined for you in the key terms list after the reading.

The second sex

WHAT IS A woman? '*Tota mulier in utero*', says one, 'woman is a womb'. But in speaking of certain women, connoisseurs declare that they are not women, although they are equipped with a uterus like the rest. All agree in recognizing the fact that females exist in the human species; today as always they make up about one half of humanity. And yet we are told that femininity is in danger; we are exhorted to be women, remain women, become women. It would appear, then, that every female human being is not necessarily a woman; to be so considered she must share in that mysterious and threatened reality known as femininity. Is this attribute something secreted by the ovaries? Or is it a **Platonic essence**, a product of the philosophic imagination? Is a rustling petticoat enough to bring it down to earth? Although some women try zealously to incarnate this essence, it is hardly patentable. It is frequently described in vague and dazzling terms that seem to have been borrowed from the vocabulary of the seers, and indeed in the times of St Thomas it was considered an essence as certainly defined as the somniferous virtue of the poppy.

But **conceptualism** has lost ground. The biological and social sciences no longer admit the existence of unchangeably fixed entities that determine given characteristics, such as those ascribed to woman, the Jew, or the Negro. Science regards any characteristic as a reaction dependent in part upon a *situation*. If today femininity no longer exists, then it never existed. But does the word *woman*, then, have no specific content? This is stoutly affirmed by those who hold to the philosophy of **the enlightenment**, of **rationalism**, of **nominalism**; women, to them, are merely the human beings arbitrarily designated by the word *woman*. Many American women particularly are prepared to think that there is no longer any place for woman as such; if a backward individual still takes herself for a woman, her friends advise her to be psychoanalysed and thus get rid of this obsession. ... Dorothy Parker has written: 'I cannot be just to books

which treat of woman as woman. ... My idea is that all of us, men as well as women, should be regarded as human beings.' But nominalism is a rather inadequate doctrine, and the anti-feminists have had no trouble in showing that women simply *are not* men. Surely woman is, like man, a human being; but such a declaration is abstract. The fact is that every concrete human being is always a singular, separate individual. To decline to accept such notions as the eternal feminine, the black soul, the Jewish character, is not to deny that Jews, Negroes, women exist today – this denial does not represent a liberation for those concerned, but rather a flight from reality. Some years ago a well-known woman writer refused to permit her portrait to appear in a series of photographs especially devoted to women writers; she wished to be counted among the men. But in order to gain this privilege she made use of her husband's influence! Women who assert that they are men lay claim none the less to masculine consideration and respect. I recall also a young **Trotskyite** standing on a platform at a boisterous meeting and getting ready to use her fists, in spite of her evident fragility. She was denying her feminine weakness; but it was for love of a militant male whose equal she wished to be. The attitude of defiance of many American women proves that they are haunted by a sense of their femininity. In truth, to go for a walk with one's eyes open is enough to demonstrate that humanity is divided into two classes of individuals whose clothes, faces, bodies, smiles, gaits, interests, and occupations are manifestly different. Perhaps these differences are superficial, perhaps they are destined to disappear. What is certain is that they do most obviously exist.

If her functioning as a female is not enough to define woman, if we decline also to explain her through 'the eternal feminine', and if nevertheless we admit, provisionally, that women do exist, then we must face the question: what is a woman?

To state the question is, to me, to suggest, at once, a preliminary answer. The fact that I ask it is in itself significant. A man would never set out to write a book on the peculiar situation of the human male. But if I wish to define myself, I must first of all say: 'I am a woman'; on this truth must be based all further discussion. A man never begins by presenting himself as an individual of a certain sex; it goes without saying that he is a man. The terms *masculine* and *feminine* are used symmetrically only as a matter of form, as on legal papers. In actuality the relation of the two sexes is not quite like that of two electrical poles, for man represents both the positive and the neutral, as is indicated by the common use of *man* to designate human beings in general; whereas woman represents only the negative, defined by limiting criteria, without reciprocity. In the midst of an abstract discussion it is vexing to hear a man say: 'You think thus and so because you are a woman'; but I know that my only defence is to reply: 'I think thus and so because it is true,' thereby removing my subjective self from the argument. It would be out of the question to reply: 'And you think the contrary because you are a man', for it is understood that the fact of being a man is no peculiarity. A man is in the right in being a man; it is the woman who is in the wrong. It amounts to this: just as for the ancients there was an absolute vertical with reference to which the oblique was defined, so there is an absolute human type, the masculine. Woman has ovaries, a uterus: these peculiarities imprison her in her **subjectivity**, circumscribe her within the limits of her own nature. It is often said that she thinks with her glands. Man superbly ignores the fact that his anatomy also includes glands, such as the testicles, and that they secrete hormones. He thinks of his body as a direct and normal connection with the world, which he believes he apprehends objectively, whereas he regards the body of woman as a hindrance, a prison, weighted down by everything peculiar to it. 'The female is a female by virtue of a certain *lack* of qualities,' said Aristotle; 'we should regard the female nature as afflicted with a natural defectiveness.' And St Thomas for his part pronounced woman to be an 'imperfect man', an 'incidental' being. This is symbolized in Genesis where Eve is depicted as made from what Bossuet called 'a supernumerary bone' of Adam.

This humanity is male and man defines woman not in herself but as relative to him; she is not regarded as an **autonomous** being. ... She is simply what man decrees; thus she is called 'the sex', by which is meant that she appears essentially to the male as a sexual being. For him she is sex – absolute sex, no less. She is defined and differentiated with reference to man and not he with reference to her; she is the incidental, the inessential as opposed to the essential. He is the Subject, he is the Absolute – she is the Other. ...

Why is it that women do not dispute male sovereignty? No subject will readily volunteer to become the object, the inessential; it is not the Other who, in defining himself as the Other, establishes the One. The Other is posed as such by the One In defining himself as the One. But if the Other is not to regain the status of being the One, he must be submissive enough to accept this alien point of view. Whence comes this submission in the case of woman? ...

The reason for this is that women lack concrete means for organizing themselves into a unit which can stand face to face with the correlative unit. They have no past, no history, no religion of their own; and they have no such solidarity of work and interest as that of the **proletariat**. They are not even promiscuously herded together in the way that creates community feeling among the American Negroes, the ghetto Jews, the workers of Saint-Denis, or the factory hands of Renault. They live dispersed among the males, attached through residence, housework, economic condition, and social standing to certain men – fathers or husbands – more firmly than they are to other women. If they belong to the **bourgeoisie**, they feel solidarity with men of that class, not with proletarian women; if they are white, their allegiance is to white men, not to Negro women. The proletariat can propose to massacre the ruling class, and a sufficiently fanatical Jew or Negro might dream of getting sole possession of the atomic bomb and making humanity wholly Jewish or black; but woman cannot even dream of exterminating the males. The bond that unites her to her oppressors is not comparable to any other. The division of the sexes is a biological fact, not an event in human history. Male and female stand opposed within a primordial *Mitsein*, and woman has not broken it. The couple is a fundamental unity with its two halves riveted together, and the cleavage of society along the line of sex is impossible. Here is to be found the basic trait of woman: she is the Other in a totality of which the two components are necessary to one another. ...

Now, woman has always been man's dependent, if not his slave; the two sexes have never shared the world in equality. And even today woman is heavily handicapped, though her situation is beginning to change. Almost nowhere is her legal status the same as man's, and frequently it is much to her disadvantage. Even when her rights are legally recognized in the abstract, long-standing custom prevents their full expression in the mores. In the economic sphere men and women can almost be said to make up two castes; other things being equal, the former hold the better jobs, get higher wages, and have more opportunity for success than their new competitors. In industry and politics men have a great many more positions and they monopolize the most important posts. In addition to all this, they enjoy a traditional prestige that the education of children tends in every way to support, for the present enshrines the past – and in the past all history has been made by men. At the present time, when women are beginning to take part in the affairs of the world, it is still a world that belongs to men – they have no doubt of it at all and women have scarcely any. To decline to be the Other, to refuse to be a party to the deal – this would be for women to renounce all the advantages conferred upon them by their alliance with the superior caste. Man-the-sovereign will provide woman-the-liege with material protection and will undertake the moral justification of her existence; thus she can evade at once both economic risk and the **metaphysical** risk of a liberty in which ends and aims must be contrived without assistance. Indeed, along with the ethical urge of each individual to affirm his subjective existence, there is also the temptation to forgo liberty and become a thing. This is an inauspicious road, for he who takes it – passive, lost, ruined – because henceforth the creature of another's will, frustrated in his transcendence and deprived of every value. But it is an easy road; on it one avoids the strain involved in undertaking an authentic existence. When man makes of woman the *Other*, he may, then, expect to manifest deep-seated tendencies towards complicity. Thus, woman may fail to lay claim to the status of subject because she lacks definite resources, because she feels the necessary bond that ties her to man regardless of reciprocity, and because she is often very well pleased with her role as the *Other*. ...

Now, what peculiarly signalizes the situation of woman is that she – a free and autonomous being like all human creatures – nevertheless finds herself living in a world where men compel her to assume the status of the Other. ... How can a human being in women's situation attain fulfilment? What roads are open to her? Which are blocked? How can independence be recovered in a state of dependency? What circumstances limit women's liberty and how can they be overcome? ...

Quite evidently this problem would be without significance if we were to believe that woman's destiny is inevitably determined by physiological, psychological, or economic forces. ...

One is not born, but rather becomes, a woman. No biological, psychological, or economic fate determines the figure that the human female presents in society; it is civilization as a whole that produces this creature which is described as feminine.

Key terms

The following key terms appear in the text above. They have been defined below to aid with the reading of this item.

Platonic essence the ancient Greek philosopher Plato believed that all humans, creatures and objects were vague approximations of a 'pure' archetype that underpinned their beings. This view suggests an archetype of 'woman', with fixed and unchanging 'womanly' qualities, which the behaviour of 'real' women would reflect

conceptualism the belief that the archetype suggested by 'Platonic essence' (above) is the product of philosophical imagination. In other words, no 'real' woman actually conforms to a womanly archetype, but her behaviour is measured by its imagined existence

the enlightenment a belief in the ability of science and reason to create human progress coupled with a questioning of tradition and authority – usually associated with an eighteenth-century philosophical movement

rationalism the belief that science and reason, rather than tradition and superstition, are the keys to understanding the natural and social worlds

nominalism the belief that the naming of an object or a person does not imbue them with certain qualities. In other words, although the word 'woman' has, in the past, been associated with certain qualities and behaviours, the term's definition can be changed

Trotskyite a follower of the views of Leon Trotsky, a Marxist, who believed that conflict between the bourgeoisie and proletariat could be fomented to bring about a revolution sooner than historical forces would otherwise allow

subjectivity viewing other people and events entirely through the lens of one's own perspective, rather than being able to view them in a neutral or 'objective' way

autonomous independent; free to choose

proletariat a Marxist term referring to the urban working class

bourgeoisie a Marxist term referring to the middle class

metaphysical 'metaphysics' is the philosopher's term for the process of thinking about 'thinking' and 'imagination'

Questions

1 Dorothy Parker writes: 'My idea is that all of us, men as well as women, should be regarded as human beings.' Why does de Beauvoir insist that this strategy will not work?

2 De Beauvoir argues that women are 'the Other' to man and that this creates their subordinate status. Give three examples of evidence she provides to support her case.

3 Why does de Beauvoir think some women are reluctant to renounce their status as a subordinate 'Other' and seek social and economic equality?

Reading 6.2 **Sex, gender and society**

Ann Oakley (from) *Sex, Gender and Society* (1972) Avebury: Ashgate, pp. 158, 189–92 and 200–1.

Editorial comments

British feminist sociologist Ann Oakley's early 1970s' work was part of the first visible 'second wave' of feminist sociology. She argues, after Simone de Beauvoir, that 'gender' is distinct from 'sex', citing studies of human anatomy and biology that show men and women to be more alike than different.

She counters the often-asserted argument that women's social role is connected with their child-bearing capacities, pointing out that women in contemporary Western societies are on average likely to spend only 3 per cent of their lifetime directly engaged with bearing children. This being so, there is no reason why they should be permanently associated with this activity.

Sex, gender and society

'SEX' IS A biological term: 'gender' a psychological and cultural one. Common sense suggests that they are merely two ways of looking at the same division and that someone who belongs to, say, the female sex will automatically belong to the corresponding (feminine) gender. In reality this is not so. To be a man or a woman, a boy or a girl, is as much a function of dress, gesture, occupation, social network and personality, as it is of possessing a particular set of genitals.

This rather surprising contention is supported by a number of facts. First, **anthropologists** have reported wide variation in the way different cultures define gender. It is true that every society uses biological sex as a criterion for the ascription of gender but, beyond that simple starting point, no two cultures would agree completely on what distinguishes one gender from the other. Needless to say, every society believes that its own definitions of gender correspond to the biological duality of sex. ...

On the whole, Western society is organized around the assumption that the differences between the sexes are more important than any qualities they have in common. When people try to justify this assumption in terms of 'natural' differences, two separate processes become confused: the tendency to differentiate by sex, and the tendency to differentiate in a particular way by sex. The first is genuinely a constant feature of human society but the second is not, and its inconstancy marks the division between 'sex' and 'gender': sex differences may be 'natural', but gender differences have their source in culture, not nature. Much of the confusion in the debate about sex roles comes from the fact that we tend to speak of 'sex differences' when we are really talking about differences of gender. Because of this the rationale of a society organized around sex differences is never made clear and the idea of a society based on liberation from conventional gender roles is written off as an impossibility.

The aura of naturalness and inevitably that surrounds gender-differentiation in modern society comes, then, not from biological necessity but simply from the beliefs people hold about it. In particular, most people believe that there are inborn differences between the sexes; that differentiation increases social efficiency; and that differentiation is a **natural law**. ...

In reality, of course, as opposed to popular myth, the biological differences between the sexes are often no more significant than those between individuals. Biological variability between individuals increases the further up the evolutionary scale one goes, so that a very wide range of size and function is found in most human organs, tissues and secretions.

The female clitoris and the male penis vary enormously in size, and so do the stomach, the oesophagus, the duodenum, the colon, the liver, the bladder, the heart and the heart rate, the distribution of muscle and fat, the chemical make-up of blood and saliva, the weight and shape of the thyroid gland, and so on. Sometimes the range of differences is not just 50% or 100% but 10 or 50 fold. For example, the size of normal ovaries varies from 2 grams to 10 grams;

normal heart rates of normal males range from 45 to 105 beats per minute, and the heart's pumping capacity may be normally 3.16 litres of blood per minute or 10.8l. On all these measures females vary as much as males, so a significant proportion of males and females are in the same group with respect to size, height, heart rate and hormone levels, to name a few of the parameters. Even in the form of the external genitals there is a range extending from very female to very male, and it is along this range that all individuals, male and female, normal and abnormal, fall. One expert on intersexuality has said that it is impossible to define male and female genital **morphologies** as distinct: they exist as a continuum of possible developments and are thus a constant reminder, not of the biological polarity of male and female, but of their biological identity. ...

The argument for the 'social efficiency' of our present gender roles centres round woman's place as housewife and mother. There is also the more vaguely conceived belief that any tampering with these roles would diminish happiness, but this type of argument has a blatantly disreputable history and should have been discarded long ago. 'Happiness' can be a cover-term for conservatism, and countless evils can be sanctioned in the name of some supposed short-term psychic gain. The most famous historical example is the subjection of negroes to slavery. It is frequently said that too much equality, too little differentiation, threatens the success of marriage. Only if the sexes are complementary (that is, differentiated) can the intense emotional relationship of modern marriage survive. In effect this means that the simple distinction between male and female is elaborated into one between masculine and feminine, with husband and wife differing in their power, their ability to take decisions, their relations with the world outside the home, their leisure interests, and so on. It is now considered all right for wives to work outside the home, but only if they do not compete with their husbands for success in their careers or for earning power: marriage manuals advise working wives to be careful to preserve the traditional balance of power in the home, so as not to 'demasculinize' their husbands (and 'defeminize' themselves). ...

Gender-differentiation persists, then, in industrial society, basically because of the importance people continue to attach to masculinity and femininity. They see a whole mass of distinctions between male and female as necessary to social life. But is our form of gender-differentiation actually related to any goal of social or economic efficiency? Moreover, do men and women like being 'masculine' and 'feminine': are they happy in their gender identities? What difference does sex make? What difference should it make?

In answering these questions, some facts about our own industrial society should be borne in mind. (1) The average woman has between two and three children, and there is a population problem of immense proportions on the horizon. (2) The majority of mothers do not breast-feed their babies – that is, they choose not to. There has been a 30–40% drop in the incidence of breast-feeding in many countries over recent decades, and something like 70–80% of all babies in industrialized cultures are weaned from the breast by the time they leave the maternity hospital. (3) The life span of women is now about seventy-five years, of which probably less than two or three years is spent in a state of pregnancy or lactation. The average woman spends about 6% of her fertile years – or about 3% of her total life span – bound by the reproductive tie. (4) There are no known medical reasons (despite a great deal of research) why pregnancy should interfere with a woman's other activities, whatever these are, for the sake of her health or that of the child. Even assuming that a woman withdraws from other activity during pregnancy and lactation, about 97% of her lifetime remains.

Key terms

The following key terms appear in the text above. They have been defined below to aid with the reading of this item.

anthropologists 'anthropology' is the study of human cultures

natural law unchangeable 'fact' set down by 'nature'

morphologies 'morphology' is the study of bodily forms

Questions

1 How do 'sex' and 'gender' differ? How are they linked?

2 Oakley argues that biological differences between the sexes are of little significance. Use the text to find two pieces of evidence that support her case.

3 How do these extracts from *Sex, Gender and Society* support Simone de Beauvoir's assertion in reading 6.1 that: 'One is not born, but rather becomes, a woman'?

Reading 6.3 **The battle of the sexes**

Steve Jones (from) *The Language of the Genes* (1994) London: Flamingo, pp. 104–13.

Editorial comments

Professor of genetics Steve Jones argues that 'sex' and 'sexual behaviour' are determined at least in part by genetic inheritance and the process of evolution. This underpins the construction of 'gender' and has ramifications for male and female life-patterns. Jones observes what he claims are the influences of genetic and evolutionary inheritances in the behaviour of men and women in contemporary societies.

The battle of the sexes

ALTHOUGH THE MACHINERY for deciding the sex of a fertilized egg is simple, the road to adult gender is a complicated and difficult one. Sexuality is a flexible thing. In some creatures, this is obvious. In crocodiles, sex is determined by the temperature at which the eggs develop, so that females must lay their clutches in a place with a temperature range which allows both males and females to be produced. In certain fish, embarrassment – or social pressure – is important. A shoal of females is guarded by a male. If he is removed there is a period of confusion, until one of the females changes sex and assumes his role.

Sex determination is hence less rigidly programmed than might at first appear. The nature of the switch from female to male varies from species to species. Even in those, like ourselves, where it is determined early in development there are many chances to take one turning rather than the other on the road to adulthood. The male-determining gene switches on a cascade of different hormones. Sometimes, these go wrong, and there is a whole range of hermaphrodites and intersexes which are due to failures in one step or the other in the sexual chain.

Once sexuality gets started enormous consequences flow from it. Most of natural history is the scientific study of sex, as the characters which differentiate birds, insects and flowers from each other are largely associated with reproduction. The diversity of sexual choices in the living world means that comparing the sex lives of different creatures must say a lot about how sex evolved and why animals behave the way they do. Although humans are in many ways distinct from the rest of creation, it might be possible to learn something about our own reproductive habits by looking at those of other species.

Many people have attempted to draw sweeping conclusions about humankind from studies of the private lives of monkeys and apes. It is always dangerous, and usually futile, to try to explain human behaviour in the simple terms which apply to animals. Attempts to do so usually fall into the 'pathetic fallacy', the literary trap which sees emotions mirrored in the weather or the landscape. Occasionally – very occasionally, as in *Wuthering Heights* – this works, but it usually ends in bathos. **Anthropology** has the same problem. It is fatally easy to read into the animal world what we would like to see in our own, to explain the human condition as an inevitable consequence of our biology. Even Charles Darwin, a veritable Brontë among sociobiologists, was at fault. Hidden in his unpublished notebooks is the damning phrase 'Origin of Man now proved – metaphysics must flourish – he who understands baboons will do more towards metaphysics than Locke.'

Metaphysics is one thing, sex another. The Nobel Prize-willing animal **behaviourist** Konrad Lorenz saw us as 'killer apes' anxious to pass on our own genes by murdering the opposition, which may have explained his own early flirtation with the Nazis; and any decent airport has a row of paperbacks whose embossed covers purport to explain human nature as emerging from a history as primates with one or other sexual and social preference. Until recently the study of sexual behaviour was little more than a set of unconnected anecdotes. It has been transformed by the rebirth of one of the oldest techniques in biology. Comparative anatomy is what convinced Darwin that men and women are related to monkeys and apes. Now there is a new science of comparative behaviour which reveals a great deal about how and why sexual conduct evolved.

As many people know to their cost, sex is filled with strife. The very existence of males and females is the resolution of a war to pass on cytoplasmic genes. There is also conflict between males to find a mate and between males and females as they invest time and effort in bringing up the young. Sometimes the disputes are obvious. There is a struggle between males, leading to the evolution of spectacular organs such as red deer's antlers, which are used by the winners to monopolize the females. Other characters – such as a baboon's brightly coloured face – are more subtle statements of male talent and may evolve because they are preferred by the opposite sex.

There is little evidence (in spite of much prurient speculation about beards, breasts and buttocks) that humans have attributes of this kind but, as in most animals, conflict between human males is greater than between females. Being a man is a dangerous thing. At birth there are about 105 males to every 100 females, but this drops to 103 to 100 at the age of sixteen and by the age of seventy there are twice as many women as men. Men have more accidents, more infectious diseases and kill each other more often than do women. The murder rate, an almost exclusively male preserve, peaks at the age of twenty-five both in London and in Detroit (although the actual rate in the latter is forty times higher than in London). This is close to the prime age of reproduction. Oddly enough, eunuchs and monks live for longer than do males condemned to a normal sex life. ...

The human mating system is, of course, flexible and can shift quickly (as in the recent change towards serial monogamy – constancy within a relationship, but more than one relationship in a lifetime). There seem to be some general rules. Strict monogamy is rare. In most societies, men have more than one mate during their lives. Polygamy (one male with several wives at once) is far more common than polyandry, the opposite pattern, although this exists in Tibet. In polygamous societies, as a few men have many wives some must have none.

The primates illustrate other skirmishes in the battle of the sexes. Some suggest a more salacious past for humankind than does the modest difference in the size of men and women. The struggle between males does not stop once mating has taken place. There is competition between sperm, too. Often a female will use the sperm of the male she mated with last, which means that a successful sperm donor must ensure that no other male mates with her until the eggs are fertilized. This is why dogs stay paired after copulation. The male is guarding the female against intruders.

An even less subtle way of ensuring the success of one's own sperm is to flood out the contribution of the preceding male. There is, among different species of primate, quite a good fit between the size of the testes and the extent of male promiscuity. Chimpanzees, the Lotharios of the primate world, have enormous testes while gorillas, in spite of rumour to the contrary, are far less well endowed. Humans, surprisingly enough, are not too different from chimps in this respect – which may say some startling things about our past. Real enthusiasts for evolutionary explanations point that men produce more sperm when returning to their partner after a long absence, possibly to overwhelm any alien sperm which may have intruded. There is also the question – as yet unanswered by science – as to why, in penis size, man stands alone. There are limits to what biology can

explain and this may be beyond them, although it does seem that there is a new genre of evolutionary pornography just waiting to be written. ...

Charles Darwin noticed that sexual selection (as he called it) might do much more than improve a male's ability to defeat his ardent competitors. He was much concerned with the evolution of characters with no obvious biological advantage (such as the peacock's tail – or the large human penis, for that matter). The struggle for sex might, Darwin thought, have more subtle consequences than just the evolution of large and aggressive males. If females prefer, for one reason or another, a particular male attribute (such as a brightly coloured tail), then males who have it will reproduce more successfully. The bright tail or its equivalent will become more common in later generations and the showiest males will once again be preferred by the females. In time there may evolve bizarre structures which are so expensive to the unfortunate males who carry them that they can evolve no further. Female choice may, Darwin suggested, be as important a part of the sexual equation as is male aggression.

In his book on the subject, *Sexual Selection and the Descent of Man*, he went further. He suggested that mating preferences explained why human races looked so different. It was not that they had evolved to fit the place in which they live, but as a consequence of arbitrary choice of a mate. In different places, those looking for a partner may have made different – and quite capricious – choices. In time, the people of the world diverged: for example, Darwin speculated, those with darker skins might have been seen as more attractive in Africa and those with lighter in Europe. There is certainly plenty of evidence that people tend to marry others who are similar to themselves in intelligence, colour and – strongest of all – length of the middle finger, but there is as yet no real evidence that such choices are important in evolution. ...

Any discussion of the evolution of sex seems doomed to stray for a time on to such untamed shores of speculation. One theory of why males may carry eccentric characters is known as the handicap principle. It claims that they evolve cripplingly expensive ornaments to demonstrate to potential spouses that their genes are good enough to bear the cost. This is, at least, an amusing idea. It has been used to explain bizarre patterns of human behaviour such as drug abuse. Perhaps men take alcohol, tobacco or stronger drugs to demonstrate to women how tough they are, how their constitutions can cope with mistreatment and how they might make excellent fathers as a result. One of the most baffling findings of modern anthropology is the discovery of small tubes in the tombs of Maya Indians. Handicappers believe that these were used to give ritual enemas of toxic drugs to the most powerful men, guaranteeing instant intoxication and a widely admired statement of sexual prowess. The habit has not yet spread to the streets of New York.

Conflict between males for the attention of females is often obvious and may be painfully close to the experience of the biologists who study it. There are also plenty of chances for conflict between males and females. In some animals, the reluctance of females to accept a new mate, however persistent he might be, arises because males invest less in bringing up offspring. It pays them to mate and run; to try and father as many children with as many females as possible. Females need to be more cautious. As it costs so much to produce and bring up a child they may choose the male who is likely to be the best father and reject the rest.

This conflict of interest is sometimes brutally obvious. In many creatures males kill a mother's offspring by another male with the aim of making her available to themselves. In the Langur Monkeys of India, most of the young die for this reason. There is even a form of pre-natal cannibalism. Pregnant female mice and horses exposed to a new male reabsorb their foetuses, a behaviour which may have evolved because of the near certainty that if the offspring are born they will be killed.

Humans reveal the intersexual conflict in less blatant ways. Their battle is an economic rather than a mortal one. If tribal people are any guide, there is more polygamy in societies which have invented private property, as women prefer well endowed mates. When wealth is concentrated into few hands life becomes more like that of a gorilla, with the richest males monopolizing the females. For example, the philoprogenitive (and opulent) Moulay Ismail the Bloodthirsty of Morocco admitted to 888 children. Although we in the West now seem to be moving towards the chimpanzees, with most men having at least a chance of finding Ms Right, in some societies mating success is still related to wealth. Among the Kipsigis people of south-west Kenya women prefer rich husbands. A wealthy man may have as many as a dozen wives and eighty children and the more land a man has the more wives he is likely to possess. Many of the poorest males leave the community as teenagers and have no children at all. The women nearly all have families of about the same size. There is an economic conflict between the sexes with men providing the capital and women choosing where to invest. In Britain, too, men from higher social groups have many more partners than do those who are less well off.

When one people conquers another it is the men who capitalize on their dominant position to find new mates. In the 'Cape Coloured' population of South Africa (which is intermediate in appearance between Africans and Europeans) most of the genes are halfway between those of modern black and white South Africans. However, nearly all the DNA of their Y chromosomes are of the European type, showing how white males took advantage of their economic domination over black females in earlier centuries.

A battle between the sexes may help to explain another unusual attribute of human reproduction. Women are the only female primates who do not make it obvious when they are most fertile. In dogs and many other mammals the female goes 'on heat'. Most female primates advertise the two or three days in each cycle when they are most likely to conceive. Often, this is accompanied by a frenzy of copulation with a series of males. Before modern medicine, most women (and all men) were unaware of when the fertile period was. Women's reproductive coyness may perhaps reflect the change in the economic relation of the sexes which came with the beginnings of society. It might be an attempt to resolve the conflict between male promiscuity and the female's need to ensure the care of her offspring. By concealing when she is fertile she ensures constant attention from her mate. If he is not sure when she can conceive then he dare not leave her for a new woman in case another male takes advantage of his absence. This is, of course, historical speculation with no direct evidence for or against it.

Reference

Darwin, C. (orig. pub. 1871) *The Descent of Man and Selection in Relation to Sex*, Amherst, NY: Prometheus.

Key terms

The following key terms appear in the text above. They have been defined below to aid with the reading of this item.

anthropology the study of human cultures

metaphysics the philosopher's term for the process of thinking about 'thinking' and 'imagination'

behaviourist 'behaviourism' is the belief that objective observation of humans and creatures under fixed conditions (e.g. in a laboratory) can aid understanding of behaviours

Questions

1 Jones warns against drawing too great a parallel between the behaviour of animals and that of humans. Why?

2 How do Jones' comments that males need to 'mate and run' whilst females need to be 'more cautious'

support traditional views on appropriate sexual behaviour? Does the existence of effective contraception undermine his theory?

3 Jones describes and interprets male and female sexual behaviour in terms of male competition for the attention of females and female discernment. How else might the behaviours he described be interpreted? How, for example, might the idea that men

use alcohol and drugs to impress women be challenged? How might female reluctance to accept the advances of a male be alternatively interpreted?

4 What is the importance for sociologists of Jones' statement, at the close of this extract: 'This is, of course, historical speculation with no direct evidence for or against it'?

Reading 6.4 **A feminist social science**

Liz Stanley and Sue Wise (from) *Breaking Out Again: Feminist ontology and epistemology,* 2nd edn. (1993) London: Routledge, pp. 164–6.

Editorial comments

Feminist social scientists Liz Stanley and Sue Wise argue that traditional 'malestream' sociological research methods are simply not geared to explaining women's lives and in some cases actively work to exclude women's experiences and ideas. When this is the case, sociology simply acts as a prop to existing myths about women's supposed capabilities and life-patterns.

Stanley and Wise want to help create an inclusive social science that speaks as much to women's lives, as men's. They argue that this may begin to overcome inequalities of gender because when women understand how and why oppression occurs, they can more effectively combat it.

Importantly, Stanley and Wise write as 'we'. This is because they want to challenge the accepted sociological practice of writing in the 'objective' third person. Feminist sociologists tend to be wary of supposed 'objectivity'. Many, including Stanley and Wise, argue that 'objectivity' is a male-centred concept and that supposed objective research is likely to support existing male structures of power.

A feminist social science

WE BELIEVE THAT a feminist social science should begin with the recognition that 'the personal', direct experience, underlies all behaviours and actions. We need to find out what it is that we know and what it is that we experience. We need to reclaim, name and rename our experiences and our knowledge of the social world we live in and daily construct. We conceptualize this world through a language provided for us by sexist society, and by a thoroughly **androcentric** social science. We need to reject this imposed language and to construct our own social science, a social science which starts from women's experience of women's reality. Without doing this we can have no truly feminist social science; we can only have a social science in which women's experiences are researched and analysed using the conceptual procedures, the methods of research, and the research models provided by sexism.

The kind of feminist social science and research we envisage is not one which is concerned only with what goes on in our heads, with a psychology of inner thoughts and feelings. Women, like all other people, are *social* beings. We live in a social world with other social beings; and merely living requires that we

behave in social ways. We interact with other people at all times, either physically or in our minds. It is all of these *social* actions and reactions which should properly be the concern of feminist social science.

Much contemporary social science appears to us over-concerned with predicting the motives and feelings of the researched. However, social scientists frequently cannot or will not enter into the world as it is experienced by the people who are its subjects. Virginia Woolf (1977, orig. pub. 1931) has expressed something of our feelings about this. Discussing her attempt to understand the experiences of guildswomen at a conference of co-operative working women, she wrote that, however hard she attempted to participate in these women's emotions, she continued to feel that she was a benevolent spectator, irretrievably cut-off from them. She goes on to argue that 'fictitious sympathy' differs from 'real sympathy' and is defective because it isn't based upon *sharing* the same important emotions; and the only way to share emotions is to share experiences.

The basis of our objections to social science attempts to deduce or predict feelings and emotions in that these derive from the 'fictitious sympathy' of people who remain outside of the experiences they write about and claim competence in. Instead of writing about how they know what they claim to know (which would necessitate locating the social scientist *within* the research process) they write about the experiences of others as though these were directly available to them. That these are necessarily transformed in a researcher's construction of them is ignored.

Feminist research as we envisage it wouldn't take this false sympathy as its basis. It would instead explore the basis of our everyday knowledge as women, as feminists, *and* as social scientists. As we do this we must make available to other people the reasoning procedures which underlie the knowledge produced out of research. We must tap our experiences of 'being a researcher', and as feminist researchers with feminist consciousness this involves tapping our experiences as *feminists* in any social situation.

This kind of research is necessary and even crucial to the feminist enterprise. We see it as crucial to an understanding of both women's oppression and women's liberation; and we insist that feminist social science should be concerned with everyday life because of this. But there is another reason for doing so as well. 'Everyday life' is what we spent our lives doing; is what we are involved in all of our waking, and a large part of our sleeping, hours. What all people spend most of their time doing must obviously be the subject of research. What women spend most of their time doing must obviously be the subject of feminist research.

We need to know how, in minute detail, all facets of the oppressions of all women occur. To talk blithely of 'the family', 'capitalism' or 'men' as the reasons for women's oppressions may in a sense be true. But this merely re-states the problem. It doesn't tell us the mechanisms, the experiences, the behaviours, the looks, conversations, which are involved. Nor does 'the abolition of the family', 'the over-throw of capitalism' or 'no more men' give us any answer, any solution to these problems.

If we are to resist oppression, then we need the *means* to do so. The means to resist oppression, we believe, are to be found where all of our oppressions are themselves to be found. Without knowing *how* oppression occurs we cannot possibly know *why* it occurs; and without knowing how and why it occurs we cannot find out how to avoid its occurrence, how it is that liberation might be achieved. Liberation has to start somewhere; we cannot leap into a liberated world overnight. We must necessarily effect many small liberations in many small and apparently insignificant aspects of our lives, or we shall never begin 'the revolution'.

Reference

Woolf, V. (1977, orig. pub. 1931) 'Introductory letter', in Davin, A. (ed.) *Life As We Have Known It*, London: Virago.

Key term

The following key term appears in the text above. It has been defined below to aid with the reading of this item.

androcentric having a male focus in sociological or other research

Questions

1 Why do feminist social scientists claim that sociology is 'androcentric'? Give examples of 'andocentrism' in any social science research you have studied.

2 Why, according to Stanley and Wise, is feminist-style research ultimately necessary to women's liberation?

3 Stanley and Wise refer to first-wave feminist writer Virginia Woolf's idea that 'fictitious sympathy' falsifies the research process. Define 'fictitious sympathy' in your own words.

4 Choosing a reading about gender from elsewhere in this book, describe how the criticism of 'fictitious sympathy' could be applied.

Reading 6.5 **Feminism in action**

Pragna Patel (from) 'Third wave feminism and black women's activism', in Heidi Safia Mirza (ed.) *Black British Feminism: a reader* (1997) London: Routledge, pp. 256–60.

Editorial comments

Pragna Patel is a long-standing member of the black feminist campaigning group Southall Black Sisters (SBS). This reading documents some of the recent work of SBS on domestic violence and associated reforms of policing methods and the judicial system. Patel comments on the way in which this work has effected new alliances amongst feminist campaigners with differing and even contradictory views on the causes of women's oppression.

Working with women from differing ethnic, cultural and socio-economic backgrounds means that issues of 'race' and 'class' are central to Patel's thinking and inform her actions. Her work also reflects the feminist view that social theory and social practice should emerge together.

Third wave feminism and black women's activism

WHAT FOLLOWS [retraces] some of the campaigns of Southall Black Sisters (SBS) and our sister organization, Brent Asian Women's Refuge. Our struggles have, out of necessity, arisen from the routine experiences of many Asian, Africa, Caribbean and other women who come to these centres with stories of violence, persecution, imprisonment, poverty and homelessness experienced at the hands of their husbands, families and/or the state. In attempting to meet the challenges they pose in their demands for justice for themselves and for women generally, we have had to organize autonomously. But we have always endeavoured to situate our practice within wider anti-racist and socialist movements, involving alliances and coalitions within and across the minority and majority divides. This has not always been easy, but it is the only way we know in which a new and empowering politics can be forged.

By organizing in women's groups and refuges, many of us have fought for **autonomous** spaces and for the right for our own voices to be heard in order to break free from the **patriarchal** stranglehold of the family. In the process we have also had to challenge the attitudes of the wider society, as well as the theory and practice of social policy and legislation which seeks to restrict our freedom to make informed choices about our lives. Our organizations and our practice are critical in unmasking the failures, not only of our communities and the state and wider society, but perhaps more tellingly, of so-called multi-culturalist and anti-racist policies.

Throughout our campaigns on domestic violence, whilst countering racist stereotypes about the 'problematic' nature of South Asian families, SBS has sought to highlight not only the familiar economic and legal obstacles faced by all women struggling to live free of abuse, but also the particular plight of Asian women; language barriers, racism, and the specific role of culture and religion which can be used to sanction their subordinate role and to circumscribe their responses. Culture and religion in all societies act to confer legitimacy upon gender inequalities, but these cultural constraints affect some women more than others in communities where 'culture' carries the burden of protecting minority identities in the face of external hostility. We have had to formulate demands and strategies which recognize the plurality of our experiences, without suppressing anything for the sake of political expediency. Alliances have been crucial in this, not only in gaining wider support, but also in breaking down mutual suspicion and stereotypes, and to ensure that some rights are not gained at the expense of others.

We began our protests in the early 1980s over the murder of Mrs Dhillon and her three daughters by her husband who burnt them to death. In 1984 we took to the streets in response to the death of Krishna Sharma, who committed suicide as a result of her husband's assaults. Organizing with other women in very public ways, through demonstrations and pickets, we broke the silence of the community. Until that point there had been not a single voice of protest from either progressive or conservative elements within the community. The women who led the demonstrations had themselves fled their own families in Southall, but returned to join us with scarves wrapped around their faces so that they might escape recognition. We demanded and won the support of many white women in the wider feminist movement, although initially they were hesitant in offering support for fear of being labelled 'racist'! One of our slogans – 'self-defence is no offence' – was appropriated from the anti-racist 'street-fighting' traditions but, ironically it has now become the much quoted slogan of the wider women's movement against male violence in Britain. The form of our protests drew directly from the varied and positive feminist traditions of the Indian sub-continent. We picketed directly outside Krishna Sharma's house, turning accepted notions of honour and shame on their heads. It is the perpetrators of violence, we shouted, who should be shamed and disrobed of their honour by the rest of the community, not the women who are forced to submit. Another slogan – 'black women's tradition, struggle not submission' – was first coined on this demonstration, and that, too, has been adapted to become the rallying cry of feminists against male violence in this country.

The lessons of those early years has ensured that we have understood the importance of campaigns and direct action as an essential means of articulating the needs of the women who turn to us daily. From the murder of Balwant Kaur by her husband at the Brent refuge in 1985, to the life imprisonment of Kiranjit Ahluwalia for killing her violent husband in 1989, our response has been driven by a recognition that those tragedies reflected, albeit in extreme forms, the day-to-day experiences of many Asian women facing violence in the home. Over the years we have managed to retain a campaigning edge to our work, while also providing day-to-day services.

The Kiranjit Ahluwalia campaign

The campaign to free Kiranjit Ahluwalia following her murder conviction in December 1989 illustrated the need for, and the potential impact of, alliances as a form of political action. We had to raise the specificity of her experiences as an Asian woman, drawing on her own depiction of her life, but we also had to draw out the connections with the experiences of other women in order to make demands relevant to all women in this society. Black and white, young and old, activists and non-activists, we found ourselves involved in one of the main empowering mobilizations of women against injustice seen for a long time. The women who use our centre and refuge wept and laughed with joy at Kiranjit's eventual release. Many from across the religious, caste and class divisions claimed her personal triumphs as their own personal and collective victory.

In July 1991, Sara Thornton lost her appeal to overturn her murder conviction because the legal system was not then ready to accept a feminist critique of the **homicide** laws. Her hunger strike and the consequent publicity, against the background of the case of Joseph McGrail who was freed after kicking his alcoholic wife to death, struck a chord with the public which was to change the course of the Kiranjit Ahluwalia campaign. In the face of government intransigence, there was growing support for our critique of the legal system's untenable position on 'battered women'. Every day yielded more voices of support, ranging from almost all sections of the media and

lawyers, civil servants, members of Parliament across the political divides, academics, activists and the general public. On our part, we were able to mobilize women in SBS and at the refuge; women who had experienced violence and who understood Kiranjit's tragic act.

Our main allies were radical feminists, with their long and rich history in campaigning around violence against women, and Asian women, particularly those working in refuges and women's centres. The unity we forged had two main aims: to ensure the release of battered women who kill their tormentors and who are unjustly incarcerated, and to demand a reform of the homicide legislation responsible for their imprisonment. There are many points of contention within the alliance as to the nature of the demands we ought to make of the state. Should we agitate for a reform of the existing laws as a tactical demand, or should we campaign for entirely new homicide laws that more accurately reflect women's daily experience of violence? Should we aim for new laws which are specific to women, or should they subsume areas such as racial violence and harassment? These tensions were never entirely resolved, nor could they have been, but despite divergent and sometimes irreconcilable views, we have been able to sustain the alliance.

Recently our campaign for the reform of homicide legislation, and more generally for changes in the criminal justice system, have led us into a new temporary alliance with more long-established women's organizations with a far from radical image, such as the Townswomen's Guild and the Women's Institute. Although we have only been able to come together on the narrow issue of changing the **law of provocation**, it is, nevertheless, a tactically important alliance of wider political significance. Conservative and liberal women from these groups have joined us in mutual recognition of the fact that the law fails women. The outcome in this instance is less important than the process by which consciousness around domestic violence can continue to grow. The established women's groups are extremely nervous about the radical elements within the alliance, but they are still soldiering on with us to organize a mass lobby at the Houses of Parliament, and a letter-writing campaign to the Home Secretary. The alliance has already led to the right-wing Home Secretary, Michael Howard, developing a defensive posture when responding to letters by members of the Women's Institute and the Townswomen's Guild. A few years ago we would not have dared participate in such a forum, fearing that our politics or terms of reference might be compromised by such co-operation. We are now much more confident about the nature and boundaries of our participation in political alliances with other women's groups.

Since the Kiranjit Ahluwalia campaign we have witnessed a resurgence in campaigns around violence against women in the South Asian and other minority communities, often in consultation with one another. These campaigns seek to redefine the relationship of women to the criminal justice system and to change the language of wider movements. So, the term 'miscarriage of justice', which initially meant the wrongful conviction and punishment of those who are innocent, has been extended to include those who are routinely failed by the criminal justice system in other ways, through the failure of the police and the prosecuting authorities to protect women from abusive partners, to the transgressions of women which the law is unable to comprehend in its wider context. Internationally, too, the debates around domestic violence and other forms of male violence are defining women's rights as human rights, and issues like rape as crimes against humanity. These developments open up the potential for creating women's alliances which transcend artificial national boundaries.

By virtue of campaigns like ours, the law has been forced to take into account the social conditions and pressures which push women into contact or conflict with the criminal justice system. The years of hard campaigning by feminists against male violence are beginning to bear some fruit within the legal system, although contradictions remain. Gains in some areas of the law are offset by losses in others, and there is no room for complacency. In the Kiranjit Ahluwalia case, the legal definition of provocation has shifted to reflect the inability of some women to retaliate immediately after an assault or threat, and expert evidence to show the psychological impact of cumulative provocation was admitted for the first time. However, the attempt to fit complex realities into neat legal definitions can constrict women in ways which deny their anger and agency, rendering them less threatening to the status quo. Thus the '**battered women syn-**drome' has been used to explain women's inaction in the face of repeated violence, but in the process the experience of women is medicalized and relegated to the realms of mental disorder. In other words, women are not 'permitted' to be angry or to locate their actions in a socio-economic context or in the failures of the institution of the family.

As feminists we have to be careful about the uncritical acceptance of superficially attractive solutions offered by the state in response to our campaigns and demands. For example, recent shifts in police attitudes and practices on domestic violence may appear to have 'solved' the problem of previous police indifference. The domestic violence units and multi-agency forums which are the practical outcome of these shifts in police strategy have done nothing to bring the issue of police accountability any closer to being addressed. In our experience the police still continue to fail women in their response to women's calls for help, and this should not inspire any confidence in the view that the police are now 'on our side'.

Similarly, as feminists we have to be careful not to separate ourselves off from other human and civil rights demands that at first sight may not appear to be a feminist concern. For instance, the abolition of the right to silence will have a profound effect on the rights of many: blacks, lesbians and gays, new age travellers and women. Kiranjit Ahluwalia exercised her right to silence at her original criminal trial, but had she been forced into the witness box in the vulnerable, confused and frightened state she was then in, the outcome of her appeal might have been very different. The legal system is not like an onion which, if peeled, might reveal an egalitarian core. The institutions of the state represent and articulate vested interests, constantly shifting ground the better to maintain the status quo. Any gains we make can be reversed or diluted in the face of power and privilege.

Key terms

The following key terms appear in the text above. They have been defined below to aid with the reading of this item.

autonomous independent; free to choose

patriarchal 'patriarchy' is a system of male oppression of women, identified by feminists

homicide unlawful killing of another person

law of provocation the idea that one person who has unlawfully killed another can plead that they did it in self-defence after being provoked by the other's actions

'battered woman syndrome' the view that women who are physically abused by their partner become psychologically damaged and are thus unable to leave the abusive relationship

Questions

1 The campaigning group Southall Black Sisters (SBS) addresses issues of 'race' and 'ethnicity' as well as 'gender'. Give examples from the text that show how these concerns are integrated in their work.

2 Feminists and women from widely differing backgrounds with widely differing perspectives are working together on the domestic violence campaigns that Patel describes. Give examples from the text that show how they have been able to surmount their differences and work together.

3 Do Patel's comments on the recent work of SBS demonstrate a link between sociological thinking and the potential for social and/or legislative change? Give reasons for your answer.

Reading 6.6 **New developments in gender relations**

Sylvia Walby (from) *Gender Transformations* (1997) London: Routledge, pp. 1–7.

Editorial comments

Feminist sociologist Sylvia Walby's work on the nature of patriarchy – set out in her books *Patriarchy At Work* (1986) and *Theorising Patriarchy* (1990) – is developed in *Gender Transformations* (1997).

Walby argues that whilst women in Britain may now have more freedom than ever before, they are still subject to forms of patriarchy. This means, for example, that while more women are now in paid work than ever before, occupational and industrial segregation tend to keep those jobs low-paid and part-time. Walby's view is that whilst women are more able to determine their individual life-courses, as regards their personal relationships and domestic environments, they are still subject to an oppressive public patriarchy.

References

Walby, S. (1986) *Patriarchy At Work: Patriarchal and capitalist relations in employment,* Cambridge: Polity.

Walby, S. (1990) *Theorising Patriarchy,* Oxford: Blackwell.

Gender transformations

Fundamental transformations

FUNDAMENTAL TRANSFORMATIONS OF gender relations in the contemporary Western world are affecting the economy and all forms of social relations. The driving forces behind these changes are the increase in women's education and paid employment and new forms of political representation of women's interests. These changes have implications not only for women's positions in wider society, in all their diversity, but also for the overall economy and polity.

For example, women are now almost half of all workers in the contemporary UK. In 1995 they were 49.6 per cent of employees in employment and indeed in one-third of local labour markets women were the majority of those in work. This is a major transformation of gender relations in employment. These transformations are having far-reaching implications not only for gender relations but for social relations in society as a whole, including class relations. However, much of this new employment of women is not performed under conditions equal to those of men. Another example is in education, where girls are passing more exams at schools than boys, creating new possibilities for young women. However, these are achievements for younger women, and older women have significantly fewer qualifications than their male peers.

The system of gender relations is changing, from one which was based on women being largely confined to the domestic sphere, to one in which women are present in the public sphere, but still frequently segregated into unequal positions. This change ultimately derives from the winning of political citizenship by first-wave feminism in the early twentieth century in the context of an increasing demand for women's labour in a developing economy and women's access to education at all levels. The patterns of inequality between women and men have changed as a result, but in complex ways, not simply for better or worse.

Gender restructuring affects women differently according their position, not only in class and ethnic relations, but also within different household forms. Diversity among women is a result not only of class and ethnicity, but also of changes in the forms of **patriarchy**, of **gender regime**, giving rise to significant generational differences.

Convergence and polarization in gender relations

Both convergence and polarization mark the contemporary restructuring of gender relations. Convergence between the genders is occurring among some young people especially where increased access to education and the labour market for some young women has reduced the differences and inequality between the sexes in qualifications and work. Polarization is occurring between women of different generations, as young women gain qualifications and labour market positions which are out of reach to older women who built their lives around a different set of patriarchal opportunity structures. Those younger women who do not achieve educational qualifications and entry to good jobs are also disadvantaged, and are especially poor if they become mothers without a supporting partner. To a significant extent women are polarizing between those, typically younger, educated and employed, who engage in new patterns of gender relations somewhat convergent with those of men, and those, particularly disadvantaged women, typically older and less educated, who built their life trajectories around patterns of **private patriarchy**. These new patterns are intertwined with diversities and inequalities generated by social divisions including class, ethnicity and region.

New developments in gender relations

Changes have been taking place unevenly in different aspects of gender relations, in the six patriarchal structures outlined in *Theorising Patriarchy*. The leading change has been the increase in women in education and paid employment, though this is tempered by the variable ways in which women are involved, for instance, the poor conditions of the nearly half of employed women who work part-time and by the tenacity of occupational and industrial segregation. The wages gap between women and men full-time workers has narrowed, though not that for part-timers. There has been a dramatic closing of the gap in educational qualifications of young men and women, both at school and university.

The structure of the typical household has changed, with an increasing propensity for women to live and to rear children outside of marriage, especially as a result of increased rates of divorce and cohabitation. The divorce rate in the UK has risen from 0.5 per 1,000 in 1960, to 3.1 per 1,000 in 1993, and is now the highest in the European Union. The proportion of women aged 18–49 who are married has declined from 74 per cent in 1979 to 57 per cent in 1994. The proportion of families headed by a lone parent has increased from 8 per cent in 1971 to 23 per cent in 1994. Women are more independent from men, but poorer. The meaning of this, in terms of equality and justice for women, is hard to assess, especially since these meanings are culturally and ethnically specific. Different ethnic groups have varied patterns, with South Asian households in the UK the most likely to contain a married couple, and Afro-Caribbean households, followed by White, least likely to contain a married couple.

The political advocacy and representation of women's interests is also subject to complex changes. Since the winning of political citizenship in the early twentieth century not only has there been a significant reduction in legislation which restricts women's activities, but also, since the 1970s a major development of equal opportunities legislation, underpinned by the treaties of the European Union. Further, in **social movements** and the **voluntary sector** women are significant actors (Miller, Wilford and Donaghue, 1996), whether these movements are clearly of relevance to women as in many feminist organizations, such as the refuge movement for battered women (Charles, 1995), or more indirectly so much as the Greenham protest against cruise missiles and militarism (Roseneil, 1995), the poll tax protests

(Bagguley, 1995), and environmentalism (Plumwood, 1993). Women are also involved in many voluntary associations such as the Mothers Union, Town's Women's Guild, the Women's Institutes, the National Commission for Women and the National Association of Women's Organizations.

However, women are still significantly underrepresented in the state and many forms of public life. ... In senior law and order positions women are notable by their absence – no women Chief Constables until the 1990s, very few senior judges – in 1994, only 4 per cent of High Court judges were women and 6 per cent of circuit judges – while in the lower level of the magistrates' courts women were 47 per cent of lay magistrates. In 1993 only 28 per cent of public appointments in the UK were held by women, though this is an increase on 19 per cent in 1986. Among ambassadors or heads of overseas missions there were only three women in 150 such posts. In the corporate sector there are few women chief executives of the large companies. In the second chamber of the British Parliament, the House of Lords, there are very few women as a consequence of the inheritance of titles. There are few women heading the many **quangos**, or quasi-governmental bodies.

Political pressure during the last two decades has led to significantly more interventionist forms of policing of male violence against women and children including rape, domestic violence and child sex abuse. Pressure, largely from feminists, made male violence into a public issue, leading to some significant reforms, such as special training for police dealing with these cases and special units within police stations – for example 'rape suites' (Dobash and Dobash, 1992; Hanmer, Radford and Stanko, 1989). However, while there has been an increased number of rapes reported to and recorded by the police, the number of convictions in the courts, while increasing, has risen much more slowly: that is, while there is an increasing rate of reporting of rape, there is a declining rate of conviction (Soothill and Walby, 1991). There is a significant increase in the number of employers with policies and procedures to deal with sexual harassment, following some headline cases in industrial tribunals, but it is hard to assess their impact. In areas such as male violence against women, the existing data makes it hard to interpret changes. There has been a greater public awareness of the impact of sexual harassment in the workplace on women's employment, but we have little evidence on the extent of changes in this. The reported rates of violence against women are increasing but, given the rate of reporting is low, it is not clear whether this reflects a real increase in the rate of such violence, or merely an increased propensity to report and for the police to record such crimes (Soothill and Walby, 1991).

The forms of sexuality and its representations have changed in complex ways over the last couple of decades. There has been a decline in the discourse and practise of confining sexuality to marriage and an increase in its public presence. Examples include: the increase in extra-marital sexual relations (Lawson and Samson, 1988); increased circulation of pornographic imagery, such as the development of the 'Page 3' first in the *Sun* and then other newspapers; public discussion of the means to control the spread of AIDS; public discussion of the affairs and duties of marriage among royalty.

Cultural representations have changed in complex ways (Franklin, Lury and Stacey, 1991). There is a greater representation of women in positions of authority in some media, such as newscasters, while there has been a backlash against the use of 'politically correct' language. Issues which were previously regarded as private matters are increasingly being represented and debated in the public arena. For instance, in the 1950s and 1960s rape and other forms of sexual attack were seldom reported in the press, while since the 1970s and the development of the tabloids these have increasingly become exposed to the public gaze, albeit in often sensationalist forms, which provide misleading images of the typical pattern of men's attacks on women (Soothill and Walby, 1991). There have become struggles within the Christian churches over whether women can become priests and vicars, with the winning of the right of women to be ordained in the Church of England.

These are tremendous changes in the lives of women and men over the last 20 years or so. There are many areas where some women have gained increasing access to the public domain leading to significantly increased opportunities, but the picture is complicated by the development of new forms of inequality and by the diversity between women.

Theorizing the diversity of gender regimes

The understanding of the significance of such diversity and inequality has been a driving force in contemporary social theory. ...

In order to grasp the different patterns of gender relations we need to have concepts at different levels of abstraction and which capture the major forms of gender system. In earlier work I have used the notions of 'system of patriarchy'; 'forms of patriarchy'; 'structures of patriarchy'; and 'patriarchal practices' to catch these different levels. A system of patriarchy was conceptualized as a system of social structures and practices in which men dominate, oppress and exploit women. The six structures of patriarchy are: household production; patriarchal relations in paid work; patriarchal relations in the state; male violence; patriarchal relations in sexuality; and patriarchal relations in cultural institutions (Walby, 1990).

There are different forms of gender regime or patriarchy as a result of different articulations and combinations of these structures. These gender regimes are systems of interrelated gendered structures. In earlier work I identified a continuum between two main types of patriarchy: private and **public**. This may be more elegantly described as more domestic and more public gender regimes. The use of the terms 'gender regime' as well as that of 'system of patriarchy' in this book should not be interpreted as suggesting that systematic gender inequality of patriarchy is over. The domestic gender regime is based upon household production as the main structure and site of women's work activity and the exploitation of her labour and sexuality and upon the exclusion of women from the public. The public gender regime is based, not on excluding women from the public, but on the segregation and subordination of women within the structures of paid employment and the state, as well as within culture, sexuality and violence. The household does not cease to be a relevant structure in the public form, but is no longer the chief one. In the domestic form the beneficiaries are primarily the individual husbands and fathers of the women in the household, while in the public form there is a more collective appropriation. In the domestic form the principal patriarchal strategy is exclusionary, excluding women from the public arena; in the public it is segregationist and subordinating. In both forms all six structures are relevant, but they have a different relationship to each other. In order to understand any particular instances of gender regime it is always necessary to understand the mutual structuring of class and ethnic relations with gender.

In order to analyse the diversity of gender relations and gender inequality it is important to separate analytically the form of gender regime from the degree of gender inequality. Whether a move to a more public form of gender regime leads to a reduction of gender inequality is an empirical question rather than one to be determined in an **a priori** fashion.

Different forms of gender regime coexist as a result of the diversity in gender relations consequent upon age, class, ethnicity and region. As a result of the recent changes older women will be more likely than younger women to be involved in a more domestic gender regime. Women whose own occupations place them in higher socio-economic groups are more likely to be in a more public form. Women of Pakistani and Bangladeshi descent are more likely to be in a domestic form and black Caribbean women more likely to be in a more public form that white women. There are complex interactions between these different forms of gender regime, as well as between gender, ethnicity and class.

Social theories which utilize concepts of structure are not infrequently accused of being rigid, and of underestimating the significance of social action. However, this is not a necessary feature of such accounts. I hold that political action is crucial to changes and the maintenance of gendered structures. For instance, the origin of the variety of patterns of **occupational segregation** cannot be understood outside of an understanding of the balance of gender and class forces in particular locations, as was argued in *Patriarchy at Work* (Walby, 1986). The transforma-tion from a private to public form of patriarchy, of a domestic to a more public gender regime, was due to the impact of first-wave feminism in a context of increased demand for women's labour (see *Theorising Patriarchy* – Walby, 1990). The significance of politics for the analysis of gender relations is not to be underestimated.

Social structures are constantly recreated and changed by the social actions of which they are composed, even though they may appear to any historical individual as a rigid institutional force.

References

Bagguley, P. (1995) 'Protest, poverty and power', in *Sociological Review, 43* (4).

Charles, N. (1995) 'Feminist politics, domestic violence and the state', in *Sociological Review, 43* (4).

Dobash, R. and Dobash, R. (1992) *Women, Violence and Social Change*, London: Routledge.

Franklin, S., Lury, C. and Stacey, J. (eds.) (1991) *Off-Centre: Feminism and cultural studies*, London: HarperCollins.

Hanmer, J., Radford, J. and Stanko, E. (1989) *Women, Policing and Male Violence: International perspectives*, London: Routledge.

Lawson, A. and Samson, C. (1988) 'Age, gender and adultery', in *British Journal of Sociology, 39* (3).

Miller, R., Wilford, R. and Donaghue, F. (1996) *Women and Political Participation in Northern Ireland*, Aldershot: Avebury.

Plumwood, V. (1993) *Feminism and the Mastery of Nature*, London: Routledge.

Roseneil, S. (1995) *Disarming Patriarchy: Feminism and political action at Greenham*, Buckingham: Open University Press.

Soothill, K. and Walby, S. (1991) *Sex Crime in the News*, London: Routledge.

Walby, S. (1986) *Patriarchy At Work: Patriarchal and capitalist relations in employment*, Cambridge: Polity.

Walby, S. (1990) *Theorising Patriarchy*, Oxford: Blackwell.

Key terms

The following key terms appear in the text above. They have been defined below to aid with the reading of this item.

patriarchy a system of male oppression of women, identified by feminists

gender regime Walby uses this term interchangeably with the term 'patriarchy' (see above)

private patriarchy the operation of patriarchy in domestic and personal settings – e.g. in women's roles within their relationships with male partners

social movements campaigning political activity undertaken by an affiliation of groups and individuals concerned with a broad issue – e.g. gay rights or feminism

voluntary sector the part of the economy concerned with organizing and administering community groups and charities

quangos quasi-governmental bodies set up to deliberate on issues of public concern. Quango members are appointed by the government and tend to support their views

public patriarchy the operation of patriarchy in workplace settings and other settings outside the home – e.g. in women's pay and working conditions which may be unequal to those of some men

a priori a philosophical term describing something that is assumed to be true, or is 'taken for granted', rather than being based on experience

occupational segregation sociological research undertaken by Walby and others has demonstrated that women and men tend to be employed in different sectors of the economy, and at different (on the whole, lower) levels than their male counterparts in the same industries

Questions

1 Give three examples of recent change in the social and economic position of women, quoting statistics where possible.

2 How do 'public patriarchy' and 'private patriarchy' differ?

3 Walby argues that the position of women is not better than it has been, nor worse, just different. Why is it impossible for her to draw an overall 'better' or 'worse' conclusion?

Reading 6.7 **Men, masculinity and feminism**

Johnathan Rutherford (from) *Forever England: Reflections on race, masculinity and empire* (1997) London: Lawrence & Wishart, pp. 142–6.

Editorial comments

Sociologist Johnathan Rutherford reflects on the economic changes that have brought relative insecurity to men who might once have worked '9–5' in a 'job for life'. Whilst work of this nature is now an endangered species, there has been an expansion in part-time jobs. These jobs have, in the main, been absorbed by women workers. As women have moved into the labour market they have become economically independent, to a degree. This has sometimes enabled them to call a halt to unsatisfactory personal relationships with men. As Rutherford points out, it is women who, in the main, initiate divorce.

Some men have perceived a threat from the widespread adoption of feminist attitudes by women who now expect a much greater degree of sexual equality, both in working life and private life. Such men have been vocal in their opposition to what they see as the passing of a man's world.

Behind the painted smile

IN THE POST-FEMINIST era of the 1990s, there has been a growing disaffection amongst middle-class men with the idea of sexual equality. The massive expansion of part-time jobs for women and the pattern of women divorcing men, have created a new wave of doubt and uncertainty in men's private lives. Organizations like 'Families need Fathers', campaigning against the divorce laws and for men's right to custody of their children, had already carved out a political space for a men's anti-feminist politics during the 1980s. Middle class men began to experience a relative loss in their social prestige and economic status. An era of economic insecurity has been precipitated by **globalization, technology-driven job losses and economic recession**. Careers are being superseded by short-term contracts, freelancing, part-time work and piece-work at home. For growing numbers in full-time employment, conditions of work are too insecure and idiosyncratic to be called jobs. Throughout the golden age of postwar consumer capitalism, full-time, tenured employment underpinned the middle-class nuclear family and its twenty-five year mortgage. By the year 2000 it will have become a minority form of work. In apparent contradiction to this trend, negative equity and falling salaries have propelled men into working longer hours. The impact of this new work order on a generation of thirty- and forty-something men, who inherited their fathers' expectations of a career for life, threatens to undermine their role of head of household. At the same time it is destroying work as the principal source of their masculine self-esteem and personal integrity.

The decline in male jobs has been accompanied by changing masculine sensibilities, as increasing numbers of men invest more time in domestic life and their children. However, this turn to the home has served to heighten male insecurity as women's increased independence has led to their greater willingness to leave men. By 1993, two and a half times more divorces were granted to women than to men. It is a state of affairs which led David Thomas to declare in his book *Not Guilty: In defence of the modern man*: 'The fact is, people are in pain. And right now, the ones who wear trousers and stand up to piss don't seem to count for much when it comes to being healed.' But this notion that men are the new victims has little grounding in social and economic reality. In August 1993, The National Child Development Study, which had been following the lives of 11,500 men and women born in one week in March 1958, presented a report to the annual British Association meeting in Keele. It argued that, 'Marital breakdowns are creating a new underclass of women who are trapped in a downward economic spiral.' It added, 'There are few signs that men had metamorphosed into the caring and labour-sharing breed that the media was trumpeting in the early 1990s.' In December 1993 the market research group Mintel published *Women 2000*, a survey of 1500 men and women. It came to similar conclusions. Only one man in a hundred, it claimed, did his 'fair share of the housework'. While two men in ten said they took an equal share in the cooking, only one in ten women thought they did. Over half of the women interviewed had full time jobs, but they were paid, on average, 29 per cent less than men in comparable jobs and were significantly less likely to have a company pension. Only 20 per cent of the working women claimed their male partners equally shared any single domestic task. Mintel's consumer manager Angela Hughes told *The Guardian*: 'Men seem to set out with good intentions to share the domestic chores but the catalyst appears to be the arrival of children. At this stage, the man appears to abdicate responsibility for his share, regardless of whether his partner is working. The surveys indicate that the downturn in men's fortunes are unrelated to any tangible increase in female equality. Men may be doing badly, but women are still worse off.

The most publicized anti-feminist diatribe was published in 1992 by a journalist, Neil Lyndon. His book, *No More Sex War: The failures of feminism*, argued that the women's liberation movement had been 'fundamentally false in logic, thoroughly false in history and poisonous in effect'. Lyndon's career as a spokesman for a male backlash against feminism began with an article in the *Sunday Times Magazine* in 1991. 'It is hard to think,' he declared, 'of one example of systemic and institutionalized discrimination against women in Britain today.' He argued that the liberation of women in the past twenty-five years had been a consequence of the new technologies of contraception and the right to abortion. Feminism had merely served to entrench gender stereotypes and promote antagonism and sex war between men and women. The effect of this revolution on his own life can be gauged by an article written by his wife, Deirdre Lyndon, which appeared in the *Daily Mail* on 21 September, 1992 (reprinted in *The Guardian*, the following day). Her opening sentence – 'This is the book that killed my marriage' – summed up the consequence of what had become her husband's obsessive loathing of feminism: 'I kept urging Neil to temper his arguments. ... "It's not feminists you're attacking," I would say. "Surely it's only militant feminists?" But it became clear that it was indeed all feminists and that, to some extent, the war was indeed being waged on women.' Lyndon moved out of the family home and began a relationship with another woman who had been acting as his part-time secretary. In trying to understand her husband's 'politics of hatred', Deirdre Lyndon suggested he had moved out because 'he needed to shred all the strands of domesticity to write this book'. She added: 'In some ways I think Neill wants to strip women of motherhood.'

Deidre Lyndon had put her finger on the primary target of anti-feminist rhetoric. Men's confusion over their role in society and feelings of impotence have encouraged the search for a scapegoat in mothers and motherhood. For Lyndon, society's neglect of the needs of men is epitomised in men's exclusion from their own homes and children: 'If our society is a patriarchy, why does it allow no statutory right to paternity leave?' For anti-feminists, the problem men face, and the predicament of society and culture, is the declining authority of the father and the subsequent prevalence of female-led one-parent families. 1992 witnessed the emergence of another symptom: male reaction to the apparent feminization of society; 'the 'Wild Men', an import from the US, inspired by Robert Bly's book, *Iron John*. This 'mytho-poetic' men's movement was the first popular development in men's sexual politics since 'Men against Sexism' began in the 1970s. While the latter had taken its inspiration from the Women's Liberation Movement – men rejecting the masculinity of their fathers and embracing their more 'feminine' feelings – the 'Wild Men' were intent upon reclaiming their fathers and their own male potency. The caring and sharing New Man of the mid-1980s, a product of its consumer boom, had reflected the changing sensibilities of post 1960s middle-class masculinities. But for Bly, the archetypal 'soft' man only proved that men had lost touch with their inner virility. Men's waged work outside the home had broken the bond between father and son. Boys raised exclusively by their mothers learnt to see their father through her eyes: 'If the son learns feeling primarily from the mother, then he will probably see his own masculinity from the feminine point of view as well.' According to Bly, modern men are mother's boys. Unable to grow up and relate to women as adults, they become trapped in compliant relationships leaving them feeling powerless and manipulated. The New Man of the 1980s is Bly's 'naïve man'. He can be receptive, can feel the other's pain, but he cannot say what he wants, he is too frightened to say 'no'. The 'naïve man' has no resolve. Bly argues that beneath his nice exterior is a man full of **misogynistic** anger.

Bly declares this unmanliness to be a crisis of men's relationship with their fathers: 'Not seeing your father when you are small, never being with him, having a remote father, an absent father, a workaholic father, is an injury.' Abandoned to their mothers, boys do not acquire the self-preservating aggression which sustains the boundaries of selfhood. 'A grown man six feet tall will allow another person to cross his boundaries, enter his psychic house, verbally abuse him, carry away his treasures, and slam the door behind; the invaded man will stand there with an ingratiating, confused smile on his face.' The purpose of the Wild Men movement was to rediscover the father within and tap his power. Groups of men attended weekend gatherings in the countryside, using ritualized dancing, drum banging and male bonding to make cathartic, primeval attempts to harness their 'masculine free spirit'. Despite widespread but mostly sceptical British press interest, Bly's simple assertion that men had a fundamental problem in being men found a ready constituency amongst a middle-class disoriented and demoralized by the new work order and the erosion of traditional masculine certitudes. The journalist Andrew Anthony attended one gathering. The profile of the one hundred men attending was remarkably homogeneous; 'Aged between late twenties and early fifties, they are all – with only one exception – white, heterosexual, overwhelmingly middle-class, highly educated, articulate and socially aware.' Anthony described the pro-feminist commitments many of the men professed, but noted how little time was spent talking about wives and girlfriends. However, men were not so reticent to talk about their mothers. 'When one fortysomething man confesses his anger at his mother's incessant demeaning of his absent father and half-jokes: "You can't hit a 75-year-old woman, even if she is your mother," the laughter and palpable sense of endorsement is universal and just a little disturbing.'

Bly stressed that blame for men's failure to be manly did not lie with women. The problem lay with fathers not doing their job of parenting. By the mytho-poetic movement he spawned, focusing on men's feelings of humiliation and shame and seeing these as a consequence of a mother-dominated family, inevitably fed into the language of women-blaming. In spite of his progressive intentions, Bly provided one impetus for a growing masculine language of complaint, directed at female power and authority in the home. Men's childhood experience of the domestic power of their mothers, refracted by a culture which disparaged male emotional dependency, readily fuelled the rhetoric of anti-feminism amongst otherwise liberal men.

References

Bly, R. (1991) *Iron John*, Shaftesbury: Element Books.

Lyndon, N. (1992) *No More Sex War: The failures of feminism*, London: Sinclair-Stevenson.

Thomas, D. (1993) *Not Guilty: In defence of the modern man*, London: Weidenfield & Nicolson.

Key terms

The following key terms appear in the text above. They have been defined below to aid with the reading of this item.

globalization an economic environment in which companies trade on an international basis, moving production of goods to wherever labour is cheapest. This often means job losses in industrialized countries, where labour is expensive

technology-driven job losses computers and other machines can now do the work of some people, hence those workers become redundant

economic recession a downturn in economic growth which tends to mean that industries shed jobs and people have less money to spend

misogynistic a 'misogynist' is a compulsive woman-hater

Questions

1 How have men's traditional social and economic positions been eroded in the postwar period?

2 Why do lone-parent families headed by women represent a social evil for writers like Lyndon and Bly?

3 How would you challenge the arguments put forward by anti-feminist writers that 'feminism has gone too far'?

Reading 6.8 **Sex and gender: a contemporary view**

Ann Oakley (from) 'A brief history of gender', in Ann Oakley and Juliet Mitchell (eds) *Who's Afraid of Feminism? Seeing through the backlash* (1997) Harmondsworth: Penguin, pp. 48–50.

Editorial comments

Feminist sociologist Ann Oakley describes very recent thinking on 'sex' and 'gender' in this reading. Her contention is that 'sex' – formerly seen as a fixed state centred on genital and biological characteristics – is, in fact, as variable a term as 'gender'. She argues that just as 'gender' is not 'natural', neither is 'sex'.

Earlier distinctions between 'sex' and 'gender' which supposed the former to be fixed and the latter a social construction, falsely made 'sex' the province of natural scientists. Oakley refers to these scientists as 'asocial' because they tend to imagine that 'sex' is a 'fact' and do not examine its social nature. 'Sex' is not a 'fact', however, and must be subject to the same process of sociological analysis as 'gender'. This will aid understanding of men's and women's relative social and economic positions because 'sex' has until now been used to suggest to both that certain aspects of their behaviour are unchangeable.

Histories of sex and gender

THE FIRST USAGE of the term 'gender' in the 1970s took cultural variability as its main difference from sex. Sex was the fixed star; the emphasis was on the non-**essentialism** of gender. Gender differences were not/are not 'true' differences; they were/are not 'absolute, abstract or irreducible'; no 'essence' is involved. Another interesting twist to the sex–gender argument is provided by recent historical and socio-logical work showing that cultural construction applies also to sex. This means that the essential distinction between sex and gender collapses. Even the binary distinction of sex itself – female or male – disappears when you look hard enough.

Thomas Laqueur (1990) found it difficult to read ancient, medieval and Renaissance texts about the body through the **epistemological** lens of the Enlightenment, which says the physical world of the body is 'real', while its cultural meanings are **epiphenomenal**. Before the seventeenth century, sex (the body) was the epi-phenomenon and gender was 'real'; sex was a sociological and not an ontological cate-gory. For 2000 years female and male bodies were not conceptualized in terms of difference. Medical texts described female and male bodies as funda-mentally the same, with one difference: women's gen-itals were inside their bodies and men's were outside. In this 'one sex' model women were simply men turned inside out and the lack of specific terms for women's organs (vagina, ovary, clitoris) reflected not a disregard for their importance, but an assumption that in this men and women were equal, that is like men. One consequence of understanding the way in which sex is culturally constructed is that 'almost everything one wants to say about sex ... already has in it a claim about gender. Sex ... is explicable only within the context of battles over gender and power.'

Laqueur's elegant exposition of the transition from a 'one sex' to a 'two sex' model is the kind of his-tory one needs to give depth to naïve understand-ings. The same could be said of Vern and Bonnie Bullough's (1993) treatise on *Cross-dressing, Sex and Gender*, which exposes the fiction of **transgen-derism** as a modern phenomenon. They show that gender-crossing is so historically and cross-culturally ubiquitous that genitalia can hardly be considered essential insignia of gender. As with everything else, however, there is little symmetry here. Women cross-dressers assume the characteristics of men as the norm, whereas male cross-dressers fit themselves into the residual category of what is left once men have defined masculinity.

Because 'gender' was originally the inverse of the essentialist term 'sex', its own usage was bound to iterate the intellectual shifts in how people perceived nature. In her book on the archaeology of sex hor-mones, Nellie Oudshoorn (1994) points out another important problem with gender; that it left sex to the medical scientists. The social scientists dealt with gen-der, and the asocial scientists with sex. A further, unhelpful binary distinction was created.

These arguments about the shifting stars of both sex and gender were prefigured in American anthro-pologist Sherry Ortner's well-known paper 'Is Female to Male as Nature is to Culture?', which was first pub-lished in 1974. Ortner contended that the sociology of women's bodies suggests a position closer to the natural world than to the cultural one. She remarked that 'the whole schema is a construct of culture rather than a fact of nature'. This is another way of express-ing the sentiment that gender leads directly to women rather than men, and/but most statements about women's sex are also statements about gender.

The feminist discovery of gender in the 1970s saw biological essentialism as a primary legacy of Western culture. What Sandra Bem (1993) has deemed 'gen-der polarization' gives to cultural processes and fac-tors the same dichotomy with which culture constructs biology: because there are two sexes, there must be two genders. There is a whole set of **dualisms** here: nature/culture, sex/gender, private/public, reproduc-tion/production. Dualistic assumptions about gender can preclude consideration of other relevant cate-gories (race, class, age, etc.). In other words, gender as an 'untheorized binary variable' is not helpful. As Barrie Thorne (1990) notes, the evidence is persua-sive for distinguishing conceptually between biological sex, cultural gender and sexuality (desire), but it should not be assumed that these are easily separa-ble: 'One of our central tasks is to clarify their com-plex, often ambiguous relationships. ... We should muse about why, after all our careful distinctions, *we so easily slip into interchangeable use of sex, gender and sexual.*' (Italics added.)

References

Bem, S. (1993) *The Lenses of Gender*, New Haven: Yale University Press.

Bullough, B. and Bullough, V. (1993) *Cross-dressing, Sex and Gender*, Philadelphia: University of Pennsylvania Press.

Laqueur, T. (1990) *Making Sex: Body and gender from the Greeks to Freud*, Cambridge, MA: Harvard University Press.

Ortner, S. (1974) 'Is female to male as nature is to culture?', in Rosaldo, M. and Lamphere, L. (eds) *Woman, Culture and Society*, Stanford, CA: California University Press.

Oudshoorn, N. (1994) *Beyond the Natural Body: an archaeology of sex hormones*, London: Routledge.

Thorne, B. (1990) 'Children and gender: constructions of difference', in Rhode, D. (ed.) *Theoretical Perspectives on Sexual Difference*, New Haven: Yale University Press.

Key terms

The following key terms appear in the text above. They have been defined below to aid with the reading of this item.

(biological) **essentialism** the belief that the biological and genital characteristics of men and women are fixed and create gendered behaviours

epistemological 'epistemology' is the study of knowledge. Put another way, people are taught to think in a certain, orthodox fashion and this colours their understanding of the world around them

epiphenomenal existing in addition to 'real' meaning. In other words, certain 'facts' are fixed and unchangeable but a layer of further ideas is presented in response to a given phenomenon. In this case, the idea under examination is that 'sex' is fixed and 'gender' a changeable phenomenon

transgenderism this encompasses 'cross-dressing', or 'transvestism', and sex changes

dualisms Western industrial societies have organized their manner of thinking around the existence of 'opposites' – e.g. 'man' is seen to be the opposite of 'woman' and vice versa

Questions

1 Ann Oakley cites the work of Thomas Laqueur on the history of 'sex'. How does his research prove her point that 'sex' is not fixed and unchanging?

2 Oakley points out, after Nellie Oudshoorn, that whilst 'gender' has been the subject of examination by social scientists, 'sex' tended to be left to the 'asocial scientists'. Why does she think this distinction is 'unhelpful'?

3 In your view, must there be two genders, just because there are two sexes? Could it ever be said that there are more than two sexes?

Further reading

The following texts may represent a useful starting point for the further investigations of the ideas contained within this chapter.

Primary texts

To trace the use of the concept of 'gender' as a tool for sociological analysis, see:

Oakley, A. (1997) 'A brief history of gender', in Oakley, A. and Mitchell, J. (eds) *Who's Afraid of Feminism? Seeing through the backlash*, Harmondsworth: Penguin.

Note: This is not an introductory text, but it is a comprehensive summary.

To follow up the feminist ideas introduced by Abbott and Wallace (1997), see:

Whelehan, I. (1995) *Modern Feminist Thought: From the second wave to 'post feminism'*, Edinburgh: Edinburgh University Press.

Secondary texts

A clear summary of the 'sex' and 'gender' debate can be found in:

Bilton, T. *et al.* (1997) 'Gender relations', in *Introductory Sociology*, 3rd edn, Basingstoke: Macmillan.

For a comprehensive introduction to feminist issues in sociology, see:

Abbott, P. and Wallace, C. (1997) *An Introduction to Sociology: Feminist perspectives*, 2nd edn, London: Routledge.

Coursework suggestions

1 **Investigate the campaigning work of one 'feminist' women's organization like Southall Black Sisters, and one 'traditional' women's organization like the Townswomen's Guild or the Women's Institute.**

 You may want to attend a meeting of each organization and interview members. Compare the similarities and differences between their ideas on what women want and what they want to achieve for women. What does this tell you about their ideas on the nature of either 'sex' or 'gender', or both?

2 **Observe and interview men and women studying for, or working in, non-traditional subject areas or occupations.**

 Note their own feelings and the feelings of others about their work. Use sociological analysis to explain the reactions you record. Contextualize your findings with reference to research on occupational segregation.

3 **Identify and challenge the assumptions about 'sex' and 'gender' contained in research conducted by evolutionists, geneticists and other natural scientists.**

 Read an essay or a popular science book like Steve Jones' *The Language of the Genes* and identify any ideas about 'sex' and 'gender' that are presented as fact but which might be challenged by sociologists. Then arrange a visit to the science department in your school or college, or to a local science laboratory, and conduct an interview with a science teacher or researcher, allowing them to present their views on 'sex' or 'gender' as 'facts' that underlie cultural influences on human behaviour. Use sociological evidence to challenge their arguments.

7

Stratification: 'race' and ethnicity

Chapter summary

Reading 7.1 **Racism in the UK** *page 173*
Richard Skellington outlines social attitudes towards racial issues in contemporary British society. This reading presents evidence from multi-ethnic surveys which shows the persistence of racism, citing data reporting two-thirds of the population as being racist.

Reading 7.2 **Early twentieth-century migration to Britain** *page 176*
John Solomos examines the presence of black people in the UK via social and state perceptions of migration at the beginning of the century.

Reading 7.3 **The 'Chicago School', symbolic interactionism and 'race'** *page 178*
Barbara Lal provides an overview in this reading of early twentieth-century Chicago sociologists and their insights into urban 'race' and ethnicity issues, such as the understanding of 'dualisms'.

Reading 7.4 **Colonial immigrants and status** *page 182*
John Rex and Sally Tomlinson offer a structural account – based on a Weberian framework – of the status situations of migrants in America and the UK.

Reading 7.5 **Marxism, ideology and migrant labour** *page 185*
Robert Miles uses a Marxist analysis to examine the specific racial disadvantages that African-Caribbean and Asian workers experience in the UK.

Reading 7.6 **Ethnicity and intelligence** *page 189*
Richard Herrnstein and Charles Murray use a New Right perspective to explore the concept of racial difference. They argue that individual 'races' possess different IQ capabilities and that this can affect their position in the socio-economic structure.

Reading 7.7 **Post-modern racial identities** *page 191*
Tariq Modood uses quantitative research methodology to investigate the post-modernist question of 'identity', by examining how different ethnic minority groups perceive their own ethnicity.

Reading 7.8 **Feminism – a black and white issue** *page 195*
Caroline Knowles and Sharmila Mercer focus on the way in which black feminism separates itself from white feminism, based on the assumption that black women suffer the inequalities caused by perceptions of 'race', alongside gender and class discrimination.

Introduction: Reading the sociology of 'race' and ethnicity

The readings contained within this chapter are presented in terms of the historical development of issues about racial inequality in contemporary Western industrial society, either through empirical research or theoretical perspectives. Discrimination and disadvantage based on 'race' and/or ethnicity are accepted by the extracts to be a feature of society, however the way in which this inequality is explained is not agreed upon. Sociological perspectives which examine 'race relations' can be broadly separated into classical approaches, such as Marxist and Weberian, and contemporary approaches, such as the New Right and post-modernism. This dichotomy reflects the different concerns examined by historically established and more recent theories; for example Marxists focus on the class position of ethnic minority workers, while post-modernists explore the concept of racial identity, two very diverse areas of 'race relations'.

It is widely accepted that the migration, after 1945, of 'old colonial black' citizens to the UK, and their consequent settlement, resulted in racially discriminatory social attitudes and policies among Britain's white population. Despite being invited to the UK to fill postwar labour shortages and the fact that they were relatively few in number (white European migrants from Ireland and Poland far outnumbered black migrants), immigration legislation became progressively more racist, controlling the number of black migrants able to enter the country (see Solomos, 1993

– reading 7.2). Black people were seen as a problem which needed restricting, which was reflected in the British Nationality Act of 1948. Racist assumptions voiced 50 years ago in parliamentary policy, and continued racialism in social attitudes (see Skellington, 1996 – reading 7.1), have resulted in the British government sustaining and reinforcing immigration legislation which limits the entry of black ethnic minorities, for example the passing of the Asylums and Immigration Act 1996. The UK may have anti-discrimination legislation on 'race', such as the Race Relations Act 1976, but this has done little to balance racist ideologies which persist in social policy.

Social scientific examination of racial issues began when scientific explanations of 'race' differences were discredited. Robert Park established a study of 'race relations' in 1920s' America based on a symbolic interactionist approach (see Lal, 1988 – reading 7.3). His work investigated the cultural backgrounds, family relationships, socio-economic inequalities and political isolation of black Americans. Park's work enabled society to see that 'race' was a label used to attach cultural and social meanings to particular groups identified as having particular physical traits.

Popular conceptions of 'race' in the UK, however, remained firmly based on the perceptions of 1940s' immigration. In fact the first theorizing and research into 'race relations' in the UK focused on migration issues. Marxist and Weberian perspectives were largely developed to examine this and related areas, such as employment, focusing strongly on class. It was not, however, until the 1970s that a clear theoretical approach on UK 'race relations' emerged in the research of John Rex. Rex defined 'race' and ethnicity through a Weberian understanding of conflict over scarce resources and conditions of exploitation and occupational segregation. In his work with Tomlinson (1979) it was discovered that immigrants formed an 'underclass', a social disadvantaged group below the working class. Rex and Tomlinson (reading 7.4) may have been criticized for their 'sub-cultural' analysis, but their examination of a British black underclass raised the issue of politics and racism in contemporary society.

The Marxist reliance on class as the main determinant of social position, its lack of reflection over the role of slavery/colonialism in capitalism and its use of racist imagery resulted in Robert Miles (1982 – reading 7.5) providing an 'up-dated' Marxist analysis of 'race'. Miles examined the ideological, political, as well as the class-based origins of 'racial identities'. He argued that racism is an integral part of capitalism, in that the state constructs racial identities in order to fragment the working class and thereby reduce class conflict. His ideological theory of 'race' is reminiscent of Park's work, but the application is truly Marxist.

Contemporary theories, such as the New Right perspective, post-modernism and black feminism have emerged to provide a much broader understanding of 'race' and ethnicity in modern industrial societies. These approaches have focused respectively on the interconnections between 'race' and nationhood (Herrnstein and Murray, 1996 – reading 7.6), racial identities (Modood, 1997 – reading 7.7) and black female separatism (Knowles and Mercer, 1994 – reading 7.8). The New Right publication by Herrnstein and Murray (reading 7.6) attempted to argue that lower intelligence is a result of genetic make-up and that this causes poor social positioning. This concept was then taken one step further by claiming that black people have higher levels of unemployment and poverty as a direct consequence of low IQs. Despite Herrnstein and Murray separating themselves from the logical conclusion of their work (i.e. that black people's genes cause social problems) by stating that each person should be judged as an individual, their book was subject to outrage because of its racist connotations and lack of scientific support. The New Right perspective is also associated with ideas of national identity, emphasizing the cultural difference of ethnic minorities as a negative trait. However, there is an evident flaw in this argument in that no culture is completely separate from others.

Post-modernism offers a critique of one-dimensional modernist theories, such as the New Right perspective, by allowing a multi-dimensional account of racial inequality. Post-modern approaches stress difference and diversity, attack essentialism, reject the presentation of racialized minorities as victims and analyse discourse. One area of 'race relations' where all these elements have become evident is in the study of identity. It is argued that globalization has brought diverse groups into contact, resulting in individual 'pick 'n' mix' identities (see Modood, reading 7.7). However, critics of post-modernism suggest that it can ignore traditional cultural values, socio-economic differentiations and even racism itself. This said, it still presents a challenging new perspective, as does black feminism.

The racialization of gender has highlighted the specific forms of disadvantage faced by black women. Black feminism has distanced itself from feminism in general by challenging the basis of white feminist perspectives (see Knowles and Mercer, reading 7.8). It is argued that the family does not oppress black women, as it does white women, because black women are less dependent on men. It is also argued that black women have to protect their reproductive rights, an issue which white women cannot relate to. Consequently, patriarchy is not seen as a central issue to their theories, because black men have to face disadvantage through racialism and are therefore more aware of inequality issues. It is clear that black women face different oppression to white women: 'race', class and gender stereotypes have to be faced daily, which supports an approach which examines the position of black women separately to that of white women.

The diverse range of theories and research examined in this chapter provides detailed information on the study of 'race relations', providing another exam-

ple of social inequality in contemporary Western industrial societies. Contemporary theories have progressed a great deal from their classical predecessors (although the recent return to biological assumptions of 'race' by Herrnstein and Murray has surprised the sociological community), providing complex and variable analyses of 'race' and ethnicity.

Reading 7.1 **Racism in the UK**

Richard Skellington (from) *'Race' in Britain Today* (1996) London: Sage, pp. 230–3.

Editorial comments

Skellington provides a clear and fluent overview of contemporary research into social attitudes on 'race' related issues in the UK. He uses a variety of data,

such as the British Social Attitudes surveys and National Opinion Polls, to assess whether racism remains prevalent in the thoughts of the British population. It appears that although attitudes towards ethnic minority groups are becoming more liberal, racial prejudice continues to exist at an alarming level in modern Britain.

Racial attitudes in Britain

The pervasiveness and deep rootedness of racism requires us to be continually vigilant and to understand that, simply because it no longer finds the same expression, it has not been erased.
(Commission for Racial Equality, 1991)

In 1984 the first British social attitudes survey described a British society that was seen by more than 90 per cent of the adult population to be racially prejudiced against its black and Asian members. More than one-third classified themselves as racially prejudiced: 42 per cent thought **racial prejudice** would be worse in five years' time. Two years later, the 1986 British social attitudes report offered an equally pessimistic picture of the perceived extent of racial prejudice for the 1990s. In July 1991 the Runnymede Trust and National Opinion Poll (NOP) produced the findings of the largest national study of attitudes to racism conducted in Britain since the British social attitudes studies of the mid-1980s and the Policy Studies Institute's third national survey.

Two out of every three white people thought Britain was a very or fairly racist society compared with four out of five Afro-Caribbeans and 56 per cent of Asians. Almost half the white respondents agreed with the proposition that 'non-white' people were treated worse than white people by the police, a similar response to the Asian sample. This compared with three-quarters of the Afro-Caribbean respondents. Two-thirds of Afro-Caribbeans believed employers discriminated in favour of white workers, compared with four out of ten from white and Asian samples. All these

figures were significantly higher than those reported by the PSI in their third national survey. The 1991 survey disclosed that over 60 per cent of Afro-Caribbeans thought that British laws against racial discrimination were not tough enough, compared with 45 per cent of Asians and 51 per cent of whites. It concluded that confidence in black and Asian people getting fair treatment from the police and the courts had 'plummeted in the past decade' (see Figure 1).

Most whites surveyed thought that social security offices, council housing departments and schools treated non-whites the same as or better than white people. However, while only 13 per cent and 18 per cent of whites and Asians thought that non-whites received worse treatment in schools, the figure for Afro-Caribbeans, at 38 per cent, was much higher. One in four white people believed that social security offices gave preferential treatment to non-white people: one in five did not want a neighbour of a different 'race'.

All groups over-estimated the numbers of black or Asian people living in Britain. The true figure was around 2.6 million. Over half the white sample thought the true figure was 5 million: a quarter thought it was 10 million.

The survey also revealed that over one-fifth of Afro-Caribbeans said they would be fairly or very unlikely to vote 'if there were a general election tomorrow', twice as many as those from the other groups.

Finally, the survey found that racial prejudice amongst white people correlated highly with social

Figure 1 Attitudes concerning racism in Britain *(Independent on Sunday, 7 July 1991)*

RACISM IN BRITAIN

Do you think Britain as a society is:

	□	■	▩
Very racist	10	26	6
Fairly racist	57	53	50
Fairly non-racist	26	14	28
Completely non-racist	4	3	6

Compared with ten years ago, do you think Britain today is:

	□	■	▩
Much more racist	11	9	9
A little more racist	17	10	18
About the same	28	25	20
A little less racist	33	39	28
Much less racist	6	9	8

Key:
□ Whites ■ Afro-Caribbeans ▩ Asians
All figures are percentages

TREATMENT BY AUTHORITIES

Do you think non-whites are treated better, worse or the same as whites by:

Employers	□	■	▩
Better	9	1	3
Worse	39	67	42
Same	44	22	44
The Police	□	■	▩
Better	7	0	2
Worse	48	75	45
Same	36	16	40
Schools	□	■	▩
Better	14	1	2
Worse	13	38	15
Same	61	48	74
The Courts	□	■	▩
Better	10	1	2
Worse	24	57	19
Same	55	26	53

RACE RELATIONS

Do you agree or disagree with the following statements:

People should only marry within their own ethnic group

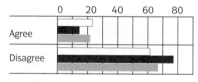

People of different races should keep to themselves

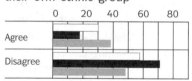

Asian people work harder than white people

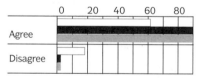

I would happily have people of a different race living next door to me

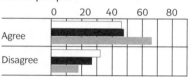

Immigration has enriched the quality of life in Britain

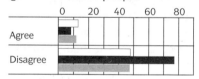

White people are more intelligent than black people

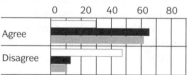

DISCRIMINATION LAWS

What do you think of the British laws against racial discrimination?

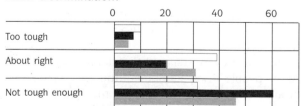

NUMBER OF NON-WHITES

How many blacks or Asians do you think there are in Britain (population 56 million)?

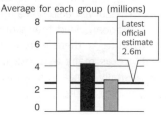

VOTING INTENTIONS

If there were a general election tomorrow:
How likely is it that you would vote?

	□	■	▩
Certain	63	45	53
Very/fairly likely	23	23	30
Fairly/very unlikely	11	22	13
Wouldn't/not registered	3	10	3

Which party would you vote for?

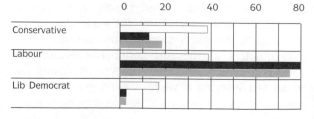

class and age. There were also indicators that racial prejudice against Asian people was stronger than against Afro-Caribbean groups.

Developments since 1992

A range of surveys has assessed the general attitudes of the British people towards 'race' and **racism** since 1991, with conflicting and often contradictory findings. The ninth British Social Attitudes survey (BSA) revealed that racism was still perceived to be widespread, but that it was beginning to decline. Over 50 per cent of those surveyed believed there was a lot of prejudice against Afro-Caribbeans and slightly more against Asians. The study reported a small decrease in reported prejudice. It did, however, reveal that over one-third of the sample were either 'very prejudiced' or 'a little prejudiced' against minority ethnic groups. The 1992 BSA, for the first time, revealed that more people were optimistic about the future of 'race' relations in Britain than were pessimistic. Moreover, people who believed themselves to be free from the effects of racial prejudice had also increased. The BSA confirmed, however, that the public still perceived Britain as a racially prejudiced society. This finding might be related to increasing media coverage of the extent of 'racial violence' and harassment in British society. The BSA reported that three quarters of the sample supported anti-discrimination legislation.

In 1993, further analysis into British racism, by Gallup for the American Jewish Committee, focused more upon the attitudes of specific minority ethnic groups, and also examined the range of attitudes between minority ethnic groups. This survey revealed a more disturbing report about the levels of racism. Gallup showed that 25 per cent of Britons would object to living next to non-white people, 10 per cent wanted anti-discrimination laws to be abolished and 45 per cent thought that anti-Semitism was not a problem. The survey, based on a sample of 959 people, found that 20 per cent would not want Chinese neighbours, 25 per cent would not want African, 27 per cent would not want West Indian, and 30 per cent would not want Pakistani (the terms used are Gallup's). The 'most **racist** respondents' tended to be from working class, elderly and least educated backgrounds. Over three-quarters of respondents felt that race relations in Britain were 'only fair' or 'poor'. Over 40 per cent thought that anti-racist laws should be strengthened.

The BSA surveys of 1993 and 1994 tended to support the BSA 1992 survey trends of a society taking a slightly more liberal turn in attitudes during the 1990s, despite the reported increase in racial violence and harassment. They perhaps underestimate the political shifts to far right agendas. The surveys also confirmed an increasing awareness and acceptance of the extent to which Britain was a racist society. In 1992 Yasmin Alibhai-Brown observed that 'racism has got worse and society cares less' (*Guardian*, 29 January 1992). She returned to her theme in 1993:

> It must be because it is fashionable to attribute a problem to individual failure rather than social and political forces ... [that there] is a backlash against any attempt to tackle inequality. The attacks follow a pattern: derision on the one hand and cataclysmic warnings on the other. ... Anyone who pushes for equality, or criticizes the male Anglo-Saxon world is ... discredited and silenced.
> *(The Guardian, 11 August 1993)*

A representative multi-ethnic survey in July 1995, in which 1,042 adults aged 18 and over were interviewed in 52 randomly selected constituencies, revealed that two-thirds of the population admitted to being racist, and only one in ten said that people they knew were not racist. The majority of the sample – weighted to the profile of adults aged 18 and over – reported supporting a variety of repatriation strategies for non-whites. Over half the sample believed there was **racial discrimination** in the labour market. Just under half of the black and Asian respondents reported that 'coloured people felt British'. On the more positive side, the younger respondents were reported to be more open-minded about racial differences.

Reference

Commission for Racial Equality (CRE) (1991) *Annual Report 1990*, London: CRE.

Key terms

The following key terms appear in the text above. They have been defined below to aid with the reading of this item.

racial prejudice, racism, racist holding a blinkered or hostile attitude towards a group who have different cultural or physical features to your own

racial discrimination the behavioural manifestation of racial prejudice; acting out of racist beliefs

Questions

1 Explain the relationship between social class and racial prejudice.

2 Assess the contribution of anti-discriminatory legislation on 'race relations' to social attitudes on minority ethnic groups.

3 Outline sociological explanations given for continued racial prejudice and discrimination in the UK.

Reading 7.2 **Early twentieth-century migration to Britain**

John Solomos (from) *Race and Racism in Britain* (1993) London: Macmillan, pp. 47–51.

Editorial comments

Contemporary sociologist John Solomos provides a lucid and concise historical account of 'race' and labour relations in the early part of twentieth-century Britain. His research examines social reactions to the presence of black people in the UK and the resulting discriminatory state legislation, such as the British Nationality Act 1948, which restricted the entry of British colonial subjects considered to be of a different 'race'. Solomos highlights the racist nature of postwar political debates arguing for the control of 'coloured' migrants to supposedly protect the British way of life.

Race and labour in the early twentieth century

THE HISTORICAL PRESENCE of black communities within Britain can be traced back over several centuries. Black communities and individuals were a feature of British society and culture for centuries before the arrival of Asian and Afro-Caribbean immigrants after 1945. By the end of the nineteenth century black seamen had settled in Liverpool, London, Cardiff, Bristol and other port towns.

This is not the place to go into the details of this history, which has recently been the subject of a number of important and insightful studies. But we should look at some aspects of the politics of black **migration** and settlement in Britain in the early twentieth century, since it was during this period that the terms of political debate and domestic **ideologies** and policies towards 'coloured' workers and their communities began to be formed.

Indeed it was during this period that the issue of racial difference began to play a central role in the politics of immigration. This was the case despite the relatively small size of the black population and the fact that they possessed the formal right to citizenship. According to Harris (1988) a central theme in debates about the black communities during the interwar period related to the supposed social problems which their presence gave rise to:

> Social decay was supposed to be connected with the presence of a 'Negro' population of Somalis, Arabs, West Indians, West Africans and so on who constituted an almost insignificant percentage of the population of the sea-port towns.
> *(Harris, 1988)*

Such issues were to become a more central feature of political debate from 1945, yet it is clear that their origins can be traced, to some extent, to the interwar years and the commonly held image of black communities in the port towns and beyond.

Part of the history of the interwar years period is being uncovered by the research of scholars such as Fryer, Rich and Harris, and by the increased interest in the history of the black presence in British society. Much more research needs to be done, but its importance for any rounded analysis of the politics of race and racism in British political life is already clear.

Yet the preoccupation of the bulk of studies in this field remains with the period since 1945 and is stubbornly ahistorical, even when written from a radical perspective. This means that many important connections and continuities in the history of race and racism in British society are hardly discussed.

Let us take an example of the consequences of such an approach, and its limitation. [I have already discussed] the policy of the British state towards the entry into Britain of people who were, by law, aliens, that is non-British citizens. Yet it is also clear that the legislation effected by the state was also used to deal with, and contained provisions concerning, certain categories of British subjects, specifically seamen recruited in different parts of the Empire, particularly from India and the Caribbean. Despite being British subjects, Indian seamen (widely known as lascars) had been subject to discriminatory treatment by the state since the nineteenth century, if not before, partly in order to limit their settlement in Britain when the passage that they had worked terminated in Britain.

An Act of 1813 required the East India Company to provide subsistence for Indian sailors in Britain until they returned to India, while an Act of 1823 stipulated that Indian seamen were not British subjects and prohibited them from becoming British subjects. These powers were consolidated in the Merchant Shipping Act 1894 which set out articles of agreement to be signed by Asian seamen and masters binding the former to return to their country of origin and giving the Secretary of State the power to **repatriate** those who attempted to become resident in Britain. These attempts were only partially successful, as the continuing presence of Asian and Caribbean people in British seaports proved.

After 1918 the British state reinforced discriminatory practices and made further efforts to prevent

British subjects considered to be of a different race from settling in Britain. This occurred in the context of the ending of the First World War, during which time there had been an increase in the number of British subjects from the Empire employed as seamen. Concerning discriminatory practices, Section 5 (2) of the Aliens Restriction (Amendment) Act 1919 legalized different rates of pay for British subjects employed as seamen according to their race. Additionally there was a slump in employment in the shipping industry after 1918 and the relevant trade unions campaigned to restrict employment to 'white' seamen. In the resulting competition for work, Indian, Chinese and Caribbean seamen resident in Britain became the victims of racist violence in Cardiff, Liverpool and Glasgow. In Cardiff the police sought to 'repatriate' these seamen. The Home Office pointed out that they were British subjects and therefore were not subject to enforced expulsion from Britain, but arrangements were made for the return of as many seamen as might be 'persuaded' to go. This initiative by the state was largely unsuccessful.

Subsequently a further initiative was taken using Article 11 of the Aliens Order 1920. By referring to this Article the Special Restrictions (Coloured Alien Seamen) Order 1925 was drafted. The Order formally applied to colonial seamen (who had previously been entitled to sign off from a ship in a British port and to seek residence there) who did not possess satisfactory documentary evidence of being British subjects. These seamen were required to obtain the permission of an immigration officer to land and were subject to removal from Britain. In practice the police, the Aliens Department and immigration officers forced 'coloured' British subjects possessing the required documentation to register under the Order, an action that deprived them of the legal status of British subjects and thereby rendered them subject to the pow-

ers of the Alien Restriction (Amendment) Act 1919 and the Aliens Order 1920 – including the requirement that they register with the police, to whom they were required to report any change of address – and to the possibility of deportation. Joshua and Wallace comment that:

> The Order was specifically designed to restrict the entry and settlement of black colonial British citizens. But, because the Conservative government did not wish to undermine the notion of a British subject which was at the heart of the Empire, the Order could not achieve its ends through a series of legalistic contortions and double standards.
> *(Joshua and Wallace, 1983)*

The concern of the state, both at the local and national level, was multi-faceted. It was responding to local **racist** agitation and violence against those defined as 'coloured' seamen, action that was grounded in the inability of the economic system to provide full employment. But it was also grounded in a wider, racist concern that followed from the settlement of these seamen in Britain, specifically the growth of a population that resulted from sexual relations between these seamen and indigenous women.

In the same way as after 1945, the two most common responses to black **immigration** and settlement were reflected in political debates about the need to control the arrival of this group of **migrants** and in calls for the repatriation of those who had already settled in Britain. Partly through the violent conflicts which occurred with some regularity in some of the port towns, but largely through the mobilization of images of the black communities as a source of social problems, even the relatively small-scale black settlements that took shape in the interwar period were perceived as 'alien' and a possible threat to the British way of life.

References

Harris, C. (1988) 'Images of blacks in Britain: 1930–60', in Allen, S. and Macey, M. (eds) *Race and Social Policy*, London: Economic and Social Research Council.

Joshua, H. and Wallace, T. (1983) *To Ride the Storm: the 1980 Bristol 'riot' and the state*, London: Heinemann.

Key terms

The following key terms appear in the text above. They have been defined below to aid with the reading of this item.

migration moving to, and settling permanently in, a country other than that in which you were born and raised

ideologies systematic collections of beliefs which serve the interests of a specific social group

repatriate to return people to their country of origin

racist holding a blinkered or hostile attitude towards a group who have different cultural or physical features from your own

immigration entering a country other than the one in which you were born and raised, in order to settle there permanently

migrants individuals who move to, and settle permanently in, a country other than the one in which they were born and raised

Questions

1 Discuss the effect of colonialism on social attitudes towards minority ethnic groups in Britain.

2 Examine the contribution of the migration to Britain in the 1940s of different ethnic groups towards the creation of racially discriminatory immigration legislation.

3 Explain why 'coloured' migrants, rather than 'white' migrants, were seen as a threat to social order in the 1940s and 1950s.

Reading 7.3 **The 'Chicago School', symbolic interactionism and 'race'**

Barbara Lal (from) 'The "Chicago School" of American sociology, symbolic interactionism, and race relations theory', in J. Rex and D. Mason (eds) *Theories of Race and Ethnic Relations* (1988) Cambridge: Cambridge University Press, pp. 285–95.

Editorial comments

Barbara Lal focuses on the most important 'race' related ideas of the 'Chicago School', which are often neglected in studies of 'race' and ethnic relations. She argues that the symbolic interactionist approach used first by Robert Park, and later by Blumer and Duster, effectively raised unexplored issues, such as ethnic minority adjustment to urban life and the development of strategies by minority ethnic groups for social mobility. Lal highlights the differences between a flexible approach, like symbolic interactionism, and a rigid structural model, such as Marxism, to show the value of the former to the understanding of ethnic relations in Western industrial society.

The 'Chicago School' on 'race relations'

PARK SUGGESTED THAT **race prejudice** is not an attribute of individuals but a property of the shifting relationship between racial groups. He argued that race prejudice is aroused, and **racial conflict** occurs, when there is a real or imaginary threat to an existing pattern of **'social accommodation'**. By 'social accommodation' Park meant 'a process of adjustment, that is, an organization of elements more or less antagonistic to each other but united for the moment'. 'Social accommodation' describes a relationship in which there is consensus, however short-lived, about matters of obligation, duty, appropriate attitudes of deference, and 'respective spheres of action'. Social distances are preserved through the monopolization of particular kinds of experience and the restriction of access to the lifestyles enjoyed by a dominant group. Conventions and etiquette are internalized and reinforce social distances, as Bertram Doyle's monograph, *The Etiquette of Race Relations in the South*, suggests. It is only in the process of **'social assimilation'** that social distances give way to social solidarity based upon participation in a common cultural life in which there is unrestricted access to the range of experience previously monopolized by a dominant group.

Park and Burgess insisted upon differentiating between the objectives of 'competition' which they believed to be economic or material advantage, and the objectives of conflict, which they took to be status and the enlargement of spheres of privilege in a pattern of social accommodation. Park argued that status, which has to do with self-conception, social control and how one sees one's group in relation to other groups, is usually of greater importance in influencing collective action than the distribution of material rewards (although he acknowledged that the two are interrelated). 'In general we may say that competition determines the position of the individual in the community; conflict fixes his place in society. ... Status, subordination and superordination, control – these are the distinctive marks of a society'.

Park thought that cities are most often the context in which 'race problems' emerge because it is here that racial groups which were either previously isolated, or which enjoyed (or suffered) a fixed 'place' in an existing mode of social accommodation, meet as competitors for jobs and housing and become antagonists in a process of social conflict aimed at preserving or changing their group's status. In cities new situations require that groups fit their lines of action together in new ways. Moreover, Park, like Simmel, believed that a money economy offered new possibilities for a subordinate group to improve its status and widen its sphere of influence.

In cities, both formal organizations and informal institutions, such as boarding houses, contribute to the development of a type of conflict group that Park referred to as 'publics'. Publics are groups that are differentiated from one another in terms of membership and often of goals but which are agreed about the procedures for gaining goals and negotiating about the division of scarce resources. 'Crowds' and 'social movements' are also features of urban life, but unlike publics have no traditions and no permanent organizations; they exert control over their participants but generally do not achieve their goals on the basis of negotiation with other groups.

Finally, Park was very definite about the role of historical evidence in social research generally, and in race relations in particular. He observed that 'opinions, creeds and doctrines become intelligible when we know their history; when we know, in other words, the experiences out of which they have sprung. ... Not merely events, but institutions as well become intelligible when we know their histories, and particularly when we know the individual experiences of men and women in which they have their origin and on which they finally rest.'

The ideas of 'race prejudice as a sense of group position' and the 'process of collective definitions', which are introduced into the race relations literature by Herbert Blumer and Troy Duster, build upon Park's perspective on race prejudice and race conflict. In his essay 'Race Prejudice as a Sense of Group Position', first published in 1958, Herbert Blumer agrees with Park's view that race prejudice is 'fundamentally a matter of the relationship between racial groups' rather than between individuals, and he reiterates the conditions that Park suggested give rise to or intensify race prejudices. In a later essay, 'The Future of the Color line', published in 1965, Blumer includes alongside what he calls a 'domination–subordination' axis of the relationship between racial groups an 'inclusion–exclusion' axis.

However, in these and also in later essays, Blumer modifies and extends Park's ideas in several ways. First, Park tended to emphasize personal experience and 'equal status contacts' within a 'bi-racially organized society' as a likely mechanism of social change between racial groups, despite his theoretical interest in the role of publics and collective behaviour in the process of change. Blumer, on the other hand, locates change in the public and in the intervention of politically powerful leaders, especially those of the dominant group. Political leaders may initiate social change by altering the objective conditions under which racist groups co-exist, or by changing the imagery of these groups and hence the 'collective definitions' which he and Troy Duster claim to be the fulcrum of race relations. For example, in his essay 'Industrialization and Race Relations', Blumer insists that 'political pressures' rather than 'inner considerations of industrial efficiency' are likely to lead to changes in a prevailing pattern of race relations. Thus, he notes of the

American South that changes 'have not sprouted indigenously in Southern industry or for that matter Southern society' but have instead emanated from the Federal Government.

A second way in which Blumer and his colleague Troy Duster develop the previous work of Park is by focusing upon the process of '**collective definition**'. ...

In addition to noting that racial groups interact in a variety of situations, all of which must be studied by students of race relations, Blumer and Duster contend that there are 'variable interpretations' of human experience and that 'It is the variable interpretation of these human experiences that is the starting point of social theory'. In addition, they suggest that the relationship between the mass media and the process of collective definitions be looked at.

The third contribution which Blumer and Duster make to the study of race relations, and which is an inherent part of their theory of collective definition, has to do with what they term '**dualisms**'. The problem of dualisms refers to subordinate groups vacillating between an insistence upon their own 'specialness' and thus reinforcing solidarity among group members, or emulating the behaviour of a dominant group in an effort to improve the rank order of the group as a whole. 'The conflict for groups (and individuals inside these groups) at the base of the social, economic and political structure, most simply put, is whether to celebrate and retain their "likeness" (which some may come to feel consigns them to the base), or whether to emulate and assimilate.' These two contradictory attitudes may be held by different members of the group at the same time.

Blumer and Duster suggest that a trend towards emulation usually occurs under favourable economic conditions, when members of the subordinate group might reasonably hope to improve their lives and their status by economic activity which results in increased rewards. On the other hand, an insistence upon 'specialness' usually occurs when economic mobility is not likely and the group members instead opt for an improvement of their lives through political action. Blumer and Duster later talk about this dualism as 'two major divergent directions of effort' which they call the 'assimilationist' orientation and the 'separatist' orientation.

Blumer and Duster see the duality of emulation/ assimilation and specialness/separateness as a useful way of describing the internal discussions within the subordinate group which contribute to the stability of, or to shifts in, collective definitions. For example, they use this conception of dualism to explain changes in the outlook of American blacks between 1920 and 1980.

I would like to suggest that the opposing

orientations that Blumer and Duster depict as dualisms have also been commented upon by the historians August Meier and Allan Spear. In his study, *Negro Thought in America, 1880–1915*, Meier documents the vacillation among black leaders between ideologies of 'accommodation' and those of 'integration' between 1880 and 1915. Meier contends that ideologies of accommodation and the growth of separate black institutions (which through the passage of time took on their own characteristics and therefore emerged as specifically 'black' institutions) were a response to the antagonism of white Americans to black aspirations – aspirations which did not differ much from those of the prevailing 'white' culture. However, Afro-Americans discovered the benefits of a separate ideology and organizational life, once articulated and established, in advancing group interests.

Similarly, Spear's work suggests that the growth of Chicago's physical black ghetto hastened the growth of the institutional ghetto, that is to say, the development of black churches, hospitals, newspapers and self-help organizations. Spear agrees with Meier that only after the exclusion of black people from jobs, housing, educational facilities and other aspects of white institutional life did black leaders opt for separatist policies, which represented a strategy for survival.

Moreover, as I have pointed out in my discussion of what I call 'the ethnicity paradox' and 'culture-building', a duality similar to that noted by Blumer and Duster had already been discussed by Park and Thomas in their work on immigrants and blacks. What I mean by an 'ethnicity paradox' is the finding that in American society participation in ethnic institutions and the celebration of separate groups' identities, while valued in and of themselves, are at the same time strategic devices for facilitating participation in all areas of social life and a fair share of scarce resources in the wider community.

The idea that immigrant institutions and, in particular, the immigrant neighbourhood, served to ease the immigrant's transition to American urban life, although not without its critics, has since become a familiar interpretation in the study of immigrant history. However, Park also anticipated the relationship between this finding and subsequent analyses which see the self-conscious creation of a genuine black culture, separatist ideologies and separate institutions as a pre-requisite for the political mobilization of blacks in pursuit of their shared interests.

To sum up: rather than being a response to a specific state of the economy, as Blumer and Duster suggest, dualisms, and in particular an insistence upon specialness/separateness, are strategic devices to facilitate an improvement in the collective status of the group as a whole and to secure a larger share of scarce resources. ...

The following brief discussion of three of the differences within symbolic interactionist thinking about race relations provides a convenient way of also exploring some of the more frequent criticisms of this perspective and method by non-interactionists.

One major source of disagreement has to do with the nature of sociological explanation and, in particular, with the level of generality to which findings in sociological inquiry should aspire. This difference is explored by Bernard Melzer and James Petras in their essay 'The Chicago and Iowa Schools of Symbolic Interactionism', in which they argue that Manfred Kuhn developed his variant of symbolic interactionism in order to re-cast Mead's social psychology so that it would fulfil a 'nomothetic (or generalizing) function' rather than an 'ideographic (or nongeneralizing) function'. Arthur Brittan, another sociologist sympathetic to **symbolic interactionism**, warns against 'over-emphasis on the situation', and on meanings, such that 'we allow ourselves to be taken in by a completely relativistic account of social interaction, in which episodes are elevated to the status of the prime unit of methodological and theoretical interest'.

In the area of race relations, Blumer and Duster's insistence that sociologists pay attention to the variety and complexity of racial groups' experience of each other reveals the tension inherent in a perspective and method which seeks to discover general, 'collective' orientations and patterns of association and, at the same time, to respect the particular instances in which social interaction between racial groups occurs. Blumer and Duster resolve the tension between the 'collective', or the general, and the 'particular' by arguing that 'Race relations, certainly in their problematic form, do operate inside of an essentially common and constant framework. Thus while the variability that is suggested by the process of definition may, and indeed does, take place, it is held within the framework and takes place along the line that is set by the framework'; and, later, 'the defining process is relentlessly brought inside a common framework, a framework which forces the definitions to deal with the basic orientations of racial groups'. What their outlook implies in terms of fieldwork, the analysis of human documents and the sociological interpretation of ongoing group life is suggested by monographs, such as *Black Metropolis, The Negro Family in Chicago, Negro Politicians, In the Shadow of the Plantation* and *The Etiquette of Race Relations in the South*, in which a variety of racial 'experiencing' is analysed in terms of the fundamental hierarchy of colour, or what Blumer has also referred to as 'the color line' and its accompanying 'sense of group position'.

What these monographs further suggest is that although symbolic interactionists do not generally aspire to explain race relations (or any other aspect of social life) through the discovery of general laws of behaviour or by generating universal hypotheses on which to base predictions about their future, their construction of 'sensitizing' concepts has enabled their analyses of group life to uncover some interesting patterns of association between racial groups. 'Collective definitions', 'dualisms', 'the ethnicity paradox', 'race prejudice as a sense of group position', 'the city as a spatial pattern and a moral order', all make sense of empirical data in the study of race and ethnic relations. I would argue that these sensitizing concepts are good examples of what John Lofland calls 'mini-concepts' and that these are amenable, by and large, to the types of research procedures outlined by Barry Glaser and Anselm Strauss. Moreover, it is precisely because these sensitizing or mini-concepts are tied to actual instances of racial experiencing that they are sometimes used by, and might be useful to, social geographers, social historians and anthropologists as well as sociologists.

A second problematic area which divides symbolic interactionists from one another, as well as dividing them from many of their critics, has to do with assessing the importance of social class as a determinant both of the situations in which racist groups experience each other and of the meanings which racial groups bring into play in resolving these situations through joint action. The conclusion that symbolic interactionism overlooks the significance of social class in the determination of 'objective' historical conditions and 'subjective' consciousness is one expression of a more widespread criticism based upon symbolic interactionism's purported 'avoidance of macrostructural emphasis in favor of its microscopic interactional one'.

Park preferred the category of occupation to that of class. More importantly, as I have already suggested, he saw 'status' based upon colour as the most significant feature of the interaction between racial groups. This outlook is generally shared by Blumer and Everett Hughes. Among Park's students, however, colour coupled with class became of increasing importance. Elsewhere, following a suggestion made to me by the historian Stanley Engermann, I explore the view that the Great Depression played a significant part in this theoretical development.

A third and related division within the ranks of symbolic interactionists has to do with the extent to which the actor and his interpretation of the situation, as opposed to disembodied variables such as social class, social role or social institutions, are kept at the centre, rather than at the periphery, of sociological analysis. Such a difference in emphasis is noticeable in a comparison of Blumer's outlook with *some* (but by no means all) of the essays of Hughes.

Thus, for example, in an early monograph Hughes observed that 'institutions are just those social forms which grow up where men collectively face problems which are never completely settled. ... It seems likely that when they do so, and continue to do so for long enough, they produce relationships and ideas which succeeding generations accept somewhat involuntarily'. Ironically, in some of his later writings on social institutions, Hughes adopts a functionalist approach which contradicts his earlier preference for keeping the actor at the centre of the analysis and which influenced some members of a later generation of Chicago scholars.

Key terms

The following key terms appear in the text above. They have been defined below to aid with the reading of this item.

race prejudice hostile feelings towards members of a group considered to be 'racially' different, i.e. possessing different cultural and/or physical characteristics

racial conflict verbal and/or physical hostility between two or more groups identified as 'racially' different, i.e. possessing different cultural and/or physical characteristics

social accommodation acceptance – through a process of adjustment – of social groups perceived as being of a different culture or 'race'

social assimilation social groups perceived as being culturally or racially different becoming more alike

collective definition the way in which groups see themselves and the way they act towards each other on that basis

dualisms the emphasis by a group of their differences and similarities to the dominant group in that society

symbolic interactionism a perspective based on the idea that people communicate using symbols, such as language, in order to understand the meaning of actions

Questions

1 Assess the Chicago School's contribution to the understanding of 'race relations' in modern Western industrial society.

2 Explain what 'strategies for social mobility' were employed by ethnic minorities in adjusting to urban life.

3 Compare and contrast structuralist and behaviourist approaches in explaining racial disadvantage in modern Britain.

Reading 7.4 **Colonial immigrants and status**

John Rex and Sally Tomlinson (from) *Colonial Immigrants in a British City: a class analysis* (1979) London: Routledge & Kegan Paul, pp. 14–19.

Editorial comments

Rex and Tomlinson's research into colonial immigrants in Handsworth, Birmingham, is a 'classic' of our time. Their findings raised the issue of black minorities constituting an 'underclass' in the UK. A Weberian approach was used to argue that the disadvantaged position of minority ethnic groups placed them in an inferior situation to whites in employment. In this extract, Rex and Tomlinson explain British developments in the study of 'race relations', making particular reference to their own empirical research of the working class in Handsworth.

A class analysis of colonial immigrants

... WE MAY APPROACH the study of immigrant assimilation in Britain by asking the following questions. How far do immigrants on the average enjoy the same rights as their fellow workers and neighbours in British cities? How far is the group-consciousness, sense of identity and group attachment of the immigrant minority still organized on an ethnic or colonial basis, and how far have individual members transferred their attachments to class and status-based British groups? How far is the maintenance of ethnic group identity compatible with the attainment of equal rights; that is to say, is it possible for the immigrant to gain acceptance and equality of treatment, while at the same time preserving a distinct social and cultural identity? And, finally, how far does the class-consciousness of the British social classes exclude the immigrant as a potential member?

Since no one would disagree with the proposition that class conflict in the labour market is a prime determinant of a working man's total life situation, we should begin by considering the evidence on the employment of immigrants. Ideally this should include knowledge of employment before migration, of his degree of commitment to his country of origin, including his aspirations to mobility there, and of the degree to which he sees his stay in Great Britain as temporary, before we even begin to turn to the evidence on assimilation into the British working class or acceptance into any other part of the class structure.

The history of **colonialism** in the West Indies has many features which are different from that of colonialism in the Indian subcontinent. Basically this difference turns upon the fact that the West Indies became far more totally dependent, culturally speaking, on Britain than did the Indian territories. Thus West Indians would seem, on the face of it, more likely to regard migration to work in Britain itself as a migration which involved crossing no cultural boundaries, and which might be conceived of simply as economically advantageous job mobility, akin to the urban migration of American blacks from the Deep South.

We should expect, therefore, that West Indians would not see their migration simply as temporary, since there would be little chance, relatively speaking, of putting to use in the West Indian context any capital or skills which they had acquired in British cities. This, however, is a matter of hypothetical speculation only, and needs to be tested against the actual evidence of the extent to which migrants maintain their links with their homelands, send remittances home, or have plans to return temporarily or for holidays.

By contrast, Indian, Pakistani and Bangladeshi migrants have often been seen as temporary sojourners in the country of their migration. They have come from socio-economic systems in which, although the overwhelming majority of the population live in abject poverty, there are, or at least appear to be, opportunities for economic and status advancement for those who accumulate capital. If this is true, we should expect the primary interest of the worker during his migration to be one of accumulating wealth at any cost in the hope of an eventual return home. Again, however, this is all a matter of prima facie supposition and the actual evidence which we have to consider regarding return to the homeland may give an altogether more complex picture. As we shall see, during the last hundred years of Empire, Indians played a number of different roles throughout the Empire from Fiji to British Columbia, and when migration to Britain occurred, there were established patterns amongst migrating Indians of living permanently in the Indian diaspora.

In any case, of course, one should expect that, even though there might be a majority tendency in any particular immigrant group to become committed to British society, some might wish to return; while on the other hand, even though another migrant group might regard itself only as temporary, some members will form attachments which tend to make their stay more permanent. Thus, while some adult immigrants might still think of return, their English-educated children may be more attracted by economic opportunities in Great Britain and more likely to stay. Some immigrants may become secularized in urban society, so that they find it increasingly difficult to meet the traditional demands of their home culture. Some will find that the class structure of British society provides opportunities for them which are not available to other immigrants. And, finally, there may be paradoxical developments, as when the children of immigrants aim to return to their parents' home, precisely because they have developed aspirations to acceptance and mobility in British society, but have been frustrated in these.

Much of the data which we have are necessarily set out in terms of a comparison between average West Indian and average Asian (particularly Indian) immigrants. Ideally, of course, these groups should be further sub-divided in terms of their class situation in their homeland, their exposure to British education, their position in the British class structure, and, according to a number of different indices, the perceived permanence of migration. Unfortunately, so far as the survey work reported below is concerned, the numbers in each sub-group, drawn in class terms from our sample, are too small for us to make significant generalizations from them, but we have attempted whenever possible to break down the wide distinction between Asian and West Indian into smaller groupings. ...

The first index for comparison between different immigrant groups and between each of them and their equivalents among native workers is that which indicates how far they can enter employment at all, and it is clear that, overall, black workers are at some disadvantage in this respect. The prime problem, however, is not whether or not immigrants obtain jobs, but what sort of jobs they obtain. Here evidence on West Indian employment up to the early 1960s suggests that West Indian workers tended to go to jobs and to areas where they were not in competition with local workers, and this was probably even more true of Asians. This conclusion fits well enough in general terms with the theory of dual or split labour markets. According to this theory it is normal in industrial society for two distinct labour markets to develop. One is open to candidates who have contacts (indeed it may not strictly speaking be a market at all, but simply a system of internal promotion within an organization) and who, when appointed, have long-term tenure, a great measure of trade-union protection, welfare benefits, high wages and also possibly some degree of humanization of their relations with their employers. In the other labour market all the opposite conditions hold. There is a frequent rotation of employees, much short-term and part-time employment, little in the way of welfare benefits, poor trade-union protection and a tendency for work to be

regarded purely as a matter of disutility, a means of earning money to be used in more significant life contexts. Thus, at the heart of modern industrial society, in the employment relation itself one finds something which may have more general validity, the notion of a working class which has won a secure contractual relationship with those who run the economy, and an '**underclass**' which enjoys no such security but which sees the economy as an alien system with which one has necessarily to communicate in order to earn a living. It is perhaps also worth noting that so far as employment is concerned, women workers share the immigrants' situation, but, because of their familial links, they remain related to mainstream working-class positions in a way in which immigrants are not.

It is not possible, of course, to classify workers precisely according to whether they are in the privileged or underprivileged sector of the labour market, because jobs do not come with labels on them. It is, however, possibly to classify workers according to a number of related indices such as unemployment history, number of hours worked, frequency of shift work, job satisfaction and so on. From these indices it will be possible to see the extent to which immigrant workers are confined to the underparts of the labour market. It is also against this background that the relevance of more orthodox comparisons of occupational and industrial classifications have to be assessed.

Trade-union membership is another matter of some importance. It signifies two things in particular. On the one hand it indicates whether or not immigrants are being employed as blacklegs to undercut native working-class standards. On the other hand it shows the extent to which immigrants have affiliated themselves to the core organizations of the working class. Such evidence as there is has not shown an unwillingness on the part of immigrants to join trades unions. On the contrary, Castles and Kosack, for example, have shown from a review of the evidence on immigrants in industrial disputes that immigrants have not merely used trade unionism for their own purposes, but have been very active in industrial conflicts in which the interests of all workers are threatened. On the other hand, they show that unions have not always been active and effective in dealing with purely immigrant grievances.

If it is shown that immigrants are often members of the major general unions, the significance of this evidence is not always clear. Immigrants may be members of these unions and satisfied with them in general terms. But the union may not have been subjected to a very severe test. A general union may, in fact, cover both sections of the labour market referred to above, but devote its major energies to the defence of its more privileged members. This will leave its less privileged members satisfied providing that they are not asking too much. It might even be the case that in giving its privileged members security the union gives the underprivileged a certain vicarious satisfaction in being members of such a powerful organization. The crunch comes, however, when the workers in the underprivileged sector demand improved conditions in their jobs, stricter control of their own elected shop-stewards and, by no means least important, a willingness on the part of the union and its shop-stewards in the privileged sector of the labour market to permit mobility and promotion. ... The population of workers which we describe is in relatively underprivileged employment, is relatively strongly unionized, but on the whole has not yet pressed the unions to a point at which their willingness to give immigrants their full protection is tested. We have not, ourselves, been able to carry out a plant-based study which might have given some detailed indications of the sorts of problems likely to be encountered, but we have reviewed some of the evidence on industrial disputes in the region which centres on these issues.

One particular facet of the employment problem, however, is that which concerns the fate of immigrant-descended children when they leave British schools and enter the labour market. There they are affected by three sets of factors. One is that, since industrial rationalization is often accomplished by a reduction in the labour force through early retirement of other workers, fewer and fewer jobs are available for the young in these rationalized industries. A second factor is that all immigrants find themselves disadvantaged in the labour market. A third is that the children of some immigrant groups suffer disadvantage in schools which puts them at a further disadvantage in the labour market. Little wonder, then, that 'immigrant youth employment' gives such cause for concern. Little wonder also that unemployed young immigrant workers are amongst the most alienated and militant elements in the total working-class population.

The population with which we have been dealing, in focusing our study on the Handsworth area of Birmingham, is a working-class population, and we have little evidence, therefore, of the experience of middle-class immigrants from the **New Commonwealth**. Obviously professional men and women such as doctors and teachers face quite different problems of acceptance, on which we offer no evidence here. Significantly, however, very few West Indian and Asian professional men live in Handsworth. More common are shop-keepers, but here we should be careful to distinguish between those who have simply succeeded as British shop-keepers, and those who service the immigrant community.

One further overwhelming factor to be borne in

mind in assessing the degree of assimilation or integration of immigrants is, of course, that, even though most of the population which we have studied is stably employed, this by no means implies that they have attained equality with their British peers, or that there is no discrimination. There are many industries and occupations in which discrimination has not been reported, simply because it is so taken for granted on all sides that immigrants do not apply. This is not merely true of middle-class occupations, but also of whole industries employing unskilled and semi-skilled workers. Thus in giving evidence to the Parliamentary Select Committee on Race Relations and Immigration Employment on behalf of the Race Relations Board, Sir Roy Wilson referred to: 'the dock industry where it is well-known that in some areas of the industry it is extremely difficult for anyone who is not a member of a docker's family to enter into this type of employment'. This may be an extreme case, but clearly it would be possible for immigrants to be an underclass in the employment situation without any evident protest, simply because facts like that mentioned by Sir Roy Wilson were taken for granted.

One last point to be noted about the field of employment is that it is not one which is directly affected by government action in the way that housing and education are. On the whole, governments do not create at least long-term permanent employment. They may stimulate the economy to reach overall levels of employment and they try to improve skills and match supply and demand of labour. They also intervene, when other means have failed, to regulate industrial disputes. In contrast, in the sphere of housing in Britain, local government creates and manages a large part of the housing stock, and, in the field of education, provides the overwhelming majority of the schools.

Still less does officially provided race relations machinery affect the employment situation. The evidence presented to the Parliamentary Select Committee by the Race Relations Board shows that the number of cases of discrimination proved either to the satisfaction of internal industrial machinery or to the Board itself was insignificant. The Board itself did not believe that this number gave any indication of the extent of discrimination or disadvantage. Thus the location of discrimination and disadvantage involves studying far more than reported cases of discrimination. It involves the study of the consequences of thousands of acts, which, whatever their intent, are discriminatory against immigrant populations in their effect.

What we are concerned with in the study of employment amongst immigrant workers and their children is their relationship to three different possible social structures or social functions. We are concerned with any continuing link with the socio-economic system and the class and status structure of their country of origin. We are concerned with the extent to which their average fate in the British labour market approximates to that of their British peers. Finally, we are concerned to discover whether there is any tendency at all for the formation of specifically immigrant underclass groupings marked by a separate fate and by the emergence of incipient immigrant labour organization. Subsequently to answering these questions we should also ask whether, as in the case with British trades unions, there is a tendency for immigrant workers' organizations to become the core of more comprehensive political and cultural groupings.

Key terms

The following key terms appear in the text above. They have been defined below to aid with the reading of this item.

colonialism control by European countries of most of Asia, Africa and Latin America dominant between the late nineteenth century and early twentieth century

underclass a concept applied to groups at the bottom of a class-based stratification system

New Commonwealth a political association consisting of Britain and states that were formerly British colonies

Questions

1 On the basis of what you have read, explain what Rex and Tomlinson mean when, elsewhere, they have suggested: 'The British are largely ethnically homogeneous, but class divisions lead to a confrontation between two cultures or between a national ruling class culture and a multitude of local and regional ones'.

2 Account for the lack of assimilation of immigrants groups into the capitalist system.

3 Outline and explain one area in which minority ethnic groups generally face social inequality in contemporary Britain.

Reading 7.5 **Marxism, ideology and migrant labour**

Robert Miles (from) *Racism and Migrant Labour* (1982) London: Routledge, pp. 167–73.

Editorial comments

This Marxist reading from Robert Miles' famous work on migrant labour in Europe, initiated much theoretical investigation into 'race' and ethnicity within a contemporary framework. He argued that 'race' exists as a socially constructed ideology, located within capitalist class relations to promote false class consciousness (an idea later utilized by the Centre for Contemporary Cultural Studies). Racial identities were seen to fragment the working class and thereby reduce any tendency towards class conflict. Miles examined the capitalist exploitation of the labour of racialized groups, but as a consequence of his Marxist framework he does marginalize the concept of 'race'.

Racial categorization of migrant labour: the British case

ALTHOUGH THE MATERIAL demands of British capital was the determinate factor in stimulating the labour migration from the New Commonwealth in the 1950s and 1960s, we cannot establish an equally clear and singularly determinate economic motive for the subsequent political and **ideological** reaction to the migration. It is important to try to establish by reference to historical analysis the sense in which this reaction (which I typify as racial categorization) was independent of directly economic pressures and the sense in which it was grounded in (but even then not necessarily directly determined by) such material factors.

As already indicated, the migrants from the Caribbean and the Indian sub-continent did not enter a neutral political and ideological context when they came to Britain. On the one hand, they entered a politico-legal context which defined them as British citizens while, on the other, they entered an ideological context shaped in part by the need to justify and rationalize the colonial exploitation of the previous three centuries. As we have seen, the ideology of racism was crucially structured (but not solely determined) by these processes. Herein lies one instance of the **relative autonomy** of racism as an element of the ideological process of racialization. Racist imagery was therefore available as an element of British national culture, available to be reproduced to categorize these migrants whose labour power was so urgently required on London Transport and in the textile mills of Lancashire. The interesting and decisive question concerns who it was who articulated that racist ideology, and for what reason. The former question is perhaps more easily answered than the second.

Sections of the working class in certain of the major English conurbations became active in anti-immigration organizations, but they were not without direct support amongst the dominant class in the late 1950s. A small number of Conservative politicians were very vocal in their opposition to New Commonwealth migration, but the role of employers is not clear for, as Freeman and Spencer have pointed out: 'The evidence is ambiguous. There was high black (and white) employment in 1961–2, but there were also specific labour shortages, particularly in the public service industries.' What is not questionable is that by the early 1960s there was in existence within both the working class and the ruling class a political movement of opposition to New Commonwealth migration and that that movement gave expression to racist sentiment and belief. Its most obvious and immediate effect was the introduction of racist immigration control in 1962. There is little point in outlining the subsequent development and success of this movement here because it only involves repeating what others have clearly established. What is worth dwelling on is the nature and significance of this political and ideological reaction to labour migration from the New Commonwealth and the terms with which we should attempt to analyse it.

Much of the reaction does not seem to have been expressed in the form of the articulation of an explicitly racist ideology like that formulated by the amateur scientists of the nineteenth century, although the activities of the various fascist groups constitute a significant exception. Rather, racist images and beliefs are expressed in a piecemeal and often inconsistent form. Nevertheless, the language of 'race' was and is used to refer to and describe these migrants, the object of much of the political agitation is to ensure that they are less favourably treated (or even 'repatriated') than the rest of the working class, and the practice of racial discrimination is widespread in the allocation of jobs and housing. The result has been a racialization of migrant labour (see Figure 1). Migrants came to Britain to sell their labour power. They were met with an increasingly negative political and ideological reaction, particularly in the 1960s and 1970s, which succeeded in applying the label of 'race' to the migrants. Consequently, they were negatively racialized and were thereby assigned a special position in ideological relations (as well as simultaneously being assigned to a specific position in economic and political relations).

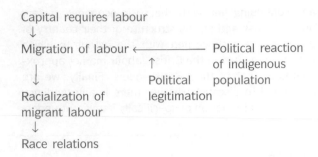

Figure 1 Racialization of migrant labour

This specific position is signalled in the 'everyday world' by the notion of 'race relations'. What is at issue here is not so much that 'race relations' are defined as problematic by the state and by sections of both the ruling and the working class, but more the fact that the notion is employed at all. One can easily demonstrate the specificity of the employment of the notion by pointing out that neither the Irish nor the Jewish migrations of the nineteenth century were defined as creating 'race relations' situations in Britain (although they were racialized to a significant degree). Moreover, one can point to the fact that entry of Vietnamese in the late 1970s did not come to be defined as likely to 'worsen race relations', but they rather were defined as political refugees, a significant contrast to the reaction to the Kenyan and Ugandan 'Asians' in 1968 and 1972 who were also, in fact, political refugees. The notion of 'race relations' is a phenomenal, social construction, a way not so much of interpreting social relations, but of constructing social relations in a particular ideological form. The reproduction of the notion ensures that social significance continues to be attributed to **phenotypical** variation such as to have an ongoing determinate effect on political and economic relations both within and between classes. That the persons so labelled were and are migrants, locked into the demands of the capitalist mode of production, is therefore obscured by their being constructed as distinct 'races' by the majority of the British population at all levels of the class structure.

This ideological process of racialization is not to be understood as an illusory process. As a social process, it is real not only in the sense that the label of 'race' is constructed and applied in the social world but also in the sense that its application has its own determinate effects. Those effects can decisively shape the form and direction of class struggles. The process of class fractionalization is paralleled by the production and reproduction of particular political interests which are expressed in a specific ideological form. The imposition of racist immigration controls stimulates resistance from those affected by them. Discrimination in employment, racist police practice and political attacks inspired by fascist political parties all similarly and necessarily bring about a distinct political consciousness and political practice from those subject to these processes. For Caribbean, Indian and Pakistani migrants, this constitutes the substance and reinforcement of fractionalization within the British working class. And, indeed, sections of the working class have had their own, independent effect on establishing and reinforcing this fractionalization because of the racial discrimination practised by trade union officials and members and because of working-class support for and membership of the National Front and British Movement, etc. This economic and political division within the working class therefore spawns a set of distinct political interests and strategies which can take a multitude of forms, including everything from self-defence groups to English-language classes, from revolutionary sects to community associations (although the formation of many of these can also be encouraged by distinct cultural interests).

The emergence of these particular interests and the necessity for a distinct political practice by the class fraction so created mirrors the racial categorization. Indeed, the political and ideological boundary can be actively reinforced by the explicit utilization and re-evaluation of the notion of 'race', as illustrated in the formation of political organizations which have as one aim the developing of a positive identity for the 'black race'. In this way, the language of 'race' (once having been positively re-defined), can come to be utilized as a solidaristic and unifying force. But equally, if not more, likely is a decision not to become involved in the political organizations of the working class, or, if they are joined for pragmatic reasons, not to participate actively within them. Whichever strategy is 'chosen', it must always be analysed not in isolation, but in relation to the original expression of racism and the accompanying exclusionary activities. And although particular political interests are constructed which are specifically those of a racialized class fraction because of racism and racial discrimination, they are also general class interests because the fractionalization constitutes another obstruction to the emergence of that class as a more unitary political force.

To this point in this section, I have argued that those who migrated to Britain in the 1950s and 1960s were faced with a negative response which can be described as racialization because sections of all classes focused their ideological and political reaction upon the migrant's phenotypical characteristics. But this process occurred within certain material parameters and cannot be explained solely in terms of the simple reproduction of a racist ideology constructed in an earlier period, as some have done.

There are two senses in which racialization is anchored in **material relations** which I wish to mention here. The first is that the object of the process of rationalization is not a group of people in the abstract, but a group of people who occupy a specific position in production relations. The migrants of the 1950s and early 1960s were a replacement labour force, coming to Britain to occupy positions vacated by individuals who had moved into other sectors of wage-labour employment. In this period, racial discrimination could not have been the major factor in allocating migrants to a position in production relations. Rather, employers were recruiting migrants primarily because there was no other source of labour available to them. But it soon became obvious that racial discrimination by employers served as a constraint when those migrants sought promotion or employment in sectors where there was no such shortage of labour. Thus, racialization (in the form of direct discrimination) has served to reinforce and maintain the economic stratification of wage labour: the racialization of the migrants is simultaneously their confinement to certain ranks of wage labour, namely manual labour and often predominantly in semi- or unskilled jobs.

Indeed, the extent of this confinement has encouraged some interest in the applicability or otherwise of the concept of a dual labour market to describe this situation in Britain. The concept derives from research in the USA and refers to the existence of two distinct labour markets, one characterized by low wages, poor working conditions, unstable employment and few opportunities for advancement and the other by precisely the opposite characteristics. Moreover, the persons who occupy these two distinct markets tend to be distinguished by other characteristics; for example, those occupying the former labour market tend to be female and/or 'black'. Bosanquet and Doeringer concluded from British data that there was a close similarity with the situation in the USA.

Although it is unlikely that migrants constitute the sole source of labour in the 'disadvantaged market' in Britain, the fact that they are rarely employed outside it is testimony to the significance of racial discrimination. Moreover, the fact of this concentration has its own ideological effect in that it appears (i.e. can be interpreted) to demonstrate the 'suitability' of 'racialized' labour for only low skilled, low paid manual jobs. Thereby, phenotypical appearance can be equated with a disadvantaged position in production relations: the negative connotations of 'blackness' come to overlap with and reinforce the negative connotations of much semi- and unskilled manual work and so adds another level of meaning to the already existing fractionalization of wage labour.

The second concerns the ideological significance of the struggle over the distribution of scarce resources within the working class in the urban context, particularly in those areas undergoing material decline. With Annie Phizacklea, I have argued elsewhere that material decline constitutes an important underlying dynamic to the articulation of racism within the working class. In most of the major English conurbations there are areas of declining capitalist production which are also characterized by poor housing conditions, inadequate provision of social and other services and other measures of deprivation. These are also areas which for various reasons have often been chosen by migrant labourers and their families as areas of residential settlement. The coincidence of their settlement with material decline, combined with their demand for access to resources (especially housing) which are in short supply has, in the context of the racist legacy of colonialism, served as a direct stimulus to the articulation and reproduction of racism within the working-class resident in such areas. Such racism, born of the direct experience of material decline via 'common sense' reasoning (the coincidence of decline and residential settlement being interpreted causally, leading to the conclusion that 'the blacks cause decline') is arguably that which served as the initial current from within the working class in the late 1950s and early 1960s which resulted in the formation of immigration control associations. This was a crucial stage in the racialization of British politics because British governments interpreted their appearance with electoral significance and so set about appeasing this racism. Moreover, it is probably upon this form of racism that fascist political organizations subsequently developed in English urban areas in the 1970s when Labour and Conservative governments failed to solve the 'inner city crisis' and baulked at following the racist policy of immigration control to the logical conclusion of compulsory '**repatriation**'.

In both of these instances cited, the process of racialization is locked into and has its own effects upon the reproduction of material inequality and disadvantage within the working class. This process is simultaneously the reproduction of inequality per se and of the allocation of persons to different positions in the structure of inequality, with ideological and political significance coming to be attached to phenotypical differences. A consequence is that the material disadvantage of the migrant appears as disadvantage caused by 'race'. ... The disadvantage results from the combination of positions of material inequality structured by capital (low wages result from an attempt to maintain profitability) with a particular process of allocation of persons to those positions, the process consisting in part of the reproduction of racism as an ideology and the practice of discrimination. The disadvantage and the ideological form in which it appears must therefore always be analysed and presented as a social (i.e. human) construction and not as a biological determinant.

Key terms

The following key terms appear in the text above. They have been defined below to aid with the reading of this item.

ideological the outcome of a set of beliefs that serve the interests of a particular social group

relative autonomy also known as cultural Marxism, because racism is used to strengthen cultural hegemony, with 'race' being seen as having some degree of freedom from class relations

phenotypical relating to physical characteristic, e.g. skin colour

material relations the relationship to the means of production

repatriation returning people to their country of origin

Questions

1 Evaluate Miles' argument that 'race' is a socially constructed ideology which supports capitalist class relations.

2 Explain the process of 'racialization' in the UK since the 1950s.

3 Using Miles' Marxist framework, outline the reaction of capitalists to immigration control.

Reading 7.6 **Ethnicity and intelligence**

Richard Herrnstein and Charles Murray (from) *The Bell Curve* (1996) New York: Free Press, pp. 270–2, 276–80 and 292–3.

Editorial comments

Herrnstein and Murray were aware of the controversial nature of their material when *The Bell Curve* was first published in 1994. Their argument, that cognitive ability varies according to genotypical ethnic differences, carried such hugely racist connotations (that black people are at the bottom of the socio-economic structure because of a lower genetically based IQ than whites) that social scientists reacted with bewildered shock. Herrnstein and Murray's ideas have no scientific basis or support, yet New Right theorists appear to continue undaunted in their support for what can only be termed racist propaganda.

Ethnic differences in cognitive ability

ETHNIC DIFFERENCES IN measured **cognitive ability** have been found since intelligence tests were invented. The battle over the meaning of these differences is largely responsible for today's controversy over intelligence testing itself. That many readers have turned first to this chapter indicates how sensitive the issue has become.

Our primary purpose is to lay out a set of statements, as precise as the state of knowledge permits, about what is currently known about the size, nature, validity, and persistence of ethnic differences on measures of cognitive ability. A secondary purpose is to try to induce clarity in ways of thinking about ethnic differences, for discussions about such differences tend to run away with themselves, blending issues of fact, theory, ethics, and public policy that need to be separated.

The first thing to remember is that the differences among individuals are far greater than the differences between groups. If all the ethnic differences in intelligence evaporated overnight, most of the intellectual variation in America would endure. The remaining inequality would still strain the political process, because differences in cognitive ability are problematic even in ethnically homogeneous societies. But the politics of cognitive inequality get hotter – sometimes too hot to handle – when they are attached to the politics of ethnicity. We believe that the best way to keep the temperature down is to work through the main facts carefully and methodically. ...

We frequently use the word *ethnic* rather than *race*, because race is such a difficult concept to employ in the American context. What does it mean to be 'black' in America, in racial terms, when the word black (or African-American) can be used for people whose ancestry is more European than African? How are we to classify a person whose parents hail from Panama but whose ancestry is predominantly African? Is he a Latino? A black? The rule we follow here is to classify people according to the way they classify themselves. The studies of 'blacks' or 'Latinos' or 'Asians' who live in America generally denote people who *say* they are black, Latino, or Asian – no more, no less. ...

It would be disingenuous to leave the racial issue at that, however, for race is often on people's minds when they think about IQ. Thus we will eventually comment on cognitive differences among races as they might derive from genetic differences, telling a story that is interesting but still riddled with more questions than answers. This prompts a second point to be understood at the outset: There are differences between races, and they are the rule, not the exception. That assertion may seem controversial to some readers, but it verges on **tautology**: Races are by definition groups of people who differ in characteristic ways. Intellectual fashion has dictated that all differences must be denied except the absolutely undeniable differences in appearance, but nothing in biology says this should be so. On the contrary, race differences are varied and complex – and they make the human species more adaptable and more interesting. ...

Do blacks score differently from whites on standardized tests of cognitive ability?

If the samples are chosen to be representative of the American population, the answer has been yes for every known test of cognitive ability that meets basic psychometric standards of **reliability** and **validity**. The answer is also yes for almost all of the studies in which the black and white samples are matched on some special characteristic – samples of juvenile delinquents, for example, or of graduate students – but there are exceptions. The implication of this effect of selecting the groups to be compared is discussed later. Since black–white differences are the ones that strain discourse most severely, we will probe deeply into the evidence and its meaning.

How large is the black–white difference?

The usual answer to this question is one **standard deviation**. In discussing IQ tests, for example, the black mean is commonly given as 85, the white mean as 100, and the standard deviation as 15. But the differences observed in any given study seldom conform exactly to one standard deviation. ...

When we focus on the studies that meet stricter criteria, the range of values for the B/W [black/white] difference narrows accordingly. The range of results is considerably reduced, for example, for studies that have taken place since 1940 (after testing's most formative period), outside the South (where the largest B/W differences are found), with subjects older than age 6 (after scores have become more stable), using full test batteries from one of the major IQ tests, and with standard deviations reported for that specific test administration. Of the forty-five studies meeting these criteria, all but nine of the B/W differences are clustered between 0.5 and 1.5 standard deviations. The mean difference was 1.06 standard deviations, and all but eight of the thirty-one reported a B/W difference greater than 0.8 standard deviations.

Still more rigorous selection criteria do not diminish the size of the gap. For example, with tests given outside the South only after 1960, when people were increasingly sensitized to racial issues, the number of studies is reduced to twenty-four, but the mean difference is 1.10 standard deviations. ...

For any equal number of blacks and whites, a large proportion have IQs that can be matched up. This is the distribution to keep in mind whenever thinking about individuals.

But an additional complication has to be taken into account: In the United States, there are about six whites for every black. This means that the IQ overlap of the two populations as they actually exist in the United States look very different. ...

... A B/W difference can be problematic to American society as a whole. At the lower end of the IQ range, there are approximately equal numbers of blacks and whites. But throughout the upper half of the range, the disproportions between the number of whites and blacks at any given IQ level are huge. To the extent that the difference represents an authentic difference in cognitive functioning, the social consequences are potentially huge as well. ...

Let us assume that during the past two decades black and white cognitive ability as measured by IQ has in fact converted by an amount that is consistent with the convergence in educational aptitude measures – a narrowing of approximately 0.15 to 0.25 standard deviation units, or the equivalent of two to three IQ points overall. Why have the scores converged? The answer calls for speculation.

We take for granted that individual variations in cognitive ability depend on both genes and environment. In a period as short as twenty years, environmental changes are likely to provide the main reason for the narrowing racial gap in scores. Real and important though the problems of the underclass are, and acknowledging that the underclass is disproportionately black, living conditions have improved for most African-Americans since the 1950s – socially, economically, and educationally.

Consider the schools that blacks attend, for example. Some schools in the inner cities are worse than they were thirty years ago, but proportionately few blacks live in these worst-of-the-worst areas. Throughout the South and in much of the rest of the country, many black children as recently as the 1950s attended ramshackle schools with undertrained teachers and meagre teaching materials. Any comparison between the schools that most blacks attend now and the ones they attended in the 1950s favours contemporary schools. Assuming that education affects cognitive capacity, the rising investment in education disproportionately benefits the cognitive levels at the lower end of the socio-economic spectrum.

The argument can be repeated for public health. If nutrition, shelter, and health care affect intellectual development, then rising standards of living are disproportionately going to show up in rising scores for the economically disadvantaged rather than for the upper classes. For travel and its educational benefits, the argument also applies. Not so long ago, many less advantaged people spent their lives within a few miles of their birthplaces. Today, Americans of nearly all walks of life crowd the interstate roads and the airports. Finally, for that most contemporary form of vicarious travel – the popular media – the levelling is still more dramatic. The modern media can bring the world to everyone in ways that were once open only to the rich.

Because blacks are shifted toward the lower end of the socio-economic range, such improvements benefit them, on average, more than whites. If the improvements affect cognitive development, the black–white gap should have contracted. Beyond this socio-economic levelling, there might also have been a levelling due to diminishing racism. The legacy of historic racism may still be taking its toll on cognitive development, but we must allow the possibility that it has lessened, at least for new generations. This too might account for some narrowing of the black–white gap.

Key terms

The following key terms appear in the text above. They have been defined below to aid with the reading of this item.

cognitive ability aptitude for thinking

tautology repetition of same thing in other words in the same sentence

reliability the ability of a test to attain the same results if repeated in exactly the same way

validity the ability of a test to measure what it sets out to measure

standard deviation the degree to which a variable differs from the norm

Questions

1 Assess the contribution of Herrnstein and Murray's theory to the understanding of racial disadvantage in America.

2 Evaluate the strengths and weaknesses of a biological explanation of racial inequality in contemporary Britain.

3 In what ways could the New Right theory be seen to support racist assumptions?

Reading 7.7 **Post-modern racial identities**

Tariq Modood (from) 'Culture and identity', in Modood, T *et al., Diversity and Disadvantage: Ethnic minorities in Britain* (1997) London: Policy Studies Institute, pp. 291–7.

Editorial comments

In this reading, Modood explores the issue of ethnic identity in contemporary Britain. He argues that an 'ethnic assertiveness' exists, which has emerged from ethnic minority people feeling that they are not respected, consisting of 'positive' images to counterpoise traditional ethnic stereotypes. He points out that these identities are not static nor stable, but change through the sharing of social space with others.

Modood presents a qualitative post-modern discussion of how ethnic groups understand their own identity and how these perceptions change and vary between and within the groups.

Describing oneself

HOW DO ETHNIC minority people think of themselves? How salient is their ethnic background in their conception of themselves; and what is the relative importance of different components of ethnicity – 'racial' grouping, skin-colour, extra-British origins, religion – in the self-image of ethnic minority persons?

These matters are of course highly complex and not at all easy for a survey of this kind to elicit data on. For a start, it is obvious that they are matters to which people may not have given much explicit thought or have a limited degree of self-consciousness about, and so their answers may be of a poor quality or may require a length of interview time not available in a survey covering so many different topics. Moreover, they are matters which are highly context-dependent. Some things may be much more salient in some contexts than others; indeed, the topic may make sense only when a context is chosen for purposes of illustration and yet will influence the answers elicited.

We decided therefore to create a question which outlined a specific, if rather unusual, situation, but which at the same time was as context-free as possible. Or, more precisely, a situation as independent as possible from social structure, social roles, community life or a pre-existing relationship. We asked interviewees to:

> suppose you were describing yourself on the phone to a new acquaintance of your own sex from a country you have never been to. Which of these would tell them something important about you. ...

The interviewer then read out 12 personal attributes, and the interviewee was asked to say 'yes' or 'no' to each (they could therefore say 'yes' or 'no' to as many as they liked). In this way a non-threatening situation of potential friendship was projected and complications to do with sexual norms and behaviour minimized. While the scenario the question depicts is somewhat unusual, it is meant to approximate to a neutral context, or at least a context where the British social pressures to project a particular identity or group label are not emphasized.

One important attribute deliberately omitted was

Table 1 Elements of self-description

percentages

	Caribbean	Indian	African Asian	Pakistani	Bangladeshi	Chinese
These would tell a new acquaintance something important about me						
Nationality	81	78	69	74	63	77
White, black, Asian etc	76	68	60	56	64	74
Country your family came from	63	67	62	67	76	65
Age	61	57	50	65	57	50
Job	56	57	65	64	54	61
Education	47	49	60	57	53	54
Height	31	30	26	26	26	13
Colour of hair or eyes	30	25	24	26	19	13
Level of income	16	19	17	19	14	6
Father's job	10	14	15	19	7	7
Weighted count	765	606	290	297	141	183
Unweighted count	580	595	361	538	289	101

Table 2 Religion and colour in self-description

percentages

	Caribbean	Indian	African Asian	Pakistani	Bangladeshi	Chinese
These would tell a new acquaintance something about me						
Religion	44	73	68	83	75	25
Skin colour	61	37	29	31	21	15
Weighted count	765	606	290	397	141	183
Unweighted count	580	595	361	538	289	101

gender. It was assumed that nearly everybody would in fact regard their sex as something important about themselves, but that as some respondents would assume that the other person (who by definition is of the same sex as the interviewee) would know their sex (at the very least, have a good idea by the sound of their voice over the telephone), nothing useful would be gained by respondents saying 'yes' or 'no' to a gender item in the list of personal attributes. Most people would say 'yes', but if they did not, it would be difficult to interpret the 'no' as important.

The answers suggest that their ethnicity is of considerable importance to minority persons in their self-descriptions. Most of the ethnicity items in fact received the most number of 'yes' by each of the minority groups. With ten of the 12 items, there is a common pattern in the frequency of positive answers which can be banded into four, as in Table 1. **Nationality**, 'broad ethnicity' and country of family origins were almost uniformly the items thought most important to mention about themselves to a new acquaintance in an unknown country; two-thirds or more of respondents from each ethnic group chose these items, except that fewer Pakistanis would mention their broad ethnicity, and fewer Chinese would mention the country their family came from. Roughly about half in each group would mention their age, job and education; less than a third would mention their height or the colour of their hair or eyes; and less than a fifth would mention their level of income or their father's job. This leaves two items on which there was a division in the responses of ethnic groups. The two items are religion and skin colour, responses to which are to be found in Table 2. In each case there is a three-way pattern. While well over two-thirds of the South Asians would mention religion, making it their first or second most mentioned item, less than half of Caribbeans would do so, and only a quarter of the Chinese. Six out of ten Caribbeans would, however, mention their skin colour, while about a third or less of the South Asian groups would do so, and few Chinese would.

Bearing in mind that the context is of personal information to someone from another country who does not know what you look like, it is perhaps not surprising that nationality received the primacy that it did. Nevertheless, it is still of some interest that it should do so, as in our development work we found some evidence of a reluctance among British Caribbeans and British Asians in calling themselves 'British' in a British context but finding it easier to do so when abroad. Nor is it surprising that the level of one's income or one's father's occupation should not be thought as likely for inclusion in the hypothetical telephone conversation. It is, however, of some importance that two-thirds or more of interviewees thought their ethnic and family origins as important things to mention about themselves in such a conversation, more important than their job or education, or even their age – surely an important basis of relating to persons and forming friendships. In all groups, however, those in higher occupational classes mentioned their job more often than any other item.

Perhaps the most significant finding was the primacy of religion in self-description in personal contexts for South Asians, in contrast to skin colour which was of little more significance than height. On the other hand, skin colour was of considerable importance to the Caribbeans. These findings are strengthened by responses to the question as to which two of the 12 features were most important. Nationality continued to be stressed, but in the case of South Asians religion was held to be equally or more important, while relatively few Caribbeans (12 per cent) chose it as among the most important and hardly any Chinese at all. Similarly, skin colour emerges as the third most important item for the Caribbeans but insignificant for the Asians.

Respondents were also asked how 'a white person who knew and liked you would describe you to another white person'. The difference from self-description was not great. The item which was most affected was skin colour, which for South Asians moved from 30 per cent to 45 per cent; even so, only 10 per cent of South Asians thought it was one of the most important items likely to be mentioned about them. As in the self-descriptions, religion continued to be the most highlighted item for South Asians, except for African Asians, for whom job continued to enjoy primacy.

Asians thinking of themselves as 'black'

From the 1960s onwards many anti-racists and sociologists have argued that, as racial discrimination was a commonly experienced problem by those whom white people thought of as 'coloured' or 'black', analysis and anti-racist action would be enhanced if all potential victims of white racism were to be described primarily as 'black'. Some analysts acknowledged that not all of the victims, especially among South Asians, would go along with their suggestion, a few protested that the suggestion was a form of political coercion not worthy of anti-racism, but most expressed confidence that enough people would be persuaded by their point of view. The only test of South Asian opinion has been a telephone poll on a BBC South Asian television programme, *Network East*, in March 1989. After opposing points of view were put, viewers were invited to telephone; nearly two-thirds of the more than 3000 who rang in rejected the term 'black' for Asians. It has been suggested, however, that the majority of Asians do think of themselves as 'black', but this cannot be elicited in questioning which is insensitive to the fact that this is an identity which comes alive only in some contexts and not in others, that it is a 'situational identity'. Others have suggested that it is a political identity forged by working-class Asians through anti-racist and class struggle, or more found among younger Asians, and that the opposition to the self-label 'black' is from middle class Asians or, alternatively, from Muslims.

In our development work we found even less use of 'black' by South Asians than in the *Network East* poll, even though it was prevalent among Caribbeans in the same localities. It was found that the Punjabi Indians, especially the young and British-born, were more likely than other Asians to argue, sometimes passionately, for political 'blackness' as the basis of anti-racist unity among the victims of racism and to prevent a divisive emphasis on separate cultural identities.

We decided to survey South Asian and Chinese opinion on this topic by asking them: 'Do you ever think of yourself as being black?' The answers, as presented in Table 3, show that about a fifth of South Asians answered 'yes' (only one Chinese person out of 118 so answered). As can be seen, there was only slight variation between South Asian groups: Indians were slightly more likely, Bangladeshis least likely to respond in the affirmative. Some other variations are worth mentioning too. Contrary to the expectations created by our developmental fieldwork, 16–34-year olds, as well as the over fifties were slightly less likely to consider themselves black as were women. The unemployed were less likely than the employed, but differences between occupational classes were negligible. Those without qualifications were more likely than those with qualifications, and migrants, especially those of more than 25 years residence, were more likely than the British-born to identify themselves as black. Those resident in wards of high minority density were a little less likely to think of themselves as black than those in wards with lower concentrations of ethnic minorities. The biggest variations were regional. About a third of South Asians

Table 3 'Black' as an element of self-conception of South Asians

column percentages

	Indian	African Asian	Pakistani	Bangladeshi
Do you ever think of yourself as being black?				
Yes	26	21	23	18
No	68	75	68	74
Can't say	6	4	9	8
Weighted count	497	337	334	120
Unweighted count	493	310	450	252

Table 4 South Asians: 'On what occasions do you think of yourself as black?'

1 *'All the time, I am black.'*	125
Further example: *'All the time, I wouldn't class myself as anything else.'*	
2 *Because I am Asian, or when I am with Asian people, or participate in Asian community events.*	71
Further examples: *'When I'm out with Asian mates.'*	
'When I'm put into a position when my culture, creed, is under discussion. All the time.'	
3 When in public places where there are many white people	43
4 When applying for jobs or at work.	43
5 *Because I am not white.*	34
Example: *'I'm never going to be white.'*	
6 *When I am being racially harassed or suspect prejudice.*	31
Example: *'When a white person swears and calls you a name, then you become conscious of colour.'*	
7 *'It's what others calls us in this country.'*	18
8 In a discussion about race relations.	8

Items without quote marks are paraphrases or composite quotes from more than one respondent.

in the West Midlands and the North West identified with 'black', but less than half this proportion in the South East and even less in London.

It has been mentioned that it has been argued that blackness for Asians is a situational identity. We wanted to test this idea and identify the kinds of situation in which this identity becomes prominent for South Asians. The interviewer asked 'On what occasions do you think of yourself as black?' and was instructed to probe fully and record verbatim. The answers, sorted into a number of categories, are presented in Table 4. A few respondents gave answers that had too little support from other respondents and are not included, and some respondents gave an answer with more than one aspect, in which case each aspect has been included. Other respondents gave a 'don't know'. The answers in Table 4 do not therefore add up to the total number of affirmative responses. One of the most frequent responses was 'all/most of the time'; another was 'because I am black'; and a third one was a combination of these two. We have therefore taken these three answers together, for they each represent the same total acceptance of a black identity. As such they repre-

sent the most common response. Others said they thought themselves black because they were Asian or when they were participating in events to do with their cultural background. While the first is not situational and the latter is, we have combined these two types of answer because in practice they were sometimes difficult to separate, as in the following example:

I know I am Asian and Indian all the time because I always wear saris and whenever I go out to the shops or I'm in public I know I look different because of my clothes and culture.

This quotation also illustrates a third category: those who felt 'black' when in public places where there are many white people. This category of answer was common as references to applying for jobs or one's work. One other situation that was of some importance was where respondents were being racially harassed or suspected that they were being given the cold shoulder because of their race. A significant number also explained their idea of blackness by reference to not being white, and some referred to how they were labelled by others and to discussions about 'race' with friends and family.

It is interesting that some contexts hardly got mentioned at all. For example, only two persons mentioned looking for accommodation and only one dealing with officialdom, as more might well have done, especially in relation to immigration, permission to stay in Britain and nationality procedures, or the police or other aspects of the criminal justice system. Nor, given that 'black' as an inclusive categorization was developed to express and build a political solidarity between people of Caribbean and South Asian origin, is there any explicit mention of Caribbeans or of solidarity. Indeed, what is most striking is that the majority of this group of Asians did not refer to situations at all. They answered 'all or most of the time' or gave an extremely common situation ('when in public places'), or they answered the 'when' question by a 'why' answer. For answers 1, 5, 7 and partly 2, representing about tow-thirds of the answers, do not list types of situation; rather they are statements about the respondents themselves or clarify what they mean by 'blackness'. For many, then, blackness, especially for those who gave the most emphatic answers ('all the time'), is not an identity which relates to some but not other contexts, but is perceived to be a fundamental aspect of themselves (at least in Britain). This tallies with our development fieldwork in which we found that while only a minority of Asians thought of themselves as 'black', for those who did this was an important identity, often subsuming all others.

What was less clear in our development work, is that for some Asian people, not only is 'blackness' compatible with their ethnicity and culture, it is also rooted in their sense of being and/or being treated as Asians, that is to say, as people having a certain physical appearance ('not white') and of being visibly cultural outsiders (wearing a sari, for example). For some Asians identification with blackness is not just a product of the suspicion of **discrimination** and explicit racial abuse, it is also produced by the experience of being made self-conscious about being *Asian*. This is particularly interesting because it means that even some of those Asians who think of themselves as black do not take the view that skin colour is the attribute of blackness. Rather they think that their cultural attributes are, both in their own eyes and in those of white people, part of their stigmatization, part of their racial identity. This complex understanding of how some South Asians perceive they are 'racialized' is consistent with the discussion in the employment chapter with what the victims of perceived discrimination said they believed was the ground of the discrimination against them.

An anomaly that emerges from these questions, however, is the discrepancy between the South Asians who thought that white people saw them in terms of skin colour (45 per cent), the South Asians who themselves would include skin colour in self-descriptions (30 per cent), and the South Asians who thought there were sometimes occasions when they thought of themselves as black (22 per cent). In our development work we found that some South Asians referred to themselves and other South Asians as 'brown'. It may be, therefore, that while most Asians do not see their ethnicity in terms of a 'colour', those who do are as likely to think of themselves as 'brown' as much as 'black'.

Key terms

The following key terms appear in the text above. They have been defined below to aid with the reading of this item.

nationality the sharing of a culture

(racial) **discrimination** the behavioural manifestation of racial prejudice; acting out of racist beliefs

Questions

1 Assess the post-modernist argument that racial identity cannot be a fixed or static concept in a constantly changing social world.

2 Using the evidence provided by Modood outline how different ethnic minority groups perceive their own identity.

3 What strengths and weaknesses can be identified in the research methodology used for collecting data on the subjective issue of racial identity?

Reading 7.8 **Feminism – a black and white issue**

Caroline Knowles and Sharmila Mercer (from) 'Feminism and antiracism: an exploration of the political possibilities', in A. Cambridge and S. Feuchtwang (eds) *Anti-Racist Strategies* (1990) Avebury: Ashgate.

Editorial comments

Knowles and Mercer present a feminist analysis of 'race' and gender, supporting the position that only temporary relationships exist between the two, which emerge only in specific circumstances. This reading consequently argues that women and minority ethnic groups are not inevitably oppressed, because the terms 'woman' and 'race' are social constructs with relative meanings. Knowles and Mercer believe that the concept of 'woman' has been divided into black and white, by many black feminists, to show the difference of experience and issues for black women compared to white women. The extract highlights some issues that directly affect black women, such as

reproduction, but which have not been represented in British (white) feminism. Knowles and Mercer suggest that 'feminism' may have ignored the 'race dimension' of gender inequality, because the relationship between 'race' and gender as forms of stratification is not clear.

Feminism and antiracism

Feminism

DESPITE THE POLITICAL and theoretical diversity of feminism, feminists have in common a recognition of themselves as a social category separating them from and placing them in opposition to others. We also have a **collective identity** in public imagery. Although we are suggesting that the content of feminist politics is a site of struggle, it is possible to identify a general direction and set of objectives, the content of which needs to be spelled out in each case. In this context a feminist perspective is one which prioritizes the identification of, and opposition to, actions, practices or procedures which have the effect of excluding women or disadvantaging them relative to men. Sexism in this context is a series of effects, not intentions (though it might also be this) which can be identified, monitored and challenged. Sexism need not be considered the prerogative of men, capitalism or the state. It need not have a cause, only a multiplicity of effects resulting from the actions and practices of diverse agencies. Sexism is evident in the construction of womanhood by, for example, a diversity of agencies promoting particular health and educative norms in the conduct of family life with which women come into contact.

The dissection of the feminist constituency by race has, in debates in *Feminist Review*, *Spare Rib* [and] *Race and Class* ... occurred along three dimensions which establish the specificity of black women. The black female constituency as an object of political analysis is demarcated by the experience of race and gender oppression, a common history of revolt and its analytical distinctiveness in feminist discourse organized around the family, patriarchy and reproduction. We propose to examine each of these in turn and see what is at stake in their use.

The family, **patriarchy** and reproduction are the main general terms around which an understanding of female oppression is organized in white feminist discourse. It is precisely around this kind of an issue that an understanding of the *unitary* nature of female oppression, so rightly offensive to black feminists, has been built. The response of feminists has been to establish the specificity of black women and their rela-

tionship to the family, patriarchy and reproduction. Therein lies a paradox. 'Black women' is a term which is used by black feminists to incorporate a diversity of lifestyles and yet it is also retained as an undifferentiated category for analysis on the grounds that black women are united by the forces of racism.

Family

Debates about the status of the family for black and white women focus on the extent to which it operates as a force for exploitation and oppression. What black feminists have rightly designated 'white feminism' (because of the narrowness of its focus) maintains that the family is one of the key sites of female oppression. Black feminists, on the other hand, maintain that the black family is a qualitatively different proposition from the family structures in which white women are involved. Black women, argues Carby, are less dependent on men and are not oppressed by the family. Indeed, black feminist analysis of the family is that it is part of the resistance (to racist oppression) rather than collusion in it. White feminists have responded to this by acknowledging that black women in Britain live within different kinds of family arrangements. Barrett and McIntosh, for example, regard this admission as an attempt to deal with what they consider the rather narrow ethnocentrism of the women's movement. They nevertheless maintain that the family is still a site for the perpetuation of gender inequalities which many black women may wish to escape. To support this they quote the views of some Indian women reported in *Manushi* magazine. This leads them to comment that opposition to immigration laws and procedures which split up families may be problematic for feminists because it involves enforcing nuclear family, heterosexist norms. This is clearly an area where feminist and antiracist objectives come into conflict. Immigration procedures operate in a racist manner in singling out black families for harassment, and feminists may justly be accused of racism in supporting, for whatever reasons, actions which, in challenging the family, specifically disadvantage black families.

It seems to us that the term 'family' lends itself to infinite variation, that it contains within it choice and flexibility for negotiation between its members over the conditions in which they inhabit a common living space. We are here using the term 'family' to indicate any living arrangement which is referred to as a family. The position of black women in their families, once we reject the stereotypes of the Afro-Caribbean one-parent family and the Asian woman without rights of disposal over her body and labour power, is infinitely varied. We therefore support the black feminist challenge to the unitary nature of the family as a site of female oppression, but argue that the family cannot just be divided into black and white. Nor does this distinction – between black and white families – correspond to distinctions made between families by agencies in the public domain. The black family, like the white family, does not take a particular form. The term 'black family' is in fact a political construct. It designates a constituency to be mobilized in political struggle – against racism – part of which must be reclaimed by black women from the clutches of another set of political claims – white feminism.

Reproduction

Black women have also sought to establish their analytical distinctiveness from white women over the issue of reproduction. They point out that, while white women have prioritized struggles to defend limited abortion rights, black women are fending off the willingness of medical agencies to curtail their fertility. The use on black women of Depo-Provera, a contraceptive drug injected into the muscle which has been known to cause sterility, is often cited to support a different attitude by medical agencies to black and white mothers. Both struggles, in fact, are about the rights of women over their own reproductive capacities. It is also entirely possible that the manner in which medical agencies, who control access to abortion, sterilization and fertilization (with it *in vitro* fertilization techniques), deal with women's requests is informed by their conception of adequacy in mothering. Such delicate assessments are capable of being made in ways which disadvantage black women.

Reproduction is doubtless an arena in which racial differences between women are a focus for unequal treatment. Further research would identify the practices through which such inequalities are produced. This approach side-steps concerns over the use of Depo-Provera until we are able to establish on whom it is used in Britain. (We suspect, from discussions with community nurses, that it is used on women not trusted by medical agencies to control their own fertility. Some of these women may be black, but others will be white and judged deficient as mothers because of handicap or presumed low intelligence.) We do not know how Depo-Provera is used in Britain, yet it always features in arguments about race and reproduction. As such, it is a fairly shaky basis on which to demarcate a unitary black female constituency. We do know that it is used on black women in third-world countries, as are other drugs which do not meet the necessary safety standards in Britain, but this needs to be taken up and challenged with the agencies responsible for their use and distribution in the third world. Learning about the use of a drug like Depo-Provera in a third-world country will indicate how black women are perceived and treated in that particular social context, but it is difficult to see what this might tell us about the position of black women in Britain.

Patriarchy

Patriarchy is the final analytical construct we wish to discuss over which black feminists have distanced themselves from the women's movement. Since the 1970s the use of the term 'patriarchy' in the context of women's politics and academic debate has become increasingly elaborate. The impetus for this has been provided by the critiques of black feminists who, like Carby, suggest that because of racism black men do not benefit from patriarchal social structures in the same way as white men and that benefit from patriarchy does not distinguish black men from black women. 'Black women have been dominated "patriarchally" in different ways by men of different "colours"'. This has encouraged white feminists to be more cautious of their use of this term as indicative of the female condition and a commonality among women. Yet few white feminist writers are prepared to jettison patriarchy as a central analytical concept. This is because, in their view, it ultimately unites all women in a common sisterhood as undifferentially oppressed subjects, all of whom have in common a disadvantaged relation to men, and it is precisely this unity which provides the force for resistance. This is certainly true of Barrett and McIntosh in their replies to criticism by black feminists in *Feminist Review*. They see the concept of patriarchy as 'one with a valuable but specific purchase'. They reject it as a noun but retain it as an adjective, descriptive of certain types of social relations 'characterized by the personal, often physical, exploitation of a servility whose causes are usually economic and always strictly regulated through a hierarchical order'. Patriarchy is retained as an analytical concept and with it a privileging of gender over other social divisions. It is this which black feminists find most offensive: the privileging of gender over race in a permanent hierarchy of social divisions. Having established the primacy of gender, it remains only to establish how this is dissected by race. This is the task which Barrett and McIntosh, as well as many other white feminists, prioritize. Thus racial divisions are relegated to a secondary importance.

The establishing of a primacy of one form of social division over another in effect is establishing which form of oppression, gender or racial oppression, has primacy as a political issue. We shall argue later that this is not an issue which can be decided once and for all. Rival primacies involve difficult negotiations between the politics of gender equality and the politics of racial equality, or which constituency has priority, black people or women. These priorities can only be established in relation to specific issues and the political configurations in which they occur.

Oppression

A black female constituency is further demarcated in many black feminist accounts by the experience of oppression. It is this which, it is suggested, unites black women and places them in opposition to white women. The experience of which black women speak arises from being both black and female in a white society which, it is argued, is by definition racist. Oppression is organized around race and gender divisions, with race divisions being accorded a permanent primacy in the establishment of political priorities. This is the opposite of the white feminist position which asserts the primacy of gender. Racial oppression is presented as the result of forms of interaction between black women (and black men) and British society and a range of British social institutions in particular. Racial oppression – it is supposed – is obviously something which black women share with black men. … And this poses difficulties in the construction of a feminist politics which, in general, seeks not only to exclude men but place them in an antagonistic relationship to women.

Racial oppression, for us, is a vague formulation which needs to be **deconstructed** and '**operationalized**' in terms of its detailed practices. We think of racial disadvantage, racism or racial inequality in terms of practices, procedures and actions which have the effect of excluding, providing unequal access for or in some way disadvantaging black people. This is similar to the conception of gender inequality we outlined earlier. The practices and procedures which constitute racism and sexism are likely to be different and there is no particular relationship between the two. Our notion of race and gender oppression is also significantly different from that of authors such as Carby and Bourne in that it does not attempt to identify a single cause or source of disadvantage.

Accounts such as Carby's and Bourne's identify a general set of processes in which disadvantage is inevitably and permanently inscribed. Capitalism, colonialism and patriarchal social systems are frequently identified as producing inherent race and gender inequalities which, in various ways, serve the needs of the systems they perpetuate. The grim inevitably of sexism and racism is the message of these accounts which deal with 'state racism' and 'institutionalized sexism'. Opposition to these general 'isms' is necessarily all-embracing, reaching beyond the manifestations of the problem to the structures of the system itself. Thus, ultimately, all forms of struggle are focused on capitalism and its political organization, the 'state'. But when, as we are suggesting, racism and sexism are viewed as a series of effects which do not have a single cause, a different kind of politics is established. There is no need to accept these inequalities as inevitable or to develop strategies which strike at the very root of capitalist and patriarchal relations. We need only to identify the practices and procedures throughout a range of social institutions (some of which may belong to what is referred to as the 'state' and others of which may not) which have the effect of producing racial and gender disadvantage. These can then be monitored and challenged by feminists and antiracists. The advantage of our approach over the ones we criticize is that it allows small-scale direct political challenges to the concrete practices which produce race and gender inequalities. We argue strongly for a deconstructionist approach to any notion of oppression which is used to account for the position of women and black people. We do not wish to participate simply in the elaboration of accounts of our own oppression. Neither do we wish to celebrate that oppression with meetings and rallies. We prefer a mode of politics which engages with the details of the oppression and which is capable of ending it.

A prominent feature of many accounts of race and gender is the presentation of oppression as an 'experience'. Such accounts often convey the impression that experience occurs in an unmediated encounter between particular categories of the population and their social and political environment. White women will, the argument goes, experience sexism just as black women will experience sexism and racism. But what is experience? Can the constituency exposed to it support the claims made upon it to engage in political struggle? Experience is being used to demarcate qualification for membership of particular political struggles. Black people are therefore expected to experience racism. Those who deny its existence are accused of false consciousness.

We argue, on the contrary, that experience has no such immediacy. Experience is organized by our understanding of the manner in which our social environment is organized. 'Racism' and 'sexism' are political constructs. They are ways of interpreting behaviour and events and require political education. The use of experience as a condition of political involvement has also to face up to the argument that experience can be as different as different people claim it to be. There may, therefore, be no end to the divisions and distinctions claimed by an apparently unitary constituency. Women will experience their femininity in different ways depending partly on the combination of circumstances in which their lives are enmeshed. It is therefore unlikely that all black women, or even all black women in Britain, will experience racism and sexism in a uniform manner. This makes the task of spokespeople very difficult. Those who speak on behalf of black women need to be aware that their accounts of oppression, grounded in experience, are open to counterclaim by other black women. We are made particularly aware of this when Parmar and Carby claim to speak on behalf of 'black women' irrespective of country of residence and differing socio-political circumstances.

Afro-American and black British women need to recognize that African women may not share their conception of femininity nor their notion of oppression. This point is illustrated by the example of a Nigerian feminist group started in 1982, 'Women in Nigeria'. In developing a notion of black women's oppression in Nigeria, this group obviously did not attach the same importance to racism as black British or black American women who live in a hostile environment. Neither did they challenge marriage or the family as legitimate forms of social organization. They did not see the family as oppressive to women and it was not considered acceptable to live outside family structures. Their concerns focused on the need for land reforms, rural development and the need to examine relations between women (co-wives) in **polygamous marriages**. Interestingly, they also made no attempt to differentiate their position or interests from the minority of white American and European women who also operated in this group, because they were setting the political agenda on behalf of all the group.

Political organizations frequently guard against the expression of a diversity of experience by their members through establishing a set of discursive constraints within which they operate. These organize their agenda-setting exercises and the manner in which they are able to prioritize and deal with issues. 'Experience' for group members then becomes organized in terms of these discursive priorities which are, to some extent, a guarantee against the diversity offered by the politics of experience.

Can experience serve as the basis for political organization? We have already indicated that experience is used as a political device to demarcate a constituency; to establish who may legitimately be involved in a particular struggle. Qualification for membership is an important part of feminist and antiracist political organization in Britain and elsewhere. We will later argue that political struggles could more effectively be built around issues, and not biogenetic categories of the population, but we maintain that black people have better access than anyone else to understanding the various effects we refer to as racism, just as women have better access to understanding the effects of sexism. With the aid of a political education, they are more likely than others to feel its effects and are therefore in a better position to direct political initiatives against it. We completely agree, therefore, that black people must have a privileged position in any antiracist struggle, but insist that within the category 'black' there will be those who have a particular grasp on specific issues (for example, women who have been subject to deportation) and because of this are more likely than others to understand what is involved in opposing particular practices, and their expertise should be recognized in any strategies adopted to counter this particular form of racism. We return to this point in our discussion of political constituency and representation, but it is worth emphasizing here that our prioritization of issues, as the basis for political constituencies and opening up struggles to all who wish to participate, does not challenge the importance within them of those who feel the effects of particular discriminatory practices.

Key terms

The following key terms appear in the text above. They have been defined below to aid with the reading of this item.

collective identity the characteristics shared by a group of people who see themselves as similar

patriarchy male domination and control of society

deconstructed when a text or idea has been analysed to demonstrate its ambiguity

operationalized the process by which an hypothesis has been turned into a practical research instrument

polygamous marriages socially acceptable unions in which an individual has more than one spouse at the same time

Questions

1 Assess the claim that black women have a completely different experience from white women in the UK.

2 Put into your own words the black feminist argument that racism stops black men benefiting from patriarchy in the same way as white men.

3 Explain why Knowles and Mercer do not accept that racism and sexism are inevitable.

Further reading

The following texts may represent a useful starting point for further investigation of the ideas contained within this chapter.

Primary texts

Anthias, F. and Yuval-Davis, N. (1993) *Racialized Boundaries,* London: Routledge.

Bradley, H. (1996) *Fractured Identities,* Cambridge: Polity.

Centre for Contemporary Cultural Studies (1982) *The Empire Strikes Back: Race and racism in '70s Britain,* London: CCCS/Hutchinson.

Gilroy, P. (1987) *There Ain't No Black in the Union Jack,* London: Hutchinson.

Mason, D. (1995) *Race and Ethnicity in Modern Britain,* Oxford: Oxford University Press.

Park, R. (1950) *Race and Culture,* New York: Free Press.

Small, S. (1994) *Racialised Barriers,* London: Routledge.

Secondary texts

Kirby, M., Kidd, W., Koubel, F., Barter, J., Hope, T., Kirton, A., Madry, N., Manning, P., Triggs, K. (1997) *Sociology in Perspective,* Oxford: Heinemann Educational.

Taylor, T., Richardson, J., Yeo, A., Marsh, I., Trobe, K., Pilkington, A. (1996) *Sociology in Focus,* Ormskirk: Causeway Press.

Coursework suggestions

1 Test the hypothesis that ethnic minority groups are disadvantaged in the labour market in modern Britain

There is sociological evidence to show that some minority ethnic groups, such as Bangladeshis, tend to occupy jobs in the lower occupational groupings. Many theoretical perspectives have been put forward to explain this disproportionate representation compared with whites. However, it must be acknowledged that other ethnic minority groups, such as Indians, have succeeded in the UK labour market, entering some professional occupations in greater numbers than whites.

In this piece of coursework you could examine secondary data on differentiations in the labour market based on ethnicity, seeking information from sources such as the Labour Force Surveys. You may also decide to interview a sample from a chosen population e.g. full-time working men and women from all ethnic groups between the ages of 18 and 65 in your town, to discover their beliefs on the issue. The context of this study would involve a critical evaluation of the relevant theories and studies – for example, Marxist explanations of racial ideologies and their affect on class position.

2 Test the hypothesis that racialism exists in modern Britain despite legislation outlawing racial discrimination in the 1960s

The British government passed protective 'race relations' legislation in 1965 making it illegal to discriminate on the grounds of colour, 'race', or ethnic origin in the provision of goods, facilities and/or services. In 1976 the government reinforced this law, making racial discrimination illegal, irrespective of intention. However, it is evident that racial disharmony continues to exist, with cases of racial discrimination being reported regularly in the media.

In this piece of coursework you could conduct a social survey to establish whether racial discrimination exists. You may decide to question a sample of minority ethnic group members to see if they have experienced racial discrimination in a specific area – for example, employment. You could also provide a critical analysis of all government legislation focusing on 'race relations', such as the 1981 Nationality Act, to establish government attitudes towards ethnic minorities and their treatment in the UK. You would also need to examine any relevant studies and/or theories for your context.

8

Family

Chapter summary

Reading 8.1 **Marxist views of the development of modern family structures** *page 203*
Friedrich Engels, using a Marxist approach, draws on historical and anthropological evidence to demonstrate the material basis of the development of different family structures and how this leads to the oppression of women.

Reading 8.2 **Functionalist views on the roles of the family** *page 206*
Talcott Parsons explores the importance of the family as an agent of primary socialization as children progress through a number of developmental phases.

Reading 8.3 **The growth of the symmetrical family** *page 208*
M. Young and P. Willmott demonstrate their view that the structure of working-class families began to change significantly in the 1960s, moving from a largely extended family network, where men and women had very different roles within and outside of the family, towards a more nuclear system of greater closeness and equality.

Reading 8.4 **Feminist views on the symmetrical family and the role of the housewife** *page 211*
Ann Oakley seeks to introduce and popularize a specifically feminist critique of the more traditional views of the family, at least partly through her attack on the concept of the symmetrical family and her notion of housework as 'real' work.

Reading 8.5 **The importance of familiar ideology – is the family in crisis?** *page 214*
Diana Gittins explores a more theoretical feminist analysis of the family, concentrating particularly on the debate about the decline of the family and the importance of our concepts of ideal family life in relation to the breakdown of society itself.

Reading 8.6 **Theories of abuse in the family** *page 217*
Faith Robertson Elliot examines the ways that feminist writers in particular have sought to understand the darker and abusive side of family life and seeks to show how such an approach brings insights that other theories cannot offer.

Reading 8.7 **The relationship between family and definitions of gender and sexuality** *page 223*
Still focusing on the themes of gender roles within the family, D. H. Morgan adopts a more post-modern approach in his view that both private and public situations are gendered for both men and women. He then examines the ways that gender is constructed, obscured or modified by our position in the family and, more problematically, how the family can construct, obscure or modify gender roles.

Reading 8.8 **The post-modern family?** *page 227*
D. Cheale suggests that current changes in family structure can only be explained through an understanding of post-modern theory, which presents family diversity as part of wider and increasingly rapid cultural changes.

Introduction: Reading the sociology of the family

The family is generally seen by non-sociologists as a 'natural' phenomenon – maybe the only natural one – where men and women reproduce and bring up their children in a simple way. Mothers, as producers and early feeders of young children, adopt a caring and nurturing role, while men – who are both stronger and less emotionally involved with the children – provide food for their mate and offspring and offer vary-ing levels of emotional support and commitment. Evidence of the sexual behaviour of animals and concepts of ideal relationships in our own society offer considerable support to this view.

However, as with so many other institutions, the sociological approach leads us to question many of our taken-for-granted assumptions about family life. Early studies did, to some extent, accept the existence of a sexual division of labour where childcare in particular was seen as an important role for women. However, as numerous anthropological studies have shown, the enormous variety of familial arrangements throughout the world demonstrates just how varied the impact of child-bearing (or not) can be on both women and men.

When Engels (1884) (**reading 8.1**) wrote about the development of modern family structures, he drew on a wide range of anthropological sources to try to demonstrate that what we call the nuclear family (two parents plus offspring) is a result of economic rather than biological factors. The historical and materialist approach to the family looks at how families developed in response to changes in people's way of living rather than just as a 'natural' outcome of biological needs. It seems that this way of seeing family structures, although not shared fully by all the writers in this chapter, does underpin many of the later sociological theories of family life.

While they may not share Engels' view of the economic basis of family organization, sociologists do see the family as something that is constructed by society rather than being something that develops naturally from the biological natures of men and women – in other words a distinctly sociological approach to our understanding of structures and change in family life. Current changes, such as evidence of increasing diversity in the structure of the family, are therefore investigated in terms of their relation to changes in society and/or the roles of men and women rather than echoing the melodramatic cries of doom and decay which fill our newspapers and – apparently – the minds of many of our political leaders in response to certain increases in single parenting and divorce rates.

Parsons' (1955) view of the family as a subsystem of society (see **reading 8.2**) moved most sociological family analysis in the 1950s from purely psychological/biological parameters to the truly sociological. He demonstrated the importance of socialization and the learning of social roles, not just in childhood but throughout our lives. Looking mainly at the American family and drawing on ideas from the father of psychoanalysis, Sigmund Freud, Parsons argued that the differences in the roles of mother and father were evidence of the specialized division of labour in modern societies. He suggested that children have no inherent abilities apart from those needed for immediate survival. Therefore a child has to learn how to get his (as Parsons insists it should be) needs gratified, as well as learning to love those who gratify these needs. In this way each child learns how to be a member of their own society and develops the ability to form emotional relationships.

The working-class family in Britain was also examined in detail by writers such as Young and Willmott (1957, 1975), throughout the 1950s and into the 1970s. They identified significant changes in family structure and conjugal roles (see **reading 8.3**). In particular they

found that the family was moving towards a position of symmetry between husband and wife. They suggested that as families became smaller and more affluent and as more married women chose to work outside the home, men became increasingly involved in housework and childcare and women became more involved in sharing the decisions about home life.

Such a positive view of family life has much to do with the functionalist approach outlined earlier, but some of this complaisance was shattered both by increasing evidence of family breakdown and divorce and the rise of feminist analyses of family life. Ann Oakley (1974) (**reading 8.4**) was only one of a number of feminists – although among the first in Britain – to question the idea that men and women gained the same from, and contributed equally to, the running of the family.

Concentrating on the notion of patriarchy – the man's dominance in the family over his wife and children and throughout society in general – feminists showed that the family was not always a haven for either women or children. They also challenged the view that increasing divorce rates pointed to a breakdown in family life or in society in general, as many with a more traditional – or nostalgic – view of families tended to claim.

Writers such as F. R. Elliot (1996) (**reading 8.6**) have suggested that abuse in the family was widespread. As a feminist, she challenged psychological views that male abuse of children (and women) is the result of individual pathology and also questioned non-feminist sociological views that such abuse was a result of social deprivation. Instead, feminists such as D. Gittins (1993) (**reading 8.5**), as well as Elliot herself, generally see the family as an expression of male power, which legitimates the abuse of children (and women) in ways that would not be tolerated in wider society.

Other recent writers have begun to look at roles within the family in a more radical way. Resurrecting the nature–nurture debate, some writers argue that it is our taken-for-granted assumptions about roles in the family that create our gender identity (see **reading 8.7**). In other words, biological sex has very little to do with either gendered behaviour or sexual orientation. We still tend to assume that mothers love their children and that fathers are more interested in providing for their families than in becoming involved in the emotional side of any family relationships. Increasing diversity in family structure and roles as well as sexual relationships suggests that such assumptions can no longer be taken for granted. An explanation for such fluidity and diversity can be understood, it is argued, through an exploration of post-modernism. This is the idea that we no longer live in a world of rationality, certainty or unchanging morality (which were the key beliefs of modernity), since people as much as institutions and relationships can and do change rapidly. We cannot expect parents to remain with their children while they grow up. Neither can we make predictions about the sex of our children's future lovers nor the manner of the relationships they may form in the future or be involved in today. This means that diversity and change replace certainty and stability as ways of understanding both the family and society (see **reading 8.8**).

Therefore, current debates in the sociology of the family relate closely to issues of gender and sexuality and to our understanding of sociological theories in general and feminism and post-modernism in particular.

Reference

Young, M. and Willmott, P. (1957) *Family and Kinship in East London*, Harmondsworth: Penguin.

Reading 8.1 **Marxist views of the development of modern family structures**

Friedrich Engels (from) *The Origin of the Family, Private Property and the State* (1946, originally published in 1884) London: Lawrence & Wishart. [This extract is taken from the 1985 Penguin edition, pp. 105–8 and 110–14.]

Editorial comments

Marx's colleague and collaborator, Friedrich Engels, shows how a Marxist approach draws on historical and anthropological evidence to demonstrate the material basis of family structures. His main argument is that the form of privatized 'bourgeois' family found most commonly in Western societies in the nineteenth century was organized specifically for the transmission of a man's property to his own offspring and the subjugation of his wife.

Although some of his anthropological material remains poorly supported by evidence, he does offer enough insights to argue convincingly that the progress from the 'primitive promiscuous hordes' through different forms of group marriage to the pairing family developed mainly as a result of changes in material circumstances, including how settled tribes were and how much land was actually owned by anyone. The final stage occurred mainly as a result of the development of capitalism (the bourgeois family) and is not only monogamous (at least for the wife) but based solely on the need for female dependence to ensure her fidelity. Thus – in this patriarchal family – men have almost total power over women. The only solution, therefore, is to get women into the workforce on an equal footing to men, which Engels believed could only happen in a communist society. Unsurprisingly, many modern feminist writers have incorporated at least part of these views into their theories of family structure.

The family

WE HAVE THREE principal forms of marriage which correspond broadly to the three principal stages of human development: for the period of savagery, group marriage; for barbarism, pairing marriage; for civilization, monogamy supplemented by adultery and prostitution. Between pairing marriage and monogamy intervenes a period in the upper stage of barbarism when men have female slaves at their command and **pologamy** is practised.

The progress which manifests itself in these successive forms is connected with the peculiarity that women, but not men, are increasingly deprived of the sexual freedom of group marriage. In fact, for men group marriage actually still exists even to this day. What for the woman is a crime entailing grave legal and social consequences is considered honourable in a man or, at the worst, a slight moral blemish which

he cheerfully bears. But the more the **hetaerism** of the past is changed in our time by capitalist commodity production and brought into conformity with it, the more, that is to say, it is transformed into undisguised prostitution, the more demoralizing are its effects. And it demoralizes men far more than women. Among women, prostitution degrades only the unfortunate ones who become its victims, and even these by no means to the extent commonly believed. But it degrades the character of the whole male world. ...

We are now approaching a social revolution in which the economic foundations of monogamy as they have existed hitherto will disappear just as surely as those of its complement – prostitution. Monogamy arose from the concentration of considerable wealth in the hands of a single individual – a man – and from the need to bequeath this wealth to the children of that man and of no other. For this purpose, the monogamy of the woman was required, not that of the man, so this monogamy of the woman did not in any way interfere with open or concealed polygamy on the part of the man. But by transforming by far the greater portion, at any rate, of permanent, heritable wealth – the means of production – into social property, the coming social revolution will reduce to a minimum all this anxiety about bequeathing and inheriting. Having arisen from economic causes, will monogamy then disappear when these causes disappear?

One might answer, not without reason: far from disappearing, it will on the contrary begin to be realized completely. For with the transformation of the means of production into social property there will disappear also wage labour, the proletariat, and therefore the necessity for a certain – statistically calculable – number of women to surrender themselves for money. Prostitution disappears: monogamy, instead of collapsing, at last becomes a reality – also for men.

In any case, therefore, the position of men will be very much altered. But the position of women, of *all* women, also undergoes significant change. With the transfer of the means of production into common ownership, the single family ceases to be the economic unit of society. Private housekeeping is transformed into a social industry. The care and education of the children becomes a public affair; society looks after all children alike, whether they are legitimate or not. This removes all the anxiety about the 'consequences', which today is the most essential social – moral as well as economic – factor that prevents a girl from giving herself completely to the man she loves. Will not that suffice to bring about the gradual growth of unconstrained sexual intercourse and with it a more tolerant public opinion in regard to a maiden's honour and a woman's shame? And finally, have we not seen that in the modern world monogamy and prostitution are indeed contradictions, but inseparable contradictions, poles of the same state of society? Can prostitution disappear without dragging monogamy with it into the abyss?

Here a new element comes into play, an element which at the time when monogamy was developing existed at most in embryo – individual sex love.

Before the Middle Ages we cannot speak of individual sex love. That personal beauty, close intimacy, similarity of tastes and so forth awakened in people of opposite sex the desire for sexual intercourse, that men and women were not totally indifferent regarding the partner with whom they entered into this most intimate relationship – that goes without saying. But it is still a very long way to our sexual love. Throughout the whole of antiquity, marriages were

arranged by the parents, and the partners calmly accepted their choice. What little love there was between husband and wife in antiquity is not so much subjective inclination as objective duty, not the cause of the marriage but its corollary. Love relationships in the modern sense only occur in antiquity outside official society. ... Except among slaves, we find love affairs only as products of the disintegration of the old world and carried on with women who also stand outside official society, with *hetaerae* – that is, with foreigners or freed slaves: in Athens from the eve of its decline, in Rome under the Caesars. If there were any real love affairs between free men and free women, these occurred only in the course of adultery. ...

Our sex love differs essentially from the simple sexual desire, the Eros, of the ancients. In the first place, it assumes that the person loved returns the love; to this extent the woman is on an equal footing with the man, whereas in the Eros of antiquity she was often not even asked. Secondly, our sex love has a degree of intensity and duration which makes both lovers feel that non-possession and separation are a great, if not the greatest, calamity; to possess one another, they risk high stakes, even life itself. In the ancient world this happened only, if at all, in adultery. And finally, there arises a new moral standard in the judgement of a sexual relationship. We do not only ask, was it within or outside marriage, but also, did it spring from love and reciprocated love or not? Of course, this new standard has fared no better in feudal or bourgeois practice than all the other standards of morality – it is ignored. But neither does it fare any worse. It is recognized, like all the rest, in theory, on paper. And for the present more than this cannot be expected. ...

In the vast majority of cases marriage remained up to the close of the Middle Ages what it had been from the start – a matter which was not decided by the partners. In the beginning, people were already born married – married to an entire group of the opposite sex. In the later forms of group marriage similar relations probably existed, but with the group continually contracting. In the pairing marriage it was customary for the mothers to settle the marriages of their children; here, too, the decisive considerations are the new ties of kinship which are to give the young pair a stronger position in the gens and tribe. And when, with the preponderance of private over communal property and the interest in its bequeathal father right and monogamy gained supremacy, the dependence of marriages on economic considerations became complete. The *form* of marriage by purchase disappears; the actual practice is steadily extended until not only the woman but also the man acquires a price – not according to his personal qualities but according to his property. That the mutual affection of the people concerned should be the one paramount reason for marriage, outweighing everything else, was and always had been absolutely unheard of in the practice of the ruling classes; that sort of thing only happened in romance – or among the oppressed classes, who did not count.

Such was the state of things encountered by capitalist production when it began to prepare itself, after the epoch of geographical discoveries, to win world power by world trade and manufacture. One would suppose that this manner of marriage exactly suited it, and so it did. And yet – there are no limits to the irony of history – capitalist production itself was to make the decisive breach in it. By changing all things into commodities, it dissolved all inherited and traditional relationships, and in place of time-honoured custom and historic right, it set up purchase and sale, 'free' contract. ...

But a contract requires people who can dispose freely of their persons, actions, and possessions and meet each other on the footing of equal rights. To create these 'free' and 'equal' people was one of the main tasks of capitalist production. ... But how did this fit in with the hitherto existing practice in the arrangement of marriages? Marriage according to the bourgeois conception was a contract, a legal transaction, and the most important one of all because it disposed of two human beings, body and mind, for life. Formally, it is true, the contract at that time was entered into voluntarily; without the assent of the persons concerned, nothing could be done. But everyone knew only too well how this assent was obtained and who were the real contracting parties in the marriage. But if real freedom of decision was required for all other contracts, then why not for this? Had not the two young people to be coupled also the right to dispose freely of themselves, of their bodies and organs? Had not chivalry brought sex love into fashion, and was not its proper bourgeois form, in contrast to chivalry's adulterous love, the love of husband and wife? And if it was the duty of married people to love each other, was it not equally the duty of lovers to marry each other and nobody else? Did not this right of the lovers stand higher than the right of parents, relations, and other traditional marriage brokers and matchmakers? If the right of free, personal discrimination broke boldly into the Church and religion, how should it halt before the intolerable claim of the older generation to dispose of the body, soul, property, happiness, and unhappiness of the younger generation?

These questions inevitably arose at a time which was loosening all the old ties of society and undermining all traditional conceptions. ...

So it came about that the rising bourgeoisie, especially in Protestant countries where existing conditions had been most severely shaken, increasingly recognized freedom of contract also in marriage, and carried it into effect in the manner described. Marriage remained class marriage, but within the class the partners were conceded at a certain degree of freedom of choice. And on paper, in ethical theory and in poetic description, nothing was more immutably established than that every marriage is immoral which does not rest on mutual sexual love and really free agreement of husband and wife. In short, the love marriage was proclaimed as a human right, and indeed not only as a *droit de l'homme*, one of the rights of man, but also, for once in a way, as *droit de la femme*, one of the rights of women.

This human right, however, differed in one respect from all other so-called human rights. While the latter in practice remain restricted to the ruling class (the bourgeoisie) and are directly or indirectly curtailed for the oppressed class (the proletariat), in the case of the former the irony of history plays another of its tricks. The ruling class remains dominated by the familiar economic influences and therefore only in exceptional cases does it provide instances of really freely contracted marriages, while among the oppressed class, as we have seen, these marriages are the rule.

Full freedom of marriage can therefore only be generally established when the absolution of capitalist production and of the property relations created by it has removed all the accompanying economic considerations which still exert such a powerful influence on the choice of a marriage partner. For then there is no other motive left except mutual inclination. ...

What we can now conjecture about the way in which sexual relations will be ordered after the impending overthrow of capitalist production is mainly of a negative character, limited for the most part to what will disappear. But what will there be new? That will be answered when a new generation has grown up: a generation of men who never in their lives have known what it is to buy a woman's surrender with money or any other social instrument of power; a generation of women who have never known what it is to give themselves to a man from any other considerations than real love or to refuse to give themselves to their lover from fear of the economic consequences. When these people are in the world, they will care precious little what anybody today thinks they ought to do; they will make their own practice and their corresponding public opinion about the practice of each individual – and that will be the end of it.

Key terms

The following key terms appear in the text above. They have been defined below to aid with the reading of this item.

polygamy having more than one husband or wife

hetaerism a socially accepted form of female prostitution in Ancient Greece

Questions

1 Explain how common ownership (communism) can change the family unit and the positions of the men and women within it.

2 Why does Engels believe that 'individual sex love' has frequently been separate from marriage?

3 Why might feminists support many of Engels' views about the role of women?

4 How might sociobiologists challenge Engels' view that forms of marriage and family structure are mainly a result of economic rather than biological factors?

Reading 8.2 **Functionalist views on the roles of the family**

Talcott Parsons (from) 'Family structure and the socialization of the child', in T. Parsons and R. F. Bales (eds) *Family Socialization and Interaction Process* (1955) New York: Free Press, pp. 35–8.

Editorial comments

Talcott Parsons, the most famous and influential American sociologist of the early postwar years, shows the importance of the family as an agent of primary socialization as children progress through a number of developmental phases. In each case the roles of mother, father, son and daughter are clearly seen as highly differentiated (each having different roles and functions). Parsons draws on a range of sources – particularly the views of the 'father of psychoanalysis', Sigmund Freud and his theory of the development of the personality through different stages of what he termed 'psychosexual development'.

Parsons also stressed the idea that the family is only one subsystem within the system that we call society. In turn, there are a number of subsystems within the family, such as the mother–child subsystem and the marriage pair subsystem, which can be examined both separately and through their contribution to the family as a whole. What links all these subsystems together, both in the family and in the wider society, is a value consensus on what is good and important. He also stresses that while the family allows children to develop their personality and their roles within the family, it is also important for children to learn their wider roles in society, especially from friends and at school, in order for them to perform fully developed adult roles in society.

Family structure and the socialization of the child

... WE MUST NOT forget that the nuclear family is *never*, most certainly not in the American case, an independent society, but a small and highly differentiated subsystem of a society. This fact is crucially relevant to our interests at two points. First the parents, as **socializing** agents, occupy not merely their familiar roles, but these articulate, i.e. interpenetrate, with their roles in other structures of the society, and this fact is a necessary condition, as we hope to show, of their functioning effectively as socializing agents, i.e. as parents, at all. Secondly, the child is never socialized only for and into his family of orientation, but into structures which extend beyond this family, through interpenetrating with it. These include the school and **peer group** in later childhood and the family of procreation which the child will help to form by his marriage, as well as occupational roles in adulthood.

Our attention will be focused on the contemporary American family. We do not, however, believe that the essential theoretical outline of our analysis is narrowly '**culture-bound**'.

Theoretically we will take our tools from a number of different sources. The analysis of family structure will come most directly from observation and analysis of the American family and from the relevant sociological theory. This is of course buttressed by considerable attention to the data of comparative kinship, and by consideration of small group structure and interaction process, taken particularly, though not exclusively, from the work of Bales and his associates.

On the more psychological side a most important set of reference points is derived from Freud's account of the stages of psycho-sexual development, as this has been developed and refined in subsequent work in psychoanalytic theory. In addition to that there has been extensive use made of psychological knowledge of the processes and mechanisms in the field of general and child psychology, and in personality theory. Finally, in the analysis of the processes which link family structure with the development of personality, an essential set of keys has been found in the analysis of therapy as a process of social control, and in relation to theories of the direction of deviant behaviour, and of the mechanisms of social control.

With increasing emphasis recent analytical work has borne in upon us the extreme importance of the fact that any large-scale social system (a society) should be considered not in a 'monolithic' way, but as an intricate network of interdependent and interpenetrating subsystems. This has been one of the most important contributions of the concept of role, to throw into relief the fact that the same individual participates in *many* social systems, not merely one; he has multiple roles. Systematic application of this generalization will be one of the central themes of our analysis of the process of **socialization**. The child may be likened to a pebble 'thrown' by the fact of birth into the social 'pond'. The effect of this event is at first concentrated at the particular point of entrance, but as he grows up, his changing place in the society resembles the successively widening waves which radiate from his initial position in his family of orientation. The process is inherently time-bound. He cannot participate in wider circles until he has fulfilled certain of the conditions of full participation in the narrower ones. But the metaphor breaks down in that not only his relationships outside the family but within its innermost core are transformed in a kind of 'spiral' process.

From this point of view the nuclear family must be placed relative to other subsystems in a series. That it is itself a subsystem of a larger system is of course a sociological commonplace. But to break it in turn down into subsystems is a less familiar way of looking at it. Yet we will treat the family in this way and say that, in certain crucially important respects, the very young child does not participate in, is not fully a 'member' of, his whole family, but only of a sub-system in it, the mother–child subsystem. The marriage pair constitute another subsystem as may, for certain purposes, also the child with all his siblings, all the males in the family, all the females, etc. In fact *any* combination of two or more members as differentiated from one or more other members *may* be treated as a *social* system which is a subsystem of the family as a whole. The smaller the family of course the smaller the number of possible subsystems, and this is a very important fact about our own small family type.

There are, of course, many different aspects of the organization of the relations of subsystems of the family or any other social system to each other. One set of relations is, however, particularly crucial for our purposes. This is a certain relation between different modes and levels of specialization and differentiation of role. The family is significant as a type that in its internal structure represents a very elementary level of differentiation of roles so far as social systems go and this is even more the case with its mother–child subsystem. At the same time the family must be sufficiently 'diffuse' in function in the larger system of which it is a part to meet all the essential needs of a highly undifferentiated class of members, its small children. Hence, though families are very numerous, they are very much more alike in basic structure than are most other types of subsystem of a larger society.

The structures articulating with the family, however, must be more differentiated than is the family itself. The family offers a wide enough range of role-participations only for the young child. He must learn, by actual participation, progressively more roles than his family of orientation can offer him. It is at this point that peer group and school assume paramount importance.

Participation in a wider society, the more so the more complex its structure, thus involves participation in an ever-widening circle of subsystems of the society. The role-repertoire of the normal adult may be regarded as a point at which the increasing complexity of differentiation from the mother–child starting point, and differentiation of the society as a system into specialized subsystems, attain some sort of meeting point which is compatible with the functional needs of adult personalities.

Key terms

The following key terms appear in the text above. They have been defined below to aid with the reading of this item.

socializing, socialization learning the norms and values of our society

peer group friends and acquaintances of similar age and status to oneself

culture-bound applicable to only one society or social group

monolithic influences only operating in one direction

Questions

1 What, or who, does Parsons see as the main agents of primary socialization?

2 Explain Parsons' view that society is made of a number of different subsystems.

3 What does he consider to be the main roles played by the different subsystems within the family?

4 Using these readings and any other knowledge you have, discuss the view that children need to be socialized into different roles outside of the family as well as within it. Why can the family not teach us all we need to know?

Reading 8.3 **The growth of the symmetrical family**

M. Young and P. Willmott (from) *The Symmetrical Family* (1975) London: Routledge, pp. 84–94.

Editorial comments

From their own research in Bethnal Green in East London, Young and Willmott argue that the structure of working-class families began to change significantly in the 1960s. It moved from a largely extended family network, where men and women had very different roles within and outside of the family (segregated conjugal roles), towards a more nuclear system of greater closeness and equality. The symmetrical family – where the roles of husband and wife are similar in terms of their contribution to economic and domestic arrangements – developed mainly as a result of three key factors:

- geographical mobility as families moved out of inner-city areas and into the suburbs, leaving their families of origin behind
- the reduction of family size due to improved contraception
- more married women taking employment outside the home.

One major consequence of these changes was the greater time spent at home and increased domestic contributions made by men, so that both partners worked both inside and outside the home, spending more time together, more time with their children (joint conjugal roles) and less time with their own parents and other kin members.

The growth of the symmetrical family

The move towards symmetry

WE HAVE ALREADY started speaking about ... the growth of a financial partnership, and we should now say something about the sources of this change and about other manifestations of the new spirit, which was first evident in the middle classes. ... The rising middle classes, far from losing their worldly goods, were on the contrary adding to them. The man was as much the master in the families benefiting most from Victorian prosperity. ... His wife could be an ornament to his property as well as part of it. She was the mistress of a bevy of maids who needed to be closely supervised if the sort of standards extolled by a Mrs Beeton were to be maintained.

The man's physical comfort, the general good order of the house and the sense of spiritual contentment gained from a consciousness of his own goodness depended upon the circumspection and the affection with which he treated his wife.

But in these same circles the new feminism, nourished by the evangelical insistence on the spiritual worth of the humblest, was beginning to grow. Just as poorer men have struggled to gain some of the privileges of the rich, so have women struggled to secure some of the privileges that formerly belonged to men alone. Feminism was in the long run an influence almost as decisive as technology upon the growth of symmetry inside the family. Once it began to be denied that power should be ascribed to rulers solely by their birth into the station of life of a particular family, once elementary democratic rights had been granted to men, or some of them, once slavery had been abolished, once the claims of the new individualism had been acknowledged for men, the same arguments could be used against men by champions of people born into a particular sex and so condemned, by their **chromosomes** alone, to inferiority in society. The position of women in law was at that time worse than that of slaves. They could not own property. They could not, however much revulsion they might feel, refuse their masters the last familiarity. They had no legal rights to separation from their men nor over their children. However severely a husband beat his wife, she could not, until a reform in the law, free herself from her tormentor. If she ran away she could without right of asylum be forced to return, and, until 1891, he could use physical force to get her back. ...

One by one, leading up to 1928 when women were given votes on the same terms as men, some legal disabilities were removed. Success was achieved because Mill and such unusual men as were of his persuasion were joined by representatives of the under-privileged. An extraordinary band of women, who had gained an education, if only by their own efforts, Miss Nightingale and Miss Hill, Miss Buss and Miss Beale, Miss Davies and Miss Garrett, many of them refusing to be bound in matrimony to any of their sex's oppressors, led a series of campaigns in the face of far more **obloquy** than the modern pro- ponents of Women's Liberation. To give one exam- ple, Josephine Butler led a bitter and long drawn out campaign against the Contagious Diseases Act which imposed upon prostitutes in garrison towns in England and Ireland compulsory medical examination and compulsory treatment at the hands of male doctors. ... Josephine Butler was, after twenty years, success- ful in getting the Contagious Diseases Act repealed, and eventually, in 1907, without destroying the family, a man was allowed to marry his deceased wife's sister, and by 1921 a woman even her deceased husband's brother.

Important as the legal reforms were – perhaps none more so than the placing of the same duty upon par- ents to send their daughters to school as their sons – they were less a tribute to feminism than was another change which owed little to the State, the reduction in the size of the family. Most women, who had spent the best part of a lifetime in child-bearing and rearing with all its pain and toil, had probably always regarded it as wearisome. But the man, espe- cially if he was humble, delayed in his reaction. He did not choose to co-operate with his wife in restraint or constraint even if she had got so far as to break free herself from a fatalistic view of her own mater- nal destiny. Family planning has run repeatedly into opposition from men in the developing countries who, in this respect, are repeating the experience of their sex in England. ...

The old attitude persists in the assignment of responsibility for the precautions. Even in 1971 Gorer spoke of the 'widespread, if not very articulate belief among the working classes that it is the husband's prerogative to determine whether any form of birth control should be used and that it is unseemly, almost unwomanly, for the wife to take the initiative'. ... The sheath or condom was still the favoured method amongst working-class people. Mutual discussion between the couple has also remained less common.

... The initiative has continued to be to a large extent with the man, as it was before.

But the vital statistics show that, however deep- lying men's attitudes, they did eventually *shift*. There were three main influences on the adoption of birth control. The first was the long-term pressure of increasing population, which may have led some people in competition with others for scarce jobs, especially when they had to wait before securing advancement, to act prudently and defer marriage. A second, of greater importance, was the fall in infant and child mortality which first affected the middle classes. ... The third influence was more specific in time. The Bradlaugh-Besant trial of 1877, publicized methods of birth control and to some extent made it respectable [and] more acceptable in the economic depression which followed it and which would have cut down the standard of living of the middle classes still more if they had not taken steps to sustain it.

The middle classes were the first to be prompted by any of these influences, and they were the first to control births within marriage rather than by the more traditional way of postponing it. ...

In time the pattern at the bottom began to change. The gap narrowed. The social classes converged. In the inter-war period, in particular, while family size generally continued to fall more sharply than ever, the reduction was now relatively greater among the wives of manual workers than among the middle classes. Class differences in family size are not, therefore, as marked as in the past. Average family size fell from nearly six at about the middle of the nineteenth century to just over two in 1970, which has been made possible by the spread of contraceptive prac- tices – from the professional class to other non-man- ual workers, and thence to the skilled, semi-skilled and unskilled.

There may have been yet another change. It seems that in recent decades among at least some sections of the middle classes couples have been having rather *more* children. The evidence is not at all conclusive, but it does suggest that, although class differences in family size are generally smaller than they were, the couples having the largest families have in recent decades been some of those from the top of the occu- pational scale along with those at the bottom. ...

Stress on the conjugal family

The size of families would not have been limited unless husbands were prepared to co-operate, and if the size of families had not been limited husbands would not have found their homes as congenial as they have eventually done. The result would not have been achieved as fully as it has without the separation of the immediate, or nuclear, family from the extended family. We believe that this extended family had a particular pattern to it, being mother centred, because it was largely created as a protective device against the insecurities inherent for women. ...

The thesis, drawn out through several books, was that when husbands could not be relied upon, women, after a time-lag for acclimatization to city life, eventually built up an organization in their own defence and in the defence of their children. This they did in what became a common mode of reaction in many societies where the **conjugal tie** was weak, from the West Indies and the Southern States to the Republic of South Africa and the industrial cities of Europe and North America. They created an informal women's trade union. ... Ever since the father had to move out of the home to work, it has been easier for daughters to build on this tie [between the mother and her daughter] because they have in their mothers a model whom they can copy. This bond was accentuated well into adult life. Daughters lived near their mothers, or with them, even after they were married.

Propinquity made support easier. Mothers could give their daughters and their grandchildren a feeling of security. More tangibly, they could look after the children if the daughter got the chance of a job, and could pass on money or gifts in kind in their capacity as co-ordinators for the extended families which they headed. The more people that belonged to it, that is, the more daughters and daughter substitutes there were, the more effective was the large family as an insurance. If someone was down on her or his luck, someone else might be in the opposite state, and therefore able to contribute, directly or through the intermediary of the grandmothers, to the welfare of the needy. The trade union also worked better as a friendly society if different people in it were at different phases in the life cycle of poverty and prosperity. A person in an up phase could help another in a down. When people were old the flow of services as well as income would be reversed, and the young do for the old what the old had done for the young.

This sort of structure – weak on the family of marriage, strong on the family of origin – tended to perpetuate itself. Husbands were often squeezed out of the warmth of the female circle, and took to the pub as their defence against the defence. They had to put up with mothers-in-law who were constantly interfering, as the man might see it, with the arrangements in his own home. His wife could seem more her daughter than his wife, and both of them belonged to a group which did not award men a high place in its order of values. He could find himself undermined, in a hundred ways, subtle and unsubtle. He could be

pushed into becoming an absentee father, so bringing on the insecurity which the extended family in this form was established to counter.

If so self-reinforcing, why has the system of balances and counter-balances been transformed? If we had to plump, we would give special prominence to the higher standard of life and to migration. ...

As for homes, new ones have been built for immediate families with young children in them, not for extended families in housing clusters like those that are common in Africa and Asia. There is no modern counterpart of the extended family compound found in the 'turnings' and courts of London. The young couples have had to, or have chosen to, move to new houses and away from relatives. Husbands have often been the most willing because it meant that their wives would be wrested away from the influence of their Mums. ... Even where the generations have not been physically separated, the declining influence of grandmothers – for instance, in finding rented housing for their daughters or in advising them on health and child care – has helped to turn the trio of mother–daughter–husband into a duet.

Less segregation of roles

These various historical processes are still working their way through the social structure which means that, in many if not all respects, they have had a fuller effect on the families of richer than poorer people, and of younger rather than older. ... But the great majority of married people in our sample were members of the dominant type of new family.

In [the past] there was segregation of roles [within families] in many more ways than those to do with money. If husbands did any 'work' at all at home the tasks that they, and their wives, thought proper to them were those to which male strength and male manual skill lent themselves. It was not a man's place to do woman's work any more than the other way round. All that has now changed. Wives are working outside the home in what is much less of a man's world than it used to be.

Husbands also do a lot of work in the home, including many jobs which are not at all traditional men's ones – which is one reason why the distinction between work and leisure is now a great deal less clear for men than it used to be. It never was very distinct for women. There is now no sort of work in the home strictly reserved for 'the wives': even clothes-washing and bed-making, still ordinarily thought of as women's jobs, were frequently mentioned by husbands as things they did as well. The extent of the sharing is probably still increasing.

Key terms

The following key terms appear in the text above. They have been defined below to aid with the reading of this item.

chromosomes carriers of basic genetic information which determine things about us such as our sex

obloquy abuse or blame

conjugal tie relationship between husband and wife

propinquity nearness

Questions

1 Which legal changes particularly improved the position of women in the nineteenth century?

2 Explain all the other factors identified by Young and Willmott which have improved the role of women and girls in the family.

3 How and why have class differences between families decreased and what have been the effects of this?

4 Explain the main factors associated with the idea of symmetry. To what extent does this reflect arrangements in any two-parent households with which you are familiar?

Reading 8.4 **Feminist views on the symmetrical family and the role of the housewife**

Ann Oakley (from) *Housewife* (1974) London: Allen Lane, pp. 60–70.

Editorial comments

Oakley was one the earliest writers to popularize a specifically feminist critique of the family, at least partly through her attack on the concept of the symmetrical family. While more women were finding paid employment outside the home, it was obvious that in terms of both earning potential and power, they did not generally occupy positions in any way similar to men. Furthermore, the concept of symmetry in the home (i.e. men and women making equal contributions to household chores and childcare) did not stand up to any sort of empirical scrutiny. Her own research showed not only that housework is more alienating than the worst factory work, but also that, overall, men do not contribute to the running of the household to anywhere the extent that women do.

Oakley suggests that women still retain a limited and limiting home-centred position, especially in strongly working-class communities. She also points out that even when both partners in a relationship work outside the home they tend to do different jobs and the responsibility for domestic matters still generally falls to the wife. Furthermore, although the family is now more home-centred than ever before, the demands on women as child-rearers and home-makers are also far more complex and exacting than in the past.

The situation of women today

THE TWO THEMES which underlie the continuing social differentiation of women from men (women's situation) are (1) **domesticity** as a defining feature of women's situation, and (2) **ambivalence** in the cultural values applied to women's roles. Since the social stereotype of women portrays them as domesticated, a view of women as people is always mixed with a perception of their social difference from men: they are housewives.

Domesticity: within the family

As a consequence of industrialization, the home means 'family' rather than 'work'. Our language contains the phrase 'a family man', but there is no corresponding phrase for women. It would be socially redundant: the family *means* women. Women bear children, women rear children, women are in the home as housewives: if the home means the family, then the family *is* women.

What kind of family is this?

Compared with other family systems throughout history and in different cultures, it is small, mobile and non-productive. On one level it is functionless: it has no broad economic or political or social significance. But on another level, its functions are crucial.

The family produces people. It does this in two ways – by socializing children, and by stabilizing adult personalities in the socially approved moulds of wife-mother-housewife and husband-father. The production of people is not a new function for 'the' family as such, but its significance in the case of the modern family is enlarged through the family's loss of its other, pre-industrial functions. Because women are the childbearers, the modern emphasis on people-production also affects women directly. This connection is clarified when the importance of gender – femininity and masculinity – in the structure of the modern family is understood.

Gender differentiation between the roles of female and male is the axis of the modern family's structure. Husband and wife are not the same sort of role, nor are father and mother, nor are housewife and non-housewife. The modern family stresses two sorts of bond: a cross-sex bond (marriage) and a cross-generational bond (the parent–child relationship). They share the same pattern of gender role-differentiation, and a clue to the nature of this differentiation is given by linguistic usage. The following are the conventional couplets: husband and wife, mother and father, man and wife. In each case a reversal sounds odd: wife and husband, father and mother, wife and man. The last couplet has the oddest ring, because a reversal of terms destroys the meaning of the phrase, which is man (person) and wife (female-person-in-the-possession-and-under-the-control-of-man). As it indicates, marriage is a situation of inequality: in marriage, women are not equal with men. This is because marriage defines a woman's place in society as it does not a man's. 'Differentiation' is a neutral word. The contrast between the roles of female and male in the family is not simply one of differentiation but of opposition. The order of terms in the couplet 'husband and wife' indicates a **patriarchal structure**. The only couplet in which the female role conventionally takes precedence over the male role is the parental one – 'mother and father'. This is simply because the woman in the family is the childrearing parent.

In *Coal is Our Life*, a description of a British coalmining community written in 1956, there is a very good illustration of how gender differentiation structures marriage and family life. … 'Man and Wife' in Ashton are strangers to each other. Their relationship lacks intimacy; they have little to say to each other and sex is rarely satisfactory. Yet (or perhaps therefore) total disintegration of marriage is uncommon: husband and wife have not got close enough to want to be apart. Marriage is a matter simply of 'carrying on' – a goal guaranteed 'so long as the man works and gives his wife and family sufficient, and the woman uses the family's wage "wisely" and gives her husband the few things he demands'. …

The Ashton pattern of rigidly segregated marital roles is found mostly in working-class communities today. This is not coincidental. Social recognition as individuals is conferred in Western culture on men and women chiefly through education and training and, to

some extent, in the world of paid work. Working-class women lack the access to these areas that middle-class women have, and a dogmatic insistence on the place of women in marriage is therefore less likely to be diluted by a belief (albeit superficial) in sex equality.

… Although the behaviour of husband and wife is extreme in its emphasis on the importance of gender, the man and the woman are both playing their socially approved roles. … In recent years, negative sanctions on married women's employment have diminished, but in the area of women's domestic roles traditional ideas have shown no corresponding tendency to change. It is not enough for a married couple to say, 'We are not like that: we do things differently,' for the woman to work as an electrical engineer, and for the man to rear the children, cook meals, and cite his wife as salary-earner on credit applications. The objection will be raised that they are husband and wife.

The family defines people's identities. It is not merely actual – female and male living together with their children – but ideological. To locate a person as a member of a family is to bestow automatically on that person a socially given identity: man-husband-father, woman-wife-mother-housewife, and child-son/daughter.

A number of social developments this century have amplified the importance of gender in the family, and thus the importance of domesticity in women. One of these is the increased emotional investment of society in the family, and therefore of *people* in the family. The family has become increasingly the locus of all meaningful personal life. 'Familism', the sociological name for this orientation towards the family, entails a style of life decisively centred on the small family of two parents and children: a major emotional investment in family relationships, which are, for all family members, their chief source of social and psychological support. Although the reduction in family size since industrialization has probably been exaggerated, some narrowing down of family relationships to the nucleus of parents and children has taken place. Certainly it is this unit which now represents the sentimental ideal: the cornflakes-advertisement pattern of father, mother, boy and girl (suggesting a symmetry which contrasts with the actual differentiation between mother and father roles).

If society has grown more 'family-oriented' the family itself has identified more and more squarely with its physical location, the home. 'Home' and 'family' are now virtually interchangeable terms. A central value of the modern family is dedication to the goal of a steadily rising standard of living. The cost of the home has enlarged to absorb an increasing proportion of every family's income.

Before the First World War, the working-class home typically consisted of one or two rooms, crammed together with other homes sharing grossly inadequate sanitary arrangements. Since then, improvements in sanitation, in water supply, in other amenities, and also in the general standard of home building, have led to a visible improvement in the physical aspects of family life. There has been a tendency for the size of the working-class home to increase, and for the decoration and equipment of homes generally to become more elaborate and less differentiated by social class. ... The size of the family may have decreased, but a raised involvement in home life has demanded more of women's time. 'Consumerism', the involvement of society in the family, the involvement of the family in the physical aspects of living, has elevated the importance of housewifery. New domestic equipment constantly requires the acquisition of yet more equipment, for technical as well as status reasons. ...

Women's roles as mothers have also been subject to amplification. Childhood is not what it used to be – and still is in many societies – a short, rather little-valued prelude to the all important business of adulthood. Modern industrial society is demonstrably child-oriented: childhood is prolonged well past puberty, rather than attenuated well before it: startling discontinuities separate child role from adult role; children are, throughout their years of dependence, and in contrast to adults, inviolable, innocent, precious creatures. The intrinsic worth of every human being is epitomized, if not always exemplified, in the state of childhood: children are good.

This view of the child accords with the high value ostensibly placed on individuality in Western society. It also owes much to the development of child psychology as a separate scientific discipline. ... The emergence of psychoanalysis in the first decades of this century gave to childhood a lasting importance.

These developments have two main implications for women as childrearers. Firstly, knowledge about childhood as a critical period in the formation of adult character makes 'successful' performance of the maternal role crucial. ...

The second important implication is the need for women as childrearers to be in touch with the standards of childcare – and the needs of children – specified by the experts. Until late in Western history the only experts in childcare and child behaviour outside the family were the midwife and the teacher. Now the world is full of experts. The basic structure for the dissemination to women of knowledge about childcare includes antenatal, postnatal and child-welfare clinics and classes, health visitors, maternity hospitals, and child-health specialists. ...

The discovery of the child's importance has affected women more than it has men. ... In the modern family, the terms 'mother' and 'father' denote roles which are qualitatively different. A child's two parents are not interchangeable: the mother is the caretaker of the child, and the father its breadwinner.

... The father's role towards children derives directly from his occupational role, with the child's material welfare depending, in the first instance, on the father's willingness to neglect it. The physical aspects of childcare are not emphasized; and when the father does take over these duties, he is said to be acting as a 'substitute mother' or as 'mother's helper'. ... Implicit in this differentiation of parental roles is the command, for the male parent, 'Self first, child second'. In the case of the female parent, the formula is reversed to read, 'Child first, self second'. Women abdicate their personhood for the sake of their maternity. ...

In the family role of women 'mothering' is thus seen as an essential ingredient, its absence **pathogenic**, threatening the whole purpose of the family – the production of healthy children. The same aura of pathogenicity is attached to women's deviation from conventional wife and mother roles. ... Correspondingly, a 'normal' woman 'can best fulfil her role as a woman when she can be the wife to a man "who is somebody" – one sure of his sexual identity and worth. ... Then she is prepared to surrender her self-containment, her own masculine instrumentality and detachment.'

The family as an institution is a prescription for gender-role normalcy: one woman, one man, and one or more children. Families with adopted children count, but single-parent families do not. They represent a social situation full of ambiguities, and are stigmatized and ostracized. There are strong economic, childcare, and social pressures for the normalization of the family unit. Within the gender-role structure of the family, women are reduced to a common social type: the housewife-wife-mother. The woman doctor, shop assistant, professional engineer, primary schoolteacher, ballet dancer, factory worker, all become Mrs X, the mother of Mr Y's children, the supporter of Mr Y's career/job, the washer of his clothes, the caretaker and creator of his home, the centre and symbol of his family life.

Reference

Dennis, N., Henriques, F. and Slaughter, C. (1956) *Coal is our Life*, London: Eyre & Spottiswoode.

Key terms

The following key terms appear in the text above. They have been defined below to aid with the reading of this item.

domesticity work done in the home

ambivalence having conflicting feelings

patriarchal structure a society characterized by the dominance of men

pathogenic sick

Questions

1 Why do the phrases 'wife and husband' and 'wife and man' sound strange?

2 How can the family be seen to define people's roles both actually and ideologically?

3 How has the position of children changed in modern industrial societies?

4 What does Oakley see as the main effects of a more home-centred family on both men and women? Is this family structure symmetrical?

Reading 8.5 **The importance of familiar ideology – is the family in crisis?**

D. Gittins (from) *The Family in Question: Changing households and familiar ideologies* (1993) 2nd edn, Basingstoke: Macmillan, pp. 155–62 and 167–8.

Editorial comments

Gittins applies a more theoretical feminist analysis of the family than Oakley (reading 8.4), concentrating particularly on the debate about the decline of the family. A single definition of the family is almost unattainable, but, Gittins argues, we tend to see 'the family' as being in some sort of crisis if it does not largely conform the what she calls 'familiar ideology' – the ideal of happy, nuclear and patriarchal (male-dominated) families. She also points out that much of our social organization is based on these assumptions of family life, so that large-scale changes such as high rates of divorce can be seen by some as indicating the breakdown of society itself.

Against this view, Gittins argues that the family has been presented as the best social organization for bringing up children since the late eighteenth century, often reinforced by both religious and scientific ideas. Differences between men and women were (and often still are) seen as natural, making women inevitably dependent on a stronger male. Even though most now work outside the home, women are still seen as being responsible for the domestic aspects of family life. These views combine to suggest that single parenthood (or non-parenthood) may lead to the breakdown of society, even though such a state was common in the past due to early death, which broke up good and bad marriages alike. She argues that family structures are now widely varied and we should accept this and concentrate on the real problems of society such as the destruction of the environment, child abuse, AIDS and the increasing number of very elderly people in our society.

Is the family in a state of crisis?

CONCERN THAT 'the family' is in a state of crisis is not a new phenomenon. It was of grave concern to many middle-class legislators and reformers of various political hues in the nineteenth century; it was a concern during the inter-war period, and in the past decade has re-emerged as a contentious political issue. It causes most concern during periods of economic recession, when there is a change in the rate of population growth, and/or during times when fear of political unrest and upheaval is acute. The three, of course, often go together, and all provide an insight into why 'the family' becomes a political issue during such periods.

There is no clear, unambiguous definition of what a family is – indeed, it has been argued that the family is little more than an ideology that influences and informs the ways in which people interact and co-reside with one another. Yet if we take it as an ideology, it is one that permeates virtually every social institution in modern industrial society. ... The notion of family informs the education system, the business world, asylums, the media and the political system itself. So when concern about the 'crisis in the family' becomes a recurrent theme, what is more probably being expressed is a fear that *society itself* is in a state of crisis. How has this come about? If the concept of family is so broad, is it then a useless concept for understanding how people live and work together? Do we need new concepts?

Deconstructing the concept of family shows that inherent in it are a number of quite distinct ideas and phenomena. Co-residence; marriage; power relations between men and women; power relations between adults and children; domestic labour; sexuality and sexual relations; procreation; motherhood and mothering; fatherhood; sibling relationships; definitions of kinship, gender, authority, dependence, service; economic relations – all these can be seen as important and implicit and explicit in definitions of the family. These are also a lot of subcategories to fit into one concept. It is hardly surprising, therefore, that people have disagreed so radically in their interpretations of whether or not families are in a state of crisis, whether they are a 'good' or a 'bad' thing, whether or not they are a constant attribute of modern industrial society. The interpretations and definitions that can be made of the family are so wide and all-encompassing that as such the concept is of very limited analytical value indeed.

Any study of, or reference to, the family needs to differentiate clearly between the **ideology** and the actual ways in which individuals interact, co-reside, have sexual relations, have babies, marry, divorce, work, rear children, move away, and so on. Obviously an ideology influences the ways people interpret their lives, though there has never been a clear way of showing just how influential ideologies are on patterns of behaviour. Ideology cannot exist in limbo; it must have some relation to people's material existence or at least be perceived as having such a relation, otherwise it would be irrelevant. Separating ideology from patterns of behaviour is thus arguably a **hypothetical** exercise, because the two must always be related in some way or other. Nevertheless, analysing them as logically distinct is a useful way of disentangling some of the complexities inherent in the concept of family, and enables us to see more clearly whether the alleged crisis in the family is more of a belief that an ideology is under threat than an accurate reflection of dramatic changes in people's behaviour patterns.

The ideology of the family is an historical creation. The very concept of family was not used in the way it is today until the late eighteenth century. Its development as a concept and an ideology was an inherent part of the development of the industrial bourgeoisie during the later stages of capitalist development. It is possible to see its growing influence in the way in which society was conceptualized as a fusion between earlier religious patriarchal ideology and the secularization of society with the growth of scientific rationalism. ...

Women in western patriarchy have always been a lesser form of being, the originator of man's fall from divine grace, temptresses, sinners, more subject to lust, and only capable of salvation through deference, obedience to male authority, and motherhood. ...

From the seventeenth century onwards, the development of science and scientific paradigms for interpreting the world perpetuated fundamental beliefs about authority and gender, except that they increasingly became expressed in terms of 'nature' rather than through direct reference to God. Men were seen as 'naturally' authoritative, stronger, more intelligent, and women were 'naturally' deferential, weak, passive and intuitive. Men, therefore, were suited to govern, to make decisions, to direct women and children, and these patriarchal assumptions became an integral part of science, of the ways in which governments and government policies were perceived and formulated. ...

An earlier religious patriarchal ideology had been symbolized as, and enshrined in, the Church, so secular scientific ideology became symbolized as, and enshrined in, the family. ...

Middle-class family ideology was informed and influenced by patriarchal **discourses** from both religion and science. ... The family was a historical, class-specific ideology premised on earlier patriarchal religious ideals and beliefs. ... But the all-encompassing and yet elusive concept of family makes it appear both as a universally shared experience and a goal which all can, and should, achieve – regardless of economic circumstances – even if its realization remains obscure.

Its strength and endurance as an ideology lies in its appearance as a universal experience not specific to a particular class. In this way it comes to have what amounts to a religious character: it is (in theory) open to all and, through 'good works', that is a well-ordered family life, salvation can be achieved by all. Yet its premises are conservative because they are based on notions of authority, service, dependence and deference, in short, it is founded on inequality. From the Victorian era onwards, perceived social threats and radical movements have been seen as both a threat *to* the family, and *a result of* a crisis in the family.

Since Victorian times, of course, some of the specific content of family ideology has changed. Ideas and ideals about sexuality have altered; women are now expected to enjoy (hetero)sexual relationships, men are encouraged to 'help' in the home and take an active interest in their children – though are stigmatized if they want to take *full* responsibility. Children are allowed more freedom of expression, and while married women working is not actively encouraged (except when there is a labour shortage, as in the Second World War), it is not seen as so serious a threat as it was during Victorian times. ...

Family ideology has increasingly purported to be **egalitarian**, yet it remains based on notions of gender, age and authority that are by definition unequal. The ideal that families are egalitarian, like the ideal that class no longer divides society, has enjoyed considerable support, even if it seldom tallies with reality. Is the problem perhaps that patterns of behaviour have altered and that it is these that are in a state of crisis because they no longer relate in any important way to the ideology? ...

The areas where families are most often seen as both villains and victims of alleged crisis relate to divorce, child abuse and delinquency. Above all else, rising rates of divorce have been used to 'show' that marriages are less stable and thus families are less secure and united. Yet, if anything, families were just as unstable in the past – death broke up *both* good *and* bad marriages in a totally arbitrary way. The consequence was high rates of widowhood, orphanage, remarriage, and single-parent families.

Families were also broken by separation in the past, except that because divorce was impossible for all except the very wealthy, those left behind had no rights to protection or maintenance. The rise in divorce rates in modern society reflects first and foremost a legal change in the accessibility of the population to formal separation and divorce. It means that wives and children have somewhat better guarantees of economic support than they once had – though recent legislation is eroding this.

Moreover, the dramatic increase in the duration of people's life expectancy has meant that marriages that remain intact last on average for much longer periods of time than in the past. ...

More is expected of, and from, marriage than in the past. Family ideology over the past 150 years has laid greater emphasis on the romantic and compassionate ideal of marriage while disguising its fundamental economic and inegalitarian aspects. Where not long ago marriage was presented as a working partnership with the husband the acknowledged head, the primary purpose of which was to produce children, it has been presented increasingly as a loving relationship between two equal partners whose aim is to create domestic harmony through co-operation, mutual sexual gratification, and the careful and loving rearing of two or three children. It has been further defined as a private and exclusive relationship. ... As an ideal, and one which has to survive a long test of time, this is a tall order and one that is unlikely to survive in reality for long. ...

Family ideology implicitly presupposes a relatively secure economic base: the husband should be *able* to support the family by his income alone, the household income should *provide* adequate shelter, food, comfort, space, and consumer durables, the wife should be *able* to cease paid work, when she has small children. In other words, the poorer a family–household's resources, the wider the gap will be between the ideal of what a family should be and what it has to be in reality. ... Everyone is supposed to aspire to a certain kind of family life, while the realities of economic inequality make it virtually impossible for the poor to achieve the ideal.

By insisting that happy marriages and happy families are made by individuals through love, devotion and hard work, the reality of the economic and patriarchal bases of marriage and family life are disguised and ignored. Thus crises of family violence, sexual abuse and delinquency are not attributed to poverty or unequal relations between men and women and parents and children, but to individuals' – and most frequently, women's – failings *within* their families. Just as nineteenth-century social reformers advocated teaching working-class wives the importance of thrift and good housekeeping as a 'solution' to their poverty, so contemporary social reformers advocate individual solutions like marriage therapy and child guidance rather than seeing the political and economic origins of such problems. ...

There is a crisis in society. More than ever society is faced with numerous serious crises – including poverty and unemployment, homelessness, AIDS, ecological disasters, widespread child abuse, the ever growing numbers of the elderly, and so on. To treat these as family problems, however, is to treat effects as causes. Everybody lives in some form of family household; everybody has some form of problem. Attributing problems of delinquency or incest or emotional problems to the individual's family – though these problems become *manifest* there – is obviating the social nature of most problems and results in blaming individuals for social crises.

For if one thing should have become obvious by now, it is that to speak in terms of 'the' family is totally misleading. There is no such thing. While everybody at some point will share space, time, skills, sexuality, affection and love with others, the ways in which individuals live, struggle and interact together are too varied to be able to encase these activities into a term such as 'the family'. ...

Yet the ideology of the family would have us believe that there is one type of family, one correct way in which individuals should live and interact together, just as Christian theology insists that there is one god, one saviour, one path to salvation. An ideology that claims there is only one type of family can never be matched in reality, for it presents an ideal to which only some can approximate, and others not at all. It is this attribute of family ideology which makes people believe there is a crisis in the family while the real problem is the gap between the ideology and reality.

Discarding family ideology would abolish the idea that there is a crisis in the family and reveal the realities of social problems and crises. Without such an ideology people would expect less from marriage and childrearing and would be less likely to become disillusioned – which is not to say that everyone would consequently become 'happier'. But they would be less likely to expect an unrealistic degree of bliss and contentment from a mythical marriage and family; they could begin to think of new and different ways of coping and co-operating with others in a variety of ways. It would mean, however, that people began to see the real nature of social and economic problems and not perceive them as individual/family failings and guilt. It might well mean that people started challenging social, economic and political injustice more directly – rather than blaming themselves or their spouse or children. It would mean challenging patriarchal ideology and thus challenging the inequalities between men, women and children.

Family ideology has been a vital means – the vital means – of holding together and legitimizing the exist-

ing social, economic, political and gender systems. Challenging the ideology thus means challenging the whole social system, but it would not mean that as a result people ceased living and interacting together in some form of family household. It would mean a radical reappraising of such arrangements. Family households are a vital and integral part of any society in some shape or form. Family ideology is not. There is no ideal family. When politicians articulate a fear that there is a crisis in the family, they are not worried about divorce or rape or incest as such, but rather that the *ideology* is being challenged, and that were this to gain momentum people might start to question the legitimacy of the existing socio-economic, political and patriarchal systems. Without family ideology modern industrial society and its political system might be very different indeed. Without family ideology it would be possible to reconsider and reconstruct the realities of relationships between men, women and children and to work towards more equal and more caring ways of living and working together.

Key terms

The following key terms appear in the text above. They have been defined below to aid with the reading of this item.

deconstructing breaking down a concept to look at its underlying components in more detail

ideology the ideas and expectations that we share about social institutions such as families

hypothetical a theoretical exercise rather than a real process

discourses ways of talking (and thinking) about the world

egalitarian a system where everyone has equal rights and status

Questions

1 What does Gittins see as the main components of the family?

2 How does she suggest that the ideology of the family has changed through history?

3 Explain and evaluate Gittins' views on divorce.

4 Using the text and any other knowledge you have, explain and assess the idea that the ideology of the family can be used to legitimate the inequality and exploitation of women and children.

Reading 8.6 **Theories of abuse in the family**

Faith Robertson Elliot (from) *Gender, Family and Society* (1996) Basingstoke: Macmillan, pp. 167–82.

Editorial comments

For functionalists, and for many of those who wish to present a positive view of family life, the family can be seen as what Shorter (1977) called 'a haven in a heartless world'. Black feminist writers such as bell hooks (1982) write genuinely of the role of the black family as a haven from racism in a mainly white society. Furthermore, many people have grown up in

happy, safe and functional families and there is a great deal to support the idea that more research into functional families may prove beneficial for future policies.

However, as with many other writers, Faith Robertson Elliot is not prepared to ignore the darker side of family life and the abuses that may go on within it. Instead she looks at statistics that demonstrate far higher levels of child abuse in the family than we would perhaps be comfortable with, although clearly the definition affects the measurements. She also explores the advantages and shortcomings of psychological, sociological and feminist explanations of child abuse. From this she concludes that feminist analysis challenges the notion of a 'safe haven' in the family home for far too many children, and women, today.

References

hooks, b. (1982) *Ain't I a Woman? Black women and feminism*, Boston: South End Press.

Shorter, E. (1977) *The Making of the Modern Family*, London: Fontana.

Perspectives on familial violence/sexual abuse

PSYCHOLOGY AND PSYCHIATRY, conventional (non-feminist) sociology and feminism provide us with three very different interpretations of violence and sexual abuse in family life. Psychological perspectives locate familial violence/sexual abuse in individual **pathologies**. Non-feminist sociology locates familial violence/sexual abuse in a range of socio-structural processes, including 'deviant' subcultures, the structure of family life, class inequality and even, on occasion, gender structures. Feminist approaches also locate familial violence and sexual abuse in socio-structural processes. However, they place gender structures at the centre of their analysis, define these structures as patriarchal and conceptualize violence and sexual abuse in intimate relationships as violence against women rather than as family violence.

Psychopathological perspectives

Most early research on violence and sexual abuse in family life was conducted by psychologists and mental health therapists ... almost all the psychological literature is informed by the presumption that violence and sexual abuse are exceptional and pathological behaviours and are rooted in the defective personalities of the individual concerned.

Review of this literature show that it presents men who batter their sexual partners as holding rigid views of men's and women's roles, as insecure in their masculine identity and as using violence as a means of demonstrating power and adequacy; as morbidly jealous, sadistic, passive-aggressive, addiction-prone and pathologically dependent; as having poor communication skills, low frustration tolerance, weak impulse control and a proneness to immature outbursts of anger; and as suffering from low self-esteem, feelings of helplessness, powerlessness and inadequacy, fear of intimacy and fear of abandonment, depression and stress.

The catalogue of psychopathologies ascribed to parents (fathers and mothers) who physically abuse their children and to incestuous fathers is also long and diverse. Parents who abuse their children are described in some studies as low in impulse control, grossly immature and chronically aggressive, in others as rigid, cold and detached, and in yet others as excessively anxious, chronically depressed and guilt-prone; some studies find that they have low intelligence while others find that they display the full range of intelligence. Incestuous fathers have been seen as passive, inadequate and pathetic when faced with authority but as exercising an unusual degree of domination over their families, as socially introverted and over invested in their families, and as suffering from feelings of phallic inadequacy and/or impaired impulse control.

In pathological models, the 'victims' of violence and sexual abuse become precipitators of their own victimization and, like perpetrators, are said to be psychologically flawed. Thus, in studies of violence and sexual coercion in intimate relationships, women may be presented as suffering from psychological inadequacies which provoke men to violence, render them incapable of taking effective action in response to violence or make them addicted to the drama, chaos and excitement of violence and danger. Women have also been depicted as an important element in men's sexual abuse of children. They have been portrayed as denying their husbands sex, as unable to maintain a nurturing, affectionate relationship with their husbands and daughters, and as physically absent from the household. Whatever the cause of these circumstances – pregnancy, illness, exhaustion, imputed personality defect, the necessity of taking on a breadwinning role or the sexual boorishness, impotence or drunkenness of the husband – men's sexual desires tend to be privileged and mothers are seen as forsaking their wifely and maternal roles and so producing an incestuous situation.

Abused children do not escape this pathologizing. Accounts of children's contribution to their sexual victimization fall into two categories: the first sees the child as a seductress who actively arouses or seeks the sexual attentions of adults, the second accords the child a less active role but nevertheless interprets a lengthy liaison as indicating the child's collusion. In such accounts children may be depicted as seducing their fathers by their unusual attractiveness and charm, as having an abnormal desire for adult attention or sexual excitement, as experiencing emotional needs which have not been met in conventional ways or as simply frightened, lonely, withdrawn, dependent or compliant.

... The dominant explanation derives from psycho-analytic and psychological theories of the importance of early childhood experiences in personality development. The earliest versions of this argument focused on the psychodynamics of the mother–child relationship and had a distinctly Freudian orientation. More recently, a cognitive–behavioural approach in which both violent and sexually abusive behaviour are conceptualized as learned behaviours has been advanced. For example, violent or abusive behaviour has been linked with childhood experiences of violence and/or sexual abuse and women's failure to leave an abusive relationship has been conceptualized as learned helplessness.

The arguments so far discussed focus on the internal pathology of individual perpetrators and their 'victims'. However, attempts have been made to move the focus of analysis away from the individual and towards the network of family relationships within which violence or sexual abuse occur. This family systems approach conceptualizes families as systems which, when functioning normally, maintain a **homeostatic** state and meet the needs of family members. It then conceptualizes violence and sexual abuse as arising out of disturbances in family relationships that impair the ability of the family to meet the needs of its members. Thus, accounts of violence against wives speak of mutual psychic imbalances that create violence-prone systems. ...

In family systems theory, the entire family is disturbed and violence/sexual abuse are symptoms of this underlying dysfunctionality. This thesis locates violence and sexual abuse within the network of family relationships and implicates *the relationship* between wives and husbands, or between parents and children or even between siblings. However, despite the affiliation to relationship concepts, violence and sexual abuse are constructed as psychological diseases.

In sum, psychopathological explanations locate familial violence within the individuals concerned and explain it in terms of personal pathologies. They treat violence and abuse as not fully social behaviours, may be as much concerned with the pathology of the 'victim' as with the pathology of the offender, and render the social and cultural context invisible. Further, whether the phenomenon being discussed is the battering of wives or children, the sexual coercion of wives or the sexual abuse of children, the failure to conform appropriately to traditional images of masculinity and femininity is a recurring theme. ...

This model of violence and sexual abuse in the family has been tremendously influential. ... However, non-feminist and feminist sociologists alike have argued, though from different standpoints, that it is fatally flawed.

First, the methodology of studies in this tradition has been scathingly criticized. It has been argued that they are based on small and unrepresentative samples, have not used control groups, fail to define the imputed personality flaws so that there is no way of knowing precisely what is being referred to, and are informed not by specific hypotheses drawn from past research, but by the excuses and rationalizations of offenders, the subjective values and interpretations of the researchers and the commonsense assumptions of everyday thought.

Second, many of its findings have been challenged. Reviews of this literature show that it has attributed a bewildering and contradictory range of personality characteristics to offenders and their victims and has not identified a personality profile that is specific to violent or incestuous men, women or families. Further, it has been suggested that the personality characteristics attributed to abusers may be the consequence of being labelled an abuser rather than the cause of abuse and that the imputed characteristics of victims of abuse may be the consequence rather than the cause of victimization. Furthermore, and devastatingly, survey evidence of the frequency of violence and sexual abuse has been used to argue that they are not exceptional and abnormal behaviours but are widespread. ...

A third set of criticisms are concerned with the conceptual basis of the psychopathological thesis and its failure to locate familial violence and sexual abuse in social structures. Some writers have argued that links are not made between violent/sexually exploitative behaviour and class structures, others that links are not made with the social organization of masculinity. Because violence and sexual abuse are attributed to personality defects, the psychopathological thesis, it is argued, studies offenders and their victims as though they exist in a social vacuum. It fails to confront the power dynamics of either man–woman or parent–child relations or to explore the class and ethnic structures in which these relationships are located.

Fourth, and relatedly, the psychopathological thesis is challenged by feminist scholars as sexist. Feminist writers have argued that the catalogue of personality defects from which offenders, their victims and their families are deemed to suffer is based on traditional stereotypes of masculinity and femininity and the construction of departure from these stereotypes as deviant. Further, the implication of women and children in responsibility for their own victimization is consistently seen by feminist and feminist-influenced researchers as buying into men's self-serving characterizations of women's behaviour and as defining as understandable if unfortunate men's violence against women and sexual abuse of children. ...

Non-feminist sociological perspectives

Whereas psychopathological discourses locate violence and sexual abuse in the psychic processes of the individual, sociological discourses focus on socially structured forces. They presume that the causes of violent and abusive behaviour, the way in which they are defined and identified, and the forms of social regulation to which they are subject are to be explained in terms of the material and cultural forces which structure social life.

Sub-cultural explanations

Early sociological accounts of the various manifestations of violence and sexual abuse in family life posited a close connection between their occurrence and social and economic deprivation. Poverty, bad and overcrowded housing, limited educational resources, unemployment and poor job opportunities, it was variously suggested, create a sense of frustration and repression which predispose families to abusive behaviour. The physical and sexual abuse of children and violence in sexual partnerships were thus defined as sub-cultural phenomena. ...

These arguments move the debate beyond an individualistic orientation and focus on deprived sub-cultures and environments. They were deployed particularly, though not exclusively, in the analysis of child physical abuse and drew upon empirical findings based on reported child abuse which seemed to show that abusive families are heavily concentrated in the poorest social groups. However, this sub-cultural thesis has been heavily criticized on a number of counts. It has been argued that it (i) fails to take account of the prevalence of abusive behaviour in all social groups and implicitly treats some groups as 'healthy' and others as 'pathological'; (ii) is unheeding of the selective processes which label poor working-class families but not middle-class families abusive; (iii) does not explain gender differences in the perpetration of abuse and (iv), in locating problems of familial violence and sexual abuse primarily *within* particular sub-cultures or structures, fails to examine the links between these sub-structures and wider political, economic and historical structures.

Structural explanations

Structural explanations shift the debate away from notions of the pathological sub-culture and seek to explain physical and sexual abuse in family relationships in terms of the social, economic and ideological structures of the society as a whole.

... The physical abuse of children is one element in a larger phenomenon of child maltreatment ... (and) the position of families in the social structure is a key determinant of the degree of stress and frustration they experience. Poverty and deprivation represent structured obstacles to development and evoke reactive personal violence by individuals against individuals. However, concentrations of poverty, and consequently of child maltreatment, in particular sub-groups of a society are to be explained in terms of class inequalities in the control and distribution of resources, which produce deprived groups in the first place, and of social policies and philosophies which consistently fail to take account of their needs.

... Researchers contend that violence in family life is so pervasive that it must be seen as a 'normal' part of family life and explained in terms of 'normal' processes. ...

First, family life exists within a cultural context in which certain forms of violence are tolerated and even mandated. The widespread acceptance of physical punishment as a means of disciplining children represents, they argue, permission for family members to use forms of violence on each other that would not be allowed elsewhere. ...

Second, these researchers maintain that the structures of family life breed stress and conflict. The family, they argue, is a social institution in which interaction is intense and wide ranging. ... At the same time, family life is, they argue, confining: the child's membership of the family is involuntary and rarely terminable, the sexes and generations are in a singularly close relationship but their interests may be widely divergent, and roles are assigned on the basis of sex and age rather than interest or competence. ... The private nature of modern family life reduces the likelihood of intervention by neighbours, the police and the courts and makes it possible for family members to 'get away with' levels of violence not generally considered acceptable.

Third, researchers suggest that structured inequalities between women and men and parents and children lead to differential vulnerability to violence. ... Women and children may be the most frequent victims of family violence because they do not have the resources either to escape from, or inflict costs on, their attackers.

... Researchers identify as a critical factor in the generation of violence a disjunction between cultural values which emphasize material success and structural conditions which limit opportunities for success. Cultural expectations of male success include the expectation that men be family breadwinners, heads of households and masters in their own home but that, in poor socio-economic groups, resources for the achievement of success are limited. The result is likely to be frustration and therefore aggression and violence. ... Where occupational opportunities are blocked, this sub-cultural pattern may substitute for occupational success in defining masculinity.

This wide-ranging, multi-factorial analysis seeks to

provide an explanation of all forms of violence in the family. It is an ambitious project. Yet it is ultimately unsatisfactory. First, its approach to explanation is **ad hoc**. ... Researchers have compiled a seemingly endless array of potentially significant factors and empirical generalizations but fail to specify how they interact and connect to produce violent behaviours. Second, they do not address the question of rape, sexual assault and the sexual abuse of children and thus leave out of the picture an important set of exploitative behaviours. Third, their argument is criticized by feminist scholars because it takes 'the family' rather than gender inequality as its unit of analysis and defines violence in intimate relationships as family violence rather than as men's violence. ... It thus addresses gender inequality as simply one factor among many, and minimizes the importance of men's power in structuring family relationships and generating violence.

Feminist perspectives

In contrast with conventional sociological analysis, feminist accounts of violence and sexual abuse in family life place gender relationships at the centre of their analysis, see the problem to be explained as men's violence against women and focus on the way in which women define and experience men's violence. ... This thesis rests on two major and interlinked arguments.

First, it is argued that male domination, though sustained and legitimated in a variety of ways, is ultimately sustained by force. For example, for centuries the authority which was vested in husbands as heads of households included the legal right to chastize their wives for their 'lawful protection'. Further, the chastisement of wives, though no longer formally enshrined in legal norms, is still used by husbands to sustain their 'rights' and has widespread cultural support. ... Violence is used to silence women, to win arguments, to express dissatisfaction, to determine future behaviour and to demonstrate dominance.

Second, sexuality is said to be the primary sphere of male power, the solid base from which men establish control over women. This thesis begins with the argument that in nearly all societies and periods of history male sexual desire is defined in terms of (i) virility, conquest and power and (ii) a biologically-driven urgency and compulsivity. In early radical-feminist writings men's sexuality is portrayed as directed to the conquest of women and as involving possession, control, abuse and domination. Male sexual discourse proclaims 'that male sexuality is innately active, aggressive and insatiable' and that women are 'sexual commodities' whom men have a right to use how and whenever they can. Male sexual discourse constitutes an 'ideology of rape' and creates a social structure in which men set out to conquer, invade and plunder women's bodies. The social construction of masculinity valorizes assertiveness and power, turns its face from emotional intimacy and glories in sexual conquest as a symbol of male prowess.

Feminist discourse suggests that aggression and abuse are inherent in this construction of masculinity and seeks to show that wife-battering and killing, date rape and marital rape and child sexual abuse are extreme forms of the sexual aggression which women and children routinely experience. ... Further, feminist researchers have shown that the beliefs which surround men's sexuality – such as the belief that men are driven by urgent sexual desire or the belief that only women who ask for it get raped – place the responsibility for avoiding violence and rape and for protecting children on women, lead to victim-blaming and act as a form of social control. The constant threat of male sexual aggression, it is argued, limits women's movements and encounters with other people, prescribes the way they dress and present themselves to the world and renders them dependent on the goodwill of a male protector. ...

Furthermore, feminist analysis suggests that male violence has institutional support. Men's violence and sexual abuse, it is argued, are supported by everyday myths and assumptions which minimize sexual violence, remove responsibility from men for their actions and make individual pathologies the explanation of violence. ...

Finally, feminist analysis challenges as a myth cultural beliefs in the security and safety of 'the home'. Marriage is a social structure that gives husbands the right to the domestic and sexual services of their wives, places wives under the control and direction of their husbands, and subjects women to the use of intimidation, coercion and violence as strategies for maintaining male rights and privileges. ... The dominance of beliefs in the safety and privacy of the family not only obscures the reality of family violence but limits public surveillance and cuts women off from public protection.

[Feminist discourses] move discussion of the causes of men's physical and sexual abuse of women and children away from the particular circumstances of individual abusers and towards the delineation of a patriarchal culture which defines masculinity in terms of aggression and sexual predatoriness. It seeks to explain not why a particular man abuses his partner or child but why men as a sex–class category are the primary perpetrators of violence and why so little is done about it. It shows that images of masculinity as aggressive and biologically driven permeate popular and élitist culture, sexual liberation ideologies and psychiatric and psychological theory, inform the way in which legal and welfare institutions respond to sexual violence and are reflected in and supported by a pornographic industry in which women are always and immutably demeaned.

However, two decades of debate have pointed to difficulties in early radical-feminist theorizing and have led to its modification.

In the first place, though the connections between 'normal' masculinity and wife-battering, rape and child sexual abuse are clear, it is also evident that these behaviours are defined by men themselves as deviant. They tend to be regarded as seamy and reprehensible even when, as in the nineteenth century, they are apparently sanctioned by legal norms. Our theoretical models must therefore seek to show where the boundaries are drawn between 'normal' and 'deviant' masculinities and to delineate the circumstances in which these boundaries are transgressed. ...

Second, feminism has been reluctant to confront the reality of women's violence. Thus women's violence against men tends to be viewed as rare and/or defensive, an argument that, on the one hand, obscures the extent of women's violence and, on the other, slides into exonerating it. There is a growing awareness of violence in lesbian relationships but research and theorizing remain tentative. Women's physical and sexual abuse of children (and indeed men's physical abuse of children) is not prominent in feminist analysis. When it is addressed, it tends to be explained in terms of the power relations between women and men and/or of class disadvantage. Thus women's 'failure' to protect their children from male violence may be attributed to their relative powerlessness and their abuse of children to the stress generated by their exclusive, wide-ranging and burdensome responsibility for childcare, isolation from supportive kin and neighbourhood networks or poverty and deprivation. However, this argument does not take account of the normative appearance by women as well as men of physical punishment as an appropriate way of disciplining children [and] it fails to confront the issue of age domination. ... The abuse of children is thus an abuse of adult/parental power and cannot be reduced to the dynamics of male–female relationships.

Third, the image of a monolithic and unvarying masculinity and femininity that emerges from most early radical-feminist accounts of male violence has been challenged. As some writers have observed, ethnographic evidence of the existence in pre-industrial societies of non-aggressive masculinities and even of rape-free cultures points to cross-cultural variation in the social construction of masculinity. Further, the history of Anglo-Saxon sexuality points to historically varying and contradictory tendencies in our sexual scripts. The predatory male sexuality which feminist writers depict describes the sexuality of the permissive revolution, but is condemned in the Christian tradition as 'lust'. It stands in opposition to notions of 'married love' as involving commitment, mutual affection, fidelity, trust and respect which were central to the Puritan tradition and which, some writers have argued, underpinned the emergence of the modern Western conjugal family. Finally, Marxist and 'black' feminists have consistently and convincingly argued that class and ethnic inequality interact with, and cross-cut, patriarchal relations to shape male power, the construction of masculinity/femininity and violence against women in complex and varying ways. These and similar accounts of the varying and changing construction of sexuality are leading radical feminism to the adoption of a mode of analysis – exemplified in a recent collection of readings on **femicide** – which, while retaining the notion that patriarchy is universal and is universally sustained by force, recognizes that male violence takes forms that are specific to particular cultural, political and economic contexts.

Key terms

The following key terms appear in the text above. They have been defined below to aid with the reading of this item.

pathologies illnesses

homeostatic self regulating or self balancing

ad hoc for only one situation – cannot be used more generally

femicide murder of women

Questions

1 Summarize and discuss psychological explanations of child abuse in the family. Who or what is seen to cause the abuse to take place?

2 Summarize and discuss subcultural and structural explanations of child abuse in the family. Who or what is seen to cause the abuse to take place?

3 Summarize and discuss feminist explanations of child abuse in the family. Who or what is seen to cause the abuse to take place?

4 Which view does Elliot support? Do you agree with her? Give your reasons.

Reading 8.7 **The relationship between family and definitions of gender and sexuality**

D. H. Morgan (from) *Family Connections: an introduction to family studies* (1996) Cambridge: Polity, pp. 72–85.

Editorial comments

Morgan adopts a post-modern approach towards gender. He rejects the widely held view that our position in the family is the result of our biology and suggests that gender roles are constructed by the family itself.

He argues that both private and public situations are gendered for men and women. Even more controversially, he suggests that changing gender roles also influence the structure of the family.

Not only is there an assumption of the male as breadwinner but also the assumption that any long-term male in a relationship will be the father of any children involved. He suggests that different perspectives on the relationships between family and gender can highlight the ways in which women and men can exploit others through gender, sexuality and family life. Furthermore, he proposes that the relationship between family and gender is now highly diverse and complex owing to considerable changes both within and outside the family.

Gender

A simple model

THE MODEL CONSISTS of two terms, 'family' and 'gender'. The relationships between these two terms may be *constructing*, of *obscuring* or of *modifying*:

> FAMILY constructs GENDER
> FAMILY obscures GENDER
> FAMILY modifies GENDER
>
> GENDER constructs FAMILY
> GENDER obscures FAMILY
> GENDER modifies FAMILY
> …

Family constructs gender

The notion that it is the family and family relationships that construct gender identities is very widespread and, on the surface, very persuasive. Justifications for differential pay or employment practices were often presented with reference to women's 'family responsibilities' or to the idea of 'the family wage'. Such ideological constructions are often seen as crucial in understanding a woman's relatively disadvantaged position in the labour market.

Beginning with definitions of 'the family' we find that these nearly always revolve around definitions of parenthood and marriage, themselves often broken down into clear gendered identities. Marriage is constructed as a heterosexual relationship which is formally recognized and parenthood is developed from or associated with the idea of marriage. The very constituent elements of everyday understandings of the family cannot be detached from issues of gender. …

It does not matter that many households may be headed by a woman and many others are, in various ways, dual-earner households. It is not always the realities of domestic life that shape gendered identities but the constructions of family that are important: the family may only appear to be the crucible within which gendered identities are forged.

Classically, much sociological and sociopsychological analysis was devoted to accounts of the ways in which gendered identities were reproduced through the agencies of socialization located, primarily, within the family and family relationships. Such analyses, it has been argued, are better at explaining how gendered identities are reproduced over time than they are at accounting for their origins; they tend to give an **overdeterministic** picture which is weaker when it comes to explaining changes in the gender order; and they are not particularly effective when it comes to assessing the part played by other institutions and processes in the construction of gendered identities.

If we are to retain some sense of the socialization process as contributing to gender identities our focus should be upon the totality of family-based practices and not simply upon those practices which might be overtly identified as 'primary socialization'. Among such practices, a key place must be occupied by the sexual division of labour and understandings of family responsibilities over the life-course. These are patterns which have proved to be remarkably resilient. … Further analysis has focused upon the complex juggling acts, the 'coping strategies', that women have to perform in order to balance domestic obligations and employment commitments. Men are not conventionally called upon to engage in such strategies. However, this is not simply a question of who *does* what. It is also a question of who *is* what, and much feminist analysis has explored the relationships between these various juggling acts that women are expected to perform and the fragmented existence that often follows from this and the very construction, with both positive and negative connotations, of female self and identity.

There are links here with the question of socialization. The patterns of sexual divisions within the home, and the construction of the divisions between home and work, are amongst the most obvious and, one must assume, taken-for-granted features of everyday domestic life, observed and sometimes adopted by children as they grow up. Moreover, the differential expectations of children in terms of their contributions to domestic labour affects their sense of gender identity.

... Women see housework and child care as *their* work. These are activities which they *own*. All the moral qualities which are, or were, associated with the world of employment, with having and keeping a job, are also to be found in analyses of women's household responsibilities.

Questions framed in terms of the sexual division of labour within the household run the risk of obscuring issues of power in the analysis of domestic relationships. To put the matter somewhat starkly, the descriptions of who does what within the home may obscure questions of who decides for whom. Power arises out of the unequal distribution of resources within the home; also, inequalities in terms of power, favouring the man, shape these distributions of resources. Yet, as will be argued later, matters are rarely as straightforward as this and increasingly scholars have been analysing the complex intersections of gender and power in the context of the home.

We cannot, therefore, conclude that family and marital relationships are automatically disempowering for women and empowering for men. It may be suggested that where the experience of power is generally consistent with gendered expectations, then these experiences of power will play an important part in the shaping of wider gender identities. The working man who is emotionally dependent upon his partner and the housebound woman who has clearly marked out areas of control and responsibility have their wider gender identities confirmed. Different and complex mixes of powerfulness and powerlessness, therefore, provide important strands in the construction, and undermining, of gendered identities through family relationships.

An important way in which family and marital relationships can construct gendered identities is around sexuality. The simplest case may illustrate the point. In a context where marriage is defined as the only legitimate site for sexual expression and where, also, legitimate sex is defined in terms of heterosexual 'penetrative' sex, then it could be argued that here marriage constructs gender in a direct way. ... The **nexus** linking marriage, sexuality and reproduction is also one which generates and reproduces gendered identities.

Despite greater freedom of sexual expression and sexual representation, this model of sexuality still remains a dominant one and hence the links between marriage, sexuality and the production of gendered identities remain strong. ...

There may be an extent to which greater sexual freedom may have strengthened or at least redefined the ways in which the marital relationship constructs gender identities. With a greater openness about sexual expression in marriage comes an obligation on the part of the spouses to satisfy each other. ...

There is another, darker, side to these links between sexuality, power, family and gender identity and this is to do with sexual abuse and violence within domestic relationships. Many of these violences follow and reinforce lines of gendered power and identity. ...

There do appear to be some very strong ways in which ideas of marriage and the family reinforce or reproduce constructions of gender. Issues of the very definition of marriage, of divisions of labour, of power, sexuality and violence all interact with each other to underline or reinforce themes of gender difference and gender inequality. However, there are further complexities to be explored.

Family obscures gender

Family relations may obscure, rather than directly construct, gender identities. For example, dominant models of marriage may construct relatively ungendered narratives about domestic life. In modern times, an understanding of marriage in relational, as opposed to institutional, terms may serve to obscure gender differences. There has been a rise of a dominant discourse about the centrality of interpersonal relationships understood not simply as the formal linking of two or more people but as the deeper psychological and interpersonal interweaving of two biographies. With the rise of this more complex understanding of relationships, there has also been a widespread understanding that marriage represents a central, if not the only, adult relationship which is expected to manifest all these characteristics. People are expected to work at their marriages, the marital relationship is constructed as a desirable end in itself and sexual expression is seen as a key element in the growth and maintenance of marriage.

These narratives about the growing relational character of marriage obscure both some persisting and deep-rooted institutional features and questions of gender differences. Deep understanding of marriage as *the* relationship presupposes some measures of equality, in theory if not in practice, between the partners. *Sexual* differences may be important within marriage given the centrality of heterosexual love and the different psychobiological experiences in childhood, while *gender* differences are assumed to decline in importance. Thus in many middle-class marriages, it may be assumed, women are faced with the complex work of reconciling this ideology of equality with the reality of deep gendered differences in, say, the understanding of a 'career' and what this may mean for domestic identities.

… Earlier understandings saw the active business of parent work as being especially the province of mothers, while issues to do with status, control and linkages to the outside world were the responsibilities of fathers. While the evolving notion of parenting, informed by professional advice and popular manuals, places particular and novel demands and responsibilities on women, it also quite specifically seeks to draw men into the active side of parent work. …

Sociology and social science in general have played a part in the elaboration and perpetuation of some relatively ungendered images of marriage and parenting. Similar observations may be made about some constructions of child abuse which ignore or obscure questions of gender. Many of the key terms – 'companionate marriage', 'the symmetrical family' etc – have developed from sociological work, while other terms, not specifically anchored to family studies, may also be deployed in ways to obscure gender differences within the home. …

Family modifies gender

Feminist and critical studies of family life have, cumulatively, developed a coherent and complex picture of the various ways in which family relationships and values construct or obscure gender. Somewhat less heralded are the ways in which family relationships may themselves become a source of change within the wider gender order.

In part this is to do with the relative autonomy of domestic life within the wider social system: notions of privacy, however limited and ambiguous, do help to ensure some degree of leeway within family practices. Further, gender is all pervasive and exists at all levels yet we cannot simply move between levels, reading off 'patriarchy' from the particularities of domestic encounters. …

Day-to-day encounters within domestic life may always be gendered but they are rarely simply just about gender and it is out of the complex, and sometimes contradictory, unity of gendered family identities that possibilities of change and modification emerge.

It is possible, therefore, to see the family or household as a site for the meeting and working through of a variety of contradictions around gender identities and the gender order. Thus some of the complexities and contradictions of power may meet within the household. A man, feeling that he has little real power in the public world of employment, may become envious of the apparent power and control which he sees in the daily life of his partner. Women, juggling domestic and employment responsibilities and sharing the experiences of marriage and parenting with other women, may come to develop ironic or critical perspectives on their own domestic situations. …

Changes in the occupational structure have their impact upon the gender order in part directly, through a restructuring of the labour market, but in part indirectly as mediated through domestic relationships. Thus the growing participation of women in the labour market at all levels increasingly produces the possibilities of discrepancies in terms of occupational status between women and men, in some cases with the former higher than the latter. Some accommodations to these discrepancies may reinforce prevailing gender patterns but others may allow for some degree of change or modification. …

Individuals within family situations are capable of evaluating and responding imaginatively to the forces and processes that confront them. Gender is not wholly 'given'. Insofar as family relationships constitute one major arena where women and men meet and interact, it is not surprising that it is here also that some people may seek to bring about modifications in their day-to-day workings of gendered themes. A minority of men head single-parent households and elsewhere women and men may work together in order to develop non-sexist or less sexist patterns of child-rearing. Individuals may explore possibilities of role reversals or more equitable divisions of labour. Men may confront their violences and seek out ways of dealing with them.

… The impact of changes within domestic and interpersonal relations and changes in the wider structuring of gender relationships is not automatic and we need more investigation into how such changes actually come about.

Gender constructs family

It may be agreed that the family cannot be seen as the sole site for the generation of gender hierarchies or the sole arena within which such differences are played out. Further, to a very large extent, family relationships are shaped by gender or patriarchal relationships. To put the matter more strongly, it is impossible to write or think about family without also thinking about gender. The reverse is less obviously true.

As we have seen, the key terms that are used in family discourse are gendered. Further, the pairing of many of these terms encourages us to hear them in terms of difference and opposition. Other oppositions and divisions, with a currency wider than the family and which have strong gendered connotations, also impinge upon constructions and understandings of family life. The distinction between public and private is one such opposition. Supposed overlaps between public/private, men/women and work/home are not complete, fixed or unambiguous. Nevertheless, they continue to be influential. Even if it becomes increasingly difficult to pronounce the phrase 'a woman's place is in the home' without irony or modification, it is still the case that the home and domesticity continue to be understood in feminine terms. 'Househusband' still has an unfamiliar ring or a sense of a striving for political correctness; 'houseperson' even more so. ...

There is an interesting contradiction here. The terms which we possess in order to describe family relationships are key terms in mapping out gender relationships. Who speaks of family also speaks of gender. Yet these terms are, formally, equally weighted and evenly balanced: husband, wife, mother, daughter and so on. Yet, as the discussion around the distinctions public/private and rational/emotional suggest, the family becomes a special sphere for women.

Men often get edited out of the account. Thus insofar as gender constructs family it does so in a complex and double way through the solidifying of gender oppositions and through the feminization of the home and domestic activities.

Within the array of gendered terms associated with the family it is doubtful whether there is a more central term than 'mother'. This is a term which is defined both around the theme of sexual difference and also around constructions of the public and the private and the rational and the emotional. Indeed, it could be said that families were 'mothered' rather than 'gendered'. The bond between the mother and the child is being constructed as having at least one foot firmly within the natural order. Mothers who voluntarily relinquish the custody of their children are defined as having *abandoned* these offspring. Fathers who leave the mother with their children may be understood as having behaved badly but they are not generally seen as behaving 'unnaturally'. ...

Gender obscures family

... Feminist scholarship has been successful in identifying the all-pervasive character of patriarchy and gendered social relations which entered into the most intimate interpersonal relationships and the most apparently innocent representation. ...

This gendered perspective has been especially strong in the context of the analysis of family and domestic relationships so much so, indeed, that it may be possible to speak of an 'over-gendered conception of the family'. This is not to say that it is possible to talk about family processes without bringing in issues of gender but it is to argue that these processes bring in themes other than gender. A chief candidate here is that of age and generation. Recent interests in age – especially childhood and children – should have the effect of allowing for a more systematic exploration of age as a key strand in family analysis. ...

It is possible to argue that an over-gendered construction of the family may have the consequence of obscuring those aspects of family life which, while being of considerable importance, do not readily fall within the framework of gender analysis. ... To argue in these terms is not to say that there are areas of 'family' which should be kept safe from gendered analysis but simply to say that a complete account of family life cannot stop with questions of gender.

Gender modifies family

The impact of changing relations between women and men at a more general level upon family and household relationships has been well explored. Pride of place is usually given to changes in the labour market both in terms of the overall expansion of opportunities for women, especially married women, and in terms of the particular opening up of areas formerly closed. In terms of their impact upon family relationships the most important would seem to be the steady erosion of the male breadwinner model; the provision for women of alternative sources of income and identity outside the home; the impact upon domestic timetables and the negotiation of time within the household; and the provision of greater opportunities for, if not the actuality of, greater male participation in the home. ...

One more ambiguous area is to do with female sexuality and personal identity. The double-edged impact of the 'sexual revolution' or 'permissiveness' upon women has often been noted. However, a major theme in modern societies has been the linking of heterosexual attractiveness with personal identity and a project of the feminine self. Women were encouraged to think of themselves not simply as wives or as mothers but as individual women who could express their femininity through bodily discipline and careful grooming. Men have not been immune to these influences either. Of particular importance was the 'democratization' of this process. ...

This discussion of some possible linkages between female sexuality, consumerism and a sense of self highlights some possible ambiguities in the analysis of factors assumed to impact on family relationships. A more liberal interpretation might argue that the cumulative effect of all these changes – political, in the market-place, in terms of freer sexuality and so on – can be liberating in the sense of a gradual enlargement of the field of choice for women. A more sceptical approach might see these changes in the gender order as being of limited significance with an effect that is overall supportive of marriage and the family with all their oppressive and patriarchal features now better concealed but definitely present. Somewhere between these two interpretations would be one which focuses upon the possible contradictions that such changes highlight, contradictions which may give rise to pressures for further change.

Changes in the gender order with their possible impacts upon family relationships are not simply the product of socio-economic changes but also of more direct sexual politics. Certainly, the post-1960s feminist movements, while addressing themselves to the gender order as a whole, paid particular attention to many of the oppressive features of family living. Recent debates about the alleged decline of the family have often cited 'Women's Lib' as a direct or an indirect cause, although this is not necessarily anything new. ...

It was largely the work of feminist writers that put questions of violences against wives on to the political agenda and that developed institutions or practices to deal with the consequences of such violences. Such a critique called into question much that had been taken for granted, namely the idea of the home as a safe haven, notions of domestic privacy and of the rights and expectations of husbands. It, together with subsequent debates around child abuse, provided some legitimation for external intervention into domestic life and some measure of demystification of the domestic relationship. A more recent illustration would be debates and legislation concerning rape within marriage.

To conclude this section we may cite changes in patterns of divorce, especially since the Second World War, as changes which link issues of family and gender together in complex and diverse ways. ... The evaluation of the significance of these trends remains controversial; what remains clear also is that here we have some major changes in family living that have been partly shaped by wider changes in the relationships between the expectations of women and men

Key terms

The following key terms appear in the text above. They have been defined below to aid with the reading of this item.

overdeterministic overstating the power of society or other factors to decide how we can and should behave

nexus social network

Questions

1 In your own words, summarize Morgan's main argument about the different ways that the rela-

tionship between gender and family can be understood.

2 Explain and discuss the view that the family constructs gender roles for both males and females

3 How could the family obscure or modify gender?

4 Explain and evaluate the view that gender can construct, obscure or modify families. Which (if any) of these do you agree with and why?

Reading 8.8 **The post-modern family?**

D. Cheale (from) *Family and the State of Theory* (1991) Hemel Hempstead: Harvester Wheatsheaf, pp. 141–9.

Editorial comments

Cheale outlines some of the key aspects of post-modern theory and shows how it can help to explain recent rapid changes and diversity in family structure. The main underlying concepts of post-modernism he examines are:

1 the end of progress and the idea that we have lost faith in the future

2 the media-saturation of society which means that

we use the media a great deal to define our concepts of society, especially family life

3 a decline in emotional family commitment, as parents and other carers are unable to relate to the rapidly changing world their children are experiencing.

His conclusion from this analysis of the post-modern world is that the chaos and rapid changes found in many family relationships can only really be explained by looking at the considerable differences and diversity found in culture overall, and the lack of confidence in the family and society at large that this might be causing.

Family and the state of theory

Something is happening

CHANGES IN FAMILY theories often follow changes in family life. In the search for new understandings sociologists have explored a number of new approaches, including a variety of redefinitions of 'family'. In all this blooming, buzzing confusion there is no clear line of theoretical development, nor should we expect to find one. Nevertheless, there is a tendency in some of the most recent writings for discussions of theoretical possibilities to crystallize into two contrasting views of the state of theory. These come together in the modernism/post-modernism debate over the future of social life and the future of the social sciences. In [this reading] we will be concerned with the future of family life.

The theoretical framework of modernism includes the theory of modernity, and related concepts of processes of modernization and anti-modernist reactions. The unifying theme here is that of the *rationalization* of social life. The progressive **rational** organization of human affairs is thought to be due to the **emancipation** of human beings from arbitrary limits of poverty and ignorance. As a result, people become free to order their activities guided by the powers of reason. Accounts of the standardization of the life course illustrate this idea very well. It is held that the timing and spacing of family transitions in the western societies has become more orderly. It is also thought that this has occurred not so much because of intensified **normative controls** of the traditional sort, but because individuals have chosen common patterns of life course management under conditions of material improvement and institutional bureaucratization.

But this grand vision of human progress has been disturbed in recent years. There is a bewildering variety of alternative life-styles. Also, disorderly sequences of transitions have become more prevalent. Parenthood may come before marriage, and individuals may cycle into and out of marriage and family formation many times, without ever completing the task of raising their children into independent adults.

In addition to the practical difficulty of providing explanatory models for these more complex patterns, there is a deeper problem for social theory. Are these recent changes simply a short-term interruption to the secular trend of western modernization? Or are they the beginning of a cultural transformation, to which the classical sociological theories of social order will no longer apply?

Post-modernist theorists agree with the second of these statements [while] modernist theorists generally disagree with claims of such a break. They do so by arguing for either a dualistic or a cyclical model of modernization. On the one hand, it is thought that there are secular tendencies toward greater collective control and social order, achieved through the expansion of powerful institutions such as the state. On the other hand, it is thought that the changes required by a modern society engaged in the progressive transformation of itself entail the frequent destruction of existing social forms, which have become outmoded. … Tendencies towards disorganization are held to be counteracted by creative forces of reorganization, which recombine the fragments of the old order in new and more advantageous ways. …

Burgess and Locke (1945) argued that the American family was in a state of transition – from *institution* to *companionship*. In the past, they thought, a stable and secure family life was guaranteed by external pressures of law, custom and public opinion. Those controls were reinforced inside the family by the authority of the male family head, the rigid discipline exercised by parents over their children, and elaborate private and public rituals. That system of control, they argued, had broken down in America in the twentieth century. This was due to a complex combination of causes. …

Burgess claimed that the result of all these changes was family disorganization: that is, a situation characterized by normative uncertainty, behavioural fluidity and relationship disintegration. But he was not pessimistic. Burgess believed that *disorganization* was always followed eventually by *reorganization*. Since he thought that the external, institutional supports for family life had declined, Burgess located the potential for reorganization in the desires and capacities of individuals to construct meaningful lives for themselves. Family life, he thought, was being reconstituted on the basis of interpersonal relationships of mutual affection and understanding. The result of that process would be the companionship family.

Significantly, Burgess seems to have believed it was unlikely that individuals could reconstitute family life on their own. He thought that individuals' limited resources of self-understanding and social skills would have to be supplemented and upgraded by the knowledge generated from social scientific research. Translated by family experts into practical techniques, this knowledge was to be communicated and implemented by a variety of social agencies. Burgess was deeply concerned with advancing the programmes of child guidance clinics, marriage counselling centres, psychiatrists and clinical psychologists in their efforts to treat the behaviour problems of children and adults. He also stressed the preventative value of family studies courses for college students.

Today it is the existence of the companionship family that is in question. Perhaps Burgess and Locke (1945) would not have been too surprised at this. They pointed out that ties of affection are not as strong as ties of duty, when the latter are publicly enforced. They also noted the greater vulnerability of the socially isolated companionship family, especially to the effects of economic insecurity.

... What is new today – and what may justify applying the term 'post-modern' to our present condition – is that human service programmes that Burgess recommended no longer work in precisely the way he envisaged. He seems to have simply assumed that therapeutic agencies would inevitably be committed to the values of familism, and in particular to the preservation of the family as a unity of interacting personalities. But today it is the values of individualism and emancipation from social limitations that are increasingly evident in the work of human service practitioners. ... Today, feminist therapists and workers in women's shelters often see it as their responsibility to provide women with personal resources with which to *leave their families.*

The post-modern family?

Post-modernist theorists have begun to grapple with the possibility that many of the features of social life that were taken for granted for a long time will have to be rethought. This is not simply a question of rethinking specific social arrangements, such as family life, or even the sex/gender role system. Rather, post-modernism poses the question of a general rethinking of 'the social' and of 'theory'. Post-modernism is an elusive approach to the study of human existence, which has only recently begun to be incorporated into the sociology of social life. ...

Post-modernist thought begins with experiences of pluralism, disorder and fragmentation in contemporary culture that are not predicted by the modern paradigm of universal reason. Post-modernists go on to argue that if modernity, and hence our concepts of reason and progress, have in some sense failed, then presumably a very different set of principles must be at work in the world. Unlike the modernist theorists, however, the post-modernists do not think these alternative principles will eventually produce a total reorganization of social life. Rather, they are inclined to believe that what is most characteristic of the post-modern era is its continuous production of instability. This production of instability – in science, art and literature as well as in lifestyles and family relationships – is described by a set of ideas that are unlike the standard theories of social evolution (such as that of Talcott Parsons), which presupposed convergence to equilibrium. ...

The end of progress
Faith in modernity has included the belief in a continuous upward path of improvement for all that leads to an ever more glorious feature of popular well-being and social harmony. This romantic view of modernity has been severely eroded by recent events in the western societies. There is growing realization that economic growth and the expansion of the welfare state since the end of the Second World War did not solve all social ills. Many individuals remain trapped in poverty and ignorance, and for some social groups – such as American blacks – conditions have got measurably worse. Stories about increasing numbers of children growing up in poverty reach us from many different directions, like a bad echo from the nineteenth century.

Social change continues, of course – at an ever more rapid pace – but it is thought that it does so in ways that bring only dubious benefits, or benefits for some but not others, or benefits that have side-effects whose accumulation will eventually cost us dearly. It therefore appears to some observers that, in the western societies at least, progress has come to an end and with it modernity. If that is the case, then what does the post modern family look like?

Norman Denzin (1987) argues that the traditional concept of a family can no longer be applied to the post-modern situation. The modern nuclear family, in which children were cared for by two parents within a protective and emotionally secure environment, is no longer the norm in America, he believes. He therefore proposes a definition of a new type of family for the post-modern period. His bleak assessment is that 'It is a single-parent family, headed by a teenage mother, who may be drawn to drug abuse and alcoholism. She and her children live in a household that is prone to be violent.'

In addition to these structural and interactional features, Denzin refers to two other aspects of post-modern family life. ... First, Denzin suggests that increasing numbers of children are now cared for by someone other than a parent. The daycare setting is therefore an important factor in contemporary child development. Second, there is the presence of the television set in the home, which is left on for up to seven hours a day. It is from television that children learn cultural myths today, Denzin insists. He concludes that the post-modern child 'is cared for by the television set, in conjunction with the day-care center'. The mass media and daycare providers also figure prominently in other accounts of post-modernization.

Simulations and the death of the subject

Post-modernist theories of popular culture attach considerable importance to the ways in which mass-mediated meanings penetrate all corners of contemporary social life. Jean Baudrillard, especially, argues that the media's insatiable urge to communicate creates an excess of cultural products. This excess of meanings erases all boundaries, and it produces a de-differentiated mass society. One aspect of this situation is the disappearance of any separation between public and private spheres. This is because intimate details of private lives are picked up by journalists and talk-show hosts, processed through electronic networks, and relayed into millions of homes through television and newspapers.

Denzin (1987) is concerned that 'television set family myths', which are portrayed in soap operas and situation comedies, are out of touch with the realities of family life for most people. They are 'cultural fantasies', which do not provide practical guidelines for how to live today. The television 'families' that fascinate mass audiences are, in Baudrillard's terminology, *simulations* (1988). These images are not real families, nor are they signs that refer to real families. Nevertheless, these imaginary families are 'real' to millions of viewers, who discuss the events of their lives at work the next day just as they discuss the details of their own lives. ...

Hyperreal mediated fantasies are of particular interest to feminist theorists, who detect in them sites for the ideological construction of male-dominated heterosexual couples. Popular romance narratives have drawn especial attention. The precise subjective effects produced by reading these texts are important issues in contemporary social theory. Post-modernist interpretations of romance narratives see them as constituting the 'subjectivity' of the individual, or in other words as creating the individual's sense of self. Of course, romance stories are only one source of subjectivity. They are therefore described as existing in (partially) contradictory relations to other constitutive sources, such as everyday family life. These other sources are also thought to contain contradictory experiences, such as love and fear, submission and autonomy, sexual desire and asexual care-giving. The self, or 'subject', produced by this complex of experiences is seen not as a coherent, stable essence, but as a fragmented participant in various discourses. ...

The claim that individuals do not now (and perhaps never did) possess a stable inner identity is sometimes expressed in the phrase 'the death of the subject'. Behind this phrase lies the argument that individuals who do not possess a coherent sense of their own identity will not be able to act consistently upon, or especially against, their environment. It is at this point that the sociology of the family comes back in. The shifting contexts of childhood socialization in post-modern society are sometimes thought to contribute to subjective instability.

References

Baudrillard, J. (1988) *Selected Writings*, Stanford: Stanford University Press.

Burgess, E. (1973) *On Community, Family and Delinquency*, Chicago and London: University of Chicago Press.

Burgess, E. and Locke, H. (1945) *The Family*, New York: American Book Company.

Denzin, N. (1986) 'Postmodern •social theory', *Sociology Theory, 4*.

Denzin, N. (1987) 'Postmodern children', *Society, 24*.

Key terms

The following key terms appear in the text above. They have been defined below to aid with the reading of this item.

rational based on reason rather than belief or emotion

emancipation political or personal freedom

normative controls social controls based on assumptions of right and wrong and what behaviour is acceptable or not

Questions

1 Explain the view presented by Burgess, within the reading, that disorganization is always followed by reorganization. How does this relate to the current evidence of family diversity?

2 What does Cheale see as the main characteristics of the post-modern family?

3 Why might people find it more difficult than in the past to construct their identities through family relationships?

Further reading

The following texts may represent a useful starting point for further investigation of the ideas contained within this chapter.

Primary texts

Abbot, P. and Wallace, C. (1992) *The Family and the New Right*, London: Pluto Press.

Barrett, M. and McIntosh, M. (1991) *The Anti-Social Family*, 2nd edn, London: Verso.

Leonard, D. and Hood-Williams, S. (eds) (1988) *Families*, Walton-on-Thames: Nelson.

Young, M. and Willmott, P. (1957) *Family and Kinship in East London*, Harmondsworth: Penguin.

Secondary texts

Abercrombie, N. and Warde, A. (eds) (1994) *Family, Households and the Life-Course*, Lancaster: Framework Press.

Jorgensen, N. (1997) *Investigating Families and Households*, in the Sociology in Action series, London: Collins Educational.

Muncie, J., Wetherell, M., Dallos, R. and Cochrane, A. (eds) (1995) *Understanding the Family*, London: Sage.

Rapoport, R. N., Fogarty, M. P. and Rapoport, R. (eds) (1982) *Families in Britain*, London: Routledge & Kegan Paul.

Wilson, A. (1985) *Family*, in the Society Now series, London: Routledge.

Coursework suggestions

1 Carry out research to explore the allocation of domestic tasks in two-parent, dual-income families

The best way to approach this is to identify a number of such families and ask each partner to keep a detailed time budget for a week itemizing how they spend their time in terms of activities related to paid employment, leisure, domestic tasks and any other aspects of personal life that you consider relevant. This should help you to identify the extent to which their involvement in the domestic aspects of life is truly symmetrical.

2 Investigate post-modern ideas about families and other aspects of society today

Through self-report studies and interviews, look at the life histories of a number of different adults to identify changes in their personal relationships over time.

3 Investigate attitudes towards cohabitation, divorce, adultery and pre-marital sex between men and women and different age groups and ethnic groups to see if any patterns can be identified

Questionnaires and attitude surveys are the best way to identify such patterns. These could be followed up with some unstructured interviews to investigate more fully why such differences might exist.

9

Education and training

Chapter summary

Reading 9.1 **Compensatory education** *page 235*
'Education cannot compensate for society.' Basil Bernstein gives an excellent critique of the concept of compensatory education and related research. The reading provides an opportunity to consider the continuities and changes in educational policy since the 1970s.

Reading 9.2 **How schools produce an amenable and fragmented labour force** *page 237*
Bowles and Gintis' classic study uses the concept of the 'correspondence principle' to explain the link between the social relations of schools and those of capitalist production. Viewed in this way, schools function not to counter inequalities but to reproduce them.

Reading 9.3 **New schools for new times?** *page 241*
Whitty *et al.* examine whether the re-structuring of education along market lines is a post-modern phenomenon.

Reading 9.4 **Access to higher education** *page 245*
Tariq Modood uses UCCA and PCAS data to refute claims about the under-representation of ethnic minorities in higher education.

Reading 9.5 **Power and discourse in primary classrooms** *page 249*
Debbie Epstein provides an accessible and interesting explanation of Foucault's key concepts, using them to explain some of the issues important to her study of anti-racism in primary classrooms.

Reading 9.6 **Schooling and sexualities** *page 252*
Mairtin Mac an Ghaill focuses on how young gay men perceive the role of schools in their oppression and how they responded to the 'compulsory hetero-sexuality' that pervaded their everyday school life.

Reading 9.7 **Acting powerfully: habitus in the primary classroom** *page 257*
Through the lens of habitus, Diane Reay, seeks to explore how differences of gender, 'race' and class are produced by children in two primary schools whose social class intake is different.

Reading 9.8 **De-constructing black educational under-achievement** *page 261*
How can young African-Caribbean women's strategies to succeed in education be re-defined – away from conformity and buying into the system – into evidence of a covert social movement for change? Heidi Safia Mirza focuses on black supplementary schools, which provide an alternative world of different meanings and shared 'ways of knowing'.

Introduction: Reading the sociology of education and training

The sociology of education is a relatively recent branch of sociology. Karabel and Halsey (1977) note that sociologists were in the forefront of the attempt to make the study of education a scientific endeavour in the 1950s. This is not to say, however, that education was ignored by the founding fathers of sociology. Durkheim in particular wrote an important history of French education. It is interesting to consider how the founding fathers' ideas, particularly those of Durkheim and Marx have been influential in, and have developed through, the work of sociologists of education since the 1950s.

The eight readings in this chapter have been chosen to illustrate such interesting, new developments in the sociology of education. They have also been chosen to show the way concepts and research findings are developed, with old perspectives challenged and new perspectives emerging.

Reading 9.1 is an important critique of the focus of what has become known as the 'old sociology of education'. As Bernstein usefully points out, much of the early sociology of education took as its focus deficits in the cultural background of pupils and their families and communities as an explanation of working-class under-achievement. This led to the term 'compensatory education' – the assumption being that schools could compensate in some way for such deficits. Bernstein's own work on linguistic codes (1977), which owes a strong debt to Durkheim (1938), was often incorrectly used to support the concept of compensatory education.

Bernstein signalled a new focus for sociologists of education towards the internal organization and the educational context of the school, and in particular what counts as valid school knowledge. This approach of the early 1970s became known as the 'new sociology of education', best exemplified by the work of the contributors to *Knowledge and Control*, edited by Young (1971), and also by phenomenologists in their work on the 'social construction of reality', that is, how teachers and pupils create, through interaction, their social worlds in schools and classrooms.

The mid-1970s saw a number of important Marxist contributions to the sociology of education, of which the work of Bowles and Gintis (1976) (**reading 9.2**) is an excellent example. They presented a Marxist account of the functions of schooling in a capitalist society as not working to counter inequalities but to reproduce them. This work was strongly influenced by Louis Althusser (1971) the French structuralist Marxist, particularly his work on the role of education as the dominant ideological state apparatus. The rather over-deterministic analysis of Bowles and Gintis, which regarded pupils as passively accepting the reproduction process, was challenged in the UK by the work of humanist Marxist sociologist Paul Willis (1977) and feminist Angela McRobbie (1978). Their ethnographic research showed much more complex processes at work in the reproductive role of schooling. They were interested in cultural as well as social reproduction and McRobbie looked at the influences of gender as well as social class. Pupils' cultural responses to schooling, their counter-school culture, served both to liberate but then to trap them into low-paid manual occupations. Reproduction – as they found out – was not a smooth and unchallenged process.

Between 1979 and 1997, successive Conservative governments consistently – if not coherently – introduced educational policies aimed at re-structuring education along market lines. The Education Reform Act (1988) was a complex and radical piece of legislation which introduced, amongst other things, the National Curriculum and Local Management of Schools (LMS). Such reforms produced an increased sociological interest in education policy analysis. Empirical studies charted the experiences and actions of policy makers, teachers and pupils at ground level

– e.g. Edwards, Fitz, and Whitty (1989) studied the assisted places scheme; Whitty, Edwards and Gerwitz (1993), City Technology Colleges; and Halpin, Fitz and Power (1993) grant-maintained schools. Bowe, Ball with Gold (1992) took a new and exciting critical and post-structural approach to the effects of the National Curriculum and LMS on schools. They researched how teachers and departments in four secondary comprehensive schools and two local education authorities responded to the Education Reform Act (1988). They were interested in how the National Curriculum was created and re-created in schools by teachers according to their institutional realities or the micro politics of schools. Micro politics is a term used by Ball (1987) to describe how each school has its own priorities, agendas and politics at a local level. These influence how policies initiated by the central state – like the National Curriculum – are interpreted. Some concern has been expressed about the focused nature of these single policy studies, that they ignore the 'bigger picture' (Ozga, 1990) that is the wider social and political context. In **reading 9.3**, Whitty *et al.* (1993) take up this challenge and consider how the establishment of City Technology Colleges, and the market form of education, relate to the bigger picture of social, political and economic changes in society, including post-modernity.

Which social groups are under-represented in higher education is an issue of on going debate and interest. This has interested sociologists of education since the 1950s, especially those in the political arithmetic tradition. This approach is derived from social mobility studies and is aimed at calculating the chances of reaching different levels in an educational system, for pupils of different social class origins. Egerton and Halsey (1993) found that while absolute access to higher education has increased for all, the service class has maintained its relative advantage in access to both university and polytechnic. In **reading 9.4**, Tariq Modood (1993) counters their rather pessimistic finding by focussing on the representation of ethnic minorities in higher education and providing some modest grounds for optimism. His study provides evidence to counter the prevailing discourses of black under-achievement. He points to the problem of the under-representation of the less-motivated white working class and the necessity for policy measures that target this group.

The late 1980s and early 1990s saw the development of exciting new perspectives in the sociology of education, namely post-structuralism and post-modernism. A good outline of the difference between modernist and post-modernist education is provided in **reading 9.3**. In the final chapter of their excellent research on City Technology Colleges, Whitty *et al.* consider whether such colleges are a post-modern phenomena. The ideas of Michel Foucault have also become very influential in the sociology of education. Ball (1990) considers a Foucauldian analysis of education important because it may 'unmask the politics that underlie some of the apparent neutrality of educational reform'. In **reading 9.5**, Debbie Epstein (1993) provides us with an accessible account of some of the key concepts in his work. In this extract she explains and critiques the concept of discourse, and applies it to some of the key issues in her study of effective anti-racist strategies in primary classrooms.

Mairtin Mac an Ghaill (1994) also draws critically on the work of Michel Foucault. He feels that Foucault's complex concept of power has been usefully used by feminist deconstructionists to move beyond social reproduction models, which assume that teachers and pupils are unitary subjects occupying predictable power positions. **Reading 9.6** provides an important, but relatively under-researched, area: male gay students' experiences of schooling, particularly of 'compulsory heterosexuality'.

Returning to the work of Bourdieu (1977, 1984), Diane Reay (1995) – in **reading 9.7** – develops the concept of 'habitus' and uses it as a lens to explore how differences of gender, 'race' and class are produced by children in primary classrooms. Habitus is an exciting if somewhat difficult concept. It is Bourdieu's attempt to overcome the on-going problem of reconciling structure and agency. He developed the concept to demonstrate how not only is the body in the social world, but the social world is in the body. He feels this is expressed through ways of being – that is, speaking, standing, walking, as well as thinking and feeling. Reay's research in two very different primary schools in London is an interesting and useful operationalization of the concept.

Finally, in **reading 9.8**, Heidi Safia Mirza (1997) contributes to the on-going debate about black female educational under-achievement and provides an alternative analysis. She is critical of social reproduction theories which analyse such success as 'resistance through accommodation'. Rather she argues their desire for success is much more strategic and subversive. She provides a compelling case for black women's educational success to be seen as part of a transformative social movement.

References

Althusser, L. (1971) 'Ideology and ideological state apparatuses', in *Lenin and Philosophy and Other Essays*, London: New Left Books.

Ball, S. J. (1987) *The Micro-Politics of the School*, London: Methuen.

Ball, S. J. (ed.) (1990) *Foucault and Education: Disciplines and Knowledge*, London: Routledge

Bernstein, B. (1977) *Class Codes and Control*, vol. 3, London: Routledge & Kegan Paul.

Bourdieu, P. and Passeron, J. C. (1977) *Reproduction in Education, Society and Culture*, London: Sage.

Bourdieu, P. (1984) *Distinction: a social critique of the judgement of taste*, London: Routledge Kegan Paul.

Bowe, R., Ball, S. with Gold, A. (1992) *Reforming Education and Changing Schools: Case studies in policy sociology*, London: Routledge.

Durkheim, E. (1938) *L'Evolution Pedagogique en France*, Paris: Alcan; translated by Collins, P. as *The Evolution of Educational Thought: Lectures on the formation and development of secondary education in France*, London: Routledge & Kegan Paul.

Edwards, T., Fitz, J. and Whitty, G. (1989) *The State and Private Education: an evaluation of the assisted places scheme*, London: The Falmer Press.

Egerton, M. and Halsey, A. H. (1993) 'Trends by social class and gender in access to higher education in Britain', *Oxford Review of Education*, vol. 19, no. 2.

Halpin, D., Fitz, J. and Power, S. (1993) *Education and the Market Place: Grant-maintained schools*, London: Kogan Page.

Karabel, J. and Halsey, A. H. (1977) *Power and Ideology in Education*, Oxford: Oxford University Press.

McRobbie, A. (1978) 'Working-class girls and the culture of femininity', in Women's Study Group, *Women Take Issue: Aspects of women's subordination*, Birmingham: Centre for Contemporary Cultural Studies.

Ozga. J (1990) 'Policy research and policy theory', *Journal of Education Policy*, 5, no. 1, 359–63.

Whitty, G., Edwards, T. and Gerwitz, S. (1993) *Specialization and Choice in Urban Education: The City Technology College experiment*, London: Routledge.

Willis, P. (1977) *Learning to Labour*, Farnborough: Saxon House.

Young, M. F. D. (ed.) (1971) *Knowledge and Control: New directions for the sociology of education*, London: Collier Macmillan.

Reading 9.1 **Compensatory education**

Basil Bernstein (from) 'Education cannot compensate for society', *New Society,* 26 February 1970; reprinted in *School and Society: a sociological reader* (1971) Open University set book, London: Routledge & Kegan Paul, pp. 61–3.

Editorial comments

In this extract Basil Bernstein provides an excellent critique of the concept of compensatory education and related research. This provides the opportunity to consider how his own work on linguistic codes may have been misunderstood in this context. It also allows us to consider the continuities and discontinuities in sociological explanations of working-class and ethnic minority under-achievement, and related educational policy, since the 1970s.

Education cannot compensate for society

TO BEGIN WITH, I find the term, 'compensatory education', a curious one for a number of reasons. I do not understand how we can talk about offering compensatory education to children who in the first place have not, as yet, been offered an adequate education environment. The Newsom Report on secondary schools showed that 79 per cent of all secondary modern schools in slum and problem areas were materially grossly inadequate, and that the holding power of these schools over the teachers was horrifyingly low. The same report also showed very clearly the depression in the reading scores of these children, compared with the reading scores of children who were at school in areas which were neither problem nor slum. This does not conflict with the finding that, on average, for the country as a whole, there has been an improvement in children's reading ability. The Plowden Report on the primary schools was rather more coy about all the above points, but we have little reason to believe that the situation is very much better for primary schools in similar areas.

Thus we offer a large number of children, both at the primary and secondary levels, materially inadequate schools and a higher turnover of teaching staff; and we further expect a small group of dedicated teachers to cope. The strain on these teachers inevitably produces fatigue and illness and it is not uncommon to find, in any week, teachers having to deal with doubled-up classes of 80 children. And we wonder why the children display very early in their educational life a range of learning difficulties.

At the same time, the organization of schools creates delicate overt and covert streaming arrangements which neatly lower the expectations and motivations of both teachers and taught. A vicious spiral is set up, with an all too determinate outcome. It would seem, then, that we have failed to provide, on the scale required, an *initial* satisfactory educational environment.

The concept, 'compensatory education', serves to direct attention away from the internal organization and the educational context of the school, and focus our attention on the families and children. 'Compensatory education' implies that something is lacking in the family, and so in the child. As a result, the children are unable to benefit from schools.

It follows, then, that the school has to 'compensate' for the something which is missing in the family, and the children are looked at as deficit systems. If only the parents were interested in the goodies we offer, if only they were like middle-class parents, then we could do our job. Once the problem is seen even implicitly in this way, then it becomes appropriate to coin the terms 'cultural deprivation', 'linguistic deprivation', and so on. And then these labels do their own sad work.

If children are labelled 'culturally deprived', then it follows that the parents are inadequate; the spontaneous realizations of their culture, its images and symbolic representations, are of reduced value and significance. Teachers will have lower expectations of the children, which the children will undoubtedly fulfil. All that informs the child, that gives meaning and purpose to him outside of the school, ceases to be valid or accorded significance and opportunity for enhancement within the school. He has to orient towards a different structure of meaning, whether it is in the form of reading books (*Janet and John*), in the form of language use and dialect, or in the patterns of social relationships.

Alternatively the meaning structure of the school is explained to the parents and imposed on, rather than integrated within, the form and content of their world. A wedge is progressively driven between the child as a member of a family and community, and the child as a member of a school. Either way the child is expected, and his parents as well, to drop their social identity, their way of life and its symbolic representations, at the school gate. For, by definition, their culture is deprived, and the parents are inadequate in both the moral and the skill orders they transmit.

I do not mean by this that in these circumstances no satisfactory home–school relations can take place or do take place: I mean rather that the best thing is for the parents to be brought *within* the educational experience of the schoolchild by doing what they can do, and this with confidence. There are many ways in which parents can help the child in this learning, which are within the parents' spheres of competence. If this happens, then the parents can feel adequate and confident both in relation to the child and the school. This may mean that the contents of the learning in school should be drawn much more from the child's experience in his family and community.

So far I have criticized the use of the concept of 'compensatory education' because it distracts attention from the deficiencies in the school itself and focuses upon deficiences within the community, family and child. We can add to these criticisms a third.

This concept points to the overwhelming significance of the early years of the child's life in the shaping of his later development. Clearly there is much evidence to support this view and to support its implication that we should create an extensive nursery-school system. However, it would be foolhardy indeed to write off the post-seven-years-of-age educational experience as having little influence.

Minimally, what is required *initially* is to consider the whole age period up to the conclusion of the primary stages as a unity. This would require considering our approach, at any *one* age, in the context of the whole of the primary stage. This implies a systematic, rather than a piecemeal, approach. I am arguing here for taking as the unit, not a particular period in the life of the child – for example, three to five years, or five to seven years – but taking as the unit a stage of education: the primary stage. We should see all we do in terms of the sequencing of learning, the development of sensitivities within the context of the primary stage. In order to accomplish this, the present social and educational division between infant and junior stages must be weakened, as well as the insulation between primary and secondary stages. Otherwise gains at any one age, for the child, may well be vitiated by losses at a later age.

We should stop thinking in terms of 'compensatory education' but consider, instead, most seriously and systematically the conditions and contexts of the educational environment.

The very form our research takes tends to confirm the beliefs underlying the organization, transmission and evaluation of knowledge by the school. Research proceeds by assessing the criteria of attainment that schools hold, and then measures the competence of different social groups in reaching these criteria. We take one group of children, whom we know beforehand possess attributes favourable to school achievement; and a second group of children, whom we know beforehand lack these attributes. Then we evaluate one group in terms of what it *lacks* when compared with another. In this way research, unwittingly, underscores the notion of *deficit* and confirms the status quo of a given organization, transmission and, in particular, evaluation of knowledge. Research very rarely challenges or exposes the social assumptions underlying what counts as valid knowledge, or what counts as a valid realization of that knowledge. There are exceptions in the area of curriculum development; but, even here, the work often has no built-in attempt to evaluate the changes. This holds particularly for **educational priority area** 'feasibility' projects.

Finally, we do not face up to the basic question: What is the potential for change within educational institutions as they are presently constituted? A lot of activity does not necessarily mean *action*.

I have taken so much space discussing the new educational concepts and categories because, in a small way, the work I have been doing had inadvertently contributed towards their formulation. It might be, and has been said, that my research – through focusing upon the subculture and forms of family socialization – has also distracted attention from the conditions and contexts of learning in school. The focus on usage of language has sometimes led people to divorce the use of language from the substratum of cultural meanings which are initially responsible for the language use. The concept, 'restricted code', to describe working-class speech, has been equated with 'linguistic deprivation' or even with the 'non-verbal' child.

We can distinguish between uses of language which can be called 'context-bound' and uses of language which are less context-bound. Consider, for example, the two following stories which the linguist, Peter Hawkins, constructed as a result of his analysis of the speech of middle-class and working-class five-year-old children. The children were given a series of four pictures which told a story and they were invited to tell the story. The first picture shows some boys playing football; in the second the ball goes through the window of a house: the third shows a man making a threatening gesture; and in the fourth a woman looks out of a window and the children are moving away. Here are the two stories:

1 Three boys are playing football and one boy kicks the ball and it goes through the window the ball breaks the window and the boys are looking at it and a man comes out and shouts at them because they've broken the window so they run away and then that lady looks out of her window and she tells the boys off. (No. of nouns: 13. No. of pronouns: 6.)

2 They're playing football and he kicks it and it goes through there it breaks the window and they're looking at it and he comes out and shouts at them because they've broken it so they run away and then she looks out and she tells them off. (No. of nouns: 2. No. of pronouns: 14.)

With the first story, the reader does not have to have the four pictures which were used as the basis for the story, whereas in the case of the second story the reader would require the initial pictures in order to make sense of the story. The first story is free of the context which generated it, whereas the second story is much more closely tied to its context. As a result, the meanings of the second story are implicit, whereas the meanings of the first story are explicit.

It is not that the working-class children do not have, in their passive vocabulary, the vocabulary used by the middle-class children. Nor is it the case that the children differ in their tacit understanding of the linguistic rule system. Rather, what we have here are differences in the use of language arising out of a specific context. One child makes explicit the meanings which he is realizing through language for the person he is telling the story to, whereas the second child does not to the same extent.

The first child takes very little for granted, whereas the second child takes a great deal for granted. Thus, for the first child, the task was seen as a context in which his meanings were required *to be made* explicit, whereas the task for the second child was not seen as a task which required such explication of meaning. It would not be difficult to imagine a context where the first child would produce speech rather like the second.

What we are dealing with here are differences between the children in the way they realize, in language use, what is apparently the same context. We could say that the speech of the first child generated universalistic meanings, in the sense that the meanings are freed from the context and so understandable by all; whereas the speech of the second child generated particularistic meanings, in the sense that the meanings are closely tied to the context and would be only fully understood by others if they had access to the context which originally generated the speech. Thus universalistic meanings are less bound to a given context, whereas particularistic meanings are severely context-bound.

Key term

The following key term appears in the text above. It has been defined below to aid with the reading of this item.

educational priority area an area – usually an inner-city area – designated for extra educational resources, to compensate for a materially poor environment. Educational priority areas were established on the recommendation of the Plowden Report in 1967

Questions

1 Why is Bernstein critical of 'compensatory education' and related research?

2 Bernstein feels that his own work on linguistic codes has been misunderstood. From his position in this extract, do you think he is viewing working-class children as linguistically deprived or criticizing an educational system that gives privileges to middle-class linguistic codes? Give reasons for your answer and indicate possible reasons for the misunderstandings.

3 Describe what has changed and what has remained the same in sociological explanations of working-class and ethnic minority under-achievement since 1970.

4 Has the concept of compensatory education disappeared completely from educational policy in the late 1990s? Give evidence for your answer.

5 What does Bernstein suggest should be the new focus of the sociology of education in 1970? Did this occur?

Reading 9.2 **How schools produce an amenable and fragmented labour force**

Samuel Bowles and Herbert Gintis (from) *Schooling in Capitalist America: Educational reform and the contradictions of economic life* (1976) London: Routledge & Kegan Paul, pp. 126–33.

Editorial comments

The main aim of education in capitalist society – as outlined in this classic study – is to reproduce the social relations of the workplace. Bowles and Gintis believe this is achieved through a 'correspondence' between the social relations of the workplace and those of schools. Schools play a crucial role in reproducing the class structure of society by developing in students the necessary attributes to maintain a hierarchical division of labour.

Schooling in capitalist America

Reproducing consciousness

ECONOMIC LIFE EXHIBITS a complex and relatively stable pattern of power and property relationships. The perpetuation of these social relationships, even over relatively short periods, is by no means automatic. As with a living organism, stability in the economic sphere is the result of explicit mechanisms constituted to maintain and extend the dominant patterns of power and privilege. We call the sum total of these mechanisms and their actions the **reproduction process**.

Amidst the sundry social relations experienced in daily life, a few stand out as central to our analysis of education. These are precisely the social relationships which are necessary to the security of capitalist profits and the stability of the capitalist division of labour. They include the patterns of dominance and subordinacy in the production process, the distribution of ownership of productive resources, and the degrees of social distance and solidarity among various fragments of the working population – men and women, blacks and whites, and white- and blue-collar workers, to mention some of the most salient.

What are the mechanisms of reproduction of these aspects of the **social relations of production** in the United States? To an extent, stability is embodied in law and backed by the coercive power of the state. Our jails are filled with individuals who have operated outside the framework of the private-ownership market system. The modern urban police force as well as the National Guard originated, in large part, in response to the fear of social upheaval evoked by militant labour action. Legal sanction, within the framework of the laws of private property, also channels the actions of groups (e.g., unions) into conformity with dominant power relationships. Similarly, force is used to stabilize the division of labour and its rewards within an enterprise: Dissenting workers are subject to dismissal and directors failing to conform to 'capitalist rationality' will be replaced.

But to attribute reproduction to force alone borders on the absurd. Under normal conditions, the effectiveness of coercion depends at the very least on the inability or unwillingness of those subjected to it to join together in opposing it. Laws generally considered illegitimate tend to lose their coercive power, and undisguised force too frequently applied tends to be self-defeating. The consolidation and extension of capitalism has engendered struggles of furious intensity. Yet instances of force deployed against a united and active opposition are sporadic and have usually

given way to détente in one form or another through a combination of compromise, structural change, and ideological accommodation. Thus it is clear that the **consciousness** of workers – beliefs, values, self-concepts, types of solidarity and fragmentation, as well as modes of personal behaviour and development – are integral to the perpetuation, validation, and smooth operation of economic institutions. The reproduction of the social relations of production depends on the reproduction of consciousness.

Under what conditions will individuals accept the pattern of social relationships that frame their lives? Believing that the long-term development of the existing system holds the prospect of fulfilling their needs, individuals and groups might actively embrace these social relationships. Failing this, and lacking a vision of an alternative that might significantly improve their situation, they might fatalistically accept their condition. Even with such a vision they might passively submit to the framework of economic life and seek individual solutions to social problems if they believe that the possibilities for realizing change are remote. The issue of the reproduction of consciousness enters each of these assessments.

The economic system will be embraced when, first, the perceived needs of individuals are congruent with the types of satisfaction the economic system can objectively provide. While perceived needs may be, in part, biologically determined, for the most part needs arise through the aggregate experiences of individuals in the society. Thus the social relations of production are reproduced in part through a harmony between the needs which the social system generates and the means at its disposal for satisfying these needs.

Second, the view that fundamental social change is not feasible, unoperational, and utopian is normally supported by a complex web of ideological perspectives deeply embedded in the cultural and scientific life of the community and reflected in the consciousness of its members. But fostering the 'consciousness of inevitability' is not the office of the cultural system alone. There must also exist mechanisms that systematically thwart the spontaneous development of social experiences that would contradict these beliefs.

Belief in the futility of organizing for fundamental social change is further facilitated by social distinctions which fragment the conditions of life for subordinate classes. The strategy of 'divide and conquer' has enabled dominant classes to maintain their power since the dawn of civilization. Once again, the splintered consciousness of a subordinate class is not the product of cultural phenomena alone, but must be reproduced through the experiences of daily life.

Consciousness develops through the individual's direct perception of and participation in social life. Indeed, everyday experience itself often acts as an inertial stabilizing force. For instance, when the working population is effectively stratified, individual needs and self-concepts develop in a correspondingly fragmented manner. Youth of different racial, sexual, ethnic, or economic characteristics directly perceive the economic positions and prerogatives of 'their kind of people'. By adjusting their aspiration accordingly, they not only reproduce stratification on the level of personal consciousness, but bring their needs into (at least partial) harmony with the fragmented conditions of economic life. Similarly, individuals tend to channel the development of their personal powers – cognitive, emotional, physical, aesthetic, and spiritual – in directions where they will have an opportunity to exercise them. Thus the alienated character of work, for example, leads people to guide their creative potentials to areas outside of economic activity: consumption, travel, sexuality, and family life. So needs and need-satisfaction again tend to fall into congruence and **alienated labour** is reproduced on the level of personal consciousness. ...

Power relations and hiring criteria within the enterprise are organized so as to reproduce the workers' self-concepts, the legitimacy of their assignments within the hierarchy, a sense of the technological inevitability of the hierarchical division of labour itself, and the social distance among groups of workers in the organization. Indeed, while token gestures towards workers' self-management may be a successful motivational gimmick, any delegation of real power to workers becomes a threat to profits because it tends to undermine patterns of consciousness compatible with capitalist control. By generating new needs and possibilities, by demonstrating the feasibility of a more thoroughgoing economic democracy, by increasing worker solidarity, an integrated and politically conscious program of worker involvement in decision-making may undermine the power structure of the enterprise. Management will accede to such changes only under extreme duress of worker rebellion and rapidly disintegrating morale, if at all.

But the reproduction of consciousness cannot be insured by these direct mechanisms alone. The initiation of youth into the economic system is further facilitated by a series of institutions, including the family and the educational system, that are more immediately related to the formation of personality and consciousness. Education works primarily through the institutional relations to which students are subjected. Thus schooling fosters and rewards the development of certain capacities and the expression of certain needs, while thwarting and penalizing others. Through these institutional relationships, the educational system tailors the self-concepts, aspirations, and social class identifications of individuals to the requirements of the social division of labour. ...

[There are] two main objectives of dominant classes in educational policy: the production of labour power and the reproduction of those institutions and social relationships which facilitate the translation of labour power into profits ... educational institutions are structured to meet these objectives. First, schooling produces many of the technical and cognitive skills required for adequate job performance. Second, the educational system helps legitimate economic inequality. ... Third, the school produces, rewards, and labels personal characteristics relevant to the staffing of positions in the hierarchy. Fourth, the educational system, through the pattern of status distinctions it fosters, reinforces the stratified consciousness on which the fragmentation of subordinate economic classes is based. ...

The correspondence principle

The educational system helps integrate youth into the economic system, we believe, through a structural correspondence between its social relations and those of production. The structure of social relations in education not only inures the student to the discipline of the work place, but develops the types of personal demeanor, modes of self-presentation, self-image, and social-class identifications which are the crucial ingredients of job adequacy. Specifically, the social relationships of education – the relationships between administrators and teachers, teachers and students, students and students, and students and their work – replicate the hierarchical division of labour. Hierarchical relations are reflected in the vertical authority lines from administrators to teachers to students. Alienated labour is reflected in the student's lack of control over his or her education, the alienation of the student from the curriculum content, and the motivation of school work through a system of grades and other external rewards rather than the student's integration with either the process (learning) or the outcome (knowledge) of the educational 'production process'. Fragmentation in work is reflected in the institutionalized and often destructive competition among students through continual and ostensibly meritocratic ranking and evaluation. By attuning young people to a set of social relationships similar to those of the work place, schooling attempts to gear the development of a personal needs to its requirements.

But the correspondence of schooling with the social relations of production goes beyond this aggregate level. Different levels of education feed workers into different levels within the occupational structure and, correspondingly, tend toward an internal organization comparable to levels in the hierarchical division of labour. As we have seen, the lowest levels in the hierarchy of the enterprise emphasize rule-following, middle levels, dependability, and the capacity to operate without direct and continuous supervision while the higher levels stress the internalization of the norms of the enterprise. Similarly, in education, lower levels (junior and senior high school) tend to severely limit and channel the activities of students. Somewhat higher up the educational ladder, teacher and community colleges allow for more independent activity and less overall supervision. At the top, the elite four-year colleges emphasize social relationships conformable with the higher levels in the production hierarchy. Thus schools continually maintain their hold on students. As they 'master' one type of behavioural regulation, they are either allowed to progress to the next or are channelled into the corresponding level in the hierarchy of production. Even within a single school, the social relationships of different tracks tend to conform to different behavioural norms. Thus in high school, vocational and general tracks emphasize rule-following and close supervision, while the college tracks tends toward a more open atmosphere emphasizing the internalization of norms.

These differences in the social relationships among and within schools, in part, reflect both the social backgrounds of the student body and their likely future economic positions. Thus blacks and other minorities are concentrated in schools whose repressive, arbitrary, generally chaotic internal order, coercive authority structures, and minimal possibilities for advancement mirror the characteristics of inferior job situations. Similarly, predominantly working-class schools tend to emphasize behavioural control and rule-following, while schools in well-to-do suburbs employ relatively open systems that favour greater student participation, less direct supervision, more student electives, and, in general, a value system stressing internalized standards of control.

The differential socialization patterns of schools attended by students of different social classes do not arise by accident. Rather, they reflect the fact that the educational objectives and expectations of administrators, teachers, and parents (as well as the responsiveness of students to various patterns of teaching and control) differ for students of different social classes. At crucial turning points in the history of US education, changes in the social relations of schooling have been dictated in the interests of a more harmonious reproduction of the class structure. But in the day-to-day operation of the schools, the consciousness of different occupational strata, derived from their cultural milieu and work experience, is crucial to the maintenance of the correspondences we have described. That working-class parents seem to favour stricter educational methods is a reflection of their own work experiences, which have demonstrated that submission to authority is an essential ingredient in one's ability to get and hold a steady, well-paying job. That professional and self-employed parents prefer a more open atmosphere and a greater emphasis on motivational control is similarly a reflection of their position in the social division of labour. When given the opportunity, higher-status parents are far more likely than their lower-status neighbours to choose 'open classrooms' for their children.

Differences in the social relationships of schooling are further reinforced by inequalities in financial resources. The paucity of financial support for the education of children from minority groups and low-income families leaves more resources to be devoted to the children of those with more commanding roles in the economy; it also forces upon the teachers and school administrators in the working-class schools a type of social relationships that fairly closely mirrors that of the factory. Financial considerations in poorly supported schools militate against small intimate classes, multiple elective courses, and specialized teachers (except for disciplinary personnel). They preclude the amounts of free time for teachers and free space required for a more open, flexible educational environment. The well-financed schools attended by the children of the rich can offer much greater opportunities for the development of the capacity for sustained independent work and all the other characteristics required for adequate job performance in the upper levels of the occupational hierarchy.

Key terms

The following key terms appear in the text above. They have been defined below to aid with the reading of this item.

reproduction process the mechanisms by which the conditions of capitalist economic power, as the basis of the social structure, are reproduced by the two main social classes over time. For example, the processes by which working-class kids get working-class jobs and middle-class kids get middle-class jobs

social relations of production relations in the production sphere between workers and capitalists

consciousness an awareness of one's own political power

alienated labour this describes the unfulfilling relationship of workers to the products they produce, derived from the exploitative nature of capitalism

Questions

1 Bowles and Gintis outline four ways in which educational institutions are structured to reproduce the social relations of production. Provide a concrete recent example of each of these in the British educational system.

2 How does education, according to Bowles and Gintis, contribute to 'divide and conquer' strategies, which enable the dominant classes to maintain their power? Relate the recent marketization of education to such strategies.

3 Is the correspondence between the needs of the economy and the different types of schools as neat and smooth a process as Bowles and Gintis claim? Give evidence for your answer.

4 Comment on the assertion that 'higher-status parents are far more likely than their lower-status neighbours to choose "open classrooms" for their children'.

5 Using your own experience of education, together with library research, describe how the relationship between employers and schools in the UK has changed since 1976, when Bowles and Gintis wrote their book. Does this add support for or against their correspondence principle?

Reading 9.3 **New schools for new times?**

Whitty, G., Edwards, T. and Gerwitz, S. (from) *Specialization and Choice in Urban Education: The City Technology College experiment* (1993) London: Routledge, pp. 170–7.

Editorial comments

City Technology Colleges were set up by the Thatcher government in 1986. They were designed to be state funded but independently run, with a technological, scientific and practical curriculum. This was to be a new market choice for all inner city children. Witty *et al.* interviewed the initiative's political architects and also staff, pupils and parents in CTCs and some nearby comprehensive schools. In their final chapter they ask (and answer briefly): 'how does the establishment of CTCs relate to the bigger picture of globalization, marketization, post- or neo-Fordism and post-modernism?' This extract examines whether the re-structuring of education along market lines is a post-modern phenomenon.

New schools for new times?

A post-modern phenomenon?

JANE KENWAY (1992) has brought together a number of theories underlying the idea of 'new times' to argue that, in education as elsewhere, modern societies *are* now entering a qualitatively new era. She suggests that accounts that concentrate solely on institutional changes pay insufficient attention to other cultural shifts which help to explain why markets in education have found such a receptive audience. For Kenway, 'the rapid rise of the market form in education is best understood as a post-modern phenomenon' (Kenway, 1992). In post-modernity, the significant **nexus** is that between the global and the local, limiting even the scope of the national state. She sees the new technology as a key element in the development of new and commodified cultural forms. What she calls the 'markets/education/technology triad' is a crucial feature of post-modernity, a triad in which CTCs could clearly be located. Kenway's account of post-modernity is, as she readily admits, a pessimistic one in which 'transnational corporations and their myriad subsidiaries ... shape and reshape our individual and collective identities as we plug in ... to their cultural and economic communications networks' (Kenway, 1992). The picture is one in which notions of 'difference', far from being eradicated by the 'globalization of culture', are assembled, displayed, celebrated, commodified and exploited.

Yet there are other accounts of post-modernity where the rhetoric of 'new times' offers positive images of choice and diversity. In this context, CTCs and other current developments might be regarded as part of a wider retreat from modern, bureaucratized state education systems – the so-called 'one best system' in the USA, for example (Glenn, 1988; Chubb and Moe, 1990) – that are perceived as having failed to fulfil their promise and now seem inappropriate to the heterogeneous societies of the late twentieth century. Thus, part of the appeal of current education policies lies in the claim that different types of schools will be responsive to the needs of particular communities and interest groups that exist as a result of the complex patterns of political, economic and cultural differentiation in contemporary society which have replaced the traditional class divisions upon which comprehensive education was predicated. While this process of differentiation is partly about creating new markets for new products, the multiplicity of lines of social fissure that are emerging may be associated with deeper changes in modes of social solidarity. In so far as these divisions and associated identities are experienced as real, they are likely to generate aspirations that will differ from traditional ones.

This has contributed to more optimistic readings of post-modernity than the one to which Kenway subscribes. Compared with the oppressive uniformity of much modernist thinking, it is possible to regard post-modernism as 'a form of liberation, in which the fragmentation and plurality of cultures and social groups allow a hundred flowers to bloom' (Thompson, 1992). Thus, many feminists have seen attractions in the shift towards the pluralist models of society and culture associated with post-modernism and post-modernity (Flax, 1987). The possibilities for community, rather than bureaucratic, control of welfare are also viewed positively by some ethnic minority groups. In the USA, the recent reforms of the school system in Chicago sought to dismantle the vast bureaucracy under which the Chicago School District was perceived by many commentators to be failing the majority of its pupils even when controlled by black politicians. The devolution and choice policies were enacted as a result of a curious alliance between New Right advocates of school choice, black groups seeking to establish community control of their local schools, together with disillusioned white liberals and some former student radicals of the 1960s (Hess, 1990).

Support for schools run on a variety of principles, rather than those of the 'one best system', might then be seen as recognizing a widespread collapse of a commitment to modernity. Or, put another way, a rejection of the totalizing narratives of the Enlightenment Project and their replacement by 'a set of cultural projects united [only] by a self-proclaimed commitment to heterogeneity, fragmentation and difference'; social development is no longer seen as 'the fulfilment of some grand historical narrative' but as 'a pragmatic matter of inventing new rules whose validity will reside in their effectivity rather than in their compatibility with some legitimating discourse' (Boyne and Rattansi, 1990). The notion of '**unprincipled alliances**', which at one time might have prevented such a political configuration as emerged in Chicago, is less appropriate in a context of postmodernity, which is seen by Lyotard (1986) as a pluralist, pragmatic and restless set of partially differentiated social orders. If large-scale attempts at

social engineering have been perceived as failing, less ambitious aspirations may now be in order.

In Britain, the Labour Party's traditional social democratic policies have also been perceived as unduly bureaucratic and alienating by many black parents, who it is sometimes claimed welcome the new opportunities offered by the Reform Act to be closer to their children's schools (Phillips, 1988). While they do not necessarily endorse the Thatcherite dream in its entirety, some aspects of it may well connect to the aspirations of groups who find little to identify with in the grand master narratives associated with class-based politics. Policies which seem to emphasize heterogeneity, fragmentation and difference may thus represent more than a passing fashion among **neo-liberal** politicians and resonate with changing notions of an open, democratic society as well as with a market ideology. Put in those terms, it is understandable that current policies have a potential appeal far beyond the coteries of the New Right.

Even on the Left, there has been some support for more specialized and diverse forms of secondary schooling. In *Parents in Partnership*, issued during the 1989 county council elections, the Labour Party proposed that schools should 'develop a distinctive character within the comprehensive principle'. The party considered using education support grants and local management of schools to encourage specialization, with parents and children 'able to choose schools which offer the type of education most suitable to their interests and abilities' (*Times Educational Supplement*, 21 April 1989). The same idea was taken further by Peter Wilby who argued that 'young minds need magnets' (*The Independent*, 15 June 1989) and that comprehensive schools had lost their way through being preoccupied with a balanced curriculum, which forced on the goats a second-rate version of what the sheep got. More curriculum specialization was therefore desirable. While the idea of magnet schools remained highly contested, and failed to gain backing from the Labour front bench, a commitment to cultural diversity within the comprehensive principle did gain official acceptance through support for the development of Muslim voluntary-aided schools alongside those sponsored by the Anglican and Catholic Churches.

Reworking old themes?

To some extent, CTCs and associated policies may then seem to be part of a wider set of changes. If we equate curriculum specialization with niche marketing, CTCs appear to display some of the characteristics of post-Fordism, while their relationship to government is consistent with emergent forms of public administration more generally. Yet, notwithstanding Valerie Bragg's conscious attempts to make Kingshurst look more like a business organization than a school (*BBC Radio 4*, 6 June 1989), CTCs are still readily identifiable as secondary schools, with more similarities to local comprehensive schools than differences. This does not suggest a radical break with the concerns of modernity. Just as some commentators see changes in ways of managing production as **neo-Fordism** rather than **post-Fordism** – and new institutional forms as merely a new way of managing the modernist project – so much of CTC thinking can also be seen as a variation on a familiar theme. Furthermore, there are serious problems in trying to see the sort of diversity sponsored by CTCs and other recent reforms as a post-modern phenomenon in the strong sense of reflecting deep-seated changes in the nature of society. ...

Some aspects of CTCs are the very epitome of the modernist project. This was apparent in the way their 'high tech' image was invoked in the early publicity. At least as much as comprehensive schools, CTCs seemed to express an underlying faith in technical rationality as the basis for solving social, economic and educational problems. Even in the new White Paper devoted to 'Choice and Diversity', this modernist project predominates. It is 'specialization' rather than 'diversity' that is given prominence. Although the proposed legislation is to be 'drawn widely enough to encourage more schools to specialize in other fields too', the emphasis throughout is on technology, which will help 'to break down the divide between academic and vocational studies' and 'equip young people with the technological skills essential to a successful economy' (DFE, 1992). Indeed, the justification for specialization is that 'other leading industrialized nations combine the attainment of high standards with a degree of specialization' (DFE, 1992).

Furthermore, although CTCs may have particular attractions for some members of the minority ethnic population, the ethos of CTCs is often **assimilationist** rather than one that actively fosters cultural pluralism. Indeed, one of the publicly made criticisms of Harris CTC by former Sylvan pupils was that 'they're leaving out the black people – in Sylvan they taught us about Rastas, black history and culture' (*Daily Telegraph*, 4 July 1991). Although Muslim leaders have interpreted clauses of the 1992 White Paper as heralding the possibility of state-funded Islamic schools through the 'opting-in' of existing private schools (*Observer*, 2 August 1992), the message in the White Paper is highly tentative and constrained:

> The Secretary of State ... [will take steps that] will help to create opportunities for new GM schools to be created in response to parental demand and on the basis of local proposals.
> (DFE, 1992)

> The Government wishes to see the role of the Churches and other voluntary bodies in education preserved and enhanced.
> (DFE 1992: 32)

Certainly, the notion of curriculum specialization, at least in technology, is much more clearly spelled out than that of diversity. Indeed, the chapter of the White Paper entitled 'Specialization and Diversity in Schools' is almost entirely about specialization.

Nevertheless, the rhetoric of specialization and diversity is given an added appeal by the suggestion that it will not entail selection and hierarchy. Early in our research, a former government minister characterized the drift away from comprehensive education towards more specialized and differentiated types of schools, not as a return to élitist approaches to educational provision, but as happening 'without any one [type of school] being regarded as inferior to the others' (Dunn, cited in *Education*, 8 July 1988) – a situation which he apparently believed existed in Germany. Similarly, in the 1992 White Paper, the government stresses specialization rather than selection and tells us that it is not its intention either to encourage or to discourage applications to make a school selective:

> The fact that a school is strong in a particular field may increase the demand to attend, but it does not necessarily follow that selective entry criteria have to be imposed by the school. The selection that takes place is parent-driven. ... Parents can choose the school they believe best suited to the particular interests and aptitudes of their children.
> (DFE, 1992)

The emphasis here is on choice rather than selection, but none of the government's rhetoric recognizes the reality of what happens, either overtly or covertly, when schools are massively oversubscribed. Yet, the White Paper goes on to say that

> The Government is committed to parity of esteem between academic, technological and creative skills, with all children – whatever their aptitude and in whatever type of school – being taught the National Curriculum to the same high standards. The Government wants to ensure that there are no tiers of schools within the maintained system [*sic*] but rather parity of esteem between different schools, in order to offer parents a wealth of choice.
> (DFE, 1992)

The impression given is that each school is to be judged on its merits, rather than as embodying the characteristics of a hierarchically arranged series of 'types'. Yet we saw earlier that parents choosing CTCs are frequently concerned with the extent to which this 'new choice of school' is similar to independent and grammar schools and different from mainstream comprehensive schools. Furthermore, looking at the reality of those reforms that have already taken place, Walford and Miller (1991) claim that, while comprehensive schools attempted to overcome the historic links between diversity of provision and inequalities of class and gender, 'City Technology Colleges have played a major part in re-legitimizing inequality of provision for different pupils'. Indeed, they argue that the 'inevitable result' of the concept of CTCs, especially when coupled with grant-maintained schools and LMS, is 'a hierarchy of schools with the private sector at the head, the CTCs and GMSs next, and the various locally managed LEA schools following' (Walford and Miller, 1991). ...

The 1992 White Paper rejects such pessimism and dismisses the relevance of the experience of the **tripartite system** of the 1950s and 1960s by arguing that we now live in 'a different educational world' with the National Curriculum ensuring equality of opportunity (DFE, 1992). However, the particular form of national curriculum introduced by the Thatcher government, and the arrangements for testing the outcomes, are likely to arrange schools and pupils in a hierarchy through the combined effects of LMS, competition among schools for pupils and the publication of assessment scores. This will leave the most disadvantaged and demotivated pupils concentrated in schools with low aggregate test scores and declining resources and low teacher morale. Resource differences between schools will thereby increase and their capacity to deliver any curriculum adequately will vary considerably.

There is certainly little evidence yet that, taken as a whole, the Education Reform Act 1988 is helping to provide a structure that will encompass diversity and ensure equality of opportunity for all pupils. Rather, there is some evidence that its emphasis on parental choice will further disadvantage those unable to compete in the market, by increasing the differences between popular and less popular schools. This could have disastrous consequences for some sections of the predominantly working-class and black populations who inhabit the inner cities. While they never gained an equitable share of educational resources under social democratic policies, the abandonment of planning in favour of a quasi-market seems unlikely to provide a fairer outcome. Indeed, there is a real possibility that an educational underclass will emerge in Britain's inner cities.

References

Boyne, R. and Rattansi, A. (eds) (1990) *Post-modernism and Society*, London: Macmillan.

Chubb, M. and Moe, T. (1990) *Politics, Markets and America's Schools*, Washington, DC: Brookings Institution.

Department for Education (DFE) (1992) *Choice and Diversity: a new framework for schools*, London: HMSO.

Flax, J. (1987) 'Post-modernism and gender relations in feminist theory', *Signs, 12*, 4:621–43.

Glenn, C. (1988) *The Myth of the Common School*, Amherst, Mass.: University of Massachusetts Press.

Hess, A. (1990) *Chicago School Reform: How it is and how it came to be*, Chicago: Panel on Public School Policy and Finance.

Kenway, J. (1992) 'Marketing education in the post-modern age', a paper presented at the American Educational Research Association annual meeting, San Francisco, 20–24th April.

Lyotard, J. F. (1986) *The Post-modern Condition*, Manchester: Manchester University Press.

Phillips, M. (1988) 'Why black people are backing Baker', *The Guardian*, 9 September.

Thompson, K. (1992) 'Social pluralism and post-modernity', in Hall, S., Held, D. and Mcgrew, T. (eds) *Modernity and its Futures*, Cambridge: Polity Press.

Walford, G. and Miller, H. (1991) *City Technology College*, Milton Keynes: Open University Press.

Key terms

The following key terms appear in the text above. They have been defined below to aid with the reading of this item.

nexus connection or link

unprincipled alliances groups with very different philosophies joining forces to pursue some mutual gain

neo-liberal a belief in the market as an equitable method of organizing social welfare and education. In relation to education, neo-liberals believe in a move away from monopolistic state provision, to make schools more entrepreneurial and efficient, and to provide freedom of choice for parents and their children

neo-Fordism and **post-Fordism** neo-Fordism implies more continuity with Fordist production methods than post-Fordism which implies a complete change or break with Fordist methods of production

assimilationist involving a process whereby ethnic minority pupils should adopt the dominant cultural values of the host society and blend in

tripartite system the education system established by the 1944 Education Act for England and Wales, with three types of secondary school, secondary modern, grammar and technical schools

Questions

1 What are the key features of modernism and post-modernism outlined in the reading?

2 In what ways might comprehensive schools be regarded as modernist and City Technology Colleges post-modernist, according to the models of post-modernity offered in the reading? Do you agree with this claim?

3 Why might markets in education appeal to feminists and ethnic minority groups?

4 What evidence is there for and against the assertion that old educational inequalities remain unchanged by recent market reforms?

Reading 9.4 **Access to higher education**

Tariq Modood (from) 'The number of ethnic minority students in British higher education: some grounds for optimism', *Oxford Review of Education* (1993) vol. 19, no. 2, pp. 175–80.

Editorial comments

Modood's analysis of UCCA (Universities Central Council for Admissions) and PCAS (Polytechnics Central Admissions System) data refutes the claim that ethnic minorities are under-represented in higher education. The picture he provides is complex, with the over-representation of some groups and the under-representation of others. He indicates a tendency for ethnic minorities to be concentrated in the new universities especially in London and the Midlands. This extract focuses on selection bias and considers UCCA's explanations for the hierarchy that exists for selecting undergraduates for universities.

Ethnic minority students in British higher education

Rates of success

PERHAPS THE ISSUE that will now come to the fore will not be representation but selection-bias, especially in the UCCA sector. Table 1, depicting success-rates in the PCAS in 1990 and 1991 show Afro-Caribbean men the most successful (nearly half of all applicants were admitted) and white women the least successful (only just over a third of applicants were admitted). This may of course reflect the fact that less of the former and more of the latter may have got university places instead. Nevertheless, with nearly all minority groups doing better than average, and whites only slightly worse than the average, the figures do not suggest that there is an issue of bias against minorities in the selection process, if admissions are a reliable guide to offers made, taking the system as a whole (the situation could be different in respect of particular institutions, faculties or department).

The situation with UCCA is, however, different. Tables 2 and 3 give a breakdown of the acceptance-rates of the different groups by A-level points score, from which it is clear that there are significant differences between groups. At the top end of A-level performance, the selection rates are similar for all groups, at just over 90%, with the Chinese above the average and Africans just below it. But the overall pattern is that, with almost identical scores, Chinese and white applicants are more likely to and the Caribbeans least likely to be admitted. Thus, in the middle of the A-level range, with applicants between 20–16 points, the average success rate is about 60 per cent, this also being the rate for whites, while for Chinese it can be 10 per cent higher, which can also be the case for some other Asian groups, though they are more likely to be nearer or just below the average, as are the Africans, but the Caribbeans are likely to be below the average (in 1991 they were 13 per

Table 1 Success rates in PCAS, 1990 and 1991

	Men (%)	Women (%)	Total (%)
Asian–Bangladeshi	47.0	35.6	42.7
Asian–Chinese	41.0	44.6	42.8
Asian–Indian	47.5	45.6	46.6
Asian–Pakistani	47.0	39.5	43.3
Asian–other	42.4	41.7	42.2
Black-African	42.0	39.7	41.0
Black-Caribbean	49.6	43.2	45.5
Black-other	40.6	39.1	39.7
White	43.4	35.0	39.2
Other	43.8	37.4	40.5
Total	43.7	35.9	39.9

Table 2 Acceptance rates for those with A levels, 1990 (*from Table 11C, UCCA*)

| | Two or more A-level passes or the equivalent-points scores | | | | | | |
	30–26	25–21	20–16	15–11	10–6	5 or fewer	Total (%)
Asian–Bangladeshi	98.1	74.4	67.1	50.0	31.2	10.5	46.6
Asian–Chinese	90.8	88.7	65.5	42.0	23.6	7.5	49.6
Asian–Indian	94.8	83.5	56.6	33.9	16.6	9.1	45.2
Asian–Pakistani	89.4	81.3	52.8	32.7	20.0	11.6	38.4
Asian–other	88.7	85.3	66.8	46.8	20.2	17.1	48.8
Black	85.7	77.5	55.3	30.0	18.4	9.8	30.1
White	90.1	82.8	59.2	35.0	22.0	17.1	53.3
Other	90.9	86.2	57.2	36.2	19.8	16.0	48.3
Not known	89.1	77.1	55.5	41.4	26.7	15.9	44.8
Total applicants	90.2	82.7	59.0	35.3	21.8	16.1	52.1

Table 3 Acceptance rates for those with A levels, 1991 (*from Table 11C, UCCA*)

| | Two or more A-level passes or the equivalent-points scores | | | | | | |
	30–26	25–21	20–16	15–11	10–6	5 or fewer	Total (%)
Asian–Bangladeshi	90.5	78.4	58.9	32.4	28.9	19.0	44.7
Asian–Chinese	95.0	86.8	69.8	46.9	25.4	22.2	53.4
Asian–Indian	92.0	87.8	60.9	32.8	17.3	10.3	46.3
Asian–Pakistani	91.9	83.3	58.5	38.2	19.2	12.7	40.7
Asian–other	89.5	89.2	61.4	49.3	33.8	20.5	53.3
Black–African	88.1	74.3	59.7	34.5	21.6	10.0	34.3
Black–Caribbean	90.9	76.0	45.9	32.3	16.5	12.0	28.1
Black–other	89.7	79.5	58.5	38.1	19.3	18.8	38.8
White	90.7	83.4	59.4	36.2	23.0	17.5	54.2
Other	88.0	80.5	59.5	33.2	20.6	12.2	48.2
Not known	84.2	78.5	59.1	40.7	27.3	29.2	49.6
Total applicants	90.7	82.5	59.4	36.3	22.8	17.1	53.2

cent below it). At the lower end of the scale, the gap in acceptance-rates between groups is once again closer, though by no means consistent between the two years, except that blacks are towards the bottom, but so are Indians (and Pakistanis, in the 5 A-level points or less category). If these variations in success-rates where applicants have almost identical scores are not problematic enough, the overall acceptance rates show a very definite hierarchy with whites at the top, closely followed by the Chinese, with the Indians and Bangladeshis 5–10 per cent below, Pakistanis about 15 per cent, Africans around 20 per cent below and Caribbeans 25 per cent below. As the overall white acceptance rate was not much over 50 per cent,

this means that only about half as many Caribbean applicants are likely to succeed compared to whites. Moreover, there can be significant variations between institutions: for example, in the unnamed eight universities, the rates of acceptance for Pakistanis and Bangladeshis is very similar to blacks, and in two cases worse (Taylor, 1992).

What is to explain the differential acceptance-rates at similar scores and the differences in the overall acceptance-rates? UCCA offer five reasons. They point, first, to the low applications from ethnic minorities for courses with low entrance requirements, notably teacher training courses, which at 12.6 have the lowest mean points score of accepted applicants. Second, and conversely, more than 20 per cent of applications from ethnic minorities are to medicine and law, three times that of whites, and yet these are the hardest subjects in which to gain acceptance (a mean of 26.7 and 25.5 A-level points respectively). Third, ethnic minorities are more likely to apply to a limited set of universities. For while only a third of whites are likely to apply to a university in their home region, 44 per cent of Asian applicants and 52 per cent of black applicants did so in 1991. As a result, because of the residential distribution of ethnic minorities, in 1992 41 per cent of Asian and 50 per cent of black applicants applied to the 35 institutions in London and the South-East, compared to 20 per cent of white applicants. Of course, each of these three factors means that ethnic minorities are in a situation of more intense competition than their white peers and that some who were not admitted would have been if they had applied for different courses or to other universities. Fourth, UCCA point out that 12 per cent (in 1991) of applicants with two or more A levels had re-sat some or all of their examinations to get their final grades; ethnic minorities were more than twice as likely (up to three times as likely in 1990) as whites to be in this category and 'this will undoubtedly affect adversely their chances of acceptance, since selectors tend to give less weight to qualifications obtained after more than one sitting.' In its 1989–90 report, UCCA point out also that ethnic minority applicants have a lower average A-level score than whites (Table 4).

It is of course difficult to estimate to what extent these five factors explain the differential selection-rates, and to what extent an issue of racial bias remains (UCCA take the view that 'any apparent racial bias largely disappears'). Certainly, each of the factors is relevant, though it is interesting to see that the explanation moves from the contingencies of more intense competition through accidents of circumstances (preference for medical subjects and law; for local institutions), to potential academic bias (a lower evaluation of A-level grades achieved through resits),

Table 4 Average A-level scores of applicants, UCCA 1990

Ethnic group	Average points score
Asian–Bangladeshi	16.4
Chinese	16.8
Indian	17.0
Pakistani	15.7
Other	17.4
Black	14.0
White	18.0

to educational disadvantage (comparative A-level scores). The last two bring us squarely to the wider issues of **structural inequality**, access and the sociology of education. The University of Warwick analysis commissioned by the CVCP, referred to earlier, pursues this line further. From the extra 1990 data supplied by UCCA to the University of Warwick, it is possible to see the contribution of the wider structural conditions to the end result. For example, applicants to university from further and higher education colleges are considerably less likely to be successful in admission than those from schools; yet all ethnic minorities rely on this route to at least twice the extent of whites (17%), and nearly three times so in the case of blacks (48%) (Taylor, 1992). The highest rates of acceptances are enjoyed by applicants from independent schools, a sector in which ethnic minorities, especially blacks and Pakistanis, are under-represented (though the ethnic minority applicants from this sector enjoy higher rates of acceptance than their white peers). Applicants with non-A level or equivalent qualifications have low rates of success and 34% of all black applicants are in this category, while about half of that percentage of Pakistanis and Bangladeshis, though only 7% of whites (Taylor, 1992). The University of Warwick analysis does not refer to mature students, but while each of the factors just considered would explain some of the difference in acceptance-rates and representation levels between the UCCA and the PCAS sectors; also relevant must be the fact that while new entrants over the age of 21 now make up half of all admissions to higher education, over 80% of them continue to be in polytechnics and colleges, and a greater proportion are likely to be black compared to other groups.

These factors are of course features of social class. It is therefore not surprising that the additional UCCA data show that, by and large in terms of parental social class, ethnic minorities are less represented in the professional and intermediate classes, and that the acceptance rate for these parental social classes is consistently higher (though not equal between groups) than for those coming from the skilled and unskilled working classes (Taylor, 1992). Yet, what is more striking about this data are the ways in which dimensions of race and ethnicity upset the overall pattern of class. For example, the minority group which is the most successful in UCCA in terms of level of representation and rate of acceptance, the Chinese, has only a 5% representation in the professional class, a full half less than that of the next least professional groups (Pakistani and black), and without any proportionate increase in the size of the intermediate class to compensate. Or, that, in distinction to all other groups, the rates of acceptance of blacks is unaffected by parental social class. The biggest anomaly for capturing differences by race and ethnicity within class analysis is the pervading underlying fact that groups with more disadvantaged class profiles than whites, a contrast which was probably even more severe in previous years and decades, produce much larger proportions of applicants and admissions in the national higher education system. The fact that despite all of the social and institutional (not to mention cultural) disadvantages stacked against them, some ethnic minorities are using higher education to alter their own class composition, offers one, if small, counter-example to the view that class inequalities in higher education remain unchanged, and that education has failed to operate as a force for '**class abatement**'.

Moreover, just as what may be called racial disadvantage or racial bias is intricately connected to social processes, institutional norms and evaluation which do not directly have anything racial about them (but can be indirectly racially discriminating in virtue of their consequences), so similarly, in so far as there is an attitudinal racial bias at work in the university admissions process, it is unlikely to be, or to be merely, crudely 'racial' but will take the form of unfavourable evaluations which include and exacerbate cultural, religious and class bias. Thus, a stereotype of one group will focus on its narrow-mindedness and traditionalism on gender, another group may be imagined as having a mathematical excellence, another a sporting prowess; individuals of one group may be approached with the presumption that they are too aggressive, of another that they are too deferential; of one that it may have literary flair but not rational discipline, and of another the opposite; too protected by family structures or too knocked about by the 'inner-city'; and they may all be deemed to lack appropriate communication skills. Such stereotypes, which of course must have some basis in group differences, flow into outcomes which in turn reinforce stereotypical generalizations. If racial attitudinal bias is complex and interwoven with other kinds of evaluations, as racial institutional bias has been seen to be connected to the non-racial, then it follows that the bias and its effect will vary from ethnic group to group. Not only is there no simple racial bias which affects all non-white groups in the same way, but the bias against an ethnicity can certainly be overcome by extra qualifications or a higher parental social class. It may seem therefore that even in a situation of racial prejudice, the real causality lies with broader social processes. So that even where, say, a white middle-class individual will achieve greater systemic success than a white working-class person as well as a middle-class ethnic minority one; and even where the system prefers a working-class white to an equally qualified middle-class minority person; the class inequalities will have done their work to ensure that

the working-class white individual is unlikely to be as well qualified as the ethnic minority middle-class person. Yet, that social class, however defined, is not all powerful has already been alluded to: virtually all working-class minority groups achieve better examination results than their white working-class peers. It may just be that the explanation does not lie in any long-term ethnicity, but in what we may call a certain 'mentality', associated with economic migrants amongst others, comprising of an over-riding ambition to better oneself and one's family, matched by appropriately high levels of **deferred gratification**; at the very least we have a situation where such advantages, be they of ethnicity or immigration, are converted into those of social class. This by itself does not eliminate racial bias, but does considerably lessen its impact. The situation is further complicated when different groups pursue this strategy to a different degree. The evidence from UCCA and PCAS suggests a complexity of just this sort with the Chinese and Indian situation rather different from that of the Afro-Caribbeans, with that of the Africans, Pakistanis and Bangladeshis sharing some features with the former and some with the latter (complicated further for some groups by gender). The level of representation is not the primary issue in respect of most of these groups. Yet, while, without exception, they seem to be already much more committed than their white counterparts to staying on in school and further education beyond the age of 16 (*The Guardian*, 23, June 1992), to persevere with examinations, including resits, and to entry into higher education, especially on vocational or career-relevant courses, they nevertheless offer considerable potential for further increases in the participation rate in higher education. They form highly targetable groups which already have the desire and motivation to enter higher education, but it would be foolish to ignore more class-based problems of access, and to ignore the under-representation of the less motivated, which means primarily the white working class. The class disadvantages of the under-represented ethnic groups suggest that focusing on the former may be the appropriate basis for access measures; whether the priority should be specific ethnicities or class, it does seem that action targeted at non-whites as such will not be the most successful in improving the access of under-represented ethnic groups, and that more complex approaches may be required.

Conclusion

The numbers of ethnic minorities admitted through PCAS and UCCA in 1990 and 1991 refute the long-standing claim of under-representation, but reveal that there are significant differences between groups, between institutions and between subjects. In the

PCAS system (the 'new universities'), Africans have a representation of more than 300 per cent, closely followed by Indians, East African Asians and Chinese; even black Caribbeans and Pakistanis are over-represented, so that only the Bangladeshis and the 'other blacks' have an under-representation greater than that for whites. The concentration in certain polytechnics (in five polytechnics 40 per cent or more admissions are minority ethnic) is regional rather than in lower-ranking institutions, and while minorities are over-represented in some subjects (e.g. business, engineering, law and medicine), and under-representated in others (e.g. languages, humanities and arts), the concentration is not necessarily in 'low-status' subjects. While most minorities are not under-represented in the UCCA sector, in total the minorities are there in only half the proportion they are in the other sector, and Afro-Caribbeans and Bangladeshis are significantly under-represented.

Reference

Taylor, P. (1992) 'Ethnic group data for university entry', project report for CVCP Working Group on Ethnic Data, University of Warwick.

Key terms

The following key terms appear in the text above. They have been defined below to aid with the reading of this item.

structural inequality inequalities arising from the way in which society is organized, for example, employment practices, legislation and the distribution of wealth

class abatement the lessening of social class inequalities through education

deferred gratification putting off immediate material satisfaction in order to pursue a long-term educational goal

Questions

1 Evaluate the explanations offered by UCCA for differential acceptance rates. How do the last two explanations relate to structural inequality?

2 Why do you think ethnic minority students may prefer to apply to their local university or a university situated in an area with a high concentration of ethnic minorities? How might this be to their disadvantage?

3 Which groups should be targeted to improve representation amongst the most under-represented in higher education, according to Modood? Suggest ways in which this might be achieved.

4 Do you think Modood has a sound basis for optimism? Give reasons for your answer.

Reading 9.5 **Power and discourse in primary classrooms**

Debbie Epstein (from) *Changing Classroom Cultures: Anti-racism, politics and schools* (1993) Stoke-on-Trent: Trentham Books, pp. 9–13.

Editorial comments

Debbie Epstein discusses the usefulness and limitations of Foucault's conception of power/knowledge or discourse. Her study – a piece of action research – explores, through case studies, possible strategies for effective anti-racist education. She also considers macro and micro political factors that have influenced the development of anti-racist education.

Power, race and racism

Social relations and discourse

SOCIAL RELATIONS ARE organized through a number of institutions and social structures, of which the education system is one (others include the family, the law, the political system, and so on). Within each of these social institutions there are a number of different possible ways of behaving and of understanding the nature of the institution. These different versions of the particular institution are in competition with each other for dominance and, at different times and in different places, different versions will be more or less successful. Indeed, contradictions and conflict are part of the network of social relations with which we all live. If we take the example of education, we can see that the different sides of current struggles around teaching methods (for example, over the use of 'real books' to teach reading) represent a struggle between different understandings of what it means to teach and to learn and different notions of what schooling is for and about.

These competing understandings are expressed through language and through the ways in which institutions like schools are actually organized. The French philosopher, Michel Foucault, used the terms '**discourse**' (taken from the field of linguistics) and '**discursive practices**' to describe these understandings and their expression through language, organizational forms and ways of behaving. The various discourses which are available in relation to particular social institutions and structures provide us with different possible ways of behaving and understanding the world as well as limiting (but not determining) what can be done and said. We are positioned in various discourses as well as taking up positions ourselves. For example, we identify ourselves and are identified as heterosexual, lesbian or gay and could not do so if categorizing discourses of sexuality did not exist. In this limited sense, we can be said to be 'produced' by discourses and discursive practices.

In *Discipline and Punish* (1977), Foucault discusses the ways in which schools have arisen as a site of discipline and surveillance of children, saying that:

> A relation of surveillance, defined and regulated is inscribed at the heart of the practice of teaching, not as an additional or adjacent part, but as a mechanism that is inherent to it and which increases its efficiency.

Following Foucault, Valerie Walkerdine (1985) argues that discourses in schooling both regulate and produce the child as a 'rational, independent, autonomous [individual] as a quasi-natural phenomenon who progresses through a universalized developmental sequence towards the possibility of rational argument'. In this context, she suggests that schooling not only 'defines ... what knowledge is, but also defines and regulates what 'a child is'. Schools, then, are sites of struggles, not only about knowledge, but also about ideologies of childhood, about what it means to be a teacher and to be gendered. Consequently, there are, within schooling, a number of different, sometimes contradictory, discourses available through which teachers and children are produced and produce themselves.

It is possible, for example, to imagine teachers behaving in a number of different ways in relation to students, and these ways may come from a number of different discourses. The most obvious discourse of teaching might be called the 'instructional discourse'. Within it, teachers pass on information, demonstrate how to do things, and so on. Within this discourse it would be impossible to imagine a teacher knowing less than pupils in her/his class about a topic being taught. However, teachers also operate, especially in the early years of schooling, within what might be called a 'mothering discourse'. In this context, teachers might offer comfort to children who are distressed or look after them in physical ways, such as changing their undergarments if they have 'wet' themselves. It would not, however, be open to a teacher to undertake all the functions of mothering and remain in the role of teacher, and even very young children are aware of the differences in expected behaviours. One little girl, when she was six and a pupil in the school where her mother taught, resolved the conflict of discourses by regularly calling her mother 'Mrs Mummy' when at school. There are, of course, many other discourses within which teachers can and do operate – for example, those of social work, policing and so on.

The question of which discourses are dominant is not a neutral one, for the social meanings given to different discursive practices will vary according to one's position within a particular set of social relations. What seems like common-sense will, in general, represent the interests of dominant groups in society, while what seems 'biased' or 'extreme' may well be those discourses which seek to oppose those interests (although subordinated groups develop their own versions of common-sense). In education, for example, it may seem perfectly reasonable to assume that it is desirable to give a 'balanced' view of controversial and political questions and this is often argued against anti-racist and anti-sexist education. However subjects which are controversial change over time. For example, until relatively recently the teaching of evolutionary theory rather than the creation story as given in Genesis was considered both subversive and controversial. Furthermore, the demands of 'balance' seem rather different depending on one's position in relation to the issue. For example, 'balance' in relation to teaching about South Africa would probably seem very different to Nelson Mandela and to President de Klerk. Equally, it might be salutary to ask oneself what 'balance' might mean in relation to teaching about child sexual abuse.

Questions of power

The concept of power is important in any discussion of social relations. In certain conceptualizations of power, it is reified and written about as if it were something held by certain groups and people and not others. For example, Mullard (1981) writes:

> Neither West Indians, Pakistanis, Indians, nor Africans, nor blacks as a whole, possess anything like the same amounts of power as the white dominant 'British' group. ...
>
> Power is held by white groups in society; ... Real power in a capitalist society and ... a racist society is indivisible.

Similarly, when Catherine McKinnon (1987) talks of 'the existing *distributions* of power', the implication is that power exists in forms which enable distribution. I would argue that power cannot be and is not distributed in the same way as, for example, slices of cake. Nevertheless, it is important to recognize that power can be and is distributed through the ways in which institutions like schools are organized and tends to accrue to certain groups of people – most obviously white, middle-class, heterosexual men.

Foucault (1979) argues that power is constructed through 'juridico-political discourse' and other professional discourses. He suggests, further, that:

> Power is everywhere; not because it embraces everything, but because it comes from everywhere. ... [P]ower is not an institution, and not a structure; neither is it a certain strength we are endowed with; it is the name that one attributes to a complex strategical situation in a particular society.

Foucault links power inextricably with knowledge, arguing that power cannot be regarded simply as the operation of repression, law and coercion. He suggests that power works not only in these negative senses but also produces ways of understanding the world (that is, knowledge) and that individuals, their knowledge and identities are also produced through their positioning in discourses and hence through power relations.

Foucault's critique of the reification of power is correct. Power is not a 'thing' which exists outside of social relationships. It is constructed and reconstructed in and through them constantly. Neither is it held uniformly by one dominant group in society. One has only to consider the power that a woman can develop in a heterosexual relationship or the position of, for example, a black man and a white woman in relation to each other, to realize that power relationships are more complex than binary notions of either race or gender would suggest.

However, Foucault's position on the construction of power through discourse is also less than satisfactory. He does not offer an adequate account of how discourses come into being or change. Because they exist already and counter (or, as he calls them, 'reverse') discourses always hark back to the dominant, discourses appear to be socially given and transformative resistance to them seems difficult, if not impossible. For example, discourses of gay liberation exist in relation to hexterosexuality and those of anti-racism in relation to racist discourses.

According to Foucault, we are produced as subjects within particular discourses, but he does not pay attention to the ways in which we ourselves produce the discourses in which we are inscribed in certain subject positions – whether they be relatively powerful or powerless. Neither does Foucault offer a full account for the concentration of power in hierarchies, which we can observe in social institutions like schools, nor for the difficulty which people belonging to certain groups (like black women, black men or white women) have in occupying subject positions of power in such institutions. Thus Foucault does not explain adequately the role that institutional structures have in maintaining power relations.

In using the concept of power I would, therefore, wish to pay attention to the complexity of power relationships raised by Foucault's discussion of discourses. I would wish particularly to note that power is not always wielded through coercion, but often through discursive practices which people, as active agents within these practices, either consent to or resist. It is, however, not always clear what constitutes consent or resistance. For example, academic success on the part of young black women in schools may appear to be consent to discourses of school, but can also be conceived of as resistance to discourses which place black students as 'under-achievers'.

Neither should we forget that power is also often wielded through the forces of coercion (for example, by the police and the weight of institutional hierarchies). It is important to hold on to notions of material existence, a kind of 'reality' which imposes itself on people, in order to avoid falling into **relativism**. It is more difficult for some people to occupy powerful positions than others. This is due not just to discourse but to the material realities through which the dice are loaded against some. For example, it is more difficult for a white woman, a black woman or black man to become a head of a school than it is for a white man.

It is also important to note that we may occupy positions within different and contradictory discourses, being, at one and the same time, in positions of relative power and relative powerlessness. For example, an anti-racist teacher in a state school will be relatively powerful in relation to her/his pupils, but relatively powerless in relation to people such as inspectors, the head of the school or local councillors, especially if the latter are supportive of dominant, racist discourses.

References

Foucault, M. (1977) *Discipline and Punish: The birth of the prison*, Harmondsworth: Penguin.

Foucault, M. (1979) *The History of Sexuality: Vol. 1: an introduction*, Harmondsworth: Penguin.

McKinnon, C. A. (1987) 'Feminism, Marxism, method and the state: towards feminist jurisprudence', in Harding, S. (ed.) *Feminism and Methodology*, Bloomington and Milton Keynes: Indiana University Press and Open University Press.

Mullard, C. (1981) 'Multiracial education in Britain: from assimilation to cultural pluralism', in Tierney, J. (ed.) *Race, Migration and Schooling*, London: Holt, Rinehart & Winston.

Walkerdine, V. (1985) 'On the regulation of speaking and silence: subjectivity, class and gender in contemporary schooling', in Steedman, C., Urwin, C. and Walkerdine, V. (eds) *Language, Gender and Childhood*, London: Routledge & Kegan Paul.

Key terms

The following key terms appear in the text above. They have been defined below to aid with the reading of this item.

discourse ways of speaking and thinking about the world that involve power and knowledge

discursive practices the ways of behaving, language and school organization produced by particular discourses

relativism the belief that knowledge is only ever relative, never absolute

Questions

1 Is education merely composed of a set of competing discourses in which teachers and pupils are positioned and position themselves? Give evidence for your answer.

2 How are African-Caribbean boys and girls positioned within current educational discourses of educational achievement? How might they position themselves? (You may like to draw on reading 9.8 for your answer.)

3 Describe how schools operate as sites of the discipline and surveillance of pupils in relation to attendance or behaviour. What are the ways in which pupils construct counter-discourses?

4 Consider Epstein's criticisms of Foucault. How might Marxist sociologists explain how discourses change and how power is maintained?

Reading 9.6 **Schooling and sexualities**

Mairtin Mac an Ghaill (from) *The Making of Men: Masculinities, sexualities and schooling* (1994) Buckingham, Open University Press, pp. 160–6.

Editorial comments

Mac an Ghaill starts with a true story. One of his male A level students gave him a bunch of flowers in the playground because he had passed his exams. As a result, the student got into a fight, responding to homophobic abuse from other students. Mac an Ghaill was asked to report to the headteacher's office to account for the event. He defended himself; the fight was not his fault. Then he realized that it was not the physical violence of the fight but the exchange of flowers between two males that was so threatening to the school. He felt that this response was symbolic of the problematic nature of modes of masculinity in school life.

His ethnography of Parnell school examines how schools construct and regulate masculinities and how female students experience these masculinities. Encouraged by young gay students in the school, Mac an Ghaill extended his research to include the experiences of young gay students and their responses to 'compulsory heterosexuality'.

Schooling, sexuality and male power

Sexual structuring – sexual typification: 'the enemy within'

INTERVIEWS WITH THE students' teachers focused on the wider issue of masculinity and schooling. Male teachers made a point of informing me that they found the subject matter difficult to discuss. They were particularly reticent about discussing homosexuality, claiming that it was not relevant as a curriculum issue, although they stressed that there were 'a few effeminate boys each year in their institutions'. In contrast to the students, most of the male and female teachers' explanations of homosexuality were rooted in essentialism; that is, that gayness is a universal category into which people are born.

Plummer (1989) informs us how meanings around homosexuality have changed in recent times: 'from a sick condition in the fifties, criminalized and medicalized, to a positive liberated identity in the seventies, to an AIDS-linked identity in the eighties'. The teachers selectively chose negative behavioural ascriptions as part of their social pathological discourse on gays. They employed a number of reactionary 'common-sense' representations of adolescent homosexuality, which included effeminate boys, mother-dominated males, arrested sexual development, predatory sexual practices, psychological sickness and disease-related behaviour. These images are resonant of nineteenth-century religious, legislative and medical discourses (Foucault, 1979). They have been particularly pervasive in England throughout the 1980s with the political shift and appeal to authoritarian popularism by the New Right moralists (Hall, 1983; Watney, 1993).

Most of the teachers operated with crude conceptions of straight–gay identities in terms of a superiority–inferiority couplet. Some of the liberal teachers, particularly those who worked in pastoral care posts, tended to emphasize sexual differences rather than sexual superiority. Nevertheless, all of them shared the dominant **homophobic** conception that heterosexuality is intrinsically different to homosexuality and that these sexual differences are primarily causal of social behaviour (see Barker, 1981, on the new racism). Furthermore, none of the teachers felt competent to counsel lesbian or gay young people. Many of them informed me that Clause 28 and the 1986 Education Act would prevent them from taking a positive curriculum approach to homosexuality.

The students have grown up in a society in which there are no positive images of gay or lesbian people. There is no acknowledgement of gay and lesbian history, sensibility, lifestyle and community. There is no recognition of gay or lesbian achievement. For example, the research showed that when texts written by gays or lesbians were read in class, no reference was made to the authors' sexual orientation. In fact, in lessons homosexuality was rarely discussed and, on the few occasions when it was introduced, it was presented in a negative way, most recently in relation to AIDS. A similar situation was found in curriculum analysis in North America (see Warren, 1984; Johnson, 1989).

For the students, this silence – reflecting that in the wider society – pervaded the whole of the formal curriculum, serving to reproduce and legitimate dominant heterosexual hierarchies. From this perspective, heterosexuality was presented as natural, normal and universal, simply because there are no alternative ways of being. The students emphasized the personal isolation, confusion, marginalization and alienation that this engendered. Most significantly, without a positive reference group, they tended to internalize ambivalent negative messages about themselves as gay men. These experiences are recalled by Lilley (1985), who describes how:

> Some teachers remain to be convinced that the problem is a serious one. While giving a vague intellectual assent to the proposition of equal rights, they cannot feel that much harm is done. Let me assure them, and I can say this from my personal experience and my knowledge of scores of ex-pupils, that going through the school system as a gay person is a terrible ordeal, one full of loneliness, anxiety and isolation, and one suffered by a tenth of the population. The usual fears and worries of adolescence are magnified ten-fold.

Barrat (1986) makes a distinction between the psychological view of typification with its focus on individuals' attitudes, such as prejudice, and the sociological view that locates typifications within the wider context of society, and emphasizes the ideological function that they serve in reproducing dominant power relations. Referring to the work of Perkins (1979), Barrat argues that: 'Even though we may not "believe" the stereotype [typification] it remains as part of our consciousness and works as a short-hand technique for conveying a complex idea'. Hooks (1992) has described the 'inner logic' of stereotypes (typifications) as specific forms of representation:

> Stereotypes, however inaccurate, are one form of representation. Like fictions, they are created to serve as substitutions, standing in for what is real. They are there not to tell it like it is but to invite and encourage pretence. They are a fantasy, a projection onto the Other that makes them less threatening. Stereotypes abound where there is distance. They are an invention, a pretence that one knows when the steps that would make real knowing possible cannot be taken – are not allowed.

It is argued here that the material and social construction of the 'modern homosexual' in the 1990s is pregnant with symbolic meanings within the collective heterosexual imagination, which is linked to the wider socio-economic, historical, gender and moral order (Matthews, 1989).

The students recalled how they have come to see that the absence of gays and lesbians from the curriculum is not an arbitrary oversight, but a systematic policy of omission. They felt that gays and lesbians had been removed insidiously from school view. The students explained how they have shifted from individual-based explanations of this removal with an emphasis on sexuality as a problem, to socio-cultural-based explanations of their sexual subordination, in which schools are seen as central to gay and lesbian oppression. They have become aware of how dominant systems of representation and typification, as Barrat suggests, function to maintain wider power relations.

M.M.: Why do you think that teachers have these views of gays?

Peter: Because they want to control you and to control how all people behave. So they label us as bad and themselves as good. It's a bit like the 'cowboys and Indians' stereotypes, turning people against each other.

Rajinder: Gays and lesbians are seen as a big threat to this society. They are seen by straight people as challenging the way that things are supposed to happen. That is a man meets a woman, they settle down, get a house if they can and live happily producing and bringing up the next generation. Gays and lesbians are seen as a big threat to all of this. Male straights fantasize that we are having a better time sexually than them and we aren't even paying the price. We have sex and our freedom, that's the way they see it. We are the enemy within.

M.M.: Why is that?

Rajinder: Like I said, firstly because it allows an alternative lifestyle and suggests that marriage is not the only way of living your life happily. Secondly, it challenges ideas about what is normal. If I am living happily with my boyfriend, then that can be seen to be normal for me. And then straight people may see me as happier than them. So my lifestyle becomes a threat to unhappy marriages and there's lots of them about. Lesbians are even more of a threat because for a lot of women they would be better off living with other women than straight men.

Colin: Also marriage controls women. They have to stay at home while their husbands go out to work or at least they're supposed to or do both.

Joseph: Sexuality is very difficult to talk about. It's difficult to know what it is really, when it's present and when it's not. I think that's why it's seen as dangerous. Men and women have different positions in the world with men who are supposed to be the rulers. Then we [gays] come along. I suppose we are seen as a threat to that power. If there are different ways of being men, then it may mean that there's different ways of being women that are equal. Then there are no set roles to justify why men must rule are there?

Joseph's comments reflect Wood's (1984) account of the elusiveness of sexuality. According to Wood:

Sexuality has no essence, nor can it be put in a field all of its own. Rather, in our society, it is channelled into many areas, into leisure, consumption and sport. It may be possible to investigate how this channelling contributes to the moral regulation of people if we pay close attention, first to the actual practice of genders.

(Wood, 1984)

Sex/gender regimes

As the students moved into the sixth-form and further education colleges, they began to read their secondary schooling in terms of 'learning to be a man'. Now they could see more directly the prescribed boundaries of what constitutes acceptable male and female behaviour in which the teacher–student and student–student relations were embedded. They had become aware of how **compulsory heterosexuality** pervaded their everyday lives (Rich, 1981). The moral order was policed by visible and invisible processes of institutional and self-surveillance that were pervasive throughout their schools and colleges. The sexual and gender imperatives of performing like a man found expression in the official and hidden curriculum – in classrooms, assemblies, counselling, cloakrooms, toilets, playgrounds and leisure activities.

In his study of male youth sub-cultures in an Australian inner-city school, Walker (1988) describes how:

The specific practices of playing football, drinking, marauding around town, and so on, constituted as it were, almost a quantitative index of manhood: prowess in these culturally exalted forms of masculinity (Carrigan et al., 1985) made you more of a man.

Sean's comments provides evidence to support Walker's findings. Sean was an outstanding footballer at secondary school and captain of the first XI team. He came to identify the codes through which male teachers and male students colluded in constructing dominant forms of straight masculinity, which served to devalue, marginalize and threaten femininities and subordinated masculinities. Of specific significance here was the exchange value of the 'straight male body' as a form of high-status physical capital in the competitive school marketplace (Bourdieu, 1978; Featherstone et al., 1991; Hargreaves, 1991).

Sean: I always loved football but there was something about it that I didn't like. I really enjoyed playing the game but it was all the rest of it. You see it wasn't just a game. I came to see that it was about proving yourself as a man. All the boys together, acting tough, bragging about sexual conquests, putting down women and all the macho fooling around in the showers. They had to keep telling each other that they were real men. We had the fit bodies, we had the strength, we had the power. The male teachers and pupils measured everyone against us, though this was usually hidden.

M.M.: What was the main reason you gave it up?

Sean: Schools are incredible on sport. There was more competition there than in the academic stuff. But it just got to me. The teachers were kind of selling our bodies; the school living off them. The sports teachers weren't interested in me, just using my body. And I thought to myself if they only knew, this isn't even a straight body.

M.M.: What do you think would happen?

Sean: They would be completely confused. You see they really fantasize about strength, posture and all that. And gays are supposed to be weak. I don't think it would do much for the school's reputation having a gay sports day, do you?

The students were surprised at the way in which male teachers and male students conflated assumed gay behaviour with femininity in order to traduce the former. They have developed a highly sophisticated understanding of the ambivalent **misogyny** which is endemic in male straight culture with its internal contradictions. Furthermore, they point to the need to acknowledge that sexuality and gendered identities are not totally separate, as Edwards (1990) argues is usually assumed. There was disagreement concerning the class basis of these sexist and homophobic values and practices. Rajinder pointed to the central role of the state in constructing differential experiences of the sex/gender hierarchical order between and within black and white lesbian and gay groups. He asked me to include the following quotation from Edgar (1981), which he felt represented his political understanding of the interrelationship of different forms of oppression and common strategies of resistance to them:

> Without Black Brotherhood, there would have been no sisterhood: without Black Power and Black Pride there would have been no Gay Power and Gay Pride. The movement against the abuse of powers of the State ... derived much of its strength and purpose from the exposure of the FBI's surveillance and harassment of the Black Panthers and Black Muslims ... only the Environmental movement did not have the Black Movement as a central organizational fact or as a defining metaphor and inspiration.

Adrian: It's strange really because heterosexual men are supposed to be attracted to women, so you would think that they would respect them. But the worst thing that they think they can call a gay man is a girl.

Joseph: They see themselves as powerful and superior and then the rest, women and us, are lumped together as inferior but at the same time they are sexually attracted to women!

Gerard: I think that the macho types are mainly from the working class. The middle-class men don't treat women in such a sexist way. I think also that it's easier about coming out and being open about being gay in middle-class areas.

Rajinder: That is not true. When straight men discriminate against women and gays, I don't think it's really about sex at one level. It's mainly about power and the middle classes have the power to control your life. It's the same with me being an Asian gay; I get a lot more problems from whites. If I come out the racism will increase. When I told a teacher I was gay, he came out with all his racist ideas about my parents with their culture not being able to accept it. He meant that he couldn't accept it. Again black lesbians will experience other types of discrimination. Power is used in different ways against people.

M.M.: Could you expand on that?

Rajinder: I used to think that a lot of discrimination against blacks, gays or women was more at the level of individuals. I mean I always knew about institutional racism and sexism but I have learnt a lot with us talking together about wider structures. My experiences as a black gay are primarily determined by the police and the courts, immigration policy, the control of blacks in the inner-city and the way black and white women are divided up and systematically treated differently by these institutions.

M.M.: Do you think that many people see this?

Rajinder: No, that's the problem. It's the arguments that we are always having. Like when Gerard says working-class men are more sexist. Yes, I can see what he is saying, but the people who make the policies, make the rules – who are mainly men – are middle-class and they are the real threat because they create the conditions in which the working-class men behave with their tabloids and all the rest of it. It's like we know why black or Irish immigrant men can seem more sexist to the English. Like our marriages, which they always point to, may seem reactionary to them and they may be, but the white liberal does not understand that in a highly racist society marriage can have a different meaning for different social groups. It can be seen to act as a means of solidarity between the community. I understand that, although I still don't agree with it. But if you are really interested in understanding gender and sexual relations, you have to look at the wider power bases don't you? Otherwise you end up divided against each other and not fighting the real enemy. It's like with gays, some of them can't see how badly this society treats women. We have a lot in common.

For the students, the assimilation of non-macho behaviour to feminine behaviour was illustrated in relation to the ubiquity of the term 'poof', which in 'denoting lack of guts, suggests femininity – weakness, softness and inferiority' (Lees, 1987). The label has several shifting meanings; sometimes it is used with an explicit sexual connotation, while at other times it is used as a general term of abuse. The notoriety and frequency of use of the label caused much distress to the students throughout their schooling as a major source of derision of their growing awareness of their sexuality.

In the following incident, Adrian describes how official moral codes are covertly transmitted in schools and the resulting differential effects on different students. At his school, a first-year boy was overheard by a member of staff, referring to another male teacher as a 'poof'. The student was reported to the headteacher. The next day at assembly the boy was caned in front of the whole school and given a lecture on respect for teachers without which, they were told, no institution could survive. The headteacher made no reference to what the student had said but claimed that it was the worst thing that he had heard in all his years as a teacher. During the following week, rumours were passed among the students of exaggerated stories with sexual connotations. The unintended effect of the headteacher's response was to highlight the presumed sexual nature of the incident. Adrian asked the first-year student what he had said, and he repeated that he had called one of the teacher's a 'poof'. When Adrian had asked him why he had called him this, the student replied, 'because he had seen the teacher kissing a woman on the bus'.

Adrian: Amazingly, no-one had even asked the kid what he meant. One of the teachers had told us that the staff assumed that he meant homosexual, their definition. But he was going through an 'anti-girls phase'! He knew that 'poof' meant something bad, so he assumed that kissing girls was what 'poofs' did. When things like this happened, it really frightened me. I thought all these teachers are punishing him and he only used the word. What would they do to me because I thought I might be gay? I couldn't sleep for weeks. I couldn't sleep with all the nightmares. I thought they were coming for me and how ashamed my family would be. It was just before my exams that I failed. I had a nervous breakdown. I can still hear the Head saying, 'this is the worst thing I've ever heard'. There was no-one to talk to, no-one to trust.

For gays and lesbians, as for other oppressed groups in England, including women and the black, Irish and Jewish communities, dominant state discourses play a central role in the maintenance and reproduction of social and sexual hierarchies (Foucault, 1979; Walkerdine, 1981). Unlike black students of Asian and African Caribbean origin, who use counter-discourses as an effective form of contestation and resistance to institutional incorporation into white cultural identities, young lesbians and gays tend to be more isolated from each other at school, and consequently are unable to develop these particular coping and survival discursive strategies (Mac an Ghaill, 1988; see Giddens, 1979).

References

Barker, M. (1981) *The New Racism*, London: Junction Books.

Barrat, D. (1986) *Media Sociology*, London: Tavistock.

Bourdieu, P. (1978) 'Sport and social class', *Social Science Information*, 17, pp. 819–40.

Carrigan, T., Connell, R. W. and Lee, J. (1985) 'Hard and heavy phenomena: the sociology of masculinity', *Theory and Society*, 14, pp. 551–604.

Edgar, D. (1981) 'Reagan's hidden agenda', *Race and Class*, 22 (3), pp. 207–23.

Edwards, T. (1990) 'Beyond sex and gender: masculinity, homosexuality and social theory', in Hearth, J. and Morgans, D. (eds) *Men, Masculinities and Social Theory*, London: Unwin Hyman.

Featherstone, M., Hepworth, M. and Turner, B. S. (1991) *The Body: Social process and cultural theory*, London: Sage.

Foucault, M. (1979) *The History of Sexuality: Vol. 1: an introduction*, Harmondsworth: Penguin.

Giddens, A. (1979) *Central Problems in Social Theory*, London: Macmillan.

Hall, S. (1983) 'The great moving right show', in Hall, S. and Jacques, M. (eds) *The Politics of Thatcherism*, London: Lawrence & Wishart.

Hargreaves, J. (1991) *Sport, Power and Culture: a social and historical analysis of popular sport in Britain*, Cambridge: Polity Press.

hooks, b. (1992) 'Representing blackness in white imagination', in Grossberg, L., Nelson, G. and Treichler, P. (eds) *Cultural Studies*, London: Routledge.

Johnson, A. (1989) 'Lesbians and gays in the schools: teachers, students and courses of study', in *Off Our Backs*, New York: Woman's World.

Lees, S. (1987) 'The structure of sexual relations in school', in Arnot, M. and Weiner, G. (eds) *Gender and the Politics of Schooling*, Milton Keynes, Open University Press.

Lilley, M. (1985) 'Gay Pupils', *Times Educational Supplement*, 5 April, p. 18.

Mac an Ghaill, M. (1988) *Young, Gifted and Black: Student–teacher relations in the schooling of black youth*, Milton Keynes: Open University Press.

Matthews, J. J. (1989) *Good and Mad Women: The historical construction of feminism in twentieth-century Australia*, London: Allen & Unwin.

Perkins, T. E. (1979) 'Re-thinking stereotypes', in Barrett, M., Corrigan, P., Khun, A. and Wolfe, J. (eds) *Ideology and Cultural Production*, London: Croom Helm.

Plummer, K. (1989) 'Being Gay: the social construction of homosexuality', *Gay Times*, March, pp. 26–8.

Rich, A. (1981) 'Compulsory heterosexuality and lesbian existence', *Signs, 5* (4) pp. 631–60.

Walker, J. (1988) *Louts and Legends: Male youth cultures in an inner city school*, London: Allen & Unwin.

Walkerdine, V. (1981) 'Sex, power and pedagogies', *Screen Education, 38*, pp. 14–26.

Warren, H. (1984) *Talking About School*, London: Gay Teacher's Project.

Watney, S. (1993) 'Simon Watney column: sex education', *Gay Times*, 2 February.

Wood, J. (1984) 'Groping towards sexism: boys' sex talk', in McRobbie, A. and Nava, M. (eds) *Gender and Generation*, London: Macmillan.

Key terms

The following key terms appear in the text above. They have been defined below to aid with the reading of this item.

homophobic 'homophobia' is the fear of gay men and lesbians

compulsory heterosexuality when heterosexual behaviour is rewarded and behaviour associated with other sexualities is punished

misogyny hatred of women

Questions

1 What reasons are suggested to explain why gay sexuality is so threatening and regarded as the 'enemy within'? Comment on these reasons.

2 From your own experience, describe some of the processes that produce and enforce compulsory heterosexuality in schools and colleges. How might they be resisted?

3 How does the extract suggest the different oppressions of 'race', gender, sexuality and social class work together? Can you provide other examples of this?

4 What sort of educational changes and policies may be necessary to help create an educational atmosphere in which all pupils are able to recognize with confidence their developing sexuality?

5 Why might researching gay sexuality in schools be difficult?

Reading 9.7 **Acting powerfully: habitus in the primary classroom**

Diane Reay (from) '"They employ cleaners to do that": habitus in the primary classroom', *British Journal of Sociology of Education* (1995) vol. 16, no. 3, pp. 362–6.

Editorial comments

Diane Reay uses Pierre Bourdieu's concept of 'habitus' to explore the behaviour of children in two London primary schools. Milner school has a working-class, multi-ethnic intake while Oak Park is white and middle-class. The concept of habitus is useful because it attempts to reconcile structure and agency – particularly how individuals are moulded by, but also change, social structure. Habitus is an internalized framework, a master-plan or grammar, which defines the opportunities and constraints of our actions. Bourdieu used the concept in relation to social class, but Reay extends it to include 'race' and gender by exploring domination in everyday practice.

Acting powerfully: children in the classroom

VERY TENTATIVELY I have explored the presence of habitus in the children's practices in the classroom. I have utilized Cicourel's suggestion that habitus can be used as a tool for examining domination as everyday practice (Cicourel, 1993a) in my own analysis. The lengthy vignette detailed below was my first attempt to link habitus to the data I collected on domination as everyday practice. On one of the first days I went into Oak Park I found myself gravitating to the back of the classroom where four girls were preoccupied with the computer program they were working on. I quietly drew up a chair next to them and sat down. It was a program on the Tudors that I was familiar with from my time spent in Milner. The programme was based on the life of Bess, a servant girl, who worked for the landed gentry. Negar was giving the instructions, Sarah was methodically typing them in, while Nancy and Sophie were providing ideas and suggestions. 'Tell her to go upstairs and hurry up'. 'OK I'll type in "go up", that's if she's not too stupid to understand'. Negar typed in 'go up' then started to tap in 'please' 'Don't be silly' said Sophie leaning over and putting her finger on the delete button. 'We don't have to say please or thank you. She's just a servant'. A few minutes later Nancy mischievously said 'Make her run'. Bess was in her mistress' bedroom by now. 'Great idea' said Negar 'make her run downstairs' Sarah typed in 'run'. Sophie, who seemed to be getting heady on the prevailing sense of power and control became impatient with Sarah's typing speed, leaned over and typed in 'run quicker or else'. It was at that point that they noticed me scribbling away. Nancy beamed, noticed my bemused look and by way of explanation told me 'We have to give her orders and be a bit rude because she's the servant'.

It was at that point that I realized that they were doing something quite normal. They were inserting themselves into the game as Bess's mistress. Bourdieu writes in terms of habitus as 'the internalization of the probabilities of access to goods, services and powers' (Bourdieu, 1992). The responses of the children in the two schools to the computer program illustrated very different relationships to 'goods, services and powers'. At Milner where the children had positioned themselves as Bess or else as a stranger in the house I had never even considered the possibility of taking on the role of authority figure. Neither had the children, my field notes have comments such as 'Our bedroom's not very nice is it' and 'Where shall we go next?'. They had either identified themselves as visitors or with Bess herself. But that was not the most

logical relationship to assume. Computer programs work on the basis of being given orders and that was what the four girls at Oak Park were doing. They had naturally, unthinkingly assumed the role of mistress and entered into relations of ruling with Bess (Bourdieu, 1992).

I acknowledge the shortcomings of an example which explicates domination as everyday practice in relation to a fictional character and accept that a flesh and blood Bess would not be treated in the same way. However, what the girls did demonstrate was a very different habitus to the one children played out in Milner classrooms, one that provided very different **dispositions** and concomitantly very different possibilities to the ones conceived of in Milner. They were demonstrating a particular understanding of the division of labour and their place within it that lay outside the habitus of the children at Milner. Implicit in their dispositions was a conceptualization of themselves as the kind of people who paid for the services of others. They were also displaying the communicative competence that is integral to the understanding and use of symbolic power. Their habitus revealed that, already at the age of 10, they had learnt 'how to be assertive, use demonstratives, produce requests and imperatives' (Cicourel, 1993b). The combination of the socialization the four girls brought with them to the classroom, plus the ongoing peer group socialization happening within it, seemed to be teaching them to assume positions of power, at least in relation to other, less privileged females.

Dispositions in the two schools: differentiation by gender and social class

However, there were further examples of dispositions acted out in Oak Park that displayed a different relationship to the division of labour to that evident in Milner classrooms. Initially, I took the 'tidying up' in Milner for granted. The good natured scramble when their teacher asked children to tidy up was very familiar – girls rushing around helpfully putting lids on felt tips, pushing chairs in, placing books back on shelves, a few over enthusiastic boys throwing themselves under tables only to emerge moments later clutching a few scraps of paper, the odd boy sidling about doing very little and being 'told on' by an indignant girl were events I had experienced innumerable times myself as a primary school teacher. I comment in my field notes:

> Tidy up time seems like pandemonium but miraculously, and accelerated by the occasional yell from Mandy, the job gets done.
> *(Milner, March 1993)*

In Oak Park there was no taking the process for granted. To my surprise most of the children did not want to tidy up. In fact some of them flatly refused to. In my field notes from November 1993 I have written:

> Five minutes before afternoon play Julia tells the class to tidy up. There is little response, children are mostly engrossed in finishing off work. Riva and Sophia rush up to the front to ask if they can stay in to finish their story. Thirty seconds later, Julia raises her voice, 'Now, or you'll miss your playtime' and children start to put their own things away and move towards the door. Julia shouts out 'I don't want to find any pens or pencils on the floor today'. After reminding Robyn's table to push their chairs in, I notice a group of children clustered around Moya. She is sobbing, slumped over her table. I go to ask what the matter is. She just continues crying. Sophie says 'It's that' and points to a pile of pencil trimmings on the floor under Moya's chair. 'She says they're not hers so she's not getting them up'. 'Ok' I reply 'You and I can get them up, can you get a dustpan and brush'? 'No, I'm not doing it'. I look round for help 'Can someone get me a dustpan and brush'? No one can so I go and do the job myself.

Surprised I went and asked a group of children after break why they were not prepared to tidy up. Susie said 'It's not our job', while Oliver interjected 'They employ cleaners to do that'.

Such **social distinctions** were not a normal part of sense making in Milner classrooms. There these 'cleaners' were children's mothers not to be conceptualized as socially distant from the children's world. Tidying up and helping generally were activities working-class girls in Milner felt 'at home with' (Bourdieu, 1981). In Oak Park such activities were both actively and passively resisted not only by the boys but by many of the girls as well. What we learn from these two lengthy vignettes is that the process of **cultural capital** production generated by habitus is not only a process of generating educational attainment. It is also one of producing social distinction. Lamont & Lareau argue that a new productive way of conceptualizing cultural capital is as a form of social and cultural exclusion (Lamont & Lareau, 1988). These children's performance in the classroom was not just about working towards academic success, it was also about producing social differentiation. They were working on their social status in the classroom alongside, and even in the process of attending to the school curriculum. They were constructing themselves as the kind of people who are different to their 'Bess' or the cleaners.

Some of the children were also constructing themselves as 'equals' of the teachers. These dispositions were due to the interaction of privileged habitus and a particular educational field. The children's dispositions were simultaneously due to their own work while being reliant on teachers' practices. How much their performance in the classroom could also be viewed in terms of the accomplishment of maternal work is difficult to disentangle. However, to some extent their behaviour reflects the sense of entitlement to question and criticize many of their mothers displayed. In the staff room, the teacher laughingly tells me that the children 'are fairly empowered' and relays an incident that happened earlier in the week. She was discussing the arrangements for the class assembly. Sophie puts up her hand to query the ordering of events. 'Mrs Symmonds I think it's best if we have the music first because we can put the music stands on the stage beforehand then take them off before we do the drama'. The teacher said she replied 'Quite right, Sophie, a much better idea'. The teacher then told me about the message, left on her desk by another girl, which said 'If you want to do some formal English I have some books from my tutor which might be useful', while Katie came up to tell the teacher about 'a good idea I've had for a Maths activity'. In my fieldnotes I have noted an exchange between Sophie and Mrs Symmonds. Mrs Symmonds is illustrating how to do long division by working out an example on the blackboard:

Sophie: Mrs Symmonds, that's not right, it comes to 126 not 136.
Mrs Symmonds: Quite right, Sophie, well spotted.

Sophie displayed many of the characteristics of Walkerdine's Charlotte. She is active and challenging in the classroom context, displaying flair, creativity and 'real learning' (Walkerdine, 1990). Her practices in the classroom produced natural distinction (Bourdieu, 1990). Nowhere in the fieldnotes from Milner is there similar evidence of pupils either acting as 'advisors' and 'curriculum consultants' to the teacher, or challenging the teacher's knowledge. There are many examples of helpfulness and some of challenges to the teacher's authority (from boys) in Milner, but nowhere is there any implicit assumption of equality or of 'knowing better' than the teacher.

Instead, in Milner there were narratives of helping which were largely absent in Oak Park. These narratives were gendered, they were mostly in the tales girls told me about social interaction in the classroom, in their explanations of what 'goes on'. Habitus could be found in 'a system of dispositions to a certain practice' (Bourdieu, 1990) that was powerfully structured by gender. On the class outing to an urban farm, Rosetta, who is holding my hand as we walk along, explains about Daisy, a new arrival in the classroom. She tells me how Daisy is not used to doing work in

English 'But I help her'. On another trip, this time to the library Lucy and Charlene both hold my hand. They are discussing the boys in the class, mostly in disparaging terms, 'some of them are silly'. However, Lucy explains that Stuart frequently sits with them and 'we help him with his work'. Their claims to help were supported by my observations in the classroom:

> Lucy has finished her work before anyone else again. She puts her books away and goes across to the book corner, I think to choose a book but has ended up tidying up the books on the display shelf. Mandy is still engrossed in explaining decomposition of number to a group of children experiencing difficulties with Maths. Delroy is fidgeting around across the table from me. He screws up his nose and tells me 'I can't do these sums'. As I lean over to look at what he's doing, Lucy comes across. He glances up at her and says 'These sums are hard'. She looks intently at his page, pulls up a chair and starts to help.
> *(Fieldnotes, May 1993)*

This theme of helping was also commented on by Milner mothers in their interviews:

> I find they do it a lot at Milner, someone helps somebody else who can't do it, like in these reading groups they've got.
> *(Elaine, Milner)*

> She's always helping the others do their work not because she has to but because that's what she wants to do, but last week when she was telling me about helping this kid, I did worry. It's funny this has brought it all back. I thought then at the time is it helping her helping other children. Why should she be teaching not learning?
> *(Jisa, Milner)*

Walkerdine & Lucey write of the issue of who helps who, and who needs help, being a recurring theme in working-class girls' accounts. They found most of the working-class girls in their sample:

> *Put themselves forward* as helpers.
> *(Walkerdine & Lucey, 1989, authors' emphasis)*

Underpinning this disposition to help were school practices in Milner. Milner, like Lise Bird's New Zealand primary school, was an educational setting in which important aspects of classroom organization were based on pupils supporting each others' learning (Bird, 1992). In particular, children were encouraged to hear each other read during the daily reading time. The educational field these children found themselves in, reinforced the disposition girls, in particular, brought with them to the classroom context. The reality was that it was predominantly girls hearing other girls and some boys read. The gendered nature of 'helpfulness' is borne out by Christine's explanation of why Matthew was 'getting into trouble' in the classroom on a regular basis:

> He actually said to me 'It's really boring, I have to listen to other children read'.
> *(Christine, Milner)*

Clearly helpfulness is a consequence of the interaction between the girls' own dispositions and teachers' practices. Although Lisa displays serious reservations about the efficacy of helpfulness for academic success, only Julie spells out what she perceives to be the costs for bright girls:

> If they are bright they are told to help other children. Kids don't want that, they're not paid to help others. If they are bright let them get on with something else. They should be given something harder while the teacher helps those who can't read or write.

Most of the other Milner mothers, who mentioned the issue, unquestioningly viewed helping as a normal feature of classroom life. In contrast, from my interview with mothers in Oak Park, the possibility of basing classroom organization on pupil practices of helping seemed remote. The pressure for academic success in Oak Park precluded classroom practices of helping being acceptable to mothers, instead mothers talked in terms of extension work: 'There is an awful lot of extension work built into the curriculum' (Pamela) and:

> I've found in Oak Park that they always give children extra work if they've finished early. With Richard his teacher will let him branch out in a different direction. There's a tendency not to let a child develop too far above the general level in the class but to give them something that pushes them to the side more and I think that's very good. That was done with Petra quite a lot, there she would go on and do a Maths investigation on a related topic that pushed her in a different direction. That's certainly the approach that Phillip's teacher took as well.
> *(Laura, Oak Park)*

Only a fifth of Walkerdine & Lucey's middle-class girls talked in terms of helping and there was a similar distribution in Oak Park where the norm among both sexes was more one of competitiveness than one of helping. The helping behaviour of girls in Milner and the much lower incidence of helping behaviour in Oak Park demonstrates the way gendered habitus is mediated by social class.

References

Bird, L. (1992) 'Girls taking positions of authority in primary schools', in Middleton, S. and Jones, A. (eds) *Women and Education in Aotearoa, 2*, Auckland: Bridget Williams Books.

Bourdieu, P. (1981) 'Men and machines', in Knorr Cetina, K. and Cicourel, A. V. (eds) *Advances in Social Theory and Methodology: Towards an integration of macro and micro sociologies*, London: Routledge & Kegan Paul.

Bourdieu, P. (1990) *In Other Words: Essays towards reflexive sociology*, Cambridge: Polity Press.

Bourdieu, P. (1992) *Language and Symbolic Power*, Cambridge: Polity Press.

Cicourel, A. V. (1993a) 'Aspects of structural and processual theories of knowledge', in Calhoun, C., La Puma, E. and Postone, M. (eds) *Bourdieu: Critical perspectives*, Cambridge: Polity Press.

Cicourel, A. V. (1993b) 'Development and adult aspects of habitus', in Gebauer, G. and Wolf, C. (eds) *Praxis and Asthetik: Neue Perspektiven im Denken Pierre Bourdieus*, Frankfurt am Main, Suhrkamp.

Lamont, M. and Lareau, A. (1988) 'Cultural capital: allusions, gaps and glissandos in recent theoretical developments', *Sociological Theory*, 6, pp. 153–68.

Walkerdine, V. and Lucey, H. (1989) *Democracy in the Kitchen: Regulating mothers and socialising daughters*, London: Virago.

Walkerdine, V. (1990) *Schoolgirl Fictions*, London: Verso.

Key terms

The following key terms appear in the text above. They have been defined below to aid with the reading of this item.

dispositions tendencies or inclinations

social distinctions markers of social differences. Bourdieu was interested in the ways different social classes distinguish themselves from others by their 'taste' or patterns of consumption, e.g. clothes, food, cars and computer games, etc.

cultural capital the skills and knowledge, language, manners, style of the dominant culture. Possession of cultural capital places middle-class children at an advantage in the educational system

Questions

1 Describe how the children at Milner and Oak Park used the computer program differently. How might this illustrate the concept of habitus and relations of ruling?

2 What other behaviour in the two classrooms produced social distinction as well as differences in academic success?

3 Does the gendered nature of 'helpfulness' work to the detriment of girls at Milner School?

4 To what extent might the habitus of the classroom reflect the habitus of the homes of the pupils in the two schools? How might this be investigated further?

5 What criticisms can be made of Reay's explorations of habitus in two primary classrooms?

Reading 9.8 **Deconstructing black educational under-achievement**

Heidi Safia Mirza (from) 'Black women in education: a collective movement for social change', in *Black British Feminism: a reader* (1997) London: Routledge, pp. 270–6.

Editorial comments

Developing earlier research on black girls relative success at school Heidi Safia Mirza argues that this success constitutes a covert social movement for change. Statistics (see Madood, reading 9.4) indicate that, in the new universities, black students and particularly black female students are over-represented. This success can be read as conformist, as buying into the system or, alternatively, as subversive and transformative because black women are refusing to be unsuccessful. She takes issue with Gilroy's assertion that black struggles for educational opportunities are fragile collectivities without the political stability to make them agents of social change. She provides an alternative black feminist analysis.

Black women in education

Evidence of collective educational urgency

BLACK WOMEN DO buy into the educational system. They do relatively well at school, relative that is to their male and female working-class peers as measured in terms of *average* exam performance at GCSE level. This phenomenon was first documented over ten years ago in 1985 in the Swann Report and confirmed by the ILEA in 1987 (Mirza, 1992). More recently the findings of the 1992 National Youth Cohort Study appear to confirm this (Drew *et al.*, 1992).

In my own research for *Young, Female and Black* (Mirza, 1992), which was a small local study of two inner city working-class schools, I also found black girls do as well as, if not better than, their peers in average exam performance. I found young black women collectively identified with the notion of credentialism. They subscribed to the meritocratic ideal, which within the parameters of their circumstances meant 'getting on'. In difficult and disruptive conditions the majority of young black women would sit in the back of the class getting on with their own work. However, whatever the young black women's achievements they were always within the constraints of the class conditions of inner city schooling.

What is clear from all the studies on race and education is that black girls have to stay on longer at school to achieve their long-term educational aspirations. In order to overcome obstacles of racism and sexism in school large numbers stay on in order to get the opportunities that enable them to take a 'backdoor' route into further and higher education. Young women do this by strategically rationalizing their educational opportunities. They opt for accessible careers (gendered and racialized jobs) which give them the opportunity to get onto a college course. Their career aspirations were tied to their educational motivation and by the prospect of upward mobility. A job was an expression of their desire to move ahead within the educational process. The young black women chose 'realistic careers' that they knew to be accessible and (historically) available to them. For example, social work and other caring jobs such as nursing or office work. The occupations they chose always required a course or several courses of rigorous professional training, and is why they choose them. Thus while it may appear young black women are reproducing stereotypes of black women's work, they are in effect expressing their meritocratic values within the limits of opportunities allowed to them in a racially and sexually-divisive educational and economic system. They are in effect subversively and collectively employing a 'backdoor' entry to further and higher education.

This picture of collective educational urgency among young black women to enter colleges of further and higher education is confirmed by national statistics. The 1993 Labour Force survey shows 61 per cent of all black women (aged 16–59) to have higher and other qualifications (*Employment Gazette*, 1993). Figures for 1995 show that 52 per cent of all black women (aged 16–24) are in full-time education, compared to 28 per cent of white women, 36 per cent of black men, and 31 per cent of white men (*Employment Gazette*, 1995). Similarly a recent study for the Policy Studies Institute shows that in relation to their respective population sizes, ethnic minority groups, overall, are over-represented in higher education (Modood and Shiner, 1994). This over-representation was especially apparent in the new universities. Here people of Caribbean origin were over-represented by 43 per cent, Asians by 162 per cent and Africans by 223 per cent! This compared to the white population which was underrepresented by 7 per cent.

But educational urgency does not stop there. As mothers black women strategically negotiate the educational advantage of their children within the constraints offered by the decaying urban education system and limited access to cultural capital (Reay, 1997). Black women are disproportionately involved in the setting up and running of black supplementary schools. They invest in the education of the next generation. In on-going research on black supplementary schools, Diane Reay and myself have done a preliminary survey of black schools in London (Reay and Mirza, forthcoming 1998). So far we found sixty officially documented black schools within four London boroughs, but we believe we only scratched the surface. Through networks and word of mouth we hear of more and more every day. Sometimes there would be several on one council estate. They appear to spring up 'unoffically' in houses, community centres, and unused school rooms. Of those we found, 65 per cent were run by women; and of those run by men, women's involvement as teachers and mentors was the overwhelming majority input.

Is black female educational urgency a new social movement?

It could be argued, as indeed I wish to suggest here, that the extent, direction and intensity of the black female positive orientation to education is significant enough to qualify their collective action as a transformative social movement. However, Paul Gilroy does not think so. He describes the black struggles for educational opportunities as constituting 'fragile collectivities'. He argues such movements are symptoms of 'resistance to domination', defensive organizations, with their roots in a radical sense of powerlessness. As they cannot make the transition to 'stable forms of politics' they are not agents for social change (Gilroy, 1987).

However, I believe an analysis of female collective action offers a new direction in the investigation of black social movements. As Gilroy's argument demonstrates, black female agency has remained invisible in the **masculinist discourse** of 'race' and social change. There has clearly been a black and male monopoly of the 'black subject' (West, 1990). In the masculinist discourse on race and social change the assumption is that 'race' is contested and fought over in the masculine arena of the streets – among the (male) youth in the city (e.g. Solomos, 1988; Keith, 1993, 1995; Solomos and Back, 1995). Urban social movements, we are told, mobilize in protest, riots, local politics, and community organizations. We are told it is their action, and not the subversive and covert action of women that gives rise to so called 'neo-populist liberatory authentic politics' (Gilroy, 1987). This is the masculinist version of radical social change; visible, radical, confrontational, collective action, powerfully expressed in the politics of the inner city, where class consciousness evolves in response to urban struggle.

Thus notions of resistance which are employed in this male discourse of social change to signify and celebrate black struggle, remain entrenched in ideology that privileges dominance. The black feminist theorist Patricia Hill Collins tells us black women writers have rejected notions of power based on domination in favour of a notion of power based on a vision of self-actualization, self-definition and self-determination (Collins, 1991). However, the political language of 'community' around which black social movements are traditionally articulated in the masculinist discourse remains a relational idea. It suggests the notion of antagonism and oppositionality – of domination and subordination – between one community and another (Young, 1990). But what if, for black women, community identity is not relational and antagonistic but inclusive with regard to the mainstream? This could be a possibility; there must be another way of understanding our lives other than always in relation to the 'other'. There is after all more to life than opposition to racism (Mirza, 1995).

Black women's activism: strategies for transformation

Mapping the hidden histories, subjugated knowledges, the counter memories of black women educators in black supplementary schools, reveals the possibilities for covert social movements to achieve social change. Black supplementary schools, as organic grassroots organizations, are not simply a response to mainstream educational exclusion and poor practice, as they are so often described. They are far more radical and subversive than their quiet conformist exterior suggests. It is little wonder they are viewed suspiciously by uninformed observers as 'black power places'!

Such schools provide an alternative world with different meanings and shared 'ways of knowing'. As one mother said, 'There is white bias everywhere except at Saturday school'. It is a place where whiteness is displaced and blackness becomes the unspoken norm. It is a place of refusal and difference; a place of belonging.

In the four supplementary schools in our research black children discovered 'really useful knowledge' (Johnson, 1988) which allowed them 'to step outside the white hermeneutic circle and into the black' (Gates, quoted in Casey, 1993). Each of the four schools in our study was distinct, but they were underpinned by two main pedagogies. Some focused more on black images, black history and black role models. Others focused more on back to basics, the formal teaching of the 3 Rs. Some did both.

In the same way as the schools were paradoxically radical and conservative in their aims, so too were the teachers both radical and conservative in their **praxis**. On the one hand, the women, who were for the most part voluntary unpaid teachers, talked of their 'joy' of what they do, the 'gift of giving back', of their work to 'raise the race'. Many had been giving up their weekends for twenty years. Others had become ill from overwork and dedication.

On the other hand, the same teachers saw themselves as complimenting mainstream education. They were concerned about 'fitting in', assisting parents with home–school relations and getting the children to do better. On the surface these schools appeared conformist and conservative, with their focus on formality and buying into the liberal democratic ideal of meritocracy.

But as Casey writes in her excellent book, *I Answer with My Life* (1993) in a racist society a black person is located very differently than a white person.

> In a racist society for a black child to become educated is to contradict the whole system of racist signification ... to succeed in studying white knowledge is to undo the system itself ... to refute its reproduction of black inferiority materially and symbolically.
> *(Casey 1993: 123)*

Thus it could be argued, as I am doing here, that in certain circumstances, *doing well can become a radical strategy*. An act of social transformation.

The black women educators did not accept the dominant discourse. In their space on the margin they have evolved a system of strategic rationalization of the dominant discourse. They operate within, between, under, and alongside the mainstream educational and labour market structures, subverting, renaming and reclaiming opportunities for their children through their transformative pedagogy of 'raising the race' – a **radical pedagogy**, that ironically appears conservative on the surface with its focus on inclusion and dialogue with the mainstream.

Patricia Hill Collins (1991) calls our attention to the dual nature of black women's activist traditions in their attempt to bring about social change. She suggests black women engage in activism that is both conservative and radical. Black women create culture and provide for their families. Fostering self-evaluation and self-reliance, patterns of consciousness and self-expression shape their cultures of difference. This struggle for group survival may appear conservative with its emphasis on preserving customs and cultural maintenance. Collins argues this struggle for group survival is in contrast to the radical tradition of black women's engaged activism. Because black communities and families are so profoundly affected by the political, economic and social institutions they are situated in, black women also find themselves working for radical institutional transformation through legal and civil action in terms of the traditional and valorized (masculine) form of visible social action.

However, it is in the uncharted struggle for group survival that black women in supplementary schools are located. Rose, a mother in one of the schools, tells us:

> We always have a session which is about giving children a voice. We teach them to speak, to develop a voice that can be heard. We tell them to be proud of what they are, to be strong about speaking out. I think perhaps that is the most important thing we do, helping them develop a voice that gets heard because it is easy for black children not to be listened to in school, to be thought of as a nuisance when they say something. I think in Saturday school it is quite clear that they are expected, entitled to speak out.
>
> *(Rose, in Reay and Mirza, forthcoming 1998)*

Charity's narrative on how Colibri was started includes similar themes of activism, community and commitment that characterize the struggle for group survival and the desire for social change:

> There was a group of about six parents who like myself, as a black teacher, were dissatisfied with what was happening to black pupils. They felt if they had been in the Caribbean their children would be much further on academically and they decided something had to be done, schools weren't doing

anything, so it had to be them. I really wish someone had the time to chart the enormous amount of work they put in those first few years. It was immense. The school started off in someone's front room on Saturday mornings. The parents doing all the teaching themselves to start with and it was very much focused on what was their main concern; their children not being able to read and write properly. Then these parents found the group of children grew from 10 to 15 and soon it was 20 and at this point it was unmanageable running a Saturday school in someone's front room so they petitioned the council for accommodation and finally got one of the council's derelict properties. They spent their spare time shovelling rubbish out of the room, tramps had been living there. Also doing building, repair work, getting groups of parents together to decorate. They pulled together and did all this work themselves, used the expertise they had to get the school on its feet.

> *(Charity, in Reay and Mirza, forthcoming 1998)*

What the black women appeared to have learnt is an awareness of the need for social support and collaborative action through their experience of marginality in a white racist society. From this awakening of consciousness and socio-analysis (Bourdieu, 1990) the women created their own cultural capital. Their habitus embodied 'real intelligence' in their ways of knowing and understanding (Luttrell, 1992). As their words show, this ultimately led to collective action and social change.

Conclusion

In conclusion the question we must return to is this: Is the coherent educational urgency uncovered among black women a radical social movement with transformative possibilities from the margin or, as some suggest, no more than a conservative act?

Research on black women in education shows there is much evidence to suggest black women do not accept the dominant discourse, nor do they construct their identities in opposition to the dominant discourse. They redefine the world, have their own values, codes and understandings, *refuse* (not resist) the gaze of the other. As Spivak says: 'Marginal groups do not wish to claim centrality but redefine the big word human in terms of the marginal' (Spivak, quoted in hooks, 1991). Black women live in counter hegemonic marginal spaces where, as hooks describes: 'Radical black subjectivity is seen not overseen by any authoritative other claiming to know us better than we know ourselves' (hooks, 1991).

For black women strategies for everyday survival consist of trying to create spheres of influence that are separate from but engaged with existing structures of oppression. Being successful and gaining authority and power within institutions that have traditionally not allowed black women formal authority or real power enables them to indirectly subvert oppressive structures by changing them. By saying this I do not wish to argue that black women are simply empowered through their educational achievement. Empowerment assumes a notion of power that is relational. It suggests the positive power of a collectivity or individual to challenge basic power relations in society (Yuval-Davis, 1994). The assumption here is that black women's actions empower them, but any gains are always oppositional and in relation to the hegemonic culture (Steady, 1993). What I have tried to show instead is that black women are not simply resisting, but have evolved a system of strategic rationalization which has its own logic, values and codes. Black women struggle for educational inclusion in order to transform their opportunities and so in the process subvert racist expectations and beliefs. By entering into dialogue with others they are not conservative or colluding with the mainstream. They are collectively opening up transformative possibilities for their community through their pragmatic recognition of the power of education to transform and change the hegemonic discourse (McLaren, 1994; hooks, 1994).

So, finally, can I claim black women's educational urgency and desire to do well within the system is radical and subversive? To answer the question I leave you with the words of a black woman university student:

> When not given success we need to be successful ... that is the most radical thing you can do.
> *(Alisha, in Mirza, 1994)*

References

Bourdieu, P. (1990) *In Other Words: Essays towards reflexive sociology*, Cambridge: Polity Press.

Casey, K. (1993) *I Answer With My Life: Life histories of women teachers working for social change*, New York: Routledge.

Collins, P. H. (1991) *Black Feminist Thought: Knowledge, consciousness and the politics of empowerment*, London: Routledge.

Drew, D., Gray, J. and Sime, N. (1992) 'Against the odds: the education and labour market experiences of young black people', Employment Department, *Youth Cohort Series Report*, no. 19, June, London: HMSO.

Employment Gazette (1993) 'Ethnic Origins and the Labour Market', Employment Department, February, London: HMSO.

Employment Gazette (1995) 'Ethnic Minorities', Employment Department, June, London: HMSO.

Gilroy, P. (1987) *There Ain't No Black in the Union Jack*, London: Hutchinson.

hooks, b. (1991) *Yearning: Race, gender and cultural politics*, London: Turnaround.

hooks, b. (1994) *Teaching to Transgress: Education and the practice of freedom*, London: Routledge.

Johnson, R. (1988) 'Really useful knowledge, 1790–1850: memories for education in the 1980s', in Lovett, T. (ed.) *Radical Approaches to Education: a reader*, New York: Routledge.

Keith, M. (1993) *Race, Riots and Policing: Lore and disorder in a multiracist society*, London: UCL Press.

Keith, M. (1995) 'Shouts of the street: identity and spaces of authenticity', *Social Identities*, vol. 1, no. 2, August, pp. 297–315.

Luttrell, W. (1992) 'Working-class women's ways of knowing: effects of race, gender and class', in Wrigley, J. (ed.) *Education and Gender Equality*, London: Falmer Press.

McLaren, P. (1994) 'Multiculturalism and the postmodern critique: towards a pedagogy of resistance and transformation', in Giroux, H. and McLaren, P. (eds) *Between the Borders: Pedagogy and the politics of cultural change*, London: Routledge.

Mirza, H. S. (1992) *Young, Female and Black*, London: Routledge.

Mirza, H. S. (1994) 'Making sense of the black female student experience in higher education', a paper given at the Society for Research in Higher Education (SRHE) conference, 'The Student Experience', University of York, December.

Mirza, H. S. (1995) 'Black women in higher education: defining a space/finding a place', in Morley, L. and Walsh, V. (eds) *Feminist Academics: Creative agents for change*, London: Taylor & Francis.

Modood, T. and Shiner, M. (1994) *Ethnic Minorities and Higher Education: Why are there differential rates of entry?* London: PSI Publishing.

Reay, D. (1997) *Class Work: Mothers involvement in their children's primary schooling*, London: Taylor & Francis.

Reay, D. and Mirza, H. S. (1998) 'Uncovering genealogies of the margin: black supplementary schooling', *British Journal of Sociology of Education*.

Solomos, J. (1988) *Black Youth, Racism and the State*, Cambridge: Cambridge University Press.

Solomos, J. and Back, L. (1995) *Race, Politics and Social Change*, London: Routledge.

Steady, F. C. (1993) 'Women and collective action: female models in transition', in James, S. M. and Busia,

A. P. (eds) *Theorising Black Feminisms: The visionary pragmatism of black women*, London: Routledge.

West, C. (1990) 'The new cultural politics of difference', in Ferguson, R., Gever, M., Min-ha, T. and West, C. (eds) *Out There: Marginalization and contemporary cultures*, New York: New Museum of Contemporary Art.

Young, I. M. (1990) 'The ideal of the community and the politics of difference', in Nicholson, L. (ed.) *Feminism/Post-modernism*, London: Routledge.

Yuval-Davis, N. (1994) 'Women, ethnicity and empowerment', in Bhavani, K. and Phoenix, A. (eds) *Shifting Identities, Shifting Racisms*, London: Sage.

Key terms

The following key terms appear in the text above. They have been defined below to aid with the reading of this item.

masculinist discourse masculine power/knowledges which are ways of thinking and speaking about the world that exclude feminist power/knowledges

praxis people's actions that are a result of the interaction of theory and practice. For example, black women's work in supplementary schools

radical pedagogy ways of teaching and learning that raise political consciousness of oppression and ways of fighting it

Questions

1 Evaluate the evidence that Mirza provides for black women's educational success as part of a transformative social movement.

2 What are the strategies described that black women employ for 'raising the race'. Suggest possible reasons why these are not used to the same extent by black men.

3 In what ways can Gilroy's analysis of black struggles for educational opportunities be described as masculinist?

4 Would supplementary schools for white working-class pupils work in the same way? Justify your answer.

Further reading

The following texts may represent a useful starting point for further investigation of the ideas contained within this chapter.

Primary texts

Sewell, T. (1997) *Black Masculinities and Schooling: How black boys survive modern schooling*, Stoke-on-Trent: Trentham Books.

Epstein, D. and Johnston, R. (1998) *Schooling Sexualities*, Milton Keynes: Open University Press.

Secondary texts

Gillborn, D. and Gipps, C. (1996) *Recent Research on the Achievements of Ethnic Minority Pupils*, London: Ofsted.

Heaton, T. and Lawson, T. (1996) *Education and Training*, Basingstoke: Macmillan.

Coursework suggestions

1 **Investigate the concept of compulsory heterosexuality in your school or college**

To do this you could organize a focus group (a taped discussion group) with some A level students. Read them the 'bunch of flowers story' at the beginning of reading 9.6 and tape the discussion that follows. You could also add in some questions or statements of your own. You would then need to transcribe all or parts of the tape. The data produced from the focus group could form the basis of a questionnaire or questions for in-depth interviews. Investigating sexualities is interesting but controversial and sensitive. Discuss your research plans carefully with your teacher first.

2 **Develop Diane Reay's work on habitus (reading 9.7) by investigating students' attitudes to helping in the classroom, particularly to clearing up after lessons**

This could involve participant observation in some very different classrooms, followed up by a questionnaire or in-depth interviews. You will have to choose your classrooms and sample carefully if you want to establish whether attitudes to 'helping in the classroom and clearing up' are affected by social class, gender and age. How do your findings compare to Diane Reay's?

10

Work, organizations and leisure

Chapter summary

Reading 10.1 **The political economy of the world's capitalisms** *page 270*

This reading is taken from Will Hutton's book *The State We're In,* an extremely influential critique of New Right political economy. He argues that the dominant American model adopted by the Thatcherites had disastrous consequences and instead suggests that there is a choice to be made between different capitalisms.

Reading 10.2 **Americanism and Fordism** *page 276*

Much of the contemporary talk of Fordism ignores the work done by Antonio Gramsci, who outlined the way in which Fordism was as much about the creation of a new way of life as it was about new production techniques. This overall analysis of the effect of new technologies has spread into the notion of post-Fordist society, which also encompasses more than the adoption of new production techniques.

Reading 10.3 **Fordism and post-Fordism** *page 280*

Krishan Kumar provides a clear summary of the main variants of the argument that we have moved from Fordism to post-Fordism, including the concentration on the development of the Third Italy. He also covers the more critical work of the French Regulation School with their notion of neo-Fordism

Reading 10.4 **From societies to flows** *page 285*

In *Economies of Signs and Space,* Lash and Urry focus on the cultural aspects of the phenomena of globalization. They argue that the idea of societies that are immune to outside influences, and which therefore have some control over their own social structures, is over and instead we need to reconceptualize sociology and the social sciences as the study of the various flows around the world that exist today and the implications of these flows.

Reading 10.5 **Capitalism, patriarchy and gender inequalities** *page 289*

One of the key arguments within the feminist movement concerns the origin of gender inequalities and this was usually a debate with two potential culprits: capitalism and patriarchy. Here Heidi Hartmann develops her argument that patriarchal relations pre-date capitalism but that capitalism built upon these, leading to the institution of gender inequalities in capitalist work organization.

Reading 10.6 **The labour process and the politics of production** *page 294*

Labour process theory, as originated by Harry Braverman, focused very much on objective processes within the workplace, whereas the starting point of Michael Burawoy's analysis is the subjective element in exploring the actuality of what goes on inside factories, with the development of his concept of 'factory regime'.

Reading 10.7 **The McDonaldization of society** *page 298*

George Ritzer argues that the principles of the fast-food restaurant are the most influential organizational model on offer today and that therefore McDonaldization is the latest version of the process of rationalization identified by Weber. This reading contains his own account of the wide-ranging influence of this model and some of the implications for wider society.

Reading 10.8 **The Devil makes work** *page 303*

The title of Clarke and Critcher's book *The Devil Makes Work,* alludes to the famous saying 'the Devil makes work for idle hands' and this is linked to their central thesis – namely that the development of leisure has not been characterized by evolution or progress but was a development that occurred out of social and political conflict and that the content of leisure has also been strictly controlled so that workers were only allowed to engage in *appropriate* leisure.

Introduction: Reading the sociology of work, organizations and leisure

Between the end of World War II and the early 1970s society could be characterized as planned, both in the political and economic sense. The state was important both economically and socially through the welfare state.

By the 1970s this model was beginning to fall into crisis and in the UK was followed by the New Right model which explicitly rejected state planning and argued instead for the adoption of free-market policies and the encouragement of the 'enterprise culture'. This policy was implemented for 18 years and is now itself falling into extreme unpopularity. This leads to the obvious question: what path will society take now? The question of economic organization will remain central to this for as long as we need to work to produce the things that we need. It is therefore the case that in the 1980s and 1990s economic sociology has been dominated by a variety of analyses which attempt to consider the shape of future developments on the basis of models that suggest that we have witnessed sharp changes which affect not only work but also other sectors of society.

Will Hutton (1996) offers his own critique of New Right thinking in *The State We're In* (**reading 10.1**), arguing that the central problem of the UK economy was the domination of finance capital and that, in so far as New Right reforms pushed us more towards the American model of capitalism, more problems would arise. He argues that there are, however, at least three very different models of capitalism which a society could choose to follow and in the extract in this book he looks at some of the key differences between the American, the German and the Japanese models of capitalism.

The most notable debate about the nature of the times we are living through has been characterized as the argument that we are moving from Fordist to post-Fordist times. The analysis of Fordism was first developed by Antonio Gramsci (1971) (**reading 10.2**) who suggested that it represented attempts to develop a new way of living based on mass production and a much more planned society. The issue was no doubt interesting to a Marxist concerned not only with the question of how one could plan society but also with the dynamic realities of capitalism.

The characteristics of Fordism are the application of scientific management (i.e. procedures designed to measure and strictly regulate the effort and output of workers) to achieve greater productivity and with the application of economies of scale (where producing things on a large-scale reduces the unit cost) to make mass production a reality. Along with this went a number of other important developments. Firstly, in order to protect the large sums invested in mass production there was the desire to avoid the booms and slumps which were evident in capitalism (and were at the time shown in the Great Depression of 1929–32). This required thinking about state planning of economic matters – an issue on which the experience of government direction of the economy in the two World Wars provided some ideas. It is also clear that in order to sustain mass production, mass consumption was necessary and this necessitated a number of developments, including the welfare state, to reduce unemployment and to provide everyone with income at a certain level.

This model became the generally adopted model of capitalism after World War II, leading in the UK to the adoption of Keynesian demand management policies (where the government actively intervened in the economy to regulate the overall level of demand) and the Beveridge blueprint for the welfare state.

However, by the early 1970s this Keynesian model was falling into crisis. A number of indicators of this can be found, notably in the move to flexible exchange rates and the economic recessions from the mid-1970s onwards. The question arose of whether this was a crisis that would result in the growth of a qualitatively different form of capitalist organization and it is those who answer in the positive who have developed the notion of a post-Fordist society. This view is generally associated with radical, sometimes Marxist, writers who start out by considering the way in which adopting a particular form of production technology has implications for structures in the rest of society. The suggestion is therefore that around the 1970s the Fordist-organized model of capitalism began to fall into crisis and is being replaced with a new post-Fordist model based on labour flexibility, production fragmentation and product specialization in the workplace and that this will have key implications for other activities in society, notably politics, the state and the question of the agency of social and political change. Kumar (1995) outlines the many varieties of this type of analysis in **reading 10.3**, as well as the more radical viewpoint of the French Regulation School thinkers with their analysis of the rise of neo-Fordism.

As well as an extract from Gramsci (1971) – looking at the way Henry Ford sought not only to regulate the life of his workers in the workplace but also outside as well, with the employment of detectives to spy on his workers sex lives and to see if they were drinking too heavily – we also include an extract from Lash and Urry (1994) who talk of the implications of the move from organized to disorganized capitalism. In reading 10.4 – focusing on the implications of the processes of globalization – they argue that the social scientific concentration on societies as stable social structures is being undermined by these processes, and they argue for a need to concentrate instead on these global flows in order to understand social life today.

The issue of gender inequalities in the workplace has been an important debate among feminist and Marxist sociologists. The implication of some Marxist writers was that gender inequalities arose with capitalism and that therefore once capitalism was overthrown then they would disappear. This notion that socialism was the answer to gender inequality was not accepted by radical feminists who argued that the system of patriarchy which led to the oppression of women predated capitalism and would therefore not logically end with it. Heidi Hartmann (1982) offers, in reading 10.5, an attempted synthesis of these two positions by showing the way in which an examination of the anthropological arguments about the origins of gender inequality – alongside an examination of how these were transformed by capitalism – can be used to explain gender inequalities at work today. Her work along with the work of Sylvia Walby (1990), provides the basis of the dual-system approach, which argues that in order to explain gender inequalities it is necessary to consider both the role of capitalism and patriarchy.

One of the key developments in relation to an understanding of the sociology of work and workers is the labour process approach developed by Harry Braverman (1974). He argued that capitalism deskilled workers by separating off the processes of conception and execution and therefore reducing the skill level needed in general workers, in order to cheapen their wage rate and thereby increase profits. Since that time, labour process theory has been a central part of Marxist analyses of the workplace. However, one of the key criticisms of Braverman was that he only really considered workers' relations to their bosses in terms of objective criteria, whereas Marx had also considered the importance of the subjective class consciousness of workers. This notion of consciousness is central to the concept of hegemony – also developed by Antonio Gramsci – and it is this that informs the alternative notion of the labour process outlined by Michael Burawoy (1985). In reading 10.6, Burawoy argues that we need to look at the way relations inside a workplace (what he calls the 'factory regime') contribute, along with an analysis of the labour process, to an overall understanding of workplace relations. He also considers the variety of production regimes which can be found under capitalism and state socialism.

In the sphere of the study of organizations one of the most important classical contributions – which

arguably led to the founding of the specialized sociological study of organizations – was Weber's theory of rationalization. Weber argued that the development of rational ways of operating, including the development of organizations, would allow much more efficiency in economic operations, but he also argued that there was a danger that such ways would come to constitute an 'iron cage' which would suffocate individual freedom. This idea has had a number of applications and one of the latest is George Ritzer's (1993) argument that the key principles underlining organizational developments in the contemporary USA, and indeed the world, are those developed and applied by the fast-food giants McDonald's (see reading 10.7). As with Weber, he is ambivalent about the potential of this development and in this extract he does point to some of the potential positive developments of this change while overall adopting a fairly critical tone in terms of the implications for society.

In relation to the study of leisure the early evolutionary progress theories suggested that somehow leisure had evolved and that as time went on more and more time would be devoted to leisure as less and less time was devoted to work. This rather simplistic and optimistic picture has, like much of those early evolutionary functionalist-inspired views, not come to pass. Clarke and Critcher (1985) (reading 10.8) offer an alternative analysis of the development of leisure, informed by notions of cultural politics and social and political struggles. There are discussions here of the way in which capitalists wished to exert some control over the way the workers used their leisure time and this provides echoes of how similar concerns developed, much later, with the interventions of Henry Ford (as discussed by Antonio Gramsci in reading 10.2).

It is undoubtedly true that since the 1970s something fairly dramatic has happened to the economic spheres of society and at the time of writing the Asian tiger economies, which had been praised as the latest boom to hit town, are now revealed as economic basket cases, requiring urgent intervention from the International Monetary Fund (IMF). It is also the case – as the *Economist* magazine has revealed – that the black economy in Russia is the same size as the official economy, revealing the emergence of a sizeable element of the global economy in the hands of gangsters and crooks. Fukuyama's (1992) capitalist victory note about the 'end of history' seems inappropriately optimistic now and the debates about the direction the world economy is taking and the implications of this for the rest of social life, which form the centrepiece of this chapter, seem even more important today than five years ago.

They also seem considerably more stimulating than rather out-dated rehearsals of the Taylor versus

Braverman argument about the merits of scientific management – an argument still valid, but needing to be supplemented by the widening out of the debate and the greater number of theoretically informed participants in this debate.

References

Braverman, H. (1974) *Labour and Monopoly Capital*, London: Monthly Review Press.

Fukuyama, F. (1992) *The End of History and the Last Man*, Harmondsworth: Penguin.

Walby, S. (1990) *Theorising Patriarchy*, Oxford: Blackwell.

Reading 10.1 **The political economy of the world's capitalisms**

Will Hutton (from) *The State We're In* (1996) London: Vintage, pp. 257–9, 262–4, 266–74, 277 and 281–4.

Editorial comments

Will Hutton's book presents a clear critique of the effectiveness of the free-market policies adopted by the New Right. These policies, he argues, have led to economic decline and – because they are guided by short-term considerations of profit and loss – they do not offer a basis for economic renewal. He offers instead the model of German capitalism, based on much more government intervention and long-term aims, as the basis for economic renewal. His argument touches upon the social consequences of the failure of Thatcherite economic performance on society. This extract particularly focuses on his argument that there are important differences among the world's capitalisms.

The political economy of the world's capitalisms

EUROPEAN, AMERICAN AND Japanese capitalism each have distinctive characteristics. They are all, of course, based on private property and the legal right to make private profits by production and exchange in markets; and they all possess stock markets, income tax and social security systems that make them seem part of the same generic type of society. These features have persuaded some to argue that Western capitalism is converging towards an Anglo-American norm – but that is gravely to misread the depth of the institutional and cultural differences between capitalisms.

For the similarities disguise vast differences between the social and economic purpose of apparently similar institutions, so that each capitalist structure ends up with very different specific capacities and cultures which are very hard to change. ...

The US model

American capitalism is commonly regarded as the most individualistic and libertarian of all. Its financial system is highly market based; the returns it requires are very high; and it is therefore important that US corporations can hire and fire their workforces freely to produce the profits their shareholders demand. Unions are weak, employment regulation is minimal and the turnover of workers is high as companies trim their staff to market demands. One worker in five expects to lose his or her job within the next year, according to a 1993 survey, and another 20 per cent expected a spell of temporary unemployment (Freeman, 1994).

There is little spending on social welfare and levels of corporate and personal taxation are low. Welfare entitlements are tightly monitored and means-tested; social security contributions are at the lower end of the international scale. However the US has proved an effective generator of jobs – although by European standards they are astonishingly poorly-paid, with the bottom tenth of the workforce earning 38 per cent of median earnings (compared with the European average of 67 per cent of median earnings). Workers are assumed to be willing to move home in order to work, and to accept low wages with social security acting only as a safety-net of last resort. Unemployment insurance lasts for a mere six months and replaces only 36 per cent of average earnings.

There are few co-operative industrial combines along Japanese and East Asian lines. There is tough anti-monopoly legislation, and the typical firm is owned by stock-holders, a majority of them financial institutions like pension funds, who trade their shares on the stock market while the company operates in a highly competitive arena for its sales. All companies can expect to be taken over or merged when predatory companies buy their shares on the stock market, and this puts a high premium on maintaining the growth of short-term profits and dividend pay-outs to sustain the share price at all costs. Firms' relations with their suppliers are strictly market-driven, with contracts put out to tender and allocated to the lowest bidder. There is little or no public ownership; whatever social objectives are deemed essential are prosecuted through federal and state regulatory authorities. The system is outwardly almost purely capitalist, its apologists celebrating its job-creating and innovative qualities and critics inveighing against its promotion of consumption over longterm investment, its systemic inequality and lack of social provision.

The US has, in fact, retained important institutional shelters against the full blast of competition and these have become ways of expressing co-operative common purpose. At the **federal** level many of these institutions were inaugurated during President Roosevelt's **New Deal** which, along with a security safety net and creative make-work programmes, put in place a system of financial regulation, innovative government financial institutions and a system of deposit insurance that has helped mitigate the worst proclivities of the US financial system to this day. ...

The US may be the home of pristine capitalism but it is qualified by a vigorous public and private morality. This is the home of the most aggressive venture capital industry on earth; but also of the largest private charitable foundations. Bill Gates, chairman of computer giant, Microsoft, followed Ford, Rockefeller and others in giving up almost all of his fortune to a private foundation. The Protestant ethic, although weakening, remains an important underpinning of the US value system and a source of co-operative economic strength.

Social market Europe

The second distinctive species of capitalism is that of Germany, its neighbours in the European Union and of Scandinavia. This is broadly the world of the **social market**, and once again the political, economic and social institutions hang together to form an interdependent web. Capital and labour operate in partnership; the financial system is less market-based than in the US and thus more committed to the enterprises it finances; the welfare structure is more all-encompassing and inclusive and the political system has a high degree of formal power sharing. Yet this social web still vibrates to the signals sent by the price mechanism; it may be regulated, but it conforms to market imperatives. It is a social *market*.

The great benefit of the system is that its institutional structures favour co-operation, high productivity and

investment. The disadvantage is that when the external environment becomes more uncertain, the system finds restructuring more difficult because the centres of power are more diffuse and the bureaucratic regulatory network can slow down firms' responses. None the less restructuring is achievable eventually. In the recent German recession Volkswagen was able to negotiate wage cuts and reduce working hours in agreement with its unions, and Daimler Benz slashed its labour costs by over DM1.5 billion within a year.

At the heart of the European model is the notion of a rule-governed, competitive market whose power to generate wealth is intimately linked with social cohesion. The partnership between capital and labour embodied in *mitbestimmung* (or co-decision making) at both board and works council level in Germany represents a bargain between manager and unions. Unions forgo the right to strike and to pursue their self-interest regardless of the firm's plight; but management eschews the right to run the business autocratically in favour of the shareholders' narrow interests. Instead there is a compromise in favour of concerted and co-operative behaviour aimed at boosting production and investment.

Labour has to recognize the legitimacy of capital; and capital the rights of labour. Seventy-five per cent of German workers are covered by union-negotiated industry-wide wage agreements – which is a major concession by management; on the other hand the agreements are legally binding and a strike can only be called once the contract has expired – a major concession by labour. If the big unions represent a majority of workers, so the employers' organizations represent most of German industry. Both capital and labour are represented by all-encompassing self-governing organizations which are allowed to manage wages and industrial relations. As a result labour turnover rates are lower than in the US and wages considerably higher.

This collaboration is interdependent with the rest of the economic, social and political system. In order for managers and workers to run enterprises collaboratively, financial stakeholders have to concede that they cannot maximize their returns in the short run. ...

This stability of ownership and financial support is matched by a welfare system – the *sozialstaat* – which offers a high degree of social protection, the visible expression of social solidarity. Pensions and unemployment benefit are high in relation to average earnings, and the universal health and education systems underwrite Germany's famous sense of social well-being. ...

One of the inevitable consequences of the system is high social overheads for both employers and employees. Health, pension, and unemployment insurance together with taxation make up one of the highest tax burdens in the industrialized world; but, as Wolfgang Streeck argues, the 'social production' of skilled workers, powerful unions and the strong welfare system help to raise the general strength of the economy. ...

The usefulness of Germany's system of decentralized power is revealed in the strength of the famous *Mittelstand* – the medium-sized business sector that is proportionally nearly twice the size of its counterpart in Britain. These family-owned companies are the backbone of German industry, but they owe their strength as much to the institutional support around them as to the dynamism of their flexible and innovative owners. ...

Under the pressure of globalization and intense cost competition the *Mittelstand* has begun to lose ground, and there are fears that large German firms are being compelled to get their supplies in low-cost countries while overseas producers – notably the Japanese – are winning business in the *Mittelstand*'s heartland. German banks, under the same pressures, are allegedly becoming more short-term in their time horizons. Even more threatening is the rise of so-called lean production in which large firms, determined to emulate the Japanese and contain costs by subcontracting out work and insisting on **'just-in-time'** delivery to cut inventories, are asking suppliers to be ever more flexible. This requires heavy new investment even as prices are being pared to the bone, and many companies lack the financial muscle to adopt a more hard-nosed relationship with major buyers. Yet in front of these challenges the German instinct is not to abandon but to update and renew its institutional network – intensifying its training effort, improving systems of technology transfer and developing new networks to share market information. Above all the banks intend to stand by their industrial companies.

Underpinning the notion of the social market is a complex value system that emphasizes both the values of order and solidarity. From the Prussian tradition comes a sense of the need for discipline and for a regulated order in human affairs; from Catholicism the tradition of social solidarity and 'subsidiarity' – the location of decision making as close as possible to those who are affected by it. These twin streams in German thinking unite with a third: an accent on the real values of production over those of finance. ...

The social market is a self-conscious way for a capitalist economy to blend the gains from competition with those from co-operation – and the new world of 'lean production', where so much depends on the collaboration between firms and their sub-contractors, will emphasize its strengths. Far from capitulating to the British and American style of capitalism, the social market economy is in the throes of adapting to changed conditions in a unique way. France has set out to copy its main strengths, and Eastern Europe and even the former Soviet Union are looking to this model as their disillusion with the Anglo-Saxon variant grows. It has not failed; the question is how far it can succeed in the new environment.

East Asian capitalism – 'peoplism'

The third distinctive form of world capitalism, and currently the most dynamic, is that of Japan, the East Asian tigers and the emergent Chinese genre. Although again there are variants within this wider culture, there is enough common ground to attempt a descriptive synthesis under a common label. Here the attempt to capture the gains from co-operation in a competitive environment has been taken to its most extreme. East Asian and particularly Japanese capitalist structures emphasise trust, continuity, reputation and cooperation in economic relationships. Competition is ferocious, but co-operation is extensive; the juxtaposition of apparently inconsistent forms of behaviour may strike those schooled in Anglo-American capitalism as irrational, but for the Japanese the tension actually enhances the strength of each. There is even a widely quoted phrase for it – *kyoryoku shi nagara kyosa* – literally 'co-operating while competing', so that out of the subsequent chaos comes harmony.

As a result human relations and the necessity of nurturing them are centre stage; the dominant factor of production is labour, so that one Japanese analyst has been moved to call the system 'peoplism'. This is probably overstating the humanity of an economy which demands long hours and often demeaning working conditions (Kamata, 1984), but it none the less captures the important stress on personal networks and human relationships. Contracts are even less price mediated than in the European social market economy; wealth creation and productivity are seen to come from co-operative longterm relationships for which the Japanese are justly famous, and which Alan Blinder (1982) calls a 'relational market'. With Japan and East Asia growing explosively, its institutional structure and value system commands increasing respect and even fear; for example, if Japan maintains its current rates of investment as a proportion of national output, nearly a third as high again as the US, then it will be the largest economy in the world by 2005 while East Asia as a whole will become the dominant force in world output and trade by the first decade of the next century.

Given Japan's track record it is unsurprising that the Japanese model has been extensively copied. Its regulated financial system is the least market-based, most traditional, above all most committed to its customers, of all the three principal capitalist variants.

Firms' shares are held tightly in a system of cross-holdings with sister firms in other industry groups, the *kigyo shudan* and *keiretsu*, and the required returns are low. Secure financial backing has allowed Japanese firms to cultivate an extraordinary series of innovations in working practices with both shop floor workers and suppliers – and these efficiencies have placed the economy firmly in a virtuous circle in which growth, investment, financial commitment, worker/supplier productivity and continual quality upgrading become mutually reinforcing.

The firm is the core social unit of which individuals are *members* rather than simply workers. Unions are organized around the firm, which promises life-time employment, social protection and a pension, and the firm expects commitment in return. Taxation is at the lower end of the international scale, but so is income inequality; senior managers earn a mere two or three times the average wage. The culture is firmly production-oriented, rooted in Japan's anxiety to catch up with the West which was intensified by the trauma of losing the Second World War.

The state is the architect of these institutional relationships; it seeks to build consensus and then guides firms and the financial system in the direction established by the consensus. In this respect it is nearer to the German social market state, and British notions of parliamentary sovereignty and top-down governance are strikingly at odds with the Japanese conception of government by consent. The boundaries between government, society and economy are remarkably porous, and there is great emphasis on inclusiveness, on respect for various points of view and on the achievement of harmony, while at the same time ensuring that business objectives are at the heart of Japan plc's concerns. On the other hand it means that the country has no hard centre, and fraud and corruption are widespread. Responsibility is diffuse and accountability low. ...

Competition, in a sense, is confined to the market where goods and services are offered to the final consumer but in all the intervening stages of production there is an accent on nurturing longterm relationships and capturing the gains from co-operation that game theory and New Keynesian economics promise.

There are four overlapping series of relationships – with finance, employees and subcontractors and, of course, with government. ... Shares, which in the Anglo-Saxon tradition are titles to a claim on the company's profits in the form of dividends and which are expected to be bought and sold on the stock market, are in Japan tokens of a longterm commitment. ...

The role of shares as tokens of relationship also extends into production and to the tiers of subcontractors who, by allowing great flexibility of production, have allowed the Japanese economy to pioneer the new techniques of lean production. While US manufacturers effectively auction their sub-contract work, Japanese industrialists enmesh themselves in a network of cross-shareholdings with their subcontractors. These non-financial *kieretsu* cross-shareholdings make up another 30 per cent of the Tokyo stock exchange, complementing the 40 per cent held by the *kigyo shudan*, indicating just how large the 'relational market' in Japan has become. ...

Lifetime employment also carries a message about those who are unemployed; to lose your job implies that the original firm was in some way unhappy with you as a worker, that you are a 'lemon': an undesirable worker. Workers are under pressure not to lose their jobs, which means that their income in the long run will depend on the welfare of the firm which they will not want to leave. Hence the willingness to co-operate in teams to improve productivity, rather than piggy-backing on others' efforts. The same applies at the top end of the scale: chief executives will have peers who have been in the firm as long as they have so, as Ronald Dore (Aoki and Dore, 1994) argues, they will be aware of the general opinion that two or three of their contemporaries 'could have done the job just or almost just as well. This knowledge, on the part of CEOs, acts as a useful curb on both greed and megalomania'.

The firm has become the core social unit in Japanese society. It trains and retrains its workers. It offers them a measure of social security. It is the adaptive and creative organization which constructs networks of finance, teams of workers, and relationships with subcontracting firms that are at the heart of the Japanese system. Paramount above all else is the desire continually to upgrade ...

This private institutional network is backed by a public infrastructure that supports economic growth and domestic industry. ...

The constitution of the Japanese firm and its relationship with government, finance and workforce is not a 'natural' evolution. It has developed from a series of experiments about what works best, fired by an overwhelming sense that the country had to catch up – a determination only strengthened by losing the war. Britain, by contrast, was the first country to industrialize. It has never lost a war. The British élite has no sense it needs to catch up, that its system doesn't work and cannot recognize that what passes for timeless economic truth is no more than a particular economic ideology. Britain's chances of reproducing what is happening in East Asia seem negligible. ...

Britain

The contrast between British capitalism and its rivals is marked. The financial system demands the same

A comparison of four systems

Characteristic	American capitalism	Japanese capitalism	European social market	British capitalism
Basic principle				
Dominant factor of production	capital	labour	partnership	capital
'Public' tradition	medium	high	high	low
Centralization	low	medium	medium	high
Reliance on price-mediated markets	high	low	medium	high
Supply relations	arms-length price-driven	close enduring	bureaucracy planned	arms-length price-driven
Industrial groups	partial, defence, etc.	very high	high	low
Extent privatized	high	high	medium	high
Financial system				
Market structure	anonymous securitized	personal committed	bureaucracy committed	uncommitted marketized
Banking system	advanced marketized regional	traditional regulated concentrated	traditional regulated regional	advanced marketized centralized
Stock market	v. important	unimportant	unimportant	v. important
Required returns	high	low	medium	high
Labour market				
Job security	low	high	high	low
Labour mobility	high	low	medium	medium
Labour/management	adversarial	co-operative	co-operative	adversarial
Pay differential	large	small	medium	large
Turnover	high	low	medium	medium
Skills	medium	high	high	poor
Union structure	sector-based	firm-based	industry-wide	craft
Strength	low	low	high	low
The firm				
Main goal	profits	market share stable jobs	market share fulfilment	profits
Role top manager	boss-king autocratic	consensus	consensus	boss-king hierarchy
Social overheads	low	low	high	medium, down
Welfare system				
Basic principle	liberal	corporatist	corporatist social democracy	mixed
Universal transfers	low	medium	high	medium, down
Means-testing	high	medium	low	medium, up
Degree education tiered by class	high	medium	medium	high
Private welfare	high	medium	low	medium, up
Government policies				
Role of government	limited adversarial	extensive co-operative	encompassing	strong adversarial
Openness to trade	quite open	least open	quite open	open
Industrial policy	little	high	high	non-existent
Top income tax	low	low	high	medium

(adapted and extended from Alan Blinder, 1982)

high returns from companies, with the same lack of commitment, as in the US; but there is not even the saving grace of statutory regulation and strong regional or state banks to moderate the consequences of such pressure: centralization in London means that the entire economy suffers.

The labour market has many of the worst features of the US – ranging from high turnover to inequality of income – but without the compensating virtues of mobility and managerial dynamism. Nor is there an institutional structure which would allow firms to develop the co-operative, community-based capitalism of Japan and East Asia; examples of such networks are rare and are the exceptions that prove the rule. Arms-length, price-mediated relationships extend all the way from the shop floor to the Stock Exchange. The British medium-sized business sector – the equivalent of the *Mittelstand* – is fragile and small in size.

The accompanying table sets out the principal features of the four capitalist systems. It is not exhaustive and merely attempts to isolate the key features of each variant. Each is an interdependent whole, in which the character of one set of institutions interacts with the others; each shapes and is in turn shaped by the whole system. In Britain, profit-maximizing firms that give the building of market share a low priority have to be run autocratically in order to produce the kind of shareholder returns that the financial system demands – and that in turn has consequences for the way the labour market is run: the less committed the financial system, the less firms are able to offer lifetime employment and the less willing they are to undertake training.

Firms whose relations with their workers and suppliers are mediated solely by price have to have low social overheads in order to maintain their competitive position; as a result the welfare system in Britain and America is necessarily less ambitious than it is in social market Europe. The same unwillingness to see the firm as an organic enterprise involving all its stakeholders extends to their attributes to the wider society: British firms resent levies to pay for training, for example, both because they seem to make their operations less competitive and because they are an attempt to impose obligations they do not feel they have. In this kind of market economy everybody looks after themselves.

None the less Britain does have the legacy of the social settlement of 1945. While welfare falls below mainland European levels it is still significantly more universal in scope and generous than in the US. The result is that the country once again gets the worst of both worlds; it has neither low enough taxes nor strong enough institutions of social solidarity and so falls between the American and European stools. The introduction of market principles into education, health, criminal justice, housing, television, pensions and social provision is actively eroding social cohesion, and undermining society.

The tradition of public spirit, common interest and national purpose which variously imbues social market Europe, the US and East Asian capitalism is absent in Britain. The private realm and the market are celebrated as the only efficient and responsive forms of organization, while notions of public and common interest are dismissed as 'bureaucratic', 'interventionist' or 'socialist'. Nor is it easy to mobilize the country in the name of national purpose when it is not clear what united purpose an increasingly divided and atomized society might have. The financial markets have no common cause with the medium-sized business sector, and neither have any sense of solidarity with the growing numbers of the excluded and marginalized. Nor is the parliamentary system a potential source of integration and national leadership.

The failure of this institutional matrix and value system to fit into the rest of Western Europe is clear, but in a world where the risk of trade tensions, financial instability and regional trade controls is growing it is apparent that Britain has no option but to stay a member of the European bloc. If that membership is not going to continue to be a source of tension, the structures of British capitalism will have to change. The élite do not want this to happen, yet change they must. How is change to be brought about? And what are the chances of success?

References

Aoki, M. and Dore, R. (eds) (1994) *The Japanese Firm*, Oxford: Clarendon.

Blinder, A. (1982) 'Should the former socialist economies look east or west for a model?', paper presented to the 10th World Congress of the International Economic Association in Moscow, August 1982.

Freeman, R. (1994) 'Jobs in the USA', *New Economy*, Spring.

Kamata, S. (1984) *Japan in the Passing Lane*, London: Unwin.

Key terms

The following key terms appear in the text above. They have been defined below to aid with the reading of this item.

federal the national level in the USA, as opposed to the individual states which form the United States. The political system of the USA is federal, which means more autonomy is given to individual states and less power to central government than in comparable regimes such as the UK. The German political system is also strongly federalist

New Deal the policy adopted in America in the 1930s after the Great Crash of 1929 which did involve some state intervention in the economy and some social welfare provision

social market an alternative notion of capitalism to the free market, where social imperatives such as social cohesion are seen to have a higher value and where partnership is seen as more important

just-in-time processes that originated in Japanese industry, whereby component parts are supplied just in time to be used. As a result the costs of storage space are minimized and overall costs reduced

Questions

1 Identify the four types of capitalism identified by Hutton.

2 What threat to the continued existence of the German social market model is identified by Hutton?

3 Summarize in your own words the differences between the four types of capitalism identified by Hutton in the table in this reading.

4 Suggest which overall approach seems to underline the economic policies of the present UK government.

5 How far do you agree with Hutton's analysis that Britain 'gets the worst of both worlds'?

Reading 10.2 **Americanism and Fordism**

Antonio Gramsci (from) 'Americanism and Fordism', in A. Gramsci, *Selections from the Prison Notebooks* (1971) London: Lawrence & Wishart, p. 299–304 and 308–12.

Editorial comments

Much contemporary debate surrounds the notion that we have moved from Fordist society to post-Fordist society. This analysis builds upon the original analysis of Fordism outlined by Antonio Gramsci in a fascist jail around 1931. (Being imprisoned and wishing to avoid the attentions of the fascist censor explains some of the somewhat obscure language used.) In this article, he examines the implications of the rise of mass production not only in terms of the economy but also in its social effects and the way Fordism was about creating a new type of man. The article provides a classical example of the application of Marxism to a concrete historical development.

Americanism and Fordism

IN THE **POSTWAR period** there has been a crisis of morals of unique proportions, but it took place in opposition to a form of coercion which had not been imposed in order to create habits suited to forms of work but arose from the necessities, admitted as transitory, of wartime life and life in the trenches. This pressure involved a particular repression of sexual instincts, even the most normal, among great masses of young people, and the crisis which broke out with the return to normal life was made even more violent by the disappearance of so many young men and by a permanent disequilibrium in the numerical proportions of individuals of the two sexes. The institutions connected with sexual life were profoundly shaken and new forms of enlightened utopias developed around the sexual question. The crisis was made even more violent, and still is, by the fact that it affected all strata of the population and came into conflict with the necessities of the new methods of work which were meanwhile beginning to impose themselves.

(**Taylorism** and rationalisation in general.) These new methods demand a rigorous discipline of the sexual instincts (at the level of the nervous system) and with it a strengthening of the 'family' in the wide sense (rather than a particular form of the familial system) and of the regulation and stability of sexual relations.

It is worth insisting on the fact that in the sexual field the most depraving and 'regressive' ideological factor is the enlightened and libertarian conception proper to those classes which are not tightly bound to productive work and spread by them among the working classes. This element becomes particularly serious in a state where the working masses are no longer subject to coercive pressure from a superior class and where the new methods of production and work have to be acquired by means of reciprocal persuasion and by convictions proposed and accepted by each individual. A two-fold situation can then create itself in which there is an inherent conflict between the 'verbal' ideology which recognizes the new necessities and the real 'animal' practice which prevents physical bodies from effectively acquiring the new attitudes. In this case one gets the formation of what can be called a situation of totalitarian social hypocrisy. Why totalitarian? In other situations the popular strata are compelled to practise 'virtue'. Those who preach it do not practice it, although they pay it verbal homage. The hypocrisy is therefore a question of strata: it is not total. This is a situation which cannot last, and is certain to lead to a crisis of libertinism, but only when the masses have already assimilated 'virtue' in the form of more or less permanent habits, that is with ever-decreasing oscillations. On the other hand, in the case where no coercive pressure is exercised by a superior class, 'virtue' is affirmed in generic terms but is not practised either through conviction or through coercion, with the result that the psychophysical attitudes necessary for the new methods of work are not acquired. The crisis can become 'permanent' – that is, potentially catastrophic – since it can be resolved only by coercion. This coercion is a new type, in that it is exercised by the *élite* of a class over the rest of that same class. It can also only be self-coercion and therefore self-discipline. In any case in the sphere of sexual relations what can be opposed to this function of the *élites* is the enlightened and libertarian mentality. The struggle against the libertarian conception means therefore precisely creating the *élites* necessary for the historical task, or at least developing them so that their function is extended to cover all spheres of human activity.

Rationalization of production and work

... These activities were less disconnected than might appear, since the new methods of work are inseparable from a specific mode of living and of thinking and feeling life. One cannot have success in one field without tangible results in the other. In America rationalization of work and prohibition are undoubtedly connected. The enquiries conducted by the industrialists into the workers' private lives and the inspection services created by some firms to control the 'morality' of their workers are necessities of the new methods of work. People who laugh at these initiatives (failures though they were) and see in them only a hypocritical manifestation of 'puritanism' thereby deny themselves any possibility of understanding the importance, significance and objective import of the American phenomenon, which is *also* the biggest collective effort to date to create, with unprecedented speed, and with a consciousness of purpose unmatched in history, a new type of worker and of man. The expression 'consciousness of purpose' might appear humorous to say the least to anyone who recalls Taylor's phrase about the 'trained gorilla' (1911). Taylor is in fact expressing with brutal cynicism the purpose of American society – developing in the worker to the highest degree automatic and mechanical attitudes, breaking up the old psychophysical nexus of qualified professional work, which demands a certain active participation of intelligence, fantasy and initiative on the part of the worker, and reducing productive operations exclusively to the mechanical, physical aspect. But these things, in reality, are not original or novel: they represent simply the most recent phase of a long process which began with industrialism itself. This phase is more intense than preceding phases, and manifests itself in more brutal forms, but it is a phase which will itself be superseded by the creation of a psycho-physical nexus of a new type, both different from its predecessors and undoubtedly *superior*. A forced selection will ineluctably take place; a part of the old working class will be pitilessly eliminated from the world of labour, and perhaps from the world *tout court*.

It is from this point of view that one should study the 'puritanical' initiative of American industrialists like Ford. It is certain that they are not concerned with the 'humanity' or the 'spirituality' of the worker, which are immediately smashed. This 'humanity and spirituality' cannot be realized except in the world of production and work and in productive 'creation'. They exist most in the artisan, in the 'demiurge', when the worker's personality was reflected whole in the object created and when the link between art and labour was still very strong. But it is precisely against this 'humanism' that the new industrialism is fighting. 'Puritanical' initiatives simply have the purpose of preserving, outside of work, a certain psycho-physical equilibrium which prevents the physiological collapse of the worker, exhausted by the new method of production. This equilibrium can only be something purely external and mechanical, but it can become internalized if it is proposed by the worker himself, and not imposed from the outside, if it is proposed by a new form of society, with appropriate and original methods. American industrialists are concerned to maintain the continuity of the physical and muscular-nervous efficiency of the worker. It is in their interests to have a stable, skilled labour force, a permanently well-adjusted complex, because the human complex (the collective worker) of an enterprise is also a machine which cannot, without considerable loss, be taken to pieces too often and renewed with single new parts.

The element of so-called high wages also depends on this necessity. It is the instrument used to select and maintain in stability a skilled labour force suited to the system of production and work. But high wages are a double-edged weapon. It is necessary for the worker to spend his extra money 'rationally' to maintain, renew and, if possible, increase his muscular-nervous efficiency and not to corrode or destroy it. Thus the struggle against alcohol, the most dangerous agent of destruction of labouring power, becomes a function of the state. It is possible for other 'puritanical' struggles as well to become functions of the state if the private initiative of the industrialists proves insufficient or if a moral crisis breaks out among the working masses which is too profound and too widespread, as might happen as a result of a long and widespread crisis of unemployment.

The sexual question is again connected with that of alcohol. Abuse and irregularity of sexual functions is, after alcoholism, the most dangerous enemy of nervous energies, and it is commonly observed that 'obsessional' work provokes alcoholic and sexual depravation. The attempts made by Ford, with the aid of a body of inspectors, to intervene in the private lives of his employees and to control how they spent their wages and how they lived is an indication of these tendencies. Though these tendencies are still only 'private' or only latent, they could become, at a certain point, state ideology, inserting themselves into traditional puritanism and presenting themselves as a renaissance of the pioneer morality and as the 'true' America (etc.). The most noteworthy fact in the American phenomenon in relation to these manifestations is the gap which has been formed and is likely to be increasingly accentuated, between the morality and way of life of the workers and those of other strata of the population. ...

Taylorism and the mechanization of the worker

Taylorism supposedly produces a gap between manual labour and the 'human content' of work. On this subject some useful observations can be made on the basis of past history and specifically of those professions thought of as amongst the most intellectual, that is to say the professions connected with the reproduction of texts for publication or other forms of diffusion and transmission: the scribes of the days before the invention of printing, compositors on hand presses, linotype operators, stenographers and typists. If one thinks about it, it is clear that in these trades the process of adaptation to mechanization is more difficult than elsewhere. Why? Because it is so hard to reach the height of professional qualification when this requires of the worker that he should 'forget' or not think about the intellectual content of the text he is reproducing: this in order to be able, if he is a scribe, to fix his attention exclusively on the calligraphic form of the single letters; or to be able to break down phrases into 'abstract' words and then words into characters, and rapidly select the pieces of lead in the cases; or to be able to break down not single words but groups of words, in the context of

discourse, and group them mechanically into shorthand notation; or to acquire speed in typing, etc. The worker's interest in the intellectual content of the text can be measured from his mistakes. In other words, it is a professional failing. Conversely his qualification is commensurate with his lack of intellectual interest, i.e. the extent to which he has become 'mechanized'. The mediaeval copyist who was interested in the text changed the spelling, the morphology and the syntax of the text he was copying; he missed out entire passages which because of his meagre culture he could not understand; the train of thoughts aroused in his mind by his interest in the text led him to interpolate glosses and observations; if his language or dialect was different from that of the text he would introduce nuances deriving from his own speech: he was a bad scribe because in reality he was 'remaking' the text. The slow speed of the art of writing in the Middle Ages explains many of these weaknesses: there was too much time in which to reflect, and consequently 'mechanization' was more difficult. The compositor has to be much quicker; he has to keep his hands and eyes constantly in movement, and this makes his mechanization easier. But if one really thinks about it, the effort that these workers have to make in order to isolate from the often fascinating intellectual content of a text (and the more fascinating it is the less work is done and the less well) its written symbolization, this perhaps is the greatest effort that can be required in any trade. However it is done, and it is not the spiritual death of man. Once the process of adaptation has been completed, what really happens is that the brain of the worker, far from being mummified, reaches a state of complete freedom. The only thing that is completely mechanicized is the physical gesture; the memory of the trade, reduced to simple gestures repeated at an intense rhythm, 'nestles' in the muscular and nervous centres and leaves the brain free and unencumbered for other occupations. One can walk without having to think about all the movements needed in order to move, in perfect synchronization, all the parts of the body, in the specific way that is necessary for walking. The same thing happens and will go on happening in industry with the basic gestures of the trade. One walks automatically, and at the same time thinks about whatever one chooses. American industrialists have understood all too well this dialectic inherent in the new industrial methods. They have understood that 'trained gorilla' is just a phrase, that 'unfortunately' the worker remains a man and even that during his work he thinks more, or at least has greater opportunities for thinking, once he has overcome the crisis of adaptation without being eliminated: and not only does the worker think, but the fact that he gets no immediate satisfaction from his work and realizes that they are trying to reduce him to a trained gorilla, can lead him into a train of thought that is far from conformist. That the industrialists are concerned about such things is made clear from a whole series of cautionary measures and 'educative' initatives which are well brought out in Ford's books.

High wages

It is an obvious reflection that so-called high wages are a transitory form of remuneration. Adaptation to the new methods of production and work cannot take place simply through social compulsion. ... Coercion has therefore to be ingeniously combined with persuasion and consent. This effect can be achieved, in forms proper to the society in question, by higher remuneration such as to permit a particular living standard which can maintain and restore the strength that has been worn down by the new form of toil. But no sooner have the new methods of work and production been generalized and diffused, the new type of worker been created universally and the apparatus of material production further perfected, no sooner has this happened than the excessive 'turnover' has automatically to be restricted by widespread unemployment, and high wages disappear. ...

The whole Fordian ideology of high wages is a phenomenon derived from an objective necessity of modern industry when it has reached a certain stage of development. It is not a primary phenomenon which does not however exonerate one from studying its importance and the repercussions that the ideology can have on its own account. Meanwhile, what is meant by 'high wages'? Are the wages paid by Ford high only in relation to the average American wage? Or are they high as a price to be paid for the labouring power expended by Ford's employees in production and with those methods of work? It doesn't seem that any systematic research has been done on this, but that alone could provide a conclusive answer. The research is difficult, but the reasons why it is difficult are in themselves an indirect answer to the problem. The answer is difficult because the skilled labour force at Ford is extremely unstable and as a result it is not possible to establish an average for 'rational' turnover among Ford workers for the purpose of comparison with the average in other industries. But why is it unstable? Why on earth should a worker prefer lower wages than those paid by Ford? Does this not mean that the so-called 'high wages' are less capable of reconstituting the labour power expended than the lower wages paid by other firms? The instability of the labour force demonstrates that as far as Ford's is concerned the normal conditions of workers' competition for jobs (wage differentials) are effective only to a limited degree. The different level of average wages is not effective, nor is the pressure of the reserve army of the unemployed. This means that in dealing with Ford a new element must be looked for, and this new element will be the origin both of the high wages and of the other phenomena referred to (instability, etc.). The new element must be looked for in this fact alone: that Ford's industry requires a discrimination, a qualification, in its workers, which other industries do not yet call for, a new type of qualification, a form of consumption of labour power and a quantity of power consumed in average hours which are the same numerically but which are more wearying and exhausting than elsewhere and which, in the given conditions of society as it is, the wages are not sufficient to recompense and make up for.

Once these reasons have been established, the problem arises: whether the type of industry and organization of work and production typical of Ford is rational; whether, that is, it can and should be generalized, or whether, on the other hand, we are not dealing with a malignant phenomenon which must be fought against through trade-union action and through legislation? In other words, whether it is possible, with the material and moral pressure of society and of the State, to lead the workers as a mass to undergo the entire process of psycho-physical transformation so that the average type of Ford worker becomes the average type of worker in general? Or whether this is impossible because it would lead to physical degeneration and to deterioration of the species, with the consequent destruction of all labour power? It seems possible to reply that the Ford method is rational, that is, that it should be generalized; but that a long process is needed for this, during which a change must take place in social conditions and in the way of life and the habits of individuals. This, however, cannot take place through coercion alone, but only through tempering compulsion (self-discipline) with persuasion. Persuasion should also take the form of high wages, which offer the possibility of a better standard of living, or more exactly perhaps, the possibility of realising a standard of living which is adequate to the new methods of production and work which demand a particular degree of expenditure of muscular and nervous energy.

To a limited but none the less important degree, phenomena similar to those created on a large scale by **Fordism** have been and still are occurring in certain branches of industry and in certain not yet 'Fordised' establishments.

Reference

Taylor, F. W. (1911) *The Principles of Scientific Management*, New York: Harper & Row.

Key terms

The following key terms appear in the text above. They have been defined below to aid with the reading of this item.

postwar period this article was written in 1931, so 'postwar' here refers to the period after World War I

Taylorism name given to the ideas of Frederick Taylor, one of the originators of scientific management, based on a strict measurement and control of the effort of the worker

Fordism the term coined by Gramsci to characterize the effect on society of the ideas of Henry Ford, who not only implemented new production techniques – notably the mass assembly line – but was also concerned with the life of his workers outside the work-

place, in particular their family and social lives. The term therefore means much more than simply the adoption of a new production technique

Questions

1 In what ways did Ford impinge on the private lives of his employees and why does Gramsci think he did this?

2 Why were the high wages paid in classical Fordist enterprises limited in their effect?

3 How do these new developments affect the prevailing notions of sexuality and family life?

4 Suggest examples of the way in which job requirements today impose restrictions on the lives of employees.

5 To what extent do you agree with the assertion that 'new methods of work are inseparable from a specific mode of living and of thinking and feeling life'?

Reading 10.3 **Fordism and post-Fordism**

Krishan Kumar (from) *From Post-Industrial to Post-Modern Society* (1995) Oxford: Blackwell, pp. 37–8, 41–3, 47, 50–2, 54–7 and 59–60.

Editorial comments

One of the key debates within the sociology of work concerns the question of whether the principles of work organization and its relations and regulation known as Fordism have exhausted themselves, leading to a new era known as post-Fordism. In this reading, Kumar discusses the variety of versions of this argument and also passes some critical comments on them.

Fordism and post-Fordism

The Third Italy

DURING THE 1970S and 1980s, Italian and other observers began to document and discuss a phenomenon that they came to call *la Terza Italia*, the Third Italy. The Third Italy was distinguished from, on the one hand, the First Italy of large-scale mass production, concentrated in the industrial triangle of Turin, Milan and Genoa; and, on the other hand, the Second Italy of the *mezzogiorno*, the economically undeveloped South. The Third Italy was, by contrast, a dynamic area of small firms and workshops in the central and north-eastern regions of the country: Tuscany, Umbria, the Marche, Emilia-Romagna, Veneto, Friuli, Trentino-Alto Adige.

In these regions, small workshops and factories employing usually no more than 5–50 workers, and often less than 10, had come to constitute the core

of thriving 'industrial districts'. Each region specialized in a range of loosely related products. Tuscany specialized in textiles and ceramics; Emilia-Romagna produced knitwear, ceramic tiles, automatic machines and farm machinery; in the Marche, shoes were the main product; Veneto also produced shoes as well as ceramics and plastic furniture.

The main features of production in the Third Italy were what one of its leading students has called 'productive decentralization and social integration'. ...

The Third Italy, for its apologists, is not simply an economic phenomenon. It is also a social, cultural and political phenomenon of the first importance. It points towards the possibility, for almost the first time in the history of industrialism, of the reunification of mental and manual labour, and of work and the community. 'If', says Charles Sabel of the skilled workers in the small firms,

You had thought so long about Rousseau's artisan clockmakers at Neuchâtel or Marx's idea of labour as joyful, self-creative association that you had begun to doubt their possibility, then you might, watching these craftsmen at work, forgive yourself the sudden conviction that something more utopian than the present factory system is practical after all. *(Sabel, 1984)*

... The Italian example is therefore conceivably the harbinger of new times, a new kind of future for industrial societies. This is not, it must again be stressed, necessarily something that all welcome. For some it is a matter of the greatest apprehension. The critics of the Third Italy see in it a warning of the onset of a new, harsher phase of capitalism. But many of them accept that, taken with other examples from other parts of the industrial world, the Italian case is a revealing symptom of a possible movement to a new phase of industrial history. The industrial societies are becoming 'post-Fordist'. We have so far, in concentrating on the Italian example, considered post-Fordist features only implicitly. We need now to look at the theory in its most general form.

Flexible specialization: the second industrial divide?

... For all thinkers, flexible specialization has been at the heart of the theory of post-Fordism. It combines the capability of the new technology with the idea of a fundamental shift in the nature of the market in late twentieth century industrial society. For some, it points to the way out of the global economic crisis of the 1970s and 1980s. In their much-discussed book, *The Second Industrial Divide*, Michael Piore and Charles Sabel argue that 'we are living through a second industrial divide' in our time, a transition comparable to the first industrial divide that saw the rise of mass production in the later nineteenth century (Piore and Sabel, 1984). The way ahead is not certain – alternative strategies are possible – but they see some real hope in the current revival of craft production. Craft production, the suppressed alternative to mass production and for long a minor current in its stream, is once more showing itself to be a real possibility. Its return in more propitious circumstances could mean not just economic but social and political gains.

The computer, Piore and Sabel claim, 'is a machine that meets Marx's definition of an artisan tool: it is an instrument that responds to and extends the productive capacities of the user'. Put to the purposes of flexible specialization, it 'restores human control over the production process' (Piore and Sabel, 1984). The advent of flexible specialization thus means greater involvement and enhanced work satisfaction for the bulk of workers. Flexible specialization puts a premium on craft skills, and it also depends on collaboration between all grades of workers in the enterprise. Moreover, as in the industrial districts of the Third Italy, it can also bring about a closer integration between economic production and the general life of the local community. ...

'New Times'

Post-Fordist theories – following in the footsteps of Antonio Gramsci's influential treatment of Fordism in the *Prison Notebooks* – usually have a left-wing provenance. They are attempts by radical theorists to come to terms with what are seen as fundamental and far-reaching changes in the nature of contemporary capitalism. Many thinkers remain hopeful that, despite what these changes might suggest about capitalism's capacity to renew itself, there may still be some scope for the realization of socialist aims, as historically conceived. But a basic ambivalence remains. Post-Fordist capitalism is still, after all, capitalism. It is driven as insistently as ever before by the motor of the accumulation process. The restructuring implicit in post-Fordism is intended to strengthen, not weaken, capitalism. There may be some unexpected bonuses for radicals – the revival of craft skills, a service class not necessarily wedded to capitalism and willing to challenge it at certain points – but these clearly have to be assessed in the context of a global economic system whose outstanding feature is dominance by **transnational corporations** of unprecedented wealth and power.

This ambivalence is most acutely to be felt in the variety of post-Fordist theory presented by British Marxists under the banner of 'New Times'. First stated in a series of articles in the journal *Marxism Today*, the perspective was later substantially adopted by the executive committee of the British Communist Party and published by them as *The Manifesto for New Times* (June 1989). Subsequently many of the original articles, accompanied by extracts from the *Manifesto* and together with critical responses, were brought together in a book, *New Times* (Hall and Jacques, 1989).

Gramsci, in his 'Americanism and Fordism' (c.1931), had defined Fordism in the broadest possible terms. Fordism had introduced a new epoch in capitalist civilization. ...

Post-Fordists of the 'New Times' school have been similarly wide-ranging in their accounts of the new times. As with other post-Fordists, they single out flexible specialization as the force that is 'orchestrating and driving on the evolution of the new world'. But in the spirit of Gramsci they argue that 'diversity, differentiation and fragmentation' – the hallmarks of post-Fordism – are replacing 'homogeneity, standardization and the economies and organizations of scale' in more than simply the economic sphere.

> Just as Fordism represented, not simply a form of economic organization but a whole culture ... so post-Fordism is also shorthand for a much wider and deeper social and cultural development ... The transition, then, is epochal – not in the sense of the classic transition from feudalism to capitalism, but as fundamental and far-reaching as, say, the transition in the closing stages of the 19th century from the 'entrepreneurial' to the advanced or organized stage within capitalism.
>
> *(Hall and Jacques, 1989)*

Various attempts have been made to express schematically the differences between **Fordism** and post-Fordism, in all their various dimensions. Put simply, the changes are generally said to be as follows.

In the *economy:* the rise of a global market and of global corporations, and the decline of national enterprises and the nation state as the effective units of production and regulation; flexible specialization and the dispersal and decentralization of production, replacing mass marketing and mass production; flatter hierarchies and an emphasis on communication rather than command in organizations; vertical and horizontal disintegration, and an increase in subcontracting, franchising, internal marketing within firms, and the hiving-off of functions; rise in the number of flexi-time, part-time, temporary, self-employed and home workers.

In *politics and industrial relations*: the fragmentation of social classes, the decline of national class-based political parties and class voting, and the rise of social movements and 'networks' based on region, race or gender or on single-issue politics (for example, the anti-nuclear movement); 'peripheral', sub- and supra-national movements; the decline of mass unions and centralized wage bargaining and the rise of localized, plant-based bargaining; a labour force divided into core and periphery; the end of the class compromise of **corporatism**; the break-up of standardized, collectivist welfare provision, and the rise of consumer choice and private provision in welfare.

In *culture and ideology*: the rise and promotion of individualist modes of thought and behaviour; a culture of entrepreneurialism; the end of universalism and standardization in education, and the rise of modularity and pupil- and parent-choice; fragmentation and pluralism in values and life-styles; postmodernist eclecticism, and populist approaches to culture; privatization in domestic life and leisure pursuits. ...

New Times, old story?

It would be easy to condemn post-Fordism, especially in its New Times form, as a 'Thatcherism (or Reaganism) of the Left'. It has been accused of promoting 'designer socialism', of being, indeed, 'the socialism of designers', a vision of the future as it looks to the new service class based in the media, the universities and the information technology industries (Rustin 1989). The language it uses, the language of individualism, choice and diversity, can be said to pay excessive homage to the vocabulary of the New Right. When a New Times theorist speaks of 'consuming as a source of power and pleasure', and of 'the hyper-eroticisation of a visit to the shops' (Mort 1989), it is difficult not to feel that even where the language is used ironically there has been a considerable shift towards the perspective of the Left's traditional antagonists. 'For socialists', as Michael Rustin says, 'there has to be more to life than shopping ...' (Rustin 1989).

More serious is the accusation that not only have some sections of the Left conceded too much to the New Right, they have failed to see that the principal elements of what they embrace are precisely the source of the current strength of the Right and the basis of its repeated electoral success. 'Thatcherism', says Rustin, 'may be understood as a strategy of post-Fordism initiated from the perspective of the right. That is to say, a determined attempt to use the advantages of new technology, mobility of capital and labour, the centrality of consumption, and more decentralized forms of organization, to strengthen capital and to attack the corporate structures of labour' (Rustin 1989).

Other critics have observed that one of the key components of post-Fordist analysis, the break up of mass production and of the mass homogeneous working class formed around it, provides the central building block of New Right strategy. ...

This is, as it were, the complaint of the old Left against the New. There is, however, another variety of contemporary left-wing thinking which, like the New Times group, accepts that there is a crisis of Fordism but sees its resolution in different terms. The so-called 'Regulation School' of French theorists do not see, not yet at any rate, a passage into a potentially hopeful post-Fordist society. What others characterize as post-Fordist they rather regard as 'neo-Fordist' strategies designed to enable capitalism to overcome its current crisis.

The Regulationists – chief among whom are Michel Aglietta, Robert Boyer and Alain Lipietz – see the history of capitalism as marked by successive 'modes of development' in which a particular 'regime of accumulation' is guided by a particular 'mode of regulation'. That is to say, at any given time the capitalist's efforts to extract surplus-value at an increasing rate is dependent on the particular constellation of class forces – especially in the work-place – and the institutional arrangements governing relations between firms and between capital and labour. In the nineteenth century, effective craft control on the shop floor and largely unregulated competition between a multitude of firms made for a regime of accumulation that was marked by 'extensive' growth: a form of growth largely dependent not on technical innovation or increases in productivity but on large reserves of cheap labour and simple geographical expansion of the system.

With the advent of scientific management (Taylorism) and the automated factory (Fordism) in the 1920s – and 'Fordism is nothing more than Taylorism plus mechanization' – a new regime of accumulation and a new mode of regulation supervened. The regime of accumulation was now characterized by 'intensive' growth: that is, growth came predominantly through investment in fixed capital embodying technical advance. This created the potential both for regular increases in productivity and for mass consumption. The new mode of regulation was slower to develop – it needed the slump and social upheaval of the 1930s to speed it on – but it was more or less established throughout the industrial world following the Second World War. As opposed to the competitive mode of the nineteenth century, it can be called the monopoly mode. Its basis was the scientific management of organizations, oligopolistic price arrangements between firms, and the determination of wages and levels of consumption through a complex system of employer-labour and governmental institutions (Keynesian fiscal policies buttressed by the welfare state).

It is this Taylorist–Fordist mode of development – responsible for the great postwar boom and prevalent until the late 1960s – that is now, according to the Regulationists, in crisis. It has exhausted its potential for growth. This is shown especially in declining productivity, as Taylorist–Fordist intensifications of the labour process bring diminishing returns, partly through increased worker alienation and resistance. Since the late 1960s there has been a sharp fall in the rate of profit throughout the capitalist world.

The Regulationists' own solution to the crisis, as they interpret it, is a return, in a more explicit and thoroughgoing way, to the 'class compromise' (or 'social contract') of the postwar era that made possible the period of sustained growth. In present conditions this would involve, they accept, nothing less than an anti-Taylorist, post-Fordist revolution. Workers would be made formal participants in decision-making; their commitment to the system would be sought by enriched forms of work and guarantees of job security and welfare benefits. This would break the current blockage on increased productivity, and both capital and labour would benefit from a faster growing economy.

Instead, according to the Regulationists, what has happened is the attempt by capital to resolve the crisis by establishing a system of 'global Fordism'. This has taken the form of a series of 'neo-Fordist' strategies. Production has been decentralized, not simply nationally but internationally, by removing it to the cheap-wage regions of the world – the newly industrializing countries of East Asia and South America, and certain parts of southern Europe. The central control and research functions meanwhile remain in the metropolises of the advanced industrial countries. Flexible specialization and devolved management have also been employed as part of a strategy to lessen the burdens of firms and to bypass or break strong labour organizations. So 'post-Fordist' elements in the First World co-exist alongside classic Fordism and 'peripheral Fordism' in the Third World. Actually there are not three worlds (especially after the collapse of state socialism in eastern Europe); there are only segments of a global capitalist system trying to maintain its dynamism in a period of crisis.

The Regulation theorists have their own shortcomings – among other things, an overestimation of the 'Taylorist–Fordist watershed' in capitalist development – but in their account of the contemporary world there is much that is convincing. Above all they allow us to consider many allegedly post-Fordist developments in a new light. Unlike many of the old Left they do not dismiss the changes as merely superficial variations on an old theme. Something new *is* afoot, even if it does not bear the interpretation of many of the more optimistic adherents of the post-Fordist idea. The new features demand a framework of understanding that is cast on the widest possible (world) plane, not narrowly focused on the advanced industrial nations. In that light much that appears post-Fordist can be shown to carry the stamp of a system of production that remains substantially Fordist, even though it is under considerable strain – and, according to the Regulationists, in its global form ultimately burdened by the same contradictions that afflicted classic Fordism.

The Regulationist critique chimes in well with the general charge made against post-Fordist theory: namely, that it mistakes effects for causes, that what it sees as the primary facts are derivative or dependent products of less visible processes. Post-Fordism has for instance made much of the rise or revival of localism and particularism, the cultivation of identity through attachment to place and to local cultures and traditions. It not merely picks out but celebrates the ethnic revival, the rise of 'peripheral nationalisms', the struggles to conserve local ways and local histories. ...

The most fundamental charge against the post-Fordists is that they have mythologized Fordism itself.

They have merged Taylorism and Fordism, identified both with mass production, and assumed the dominance of this unified formation in the industrial systems of the advanced economies in the first half of the twentieth century. Now, post-Fordists argue, mass production industries have run up against a wall; Taylorist methods of work organization have met with increasing resistance from workers; and new kinds of industries, based on the principles of flexibility and local production, are emerging to challenge the old mass centralized forms. A new system is coming into being, sufficiently different in kind from the old to warrant the name 'post-Fordist'. Its birth-pangs are evident not only in the industrial system itself, narrowly defined, but in wide-ranging changes in politics, culture and social institutions.

But, respond the critics, this model collapses at virtually every important point. Taylorism is a different thing from Fordism; it was and is capable of application not just to mass production but to small- and medium-batch production. It can even be applied to the new forms of teamworking in supposedly 'post-Fordist' enterprises. Mass production, whatever its strategic importance in the economy, was never, nor could it be, the dominant form of industrial production. Small firms and 'craft production' – not of course necessarily the same thing – always persisted alongside mass production, as had been the case since the Industrial Revolution; they performed then as now not vestigial but indispensable functions. There is no revival or renaissance of these forms, merely continuation. The opposition, 'mass production versus flexible specialization', is false: even the car industry, supposedly the very type of mass production, employs both methods. The assembly-line itself, the very symbol of Fordism, was never present in more than a minority of plants in the advanced economies.

The most serious criticism argues that the post-Fordists mistake the very nature of the Fordist revolution. They fail to see that what they call 'the crisis of Fordism' and its resolution into post-Fordist forms are in fact part of a continuing evolution – or rather, part of the 'permanent revolution' that is Fordism. Fordism cannot simply be equated with 'inflexibility', the assembly-line, and mass production. As Simon Clarke, following Gramsci, emphasizes, Fordism was not just a new technology; it was the systematic application of new techniques – social as well as scientific in the technical sense – to the organization of production in all its spheres, including the regulation of the relation between management and workers. In this sense it continued the basic drive of the Industrial Revolution: 'it marked the culmination of the penetration of capital into production, which means that Fordism is synonymous with capitalist production *as such*'.

Far from giving rise to 'inflexibility', the principles of Fordism have proved applicable in 'an extraordinarily wide range of technical contexts'. What Henry Ford actually introduced was *flexibility* in mass production, hence paving the way for constant technological dynamism and maximum adaptability of production methods. The fact that Ford himself was, in the 1930s, the victim of his own revolution did not prevent further conquests by Fordism under new leaders, for instance Albert Sloan of General Motors. And this has been the case ever since: Fordism has manifested itself in a number of technological and organizational guises. What has been hailed as 'neo-Fordist' or 'post-Fordist' is merely the latest, and is unlikely to be the last.

References

Communist Party of Great Britain (1989) 'Manifesto for New Times', *Marxism Today*, June.

Gramsci, A. (1971) *Selections from the Prison Notebooks*, London: Lawrence & Wishart.

Hall, S. and Jacques, M. (eds) (1989) *New Times*, London: Lawrence & Wishart.

Mort, F. (1989) 'The politics of consumption', in Hall, S. and Jacques, M. (eds) *New Times*, London: Lawrence & Wishart.

Murray, R. (1989) 'Fordism and post-Fordism', in Hall, S. and Jacques, M. (eds) *New Times*, London: Lawrence & Wishart.

Piore, M. and Sabel, C. (1984) *The Second Industrial Divide*, New York: Basic Books.

Rustin, M. (1989) 'The politics of post-Fordism: or, the trouble with "New Times"', *New Left Review*, 175.

Sabel, C. (1984) *Work and Politics: The division of labour in industry*, Cambridge: Cambridge University Press.

Key terms

The following key terms appear in the text above. They have been defined below to aid with the reading of this item.

transnational corporations companies whose production and operations are not limited by being confined to one particular geographical area but who operate around the globe

Fordism the term developed by Antonio Gramsci (see reading 10.2) to describe the social and political implications of the rise of mass production, embodied most famously by the development of the Ford motor company

corporatism a system where negotiations and

organization is undertaken on behalf of groups, notably: workers, employers and the state – leading to the classical tripartite (three parties) corporatism. This is seen as characteristic of the period from the end of World War II until the early 1970s, when these arrangements began to break down

Questions

1 In what ways does 'The Third Italy' differ from classical Taylorism and Fordism?

2 What are the main characteristics of 'flexible specialization'?

3 Explain in your own words the characteristics of, and differences between, Fordism and post-Fordism.

4 How is the analysis of the 'Regulation School' distinct from post-Fordist analysis?

5 Suggest examples of firms that use the principles of flexible specialization.

6 To what extent do you agree that 'post-Fordists mistake the very nature of the Fordist revolution'?

Reading 10.4 **From societies to flows**

S. Lash and J. Urry (from) *Economies of Signs and Space* (1994) London: Sage, pp. 319–26.

Editorial comments

In their earlier book, *The End of Organized Capitalism*, Lash and Urry (1987) argued that the period after World War II – characterized by mass production, corporatist industrial relations and cultural modernism – was coming to an end. This was being replaced by disorganized capitalism – characterized by globaliza-

tion, flexible specialization, the atomization of the working class and the rise of new political structures based on new social movements. In this second book they concentrate much more on the process of globalization and the impact of the growth of trading in signs (such as information) and the implications of this for work, politics and, importantly, for cultural life. This extract comes from the concluding chapter of the book.

Reference

Lash, S. and Urry, J. (1987) *The End of Organized Capitalism*, Cambridge: Polity.

Economies of signs and space

IT HAS BEEN common for analysts of post-industrialism, of reflexive modernity, to speak of the decline of importance of class structure or consciousness in voting behaviour, the proclivity to join unions, the taking on of a working-class lifestyle and the like. The analyses in this book take this perhaps a step further and suggest an inversion of the Marxist thesis; they suggest that in informationalized and reflexive modernity it is consciousness or **reflexivity** which is determinant of class structure. This provisional argument can be seen in four ways.

First, access to information and communication networks, as conditions of reflexivity, is a crucial determinant of class position. The 'wild zones' of very sparse lines, flows and networks tend to be where the underclasses, or at least the bottom third, of the 'two-thirds societies' are found. That is, place in the 'mode of information' rather than in the mode of production is the crucial factor in class position. Similarly the unusually densely networked centres of the global cities tend to be where the top fractions, in the corporation headquarters, business and finance and legal

services, of today's new informational bourgeoisie are primarily located.

Second, where reflexivity is found will determine the shape of class structure. Thus where information structures favour reflexive production – through their articulation with production systems – in Germany and Japan, industry is competitive and there is a proportionally quite large (industrial) working class. The deficit of reflexivity in production in the UK and USA has via loss in competitiveness led to a class structure in which the rump of a working class is now quite small. Concomitantly the persistence of reflexive consumption in the market-driven Anglo-American world will mean a much larger advanced consumer services sector, including many professionals employed in the expert systems upon which reflexive and individualized consumers are dependent. This will be part of a 'swollen' professional middle class in the Anglo-American world by comparison with **corporatist** Germany and Japan.

Third, reflexive production in corporatist countries (Germany, Japan) will continue largely to mean the application of information technology in machine building, while in **neo-liberal** countries (USA, UK, France) it involves working in the informational sectors themselves. The corporatist countries will continue to have a large 'middle mass', of which the highly skilled working class makes up a large part. Neo-liberal nations have a much smaller middle mass – indeed a sizeable portion of the working class proper will work in exporting say Japanese products from inwards investing firms in Britain. Such nations will have exacerbated class polarization of the university-educated information and advanced service sector professionals and a large number of 'junk jobs' in the downgraded services and manufacturing sectors at the bottom end of the social stratification ladder. This will itself be further exacerbated by expected increases in immigration, by the so-called 'browning' of the USA and western Europe.

And finally, the corporatist countries with their large middle mass will continue to have smaller disparities in class stratification. But the same collective institutions that favour growth and class equality – through their reflexive exclusion of 'the other' – create much greater inequalities in regard to gender and ethnicity. Such statist-corporatist measures exclude ethnic minorities from corporate membership and national citizenship altogether. Thus the other side of the high-value-added labour of the corporatist middle mass of men is a low labour force participation rate for women.

We have thus endeavoured to recast the categories by which contemporary societies are to be investigated. There are a number of conceptual innovations which imply the reordering of much of the conventional basis of Western social science. ...

So far we have suggested that social science has been organized in terms of the concept of the individual 'society'. There has though been an alternative approach which has talked very generally about certain categories of society, such as industrial, capitalist, organized capitalist, late capitalist, post-industrial, post-Fordist and so on. Although some of these categories are helpful they lead analysts to minimize really important differences between societies, both historically and in the contemporary world. In this book we have demonstrated that there are major differences in the form of accumulation and in the pattern of services as between Germany, Japan, certain Scandinavian countries, and the UK and USA. Indeed as with *The End of Organized Capitalism* (Lash and Urry, 1987) we tried to demonstrate the importance of 'cross-societal' analysis, to show that there are major differences between apparently similar advanced capitalist societies. But we have not engaged in such comparative analysis simply to show that there are differences between societies because

that would have been to return to the kind of 'society-centric' formulation criticized above. Rather we have shown that such differences are the complex product of the interplay between each society's history *and* the current flows of capital, technologies, people, ideas and images, where those flows are also seen as having a history and a geography and where there are certain local nodes in particular societies involved in the propagation or reproduction of particular flows.

So although in a loose sense we might wish to characterize a number of societies mainly in the north Atlantic rim as the product of 'disorganized capitalism', that they are post-industrial, postmodern and post-Fordist, there are some striking differences between them. However, there is not a complete arbitrariness of form. For example, there are three main routes to reflexive accumulation, the Japanese, the German and the advanced sectors model.

This though leads onto a further theme, namely the importance attached to individual and institutionalized reflexivity. In relationship to accumulation the processes by which information was generated, distributed and passed on were shown to be of central importance. We saw not only significant differences between the three routes to reflexive accumulation but also that the kind of information itself differed, being much more practical in the German case, more abstract in the advanced sectors, and more the result of shopfloor discussion in the Japanese case.

So how reflexivity is systematized varies between what appear to be similar societies. Although they are all loosely post-industrial, Germany remains peculiarly retarded in its development. This is partly because of its family structures, and partly because of the very success of German manufacturing based upon training and craft apprenticeships. The US and UK are more obviously post-industrial and postmodern, while Scandinavia has developed as a kind of public post-industrial society. In the UK and US the growth of advanced producer and consumer service industries and hence the huge institutionalization of reflexivity has produced an economy in which services dominate manufacturing. In such societies individual reflexivity is institutionalized through the development of various complex services including even 'therapy services'.

Overall we have emphasized that reflexivity is not merely a matter of cognition or of ethics, but also of aesthetics. Such aesthetic or hermeneutic reflexivity, in its interpretive relation to social conditions and the self, is active in production and consumption, in critique and as a foundation for community. More generally, the development of multiple forms of a modernizing reflexivity counters the postmodern dystopia favoured by some analysts. There are of course some immensely powerful transformations of mobility in disorganized capitalism – indeed this book is a systematic attempt to chart these – but the processes involved are more contradictory than the 'dystopic' postmodern account would suggest. Not only are there mobile objects, and this includes capital, technologies, labour-power and images, but there are also reflexive subjects, individually able to monitor their actions and increasingly embedded within systems which are themselves reflexive, cognitively, morally or aesthetically.

The term 'disorganized capitalism' has been employed here. It is not a characterization of individual societies but refers rather to the entire epoch in which a number of putative trends have been developing. There is an asymmetry about organized and disorganized capitalism.

The former refers to individual societies, to a particular configuration of economic, social, political and cultural relations at the level of the *individual* society. It refers to the no more than a dozen or so organized capitalist societies, which were all located within the north Atlantic rim. Although there were some substantial differences between them, as we analysed in *The End of Organized Capitalism* (Lash and Urry, 1987), each of them was characterizable as an organized capitalist society. Beyond them there were scores of other 'more-or-less' societies in colonial and semi-colonial relations with this organized core.

Disorganized capitalism is an epoch in which various processes and flows have transformed this pattern of a dozen or so organized capitalist societies constituting the core within the north Atlantic rim. The processes and flows which have ushered in such a disorganized capitalism include the following: the flowing of capital and technologies to 170 or so individual 'self-governing' capitalist countries each concerned to defend 'its' territory; time-space compression in financial markets and the development of a system of global cities; the growth in importance of internationalized producer services; the generalization of risks which know no national boundaries and of the fear of such risks; the putative globalizing of culture and communication structures partly breaking free of particular territories; the proliferation of forms of reflexivity, individual and institutionalized, cognitive and especially aesthetic; huge increases of personal mobility across the globe, of tourists, migrants and refugees; the development of a service class with cosmopolitan tastes especially for endlessly 'fashionable' consumer services provided by one or other category of migrant; the declining effectivity and legitimacy of nation-states which are unable to control such disorganized capitalist flows; and the emergence of 'neo-worlds', the kinds of socially and regionally re-engineered cultural spaces which are the typical homelands for cosmopolitan postmodern individuals. Luke

summarizes the shifts involved: from place to flow, from spaces to streams, from organized hierarchies to disorganization (1992). Social classes, which are conventionally taken as focussed around place, national spaces and organized hierarchies, are one of the victims of such disorganization. They are simultaneously localized and globalized, transformed by the flows of people, images and information. Classes in the sense of hierarchically organized national entities are rapidly disssolving, at the very same time that social and spatial inequalities rapidly increase.

What then are the consequences of such forms of disorganization for social and political life at the turn of the millennium? Do the flows of social life provide such rich possibilities that apocalyptic terrors of the future are unjustified and inappropriate? The marriage of the computer and the telecommunications revolution results in movements of information at the speed of light and to enormous audiences, and this might be thought to decentralize both knowledge and power and to enable 'new sociations' to develop away from the 'traditional' institutions of social life. Wriston argues how:

> an international communications system, incorporating technologies from mobile telephones to communication satellites, deprives governments of the ability to keep secrets from the world, or from their own people, [hence] power changes hand [since] the world is watching, and the power of world opinion is transmitted and focussed and reported by the telecom network.
> *(1992)*

The 'de-traditionalization' of the British monarchy is perhaps the clearest example of this. Another instance is the way in which, prior to the Gulf War, Kuwait was transformed from a place in space to be annexed by Iraq into a flow as its assets were transformed into streams of electronic communication on the screens of the world's financial institutions.

Or alternatively will these flows create nightmare scenarios, of increasingly extensive 'wild zones' consisting of collapsing empires (USSR), imploding nation-states (Yugoslavia), ungovernable First World cities (Los Angeles), tracts of desertification (south east Africa) and countries dominated by narco-capitalism (Colombia). Such wild zones are characterized by a collapsing (or collapsed) civil society, a weakly developed 'civilizing process', and flight to 'tame zones' for those that are able to escape. Such tame zones are areas of economic, political and cultural security, often with strong boundaries separating them off from the wild zones of disorganized capitalism. Such divisions can of course be seen within local areas where electronic surveillance techniques keep the one-thirds and the two-thirds societies apart.

So there are quite different possibilities envisaged

here, of a kind of disorganized decentralization, or an apocalypse now; of a generally benign redistribution of information, knowledge and power, or a terrifying crisis of ungovernability spreading over significant parts of the globe. There are many aspects of these contrasting visions. We will note three, those focused around information, the state and place.

The growth of information may be seen as liberating or as repressive. On the one hand, the use of new forms of information technology may facilitate the development of small communitarian public spheres. A new logic of place and practical will-formation could develop on the basis of decentralized data banks, interactive communication systems and community-based multi-media centres. New sociations can generate new skills and new loci of power away from the traditional institutions of class, family, education, politics, monarchy and so on.

Or on the other hand, information technology can lead to new forms of control and erode the critical crafts of reading and writing. What Agger (1989) terms 'fast capitalism' undermines the power of the book and a kind of Foucauldian power/knowledge dystopia may develop in which even moral and practical knowledge is transformed into cognitive and technical systems which normalize and regulate what was previously private. A visual culture is publicly controllable in a way in which a literary culture is not.

Likewise the potential evolution of the state can be viewed positively or negatively. The modernist nation-state, which resulted in the achievements of both liberal and social democracy *and* of the 'holocaust', is being 'hollowed out'. Its powers are being delegated upwards to supraregional or international bodies, downwards to regional or local states or to the private sector, inwards to alternative elements controlling the means of physical coercion, and outwards to relatively autonomous cross-national alliances. Such a hollowed-out state has its powers weakened at the same time that its legitimacy is challenged. This occurs partly because of its shortcomings in the face of the flows previously discussed and especially its inability to control the information flows within its national boundaries, and partly because it has difficulty in justifying its actions as being in accordance with the apparently omnipotent 'market'. So states are faced by a tremendous postmodern complexity. Partly this might be seen positively, as indicating the demise of the kinds of bureaucratically organized states which have waged wars, incarcerated citizens and administered large populations for most of this century. The demise of the nation-state might favour the proliferation of local and regional states which could more effectively respond to the wishes of its citizens, a much more localist and pluralist democracy. Or such developments might be viewed as reinforcing a nightmarish

dystopia. The absence of a national context for policy will result in enormous social and spatial inequalities, of ungovernable wild zones next to highly disciplined tame zones, where each reinforces the other, and where there is no strong national authority able to impose more uniform civilized conditions of existence. The absence of national social classes means that there is little to counter such disorganization. At the same time the cosmopolitan participants in various neo-worlds can speed between the tame zones leaving other travellers to make out in the wild zones, perhaps encountering each other in 'empty meeting grounds'.

Finally, flows impact most significantly on places. How can spatial meanings be attached to or develop within an experience in which 'the space of flows … supersedes the space of places'? (Henderson and Castells 1987). Do places vanish, rendered invisible by the overwhelming rush of capital, images, ideas, technologies and people? Does not this intense mobility of objects and subjects produce placelessness, where only the most superficial of differences stand out against the onward rush of flows? Meyrowitz suggests that many people:

> no longer seem to 'know their place' because the traditionally interlocking components of 'place' have been split apart by electronic media … Our world may suddenly seem senseless to many people because, for the first time in modern history, it is relatively placeless.
> (1985)

Alternatively it may be argued these flows are themselves organized, they are not literally undiscriminating, and so places attract and they repel. Of course by place we mean in part image but even so places might not be seen as simply swamped by a meaningless placenessness. They are remade or reimagined, often to attract flows of tourists or entrepreneurs (a tame zone), or to repel migrants or low-wage capital (to a wild zone). But places have always been remade. There is nothing surprising about this. What is distinct about the contemporary remaking of place are the following: the importance of image and especially of an (aesthetic) reflexivity of place; the impact of global flows and especially of information, image and voluntary visitors which cause places to be remade with increasing rapidity; and the relative weakness of national states (and national classes) in the face of such flows and their effects on the extraordinary remaking of place. As Marx might have said more generally, 'all that is built or all that is "natural" melts into image' in the contemporary global economies of signs and space.

References

Agger, B. (1989) *Fast Capitalism*, Urbana, Ill.: University of Illinois Press.

Henderson, J. and Castells, M. (eds) (1987) *Global Restructuring and Territorial Development*, Beverley Hills: Sage.

Lash, S. and Urry, J. (1987) *The End of Organized Capitalism*, Cambridge: Polity.

Luke, T. (1992) 'New world order or neo-world orders: power, politics and ideology in the informationalizing global order', a paper for the Theory, Culture and Society 10th anniversary conference, 16–19 August.

Meyrowitz, J. (1985) *No Sense of Place*, Oxford: Oxford University Press.

Wriston, W. (1992) 'The twilight of sovereignty', *Royal Society of Arts Journal, 140*, August–September.

Key terms

The following key terms appear in the text above. They have been defined below to aid with the reading of this item.

reflexivity the notion that we are aware of ourselves and, through that awareness, monitor our own actions and reflect on them

corporatist relating to the regulation of the economy and society through corporate means. In practice this meant decisions reached in meetings between the government, representatives of employers and representatives of employees

neo-liberal free-market based. The authors use this term to describe societies such as the USA and the UK

Questions

1 How do the authors react to the Marxist argument that class structure determines class consciousness?

2 Explain the contrast drawn by the authors between Anglo-American production systems and German-Japanese production systems.

3 Why do the authors feel that an approach based on 'cross-societal analysis' is now necessary?

4 What are the key characteristics of disorganized capitalism?

5 To what extent do you agree that social science must no longer concentrate on societies but instead on flows?

Reading 10.5 **Capitalism, patriarchy and gender inequalities**

Heidi Hartmann (from) 'Capitalism, patriarchy, and job segregation by sex', in A. Giddens and D. Held (eds) *Classes, Power and Conflict* (1982) London: Macmillan, pp. 446–50, 454–60 and 468 9.

Editorial comments

Hartmann argues that there was a patriarchal system in operation before capitalism where men dominated the labour of women and children and that it is here that we need to look for the origins of modern-day gender inequalities. In this reading, she surveys anthropological perspectives on the emergence of sexual stratification and goes on to consider how the emergence of capitalism built upon these pre-existing inequalities, leading to more contemporary forms of inequality such as sex segregation.

Patriarchy and the division of labour

THE DIVISION OF labour by sex appears to have been universal throughout human history. In our society the sexual division of labour is hierarchical, with men on top and women on the bottom. Anthropology and history suggest, however, that this division was not always a hierarchical one. The development and importance of a sex-ordered division of labour is the subject of this paper. It is my contention that the roots of women's present social status lie in this sex-ordered division of labour. It is my belief that not only must the hierarchical nature of the division of labour between the sexes be eliminated, but the very division of labour between the sexes itself must be eliminated if women are to attain equal social status with men and if women and men are to attain the full development of their human potentials.

The primary questions for investigation would seem to be, then, first, how a more sexually egalitarian division became a less egalitarian one, and second, how this hierarchical division of labour became extended to wage labour in the modern period. Many anthropological studies suggest that the first process, sexual stratification, occurred together with the increasing productiveness, specialization, and complexity of society; for example, through the establishment of settled agriculture, private property, or the state. It occurred as human society emerged from the primitive and became 'civilized'. In this perspective capitalism is a relative latecomer, whereas patriarchy, the hierarchical relation between men and women in which men are dominant and women are subordinate, was an early arrival.

I want to argue that, before capitalism, a patriarchal system was established in which men controlled the labour of women and children in the family, and that in so doing men learned the techniques of hierarchical organization and control. With the advent of **public–private separations** such as those created by the emergence of state apparatus and economic systems based on wider exchange and larger production units, the problem for men became one of maintaining their control over the labour power of women. In other words, a direct personal system of control was translated into an indirect, impersonal system of control, mediated by society-wide institutions. The mechanisms available to men were (1) the traditional division of labour between the sexes, and (2) techniques of hierarchical organization and control. These mechanisms were crucial in the second process, the extension of a sex-ordered division of labour to the wage-labour system, during the period of the emergence of capitalism in Western Europe and the United States.

The emergence of capitalism in the fifteenth to eighteenth centuries threatened patriarchal control based on institutional authority as it destroyed many old institutions and created new ones, such as a 'free' market in labour. It threatened to bring all women and children into the labour force and hence to destroy the family and the basis of the power of men over women (i.e., the control over their labour power in the family). If the theoretical tendency of pure capitalism would have been to eradicate all arbitrary differences of status among labourers, to make all labourers equal in the marketplace, why are women still in an inferior position to men in the labour market? The possible answers are legion; they range from neoclassical views that the process is not complete or is hampered by market imperfections to the radical view that production requires hierarchy even if the market nominally requires 'equality'. All of these explanations, it seems to me, ignore the role of men – ordinary men, men as men, men as workers – in maintaining women's inferiority in the labour market. The radical view, in particular, emphasizes the role of men as capitalists in creating hierarchies in the production process in order to maintain their power. Capitalists do this by segmenting the labour market

(along race, sex, and ethnic lines among others) and playing workers off against each other. In this paper I argue that male workers have played and continue to play a crucial role in maintaining sexual divisions in the labour process.

Job segregation by sex, I will argue, is the primary mechanism in capitalist society that maintains the superiority of men over women, because it enforces lower wages for women in the labour market. Low wages keep women dependent on men because they encourage women to marry. Married women must perform domestic chores for their husbands. Men benefit, then, from both higher wages and the domestic division of labour. This domestic division of labour, in turn, acts to weaken women's position in the labour market. Thus, the hierarchical domestic division of labour is perpetuated by the labour market, and vice versa. This process is the present outcome of the continuing interaction of two interlocking systems, capitalism and patriarchy. Patriarchy, far from being vanquished by capitalism, is still very virile; it shapes the form modern capitalism takes, just as the development of capitalism has transformed patriarchal institutions. The resulting mutual accommodation between patriarchy and capitalism has created a vicious circle for women.

My argument contrasts with the traditional views of both neoclassical and Marxist economists. Both ignore patriarchy, a social system with a material base. The **neoclassical economists** tend to exonerate the capitalist system, attributing job segregation to exogenous *ideological* factors, like sexist attitudes. Marxist economists tend to attribute job segregation to capitalists, ignoring the part played by male workers and the effect of centuries of patriarchal social relations. In this paper I hope to redress the balance. The line of argument I have outlined here and will develop further below is perhaps incapable of proof. This paper, I hope, will establish its plausibility rather than its incontrovertability.

Anthropological perspectives on the division of labour by sex

Some anthropologists explain male dominance by arguing that it existed from the very beginning of human society. Sherry Ortner (1992) suggests that indeed 'female is to male as nature is to culture'. According to Ortner, culture devalues nature; females are associated with nature, are considered closer to nature in all cultures, and are thus devalued. Her view is compatible with that of Rosaldo (1974), who emphasizes the public-private split, and that of Lévi-Strauss, who assumes the subordination of women during the process of the creation of society.

According to Lévi-Strauss, culture began with the exchange of women by men to cement bonds between families – thereby creating *society* (1971). In fact, Lévi-Strauss sees a fundamental tension between the family (i.e., the domestic realm in which women reside closer to nature) and society, which requires that families break down their autonomy to exchange with one another. The exchange of women is a mechanism that enforces the interdependence of families and that creates society. ... Thus the existence of a sexual division of labour is a universal of human society, though the exact division of the tasks by sex varies enormously. Moreover, following Lévi-Strauss, because it is men who exchange women and women who are exchanged in creating social bonds, men benefit more than women from these social bonds, and the division of labour between the sexes is a hierarchical one.

While this first school of anthropological thought, the 'universalists', is based primarily on Lévi-Strauss and the exchange of women, Chodorow, following Rosaldo and Ortner, emphasizes women's confinement to the domestic sphere. Chodorow locates this confinement in the mothering role. She constructs the universality of patriarchy on the universal fact that women mother. Female mothering reproduces itself via the creation of gender-specific personality structures.

Two other major schools of thought on the origins of the sexual division of labour merit attention. Both reject the universality, at least in theory if not in practice, of the sex-ordered division of labour. One is the 'feminist-revisionist' school which argues that we cannot be certain that the division of labour is male supremacist; it may be separate but equal (as Lévi-Strauss occasionally seems to indicate), but we will never know because of the bias of the observers which makes comparisons impossible. ...

The second school also rejects the universality of sex-ordered division of labour but, unlike relativists, seeks to compare societies to isolate the variables which coincide with greater or lesser autonomy of women. This school, the 'variationist', is subdivided according to the characteristics members emphasize: the contribution of women to subsistence and their control over their contribution, the organization of tribal versus state societies, the requirements of the mode of production, the emergence of wealth and private property, the boundaries of the private and public spheres. ...

... Several studies from the third school of anthropology, the variationist school, ... suggest that increased sexual stratification occurs along with a general process of social stratification (which at least in some versions seems to depend on and foster an increase in social surplus – to support the higher groups in the hierarchy). As a result, a decrease in the social status of woman occurs when (1) she loses control of subsistence through a change in production methods and devaluation of her share of the division of labour; (2) her work becomes private and family centered rather than social and kin focused; and/or (3) some men assert their power over other men through the state mechanism by elevating these subordinate men in their families, using the nuclear family against the kin group. In this way the division of labour between men and women becomes a more hierarchical one. Control over women is maintained directly in the family by the man, but it is sustained by social institutions, such as the state and religion.

The work in this school of anthropology suggests that patriarchy did not always exist, but rather that it emerged as social conditions changed. Moreover, men participated in this transformation. Because it benefited men relative to women, men have had a stake in reproducing patriarchy. Although there is a great deal of controversy among anthropologists about the origins of patriarchy, and more work needs to be done to establish the validity of this interpretation, I believe the weight of the evidence supports it. In any case, most anthropologists agree that patriarchy emerged long before capitalism, even if they disagree about its origins.

In England, as we have seen, the formation of the state marks the end of Anglo-Saxon tribal society and the beginning of feudal society. Throughout feudal society the tendencies toward the privatization of family life and the increase of male power within the family appear to strengthen, as does their institutional support from church and state. By the time of the emergence of capitalism in the fifteenth through eighteenth centuries, the nuclear, patriarchal peasant family had become the basic production unit in society.

The emergence of capitalism and the Industrial Revolution in England and the United States

The key process in the emergence of capitalism was primitive accumulation, the prior accumulation that was necessary for capitalism to establish itself. Primitive accumulation was a twofold process which set the preconditions for the expansion of the scale of production: first, free labourers had to be accumulated; second, large amounts of capital had to be accumulated. The first was achieved through **enclosures** and the removal of people from the land, their subsistence base, so that they were forced to work for wages. The second was achieved through both the growth of smaller capitals in farms and shops amassed through banking facilities, and vast increases in merchant capital, the profits from the slave trade, and colonial exploitation.

The creation of a wage-labour force and the increase

in the scale of production that occurred with the emergence of capitalism had in some ways a more severe impact on women than on men. To understand this impact let us look at the work of women before this transition occurred and the changes which took place as it occurred. In the 1500s and 1600s, agriculture, woollen textiles (carried on as a by-industry of agriculture), and the various crafts and trades in the towns were the major sources of livelihood for the English population. In the rural areas men worked in the fields on small farms they owned or rented and women tended the household plots, small gardens and orchards, animals, and dairies. The women also spun and wove. A portion of these products were sold in small markets to supply the villages, towns, and cities, and in this way women supplied a considerable proportion of their families' cash income, as well as their subsistence in kind. In addition to the tenants and farmers, there was a small wage-earning class of men and women who worked on the larger farms. Occasionally tenants and their wives worked for wages as well, the men more often than the women. As small farmers and cottagers were displaced by larger farmers in the seventeenth and eighteenth centuries, their wives lost their main sources of support, while the men were able to continue as wage labourers to some extent. Thus women, deprived of these essential household plots, suffered relatively greater unemployment, and the families as a whole were deprived of a large part of their subsistence.

In the 1700s, the demand for cotton textiles grew, and English merchants found they could utilize the labour of the English agricultural population, who were already familiar with the arts of spinning and weaving. The merchants distributed materials to be spun and woven, creating a domestic industrial system which occupied many displaced farm families. This putting-out system, however, proved inadequate. The complexities of distribution and collection and, perhaps more important, the control the workers had over the production process (they could take time off, work intermittently, steal materials) prevented an increase in the supply of textiles sufficient to meet the merchants' needs. To solve these problems first spinning, in the late 1700s, and then weaving, in the early 1800s, were organized into factories. The textile factories were located in the rural areas, at first, in order both to take advantage of the labour of children and women, by escaping the restrictions of the guilds in the cities, and to utilize waterpower. When spinning was industrialized, women spinners at home suffered greater unemployment, while the demand for male handloom weavers increased. When weaving was mechanized, the need for handloom weavers fell off as well.

In this way, domestic industry, created by emerging capitalism, was later superseded and destroyed by the progress of capitalist industrialization. In the process, women, children, and men in the rural areas all suffered dislocation and disruption, but they experienced this in different ways. Women, forced into unemployment by the capitalization of agriculture more frequently than men; were more available to labour, both in the domestic putting-out system and in the early factories. It is often argued both that men resisted going into the factories because they did not want to lose their independence and that women and children were more docile and malleable. If this was in fact the case, it would appear that these 'character traits' of women and men were already established before the advent of the capitalistic organization of industry, and that they would have grown out of the authority structure prevailing in the previous period of small-scale, family agriculture. Many historians suggest that within the family men were the heads of households, and women, even though they contributed a large part of their families' subsistence, were subordinate.

We may never know the facts of the authority structure within the preindustrial family, since much of what we know is from prescriptive literature or otherwise class biased, and little is known about the point of view of the people themselves. Nevertheless, the evidence on family life and on relative wages and levels of living suggests that women were subordinate within the family. This conclusion is consonant with the anthropological literature, which describes the emergence of patriarchial social relations along with early societal stratification. Moreover, the history of the early factories suggests that capitalists took advantage of this authority structure, finding women and children more vulnerable, both because of familial relations and because they were simply more desperate economically due to the changes in agriculture which left them unemployed.

The transition to capitalism in the cities and towns was experienced somewhat differently than in the rural areas, but it tends to substantiate the line of argument just set out: men and women had different places in the familial authority structure, and capitalism proceeded in a way that built on that authority structure. In the towns and cities before the transition to capitalism a system of family industry prevailed: a family of artisans worked together at home to produce goods for exchange. Adults were organized in guilds, which had social and religious functions as well as industrial ones. Within trades carried on as family industries women and men generally performed different tasks: in general, the men worked at what were considered more skilled tasks, the women at processing the raw materials or finishing the end product. Men, usually the heads of the production units, had the status of master artisans. For though women usually belonged to their husbands' guilds, they did so as appendages; girls were rarely apprenticed to a trade and thus rarely become journeymen or masters. Married women participated in the production process and probably acquired important skills, but they usually controlled the production process only if they were widowed, when guilds often gave them the right to hire apprentices and journeymen. Young men may have married within their guilds (i.e., the daughters of artisans in the same trade). In fact, young women and girls had a unique and very important role as extra or casual labourers in a system where the guilds prohibited hiring additional workers from outside the family, and undoubtedly they learned skills which were useful when they married. Nevertheless, girls appear not to have been trained as carefully as boys were and, as adults, not to have attained the same status in the guilds. ...

The capitalistic organization of industry, in removing work from the home, served to increase the subordination of women, since it served to increase the relative importance of the area of men's domination. But it is important to remember that men's domination was already established and that it clearly influenced the direction and shape that capitalist development took. ...

When women participated in the wage-labour market, they did so in a position as clearly limited by patriarchy as it was by capitalism. Men's control over women's labour was altered by the wage-labour system, but it was not eliminated. In the labour market the dominant position of men was maintained by sex-ordered job segregation. Women's jobs were lower paid, considered less skilled, and often involved less exercise of authority or control. Men acted to enforce job segregation in the labour market; they utilized trade-union associations and strengthened the domestic division of labour, which required women to do housework, child care, and related chores. Women's subordinate position in the labour market reinforced their subordinate position in the family, and that in turn reinforced their labour-market position. ...

Conclusion

The present status of women in the labour market and the current arrangement of sex-segregated jobs is the result of a long process of interaction between patriarchy and capitalism. I have emphasized the actions of male workers throughout this process because I believe that emphasis to be correct. Men will have to be forced to give up their favored positions in the division of labour – in the labour market and at home – both if women's subordination is to end and if men are to begin to escape class oppression and exploitation. Capitalists have indeed used women as unskilled, underpaid labour to undercut male workers, yet this is only a case of the chickens coming home to roost – a case of men's co-optation by an support for patriarchal society, with its hierarchy among men, being turned back on themselves with a vengeance. Capitalism grew on top of patriarchy; patriarchal capitalism is stratified society par excellence. If non-ruling-class men are to be free they will have to recognize their co-optation by patriarchal capitalism and relinquish their patriarchal benefits. If women are to be free, they must fight against both patriarchal power and capitalist organization of society.

References

Levi-Strauss, C. (1971) 'The family', in Shapiro, H. (ed.) *Man, Culture and Society*, New York: Oxford University Press.

Ortner, S. (1972) 'Is female to male as nature is to culture?', *Feminist Studies*, vol. 1, no. 2.

Rosaldo, M. (1974) 'Woman, culture and society: a theoretical overview', in Rosaldo, M. and Lamphere, L. (eds) *Woman, Culture and Society*, Stanford: Stanford University Press.

Key terms

The following key terms appear in the text above. They have been defined below to aid with the reading of this item.

public-private separations the idea that we can distinguish between the private arena in society, notably inside the family, and the public arena in society – comprising of all other institutions. The suggestion is that while men were free to operate in both spheres of society, women were for a long period confined to the private sphere, where they were further subjugated by being under the legally enforced authority of a male (either father or husband)

job segregation the idea that the kind of jobs available to women are different and usually inferior, in terms of conditions, to those available to men

neoclassical economists supporters of the free-market economy

enclosures areas of common land that were fenced in and turned into private property. Once land was enclosed poor peasants no longer had access to it and were forced to look for other ways of earning money, notably through paid employment

Questions

1 What, according to the author, is the basis of men's power over women?

2 What are the key effects of job segregation by sex?

3 In what ways did the emergence of capitalism affect gender inequalities?

4 Suggest three examples of the way sex segregation in contemporary society reinforces gender inequalities.

5 Assess the relative merits of the differing anthropological arguments given for the origin of sex inequalities.

6 How far do sociological arguments support the proposition that male workers play a crucial role in maintaining sexual divisions in the labour process?

Reading 10.6 **The labour process and the politics of production**

Michael Burawoy (from) *The Politics of Production* (1985) London: Verso, pp. 5–8 and 10–14.

Editorial comments

One of the key approaches within Marxist industrial sociology is the labour process approach developed by Harry Braverman (1974). Michael Burawoy is famous for his studies of the labour process and the way he has developed this approach through a critical appreciation of the work of Braverman. Crucially he argues that Braverman took a very objectivist view of workers, ignoring their subjective attitudes which he himself feels are crucial. Here he utilizes the Gramscian concept of hegemony to develop an analysis of the way the labour process is affected by the politics of production and by the ebb and flow of subjective factors in the workplace. In this reading, he outlines the basis of labour process theory, including his differences with Braverman, as a basis for outlining his own approach.

Reference

Braverman, H (1974) *Labour and Monopoly Capital*, New York: Monthly Review Press.

Bringing workers back in

THIS IS AN unfashionable book. It defends an unfashionable thesis about an unfashionable class formed in an unfashionable place. The class is the industrial proletariat. The place is the point of production. And the thesis has two parts. First, I argue that the industrial working class has made significant and self-conscious interventions in history. Second, I argue that these interventions were and continue to be shaped by the process of production. This thesis is in contention with contemporary trends, both within and beyond Marxism, which either abandon the working class for **new social movements** or consider it to be just one of a number of collective actors formed in the public sphere. Found on both sides of the Atlantic, the 'newer left', as it has been called, challenges two central Marxist propositions: the privileged status of the working class, and the primacy of production. Can one recognize what underlies these critiques and still be a Marxist? My answer is yes.

Within these emerging political and intellectual currents, the postulate of the revolutionary working class is held to be theoretically and philosophically overburdened. From the beginning the working class could only give lie to the mission, assigned by Marxists, of emancipating itself and therewith the whole of humanity. 'Marxism has been the greatest fantasy of our century' (Kolakowski, 1978). We must cry farewell to the working class, embracing the new social movements which spring from **civil society**, understood as the forgotten space between state and economy. From here community struggles, the feminist movement, the ecology movement, the civil rights movement and the peace movement burgeon forth as the progressive movements of the 1980s. If they have a limited vision this is all to the good, since transcendental tasks, such as the one that Marxists assigned to the working class, are the back door or even the front door to totalitarianism.

If messianic radicalism is now philosophically, theoretically and politically unacceptable, why can we not simply reduce the burden on the working class to one appropriate to its real rather than imagined interventions in history? The answer, it seems, is that the working class not only has lost its revolutionary temper, if it ever had one, but also is a dying class. The post-industrial society ushers in 'deindustrialization' and with it a shrinking, weakening industrial working class. In its place new classes, such as intellectuals, emerge as agents for alternative visions of the future. Another strategy is to reduce socialism to social democracy, and social democracy to a question of numbers. On careful investigation it now turns out that there were never enough proletarians for socialist parties to become effective forces through electoral means. Coalition politics between the working class and allied classes, and therefore the compromise of socialist goals, were always and inevitably part of capitalist democracy. This provides the basis for a movement to the right in the name of electoral politics.

Contemporary historical studies reproduce this drift. Marxism is fleetingly raised from the floor only to be knocked out of the ring. Marx mistakenly projected the model of a revolutionary bourgeoisie onto the working class, which could never achieve the transformative power of its overlord. Paradoxically, the peasantry – which Marx, at least in conventional interpretations, condemned to the proverbial sack of potatoes – is resurrected as the last heroic class capable of fuelling revolution. Revolutions become a thing of the past, save perhaps in the beleaguered Third World. Certainly the working class plays no leading role in them. Instead the state becomes an actor in its own right with its own interests, something to be not transformed or destroyed but manipulated and bargained with. States are here to stay, so we must learn to live with them.

Equally damning for the postulate of a revolutionary proletariat are the studies of workers in their brief moments of heroism. These studies have unearthed the swan songs of artisans in their battle to defend their skills against the encroachment of capital – a battle they seemed destined to lose, but which momentarily threw up radical visions. We are left rescuing the pristine artisans of the past in those moments of tragedy and ecstasy, as an exhortation to the hollow walls of the present. Now we face an atomized, fragmented, objectified working class. Labour historian and prophet of work degradation join hands in orchestrating the proletariat's last dance – in a conspiracy upset only by the authors refusal to be implicated and by their surges of utopianism.

This, then, is the polemical context of this book – the emergence of perspectives that conjure away the working class. A pathos has engulfed Marxist and 'post-Marxist' thought, reconstructing history in its own image and projecting those reconstructions into the future. It would be foolhardy to place oneself outside the course of history, to swim directly against a tide which is dashing the revolutionary proletariat onto the rocks of history or sweeping it out to sea, never to be seen again. I am not, therefore, going to restore the working class to its messianic role, but nor do I intend to abandon it to the vicissitudes of some putative logic of history. I am not going to replace one metaphysical imputation (the working class as saviour of humanity) with its opposite (the working class as incapable of shaping its own destiny). As we shall see when we undertake sociological analyses in comparative and historical dimensions, the record of the industrial working class is not as insignificant as

its detractors would lead us to believe. As to the question of deindustrialization, I do not deny its importance in advanced capitalist countries: it might indeed be happening on a world scale too. Of greater significance, however, is the international *recomposition* of the industrial working class – which entails that the conditions for the renewal of working-class radicalism are to be found in the industrially advancing areas of Latin America, Africa and Eastern Europe. In other words, the quiescence of industrial workers in some of the most advanced capitalist countries should not be projected into the past and the future or generalized to other countries. Just as revolutionary impulses are not innate characteristics of the working class, so resignation to the status quo is neither natural nor inevitable but is produced by specific conditions. ...

I defend the thesis that the process of production decisively shapes the development of working-class struggles. This thesis can be sustained only if the process of production is seen to have two political moments. First, the organization of work has political and ideological *effects* – that is, as men and women transform raw materials into useful things, they also reproduce particular social relations as well as an experience of those relations. Second, alongside the organization of work – that is, the *labour process* – there are distinctive political and ideological *apparatuses of production* which regulate production relations. The notion of *production regime* or, more specifically, factory regime embraces both these dimensions of production politics. ...

At this point, it may assist the reader if I trace the genesis of the concept of production politics. It first emerged while I was machining parts of diesel engines at the South Chicago division of the multi-national corporation Allied. During my ten-month stint as a miscellaneous machine operator, from June 1974 to April 1975, Harry Braverman (1974) published his pathbreaking *Labour and Monopoly Capital*. At the time it failed to speak to my experiences on the shopfloor, to get at what work meant to me and my fellow operators. We were constructing a shopfloor life of our own that took for granted what Braverman bemoaned: the separation of conception and execution. Our jobs may have had little skill in Braverman's sense, but they involved ingenuity enough. They absorbed our attention and sometimes even left us too much autonomy. Uncertainty could be as nerve-wracking as it was seductive. Objectification of work, if that is what we were experiencing, is very much a subjective process – it cannot be reduced to some inexorable laws of capitalism. We participated in and strategized our own subordination. We were active accomplices in our own exploitation. That, and not the destruction of subjectivity, was what was so remarkable.

It was not Braverman who offered insights into my

daily life but, curiously, the abstract theories of politics and ideology found in Gramsci, Poulantzas and Althusser – very much in fashion at the time. Their analyses of hegemony – the presentation of the interests of the dominant classes as the interests of all, the constitution of the popular class state, the construction of the power bloc, the disorganization of the subordinate classes, the relative autonomy of the law, and so forth – all appeared as germane to the factory as to the sphere of public power. Thus, collective bargaining concretely coordinated the interests of workers and management, the grievance machinery constituted workers as industrial citizens with rights and obligations, and the internal labour market produced a possessive individualism right there on the shopfloor. These institutions materialized a balance of power, which first and foremost set limits on workers' struggles but also restrained management from its authoritarian impulses. The **regulating institutions** afforded an arena of self-activity, free from managerial depredations, that gave workers the opportunity to construct effective working relations and drew them into the pursuit of capitalist profit. Cooperation revolved around 'making out', a 'game' in which the goal was to make a certain quota, and whose rules were recognized and defended by workers and management alike. Originally constructed to alleviate boredom and to introduce some meaning into eight hours of drilling, milling or turning, this 'making out' had the effect of generating consent to its rules and of obscuring the conditions that framed them. Coercion was applied only when the rules were violated, and even then within bounds that were themselves part of a larger game. In short, as we slaved away on our machines trying to make our quotas we manufactured not only parts of diesel engines, not only relations of cooperation and domination, but also consent to those activities and relations.

I christened the regulating institutions that embodied and guaranteed this **hegemonic** order the 'internal state', underlining the analogies with the 'external state'. However, once the central point had been made that there was a politics outside the state – that is, a production politics as well as a state politics – the concept of 'internal state' was of limited analytical use. It had to go for at least two reasons. First, it blurred the essential association of the state with the monopoly of the means of organized coercion, guaranteed by armed bodies of men and women. The state remains the decisive nucleus of power in capitalist societies in that it guarantees the constellations of power outside the state, in the family, the factory, the community, and so on. In this sense state politics is 'global' politics; it is the politics of politics. The second reason for abandoning the concept of 'internal state' was its unjustified focus on the factory. There

was no obvious warrant for referring to factory apparatuses as an 'internal state' while denying such a designation for family apparatuses. I therefore stuck to the idea of politics of production, whose locus and object were not an 'internal state' but simply the political apparatuses of production. The concept of factory regime encompasses these apparatuses and the political effects of the labour process.

The similarities and differences between workplace and state apparatuses led inexorably to the question of their interrelationship. Allied turned out to be the same plant that Donald Roy, a famous industrial sociologist, had studied in meticulous detail while he was a radial drill operator thirty years earlier. I was therefore able to map changes in the factory regime during the post-war period, but I never succeeded in isolating secular changes due to the development of new forms of state regulation of production apparatuses from changes specific to the enterprise, particularly its changing market context. Indeed, I tended to stress the absorption of Roy's Geer Company into the multinational Allied – that is, the firm's passage from the competitive to the corporate sector – as the major explanation for the movement along the axis from despotic to hegemonic regimes.

Undoubtedly the major inspiration for linking production politics and state politics came from Miklós Haraszti's extraordinary sociography of Red Star Tractor Factory in Budapest, where he worked as a mill operator in 1971. The same stroke of luck that had landed me in Donald Roy's factory also landed me in a machine shop which, in terms of work organization, technology and payment system, bore a remarkable resemblance to the one at Red Star. And yet the production politics could not have been more different. Whereas the hegemonic regime at Allied relied on the relative autonomy of the factory apparatuses, restricting managerial interventions while regulating working-class struggles, the despotic regime at Red Star gave management a coercive instrument of untrammelled domination over the workforce. The importance of the relationship between state and factory was immediately obvious. At Allied, the factory apparatuses and state apparatuses were institutionally separated; at Red Star they were fused. To be sure, the state intervened to shape the form of factory apparatuses at Allied, but it was not physically present at the point of production. At Red Star, management, party and trade union were arms of the state at the point of production.

I called the regime at Red Star despotic because coercion prevailed over consent. I called it bureaucratic despotism because it was constituted by the administrative hierarchy of the state. Market despotism, by contrast, is constituted by the economic whip of the market, and the state regulates only the external conditions of market relations – that is, the state protects market relations and labour mobility among firms. Under market despotism, Marx's prototypical factory regime for modern industry, the state is separated from and does not directly shape the form of the factory regime; whereas, under the hegemonic regime, the state and factory apparatuses are also institutionally separated but the state shapes the factory apparatuses by stipulating, for example, mechanisms for the conduct and resolution of struggle at the point of production. Our three types of regime may be presented in the following table.

		Separation	Fusion
Intervention of state in factory regime	Direct	HEGEMONIC	BUREAUCRATIC DESPOTIC
	Indirect	MARKET DESPOTIC	COLLECTIVE SELF-MANAGEMENT

Institutional relationship between apparatuses of factory and of state

The fourth cell – collective self-management – combines a different form of state-factory relations, in which factory apparatuses are managed by workers themselves. However, the state, or at least some central administrative organ, stipulates the conditions under which factories become self-regulating – that is, it stipulates what is to be produced with what materials obtained from what source. Moreover, this central planning agency is subject to influence from below through institutionalized mechanisms of participation by factory councils.

The above table provides the point of departure for this book. What significance can we attach to four types of factory regime inferred from a study of just two machine shops?! In particular, is there any relationship between market despotism, hegemonic systems and bureaucratic despotism on one side and early capitalism, advanced capitalism and **state socialism** on the other? If so, what is it? What other types of factory regime can be found under capitalism and socialism in both **core and peripheral countries**? What are the conditions of their reproduction and transformation? What are the consequences, in particular for class struggles, of the different regimes? Can we isolate their effects from those of other institutions? And what can we say about the transition from one system of politics (combination/articulation of production politics and state politics) to another?

How much is this shaped by tendencies inherent to those systems, and how much by political and economic factors of an international character? We can begin to answer these questions only by situating regimes in their historical contexts of specific economies and states.

Before proceeding to these questions, we must be careful not to detach the political apparatuses of production from their material base – from the labour process. ... For Braverman, the generic notion of the labour process involves a combination of two sets of activities: mental and manual labour. The hallmark of capitalism is their separation, which appears to the worker as domination. Here we shall pursue a slightly different course, defining the labour process by the social relations into which men and women enter in order to produce useful things. I call these social relations between and among workers and managers *relations in production*. These must be distinguished from the *relations of exploitation* between labour and capital. Whereas the former refer to the organization of tasks, the latter refer to the relations through which surplus is pumped out of the direct producer. It should be noted that relations of exploitation are part of the *relations of production*, which also include the relations among the units which organize exploitation. Thus, relations of production include both the appropriation and the distribution of surplus. Whereas the relations of production uniquely define a mode of production, the same relations in production – the same labour process – may be found in different modes of production. Hence we refer not to the capitalist labour process but to the labour process in capitalist society.

Once a notion of the labour process as the unity/separation of conception and execution is replaced with a relational notion, the emphasis shifts from a question of *domination* to one of *reproducing* social relations. This is precisely the theoretical inspiration behind the concept of production apparatuses, although there is no one-to-one correspondence between institution and function. Thus, state apparatuses also reproduce relations in production and relations of exploitation, just as production apparatuses can reproduce relations of domination, such as gender and race relations, originating outside production.

Whereas my discussion of Braverman's work stresses the directly political and ideological *effects of the labour process*, the succeeding parts of the book deal with struggles as they are also shaped by different types of *production apparatuses*. I will be at pains to demonstrate that the labour process is only one of a number of factors that condition their form.

References

Braverman, H. (1974) *Labour and Monopoly Capital*, New York: Monthly Review Press.

Kolakowski, L. (1978) *Main Currents of Marxism*, vol. 3., Oxford: Oxford University Press

Key terms

The following key terms appear in the text above. They have been defined below to aid with the reading of this item.

new social movements movements such as the women's liberation movement, the black civil rights movements and other more recent political movements whose basis of organization is not the production process, and which are often therefore contrasted with class-based movements

civil society all the institutions in a society other than the state

regulating institutions the term used to convey the idea that society is regulated and that the key to this is production relations and the way they have a political and ideological aspect to them

hegemonic derived from the work of Antonio Gramsci, this term is used to suggest the way that some ideas become dominant in society. It also implies the partial acceptance of those ideas, in contrast to the despotic imposition of power

state socialism Burawoy uses this term to describe the states of Eastern Europe

core and peripheral countries a categorization developed by dependency theorists to argue that placement in the world economy has some effect on national development or underdevelopment, but also later developed to argue that workforces in any one sector can face such divisions, often seen as between full-time (male) workers and part-time or temporary (female) workers

Questions

1 Explain in your own words what the author means by 'the process of production decisively shapes the development of working-class struggles'.

2 What does the author mean by distinguishing between the 'labour process' and the 'factory regime'?

3 Why does the author argue that objectification of work is very much a subjective process?

4 Suggest two contemporary examples of the kind of strategy that Burawoy outlines at the start of this reading and which he argues is mistaken in some respects.

5 How far do you agree that consent is becoming more important in relations of production?

Reading 10.7 **The McDonaldization of society**

George Ritzer (from) *The McDonaldization of Society* (1993) Thousand Oaks: Pine Forge Press, pp. 4–13.

Editorial comments

George Ritzer applies Weber's theory of rationalization to contemporary American society and argues that fast-food chains can be seen as the key contemporary archetype of that process. In this reading, Ritzer provides both some information about McDonald's to back up his argument, and the links to the insights developed by Weber in his original exposition of the theory of rationalization.

The McDonaldization of society

McDonald's as 'Americana', sacred 'icon', and at 35,000 feet

MCDONALD'S AS WELL as its many clones have become ubiquitous and immediately recognizable symbols throughout the United States as well as much of the rest of the world. For example, when plans were afoot to raze Ray Kroc's first McDonald's outlet, hundreds of letters poured into McDonald's headquarters, including the following:

Please don't tear it down! … Your company's name is a household word, not only in the United States of America, but all over the world. To destroy this major artifact of contemporary culture would, indeed, destroy part of the faith the people of the world have in your company.

In the end, the outlet was not torn down, but rather turned into a museum! Said a McDonald's executive, explaining the move, 'McDonald's … is really a part of Americana'. Similarly, when Pizza Hut opened in

Moscow in 1990, a Russian student said, 'It's a piece of America'.

In fact, McDonald's is such a powerful symbol that we have come to give many businesses nicknames beginning with *Mc* in order to indicate that they follow the McDonald's model. Examples include '*Mc*Dentists' and '*Mc*Doctors' (for drive-in clinics designed to deal quickly and efficiently with minor dental and medical problems), '*Mc*Child' Care Centers (for child care centres like Kinder-Care), '*Mc*Stables' (for the nationwide racehorse training operation of Wayne Lucas), and '*Mc*Paper' (for the newspaper *USA TODAY* and its short news articles often called 'News *Mc*Nuggets'). When *USA TODAY* began an aborted television program modelled after the newspaper, some began to call it 'News *Mc*Rather'.

McDonald's has come to occupy a central place in popular culture. It can be a big event when a new McDonald's opens in a small town. Said one Maryland high school student at such an event, 'Nothing this exciting ever happens in Dale City'. Newspapers cover fast-food business developments; the opening of the McDonald's in Beijing was big news. McDonald's is spoofed or treated with reverence on television programs and in the movies. A skit on the television show *Saturday Night Live* makes fun of the specialization of such businesses by detailing the trials and tribulations of a franchise that sells nothing but Scotch tape. The movie *Coming to America* casts Eddie Murphy as an African prince whose introduction to America includes a job at 'McDowell's', a thinly disguised McDonald's. In *Moscow on the Hudson*, Robin Williams, newly arrived from Russia, obtains a job at McDonald's. H. G. Wells, a central character in the movie *Time After Time*, finds himself transported to the modern world of McDonald's, where he tries to order the tea he was accustomed to drinking in Victorian England. In *Sleeper*, Woody Allen awakens in the future only to encounter a McDonald's. Finally, *Tin Men*, which shows the passage from the era of the Cadillac to that of the Volkswagen, ends with the heroes driving off into a future represented by a huge golden arch looming in the distance.

Many people identify strongly with McDonald's; in fact to some it has become a sacred institution. On the opening of the McDonald's in Moscow, one journalist described it as the 'ultimate **icon** of Americana', while a worker spoke of it 'as if it were the Cathedral in Chartres ... a place to experience "celestial joy"'. Kowinski argues that shopping malls – which we will show to be crucial to McDonaldization – are the modern 'cathedrals of consumption' to which we go to practice our 'consumer religion'. Similarly, a visit to what we shall see is another central element of our McDonaldized society, Walt Disney World, has been described as 'the middle-class haj, the compulsory visit to the sunbaked holy city'.

McDonald's has achieved its exalted position as a result of the fact that virtually all Americans, and many of those from other countries, have passed through its golden arches, often on innumerable occasions. Furthermore, we have all been bombarded by commercials extolling McDonald's virtues. These commercials have been tailored to different audiences. Some are aimed at young children watching Saturday morning cartoons. Others point toward young adults watching prime-time programs. Still others are oriented toward grandparents who might be coaxed into taking their grandchildren to McDonald's. In addition, McDonald's commercials change as the chain introduces new foods (such as breakfast burritos), creates new contests, and ties its products to things such as new motion pictures. These ever-present commercials, combined with the fact that we cannot drive very far without having a McDonald's pop into view, have served to embed McDonald's deep into our consciousness. In a survey taken in 1986, 96 per cent of the schoolchildren polled were able to identify Ronald McDonald, making him second only to Santa Claus in name recognition.

Over the years McDonald's has appealed to us on a variety of different grounds. The restaurants themselves are depicted as spick-and-span, the food is said to be fresh and nutritious, the employees are shown to be young and eager, the managers appear gentle and caring, and the dining experience itself seems to be fun-filled. We are even led to believe that we contribute, at least indirectly, to charities by supporting the company that supports Ronald McDonald homes for sick children.

McDonald's has continually extended its reach, within American society and beyond. It began as a suburban and medium-sized-town phenomenon, but in recent years it has moved into big cities not only in the United States, but also in many other parts of the world. Fast-food outlets can now be found in New York's Times Square as well as on the Champs Élysées in Paris. They have also now migrated into smaller towns that supposedly could not support such a restaurant. At first, McDonald's and its fast-food clones settled on specific strips of road, such as Route 161 in Columbus, Ohio. Said one local resident, 'You want something for the stomach? ... Drive that car down Route 161 and you'll see more eating than you ever saw in your life'. Although such strips continue to flourish, fast-food restaurants are now far more geographically dispersed.

Another significant expansion has occurred more recently as fast-food restaurants have moved onto college campuses, instead of being content, as they have in the past, merely to dominate the strips that surround many campuses. Installed on college campuses with the seeming approval of college administrations, McDonald's is in a position to further influence the lifestyle of the younger generation.

Another, even more recent, incursion has occurred: Fast-food restaurants are taking over the restaurant business on the nation's highways. Now we no longer need to leave the road to dine in our favourite fast-food restaurant. We can stop for fast food and then proceed with our trip, which is likely to end in another community that has about the same density and mix of fast-food restaurants as the locale we left behind. Also in the travel realm, fast-food restaurants are more and more apt to be found in railway stations and airports and even on the tray tables of inflight meals. The following advertisement appeared on September 17, 1991, in the *Washington Post* (and *The New York Times*): 'Where else at 35,000 feet can you get a McDonald's meal like this for your kids? Only on United's Orlando flights'. Thus, children can now get McDonald's fare on United Airline's flights to Orlando. How soon before adults can have the same option? How much longer before such meals will be available on all United flights? On all flights everywhere by every carrier?

In other sectors of society, the influence of fast-food restaurants has been more subtle, but no less profound. Few high schools and grade schools have in-house fast-food restaurants, but many have had to alter school cafeteria menus and procedures so that fast food is readily and continually available to children and teenagers. Apples, yogurt, and milk may go straight into the trash can, but hamburgers, fries, and shakes are devoured. Things may be about to change dramatically, however, since Domino's, in conjunction with Marriott, has recently signed an agreement to market Domino's pizza in school cafeterias that are run by Marriott, which presently serves 200 school systems in 20 states and about a 120 million meals a year. The effort to hook schoolchildren on fast food, long a goal of advertisements aimed at this population, reached something of a peak in Illinois where McDonald's outlets operated a program called 'A for Cheeseburger'. Students who received an A on their report cards were rewarded with a free cheeseburger, thereby linking success in school with McDonald's.

The military has been pressed into offering fast-food menus on its bases and on its ships. Despite the criticisms by physicians and nutritionists, fast-food outlets are increasingly turning up *inside* hospitals. No homes have a McDonald's of their own, but dining within the home has been influenced by the fast-food restaurant. Home-cooked meals often resemble those available in fast-food restaurants. Frozen, microwavable, and preprepared foods, also bearing a striking resemblance to McDonald's meals and increasingly modelled after them, often find their way to the dinner table. Then there is the home delivery of fast foods, especially pizza, as revolutionized by Domino's.

Dunkin' Donuts, 'Critter Watch', and 'the McDonald's of sex'

Clearly, McDonald's has not been alone in pressing the fast-food model on American society and the rest of the world. Other fast-food giants, such as Burger King, Wendy's, Hardee's, Arby's, Big-Boy, Dairy Queen, TCBY, Denny's, Sizzler, Kentucky Fried Chicken, Popeye's, Taco Bell, Chi Chi's, Pizza Hut, Domino's, Long John Silver, Baskin-Robbins, and Dunkin' Donuts, have played a key role, as have the innumerable other businesses built on the principles of the fast-food restaurant.

Even the derivatives of McDonald's are, in turn, having their own influence. For example, the success of *USA TODAY* has led to changes in many newspapers across the nation, for example, shorter stories and colour weather maps. As one *USA TODAY* editor put it, 'The same newspaper editors who call us McPaper have been stealing our McNuggets'. The influence of *USA TODAY* is blatantly manifest in the *Boca Raton News*, a Knight-Ridder newspaper. This newspaper is described as 'a sort of smorgasbord of snippets, a newspaper that slices and dices the news into even smaller portions than does *USA TODAY*, spicing it with colour graphics and fun facts and cute features like "Today's Hero" and "Critter Watch"'. As in *USA TODAY*, stories in the *Boca Raton News* usually do not jump from one page to another; they start and finish on the same page. In order to meet this need, long and complex stories often have to be reduced to a few paragraphs. Much of a story's context, and much of what the principals have to say, is severely cut back or omitted entirely. With its emphasis on light and celebrity news, its colour maps and graphics, the main function of the newspaper seems to be to entertain.

One issue to be addressed in this book is whether McDonaldization *is* inexorable and will therefore come to insinuate itself into every aspect of our society and our lives. In the movie *Sleeper*, Woody Allen not only created a futuristic world in which McDonald's was an important and highly visible element, but he also envisioned a society in which even sex underwent the process of McDonaldization. The denizens of his future world were able to enter a machine called an 'orgasmatron' that allowed them to experience an orgasm without going through the muss and fuss of sexual intercourse.

In fact, sex, like virtually every other sector of society, has undergone a process of McDonaldization. 'Dial-a-porn' allows us to have intimate, sexually explicit, even obscene, conversations with people we have never met and probably never will meet. There is great specialization here, and dialing numbers like

555-FOXX will lead to a very different phone message than dialing 555-SEXY. Escort services advertise a wide range of available sex partners. Highly specialized pornographic movies (heterosexual, homosexual, sex with children, sex with animals) can be seen at urban multiplexes and are available at local video stores for viewing in the comfort of our living rooms. Various technologies (vibrators, as an example) enhance the ability of people to have sex on their own without the bother of having to deal with a human partner. In New York City, an official called a three-story pornographic center 'the McDonald's of sex' because of its 'cookie-cutter cleanliness and compliance with the law'. The McDonaldization of sex suggests that no aspect of our lives is safe from it.

The Dimensions of McDonaldization: From Drive-Throughs to Uncomfortable Seats

Even if some domains are able to resist McDonaldization, this book intends to demonstrate that many other aspects of society are being, or will be, McDonaldized. This raises the issue of why the McDonald's model has proven so irresistible. Four basic and alluring dimensions lie at the heart of the success of the McDonald's model and, more generally, of the process of McDonaldization.

First, McDonald's offers *efficiency*. That is, the McDonald's system offers us the optimum method for getting from one point to another. Most generally, this means that McDonald's proffers the best available means of getting us from a state of being hungry to a state of being full. (Similarly, Woody Allen's orgasmatron offered an efficient method for getting us from quiescence to sexual stimulation to sexual gratification.) Other institutions, fashioned on the McDonald's model, offer us similar efficiency in losing weight, lubricating our cars, filling eye-glass prescriptions, or completing income tax forms. In a fast-paced society in which both parents are likely to work, or where there may be only a single parent, efficiently satisfying the hunger and many other needs of people is very attractive. In a highly mobile society in which people are rushing, usually by car, from one spot to another, the efficiency of a fast-food meal, perhaps without leaving one's car while passing by the drive-through window, often proves impossible to resist. The fast-food model offers us, or at least appears to offer us, an efficient method for satisfying many of our needs.

Second, McDonald's offers us food and service that can be easily *quantified* and *calculated*. In effect, McDonald's seems to offer us 'more bang for the buck'. (One of its recent innovations, in response to the growth of other fast-food franchises, is to proffer 'value meals' at discounted prices.) We often feel that we are getting a *lot* of food for a modest amount of money. Quantity has become equivalent to quality; a lot of something means it must be good. As two observers of contemporary American culture put it, 'As a culture, we tend to believe – deeply – that in general "bigger is better."' Thus, we order the *Quarter Pounder*; the *Big* Mac, the *large* fries. We can quantify all of these things and feel that we are getting a lot of food, and, in return, we appear to be shelling out only a nominal sum of money. This calculus, of course, ignores an important point: the mushrooming of fast-food outlets, and the spread of the model to many other businesses, indicates that our calculation is illusory and it is the owners who are getting the best of the deal.

There is another kind of calculation involved in the success of McDonald's – a calculation involving time. People often, at least implicitly, calculate how much time it will take them to drive to McDonald's, eat their food, and return home and then compare that interval to the amount of time required to prepare the food at home. They often conclude, rightly or wrongly, that it will take less time to go and eat at the fast-food restaurant than to eat at home. This time calculation is a key factor in the success of Domino's and other home-delivery franchises, because to patronize them people do not even need to leave their homes. To take another notable example, Lens Crafters promises us 'Glasses fast, glasses in one hour'. Some McDonaldized institutions have come to combine the emphases on time and money. Domino's promises pizza delivery in one-half hour, or the pizza is free. Pizza Hut will serve us a personal pan pizza in five minutes, or it, too, will be free.

Third, McDonald's offers us *predictability*. We know that the Egg McMuffin we eat in New York will be, for all intents and purposes, identical to those we have eaten in Chicago and Los Angeles. We also know that the one we order next week or next year will be identical to the one we eat today. There is great comfort in knowing that McDonald's offers no surprises, that the food we eat at one time or in one place will be identical to the food we eat at another time or in another place. We know that the next Egg McMuffin we eat will not be awful, but we also know that it will not be exceptionally delicious. The success of the McDonald's model indicates that many people have come to prefer a world in which there are no surprises.

Fourth and finally, *control*, especially through the *substitution of nonhuman for human technology*, is exerted over the human beings who enter the world of McDonald's. The humans who work in fast-food restaurants are trained to do a very limited number of things in precisely the way they are told to do them. Managers and inspectors make sure that workers toe the line. The human beings who eat in fast-food restaurants are also controlled, albeit (usually) more subtly and indirectly. Lines, limited menus, few options, and uncomfortable seats all lead diners to do what the management wishes them to do – eat quickly and leave. Further, the drive-through (and in some cases walk-through) window leads diners to first leave and then eat rapidly. This attribute has most recently been extended by the Domino's model, according to which customers are expected to *never* come, yet still eat speedily.

McDonald's also controls people by using non-human technology to replace human workers. Human workers, no matter how well they are programmed and controlled, can foul up the operation of the system. A slow or indolent worker can make the preparation and delivery of a Big Mac inefficient. A worker who refuses to follow the rules can leave the pickles or special sauce off a hamburger, thereby making for unpredictability. And a distracted worker can put too few fries in the box, making an order of large fries seem awfully skimpy. For these and other reasons, McDonald's is compelled to steadily replace human beings with nonhuman technologies, such as the soft-drink dispenser that shuts itself off when the glass is full, the french-fry machine that rings when the fries are crisp, the preprogrammed cash register that eliminates the need for the cashier to calculate prices and amounts, and, perhaps at some future time, the robot capable of making hamburgers. (Experimental robots of this type already exist.) All of these technologies permit greater control over the human beings involved in the fastfood restaurant. The result is that McDonald's is able to reassure customers about the nature of the employee to be encountered and the nature of the service to be obtained.

In sum, McDonald's (and the McDonald's model) has succeeded because it offers the consumer efficiency and predictability, and because it seems to offer the diner a lot of food for little money and a slight expenditure of effort. It has also flourished because it has been able to exert greater control through nonhuman technologies over both employees and customers, leading them to behave the way the organization wishes them to. The substitution of nonhuman for human technologies has also allowed the fast-food restaurant to deliver its fare increasingly more efficiently and predictably. Thus, there are good, solid reasons why McDonald's has succeeded so phenomenally and why the process of McDonaldization continues unabated.

A critique of McDonaldization: the irrationality of rationality

There is a downside to all of this. We can think of efficiency, predictability, calculability, and control through nonhuman technology as the basic compo-

nents of a *rational* system. However, rational systems often spawn irrationalities. The downside of McDonaldization will be dealt with most systematically under the heading of the *irrationality of **rationality***. Another way of saying this is that rational systems serve to deny human reason; rational systems can be unreasonable.

For example, the fast-food restaurant is often a **dehumanizing** setting in which to eat or work. People lining up for a burger, or waiting in the drive-through line, often feel as if they are dining on an assembly line, and those who prepare the burgers often appear to be working on a burger assembly line. Assembly lines are hardly human settings in which to eat, and they have been shown to be inhuman settings in which to work. As we will see, dehumanization is only one of many ways in which the highly rationalized fast-food restaurant is extremely irrational.

Of course, the criticisms of the irrationality of the fast-food restaurant will be extended to all facets of our McDonaldizing world. This extension has recently been underscored and legitimated at the opening of Euro DisneyLand outside Paris. A French socialist politician acknowledged the link between Disney and McDonald's as well as their common negative effects when he said that Euro Disney will 'bombard France with uprooted creations that are to culture what fast food is to gastronomy'.

Such critiques lead to a question: Is the headlong rush toward McDonaldization around the world advantageous or not? There are great gains to be made from McDonaldization, some of which will be discussed below. But there are also great costs and enormous risks, which this book will focus on. Ultimately, we must ask whether the creation of these rationalized systems creates an even greater number of irrationalities. At the minimum, we need to be aware of the costs associated with McDonaldization. McDonald's and other purveyors of the fast-food model spend billions of dollars each year outlining the benefits to be derived from their system. However, the critics of the system have few outlets for their ideas. There are no commercials on Saturday morning between cartoons warning children of the dangers associated with fast-food restaurants. Although few children are likely to read this book, it is aimed, at least in part, at their parents (or parents-to-be) in the hope that it will serve as a caution that might be passed on to their children.

A legitimate question may be raised about this analysis: Is this critique of McDonaldization animated by a romanticization of the past and an impossible desire to return to a world that no longer exists? For some critics, this is certainly the case. They remember the time when life was slower, less efficient, had more surprises, when people were freer, and when one was more likely to deal with a human being than a robot or a computer. Although they have a point, these critics have undoubtedly exaggerated the positive aspects of a world before McDonald's, and they have certainly tended to forget the liabilities associated with such a world. More importantly, they do not seem to realize that we are *not* returning to such a world. The increase in the number of people, the acceleration in technological change, the increasing pace of life – all this and more make it impossible to go back to a nonrationalized world, if it ever existed, of home-cooked meals, traditional restaurant dinners, high-quality foods, meals loaded with surprises, and restaurants populated only by workers free to fully express their creativity.

While one basis for a critique of McDonaldization is the past, another is the future. The future in this sense is what people have the potential to be if they are unfettered by the constraints of rational systems. This critique holds that people have the potential to be far more thoughtful, skillful, creative, and well-rounded than they now are, yet they are unable to express this potential because of the constraints of a rationalized world. If the world were less rationalized, or even derationalized, people would be better able to live up to their human potential. This critique is based not on what people were like in the past, but on what they could be like in the future, if only the constraints of McDonaldized systems were eliminated, or at least eased substantially. The criticisms to be put forth … are animated by the latter, future-oriented perspective rather than by a romanticization of the past and a desire to return to it.

Key terms

The following key terms appear in the text above. They have been defined below to aid with the reading of this item.

icon a cultural symbol that assumes some importance

rationality the belief that through logical and scientific investigation of phenomena it is possible to understand the world and use that knowledge to produce a better world. It is also the case that Max Weber in his writings on bureaucracy saw the potential downsides of this and likened it to the possibility of human beings becoming trapped inside an 'iron cage' of bureaucracy

dehumanizing treating people in a way that denies their individuality or importance. People become merely a number, a worker or a customer, rather than being seen as a full human being

Questions

1 Who was the only name recognized more than Ronald McDonald by American schoolchildren?

2 According to the author, in what ways has the process of McDonaldization affected education?

3 What, according to the author, are the four basic elements of the allure of the McDonald's model?

4 Explain what the author means by the irrationality of rationality.

5 How far do you agree that society is now dominated by the irrationality of rationality?

Reading 10.8 **The Devil makes work**

J. Clarke and C. Critcher (from) *The Devil Makes Work* (1985) London: Macmillan, pp. 94–9.

Editorial comments

Clarke and Critcher present a neo-Marxist account of the rise and nature of leisure in contemporary Britain, arguing against the interpretations offered by others – especially those who argue that this was an inevitable result of progress (particularly as argued by Young and Willmott in *The Symmetrical Family*). Instead, they present the emergence of leisure as the result of conflicts to rationalize work and to remove all satisfaction from it, but also to control the nature of enjoyment gained in free time. This presents a kind of historical cultural politics of leisure. In this reading, they summarize both their criticisms of others and their own theoretical outlook.

The Devil makes work

IN THE FIRST part of this book, our concern has been to establish how a critical – and more adequate – approach to the study of leisure can be constructed. We set about this, on the one hand, through a critical encounter with existing sociological theories of leisure, and, on the other, through providing a history attentive to some of the major structural and cultural conflicts through which leisure has been created. Our intention here is to pull together the themes which have emerged from these two routes, and in doing so, to establish more sharply the essential elements of our own approach to the study of leisure. The general conclusions which can be drawn from our theoretical and historical arguments provide the preconditions for our analysis of leisure in contemporary Britain ...

One conclusion drawn from our discussion of theories of leisure was that the conception of contemporary leisure as the product of a history of steady growth was untenable. We attempted to show [earlier in the book] how 'leisure' has been the outcome of complex historical conflicts. These conflicts are concealed by the ideology of history as a smooth progression. Instead, we have seen that the existence of leisure as a 'separate sphere' of social life is dependent on the major reorganization of *work* which took place in the period of capitalist industrialization. This separation of leisure had to be enforced – the nineteenth century experienced a variety of efforts to inculcate good work habits and to eradicate irrational leisure patterns which threatened the development of an orderly workforce.

Nor can the boundaries of this separation of employment and leisure be viewed as the natural outcome of 'progress'. The length of the working day, week and year were, and have remained, focal points of conflict between employers and workers' organizations – even though they are now less dramatically visible than conflicts over pay and working conditions. One of the principal successes of capitalism in conflicts over leisure is not the establishment of any *particular* leisure behaviour, but the establishment of this demarcation between work (employment) and leisure. The acceptance of this distinction as 'natural' and 'inevitable' necessarily produces a splitting of needs, desires and expectations about life. The identification of leisure as the sphere in which needs are satisfied and pleasures found simultaneously makes work *less* susceptible to criticism as unsatisfactory and *more* salient as that which has to be tolerated to 'earn' the freedom of leisure. **Instrumentalism** about work is built into this enforced separation: 'leisure' is the prize to be won.

However, the identification of leisure with freedom, choice and satisfied needs is also misleading. While the demarcation of leisure from employment has been a focal point of conflict, so has the content of that 'free time'. The suppression of immoral, irrational and generally 'dangerous' activities; the permanent 'policing' of public space; the control of 'standards' in family life; and the provision of 'improving' alternatives, have all been elements in the struggle to control the uses of free time.

But the 'cultural politics' of leisure are not only contained in these efforts to *control*, they must also include the active attempts to make concessions to the needs and interests of subordinate groups. It is important to recognize that provision, through both commercial and state forms, is not simply a direct imposition. Provision attempts to meet the demands of social groups. As with the case of music hall at the end of the nineteenth century, the aim is to meet the needs of social groups, to take account of their interests, and to turn that concession to economic or political advantage. Again, we must emphasize that these processes of economic and political *concession* are less concerned about the specific activities being provided than with ensuring that the *form* in which they are provided is regulated. If the working class wants alcohol and music, it shall have them – but only to be consumed under certain conditions.

While the demarcation of employment and leisure was capitalism's first achievement, the establishment of leisure – as – consumption, the limiting of the *forms* of leisure organization, has also been of considerable significance.

One of the most striking features of historical development is the increasing equation which is drawn between leisure and consumption, and in particular, the increasing dominance of commercial provision. This has affected not only the *logic* of provision (is servicing this need likely to be *profitable*?) it has also affected the sorts of social relationships which characterize leisure.

We want to suggest that it is possible to think of three possible sorts of relationship between a **citizen** and a cultural institution: those of member, customer and consumer. The *member* has an active commitment to the institution, which is run on his or her behalf, and over which the membership exercises collective control. The *customer*'s stake is that of habit. Mutual expectations arise, and a contract of sorts is evolved, which both sides are reluctant to abandon. The *consumer*, however, has neither the commitment of the member, nor the informal contract of the customer. His or her expectations are altogether more specific: the maximisation of immediate satisfaction. If goods or services are not provided in the manner or at the price required, then the consumer will go elsewhere.

If we take an activity like shopping – each of these three relationships is *possible*: member of the Co-op, customer of the cornershop, consumer at the supermarket. But the dominant tendency has been towards the last of these, forced on by the economic logic of profitability for which the ties of membership or custom are 'irrational' barriers to rational economic organization. So, for example, in the pressure of competition from large scale commercial retailing organizations, the Co-op has moved closer to consumer relationships, reducing the significance of membership to stamps and divi-books. Cornershops – and their specific local relationships – have also been squeezed by the power of economic concentration in the retailing business. Even where the rhetoric of 'membership' is revived (from sports centres to video-clubs), the desired relationship is that of the consumer: membership in these circumstances carries only market advantage (cheaper prices) rather than any active involvement in decision making and control.

For the economist (and particularly the **monetarist**), this growth of the consumer relationship represents a substantial gain. The market allows the exercise of rationally calculated choice on the part of the citizen, and 'consumer sovereignty' ensures that needs will be met through the supply of appropriate goods and services. For cultural critics, this apparent gain involves a qualitative loss – the disappearance of the potential for other kinds of relationships. The much vaunted democracy of the market-place (where rational individuals exercise their free choices) rests on the rather less democratic foundations of the profoundly unequal distribution of wealth and income. Even where the necessary membership card for the market society is obtained, the powers involved in consumer sovereignty are of a specific kind. The sanctions possessed by the consumer are entirely *negative* (we can choose not to buy), and depend for their existence on viable alternative sources of supply. And these 'alternatives' are increasingly to be found only in the form of other major companies engaged in the leisure business.

We have argued that one other central feature of the development of leisure is the sharp distinction that is constructed between employment and leisure. This separation is organized along a number of social axes. First, it involves a distinction in the sorts of relationships which characterise these two spheres – the difference between employee, subject to occupational constraints, and the variety of social roles which may be performed outside the place of employment. This distinction is commonplace to studies of leisure, but the attention it receives can distract attention from two other dimensions of this separation – those of time and space.

The distinction between employment and leisure creates two relatively distinct sets of time – on the one hand, that part surrendered to an employer in exchange for earnings; on the other, that reserved to oneself (and the others with whom one chooses to pass it). This pattern of weekdays *versus* evenings and weekends has come to be expected as the natural pattern of demarcation, although it, too, is the outcome of conflicts over the allocation of time to employment.

The development of capitalism also produced a geographical segregation of employment and leisure, such that paid work mostly takes place away from the home. This separation of production from the household has been intensified by subsequent developments in the planning of residential, office and industrial building, with an increasing tendency to segregate residential districts away from city centres and industrial areas.

Nevertheless, this pattern of segregation (of roles, of time and of space) only holds good for the dichotomy between paid work and employment. It leaves out of account the sexual division of labour and the way that division affects domestic work. For women in the home, roles, time and space are not demarcated by this separation. Women's familial roles contain personal dimensions (wife, mother, lover) which are inseparable from their implications of domestic duties (cook, washer, nurse, child minder). Similarly, time 'at home' carries no definitive demarcations: no factory hooter, school bell or office clock to mark the end of the working day; and equally, no factory gates or office door to walk through to enter the different time and place of leisure. This private work of reproduction is the hidden or reverse side of the public world of capitalist production – shaped by it, but not subject to its 'natural' demarcations of role, time and place.

Ideals of a 'woman's place' have this precise *spatial* confinement in mind – the woman bound by ties of love, obligation, obedience and duty to the home. But no more than any of the other demarcations that we have encountered, is this boundary fixed, natural or inevitable. The past century has seen numerous attempts to enforce or cajole women to occupy a woman's place, usually supported by efforts to educate women as to their biological imperatives. At other times, the bounds of this biology have been loosened in the face of the demands for productive labour. In both world wars, the recruitment of women as wage labour was supported by expanded provision of collective child-care, state laundries, and restaurants, which promised, temporarily, alternatives to the privatized pattern of domestic labour. Over this boundary, too, there have been conflicts ranging from the struggles to impose the idea of most paid work as male in the early nineteenth century, through to contemporary campaigns around state facilities, such as crèches and nurseries.

Between the places of paid work and domesticity, lies the contested ground of public space. Since the enclosure of common lands, there have been conflicts over the availability and use of parks, footpaths, streets and the countryside. It is here that the state has played its most active role in organizing leisure. At one point, it clears the streets of 'nuisances'; at another, it provides public spaces for the purposes of rational recreation. It defines and adjudicates the 'rights' to public space, and polices the uses to which that space is put. The history of that adjudication and policing has been one in which the formal rights inscribed in law have always taken precedence over the informal and 'customary' rights of popular culture. Yet, for those subordinate groups who own little 'private space', streets, paths and open spaces have been essential ingredients of leisure practices. 'Gossiping', 'doing nothing', 'hanging about' may not be clearly expressed 'leisure needs', but they have remained strikingly stable uses which popular cultures have made of public space.

Through these points, it is possible to understand why leisure is persistently ambiguous. It is the site of a number of conflicts – over time and space; over control of resources; over the character of social relationships; over the boundary between public and private; and over the tension between control and autonomy. What we now experience as 'leisure' is the current outcome of these historical struggles between contending social interests.

Discussions of the Leisure Society and the Future of Work, which are so visible in the 1980s, indicate that these conflicts are not yet over. But all too often, the structures within which leisure takes shape – the nature of work. Its social distribution, the inequalities of wealth, power and other resources associated with it in the system of capitalism – are left to one side in these discussions. Leisure is yet again identified as the necessary consequence of economic growth and technological change. At the same time, leisure as the site of cultural conflict – of competing demands, definitions and ideologies of what is and should be – is also left out of account. The best, it seems, that can be offered is a wider range of market choice, and the servicing of 'deprived' minorities by the state.

Just as our account of the history of leisure paid attention to how social conflicts dictated the pattern which did emerge (and therefore what other possibilities were excluded), so our understanding of the contemporary trends and patterns of leisure must try to question the current assumptions of benign progress. In what follows, we shall be reviving our interest in the structural organization of, and cultural conflicts over, leisure in contemporary Britain.

Key terms

The following key terms appear in the text above. They have been defined below to aid with the reading of this item.

instrumentalism treating something merely as an instrument to achieve something else rather than for any pleasure of intrinsic satisfaction to be derived from it. In this case, when the authors talk about work they mean treating work merely as a means to get money rather than for any satisfaction to be derived from the work itself

citizen a member of a society with certain basic rights

monetarist a supporter of the economic doctrine of monetarism, which is the main form of economic doctrine supported by the New Right

Questions

1 What, according to the authors, is the main problem with the idea of the democracy of the marketplace?

2 Summarize the conflicts which the authors see as central to the emergence of the character of leisure in contemporary society.

3 In what ways does the issue of the demarcation of work and leisure differ for males and females?

4 Suggest contemporary examples of the way leisure is structurally organized and the result of cultural conflict.

5 To what extent do sociological arguments support the assertion that the separation of work and leisure cannot be viewed as natural or inevitable?

Further reading

The following texts may represent a useful starting point for further investigation of the ideas contained within this chapter.

Clegg, S. (1990) *Modern Organizations*, London: Sage.

Grint, K. (1991) *The Sociology of Work*, Cambridge: Polity.

Madry, N. and Kirby, M. (1996) *Investigating Work, Unemployment and Leisure*, London: Collins Educational.

Watson, T. (1995) *Sociology, Work and Industry*, 3rd edn, London: Routledge.

Coursework suggestions

1 Investigate the extent to which students' leisure interests and participation are affected by the need to hold part-time jobs.

2 Conduct a survey on fast-food provision in your area to test out the thesis of the McDonaldization of society.

3 Consider whether it is possible to identify patterns of gender segregation in the workplaces in your local area.

11

Culture and identity

Chapter summary

Reading 11.1 **Relativism and culture** *page 311*
Richard Hoggart develops a critique of relativist approaches to the discussion of culture.

Reading 11.2 **Television, ethnicity and cultural change** *page 312*
Marie Gillespie explores the ways in which mainstream culture can interact with ethnicity.

Reading 11.3 **Gender and the look of love**
page 314
Suzanne Moore examines the implications of the sexualization of the male body for cultural theory.

Reading 11.4 **Popular culture as the culture of the subordinate** *page 316*
John Fiske provides an example of culturalism – an important theoretical approach in the sociology of culture and identity.

Reading 11.5 **Youth subcultures and retro styles**
page 318
Paul Willis describes the influence of retro fashion and the 'symbolic creativity' of young people.

Reading 11.6 **Cultures of consumption** *page 319*
Frank Mort provides a post-structuralist analysis of the development of men's fashion and lifestyle industries in the 1980s.

Reading 11.7 **Baudrillard and post-modern culture** *page 321*
Douglas Kellner summarizes some of the key points in Baudrillard's post-modern analysis of contemporary culture and includes some of his own reservations.

Reading 11.8 **The political economy of popular culture** *page 323*
Peter Golding and Graham Murdock provide an example of the critique of culturalist and post-modern approaches offered by political economy theorists.

Introduction: Reading the sociology of culture and identity

Culture is the glue that holds society together. When sociologists use the term 'culture' they refer not only to examples of 'high culture' – a Mozart opera or a novel by Charles Dickens – but to all the products or consequences of social relationships and interaction between human beings. In particular, sociologists refer to norms (specific rules) and values (general principles) as important features of every society's culture. Norms and values represent the 'glue' that binds society together because most members of society, most of the time, acknowledge them and conform to their guidelines. And, of course, much of how we see ourselves as individuals, and how others see us, is shaped by these cultural norms and values, too. This is why sociologists study culture *and* identity.

However, while it is true that a shared culture holds society together, it is not the case that *all* culture is shared by *all* social groups. Different social groups will generate distinct subcultures and identities within the main culture of society, according to their particular circumstances and outlooks. Differences will emerge between social groups in the way culture is evaluated and understood. The sociological study of culture quickly reveals that culture is inextricably linked to power. Some social groups may enjoy more power than others and will try to exploit this advantage in imposing their cultural preferences and their definitions of culture upon others. The readings contained in this chapter provide examples of the different ways in which sociologists have attempted to describe and explain these processes.

A consistent theme running throughout sociology is the importance of stratification in shaping opportunities and experiences for people. This is as true of culture and identity as any other topic. The readings included here illustrate the importance of the key dimensions of inequality in society – gender, ethnicity, social class and age – in shaping both the way popular culture is created and the way it is consumed. However, these readings also underline just how complex processes of cultural production, cultural definition and cultural consumption actually are. Perhaps this is why the various sociological perspectives represented in these readings differ in the ways they approach the analysis of culture and identity. Each focuses upon particular aspects of highly complex processes.

Before commencing the study of the sociology of culture it is necessary to consider whether or not it is possible to draw hard and fast conclusions or make objective judgements about cultural standards. Just what counts as 'good' or 'bad' in relation to culture? Employing a sociological perspective, it is tempting to suggest that with regard to culture, 'objective' judgements cannot be made. Surely, sociology teaches us that all such judgements reflect the values and, perhaps, interests of those making them. Cultural standards, for example, often reflect the distribution of power – those with power in society (including élite groups within education, the media, and the cultural industries) – enjoy the capacity to impose 'their' cultural standards. Similarly, it is often argued that we should avoid condemning mass popular cultural tastes because this would involve imposing our 'standards'. Who is to say that the Spice Girls produce pop trivia, inferior in quality to, for example, Blur? These are relativist arguments in which cultural definitions and standards are understood to be relative to particular social groups and societies at particular times in history.

Yet, there are dangers in uncritically adopting a relativist position as **reading 11.1** underlines. Richard Hoggart (1996) spent much of his career trying to insist that the popular culture of English working-class communities was worthy of serious academic study. He is often regarded as one of the founders of cultural studies as a discipline. Nevertheless, he is very reluctant to embrace an uncritical relativism in which one cultural product is regarded as just as 'good' or 'bad' as any other; a view in which it is assumed that it is impossible to insist that Shakespeare is 'better' than the Teletubbies. On the contrary, Hoggart argues that the spread of relativism through society serves the interests of the market and commercialism because it encourages us to consume commercial culture in an uncritical way.

In marked contrast, **reading 11.2** discusses the relationship between ethnicity and popular culture in the context of the development of global communication technologies. Marie Gillespie's ethnographic work in Southall (1995), within the Punjabi community, presents a very different picture of the potential of commercial culture and of the skills of young people as consumers of popular culture. Gillespie shows that modern technology can be used to preserve elements of tradition because the camcorder can unite kin across the world and all members of Punjabi families,

older and younger, can share the enjoyment of Indian cinema on video or cable television. At the same time, young Punjabis living in west London can enjoy a television soap like *Neighbours*, although its subjects are white, mainly middle class Australians living in a sunny suburb, because they can relate to the way in which it deals with relations between older and younger members of families and the suggestion that gossip can act as a mechanism to control the behaviour of young people.

This represents a contrast to Hoggart's position because it suggests that commercial culture can sometimes stimulate creative cultural responses although not necessarily in ways anticipated by the market. Similarly, Suzanne Moore (1988) in her discussion of the sexualization of the male body in magazines and film (**reading 11.3**), emphasizes the capacity of women to consume this form of popular culture in a variety of ways. Earlier versions of feminist cultural theory stressed the extent to which film and magazine images were produced by men to satisfy a 'male gaze'. Moore attempts to interpret what she regards as an important change in cultural production by arguing that women can 'enjoy' the representation of men's bodies in ways which subvert patriarchal values (values legitimating male dominance), although she also notes that such patriarchal values still place some constraints upon the ways in which such pictures of men are constructed.

Culturalists believe that popular culture is generated by subordinate groups – women in their struggles against patriarchy, ethnic minorities in their resistance to racism and discrimination, the working class in its experience of exploitation and powerlessness. Each group will create popular culture as a way of expressing their resistance to the forces which oppress them. The extract from John Fiske's work (1989) (**reading 11.4**) is a good example. Note that Fiske insists that popular culture can only be defined as such if it contains elements of resistance to dominant values. Culturalists believe that often popular culture is created through a process whereby the subordinate take symbols or commodities produced by the dominant institutions in society and lend them a new meaning. The mod working-class youth subculture of the 1960s, for example, gave the Union Jack an entirely new meaning when they stitched it onto the backs of their jackets.

Culturalists such as Fiske, then, define popular culture in terms of its quality of resistance. Willis (1990), in **reading 11.5**, also approaches popular culture in terms of the activity or, as he describes it, 'symbolic creativity' of ordinary young people. However, Willis points to the trend towards the emergence of retrospective styles in young subcultural fashion. Young people now can plunder elements of style drawn from previous eras, partly because pop video and the music media provide a popular archive or ready record of what these styles were like. There is less emphasis upon patterns of collective subcultural resistance in Willis' account and more upon the *individual* ways in which clothes, hair styles, and other commodities can be used to convey meaning.

The point that sociologists of culture have paid more and more attention to consumption is a reflection of social developments during the last two decades and the enormous impact of advertising and marketing upon popular culture. For Fiske, culture cannot be called *popular* unless it includes the suggestion of resistance to dominant values. In Mort's writing on the development of men's fashions and styles (1996) (**reading 11.6**), there is an acknowledgement of the influence of styles developed within the gay community but there is much less emphasis upon popular culture as resistance. Instead, Mort draws upon post-structuralist approaches, particularly the ideas of Foucault, to explain the growing interest men were encouraged to have in themes of style and identity during the 1980s and early 1990s. Following Foucault (1979) and Bourdieu (1993), Mort points to the impact of quite disparate elements in the emergence of powerful forms of knowledge about style and identity. These include both 'taste leaders', such as certain journalists and fashion designers, particular metropolitan 'taste communities' associated with urban night life, the influence of the urban gay scene, but also, the needs of mainstream commercial enterprises.

The writing of post-modern theorists such as Baudrillard (1988) also explores the relationship between culture and consumption. As Kellner (1989) suggests, in **reading 11.7**, for Baudrillard, what marks out the working of capitalist economies in the post-modern era is the central importance of cultural industries rather than manufacture. Advanced economies now primarily trade symbols and images rather than 'things' such as washing machines. A large proportion of economic transactions everyday involve the selling of services such as advertising, design, marketing and lifestyle advice. Commodities are now selected for what they 'stand for' rather than their 'use value'. Baudrillard argues that Marx failed to appreciate the importance of this development and

that Marxist analysis is, therefore, redundant for the purposes of contemporary analysis. Baudrillard is particularly pessimistic about the capacity of subordinate groups to generate meaningful patterns of cultural resistance. So powerful are the agencies of signification (advertising, marketing, the mass media, etc.) that all patterns of resistance are quickly absorbed or incorporated to assist the marketing drives of the commercial mainstream. Thus, for example, 'oppositional' black working-class hip-hop and rap music is used to sell products to young people on television advertisements, simultaneously absorbing the threat posed by the subculture and assisting the marketing drives of wealthy corporations.

Not all theorists, however, are impressed by the growing preoccupation with fashion and consumption in cultural studies. Recently, McGuigan (1992) has criticized the tendency in cultural studies to welcome any development in popular culture as 'progressive'. Culturalists, for example, have tended to read into popular cultural fashions elements of 'resistance' to dominant values on the basis of fairly flimsy empirical evidence or none at all. **Reading 11.8** is an example of the critique which political economy theorists (researchers who emphasize the importance of understanding the forces shaping the production of cultural commodities) are now developing both of the influence of culturalism and post-modernism in sociology and cultural studies. Golding and Murdock (1991) insist that it is still important to empirically explore the ways in which access to cultural goods is stratified unequally and determined by the distribution of power in society together with the policies of the capitalist state. Political economy reminds us that we should continue to ask critical questions about the relationship between culture and the market.

References

Baudrillard, J. (1988) *Selected Writings,* Cambridge: Polity Press.

Bourdieu, P. (1993) *The Field of Cultural Production,* Cambridge: Polity Press.

Foucault, M. (1979) *The History of Sexuality: Vol 1: an introduction,* New York: Pantheon.

McGuigan, J. (1992) *Cultural Populism,* Routledge: London.

Reading 11.1 **Relativism and culture**

Richard Hoggart (from) *The Way We Live Now* (1996)
London: Pimlico Press, pp. 6–9.

Editorial comments

Hoggart was one of the first academics in the postwar period to insist that the culture of 'ordinary' working-class people deserved academic study as well as 'high' culture, such as literature or opera. However, even in his early work he expressed concerns about the erosion of 'authentic' popular culture under the influence of commercial forces. In this extract from a much more recent book written in the 1990s, Hoggart argues that capitalist societies foster relativistic outlooks in which people come to believe that cultural standards are simply a matter of individual taste. This extract is important because it prompts us to consider whether or not it is possible to make critical judgements about culture and also reminds us that commercial interests have a lot to gain from the spread of relativist perspectives.

Relativism and consumerism

... THE CONTEMPORARY GROUND-LEVEL is **relativism**. It is an amenable ground for those societies which, though not uniformly prosperous, are generally well-off to a degree which most other nations are not; those technologically advanced societies, 'open democracies', capitalist, operating ever more elaborate communication systems; consumer-driven and so run by means of persuasions of all kinds, at all levels and depths.

Such societies need relativism; it is the perfect soil for their endless and always changing urges. A society of beliefs, of different beliefs, divides, splits people into majorities and, worse, awkward minorities. Some well-heeled minorities can by now be addressed with profit. But that specialized provision is inextricably related to the fact that others, the great body of people, are more and more led towards having undifferentiated, shared, but always changing tastes.

Utterances characteristic of this overall climate can be met any day and everywhere, in shops, trains, pubs and clubs; and in Cabinet Ministers. All are pronounced as matters of obvious common sense. A Cabinet Minister is asked, apropos of the concept of the Public Service in broadcasting, about the exact definition of a public service, the public interest. With no apparent sense of hedging, he replies that, like so many other matters, such a concept 'has to be redefined in and for each generation'. So what's the definition of honesty for this generation? This year? This month? Why should any particular definition be accepted at any one time by any individual, or shared at any one time by any group?

It follows that relativism also implies levelling, the belief – if belief it is; more likely it is an assumption – that with a few obvious exceptions all are equal in all things and so all views are of equal worth. We should not have to note, but perhaps it is necessary as an agreed proper marker, that in some important respects we should indeed be thought of as equal: before God, if we recognize one; before the law; and before others – that in these things we are all initially worthy of respect. After that, the lines divide: we are not equal in beauty or sporting ability, or in the talents needed to become a pop star; or in intelligence, or, hardest of all, in virtue.

It is of the essence of a true democracy that people should be respected individually, not simply collectively. It is also of the essence of a democracy that differences and distinctions are recognized and, where relevant, honoured. A democracy should be above all a *thoughtful* type of society, in these and other respects.

Anything less than that set of basic precepts demotes a democratic to a **populist state**; populist states are by nature thoughtless rather than thoughtful. Those who work the levers of power and persuasion need, above all else, to be accepted, to be liked, to be seen as having the truth within them; they have to 'manufacture consent'. All playing-fields are level and all compasses point in the same direction, towards the same fallacious Shangri-La.

In such a society those on the Right politically can move happily. They know that, behind the slogans and the blokishness, most levelling is bogus, that 'the masses' will not invade their clubs, seek to marry their daughters, travel first-class or have access to a range of other privileges.

Many active on the Left accept the same framework either because it allows them, as it allows those on the Right, to flatter people low down in the heap, or because they are muddled enough actually to believe that all really are equal in every possible sense (apart, of the exceptions noted above, from beauty, and sporting and pop stars' talent; intelligence and virtue are less happily accommodated, maybe positively rejected from membership in this category).

Otherwise all are equal. In particular, all opinions are as good as all others; therefore head-counting will produce the 'right' answer on every conceivable issue.

To sum up so far; relativism leads to **populism** which then leads to levelling; and so to reductionism, to **quality-reductionism** of all kinds – from food to moral judgments. There are no varying perspectives, no changes of level, no goals, no aims outside this sequence; except the aim of being so far as possible like everyone else; or apparently so, for the sake of rubbing along. Even those who have proved to be exceptional in the accepted way – pop stars and sports stars – have to act on the required occasions as if they are just ordinary blokes; even though their styles of life outside such occasions are wildly unordinary. That too is not only accepted but wished for; the exceptional bloke is at bottom ordinary but also fascinatingly unordinary – as he turns up from time to time at his ordinary childhood home in his exceptional Rolls-Royce. Such individuals are not usually the focus of envy; they are liked as they are, in their exceptionalness of gifts, their apparent ordinariness of manner before their fans, and their manifestly unordinary styles of life in all else.

That sequence – relativism to populism to levelling to reductionism – leads in technically sophisticated capitalist societies to concentration. Here the power-

ful links of relativism to consumerism become clear. So as to make economies of scale and enhance profits, consumerism must persuade people to allow themselves to be seen as, to come to see themselves as, a single body with shared tastes, small to large. 'You can have the Model T in any colour – so long as it's black'. It was not accidental that that first Fordism became so emblematic. It was an early, unabashed, apparently paradoxical but actually straightforward statement of the populist/reductionist ethos. Since it was about making objects cheap, not ideas, it was not very important.

Relativist-consumerism is also by nature jerky; it cannot rest. Once it has its mass clientele and its methods of mass production it must move those masses quickly and often, or the machines will seize up and the whole process threaten to collapse. The articles produced must themselves enter and leave at faster and faster intervals like cream crackers on a conveyor-belt – a 'new' new car each year, a 'new' model of camcorder, a 'new' set of interests and notions – even if almost all of those changes are, are forced to be, marginal and cosmetic. They can be sufficient to still the itch for change in us. This is a world of short breaths and short distances, more a matter of spinning round in grooves than of taking off into the high blue yonder.

Key terms

The following key terms appear in the text above. They have been defined below to aid with the reading of this item.

relativism the view that cultural standards cannot be fixed absolutely but are 'relative' to particular periods in time, particular societies, particular social groups or even particular individuals

populist state a society in which political leaders devise policy on the basis of popular sentiment rather than political principle

populism an approach which celebrates what is widely popular rather than insisting upon the application of critical principles

quality-reductionism Hoggart's phrase to describe what he believes as the erosion of cultural standards through commercialism and relativism

Questions

1 What does this passage suggest is the relationship between relativism and consumerism?

2 Why might relativism flourish in late capitalist societies?

3 What conclusions might we draw about the connection between cultural definitions and power from this passage?

Reading 11.2 **Television, ethnicity and cultural change**

Marie Gillespie (from) *Television, Ethnicity and Cultural Change* (1995) London: Routledge, pp. 205–7.

Editorial comments

This reading explores the relationship between culture and ethnicity based on an ethnographic study of

young Punjabis living in west London in the 1980s. Gillespie describes the ways in which television, video and cinema are used by these young people in the process through which they redefine their sense of ethnicity to suit their circumstances in west London. Gillespie emphasizes the point that while contemporary communication technology exposes these young people to the images, themes and identities associated with Western commercialism (television soaps such as

Neighbours, McDonald's food, etc.), it also allows them to preserve a strong commitment to parental and traditional culture – the video and the camcorder are widely used by families to watch Indian films and to record and play video messages to and from relatives in the Punjab.

Compare Gillespie's approach to contemporary commercial culture with that of Hoggart (reading 11.1).

Television, ethnicity and cultural change

IN SOUTHALL, THE redefinition of ethnicity is enacted in young people's collective reception and appropriation of TV. **Transnational** and **diasporic media** representing several cultures are available in Southall homes, offering a range of choices of symbolic identification. This range is sometimes felt to be too wide, as when, in situations of international conflict such as the Gulf War, young people find themselves facing difficult or even painful dilemmas. On the other hand, in key respects the range is not wide enough: young people complain, for example, that too few images of 'Asian' style and beauty are available which they feel able to take as role models. Yet the very coexistence of culturally diverse media is a cultural resource. It engenders a developed consciousness of difference and a cosmopolitan stance. It encourages young people to compare, contrast and criticize the cultural and social forms represented to them by their parents, by significant others present in their daily lives and by significant others on screen. This is the kind of context in which the construction of new ethnic identities becomes both an inevitable consequence and a necessary task.

We have just seen how the aspiration towards cultural change among Southall teenagers takes its most emphatically positive form from images (and sounds) designed to market the products of US-based transnational corporations such as Coca Cola and McDonald's. This utopian 'teen dream' might easily be dismissed as gullibility. But when the responses to these ads invoke a hoped-for transcendence of ethnic – and other – difference, in a setting of consumerist freedom, they define an ideal arena, an imaginative space, within which the construction of new identities becomes possible as a real project. The relatively humdrum, material corollary of their utopian ad talk – the visit with friends to McDonald's in Hounslow – is an entirely real 'escape' into a new social and communicative space, in which young people can actively redefine their culture.

The position of young British Asians – and other minorities – has long been described in the metaphor of 'culture clash', with its implicit notion of 'culture' as a bounded, impermeable, monolithic entity. Such thinking in terms of binary oppositions is not only characteristic of academic and media accounts of cross-cultural encounters and flows, but also structures everyday perceptions of cultural interaction and change among people of all ages in Southall. The oppositions of 'east' and 'west', tradition and modernity, religious and secular, poverty and wealth are rooted in the history of imperialism and colonialism, and continue to shape people's understanding of the cultural changes in which they participate. Images of cultural 'purity', fears of cultural 'contamination' and 'weakening' abound. Young people in Southall tend to claim that, while their parents are concerned with maintaining 'the culture', they themselves are open to change. Yet in the face of news events which represent a challenge to their sense of identity, they become acutely aware of the range of options open to them and trapped in binary thinking themselves. Responses to the Gulf War, an event mediated primarily by TV, provided a paradigmatic example of this.

In this book I have used the term 'ethnicity' in the sense of an array of strategic positionings in a field of differences, and adopted a dynamic concept of culture, in the hope of challenging in some small way the limiting, paralysing or destructive effects of such binary thinking. It remains to be seen whether the collective identity which is still in the process of being developed by young British Asians will succeed in avoiding its snares.

Young Punjabi Londoners' media consumption is characterized by a reflective awareness of cultural difference even when, as in the case of *Neighbours*, they are drawn to a programme because (though they would express this differently) they perceive it to offer a complex metaphor for their own social world. A valuable parallel to my analysis of *Neighbours* in Southall is the work of Miller (1992) on the reception of the American soap *The Young and Restless* in Trinidad: it proves that ethnographic studies can indeed produce potentially generalizable results. Many of his informants offered the term *bacchanal* (scandal, confusion, disorder, exposure of truth) as a one-word characterization of Trinidad society, and referred to the soap – an imported media product – in order to exemplify what the term meant. Underlying and linking the various meanings of *bacchanal*, Miller argues, is a notion close to that of 'gossip': thus his study provides a close comparative parallel to mine. In Southall too, 'gossip' is the term which young people use to characterize the essence of their local society, as well as the essence of the soap, and of the talk which embeds the TV representation in their everyday life. Thus in Trinidad as in Southall, according to a very similar pattern, a transnational media product is **locally appropriated** in ways which encourage people to refine their conceptions of their own local culture, and at the same time redefine their collective identity in relation to representations of 'others'.

Such 'indigenization' as an effect of globalization involves enhanced cultural consciousness; but further ethnographic studies are needed to discover why particular local societies appropriate particular 'imported' media products – are they always melodramatic soaps? – in particular ways. And our conceptual vocabulary will also need revising, if we are to find better ways of describing and analysing the processes vaguely called 'hybridization', 'syncretism', 'crossover' and the like.

'Cultural translation' offers one very useful addition to our vocabulary. Growing up in Southall involves learning to translate both literally – as young people translate British TV news to their elders – and, at the same, metaphorically, as they must acquire skills in negotiating from context to context between various cultures and various positions within each. As many commentators have pointed out, the contemporary development of global communications increasingly brings together cultures which might once have been clearly distinct, calling forth a range of ambivalent responses, sometimes hardening and sometimes dissolving boundaries. The apparently marginal experience of Punjabi Londoners can thus be seen to be, in fact, central to so-called post-modern culture, in which 'translation' is becoming a common global experience. But the uneven effects of globalization, of the communicative linkage of **diaspora** cultures and of the emergence of the politics of identity as an apparent successor to class politics in contemporary societies, stand in need of further empirical research. This study at least suggests that class politics and the nation state continue to play an overriding role in structuring identities.

Reference

Miller, D. (1982) 'The young and restless in Trinidad: a case study of the local and the global in mass consumption', in Silverstone, R. and Hirsch, E. (eds) *Consuming Technologies*, London: Routledge.

Key terms

The following key terms appear in the text above. They have been defined below to aid with the reading of this item.

transnational and diasporic media mass media which can disseminate the culture of particular social groups to different parts of the world

locally appropriated the 'meaning' of particular television programmes and other cultural products being reinterpreted at a local level to help social groups express their own ideas and values

diaspora the dispersal of particular ethnic traditions and cultures through migration

Questions

1 Why is *Neighbours* so popular with young British Asians in Southall?

2 How does this reading help us to understand the impact of globalization upon local culture?

3 What does this reading tell us about:

   a processes of cultural change, **b** the relationship between ethnicity, culture and identity?

Reading 11.3 **Gender and the look of love**

Suzanne Moore (from) 'Here's looking at you, kid!', in L. Gammon and M. Marshment (eds) *The Female Gaze: Women as viewers of popular culture* (1988) London: The Women's Press, pp. 49 and 57–9.

Editorial comments

In this reading Suzanne Moore discusses what she regards as a newly emerging trend in popular culture – the sexualization of the male body. She uses this evidence to question some of the assumptions underpinning Screen theory, an approach associated with Laura Mulvey (1975) and radical feminism. Mulvey argued that film and other examples of popular culture often represented women as objects or victims to be consumed by audiences as if they were male voyeurs. Moore argues that the new emphasis upon the male body in magazines, films and pop videos suggests that women, too, can derive pleasure through a female gaze.

Reference

Mulvey, L. (1975) 'Visual pleasure and narrative cinema', in *Screen*, vol. 16, no. 3.

Here's looking at you, kid!

DWELLING AS THEY have on woman as object of the gaze, many of the theories associated with *Screen* have been vital in understanding the relations of power involved in relations of looking. Paradoxically, however, such theory has also contributed to the repression of the female gaze. For repression is about power too, and as Mary Ann Doane comments: 'In theories of repression there is no sense of the productiveness or positivity of power'.

Likewise there is no sense of the productivity of resistance: to say that women *can* and *do* look actively and erotically at images of men and other women disrupts the stifling categories of a theory which assumes that such a look is somehow always bound to be male. ...

While it is crucial to treat women's pleasure as distinct from men's, we must avoid discussing both as though they were fixed outside social conditions. For surely as social conditions change, so do our pleasures. A simple explanation for the proliferation of these new images of men may be found in more liberal attitudes to homosexuality. As homosexual discourse has become public, what was once hidden has become more explicit.

Accompanying these changes there have also been shifts in attitudes to female sexuality. In the 1970s magazines such as *Playgirl* were launched, on the assumption that women could move from being sexually passive to being sexually active by behaving like imitation men and devouring pictures of naked models in ludicrous poses with ridiculous captions. As Margaret Walters writes, 'Such magazines are trying to reduce a woman's feelings to a formula before she knows what they are or might be.' The laughter occasioned by projects such as *Viva* and *Playgirl* compensated for their failure to provide us with anything remotely erotic. If a distance between the viewer and the image is a prerequisite of pleasurable looking, it seems that in this case the gulf was so wide that it could not be filled by any amount of cheap talk about the 'liberated woman'. Ironically, part of these magazines' commercial failure was the fact that advertisers did not want to place their ads on the same page as pictures of naked men!

You're so vain

As representations of male homosexual desire become incorporated into the mainstream, they disturb the suffocating dualism of the theory which provides little pleasure for women. Yet is all this to our benefit? Well, like many of the shifts thrown up via the marketplace, I think it works in contradictory ways.

So far I have sketched out what I see as potentially positive for women, i.e. an erotic and pleasurable look. Yet not surprisingly what these representations allow, which has so long been repressed, is the 'coming out' of male narcissism. A few years ago, at a press conference in London, Schwarzenegger suggested the boom in male body building was connected to feminism: 'For years men looked at women. Now women are looking back at men.' However, it's not that simple, for, as Walters suggests, 'the male body builder is less concerned with women than with his mirror'.

This would appear to be reinforced by men-focused ads and new men's magazines, such as *Arena*, which promote a kind of 'Look, don't touch' sensibility whereby sexuality becomes a self-conscious status symbol. The idea of smooth sexual autonomy, rather than the messy world of relationships, is the one that sells all those 'personal adornment' products. We're talking strictly *market* penetration here. Listen to Tony Hodges, managing director of the agency that handled the Grey Flannel campaign, speaking about the 'New Man':

> The individual at the heart of this brand is in his early twenties, is discovering himself – discovering what women discovered years ago – that the mirror is perhaps more important than the other person.
> *(Hodges, 1987)*

Frank Mort suggests that there is positive potential in men becoming self-conscious in so far as it leads to the realization that they *can* change, rather than thinking of masculinity as an unalterable norm. Yet such superficial changes, so skilfully utilized by the advertisers, will remain precisely at the level of *image* unless they are tied to parallel social changes in male attitudes – unless men are convinced that they need, and want, to change. Caring has to mean more than caring about how one looks. Two decades of feminist demands that men should be more sensitive must surely result in something more than men with sensitive skin?

So are we to welcome this upsurge of male narcissism as a 'good thing'? Or is it just another way of excluding women? Now that men can look good and be emotional, are women expendable? Or are we just trying to pull a homosexual discourse into a heterosexual space?

Such questions arise out of contradictory cultural processes; on one hand culture promotes gay imagery and style in order to target young men as consumers, and on the other, the political climate is increasingly repressive and anti-gay. So although in some contexts the male body is being legitimated as an object of desire, explicit portrayals of the male genitals are still forbidden.

Reference

Hodges, T. (1987) interviewed in *The Media Show*, Channel 4, May.

Questions

1 On what grounds does Suzanne Moore criticize Screen theory (the concept of the male gaze)?

2 The emergence of a female gaze is regarded as a positive development in many ways but Moore also acknowledges some less positive possibilities associated with it. Summarize, in your own words, both the positive features and the less desirable consequences which Moore discusses.

3 If we accept Suzanne Moore's analysis, what are the implications for our understanding of sex role socialization and masculine identity?

Reading 11.4 **Popular culture as the culture of the subordinate**

John Fiske (from) *Reading the Popular* (1989) London: Unwin Hyman, pp. 1–4.

Editorial comments

This reading sets out the main features of an approach often described as 'culturalism'. It draws upon Gramsci's theory of hegemony (1971) and the suggestion that class conflicts are sometimes fought out through culture rather than politics or the factory floor. For Gramsci, dominant social classes enjoyed hegemony when their ideas and culture were embraced by most members of subordinate social groups. However, culturalism understands popular culture as being produced by subordinate groups in society as they attempt to resist the dominant values of capitalism. This would include, for example, groups subordinated by patriarchy, racism or their position in relation to age or sexuality, not merely social class – as Fiske tries to demonstrate in this passage. Although not explicitly mentioned, Fiske is drawing upon the concept of 'excorporation' to develop his ideas here. Subordinate groups excorporate commodities and images produced by dominant social groups and give them a new meaning by using them in different ways to resist dominant values.

Reference

Gramsci, A. (1971) *Selections From Prison Notebooks*, London: Lawrence & Wishart.

Understanding popular culture

POPULAR CULTURE IS made by various formations of **subordinated** or disempowered people out of the resources, both discursive and material, that are provided by the social system that disempowers them. It is therefore contradictory and conflictual to its core. The resources – television, records, clothes, video games, language – carry the interests of the economically and ideologically dominant; they have lines of force within them that are **hegemonic** and that work in favor of the status quo. But hegemonic power is necessary, or even possible, only because of resistance, so these resources must also carry contradictory lines of force that are taken up and activated differently by people situated differently within the social system. If the cultural commodities or texts do not contain resources out of which the people can make their own meanings of their social relations and identities, they will be rejected and will fail in the marketplace. They will not be made popular.

Popular culture is made by subordinated peoples in their own interests out of resources that also, contradictorily, serve the economic interests of the dominant. Popular culture is made from within and below, not imposed from without or above as mass cultural theorists would have it. There is always an element of popular culture that lies outside social control, that escapes or opposes hegemonic forces. Popular culture is always a culture of conflict, it always involves the struggle to make social meanings that are in the interests of the subordinate and that are not those preferred by the dominant ideology. The victories, however fleeting or limited, in this struggle produce popular pleasure, for popular pleasure is always social and political.

Popular culture is made in relationship to structures of dominance. This relationship can take two main forms – that of resistance or evasion. The girl fans of Madonna are resisting the patriarchal meanings of female sexuality and constructing their own oppositional ones; the boys in video arcades are similarly making their own resistant meanings of human–machine relations and power structures. But surfers are evading social discipline, evading ideological control and positioning. Evasion and resistance are interrelated, and neither is possible without the other: both involve the interplay of pleasure and meaning, but evasion is more pleasurable than meaningful, whereas resistance produces meanings before pleasures.

Making popular culture out of television news, for instance, is possible and pleasurable only if the subordinate can make their meanings out of it, otherwise the news would be part of dominant, hegemonic culture only. So the news of a snow storm or of Israeli troops quelling an uprising by Arab youths can be made popular only if it offers meanings that are relevant to the everyday lives of subordinate people, and these meanings will be pleasurable only if they are made *out of* the news, not *by* the news. These productive pleasures of making one's own sense are different in emphasis from the evasive, offensive pleasures of the body experienced by surfers or video game players.

Popular culture is always in process; its meanings can never be identified in a text, for texts are activated, or made meaningful, only in social relations and in **Intertextual relations**. This activation of the meaning potential of a text can occur only in the social and cultural relationships into which it enters. The social relationships of texts occur at their moment of reading as they are inserted into the everyday lives of the readers. Shopping malls are quite different texts for women and for unemployed youths, because their social relationships differ in each case: for women, malls are legitimate, unthreatening public places, that are opposed to both the street and the home; for unemployed youths, they are a place to trick 'the system', to consume the images, warmth, and places of consumerism, without buying any of its commodities. The meanings of shopping malls are made and circulated in social practices.

But they are also made intertextually: bumper stickers announcing, 'A woman's place is in the mall', coffee mugs decorated with the words 'mall rats', or T-shirts that proclaim the pathology of the 'shop-a-holic' can be used defiantly, skeptically, critically, and variously, according to their many uses – a father giving a T-shirt to his teenage daughter would set up a series of meanings that would differ significantly from those generated by it as a gift from one of her friends. The culture of shopping malls, as of Madonna, as of the beach, cannot be read off the primary texts themselves, but only in their social uses and in their relationships with other texts. The postcards we send are as much a part of the meaning of the beach as our use of it to expose ourselves to the sun and sight of others; Madonna's posters are as much a part of her meanings and pleasures as her songs and videos. The fan decorating her bedroom with Madonna icons, the wanna-bes (Madonna look-alikes) striding down the sidewalk, are agents in 'Madonna culture', their texts (the bedroom, their bodies) as signifying as any of Madonna herself.

Key terms

The following key terms appear in the text above. They have been defined below to aid with the reading of this item.

subordinated located in a position of relative powerlessness in society and subject to various kinds of discrimination or exploitation

hegemonic (forces) the channels through which powerful groups seek to promote their dominant or hegemonic ideas

intertextual relations the social relationships which give meaning to popular cultural texts such as T-shirt designs, car stickers, television programmes, magazine covers, etc.

Questions

1 How does John Fiske define popular culture?

2 Provide further examples of the ways in which items of popular culture can express a struggle between the dominant and the subordinate as described by Fiske.

3 Do you agree with Fiske that popular culture is *always* 'made by subordinated peoples in their own interests … from within and below, not imposed from without or above'? Give reasons for your answer.

Reading 11.5 **Youth subcultures and retro styles**

Paul Willis (from) *Common Culture* (1990) Buckingham: Open University Press, pp. 87–8.

Editorial comments

Paul Willis describes some of the developments which he believes explain why 'spectacular youth subcultures' (for example, skinheads, punks, etc.) no longer suddenly emerge. All young people, he believes, can engage in more individualistic 'symbolic creativity' in the way they consume commodities, particularly clothes. Leisure time provides a release from the disciplines and controls of the workplace; young people can use the ever-expanding range of consumer products generated by the market to plunder 'bits' of previous fashions in making their own more individual styles. Note that even in the case of the earlier 'working-class subcultures' Willis emphasizes the role of 'middle class' institutions such as the art school and the impetus given to subcultural style by commercial forces.

From subculture to 'retro'

THE SUCCESSION OF spectacular youth subcultures has shown particular, conspicuous, symbolic creativity in clothes. There is now a long and well-known list of youth subcultural styles, from the teddy boys and the mods, to the skins and punks, which have occupied the attention of sociologists, journalists and fashion commentators alike. The distinct styles of postwar youth subcultures have been interpreted as symbolic solutions to age and class domination, and a means of marking out and winning cultural space for young people. Such styles have been lauded for their symbolic work in borrowing and transforming everyday objects or fashion components, recoding them according to internal subcultural **grounded aesthetics**. Examples include the teds' **appropriation** of the Edwardian suit, the skins' appropriation of proletarian work clothes, or the punks' borrowing of safety pins, bin liners and zips.

While only a small minority of young people adopted the complete uniform of youth subcultures, large numbers drew on selective elements of their styles creating their own meanings and uses from them. Many subcultural styles became popularized, finding their way into mainstream working class and middle class youth culture. In this way, subcultures became a source of inspiration for the stylistic symbolic work and creativity of all young people. Punk, for example, stimulated a move back to straight-legged trousers, smaller collars and shorter hair amongst young people of all ages. The leggings/thermal underpants first worn by punk girls – which were originally cream and had to be dyed black – were soon being made up new by young market-stall holders. By the summer of 1985 they were being produced in T-shirt cotton and a wide range of colours and had become a definitive fashion item for all women under the age of 40.

But fashion trends arise not only from the street – though always in a dialectic with it. Punk, for example, emanated as much from the art school avant garde as it did from the dance halls and housing estates. Many of the stylistic innovators in punk had a firm stake in the commodity market themselves. Indeed, within most postwar youth subcultures, young people have always been directly involved in the production and selling of clothes themselves. A whole economic infrastructure of entrepreneurial activity has accompanied all the major postwar youth style explosions, creating careers for many of those involved.

Punk was perhaps the last major subculture in which there was a convergence of design, subcultural style and small innovative retail businesses. Malcolm McLaren and Vivienne Westwood's shop 'Sex' (later renamed 'Seditionaries'), set up in the Kings Road in the mid-70s, was one of the few which integrated popular street fashion with the music of the time.

Since punk the stylistic options among an increasingly self-reflexive and stylistically mobile youth have been greatly expanded with revivals of all the major subcultures occurring in the late 1970s and '80s. Punk itself reproduced the entire sartorial history of postwar working class youth culture in cut-up form, combining elements which had originally belonged to completely different epochs. The wardrobes of past subcultural styles were exhumed, re-adapted and recombined in endlessly different combinations.

Since and including the punk explosion, then, one of the most important trends in youth style has been the rehabilitation and raiding of previous sartorial styles for raw material in young people's own, current symbolic work and creativity, stylistic and cultural expression. Retro style is part of a general trend in contemporary culture which ransacks various historical moments for their key stylistic expressions and then re-inserts and recombines them in current fashion. Clothing items are worn as though in quotation marks, their wearers self-consciously evoking some past, even at the risk of stylistic mismatch and incongruity. These references to past stylistic forms have taken on a kind of iconographic status in pop culture, evoking whole periods of social history, and have been used extensively in popular music and advertising.

Key terms

The following key terms appear in the text above. They have been defined below to aid with the reading of this item.

grounded aesthetics Willis's phrase to describe the way in which ordinary people can use everyday fashion items and commodities to create their own styles

appropriation the process through which a style or image is adopted by a new social group and given a new meaning

Questions

1 How do young people express 'symbolic creativity' in their choice of clothing and leisure pursuits?

2 Although Willis distances himself from the concept of post-modern society, how might post-modern theorists interpret the evidence and examples he provides?

3 What contrasts can be made between the approach of Willis, here, and Marxist approaches?

Reading 11.6 **Cultures of consumption**

Frank Mort (from) *Cultures of Consumption: Masculinities and social space in late twentieth-century Britain* (1996) London: Routledge, pp. 8–11.

Editorial comments

Two important developments within the sociology of popular culture in the last two decades have been, firstly, the growing academic interest in consumption, and secondly, the increased attention given to changes in the main cultural definitions of masculinity. In this passage, Frank Mort draws upon the ideas of Foucault (1979) and Bourdieu (1993) to develop a post-structuralist account of the recent boom in men's fashions and associated style magazines. Applying a Foucauldian post-structuralist framework (one which emphasizes the ways in which language and knowledge organize social relationships), he argues that this

phenomenon cannot be reduced to a single structural 'cause' but, rather, is the product of the complex interplay of forms of 'professionalizing knowledge' – including, for example: the ideas of a key group of young journalists associated with the *Face* magazine; photographic and video styles first employed in the representation of men in the media serving the gay community; the values of particular urban cosmopolitan 'taste communities'; and finally, the marketing strategies of fashion companies desperate to expand a young male market for clothes, masculine cosmetics and lifestyle commodities.

References

Bourdieu, P. (1993) *The Field of Cultural Production*, Cambridge: Polity Press.

Foucault, M. (1979) *The History of Sexuality: Vol 1: an introduction*, New York: Pantheon Books.

Cultures of consumption

THE BOOK OPENS by exploring how and why the habits and behaviours of young men figured so prominently in British visions of the future of commercial society in the 1980s. For if the 'new man', as he became labelled, carried specific connotations, he was also endowed with more general significance as a beacon for the future. This icon of commercial masculinity was the product of multiple forms of knowledge and a complex set of professional alliances. ... We begin, not on the obvious terrain of mainstream advertising or large-scale manufacturing, but with a clutch of more esoteric personalities. What is uncovered is

the way in which a number of talented individualists exerted a strong sense of authority in the search for new markets. The **habitus** of these cultural professionals was overwhelmingly metropolitan. Notions of taste leadership have featured prominently in debates over the dissemination of goods. [We explore] ... the influence of the *cognoscenti*, in the context of the quest for a new type of consumer journalism for men. It uncovers a coalition between independent journalists and designers, photographers, models and urban *flâneurs*. These experts claimed to provide answers to a set of pressing questions about the disintegration of established consumer patterns and the emergence of new ones. As significant as the theories of this self-proclaimed taste-élite were the particular cultural resources they drew on to represent young men to themselves. A dense visual symbolism projected an exotic range of personas. Tracking the emergence of these representations takes us towards an exploration of the commercial cultures of sexual dissidence. For the growing visibility of the homosexual marketplace began to exercise its own influence over more mainstream versions of masculinity during the period. In the context of men's consumer journalism, one important result was the consolidation of a particular culture of homosociality, targeting the bodies and lifestyles of young men.

[We can also pursue] ... this narrative of gendered commerce into the worlds of advertising, marketing and retailing. The spectacular growth of these industries in the 1980s registered a confidence and optimism which was reflected in the expansion of their knowledge base. One important part of their programme involved developing a commercial language capable of speaking to young men. Consumption experts drew heavily on the rhetoric of style and fashion to shape this project. The resulting alliance between the mainstream and the avant-garde was a complex rather than a simple tale. Advertisers and marketers held to their own agenda for masculinity. The move into the mass market did not exemplify the 'trickle-down' theory of cultural transmission, whereby goods beginning life at the pinnacle of the taste pyramid eventually influenced more lumpen consumers. Different audiences demanded different patterns of taste.

These opening sections of the book involve an extended engagement with the commercial professions. In that sense *Cultures of Consumption* continues the concerns of my earlier work, *Dangerous Sexualities*, not in its empirical focus, but in the analysis of forms of professionalizing knowledge as discourse. Yet in dealing with what might be termed commercial rather than official experts, the historian faces a number of difficulties. At a practical level there is the problem of a lack of any codified archive. Rarely do we encounter the systematized records which are preserved for the law or medicine. There is still no effective institutional account of advertising, marketing or retailing in Britain, either from within the ranks of the entrepreneurs themselves or from academic historians. Commercial savants differ in a number of important ways from the intellectuals associated with the domains of public administration or scientific expertise. Usually cited as belonging to young or embryonic professions, their genres of knowledge are not always neatly demarcated, as in more prestigious systems. Boundaries between paradigms frequently

overlap, or are deliberately blurred. Moreover, commercial briefs are typically generated by intuitive hunches, or by the energy of particular practitioners, rather than through the supposedly more rigorous procedures of professionalizing practice. And yet, turning the pages of an advertising journal such as *Campaign* reveals a world-view quite as expansive as that encountered in *The Lancet* or in the *British Medical Journal*. *Cultures of Consumption* is very much about coming to terms with the forms of knowledge generated by these consumer professionals.

Yet, as should now be clear, the book is also about men and their relationship to consumer culture. In this respect my choice of market was not entirely innocent. Though a number of other constituencies were targeted in similar ways during the 1980s, the commercial address to men provided a way into posing a number of broader questions about contemporary changes to masculinity. After almost total neglect, this topic has begun to receive serious attention. As Lynne Segal noted, throughout the 1980s the shifting nature of men's lives, their behaviours, fears and anxieties were scrutinized with a new intensity. It was no accident that all this occurred at precisely the moment when feminism was defining men as an object of political and intellectual concern. In this context it has recently become fashionable to talk about a contemporary crisis of masculinity. While such an idea may appear overblown (often erroneously contrasting perceived present-day rapid change among men with past stability), it does pose the sharp end of questions about the shifting nature of gender relations and gendered power.

How does this debate, essentially derived from sexual politics, impinge on the sphere of commercial culture? In the most obvious sense, the probing of young men's relationship to traditionally feminine areas, such as shopping or consumer journalism, which took place during the decade, did produce an extended inquiry into the nature of masculinity. This initiative was not as new as was claimed at the time. It had its origins in earlier moments of consumer expansion, notably in the 1950s and early 1960s. But the 1980s did see an intensification of these processes. One theme to emerge out of a study of the material is a by now familiar, but nonetheless important, point. Masculinity is multiform, rather than unitary and monolithic. The object of inquiry is masculini*ties*, not masculinity. Late twentieth-century promotional culture has been extremely active in the construction of more plural versions of identity for men.

This emphasis has the capacity to produce a more subtle account of the multiple dynamics governing masculinity. But an exclusive focus on men projects a distorted picture. Equally important are the positions they occupy within the total ensemble of gender relations – understood as relations of difference and power. Masculinity needs to be interrogated in conjunction with its feminine counterparts. The history of commercial culture in the postwar period has been punctuated by gendered struggles about access to goods and the meaning of consumption. In the 1980s the formation of new consumer identities coincided with an upsurge of feminist pressure on the professional fields of advertising and marketing. Women's growing impact on these institutions – as well as that of gay men – contributed substantially to the strategy making masculinity more self-conscious. And yet the intensified scrutiny of men often resulted in the consolidation of a world-view which marginal-

ized or excluded femininity, let alone feminism. Cultural progressivism did not necessarily imply progress for women. Masculine and feminine divisions feature in the book, alongside men's differentiated power relations to each other. What is needed is a more plural model of gender, which grasps these multiple lines of force. Such arguments have been set out most cogently by Joan Scott (1988) and others in relation to the discursive production of women, but their relevance is just as important for the analysis of masculinity. They point not towards the total dissolution of gender but towards its more historically differentiated exploration, and towards a more nuanced version of sexual politics.

Reference

Scott, J. (1988) *Gender and the Politics of History*, New York: Columbia University Press.

Key terms

The following key terms appear in the text above. They have been defined below to aid with the reading of this item

habitus a set of ideas about fashion and taste which allow judgements or choices to be made

cognoscenti the well-informed or expert regarding, in this case, men's fashions

flâneurs those who 'hang around' the fashionable scene

Questions

1 Explain what Mort means when he refers to the impact of a group of 'talented individualists' exercising 'taste leadership'?

2 What has been the recent effect, according to Mort, of commercial culture upon the way in which masculinity has been understood and defined?

3 Foucault's writing often stresses the theme that new forms of knowledge emerge through the efforts of quite distinct social groups. How does this passage illustrate this idea?

4 In what ways might a Marxist analysis differ from the account presented by Mort?

Reading 11.7 **Baudrillard and post-modern culture**

Douglas Kellner (from) *Jean Baudrillard: From Marxism to postmodernism and beyond* (1989) Cambridge: Polity Press, pp. 48–50 and 52.

Editorial comments

Baudrillard is one of the leading theorists associated with the concept of the post-modern society. This passage summarizes some of the reasons why Baudrillard believes that Marxism is no longer adequate as a theory to explain developments in contemporary society.

Baudrillard believes that contemporary societies are primarily concerned with the exchange of images and symbols rather than the industrial production of manufactured commodities. Put simply, advanced Western societies now have economies in which many more people are employed in cultural and media sectors, such as advertising, public relations, marketing, design, lifestyle services and so on, rather than the production of cars or washing machines. This, he argues, requires a new type of theory. However, after summarizing Baudrillard's argument, Kellner explains why he believes a Marxist analysis is still relevant.

Beyond Marxism

IN *MIRROR*, BAUDRILLARD makes a definite break with Marxism for the first time, – though one can read his earlier works in retrospect as leading up to this

break – and presents his own theory as providing superior perspectives on contemporary society. He claims that there is as decisive and revolutionary a mutation between the classical capitalism character-ized by Marx and contemporary capitalism as between capitalism and feudalism. In short, he declares that the era of production is over, and that we have entered a new era in which radical semiurgy – that is, the production and proliferation of **signs** – has replaced production of objects as the centre of social life and as a new mode of social control. Baudrillard thus concludes that the entire Marxian analysis is no longer adequate to contemporary con-ditions, which now require passage to '*the political economy of the sign*' (Baudrillard, 1975).

In this radically new situation, 'The super-ideology of the sign and the general operationalization of the signifier – everywhere sanctioned today by the new master disciplines of **structural linguistics**, **semiol-ogy**, information theory and cybernetics – has replaced good old political economy as the theoreti-cal basis of the system' (Baudrillard, 1975). Consequently Baudrillard believes that it is old-fashioned and romantic to criticize the corruption of art, the media, sexuality, nature and so on by capi-talist market relations, when it is the code of sign value – and not exchange value or the market – that controls these spheres. He claims that '*control of the code*' and the proliferation of sign values are of more significance than control of labour and the sphere of production.

This analysis suggests that 'code' now refers to the rules, laws and structures of the political economy of the sign. Marxism, by contrast, mirrors the code of political economy, that of the imperatives, laws and structures of the capitalist system of production. On this analysis, Marxism can be seen as a reflex of a previous code, belonging to an earlier stage of history. In this context, Baudrillard's position can be read as a Left variant of theories of the post-industrial society, the **information society**, the **cybernetic society** or post-modern society in which it is claimed that socioeconomic development has moved beyond the previous stage of development and has entered a new stage in which the theories and categories of the previous stage are no longer adequate or rele-vant to the new social conditions. At stake is whether the transformation and differences are as radical as Baudrillard suggests, whether the older theories, like Marxism, are completely obsolescent, and whether we need entirely new theories and categories to make sense of the new developments.

Baudrillard argues that 'This new ideological struc-ture, that plays on the **hieroglyphs of the code**, is much more illegible than that which played on productive energy. This manipulation, that plays on the faculty of producing meaning and difference, is more radical than that which plays on labour power' (Baudrillard, 1975). Presumably, while capitalism previously channelled labour power into production and exploited productive energies of workers for profit, today signs and codes channel consciousness and behaviour into certain predetermined paths like consumption, conformity, fascination with media spec-tacles, representative democracy and so on. What I will call 'sign control' articulates differences (in class, sex, race, political affiliation and so on) and channels individuals into some predefined mode of thought and behaviour or another, closing off more radical alter-natives (symbolic exchange, as it turns out once again).

Sign control is especially efficacious because 'The form-sign applies to the whole social process and it is largely unconscious' (Baudrillard, 1975). Sign con-trol for Baudrillard is therefore unconscious, illegible and thus hard to combat. Presumably we are not aware how we are channelled into certain forms of class behaviour, consumer behaviour, conformity, sex role behaviour, ethnic behaviour and the like which are being controlled by the code (never defined, but always hegemonic and totalitarian in Baudrillard's theory). For in 'the planned cycle of consumer demand, the new strategic forces, the new structural elements – needs, knowledge, culture, information, sexuality – have all their explosive force defused' (Baudrillard, 1975). All phenomena are functionally integrated into a new 'mode of strategic control' which eliminates all contradictions, potential threats to order and social crises.

Baudrillard argues that what appears to be new, different, oppositional or subversive is merely part of a differential play of signs in a semiotic system which itself regulates and controls all **signification** and meaning. To the Marxian claims for the primacy of production and the mode of production, Baudrillard counters a concept of 'the mode of signification', which he claims is now prior to and more determi-nant than the mode of production and its laws, logic and exigencies. In order words, he claims that semi-otic control takes place through the proliferation and dissemination of signs. Signification now operates according to its own logic and laws, and absorbs everything back into its system. No behaviour can refer back to a particular use value or meaning for an individual, because all meaning and use value are prescribed in advance and circumscribed by the code. Consequently 'the sign no longer designates anything at all. It approaches its true structural limit which is to refer back only to other signs. All reality then becomes the place of a semiurgical manipulation, of a structural simulation' (Baudrillard, 1975). The entirety of Baudrillard's subsequent work to the present explores this situation, and draws out its implications. It rests henceforth on the proposition that we have entered a new stage in history, in which sign control is almost complete and totalitarian. Signs, simulations and codes have become the primary social determinants, and supposedly follow their own logic and order of signification. Consequently previous theories predicated on the logic of production, like Marxism, are no longer useful or relevant to the new social situation. ...

... Baudrillard ascribes a new role to signification as a primary mode of social determination. But does signification escape the logic of production so easily? Is it an autonomous social force with its own ends, goals, purposes and interests?

I think not. We are still in a society where the imperatives of capital and production play a crucial structuring role in politics, culture, and social and economic life through capitalist control of the media, advertising, packaging, design, architecture, urbanization, computerization and so forth. Against Baudrillard's position, I would argue that some of the most useful work in contemporary cultural and social theory has combined economic, political and cultural approaches, and that it would be perverse to dismiss political economy, production and Marxism completely from contemporary social theory. For, even minimally, such perspectives can provide illuminating approaches and concepts in dealing with a wide range of phenomena.

Baudrillard might argue against this proposal that it is impossible to combine radically different logics of production and signification, and that Marxism is intrinsically reductionistic, imperialistic and terroristic and refuses to be combined with any theories that oppose in any way its categories and logic. But just as I argued [previously] that Baudrillard's critiques of Marx's theories of use value and needs were unfair to Marx who himself anticipated many of Baudrillard's points in his critique of bourgeois political economy, so I would also argue that Marxism is not as economistic or reductive as Baudrillard claims, and that Marxists like Henri Lefebvre, Guy Debord and the Critical Theorists of the Frankfurt School anticipated many of Baudrillard's positions – though admittedly not in such an extreme, anti-Marxist form.

Reference

Baudrillard, J. (1975) *The Mirror of Production,* St. Louis: Telos.

Key terms

The following key terms appear in the text above. They have been defined below to aid with the reading of this item.

signs images or symbols

structural linguistics the study of language as a system

semiology the study of symbols or images as systems

information society, cybernetic society terms used by theorists who argue that information, particularly computerized data, is becoming more and more important in shaping social development

hieroglyphs of the code the characters or symbols used to create messages in, for example, advertising or 'spin-doctoring' in politics

signification the process through which symbols or images are created

Questions

1 What, according to Baudrillard, are the main differences between earlier forms of capitalism and the contemporary capitalism of the post-modern society?

2 What picture does Baudrillard present of the effect of the signs, images and symbols, produced by the mass media, advertising, public relations, etc., upon people living in contemporary societies?

3 Why does Kellner believe that, contrary to Baudrillard's argument, a Marxist analysis is still relevant?

Reading 11.8 **The political economy of popular culture**

Peter Golding and Graham Murdock (from) 'Culture, communications and political economy', in J. Curran and M. Gurevitch (eds) *Mass Media and Society* (1991) London: Edward Arnold, pp. 28–30.

Editorial comments

The influence of both culturalism (see reading 11.4) and post-modernism (see reading 11.7) has encouraged a fashionable interest in the study of consumption and pleasure amongst cultural theorists. A number of studies influenced by these theoretical frameworks have charted the ways in which a variety of social groups develop popular cultures through consuming commodities in pleasurable ways (see, for example, reading 11.3) which can be subversive. According to this position, cultural consumers do not always follow the patterns dictated by the commercial forces in society.

However, Golding and Murdock, two long standing political economy theorists, sound a cautionary note in this reading. We should not lose sight of the ways in which inequalities in power and resources constrain the extent to which any social group can consume in the first place, let alone derive subversive pleasures. They point out that some culturalist approaches end up by offering what amounts to a defence of the free market.

Consumption – sovereignty or struggle?

FOR POLITICAL PROPONENTS of a free market philosophy communications goods are like any other. Since the best way of ensuring adequate distribution and production of the general commodities people want is through the market, so too, the argument follows, is this true for cultural goods. It is the truth or otherwise of this proposition that provides the analytical target for a political economy of cultural consumption.

Curiously, an influential version of this free market philosophy has had considerable currency in much work within recent cultural studies. In an attempt to contest the apparent simplistic determinism of a view which sees audiences as the passive dupes of all powerful media, some writers have asserted the sovereignty of viewers and readers, to impose their own meanings and interpretations on material which is 'polysemic' – that is capable of generating a variety of meanings. This analysis has tempted writers of very varying political or social presuppositions. For **liberal pluralists** it has refurbished the view that the checks and balances of cultural supply and demand, though admittedly uneven, are far from bankrupt. The customer, though perhaps a little bruised, is still ultimately sovereign. For writers with more critical or radical instincts, it is a view which has unleashed a populist romance in which the downtrodden victims caricatured by crude **economic determinists** are revealed as heroic resistance fighters in the war against cultural deception.

Consumer sovereignty is in any total sense clearly impossible – nobody has access to a complete range of cultural goods as and when they might wish, without restriction. The task of political economy, then, is to examine the barriers which limit such freedom. It construes such barriers being of two kinds, material and cultural. We can examine each of these in turn.

Where communications goods and facilities are available only at a price there will be a finite capacity to have access to them, limited by the disposable spending power of individuals and households. Spending on services generally has grown significantly in the last generation. In 1953/4 spending on services made up 9.5 per cent of household expenditure; by 1986 this proportion had risen to 12.7 per cent (Central Statistical Office, 1990). All expenditure on personal and household services and on leisure goods and services amounted to over a third of household expenditure by 1988. Within this global figure spending within the home has risen as a proportion, linked most significantly to the television set as an increasingly dominant hub of leisure time and expenditure. On average British adults in 1990 spent 24 hours a week watching television broadcasts, and an as yet uncertainly calibrated amount of time using television for related activities, such as viewing videos or playing computer games. As the range of hardware required for such activities grows, however, so too does the demand on private expenditure necessary to participate in them.

As Table 1 shows, there is a marked difference in the ownership of home computers and videos between different income groups, a gap that is unlikely to diminish substantially due to two factors. First, income differentials themselves have sharply widened in the last decade. During the 1980s wage increases for the highest paid fifth of male workers were 42 per cent higher than for the lowest paid fifth (Low Pay Unit, 1988). In addition the gap between households dependent on social security benefits for their income and those in the labour market has also increased. Together these changes meant that between 1977 and 1987 the share of incomes (after allowing for all taxes paid and benefits received) of the poorest fifth fell from 6.4% of the total to 5.1%, while the share enjoyed by the richest fifth grew from 40% to 45% (Oppenheim, 1990). The disposable spending power of different groups in the population is thus significantly polarized. Secondly such goods require regular updating and replacement, disadvantaging groups with limited spending power and cumulatively advantaging the better off. Owning video or computer hardware requires expenditure on software, owning a phone means spending money on using it. Thus limited spending power is a deterrent not only to initial purchase but to regular use.

However not all expenditure on communications goods involves expensive acquisition of equipment. Television programmes can be viewed once you have a set to watch them on, as most people do, while many cultural materials are available as public goods; they are paid for from taxation as a common resource – public library books, for example. This is not a static situation, however. For political economists a shift in

Table 1 Ownership of communications equipment among households in different income groups (1989)

Household weekly income (£)	Percentage owning		
	phone	video	home computer
46–60	64.3	13.9	0.8
81–100	73.9	25.9	6.2
126–150	83.9	42.6	6.9
151–175	83.9	55.4	11.2
176–200	87.2	65.5	14.1
226–250	96.2	75.4	25.8
276–325	96.2	80.5	29.4
376–450	98.6	85.2	33.1
over 550	99.7	77.7	34.3
All households	86.2	56.6	16.6

Source: Family Expenditure Survey, 1989

the provision and distribution of cultural goods from being public services to private commodities signals a substantial change in the opportunity for different groups in the population to have access to them. If television channels, or individual programmes, are accessible by price, as is envisaged for much of the new television structure heralded by the 1990 Broadcasting Act, then consumption of television programmes will be significantly governed by the distribution of household incomes. Similar considerations would come into play if, for example, public libraries were to make greater use of powers to charge, as was proposed in a government green paper in 1988, even though, at the time, such proposals were shelved (Office of Arts and Libraries, 1988). By imposing the discipline of price on cultural goods they acquire an artificial scarcity which makes them akin to other goods of considerably greater scarcity. It is for this reason that the political economy of cultural consumption has to be especially concerned with material inequalities.

Critical political economy is not only concerned with material barriers to cultural consumption, however. It is also interested in the ways in which social location regulates access to the cultural competences required to interpret and use media materials in particular ways. One of the strongest empirical traditions within cultural studies – running from studies of youth subcul-

tures to research on differential 'readings' of television texts – has concerned itself with how social locations provide access to cultural repertoires and symbolic resources that sustain differences of interpretation and expression. This emphasis on social experience as a cultural resource is important, but it can be oversold. Consumption practices are clearly not completely manipulated by the strategies of the cultural industries but they are equally clearly, not completely independent of them. Rather we need to see cultural commodities as the site of a continual struggle over uses and meanings between producers and audiences and between different consumer groups.

At the same time we need to go on to explore other links between people's loction in the productive system and their communicative activity. In pursuing this project, it is important to remember that 'production' is not the same thing as paid employment, it also includes domestic labour. Women's prime responsibility for the 'shadow work' of shopping, cleaning, cooking and nurturing has fundamental consequences for their relation to the mass media. Not only are their choices often constrained by the prior demands of husbands and children, but the fact that no one else in the family is regenerating their affective resources, leads them to look for other ways of maintaining psychological support. For example, where men mostly use the telephone instrumentally, to 'get things done', women often use it expressively, to sustain social networks. What appears from the outside as trivial gossip, is experienced from the inside as an emotional life-saver.

Conclusion

People depend in large measure on the cultural industries for the images, symbols, and vocabulary with which they interpret and respond to their social environment. It is vital, therefore, that we understand these industries in a comprehensive and theoretically adequate way which enables the analysis of communications to take its place at the heart of socal and cultural research. We have argued that a critical political economy provides an approach which sustains such an analysis, and in so doing have illustrated in a preliminary way, the origins, character, and application of such an approach. Much remains to be done, both theoretically and empirically, however, before we can claim to have fully established a critical political economy of communications.

References

Central Statistical Office (1990) *Family Expenditure Survey 1989*, London: HMSO.

Low Pay Unit (1988) *The Poor Decade: Wage inequalities in the 1980s*, London: Low Pay Unit.

Office of Arts and Libraries (1988) *Financing our Public Library Service: Four subjects for debate*, Cmnd 324, London: HMSO.

Oppenheim, C. (1990) *Poverty: The facts*, London: Child Poverty Action Group.

Key terms

The following key terms appear in the text above. They have been defined below to aid with the reading of this item.

liberal pluralists social scientists who suggest that power is not concentrated in the hands of a single group in society but that in open or liberal societies the power of some groups is balanced by the power of others

economic determinists a term applied critically to those theorists who support the view that ultimately many social phenomena have an economic cause

Questions

1 Which theories do Golding and Murdock have in mind when they comment that some writers have 'asserted the sovereignty of viewers and readers, to impose their own meanings and interpretations'?

2 Why do Golding and Murdock link these theories to a 'free market philosophy'?

3 Why do Golding and Murdock believe that the 'shift in the provision of cultural goods from being public services to private commodities signals a substantial change in the opportunity for different groups in the population to have access to them'?

4 What evidence do Golding and Murdock offer to challenge the view of the cultural consumer as 'sovereign'?

Further reading

The following texts may represent a useful starting point for further investigation of the ideas contained within this chapter:

Primary texts

Fiske, J. (1989) *Reading the Popular*, London: Unwin Hyman.

Storey, J. (1993) *An Introductory Guide to Cultural Theory and Popular Culture*, Hemel Hempstead: Harvester Wheatsheaf.

Strinati, D. and Wagg, S. (eds) (1992) *Come On Down? Popular media culture*, London: Routledge.

Secondary texts

Gillespie, M. (1995) *Television, Ethnicity and Cultural Change*, London: Routledge.

Fawbert, J. (1997) 'Replica football shirts: a case of incorporation of popular dissent?', in *The Social Science Teacher*, vol. 27, no. 1.

Hall, S. and du Gay, P. (eds.) (1996) *Cultural Identity*, London: Sage.

Sugrue, B. and Taylor, C. (1996) 'Cultures and identities', in *Sociology Review*, vol. 5, no 3.

Coursework suggestions

Culture and Identity is a good area to select for project work because of the variety of empirical evidence which is readily to hand in the form of:

- cultural products (magazines, television programmes, music CDs, computer games, advertisements, etc.)
- people to interview about their ideas of identity (friends, fellow students, parents, etc.)
- cultural institutions (museums, leisure and film complexes, football grounds, dance venues, etc.)
- fashion items (clothes, hair styles, football shirts, etc.)
- official documents (produced by the Department of Culture, Media and Sport, Arts Council, etc.).

1 **The incorporation of popular dissent?**
'Soccer and terrace culture is being incorporated by the new commercial marketing forces influencing sport.' You could start to explore this hypothesis by reading the article by Jack Fawbert listed above. What methodologies might be explored to assess the view of ordinary soccer fans? Could this theme be explored using a political economy approach?

2 **Audience resistance to dominant values**
John Fiske (reading 11.4) argues that culture can only be described as popular if it contains within it possibilities for the expression of resistance to dominant values. Fiske, for example, points to the way in which aboriginal Australians enjoyed Hollywood westerns because they sided with the Red Indians against 'the white man'. Use the techniques of audience ethnography (interviewing and focus group work) to explore whether or not contemporary audiences enjoy current examples of popular culture in a way which expresses resistance to dominant values. Is it possible to enjoy Cilla Black's *Blind Date*, for example, in a subversive way?

3 **Consumerism and popular culture**
Several writers, including some of those included here, have put particular emphasis upon consumerism as a crucial dimension of contemporary popular culture. Conduct a piece of research to assess the extent to which this is the case amongst young people. One measure of consumerism might be the extent to which young people regard fashionable clothing labels as indicators of status. What quantitative and qualitative methods could be used to research this topic?

12

Deviance

Chapter summary

Reading 12.1 **The functions of crime and punishment** page 329

For Emile Durkheim, deviance – and the public punishment of deviance – functions to reinforce the stability of society since it provides an opportunity for the collective expression of norms and values: the moral sentiments of social life.

Reading 12.2 **Common sense, criminology and 'sceptical' sociology** page 332

Stanley Cohen draws a distinction between common-sense, 'positivistic' criminology and a more 'sceptical' sociological approach to the study of crime and deviance. He suggests that academic criminology, which unquestionably supports the activities of the state, is problematic for a genuinely critical or radical understanding of crime in society.

Reading 12.3 **A new criminology?** page 337

In their book *The New Criminology*, Taylor, Walton and Young set out a manifesto for what at the time represented a new approach to the sociology of crime, which drew upon both macro and micro approaches.

Reading 12.4 **Moral panics, 'mugging' and social control** page 342

Stuart Hall *et al.*, in the book *Policing the Crisis*, review their intentions for the study of the relationships between 'race', ethnicity, class and social control in society.

Reading 12.5 **New left realism** page 348

John Lea and Jock Young ask the question *What Is To Be Done About Law and Order?* and provide an answer located in the development of a 'New Left Realist' approach to criminology.

Reading 12.6 **Women, crime and the 'malestream criticism'** page 352

For Frances Heidensohn, like many other feminists, the sociological treatment of crime and deviance has, until recently, been characterized by a 'malestream' orientation – i.e. it has been largely concerned with men, at the expense of the study of women. Heidensohn attempts to address this problem.

Reading 12.7 **Visions of social control** page 356

A very recent trend in social theorizing has been the adoption of a critical approach to the history of prisons and punishment. Stanley Cohen identifies what he considers to be the nature of social control in contemporary social life.

Reading 12.8 **Crime, policing and the 'risk society'** page 360

Since the publication of Ulrich Beck's highly influential work *Risk Society*, many other sociologists have attempted to take up these ideas and use them in their work. In this case we see an application of the concept of 'risk' to contemporary policing.

Introduction: Reading the sociology of deviance

To start to think about the sociological treatment of deviance, we must be clear on a number of basic – but essential – definitions: Firstly, in the readings in this chapter whereas some thinkers write about 'crime' others write about 'deviance'. Whereas all crime is deviance, not all deviance is crime. Deviance is a broad sociological category which simply means to stray from the norms of a society – to deviate away from the expected paths of behaviour. In fact, some sociologists – in particular Emile Durkheim – have

noted that deviance does not necessarily have to be negative behaviour (as defined by the particular values of the culture in question). For example, being a great scientist or athlete is 'deviant' since the vast majority of the population – the norm – will not achieve these goals. But, obviously, given the society we live in, being a great scientist is a very different form of deviant behaviour than being, say, a bank robber – which is also criminal since it breaks formal, written laws. Equally, the punishment of the criminal is generally expected to be more harsh than the general deviant.

To continue with the theme of key definitions, the

sociological study of crime is a study of what we can call a 'social problem'. Social problems are problems as defined by the culture of a given society – usually, one could argue, as defined by the rule-makers and decision-makers of a society. 'Social problems' are different from 'sociological problems'. Social problems can be seen as undesirable features of a society which are seen to be problems to be solved – crime, unemployment, poverty are all examples of social problems. Sociological problems, however, are problems concerned with the study and analysis of social life: problems of the reliability and validity of methods, the accuracies of theories etc. Social problems – as seen in this chapter – can become the focus of sociological problems. The writers of the readings in this section are concerned with the problems of understanding the existence of crime and deviance.

Finally, a mention should be made of the relationships between sociology and criminology. As the name suggests 'criminology' is the academic study of crime. For some sociologists, criminology is simply applied sociology. For others it is a related but wider discipline encompassing ideas from many different social sciences, in particular sociology and psychology.

The origins of a truly sociological approach to the wide category of 'deviance' can be found in the work of Emile Durkheim (1972). The extracts that make up **reading 12.1** come from two different sources – an essay published originally in France in 1895 and his classic text *The Division of Labour in Society* – originally published in 1893.

For Durkheim, deviance is normal, natural, inevitable and functional in society. He argues that deviance is needed in society in order to periodically reinforce the collective sentiments of culture; in other words, it shows the 'group' how not to behave. Equally, punishment of deviant acts – and particularly criminal acts – also bonds the group together against a 'common enemy'. Thus, a small amount of deviance is needed to ensure the overall stability of the system, conceived of by Durkheim (through the functionalist sociological perspective) as an 'organic' entity.

In **reading 12.2** by Stanley Cohen (1971) we see an approach to sociology that tries to draw distinctions between sociology and both criminological and common-sense thinking. Cohen argues that whereas common-sense thought accepts – without question – the categories 'normal', 'criminal' and 'deviant', the role of the sociologist is to treat these categories and labels with a degree of scepticism. The sociologist should stand back and be critical of any attempt by those who have the power to label in society or to draw boundaries between those who are seen as 'normal' and those who are seen as 'abnormal' or 'deviant'. Equally, Cohen suggests that a great deal of criminology has been too concerned with the gathering of empirical

'facts' through the use of an uncritical positivistic methodology which are then used by the state to justify their medical model of deviant behaviour – i.e. the idea that deviants are somehow 'sick' or 'ill' and they need 'treatment'. Cohen notes that this image of deviance is popular in both political and common-sense thought.

Instead of this state-subscribed medical model of criminology, Cohen advocates the adoption of a more 'radical' sociological approach using ideas and theoretical positions drawn from both Marxist-influenced and interactionist thought.

In **reading 12.3** from *The New Criminology* by Taylor, Walton and Young (1973) we see another attempt to conceptualize possible theoretical futures for the sociological study of crime. Taylor *et al.* attempted to combine a great many theoretical and methodological interests together, within a general framework made-up of neo-Marxist and interactionist thinking. This combination of Marxism and interactionism has proved to be a highly influential 'radical' approach in this topic area, and one that has lasted in popularity and importance until – arguably – very recently, with the adoption of post-structuralist ideas from thinkers such as Michel Foucault (1991).

In **reading 12.4**, we see once more the popularity of the neo-Marxist approach. For Hall and his colleagues in *Policing the Crisis* (1978) definitions of crime and deviance – in fact the category of 'social problem' itself – are products of the ideological rule of capitalism. By labelling some behaviour and social groups as 'deviant', social control – both ideological and repressive (based upon the threat and use of force) – is more likely to be seen as justified by the population of a society.

Hall *et al.* argue that moral panics in the media can be used by capitalism to preserve ideological – or 'hegemonic' – rule. Groups can be labelled and scapegoated for the problems of capitalism itself such as crime, poverty, poor housing, unemployment etc. In the extract, Hall *et al.* discuss how deviance and crime are treated by various different ideologies in society.

In the mid-1980s, and through to the present day, we have witnessed, in British sociology, the rise of yet another neo-Marxist variation, also combined with ideas from interactionist sociology. This new version of left-wing sociology called itself 'New Left Realism' and came with a criticism of other Marxist sociologies and criminologies. Lea and Young (1993) – two key proponents of this new approach – warned against the dangers of what they called the 'left idealists' – those who saw working-class crime as a form of political struggle.

Lea and Young argued instead, that sociology needs to be 'realistic' about both the causes of, and solutions to, crime. They argue that to see working-class crime as some sort of 'Robin Hood' style action against capitalism is to do a disservice to the urban working classes themselves who are frequently the victims of crime. Instead, Lea and Young set out their version of recommendations for the future of sociology – as contained in **reading 12.5** from the second edition of their book *What Is To Be Done About Law and Order?*.

Recently, feminist sociologists have noted the exclusion of feminist ideas in sociology. As Frances Heidensohn (1996) asks in **reading 12.6**, 'what about women?' This invisibility of women in sociological thinking denies opportunities to female academics and ignores female experiences of social life.

In the past few years, sociological thinking – and in particular social theory – has expanded even further. These new theoretical directions have included often controversial ideas from post-modernist and post-structuralist thinkers. The ideas of Michel Foucault have proven to be very important in discussions of deviance. In particular, Foucault is interested in re-thinking the history of prisons and punishment – arguing that so-called 'humane treatment' of 'sick' individuals is a powerful social control mechanism hidden in the guise of 'caring' for those unable to help themselves – a theme similar to some of the points raised by Cohen in **reading 12.2**.

It is Cohen once more who we return to for **reading 12.7**. In his text *Visions of Social Control* (1985) Cohen discusses the concept of 'social control' in great depth. He imagines society as a vast web or map of social control – operating at many different levels: formal and informal; local and national; voluntary and professional. Such patterns of control operate to label or classify the population and, in doing so, to limit our behaviour in the school, at work, in the city – in all realms of social life.

Finally, despite the popularity of post-modern and post-structural ideas, many sociologists have tried to move sociological thinking away from these ideas – suggesting that they have nothing to offer sociological thought, given that by denying absolute knowledge in society and the rise of relativism (where 'anything goes'), these ideas ultimately deny the existence of sociology itself!

One contemporary approach to social theorizing which is an attempt to rescue sociology back from ideas of post-modernity, is provided by Ulrich Beck (1992) in his work *Risk Society*. Beck suggests that contemporary social life is characterized by the rise of an awareness of, and concern with, the 'risks' or 'harms' of social life. In this 'Risk Society' culture, politics, lifestyle and identity become concerned with the avoidance of these harms. Beck argues that this is very different from the 'modern' age where science and technology were seen as positive – giving 'goods' such as full employment, knowledge, consumer durables, etc. Today, Beck suggests we live not in 'post-modernity' but in a stage of 'reflexive-modernity'. **Reading 12.8** by Ericson and Haggerty (1997) is an attempt to use Beck's ideas as another, new direction for the study of crime and, in this case, the policing of crime. Like the other attempts to model and re-model the sociology of crime and deviance, time and the academic community will be the best judge.

References

Beck, U. (1992) *Risk Society: Towards a New Modernity* (orig. pub. in Germany in 1986) London: Sage.

Foucault, M. (1991) *Discipline and Punish: The birth of the prison*, new edn (orig. pub. in France in 1975) Harmondsworth: Penguin.

Reading 12.1 **The functions of crime and punishment**

Emile Durkheim (from) *Selected Writings*, A. Giddens (ed.) (1972, originally published in 1893 and 1895) Cambridge: Cambridge University Press, pp. 106–7, 123–4 and 125–8.

Editorial comments

We can argue that the starting point for a truly sociological analysis of crime – and the much broader category of deviance – was provided by one of the founders of sociology. For Durkheim, deviance is a social construction, since to deviate from the norms and values of a society is culturally relative to the particular society one has been socialized into.

Durkheim argues that deviance is both functional and dysfunctional to society. It is functional, providing it does not appear in too large quantities, since it reinforces the 'collective conscience' of a society: it provides a framework against which the group can judge its own actions. The punishment of deviance, then, also is functional because it reaffirms group identity in the face of potentially disruptive action.

Forms of social solidarity

IN THE THEORY which I have formulated, a society which was made up only of average individuals would be essentially abnormal. For there is no society which does not contain a profusion of individual anomalies, and such a universal phenomenon cannot exist without reason. *It is therefore socially normal that there should be psychologically abnormal individuals in every society*; and the normality of crime is only a particular case of this general proposition. As I expressly remarked in my book [*The Rules of Sociological Method*], the conditions of individual health and those of social health may be very different, and even contrary to one-

another. This can be accepted without difficulty, if one recognizes, as I do, that there is a deep line of demarcation between the social and the psychic. However, this opposition can be directly proved in an empirical manner, without reference to any system. A society can only survive if it is periodically renewed: that is to say, if the older generations cede place to new ones. Therefore it is necessary for the first to die. Thus the normal state of societies implies the illness of individuals; a certain rate of mortality, like a certain rate of criminality, is indispensable to collective health. ...

Repressive sanctions and mechanical solidarity

THE LINK OF **social solidarity** to which repressive law corresponds is one whose break constitutes a crime; we give this name to every act which, in any degree whatever, evokes against its author the characteristic reaction which we term 'punishment'. To seek the nature of this link is thus to ask what is the cause of punishment, or, more precisely what crime essentially consists in ...

... an act is criminal when it offends strong and defined states of the **conscience collective**. The statement of this proposition is rarely disputed, but it is ordinarily given a sense very different from that which it ought to have. We take it as if it expressed, not the essential property of crime, but one of its repercussions. We well know that crime violates very general and intense sentiments; but we believe that this generality and intensity derive from the criminal character of the act, which consequently remains to be defined. We do not deny that every delict is universally condemned, but we take as agreed that the condemnation to which it is subjected results from its delinquent character. Then, however, we are hard put to say in what its delinquent character consists. Is it to be found in an especially serious transgression? Perhaps so; but that is simply to restate the question by putting one word in place of another, for it is precisely the problem to understand what this transgression is, and particularly this specific transgression which society reproves by means of organized punishment and which constitutes criminality. It can evidently come only from one or several characteristics common to all criminological types. The only one which satisfies this condition is the very opposition between a crime, whatever it may be, and certain collective sentiments. It is, accordingly, this opposi-

tion which forms the crime, rather than being a derivation of crime. In other words, we must not say that an action shocks the *conscience collective* because it is criminal, but rather that it is criminal because it shocks the *conscience collective*. We do not condemn it because it is a crime, but it is a crime because we condemn it. As for the intrinsic nature of these sentiments, it is impossible to specify them; they have the most diverse objects and cannot be encompassed in a single formula. We cannot say that they relate to the vital interests of society, or to a minimum of justice: all such definitions are inadequate. By this alone can we recognize it: a sentiment, whatever its origin and end, is found in all minds with a certain degree of strength and clarity, and every action which violates it is a crime ...

... today, it is said, punishment has changed its character; it is no longer to avenge itself that society punishes, it is to defend itself. The suffering which it inflicts is in its hands no longer anything but a methodical means of protection. It punishes, not because chastisement offers it any intrinsic satisfaction, but so that the fear of punishment may paralyse those who contemplate evil. It is no longer anger, but a well thought-out precaution which determines repression. ...

Today, as we understand more clearly the end to be attained, we know better how to utilize the means at our disposal; we protect ourselves more systematically and, accordingly, more efficiently. But this result was also obtained previously, although in a rather imperfect manner. There is no radical division between the punishment of today and yesterday, and consequently it was not necessary for the latter to change its nature in order to accommodate itself to the role that it plays in our civilized societies. The whole difference derives from the fact that it now produces its effects with a heightened awareness of what it does. But, although the individual or social consciousness may not be without influence upon the reality that it clarifies, it has not the power to change its nature. The internal structure of the phenomenon remains the same, whether men be conscious of it or not. We may thus conclude that the essential elements of punishment are the same as of old.

And in fact, punishment has remained, at least in part, a work of vengeance. It is said that we do not make the guilty party suffer for the sake of suffering; it is nonetheless true that we find it right that he should suffer. Perhaps we are wrong, but that is not the question. We seek, at the moment, to define punishment as it is or has been, not as it ought to be. It is certain that this expression of public prosecution which finds its way again and again into the language of the courts is not a mere expression. In supposing that punishment can really serve to protect us in the future, we think that it must be above all an *expiation* of the past. This is shown by the minute precautions we take to allot punishment as exactly as possible in relation to the severity of the crime; this would be inexplicable if we did not believe that the guilty party ought to suffer because of his wrongdoing, and in the same degree. This gradation is not necessary if punishment is only a means of defence. No doubt, there would be danger for society if the most serious offences were treated as simple transgressions; but it would be greater, in the majority of cases, if the latter were treated in the same way as the former. Against an enemy, we cannot take too much precaution. Shall we say that the authors of the smallest misdeeds have less perverse natures, and that to neutralize their criminal instincts less stringent punishments will suffice? But if their inclinations are less vicious they are not on that account less intense. Robbers are as strongly inclined to rob as murderers are to murder; the resistance offered by the former is not less than that of the latter, and consequently, to control it, we would have recourse to the same means. If, as has been said, it was solely a question of putting down a noxious force by an opposing force, the intensity of the second would be measured solely by the intensity of the first, without the quality of the latter entering into the consideration. The penal scale would then encompass only a small number of gradations. Punishment would vary only as the criminal is more or less hardened, and not according to the nature of the criminal act. An incorrigible robber would be treated in the same way as an incorrigible murderer. But, in fact, if it were shown that a misdoer was completely incurable, we would still not feel bound to punish him excessively. This is proof that

we are faithful to the talion principle, although we apply it in a more refined sense than previously. We no longer measure in so material and gross a manner either the extent of the deed or of the punishment; but we still think that there ought to be an equation between the two terms, whether or not we benefit from this balance. Punishment thus remains for us what it was for our forefathers. It is still an act of vengeance since it is an expiation. What we avenge, what the criminal expiates, is the outrage to morality …

As for the social character of this reaction, it comes from the social nature of the offended sentiments. Because they are found in the consciousness of every individual, the infraction which has been committed arouses the same indignation in those who witness it or who learn of its existence. Everybody is attacked; consequently, everybody opposes the attack. Not only is the reaction general, but it is collective, which is not the same thing. It is not produced in an isolated manner in each individual, but is a total, unified response, even if this varies according to the case. In fact, in the same way as contrary sentiments repel each other, similar sentiments attract each other, and they attract as strongly as they themselves are intense. As contradiction is a threat which stirs them, it adds to their force of attraction. Never do we feel the need of the company of our compatriots so greatly as when we are in a foreign country; never does the believer feel so strongly attracted to his fellow believers as during periods of persecution. Of course, we always love the company of those who feel and think as we do, but it is with passion, and no longer solely with pleasure, that we seek it immediately after discussions where our common beliefs have been directly attacked. Crime brings together honest men and concentrates them. We have only to notice what happens, particularly in a small town, when some moral scandal has just occurred. Men stop each other on the street, they visit each other, they seek to come together to talk of the event and to wax indignant in common. From all the similar impressions which are exchanged, and the anger that is expressed, there emerges a unique emotion, more or less determinate according to the circumstances, which emanates from no specific person, but from everyone. This is the public wrath.

Moreover, this is what gives it its functions: the sentiments in question derive all their force from the fact that they are common to everyone. They are strong because they are unquestioned. It is the fact that they are universally respected which gives them the specific respect which they are accorded. Now, crime is possible only if this respect is not truly universal; consequently, it implies that they are not absolutely collective, and thus damages this unanimity which is the source of their authority. If, then, when a crime takes place, the individuals whom it offends do not unite to manifest what they share in common, and to affirm that the case is anomalous, they would be permanently shaken. They must fortify themselves by the mutual assurance that they are still in unison. The only means for this is action in common. In short, since it is the *conscience collective* which is attacked, it must be that which resists, and accordingly the resistance must be collective …

Thus, the analysis of punishment has confirmed our definition of crime. We began by establishing inductively that crime consisted essentially in an act contrary to strong and defined states of the *conscience collective*. We have just seen that all the qualities of punishment ultimately derive from this nature of crime. That is because the rules that it sanctions express the most essential social likenesses.

Key terms

The following key terms appear in the text above. They have been defined below to aid with the reading of this item.

social solidarity society being in a state of harmony; being bonded together

conscience collective the shared norms, values and moral sentiments socialized into the individual in order for society to function in a smooth and orderly fashion

Questions

1 According to Durkheim, what are the functions of deviance?

2 How does Durkheim use medical and biological images when thinking about the nature of society?

3 What are the relationships between the group, the conscience collective and punishment?

Reading 12.2 **Common sense, criminology and 'sceptical' sociology**

Stanley Cohen (from) *Images of Deviance* (1971) Harmondsworth: Penguin, pp. 9–24.

Editorial comments

The book *Images of Deviance* drew together a number of papers from leading theorists and researchers in the field of the sociological study of crime and deviance. In this extract we can see a discussion of the ways in which sociology could take its analysis of deviance further – a theme returned to in a number of the readings in this chapter, from various points in the 'history of ideas' of the sociology of crime and deviance.

Cohen suggests that sociology should be sceptical of the political justifications given by the state for the control of deviance and deviants in society. He argues that criminology – as opposed to sociology – has for too long been concerned with an empirical, positivistic and medical model of academic analysis. This extract is useful since it highlights key themes and concerns that a number of sociologists have in this topic area.

Images of deviance

THERE HAS ALWAYS been some truth in the **layman**'s charge that the sociologist's picture of the world is merely a more complicated representation of his own **common-sense** way of understanding things. One can also see why sociologists in their quest for academic respectability have bristled at such accusations and insisted on their subject's status as a 'science'. Such defensiveness, though, is not only misplaced in that the sociologist needs to break free from the chains of science, but misses the point that he has to start off with the layman's picture of the world. This is not to say that he must take this picture as the truth, but, unlike the natural scientist, he cannot afford to ignore it. He must look behind the picture and understand the processes of its creation, before trying to paint over it and superimpose his own version of what is happening.

There is perhaps no sub-field of sociology where this paradox is more clearly illustrated than in the study of crime, delinquency and other forms of deviant behaviour. A large amount of space in newspapers, magazines and television and a large amount of time in daily conversation are devoted to reporting and discussing behaviour which sociologists call deviant: behaviour which somehow departs from what a group expects to be done or what it considers the desirable way of doing things. …

By using a very broad and abstract concept of

deviance, this book does not ignore what to the public are the most serious and obvious forms of deviant behaviour. But the concept of deviance itself does not only include such 'headline social problems', nor does it by any means only include criminal or delinquent conduct. The term 'deviance' itself is to blame for carrying this narrower connotation. If we look at some words which can mean roughly the same things as the verb 'to deviate' we find some of the more generic features of the concept: alter course; stray; depart from; wander; digress; twist; drift; go astray; change; revolutionize; diversify; dodge; step aside.

The possibilities to which words such as these alert us are usually ignored, and the layman's understanding of deviance is based on the more visible types that are classified and presented to him every day. Pressed to explain the *fact* of deviation, he will probably redirect the question by talking about the *type of person* the deviant is thought to be: brutal, immature, irresponsible, vicious, inconsiderate, degenerate. These labels are the traditional ones of sin and immorality on to which newer concepts have been uneasily grafted following the increase in prestige and credibility given to psychiatrically derived vocabularies. Thus the sexual offender is not degenerate but sick: he has a 'kink', a 'warped mentality', or a 'twisted mind'. These labels are comfortable ways of looking at things, because they leave us with the satisfaction of knowing that the problem is somewhere out there. The fault lies in the individual's genetic composition, his mind, his family, his friends, or society as a whole.

This leaves the public with broadly four types of response to deviance: it can be *indifferent* – the problem doesn't concern us, 'let him do his thing'; it can *welcome* the deviance, heralding it, for example, as pointing the way for society to advance; it can be *punitive*, advocating deterrent and retributive measures, ranging from £5 fines to the death penalty; or, finally, it can be *progressive*, advocating various treatment and therapeutic measures, ostensibly designed for the deviant's 'own good'. (This last group might, of course, only look more progressive and libertarian than the third, but some of their methods, such as electric shock, brain surgery and compulsory hospitalization, could be merely authoritarian techniques of social control under the guise of benevolent science.) In any event, all these responses are evaluated in terms of their success in eradicating the deviance or controlling it within manageable proportions.

Traditionally, criminologists have accepted a view of deviance not very far from all this. They have carried out research – spending millions of pounds in the process – to demonstrate the ways in which the deviant is supposed to be different from the non-deviant. They have tried to show, for example – and less successfully than most people assume – that the deviant's personality, family experience, or attitudes to authority are significantly different from those of his normal counterpart and that these differences somehow cause his deviance. Measures of control or treatment are then usually proposed which take such differences into account. A vocal group of criminologists in America and Britain have gone a step further in proposing to extrapolate backwards from such supposed differences in order to predict and hence pick out in advance those destined to occupy deviant roles. A certain amount of controversy was aroused at the beginning of 1970 when a New York psychiatrist – formerly President Nixon's physician – proposed that psychological tests should be given to all six-year-olds in the United States to uncover their potential for future criminal behaviour. He went on to advocate massive psychological and psychiatric treatment measures for those children with criminal inclinations, suggesting further that those who persisted into their teens should be interned in special camps for conditioning. The controversy about these views – and the fact that they were apparently being received seriously by the American government – occurred mainly because of the starkness with which they were expressed. They were not at all novel, or the idiosyncratic ramblings of a cranky scientist, but, in fact, the logical conclusion of years of respectable theory and research shaped by the conception of the criminal as a particular type of person, understandable and treatable apart from his society.

What sort of strategies could lead to such proposals? Let me give a crude example of how somebody working within this particular tradition makes such connexions between research, theory and policy. Last year, an intelligent psychology student in a reputable university obtained his Ph.D. after a lengthy study of the degree to which long-term prisoners were capable of 'abstract' as opposed to 'concrete' thinking. He chose as his controls (i.e. a group drawn for comparative purposes from the normal population) men from a sheltered employment workshop in the area [!] and found that the prisoners were more likely to think in a 'concrete' way. This meant that they scored – and his logic and statistics were impeccable – less well on a test of abstractness: when presented with objects such as miniature handcuffs they were more likely to say things like 'police' than abstract notions such as 'law and order'. On the basis of this statistical demonstration our psychologist then went ahead to propose that group therapy of long-term offenders should be designed to help men think abstractly so that aims such as deterrence and rehabilitation should be meaningful to them. Presumably the next step is to design a test for schoolchildren which will weed out all the concrete thinkers and help them to come to terms with the abstractness of reality. ...

The mainstream of criminology, though, particularly in Britain, has identified with strategies, values and aims remarkably close to what the public demands and expects of them, and the implications of sociological theories have either not been made explicit or not permeated through. It would be surprising, given the close historical connexion between criminology and control or welfare concerns, to find otherwise. More often than not, these concerns have expressed themselves in 'soft' ways, and students of crime and deviance are invariably accused of being do-gooders or sentimental busybodies. In these roles, they have played an important part in removing the more barbaric irrationalities of our legal and penal system. But the welfare approach embodies a conception of deviance close to that of the general public's, and in their well-meaning attempts to educate prison officers, policemen or magistrates, criminologists are playing out the role which society happily allocates to them.

In recent years – particularly in America – there has been a two-pronged attack on this way of looking at the subject. From the theoretical side, questions have been raised about the whole concept of deviance, and a sociological truism has been reasserted: namely that deviance is not a quality inherent in any behaviour or person but rests on society's reaction to certain types of rule-breaking. The same act – shall we say a homosexual encounter – is not defined in the same way by all societies, nor are all persons breaking the rules (in this case, the rules governing sexual encounters) officially defined and classified as deviants. One must understand deviance as the product of some sort of transaction that takes place between the rule breaker and the rest of society. Similarly, a 'social problem' consists not only of a fixed and given condition but the perception and definition by certain people that this condition poses a threat which is against their interests and that something should be done about it. From the policy side, the issue about what sort of role the criminologist or student of deviance should play has also been re-analysed. Questions – always dormant – have been brought out into the open about what side he is on and what sort of value commitments his theories lead him on to. When dealing with the phenomenon of violence, for example, these answers have had to be made in contexts such as those of the American ghettos in which the distinctions between ideological and criminal action have become increasingly blurred.

These developments, which are among those characteristic of what I will call the **sceptical** approach to deviance, raise a number of important issues far beyond the scope of this introduction. Obviously also, all these issues cannot be taken up in seven disparate papers which are as much products of their authors'

individual interests as their commitment to a particular theoretical viewpoint. ...

The sceptical position in regard to crime, deviance and social problems was the common starting point for the sociologists involved in this volume. We had all been students and subsequently teachers in these areas and had completed, or were busy doing, research on topics such as drug-taking, vandalism, organized crime, sexual deviance, debt collection, the Mods and Rockers, football hooliganism, police action, juvenile delinquency, physical handicaps, approved schools, prisons, suicide and mental illness. We were all familiar with American literature on deviance, and in some cases this had directly shaped our research. In any event, we were all uneasy about the way our subject seemed to be going in Britain.

Our feelings towards official criminology ranged from distrust at its orientation towards administrative needs and impatience with its highly empirical, antitheoretical bias, to simply a mild lack of interest in the sort of studies that were being conducted. Many such studies were useful, but useful for what? We were also unhappy with the apparent attempt to define criminology as a self-contained discipline which, in Britain, was being dominated by forensic psychiatrists, clinical psychologists and criminal lawyers. In terms of having congenial people to discuss our work with, we found some of our sociological colleagues equally unhelpful. They were either mandarins who were hostile towards a committed sociology and found subjects such as delinquency nasty, distasteful or simply boring, or else self-proclaimed radicals, whose political interests went only as far as their own definition of 'political' and who were happy to consign deviants to social welfare or psychiatry. For different reasons, both groups found our subject matter too messy and devoid of significance. They shared with official criminology a depersonalized, dehumanized picture of the deviant: he was simply part of the waste products of the system, the reject from the conveyor belt. ...

1 Connecting with the public

If the sociologist sees his task as explaining the world in terms intelligible only to his fellow sociologists, then he is welcome to do so. Let him not complain, though, that politicians, policy-makers, social workers and the mythical man in the street do not listen to him. Of course, the main reason they do not listen to him is not because of a communication problem but because he has no position of power or says things contrary to their values: witness the wilfully ignorant way in which the government has handled the drug addiction problem. But we can be credible only to the extent that we are intelligible. Without our talking down or being patronizing, the accounts and theories we give of deviance should be interesting and meaningful to the layman. Conversely, the accounts of deviance given by non-sociologists – schoolteachers, journalists, barmen or policemen – should be of interest to us. ...

2 Looking at the others

I have already pointed out that a cornerstone of the sceptical viewpoint was a concern with the reactions of society to those forms of behaviour classified or classifiable as deviant. The research worker must question and not take for granted the labelling by society – or certain powerful groups in society – of certain forms of behaviour as deviant or problematic. To say that society creates its deviance and its social problems is not to say that 'it's all in the mind' and that some nasty people are going around creating deviance out of nothing, or wilfully inflating harmless conditions into social problems. But it does mean that the making of rules and the sanctioning of people who break these rules are as much a part of deviance as the action itself. The concept of crime is meaningful only in terms of certain acts being prohibited by the state, and a problem can only be a problem to somebody. So, whenever we see terms such as deviance and social problem, we must ask: 'Says who'? ...

3 Deviance as a process

Our young psychologist's discovery of criminals' concrete thought patterns was one move in the obsessive game of finding the holy grail which will tell us the secret of deviance. The deviant is seen as the product of certain forces, or the possessor of certain characteristics, and one day, given time, skill and of course research funds, we will know what these forces and characteristics are.

The only part left out of this picture is the deviant himself and the fact that he arrives at his position and becomes the sort of person he is through a series of processes observable elsewhere in life. It is these processes we are interested in, not just the initial pushes and pulls but the stages of involvement, disinvolvement, side-tracking, doubt, guilt and commitment. If psychological characteristics such as concreteness, extraversion, neuroticism and the rest are of any meaning at all, they must be related to the processes of becoming a deviant.

These processes, of course, only take place in a context. We have become very much aware that the sceptical position has exaggerated its differences from older sociological concerns by playing up the role of 'others' in creating and perpetuating deviance and playing down the structural conditions in which various forms of deviance arise in the first place. Neither societal reactions to deviance nor the process of becoming deviant can be studied apart from the economic, educational and class systems, institutions such as family and school, and leisure and patterns of power, conflict and diversity. In different ways, the papers on sabotage, soccer hooliganism and thieving highlight some of these contexts.

4 The defence of meaning

What to some of us is a very radical break from traditional perspectives is the concern to defend both a conception of deviance as meaningful action and the status of the meaning which the deviant gives to his own activities. The annihilation of meaning has occurred in two ways. The one is to use adjectives such as 'meaningless', 'senseless', 'pointless', 'aimless', or 'irrational' to describe various sorts of deviance, for example violence or vandalism. People cannot allow deviation to threaten their picture of what their society is about. Part of this picture involves recognizing and accrediting certain motives as legitimate; if these motives cannot be found, then the behaviour cannot be tolerated, it must be neutralized or annihilated. Thus vandalism, unlike theft, cannot be explained in terms of the accredited motive of acquiring material gain, so it is described as motiveless. The only way of making sense of some actions is to assume that they do not make sense. Any other assumption would be threatening. We are very much concerned with restoring meaning to behaviour which has been stripped of it in this way. ...

It should be made clear that in talking about appreciating the deviant's own account of his motives, we do not regard this as the only story. We are also wary of the trap of romanticizing deviance. To hail the schizophrenic as a saint is no less misleading than to dismiss him as the unfortunate product of a biochemical imbalance. Such romanticism is not a form of appreciation at all, because it ignores the pathos, guilt, suffering and unhappiness which might be part of his situation.

5 Deviance as continuous and permeating

Another way to emphasize the problematic nature of the concept of deviance is to note that many aspects of deviance are continuous with normal life. It is not only labelled vandals who break other people's property, not only professional con-men who con others into believing in or parting with something, not only blackmailers who use blackmail to exploit a position of strength. This is not to say that the very illegality of certain types of transactions or behaviour is not crucial. On the contrary, the labelling of actions in certain terms puts them in a class of their own. What we mean by continuity is the need to be alerted to similarities between deviant and normal transactions. ...

Deviant values are also not altogether discontinuous

with more accepted ones: the deviant might only be taking conventional values to extremes or acting out private values which are subterranean to society. The deviant might justify his behaviour by appealing to widely acceptable social motives: 'I only did it for fun', or 'everyone else is doing it'. One has to delineate the normal patterns – such as those of technology and leisure in the cases of thieving and soccer hooliganism – within which the deviance develops. ...

6 The political implications of studying deviance

A conception of deviance is not simply a shorthand description. It carries within it a range of evaluative, moral and practical implications. For too long criminologists have either ignored these implications or readily accepted the directions they pointed to. Both these strategies are theoretically and morally indefensible. Let us imagine a sociologist interested in race relations being asked by a local authority to study its race problem in order to discover the best way of getting rid of its coloured residents. Most such sociologists in Britain would refuse the job and would probably see as the major theoretical issue the reason why the city should have posed the problem in this way. Their values would commit them to such a perspective.

In some cases of deviance and social problems, the position is analogous. We would not accept a brief from a seaside resort to clear its beaches of beatniks, however much we are interested in the subject of beatniks. And if we were against laws prohibiting homosexual behaviour, we would presumably not undertake research on how to make such laws more effective. But the decisions are usually more complicated than or of a different order from these, and the position is only roughly analogous to the race relations illustration. The deviance might be of a nature or degree which we would find difficult to tolerate or accept, and indeed sceptical theorists can be accused of opting for studying forms of deviance (such as homosexuality) which are calculated anyway to elicit a progressive, liberal response. Research goals are also usually defined in more subtle ways than 'making the law more effective', and – as students of race relations have discovered – one can be 'pure' enough in one's research or even explicitly come down on one side, only to have one's findings distorted or torn from their contexts by politicians and used for the other side. In the study of crime, an additional political problem presents itself: vast amounts of the

information one might require are controlled by such bodies as the prisons, police and Home Office and are subject to sanctions such as the Official Secrets Act. Research funds also usually come from bodies with clearly defined aims, and although he who pays the piper doesn't always call the tune his directions are not easy to ignore.

All these considerations imply – at the very least – that criminologists should be more honest and explicit about what their values are and what they are aiming to do. If they want to be technologists to help solve the state's administrative and political problems, let them state this. But, however interesting and commendable such research may be, there are surely some subjects where something else is required.

We are not all agreed among ourselves about this 'something else'. In some cases there is a clear imperative to reject the officially stated aims of social control, and actively – or by implication – lend support to the deviant group. In other cases we might support official aims such as deterrence but be concerned to define the deviant as a different sort of person from that which he is supposed to be. In yet other cases we might unequivocally accept the aims and conceptions of the control system. ...

It should be made clear that in lumping together the police, the courts, correctional institutions, social work and psychiatry as forms of **social control** one is not implying some sort of blanket moral condemnation of those associated with these institutions. The term 'social control' is a neutral, analytical one which should not carry any such overtones. Not only do we recognize that, say, child care officers, approved-school housemasters, probation officers, psychiatrists are involved in genuinely helping functions under usually frustrating and intractable conditions, but we would want to give such groups some support. We do not want to keep aloof from those who are doing our dirty work for us. Our support might only take the form of buttressing a latent ideology which some of these groups have already arrived at, but such support is very much needed if the dehumanizing tendency of the social sciences (statistical reductionism, people being seen as collections of symptoms, the worship of computers) is not to be repeated in the world of policy and practice.

Sociologists are increasingly becoming traders in definitions: they hawk their versions of reality around to whoever will buy them. There is a responsibility to make such definitions not only intelligible, consistent and aesthetically satisfactory, but also human.

Key terms

The following key terms appear in the text above. They have been defined below to aid with the reading of this item.

layman one who lives in society, lacking specialized or academic knowledge of their situation, using only common-sense thought to give meaning to life

common-sense describing the thought processes of 'lay actors' in society; common sense is a form of knowledge given through the socialization process and needed in order to act in a meaningful way

sceptical/scepticism the stance advocated by Cohen for sociology to take when dealing with crime: to stand back and not treat at face value the ideas of the state

social control ensuring that members of a society keep to the norms and values of that society

Questions

1 How and why does Cohen criticize common sense and criminological thinking? Why does he argue that sociological knowledge is better?

2 How and why is Cohen critical of the medical, 'rehabilitative' and 'welfare' goals of some criminology?

3 What criticisms have been made of the sociological discussion of crime and deviance by non-sociologists? Do you agree? Give reasons for your answer.

Reading 12.3 **A new criminology?**

Ian Taylor, Paul Walton and Jock Young (from) *The New Criminology. For a social theory of deviance* (1973) London: Routledge & Kegan Paul, pp. 268–82.

Editorial comments

In this now classic text by Taylor and his colleagues we are offered a review of existing theories on crime – both sociological and non-sociological (or, in other words physiological and psychological) and suggestions for what were, at the time, ways forward for the sociological study of crime. Taylor *et al.* argued that a sociological explanation had to be 'fully social' – it had to understand the nature of criminality at both macro and micro levels. This 'new criminology', rooted in a neo-Marxist approach, was to study meanings of criminality, the labelling process involved in the social construction of deviance, the effects of social structure on class, 'race', ethnicity and crime, and analyse the political nature of crime against an exploitative society.

In this reading Taylor *et al.* set out their ideas for such a new approach.

The new criminology

THE INSULATION OF criminology from sociology in general ... is rapidly being broken down. ... We are confronted once again with the central question of man's relationship to structures of power, domination and authority – and the ability of men to confront these structures in acts of crime, deviance and dissent – social theory itself.

This book has attempted to provide an implicit account of the uneven history of criminology's relationship to the social sciences. Starting with an account of the classical utilitarian approach to the protection of the individual from excessive punishment, and moving through the varieties of biological, psychological and social positivism, we have attempted to provide an immanent critique of various positions from a vantage point which stresses the importance of the initiative of State, and its entrepreneurial representatives, in defining and sanctioning certain forms of behaviour at certain points in

time: and we have suggested that an adequately *social* theory would need to be free of the biological and psychological assumptions that have been involved in the various attempts to explain the actions of the men who do get defined and sanctioned by the state as deviant and react against those definitions, in different historical circumstances.

Thus far, the book has operated within a relatively modest or limited perspective. The sociology with which we have urged a reconciliation has remained ambiguous: we have been content to say that such a sociology must be fully social (unbroken by the assertions of biological or other non-social assumptions) and that it must be able to account (in a historically informed fashion) for men's imprisonment within social structures that constrain his possibilities. We have not been able to specify, for example, the limitations of a sociology that is itself insulated from an economic understanding of structural forces or that has been developed entirely within the confines of a developing or developed capitalist society. We have not had space enough to draw out sufficiently cross-cultural evidence about the forms assumed by criminal and deviant action, and structures of social control, in pre-capitalist societies or in societies where there is an explicit attempt to break down the culture of capitalist societies.

We have, however, attempted to open out the criminological debate by pointing to certain *formal* and *substantive* requirements of a fully social theory of deviance, a theory that can explain the forms assumed by social control and deviant action in 'developed' societies (characterized – we have argued – by the domination of a capitalist mode of production, by a division of labour involving the growth of armies of 'experts', social workers, psychiatrists and others who have been assigned a crucial role in the tasks of social definition and social control, and, currently, by the necessity to segregate out – in mental hospitals, prisons and in juvenile institutions – an increasing variety of its members as being in need of control).

We have not, at this point, gone far beyond what we might call an immanent critique of existing theory. Rather, we have been concerned to develop a model which contains all the elements, some of which are lacking in individual examples of the existing literature on crime and deviance. And, despite the fact that we have continually stressed the need for a sense of history in the kind of explanations offered out of crime, deviance and control (a sense of history that is almost totally absent in existing criminological *theory*), we have not had the space here to enter into any detailed historical explanations. It is obvious that our endeavours need now to be supplemented with a concrete application of the formal model, resulting from the immanent critique of existing thinkers, to empirical cases: and, in particular, to situations in which a different form of production, a different division of labour and a different form of crime are all alleged to obtain. Given the nature of our premises, spelt out in the substantive requirements of the theory later in this conclusion, such an onerous enterprise would only be useful if the purpose for carrying it out was clear. And one of the central purposes of this critique has been to assert the possibility – not only of a fully social *theory* – but also of a society in which men are able to assert themselves in a fully social fashion. With Marx, we have been concerned with the social arrangements that have obstructed, and the social contradictions that enhance, man's chances of achieving full sociality – a state of freedom from material necessity, and (therefore) of material incentive, a release from the constraints of forced production, an abolition of the forced division of labour, and a set of social arrangements, therefore,

in which there would be no politically, economically, and socially-induced need to criminalize deviance. We shall expand on this later: for the time being, it is clearly essential to spell out the elements of the formal model that emerge out of the immanent critique.

The *formal* requirements of this theory are concerned with the scope of the theory. It must be able to cover, and sustain the connections between:

1 The wider origins of the deviant act

The theory must be able, in other words, to place the act in terms of its wider structural origins. These 'structural' considerations will involve recognition of the intermediate structural questions that have traditionally been the domain of sociological criminology (e.g. ecological areas, subcultural location, distribution of opportunities for theft) but it would place these against the overall social context of inequalities of power, wealth and authority in the developed industrial society. Similarly, there would be consideration of the questions traditionally dealt with by psychologists concerned with the structures conducive to individual breakdown, that is with an individual's exclusion from 'normal' interaction. ...

The wider origins of the deviant act could only be understood, we would argue, in terms of the rapidly changing economic and political contingencies of advanced industrial society. At this level, the formal requirement is really for what might be called *a **political economy** of crime*.

2 Immediate origins of the deviant act

It is, of course, the case, however, that men do not experience the constraints of a society in an undifferentiated fashion. Just as subcultural theorists, operating in the anthropological tradition, have argued that the subcultural notion is useful to explain the different kinds of ways in which men resolve the problems posed by the demands of a dominant culture, so we would argue that an adequately social theory of deviance must be able to explain the different events, experiences or structural developments that precipitate the deviant act. The theory must explain the different ways in which structural demands are interpreted, reacted against, or used by men at different levels in the social structure, in such a way that an essentially deviant choice is made. The formal requirement, at this level, that is, is for a *social psychology of crime*: a social psychology which, unlike that which is implicit in the work of the social reaction theorists, recognizes that men may *consciously* choose the deviant road, as the one solution to the problems posed by existence in a contradictory society.

3 The actual act

Men may choose to engage in particular solutions to their problems, without being able to carry them out. An adequate social theory of deviance would need to be able to explain the relationship between beliefs and action, between the optimum 'rationality' that men have chosen and the behaviours they actually carry through. A working-class adolescent, for example, confronted with blockage of opportunity, with problems of status frustration, alienated from the kind of existence offered out to him in contemporary society, may want to engage in hedonistic activities (e.g. finding immediate pleasure through the use of alcohol, drugs, or in extensive sexual activities) or he may choose to kick back at a rejecting society (e.g. through acts of vandalism). ...

4 Immediate origins of social reaction

Just as the deviant act itself may be precipitated by the reactions of others (e.g. as a result of an adolescent's attempt to win acceptance as 'cool' or 'tough' in a subculture of delinquency, or from a businessman's attempt to show ability as a sharp practitioner) so the subsequent definition of the act is the product of close personal relationships. A certain behaviour may encourage a member of the actor's family or peer group to refer that actor to a doctor, to a child guidance clinic, or to a psychiatrist (because that behaviour is seen to be odd). Or another behaviour may result in the individual being reported to the police by people outside the individual's immediate family circle or friendship group (because he has been acting suspiciously, or actually been seen committing an illegal act). In both instances, there is a degree of choice on the part of the social audience: it may be thought that the behaviour *is* odd, but that it is preferable to keep it in the family; or it may be thought that although the individual *has* been acting suspiciously or has been behaving illegally, it would be too troublesome to involve the police. ...

5 Wider origins of deviant reaction

In the same way that the choices available to the deviant himself are a product of his structural location, primarily, and, secondarily, his *individual* attributes (his acceptability to significant others – both those involved in legitimate activity and those who are engaged in rule-breaking activity of one kind or another), so the social psychology of social reaction (and the lay theories of deviance behind it) is explicable only in terms of the position and the attributes of those who instigate the reaction against the deviant. It is obviously the case that members of a law-breaker's immediate family group are far less likely to react against his activity than those who are strangers to him. But it is also the case that the 'lay' theories of criminality and deviance adhered to by strangers will vary enormously: social work ideology (with its positivistic stress on reform) is continually at odds with the more classically punitive ideologies of correctional institutions and their controllers; police ideology is sometimes at odds with the philosophies of courtroom practice (in particular, the adjudicatory powers of the non-professional jury); and even amongst those without formal positions in the structure of social control (the 'public') the lay theories found to be acceptable will vary across the contours of social class, ethnic group and age. ...

... Marx's political sociology of crime was also inextricably bound up with a political critique and a clear-headed analysis of existing social arrangements. For him, crime was expression of men's situation of constraint within alienating social arrangements – and in part an indication of a struggle to overcome them. The fact that criminal action was no political answer in itself to those situations was explained in terms of the political and social possibilities of the *Lumpenproletariat* as a parasitical agency on the organized working class itself. We shall develop our earlier critiques of these two positions a little later: for the time being, it is sufficient to mention them not only as evidence of the *dilution of theory* in twentieth-century investigations of crime but also as an indictment of the *depoliticization* of the issues involved in the classical discussions in social theory on crime, accomplished and applauded by those who carry out work in the field of contemporary 'applied' criminology.

For the moment it is sufficient to assert that one of the important formal requirements of a fully social theory of deviance, that is almost totally absent in existing literature, is an effective model of the political and economic imperatives that underpin on the one hand the 'lay ideologies' and on the other the 'crusades' and initiatives that emerge periodically either to control the amount and level of deviance or else (as in the cases of prohibition, certain homosexual activity, and, most recently, certain 'crimes without victims') to remove certain behaviours from the category of 'illegal' behaviours. We are lacking a *political economy of social reaction*.

6 The outcome of the social reaction on deviant's further action

One of the most telling contributions of the social reaction theorists to an understanding of deviance was their emphasis on the need to understand deviant action as being, in part, an attempt to come to terms by the rule-breaker with the reaction against his initial infraction. As we argued [previously], one of the superficial strengths of the social reaction perspective was its ability to see the actor as using the reaction against him in a variety of ways (that is, in exercising choice). This we saw to be an advance on the deterministic view of the impact of sanctions on further behaviour in positivistic views of 'reform', 'rehabilitation', and, most particularly, 'conditioning'. We also argued, however, that the notion of secondary deviation was undialectical; that is, that it could have the same status as an explanation of what the social reaction theorists separate out as primary deviation, and that, in reality, it might be impossible to distinguish between the causes of primary and secondary deviation.

A fully social theory of deviance – premised on the notion of man as consciously involved (however inarticulately) in deviant choices – would require us to see the reaction he evolves to rejection or stigmatization (or, for that matter, sanction in the form of institutionalization) as being bound up with the conscious choices that precipitated the initial infraction. ...

A fully social explanation of the outcome of social reaction to the further actions of the apprehended deviant, therefore, would be one in which the deviant actor is always endowed with some degree of consciousness about the likelihood and consequences of reaction against him, and in which his subsequent decisions are developed from that initial degree of consciousness. All those writers who see deviants as 'naive' must now realize that they are dealing with a minority of deviants, even in situations where the degree or extent of social reaction is unexpected (because, for example, of a moral panic amongst the powerful about a particular kind of offence, or because a campaign of control has been instigated against it – as in the case of the white adolescents who received unexpectedly heavy sentences for their role during the Notting Hill race riots in 1959), it would still be important to have a social explanation of the ways in which the deviants responded to their sentences with a degree of consciousness about 'the law' which they had developed before they had had a formal contact with it.

In a fully social theory, then, the consciousness conventionally allowed deviants in the secondary deviation situation would be seen as explicable – at least in part – in terms of the actors' consciousness of the world in general.

7 The nature of the deviant process as a whole

The formal requirements of a fully social theory are formal in the sense that they refer to the *scope* of the theoretical analysis. In the real world of social action, these analytical distinctions merge, connect and often appear to be indistinguishable. We have already

indicted social reaction theory, which is in many ways the most sophisticated rejection of the simpler forms of positivism (concentrating as they do on the pathologies of the individual actor), as one-sidedly deterministic: in seeing the deviant's problems and consciousness simply as a response to apprehension and the application of social control. Positivistic explanations stand accused of being unable to approach an explanation not only of the *political economy* of crime (the background to criminal action) but also of what we have called the *political economy*, the *social psychology* and the *social dynamics* of social reaction to deviance. And most of the classical and earlier biological psychological positivists are unable to offer out even a satisfactorily social explanation of the relationship between the individual and society: the individual in these accounts appears by and large as an isolated atom unaffected by the ebb and flow of social arrangements, social change, and contradictions in what is, after all, a society of social arrangements built around the capitalist mode of production.

The central requirement of a fully social theory of deviance, however, is that these formal requirements must not be treated simply as essential factors all of which need to be present (in invariant fashion) if the theory is to be social. Rather it is that these formal requirements must all appear in the theory, as they do in the real world, in a complex, dialectical relationship to one another. ...

The new criminology

The conditions of our time are forcing a reappraisal of this compartmentalization of issues and problems. It is not just that the traditional focus of applied criminology on the socially deprived working-class adolescent is being thrown into doubt by the criminalization of vast numbers of middle-class youth (for 'offences' of a hedonistic or specifically oppositional nature). Neither is it only that the crisis of our institutions has deepened to the point where the 'master institutions' of the state, and of the political economy, are unable to disguise their own inability to adhere to their own rules and regulations. It is largely that the total interconnectedness of these problems and others is being revealed.

A criminology which is to be adequate to an understanding of these developments, and which will be able to bring politics back into the discussion of what were previously technical issues, will need to deal with the society as a totality. This 'new' criminology will in fact be an *old* criminology, in that it will face the same problems that were faced by the classical social theorists. ...

We have argued here for a political economy of criminal action, and of the reaction it excites, and for a politically-informed social psychology of these ongoing social dynamics. We have, in other words, laid claim to have constructed the formal elements of a theory that would be adequate to move criminology out of its own imprisonment in artifically segregated specifics. We have attempted to bring the parts together again in order to form the whole.

Implicitly, we have rejected that contemporary trend which may claim for itself the mantle of a new criminology, or a new deviancy theory, and which presumably claims to find a solution to our present discontents largely in the search for the sources of individual meaning. **Ethnomethodology**, however, is a historical creature too: its pedigree goes back to the phenomenological contemplations that were so prominent in an earlier period of uncertainty and doubt: the collapse of European social democracy and the rise of fascism. **Phenomenology** looks at the prison camp and searches for the *meaning* of the 'prison' rather than for its alternative; and it searches for the meaning in terms of individual definitions rather than in terms of a political explanation of the necessity to imprison. ...

It should be clear that a criminology which is not normatively committed to the abolition of inequalities of wealth and power, and in particular of inequalities in property and life-chances, is inevitably bound to fall into correctionalism. And all correctionalism is irreducibly bound up with the identification of deviance with pathology. A fully social theory of deviance must, by its nature, break entirely with correctionalism (even with social reform of the kind advocated by the Chicagoans, the Mertonians and the romantic wing of Scandinavian criminology) precisely because, as this book has attempted to show, the causes of crime must be intimately bound up with the form assumed by the social arrangements of the time. Crime is ever and always that behaviour seen to be problematic within the framework of those social arrangements: for crime to be abolished, then, those social arrangements themselves must also be subject to fundamental social change.

It has often been argued, rather misleadingly, that for Durkheim *crime* was a normal social fact (that it was thus a fundamental feature of human ontology). For us, as for Marx and for other new criminologists, *deviance* is normal – in the sense that men are now consciously involved (in the prisons that are contemporary society and in the real prisons) in asserting their human diversity. The task is not merely to 'penetrate' these problems, not merely to question the stereotypes, or to act as carriers of 'alternative phenomenological realities'. The task is to create a society in which the facts of human diversity, whether personal, organic or social, are not subject to the power to criminalize.

Key terms

The following key terms appear in the text above. They have been defined below to aid with the reading of this item.

political economy understanding the operation of power in society by reference to the structure and nature of inequality through the economic system. Marxism is a theory which has as its basis a theory of 'political economy'

ethnomethodology the branch of interactionist sociology concerned with understanding the methods used by social actors, in order to understand the taken-for-granted, common-sense rules of social behaviour

phenomenology the branch of interactionist sociology concerned with understanding how 'reality' is categorized in individual consciousness

Questions

1 Describe in your own words the aims of these 'new criminologists'.

2 Even though trying to move sociology in new directions, Taylor *et al.* still retain a commitment to Marxism. What do they say about their use of such Marxist sociology?

3 How have they used interactionist ideas in their work?

4 Do you think it is a good idea to combine macro and micro ideas like this? What benefits, and disadvantages, might it have?

Reading 12.4 **Moral panics, 'mugging' and social control**

Stuart Hall, Chas Critcher, Tony Jefferson, John Clarke and Brian Roberts (from) *Policing the Crisis: Mugging, the state and law and order* (1978) London: Macmillan, pp. 165–77.

Editorial comments

Working at the Birmingham-University-based Centre for Contemporary Cultural Studies (CCCS), Hall and his colleagues suggest that media moral panics can serve the stability of capitalism by justifying social control at times of 'legitimation crisis'. Hall *et al.* argue that at times of crisis – where the problems of capitalism become visible to those who suffer their consequences: the masses – capitalism needs to renew stability in society by using both ideological and sometimes repressive forms of social control. Thus, argue Hall *et al.*, racism in the media aimed at a fictional 'black mugger' can function to divide working-class political action between a black working class and a white working class. In such a way, the problems of capitalism are blamed upon a 'scapegoated' group.

In this reading, Hall and his colleagues survey various ideologies of crime – political explanations offered for the existence for crime – and their various ideological functions.

Explanations and ideologies

WHAT WE HAVE tried to do so far … is to reconstruct the deep-structure or social matrix of the 'traditionalist' views on crime which proved so instrumental in the public reaction to 'mugging' and which provides the support for conservative popular campaigns on crime in general. **Moral panics** come into play when this deep-structure of anxiety and traditionalism connects with the public definition of crime by the media, and is *mobilized*. Now we can at last go back to the questions we posed at the beginning concerning 'explanations and ideologies'. How is crime commonly explained? What 'vocabularies of motive', what social ideas already arranged in credible chains of explanation are drawn on, across the class and power spectrum, to provide an account of why 'mugging' suddenly occurred out of the blue? What general lay ideologies about crime inform these explanations?

First, we have to make clear what we mean by an 'explanation'. We are not here discussing fully coherent and adequately theorized explanations of crime, such as we might find in the different schools and tendencies which make up criminological theory. We shall see, at the end, that the more fragmentary, more incoherent and contradictory kinds of explanations which have explanatory power at the level of judicial reasoning, news and feature presentations in the media, public expert and **'lay' opinion**, and so on, do indeed relate to the more elaborate 'criminological theories' which have gained currency at different times in Britain, and other developed capitalist societies. But we have started, in fact, at the opposite end. When the journalist, or the judge, or the members of the ordinary public have to respond to, or explain, troubling events, like 'mugging', they tend to draw, often in a piecemeal and unreflexive manner, on the social images, the 'ideas of society', the sources of moral anxiety, the scattered meanings which frame their everyday experience in order to construct, out of them, social accounts which carry credibility. These accounts are not constructed afresh out of each individual's head. They draw on the publicly objectivized 'vocabularies of motives' already available in the public language – the available field of practical ideologies. To find an explanation for a troubling event, especially an event which threatens to undermine the very fabric of society, is of course the beginnings of a sort of 'control'. If we can only understand the *causes* of these events, then we are half-way to bringing them under our control. To give shocking and random events 'meaning' is to draw them once again into the framework of the rational order of 'things understood' – things we can work on, do something about, handle, manage.

The explanations we construct are not in the normal sense 'logical'. They are not internally consistent and coherent. They do not obey a strict logical protocol. In part this is because (as we shall see in a moment) we do not construct such 'explanations' out of nothing. We work with the elements of explanation which are already available, which lie to hand, which seem to have some relevance to the problem at hand. These bits and pieces are really the fragments of other, often earlier, more coherent and consistent theoretical elaborations which have lost their internal consistency over time, fragmented, become sedimented in ordinary **'common sense'**. Gramsci calls them *traces*: 'the historical process … has left an infinity of traces gathered together without the advantage of an inventory'. So when we use these fragments of other ideological systems to construct explanations, we are operating rather like Levi-Strauss's primitive myth-maker, the *bricoleur*, who assembles the oddments and fragments of his culture, combined in ever new ways, to construct meanings and to reduce the world to orderly shape and meaningful categories: the bricks and mortar for a 'house of theory'. It is perfectly clear, for example, that, though Britain is by now a thoroughly secularized society, in one sense, there is hardly a developed argument or an important social or moral attitude we are likely to encounter about, say, marriage or sexuality, which does not, in either a positive or negative way, draw on or refer to religious – indeed often specifically Christian – modes of thought. Christianity continues to provide 'traces' which enable secular men to 'think' their secular world. Thus, as Marx once observed, 'The tradition of all the dead generations weighs like a nightmare on the brain of the living.'

When the ordinary lay public constructs explanations, it imagines that it is doing so free from ideological and societal constraint, far away from theorizing and scientific **discourse**; but in fact, all explanations are constructed, not by being produced out of the internal fabric of the mind, but by being cast within the existing fields of explanation, the socially maintained 'vocabularies of motive', objectivated over time. It is from these larger 'systems of thought' that, in fact, their credibility as well as their coherence derives.

We can simply indicate here the three main levels at which explanations of crime arise: in the judiciary, in the media, and amongst the 'ordinary lay public'. Judges do often elaborate on the social and moral 'meaning' of the crimes they are judging or the criminals they are sentencing. But, on the whole, they do not provide very elaborated 'explanations'. Retribution, condemnation, deterrence are the primary tasks of the judge, not providing convincing explanations of crime. ...

Perhaps the most elaborated attempts to develop explanations of crime occur in the press, especially in feature articles. That, we suggested, was because it is the essential function of feature articles to probe into the backgrounds and causes of events, and to explore explanatory models. As we saw earlier, there seem to be a variety of explanatory models of crime in play in the press, though in fact the range – looked at in terms of their 'logics' rather than in terms of the specific arguments they deploy – is much more limited. Even 'environmental' explanations, which figure strongly where the Handsworth 'mugging' was concerned, really operate within a very tight set of constraints.

The range of explanatory **paradigms**, then, is very limited, and these limited basic structures of thinking about crime form the framework within which the variety of specific explanations have to be constructed. These basic paradigms operate by providing answers to a *common* set of shared questions or problems – it is these which pose the 'criminal question' for these paradigms. We have seen earlier how the debate around the Handsworth sentences was more or less polarized around the 'liberal' and 'traditionalist' positions – in the various forms of press treatment, in judicial comments, and in both the public and private letters. The reason why these two positions (and their complex concrete variants) are able to take the role of positions *within a 'debate'* is that they are fundamentally organized by, and address themselves to, the same set of questions.

Central to this set of questions is the 'nature' attributed to the criminal – his motivation or state of mind, which polarizes the liberal and traditional positions around the degree of choice involved in action, or – in more legalistic terms – the degree of responsibility the criminal has. This connects with deeper assumptions about the conception of 'human nature' which is attributed to the criminal, and thus with conceptions of the *relation* between the criminal and society. Only from these *fundamental* positions about the nature of crime, the individual and society (i.e. the underpinnings of 'causal' explanations of crime) is the final question answerable – what the society's response to crime should be: the objectives of penal policy and punishment.

We do not find elaborate and extensive responses to these questions within the various 'bits' of lay explanations which we saw earlier, but nevertheless very similar positions are *implicit* in the attribution of motive, 'nature', causation, and so on to the criminal in everyday speech. But they are not derived from criminological theorizing or judicial reasoning – they are precisely the attempt at lay explanation which must 'make sense' of crime – connect it with their experience – in common-sense terms: that is, with whatever 'bits' of cultural knowledge are at hand and seen to connect.

In this final section, we shall try to develop a typology of these explanations which will show how the answers to the different questions cohere, but, also, how what appear to be the two *polar* positions in the lexicon of crime – the liberal and traditionalist – are themselves interconnected: how they form a 'unity in difference' of the available ideologies of crime. In very simplified terms, we can identify two basic 'lay ideologies' of crime, two basic explanatory frameworks.

The *conservative* explanation of crime lays fundamental stress on the primitiveness of crime, and the state of mind leading up to it. It is predicated on the eternal struggle between Good and Evil. Human nature is fundamentally nasty, brutish and vile. But the seed of Good is planted in us all. It requires, of course, eternal vigilance on the part both of society and of conscience. All of us are involved in this perpetual spiritual warfare against the 'evil that is in us'. Most of us manage to subdue the Devil. For the explicitly religious version, the submission to the authority of God and the moral law; for the secularized version, the submission to social authority and hierarchy, are the armour-plates of conscience which help us to surmount Evil and do Good. The criminal, however, has chosen not to fight the good fight. He has embraced Evil. This puts him outside the human community, makes him something 'less than human', something pre-human, uncivilized. That is his choice; but the wages of choosing Evil are heavy. The criminal represents a threat to us all, both to our physical safety, our moral duty and our social code. We must be protected against him. And a clear warning must be delivered to all others who for the sake of gain, impulse or base motive are tempted to follow him in this path to unrighteousness. There is a sort of calculus – both divine and utilitarian – by which the greater the crime, the more severe the punishment.

The *liberal* theory of crime is different. Here, the criminal is seen as backward, or bored, or confused, or ignorant, or poor, or under-socialized: 'Forgive them, for they know not what they do.' If the conservative view of crime is pure Old Testament, the liberal view is the New Testament in the form of a social gospel. The individual agent is a weak vessel, with the power of forces larger than himself. Only the mechanisms of socialization and good fortune keep the majority of us on the straight and narrow. When these 'socializing' mechanisms break down, all of us are vulnerable to the revival of antisocial instincts and impulses. Crime is at root a 'social problem'. It arises, not from some fundamental premises of the whole moral universe, and not from some major structural fault of the social or moral system, but from particular failures, particular lapses in a structure which remains, in large measure, sound. Social problems require solutions. If the social or psychological processes can be remedied and improved, the possibility of such behaviour reoccurring can be minimized. Meanwhile, of course (here the liberal version makes its vital concession to the greater fundamental coherence of the conservative paradigm), public safety must be preserved, the guilty punished (for few are totally without responsibility) as well as rehabilitated, the innocent protected.

These are caricatures, no more. They are not intended as exhaustive sketches of the content of public consciousness about crime; and, even as sketches, they are patently [in]adequate. We offer them simply to indicate one of the most fundamental principles of structuration in the body of common attitudes widely diffused in our society on the theme of crime and punishment. They provide a line of articulation which distinguishes between the idea that crime is an evil thing, part of the dark forces of nature and human nature, beyond our rational control, against which men and society in their deep revulsion must be protected – a fundamental breach in 'the order of the moral universe' – and the idea that crime derives from the weakness and fallibility of human arrangements, whether of our society or our personalities, part of the structure of human frailty, which, in punishing, we must also rescue, buttress, protect and gradually strengthen by reform. It is hard to give these root-images any more precise legal, ideological or indeed historical content. Yet, between them, they command and construct the skeletal syntax, the elementary forms, of the collective mental discourse of a great many English people about crime and its control. ...

These two broad structures of common-sense ideas are best thought of as 'workings up' of our pretheoretical knowledge about crime. They embody the 'sum total of what everybody knows about' crime; an 'assemblage of maxims, morals, proverbial nuggets of wisdom, values and beliefs, myths and so forth, the theoretical integration of which requires considerable intellectual fortitude in itself'. These are the categories which most of us who have no professional knowledge of, or responsibility for, crime and its control, employ in order to 'think' the reality of crime which confronts us every day. These are the *practical ideologies* which supply 'the institutionally appropriate rules of conduct' for the majority. This is the level at which ideologies become real, enter experience, shape behaviour, alter conduct, structure our perception of the world – the level of ideas as a 'material force'. 'What is taken for granted as knowledge in society comes to be coextensive with the knowable, or at any rate provides the framework within which anything not yet known will come to be known in the future.' 'That atmosphere of unsystematized and unfixed inner and outer speech which endows our every instance of behaviour and action and our every "conscious" state with meaning.'

Behind and informing these practical ideologies, though in no simple one-to-one correspondence, lie the more articulated, 'worked-up', elaborated and theorized ideologies of crime which have shaped the operation of the juridical apparatuses of the state and the work of its intellectual exponents over time. Once again we can do no more than crudely sketch in some of the main positions which have emerged at this more theoretical level. The purpose of attempting this complicated – and largely unwritten – 'social history' of the theories of crime and punishment in summary form at all is twofold. First, because when we try to give the content of our two fundamental common-sense structures any greater richness of detail, then we are obliged to acknowledge that this detail, and the logics which inform them, have been imperfectly and haphazardly *borrowed* from the larger 'universes' of social discourses about crime: the theories of crime have left their 'trace', though not their 'inventory', as Gramsci remarked, on the structure of common-sense ideas about crime. But the second reason is that these theories did not elaborate themselves out of thin air; they are not only mental constructions. They arose because of the particular needs, the historical position, of the great social classes and class alliances which have had the control and containment (and thus the definition) of crime at their command – at different points through the development of the British (and related) social formation. Or, rather – since this way of putting it suggests, erroneously, that each emergent class carries its conception of law and crime 'like a number plate on its back' – they are the great constructions of crime and the law which have emerged through the struggle between the dominant and subordinate classes at particular moments and stages in the development of capitalist social formations and their civil, juridical, political and ideological structures: 'Each mode of production produces its specific legal relations, political forms, etc.' Laws, Marx stated, help to 'perpetuate a particular mode of production', though the influence they exert 'on the preservation of existing conditions of distribution and the effect they thereby exert on production has to be examined separately'. The ways of conceiving crime, society and the law, elaborated in these different theoretical perspectives, and materialized in the practices and apparatuses of the legal and criminal justice systems, remain active in structuring common sense and 'weigh on the brain of living'. Thus, unconsciously, often incoherently, in thinking the question of crime within the framework of common-sense ideas, the great majority of us have no other mental equipment or apparatus, no other social categories of thought, apart from those which have been constructed for us in other moments of time, in other spaces in the social formation. Each of the phases in the development of our social formation has thus transmitted a number of seminal ideas about crime *to* our generation; and these 'sleeping forms' are made active again whenever common-sense thinking about crime uncoils itself. The ideas and social images of crime which have thus been embodied in legal and political practices historically provide the present horizons of thought inside our consciousness; we continue to 'think' crime *in them* – they continue to think crime *through us*. ...

The conceptions of freedom, of contract, of responsibility and of 'the rational' generated in the liberal or classical revolution constitute the core of some of our most profound 'modern' ideas about law and crime. But the actual processes of the legal system, in their day-to-day manifestations, though based on these presuppositions, have been extensively modified by a subsequent change in the structure of legal ideas: the impact of positivism and the beginnings of the 'deterministic positions', which have so profoundly shaped modern notions of crime, and which were enshrined at the heart of the criminal system in what has been called the 'neo-classical revision'. The neo-classical revision was the product, not of competitive market bourgeois society, but of industrial capitalism as an increasingly organized corporate social system. Into the classical conceptions of free contract there gradually penetrated the sense of all those powerful forces which modified and constrained the free play of free wills. Bentham, whose rationality so often drove him beyond the limits which the rationality of market individualism assumed in his own time, had, as early as 1778, called for a systematic study of crime and periodical statistical returns on criminals; they would, he said, constitute 'a kind of political barometer'. And as industrial capitalism remade the world in its image, it became progressively clear that not the contracted individual but the contracted classes, and the social conditions they lived and worked in, were the shaping historical agencies. In this new framework, the 'working classes' and the 'dangerous and criminal classes' assumed a new and menacing identity: what Chevalier has called the metamorphosis of 'the criminal theme into the social theme' had commenced. The impact of Marx and Durkheim on legal ideas was a consequence of this attempt to think crime in terms of its social origins. In the neo-classical tradition, though the doctrine of 'individual responsibility' remained undiminished at its centre, men's actions gradually came to seem more and more shaped by forces which were not under his control, in societies which in their size and complexity dwarfed man's reason and will. The great English investigations into the social conditions of the industrial and criminal classes, from Mayhew to Booth, and the great amassing of 'moral statistics', using crime as a 'barometer' of social disorganization – to which the French investigators, Durkheim's forerunners, made such a contribution – began to reshape popular as well as legal conceptions of crime. The era of biological, psychological positivism and of sociological determinism – alongside the era of developed industrial capitalism – had commenced; beside the law there arose the 'science of crime' – criminology, the study of the conditions and aetiology of the criminal impulse, with its root in earlier 'moral statistics'.

We must note that the movements which shape this second transformation of legal thought and practice – like the first transformation – do not occur *within* the legal apparatus, but modify it through their impact on it from outside. As Pearson has noted, some elements of this new strain of thought about crime are visible in the work of many of the nineteenth-century 'moral investigators' of city life; but its codification and systematization took place within criminology and in its relations to (and borrowings from) other 'human sciences' – sociology, psychology and psychiatry. We cannot here leave our main theme to follow the shifts and developments in the theorizing of the aetiology of crime, but merely focus on the emergence of psychologistic and environmentalist determinism as two of the crucial tendencies along which legal practice aligned itself.

There is no direct and simple transference of these ideas into legal practice from criminology, though as Cohen has argued, the deeply *pragmatic* nature of English criminology has promoted persistent and close connections with policy-making, especially in the humanitarian reform of correctional institutions. However, the actual modification of the law to take account of this 'positivist revolution' depended on the expansion and organized intervention of professional and semi-professional agencies. The two crucial apparatuses with respect to the criminal law are the 'psychiatric professions' and the development of social-work agencies within the state. These institutions have been the 'practical bearers' of these ideologies in the modification of the law. They have been the agencies which have not only modified the *ideas* of criminal responsibility in the law, but provided practical alternatives for the disposition of the criminal – therapeutic and treatment-based alternatives to 'correctional' penal policy. If classical law was formulated within the *laissez-faire* state of early capitalism, these reformulations have taken shape within the organization of an interventionist Welfare State.

We cannot trace the complex development of these two main strands in the modification of the criminal law in this context any further. We can only note its broad parameters. First, both are organized by an *individualist* determinism – the boundaries of their theoretical horizons are largely limited to the psychological interaction of the individual and the family, though social work is theoretically more ambiguous than clinical psychiatry in this sense. Indeed, the (historically derived) individual-centred case-work orientation of social work was one of the predisposing factors leading to its being professionally submerged under what has been called the 'psychiatric deluge' – with psychiatry as social work's main 'theoretical organizer'. Both, then, occupy the same 'theoretical space' (individualism) though with rather different origins and outcomes.

Second, both have historically modified the criminal law – but as 'exemptions' from its central principles, rather than transforming those principles. They operate on the basis of demonstrating that *individual cases* do not meet the criteria of 'individual responsibility' because of *exempting factors* – the individuals have in some sense a 'diminished responsibility'. In the psychiatric instance, this is demonstrated 'clinically': the individual is in need of 'treatment'. The principles of exemption in social work are looser – they include predisposing inadequacies of various sorts; and the possibility is held out to the court that the individual will respond to rehabilitative personal contact – supervision. The only exception to this essentially *marginal* status of the liberal revisions to classical positions on crime within the legal apparatus has been restricted to the sphere of operation of the juvenile court, where children have been accepted as incapable of 'criminal responsibility' *as a social category*. This is the one element of the legal apparatus within which social-work principles have actually come to dominate classical legal principles. (Current demands for the reorganization of the court and the removal or modification of the 1969 *Children and Young Person's Act* are aimed in part at removing the 'welfarist' dominance in this sector.)

Third, we must note the reflection of this marginal position of liberalism within the law in the failure of the 'liberal imagination' fundamentally to touch and reorganize popular conceptions of crime and law. The psychiatric frame connects only in the broadest sense – in adding some materials and illustrations for the more fundamental common-sense designation of the incomprehensible as 'he must be made' – while the social-work development has, more often, been seen as 'soft' – *excusing* the criminal for his actions. Fuel has been added to this conception in the recent highly publicized 'misjudgements' and 'errors' of social workers in relation to cases of 'child-battering' and the 'sexuality' of their young charges. These instances have provided powerful ammunition to the traditionalist assault on the 'soft liberalism' of the welfare agencies.

The connections of this liberal 'reforming' ideology to the working class are extremely complex. At the most fundamental level, it has been the organized struggle of the working class which has played a crucial role in forcing the expansion of the state in a welfare-orientated direction. However, the social-policy orientation of the Labour Party (Fabian reformism) has been massively shaped by the new petty bourgeoisie. The social-democratic demands for equality, welfare and the 'caring society' have taken a form which is strongly structured by the conceptions of these 'disinterested' liberal professions and semi-professions.

Thus, at one level, there are powerful material

connections between this reformist ideology and the social-democratic reformism of much of English working-class politics – it touches crucial demands for material improvement, security in the face of the vagaries of capitalism, and the greater equality of provision of material and cultural resources, etc. But there are crucial ambiguities in the way the class experiences its own apparent achievement. Suspicions of 'state snoopers', distrust of the activities of middle-class 'do-gooders', 'bleeding heart' liberals who are over-interested in 'good causes', a Welfare State which spends their money on immigrants and 'scroungers', and which has at the same time failed to fulfil its promises to the diligent and hard working – all these recapitulate both the division of 'mental' and 'manual' labour which we noted earlier, and the internal segmenting of the working class itself: the 'respectables and the rough' and the 'racial' fractioning. This contradictory working-class attitude to 'welfare reformism' in the legal-criminal area reflects a fundamentally contradictory reality – one which differs from the promises held out by the Welfare State as the means of achieving the ideal of the 'just society'.

In addition, the liberal-reforming ideology – though it connects most concretely with these material questions – is least sure-footed on the terrain of crime. We saw earlier how each of the central themes of the traditionalist world view touched and drew into its ambit the question of crime. The liberal ideology manages no such concrete address to the working-class experience of crime – it remains distanced and abstracted. Even within the Labour Party, the otherwise solid alliance with the liberal ideology has always been profoundly ambiguous on the topic of crime – involving both 'liberalizing' legislation, e.g. on the juvenile court, but also profoundly repressive measures, e.g. the implementation of the Mountbatten report on secure accommodation for long-term prisoners. The relative weakness of the liberal position on crime, in all the different terrains we have examined (within the legal apparatus, in relation to popular consciousness, and at the level of organized politics), constitutes a crucial feature of that position – its fundamentally *defensive* nature. In relation to crime, liberal reformism remains essentially on the defensive – reasonably strong in good times, and capable for a time of setting the pace of reform, but capable also of being rapidly eroded when times are not so good, and placed under pressure by the more conventional structure of beliefs about crime. One of the most notable features of the 'mugging' episode, for example, is the fact that, under the pressure of a mounting public scare about muggings, this liberal-humanitarian-reformist perspective more or less temporarily disappears from, for example, editorials

in the newspapers, and appears in subordinated and defensive positions elsewhere. In terms of the common-sense imagination, liberal views on crime represent a fragile and compensatory structure of ideas. Under conditions of stress they do not possess enough of a social base or real ideological purchase to determine the nature of public reactions to crime, once the traditional categories of thought have been mobilized by way of social anxiety and moral entrepreneurship.

In this chapter we have tried to pull together, in an inevitably speculative way, a number of themes and problems. By trying to trace the reaction to crime from its source in the media (where it is subject to complex structuring) right through to its varied expression in 'public opinion', we have been trying to undermine two, apparently opposed, but actually *complementary*, false propositions which impair much of radical thought on the question of crime. The first is that the traditionalism of the public temper on crime is the product of a conspiracy on the part of the ruling classes and their allies in the media. The second is that there really is a single thing called 'English culture' or 'English thought', and that it is overwhelmingly conservative in its essence. Neither, we argue, adequately accounts for the contradictory character of 'English ideologies'. It is of the utmost importance, then, to try to penetrate beneath these convenient 'unities' to their underlying antagonisms. This led us to explore some of the processes by which ideas have been *hegemonized* by the ruling classes in capitalist society. Such a critique will not, of itself, rupture the structures of **hegemony**, but it forms one of the first requirements, a necessary condition, of that break. Beyond that rupture lie alternatives which are as yet only partially and fitfully glimpsed – which are present only when the dominated classes align themselves with their historical movement, and develop strategies of action and modes of thought which have broken the internal structures which maintain their subordination. In that alternative space *also* lies the termination of the existing processes of 'criminalization': an alternative view of crime and the law as the product of antagonistic social forces, and of their incidence and operation as one of the principal means by which class domination is secured. The law remains one of the central coercive institutions of the capitalist state; and it is *coupled* in the most fundamental way with the structure of crime, with the way crime is perceived, and in the way crime forces those who are subordinate in society to shelter beneath a hegemonic order:

> But when men become separated or feel themselves separated from traditional institutions, there arises, along with the spectre of the lost individual, the spectre of lost authority. Fears and anxieties run

over the intellectual landscape, like masterless dogs. Inevitably in such circumstances men's minds turn to the problem of authority.
(Nisbet, 1966)

It is with the posing of this problem – the 'problem of authority' – that our analysis can no longer remain at the level of analysing ideologies of crime. We have tried in this chapter to pose and answer questions about how complex ideologies of crime provide the basis, in certain moments, for cross-class alliances in

support of 'authority'. But authority itself is not discoverable here – the conditions and forms of its exercise, the conditions under which *support* for authority needs to be mobilized actively, cannot be formed in ideologies of crime. The 'problem of authority' directs us to a different level of analysis, a different terrain of social organization: as Gramsci put it:

> A 'crisis of authority' is spoken of: this is precisely the crisis of hegemony, or general crisis of the State.
> *(Gramsci, 1971)*

References

Gramsci, A. (1971) *Selections from the Prison Notebook*, in Hoare, Q. (ed.) London: Lawrence & Wishart (orig. written 1929–35).

Nisbet, R. (1966), *The Sociological Tradition*, New York: Basic Books.

Key terms

The following key terms appear in the text above. They have been defined below to aid with the reading of this item.

moral panics exaggerated fears caused by media sensationalized reporting

lay opinion the ideas held about society by those who live in society; lacking specialized or academic knowledge

common sense the term given to the thought processes of 'lay actors' in society; a form of knowledge given through the socialization process and needed in order to act in a meaningful way

discourse a specialized set of languages which operate to label, control and define the world

paradigms frameworks for thinking – a world-view.

hegemony a term used by the Italian neo-Marxist Gramsci to refer to a dominance of ideological thought by those in positions of power so that the world appears normal, natural and is not questioned by those who live in it

Questions

1 How are Hall *et al.* influenced by the ideas of Gramsci?

2 What do Hall *et al.* have to say about the role moral panics can play in the creation of criminality?

3 How might moral panics help capitalism?

4 What ideas have been used to legitimate – to justify – our present legal and criminal justice systems? Describe the content of these ideas in detail.

Reading 12.5 **New left realism**

John Lea and Jock Young (from) *What Is To Be Done About Law and Order? Crisis in the nineties*, 2nd edn, (1993) (originally published in 1984 as *What Is To Be Done About Law and Order? Crisis in the eighties*) London: Pluto Press, pp. 262–73

Editorial comments

This text, originally written in 1984, represented a key moment in the theoretical development of the New

Left Realist movement in criminology and the sociology of crime and deviance. Lea and Young set, in the concluding chapter of this work, a 'realist' approach to crime by highlighting what they consider to be the six most important issues in the study – and the policing – of crime in contemporary social life. These six issues cover the realities of criminal statistics; the relationships of 'race', ethnicity, class and crime; the social and cultural characteristics of both the criminal and the victim; and the practices of contemporary policing.

A realistic approach to law and order

WE HAVE ATTEMPTED in this book to outline a realistic strategy about crime and policing from a socialist perspective. ... Under the impact of the Women's Movement socialists quite correctly began to realize

the problems of violence against women and their sexual harassment. The struggle against fascism galvanized particularly by the Anti-Nazi League and continued by numerous monitoring groups brought home to the Labour movement the extent and severity of racist attacks. But concern about crime stopped at these points. There was a schizophrenia about crime on the left where crimes against women and immigrant groups were quite rightly an object of concern, but other types of crime were regarded as being of little interest or somehow excusable. Part of this mistake stems, as we have noted, from the belief that property offences are directed solely against the bourgeoisie and that violence against the person is carried out by amateur **Robin Hoods** in the course of their righteous attempt to redistribute wealth. All of this is, alas, untrue. Indeed, the irony is that precisely the same kids who break into the next-door neighbour's flat sit around the estates wearing British Movement badges and harassing Asians.

But in adopting a realistic perspective on crime we must avoid finding ourselves in the ranks of the law-and-order lobby; a correct perspective is needed, but is extremely difficult at present. There is the story of a seminar in North London where one week the students, reeling from the impact of a description of the deplorable results of imprisonment on inmates, decided to abolish prisons. But then the next week, after being, quite correctly, informed by a speaker from the Women's Movement of the viciousness of many anti-female offences, decided to rebuild them!

An important corollary of the breakdown of community is decrease in accurate knowledge about crime. In a tight-knit social setting not only is there more unanimity of communal interest and an ability to **stigmatize** offenders, there is also greater knowledge about what is going on and what deviance is about. As social splintering occurs there is a decrease in direct knowledge about crime, but, although the quality of information declines, the actual quantity increases. As has been well documented, one of the key selling-points of Western mass media is its coverage of crime and social problems. A commercially oriented media bent on maximizing sales and audience ratings supplies news coverage which, although based on a rational kernel of public fear, has few curbs on its excesses of sensationalism. The only limits on this process are good taste and the limited knowledge that journalists have of crime. Thus we come to the crux of the matter. To recapitulate, in our time, relative deprivation and hence discontent have increased. This, combined with unemployment and community breakdown, has not allowed such discontent to be channelled into political forms. Instead, the most obvious solution is that of crime. Meanwhile, community breakdown facilitates crime by drastically undermining the informal process of social control. The same forces which make for the increase in crime fuel a **moral panic** about crime. That is, the real fear about crime is intimately related to the moral hysteria about crime.

It not only provides a rational kernel for alarm, but its genesis lies at the same source; and the mass media serve and exaggerate such public fears. The demand for crime news is great; the media reporting of crime and policing foments and exaggerates this appetite. This atmosphere carries with it a corresponding politics, but the law-and-order campaigns, such a familiar monopoly of the right, are an area in which the left has had very little to say except when it is on the defensive.

Thus, at precisely the time when there is the greatest need for a rational approach to crime, the greatest level of irrationality occurs. Just at the time when there is a need for a humane and realistic political intervention from the left, such a movement is lacking. Let us conclude by spelling out the basic premises of left realism in the areas of crime and the police.

1 Crime really is a problem

In contrast to the beliefs of **left idealists**, working-class crime really is a problem for the working class. This is not to deny the impact of crimes of the powerful or indeed of the perfectly legal social problems created by capitalism. Rather, left realism notes that the working class is a victim of crime from all directions; that one sort of crime tends to compound another, as one social problem does another; and furthermore, that crime is a potent symbol of the antisocial nature of capitalism and is the most immediate way in which people experience other problems, such as unemployment or competitive individualism.

Left realism examines the problem of crime seriously; it does not enter into the moral panics of the mass media or the blatant denial of left idealism. It clearly separates out moral panic from moral realism, and moral indignation from material conflict. With this in mind, it assesses the impact of crime on different victims and sections of the population. Furthermore, it carefully appraises the impact of crime, materially, politically and ideologically, on the maintenance of capitalism. For fear of street crime helps the disintegration of the working-class community and thus engenders a breakdown in the ability to fight back. It divides the poor against the poor both in a real sense and in the distorted ideological sense repeated by the mass media that the real enemy is crime and not the inequitable nature of our society.

2 We must look at the reality behind appearances

Left realism does not simply examine crime on the level of its immediate appearances. Conventional criminology notes the antisocial nature of crime; in this it is correct, but it ignores the social basis of its genesis. Left idealism, in that it notes how crime is a form of rebellion, is also correct, but by failing to go further than a discussion of its causes, is seriously myopic about the reactionary nature of its impact and the conventional nature of its mode of operation.

It is vital to realize the contradictory nature of working-class crime. Its cause is seeing through the deception and inequality of the world; its direction is towards that of selfishness. Its cause is righteous, its direction individualistic. The political energies that could have been harnessed for a transformation of society become channelled into ensuring its inertia.

3 We must take crime control seriously

Left realism is in fundamental disagreement with conventional and left-idealist approaches to crime control. The draconian penalties advocated by the law-and-order lobby, by amplifying and hardening criminals, simply serve to make matters worse. A fundamental irony is that the policies of the 'hard-on-crime' advocates in fact only serve to increase crime. They do not take crime seriously. On the other hand, the idealists with their myopia about crime simply turn their back on the problem. They leave crime alone and help create social mores where no one seems to care.

Realism instructs us that the problem is crime and not the criminal; that the vast majority of crimes are minor, amateurish and of little consequence in isolation; and that the average offender is not committed to crime but drifts into illegality sporadically and compulsively. But if one pinprick is of little significance, a thousand, repeated daily, certainly are! For this reason the keynotes of a left realism crime control programme are as follows.

a Demarginalization: Instead of marginalizing and excluding an offender, realists would argue for alternatives to prison which help to integrate rather than separate the offender. ...

b Pre-emptive deterrence: To deter crime before it is committed is infinitely better than to attempt to intervene by punishing the culprit after the event, with the aim of deterring his future activities or perhaps those of others. ...

c The minimal use of prison: Prison should only be used in those circumstances where there is extreme danger to the community. ...

4 We must look realistically at the circumstances of both the offender and the victim

Two abstract systems of justice dominate our penal and sentencing system. One, epitomized by the adult trial (for example, in the Crown Court), has the notion of the free-willed, responsible agent. Mitigating circumstances are allowed as random, unsystematized, marginal excuses; they only peripherally enter the realm of free choice which citizens as offenders are presented as inhabiting. All people, in this scheme, are held equally responsible for their deeds, and the seriousness of the offence is judged against a scale of well-intentioned but rather ill-defined notions of social harm. The other system is quite the opposite: the individual is viewed as a product of circumstances. This mode of justice is seen in the Juvenile Court. ...

So to explain a criminal event in terms of the total system is not to excuse it. It is to provide mitigating circumstances on a systematic level which the present system of law does in an arbitrary and individualistic fashion. This is not to advocate a hard law-and-order approach, but neither is it to provide a blanket excuse, as in much socialist thinking on crime. Rather, it recognizes the vital necessity for intervention, firstly, because – as we have argued – much criminality is essentially contradictory and strong intervention can – if it comes from the right direction – 'resolve' these contradictions; secondly, because crime is a demoralizing force within the community, which saps the strength of any political organization within the most depressed areas of the city. To recognize that there is this element of choice in crime is to accept that it is necessary to counter crime with force – realistically guided by knowledge of the circumstances involved.

5 We must be realistic about policing

The paramount fact is that the police need the public and that the effectiveness of policing is dependent on the extent to which we transform, as Steve Bundred of the GLC Police Committee put it, 'the police force into a police service'. The arrogance and autonomy which the police evidence towards those who pay their salaries must be got rid of. It is essential to impose a system of positive public accountability in which the needs of the community direct the activities of the police. Arguments about the need to maintain autonomy in operational tasks should clearly note that much of what the police deem operational is in fact directly political. The police demand to keep politics out of policing is only too often an argument for giving the political decisions to them. But we must not shirk the problems of democratic control. There is no reason for suspecting that a free vote on policing would protect the ethnic minorities, would stop the harassment of the young, would be tolerant of the dosser, and would direct police attention to the corruption among local councils or corporate executives. One of our constant nightmares is that if there was a completely democratic control of police in areas such as Hackney, the resulting police force would look exactly the same as the present Hackney police force. The irrationalities engendered by the mass media, the real and divisive difficulties which people face in their everyday life, the breakdown of community and 'obvious' sources of collective interest, all militate against this. But a crucial function of party politics in a democracy is not to be a mere cipher of public opinion but to attempt to try and convert the fearful and to create the circumstances for greater rationality. We must, in this context, also be realistic about the difficult position of the police. Their capacity to clear up crime has fallen to an all-time low. In the Metropolitan Police District, Walter Easy, Head of Camden Police Support Unit, has calculated that only 6 per cent of burglaries are successfully cleared up by the police. Part of this is due to rank police inefficiency, part is the lack of co-operation of the community, but the most difficult part is the breakdown of a working-class community which could possibly provide such instruction and information. We have argued that public involvement in a politics which is concerned with control of crime and antisocial activities within their areas will be dependent on the bringing of the police within democratic control and thus enhancing the co-operation of the public. But it will also serve to recreate the community.

6 We must be realistic about the problem of crime in the present period

Although for the last century crime has been a perennial problem for working-class people, we feel that there are certain key factors about the present period which are of great importance. Firstly, the degree of relative deprivation engendered by education, the mass media, the Welfare State and the inconsistencies of the market has constantly risen. Secondly, such discontent, instead of focusing on political objectives, has constantly been splintered as a consequence of the breakdown of community and the fragmentation of employment. Such a situation of discontent without a political outlet creates a criminal response which the left are, by tradition, extraordinarily inept at dealing with. Yet the whole possibility of a new community politics which unites people at a grass-roots level depends on this. If we return to our equation that crime is a result of economic discontent without political alternatives, then the implication for socialists is clear. Not only is crime control a material necessity for the working class and therefore an essential part of any socialist programme, but the absence of an alternative politics for marginalized youth that can give their lives meaning and potential contributes substantially to the creation of crime and disorganization. ...

We must be involved, then, for material, political and ideological reasons: materially, to pursue the cause of justice in working-class communities; politically, to provide an alternative politics which will harness the energies of the marginalized, thus diminishing the causes of crime while providing a humane and efficacious crime control. Such politics of crime control are part of the wide sweep of grass-roots politics: the control of pollution, industrial safety, traffic control, environmental improvements – representing, in fact, the united interest of a divided community. In this process of seeking out a common political interest and exerting public control, we will recreate a sense of community both in consciousness and in muscle, rather than resurrect a mythical entity which has long since disappeared. Lastly, ideologically, we will combat the tendency of a divided and disillusioned public to move to the right, to construct a quasi-community out of shabby nationalism and racism, and replace the 'war against crime' notion of conventional politics with the notion that the fight against crime is one that combats the material deprivation of capitalism and the rank individualism of its values. It is with this aim in mind that we have written this book. For too long the politics of law and order have been a monopoly of the right. Yet the left have every reason materially, politically and ideologically to intervene in this area. We are too paralysed by our own preconceptions easily to take up the challenge which is demanded of us. The opportunities for an initiative from the left are enormous; we must not shirk the task.

Key terms

The following key terms appear in the text above. They have been defined below to aid with the reading of this item.

Robin Hoods New Left Realists argue that traditional Marxism is guilty of treating those who commit crime as 'romantic figures'. They see working-class criminals as 'Robin Hood' figures re-distributing wealth from the rich to the poor. New Left Realists argue that this idea ignores the fact that crime is often unpleasant and usually not seen by the criminal themselves as a fight against capitalism!

stigmatize to label negatively, to condemn

moral panic a fear in the public of a criminal group due to exaggerated and sensationalized media reporting

left idealists those who, according to the New Left Realists, are guilty of treating working-class criminals as heroes in the class struggle

Questions

1 How do Lea and Young criticize previous left-wing sociologists?

2 Why do they call their theory 'realism'?

3 What do they say about the realities of criminal statistics?

4 What recommendations do they make for the future of policing?

5 What recommendations do they make for the future of sociological thinking about crime?

Reading 12.6 **Women, crime and the 'malestream criticism'**

Frances Heidensohn (from) *Women and Crime,* 2nd edn (1996) London: Macmillan, pp. 1–12.

Editorial comments

Although feminist ideas have influenced sociological thought, many feminists still feel that sociology has a 'malestream' character – i.e. it is largely knowledge about male experiences in society, conduced by males at the expense of a true understanding of the female experience.

In this reading, Heidensohn notes how this criticism of sociology is particularly true of the sociology of crime and deviance. Women – until recently – have been invisible in much of the sociology of deviance: it was felt that women do not commit crime and thus there was no point in spending time analysing them. Heidensohn argues that sociological studies which ignore the female voice – or experience – can simply no longer be seen as valid.

Introducing women and crime

ONE OF THE most remarkable developments in publishing in recent years has been the growth in the number of books for, about and by women. In particular, handbooks and guides of every sort have appeared, encouraging women to realize themselves emotionally and educationally and imparting skills in everything from building to banking. There is too a growing range of women's studies – books designed to explain and analyse aspects of women's experience both for the concerned general reader and for the increasing numbers of students of women's studies or sex and gender courses which are now offered. ... I have tried to extend and develop an understanding of the deviance and conformity of women which will, I trust, prove useful both to students of women's studies and to the professional looking for a guide to the maze of assertions and counter-assertions about, for instance, the 'new' female criminal. ...

The issues

There are probably two observations about female criminality with which many people will be familiar. First, and much the best known, is that over long periods of time and in many differing judicial systems, women have a consistently lower rate of officially recorded crimes than men. There are many ways of presenting this, but one clear one is given by Farrington (1981) in estimating the accumulation of criminal convictions over a lifetime in England and Wales:

> This analysis shows 11.70 per cent of males convicted up to the seventeenth birthday, 21.76 per cent up to the twenty-first birthday, and 43.57 per cent at some time in their lives. For females, the corresponding figures are 2.10, 4.66 and 14.70 per cent.

In other words, females are not only much less criminal than males, they are so much less criminal that whereas convictions are, statistically at least, 'normal' for males, they are very unusual for females. Indeed Farrington predicts a lifetime prevalence for males by 1989 in excess of 50 per cent (Farrington, 1981).

The second observation which has been increasingly stressed by feminist and other commentators since the 1960s is that this low criminal-participation rate has not been sufficiently remarked upon nor studied. Feminists have seen it as another example of the characteristic '**invisibility**' of women in social science or social policy, while several non-feminist writers have pointed out that any causal explanation of crime which does not include gender-related factors cannot be valid. Female criminality is now a topic on the agenda and there have been very many more studies of it produced in the fifteen years up to 1984 than in any previous period. One purpose of this book is to present an accessible version of these findings.

While a 'hidden' group of women have, thus, to some extent, been rendered visible, this development does not, at first sight, seem to have the same broad relevance for all women as other parallel 'discoveries' have. The (re-)discovery of domestic violence in the early 1970s and the discussions of rape and of sexual harassment at work have been presented and analysed in ways which make them relevant to the oppression of all women and not just to those who are victims of these particular acts. Moreover, the first open consideration of all these issues led to a flood of revelations from women who had been silent sufferers before. In turn, there have been some changes in law, related social policies or trades union practices which acknowledge that these problems exist. Women's criminality, however, appears rather different. It does not look like a problem which connects with the experience of many women. I want now to look at what we know about female criminality and then to look at its main characteristics to see how we can understand them and make the topic a much broader and more widely relevant one than first it seems.

Crime and women

A cautionary note

Scepticism about both the validity and the reliability of criminal statistics is now more or less universal. The police themselves point to changes in recording procedures and public attitudes which can affect reporting of crime and the annual *British Criminal Statistics* publication makes a point of stressing the limitations of the data it presents (Home Office, 1983). The UK Home Office now undertakes a regular crime survey which gives a rather different picture from police records and surveys are increasingly used in Canada, the Netherlands, etc. Two principal features limit the official recording of crime: the iceberg effect and the dark figure. While the tip of the iceberg – that is, the amount of reported and recorded crime – may be visible, there are many offences which go unobserved, unreported or unrecorded. Lack of a victim, or of witnesses or of sufficient evidence may all limit or prevent recording. The amount of unrecorded crime is not known, although attempts to measure it through victim and crime surveys or **self-report studies** all indicate that it is much larger than 'crimes known'. A further problem lies in the fact that the relationship between hidden and recorded crime can change, so that an apparent increase in crime may reflect an increase in offences reported and recorded rather than an increase in crimes actually committed. This, the Home Office itself suggests, is exactly what happened with offences of burglary and theft in a dwelling in the 1970s (Home Office, 1983) in England and Wales.

Even when crimes are known to the police, only a small proportion are 'cleared up' – that is, lead to arrest, conviction and sentence or other outcome which closes the case. There thus remains a dark figure of uncleared crimes about which very little detail is available, such as the sex, age or social characteristics of the perpetrator. In looking at available official data we must bear these general limitations in mind. There are also several factors which may have particular impact on the recording of female criminality. The only certain data on the sex of offenders comes either from police statistics of cautioning, or from judicial figures of those tried in the courts, in other words, at a fairly late stage in the process from commission to conviction, and it is a criminological truism that the further away one is from the act itself the more selected is the sample of people and events. Many early studies, for example, were seriously flawed by their exclusive use of incarcerated offenders as samples of criminals.

A further difficulty lies with the unknown dimensions of possible bias in reporting and recording offences by girls and women. It has often been suggested that there is an innate '**chivalry**' which protects women from the full rigours of policing and the courts, although this is a doubtful contention. However there may be special features which affect the reporting of crimes committed by women. Pollak (1961) suggested that women's hidden crimes were massive, but he gave neither serious evidence for this contention, nor explanation for the tolerance of widespread female crime. It has also been contended that women, especially young girls, are brought before the courts for trivial activities which would be tolerated in boys. All we can say is that the propensity to report women's crimes may differ from the propensity to report those of men but to what degree we cannot say. Two further rather technical points of interpretation also need to be stressed. First, since the number of women convicted of serious offences tends to be fairly small, a small numerical increase can mean a very large percentage change which should be interpreted with great caution. Second, the small numbers involved mean that various forms of analysis routinely applied to figures for males may either not be used on females or need to be treated with scepticism because of the small numbers. Thus the 1982 *Criminal Statistics* for England and Wales devote fourteen lines to variations in known offending by male juveniles in different police force areas and only four and a half to the same phenomenon in girls. With all these reservations in mind we can now look at official crime and delinquency by females.

The female share of crime

As I have already noted, the one thing most people know about women and crime is that women's contribution to total criminality is modest. Indeed this is an area of public achievement where women hardly compete with men.

In the analysis in this section I have used recent data for England and Wales. This data provides a reasonable example and has the advantage of coming from a single jurisdiction with a reasonably standard system of reporting and recording. Similar analyses for the USA can be found in Leonard (1982) and Simon (1975). Figures for the USA are complicated by the existence of State and Federal jurisdictions and the considerable variations in criminal law and in recording violations of it to which these lead. This presentation is therefore intended to be merely an example; while there are recent changes and local variations, the patterns we shall find in recent British experience have a remarkable robustness and stability.

If we take the most recent year for which figures

are available, 1982 (all the figures in this paragraph are from Home Office, 1983), some 2 million offenders were found guilty by all courts in England and Wales. More than 1 million were found guilty of summary motoring offences. Of all those found guilty 1 in 9 was female (11 per cent). For indictable offences (that is, broadly, more serious offences) 1 in 7 was female (14 per cent). However, when figures of cautions are included – that is, where a formal warning was given and recorded by the police – the picture changes somewhat, as females are more likely to be cautioned. Thus in 1982 as in previous years a higher proportion of female offenders – 34 per cent of females but only 17 per cent of male offenders – were cautioned for indictable offences. Therefore 83 per cent of those found guilty of, or cautioned for, indictable offences were male and 17 per cent female. These represent nearly half a million males and nearly 100,000 females of whom about a third of both sexes were juveniles. For both sexes the peak age of offending is very young and related to the period of compulsory schooling – at 15 years of age for boys and 14 for girls. This proportionate share of crime has remained fairly stable during the past decade.

These ratios, although they suggest that women now take a larger part in crime than they did in the past, or in some other societies, are not very dissimilar from historically observed trends. Indeed women's low level of performance in crime has been regularly cited as the reason for the lack of attention given to them by criminologists, both because they seemed not to pose a problem and because their small numbers made study difficult. However in recent years there has been something of a moral panic created about the allegations that women's share of crime was rising faster than that of men and rising particularly fast in unfeminine and untypical offences such as robbery and violence. This phenomenon was linked to the movement for women's liberation which, it was suggested, was leading to the emancipation of women into taking a bigger share of crime. Box and Hale (1983) analysed trends over the past thirty years and showed that there had been overall a fairly stable ratio of female to male convictions since 1951 in England and Wales, although property crimes had shown some convergence, while for crimes of violence, the female contribution remained static. In reviewing the extensive popular and academic concern, they point out that most studies used absolute increases in female crime, rather than relative share, and that this leads to an exaggeration of the female contribution.

Crimes women and girls commit

Females contribute to the officially recorded tariffs of all known offences. Even where there are legal requirements, as with rape, which women cannot fulfil, they

may be charged as accomplices to a crime. Certain offences relate only to women: it is only mothers who can be charged with infanticide and offences by prostitutes involve soliciting and similar actions by females. Male homosexual relations are still much more heavily restricted by criminal sanction. But the overwhelming majority of offenders are charged with motoring offences or theft, relatively few with those where there is a discriminatory factor in the law. ... Shoplifting is in practice the only major category of crime to which women make a significant contribution. Even so, the rate of convictions in relation to population at risk has been higher in recent years for men than women ...

Women can be found in all other offence categories and so it would be wrong to say that there are 'sex-specific' crimes, or 'masculine' crimes. Rather criminal activity as officially recorded is by and large a masculine activity, but one in which women do participate. In Britain and the USA more women have been participating in the past decade, with their age-related rates growing slightly faster than those for males (2–3 per cent) while for females they averaged 3–4 per cent between 1971 and 1981. But this shift, while it increased the numbers of women going to prison, did not result in women taking a noticeably larger role in recorded criminality.

While official data is not very helpful on this, it does seem that women commit fewer serious crimes and are rather less likely to be recidivists. Men predominate in homicide – 176:8 in 1982 – and the infanticide figures hardly change the picture (three cases in 1982). Studies of cautioning and sentencing procedures suggest, for the UK at least, that the lesser showing of women is due to the more trivial nature of their offences and their comparative lack of 'form'. ...

With the defects of criminal statistics so well-known, attempts have been made by both policy-makers and academics to supplement and correct them. These attempts are of two main kinds: crime surveys and self-report studies. Crime surveys can either be large-scale attempts to measure the volume of perceived offences by questionnaire or interview, as in the British Crime Survey, or smaller studies, such as the observations of shoplifting reported above. The former are not very helpful to us since obviously, unless the victim of a crime actually saw the individual who burgled his home or picked his pocket, there would be no evidence on that individual's sex. The shoplifting studies suggest on the whole that, while official figures greatly under estimate the *incidence* of shoplifting by women they also do so in relation to men, if anything, rather more so. Pratt's study of mugging in London, based not on a sample survey of victims but on police records of details reported by victims of their attackers showed that 'the vast majority of assailants are male. In less than 2 per cent of cases were females alone involved' (Pratt, 1980).

Victim surveys in the USA have a longer history than in Britain, probably because of even greater discontent with official data. Hindelang reviewed a series of such studies to see how different a picture they gave from arrest or court data. He found that basically, there was no real difference, reported and observed female involvement was 'strikingly similar to that portrayed in arrest data'.

Self-report studies are a more rewarding area to examine, since the purpose of many has actually been to correct for the supposed 'bias' in under-reporting female crime. This was a claim made by Pollak which has been sustained by generations of criminologists ever since. Self-report studies are questionnaires administered anonymously and confidentially to various population samples which ask respondents which of a list of offences they have ever, or frequently committed. Most of them have been conducted on rather youthful groups who tend to be conveniently available, *en masse* in schools and colleges and also, of course, tend to be in the age ranges in which the peak rate of offending is found. ...

Finding a place for female crime

If we were to try to draw a portrait of a 'typical' female offender at this stage she would be a young girl, a first offender charged with shoplifting, and her likely destiny would be a caution or a non-custodial sentence. There are, of course, small groups of women who deviate from this: the regular drunk with a string of convictions, or the prostitute regularly fined for soliciting, as well as a sprinkling of women convicted of serious crimes such as murder, and offences associated with terrorism. However, while a very few female offenders have attracted unusual popular attention, the picture is not on the whole an exciting one. 'Monster' murderers or big-time gangsters are scarcely found amongst the ranks of women offenders. There is little evidence of the drama of juvenile gang activity between girls of the kind which has excited the interest of several generations of sociologists.

It is because of their lack of glamour as well as their low social threat, that as several commentators have suggested, female criminals have received so little consideration in the immense literature from sensational to serious which has been generated on the topic of crime. Yet I believe this cannot be the complete explanation. Even though women criminals may have seemed boring under-achievers compared with their male counterparts, the pattern of sex crime

ratios – that is, the relative share of males and females in crime – was far too serious an issue to ignore for so long. Baldly, no theory of criminality which ignores the overwhelming importance of gender can be valid. *Sex differences in criminality are so sustained and so marked as to be, perhaps, the most significant feature of recorded crime.*

... I simply want to point out that, paradoxically, an examination of female criminality and unofficial deviance suggests that we need to move away from studying infractions and look at conformity instead, because the most striking thing about female behaviour on the basis of all the evidence considered here is how notably conformist to social mores women are. There is no evidence that this is somehow innate in women, a feature of their sweeter 'better' natures, not as the nursery rhyme has it that little girls are 'sugar and spice and all things nice' while boys are 'snaps and snails and puppy dogs tails'. In fact some women can and do commit offences of the same kind as men, save where legal or technical barriers exist, but they do so in very much smaller numbers, at less serious levels and far less often. In consequence, there are far more men than women in prison. ...

The growth of a feminist appreciation of social divisions and forces enables a reappraisal. It is possible to break conventional moulds and link different approaches to the topic, it also means that we no longer take for granted long-current assumptions about the world. Thus I have used feminist analyses of family life to show how these have a bearing on the social constraints experienced by women. In what follows I have deliberately mixed résumés of scholarly researches with more direct descriptions by individuals and popular accounts. Crime is not just for experts who have, in any case, no purpose to their existence if they cannot convey their findings to wider and less specialized audiences. At times, therefore, the argument I convey is direct and simple. It is meant to be challenging, and I hope, arresting. There are, of course, reservations and caveats as with all such contentions: real life is far more complicated than any description or analysis can reasonably portray. The main aims that I have followed have been to convey as fully and faithfully as possible the experiences undergone by women offenders through their own and society's reactions and in the courts and prison. The questions raised by these experiences are then analysed and as far as possible, answered in a coherent fashion. There should be here something of interest and relevance and certainly to argue about for professionals who encounter female offenders and for students.

References

Box, S. and Hale, C. (1983) 'Liberation and female criminality in England and Wales', *British Journal of Criminology*, vol. 23, no. 1.

Farrington, D. P. (1981) 'The prevalence of convictions', *British Journal of Criminology*, vol. 21, no. 2.

Home Office (1983) *Criminal Statistics: England and Wales 1982*, London: HMSO.

Leonard, E. B. (1982) *Women, Crime and Society*, London: Longman.

Pollak, O. (1961) *The Criminality of Women*, New York: A. S. Barnes.

Pratt, M. (1980) *Mugging as a Social Problem*, London: Routledge & Kegan Paul.

Simon, R. J. (1975) *Women and Crime*, London: Lexington.

Key terms

The following key terms appear in the text above. They have been defined below to aid with the reading of this item.

invisibility a term used by many feminist thinkers to denote the fact that the female voice and the female experience are often hidden in sociological research

self-report studies a methodological tool used to expose the 'hidden figure' of crime – which does not appear in official crime statistics – by asking members of a society to actually admit to undetected crimes they have committed

chivalry often known as the 'chivalry factor' – the idea that the low recorded rates for female crime can be explained by the fact that the male-dominated police and courts 'let women off' more than they would men

victim surveys like self-report studies (see above) this is another tool to expose the 'hidden figure' of crime. In this case, members of society are asked to list crimes they have been a victim of, but which may not have been reported to the police

Questions

1 What does Heidensohn have to say about how women have been treated by the sociology of crime and deviance?

2 What does Heidensohn note about the nature of female criminality?

3 From what you know about the sociology of deviance so far, do you agree with Heidensohn's contention that this topic area is generally 'malestream'? Give reasons for your view.

Reading 12.7 **Visions of social control**

Stanley Cohen (from) *Visions of Social Control: Crime, punishment and classification* (1985) Cambridge: Polity Press, pp. 1–8.

Editorial comments

In this extract Cohen attempts to define the framework in which he thinks about issues of social control in contemporary social life. He starts the mapping of this framework by discussing definitions of the concept 'social control' and notes how this term has been frequently used – and abused – through decades of sociological theorizing. Cohen is principally interested in the ways in which state agencies plan to control and 'help' those defined and classified as in need of attention: those classified as 'social problems'. Cohen suggests, throughout this extract, that the process of classification of the population is itself a feature of contemporary social control. Equally, he treats with scepticism claims of 'humane treatment' and 'welfare' within professional social control agencies such as social work, psychiatry, etc.

Crime, punishment and classification

THIS IS A book about social control, that is, the organized ways in which society responds to behaviour and people it regards as deviant, problematic, worrying, threatening, troublesome or undesirable in some way or another. This response appears under many terms: punishment, deterrence, treatment, prevention, segregation, justice, **rehabilitation**, reform or social defence. It is accompanied by many ideas and emotions: hatred, revenge, retaliation, disgust, compassion, salvation, benevolence or admiration. The behaviour in question is classified under many headings: crime, delinquency, deviance, immorality, perversity, wickedness, deficiency or sickness. The people to whom the response is directed, are seen variously as monsters, fools, villains, sufferers, rebels or victims. And those who respond (by doing something or by just studying the subject – jobs which are too often confused) are known as judges, policemen, social workers, psychiatrists, psychologists, criminologists or sociologists of deviance ...

I am critical of a society which classifies too much. This book itself, however, is primarily an exercise in classification, in ways of looking, in modes of making sense. It belongs to the type of sociology which tries to make the world look different: a strange terrain appears imperceptibly to be familiar or, just as interesting, a familiar terrain begins to look a little strange. My book attempts this type of **cognitive re-mapping**. ...

Something like a definition

The term 'social control' has lately become something of a Mickey Mouse concept. In sociology textbooks, it appears as a neutral term to cover all social processes to induce conformity ranging from infant socialization through to public execution. In radical theory and rhetoric, it has become a negative term to cover not just the obviously coercive apparatus of the state, but also the putative hidden element in all state sponsored social policy, whether called health, education or welfare. Historians and political scientists restrict the concept to the repression of political opposition, while sociologists, psychologists and anthropologists invariably talk in broader and non-political terms. In everyday language, that concept has no resonant or clear meaning at all.

All this creates some terrible muddles. Historians and sociologists are locked in a protracted debate about whether the history of prisons, mental hospitals and the juvenile court can meaningfully be studied in the same framework as the history of the factory and the control of working class resistance to the state. Analysts of social policy spend time in deciding whether this or that measure by the state is 'really' social control. The question is asked, whether teachers in schools, warders in prisons, psychiatrists in clinics, social workers in welfare agencies, parents in families, policemen on the streets, and even bosses in the factories are all, after all, busy doing the 'same' thing.

The answer to these fascinating questions is, no doubt, that 'it depends' – it depends on our image of social control and on the purposes of any definition. My own purpose is to classify, assess and criticize some current changes (proposed or actual) and to comment on other similar exercises. This purpose will be served less well by any essentialist definition than simply by mapping out those 'social control matters' which this book covers.

My interest is in planned and programmed responses to expected and realized deviance rather than in the general institutions of society which pro-

duce conformity. I will use the term 'social control', then, to cover matters considerably narrower and more specific than the general sociological/anthropological terrain of all those social processes and methods through which society ensures that its members conform to expectations. These normally include **internalization**, socialization, education, peer-group pressure, public opinion and the like, as well as the operations of specialized formal agencies such as the police, the law and all other state powers. But I am interested in something a little wider and more general than the restricted criminological terrain of the formal legal-correctional **apparatus** for the control of official crime and delinquency. My focus is those organized responses to crime, delinquency and allied forms of deviant and/or socially problematic behaviour which are actually conceived of as such, whether in the reactive sense (after the putative act has taken place or the actor been identified) or in the proactive sense (to prevent the act). These responses may be sponsored directly by the state or by more autonomous professional agents in, say, social work and psychiatry. Their goals might be as specific as individual punishment and treatment or as diffuse as 'crime prevention', 'public safety' and 'community mental health'.

I will talk about 'deviance' but my material comes mainly from crime control and, moreover, from ordinary 'bread and butter' adult crime and juvenile delinquency rather than such important types as organized, political, white collar and state crime. Parallel issues arise in the control of drug abuse, mental illness and sexual deviance and where these are particularly relevant, I will draw on this literature. Another way of restricting my scope is to concentrate on certain societies, notably 'liberal capitalist' states such as the USA, Canada, Britain and other Western European countries. These have social control systems embedded in more or less highly developed commitments to 'welfare' and more or less sophisticated ideologies about 'treatment'. These are also the same societies in which these commitments and ideologies have been the object of so much scepticism over the past decade or so.

It is just these shifts in strategy and beliefs that interest me. This book is less a description of the social control apparatus as it stands, than an attempt to monitor recent visions and alleged or real master movements and predict their implications for the future: a sociological seismograph to detect fissures, cracks, quakes, tremors and false alarms. The textbook notion of 'correctional change' draws attention to movements of this sort:

(1) A transformation of the arrangements employed to deal with convicted offenders (for example, the establishment of the penitentiary system); (2) a

change in the severity of punishment dispensed to offenders (for example, an increase in the average length of time offenders spend in confinement);(3) a change in either the numbers or the proportion of convicted offenders dealt with by various components of the correctional system (for example, an increase in prison population or assignment of an increasing number of convicted offenders to pre-trial diversion programmes); and (4) a change in the prevailing ideologies employed to 'explain' or make sense of offenders and their involvement in criminality.

(Shover, 1979)

But this is a list of operational changes – shifts that are often too minor and ephemeral to be of much concern to the non-specialist. I am interested in more dramatic and profound movements, the genuine master shifts against those massively entrenched patterns of organized social control associated with the birth of the modern state: attacks on prisons and mental hospitals, the development of alternative forms of community control, attempts to bypass the whole criminal justice system, scepticism about professional competence; disenchantment with the rehabilitative ideal, the development of new forms of intervention and the ideologies which justify them. I will keep returning to the profoundly ambiguous and contradictory nature of these changes.

There are other control patterns, both of change and stability, that also deserve attention: in the form, content and administration of the criminal law; in the nature of civil law and other forms of regulation or conflict resolution; in the organization and techniques of policing. But these subjects I mention not at all or only in passing. I focus less on detection, apprehension or judicial procedure, than on 'deployment', that is, the institutional tracks into which populations about to be or already defined as deviant are directed. It is here, particularly in the iconography of prison against community, that visions, claims and changes have been most dramatic. In brief, this book is about punishment and classification.

The sociological connection

Now is the time for the obligatory self-serving section about how irrelevant, misguided or plain foolish the existing literature on the subject turns out to be.

In truth, the standard literature on social control probably *is* a little more irrelevant, misguided and foolish than it might be in most other areas of sociology. The academic, sociology-of-knowledge reasons for this, lie in the already well-chartered argument about the severance of criminology and the sociology of deviance from the mainstream of sociological concerns. This was not always so. In the classical nineteenth-century tradition of social thought, the concept

of social control was near the centre of the enterprise. The great problem of social order was how to achieve a degree of organization and regulation consistent with certain moral and political principles (for example, 'democracy' or 'civil rights') and without an excessive degree of purely coercive control.

In twentieth century, largely American, sociology this organic connection between social control and a contemplation of the state, became weaker and weaker. The concept lost its political thrust, becoming less structural and more social-psychological. That is, it became more concerned with the 'processes' (a key term) by which the individual was induced into becoming a more-or-less willing participant in the social order. The individual was seen as an actor who learnt scripts and internalized rules and roles or else was pulled or pushed back into shape by something vaguely called 'official' or 'formal' control. This was a reactive, 'trampoline' model of social control. Usually things went pretty smoothly ('consensus'), but every now and then the play broke down, the actors departed from the script and the director was challenged. Then social control was needed to get things back into order.

The social and sociological crises of the sixties were to change all this. Oppression, repression and suppression now became the normal properties of society. Consensus was either non-existent or else precariously maintained by awesome and cunningly disguised systems of social control. The individual could barely breathe, let alone 'internalize'. The struggle was to survive in the belly of that monster, the state. And those old 'deviants' – the nuts, sluts and perverts of criminology and social pathology textbooks – could emerge from their dark closets into the sociological daylight. They were now to be awarded leading roles in the rewritten drama of social reality, as exemplars (first victims and underdogs, then rebels and heroes) of the struggle against social control.

Slowly too, the 'new' sociologists of deviance then, a few years later, the 'new' criminologists came out. Leaving the deviants huddled in their closets with their custodians and healers, these intellectuals proclaimed their independence from 'correctional' interests. Their project was to distance themselves from the machine – not to make it more effective, nor even to humanize it, but to question and demystify its very moral legitimacy. Labelling theorists and their later, rather tougher successors (Marxist or radical criminologists) pushed the notion of social control towards the centre of the stage. It was not just a reactive, reparative mechanism produced when other methods failed, but an active, ever present, almost mystical force which gave crime and deviance their very shapes. Control leads to deviance, was the catechism, not deviance to control. And law and other systems of control were intimately linked with the whole business of maintaining social order, discipline and regulation.

Further, along with these largely academic developments in sociology, wider social movements, whose effects and ideologies I will examine closely, started registering these same changes. The very agents of social control themselves – the professionals who operated the machine – began to scrutinize their own roles. Successive waves of anti-psychiatrists, radical social workers, demedicalizers, deschoolers and delegalizers began to nourish and draw nourishment from those more academic reappraisals of social control. With varying degrees of commitment, credibility and success, they lent their support to movements dedicated to changing, reforming or (amazingly) even abolishing the very agencies and institutions in which they worked.

All these moves – whether within general sociology, specialized subfields such as criminology, or the control apparatus itself – contributed towards a massive theoretical and political reordering of the subject. But (as with the alleged master changes in the apparatus itself) these cognitive shifts have turned out to be much less clear than they seem at first sight. Many have been false alarms or tremors which have registered only slightly in the worlds of theory and practice. What this means – and here comes the criticism of the literature is that the sociology of social control remains a lot more retarded than these academic rumblings would lead us to expect. ...

The professional literature, however, reveals little of such nightmares and science fiction projections. Textbooks – those depositories of a discipline's folk wisdom – still use an older and blander language of social control: how norms are internalized, how consensus is achieved, how social control evolves from pre-industrial to industrial societies. Marxist theories, to be sure, confront the concept in a more critical way. But seldom in these powerful and baroque abstractions about the 'ideological' and 'repressive' state apparatus do we get much sense of what is happening in the apparatus. ...

For this sense of what the social control apparatus is actually getting up to, the specialized literature is surprisingly unhelpful. Take, for example, the realm where the most formidable and irreversible of all master shifts is alleged to be taking place – the replacement of the closed segregated institution by some form of 'open' community control. Most criminological studies here are of a uniformly low level. They fall into three categories:

1 *evangelical*, in which we are told that this or that project has achieved a breakthrough in reducing recidivism, in involving the community or whatever (and that further research is needed to confirm this result);

2 *fudgy*, in which under the heading of 'evaluation' words such as process, control group, feedback, flow-chart, objectives, goals, inputs, and system are arranged in random order (and more research is called for); and

3 *nihilistic*, in which it is shown that nothing, after all, works, everything costs the same (and more research is probably needed).

Little of this helps towards understanding the underlying picture, and much reading between the lines is required to see what these projects and programmes are about.

There are, of course, major exceptions to this dull collection. Most notably, there are the various recent schools of revisionist history about the origins of eighteenth- and nineteenth-century control institutions and systems. ... [This work] includes Rothman's pioneering history of the origins of the asylum in early nineteenth-century America and, from quite a different intellectual tradition, Foucault's extraordinary '**archaeology**' of deviancy control systems. We have here at last a vocabulary with which to comprehend more recent changes. Already, such work has been extended into the contemporary scene, for example in Scull's writings on 'decarceration' and those of Foucault's followers on the 'policing of families' and the 'advanced psychiatric society'. Less penetrating theoretically, but equally compelling polemically, are the various formulations about the 'therapeutic state', 'psychiatric despotism', the 'psychological society', and 'mind control'. Note, though, that this work, and other allied, but more ambitious social critiques, tend curiously to concentrate on psychiatry the form of intervention least visible as social control and (arguably) the least appropriate to conceive simply as social control.

The more obvious, everyday forms of control – police, prisons, courts – have been much less frequently chosen for this type of sophisticated theoretical scrutiny. They are no doubt less glamorous and romantic subjects for the social critic. There is much more fun (and theoretical mileage) in studying fashions in psychoanalytical theory, nude encounter groups, primal screaming and sensitivity training, than in peering down the corridors of a juvenile correctional institution. There are, of course, useful statistics and good ethnographies of these more mundane control agencies – police departments, juvenile courts, prisons, crime prevention programmes – but these studies tend to be fragmented and abstracted. They need locating in historical space (How did they get there?) in physical space (the city, the neighbourhood) and, above all, in social space (the network of other institutions such as school and family, broader patterns of welfare and social services, bureaucratic and professional interests).

Reference

Shover, N. (1979) *A Sociology of American Corrections*, Homewood, Ill.: Jersey Press.

Key terms

The following key terms appear in the text above. They have been defined below to aid with the reading of this item.

rehabilitation the aim of much contemporary treatment of criminal offenders: not to punish, but to 'make the offender better'

cognitive re-mapping used here to refer to the process whereby Cohen seeks to re-theorize about the issues contained within the reading; to re-think and to re-classify ideas

internalization the acceptance of social norms, values, etc. through socialization into the self

apparatus a tool to be used (e.g. 'state apparatus' – tools used by the state)

archaeology in recent times, a term used in sociology to refer to the methods of historical enquiry adopted by French post-structuralist Michel Foucault who argues that we need to go beyond, behind and under accepted histories to find the truth about marginal groups in society

Questions

1 What criticisms does Cohen make about how the term 'social control' is used? How does he use this term?

2 How does Cohen characterize previous criminological studies?

3 In what sense does Cohen seek to rewrite a history of sociological ideas and of the treatment of criminals?

4 To what extent do you agree with Cohen's image of the state as an instrument of control under the guise of trying to help those who may need it?

Reading 12.8 **Crime, policing and the 'risk society'**

Richard V. Ericson and Kevin D. Haggerty (from) *Policing the Risk Society* (1997) Oxford: Clarendon Press, pp. 3–11. Reprinted by permission of Oxford University Press.

Editorial comments

In this reading we see Ulrich Beck's idea of a *risk society* applied to issues and problems in contemporary policing.

Ericson and Haggerty are concerned to up-date the ways in which sociologists think about policing. They argue that policing is an example of what they call a model of 'risk communication' – policing is seen as a dialogue (an interaction of communication) between the police and other agencies all of whom identify, classify, manage, limit and respond to the 'risks' of social life.

A key characteristic of a risk society is the way in which knowledge is used to manage risks. Ericson and Haggerty note that in contemporary social life, a great deal of police time and resources is spent on the creation and manipulation of knowledge about crime. However, such knowledge is increasingly governed and controlled by rules and regulations dictating how knowledge can be produced and the ends to which it can be used. The manipulation of knowledge is seen to be a prime characteristic of contemporary social life at all levels and in a number of different guises.

Policing the risk society

THE POLICE PERVADE contemporary social life. They are seen daily on the streets. Their presence is felt even more strongly through hour-long television shows that feature cathected scenarios of their heroics. They are turned to for help when people experience personal troubles, accidents, and criminal victimization. They are present at community ceremonies, sporting events, parades, and demonstrations. They are featured in full-dress uniform on postcards and souvenirs, standing for what is noble about the community and nation-state. In all of these manifestations the police simultaneously reproduce and represent order. They embody central authority as peace, order, and good government.

... While research literature on policing is proliferating, it is also increasingly redundant and stagnant. There is a need to reflect critically on existing research, to provide a comprehensive theory of policing, and to undertake more-thorough analyses of the purposes and consequences of policing.

We argue that policing and the society in which it takes place are best understood in terms of a model of **risk communication**. In this book policing is conceived of not only in terms of what the public police do but also in terms of what is done in other **institutions** to identify and manage risks. Our point is that policing consists of the public police coordinating their activities with policing agents in all other institutions to provide a society-wide basis for risk management (governance) and security (guarantees against loss).

Risk refers to external danger, such as a natural disaster, technological catastrophe, or threatening behaviour by human beings. The system for communicating risk – its rules, formats, and technologies – is a part of the social meaning of risk. The risk communication system is thus a key locus for our analysis. Our research focuses on the communication systems that institutions develop to identify and manage risks, and on how the police become involved in these systems. The meaning of risk varies with the communication system used by the institutions responsible for managing it, and the police are therefore in a complex, ambiguous, shifting, and contradictory field of risk management in relation to other institutions.

Communication systems are not simply conduits through which knowledge is transferred. Rather, they have their own logics and autonomous processes. They govern institutional relations and circumscribe what individuals and their organizations are able to accomplish. There is not just an event in the world and then communication about it. The event is called into being, made visible, and responded to through the rules, formats, and technologies available in the communication system. The communication system makes things real. An understanding of the ways in which police work is done thus requires analysis of the logics and processes of the communication system the police participate in. These logics and processes *direct* how the police are organized and assessed. ...

In developing our argument we have followed an academically unconventional path. Instead of opening with the more abstract theory that informs our analysis, we begin with a critical analysis of existing research on policing. This analysis demonstrates that other researchers have almost entirely overlooked the risk communication systems of policing. However, it also identifies how existing research at least points to the fact that policing operates in terms of the rules, formats, and technologies of risk communication systems. This identification connects in turn to features of the **risk society** within which policing now takes place. The abstract theory of the risk society makes more sense after one is exposed to substantive issues of policing and risk communication addressed by the research literature. Theorizing the risk society at that later point not only adds cogency to the critique of the literature that precedes it but also provides the explanatory framework for the empirical analyses presented subsequently.

Our analysis of existing research on policing allows us to contend that police mobilization is not only a matter of intervention in the lives of individual citizens but also a response to institutional demands for knowledge of risk. As a result, the primary locus of police activity is the risk communication systems shaped by external institutions. Through these communication systems, external institutions are able to routinely access police for knowledge useful in their own risk management. This routine access makes police work highly visible and circumscribes both the autonomy of police organizations and the discretion of individual police officers.

The criminal justice system is but one of many institutions that organize themselves through risk communication systems, and it is by no means the central or most influential institution in policing. Most of the crime-related knowledge produced by the police is disseminated to other institutions (for example, those concerned with health, insurance, public welfare, financial matters, and education) for their risk management needs, rather than used for criminal prosecution and punishment. While they have considerable coercive power to produce knowledge of risk, the police mainly distribute the knowledge so obtained through risk communication systems of other institutions that govern in terms of a compliance mode. **Coercive control** gives way to contingent categorization. Policing is effected not only through territorial surveillance but also at the extraterritorial level of abstract knowledge of risk concerning securities (economic-exchange instruments), careers (life-course management), and identities (personhood).

Community policing is here analysed as a discourse that rationalizes, after the fact, the policing of risk society. Community policing turns out to be risk communication policing. It accounts for the fact that our communities are based on risk communications that give little sense of place or identity outside of institutionalized risk classifications.

... Risk society operates within a negative logic that focuses on fear and the social distribution of 'bads' more than on progress and the social distribution of 'goods'. Collective fear and foreboding underpin the value system of an unsafe society, perpetuate insecurity, and feed incessant demands for more knowledge of risk. Fear ends up proving itself, as new risk communication and management systems proliferate. The surveillance mechanisms of these systems create profiles of human populations and their risks to ascertain what is probable and possible for those populations. People are fabricated around institutionally established norms: risk is always somewhere on the continuum of imprecise normality.

Risk communication systems are entwined with privacy and trust. The more that foreboding and fear lead people to withdraw from public involvement, the more they value privacy and withdraw into privatized lifestyles. The greater the privacy, the greater the need for surveillance mechanisms to produce the knowledge necessary to trust people in otherwise anonymous institutional transactions. Paradoxically, these mechanisms intrude on privacy and are a constant reminder of the uncertainties of trust. Yet it is only in a framework of trust that patterns of risk can be adequately institutionalized and form the basis of decisions. Privacy, trust, surveillance, and risk management go hand in hand in policing the probabilities and possibilities of action.

In risk society, governance is privatized and dispersed across myriad fragmented institutions. The onus is placed on organizations and individuals to be more self-sufficient, to look after their own risk management needs. This emphasis on self-governance is underpinned by the interconnected discourses of morality, rights, responsibility, and accountability.

In the utilitarian morality of risk management, the norm or standard of acceptable risk is always both factual and moral. It signifies the typical or usual standard but also ethical constraint. Risk classifications infuse moral certainty and legitimacy into the facts they produce, allowing people to accept them as normative obligations and therefore as scripts for action. The legitimacy of utilitarian morality in risk discourse is augmented by the discourse of rights. Rights discourse has burgeoned with the decentralization of politics into risk institutions and their peculiar means of distributive justice. Rights discourse provides an ethics of the possible and probable that is embedded in legal rules of right. It forms part of the politics of difference, which contests the morality of risk classifications with respect to the security they do or do not provide. In the condition of self-governance, organizations and individuals are to contribute to the whole by being accountable for their part, including the risks they create for themselves and others. They are to be self-sufficient, to manage their own **biographies** competently, to be their own political economy. The result is not autonomy but rather the institutional structuration of organizational and individual careers for practical risk management purposes. ...

... the police participate in risk communication systems that relate to securities, careers, and identities, which are broad areas of risk management and security provision not directly associated with the policing of territories. These systems risk-profile populations for the purpose of economic exchange, life-course management, and identity management. They are based on abstract systems of trust and risk that require sophisticated surveillance mechanisms not tied to territorial boundaries. They represent institutional boundaries that traverse time and space but still keep people in their place.

Securities such as certificates, credentials, and financial instruments attest to credit, ownership, identity, and achievements. They provide security in the form of a promise to fulfil obligations and a guarantee against any loss, damage, or default that might ensue. The police are an essential component of how institutions establish trust and efficiency through their securities. In particular, the police participate in interinstitutional knowledge coordination, risk profiling, and auditing, all to verify the integrity of securities data, products, and markets.

The police also help other institutions construct the careers of the populations that concern them. In the most routine aspects of their work – for example, reporting an accident, conducting a street-stop check or an employment screening check, and recording information about criminal suspects, victims, and informants – police officers register peoples' significant accomplishments and failures, credentials and demerits, routines and accidents.

These routines of police work also help institutions to construct population identities. Even the checking off on police forms of boxes that identify, for example, age, race, gender, and ethnicity, forces people into specific institutional identities. In this book we present illustrative cases of identities policing. For example, we analyse the policing of youth. The police help to secure the social boundaries of youth by working in the interstices of institutions that deal more directly with young people. An analysis of police programmes in schools reveals that police officers function simultaneously as security officers, risk educators, informant-system operators, and counsellors, and that they mobilize students and staff to play these roles as well. Police involvement in the governance of racial and ethnic groups is also examined. In response to the urgings of other institutions, the police use racial and ethnic classifications to understand problems and to risk-profile populations. Police multicultural units select those who are in the 'other' (that is, other than 'white') category for more intensive scrutiny of the problems they experience and pose. These units also engage in extensive interinstitutional networking to foster knowledge of problems specific to racial and ethnic groups. ...

Risk society is characterized by the perpetual refinement of rules governing how knowledge is communicated. Thus the police are increasingly subject to external institutional pressures to produce and distribute knowledge in new rule-governed frameworks. For example, the criminal law dictates conditions and criteria for disclosure, as do various areas of information law regarding privacy and access to information. The need to be publicly accountable also leads the police to elaborate internal rule systems for risk communication. Rules develop to centralize the access of other institutions to police knowledge, to commodify police knowledge that is bartered or sold to external institutions, and to regulate internal systems of knowledge production and distribution. These rules protect police organizations from appearing irresponsible in the management of their knowledge assets.

The knowledge conceived, recognized, and presented through a police report depends on the format used, and is therefore always secondary to the format. Formats provide the framework through which police officers take action and regulate the actions taken. Alternative meanings tend to be seen as unrealistic, or are not seen at all. As such, risk communication formats are the focal point for an institution's selection and definition of risks. To know an institution is to know how its communication formats are used to define and select risks in ways that support and stabilize the institution. ...

The introduction of computer technology has had a significant influence on communication formats. Police officers now patrol the beat with a keyboard rather than a nightstick in hand. Every keystroke 'types' the population policed for risk management purposes. Some of these purposes are internal to the police. For example, computer terminals in patrol cars accelerate the use of street-stop surveillance, which allows the police to trace more people who appear to be out of place. Some of these purposes are external to the police. For example, police computer formats are made compatible with those of external institutions in order to increase the efficiency of risk communications to such institutions.

Every keystroke on the keyboard also 'types' police officers in terms of the quality and quantity of their knowledge production, and thereby creates the discipline that makes them useful workers, without the need for direct supervisory intervention. The computer terminal in the patrol car is a time-and-motion study that never ends. It routinely measures the police officers' activities and sorts them according to finely calibrated performance ratings and career potentials.

Regardless of the steps taken to reduce what the police call the 'paper burden', that burden continues to weigh heavily on the police because other institu-

tions demand more and more knowledge. This knowledge is demanded not only because of the risk management needs peculiar to these external institutions but also because of the increased capacity to provide it through computer technology, which makes new classifications imaginable and eases the task of altering communication formats to meet risk classification needs. The external demand for more knowledge, and the ease of computerized knowledge production, feed into the internal police compulsion to produce knowledge in case it might come in handy. What initially appears as an interesting technological convenience quickly becomes an expectation of supervisors and of police officers themselves.

Computer technology alters hierarchical structures of command and control among supervisors, police officers, and support staff. There is a blurring and levelling of some roles, with the result that no single person is easily identifiable as the decision maker. Decision making occurs within the criteria of risk communication formats, which have their own reality and autonomy at the system level. Hence the role ambiguity and alteration of hierarchy does not enhance the discretion of field-level police officers. Rather, discretion is at once circumscribed and dispersed into the risk communication systems that provide for routine surveillance of both the population of citizens and the population of police.

Our model provides a new window on policing and the constitutive mechanisms of society. A look through this window reveals many aspects of policing that have not been brought to light previously. Our new perspective allows us to show the limitations of other theories of policing and to open up new areas for empirical exploration and theoretical debate. Risk is a central feature of modernity, and this feature must be interrogated in fine detail and to the fullest possible extent. Risk institutions and their communication systems have become an important basis of society, and our empirical research on police participation in these institutions and systems substantiates this claim.

Key terms

The following key terms appear in the text above. They have been defined below to aid with the reading of this item.

risk communication discussion and dialogue aimed at identifying risks and ways of limiting/solving their impact in society

institutions features of social life that have a structure and are regular and repeated over time

risk society the idea that contemporary life is characterized by an avoidance of risks or harms

coercive control the use of violence, or rather the use

of force to control a population or smaller group

biographies the sum total of all our social experiences both unique and shared; often used in the context of a 'self-biography': to write one's own life-style/self/ identity

Questions

1 Describe in your own words the concept of a 'risk society'

2 How can the police be seen to contribute to a 'risk society'?

Further reading

The following texts may represent a useful starting point for further investigation of the ideas contained within this chapter:

Primary texts

For a wider appreciation of the work of Stan Cohen, see:

Cohen, S. (1980) *Folk Devils and Moral Panics: The creation of the mods and rockers*, Oxford: Basil Blackwell.

Cohen, S. and Taylor, L. (1971) *Psychological Survival: The experience of long-term imprisonment*, Harmondsworth: Penguin.

A classic phenomenological approach to crime and deviance is offered by the following texts:

Becker, H. S. (1973) *Outsiders: Studies in the sociology of deviance*, New York: Free Press.

Goffman, E. (1991) *Asylums: Essays on the social situation of mental patients and other inmates*, Harmondsworth: Penguin (orig. pub. 1968).

An interesting empirical study covering moral panics, street crime and crime statistics is provided by:

Pearson, G. (1983) *Hooligan: a history of respectable fears*, London: Macmillan.

Finally, a feminist perspective on crime is well represented by:

Heidensohn, F. (1989) *Crime and Society*, Basingstoke: Macmillan.

Secondary text

Moore, S. (1996) *Investigating Deviance*, 2nd edn, London: Collins Educational.

Coursework suggestions

1 **The functions of the media representation of crime**
Content analysis of the media could be undertaken – either of newspapers or television news reports – to establish how crime is reported.

Issues to consider could include:

- Does the media sensationalize crime reporting?
- What social groups appear to be targeted by the media when discussing crime?
- Are moral panics created – and if so, how?

Careful attention would need to be paid to the language used by the media when dealing with the issue of crime.

2 **Racism, the media, and crime and deviance**
Taking the ideas of the first suggestion (above) further, racism and the biased reporting of crime could be looked at in particular detail.

13

World development

Chapter summary

Reading 13.1 The new international division of labour page 368

This extract is taken from Fröbel et al.'s The New International Division of Labour where they argue that the old division based on the export of raw materials by the Third World and the production and export of manufactured goods by the First World is being replaced by a new structure which has important implications for the development of both the First and the Third Worlds.

Reading 13.2 Aid: rhetoric and reality page 372

This extract comes from Teresa Hayter and Catherine Watson's book Aid: Rhetoric and reality, a study of the activities of the World Bank and other multilateral aid agencies from a very critical radical socialist perspective. They highlight the problematic nature of the free-market economics behind such interventions and also consider the issue of the way aid is often tied to conditional clauses.

Reading 13.3 The effect of the debt crisis page 376

Susan George in her book, A Fate Worse Than Debt, examines the effects and implications of one of the most important events in the 1980s – namely the emergence of the Third World debt crisis. This extract examines the way the debt crisis emerged out of decisions taken by both governments and banks in the First World but has had major negative effects on people living in the Third World.

Reading 13.4 Poverty and world hunger page 379

Ben Jackson of the World Development Movement considers in his book, Poverty and the Planet, the way that reports of famine – and the way these are seen as sporadic events linked to unlucky circumstances – present an inaccurate picture of the causes and extent of world hunger, which leads to 35,000 children dying every day. He argues that inequality, in terms of entitlement to food rather than any shortage of food, is responsible for this continuing daily death toll.

Reading 13.5 Development and the environment page 382

In an article taken from Leslie Sklair's book, Capitalism and Development, Michael Redclift considers the way that thinking about the environment has become more central in development thinking in recent years. However, he offers a critical analysis of most approaches and argues instead for thinking about the environment to be located within a political economy approach.

Reading 13.6 The end of the Third World page 386

Nigel Harris in The End of the Third World argues that the growing internationalization of the world economy has meant that policies based on national reform, which were the crucial underpinning of the ideologies of Third World nationalism, have now been undermined, leading to the end of the Third World as a political strategy as well as a reality in terms of the increasing differentiation within the Third World.

Reading 13.7 The IMF, structural adjustment and food riots page 390

Walton and Seddon in their book, Free Markets and Food Riots, develop a detailed analysis of the emergence of the recent economic crisis which has affected societies since the 1970s and argue that one response to the structural adjustment plans imposed on Third World societies by international agencies such as the International Monetary Fund (IMF) is the widespread emergence of popular urban movements based on rioting.

Reading 13.8 Globalization in question page 396

The concept of globalization has become one of the most fashionable sociological concepts of the 1990s and its implications have important consequences in terms of nation-states and democracy. Paul Hirst and Grahame Thompson argue in 'Globalisation and the future of the nation state' that notions of globalization have been considerably overstated and instead argue that nation-states retain important powers to affect national and international developments.

Introduction: Reading world development sociology

For a long time world development sociology was dominated by the argument between those who saw the Third World as needing to follow the model presented by the First World and therefore saw the United States as their ultimate destination (modernization theory), and the more radical approaches of the 'dependency theorists' who argued that it was links with the First World that were responsible for underdevelopment rather than the development promised by modernization theorists. They therefore argued for autonomy from the First World as a precondition of genuine development. This debate which was at its height after World War II was most certainly influenced by the Cold War atmosphere and the way that this impacted upon the Third World. It is also the case that the classical versions of this argument are not particularly accepted as contemporary development theories although they are still sometimes reported as if they are in the textbooks.

Crucially, the last 20 years have seen the emergence of a much more free-market orientated approach to development with the emergence of New Right governments around the world, most notably those of Reagan in the USA and Thatcher in the UK. These governments rejected the idea of state intervention implied by the more moderate modernization theorists and suggested that policies of liberalization, involving opening up Third World countries to trade was the only route to achieve economic development.

This trend in international economic and political relations was also encouraged by the ending of fixed exchange rates in the 1970s, the move to a floating system of exchange rates and the removal of exchange controls from many countries in the 1980s. This created a situation where money could move about the globe much more freely and where fluctuating exchange rates sometimes made it profitable to do so.

In **reading 13.1**, Fröbel *et al.* (1980) consider some of the important changes that have occurred since the 1970s and outline their thesis that the key component of this has been the development of a new international division of labour. What they mean by this is the replacement of the old international division of labour based on the idea that countries in the Third World would export raw materials and countries in the First World would export manufactured goods. The new division of labour is based on the idea that the production of goods themselves can be divided among many countries through branches of the same company and that in some instances this has led to the movement of industrial production from the First World to the Third World.

As well as private sector flows between the First and the Third World another important source of funds entering this flow is government and multilateral aid. Although the name suggests that this is helpful, Teresa Hayter (1985) is associated with a radical critique of development aid, first developed in her book, *Aid as Imperialism* (Hayter, 1971). In **reading 13.2** – an extract from a book she wrote with Catherine Watson (Hayter and Watson, 1985) entitled *Aid: Rhetoric and reality* – she questions the extent to which aid agencies have really changed their policies in the light of earlier criticisms and therefore the extent to which aid is now socially concerned.

One of the most important developments in the 1980s, which has changed the nature of First World/Third World relations and drastically affected the lives of people in the Third World, is the emergence of the Third World debt crisis. In **reading 13.3** – an extract from her book *A Fate Worse Than Debt* – Susan George (1990) outlines the reasons for the development of the debt crisis and examines the scale of it, pointing out that although one trillion dollars sounds a lot it is relatively easy to get that much in debt when all the structural factors of the world economy are taken into account. She also considers the way this legacy of debt is affecting people in the Third World.

The impact of the debt crisis has all too often been written in terms of the effects on the banks and economies of the Western advanced industrialized nations, although the extent to which this was a crisis for them is most certainly open to question. What is not open to question is the detrimental effect that the structures of which the debt crisis is a symptom have had on those in the Third World. In **reading 13.4** – an extract from his book *Poverty and the Planet* – Ben Jackson (1994) of the World Development Movement outlines the way that famines and poverty are caused by these structures and have unequal effects on the citizens of Third World nations.

Another issue that has risen to the top of the political agenda in the 1980s and 1990s is an increasing concern about the state of the environment. This is most clearly a phenomena that has international implications and is therefore central to recent developments in World Development sociology. Michael Redclift (1994) presents a critique (**reading 13.5**) of the dominant approach which views environmental problems as something that can be managed, and argues that analyses such as the idea of the *Risk Society* developed by Ulrich Beck (1992) are Eurocentric. He argues instead that analysis of environmental problems can only really be understood in the context of the development of an overall political economy analysis.

A third issue which has become recently predominant is the emergence of a group of societies known as the Newly Industrializing Countries (NICs) which are sometimes seen to present a new distinctive model of development based on clear integration into the world economy. Nigel Harris (1986) argues (**reading 13.6**) that the development of this world economy has undermined the political strategy advocated by Third World nationalists (the group of people most closely associated with dependency theory), but also that the NICs' strategy has limitations, since it is often based on repression and military regimes which are unable to take development beyond a certain point. The recent collapse of the South Korean bubble has further placed great question marks over whether the NICs offer a distinct strategy of development.

The collapse of the South Korean economy has led to the intervention of the International Monetary Fund (IMF) in ways that some have seen as the USA operating to effectively destroy the notion of an alternative model of capitalist development based on Japan and South Korea. The character of IMF intervention is the central element in the analysis of recent economic development in the world economy offered by Walton and Seddon (1994) (**reading 13.7**). Operating broadly within the approach known as 'world systems theory' they argue that the current economic crisis around the world is distinctive in terms of the international character of the world economy and the increasing power of agencies such as the IMF. They are critical of their interventions and argue that plans such as the structural adjustment plans advocated by the IMF have often led to a rise in urban-based political movements protesting against the social consequences of IMF adjustment – notably the rise in food prices – by rioting.

The increasing internationalization of the world economy, and the concept of globalization which is used to describe it, has been one of the key debates of the 1990s and the concept of globalization has become increasingly fashionable in sociological circles. However, there are critical voices. In **reading 13.8**, Hirst and Thompson (1995) offer their own critical voice, suggesting that the internationalization of the world economy has not reached a state that can reasonably be described as globalization. The political implications of this are important since, as noted also by Harris (1986), it is often the case that radical governments in the Third World, and indeed in the First World, based their policies on the economic strategy of being able to control their economy.

Globalization theories suggest that the ability of national governments to have such control has been undermined. The implications of Hirst and Thompson's rejection of this view is therefore that nation-states still do retain important powers to influence national and international events. In particular they point to the importance of military power, still largely organized in national units in the world.

Overall these readings attempt to cover the key debates in world development sociology in the 1990s, covering the issues of whether it is possible to develop outside the world economy or whether Third Worldist strategies are now outdated. The readings also cover the alternative model offered of development through clear integration into the world economy – with the example of the Newly Industrializing Countries (NICs) and the slightly different capitalist model offered by the IMF and the World Bank (and the implications of their interventions in the Third World). All of this debate can be fitted inside the wider debate about the nature and the extent of globalization.

These contemporary debates have emerged as a result of concrete developments since the mid-1970s, such as the emergence of the Third World debt crisis, the growth in private commercial lending to the Third World, the changing nature of aid to the Third World and the growing importance of international agencies such as the World Bank and the IMF. While some of the readings seek to consider the reasons for these developments and look at the macro implications for the world economy, others seek to understand the implications of these developments for continuing and emerging issues in world development sociology – such as world hunger and the environment. Although there are clearly still important theoretical debates about the nature of development, and although these often build on the now somewhat outdated legacy of modernization theory versus dependency theory, they most certainly go beyond them and show that such theories alone are no longer sufficient to explain the nature and process of world development.

References

Beck, U. (1992) *Risk Society*, London: Sage.

Hayter, T. (1971) *Aid as Imperialism*, Harmondsworth: Penguin.

Reading 13.1 **The new international division of labour**

F. Fröbel, J. Heinrichs and O. Kreye (from) *The New International Division of Labour* (1980) Cambridge: Cambridge University Press, pp. 2–10 and 12–15.

Editorial comments

The authors support the idea of world systems theory, which suggests that developments in economic processes can only be understood if we see the world economy as a unified system. On this basis they argue that relations between the developed and the developing world are being transformed from being based on an old international division of labour – based on the developing countries exporting raw materials for manufacture in the developed countries – into a qualitatively different new international division of labour, the characteristics of which they describe in this extract.

The new international division of labour in the world economy

IN THE WESTERN *industrialized countries* the rate of unemployment has reached its highest level for many years. In 1975 the official rate of unemployment, which always understates the real volume of unemployment, averaged 5% for the **OECD** countries (USA = 8.5%, Japan = 1.9%, **Federal Germany** = 4.7%) and has remained at this high level with no indications that it will decrease. The number of people in OECD countries officially registered as unemployed has hovered around the fifteen million mark since 1975 and there is no reason to suppose that it will fall in the immediate future.

An increasing number of the industrial branches of the OECD countries are reporting declining output, overcapacities, short-time working and mass redundancies. For example, the garment, textile and synthetic fibres industries in the most highly industrialized countries have, almost without exception, drastically cut back the production of their respective products at the traditional manufacturing sites as production there is becoming increasingly less competitive in the world market. Employees in many branches of industry are threatened with redundancy and the devaluation of their professional skills – victims of spreading automation and, in particular, of the recent leap forward in the rationalization of the production process made possible by technical developments in the electrical engineering industry, especially the shift from electro-mechanical to electronic components in the production both of consumer goods and components to be used in other sectors of the economy.

Domestic investment in the largest industrialized countries (USA, Japan, Federal Germany, France, United Kingdom) has not only been stagnating but has even fallen in Japan and Federal Germany as a proportion of gross national product in the first half of the 1970s. In the face of the decreasing profitability of domestic investments, companies in the OECD countries have expanded and justified their policy of investment directed towards rationalisation on the grounds that they cannot expect any change in the current trends for the foreseeable future. In many countries the increase in the share of domestic investment which has been directed towards rationalization schemes over recent years has resulted in a substantial loss of local jobs, without any reduction in productive capacity.

By contrast, *foreign* investments originating from the Western industrialized countries have been steadily increasing for a number of years. An ever-increasing share of these investments is flowing into the developing countries. Foreign investment for the purpose of industrial relocation is gaining in importance, both that undertaken in industrialized countries, as well as in developing countries.

Stagnating output, short-time working and mass redundancies in numerous countries do not, however, necessarily reflect the fates of individual companies. On the contrary, many companies, both large and small, from the industrialized countries are expanding their investments, production capacities and employment abroad, especially in developing countries, whilst their investments, production capacities and employment at home are stagnating or even declining. ...

In addition, the Western industrialized countries are experiencing a long-term **fiscal crisis of the state**. High unemployment and short-time working have forced the state to increase its expenditure, while at the same time the state's tax receipts have fallen because high unemployment has reduced the revenue from personal taxation and the threat or reality of industrial relocation has reduced the ability of the state to tax private companies. It is becoming more and more difficult to provide adequate funds for public pension and health programmes. Outlays on social services are being cut, while at the same time higher social security contributions and taxes threaten employees with a decrease in real incomes. On the other hand, the state has been compelled to provide grants, loans and tax concessions to private business on an increasing scale, hoping that this will stimulate domestic investment, reduce the rate of unemployment, and thus avert the danger of potentially explosive social tensions. ...

These economic, social and political problems in each of the Western industrialized countries are occurring in the context of world-wide higher turnovers and profits by individual companies. The annual reports of most large companies show that, even in the years of the world recession, these companies have been operating very successfully.

A remarkable contrast then exists between the success of individual private companies and the failure of the economic policies of the industrialized countries to attain their declared principal policy aim, namely the reduction in unemployment. The panacea of the last few decades, high rates of growth in gross national product, no longer appears to be available. ...

The number of un- and underemployed in the *developing countries* is even greater: they constitute an enormous mass of people who are either not at all or only partially integrated as productive labour into the so-called modern sector. This reservoir of potential labour amounts to hundreds of millions of workers. It is an oversimplification to say that it is the traditionally bad living conditions in underdeveloped countries which produced an ever-increasing flow of people seeking work and incomes from the countryside into the cities, the potential sites of the industry which can grant these things. Paradoxically the cause must be looked for in the modernization of agriculture which can only attain its declared goal of increasing food production by the destruction of small subsistence farming, the traditional modest basis of survival for large sections of the rural population who are then forced to migrate to the cities where they are not usually able to obtain an income sufficient to provide them with a decent living.

The contemporary slums and similar poverty-stricken districts of the underdeveloped countries' cities are overcrowded with these landless rural immigrants. (By 1970 population *statistics from* at least ten cities in the so-called Third World showed that more than a million people in each of them were living in such areas.) Transformed into proletarianized wage workers they are forced to seek employment regardless of the level of remuneration and under the most inhuman conditions merely to ensure their sheer physical survival. They constitute a nearly inexhaustible source of the cheapest and most exploitable labour in the underdeveloped countries.

This vast industrial reserve army of extremely cheap labour feeds a process of industrialization which can be observed in many contemporary developing countries. But this process of industrialization rarely absorbs any significant proportion of the local labour-force. It is oriented to production for export, as the purchasing power of the mass of the local population is too low to constitute an effective demand on the local market for the products of the country's own industry. The markets supplied by the industrialization of the developing countries are therefore predominantly overseas, primarily in the traditional industrial countries.

This process of **export-oriented industrialization** in developing countries is not only highly dependent on foreign companies but also extremely fragmented. Only very rarely do developing countries end up with the establishment of reasonably complex industrial branches (e.g. textile and garment industry in some cases complemented by synthetic fibre production). And even in the very few developing countries where such centres of partial industrialisation have been established there are no signs that they are being supplemented by a wider industrial complex which would enable them to free themselves eventually from their dependency on the already industrialized countries for imports of capital- and other goods, and for the maintenance of their industrial installations.

However, in the overwhelming majority of developing countries not even the beginnings of this partial industrialization process can be observed, that is, a process which would at least serve to develop a few individual branches of industry. Instead, industrial production is confined to a few highly specialised manufacturing processes: inputs are imported from outside the country, are worked on by the local labour-force in 'world market factories' (for example, sewing, soldering, assembling and testing) and are then exported in their processed form. In other words, these world market factories are industrial enclaves with no connection to the local economy except for their utilization of extremely cheap labour and occasionally some local inputs (energy, water and services for example), and are isolated from the local economy in almost all other respects. ...

So far export-oriented industrialization has failed to achieve any improvement in the social conditions of the mass of the populations of the developing countries, not even as far as their most fundamental needs such as food, clothing, health, habitation and education are concerned. Nor can any improvement be expected in the foreseeable future. Quite the opposite – the social tensions and struggles between the tiny privileged minority which benefits from export-oriented industrialization, and the vast majority of the population which derives no benefits from it will intensify in the future. It is such predictable developments as these which have occasioned Business International to take account of war and revolution in many countries. The increasing militarization of the so-called Third World is a clear indication that increasingly overt and repressive force is needed to prevent the violent eruption of social tensions. South Africa, Chile and Thailand are but three especially well-known examples of military repression – but there are very many others. ...

After decades and centuries of the underdevelopment of the so-called developing countries the recent export-oriented industrialization of these countries offers but faint hope that that living standards and conditions of the mass of their populations will undergo any substantial improvements in the foreseeable future. Moreover there is no reason to assume that the main goal of the policies pursued by the governments of many developing countries is, in fact, the improvement of the material conditions of the mass of their populations. But even in those developing countries whose governments appear to be actively pursuing this goal, little progress can be discerned, except in very rare instances. ...

Even the most superficial description of the **world economy** in the 1970s cannot be confined to a consideration of the situation of the industrialized countries on one hand, and of the developing countries on the other, each looked at in artificial isolation. (The 'socialist' countries will be taken into account in our study only inasmuch as they are also integrated into the world market.) The world economy is not simply the sum total of national economies, each of which functions essentially according to its own laws of motion, with only marginal interconnections, such as those established by external trade. These national economies are, rather, organic elements of one all-embracing system, namely a world economy which is in fact a single world-wide capitalist system. As our cursory survey has already shown, the structural changes in individual national economies are interrelated within this single world economy and mutually determine one another.

The most striking manifestation of the world economy is international trade. Well over 15% of all commodities and services which are produced every year in Western industrialized and developing countries enter international trade, and this percentage has been steadily increasing for at least the last fifteen years. Recognition of this fact is a first step towards understanding the increase of world-wide economic interpenetration.

The industrialized countries handle 70% of international trade and the developing countries only 20%. Seventy per cent of exports from both developing and industrialized countries are destined for industrialized countries and only 20% for the developing countries. In other words, whereas the foreign trade of the industrialized countries is mostly with each other, the foreign trade of the developing countries is mostly with the industrialized countries, and not their fellow developing countries. Recognition of this fact is a first step towards understanding the economic dependency of the developing countries on the industrialized countries.

The developing countries' exports to the industrialized countries still consist overwhelmingly of raw materials, whereas the vast bulk of the exports of the industrialized countries to the developing countries are still manufactures. In recent years, however, there has been a marked, slow but steady increase in manufactures exported from developing countries as a proportion of total world exports of manufactured goods. ...

One, albeit incomplete, expression of this international division of labour, which has been organized by private companies in pursuit of their own profit maximisation, is foreign investment. Figures for Federal German investment show that in recent years investment abroad by Federal German companies has exceeded investment by foreign companies in Federal Germany. Taken together with the fact that investment policy in Federal Germany has concentrated on rationalization schemes for a number of years, this would suggest that Federal Germany has now apparently become less 'interesting' as a site for the expansion of industrial production. (Figures on the development of industrial assets of Federal German companies, including the re-invested profits, both at home and abroad would, in all probability, if available, demonstrate this phenomenon even more clearly.)

However, perhaps the clearest expression of the structural changes in the world economy which can be observed in the mid-1970s is the relocation of production. One form of this relocation (among other equally important ones) is the closing down of certain types of manufacturing operations in undertakings in the industrial nations and the subsequent installation of these parts of the production process in the foreign subsidiaries of the same company. The Federal German textile and garment industries represent one of the best-known examples of such relocations. Trousers for the Federal German market are no longer produced for example in Mönchengladbach, but in the Tunisian subsidiary of the same Federal German company. The process of relocation is also gaining momentum in other branches of industry. Injection pumps which were formerly made for the Federal German market by a Federal German company in Stuttgart, are now manufactured partly to the same end by the same company at a site in India. Television sets are produced on the same basis by another company in Taiwan; car radio equipment in Malaysia, car engines in Brazil, watches in Hong Kong, electronic components in Singapore and Malaysia all fall into the same category.

The Federal German worker rendered unemployed by the relocation of production has been replaced by a newly hired worker in a foreign subsidiary of 'his' or 'her' company. ...

Our earlier descriptive sketch of some typical aspects of the contemporary world economy has already indicated that the old or 'classical' international division of labour is now open for replacement. The decisive evidence for this hypothesis is the fact that developing countries have increasingly become sites for manufacturing – producing manufactured goods which are competitive on the world market. ...

This world market oriented industralization which is emerging today in many developing countries is not the result of positive decisions made by individual governments or companies. Industry only locates itself at those sites where production will yield a certain profit, sites which have been determined by five centuries of development of the world economy. In the 'classical' international division of labour which developed over this period, industrial sites for manufacturing basically only existed in Western Europe, and later in the USA and Japan. Since it is evident that the developing countries are now providing sites for the profitable manufacture of industrial products destined for the world market to an ever-increasing extent, we quickly come up against the question: What changes are responsible for this development?

Three preconditions taken together seem to be decisive for this new development.

Firstly, a practically inexhaustible reservoir of disposable labour has come into existence in the developing countries over the last few centuries. This labour-force is extremely cheap; it can be mobilized for production for practically the whole of the year, and all hours of the day, on shift work, night work and Sunday work; in many cases it can reach levels of labour productivity comparable with those of similar processes in the developed countries after a short period of training; companies can afford to exhaust the labour-force by overwork as it can easily be replaced, and they can also select their employees very specifically according to age, sex, skill, discipline and other relevant factors as there is an oversupply of people who are forced to take any job which is available.

Secondly, the division and subdivision of the production process is now so advanced that most of these fragmented operations can be carried out with minimal levels of skill easily learnt within a very short time.

Thirdly, the development of techniques of transport and communication has created the possibility, in many cases, of the complete or partial production of goods at any site in the world – a possibility no longer ruled out by technical, organizational and cost factors.

The coincidence of these three preconditions (which are supplemented by other, less important ones) has brought into existence a world market for labour and a real world industrial reserve army of workers, together with a world market for production sites. Workers in the already industrialized countries are now placed on a world-wide labour market and forced to compete for their jobs with their fellow workers in the developing countries. Today, with the development of a world-wide market in production sites, the traditional industrialized and the developing countries have to compete against one another to attract industry to their sites. ...

The term which we shall use to designate this qualitatively new development in the world economy is the *new international division of labour*. ...

This means that any company, almost irrespective of its size, which wishes to survive is now forced to initiate a transnational reorganization of production to adapt to these qualitatively new conditions.

By far the most important means by which companies have secured their continued survival in the past has been through 'investment in rationalization' – the installation of more efficient machinery and a reduction in the size and skills of the labour-force. This device alone (along with other 'classical' devices) is no longer adequate. The development of the world economy has increasingly created conditions (forcing the development of the new international division of labour) in which the survival of more and more companies can only be assured through the relocation of production to new industrial sites, where labour-power is cheap to buy, abundant and well-disciplined; in short, through the transnational reorganization of production.

Key terms

The following key terms appear in the text above. They have been defined below to aid with the reading of this item.

OECD Organization for Economic Co-operation and Development, an organization whose members are the advanced industrial nations

Federal Germany the official name of the state known as West Germany which existed until the early 1990s

fiscal crisis of the state a situation where the state faces a reduction in tax revenue together with increasing demands, particularly for welfare expenditure, leading to a crisis in state finances

export-oriented industrialization a policy adopted by many developing countries based on setting up plants to produce goods for export and using the money raised to finance further industrialization

world economy the notion that there is a unified capitalist system which operates to some extent independently of national borders and governments

Questions

1 Explain what is meant by the phrase 'relocation of production'.

2 Identify what the authors mean by the 'old international division of labour' and explain how the 'new international division of labour' differs from this old pattern.

3 What three preconditions are required for the development of this 'new international division of labour'?

4 Suggest three examples of UK industries that have suffered rationalization due to the growth of the tendency to relocate industries, outlined by the authors.

5 To what extent does evidence support the assertion that 'any company, irrespective of size, which wishes to survive is now forced to initiate a transnational reorganization of production'?

Reading 13.2 **Aid: rhetoric and reality**

Teresa Hayter and Catherine Watson (from) *Aid: Rhetoric and Reality* (1985) London: Pluto Press, pp. 238–47.

Editorial comments

In her book *Aid as Imperialism,* Teresa Hayter (1971) explored the role of the World Bank. This book set out to re-examine the role of the World Bank ten years later to see if their stated greater commitment to the alleviation of poverty had had a noticeable effect.

They argue that they have not had to change their conclusions greatly. The overall tone of the book is very critical towards the role of the World Bank in international development and in particular about the way that aid is made conditional on the acceptance of certain controversial economic doctrines. This extract takes a critical look at the forms of aid that are offered to developing countries.

Reference

Hayter, T. (1971) *Aid as Imperialism,* Harmondsworth: Penguin.

Current forms of aid from the West

Purposes

THERE IS NO doubt an element of humanitarianism, or guilt, in the provision of aid. The motives of many people engaged in the business of aid are mixed and the people themselves vary. For many of them, a concern about poverty in the Third World must be the main reason for their involvement and they may genuinely believe that their activities are beneficial to the poor. Others may have a different vision of the purposes of aid and be committed to different goals. Others, again, are probably just cynical, aware that they are doing nicely out of the gravy train provided by the aid business and unable to find another one with the same rewards. Even governments which include a provision for aid in their budgets may do so partly out of a sense of obligation and are not immune to high-minded pleas for international goodwill put forward at international forums.

But there is of course much more to it than that. Aid is also seen as a means of promoting political and strategic objectives. To the extent that it is an alternative to more violent methods of achieving these ends, it has aspects of humanitarianism. Thus McNamara, during his period at the **World Bank**, and the authors of the Brandt report, can be said to have been more progressive than Reagan or Thatcher in the simple sense that they saw economic development as a means for the containment of rebellion preferable to the use of military force. But the political and strategic goals themselves are far from progressive, even though the anti-communist crusade is carried out in the name of 'freedom and democracy'. The majority of the Third World governments supported by the West are authoritarian, often military, regimes of a brutally repressive nature. The governments that are overthrown, or subjected to '**destabilization**' through, for example, the withdrawal of aid, are usually much less repressive and they have sometimes been elected under the usual constitutional processes. The **Popular Unity government** in Chile is the most famous example; military methods were used in Chile only after Popular Unity had increased its share of the vote in the mid-term municipal elections and the prospect of defeating it by democratic means had receded. Manley's government in Jamaica, Goulart in Brazil, Cheddi Jagan in Guyana were all elected. ... The US helped to prevent the fulfilment of the undertaking in the 1954 Geneva Accords that elections would be held in the South of Vietnam; if elections were held, Eisenhower said on television, 'that dictator [Ho Chi Minh] would get 100 per cent of the votes'. When the Sandinistas announced that they were keeping to their plan to hold elections in 1985, and then that they were bringing them forward to 1984, the US government switched to another demand: that they should reduce the size of their military forces, which unfortunately they need in order to defend themselves against US-backed invasion.

These governments are less repressive than the governments commonly supported by the West precisely because they are seen to be acting in the interests of the majority of their own people, who usually give them their overwhelming support. The purpose of economic destabilization is to undermine that support by making it more difficult for left wing governments to deliver tangible benefits to their people. In Chile, military force was resorted to when destabilization had been partially successful but not successful enough, presumably, for the ruling class to risk waiting for elections. In Grenada, economic destabilisation was notably unsuccessful. But political dissension, tragically and perhaps with the help of the CIA, provided the pretext for the invasion the US had long been planning. These governments nevertheless encounter the hostility of the West precisely because they are successful and popular and provide an alternative and more attractive model of development.

This alternative model is seen as a threat to the West partly for strategic and political reasons. Although the claim that countries as small as Nicaragua and Grenada constitute a military threat to the United States is clearly ludicrous, and the idea that they might provide bases from which the Soviet Union could attack the United States is hardly less so, the Soviet Union and Cuba can provide some form of military support for struggles elsewhere. Even very small countries, such as Grenada, which do not constitute a military threat, can nevertheless provide an example to be followed by others if they are allowed to succeed. The **domino theory** is far from dead. If such models of development become widespread in the Third World, they will be the opposite of a threat to freedom and democracy, in the Third World or anywhere else. But they will threaten the political system in the imperialist heartlands. And some people, even those who would not applaud the political system in Paraguay, the Philippines or Chile, nevertheless pre-

sumably feel that the relative freedoms that exist in prosperous Western parliamentary democracies can justifiably be defended by propping up right-wing dictatorships in the Third World.

But economic considerations provide an even more compelling justification for the existence of aid. As the Brandt report (Brandt Commission, 1980) correctly points out, not only is the 'South' dependent on the 'North', but the North is dependent on the South. Anxious though the Brandt report was to change the geographical terminology, this is primarily a dependence of the major Western powers on their former colonies and semi-colonies in the Third World. Having built up a system under which the Third World provides it with cheap and abundant raw materials and primary commodities, markets for its manufactured goods and super-profits for some of its major firms and banks, the West would find it difficult to adjust to the loss of these advantages. Some raw materials crucial to Western industries are to be found only or mainly in the Third World. A large part of the proven reserves of oil are in the Third World. The Brandt report is concerned that multilateral mining companies, whose super-profits are threatened by Third World nationalism, may become reluctant to invest in new capacity. Western consumers would suffer from any diminution in the willingness of Third World countries to turn over their land to export crops in their desperate attempts to satisfy the requirements of their urban elites for Western manufactured goods. If more land was devoted to food crops for local consumption, there could be shortages of tea, coffee, bananas and other tropical crops and their prices could go up, feeding inflation; the Thatcher government's 'success' in bringing down inflation was said by the Bank of England to be mainly a consequence of the decline in the prices of commodities supplied by Third World countries.

Between a quarter and a third of the exports of developed countries and nearly 40 per cent of US exports go to the Third World. The big redundancies at British Leyland Trucks in 1984 (which were followed by its threatened total closure) and the failure of Vauxhall to reduce its losses in spite of its success on the British market were ascribed to their overdependence on Third World markets and the contraction in these markets caused by the **debt crisis**. ... [S]ome of the major multinational companies make most of their profits and in some cases most of their sales in the Third World. Left-wing governments might be more interested in a debtors' cartel, which would threaten major banks.

Methods

Aid is one means of safeguarding these interests. It does so in a number of direct and indirect ways. The most obvious is that aid is allocated between countries so as to reward friends and penalize enemies and, in some cases in which aid is provided to left-wing governments, to keep open or enlarge the possibility that they will adopt policies favourable to Western interests. At times the threat of cutting aid is used as a means of preventing governments from adopting specific policies of which Western donors disapprove; for example, trading with Cuba or nationalising some foreign asset. ...

Aid is used to open up markets. Once a country has imported a steel mill or railway equipment partly financed on 'soft' terms or with grants, it is almost bound to have a continuing need for imports from the same source. Abandoned equipment in many parts of the Third World testifies to the fact that this need is often not met. But it increases the willingness of many governments to do what is necessary to obtain the favours of the West. If the aid had not been available in the first place, the materials and skills might, in many cases, have been provided from local sources. ...

Aid also finances projects in the economic infrastructure, such as harbours and telecommunications, which are essential for the profitable operation of foreign investors but which the private sector itself will not invest in, because they are not profitable enough. This is also a means of ensuring that governments' revenues are used for these purposes, since aid seldom finances the total cost of a project or its recurring costs, and the loans must be repaid. Projects in social sectors such as education and health are sometimes justified in publications about aid as a means of ensuring that the private sector is supplied with a sufficiently healthy and competent workforce. It can also be justified as a contribution to quietening unrest, and is in that sense equivalent to reforms within industrialized countries, though on a far smaller and more haphazard scale. Projects in agriculture are in line with the interests of the increasingly powerful and expanding agribusiness firms which supply the inputs of fertilizer and improved seeds used in Green Revolution projects. They are also of course a means of helping to secure continued supplies of agricultural commodities for consumption in the West.

Aid is in a sense a transfer from taxpayers to private firms and banks, enabling them to get rid of otherwise uncompetitive products or to get their money back. For this reason it has its right-wing critics, who do not deny that aid is useful to parts of the private sector but who are opposed to public subsidies as such. This type of criticism partly accounts for the failure of the Reagan and Thatcher governments to support aid, and is related to their general hostility to all public spending, except spending on the military and the police. They are clearly also unconvinced of the

general political usefulness of aid, preferring to rely on military methods. The Thatcher government has abandoned much of the sentimental rhetoric surrounding aid and directed that it should be more closely related to British commercial interests. These governments' hostility to aid extends even to the World Bank, though they are forced to concede that the **IMF** is indispensable to the recovery of debt and must have its funds replenished to some extent. ...

The **multilateral 'aid' institutions** specialize in active intervention in the economic policy-making of Third World governments, and their aim is to buttress their efforts through the support of **bilateral donors**, other lenders, including the banks, and private investors. They are the self-appointed guardians of the profits and assets of the banks and the private sector in general.

The World Bank and the IMF are sometimes described as the police of the international financial (capitalist) order. In their efforts to ensure its survival, they devise programmes of 'adjustment' to the shocks which it administers to the economies of Third World countries. These adjustment programmes are supposed to enable countries to avoid financial and economic chaos and are presented as being in the interest of the developing as well as the developed countries. But because of the inherent difficulty of providing for the needs of the poor as well as for those of local élites and foreigners, they end up as austerity programmes whose major emphasis is, as always, on squeezing the poor: through cuts in public expenditure, increases in the prices of basic goods, and wage cuts. The prospect that they will lead to a resumption of growth in the Third World and the ability to service and repay existing debts, let alone reduce the incidence of poverty, is minimal.

Effectiveness

It is of course hard to tell whether these efforts to change the policies of governments have any effect. Recipient governments invariably claim that their policies are unaffected by aid. They would have done it anyway, they say. Government officials and politicians say, as for example Algerian officials did, that they know their own minds and cannot be pushed around. Indian officials say, implicitly, that they are cleverer than Fund, Bank and other aid officials and can out-manoeuvre them. There is much truth in these claims. Government officials elsewhere make similar claims; although not all of them are as tough or as intellectually powerful as Algerian or Indian officials, their knowledge of local conditions is necessarily greater than that of the aid agencies, and they are often more competent as well. Some of them are, in any case, former officials of the Bank or the IMF, or former employees of Wall Street banks. Governments may say they will do one thing and in fact do something else. And aid agency officials do not usually claim to be able to bring about radical shifts in policies, but merely to be attempting to move them some way in the desired direction. Thus neither in Hungary nor in Algeria would they dare to propose the wholesale privatization of state enterprises; and the degree of import liberalization pressed upon India, or the opening up to the world market urged on China, is nothing compared to the wholesale dismantling of import restrictions embarked upon in some Latin American countries. Clausen is reported in the Indian newspaper *Business Standard* as saying: 'We would never hold a gun to anyone's head' to make them accept conditions; 'I know that the political ice in some of these countries can be too thin for the right economic policies to be put into gear'. Excessive pressures may even be counterproductive from the point of view of the donors, pushing governments into open displays of defiance; governments do not wish to be seen to be bowing to the pressure of foreigners. Thus an Indian government employee, on leave of absence from the World Bank, claimed that the IMF's support for import liberalization, far from being useful, was 'an albatross around our necks'. The whole exercise, one is frequently told, is a 'sensitive' one, hence the desire for secrecy.

But it is obvious that, however limited the power of the aid agencies, they do have some effect on the balance of power within countries. For example, identical 'rural development' projects appear in Colombia, Nigeria and the Philippines. The aid agencies' success depends on identifying and supporting local allies who favour the policies of the West. Such people are to be found in every country. Their position within governments can be reinforced by the support of the aid agencies. They can argue that the money will not be forthcoming unless certain policies are adopted. Allies can be created by more or less obviously corrupt methods, ranging from the prospect of jobs in the World Bank to outright pay-offs. The financial well-being of local elites may be closely related to aid. The burgeoning urban elite of Bangladesh owes its posi-

tion almost entirely to aid; the creation of luxurious residential and shopping areas in Dhaka is the one tangible effect of all the aid money that has been poured into Bangladesh since its independence from Pakistan.

In the current world crisis and with acute balance of payments problems in most Third World countries, the position of many governments is abject. The aid agencies congratulate themselves on the current 'greater receptivity' to foreign advice among Third World governments, much as employers in the industrialized countries are able to assert their 'right to manage' because workers fear redundancy. Governments which wish to reach agreement with their bank creditors now have to go to the IMF. Having been forced to take this step, they may be more open to pressures from other quarters and the proffering of 'solutions' to their crisis in the form of import liberalization, 'reform' of their public sector, and so on.

Moreover, while the policies promoted through aid hurt many sectors of the population, especially the poor, the money is likely to benefit more crucial sources of support to the government and thus enable it to survive. Aid can bolster reactionary regimes. But the threat of its withdrawal is taken seriously by most governments. It can be especially effective as a deterrent to governments whose commitment to a radical redistribution of income in favour of the poor is not whole-hearted, such as the Manley government in Jamaica. But even governments with a clearer commitment to left-wing policies or a more radical tradition are wary of becoming embroiled with the major aid agencies. The fact that the government of Zimbabwe successfully pursued a policy of getting money from the World Bank no doubt played a part in its shift to the right. The Sandinistas in Nicaragua were determined to have nothing to do with the IMF and divided on their attitude towards the World Bank. A Filipino revolutionary, asked whether, supposing the left won power in the Philippines, they should try to get money out of the World Bank, thought it over and eventually said he would prefer 'not to ride the tiger'.

Reference

Brandt Commission (1980) *North-South: a programme for survival*, London: Pan.

Key terms

The following key terms appear in the text above. They have been defined below to aid with the reading of this item.

World Bank an international institution set up soon after World War II, charged with helping developing economies through the provision of loans. Formally known as the International Bank for Reconstruction and Development

destabilization the pursuit of policies designed to destabilize a country or its government, with the aim of achieving economic and/or political change

Popular Unity government the name of the socialist government of Salvador Allende in Chile, overthrown by a military coup in 1973 which was backed by the American CIA

domino theory the view of the US State Department that if one country is allowed to become communist it will affect others, like dominoes lined up to knock each other down

debt crisis the mid-1980s crisis caused by the rise in interest rates and consequent rise in debt repayments which led Third World countries to be unable to afford to repay their debts

IMF the International Monetary Fund – a body set up to regulate international monetary transactions, but which is increasingly becoming involved in the developing world.

multilateral aid institutions bodies that provide the developing world with aid that originates in many countries, through international agencies such as the World Bank.

bilateral donors aid provided by one country directly to another

Questions

1 Briefly explain each of the motives for giving aid that are identified by the author.

2 What proportion of the exports of developed countries go to the Third World?

3 According to the authors, in what ways does aid safeguard the interests of Western capitalism?

4 Why are there some right-wing critics of aid?

5 How far do you agree with the assertion that World Bank and IMF austerity programmes end up as 'austerity programmes whose major emphasis is, as always, on squeezing the poor'?

Reading 13.3 **The effect of the debt crisis**

Susan George (from) *A Fate Worse than Debt* (1990) Harmondsworth: Penguin, pp. 12–14, 16 and 18–24.

Editorial comments

In this extract from *A Fate Worse than Debt*, Susan George discusses the extent of the debt crisis in the Third World and considers some of the implications for the people who live there. This reading again focuses on the key role of relations between the advanced industrial nations and the developing countries and the way that the growth of debt in the 1980s has had a large and continuing impact on development. In particular, Susan George focuses on the relationship between debt and militarization, an important but often-ignored issue.

How much is $1 trillion?

WHY IS THERE such a hue and cry about Third World debt? The figures sound enormous – in early 1986 this debt topped the **trillion**-dollar mark. But is this really much money? There are several ways to measure it. For example, Third World debt acquired over the past *fifteen* years represents only one-eighth of the combined **Gross National Product** (GNP) generated *annually* by the OECD countries (the twenty-four rich nations that belong to the Organization for Economic Co-operation and Development) – now an astronomical $8 trillion. The amounts owed by developing countries also pale when compared with the public debt of the United States, which in 1986 reached $2 trillion, twice that of all Third World countries put together.

Take another yardstick: the world's top 200 transnational corporations. They now have a staggering annual turnover of more than $3 trillion – equivalent to almost 30 per cent of gross *world* product. Total Third World debt thus amounts to a mere third of the yearly sales of these top 200 firms, or about 10 per cent of the world's yearly economic activity (now estimated at about $10 trillion). So, again, why the fuss? $1 trillion may not be much money after all.

Latin America's debt provokes countless columns of doom-laden journalism, but you won't find hand-wringing articles about France's debt on the financial pages every other day, even though French public debt at the end of 1985 was over $62 billion – much more than Argentina's and about the same as that of Chile, Peru and the Philippines combined. Some nominally 'Third World' countries, particularly in Asia, also carry heavy debt loads, yet rarely appear in the headlines because, for the time being at least, they are servicing their loans without a hitch. Perhaps, then, the newspapers have been exaggerating matters and we can simply ignore reports of impending crisis. Yes and no.

The absolute Third World debt figure – say, $1 trillion, give or take a few billion – is not the problem, however astronomical it may sound. Debt produces jitters in high places and becomes a menace to the world financial system and to the general public only when it cannot be *serviced* – that is, when interest payments fall into deep arrears or stop altogether. ...

The mal-development model: a downpayment on disaster

The honest answer to the question 'What happened to the money'? is deeply embedded in post-Second World War history. Beginning in the 1950s, a new breed of economists invented the notion of development – a word that has now become well-nigh meaningless. It would take a book in itself to do justice to this all-things-to-all-people concept, and since I do not choose to write that book, I shall evade definitions and simply call the problem at hand 'the model'. ...

Industrialization: why pay less when you can pay more?

The mal-development model calls for industrialization at all costs. A major cause of debt accumulation was investment in ill-considered, ill-conceived projects, many involving bloated capital costs and healthy doses of graft. ...

In early 1986 the newspapers regaled us daily with the exploits of Ferdinand and Imelda. One remark said it all: 'Imelda Marcos makes Marie Antoinette look like a bag lady'. At a conservative estimate, this couple's Filipino translation of *après moi le déluge* cost their people *at least* 15 per cent of the country's $26 billion debt. Some of it may return to the national coffers, thanks to international co-operation with the Aquino government.

This debt was not, however, accumulated entirely to pay for Ms Marcos's astounding collection of shoes. One expensive debt-financed project is the Morong (Bataan) nuclear power plant ordered in 1976 from Westinghouse with a price tag of $2.1 billion. The debt incurred for this plant alone cost the Philippines at least $350,000 *a day* in interest payments – a figure that jumped to $500,000 in 1987 when debt to the US Ex-Im Bank fell due. The reactor is ready to go; that it is not yet operating is perhaps just as well. The building site chosen is in the middle of the Pacific 'fire-rim' earthquake zone at the foot of a volcano. The International Atomic Energy Authority noted in a 1978 report that the choice of the Morong site in a zone of such high seismic activity was 'unique in the atomic industry' and deemed the risk of a future volcanic eruption 'credible' (Watt and Taylor, 1985).

According to a report in the *New York Times*, Marcos received $80 million in commissions from Westinghouse through one of his cronies, who mysteriously snatched the nuclear-plant contract from the jaws of General Electric and got it awarded to its arch-rival Westinghouse. General Electric's much lower bid had already been approved by a panel appointed by Marcos himself and by the then head of the Philippine National Power Corp. Marcos overruled the panel's choice in favour of Westinghouse before the latter had even submitted a detailed bid. The Filipino Secretary of Industry wrote angrily to Mr Marcos that he was buying 'one reactor for the price of two'. The crony who arranged the deal, a Mr Herminio Disini, 'now lives in a castle near Vienna', according to the *New York Times* report. Westinghouse acknowledges paying a commission to a Marcos associate but says, 'Allegations of illicitly inflated costs at its nuclear power plant in the Philippines are "completely without merit"' (Butterfield, 1986).

Mrs Aquino's government has announced that in the wake of Chernobyl the plant will not go into operation anyway, which is welcome news, except that the interest is still piling up. Other countries fell into the same sort of trap – a substantial proportion of Brazil's debt (some sources claim up to $40 billion) is due to purchases of nuclear reactors, also non-operational as of this writing.

Capital flight: take the money and run

Were there other good ways of falling deep into debt besides financing current consumption and wasteful projects? Certainly. One of the best and quickest was capital flight. Money spirited out of the South in huge quantities has allowed Northern commercial banks to defy the adage about cake. It turns out the banks *can* both have and eat it because they control both ends of the financial system. First, they make the loan. Almost instantaneously, a large proportion of it returns to their coffers as deposits because corrupt government officials may transfer it there directly. National companies, heavy borrowers whose governments have guaranteed their debt, may also feel that the money they were supposed to invest at home will be happier abroad. This capital, which in fact left the debtor country long ago, will still, unfortunately, appear on the banks' books as loans on which interest is due. The banks are thus paid back twice for a single commitment – first in deposits from foreigners, then in interest. As one economist remarks, 'The most aggressive banks, such as Citibank, have probably accumulated almost as much in assets from poor countries as they have loaned to them. Their real role has been to take funds that Third World élites have stolen from their governments and to loan them back, earning a nice spread each way' (Henry, 1986).

The Bank for International Settlements (BIS) – the central banks' central bank in Basle – is not given to inflammatory statements. It none the less announced in its 1983 annual report that capital flight had been taking place on a 'massive scale'. The BIS estimates that $55 billion was wafted northwards from Latin America between 1977 and 1983. A BIS official conceded that this is a 'conservative estimate'. In 1986 Morgan Guaranty appraised capital flight from the big ten Latin American debtors (Brazil, Mexico, Venezuela, Peru, Colombia, Ecuador, Bolivia, Uruguay, Argentina and Chile) at fully 70 per cent of all their new loans from 1983 to 1985. Mexico takes the dubious first prize in this category, with new net borrowing of $9 billion during the two-year period and an estimated $16 billion worth of capital flight.

For sheer magnitude Mexico is indeed unequalled. The president of the Inter-American Development Bank, himself a Mexican, is far less conservative than the BIS. He places capital flight from Mexico between 1979 and 1983 alone at $90 billion – an amount greater than the entire Mexican debt at that time. In March 1985 a Mexico City newspaper published the names of 575 Mexicans who were all supposed to have at least $1 million deposited in foreign banks. One of the more affluent among these so-called *sacadolares* may well have been the ex-President of Mexico himself, Lopez-Portillo, who, according to James Henry, writing in the *New Republic*, is 'widely rumoured to have absconded with over one billion dollars' when he left office and moved to Rome. ...

The military model: guns, *si; butter, no*

Several countries ran up staggering debts buying toys for their generals. Debt-financed militarization has reached proportions such that the universally respected Stockholm International Peace Research Institute (SIPRI) devotes a chapter of its 1985 *Yearbook* to the phenomenon. SIPRI seeks to elucidate the connections between arsenals and high finance. Its basic question is: 'How much lower would external debt have been without arms purchases'?

Military spending for the National Security State undergirds and protects the mal-development model. SIPRI concludes that 20 per cent of Third World debt – Organization of Petroleum Exporting Countries (OPEC) excluded – can be attributed directly to arms purchases. The more affluent Middle Eastern oil producers went all out for AWACS and other costly military hardware. The economic austerity brought about by debt rescheduling has forced some cutbacks, especially since 1982, but even when military expenditures have fallen in real terms, the proportion devoted to armaments in Third World budgets has almost always remained the same or increased.

One might think that in heavily indebted societies austerity programmes would require that flab be first trimmed from defence spending, especially when a sizeable part of the population is living in hunger and misery. One might further imagine that Western agencies in a position to do so would insist on such cuts. This, unfortunately, is not the case. The IMF consistently demands that its pupils make drastic reduc-

tions in civil spending, but arms budgets remain untouched. When asked about this anomaly, Fund personnel recoil and explain in pained tones that such measures would be 'interfering in the internal affairs of sovereign nations' (which is exactly what the Fund does every working day ...).

It is precisely the poorest countries, especially those in Africa with large debts to service, that tend to spend most heavily on national security. Ethiopia, which has been waging protracted war against liberation struggles in its northern provinces (Eritrea and Tigré), is at the bottom of the African poverty barrel. Its GNP is $4.3 billion, which works out to about $110 per Ethiopian, the lowest **per capita GNP** anywhere in the world, according to World Bank figures. This does not prevent Ethiopia from spending $13 per head and per year on its military but only $7 on health and education combined. Sudan spends $15 for each Sudanese on arms, Tanzania $16, Kenya $17, Somalia $20, Zimbabwe a whopping $55 (related to the threat from South Africa). These countries carry debt loads ranging from $1.5 billion to $4 billion dollars; Sudan's is close to $11 billion.

Ten billion dollars of the total $54 billion owed by Argentina can be traced directly to military spending under the generals' regime. Before Alan García was elected President, Peru was spending a minimum of $300–$400 million yearly on arms, not counting a paltry $700 million for twenty-six French Mirage jets. Debt service and military expenditure between them accounted for over 50 per cent of the Peruvian budget. It is not coincidental that those countries that today find themselves in the deepest debt trouble were those that yesterday bought the most weapons. ...

Unless they are helping with the crops or building bridges, armies themselves are unproductive, yet cost the state dearly in both peacetime and war. In the US, for example, salaries represent $90 billion or close to 35 per cent of 1985 defence outlays. Military salaries may eat up a smaller proportion in poor countries, but still an immutable law plays havoc with Third World budgets: the more defence establishments can obtain, the more powerful they become; the more powerful they become, the more they can blackmail civilian governments into higher arms purchases – and on up the vicious spiral until the generals take over completely and can do as they please.

This law doubtless accounts as well for rates of growth in arms imports, which were particularly alarming in the decade 1972–82. During these ten years Latin America's imports increased by 13 per cent a year, while Africa bought 18.5 per cent more weapons annually (admittedly starting from a lower level). Sixty per cent of Black African countries now live under military rule. The increasing militarization of the continent has been sustained by outside financing: the huge strides in weapons procurement coincide exactly with the 'easy-money' era of 1973–82 (from the first OPEC price increase to the Mexican debt crisis). These unproductive expenditures also helped to set the stage for the African food disaster.

References

Butterfield, F. (1986) 'Marcos linked to $80 million: Westinghouse paid "commission" for nuclear plant in 76', *International Herald Tribune*, 8/9 March.

Henry, J. S. (1986) 'Where the money went', *New Republic*, 14 March.

Watt, S. and Taylor, C. (1985) 'Playing with fire', *Inside Asia*, June–August.

Key terms

The following key terms appear in the text above. They have been defined below to aid with the reading of this item.

trillion one thousand billion dollars. (A billion is one thousand million dollars)

Gross National Product (GNP) a measure of economic production

per capita GNP a measure of total economic production divided by the number of the population; used to facilitate international comparisons without being distorted by the very different population figures in different countries

Questions

1 How does the level of Third World debt compare to the debts of:
   a the OECD nations
   b the USA
   c the world's top 200 transnational corporations?

2 Summarize the main ways in which money lent to the Third World might not be used productively.

3 What problems does the author highlight in relation to loans to the Philippines?

4 What is meant by capital flight and what problems does it cause?

5 How does military expenditure contribute to Third World debt?

6 To what extent do you agree with the authors assertion that 'Debt is ... [an] outcome of the mal-development model'?

Reading 13.4 **Poverty and world hunger**

Ben Jackson (from) *Poverty and the Planet* (1994) Harmondsworth: Penguin, pp. 37–41 and 48–50.

Editorial comments

In this reading, Ben Jackson of the World Development Movement considers the issue of famine, looking at the experience of famine and exploring the reasons for the widespread existence of famine in the contemporary world. The extract considers the unequal effects of famine and the way governmental and international aid policies can contribute to this inequality.

Feeding the world

Who starves?

The image of famine as a great leveller, sweeping all before it, is a myth. Famine is not indiscriminate. It hits people in some areas more than others (and not necessarily the areas with the worst crop failure), and people in the countryside more than those in the towns. Most significantly of all, famine kills the poor and not the rich.

The eminent Indian economist Amartya Sen (1981) investigated the facts behind major famines of recent history, including the Great Bengal Famine of 1942 and famines in Ethiopia and the Sahel in the 1970s. In his mould-breaking study, *Poverty and Famines*, he concludes that 'starvation is the characteristic of some people not *having* enough to eat. It is not the characteristic of there not *being* enough food to eat'. He finds that explaining starvation in terms of food shortages is misleading, for this concentrates too much attention on production and not enough on people. Instead he stresses what he calls people's 'entitlements to food'. They get entitlements to food through growing their own, working for money so that they can buy food, trading (as herders trade their cattle for grain), or by being directly lent or given food. Famines happen when large numbers of people are deprived of entitlements and so starve to death. Sen argues that famine is much more often a case of Food Entitlement Decline (FED) than Food Availability Decline (FAD). Many more go hungry regularly because they lack entitlements (in the shape of land, jobs, or anything to trade) in the first place. ...

Hungry world

As many as a million people died in the Ethiopian famine of 1984–5. Across Africa, tens of thousands more died. Famines continue to threaten. But devastating as they are, famines are, in three senses, just the tip of the hunger iceberg.

First, disasters like drought, flood or crop failure turn into famines only where poor people in poor countries are already living close to the margins of survival. In Ethiopia, bad weather led to famine because farmers and labourers were too poor to ride it out. The government also lacked adequate resources to act as a safety-net for the drought-stricken, and used what it did have for the army and for the lavish 300-million-dollar tenth anniversary celebration of the country's revolution. ...

Second, famine tends to concentrate attention on an immediate natural catalyst, such as drought rather than on the long-term impact of environmental degradation on the poor. In Ethiopia's highlands, where 70 per cent of the people live, more than half the area shows signs of accelerated erosion, according to one report. ...

Third, most hungry people are not those affected by mass famines striking a particular area at one time. Most of those who die of starvation are victims of a quiet but ongoing 'famine' that continues day in, day out. Every few weeks this quiet hunger kills the same number of people in the Third World as the famine in Ethiopia in 1984–5. Almost thirteen million children every year, or 35,000 a day, die from malnutrition and common diseases – many of them hunger-related. According to the **World Bank**, even in 1980 as many as 340 million people did not have enough food to prevent serious health risks and stunted growth in children. The number may have doubled by now. One in three people in the Third World does not have enough to eat for an active working life.

This starvation occurs in the midst of plenty. Statistics show there is more than enough food to go round. At a global level, the UN's Food and Agriculture Organization (FAO) estimates that the world grows enough grain to provide every human being with 3,600 calories a day, well above the average 2,400 calories a day they need. Neither is hunger a simple question of there being too many mouths to feed – of pressure of population on finite resources. Between 1950 and 1983, world population increased from 2.51 billion to 4.66 billion, but agricultural production increased from an average of 248 kilograms to 310 kilograms *per head*. In a Third World country, the food that hungry people lack is usually equivalent to less than 5 per cent of the country's overall food supply, according to the World Bank. But as it points out:

> ... this does not mean, however, that a 5 per cent increase in food supplies would eliminate malnutrition. It means merely that in many countries the supply of food is not the only obstacle to food security.
>
> *(World Bank, 1986)*

Yet economists continue to focus on inefficient production methods, while environmentalists analyse the physical constraints of soil, changing climate and growing population. The basic problem is still defined as shortage rather than entitlement. The economic, technical and environmental obstacles to growing more are indeed serious problems, but they have little meaning without asking *who* is affected by them.

Peasants, ignored left and right

Devastating famines in Ethiopia, Sudan, Mozambique and other countries in 1984–5, and the repeated threats of famines since, have firmly linked Africa with hunger in the public consciousness. But even in a 'normal' year, about 100 million people, or a quarter of Africa's population, get less than 80 per cent of the daily food the UN estimates they need.

Africa is a continent dominated by peasant families tilling their own small farms, growing much of their own food in the form of maize, yams, sorghum or cassava. They may also grow cash crops, like cocoa, or extra food to sell in order to raise money for clothes, tools or children's schooling. A majority of families do have land. Unequal land distribution is not, in general, the major cause of hunger and environmental destruction in Africa; not, at least, in the way it is in Latin America and Asia. (Although it is a major cause in countries heavily settled by white colonists, including Kenya, Malawi, South Africa, and, as we see below, Zimbabwe.)

Peasant farmers account for about seven out of every ten Africans. Although poor, they produce a large proportion of the continent's wealth and a significant proportion of the crops it trades abroad. They have also developed sophisticated ways of managing the various and sometimes delicate environments of Africa. And yet the peasant majority have been widely despised, ignored and exploited, first by colonial rulers and then by African governments, aid donors and experts, who put their money on 'modernizing' Africa into development by setting up Western-style industries and big hi-tech farms. Many of these have turned into expensive and unproductive failures.

This antipathy towards the peasants has been shared by both Western capitalist-orientated and 'socialist' African countries alike. The former inherited it from colonial thinking and, for many years, the advice of the Western aid experts who regarded the peasant producer as backward and inefficient. They condemned the peasant as unresponsive to market incentives and undynamic, preferring never to take risks. Small-scale peasant agriculture had to be transformed into large-scale capitalist farms, using the most modern technology and machinery. This would, on the one hand, produce efficient big farms and, on the other hand, a ready supply of labourers for mining and industry. Africa was to repeat Europe's pattern of industrial revolution – held to be the 'natural' path for development. Peasant farmers had no place in that order. ...

The 'magic of the market': making hunger disappear?

During the 1980s African countries did, however, start to reverse the bias against agriculture and to increase prices paid to farmers. A number of countries abolished government controls holding down farm prices (including Mali, Niger, Nigeria, Somalia, Uganda and Zambia; also Madagascar and Cameroon) and some reformed or abolished their marketing boards (such as Nigeria, Senegal and Somalia). Food crisis and agricultural decline, with few hopeful signs that industry would be able to compensate, had started to persuade some African governments that change was needed. But a second major push came from the **IMF** and World Bank who insisted that farm prices be freed and state control in agriculture cut as a major part of the free-market adjustment policies demanded of debt-strapped African countries.

The World Bank says that 'taxes in many poor countries (not only Africa) discourage domestic food production and encourage food imports' (World Bank, 1989). In answer to the charge that their programmes hurt the poor, the Bank says that higher free-market crop prices help to 'raise the income of the rural poor, increase food security and generate foreign exchange'. The IMF and World Bank appear in this light not as the ogres of austerity bringing poverty in their wake, but as champions of the downtrodden peasant.

We have already seen how low farm prices, first imposed by colonial governments and maintained since, have deprived peasant farmers of a livelihood, undermined long-term management of the land and prevented Africa from feeding itself. Where IMF and

World Bank adjustment policies have tried to reverse this discrimination they have created a welcome break for Africa's rural poor. But this has led many to assume that adjustment policies are always good for the peasant farmer. Some Western free-market crusaders propose the IMF policy of 'getting the prices right' as a panacea for hunger. It is not.

Large farmers still on top

Despite the World Bank/IMF rhetoric in support of the small farmer, adjustment has in practice been biased towards the big farmer. Prices have been increased more for the crops grown by the large-scale, hi-tech commercial farms which governments and the World Bank still seem to see as the ideal goal of African agriculture, even if their anti-peasant prejudice has been tempered to some extent. For some farmers, what adjustment policies have given in better prices with one hand they have taken away with the other. For example, devaluing the currency and freeing price controls has made farm inputs, such as fertilizers and pesticides, cost more – especially in the remoter areas where some of the poorest peasants live.

In Zambia, for instance, adjustment programmes increased producer prices for maize, sunflower, groundnut, soya bean, cotton and coffee. But peasants mainly grow cassava, millet and sorghum. None of the producer prices for these crops was increased. Furthermore, a subsidy to the marketing board, NAMBOARD, to help farmers transport their crops to market was cut as part of the policy package – and yet small farmers had few other ways of getting their crops to market.

Market losers

Furthermore, while farm price rises may leave some farmers winners, there are losers too. In particular, higher farm prices for food crops are passed on to customers, some of them poor, as more expensive food in the market. The exception is where governments step in to subsidize food. But most Third World, and particularly African, governments can ill afford to do this, and anyway IMF programmes usually specifically forbid them to do so.

Price rises affect different groups of poor people differently. Poor peasant farmers find themselves better off overall, because they gain from better prices for crops they sell in the market. At the same time, higher food prices do not affect them much since they grow most of what they eat and buy little from elsewhere. But other groups of poor people with little or no land, such as landless farm workers and the poor and unemployed in the cities, have to spend a large proportion of the little money they have on food. A price rise can mean starvation.

In Latin America, where a majority of the poor live

in city slums or are farm workers on large farms, the higher farm and food prices of adjustment programmes have been devastating. Even in Africa, the problem of urban bias does not mean that all city-dwellers live a cushioned life of state-subsidized plenty; one has only to visit the slums of Lagos, Khartoum or Nairobi to see that. With unemployment often running at 40 per cent or more in African cities and no state provision for the poor, rising food prices push poor families deeper into hunger. It is little wonder that IMF-imposed price rises have sparked off food riots in cities across the Third World.

Even in the countryside, higher food prices can bring disaster for poor people if they do not grow their own food. In Bangladesh and India, for example, the rural poor get about half their food energy from bought food. If food prices go up, many cannot afford to eat. Furthermore, most poor people own little or no land and therefore cannot reap much benefit from higher farm prices. It is the big farmers who benefit from higher prices. In Bangladesh, more than three-quarters of the rice sold on the market is produced by only 15 per cent of the farms, mostly the large ones. In Africa, where higher prices have been hailed as a boon for the poor, landlessness is on the increase – in Kenya, Zimbabwe, Malawi and elsewhere. Feeble attempts in Brazil, Kenya and Thailand to include an element of land reform in adjustment programmes have buckled under political pressure from big landlords. This is in stark contrast to the resolute response of the IMF when the poor have protested that adjustment programmes have pushed up their food prices.

References

Sen, A. (1981) *Poverty and Famines*, Oxford: Clarendon Press.

World Bank (1986) *Poverty and Hunger*, Washington: World Bank.

World Bank (1989) *Development Report 1989*, Washington: World Bank.

Key terms

The following key terms appear in the text above. They have been defined below to aid with the reading of this item.

World Bank the international institution set up soon after World War II, charged with helping developing economies through the provision of loans. Formally known as the International Bank for Reconstruction and Development, it is seen – along with the IMF – as a key instrument of intervention by advanced industrial nations, usually on the basis of the promotion of free-market economics

IMF the International Monetary Fund – a body set up to regulate international monetary transactions, but which is increasingly becoming involved in the developing world

Questions

1 According to the author, in what way is famine not a 'great leveller'?

2 Why is a concentration on the concept of famine misleading in understanding world hunger?

3 How many children die every day from malnutrition and common diseases?

4 Using material from the extract and elsewhere suggest reasons why free-market adjustment policies tend to be biased toward large farmers.

5 To what extent do you agree that the problem of hunger is caused more by a lack of entitlement to food rather than shortages of food? Give reasons for your answer.

Reading 13.5 **Development and the environment**

Michael Redclift (from) 'Development and the environment: managing the contradictions?', in L. Sklair (ed.) *Capitalism and Development* (1994) London: Routledge, pp. 123–4, 127–9 and 131–6.

Editorial comments

In this reading, Michael Redclift looks at theories on development and the environment including the more structurally inclined theories of environmental degradation. He argues that there is a need to develop a political economy of the environment in order to relate changes in nature to political and ideological struggles.

Development and the environment

Managing the contradictions?

FROM THE PERSPECTIVE of the 1990s it seems extra-ordinary that the environment should have been so neglected by political economists. Who would have imagined, even five years ago, that a United Nations' conference on the *environment* would attempt to set the agenda for *development* into the next century? The United Nations Conference on Environment and Development (UNCED) meeting in Rio de Janeiro in 1992 illustrated more effectively than anything else, the enormous rift that has appeared between **North and South**. ...

In the North the virtual collapse of radical, distributive politics has left a vacuum which will be difficult to fill. Some sociologists, such as Ulrich Beck (1987, 1992) have argued that this marks an important social transition, away from distributional politics and towards the 'risk society'. If we take a closer look at environmental concerns, and politics, in the South as well as the North, it becomes clear how partial and Eurocentric is this position. The failure to grasp the global nature of environmental issues lies at the heart of the problem for radical scholarship. ...

What Humphrey and Buttel (1982) described as 'their collective celebration of Western social institutions' has caused most sociologists to regard 'energy-intensive industrial development [as] the natural end point of a universal process of social evolution and modernization'. If it *is* the end point, then, this paper argues, we are certainly witnessing a crisis, since the inability of international capitalism to regulate the world economy successfully has been eclipsed by its inability to regulate the environmental consequences of this 'development'. ... Reassessments of theory and conceptual adequacy would benefit, in my judgement, from a more systematic attempt to relate environmental change in the North to structural development processes in the South and vice versa. This absence of an international and historical dimension is apparent wherever social scientists meet together to discuss environmental issues. ...

The problem-centred solution: environmental managerialism

... Environmental management makes increasing use of techniques to evaluate the 'environmental' impact of development. The costing of environmental losses over an extended period enables calculation to be made about the weight to be attached to 'non-economic' factors, notably the maintenance of ecological diversity. Similarly, the social impact of environmental change can be assessed, in the case, for example, of resettlement programmes. Legal regulations are another dimension of the socio-economic package which usually forms part of those large-scale development projects which are admitted to have substantial environmental impacts. The emphasis throughout the project cycle is on measurability and quantification.

Environmental Managerialism rests on a set of assumptions, although these assumptions are rarely the subject of explicit discussion. The underlying belief is that there is an optimum balance of natural-resource uses, which can combine sustainability in agriculture and forestry. The object of policy is to determine where this optimum lies and to use the machinery of planning and political persuasion to help bring it about. Environmental conservation is not seen as a binding constraint on development, except in a few designated areas such as 'biosphere reserves'. Normally conservation objectives can be incorporated within the development policy package.

It is also an assumption of this approach that long-term interests in the environment are convergent, however much short-term interests might diverge. In the long term, securing environmental goals is the only guarantee of survival. In the short term the means of resolving short-term interests have to be negotiated. Environmental Managerialism is heavily prescriptive and unanalytical. When the objectives are 'agreed' and evaluation confined to the means at our disposal, there is not much room left for an analysis of conflicting outcomes or the interest of different groups in these outcomes.

The environment and capitalist development

In general little consideration is given to the impact of capitalist development on the environment. The approach which probably can count upon most support – 'Environmental Managerialism' – is concerned with objectives that, until recently, appeared to lie outside the camp of market economics, such as conservation and physical planning.

Similarly no account is taken of the structural linkages which exist between economic development and the environment in the North and the South. Policies such as the disposal of food-grain surpluses from the North (US Public Law 480 in the past; EEC food 'mountains' in the present) radically affect the environment in the South. The penetration of the South by new agricultural production technologies, marketing and contract farming, have also served to shift agriculture in parts of Latin America and Africa away from traditional, environmentally sustainable, systems towards greater specialization and economic dependency. These problems are more acute when so many countries in both continents have enormous external debts, which they are urged to repay by more specialized exports of cash crops, forest products, etc. Changes in the environments of the South need to be understood, then, in terms of the international redivision of labour. These processes carry important implications.

If we consider the historical role of the environment in capitalist development the relationship between the market and environmental management assumes much more importance. It is important to clarify this historical role in order to appreciate the part played by policy and planning responses such as those that figure within Environmental Managerialism, in long-term environmental change. ...

Structurally transformed environments

... Structurally transformed environments are ones in which the primary emphasis in development is the achievement of agricultural growth through the operation of market forces, often supported by state intervention. In some areas stimulus is provided by rapid urban growth, in others by technological breakthroughs of the '**Green Revolution**' type. The development of food production is increasingly linked to transnational corporation and the agribusiness complex based in the developed countries. In many areas the environment is only beginning to be affected by these linkages. Some areas have seen the market recede, leaving a 'vacuum' which either contributes to accelerated migration (north-east Brazil) or which the state attempts to fill for political and other reasons (Yucatan Mexico).

The class structure of structurally transformed environments is formative and social conflicts are often not institutionalized. The divisions that occur within rural areas, and between the rural poor, reflect sectoral considerations ('urban bias') as well as commodity-producing interests. Class interests are frequently mediated through nationalist, tribal or other ethnic identities.

The main feature of change in structurally transformed environments is whether agriculture is developed according to a 'market logic' determined outside the region, or according to some other 'logic' with a basis in the pre-colonial history of the area. It is much more difficult than in 'post-industrial environments' to define the parameters of environmental activity. Rather like women's labour (with which it is closely linked), the 'environment' involves different 'spheres' of activity, some within the household and some outside. The environment includes the production of commodities for exchange and for use. Not all exchanges are market exchanges and not all domestic produc-

tion affecting the environment (food, clothing, shelter, energy) is for the personal consumption of the family. Like women's labour the environment is both valorized and non-valorized in different structural contexts. The impact of the market in one sphere of environmental activity where exchange values prevail (e.g. cash cropping or forestry) has important implications for other spheres where use values predominate (food staples or firewood collection). In this case structurally transformed environments represent the meeting point of two 'spheres': one of which produces commodities from the application of labour to natural resources, while the other (simple reproduction) is concerned with the material and social reproduction of the household unit.

The implications of **sustainable development** for structurally transformed environments will vary considerably. In largely undeveloped areas, even those with fragile ecosystems like the tropical forests, sustainable development implies long-term resource efficiency for a large number of people. Most actual development in such areas involves short-term efficiency for a small number of people. Powerful commercial interests are in a position to exploit the openness of the environment to market pressures. The relatively easy access to new land, which the 'frontier' represents, together with the social fluidity of frontier societies, means that the effort to develop sustainable agriculture is rarely worthwhile. In extreme cases the environment is 'mined' to produce the required resources: timber, minerals or exotic natural species. In general the ethic of private property and the ownership of land come to assume more importance in the process of accumulation. In general, too, the interests in unsustainable production far outweigh those in conservation. This state of affairs is not a historical accident, but the result of powerful social classes acquiring ideological legitimacy from new forms of agricultural production, rather than from environmental sustainability. What we term 'the environment' is transformed in the development process from a situation in which use values predominate, through one in which exchange values assume increasing importance (structurally transformed environments) to a situation where the environment is often an area of 'collective consumption', in the public rather than the private domain (post-industrial). Of course, in most societies this process is not completed in a linear way: few 'small-scale' societies will become 'post-industrial' ones. Nevertheless, as will be argued in the next section, the way we conceive of the environment in one setting is critical for our understanding of others.

Objections to environmental managerialism

... The first objection to Environmental Managerialism is that it considers the environment *after* the 'development' objectives have been set. At best it requires a modification of these objectives to take account of ecological factors. ...

The second objection is to the way that the environmental consequences of development are separated from the social and economic ones within the Managerialist approach. Extending protection to geographical areas on ecological grounds (meeting the first and second objectives of the World Conservation Strategy 1980) is perfectly valid. Nevertheless, ecological objectives usually imply social ones. ...

The third main objection to Environmental Managerialism is that it takes as a 'given' the distributive consequences which the market produces in the course of development. Development aid offered on a bilateral basis tends often to accelerate environmental degradation in the immediate vicinity of the urban and rural poor. If environmental factors are to be given real weight in the development process then the distributive effects of development policy need to be recognized, and environmental management needs to assume redistributive functions. ...

Finally, the techniques which form part of the Environmental Managerialist package deflect attention away from the context of environmental degradation. ...

Elements in an alternative theoretical project

... We are now in a position to relate the theoretical concern with the environment to the historical/comparative framework of capitalist development. First, it is clear that the transformation of the environment under capitalism – the 'production of Nature' (Smith, 1984) – has contradictory effects. On the one hand it allows people to regulate the production of use values to meet human needs. With the development of the market, exchange values assume more importance, and benefits can be derived from the specialized production of commodities.

At the same time as societies become freer from the constraints of Nature, social control assumes more importance. Ultimately class society is created out of the differentiation of the productive process and the accompanying social differentiation. Production under capitalism produces a liberation from Nature and a transformation of the environment. Nevertheless, as labour is employed in the transformation of the environment the problem is presented of how to *sustain* development. That is, how to provide commodity production for the market and a renewal of the natural-resource base. In this case the difficulty in achieving 'sustainability' presents itself as one of the contradictions of capitalist development.

Most analysis of the development of capitalism in the productive sphere has concentrated on the use that is made of Nature. Development theory, beginning with Rosa Luxemburg (1951), has usually considered the breakdown of 'natural economy' as linked to the production of exchange values, for distant markets. Subsequently we have learnt that primitive accumulation did not disappear from underdeveloped countries, indeed it has continued to be important as a means of guaranteeing the existence of non-capitalist production within social formations dominated by capitalism.

It is increasingly clear that we need to push our analysis beyond the sphere of production alone. In considering the environment within a historical dimension we also need to consider the way that nature is transformed. This is particularly true in what I have termed structurally transformed environments. Here we can distinguish between sustainable development and the progressive depletion of resources, as reflected in the loss of soil fertility to which Marx referred in the celebrated paragraph from *Capital* (Marx, 1867). These processes, moreover, take place in a social and historical context which provides them with meaning. Hence the 'consciousness' of the environment under conditions of resource degradation is different from situations where sustainable options exist and are practised.

We can ask several questions of this process: what kinds of 'consciousness' accompany changes in the relationship between people and Nature, not simply over time (Pepper, 1984) but also within a spatial dimension? Are they determined largely by *the use* to which Nature is put or *the way* that Nature is transformed? The answers to these questions are important precisely because they will help us to understand the political conditions governing environmental interventions. The perceptions that are held of the environment by different classes and interests and the channels that exist for articulating these interests, are a necessary part of any alternative to Environmental Managerialism, as Blaikie (1984) demonstrates.

References

Beck, U. (1987) 'The anthropological shock: Chernobyl and the contours of the risk society', *Berkeley Journal of Sociology, 32*.

Beck, U. (1992) 'How modern is modern society?', *Theory, Culture and Society, 9*.

Blaikie, P. (1984) *The Political Economy of Soil Erosion in Developing Countries*, London: Longman.

Humphrey, C. R. and Buttel, F. (1982) *Environment, Energy and Society*, Basingstoke: Macmillan.

Luxemburg, R. (1951) *The Accumulation of Capital*, London: RKP.

Marx, K. (1867) *Capital*, vol. 1, Moscow: Foreign Languages Publishing House.

Pepper, D. (1984) *The Roots of Modern Environmentalism*, London: Croom Helm.

Smith, N (1984) *Uneven Development: Nature, capital and the production of space*, Oxford: Blackwell.

Key terms

The following key terms appear in the text above. They have been defined below to aid with the reading of this item.

North and South the advanced industrial nations (North) and the less developed nations (South)

Green Revolution the implementation of reforms in agriculture in developing countries, involving higher yielding varieties of crops. It was sometimes subject to criticisms that it reinforced the power of big farmers over small ones

sustainable development the idea of development that does not harm the environment and is compatible with sustaining environmental diversity. A debate surrounds exactly what this means and entails

Questions

1 What does the author feel would benefit theories and conceptual adequacy, in relation to debates about the environment?

2 Explain in your own words the meaning of the term 'environmental management'.

3 Suggest ways in which environmental management can become a form of social control.

4 To what extent do you agree with the argument that conservation requires a brake on market forces?

5 Assess the arguments for and against the proposition that 'interests in unsustainable production far outweigh those in conservation'.

Reading 13.6 **The end of the Third World**

Nigel Harris (from) *The End of the Third World* (1986) Harmondsworth: Penguin, pp. 187–8 and 191–202.

Editorial comments

Nigel Harris argues that one of the elements of the Third World as a political movement was the belief that it was possible to achieve reforms through the economic action of the national government. He argues, however that in recent years the growth of the international world economy has undermined this path and, as such, has led to the end of the Third World route to development and the end of Third Worldism as a political strategy.

The end of national reformism

THE HISTORY OF capitalism – like that of its unlovely child, nationalism – is one of geographical spread, the slow **colonization** of the globe by the market. From Lancashire, we might say with some licence, to England and north-western Europe, from North America to Latin America, south and then east Asia, from south-east Asia to Africa. In the 1950s, the same process continued, now transforming itself where it had already arrived. The commodity composition of the flows of trade between the different geographical components of the system were transformed – the patterns of skills and productivity, networks of interdependence and collaboration, physical distributions, urbanization, income distribution and social structure, all were remarkably changed. But in terms of the brute undifferentiated capacity to produce, colonization continued. From the old exchanges of raw materials for manufactured goods between the less and more developed countries, the pattern changed: the more developed countries now produced a growing volume of raw materials and agricultural goods, highly sophisticated manufactured goods, and a vast array of advanced services, while the less developed exported a growing volume of manufactured goods and some raw materials.

Nationalism was one of the main exports of the new capitalism of Western Europe. To protect a people against the depredations of the market and conquest by European states required the creation of a state, with a centralized and disciplined body of armed men capable both of warding off outsiders and dragooning the population to the tasks of accumulation. The Americas struck out first to defend themselves against the European empires, then East Europe. In the postwar period, Asia and then Africa followed suit, until all the world had acquired the machinery of local defence and work discipline, as well as the decorative forms of independent states. Up until the Second World War, it had seemed that this was progress, and that the creation of the democratic republic provided the cradle for the infant of free enterprise – the one must entail the other. ...

Governments are fully aware of the limits upon their capacity to intervene. But they also recognize that the ideological basis of their power implies that they must intervene to protect and enhance the position of their inhabitants, and that it is the tradition of every country to blame foreigners for whatever domestic misfortunes occur. **Protectionism** is cheap for the government – for it is the buyers of formerly imported goods who pay. So it is easy to understand that, no matter how disastrous long-term import controls may be economically, in political terms they are a cheap method of seeking votes. ...

The central problem of the world economy today is the phase of slump and stagnation, not change; change is part of the intrinsic nature of the system in boom or slump, and has been since its inception. It is always easier to see the negative effects of such change, even though historically it is the benefits which have loomed larger. Thus, for example, since 1880 two thirds of the jobs in more developed countries have been lost, but during the same period total employment has increased three times over. In European agriculture, 90 per cent of the jobs have been lost over the past century as the result of mechanization – the proportion of the labour force engaged in agriculture has fallen from about 50 to between 4 and 5 per cent – yet total employment as well as agricultural output have continued to expand. If slump and stagnation could be overcome, there is no reason to believe that employment would decrease whether from relocation of capacity or as a result of technical innovation. Of course, what is true for the labour force as a whole is not true for individual workers – a redundant fifty-year-old coal-miner cannot get new employment as a computer programmer. But if increased output is the result of rationalization, resources will be available to ensure the former miner need suffer no hardship. That, rather than defending an increasingly obsolete structure of employment, is the heart of the problem.

Is the growth of output in the newly industrializing countries a temporary phenomenon? The change in the structure of the world economy, integrating the activity of the more developed countries, is the source of the growth of output of the newly industrializing countries. ...

Because the process is now part of the structure, it no longer depends on those countries that are currently newly industrializing. Of course, there is a strong presumption that, once started, countries continue on the same path, changing and upgrading output as industrialization deepens (and other newer competitors take over the lower-value lines of output). But this is not necessarily so – the front-runners can fall back, become trapped in one particular specialization and stagnate there. Nor would this necessarily be the fault of the government, for the possibilities of public initiative grow weaker as the process continues. And indeed, the market can be ingenious in overcoming the obstacles put in the way of the process by the interests of government – as happened in South Korea in 1979 and 1980, when the ambitions of General Park were defeated. Despite the alarms of the early eighties, the threats from purely economic or financial sources to the newly industrializing countries did not seem unmanageable. Mexico's debts loomed dangerously large in 1985, and Singapore's growth sank to zero; no doubt others would also face turbulence. But despite vulnerabilities and dangers, general dispersal continued. Only sudden shock seemed dangerous, but that could affect a more developed country just as much as a newly industrializing one; for example, the bankrupting of a major company could begin to unravel the nets of finance uniting Wall Street and the European bourses. That was not a special feature of the redistribution of manufacturing.

The medium-term threat to the possibility of continued growth in the individual newly industrializing countries (as opposed to general geographical dispersal) came not so much from crises generated in the financial or trading system as from politics. ... In some of the newly industrializing states, the class struggle posed the main threat to the ambitions of the local ruling order. ... In reality, the dazzlingly high rates of growth of output, year in and out, were not achieved by magic, nor by governments, nor by management; they required the muscle, brain and discipline and the unremitting toil of millions of collaborating workers. This is the character omitted from the drama, the character required to create the output, but in conditions of political and social passivity, not to say apathy. The 'flexibilities' and 'structural adjustments' that sound so comfortingly remote from people, so sterile of moral content, are in fact attributes of workforces. The 'adjustments' are imposed in countries where one of the most massive and continuing sources of subsidy to the growth of capital derives from a failure to pay the full costs of the process, as seen in the workers' conditions of housing and nutrition, water and drainage, in pollution, in the exhaustion of labour, in all the casual savageries of police regimes.

The newly industrializing countries are unstable precisely because of the disciplines and sacrifices which the frenetic pace of growth has imposed upon the workforce. The condition of maintaining what stability there is now requires the continuation of high rates of growth. At each check to growth, there is some sense of foreboding in the ruling order that it could produce an explosion of popular rage. ...

The transition to a modern economy is not simply measured by the composition of the output or the skills of the workers. The mechanisms required to enforce involuntary sacrifices at a primitive phase of the growth of capital inhibit, if they do not make impossible, accumulation in a more sophisticated phase. The first can be planned by the state in detail; it is measured in crude, undifferentiated output – of coal, iron ore and steel, fertilizers. Here the state can overshadow all. Import-substitution industrialization often fits such a phase, and it does not require the conscious participation of most of the labour force. A regime whose main instrument to enforce conformity is terror for the majority and bribes for the few can keep up an impressive rate of growth of crude output regardless of what the workforce thinks – as was done in Britain in the nineteenth century, or Russia in the 1930s and 1940s (and sporadically thereafter). The cost is very high, but it can be done. However, the more variegated the output becomes, and the more intensive the skill and technology required, dependent upon continuous technical innovation and the creative participation of the workers, then the more the operation of the economy requires the deliberate, conscious and rational participation of millions of people, with their psychological involvement and responsibility. No planning system can substitute for this, and the imposition of a single centre of authority turns the system into chaos. Thus, the pursuit of growth itself forces a different kind of 'liberalization' from the one we have hitherto considered. How to make the transition from the old to the new system of production is a problem perpetually besetting Eastern Europe and Russia, for there the old system created the dominant institutions and they will not now simply allow themselves to be adjusted away. ...

Hitherto, it has been the aim of the governments of the newly industrializing countries to do all in their power to frustrate the growth of the most modest forms of worker involvement embodied in independent organization and bargaining, the first steps in the incorporation of workers in the conscious direction of the process of production. Worker involvement is seen simply as praising the government, waving flags when Ministers tour factories, a walk-on stage army to ratify the fantasies of the rulers. Yet, independent trade unions are vital for the operation of advanced economies. Everywhere in the newly industrializing countries they are banned or neutralized, from the tame CGT of Mexico and the yellow unions of Brazil (although both Mexico and Brazil also have some independent unions) to the government-controlled NTUC in Singapore and the explicit legal prohibition on the intervention of 'third parties' (that is, national trade unions) in South Korean industrial disputes. Thus, governments seek to prevent the development of just those forms of organization demanded by the operation of mature capitalism. ...

Such regimes make for fewer labour disputes, for the illusion of national unanimity is based upon the enforced silence of the majority, but they pose severe obstacles to moving on to a modern economy. They also mean that when disputes occur, they prove more intractable and violent, more swift to move on to political opposition. The 1975 dispute at Hyundai's Ulsan shipyards swiftly changed to riots; the 1980 miners' dispute led to the seizure of the town of Sabuk; the disputes in Gwang-ju led to the seizure of the province. Terrorizing the workforce so as to maintain very low wages and long hours has declining returns with a maturing economy. Liberalizing imports will not touch this problem, nor will political liberalization which stops at the gates of the factory. In fact, the emerging forces of the economy oblige employers to defeat the law if production is to proceed – as South African employers have for long been obliged to evade the apartheid provisions so that they can employ skilled black workers or negotiate with *de facto* associations of black workers. There are reports that foreign employers in Taiwan have already reached national agreements with illegal proto-unions as the only means available of easing the supply of skilled labour and standardizing incentives.

Without a relaxation of the repressive conditions governing labour and society at large, it will prove increasingly difficult to make the transition to a modern economy. The growth of capital will be punctuated by explosions of the frustrated fury of the workers, simultaneously called upon to play an increasingly responsible role but denied the legal means to do so. The selfsame problem afflicts many countries, including the Eastern European countries and South Africa. If only one of these explosions were to spill over into revolution, it would completely change the terms of reference of the argument concerning repression.

A comparable point concerns the problems thrown up by the process of the geographical dispersal of manufacturing capacity from the more developed countries. For although this is not the cause of unemployment, it is the source of a radical reduction in the power of organized labour to limit the depredations of capital. The mobility of capital means that it can escape from a national context which appears unfavourable (whether that is the result of an unsympathetic government or of strongly organized trade unions). An integrated system of manufacturing also creates a single global labour market, moving towards one price for labour in each skill grade regardless of whether the countries are more or less developed (of course, restrictions on the movement of labour inhibit this process of generalization, but only to a limited degree). This implies that groups of workers in different countries compete with each other for employment, offering employers the lowest price at a given level of labour productivity. The power of trade unions to influence this bargain without the support of the state is limited in a national context; in the international, it hardly exists for most occupations. ...

Although capital can go international, this is much more difficult for labour. It took many decades to create national trade-union structures with some power to curb competition between workers, and that was almost invariably achieved with some political assistance from the state in its own interest. Without a state and on an international plane, the task becomes daunting. Yet without measures to curb competition, the power of employers is enormously increased. They can play off groups of workers in many different countries against each other; they can organize an auction in which the lowest paid – at a given level of productivity – win, and do so in secrecy, since the competing workers have no way of knowing what the other bids are. The penalty for those who fail to work for the lowest world price of labour is unemployment. It is here that the fears in the more developed countries are most justified. After more than a century and a half in the long, slow struggle to establish order in the national labour markets, suddenly it seems world capital can escape and, furthermore, can force the reversal of all those gains. Capital has stolen a march, and labour is still far from understanding the implications of that, let alone beginning to create the appropriate institutions to counter it.

The Third World is disappearing. Not the countries themselves, nor the inhabitants, much less the poor who so powerfully coloured the original definition of the concept, but the argument. Third Worldism began as a critique of an unequal world, a programme for economic development and justice, a type of national reformism dedicated to the creation of new societies and a new world. It ends with its leading protagonists either dead, defeated or satisfied to settle simply for national power rather than international equality; the rhetoric remains, now toothless, the decoration for squabbles over the pricing of commodities or flows of capital.

The conception of an interdependent, interacting, global manufacturing system cuts across the old view of a world consisting of nation-states as well as one of groups of countries, more and less developed and centrally planned – the First, the Third and the Second Worlds. Those notions bore some relationship to an older economy, one marked by the exchange of raw materials for manufactured goods. But the new world that has superseded it is far more complex and does not lend itself to the simple identification of First and Third, haves and have-nots, rich and poor, industrialized and non-industrialized.

Yet the world order is still dominated by the culture, politics and ideology of the old pattern, a world of national egotisms where states determine what is important. Indeed, the global manufacturing system can only be identified through the prism of national shares of output; the interests of states take priority over understanding the technical geography of production. The concepts of nationalism thus organize our perception and our consciousness, and so predetermine our view of what is reality. It will be a long time before the identification of the world catches up with the reality.

The simple dichotomies of the past, First and Third World, imposed their own gross distortion. Poor and rich were never properly defined by different countries. Even the so-called poorest country has its clutch of millionaires living in the same lifestyle as their peers in the richest country. Each so-called rich country has, trapped in the cruel interstices of its economy, thousands of hungry and poor. The division between rich and poor is represented in each microcosm of the system; poverty at the global level was never a territorial concept. The 'geopoliticalization' of inequality illuminated in the first instance, but finally obfuscated. The poor of the United States were defined out of existence. The rich of India were carefully concealed from view. ...

Capitalism remained the same. The market remained the market. Only for a short time did it seem that the state had conquered the economy – to guarantee full employment in one part of the world, to force perpetual growth in the other. The period was long enough to soak into popular consciousness and the social sciences on both left and right. Conscious reform by the state, it was supposed, now replaced the blind transformations of the market. It was a half hint of socialism, a human order determined by need, but without the precondition – power in the hands of the majority. In place of popular democratic control of the means of production, much of the Third World offered old-fashioned dictatorship, the one-party state or the revolutionary military junta. The majority could not be trusted to exercise power.

National reformist aspiration grew weak as the new orders settled more comfortably into power. The old issues became less urgent. But, also, the needs of accumulation limited the potential for social reform. Furthermore, an increasingly integrated world system lays down narrower and narrower limits to the possibility of local eccentricity, including reform. In a competitive system, holding down the price of labour takes precedence over protecting it, and the domestic economy becomes increasingly a spin-off of a wider order. Such a prospect causes understandable alarm. If the state cannot control domestic affairs, regulate and order the growth of incomes and employment, and propel self-sufficient economic growth, all, it seems, becomes dangerously random.

Key terms

The following key terms appear in the text above. They have been defined below to aid with the reading of this item.

colonialization the process whereby advanced capitalist nations took control – often by force – of less developed countries and integrated them into their economies

protectionism policies designed to protect the domestic economy, largely through curbs on imports. Protectionism is associated with the United States for several periods of its history

Questions

1 Why does the author feel there are limits to the growth that can be achieved with 'terror for the majority and bribes for the few'?

2 Using information from the extract and elsewhere, discuss the changing fortunes of the Newly Industrializing Countries such as South Korea?

3 How far do you agree with the argument that the increasing mobility of capital and the fall in the power of the state lead to the power of employers becoming enormously enhanced.

4 To what extent do you agree with the authors argument that the main threat to the stability of the Newly Industrializing Countries comes from the threat of social and political revolt?

Reading 13.7 **The IMF, structural adjustment and food riots**

J. Walton and D. Seddon (from) *Free Markets and Food Riots* (1994) Oxford: Blackwell, pp. 5–7 and 10–22.

Editorial comments

The authors have studied the effect of the structural adjustment policies advocated by the International Monetary Fund (IMF) and argue that these policies have led to a growing political response, in the form of food riots – which they see as a distinctive new urban-based social movement. In this reading they consider the roots of the adoption of free-market adjustment policies, before looking at some examples of the protests which have arisen in their wake.

Global adjustment

THE ROOTS OF the current crisis lie back in the 1960s, when the industrial capitalist economies began to experience a profits squeeze reflecting a crisis of overaccumulation. Measures adopted by Western governments to help resolve the crisis included austerity measures directed primarily at reducing real wages, particularly in the public sector. According to this analysis, it was the induced recession and austerity measures of the mid-1960s, designed to restructure and rationalize working processes, which established the conditions for the subsequent crisis. The austerity measures introduced as part of the process of restructuring provoked unprecedented popular protest and a wave of strikes swept across Europe between 1968 and 1970, resulting in a rapid increase in money wages. Broadly similar developments took place in North America around the same time. The clampdown which followed was associated with a 'mini-recession' in 1970–1 and succeeded by a 'mini-boom' in 1972–3, which proved to be the final phase of the long postwar boom.

The mini-boom effectively marked the end of the an era. The US dollar devaluation of 1971, the 'oil crisis' of winter 1973–4 and an international 'crash' in the summer of 1974 brought the golden years to an abrupt and painful halt. ...

The distinctive character of the last two decades is associated with the increasing integration of capitalism on a world scale, its 'inter-nationalization'.

This has ensured that a crisis of capitalism is, increasingly, and unavoidably, a crisis on a world scale, even if that crisis is experienced unevenly and differently at different moments and in different places. For Gill and Law,

the global political economy has reached an unprecedented stage of development. The present is not like the past. Today, the security, trade, money, direct investment, communications, and cultural dimensions of global interdependence, are such that there is now an integrated global political economy, whereas in the past, there was a less

complex international political economy (and before 1500 a series of regional political economies).
(Gill and Law, 1988)

One of the major consequences of this deepening integration is a greater 'synchronicity' or 'simultaneity' of events in different parts of the world and in different countries. Evidence suggests that, from the late 1960s onwards, the advanced capitalist countries of the West in particular have become both more closely integrated and mutually interdependent. Consequently, they demonstrate, in recession and in recovery, an increasingly high degree of synchronicity in economic rhythms relative to earlier periods; only Japan stands somewhat apart. By the early 1980s the same was becoming more generally the case for the developing world as a whole, although the unevenness of capitalist development in the Third World and the continuing survival of state socialism in the Second World until the late 1980s ensured that global synchronicity was still not achieved at the beginning of the 1990s. Increasingly, however, the success booms and recessions of the advanced capitalist West have been 'passed on' to the rest of the world in a variety of ways and a consequence a major process of restructuring on a world scale has taken place. ...

The end of the Third World

Towards the end of the 1960s, as the developed capitalist economies began to move into crisis the developing countries as a whole appeared to experience a period of growth. International capital and commodity markets continued to boom and, as the **World Bank** noted in 1987,

> some developing countries liberalized their trade regimes in the mid-1960s, became exporters of manufacturers, and gained directly from the expansion in world trade. Most of the others benefited from rising demand for raw materials and foods. So, in one way or another, the developing countries that participated in the expansion of world trade experienced high output growth.
> *(World Bank 1987)*

In the early 1970s, accumulation in the developing countries as a whole was close to the 5.7 per cent rate achieved in the advanced capitalist countries; by the end of the 1970s it was running at about twice the 4 per cent a year of the advanced capitalist countries. While real GDP growth in the advanced capitalist countries was 4.7 per cent in the period 1965–73, it slumped to 2.8 per cent between 1973 and 1980; in the same period the developing countries as a whole recorded GDP growth rates of 6.5 per cent and 5.4 per cent (Mosley, Harrigan and Toye, 1991). The share of world capitalist investment in developing countries went from 16.5 per cent in 1973 to 23.25 in 1979.

It was on the basis of such data that some argued against what they termed 'The Illusion of Underdevelopment' (Warren, 1980) and for the progressive development of the Third World during the 1960s and 1970s; and indeed, significant rates of growth were recorded mainly by a select group of newly industrializing countries whose performance was taken by 'the optimists' as indicative of a general process of development and by 'the pessimists' as challenge to the supremacy of the developed world. The NICs and the OPEC countries together certainly experienced a very considerable growth; and discussions of a new international division of labour surfaced in the mid-1970s together with a call for a New International Economic Order (NIEO), at a time when the action of OPEC appeared to hold out the prospect for a real challenge from the developing countries to the prevailing dominance of the developed countries.

But for most developing countries, the 1970s were more difficult than the 1960s. It rapidly became clear during the second part of the 1970s that, not only were the developed countries becoming less prepared than ever to open themselves to a new international order as signs of recession began to increase, but the increase in oil prices achieved by the OPEC countries had generally adverse effects on the majority of non-oil-exporting developing countries. For many developing countries, particularly those strongly committed to a 'nationalist' development strategy built around import substitution, foreign exchange was a major constraint; commodity prices held up in the wake of the first oil-price increase and many developing capitalist countries began to borrow heavily (OPEC surpluses channeled through Western banks). This created the conditions for what was to emerge rapidly as 'the debt crisis', to which the response of the international financial institutions was 'stabilization' and 'adjustment'. For a time the high import demand of these countries provided much needed markets for Western commodities. But by the end of the decade this was no longer the case. While the OPEC producers and NICs surged ahead during the latter part of the 1970s, most other developing countries began to experience growing indebtedness, declining terms of trade and increased balance-of-payments problems.

This resulted in increasing differentiation within 'the Third World' and the beginning of 'the end of the Third World' (Harris, 1986): different regimes of capital accumulation and different state forms, following different policies and different trajectories. Generally, those countries experiencing strong economic growth were better able to provide the conditions under which 'vulnerable' social groups could survive and defend their living standards; those whose economic crisis only deepened during the 1980s experienced the full severity of adjustment.

If, even in the 1970s and 1980s, the developing countries as a whole performed well, in terms of various economic-performance indicators, in comparison with the industrial capitalist West, there was considerable variation within 'the Third World'. East Asia and South Asia showed the highest rates of real GDP growth, growth in exports and growth in domestic investment. The poorest performance was that of sub-Saharan Africa, with Latin America and the Caribbean, North Africa, and the Middle East little better. If growth of real per capita GDP is taken as an indicator of economic performance, it is easy to see the difference between the Asian region – particularly East Asia – and the others (see table 1).

But, increasingly through the period under consideration, it was the size and 'burden' of its foreign debt that came to characterize the severity of the crisis for any developing economy. The deepening recession in the West and the effects of increasing oil prices on the economies of oil-importing countries in Africa, Asia, and Latin America began to have their impact, and loans for development turned increasingly into debts. In the 1970s, the global economic crisis was characterized particularly by a financial crisis, with growing international financial instability and international debt. Indeed, one key aspect of the global crisis with which this book will be particularly concerned is that of the so-called 'debt crisis', which developed rapidly during the second part of the 1970s and surfaced in an acute form at the beginning of the 1980s.

It was in large part in response to the growing balance-of-payments problems experienced by an increasing number of countries, that the **International Monetary Fund** began to intervene more systematically in the fiscal policy of developing countries in particular with loans conditional on various 'stabilization' measures during the late 1970s. The perceived need to take these measures still further and to 'adjust' macro-economic policy as a whole to meet the 'new' circumstances of a world in recession led to the introduction (by the **IMF** in collaboration with the World Bank) at the beginning of the various programmes of 'stabilization' and '**structural adjustment**' that came increasingly to characterize the decade.

The debt crisis and structural adjustment

Already by the mid-1960s the burden of debt carried by the developing countries was considerable and the debt-servicing requirements worrying. According to the Pearson Commission (Pearson, 1969) by the mid-1960s debt service was eating up 87 per cent of new lending to Latin America and 73 per cent of new lending to Africa. *Business Latin America* reported in 1968 that the average debt–service ratio for Latin America was at least 14 per cent in 1966, while the Inter-American Development Bank estimated 20 per cent. But though the governments of Latin American countries were criticized by bankers as 'deadbeats' who 'year after year have had to come back to Washington for bail-out loans and foreign "stretch-outs"', the bankers were evidently prepared to consider lending money to these 'deadbeats' with debt crises. In the period between 1955 and 1970, 7 developing countries – all regarded as countries with considerable economic development potential (Argentina, Brazil, Chile, Ghana, Indonesia, Peru, and Turkey) – were involved in 17 debt reschedulings. There were also some debt reschedulings for low-income countries, including India, but these were designed to provide additional finance when official lenders could not increase new lending. The private bankers did not fear rescheduling, as long as they could continue to collect market rates of interest; indeed, the first reschedulings of bank debt in the late 1970s and early 1980s made these loans even more profitable. Also, it is clear that, in the case of default, the banks confidently expected a government rescue.

Thus, even before 1973 and the first dramatic increase in oil prices, many developing countries had heavy debts and had experienced specific debt 'crises'. But the commodity price boom of the 1970s and the reassurance that ultimately there would be no 'bad debts' among the governments of develop-

Table 1 Regional patterns of growth, 1965–2000

Region	Growth of real per capita GDP (per cent)			
	1965–73	*1973–80*	*1980–9*	*1989–2000*
Sub-Saharan Africa	3.2	0.1	−2.2	0.5
Latin America and Caribbean	3.7	2.6	−0.6	2.3
Middle East and Mediterranean	5.5	2.1	0.8	2.1
Eastern Europe	4.8	5.3	0.8	1.5
South Asia	1.2	1.7	3.2	3.2
East Asia	5.1	4.7	6.7	5.1

Source: World Bank, 1990

ing countries encouraged Western banks to increase their lending. Indeed the most eager lending was to oil-exporting countries with large populations and sizeable markets (e.g. Venezuela, Nigeria, Indonesia, Mexico).

Between 1973 and the early 1980s the principal source of external finance had become the private commercial banks offering non-concessional loans. But the international agencies appeared to speak for all when they argued (as did MacNamara in his 1977 Presidential Address) that the large growth in private commercial lending to developing countries did not make a debt crisis inevitable, and that it could be staved off by appropriate corrective actions. In 1977, the Bank was 'even more confident today than ... a year ago that the debt problem is indeed manageable' (cited in Mosley, Harrigan and Toye, 1991). Indeed, throughout the 1970s the Bank had not been much concerned about adjustment and did not oppose large-scale commercial borrowing to maintain high economic-growth rates. In fact it saw high growth as the guarantee of the continuing credit-worthiness of developing countries and it had repeatedly soothed fears about the sustainability of the recycling operation. It was not until after the second 'oil shock' in 1979–80 that the Bank publicly revived 'questions about the International financial system's ability to recycle enough funds ... to maintain import levels and economic growth rates'. ...

The growing debt crisis surfaced visibly and unavoidably in 1982 when Mexico threatened default. Certainly borrowing continued, with the middle-income economies as a whole increasing their debt/GNP ratios from 36.1 in 1980 to 46.1 in 1989 (with the lower middle-income economies rising from 37.7 to 67.7) and low-income countries other than China and India increasing their indebtedness (in terms of debt/GNP) from 27.0 in 1980 to 71.0 in 1989. But much of this borrowing was now conditional on adopting IMF and World Bank approved stabilization and structural adjustment programmes. The debt crisis, however, had a number of different dimensions. For the Western bankers and the international financial system as a whole, it was the big debtors that appeared most threatening and for whom specific 'rescue packages' were devised; but within the developing world, it was often those with smaller debts but a higher debt ratio that appeared in deepest difficulties.

For once the debt crisis surfaced in 1982, private lending dried up overnight for all developing countries that were already highly indebted; and by 1986, private lending had fallen back to a third of its 1980 level. The banks had expected the US and other governments, and the IMF, to bail them out; and indeed the IMF and the World Bank did devote billions

of dollars to rescue packages, while the Bank for International Settlements and the United States provided some 'bridge' financing; but it became rapidly apparent that the banks would effectively have to bail themselves out. ...

Adjustment was presented as the key to debt management. Between 1980 and 1986, a total of 37 SALs [structural adjustment loans] were negotiated: activity built up slowly in the first three years of operation, reached its height in 1983 and fell away rapidly between 1984 and 1986. What was stressed initially was that the SAL was a response to a once-and-for-all, exceptional crisis in the balance of payments, albeit one that would require assistance over a longer period than that for which IMF Stand-By finance was available. Such assistance was to be confined to countries both willing and able to make progress on policy reform.

By 1983, however, SALs were increasingly defended as a means of persuading more governments to *change* their economic policies – these being given a greater prominence than external factors as causes of poor performance: 'the past dozen years have underlined ... the crucial role of domestic policies in determining the performance of developing countries – particularly in the use they make of foreign finance' (World Bank, 1985). Reforms were increasingly sought in areas (e.g. institutional arrangements) which, even if successful, would have little immediate impact on the balance of payments. Instead of providing balance-of-payments assistance to countries willing to undertake structural adjustments, the Bank increasingly saw itself as using SAL funds to facilitate the countries' decision to adopt a broad programme of economic reform. **Conditionality** was now imposed less to maximize the probability of repayment of the loan than to enable the borrower to remove what the lender sees as fundamental policy-induced obstacles to economic recovery and growth. Conditionality on the part of the Bank, as opposed to that applied by the IMF was applied across a wide range of policy areas: a high percentage of SALs included conditions relating to 19 typical policy measures, while the average SAL had conditions in 10 of these 19 areas. A particular SAL could have as many as 100 separate policy conditions (the second SAL for Thailand boasted over 100 conditions). Only by responding rapidly and rigorously implementing these policies of 'adjustment', it was suggested, could developing countries receiving SALs expect to make the necessary 'transition' and achieve the conditions required for renewed growth and a resolution of their debt crisis.

Co-ordination between the IMF and the World Bank became a matter of increasing concern through the 1980s. In early 1989, two important innovations were introduced designed to improve IMF – World Bank co-ordination: the Policy Framework Paper (PFP) and the New Concordat. The PFP is a document drafted by the IMF, and amended and agreed by the Bank and the borrowing government, which sets out a joint understanding of the economic situation of the borrowing country and the policies necessary for 'successful stabilization and adjustment'. Furthermore, cross-conditionality between the Bank and the Fund, although formally it does not occur, in practice has now become reality. This arises because Bank adjustment lending normally requires an IMF stabilization loan to be in place; and if the conditions of both loans are then coordinated through a PFP – and if bilateral donors, and other multilateral donors like the European Development Fund, then follow suit by making their aid subject to the conditionality of the Fund and the Bank being observed (as has increasingly been the case during the 1980s) – then the borrower's freedom of action becomes extremely limited. Furthermore, as some commentators have remarked, 'since the Bank from 1986 has begun to speak publicly of the political aspect of structural adjustment lending, and has acknowledged its efforts to build up internal coalitions in borrowing countries in support of its policies, it is perfectly clear that the tightening of cross-conditionality has direct political implications for the countries concerned' (Mosley, Harrigan and Toye, 1991), not only restricting the room for manoeuvre for governments but giving explicit support to those within the country whose interests coincide with those of the IMF and the Bank.

Social crisis and popular unrest

Studies which showed a tendency for poverty in developing countries to worsen under adjustment were circulating within the UN 'family' of organizations from 1983. However, it was not until the mid-1980s, when the social costs of the recession and of adjustment measures were becoming undeniable, that UN agencies like UNICEF and the International Labour Office (ILO) openly argued for 'adjustment with a human face'. ... In practice, by the end of the 1980s, despite considerable discussion of adjustment with a human face and a more explicit concern with poverty alleviation (see the World Bank's *World Development Report, 1990*, which is focused on 'poverty'), relatively few examples of effective mitigation of the social costs of adjustment by combined government and agency action could be identified.

Whatever the stated concern of the Bank with compensatory programs and poverty alleviation towards the end of the 1980s and into the early 1990s, the general argument of the Bank has consistently been that early and rigorous implementation of structural adjustment effectively reduces the social costs of adjustment and ensures better economic recovery. This is, in effect, an argument for adjustment without a human face insofar as it implies greater benefits to a 'short, sharp shock' in the long run than to a gradual and more cautious approach.

In fact, in many developing countries today the combination of the recession and specific adjustment and austerity measures has been devastating. Rapid social change has been a feature of the past half-century, to be sure, and the process of class formation and transformation, the rural exodus and the growth of urban areas, has generated enormous social changes. But social change in times of prosperity generates less effective tension than change under duress in conditions of economic stringency and austerity.

By the 1980s, as the world recession turned into a global slump, the process of restructuring which accompanied the crisis and aimed to restore the basis for capital accumulation in the industrial capitalist countries increasingly affected the rest of the world. In parts of the Third World this restructuring has been accompanied by a continuing economic crisis – notably in sub-Saharan Africa, North Africa and the Middle East, and Latin America; elsewhere – notably in East Asia – relatively high rates of growth have helped overcome or postpone economic problems. ...

One effect of greater integration and synchronicity within the world economy is a greater degree of simultaneity and similarity in what might broadly be referred to as 'class struggles' around the process of capital accumulation and around government measures to resolve crises in that process and to promote renewed accumulation. It becomes less surprising then that a 'wave' of popular protest accompanies the process of structural adjustment and government austerity measures as it takes place across the developing world (and even the developed world) during the last two decades.

For the contemporary global crisis of capitalism is not only a financial-economic, but also a political-economic crisis; it is also (although this is less considered by the economists who dominate the debates on 'the world in transition') a social and cultural crisis. In the last 20 years, the world has been turned 'upside down' and a process of fundamental restructuring of social relations, ideas, and values has taken place. Increasingly, since the late 1970s, economic reforms and restructuring have been accompanied, in the West, South and East, by far-reaching changes in the nature of the state and in the definition of state – civil society relations – the very nature of politics and the significance of 'democracy' has been subject to redefinition. Rapid changes in the structure of social relations, taking place particularly at a time when the relationship between the state and civil society is undergoing fundamental restructuring and reconsideration, have given rise to new social divisions and solidarities and to new forms of identity and morality. New certainties (fundamentalisms of various kinds) have emerged just as old certainties or faiths have crumbled.

Not only economic and political structures but the very relationship between state and society have been substantially redefined as new forms of integration and disintegration have developed to lay the foundations for the world of the 1990s and beyond. Popular protest is an integral part of that process. This is not to say that the world of the 1990s and beyond will be entirely different from that of the 'post-war period', but it will be qualitatively different, not least in the degree of economic integration which will ensure that developments taking place within states will be increasingly conditioned by global forces. At the same time, resistance to certain aspects of those developments will continue to be associated with various forms of open struggle and protest.

In our view, then, it is the crisis and process of reconstruction of global capitalism that began in the late 1960s and early 1970s that has generated the economic policies of liberalization and austerity that have themselves given rise to the upsurge of popular unrest across the developing world.

References

Gill, S. and Law, D. (1988) *The Global Political Economy*, London: Harvester Wheatsheaf.

Harris, N. (1986) *The End of the Third World*, Harmondsworth: Penguin.

Mosley, P., Harrigan, J. and Toye, J. (1991) *Aid and Power*, London: Routledge.

Pearson, L. B. (1969) *Partners in Development*, London: Pall Mall.

Warren, B. (1980) *Imperialism: Pioneer of capitalism*, London: Verso.

World Bank (1985) *World Development Report 1985*, Washington: World Bank.

World Bank (1987) *World Development Report 1987*, Washington: World Bank.

World Bank (1990) *World Development Report 1990*, Washington: World Bank.

Key terms

The following key terms appear in the text above. They have been defined below to aid with the reading of this item.

World Bank the international institution set up soon after World War II, charged with helping developing economies through the provision of loans. Formally known as the International Bank for Reconstruction and Development, it is seen – along with the IMF – as a key instrument of intervention by advanced industrial nations, usually on the basis of the promotion of free-market economics

IMF the **International Monetary Fund** – a body set up to regulate international monetary transactions, but which is increasingly becoming involved in the developing world

structural adjustment a reference to the structural adjustment plans imposed on countries by the IMF as a condition for loans, usually involving liberalization and cutbacks in public expenditure

conditionality a term used to describe the situation where loans or aid are made available only on condition that certain changes are made, usually relating to economic policy

Questions

1 According to the authors, in what way is the current crisis distinct from those in previous periods?

2 Identify the factors that led to 'the end of the Third World'.

3 Identify the two regions with the highest growth in real GDP between 1980 and 1989 and the two regions with the lowest.

4 How successful was adjustment with a human face, according to the authors?

5 Using material from the extract and elsewhere, list the factors that contributed to the rise of the debt crisis.

Reading 13.8 **Globalization in question**

Paul Hirst and Grahame Thompson (from) 'Globalisation and the future of the nation state', in *Economy and Society* (1995) vol. 24, no. 3, pp. 413–19 and 422–7.

Editorial comments

In this reading the authors critically consider the extent to which globalization has actually occurred and they criticize the notion that, as a result of globalization, nation-states are now powerless in the face of all-powerful transnational forces.

Globalization and the future of the nation state

The rhetoric of 'globalization'

IT HAS NOW become fashionable to assert that the era of the **nation state** is over, that national-level governance is ineffective in the face of globalized economic and social processes. It is claimed that from the 1970s onwards we have witnessed the creation of a truly global economy, one in which world market forces are stronger than even the most powerful states. National economies are being subsumed into one global economy, in which international financial markets and transnational companies dominate. Capital is mobile and will locate wherever economic advantage dictates, but labour is both nationally located and relatively static, and it must adjust its political expectations to meet the new pressures of international competitiveness. Distinct national regimes of extensive labour rights and social protection are thus held to be obsolete. So too are monetary and fiscal policies contrary to the expectations of global markets and transnational companies. The nation state has ceased to be an services economic manager. It can only provide those social and public services international capital deems essential and at the lowest possible overhead cost. ...

Nation states in this new perspective have become the local authorities of the global system. They can no longer independently affect the level of economic activity or employment within their territories; rather, that is dictated by the choices of internationally mobile capital. The job of nation states is like that of municipalities within states heretofore: to provide the infrastructure and public goods that business needs at the lowest possible cost.

This new globalist rhetoric is based on an anti-political liberalism. Set free from politics, the new globalized economy allows companies and markets to allocate the factors of production to greatest advantage, without the distortions of state intervention. Free trade, transnational companies and world capital markets have set business free from the constraints of politics, able to provide the world's consumers with the cheapest and most efficient products.

Globalization realizes the ideals of mid-nineteenth-century freetrade liberals like Cobden and Bright. That is, a de-militarized world in which business activity is primary and political power has no other task than the protection of the world free trading system.

For the Right in the advanced industrial countries, the rhetoric of **globalization** is a godsend. It provides a new lease of life after the disastrous failure of their monetarist and radical individualist policy experiments in the 1980s. Labour rights and social welfare of the kind practised in the era of national economic management will render Western societies uncompetitive in relation to the newly industrializing economies of Asia and must be drastically reduced. For the radical Left, globalization proves the reality of the world capitalist system and the illusory nature of national reformist strategies, even if this intellectual certainty is bought at the price of political impotence.

Left and Right can thus mutually celebrate the end of the Keynesian era. National economic management, full employment and sustained growth, standardized mass production with large semi-skilled manual labour forces corporatist collaboration between industry, organized labour and the state – these factors, central to the period of the post-1945 Great Boom, created conditions that favoured the political influence of organized labour and that confined credible political policies to a centrist and reformist path. The dominance of volatile international markets, the change to flexible methods of production and the radical re-shaping of the labour force, fitful and uncertain growth in the advanced countries, the decline of organized labour and corporatist intermediation, have all, it is claimed, rendered reformist strategies obsolete and reduced the centrality of national political processes, whether competitive or co-operative. ...

These arguments have some force. There is no doubt that the salience and role of nation states has changed markedly since the Keynesian era. States are less autonomous, they have less exclusive control over the economic and social processes within their territories, and they are less able to maintain national distinctiveness and cultural homogeneity.

The changing capacities of the nation state

There are certain areas in which the role of the state has changed radically and its capacities to control its people and domestic social processes have declined as a consequence. The first of these is war. The state acquired a monopoly of the means of violence within, the better to be able to mobilize the resources of a territory for external conflict. From the sixteenth century to the present the primary defining capacity of the modern state has been the power to make war, and to draw on the lives and property of its citizens in order to do so. The Cold War kept this power alive. Mutual enmity between East and West reinforced the need for permanent mobilization against an ever-present threat of war. The development of nuclear weapons, however, has had the effect of making war between nuclear states impossible, in the traditional sense of the use of force to attain some objective. Classically, war was seen as a means of decision, victory settling an issue between states that could be resolved in no other way. Clausewitzian war was purposive, and to that degree rational, the continuation of policy by other means. Nuclear war between roughly equal combatants can only end in mutual destruction and the negation of any rational policy pursued by the officials of the participating states. As Bernard Brodie perceptively observed (immediately after Hiroshima), the sole rational political function of nuclear weapons was deterrence – the greatest military force could no longer be employed to reach a political decision but could now be effective only if it prevented its use and thus gave politicians time to devise means to bring it under political control by the mutual agreement of the nuclear states. ...

War between nuclear states became impossible, whether they were liberal or illiberal, provided their leaders were possessed of minimal rationality. Non-nuclear conflicts could only occur in peripheral regions, conflicts by proxy where the defeat of one side would not lead to the threat of nuclear war. ...

This does not mean we shall live in a peaceful world. Lesser states will fight one another. Advanced states will be threatened by terrorism. Revolutionary movements will continue to arise on the impoverished periphery, new but local 'beggars' armies' like the Zapatistas in Chiapas. Revolutionary movements will articulate specific local antagonisms, but they will no longer seem to be detachments of a single struggle united by a common anti-Capitalist and anti-Imperialist ideology. But it does mean, in the advanced states at least, that governments are unlikely to have the occasion to call extensively on the lives and property of their citizens for war. They will no longer be able to mobilize their societies and demand and create the solidarity and common identification with authority necessary to the effective pursuit of total war. War, the presence of a genuine enemy, reinforced national solidarity and made credible the claim to national cultural homogeneity.

Without the threat of war, without enemies, the state becomes less significant to the citizen. When peoples really faced enemies, invaders and conquerors, they needed their state and their fellow citizens. The liberal state, that claimed to live peacefully with its neighbours and to make limited demands on its own people could claim great legitimacy if attacked, thereby rousing its people to a degree of commitment and common effort authoritarian states could seldom match. These legitimations are gone, and with them whole classes of provision for 'national' needs justified by the possible contingency of war: 'national' industries, health and welfare to promote 'national efficiency', and social solidarity to unite rich and poor in a common struggle. Social democracy profited from industrialized conventional war because it could deliver organized labour to the all-out war effort at the price of economic and social reforms.

States in the advanced world no longer have war as a central support for their claims to 'sovereignty'. They are no longer conceivable as autonomous actors, free to pursue any external policy in the anarchical society of states. ...

The problem now is that there are no compelling models that seem to fit the emerging international system, neither Great Power conflict nor hegemonic stability are accurate accounts of the current state of affairs. Yet some *elements* of both models still have some relevance. In economic terms the old Great Powers are still in business. The G7 includes the majority of the Great Powers of 1914 – Britain and Canada, France, Germany, Italy, Japan and the USA. Only Austria-Hungary has vanished. Russia has returned to what it was in 1914, an economically backward but very considerable military power. There are no new powers to join them – China and India both possess considerable local military strength, but they are unlikely to join the club of the most powerful economies for a considerable time, if at all. The Powers remain, but all except Russia are members of a standing association of states between whom war is almost unthinkable.

Similarly, the USA retains at least a considerable portion of the hegemony it enjoyed during the *Pax Americana*. American hegemony after 1945 was both multi-dimensional and not uncontested. Some dimensions of that hegemony remain. Militarily the US remains unrivalled, which means that no other power dare use military force radically to disrupt or restructure the international economy against American interests. The US thus remains the only possible and credible guarantor of the world free trading system against extreme challenges, even if it is reluctant to play the role of routine world policeman. America also remains the largest economy in the world by far and the power-house of world demand, on which successful export-oriented states in Asia are heavily dependent. Even though the US no longer has monetary hegemony, in that it cannot pursue an autonomous monetary policy, the dollar remains the medium of world trade. There are no obvious contenders for the remaining elements of hegemony, neither the EU or Japan being capable of taking over America's world role or wishing to do so. ...

Governance and the world economy

There can be no doubt that the era in which politics could even minimally plausibly be conceived in terms of processes within nation states and their external billiard ball interactions is passing. Politics is becoming more polycentric, with states as merely one level in a complex system of overlapping and often competing agencies of governance. It is probable that the complexity of these superimposed authorities, both territorial and functional, will soon come to rival that of the Middle Ages. But this complexity and multiplicity of levels and types of governance implies a world quite different from that of the rhetoric of 'globalization', and one in which there is a distinct, significant and continuing place for the nation state. ...

Extreme 'globalization' theorists like Ohmae (1990) contend that only two forces matter in the world economy, global market forces and transnational companies, and that neither of these is or can be subject to effective public governance. The global system is governed by the logic of market competition, and public policy will be at best secondary, since no governmental agencies (national or otherwise) can match the scale of world market forces. To repeat, this view regards national governments as the municipalities of the global system, their economies are no longer 'national' in any significant sense and they can only be effective as governments if they accept their reduced role of providing locally the public services that the global economy requires of them. The question, however, is whether such a global economy exists or is coming into being. There is a vast difference between a strictly *global* economy and a highly *internationalized* economy in which most companies trade from their bases in distinct national economies. In the former national policies are futile, since economic outcomes are determined wholly by world market forces and by the internal decisions of transnational companies. In the latter national policies remain viable, indeed, essential in order to preserve the distinct styles and strengths of the national economic base and the companies that trade from it. A world economy with a high and growing degree of international

trade and investment is not necessarily a globalized economy in the former sense. In it nation states, and forms of international regulation created and sustained by nation states, still have a fundamental role in providing governance of the economy.

What kind of international economy?

The issue, therefore, turns on what type of international economy is coming into being: one that is essentially supra-national or one in which, despite high levels of international trade and investment, nationally located processes and economic actors remain central? The problems of establishing the kinds of evidence that will count in assessing this question, and of collecting that evidence, are formidable and space forbids their full consideration here. We have attempted to review the evidence for and against globalization and contend that the balance of evidence seems to favour the concept of a highly internationalized economy that is based on trade and capital exchanges between distinct national centres. The following points summarize the case against the thesis of a truly globalized economy:

- the number of genuine transnational companies (TNCs) is small; most major companies continue to operate from distinct national bases and to wish to retain a distinct national identity, even though they trade in world markets and locate a significant part of their operations abroad
- if true TNCs are rare, the major supra-national phenomenon evident at company level is the rapid growth in inter-firm partnerships and joint ventures, activities which are international but tend to lack the unity of ownership and hierarchical control characteristic of the corporation and take on characteristics more akin to those of networks, weakening both traditional foci of property rights and staff loyalty and thus subverting classic corporate ownership *and* control – thus traditional companies may be losing some of their identity from the blurring of the boundary between the firm and the wider world, and thus be rather more challenged in this regard than is the nation state
- both foreign trade flows and patterns of foreign direct investment are highly concentrated, both are overwhelmingly between the advanced industrial states and a small number of NICs; thus income and wealth remain phenomena that are nationally distributed and which are extremely unequal, so that 14 per cent of the world's population accounted for 75 per cent of investment flows in the period 1980–91 and 14 per cent of the world's population for 70 per cent of world trade in 1992: the world's economy is far from 'global'; rather, it is substantially confined to the Triad of Europe, North America and Japan

- the figures for stocks and flows of foreign direct investment (FDI) demonstrate that the alarmist version of the globalization thesis that sees capital moving inexorably from high-wage advanced countries to low-wage developing countries (and with it employment and output) is inaccurate in aggregate
- the evidence that world financial markets are beyond regulation is by no means certain, for example, extreme volatility in exchange rates is in the interest only of short-term speculators and periods of turbulence have been followed by more or less successful attempts at stabilization and regulation, as with the efforts of the G7 in the 1980s with the Louvre and Plaza accords or current debates on the need for a new Bretton Woods system of fixed exchange rates within broad bands
- many commentators assume that rapid growth trends in the developing world (particularly China and South and East Asia) will result in a radical redistribution of output and income, overwhelming the Triad in twenty to thirty years' time – the problem with such analyses is that they project current trends forward beyond the calculable, but if previous historical experience is anything to go by such growth rates (particularly in China) are probably too high to be sustained and generally they seem to depend on authoritarian governments' ability to repress the political protests of the losers in these highly uneven processes of development, and, as the Iranian revolution of 1978 indicates, this is by no means guaranteed.

The ongoing battles between the public policy of the advanced nations and the major financial markets are by no means settled, but there is no reason to believe market forces will inevitably prevail over regulatory systems, despite setbacks like the unravelling of the EMS. The reason is that most players in the international economy have an interest in financial stability. This includes most major companies, for whom the reduction in uncertainty is of obvious advantage in their planning of investment and in their production and marketing strategies. The idea, common among extreme globalization theorists, that major companies will benefit from an unregulated international environment remains a strange one. Calculable trade rules, settled and internationally common property rights, and exchange-rate stability are a level of elementary security that companies need to plan ahead and, therefore, a condition of continued investment and growth. Companies cannot create such conditions for themselves, even if they are 'transnational'. Stability in the international economy can only be had if states combine to regulate it and to agree on common objectives and standards of governance. Companies may want free trade and common regimes

of trade standards, but they can only have them if states work together to achieve common international regulation.

Equally, the notion that companies should wish to be 'transnational' in the sense of extra-territorial is also a strange one. The national economic bases from which most companies operate actually contribute to their economic efficiency and not just in the sense of providing low-cost infrastructure. Most firms are embedded in a distinct national culture of business that provides them with intangible but very real advantages. Managers and core staff have common understandings that go beyond formal training or company policies. Genuinely transnational companies, with no primary location and a multinational workforce, would have to try to create *within* the firm the cultural advantages and forms of identification that other firms get almost free from national institutions. They would have to get core workers to put the company first as a source of identification and build a cohesive non-national managerial élite that can communicate implicitly one with another. This transnationality has traditionally been achieved only by non-economic organizations with a strong ideological mission as an alternative focus of loyalty to countries and states, such as the Society of Jesus. This would be difficult for companies to match. After all, the Jesuits are culturally distinct even if multinational products of a distinctive Latin Catholic environment and education. It is difficult to make the firm the exclusive *cultural* focus of an individual's life, and for individuals to make an ongoing commitment to one company, entirely removed from national connections. The Japanese managers and core workers who see the firm as a primary and ongoing social community do this in a *national* context where this makes sense.

Companies benefit not just from national business cultures, but from nation states and national communities as social organizations. These national business systems are quite distinct from the forms of homogeneity preached by cultural nationalists, but they remain tenaciously distinctive in a way that many other forms of national culture do not. Companies benefit from being enmeshed in networks of relations with central and local governments, with trade associations, with organized labour, with specifically national financial institutions orientated towards local companies, and with national systems of skill formation and labour motivation. These networks provide information, they are a means to co-operation and co-ordination between firms to secure common objectives, and they help to make the business environment less uncertain and more stable – a national economic system provides forms of reassurance to firms against the shocks and the risks of the international economy. Such national business-orientated systems have been most evident in the developed world in Germany and Japan, both of which have had strongly solidaristic relationships between industry, labour and the state.

But national advantages are not confined to those societies whose institutions promote solidarity in order to balance co-operation and competition between firms and between the major social interests. The USA has a national business culture that emphasizes competition and the autonomy of the individual corporation, but US firms have very real benefits in remaining distinctly American that stem from the powers and functions of the national state: for example, that the dollar remains the medium of international trade, that regulatory and standard-setting bodies like the FAA and FDA are world leaders and work closely with US industry, that the US courts are a major means of defence of commercial and property rights throughout the world, that the Federal Government is a massive subsidizer of R&D and also a strong protector of the interests of US firms abroad.

The extreme globalization theorists paint a picture of a world set free for business to serve consumers. States and military power cease to matter in the face of global markets. In this view economics and politics are pulling apart, and the latter is declining at the expense of the former. As markets dominate and the results of markets are legitimated by free competition and seen to be beyond national control, so states come to have less capacity to control economic outcomes or to alter them by force. Attempts to use military force for economic objectives against the interests of world markets would be subject to devastating, if unplanned, economic sanction: plunging exchange rates, turbulent stock exchanges, declining trade, etc. War would cease to have any connection with economic rationality – most societies would have become inescapably 'industrial' rather than 'militant'. War would become the recourse of failed and economically backward societies and political forces, driven by economically irrational goals like ethnic homogeneity or religion. Such a world free for trade has been the dream of classical economic liberalism since its inception. It is also an illusion. Markets and companies cannot exist without the protection of the public power. The open international economy depends ultimately on Western (particularly US) force and upon active public regulation backed by legal enforcement.

Reference

Ohmae, K. (1990) *The Borderless World*, London: Collins.

Key terms

The following key terms appear in the text above. They have been defined below to aid with the reading of this item.

nation-state the basic political unit, where a government and a state machinery are deemed to have a monopoly of power over a certain defined territory

globalization the idea that the world is becoming more unified and that global forces – be they economic, social, political or cultural – are now undermining differences between nations

Questions

1 Explain in your own words why the authors feel that the notion of economic globalization has only limited validity.

2 How is the modern nation-state in some ways the product of international processes?

3 In what ways have the powers and role of nation-states changed since the 1960s according to the authors?

4 In what sphere do the authors argue that the power of the USA remains unrivalled, and how does this fact affect the globalization thesis?

5 Suggest reasons why the debate over the continued power of the nation-state might have important implications for the direction of development in the Third World.

6 How far do you agree that nation-states have now become like local authorities of the global system? Give reasons for your answer.

Further Reading

The following texts may represent a useful starting point for further investigation of the ideas contained within this chapter.

Brydon, L. and Legge, K. (1996) 'Gender and adjustment: pictures from Ghana', in G. Thomas-Emeagwali (ed.) *Women Pay the Price: Structural adjustment in Africa and the Caribbean*, New Jersey: Africa World Press.

Kiely, R. (1995) *Sociology and Development: The impasse and beyond*, London: UCL Press.

Thomas, A. *et al.* (1994) *The Third World Atlas*, 2nd edn, Buckingham: Open University Press.

Watkins, K. (1995) *The OXFAM Poverty Report*, Oxford: OXFAM.

Coursework suggestions

1 Conduct a case-study of the effect of IMF structural adjustment programmes on a particular country.

2 Evaluate the contrasting ideas about the meaning of the term 'sustainable development'.

3 Conduct an investigation of the effect of the recent economic crisis in East Asia on conventional development theory and in particular its impact on the idea of the Newly Industrializing Countries (NICs).

14

Health

Chapter summary

Reading 14.1 **Paradigms of knowledge: magic, religion and science** *page 404*

This extract is taken from Sir Gordon Frazer's classic anthropological 20-volume work on the study of religion. He differentiates science – the acknowledged basis of most contemporary medicine – from both magic and religion as ways of seeing the world.

Reading 14.2 **Talcott Parsons, functionalism and the sick role** *page 406*

Bryan Turner outlines Talcott Parsons' contribution to the sociology of health and illness, particularly his concept of the function of the 'sick role' and how it is used to legitimize and control illness in society.

Reading 14.3 **Iatrogenesis and medical nemesis** *page 408*

Ivan Illich challenges the claim that medicine was the main reason for improved health and declining death rates in the nineteenth century. He goes on to suggest that the medical profession (like other professions) in fact does more harm than good, while keeping doctors in business.

Reading 14.4 **Explanations of class inequalities in health** *page 412*

The Black Report into the health of a nation 30 years after the introduction of a free and universal NHS proved shocking in its evidence of extensive structured health inequalities in society. Townsend and Davidson explore explanations of class-related health inequalities.

Reading 14.5 **Women's movements for health throughout the world** *page 415*

Lesley Doyal looks at the ways that women are taking control of their own health care throughout the world. In particular, she examines the involvement of women in self-help groups in Latin America and the Caribbean as they try to control their reproductive rights and sexual autonomy in areas such as birth control, abortion and childbirth.

Reading 14.6 **'Race', ideology and health research** *page 420*

W. I. U. Ahmad outlines his view that the expanding industry concerning 'race' and health has offered relatively few advantages for ethnic minorities. In fact, the research into 'race' and health can actually make people sick, as minority ethnic groups are seen as 'other' or inferior. The health of black people has generally been seen in racial rather than medical terms, with numerous negative results – including spurious scientific and biomedical models of 'race' and ill-health, resulting in inappropriate definitions of illness (especially mental illness) among ethnic minority groups.

Reading 14.7 **Disease and disorder** *page 423*

Bryan Turner explores the view that both nature and culture affect the way that we experience our bodies, so that even death can be seen as socially organized. The concept of disease is therefore a way of exploring what we mean by the body.

Reading 14.8 **Feminism and the sociology of the body** *page 426*

Sarah Nettleton discusses how theorists of health and illness have only quite recently seen the body as a key area of study. One reason for this has been the development of feminist approaches to the study of health and illness. Feminist analysis of new reproductive technologies, in particular, has helped make the body an important area of focus for sociologists of health and illness.

Introduction: Reading the sociology of health and illness

It was really only with the work of Talcott Parsons in the 1940s that medicine became seen as an area of study for sociologists. Other factors, such as increasing longevity and the replacement of acute illnesses (such as tuberculosis) with chronic illnesses (such as heart disease and cancer) also challenged some of the basic assumptions about health and illness in modern societies. Traditionally, the history of health and illness had been linked to the history of science and scientific discoveries. Medicine as a discipline was seen as being the one true applied science, where it was possible to distinguish between health and non-health in terms of biological differences. For this reason, it became important to look at what is meant by science and how it differs from other explanations of the world – as explored by Sir Gordon Frazer (1936) in **reading 14.1**.

This debate formed a considerable part of the sociology of knowledge from the 1950s onwards, although the understanding of what knowledge is, and how it arises, has been the basis of much philosophical debate since ancient times. It also challenged the biological basis of the 'germ theory' of illness, which underpinned the biomedical model of health and illness. In other words, it questioned the view that illness is caused by a germ or virus and that such biological factors are the cause of ill-health in society and must therefore be treated by trained medical practitioners.

Parsons (1951) showed that while medical practice dealt with biological problems and their treatments (as he believed), medical relationships were largely social – see **reading 14.2**. The way a person was treated when sick and the power held by the practitioner was structured by social norms and expectations that differed between societies and in different social relationships. This really opened up the whole debate about the power of doctors and the assumptions of medicine. No one has developed this view as much as the radical liberal philosopher and sociologist, Ivan Illich (1976) (**reading 14.3**).

Again, setting a debate that many other would follow, Illich challenged two of the main claims – or, to his mind, pretensions – of the medical professions. These were that the great improvements in health and longevity in the nineteenth and twentieth centuries could be seen as a direct result of medical intervention and that doctors basically work only in the long-term interests of their patients and of society at large.

In Britain, with its extensive and free National Health Service (NHS), there have also been concerns that the far better health and longer life expectancy of those in higher social classes seemed to be, if anything, increasing as the NHS became better established – as well as increasingly expensive for whatever government was supposed to provide it – as was shown in the Black Report, from which **reading 14.4** is taken. Some of the more recent research from writers including Professor Steve Taylor (1993) at the London School of Economics links class inequalities in health to factors such as stress.

Although lacking space to examine reforms of the health-care sector in Britain in this book, it is clear that faith in the NHS is failing and that some arguments from both Conservative and Labour governments are beginning to convince many people that we can no longer afford free and comprehensive health care for all, in an increasingly ageing society.

Studies of ethnic and gender inequalities in health and health care are also critical of a number of factors in the treatment of people and not only in modern Western societies. Reflecting the critical ideas of Illich and drawing on post-modern views of the way that not only 'race', but also sex, health and illness are socially constructed, they look at how our very bodies are constructed by our social conditions. This theme is shared in the final four readings in this chapter. In **reading 14.5**, Lesley Doyal (1995) adopts a global dimension to look at the ways that women are challenging medical orthodoxy in many parts of the world, in order to re-establish some control over their biological and material functions.

In relation to cultural differences in health, W. I. U. Ahmad (1993) shows, in **reading 14.6**, how the construction of 'race' by health professionals is designed more to control and exclude minority ethnic groups in Britain than to benefit their particular problems. Like Doyal, he regards greater patient control as the only solution to the problem of inappropriate diagnosis and treatment by inadequate professionals.

Updating the debate, in **reading 14.7**, Bryan Turner (1984) draws on traditional writers such as Durkheim and Parsons, but also incorporates a post-structural dimension from writers such as Michel Foucault, where perceptions of the body (rather than merely of health and illness) are shown to be a result of both cultural and natural or biological factors. Such an assumption is shared and developed by the explicitly feminist writing from Sarah Nettleton (1995) (**reading 14.8**). She shows that feminists have been at the forefront of many of the changes in our perceptions of health, illness and the body, especially in relation to the development of new medical and reproductive technologies which are being developed to help (and control) women, rather than, it appears, to allow women or men to help themselves.

The above writers focus on the increasing medicalization of society – the way that our bodies and their functions are constructed, defined and surveyed by health professionals until we either have to seize back control over what 'they' can and cannot do to us, or we have to accept a feeling of total separation from the body we experience as our own. The main views expressed in these readings seem to suggest that medicine is nearly always bad for us, and yet many people know that they would not be alive today without medical intervention. Nevertheless, the overriding message coming from these writers is that we need to seize back control of our own bodies, or else the state will increasingly define what levels of difference are acceptable on scientific and medical grounds, making such definitions difficult if not impossible to challenge.

The readings for this chapter seek to illuminate the sociological nature of debates about health, illness, disease and health care. There is a deliberate focus on readings that reflect key issues of definition and control which are obviously also applicable to other institutions in society. Specific debates about deviance,

welfare and world sociology all offer further insights into these issues. You may find it useful to explore some of the more theoretical topics in this book on feminist, anti-racist and post-modern theories, as health is so closely linked to many other aspects of structured inequality. The sociology of health and illness, however, has a particular function in this debate as the biological causes of illness are so often taken for granted and health is therefore seen as an area to be dealt with by 'someone else'. Therein lies the danger. Many of these readings show how minority ethnic groups and women throughout the world – like many people suffering with AIDS – are beginning to take back some control over their health, their bodies and their lives.

Reference

Parsons, T. (1951) *The Social System*, London: Routledge & Kegan Paul.

Taylor, S. (1993) in Taylor, S. and Field, D. (eds) The *Sociology of Health and Health Care*, Oxford: Blackwell Science

---

Reading 14.1 **Paradigms of knowledge: magic, religion and science**

J. G. Frazer (from) *The Golden Bough, Vol. I: The magic art* (1936) London: Macmillan, pp. 220–5.

Editorial comments

The 'biomedical' model of illness is the view that illness is caused by biological factors such as bacteria or viruses and that it must therefore be treated by professionally trained medical practitioners. While this model of illness is debated among many of the other writers in this chapter, the scientific concept of health and illness remains dominant in our society, although, as a number of writers also point out or illustrate, its dominance is now certainly under attack.

In this reading, Frazer shows that science is based on faith in an ordered system – just like magic – but does not necessarily assume a relationship between correlation and causation. Medicine based on science, therefore, is founded on a view of impersonal laws (like magic) but not (unlike magic) on spurious coincidences. Nor – unlike religion – does science seek to impress or win approval from a higher being.

Magic and religion

WHEREVER SYMPATHETIC MAGIC occurs in its pure unadulterated form, it assumes that in nature one event follows another necessarily and invariably without the intervention of any spiritual or personal agency. Thus its fundamental conception is identical with that of modern science; underlying the whole system is a faith, implicit but real and firm, in the order and uniformity of nature. The magician does not doubt that the same causes will always produce the same effects, that the performance of the proper ceremony, accompanied by the appropriate spell, will inevitably be attended by the desired results, unless, indeed,

his incantations should chance to be thwarted and foiled by the more potent charms of another sorcerer. He supplicates no higher power: he sues the favour of no fickle and wayward being: he abases himself before no awful deity. Yet his power, great as he believes it to be, is by no means arbitrary and unlimited. He can wield it only so long as he strictly conforms to the rules of his art, or to what may be called the laws of nature as conceived by him. To neglect these rules, to break these laws in the smallest particular is to incur failure, and may even expose the unskilful practitioner himself to the utmost peril. If he claims a sovereignty over nature, it is a constitutional sovereignty rigorously limited in its scope and exercised in exact conformity with ancient usage. Thus the analogy between the magical and the scientific conceptions of the world is close. In both of them the succession of events is perfectly regular and certain, being determined by immutable laws, the operation of which can be foreseen and calculated precisely; the elements of caprice, of chance, and of accident are banished from the course of nature. Both of them open up a seemingly boundless vista of possibilities to him who knows the causes of things and can touch the secret springs that set in motion the vast and intricate mechanism of the world. Hence the strong attraction which magic and science alike have exercised on the human mind; hence the powerful stimulus that both have given to the pursuit of knowledge. They lure the weary enquirer, the footsore seeker, on through the wilderness of disappointment in the present by their endless promises of the future: they take him up to the top of an exceeding high mountain and shew him, beyond the dark clouds and rolling mists at his feet, a vision of the celestial city, far off, it may be, but radiant with unearthly splendour, bathed in the light of dreams.

The fatal flaw of magic lies not in its general assumption of a sequence of events determined by law, but in its total misconception of the nature of the particular laws which govern that sequence. If we analyse the various cases of sympathetic magic [earlier in Frazer's book] we shall find, as I have already indicated, that they are all mistaken applications of one or other of two great fundamental laws of thought, namely, the association of ideas by similarity and the association of ideas by contiguity in space or time. A mistaken association of similar ideas produces homoeopathic or imitative magic: a mistaken association of contiguous ideas produces contagious magic. The principles of association are excellent in themselves, and indeed absolutely essential to the working of the human mind. Legitimately applied they yield science; illegitimately applied they yield magic, the bastard sister of science. It is therefore a truism, almost a tautology, to say that all magic is necessarily false and barren; for were it ever to become true and fruitful, it would no longer be magic but science. From the earliest times man has been engaged in a search for general rules whereby to turn the order of natural phenomena to his own advantage, and in the long search he has scraped together a great hoard of such maxims, some of them golden and some of them mere dross. The true or golden rules constitute the body of applied science which we call the arts; the false are magic.

If magic is thus next of kin to science, we have still to enquire how it stands related to religion. But the view we take of that relation will necessarily be coloured by the idea which we have formed of the nature of religion itself; hence a writer may reasonably be expected to define his conception of religion before he proceeds to investigate its relation to magic. There is probably no subject in the world about which opinions differ so much as the nature of religion, and to frame a definition of it which would satisfy every one must obviously be impossible. All that a writer can do is, first, to say clearly what he means by religion, and afterwards to employ the word consistently in that sense throughout his work. By religion, then, I understand a propitiation or conciliation of powers superior to man which are believed to direct and control the course of nature and of human life. Thus defined, religion consists of two elements, a theoretical and a practical, namely, a belief in powers higher than man and an attempt to propitiate or please them. Of the two, belief clearly comes first, since we must believe in the existence of a divine being before we can attempt to please him. But unless the belief leads to a corresponding practice, it is not a religion but merely a theology ... In other words, no man is religious who does not govern his conduct in some measure by the fear or love of God. On the other hand, mere practice, divested of all in religious belief, is also not religion. Two men may behave in exactly the same way, and yet one of them may be religious and the other not. If the one acts from the love or fear of God, he is religious; if the other acts from the love or fear of man, he is moral or immoral according as his behaviour comports or conflicts with the general good. Hence belief and practice or, in theological language, faith and works are equally essential to religion, which cannot exist without both of them. But it is not necessary that religious practice should always take the form of a ritual; that is, it need not consist in the offering of sacrifice, the recitation of prayers, and other outward ceremonies. Its aim is to please the deity, and if the deity is one who delights in charity and mercy and purity more than in oblations of blood, the chanting of hymns, and the fumes of incense, his worshippers will best please him, not by prostrating themselves before him, by intoning his praises, and by filling his temples with costly gifts, but by being pure and merciful and charitable towards men, for in so doing they will imitate, so far as human infirmity allows, the perfections of the divine nature. It was this ethical side of religion which the Hebrew prophets, inspired with a noble ideal of God's goodness and holiness, were never weary of inculcating. ... And at a later time much of the force by which Christianity conquered the world was drawn from the same high conception of God's moral nature and the duty laid on men of conforming themselves to it. ...

But if religion involves, first, a belief in superhuman beings who rule the world, and, second, an attempt to win their favour, it clearly assumes that the course of nature is to some extent elastic or variable, and that we can persuade or induce the mighty beings who control it to deflect, for our benefit, the current of events from the channel in which they would otherwise flow. Now this implied elasticity or variability of nature is directly opposed to the principles of magic as well as of science, both of which assume that the processes of nature are rigid and invariable in their operation, and that they can as little be turned from their course by persuasion and entreaty as by threats and intimidation. The distinction between the two conflicting views of the universe turns on their answer to the crucial question, Are the forces which govern the world conscious and personal, or unconscious and impersonal? Religion, as a conciliation of the superhuman powers, assumes the former member of the alternative. For all conciliation implies that the being conciliated is a conscious or personal agent, that his conduct is in some measure uncertain, and that he can be prevailed upon to vary it in the desired direction by a judicious appeal to his interests, his appetites, or his emotions.

Conciliation is never employed towards things which are regarded as inanimate, nor towards persons whose behaviour in the particular circumstances is known to be determined with absolute certainty. Thus in so far as religion assumes the world to be directed by conscious agents who may be turned from their purpose by persuasion, it stands in fundamental antagonism to magic as well as to science, both of which take for granted that the course of nature is determined, not by the passions or caprice of personal beings, but by the operation of immutable laws acting mechanically. In magic, indeed, the assumption is only implicit, but in science it is explicit. It is true that magic often deals with spirits, which are personal agents of the kind assumed by religion; but whenever it does so in its proper form, it treats them exactly in the same fashion as it treats inanimate agents, that is, it constrains or coerces instead of conciliating or propitiating them as religion would do. Thus it assumes that all personal beings, whether human or divine, are in the last resort subject to those impersonal forces which control all things, but which nevertheless can be turned to account by any one who knows how to manipulate them by the appropriate ceremonies and spells.

Questions

1 Identify the main differences and similarities between magic and science as ways of explaining the world.

2 Identify the main differences and similarities between religion and science as ways of explaining the world.

3 Using the material in the text, your answers to questions 1 and 2, and other areas of knowledge – including your own personal experiences – to what extent can it be argued that science is now the only basis for modern medical practices?

Reading 14.2 **Talcott Parsons, functionalism and the sick role**

Bryan S. Turner (from) 'Parsons' contribution to medical sociology', in R. J. Holton and B. S. Turner (eds) *Talcott Parsons on Economy and Society* (1986) London: Routledge & Kegan Paul, pp. 119–23.

Editorial comments

Contemporary accounts in the sociology of health and illness are mainly critical of the nature of health and health care in society. This view falls into a number of different areas, as the readings suggest. Talcott Parsons – according to Bryan Turner's account of Parsons' highly influential work – while accepting

the biomedical model, showed that there is an important sociological aspect to ill-health. We have to be granted permission to be ill by various 'gatekeepers' (doctors especially) who permit us to be unwell for a while, as long as we seek and take their advice in an effort to 'get better' and return to our useful roles as members of society.

This view shows that there are certain norms attached to being sick, including the way that we are expected to withdraw from particular social functions for a limited period of time, but only if we are not responsible for the condition and seek and accept professional medical help in order to get well as quickly as possible. Turner also outlines some of the main criticisms and contradictions of Parsons' viewpoint, as well as how it has been developed by other sociologists.

The sick role

ALTHOUGH PARSONS' ANALYSIS of the professions is well known, his principal contribution to medical sociology was the concept of the sick role which was first stated systematically in *The Social System* (1951). The elements of the sick role are relatively simple, but the background and implications of the concept are highly complex. The central components of the sick role can be outlined succinctly. The difference between feeling sick and being sick points to the existence of a definite set of social expectations for the incumbent of a sick role, which Parsons claimed has four dimensions. The first is that it legitimates withdrawal from a number of social obligations, especially from work and family duties. There is the notion that a sick person ought to stay at home and rest. The second aspect of the role is that the person is exempted from responsibility for their condition; they cannot get well without external help and support. The third component is that the sick person has an obligation to get well; legitimation of sickness as a basis for withdrawal from social roles is conditional on the patient's acceptance of an obligation to get well by co-operating with the doctor's regimen. The final element within the role is thus an expectation that the sick person will seek out technically competent health care, typically a trained physician. The sick role in fact describes a role-set or social system of the doctor–patient relationship, which is organized in terms of the pattern-variables, which Parsons had developed in connection with the analysis of professional roles.

Although the sick-role concept may look like common sense ('When people are sick, we expect them to get better'), it is in fact a subtle and complex notion. Parsons developed the concept against an intellectual background in which the American medical establishment was beginning to take the notion of psychosomatic illness very seriously, and to realize that the social and emotional relationship between the doctor and the patient was an important aspect of the therapeutic process. Parsons himself had become aware, through the prompting of Elton Mayo, of the relevance of Freudian **psychoanalysis** for the study of sick roles, especially Freud's study of **transference**. These influences led Parsons to realize that there was an important issue of motivation in the process of becoming sick and that, given the nature of the action frame of reference with its **voluntaristic** premises, there is an important sense in which people decide to be sick. ...

It is worth emphasizing these features of Parsons' definition of the sick role in order to grasp the inno-

vatory character of his approach to the problem. The concept emerges in *The Social System* in the section on **deviance** and social control. Sickness, like crime, involves deviance from normal role expectations, and they are both forms of motivated action. The sick role legitimates this deviance, but it is also an important vehicle of social control since the aim of therapy is to return the sick person to conventional roles. Parsons' insight into illness behaviour as deviance was thus a remarkable anticipation of various deviancy-models of mental illness. ... There was thus an important link for Parsons between the role expectations of the doctor–patient relationship and problems of social control and legitimation at the level of the social order. Although Parsons is not noted for his contributions to the sociology of power, it is interesting that his discussion of sickness should have so clearly located the sick role in the context of an analysis of legitimation, social control and deviance.

Although the sick role has been recognized as an important contribution to medical sociology, it has also been subject to extensive criticism. At the core of these criticisms, there is the argument that Parsons' ideal typical model is based on a narrow, positivist model of organic disease. The model assumes that sickness is acute, the patient is passive, and the physician is competent and altruistic. The model has little relevance to chronic illness or physical disability. The relevance of the model becomes particularly problematic in areas where the use of the term 'sickness' is uncertain and unstable. These ambiguous cases would include mental illness, alcoholism, homosexuality or pregnancy. The thrust of these objections is that Parsons simply accepted conventional medical categories in the definition of what is to count as sickness. For example, although Parsons constantly drew attention to the activistic assumptions of western medicine, which postulates that in principle all disease can be cured, he did not question the medical assumption that ageing falls outside the conventional category of disease. Should ageing be regarded as a permanent sick role that legitimates withdrawal from social roles? Parsons' model is limited because it refers to acute illness (like appendicitis) where the doctor intervenes to solve a problem which is morally neutral, unambiguous and life-threatening, but short-term. The criticism of Parsons suggests that his sick-role theory accepts naively the medical model of sickness. ...

The criticisms of the sick-role concept appear often to overlook the radical implications of the model. For example, although Parsons acknowledged that sickness was ultimately rooted in biological malfunctions of the organism, the manifest content of sickness was completely social. The crucial distinction between illness and health was engagement in and withdrawal from social activities and responsibilities in familial and occupational roles. These social criteria are particularly emphatic and central in the definition of mental illness. ... Mental illness is primarily a form of deviance from conventional social expectations. Parsons was also fully aware that patients may be reluctant to get better and abandon the sick role since there were many 'secondary gains' from sickness. People choose to be ill as a defence against a social system in which they find it difficult to operate or to cope successfully. Thus, Parsons saw mental illness as a reaction of the individual to the 'strains' of the social system. In a discussion of the 'vulnerabilities of the American family', Parsons noted that sickness was an attractive solution to the structural tensions within the nuclear family. The sick role legitimizes a withdrawal from such strains and tensions within the family. ...

The idea that sickness is positively functional for the individual by permitting withdrawal has been developed by a variety of contemporary theorists, especially those with a psychoanalytic background. ... For Parsons, of course, sickness could offer only a partial solution to these critics since the incumbent of a sick role is expected to struggle for recovery.

Parsons' sick-role concept is, therefore, not simply 'founded on the narrow organic disease model of positivist medical science'. On the contrary, Parsons' conceptualization of sickness provides a wide-ranging critique of the medical model. ... Under the influence of Freudian psychoanalysis, Parsons drew the attention of sociologists to the motivational factors in sickness and recognized the 'secondary gains' of the sick role. In brief, Parsons consistently denied that sickness was exclusively a biochemical condition and argued instead that it was an institutionalized role. The implications of such a view are that the medical profession does not enjoy a monopoly of relevant skill with respect to the patient's welfare. Parsons was perfectly aware of these implications since he argued that medical education would have to change in response to changes in social conditions and would have to incorporate developments in the social sciences, especially sociology and psychology.

Reference

Parsons, T. (1951) *The Social System*, London: Routledge & Kegan Paul.

Key terms

The following key terms appear in the text above. They have been defined below to aid with the reading of this item.

psychoanalysis the study and treatment of mental disorders based on the work of Sigmund Freud

transference the use of psychoanalysis as a tool for resolving the inner dilemmas that cause mental disorders

voluntaristic the way people decide on certain courses of action

deviance social behaviour that deviates from expected norms

Questions

1 Describe in your own words the four main dimensions of the 'sick role'.

2 Explain how Parsons sees sickness as a form of deviance.

3 What are the main criticisms of the assumptions which underlie Parsons' view of illness?

4 What does Turner, the author of this extract, regard as the most radical implications of the model of the 'sick role'?

Reading 14.3 **Iatrogenesis and medical nemesis**

Ivan Illich (from) *Limits to Medicine – Medical Nemesis: The expropriation of health* (1976) London: Marion Boyars, pp. 15–17 and 22–35.

Editorial comments

While Parsons raises some interesting debates about the role of medical personnel, Ivan Illich is far more scathing about the whole medical profession. Writing from what can best be described as a radical liberal perspective, largely rooted in his work in Latin America and the poorest parts of the USA, he shows that improved survival rates are due mainly to environmental improvements such as better nutrition and sanitation, rather than medical intervention. He also regards professionals as being intent on destroying our autonomy and self-determination (medical nemesis). Their treatments can make us ill (clinical iatrogenesis), their medical definitions disguise the real causes of illness – boredom and lack of autonomy (social iatrogenesis), while their professional manner of authority denies our ability to make our own decisions about sickness and health (cultural iatrogenesis). The result is a sickness not just of the body, but of our very souls and culture, where doctors, teachers, lawyers and advertising managers tell us what and how to think and even what we should feel and consume.

The epidemics of modern medicine

Doctors' effectiveness – an illusion

THE STUDY OF the evolution of disease patterns provides evidence that during the last century doctors have affected epidemics no more profoundly than did priests during earlier times. Epidemics came and went, imprecated by both but touched by neither. They are not modified any more decisively by the rituals performed in medical clinics than by those customary at religious shrines. Discussion of the future of health care might usefully begin with the recognition of this fact.

... In England, by the middle of the nineteenth century, infectious epidemics had been replaced by major malnutrition syndromes, such as rickets and pellagra. These in turn peaked and vanished, to be replaced by the diseases of early childhood and, somewhat later, by an increase in duodenal ulcers in young men. When these declined, the modern epidemics took over: coronary heart disease, emphysema, bronchitis, obesity, hypertension, cancer (especially of the lungs), arthritis, diabetes, and so-called mental disorders. Despite intensive research, we have no complete explanation for the genesis of these changes. But two things are certain: the professional practice of physicians cannot be credited with the elimination of old forms of **mortality** or **morbidity**, nor should it be blamed for the increased expectancy of life spent in suffering from the new diseases. ...

Useless medical treatment

Awe-inspiring medical technology has combined with egalitarian rhetoric to create the impression that contemporary medicine is highly effective. Undoubtedly, during the last generation, a limited number of specific procedures have become extremely useful. But where they are not monopolized by professionals as tools of their trade, those which are applicable to widespread diseases are usually very inexpensive and require a minimum of personal skills, materials, and custodial services from hospitals. In contrast, most of today's skyrocketing medical expenditures are destined for the kind of diagnosis and treatment whose effectiveness at best is doubtful. To make this point I will distinguish between infectious and noninfectious diseases.

In the case of infectious diseases, chemotherapy has played a significant role in the control of pneumonia, gonorrhea, and syphilis. Death from pneumonia, once the 'old man's friend', declined yearly by 5 to 8 per cent after sulphonamides and antibiotics came on the market. Syphilis, yaws, and many cases of malaria and typhoid can be cured quickly and easily. The rising rate of venereal disease is due to new mores, not to ineffectual medicine. The reappearance of malaria is due to the development of pesticide-resistant mosquitoes and not to any lack of new antimalarial drugs. Immunization has almost wiped out paralytic poliomyelitis, a disease of developed countries, and vaccines have certainly contributed to the decline of whooping cough and measles, thus seeming to confirm the popular belief in 'medical progress'. But for most other infections, medicine can show no comparable results. Drug treatment has helped to reduce mortality from tuberculosis, tetanus, diphtheria, and scarlet fever, but in the total decline of mortality or morbidity from these diseases, chemotherapy played a minor and possibly insignificant role. ...

The effectiveness of medical intervention in combatting noninfectious diseases is even more questionable. In some situations and for some conditions, effective progress has indeed been demonstrated: the partial prevention of caries through fluoridation of water is possible, though at a cost not fully understood. ... Through intravenous feeding, blood transfusions, and surgical techniques, more of those who get to the hospital survive trauma, but survival rates for the most common types of cancer – those which make up 90 per cent of the cases – have remained virtually unchanged over the last twenty-five years. ... Surgery and chemotherapy for rare congenital and rheumatic heart disease have increased the chances for an active life for some of those who suffer from degenerative conditions. The medical treatment of common cardiovascular disease and the intensive treatment of heart disease, however, are effective only when rather exceptional circumstances combine that are outside the physician's control. ...

Doctor-inflicted injuries

Unfortunately, futile but otherwise harmless medical care is the least important of the damages a proliferating medical enterprise inflicts on contemporary society. The pain, dysfunction, disability, and anguish resulting from technical medical intervention now rival the morbidity due to traffic and industrial accidents and even war-related activities, and make the impact of medicine one of the most rapidly spreading epidemics of our time. Among murderous institutional torts, only modern malnutrition injures more people than **iatrogenic** disease in its various manifestations. In the most narrow sense, iatrogenic disease includes only illnesses that would not have come about if sound and professionally recommended treatment had *not* been applied. Within this definition, a patient could sue his therapist if the latter, in the course of his management, failed to apply a recommended treatment that, in the physician's opinion, would have risked making him sick. In a more general and more widely accepted sense, clinical iatrogenic disease comprises all clinical conditions for which remedies, physicians, or hospitals are the pathogens, or 'sickening' agents. I will call this plethora of therapeutic side-effects *clinical iatrogenesis*. They are as old as medicine itself, and have always been a subject of medical studies.

Medicines have always been potentially poisonous, but their unwanted side-effects have increased with their power and widespread use. Every twenty-four to thirty-six hours, from 50 to 80 per cent of adults in the United States and the United Kingdom swallow a medically prescribed chemical. Some take the wrong drug; others get an old or a contaminated batch, and others a counterfeit; others take several drugs in dangerous combinations; and still others receive injections with improperly sterilized syringes. Some drugs are addictive, others mutilating, and others mutagenic, although perhaps only in combination with food colouring or insecticides. In some patients, antibiotics alter the normal bacterial flora and induce a super-infection, permitting more resistant organisms to proliferate and invade the host. Other drugs contribute to the breeding of drug-resistant strains of bacteria. Subtle kinds of poisoning thus have spread even faster than the bewildering variety and ubiquity of nostrums. Unnecessary surgery is a standard procedure. *Disabling nondiseases* result from the medical treatment of nonexistent diseases and are on the increase: the number of children disabled in Massachusetts through the treatment of cardiac non-disease exceeds the number of children under effective treatment for real cardiac disease.

Doctor-inflicted pain and infirmity have always been a part of medical practice. Professional callousness, negligence, and sheer incompetence are age-old forms of malpractice. With the transformation of the doctor from an artisan exercising a skill on personally known individuals into a technician applying scientific rules to classes of patients, malpractice acquired an anonymous, almost respectable status. What had formerly been considered an abuse of confidence and a moral fault can now be rationalized into the occasional breakdown of equipment and operators. In a complex technological hospital, negligence becomes 'random human error' or 'system breakdown', callousness becomes 'scientific detachment', and incompetence becomes 'a lack of specialized equipment'. The depersonalization of diagnosis and therapy has changed malpractice from an ethical into a technical problem.

... The problem, however, is that most of the damage inflicted by the modern doctor ... occurs in the ordinary practice of well-trained men and women who have learned to bow to prevailing professional judgment and procedure, even though they know (or could and should know) what damage they do.

The United States Department of Health, Education, and Welfare calculates that 7 per cent of all patients suffer compensable injuries while hospitalized, though few of them do anything about it. Moreover, the frequency of reported accidents in hospitals is higher than in all industries but mines and high-rise construction. Accidents are the major cause of death in American children. In proportion to the time spent there, these accidents seem to occur more often in hospitals than in any other kind of place. One in fifty children admitted to a hospital suffers an accident which requires specific treatment. ... It has also been established that one out of every five patients admitted to a typical research hospital acquires an iatrogenic disease, sometimes trivial, usually requiring special treatment, and in one case in thirty leading to death. Half of these episodes result from complications of drug therapy; amazingly, one in ten comes from diagnostic procedures. Despite good intentions and claims to public service, a military officer with a similar record of performance would be relieved of his command, and a restaurant or amusement centre would be closed by the police.

Defenceless patients

The undesirable side-effects of approved, mistaken, callous, or contraindicated technical contacts with the medical system represent just the first level of pathogenic medicine. Such *clinical iatrogenesis* includes not only the damage that doctors inflict with the intent of curing or of exploiting the patient, but also those other torts that result from the doctor's attempt to protect himself against the possibility of a suit for malpractice. Such attempts to avoid litigation and prosecution may now do more damage than any other iatrogenic stimulus.

On a second level, medical practice sponsors sickness by reinforcing a morbid society that encourages people to become consumers of curative, preventive, industrial, and environmental medicine. On the one hand defectives survive in increasing numbers and are fit only for life under institutional care, while on the other hand, medically certified symptoms exempt people from industrial work and thereby remove them from the scene of political struggle to reshape the society that has made them sick. Second-level iatrogenesis finds its expression in various symptoms of social overmedicalization that amount to what I shall call the expropriation of health. This second level impact of medicine I designate as *social iatrogenesis*.

On a third level, the so-called health professions have an even deeper, culturally health-denying effect insofar as they destroy the potential of people to deal with their human weakness, vulnerability, and unique-ness in a personal and autonomous way. The patient in the grip of contemporary medicine is but one instance of mankind in the grip of its pernicious tech-niques. This *cultural iatrogenesis* is the ultimate back-lash of hygienic progress and consists in the paralysis of healthy responses to suffering, impairment, and death. It occurs when people accept health manage-ment designed on the engineering model, when they conspire in an attempt to produce, as if it were a commodity, something called 'better health'. This inevitably results in the managed maintenance of life on high levels of sublethal illness. This ultimate evil of medical 'progress' must be clearly distinguished from both clinical and social iatrogenesis.

On each of its three levels iatrogenesis has become medically irreversible: a feature built right into the medical endeavour. The unwanted physiological, social, and psychological by-products of diagnostic and therapeutic progress have become resistant to medical remedies. New devices, approaches, and organizational arrangements, which are conceived as remedies for clinical and social iatrogenesis, them-selves tend to become pathogens contributing to the new epidemic. Technical and managerial measures taken on any level to avoid damaging the patient by his treatment tend to engender a self-reinforcing

iatrogenic loop analogous to the escalating destruc-tion generated by the polluting procedures used as antipollution devices.

I will designate this self-reinforcing loop of negative institutional feedback by its classical Greek equivalent and call it *medical* **nemesis**. The Greeks saw gods in the forces of nature. For them, nemesis represented divine vengeance visited upon mortals who infringe on those prerogatives the gods enviously guard for them-selves. Nemesis was the inevitable punishment for attempts to be a hero rather than a human being. Like most abstract Greek nouns, Nemesis took the shape of a divinity. She represented nature's response to *hubris*: to the individual's presumption in seeking to acquire the attributes of a god. Our contemporary hygienic hubris has led to the new syndrome of medical nemesis.

By using the Greek term I want to emphasize that the corresponding phenomenon does not fit within the explanatory paradigm now offered by bureaucrats, therapists, and ideologues for the snowballing dis-economies and disutilities that, lacking all intuition, they have engineered and that they tend to call the 'counterintuitive behaviour of large systems'. By invok-ing myths and ancestral gods I should make it clear that my framework for analysis of the current break-down of medicine is foreign to the industrially deter-mined logic and ethos. I believe that the *reversal of nemesis* can come only from within man and not from yet another managed source depending once again on presumptious expertise and subsequent mystification.

Medical nemesis is resistant to medical remedies. It can be reversed only through a recovery of the will to self-care among the laity, and through the legal, political, and institutional recognition of the right to care, which imposes limits upon the professional monopoly of physicians.

Key terms

The following key terms appear in the text above. They have been defined below to aid with the reading of this item.

mortality death

morbidity long-term chronic illness

iatrogenic doctor-made

nemesis the view that certain actions return to take revenge on those who misuse them

Questions

1 Using material from the text, discuss the causes of improved mortality and morbidity rates in devel-oped countries this century.

2 Explain, with examples, the concept of clinical iatrogenesis.

3 Explain and assess the view that medical treatments cause both social iatrogenesis and cultural iatrogenesis.

4 What do you think Illich means by the term 'medical nemesis'?

Reading 14.4 **Explanations of class inequalities in health**

P. Townsend and N. Davidson (from) *Inequalities in Health – The Black Report* (1982) Norwich: HMSO, pp. 112–23.

Editorial comments

Social democracy is the view that all citizens of a civilized democratic society are entitled to a decent standard of living and level of health care provided by the state. Taking a social democratic approach to the class inequalities found in health, this reading by Townsend and Davidson examines the various explanations of the inequalities identified by the Inequalities in Health report produced under the chairmanship of Sir Peter Black in 1981. They include artefact explanations, which see health and class as variables that are most likely not causal because of the changes in the proportion of people in manual work. Theories of natural and social selection suggest that poor health causes low class position rather than any external factors.

Materialist structural explanations show that deprivation is still a factor in explaining relative ill-health even though, for most people, absolute poverty has almost disappeared. Cultural and behavioural explanations examine the lifestyle and beliefs of working-class people as higher levels of smoking and drinking are seen as leading to higher levels of early death and chronic illness among the working class. The authors concluded that all these explanations offered some insights, but their in-depth analysis of statistics for different age-groups showed convincingly that structural factors including comparative material factors were the most important.

Towards an explanation of health inequalities

DEATH RATES IN present-day Europe have reached what appear to be their lowest points in the history of human society. The twentieth century has witnessed a dramatic decline in the rate of infectious disease, as well as the introduction of powerful therapies for its treatment. Common causes of death like TB and diphtheria, often linked with poverty and material deprivation, have greatly diminished, though they have been replaced by new diseases, some of which have been linked in particular studies with affluence and material abundance. On that account inequalities in health might have been expected to diminish. But the evidence suggests that this has not been the case. In this [reading] we ask why occupational class continues to exert so significant an influence on health in Britain.

There are a number of approaches to an explanation, though none in our view provides a wholly satisfactory answer. Indeed, the variable of occupational class is in itself multifaceted, and its influence probably varies according to age or stage in the **life-cycle** and according to the natural history of disease.

Theoretical approaches

Theoretical explanations of the relationship between health and inequality might be roughly divided into four categories:

1 Artefact explanations.
2 Theories of natural or social selection.
3 Materialist or structuralist explanations.
4 Cultural/behavioural explanations.

In some respect each one of these approaches sheds light on the observed relationships between class and health in present-day Britain. We shall first describe and discuss in general terms the four approaches and then go on, by reference to the problems of different age groups, to show that any satisfactory explanation must build essentially on the ideas of the cumulative dispositions and experience of the lifetime, and of multiple causation.

The artefact explanation
This approach suggests that both health and class are artificial variables thrown up by attempts to measure social phenomena and that the relationship between them may itself be an artefact of little causal significance. Accordingly, the failure of health inequalities to diminish in recent decades is believed to be explained to a greater or lesser extent by the reduction in the proportion of the population in the poorest occupational classes. It is believed that the failure to reduce the gap *between* classes has been counterbalanced by the shrinkage in the relative size of the poorer classes themselves. The implication is that the upwardly mobile are found to have better health than those who remain, or that their health subsequently improves relative to the health of those they join. We would make two comments. One is that informed examination of successive census reports shows that the poorer occupational classes have contracted less sharply than often supposed. The other is that indicators of relatively poor progress in health apply to much larger sections of the manual

occupational classes than just those who are 'unskilled'.

Natural and social selection

Occupational class is here relegated to the state of dependent variable and health acquires the greater degree of causal significance. The occupational class structure is seen as a filter or sorter of human beings and one of the major bases of selection is health, that is, physical strength, vigour or agility. It is inferred that the Registrar General's class I has the lowest rate of premature mortality because it is made up of the strongest and most robust men and women in the population. Class V by contrast contains the weakest and most frail people. Put another way, this explanation suggests that physical weakness or poor health carries low social worth as well as low economic reward, but that these factors play no causal role in the event of high mortality. Their relationship is strictly reflective. Those men and women who by virtue of innate physical characteristics are destined to live the shortest lives also reap the most meagre rewards. This type of explanation has been invoked to explain the preponderance of individuals with severe mental disorders in social class V. It is postulated that affected people *drift* to the bottom rung of the Registrar General's occupational scale. Similar selective processes are thought to occur with other forms of disease even though the extent of drift may not be so great and there is little actual evidence of it.

Materialist or structuralist explanations

The third type of explanation emphasizes the role of economic and associated socio-structural factors in the distribution of health and well-being, and, because it is frequently misunderstood, requires fuller exposition. ... Amongst explanations which focus on the *direct* influence of poverty or economic deprivation in the production of variation in rates of mortality is the radical Marxian critique. With the benefit of a century's hind-sight the validity of much of this nineteenth-century theory of the relationship between health and material inequality has been accepted today, especially for the earlier phase of competitive industrial capitalism. Exploitation, poverty and disease have virtually become synonymous for describing conditions of life in the urban slums of Victorian and Edwardian cities, as they are today for the shanty towns of the under-developed world.

But can it be so readily applied to contemporary health experience? Can the premature mortality of the working class still be directly attributed to subsistence poverty and exploitation? It is true that a relationship between material deprivation and certain causes of disease and death is now well established, but then so is the capacity of the capitalist mode of produc-

tion to expand the level of human productivity and to raise the living standards of working people. Economic growth of the kind most readily associated with the European style of industrialization has in itself been credited with the decline in mortality from infectious disease during the nineteenth and twentieth centuries. Today death rates for all age groups in Britain are a fraction of what they were a century ago and many of the virulent infectious diseases have largely disappeared, and the 'killer' diseases of modern society – accidents, cancer and heart disease – seem less obviously linked to poverty. Against this background, the language of economic exploitation no longer seems to provide the appropriate epithet for describing 'Life and Labour' in the last two decades of the twentieth century. ...

The flaw in this line of reasoning is the assumption that material subsistence needs can be uniquely and unambiguously defined in terms independent of the overall level of economic development in a society. People may still have too little for their basic *physiological* as well as social needs. Poverty is also a relative concept, and those who are unable to share the amenities or facilities provided within a rich society, or who are unable to fulfil the social and occupational obligations placed upon them by virtue of their limited resources, can properly be regarded as poor. They may also be **relatively disadvantaged** in relation to the risks of illness or accident or the factors positively promoting health.

... The material deprivation of some sections of the population can paradoxically grow even when their income increases, relative to changing structures and amenities.

How far might differences in access to resources help to explain this? How unequal is the distribution of wealth in Britain? Historically the structure of living standards has been slow to change. Personal wealth is still concentrated in the hands of a small minority of the population ...

The Royal Commission has referred to the 'remarkable' stability of the unequal distribution of income over the past two decades. Moreover there is no doubt that the proportion as well as number of the population dependent on a subsistence or near-subsistence income from the state has grown. For some groups, and especially manual groups, relative lifetime resources will have been reduced. Earlier retirement, unemployment and redundancies, single-parent status and disablement, as well as the proportionate increase in the elderly population, all play some part in this development. ...

There is therefore a paradox: while we would not wish to assert that the evidence is consistent and complete, the proportion of the population with relatively low lifetime incomes (in the widest sense of 'income') seems to have increased in recent decades, just as the proportion assigned to classes IV and V seems to have decreased, though the latter continue to comprise more than a quarter of the population. While economic growth has improved the access of both groups to income and other resources, other groups have gained in proportion, and since neither facilities nor knowledge is a finite commodity, those with relatively low incomes (in increasing numbers) have remained relatively disadvantaged.

So it has been with health. Occupational classes IV and V may in time catch up with the contemporary levels achieved by I and II but by that time the latter groups will have forged even further ahead. There is nothing fixed about levels of physical well-being. They have improved in the past and there is every likelihood that they will improve in the future. But class inequalities persist in the distribution of health as in the distribution of income or wealth, and they persist as a form of relative deprivation.

... These dimensions of material inequality are also closely articulated with another determinant of health – education. ...

Cultural/behavioural explanations

A fourth approach is that of cultural or behavioural explanations of the distribution of health in modern industrial society. These are recognizable by the independent and autonomous causal role which they assign to ideas and behaviour in the onset of disease and the event of death. Such explanations, when applied to modern industrial societies, often focus on the individual as a unit of analysis emphasizing unthinking, reckless or irresponsible behaviour or incautious lifestyle as the moving determinant of poor health status. What is implied is that people harm themselves or their children by the excessive consumption of harmful commodities, refined foods, tobacco and alcohol, or by lack of exercise, or by their under-utilization of preventive health care, vaccination, ante-natal surveillance or contraception. Some would argue that such systematic behaviour within certain social groups is a consequence only of lack of education, or individual waywardness or thoughtlessness. Explanation takes an individual form. What is critical, it is implied, are the personal characteristics of individuals, whether innate or acquired their basic intelligence, their skills obtained through education and training, their physical and mental qualities, and their personal styles and dispositions. Others see behaviour which is conducive to good or bad health as embedded more within social structures – as illustrative of socially distinguishable styles of life, associated with, and reinforced by, class.

Certain styles of living, like a diet strong in carbohydrates, cigarette smoking and lack of participation in sporting activities, are known to cut across class. It is implied that there are individual or, at most, **subcultural** lifestyles, rooted in personal characteristics and level of education, which govern behaviour and which are therefore open to change through changes in personal activities or educational inputs. ... A balanced diet, or balanced physical activity, to promote health is easy neither to define nor measure. People who eat one type of food to excess may make up for that disadvantage in some other respect. And manual workers who are spectators rather than active sportsmen include those who have to exert physical strength and agility in their everyday jobs.

... Commercial advertisements are planned to 'educate' tastes, and the education provided in schools is not always calculated to prepare young people to ward off influences upon their consumption and behaviour which may be undesirable for health. Moreover, access to good food and sports facilities depends also on the area in which people live and the resources they can command, and not only their personal characteristics or behaviour, or education. But, in emphasizing these reservations we must also call attention to the *cumulative* importance of those contributions to personal behaviour made by genetic endowment of attributes, the influence of family upbringing and practices and the evolution of modes of self-management which contribute to wide differences in health achieved by different members of the same occupational or socio-economic class. ...

More theoretically developed as the basis for cultural/behavioural explanations is the 'culture of poverty' thesis – which has much in common with the idea of 'transmitted deprivation'. As originally proposed by Oscar Lewis, the 'culture of poverty' was intended to apply only to market-organized social structures with poorly developed public systems of health, welfare and income maintenance. Starting from a distinct cultural anthropological perspective, Lewis argued that human existence in any given environment involves a process of biological and social adaptation which gives rise to the elaboration of a structure of norms, ideas and behaviours. This culture over time acquires an integrity and a stability because of the supportive role it plays in helping individuals to understand and cope with their environment but, through its influence on socialization practices and the like, it also comes to have an important autonomous influence in the social consciousness of individuals. The integrity of the culture ensures its autonomous survival even when the material base from which it emerged has changed or been modified. It is for this reason that people cling on to outmoded ideas or old-fashioned practices which do not seem to accord with the changed material realities of modern existence. The 'culture of poverty' thesis has been widely criticized by British social scientists.

Consider, for example, the diffusion of the acceptance of the idea of family planning, which is generally agreed to have been first adopted by the professional classes, from whence it diffused to poorer classes. On the basis of the 'culture of poverty' thesis this should not have happened or, at least, there should have been more evidence of stiff resistance to the adoption of the practice. However the fact that family planning has spread rapidly to all classes is one strand of historical evidence which is felt to cast doubt on the 'culture of poverty' thesis. The implication of that example is that the beliefs and values of poorer sections of the population are less autonomous, and more dependent upon conventional or orthodox beliefs and values, than has been assumed by proponents of the thesis. Instead social scientists have felt it right to place emphasis on the material circumstances of families and their access to the means of contraception in explaining class variations in the readiness or otherwise to adopt new methods of family planning. While recognizing the force of many of their criticisms we believe it is difficult to settle questions of interpretation like that of family planning one way or the other. We are aware that even if it is difficult to make a case for separately identifiable sub-cultures that does not dispose of the possible role of cultural variations in contributing to any overall explanation of variations in health.

Choosing between such complex and sometimes competing approaches, when applied to evidence as complex as that which we have assembled, is a daunting task. We must make clear our belief that it is in some form or forms of the 'materialist' approach that the best answer lies. But there can be little doubt that amongst all the evidence there is much that is convincingly explained in alternative terms: cultural, social selection and so on. Moreover, it may well be that different kinds of factors, or forms of explanation, apply more strongly, or more appropriately, to different stages of the lifecycle.

Key terms

The following key terms appear in the text above. They have been defined below to aid with the reading of this item.

lifecycle the pattern of different stages in peoples' lives, such as birth, infancy, childhood, adolescence and old age

relatively disadvantaged having less access than others to both material rewards and safe and healthy conditions at work and at home

sub-cultural relating to groups with norms and values that differ from those of the majority

Questions

1 Explain and evaluate, with examples, what is meant by an artefact explanation of inequality.

2 Explain and evaluate, with examples, the natural and social selection explanations of health inequalities.

3 Using the text and other knowledge you have of peoples' lifestyles and beliefs, explain and evaluate cultural/behavioural explanations of health inequalities between social groups, including the 'culture of poverty' thesis.

4 Identify the main strands of material or structural explanations of inequalities in health between social classes and assess the evidence for this type of explanation.

Reading 14.5 **Women's movements for health throughout the world**

Lesley Doyal (from) *What Makes Women Sick: Gender and the political economy of health* (1995) Basingstoke: Macmillan, pp. 198–209.

Editorial comments

Writing from a Marxist feminist perspective, Doyal shows how women are fighting the medical establishment to gain some control over their reproductive and sexual behaviour. It is inspiring to find that women (and latterly men) now seek to remove the definitions of behaviour from the professionals, although it can be argued that only dire circumstances have made them do so. She found in many cases that women are challenging orthodox medical practices in their own countries and forming self-help groups to offer genuine feminist alternatives that empower women in controlling their fertility and reproduction and their needs for both physical and mental health care.

Doyal points out that challenging medical dominance and creating feminist alternatives, to reform the system and empower women, are key aspects of the fight against the medical establishment. These movements are also inevitably linked to improving the provision of the basic need for food, sanitation, decent housing and respect in both the home and the workplace.

REPRODUCTIVE RIGHTS ISSUES are now central to women's health politics in most parts of the world. Historically most initiatives have consisted of single-issue campaigns for birth control. However these are increasingly located within a broader framework that includes not just the right to prevent conception but also the right to **sexual autonomy**, to safe motherhood and to a healthy environment for child rearing. ...

Campaigning for change: unity and diversity

Most reproductive health campaigners work at community level empowering others through information, advice and care. However broader initiatives are also flourishing, as women identify and publicize the deficiencies of many family planning and abortion services, expose the hazards of some medical techniques and fight for greater participation in reproductive research and development.

In recent years many of these campaigning groups have begun to work together in regional and national alliances. The Latin American and Caribbean Women's Health Network co-ordinates many of the activities in that region, working in collaboration with Isis International. ... International advocacy for women's health is especially strong in the area of reproductive rights and two organizations offer complementary models of political action.

The International Women's Health Coalition (IWHC) is a charity 'dedicated to promoting women's reproductive health and rights in Southern countries'. It is based in New York and works in alliance with women's organizations, health professionals and government officials in third world countries and with a variety of non-governmental organizations (NGOs) in the north. Its goal is to serve as a 'catalyst for change through research, consultancy and support for women-centred reproductive health services'. ...

The Women's Global Network for Reproductive Rights (WGNRR) operates on a more decentralized model. It is an autonomous network of groups and individuals from all parts of the world, has been in existence since 1978 and currently has members in over a hundred countries. ... The WGNRR acts as a resource centre, collecting, exchanging and responding to requests for information on reproductive health issues. It organizes and participates in regional and international actions as well as responding to requests for solidarity from around the world. ...

The volume of campaigning on reproductive issues and the growing links at both national and international levels testify to the vitality of this area of women's health politics. However this should not be allowed to obscure the very varied interests of the many groups of women involved. In much of Latin America, for instance, women have been drawn into political action by their inability to obtain safe and effective contraception and by the denial of abortion rights. In many Asian countries, on the other hand, women have been politicized by their experiences of coercive policies that gave them little right to refuse contraception or sterilization.

Significant differences are also evident in debates about strategy. Some women believe that working with government agencies – with 'the state' – or with international family planning organizations can never be an appropriate means to achieve reproductive rights. They argue that only marginal gains will be made, and that these may be at the cost of legitimating existing population policies. Others believe that fundamental change is impossible without entering the corridors of power, either as workers or campaigners.

There is also disagreement among feminist health activists about the acceptability or otherwise of certain medical practices. Some argue that the **new reproductive technologies** such as in vitro fertilization (IVF) are inevitably damaging to women and that their use should be opposed under all circumstances. ... Others do not reject these technologies in principle but call for greater control by women over their development and use.

Disagreements are especially likely to emerge in sensitive areas of work that cross cultural boundaries, as the fight against genital mutilation illustrates. In recent years many women in Africa have campaigned against the public health hazards associated with female circumcision and its negative effects on women's well-being ...

While it is clear that genital mutilation can be extremely damaging to women's health, particular care is needed in the development of appropriate and effective strategies for its elimination.

Thus many groups of women are now working under the broad banner of reproductive rights. They share common goals but come from very different places, have followed a variety of routes and have very different levels of resources at their disposal. ...

Seeking sexual self-determination

A major feature separating 'new wave' reproductive rights campaigns from their predecessors has been an emerging demand for women's right to greater sexual autonomy. In developed countries campaigns for sexual freedom have a long history, especially within the lesbian and gay movements. However they have rarely been linked directly to health, and are sometimes divorced from wider social and economic issues. These important connections are now being made by many women in the context of a broader campaign for reproductive rights.

In Latin America, in particular, female sexuality has been a central concern for many women's health groups. They have emphasized the links between birth control and sexual pleasure, and campaigned for women's right to determine the nature of their own sexual lives. ...

The politics of women's sexuality was also taken up by a group of feminist researchers at the Chagas Foundation in São Paulo. Using an action research approach they worked with the Mothers Club of Diadema, whose members are mostly low-income housewives. While these women wanted basic information about bodily functioning they also wanted to explore ideas about sexual pleasure. This led to extensive debate about the reality of sex where the family shares a single room, where safe contraception is difficult to obtain and where many men put their own pleasure before that of their partner. ...

As a result of their discussions they worked together to produce a series of easily accessible pamphlets entitled *Esse Sexo que Nosso* (This Sex of Ours). After some pressure the Brazilian Ministry of Health agreed to publish 20,000 copies, which have been used for similar projects around the country.

In other parts of the world female sexuality has been less prominent in reproductive rights campaigns. ... However refusal to confront issues relating to women's sexuality is becoming increasingly untenable as the AIDS epidemic spreads. Without a clearer understanding of their own bodies and their own desires, women will be unable to achieve the sexual autonomy that will ultimately be their only means of protection against the HIV virus. It is recognition of this reality that has led women in many countries to set up groups to share their sexual knowledge and concerns. One of the most active of these is the Society for Women and AIDS in Africa, which undertakes educational activities in many parts of the continent.

The battle for birth control

Similar issues of autonomy and decision making lie at the heart of continuing campaigns for safe and effective contraception. The first large-scale efforts to achieve this goal began in Europe and the United States in the late nineteenth and early twentieth centuries. Women from many different backgrounds were involved in campaigns for the wider availability of birth control techniques. Significantly however, divisions between middle-class and working-class women and black and white women were already evident as the **eugenic implications** of some policies became clear.

Today millions of women are still without effective means of contraception and the fight to achieve this continues. However it is now clear that access alone is not enough. Women's health advocates have been highly critical both of the safety and the acceptability of many of the most commonly used methods and of the social inequalities embedded in many family planning services. Hence the emphasis in campaigning has now expanded to include not just availability but also safety and quality of care.

The hazards of the 'new' contraceptives first became apparent in developed countries during the 1970s, with the Dalkon Shield providing one of the most dramatic examples. Women in North America, Australia, New Zealand and many European countries were actively involved both in exposing its dangers and in campaigning for its removal from the market. The device was eventually withdrawn and many women who had been harmed by its use joined together to sue for compensation.

... Though dangerous drugs and devices might eventually be removed from the market in the rich countries, they continued to be exported in their millions to those areas where women had less knowledge and very little choice. In response to this unequal treatment, campaigns were mobilized both by international groups and by women in some third world countries.

... Knowing the hazards of Depo Provera, several groups recently combined together to challenge the introduction of another injectable (Net-en) into the national family planning programme. Another focus of concern has been the dangers of high-dose oestrogen/progesterone formulations (HDEP) which many women use to try to induce abortions.

International groups such as the WGNRR, the IWHC and the International Organization of Consumer Unions (IOCU) have also played a major part in the global dissemination of knowledge about birth control techniques, garnered from women in a variety of social contexts. However judgements about the value of different methods can be difficult to make, since the circumstances of individual women will affect their contraceptive preferences. ...

The work of the Women and Pharmaceuticals Project, based in Holland, has played an important part in beginning to resolve some of these difficulties.

Using both social and biological criteria they have evaluated a range of contraceptive methods in a way that is both scientific and women-centred. Their publications have been widely used in many parts of the world, not just because of the information they provide, but also because of their sophisticated analysis of the methodological issues involved in assessing medical technology from a feminist perspective.

A woman's right to choose?

But whatever the availability and effectiveness of contraception, women will always need access to safe termination of pregnancy, both as a back-up and sometimes as a preferred method of birth control. Recognition of this reality is manifest in continuing campaigns for the legalisation of abortion. In Ireland the struggle is still hard, despite pressure to harmonize with the rest of Europe. In Brazil women's groups managed to prevent the insertion of a foetal protection clause in the 1988 constitution, but the fight for decriminalization continues. In Hungary, Romania and Poland women have fought to retain abortion rights, which have come under threat as a result of the revitalization of the power of the Catholic Church, while in East Germany campaigners have tried to maintain rights threatened by unification with the West. However it is in the United States that one of the most vigorous and certainly the best documented campaigns has been fought – first to legalize abortion and then to maintain that gain.

In 1973 the US Supreme Court legalized abortion in the historic Roe v. Wade case. However, this decision has been under attack for much of the intervening period. As early as 1976 the Hyde Amendment removed Medicaid funding for abortions, except in the case of rape or severe illness. ... This was followed by attempts in many other states to stop public funding of abortion. In 1989 the Webster decision prohibited terminations both in public facilities and in private hospitals receiving public funds. Many states have also passed laws requiring parental consent for termination in minors. Thus the anti-choice movement has been successful in denying or limiting access to legal abortion for some of the most politically powerless women – those who are young, poor or living in rural areas. ...

Before 1973 women had to search for abortions wherever they could find them. In response to this dilemma a group of women in Chicago set up a counselling and referral service called Jane. Within two years they had all learned the skills necessary to perform safe, supportive, low-cost terminations during the first six weeks of pregnancy. ...

'Jane' was able to help many women, but hundreds of thousands more were left to fend for themselves, often in fear and sometimes in poverty. It is a recognition of that still very recent reality that has made so many women (and men) determined to resist those anti-abortion activists who would wish to return to it. This commitment was evident in the March for Abortion Rights held in Washington DC in 1992 and attended by about three quarters of a million supporters. ...

Thus the politics of abortion needs to be placed in a wider context if the differing interests of all those involved are to be adequately recognized. As we shall see similar complexities are apparent in the politics of maternity. Some women are fighting for access to the skills and technology necessary to ensure a safe delivery, while others are resisting what they see as the 'over medicalization' of a major event in their lives.

Controlling Birth

Maternity continues to be a primary cause of morbidity and mortality for women in many parts of the world. Not surprisingly, those most at risk are least likely to have the resources to fight for change, and for generations these deaths were largely invisible. However a number of international organizations campaigned during the 1980s to put maternal mortality on the agenda and hundreds of women's groups have now taken up the cause.

... In 1988 these concerns were taken up by delegates at the Fifth International Women and Health Meeting in Costa Rica, who launched the Campaign against Maternal Mortality and Morbidity. This international initiative is co-ordinated by the WGNRR and the Latin American and Caribbean Women's Health Network.

As part of the Campaign, 28 May was designated International Day of Action for Women's Health. This has now become an annual focus of activity for many women's health groups, especially those working outside the developed countries. Significantly it has also been adopted by WHO, marking an important link between women's health advocates working in very different environments. ...

In 1992 the scale of events was immense, with events occurring in dozens of different countries. In Nicaragua, for instance, activities were held in twenty-one towns and included video presentations, debates, theatre performances, meetings, training sessions, radio programmes and workshops. The Women's Health Network then presented the government with a petition calling among other things for the state to comply with the agreements laid down in the Constitution, the Universal Declaration of Human Rights, the Convention against Discrimination against Women and the commitments undertaken at the 1992 Safe Motherhood Conference. In the Philippines the GABRIELA Commission on Women's Health and

Reproductive Rights put up posters in different communities in metropolitan Manila, emphasizing the dangers of unwanted pregnancies. In Kampala the Safe Motherhood Project organized a workshop for market men and women to sensitize them to women's health issues, while in Equatorial Guinea the Association of Protestant Women distributed the Campaign's Call for Action in schools and hospitals.

Women in many third world countries have used the campaign to call for access to effective and appropriate obstetric care tailored to meet the circumstances of their lives. For most this means a close link between maternity services and primary health care as well as the use of traditional methods where appropriate. ...

In developed countries too maternity campaigners have called for appropriate care, but not surprisingly the detail of their demands has been very different. Most are concerned not to increase levels of obstetric intervention, but to reduce them.

Some women living in rich countries do lack medical support. This is particularly evident in the United States where lack of funding often leaves poor mothers deprived of necessary services. However the major protagonists in the politics of pregnancy have been white middle-class women who can rely on a baseline of effective care for safe delivery but wish to prevent medical intervention exceeding what they regard as reasonable for the health of mother and child. ...

Despite their apparent unanimity the women (and men) involved in the movement do have widely divergent beliefs about the significance of birthing. Some have sought 'natural' childbirth as an end in itself. This is often part of a more general 'anti-technology' stance that emphasizes the spiritual dimension of women's relationship with their own bodies and/or the centrality of the birth process in family life. Others reject such beliefs, arguing that they simply impose a different requirement on women – to give birth 'naturally' to prove their true femininity. Instead they emphasize women's right to determine their own labour – whether or not they opt for technological intervention.

Despite these differing philosophies, consumer campaigns do appear to have had a noticeable effect on medical practice in some countries. More mothers can now choose to give birth in 'home-like' surroundings. They are subjected to less intrusive procedures, are more likely to be cared for by a midwife and are not separated from their babies for lengthy periods. However these gains should not be overestimated. In many hospitals the incidence of procedures such as caesarean sections remain high and home births are rarely available. Even where care has been humanized, birth usually remains firmly under medical control. Indeed it is significant that some of the most visible innovations have occurred in the United States, where pregnant women with resources can command considerable market power. These changes have sometimes been apparent rather than real, reflecting not changes in medical philosophy but an economic imperative to keep patient numbers high as the birth rate declines.

We have seen that the global campaign for reproductive rights is a complex and multi-faceted political reality. It takes many different forms but has the common thread of a belief in women's right to determine what happens to their own bodies. This potential for collective action was amply demonstrated in the 'Women's Declaration on Population Policies', put together by over a hundred women's organizations across the globe for the International Conference on Population and Development held in Cairo in 1994.

Key terms

The following key terms appear in the text above. They have been defined below to aid with the reading of this item.

sexual autonomy control over how people are viewed and treated in terms of their sexuality and sexual behaviour

new reproductive technologies technical intervention in the reproductive process to limit or enhance fertility

eugenic implications the results of certain decisions that allow only 'desirable' groups to decide the number of children they may produce

Questions

1 Identify the key areas of medical practice which Doyal believes that women are (and should be) taking control of in their lives.

2 Outline the campaigns identified in the reading that can be seen as adopting these practices. How successful do you think they have they been to date?

3 What are the key aspects of sexual determination?

4 Using material from this text and any other information you may have, explain and evaluate the ways that women have sought to improve their autonomy in terms of birth control, abortion and maternity rights.

Reading 14.6 'Race', ideology and health research

W. I. U. Ahmad (from) 'Making black people sick: 'race', ideology and health research', in W. I. U. Ahmad (ed.) *'Race' and Health in Contemporary Britain* (1993) Buckingham: Open University Press, pp. 12–17.

Editorial comments

Examining the extensive health inequalities between ethnic groups, Ahmad shows how scientific thinking, and resulting medical practices, have affected views of ethnic minorities in Britain, and our views of others around the world. He, too, challenges the biomedical model for the way it looks only at the individual and potentially treatable causes of illness, while ignoring social or cultural aspects and implications. As life is increasingly medicalized, drugs are used to control behaviour and scientific definitions of society are paramount.

For members of ethnic minorities this has two immediate implications. Firstly, he argues that scientific 'views' of race and their resulting racism (of which eugenics and Nazi concentration camps are only the worst examples) are perpetuated in society despite having no biological foundation. Secondly, cultural behaviours that do not fit the norm are medicalized, defined as forms of mental or physical 'illness' and thus subjected to control.

'Race', medicine and ideologies of oppression

THE CONSTRUCT 'RACE' has been used to support colonization of a socially constructed 'Other', a supposedly inferior people or nation, while the construct 'biomedicine' has been employed to support the increasing colonization of human life. 'Race' has legitimated exploitation on the basis of the 'scientific' and 'natural' superiority of some over others, natural selection taking over from divine hierarchies; differential worth attached to the cultures of the conqueror and the conquered; and an undermining of the values, history, frameworks of knowledge, laws and customs of the colonized.

Biomedicine, too, can be seen as an instrument of oppression, controlling deviance and maintaining conformity – here there is agreement among a range of critiques of biomedicine, from the culturalist, the Marxist, the feminist and the social constructionist perspectives. Biomedicine depoliticizes and individualizes ill health, treats the afflicted in isolation from their social, economic, and citizenship context and thus legitimates structural inequalities and supports the status quo. It diverts attention away from the production of ill health to its distribution among individuals and, by relating it to their lifestyles, perpetuates the ideology of victim blaming.

Like 'race', it legitimates the colonization of new territories, so convincingly argued by Zola (1977). In discussing the increasing medicalization of life, he identifies four concrete ways in which medicine extends its claims of expertise:

1 Through the expansion of what in life is deemed relevant to the good practice of medicine.
2 Through the retention of absolute control over certain technical procedures.

3 Through the retention of near absolute access to certain 'taboo' areas.
4 Through the expansion of what in medicine is deemed relevant to the good practice of life.

He goes on to show how treatment of 'psychosocial' states has become a major preoccupation of medicine, where drugs are now available:

> To help us sleep or keep us awake. To stimulate our appetite or decrease it. To tone down our energy level or to increase it. To relieve our depression or activate our interests. To enhance our memory, our intelligence and our vision – spiritually or otherwise.
> *(Zola, 1977)*

Elsewhere, Zola (1972) claims that biomedicine has taken over from religion and law as the new repository of the truth, becoming the articulator and the guardian of a new, secular morality. On the emergence of biomedicine, he writes: 'Instead of a fixity of the universe, of hierarchical relations promulgated by God, we now had a universe fixed by laws ... Medical science became the ultimate articulator and conveyor of the message of Darwin and Spencer'. Social Darwinism also formed the basis of scientific racism.

Common to both is to some extent the complicity of the colonized. The legitimacy of colonial rule was rarely effectively challenged by the colonized; any rebellion was harshly crushed. Likewise, patients rarely challenge the **hegemony** of medicine or the expert status of the doctor; medicine monopolizes the definition of 'truths' about health and ill health, their causes and cures. Notions of appropriate and inappropriate behaviour in illness are dictated by medicine and relate directly to labels of 'good' and 'bad' patients. The functionalist model of the sick person stipulates conformity to the medical diagnosis and treatment as a precondition for the legitimacy of status as a 'sick person' (Parsons 1951). The function of the 'sick role' is seen by Parsons as maintaining social order and cohesion where society accepts, and sympathizes with, sick people's predicament and assists in bringing them back to 'normality' as long as they behave within the confines of the 'sick role'; normality here is a return to the sick person's role in society, that is, as parent, teacher, or whatever.

'Alternative' therapies are also marginalized, judged by the yardsticks of biomedicine (whether or not these yardsticks are appropriate); and their users and practitioners demonized. Both 'race' and medicine have a fascination with technical solutions. Medicine provides technical/scientific 'fixes' for impaired biology or diseased organisms through surgical, electrical, chemical, rhetorical, or public health interventions. The concept of 'race' led to various fixes, from 'civilizing' the savages through a long period of 'pupillage' under the rule of the civilized colonial powers before 'graduation' to self-rule, to the current fascination with equal opportunities policies as a technical activity.

Neither the structures built on the 'race' theory nor on biomedicine tolerate challenges. The freedom movements in British ex-colonies were explained in terms of 'return to savagery' and the 'end of civilization and democracy', thus legitimating their brutal suppression on the pretence of caring for the masses. Medicine's suppression of alternative therapies, and the patients who may use these, has a long history, including the ideologically motivated removal of lay midwives from maternity care during the medicalization of childbirth. The British Medical Association's (1986) *Report of the Board of Science Working Party on Alternative Therapy* confirmed the medical orthodoxy's paranoia regarding alternative therapies. Recently, attempts to 'scientify' the failure of non-orthodox cancer therapy led to heated debates and eventually acceptance of methodological flaws by the authors.

When alternative therapies are granted credibility it is through the ritual of 'scientific' evaluation, or embracing the religion of science and therefore proving a commonality with scientific medicine. Such conversions help maintain the dominance of scientific medical ideology while suggesting objectivity and openness, and are similar to bringing 'approved' black people into the folds of white institutions, to create an illusion of change while maintaining the status quo.

Racist ideology permeates British and other Western societies and their institutions although racism may be articulated and experienced in different forms. Similarly, the permeation of the **discourse**

of medicine into the collective psyche is apparent from the use of health jargon as metaphor; for example, one hears of racism being the 'cancer' of our society that needs to be 'incised' to return society to 'full health'. Health services are granted or witheld on consultants' or general practitioners' moral judgements. A prime example here is the variation in the availability of abortions between consultants and district health authorities. The common fears about black women 'over-breeding', and about poor quality of parenting in black homes have been reflected in the relatively generous availability of abortion and birth control services to black women, whereas this has been a prime site of white feminists' struggles for such services against medical orthodoxy.

Neither the construct of 'race' nor the institution of medicine has survived on the basis of some intrinsic merit or truthfulness; both are socio-political constructs supported by and supporting dominant orthodoxies and ideologies, often reinforcing and legitimating each other. Gordon (1983) illustrates this with reference to the role of medicine in racist immigration control. An analysis of medicine's claims to be scientific and of science being neutral, objective, value-free, ahistorical and universal is beyond the scope of this [reading]. However, scientific medicine needs to be acknowledged as political, often oppressively so. Medicine played a frontline role in colonialism as an essential and integral tool of colonial foreign policy – the need to institute the London and Liverpool Schools of Hygiene and Tropical Medicine signifies this. It kept the colonizers healthy and its benevolent face softened up the 'natives'. It undermined and often destroyed indigenous systems of health care with the knock-on effect of destroying morale and self worth, and created long-term dependency – a dependency all too apparent in the contemporary health care systems of many underdeveloped ex-colonies. Fanon (1978) states that the colonized people equated accepting foreign medicine with accepting foreign rule.

Earlier still, medicine 'naturalized' slavery by coining diagnostic labels such as *drapetomania* (the 'irrational' and pathological desire of slaves to run away from their masters) and *dysaethesia Aethiopica* (or rascality) …

Even in the recent past (1950s) it was suggested that mental illness among black people in America was due to political activity, for which presumably their brains were not sufficiently developed. New 'scientific' theories purported to demonstrate that while the whites possessed determination, power, self-control and rationality the black people lacked all of these. The theories were often contradictory – for example, showing black people as more sensitive and at other times as less sensitive – but they always confirmed the superiority of white people over black people.

The testing of drugs on men, women and children in the underdeveloped world before marketing in the West as well as using drugs banned in the West in the underdeveloped countries has become commonplace (Doyal 1979). Doyal cites numerous examples of this taking place in Latin America, Africa and Asia …

At the time of writing there is a renewed campaign against the policy of the multinational conglomerate, Nestlé, of aggressive marketing of baby milk in underdeveloped countries, a policy which has a disastrous history in Africa (Doyal 1979).

There are parallels with other areas of medical influence. The medicalization of sexuality, where non-heterosexuality once equalled clinical mental disorder, scientifically legitimated the oppression of gays and lesbians. This continues to the present day with the recent attempts to find genetic explanations for homosexual behaviour and more generally, gender roles. The respectable current affairs weekly, *Newsweek*, devoted eight pages to the subject in one issue and advertised it on its front cover with the heading superimposed on the picture of a child: 'Is This Child Gay? Born or Bred: The Origin of Homosexuality'. A further example of medicine expropriating the moral guardianship of society is the past treatment of unmarried mothers, including their confinement to mental institutions for 'moral imbecility', medicalizing and 'naturalizing' patriarchal gender roles.

Scully and Bart (1978) provide an excellent account of this process in gynaecology textbooks, which both reflected contemporary societal views of women's role and sexuality and structured the medicalization of womanhood. Contemporary treatment of women as patients, and gender divisions in health service employment, also provide evidence of this. The changing fashions in obstetric medicine constantly redefine the boundaries of acceptable maternity behaviour; examples include hospital versus home births, delivery positions, care regimens during pregnancy and after birth, 'active management of birth' leading to increases in induced births, and Caesarean sections.

To see the development and practice of scientific medicine as mediated through socio-political and ideological processes is not **scientific nihilism**. I am not arguing that scientific medicine can simply be reduced to ideology or social relations. That scientific medicine is value-laden is not in doubt; that it is valueless or that its ideological biases can dissolve the phenomenon itself must be contested. Nevertheless, the institution of scientific medicine and its construction of health and illness have a strong ideological basis, and oppressive relations – be they related to 'race', gender, social class or sexuality – are effortlessly reproduced through professional ideologies and institutional administrative practices …

Just as 'common-sense neutral' views about gender roles and the family legitimate gender oppression, so similarly, common-sense ideas about black people become part of the collective wisdom. This is a cyclical relationship. White racism keeps black people in low status in terms of education, employment, housing, health or position in society; this then confirms racist ideas about black inferiority. An anti-racist analysis of black people's experience of health and illness and the response of the health services requires an understanding of racism in British society and its reproduction in institutions, including in medicine.

References

Doyal, L. (1979) *The Political Economy of Health*, Basingstoke: Macmillan.

Fanon, F. (1978) 'Medicine and colonialism', in Ehrenreich, J. (ed.) *The Cultural Crisis of Modern Medicine*, New York: Monthly Review Press.

Gordon, B. (1983) 'Medicine, racism and immigration control', *Critical Social Policy*, 7.

Parsons, T. (1951) *The Social System*, London: Routledge & Kegan Paul.

Scully D. and Bart, B. (1978) 'A funny thing happened to me on the way to the orifice: women in gynaecological textbooks', in Ehrenreich, J. (ed.) *The Cultural Crisis of Modern Medicine*, New York: Monthly Review Press.

Zola, I. K. (1972) 'In the name of health and illness', *Social Science and Medicine*, 9.

Zola, I. K. (1977) 'Medicine as an institution of social control', *Sociological Review*, 20.

Key terms
The following key terms appear in the text above. They have been defined below to aid with the reading of this item.

hegemony the dominant view of the 'experts'

racist ideology the view that minority ethnic groups are inferior

discourse ways of talking and thinking about different groups and their medical condition

scientific nihilism the idea that science has no use or positive functions in society

Questions

1 Explain in your own words the four ways that society has become increasingly medicalized, according to Ahmad.

2 How does Ahmad suggest that medical views of the world have been used to 'explain' and justify or control:
a colonial rule
b 'alternative' medicine
c slavery
d black political activity
e homosexuality.

3 Using material from the text and other sources of knowledge, evaluate the claim that scientific views of the world have been used to limit the activities of minority ethnic groups in a racist society.

4 To what extent would you agree that medicine reflects and legitimates racist ideologies and practices in society?

Reading 14.7 **Disease and disorder**

Bryan S. Turner (from) *The Body and Society* (1984) Oxford, Basil Blackwell, pp. 204–9.

Editorial comments

Turner argues that people as members of society have to be seen as a result of both natural and cultural factors. Drawing on the work of both Emile Durkheim and Michel Foucault, he examines the relationship between concepts of disease and illness and the value judgements found in medical diagnoses to show how definitions of illness are closely linked to the power held by medical practitioners.

The dominance of germ-theory as the cause of disease can be seen as just one way of looking at and talking about health and illness – this is known as the medical discourse. This leads us on to conceptions of the body in our understanding of the sociology of health and illness – a view explored by many writers through the 1980s and 1990s. According to Turner, the body, and disease generally, is equated with social disorder and treated similarly through mechanisms of social control.

Disease and disorder

ONE CENTRAL ISSUE in sociology is the idea that human beings are simultaneously part of nature and part of culture. Culture shapes and mediates nature, since what appears as 'natural' in one society is not so in another. It is 'natural' for respectable Japanese to spit in public, but not to blow their noses. Alternatively, we can argue that nature constitutes a limit on human agency, since, as part of a natural environment, we are subject to growth and decay. Reproduction is a requirement for human societies if they are to survive more than one generation. This limiting boundary is of course both uncertain and flexible, because the limits on human 'natural' capacity constantly change. Modern athletes set standards which were assumed to be impossible in previous sporting epochs. More interestingly, genetic engineering is reshaping and redefining what we take 'life' to be.

Most human societies have historically defined this boundary between the human and the inhuman in terms of rituals. For the sake of argument, these rituals may be classified as rituals of inclusion and rituals of exclusion. In traditional societies, the fact of birth is not an immediate guarantee of social membership; one has to be transferred from nature to culture by rituals of social inclusion. These typically include religious rituals of initiation: baptism, circumcision and scarification. These rituals of inclusion involve cultural work upon the body and their effect is to transform the natural body into a social entity with rights and status. This transformation is brought about by washing, burning and cutting; these transformative interventions are also associated with naming, since having a name is an institutional mark of social membership, but not necessarily of personhood. Being born is not an ultimate guarantee of cultural membership of society, since infanticide was widely practised either implicitly or explicitly in most traditional subsistence societies. Slavery was another alternative and feminist theory claims that women never fully made it across the great divide that separates nature, monsters and unreason from the reality of culture and morality. There are other possibilities. To have a personal name is a good indication that one is a member of a human society. Although chairs and tables are cultural artefacts which embody human labour as commodities, they do not have personal names. Domestic dogs and cats, however, have bodies which have been transformed by human labour (breeding and training) and they are commodities which can be exchanged; they also have personal names and we ascribe character to them. Dogs can be 'neurotic' and 'badly behaved'. Are domesticated dogs part of nature or culture? Indeed, are they persons?

To be born and to be embodied do not in themselves guarantee social membership. The transfer of bodies out of culture back to nature is equally ritualized by exclusionary practices. The dead are buried, cremated or embalmed; their persons are deconstructed by rituals which indicate that they are now to some extent once more 'natural'. Of course, in some cultures a person never dies and may have a capacity for reconstruction at the Day of Judgement. Some persons such as dead saints may continue to have major social roles to play centuries after their physical departure, while most societies have ghosts of one sort or another. It is often argued that advances in modern medicine have made the division between life and death problematic, because the technical definition of death has changed with advances in medical technology. The problem, however, is not simply technical, since there is an essential difference between medical death and 'social death'. Dying is a social process, involving changes in behaviour and a process of assessment which do not necessarily correspond to the physical process of body-death. Death, like birth, has to be socially organized and, in the modern hospital, is an outcome of team activities. These questions concerning birth, dying, personhood and social membership are indications of a generic issue which hinges on the relationship between nature and culture. The argument of this [reading] is that the concept of 'disease' is the most sensitive indicator of the problematic quality of the nature/culture division and that an exploration of the nature of disease provides the best route into the question: what is the body?

Disease versus illness

In the philosophy of medicine, there has been considerable debate over the relationship between 'disease' and 'illness'. Part of my argument is that the uncertain relationship between these two concepts is a function of the paradoxical and contradictory relationship between nature and culture; the connection between the two is also related to the institutionalization of power and knowledge. We can express the problem initially be examining an expression in everyday language. Although we would have no difficulty with the sentence 'This apple is diseased', we would find it an odd use of the language for somebody to say 'This apple is ill' or 'This apple is sick'. Similarly, we might state that 'His lung is diseased', but rarely

'This person is diseased'. To have a 'diseased mind' is an expression used of some person whose behaviour falls completely outside the pale of normal human activity; such a person is a 'monster'. These everyday examples point to a position in medical philosophy which says that illness is an evaluative concept which is entirely social and practical; disease by contrast is a neutral term referring to a disturbance in an organism or, more technically, to some atypical functional deficiency. This position which sharply distinguishes between illness and disease is best represented by Christopher Boorse (1975). Boorse contrasts '**normativism**' and 'functionalism'. Thus, strong normativism argues that all judgements in the medical sciences are evaluative and lack any real descriptive content; weak normativism suggests that health judgements are a mixture of evaluative and descriptive statements. By contrast, functionalism, which Boorse supports, asserts that health and disease may be defined descriptively without reference to values in terms of natural functions which are present within the members of a species. In part, Boorse's argument rests on a distinction between theoretical and practical problems, that is we should not confuse the practical problem of a doctor treating the illness of a patient in a clinic with the theoretical problem of a pathologist analysing a disease in a laboratory context. On the basis of these arguments, Boorse (1976) came eventually to identify three separate types of 'unhealth'. These are disease, which refers to 'some deviation from a biological norm' (Boorse, 1976), illness which is a personal experience of unhealth, and sickness, which is a social role expressing the public dimension of unhealth as in the concept of 'the sick role' (Parsons, 1951).

Normativism – the position that medical judgements are simply evaluative statements – has been dominant in **anti-psychiatry** and, before turning to a critique of Boorse's defence of functionalism, it is important to consider the problem of 'mental health'. It would, of course, be perfectly possible for a Boorsean functionalist to accept that concepts of mental dysfunction are wholly evaluative while rejecting normativism when applied to diseases of the body. One illustration of normativism as a critique of the concept of 'mental illness' would be **labelling theory**. Originally used in the sociology of deviance, labelling theory has been extended to explain mental illness as stigmatized behaviour. Psychiatric labels provide an official stamp on behaviour which is regarded as socially unacceptable in the wider society and the effect of these official labels is social exclusion. It is well known, however, that labelling theory cannot genuinely explain the causes of primary deviance; it merely gives a description of labels, stigma and secondary deviance. Furthermore, psychiatric labels tend to be used as a last resort when other explanations of deviant behaviour have been exhausted. Although labelling theory has clear weaknesses, it has served a useful function as a critique of the medical model. In particular, labelling theory draws attention to the very different consequences for individual behaviour of different social labels: to call someone 'deviant' has very different consequences from calling them 'sick'. Hence the conversion of deviant categories becomes of special interest historically. Nineteenth-century inebriety was converted into the twentieth-century disease of alcoholism, while homosexuality as a sin was transformed via a disease category to simply a personal preference. Paedophilia may well become a candidate for conversion. In psychiatry, diagnostic labels and therapeutic regimes appear to be culturally relativistic and historically variable. It has proved difficult to locate mental illness within an organic category, since psychological disturbance appears to be a product of life stress and professional categorization. The solution to the problem is to argue that while diseases can be defined by neutral biological criteria, illness is essentially social since it refers to undesirable deviation from accepted social norms of health and appropriate behaviour. Diseases belong inside nature; illnesses, inside culture. Human beings, because they are ambiguously located in both nature and culture, are subject to both diseases and illnesses. The implication of this position is that we sometimes misdescribe an illness as a disease and the solution is simply to get our categories correct.

We might agree that illness is essentially a cultural phenomenon, but can we agree that disease is simply a fact of nature and not itself subject to cultural processes? The difficulty is that 'disease' is as much contested as 'illness'. The concepts of 'illness' 'disease' and 'health' inevitably involve some judgement which ultimately rests on a criterion of statistical frequency or an ideal state. The 'average individual' does not exist and biological functions can be realized by very different means. Disease is not a fact, but a relationship and the relationship is the product of classificatory processes: 'a disease pattern is a class, or niche in a framework. This framework is a means of approaching or organizing crude experience, that is, for dealing with everyday events in the most satisfactory way' (King, 1954). The discovery of a new disease is not, according to this view, epistemologically equivalent to discovering a new butterfly; a new disease is the product of a shift in explanatory frameworks or the identification of a new niche. These changes in framework are linked to changes in institutionalized medicine and to the nature of medical power. ... Disease is a system of signs which can be read and translated in a variety of ways.

The merit of Foucault's approach to medicine is that it recognizes that changes in the form of knowledge (of disease) are related to forms of power; the weakness of the philosophy of medicine is that it too frequently and too glibly separates the question 'What is disease'? from the question 'What is the function of medical knowledge in the context of medical professionalization'? The language of disease involves judgement as to what is desirable and undesirable, and the medical profession has in modern society enormous institutional purchase on what is to count as the good life. By relegating disease to nature, Boorse denies the impact of cultural values in medicine at all levels. ...

The conceptual purity is, in any case, ruled out on the grounds that the natural and cultural realms are interwoven and interlocked. The reality which human beings inhabit is socially constructed and that reality includes biology, which, although a limiting horizon, is still culturally constituted and socially transformed. To argue that disease is constituted by classification is thus to raise the question of the ontological status of the body itself.

One implication of Foucault's approach to the relationship between the order of things and the order of words is that the body is itself a cultural object which is the product of classification. ...

To approach disease sociologically, we have to combine the notions that (1) disease is a language, (2) the body is a **representation** and (3) medicine is a political practice. Disease is a social phenomenon, although there may be highly variable individual manifestations of it.

References

Boorse, C. (1975) 'On the distinction between disease and illness', *Philosophy and Public Affairs*, 5.

Boorse, C. (1976) 'What a theory of mental health should be', *Journal for the Theory of Social Behaviour*, 6.

King, L. S. (1954) 'What is disease?', *Philosophy of Science*, 21.

Parsons, T. (1951) *The Social System*, London: Routledge & Kegan Paul.

Key terms

The following key terms appear in the text above. They have been defined below to aid with the reading of this item.

normativism the view that medical diagnoses are only the result of particular value judgements

anti-psychiatry a movement that challenges biological definitions of mental disorders

labelling theory the view that all behaviour is a result of the label applied to it

representation the way the body is perceived by different people such as religious leaders, doctors or sociologists

Questions

1 Explain Turner's view that 'natural' behaviour in different societies can be understood through an examination of cultural norms and rituals of inclusion and exclusion.

2 How can dying be seen as a social process?

3 What does Turner see as the key differences between concepts of disease and illness?

4 Using material from the text and other knowledge, explain and evaluate the view that the sociology of disease rests on three concepts: that disease is a language; that the body is a representation; and that medicine is a political practice.

Reading 14.8 **Feminism and the sociology of the body**

Sarah Nettleton (from) (1995) *The Sociology of Health and Illness*, Cambridge: Polity, pp. 101 and 122–9.

Editorial comments

Continuing and up-dating the feminist viewpoint on health and illness from a post-structural perspective – which also draws on Turner's work on the body – Nettleton examines the way that the body has become the key focus for the 'medical gaze'. She suggests that in late (or post) modernity, society is now 'somatic' or body-centred in a new way. Concerns focus on how people use their bodies in terms of reproduction, abortion and sexual behaviour. This has been accompanied by an extensive increase in 'cosmetic' surgery over the past two decades, along with greater interest in the sexual body due to the AIDS epidemic.

There remain a number of different perspectives on the body. While naturalistic views regard the body as a purely biological entity, increasingly sociologists accept the view that the body is constructed to a greater extent by the expectations and actions of society. Phenomenological perspectives have focused on the subjective experience of the body, which we define as health or illness. Most current thinking presents the body as an entity that has a real existence but which is also transformed by its social existence. We are now expected to work to construct and maintain a fit and healthy body which is increasingly surveyed, monitored and regulated, so that social order is achieved through the control and regulation of reproduction and sexuality as well as medical surveillance and expectations of self-restraint.

Feminist views challenge the mechanical and technological models of the body, which still underpin much medical practice. The bodies of women are perceived as increasingly medicalized, particularly in the treatment of conception and contraception. Attempts at greater female control are often undermined by the new reproductive technologies which tend further to separate women from their bodies, but these developments also make it possible to identify the increasingly cultural aspects of apparently 'natural' states such as pregnancy, motherhood and sexuality.

The sociology of the body

WHILST MALE SOCIAL theorists have been influential in the sociology of the body, feminist sociologists were the first to recognize and make explicit the significance of the body for social theory. Feminist analyses of women's bodies have revealed the extent to which medical and scientific descriptions of the biological basis of bodies are socially constructed, and may be used for ideological purposes such as maintaining gender inequalities. They have also contributed to an appreciation of the ways in which women's bodies have long been regulated by a male-dominated medical profession. Today this regulation and control are perhaps nowhere more evident than in developments in the field of the new reproductive technologies (NRTs). ...

Feminism and bodies: perceptions and assumptions about women's bodies

The way in which cultural assumptions underlie our perception of the body is the main theme of Emily Martin's (1989) study of the *Woman in the Body*. ...

In her book Martin graphically illustrates how bodies

are described in nineteenth-century medical texts in ways that reflect the social and economic system – in that the body formed the model of industrial society.

The body resembled factories and communication systems, and certain parts carried specialized functions. In the twentieth century the development of molecular biology drew on metaphors from information science and management, the co-ordinating centre of which is the central nervous system. The dominant image of the female reproductive system is that of a signalling system which functions in a manner analogous to a radio transmitter. ...

The 'female brain-hormone-ovary system' is described in terms of a hierarchy whereby directions and orders are given and as such relate to the dominant form of organization in Western capitalist societies.

A consequence of this is that 'normal' biological processes come to be defined in negative terms. For example, the menopause is defined in terms of a breakdown in a system of authority, and menstruation is defined as a production system that has failed to produce. Women's bodies come to be seen as 'another kind of horror   the disused factory, the failed business, the idle machine' (Martin, 1989). The metaphors used reinforce the traditional roles assigned to women; they presume that if a woman menstruates, then once again she has failed to produce a baby, and the menopause renders her as unproductive and superfluous to society's requirements.

The images that the 165 women Martin interviewed had of their bodies reflected those of the doctors. This is not surprising as the language ordinary women use to construct themselves is influenced by prevailing medical, social, economic and political discourses. The central image that the women used was 'your self is separate from your body'. Associated with this were five further conceptualizations. First, 'your body is something that your self has to adjust to or cope with'. Many of the women felt at odds with their bodies and 'unpleasant' biological functions were something that had to be 'coped' with. Second, 'your body needs to be controlled by your self'. Many women spoke of differing degrees of control over their bodies which could potentially become beyond their self-control. Third, 'your body sends you signals'. Again, the women articulated how their 'separate' physical body could transmit messages to the self, and when these messages were received they tried to act upon them. Fourth, 'menstruation, menopause, labour, birthing and their component stages are states that you go through or things that happen to you (not actions you do)'. The women felt that it was something that happened to them and did not express it as an experience that unified their physical and lived body. Finally,

'menstruation, menopause and birth contractions are separate from the self. They are "*the* contractions", "*the* hot flushes" (not *mine*); they "come on"; women "get them". The women felt that things happen to their bodies which are, again, removed from the self' (Martin, 1989).

The women, however, were not simply swamped by the medical discourse, because they simultaneously drew on alternative discourses. This was especially true of working-class women. Whilst the middle-class women may have articulated a dissatisfaction with the medical model, at the same time the language of medicine was more evident in their interview data. Working-class women were less likely to use the medical metaphors of failed production and were more likely to see menopause, menstruation and childbirth as part of life. The working-class women especially draw upon a phenomenological as well as a medical model.

Martin suggests women have a view of the world that is different to that which currently dominates. This is as a consequence of the way in which women experience their bodies. Their bodily processes go with them everywhere and so they invariably transcend those **dichotomies** constructed within capitalist societies, such as home versus work, nature versus culture, women versus men, private versus public. ... Martin's analysis integrates the biological and the social and so overcomes the sex versus gender or the biology versus social dichotomy.

In this respect Martin's study fits neatly into the contemporary theoretical literature on the sociology of the body in that it combines naturalistic, constructionist and phenomenological perspectives. Furthermore, it highlights the significance of embodied social action. ... It was, of course, the feminist literature which first drew attention to the importance of the body for sociological analysis. This occurred not only as a result of academic debate but also of women's experience. Women's bodies have been increasingly medicalized, and one of the key aims of second-wave feminism was to reclaim control over the female body. This is not easy, however, as innovations in medical technology permit more and diverse forms of control over women's lives and bodies. One particularly overt example of this is in the area of the new reproductive technologies.

New reproductive technologies

The regulation of bodies and the control of reproduction are central issues within the sociology of the body. This is closely bound to the control of female sexuality which has, in different forms, existed in both religious and secular Western patriarchal societies. Reproductive technology has been used both to regulate populations and enable some women (depending on their social, economic and religious contexts) to have control over their reproduction. The presence of such technology has altered our pre-conceived notions of the boundaries between the social and the physical body. Thus the issues raised by reproductive technologies are central to any consideration of the sociology of the body. ... Technological innovations in themselves do not shape people's lives. Rather, it is the *application* of them which is inherently social.

Stanworth (1987) has grouped those technologies which aim to intervene in the process of reproduction into four categories. First, fertility control technologies such as the pill, diaphragms, intra-uterine devices and the condom; second, those which are designed to manage labour and childbirth such as foetal monitoring, episiotomies, Caesarean sections and forceps; third, screening techniques, such as ultra-sound and amniocentesis, which monitor the foetus for any 'defects'; and finally, conceptive technologies which are designed to overcome infertility. Here we will focus on the latter and in particular the more recent techniques known as 'New Reproductive Technologies' (NRTs). These include artificial insemination by donor (AID) and fertility drugs, in vitro fertilization, egg donation, embryo donation, and the low-temperature storage of gametes and embryos.

The NRTs require varying degrees of technological equipment and sophistication. AID, which has been used in Britain since the 1930s can be carried out by anyone at home. There is no need for medical intervention. Similarly, surrogacy with self-insemination can be negotiated informally. In the UK a Feminist Self-Insemination Group advised and helped women to use this low-tech method for the promotion of pregnancy. Such activities, however, are not deemed acceptable by those who prefer reproduction to be subject to medical and legal regulation. The Warnock Committee, which was set up in 1982 to look into the ethics of technologies of human reproduction, was adamant that all forms of 'artificial' modes of reproduction must only take place under medical supervision.

It is clear that there is a prevailing belief that pregnancy and childbirth must be monitored both medically and legally. The desire to regulate surrogacy is reflected in other reports produced throughout Western Europe, and that this is the outcome of suspicions about the credibility and validity of women's actions. There is a perception that if ordinary people were to make their own arrangements, this could be threatening to social order. ...

Nevertheless, people have always devised their own ways of organizing procreation, and it is likely that they always will. In-vitro fertilization is a more complex technique. It involves removing the egg from a woman which is then fertilized and returned to the woman's womb or to the womb of another, 'surrogate' mother. The first child to be born by this means in the UK was Louise Brown in 1978, hailed as the first 'test-tube baby'. This, and similar techniques, raise a number of legal and ethical issues and highlight the status of women's bodies within Western societies.

First, there is the issue of fatherhood and motherhood. Hitherto, legally we have had only two types of mother, a biological mother and a social mother, but to this we must now add a third, the surrogate – or carry – mother. The legal rule '*mater semper certa est*' (it is always certain who the mother is) can no longer be taken as an eternal truth. The case in the USA of the Sterns, who signed a contract with Mary Beth Whitehead in which she agreed to be artificially inseminated with the sperm of Mr Stern, to carry and deliver the baby, and then hand it over, illustrates the new dilemma. After the birth, Mary Beth Whitehead did not want to give up the baby. 'Experts' who contributed to the legal battle testified that she was not fit to be a mother. She was merely a surrogate, not a 'real' mother. Mr Stern, however, who donated the sperm, was taken to be the real biological father.

Another case, tells of a gay man who agreed to provide a lesbian friend with sperm and have no contact with the child. Having changed his mind, he claimed visiting rights which he was granted after winning his paternity suit. It seems that male sperm is taken to be more significant than the woman's body which nurtures the child during pregnancy and delivers the baby. Responses to the dilemmas created by the NRTs reinforce existing beliefs about the social organization of sexuality and reproduction. The ideology of motherhood is reinforced and patriarchal family life is privileged. ...

This relates to a second issue raised by the context in which NRTs are applied, and this is the status of pregnancy. Women's bodies are rendered superfluous to the creation of life. Oakley (1987) notes that the delivery of babies by Caesarean section to brain-dead women has contributed to this vision. 'It has now become technologically possible to ignore the status of pregnant women as human beings' (Oakley, 1987). Terms such as 'artificial', 'surrogacy' and 'test-tubes' have led to 'the eclipsing of the pregnant women's part in childbearing' (Stanworth, 1987). However, as Stanworth points out, such terms are misleading. The test-tube baby does not, as the term implies, grow in a test-tube but is nurtured within the womb of a woman who experiences pregnancy and childbirth; there is nothing artificial about the pregnancy which results from artificial insemination; and a 'surrogate' mother is a willing woman who is wholly involved in the pregnancy and birthing process.

Responses to NRTs are by no means **homogeneous**. Within the medical profession most doctors are keen to distance themselves from the 'eugenics model' and work instead with a 'therapeutic model' which offers treatment for those women who suffer from infertility. Infertility becomes treated as a disease and doctors offer to alleviate the problem. …

As with most issues, there is no feminist orthodoxy on NRT but rather a range of responses. For some, the creation of NRTs is seen as an end-stage in men's desire to control women and men's aspirations to appropriate reproductive power have been realized. … Others, however, have argued that it is not the technologies in themselves which are problematic, but the social context within which they are developed and applied. Rather than advocating a return to natural motherhood, women must participate in the development and evaluation of these technologies which hitherto have been left to malestream science and medicine, and so make sure that these technologies can be within the control of women. Another critical response has come from feminists who have demonstrated how the provision of NRTs contributes to social inequalities. For example, increasingly infertility clinics are available only in the private sector. …

We can see, therefore, that the recognition of the body as a site of political struggle has been a major force in the women's health movement. Knowledge of women's bodies which had been usurped by men is being regained by women. The implications of this for health and health care are significant. Individuals can no longer be treated as passive, inert objects who have no say in how they want their bodies acted upon. Bodies form a key site of political struggle and their presence forms a key dimension of the interactions between health carers and those who are being cared for.

References

Martin, E. (1989) *The Woman in the Body: a cultural analysis of reproduction*, Milton Keynes: Open University Press.

Oakley, A. (1987) 'From walking wombs to test-tube babies', in Stanworth, M. (ed.) *Reproductive Technologies: Gender, motherhood and medicine*, Cambridge: Polity.

Stanworth, M. (ed.) (1987) *Reproductive Technologies: Gender, motherhood and medicine*, Cambridge: Polity.

Key terms

The following key terms appear in the text above. They have been defined below to aid with the reading of this item.

dichotomies seeing the world in terms of opposites

homogeneous all the same

Questions

1 In what ways can the body be seen as a model or metaphor for industrialized societies?

2 Explain and discuss the key issues raised by the development of artificial insemination and surrogate motherhood.

3 Using the text and any other knowledge you have, explain and evaluate four different feminist responses to the development of new reproductive technologies.

Further reading

The following texts may represent a useful starting point for the further investigation of the ideas contained within this chapter.

Primary texts

Aggleton, P. (1990) *Health*, London: Routledge.

Morgan, M., Calnan, M. and Manning, N. (1985) *Sociological Approaches to Health and Medicine*, London: Routledge.

Taylor S. and Field, D. (eds) (1997) *The Sociology of Health and Health Care*, 2nd edn, Oxford: Blackwell Science.

Turner, B. S. with Sansom, C. (1995) *Medical Power and Social Knowledge*, 2nd edn, London: Sage.

Secondary texts

Senior, M. with Viveash, B. (1998) *Health and Illness*, in the Skills-based Sociology series, Basingstoke: Macmillan.

Trowler, P. (1996) *Investigating Health, Welfare and Poverty*, 2nd edn, in the Sociology in Action series, London: Collins Educational.

Coursework suggestions

1 **Investigate people's experiences and perceptions of their health treatment**

You could use in-depth interviews of people who have recently experienced health care, possibly comparing similar treatment in private and state hospitals. It may also be possible to get older people to compare treatment of similar problems now and in the past to see how health care has changed over time.

2 **Identify the key aspects of the sick role and carry out interviews with people who have recently been sick to test whether the concept is still valid today**

Look at how their family, friends and teachers or employers have responded to any prolonged time off work or school/college. It may be interesting to compare responses to sufferers from chronic illnesses (such as repetitive strain injury, which is often caused by use of technology at work) to responses to those with more acute illnesses (such as a broken leg) or to people with mental disorders such as depression.

3 **Examine patterns of health care among different ethnic groups in your area**

A sensitively applied semi-structured interview with a doctor's receptionist or a nurse in a local hospital may bring insights about assumptions related to ethnic differences in health. A questionnaire may be useful to identify a sample of people from different backgrounds with follow-up interviews on their experience of health care. People whose parents have difficulty with English may provide some interesting insights into problems encountered.

15

Wealth, welfare and poverty

Chapter summary

Reading 15.1 **From Poor Law to Beveridge**
page 433
Tony Cole looks at the ideas underlying both the Poor
Law Amendment Act of 1834 and developments in
the twentieth century, culminating in the Beveridge
Report – seen as the blueprint for the modern welfare
state. He also links these into the development of
sociological theory.

Reading 15.2 **Care in the Community** *page 437*
There have always been arguments against institutional care that suggested the need to integrate care
into the community. Alan Walker looks at the way the
actual implementation of this policy in the 1980s was
also affected by Thatcherite notions of the promotion
of private over public care and attempts to cut back
on state expenditure.

Reading 15.3 **Welfare regimes** *page 441*
Gøsta Esping-Andersen has developed the most
widely used contemporary analysis of the differing
approaches to welfare, which focus on the extent to
which welfare services are provided without the need
to work (de-commodification). He also goes beyond a
simple concern with state institutions to see actual
developments as dependent on other factors, notably
the level of class mobilization.

Reading 15.4 **Women and welfare states**
page 444
Lois Bryson presents an analysis of the way welfare
provision has been gendered and looks at the way this
means women experience the welfare state in a very
different way to men. She also considers some of the
issues that arise from attempts to implement equality
policies.

Reading 15.5 **Poverty and racism** *page 448*
In his analysis of poverty in the UK, Pete Alcock
argues that one of the key pressures that lead ethnic
minorities to be over-represented in poverty and
deprivation is that of racism. This extract considers
the impact of racism both within employment structures and the structures of the welfare state.

Reading 15.6 **Power, privilege and income
inequality** *page 452*
John Westergaard presents a classical Marxist analysis of the patterns of income and wealth distribution
in the 1980s and argues that these point to the continued importance of social class divisions. He argues
that the most notable absence in the arguments
of those who view classes as dissolving is their failure to analyse the power and role of the upper
class.

Reading 15.7 **Poverty and wealth** *page 455*
John Scott has consistently studied and analysed the
shape and influence of the upper class in UK society.
In this reading, he underlines his argument that the
creation of poverty and the creation of wealth need to
be analysed together.

Reading 15.8 **The class analysis of poverty**
page 460
Erik Olin Wright presents an analytical view of the
four main forms of explanations given for poverty. He
goes on to outline in more detail the class analysis of
poverty drawing on the Marxist tradition. This means
that he provides an explanation of the important distinction between oppression and exploitation.

Introduction: Reading the sociology of wealth, welfare and poverty

The origins of British sociology undoubtedly lie in the
attempt to measure the extent of poverty and to identify its causes. This information fed into proposals to
create a modern welfare state, culminating in the
Beveridge Report in 1942. Sociology has therefore
always been intimately connected with social and welfare policies and this interest continues to the present
day.

One problem which often arises in discussion of the
welfare state is the assumption that until the
Beveridge Report and the end of World War II, no

such thing existed. This is a mistaken view since the Poor Law was first passed in 1601 and there have therefore been state interventions into society, based on notions of welfare, for some considerable time.

One of the most important historical developments in the UK was the passing of the 1834 Poor Law Amendment Act. It was this which introduced significant changes to the workhouses – often against protests from local working people, who could see the way they were likely to be treated inside these fearful institutions, the workings of which were exposed in the Charles Dickens novel *Oliver Twist*. In an extract from his book on the welfare state, Tony Cole (1986) (**reading 15.1**) provides a summary of the ideas inspiring the Poor Law Amendment Act and also goes on to look at developments in the first half of the twentieth century.

It is important to be aware of what principles lay behind the Poor Law legislation. This is because it was against these that the modern welfare state was created. It is however also the case that some of these principles were later incorporated into New Right thinking, which, through the Conservative governments of the 1980s, had an impact on the welfare state.

One of the key elements of Conservative policy in the 1980s was the initiative known as 'Care in the Community'. In **reading 15.2**, Alan Walker (1989) argues that while there have always been arguments for care in the community – mainly resting on negative reactions to large-scale institutional care – there is a distinctive element to the way this policy was implemented in the 1980s, which derive from the free-market principles of the New Right. As a result of their impact on government in the 1980s it is clear that the nature of the welfare state in the UK has changed. In order to try to consider the extent to which this is the case, it is useful to engage in comparative analysis by looking at the experience of other countries.

It is such an exercise that lies at the basis of Gøsta Esping-Andersen's (1990) work. He has developed a new and influential typology of what he calls welfare regimes. He uses this term, rather than the more conventional 'welfare states', to underline his point that the nature and direction of welfare provision in any society depends on more than simply the nature of state institutions in that society. He argues that the level of class mobilization is important in leading to the level of de-commodification. His comparative analysis of advanced industrial societies has led him to argue that welfare regimes form around three clusters which he classes as conservative, liberal and social democratic regimes. The characteristics of these three types of welfare regime are discussed in **reading 15.3**, which will allow you to consider which of these

regimes contemporary UK provision most resembles.

One area of controversy relating to Esping-Andersen's analysis is the extent to which it is applicable to the experience of women who do not spend their whole lives involved in paid employment. The issue of gender inequalities in relation to the welfare state has been a long-running one, going back to some rather questionable assumptions contained within the Beveridge Report. Lois Bryson (1992) has argued that the experience of welfare is very different for men and for women and in **reading 15.4** she looks at the way that this operates, focusing both on the employment sector and the institutions of the welfare state itself.

It is also of course the case that there are inequalities relating to ethnicity in terms of the experience of welfare and life in general. This leads to ethnic minorities in this country being much more likely to suffer from poverty and deprivation. In **reading 15.5** – an extract from his study of poverty in the UK – Pete Alcock (1993) looks at the effect of racism on poverty and deprivation by considering its impact on both the employment structure and the institutions of the welfare state itself.

The third main social division, which has clear implications, both in terms of the experience of the welfare state, but also in terms of the experience of poverty or inequality, is that of social class. In **reading 15.6**, John Westergaard (1995) defends the classical Marxist argument that social class is a fundamental element of the social structure and he argues against those who see it as diminishing in importance, in particular by arguing that such analyses ignore the continued existence – and power – of an upper class in this country. His analysis provides material relating to both poverty and wealth, as does the work of John Scott (1994). It is a feature of the reorganization of the syllabus that these two elements can now be analysed together. It is certainly the case that John Scott feels they should – a point he has consistently argued. In **reading 15.7**, he makes a number of points relating to recent evidence on the wealthy in the UK.

Once we have decided how many people are in poverty (very much a matter of debate) then logically we can move on to consider the causes of poverty in order to devise programmes to eliminate it. However, we are of course faced here with another debate and in **reading 15.8** Erik Olin Wright (1994) provides an analytical summary of the four main approaches to the explanation of poverty. He goes on to outline what he calls the class analysis of poverty and provides some important information relating to the distinction between oppression and exploitation and the way that confusing these two can provide a mistaken impression of what class analysis entails.

Reading 15.1 **From Poor Law to Beveridge**

Tony Cole (from) *Whose Welfare?* (1986) London: Tavistock, pp. 13–14, 17–18, 21–2 and 24–30.

Editorial comments

In this reading, Tony Cole traces the link between the rise of sociology and the rise of social policy in the UK, through the response to the 1834 Poor Law Amendment Act, which ushered in the dreaded workhouses, and also through a consideration of the family policy evident in Victorian times. The extract goes on to look at reactions to the developments in the late nineteenth and early twentieth centuries in terms of the formation of the welfare state.

1834: sociology and social welfare – origins and foundations

The new Poor Law

SOCIOLOGISTS AND OTHERS have questioned the use of the term 'welfare' and indicated that it may be used to cover a wide range of intentions and effects. Some of the complexity of the concept is illustrated in the following criticisms made of the system of poor relief operating in England prior to the Poor Law Amendment Act, 1834:

(i)   It was not adequate to the task of relieving or preventing poverty, especially after the massive changes brought about by industrialization, urbanization, and the rapid growth of population (from an estimated 9¼ million in 1781 to 16½ million in 1831).

(ii) Despite this failure, many **ratepayers** and commentators saw its cost as a burden; an estimated 10 per cent of the population were on relief in 1803 and, in 1815, an estimated 100,000 paupers were in workhouses.

(iii) To many of the propertied classes, this burden might have been tolerable if it had acted as effective insurance against unrest among the poor but it did not. In 1830 there were agricultural riots in areas covered by the Speenhamland system.

(iv) Speenhamland itself and poor relief generally came under increasing theoretical or ideological attack. In particular, relief was said to demoralize the worker by undermining hard work and independence – the focus of this concern was nearly always on the able-bodied poor rather than the old, sick, or orphaned. These ideas are explored more later.

(v)   Poor relief and labour mobility. The economist Adam Smith saw that the expanding industrial capitalism required that village labourers be prepared to move to the growing towns and factories. He argued that the 1662 Act of Settlement, empowering **parishes** to remove newcomers from the village if they appeared likely to become chargeable on the rates, prevented many people leaving their villages to seek work elsewhere. Modern historians believe these restrictions on labour mobility were probably over-estimated, but as Fraser notes on the 1834 Report, 'What people thought was happening was, for the purpose of social policy, more important than what was actually happening' (Fraser, 1973).

…

The Poor Law Amendment Act, 1834 – agenda and proposals

In the shaping of social policy and the exercise of power generally, it is important to look at what is called agenda setting, a process which 'presents a limited range of policy options as inevitable, probable or impracticable, very much according to the current wisdom in the corridors of state' (Golding and Middleton, 1982). The 1834 Report set the agenda by omitting or understating the following issues:

(i)   It underplayed the influence squalid housing, poor sanitation, and dirty, dangerous working conditions could have on working-class life.

(ii) It dealt only minimally with poverty among the elderly, orphaned, and sick.

(iii) It assumed unemployment among the able-bodied was self-chosen and wilful rather than related to such structural factors as lack of work and economic upheaval.

The Act itself was based on three key principles:

(i)   The Poor Law should be run by a central authority. This proposal seems to run counter to the doctrine of **laissez-faire**. It was consistent, however, with another view strongly held by the Report's authors. This was a firm and optimistic belief that the new 'scientific study of society' could be rationally applied to problem solving and that bureaucratic organization was the most efficient means of pursuing this.

(ii) Relief was to be made conditional on entry into

a workhouse which would 'moralize' the pauper. Paupers were those with no livelihood and who relied on relief or begging. They were categorized as moral defectives and seen as quite distinct from the poor on low incomes.

(iii) Conditions in the workhouse were to be set at a level lower than any likely to be met outside. This so-called principle of less eligibility was designed to ensure that even the lowest wages available were more attractive than the workhouse.

The historian E. P. Thompson (1968) quotes one administrator of a Norfolk workhouse as recording that his policy of reducing inmates' diets had been less effective as a deterrent to workhouse entry than '"a minute and regular observance of routine", religious exercises, silence during meals, "prompt obedience", total separation of the sexes, separation of families, labour and total confinement'. He also forbade paupers from keeping their own possessions such as clothing or soap and noted, with satisfaction, how his policy led twelve women paupers to leave the workhouse.

In short, the Act was designed to deter paupers rather than relieve the poor. ...

Women, work, and welfare in Victorian Britain – the rise of the family wage

So far, like much history and sociology, the writing has referred to social classes or the poor but has not differentiated on grounds of gender. This must be remedied. Not only was (and is) there inequality between women and men in society but social policy has often reflected and reinforced this. It has, to some extent, been the work of feminists in these areas to 're-discover' some of the processes by which this inequality was produced and is sustained. In doing this, they have shown how these academic disciplines have often reflected the dominant male assumptions of wider society.

The industrial revolution made waged work outside the home the main or only source of household income and, with this, labour at home ('housework') lost touch with the public world of money, status and recognition (Himmelweit, 1983). Initially, men were a minority of waged workers but gradually this changed as middle-class reformers campaigned against child and female labour on 'protective' grounds. Sometimes this reforming spirit came from a Puritanical zeal which looked on the mines, for example, as 'indecent' places for women to work. Women's role in providing a moral environment at home came to be increasingly stressed and they came to be defined primarily as wives and mothers. These roles had assumptions of nurturance and dependency.

In addition to these reforming pressures, male-dominated working-class organizations sought to strengthen their position by reducing the supply of labour, that is excluding women and children. They could also then argue for the need for a higher wage to support a family. Thus was born the ideology of the family wage, the idea that there should be one wage earner per family and that he, for it was assumed to be the man, should be able to earn enough to support the others. As a consequence, of course, single men benefited but wages and opportunities for the many women who stayed in the labour market were depressed. Some feminists argue that this led to marriage and domestic labour being the only options for many working-class women. As in the exclusion of women from 'indecent' mines, we again see women's sexuality being defined by statute or economic pressure.

In the long run, it was beneficial also to the capitalist class to have their (male) employees better fed and looked after. In other words, women came to be defined in terms of reproducing the workforce, through bearing and rearing children and caring for men. Coote and Campbell (1982) argue that the consciousness of the family wage ideology still affects trade union bargaining to the detriment of demands for equal pay.

In general, we will not look in as much detail as this at employment or wage policies but the impact of the above on women's welfare is crucial. Their assumed dependence on men was, for example, later institutionalized in the National Insurance system. ...

The Poor Law era

Returning now to the period and practice of the New Poor Law, we should note the following background changes in nineteenth century Britain. There were reforms in local government, public health, factory inspection, and education. Some of these were associated with attempts to appeal to those better-off sections of the male working class who achieved the vote in 1867 and 1884. Our main theme here, however, is the operation of the Poor Law itself.

Poor Law practice – continuity and change
There was much working-class hostility to the new Act and the workhouses ('Bastilles'). As it turned out, however, there was much continuity between pre- and post-1834. Firstly, the local Poor Law guardians (mainly middle class) found that the centralized administration did not erode their power as much as they had feared. Secondly, outdoor relief continued to be given, especially in industrial areas when trade slumps made the idea of frightening the unemployed into work more than usually inappropriate.

Some historians believe that it was only in the 1860s that the Poor Law was organized on its strictly intended lines. A series of poor winters and a depression in the cotton industry led to big increases in spending on outdoor relief and charity. There was also growing concern with the condition both of children and of sick inmates of workhouses. Many commentators argued that these large institutions were breeding grounds for disease, institutional dependence, and stigma, undermining children's chances of achieving an independent life outside the workhouse. As a result, a number of changes were brought in.

Firstly, workhouse organization was tightened up. The Poor Law Board became a full department of state and, in 1871, was amalgamated with public health provision to become the Local Government Board. There were also moves to provide separate infirmaries for the sick and boarding-out arrangements for children, in theory leaving the able-bodied pauper to face the harsher workhouse test that was introduced and which lasted until the 1880s.

Secondly, concern that charity had grown indiscriminately and was demoralizing the poor gave rise to a more disciplined approach to giving. The Charity Organization Society was set up in 1869 to help regulate charity according to the Victorian virtue of self-help; charity was denied to those deemed incapable of such. The casework assessment involved in this was the forerunner of much modern social work practice and partly explains the origin of the view of social workers as agents for imposing middle-class values on the poor.

Poor Law ideals under attack

By the 1880s and 1890s, there was increasing opposition to Poor Law ideals. There was the growing organization of unskilled workers into unions, the reappearance of socialist ideas and the growth in influence of the newly enfranchized sections of the working class. Golding and Middleton (1982) note that, although class conflict and consciousness were increasing, the relatively new popular press did not express this. These papers sometimes called for reforms for 'the deserving poor' but made no criticism of overall class inequality and capitalism.

In ruling circles there was growing concern that a disaffected working class could be a threat to order and stability. Some politicians began to accept the need for reform as a ransom for the protection of privilege. In addition, whilst the new Poor Law might have been appropriate for securing the readiness to work of a large unskilled workforce new to waged labour, it was not appropriate for securing the support of an increasingly skilled workforce.

In this way welfare came to be less repressive and more ideological in its role. This distinction is based on the work of the modern French Marxist Althusser. He saw repression (by the law or armed forces) and

ideological conditioning (especially through education) as ways in which the state acts to uphold the system by which most wealth is in the hands of a minority and the majority work for them. An important part of this process is getting the subordinate class to accept their position; they are more likely to do this if welfare has narrowed some of the extremes of inequality.

Concern about national efficiency

Towards the end of the century, concern was growing that Britain's main competitors, Prussia and America, were beginning to threaten her economic and imperial power. It was argued that a strong nation needed fit, healthy workers and this might require an extension of welfare provision. Behind this also was a re-working of the theory of Social Darwinism, no longer stressing the survival of the fittest individual but rather that of the group or nation; in this way Social Darwinism took on overtly racist dimensions. ...

British welfare development also received a boost when anxieties about national decline were heightened by evidence of massive ill health during recruitment to the Boer War (1899–1902).

Most of these explanations of welfare development in Britain roughly correspond with those of post-war Marxist historian John Saville, whose theory stressed three main factors:

(i) Property owners' recognition that welfare was necessary as a ransom for their security.

(ii) Industrial capitalism's requirement of an efficient workforce.

(iii) Working-class struggle, which has been the main determinant of the pace of reform. The other factors remind us that reforms need not be against capitalist interests.

Other explanations – progress and bureaucracy?

Some writers have argued that welfare development was a humanitarian reaction to the horrors of the Poor Law. ...

Another set of explanations suggests that, from the 1834 Commissioners down to Beveridge, welfare state development has been the impetus of the administrators themselves, a kind of self-sustained bureaucratic initiative. ...

Alternatives to Poor Law provision – trade unions, friendly societies, and insurance companies

Outside the Poor Law system there were two main kinds of organized relief:

(i) Mutual aid. This was the collective provision in the form of contribution-based benefits made by the working class, or at least its better-off members. Mutual aid was largely organized through trade unions and friendly societies. The latter with four million members in 1872 was far more statistically significant, but less socially threatening to the powers-that-be than the trade unions.

(ii) Private insurance. The commercial insurance companies with their aggressive sales methods catered mainly for those who feared the stigma of a pauper funeral.

The twentieth century

… Marxists argue that many reforms can actually reinforce capitalism. They point to the many reforms introduced by Conservative and Liberal governments as evidence of this. The Liberal Government of 1906 was just such a reforming government. …

Old age pensions
Firstly, after three decades of interest and agitation, Britain finally introduced old age pensions in 1908, nearly ten years after New Zealand. The pension was means tested and small and, whilst it distinguished

between the 'deserving' and 'undeserving' (those who habitually failed to work or save), it was outside the hated Poor Law. Unlike today's pensions, it was financed out of general taxation with no contributory requirement. In those days, taxation extended far less into lower income groups and so pension funding had some vertical redistributive effect, that is from rich to poor.

The National Insurance Act, 1911
This introduced compulsory insurance (with contributions from employers, employees, and the state). Part I of the Act covered health insurance for all manual workers and non-manual workers below a certain income. It provided sick pay and free medical treatment from a 'panel' doctor for the worker but not his dependants. In Britain today, we take free GP or hospital treatment for granted but it is a benefit which in other times or places would have to be paid for; it is therefore called part of the social, as opposed to money, wage. Part II covered unemployment but included only 2¼ million, predominately male workers in a limited range of occupations.

References

Coote, A. and Campbell, B. (1982) *Sweet Freedom*, London: Picador.

Fraser, D. (1973) *The Evolution of the British Welfare State*, London: Macmillan.

Golding, P. and Middleton, S. (1982) *Images of Welfare: Press and public attitudes to poverty*, Oxford: Blackwell.

Himmelweit, S. (1983) 'Production rules OK? Waged work and the family', in L. Segal (ed.) *What is to be Done About the Family?*, Harmondsworth: Penguin.

Thompson, E. P. (1968) *The Making of the English Working Class*, Harmondsworth: Penguin.

Key terms

The following key terms appear in the text above. They have been defined below to aid with the reading of this item.

ratepayers rates were, until the 1980s, the main form of local taxation, paid on the value of property and therefore attacked by the more affluent elements, particularly when revenue from rates was spent on the poor

parishes the lowest level of local government and the unit on which administration of the Poor Law was based

laissez-faire to leave alone; a phrase associated with those who believe that the market left to its own devices will provide just outcomes and that this is, therefore, an argument against state intervention in society

Questions

1 Summarize in your own words the criticisms of the old Poor Law.

2 Why does the author feel that the 1834 Poor Law Amendment Act was designed to 'deter paupers rather than relieve the poor'?

3 Explain what is meant by the concept of the 'family wage' and why this has important implications for gender inequality.

4 In what ways might the principles underlying the 1834 Poor Law Amendment Act and the principles underlying the welfare policies of the New Right in the 1980s be seen as similar?

5 To what extent do sociological arguments support the notion that welfare development was a humanitarian reaction to the horrors of the Poor Law?

Reading 15.2 **Care in the Community**

Alan Walker (from) 'Community Care', in M. McCarthy (ed.) *The New Politics of Welfare* (1989) London: Macmillan, pp. 207–14.

Editorial comments

Alan Walker argues that the implementation of the 'Care in the Community' policy by the Thatcher governments of the 1980s represented a break with the pre-existing consensus on the provision of welfare care in the community, which has led to large-scale closure of institutions for the care of the elderly and the mentally handicapped and also represents an ideologically inspired attempt to promote private welfare provision and to reduce the role of local authorities in this area. The reading contains a detailed analysis of the development and implementation of Care in the Community, up until the end of the 1980s.

The new politics of community care

NEW IDEOLOGICALLY INSPIRED pressures arising in the late 1970s and early 1980s – budgetary and resource constraints and the cost-effectiveness imperative – combined with a major expansion of need for care, particularly among very elderly people, produced the political will to overcome both inertia and sectional interests. But the policy itself departed significantly from the, albeit weak, consensus that had existed for the previous forty years. Thus, the emphasis in policy has shifted away from care *in* the community by local authority personnel towards an even more confusing mixture of care *by* the community itself and private care, regardless of whether in domiciliary or institutional settings.

Promoting the private sector

While the primary intention of community care policy over the past nine years appears to have been the negative one of reducing the role of health and social services authorities in the provision of care, the 1980s also witnessed for the first time the active official encouragement of the private sector. This new policy direction was signalled early on in the life of the first Thatcher government when, soon after coming to power, the **DHSS** moved to encourage a switch in the provision of residential care from the public sector to the private sector.

It did so, first of all, by reducing the resources available to local authorities, by 4.7 per cent in 1979–80 and 6.7 per cent in 1980–1. Although cuts in **PSS** expenditure were carried out in the mid-1970s these fell particularly on capital, with some limited protection (2 per cent real growth per annum) being offered to current spending. In fact what happened in practice was that many local authorities took steps to protect their PSS spending, that is until the introduction of the block grant in 1981–2 and the subsequent imposition of ratecapping considerably reduced their room for manoeuvre.

Secondly, while the public sector received the stick the private sector was given the carrot. The DHSS agreed not only to meet the full cost of care in private residential and nursing homes for those on income support (then supplementary benefit) but it also allowed local offices to set limits on such board and lodging payments deemed appropriate for their area. As a result the number of residential places in private rest homes for the elderly and physically and mentally disabled nearly doubled (97 per cent) between 1979 and 1984, with expenditure on both residential and nursing homes increasing from £6 million in 1978 to £460 million in 1986. The proportion of people in private residential homes receiving help with their fees through income support payments increased from 14 per cent in 1979, to 35 per cent in 1984 and, by 1987, had reached 54 per cent.

Since this growth in spending conflicted with the government's policy of reducing public expenditure, the DHSS acted to stem the flow of resources first by freezing local limits in September 1984 and then in April 1985 imposing national limits for board and lodging payments. These limits, reviewed three times since their introduction, were in 1988 £130 for residential and £185 for nursing homes for the elderly and £160 and £200 respectively for homes for people with mental disabilities and, therefore, still continue to provide a substantial subsidy to the private sector. In addition, many local authorities use private homes on an agency basis to house some of their residents. The picture sometimes painted of DHSS ministers being taken by surprise by the unplanned expansion of the private residential sector sits rather uneasily with the purposeful encouragement given to it and the government's antagonism towards local authority spending.

Some policy analysts have mistakenly viewed the growth of the private sector of residential care as beneficial in terms of increasing choice in an expanding '**mixed economy of welfare**'. Indeed, the appeal to increased choice has proved an important source of popular legitimation for the fast expansion of the private sector. However, while it is true that there has been a rapid multiplication of private homes – estimated by the **Audit Commission** in 1986 to be doubling in size each year – genuine choice requires a range of alternatives: public sector homes, day care, the chance to remain in an ordinary home with community support. But, ironically, this choice has been restricted by the 'perverse' incentive' (Audit Commission, 1986) provided by social security. Furthermore, when it comes to entering a residential home the concept of 'choice' is rarely appropriate. The need for residential care usually arises because of a crisis of care in the informal sector, leaving little time to 'shop around'. Thus, the promise of choice held out by the supporters of the private sector is illusory.

A study of the private sector by the Centre for Policy on Ageing found that only a quarter of residents exercised any choice about the home they were admitted to, while nearly a quarter said that their admission resulted from unsolicited arrangements by a third party. Choice between private homes is severely restricted by factors such as geographical area, waiting lists and ability to pay. There is, for example, a clear North–South divide in the public/private mix of welfare. Private nursing home beds in the South-West outnumber those in the Northern region by seven times. In two regions, South-East and South-West Thames, the private sector already provides more than half the total unit health care for elderly people. According to the Audit Commission (1986) a more equitable distribution of resources for health and social services, sought through RAWP and GREA calculations, has been offset by board and lodging payments for private care.

Within local areas choice is restricted by the admission criteria applied by private homes, often excluding demented people or those who are difficult to control. Thus an ADSS (1986) survey found a tendency for private rest homes to select the less severely disabled elderly people, leaving the more severely disabled for the public sector. Also private homes often levy charges above the income support limits, requiring top-up payments, or make supplementary charges for single rooms or items such as laundry.

Once inside a private home residents cannot exercise much choice either. A recent study of homes in North Yorkshire found that 21 per cent had undergone a change of ownership in the previous 18 months. Residents have no say in such changes and are not always informed before they happen, nor do they have any choice about other changes in the character of their home.

Residents entering small homely homes may find them enlarged. Residents have no control over the

mix of residents or who shares their bedroom. As charges move ahead of (income support) limits residents may find themselves shifted into double or treble rooms, required to commit their pocket money to supplement the (income support) allowance or being subsidised by relatives – often without their knowledge.
(Bradshaw, 1988)

Questions have been raised not only about the distributional consequences of the government's policy of promoting the private sector; considerable doubts have also been raised about the quality of the care provided. As the private residential sector has mushroomed, evidence has mounted of abuse, misuse of drugs, fraud, lack of hygiene and fire hazards in some homes. Some of the worst cases of abuse have been documented by the media, such as Yorkshire Television's 1987 programme *The Granny Business*. Evidence of abuse in the private sector inevitably invites comparison with the public sector and there are similar instances of ill-treatment to be found there. However, concentrating on this sort of comparison of rogues diverts attention from the key issues: the operation of power in a residential setting, regardless of whether it is publicly or privately run, and which of the two sectors can be sufficiently regulated to ensure that no abuse of power occurs, issues we return to later.

Care in the community

At the same time as imposing severe resource constraint on local authorities and encouraging the rapid growth of the private residential and nursing home sector, the government had embarked on a radical programme of mental health hospital closure. The policy of hospital rundown, particularly of mental illness facilities, dates back to the *Hospital Plan* of 1962. However, prior to 1987 no major hospital had been closed.

There has been a steady decline in the number of patients in both mental illness and mental handicap hospitals. For example, in the ten years to 1986 the average number of daily occupied beds in mental illness hospitals fell from 109,000 to 82,500 and in mental handicap hospitals from 59,000 to 42,500. But the decline accelerated in the 1980s as the government's discharge programme took effect.

The 1981 Care in the Community initiative was specifically intended to promote the discharge of long-stay hospital patients by enabling district health authorities to transfer their funds (above and beyond joint finance) to local authorities and voluntary organizations in order to support ex-patients in the community. In addition the DHSS has exerted considerable pressure on health authorities to close hospitals within specified time limits. This contrasts with the earlier consensus period of community care policy as exemplified by the 1976 DHSS document on priorities in the health and social services: 'The closure of mental illness hospitals is *not* in itself an objective of government policy, and the White Paper stresses that hospitals should not encourage patients to leave unless there are satisfactory arrangements for their support' (DHSS, 1976).

Although the radical Conservative welfare policy has succeeded where previous consensus policies had failed in overcoming institutional inertia and professional interests in the promotion of community care, the main motivation for doing so is cost-efficiency with the effectiveness of care received in the community taking second place. This was the main thrust of the trenchant critique of the government's community care policy towards people with mental disabilities by the House of Commons Social Services Committee (1985), one of the most authoritative among several similarly critical reports in recent years.

The Social Services Committee focused attention on the disaster course that had been set by forcing a closure programme without sufficient planning preparation and consultation and, furthermore, without any agreed understanding of what the intended community care would actually entail. It was especially mindful of the danger that community care is perceived as a cheap option. In the Committee's own words: 'A decent community-based service for mentally ill or mentally handicapped people cannot be provided at the same overall cost as present services. The proposition that community care could be cost-neutral is untenable ... We are at the moment providing a mental disability service which is underfinanced and understaffed in its health and social aspects' (Social Services Committee, 1985).

The official rhetoric surrounding the government's policy may be community care, but the reality is decanting and de-hospitalization coupled with an increase in both public and private residential placements. For example, between 1976 and 1985 there was an increase of 70 per cent in the numbers of mentally handicapped people in local authority staffed homes and 154 per cent in private homes. The bulk of the increase (133 per cent) in the numbers in private homes occurred between 1981 and 1985 while most of the increase (47 per cent) among those in public sector homes took place between 1976 and 1981. So, the result of hurried de-hospitalization in the face of the underfunding of community-based services is that many people with mental disabilities have merely been shifted from one institution to another. People are ending up in residential homes when they do not need to because there is no realistic alternative and private sector places are subsidized by social security.

The Social Services Committee summed up the irresponsible nature of the government's care in the community policy in its now famous sentence: 'Any fool can close a long-stay hospital: it takes more time and trouble to do it properly and compassionately' (Social Services Committee, 1985). In trying to bring some sense to bear the Committee attempted to establish the basic principle of a community care policy and insisted that the statutory health and social services are central to the provision of community care, both of which harked back to the pre-1980s consensus.

Residualizing the social services

A series of what seemed as they occurred to be separate policy developments over the last decade or so may, with the benefit of hindsight, be seen as part of an evolving government strategy aimed at turning local authority social services from the main providers of formal care into something far more limited: the provider of those residual services which no one else could or would take on.

In 1980, in a speech to directors of social services departments, the then Secretary of State, Patrick Jenkin, outlined a supportive and decidedly residual role for the social services: 'a long stop for the very special needs going beyond the range of voluntary services'. In 1981 the White Paper on services for the elderly asserted, in a widely quoted phrase, 'care in the community must increasingly mean care *by* the community' (DHSS, 1981). The previous year, when giving evidence before the House of Commons Social Services Committee, Jenkin had justified the cuts in PSS expenditure and the closure of long-stay hospitals (outlined above) on the, unsubstantiated, assumption that the non-formal sector would expand: 'When one is comparing where one can make savings one protects the Health Service because there is no alternative, whereas in personal social services there is a substantial possibility and, indeed, probability of continuing growth in the amount of voluntary care, of neighbourhood care, of self help' (Social Services Committee, 1980). This aim of placing greater reliance on quasi-formal voluntary help and informal support was reflected in the Care in the Community (1981) and the Helping the Community to Care (1984) initiatives.

But it was Jenkin's successor as Secretary of State, Norman Fowler, in a speech to the 1984 Joint Social Services Conference in Buxton, who provided the clearest and most detailed outline of the new residual role proposed for social services. He argued that there are 'three paramount responsibilities' of social services departments: to take a comprehensive strategic view of all the sources of care available in the area; to recognize that the direct provision of services is only part of the local pattern and that in many cases other forms of provision are available; and to see a major part of their function as promoting and supporting the fullest possible participation of the other different sources of care. The fundamental role of the state, according to Fowler, is 'to back up and develop the assistance which is given by the private and voluntary support' (Fowler, 1984).

The Audit Commission's inquiry into community care came to the same conclusion as countless previous independent studies: 'Joint planning and community care policies are in some disarray. The result is poor value for money. Too many people are cared for in settings costing over £200 a week when they would receive a more appropriate care in the community at a total cost to public funds of £100–£130 a week. Conversely, people in the community may not be getting the support they need' (Audit Commission, 1986).

The Audit Commission proposed various organizational changes aimed primarily at clarifying the overlapping responsibilities of health and social services authorities. In the case of the physically and mentally disabled, local authorities were to be given lead responsibility and made responsible for their long-term care in the community, except for the most severely disabled who would be the responsibility of the NHS. The long-term care of the elderly people in the community would be financed from a single budget established by contributions from the NHS and local authorities. The budget would be under the control of a single manager who would purchase services from the appropriate public or private agency. Health authorities were to be given lead responsibility for the care of the mentally ill in the community.

The Audit Commission's critical report was much more influential with the Government than any previous one had been, including the authoritative analysis by the House of Commons Social Services Committee. The Secretary of State had been promising, for two years, the publication of a Green Paper on the personal social services. This did not materialize and, instead, in response to the debate following the Audit Commission report, Sir Roy Griffiths was appointed, in March 1987, to examine problems in the arrangements for community care between the NHS and local authorities and to explore the option of putting the whole service for elderly people 'under the control of a manager who will purchase from whichever public or private agency is appropriate'. (Sir Roy Griffiths had conducted a similar inquiry into the management of the NHS in 1983, which led to the appointment of general managers at district level.) The report of the Griffiths inquiry was published in March 1988.

References

Audit Commission (1986) *Making a Reality of Community Care*, London: HMSO.

ADSS (1986) *Who Goes Where?*, London: ADSS.

Bradshaw, J. (1988) *Financing Private Care for the Elderly*, York: Department of Social Policy and Social Work, University of York.

DHSS (1976) *Priorities for Health and Personal Social Services in England*, London: HMSO.

DHSS (1981) *Care in the Community*, London: HMSO.

Fowler, N. (1984) Speech to Joint Social Services Annual Conference, 27 September, London: DHSS.

House of Commons Social Services Committee (1980) *White Paper on Public Expenditure: The Social Services*, vol. II, HC 702, London: HMSO.

House of Commons Social Services Committee (1985) *Community Care*, HC13–1, London: HMSO.

Key terms

The following key terms appear in the text above. They have been defined below to aid with the reading of this item.

DHSS the Department of Health and Social Security, which was one government department until split into two (creating the Department of Health and the Department of Social Security) in the 1980s

PSS personal social services – a term used in government documents to cover expenditure in this area

mixed economy of welfare the idea that welfare can be provided by a number of agencies, including the state (both central and local), private providers and voluntary agencies and charities. This is sometimes referred to as 'welfare pluralism'

Audit Commission the body charged with overseeing the use of public funds

Questions

1 Explain in your own words the distinction made by the author between 'care *in* the community' and 'care *by* the community'.

2 How did the Thatcher government encourage private provision of welfare?

3 Summarize in your own words the author's criticisms of the philosophy underlying the Thatcherite implementation of the policy of Care in the Community.

4 Identify the two main client groups affected by the Care in the Community policy.

5 To what extent do you agree that a key motivation behind the development of the Care in the Community initiative was the residualization of the role of local authorities in community care?

Reading 15.3 **Welfare regimes**

Gøsta Esping-Andersen (from) *The Three Worlds of Welfare Capitalism* (1990) Cambridge: Polity, pp. 26–32.

Editorial comments

Esping-Andersen has developed an extremely influential categorization of welfare states, which considers not only the amount of welfare spending but the nature of that expenditure and the nature of the social and political mobilization of various actors in the nation concerned. Specifically he argues that it is possible to distinguish between three distinct welfare regimes that have been developed – namely the liberal, conservative and social democratic models. At the heart of his theory is the notion of de-commodification and the extent to which people are entitled to benefits as of right and which therefore comprise an element of citizenship. This provides a powerful tool for the comparative and historical analysis of the development of welfare provision in different societies.

Welfare-state regimes

AS WE SURVEY international variations in social rights and welfare-state stratification, we will find qualitatively different arrangements between state, market, and the family. The welfare-state variations we find are therefore not linearly distributed, but clustered by regime-types.

In one cluster we find the 'liberal' welfare state, in which **means-tested assistance**, modest universal transfers, or modest social-insurance plans predominate. Benefits cater mainly to a clientele of low-income, usually working-class, state dependents. In this model, the progress of social reform has been severely circumscribed by traditional, liberal work-ethic norms: it is one where the limits of welfare equal the marginal propensity to opt for welfare instead of work. Entitlement rules are therefore strict and often associated with stigma; benefits are typically modest. In turn, the state encourages the market, either passively – by guaranteeing only a minimum – or actively – by subsidizing private welfare schemes.

The consequence is that this type of regime minimizes **de-commodification**-effects, effectively contains the realm of social rights, and erects an order of stratification that is a blend of a relative equality of poverty among state-welfare recipients, market-differentiated welfare among the majorities, and a class-political dualism between the two. The archetypical examples of this model are the United States, Canada and Australia.

A second regime-type clusters nations such as Austria, France, Germany, and Italy. Here, the historical corporatist-statist legacy was upgraded to cater to the new 'post-industrial' class structure. In these conservative and strongly 'corporatist' welfare states, the liberal obsession with market efficiency and commodification was never pre-eminent and, as such, the granting of social rights was hardly ever a seriously contested issue. What predominated was the preservation of status differentials; rights, therefore, were attached to class and status. This corporatism was subsumed under a state edifice perfectly ready to displace the market as a provider of welfare; hence, private insurance and occupational fringe benefits play a truly marginal role. On the other hand, the state's emphasis on upholding status differences means that its redistributive impact is negligible.

But the corporatist regimes are also typically shaped by the Church, and hence strongly committed to the preservation of traditional familyhood. Social insurance typically excludes non-working wives, and family benefits encourage motherhood. Day care, and similar family services, are conspicuously underdeveloped; the principle of 'subsidiarity' serves to emphasize that the state will only interfere when the family's capacity to service its members is exhausted.

The third, and clearly smallest, regime-cluster is composed of those countries in which the principles of **universalism** and de-commodification of social rights were extended also to the new middle classes. We may call it the 'social democratic' regime-type since, in these nations, social democracy was clearly the dominant force behind social reform. Rather than tolerate a dualism between state and market, between working class and middle class, the social democrats pursued a welfare state that would promote an equality of the highest standards, not an equality of minimal needs as was pursued elsewhere. This implied, first, that services and benefits be upgraded to levels commensurate with even the most discriminating tastes of the new middle classes; and, second, that equality be furnished by guaranteeing workers full participation in the quality of rights enjoyed by the better-off.

This formula translates into a mix of highly de-commodifying and universalistic programmes that, nonetheless, are tailored to differentiated expectations. Thus, manual workers come to enjoy rights identical to those of salaried white-collar employees or civil servants; all strata are incorporated under one universal insurance system, yet benefits are graduated according to accustomed earnings. This model crowds out the market, and consequently constructs an essentially universal solidarity in favour of the welfare state. All benefit; all are dependent; and all will presumably feel obliged to pay.

The social democratic regime's policy of emancipation addresses both the market and the traditional family. In contrast to the corporatist-subsidiarity model, the principle is not to wait until the family's capacity to aid is exhausted, but to pre-emptively socialize the costs of familyhood. The ideal is not to maximize dependence on the family, but capacities for individual independence. In this sense, the model is a peculiar fusion of liberalism and socialism. The result is a welfare state that grants transfers directly to children, and takes direct responsibility of caring for children, the aged, and the helpless. It is, accordingly, committed to a heavy social-service burden, not only to service family needs but also to allow women to choose work rather than the household.

Perhaps the most salient characteristic of the social democratic regime is its fusion of welfare and work. It is at once genuinely committed to a full-employment guarantee, and entirely dependent on its attainment. On the one side, the right to work has equal status to the right of income protection. On the other side, the enormous costs of maintaining a solidaristic, universalistic, and de-commodifying welfare system means that it must minimize social problems and maximize revenue income. This is obviously best done with most people working, and the fewest possible living off of social transfers.

Neither of the two alternative regime-types espouse full employment as an integral part of their welfare-state commitment. In the conservative tradition, of course, women are discouraged from working; in the liberal ideal, concerns of gender matter less than the sanctity of the market. ...

The causes of welfare-state regimes

If welfare states cluster into three distinct regime-types, we face a substantially more complex task of identifying the causes of welfare-state differences. What is the explanatory power of industrialization, economic growth, capitalism, or working-class political power in accounting for regime-types? A first superficial answer would be: very little. The nations we study are all more or less similar with regard to all but the variable of working-class mobilization. And we find very powerful labour movements and parties in each of the three clusters.

A theory of welfare-state developments must clearly reconsider its causal assumptions if it wishes to explain clusters. The hope of finding one single powerful causal force must be abandoned; the task is to identify salient interaction-effects. Based on the preceding arguments, three factors in particular should be of importance: the nature of class mobilization (especially of the working class); class-political coalition structures; and the historical legacy of regime institutionalization.

As we have noted, there is absolutely no compelling reason to believe that workers will automatically and naturally forge a socialist class identity; nor is it plausible that their mobilization will look especially Swedish. The actual historical formation of working-class collectivities will diverge, and so also will their aims, ideology, and political capacities. Fundamental differences appear both in trade-unionism and party development. Unions may be sectional or in pursuit of more universal objectives; they may be denominational or secular; and they may be ideological or devoted to business-unionism. Whichever they are, it will decisively affect the articulation of political demands, class cohesion, and the scope for labour-party action. It is clear that a working-class mobilization thesis must pay attention to union structure.

The structure of trade-unionism may or may not be reflected in labour-party formation. But under what conditions are we likely to expect certain welfare-state outcomes from specific party configurations? There are many factors that conspire to make it virtually impossible to assume that any labour, or left-wing, party will ever be capable, single-handedly, of structuring a welfare state. Denominational or other divisions aside, it will be only under extraordinary historical circumstances that a labour party alone will command a parliamentary majority long enough to impose its will. We have noted that the traditional working class has hardly ever constituted an electoral majority. It follows that a theory of class mobilization must look beyond the major leftist parties. It is an historical fact that welfare-state construction has depended on political coalition-building. The structure of class coalitions is much more decisive than are the power resources of any single class.

The emergence of alternative class coalitions is, in part, determined by class formation. In the earlier phases of industrialization, the rural classes usually constituted the largest single group in the electorate. If social democrats wanted political majorities, it was here that they were forced to look for allies. One of history's many paradoxes is that the rural classes were decisive for the future of socialism. Where the rural economy was dominated by small, capital-intensive family farmers, the potential for an alliance was greater than where it rested on large pools of cheap labour. And where farmers were politically articulate and well-organized (as in Scandinavia), the capacity to negotiate political deals was vastly superior.

The role of the farmers in coalition formation and hence in welfare-state development is clear. In the Nordic countries, the necessary conditions obtained for a broad red–green alliance for a full-employment welfare state in return for farm-price subsidies. This was especially true in Norway and Sweden, where farming was highly precarious and dependent on state aid. In the United States, the New Deal was premised on a similar coalition (forged by the Democratic Party), but with the important difference that the labour-intensive South blocked a truly universalistic social security system and opposed further welfare-state developments. In contrast, the rural economy of continental Europe was very inhospitable to red–green coalitions. Often, as in Germany and Italy, much of agriculture was labour-intensive; hence the unions and left-wing parties were seen as a threat. In addition, the conservative forces on the continent had succeeded in incorporating farmers into 'reactionary' alliances, helping to consolidate the political isolation of labour.

Political dominance was, until after World War II, largely a question of rural class politics. The construction of welfare states in this period was, therefore, dictated by whichever force captured the farmers. The absence of a red–green alliance does not necessarily imply that no welfare-state reforms were possible. On the contrary, it implies which political force came to dominate their design. Great Britain is an exception to this general rule, because the political significance of the rural classes eroded before the turn of the century. In this way, Britain's coalition-logic showed at an early date the dilemma that faced most other nations later; namely, that the rising white-collar strata constitute the linchpin for political majorities. The consolidation of welfare states after World War II came to depend fundamentally on the political alliances of the new middle classes. For social democracy, the challenge was to synthesize working-class and white-collar demands without sacrificing the commitment to solidarity.

Since the new middle classes have, historically, enjoyed a relatively privileged position in the market, they have also been quite successful in meeting their welfare demands outside the state, or, as civil servants, by privileged state welfare. Their employment security has traditionally been such that full employment has been a peripheral concern. Finally, any program for drastic income-equalization is likely to be met with great hostility among a middle-class clientele. On these grounds, it would appear that the rise of the new middle classes would abort the social democratic project and strengthen a liberal welfare-state formula.

The political leanings of the new middle classes have, indeed, been decisive for welfare-state consolidation. The Scandinavian model relied almost entirely on social democracy's capacity to incorporate them into a new kind of welfare state: one that provided benefits tailored to the tastes and expectations of the middle classes, but nonetheless retained universalism of rights. Indeed, by expanding social services and public employment, the welfare state participated directly in manufacturing a middle class instrumentally devoted to social democracy.

In contrast, the Anglo-Saxon nations retained the residual welfare-state model precisely because the new middle classes were not wooed from the market to the state. In class terms, the consequence is dualism. The welfare state caters essentially to the working class and the poor. Private insurance and occupational fringe benefits cater to the middle classes. Given the electoral importance of the latter, it is quite logical that further extensions of welfare-state activities are resisted.

The third, continental European, welfare-state regime has also been patterned by the new middle classes, but in a different way. The cause is historical. Developed by conservative political forces, these regimes institutionalized a middle-class loyalty to the preservation of both occupationally segregated social-insurance programmes and, ultimately, to the political forces that brought them into being.

Key terms

The following key terms appear in the text above. They have been defined below to aid with the reading of this item.

means-tested assistance welfare programmes where resources are directed only at a certain section of the population, most notably through testing that seeks to establish whether people need assistance or not, usually by looking at the financial resources available to them

de-commodification Esping-Andersen uses this term to denote a situation where resources are made available to people without reference to the market and therefore by virtue of citizenship, not through working

universalism welfare programmes where all citizens are entitled to benefit. For example, in the UK Child Benefit is paid to all parents regardless of their level of income

Questions

1 Identify the key characteristics of the three welfare-state regimes identified by the author.

2 What key factors affect the direction in which welfare-state regimes develop?

3 Suggest where the contemporary UK might be placed in terms of Esping-Andersen's welfare-state regimes. How does this compare to the welfare-state regimes in the UK in the 1950s and 1960s?

4 How far do sociological arguments and evidence support the notion that the welfare state is a system of stratification in its own right?

5 To what extent do you agree that changes in the class structure have undermined the basis for the universalistic welfare-state regime?

Reading 15.4 **Women and welfare states**

Lois Bryson (from) *Welfare and the State* (1992) London: Macmillan, pp. 192–6 and 207–11.

Editorial comments

The central point of Lois Bryson's book is that while there are benefits from the way the welfare state modifies the distribution pattern of the market, nonetheless important inequalities remain, including the fact that by and large men benefit more from it than women. This extract outlines the experience of the welfare state by women and shows some of the ways that these inequalities manifest themselves in relation to gender.

Women's welfare state

Women's economic position

GIVEN THAT WOMEN were historically denied property rights and systematically excluded from the better jobs in the paid workforce, it is only to be expected that women will be poorer than men. Over recent years this fact has been publicly 'discovered' and hailed as a new phenomenon: the feminization of poverty. The term has been taken up with considerable enthusiasm, presumably because of its evocation of an undeniable situation. While to talk of the feminization of poverty does direct attention to women's situation, to the extent that this implies that this is a new phenomenon, it almost certainly is inaccurate. Even though, in the past, we have mostly lacked the 'herstory' to demonstrate it, it seems clear that women have, throughout history, borne the major 'burden of poverty, the exhausting labour of the micro-administration of insufficient resources for their families and themselves' (Rose, 1983).

Women's relative economic position is masked in two-parent households by the tendency of statistics not to deal with access to the family income, but to assume equality of access. Research on the topic of family finances has, however, demonstrated that in general women do not have equal access to, nor control over, family finances. Research has also repeatedly shown that some women who move out of a marital relationship, even though their apparent access to family income diminishes and they are close to, or below, the poverty-line as sole parents, report an improvement of their economic, as well as their social circumstances. Graham, in reviewing successive studies over the past twenty or so years in Britain, found that the proportion indicating an improvement in their economic situation ranges from one-fifth to two-thirds (Graham, 1987). On this basis, it is clear that many women experience poverty within marriage.

However, it is only when women move out of a couple-relationship, to head their own family, that their poverty gains recognition. The female-headed sole parent family, particularly where the mother is dependent on social welfare benefits, shows up in national statistics in most countries as the most disadvantaged household type. With the numbers of such families generally increasing, this has aroused concern often in the form of anxiety about the 'breakdown of the family'. Given the evidence about women's financial status within marriage, this newfound concern for women's poverty smacks of what Barrett and McIntosh (1982) identify as 'familism'. Familism accepts the 'naturalness' of the traditional bourgeois family, with its male breadwinner, and implies that this form best secures the protection of women and children.

While rates of sole-parent families remain low in some countries – such as Israel, with only about 4 per cent (mostly widows), and Japan – the trend in most industrialized countries is for an increasing proportion. The proportion of single-parent households has virtually doubled in the USA, Sweden, Australia, France and West Germany, for example, over the last two decades. The rate of increase in Britain has been somewhat slower. Sweden, with around 30 per cent of families headed by a sole parent (in 1985), has the highest proportion. Next comes the USA with 22 per cent. Australia has a rate of 14.4 per cent, which is similar to a number of countries including Canada and France, while the British rate at 13 per cent is slightly lower. The US figure masks significant differences between Black and non-Black families. For the non-Black population the rate of one-parent families is 14 per cent. For Black families the figures reach 65 per cent. This must be linked with the low, marginal and economically insecure position of Black men, at the same time as the welfare state makes available a form (however inadequate) of financial support for mothers and their children. Research suggests that the economic effects of race are broadly similar to this for Afro-Caribbean families in Britain and for Aboriginal women in Australia.

Sole parents are much more likely to be mothers than fathers. Over 80 per cent of one-parent families are headed by mothers in virtually all countries. In France and West Germany the figure reaches more than 90 per cent. It is these female-headed families which are likely to be the poorest families. Of the nine countries which Kamerman (1984) studied, only in Sweden, and to a lesser extent France, with their well-developed family support policies, did unemployed single mothers come close to receiving the average weekly earnings of a production worker. Nonetheless, even in Sweden, to the extent that poverty is identified, it falls disproportionately on women, particularly female sole parents.

In the USA in 1987 female heads of households had an annual income of $US13,660 compared with $US24,556 for male heads of households. They made up about half of all families with children in poverty, despite the fact that they represented only one-fifth of such families. Also, two-thirds of all adults in the USA who lived below the official poverty-line were women. In Britain, although sole-parent families make up only 13 per cent of all households with dependent children, as in the USA, they make up about half of all families in poverty.

Unlike Sweden, where almost 90 per cent of female sole parents are in the labour force, in Australia almost the same proportion (89 per cent) were in receipt of social security benefits in 1985. At the same time, about 43 per cent of all sole parents fell below the officially-recognized poverty line. However, this situation of sole parents improved somewhat in response to a three-pronged government policy instituted in 1987. There was a concerted attempt to get sole parents into the labour force; an additional benefit in respect of children was made available to families with low incomes; and a national child support scheme made compulsory a contribution towards child maintenance from **non-custodial parents**. These policies, over a two-year period, significantly improved the financial circumstances of female-headed families. Though these particular policies did have many negative elements, including strict targeting of assistance and the failure to alter macro-economic circumstances which affect women, the speed with which an impression was made on the problem of sole-parent poverty illustrates the effective role that governments can quite readily play in redressing aspects of inequality.

While the evidence is overwhelming that women as sole parents are poor, the broader dimensions of women's inferior economic position are established by also considering women within couple-households. Hobson investigated this recently, drawing on information from the Luxembourg Income Study. Her study included nine **OECD** countries and compared husbands' and wives' income to assess the dependency level, which is essentially the 'gap between the wife's and husband's proportion of family income' (Hobson, 1990). The extent of wives' dependency varied, with Holland and Switzerland having the highest levels of total financial dependence, with 68.2 and 52.9 per cent respectively. However, even for Sweden, the country with the lowest levels of total dependence, wives' economic situations were significantly worse than their husbands' (see Table 1). In only 11.6 per cent of families was the wife's contribution to the family income equivalent to the husbands' (or greater) and in a similar proportion of families, the wife was totally dependent.

Even where wives were employed, their contribution to the family income was much lower than their husbands'. In Switzerland employed married women's contribution to the family income was only about half that of their husbands. An anomalous finding was that in Holland, with the largest proportion of totally dependent wives, where wives were actually in paid employment, their incomes came closer to their husbands' than for any country – that is, within 20 per cent (see Table 1). A rough summary for all nine countries suggests that for women in paid employment, less than 10 per cent earn the equivalent of their husbands and on average they contribute one-third less to the family income, leaving a large dependency-gap. It is in the context of this weak economic bargaining situation that we must view the research that has shown that women do not usually have equal control of family finances. However, we must also recognize that even this degree of relative independence is recent. ...

Child care

Estimates of loss of income to women from child-bearing show quite startling results. A UK study using 1980 data estimated a lifetime loss for a woman bearing and raising two children of £122,000. This is equivalent to $A370,000 and is very similar to one

Table 1 Women's economic dependency in several Western societies (*percentages*)

Country	Dependency level	Dependent working women	Total dependency	No dependency
Sweden (1981)	40.6	33.4	11.2	11.6
USA (1979)	58.8	36.6	35.5	6.7
USA (1986)	49.8	29.3	29.4	9.6
Holland (1984)	74.7	20.3	68.2	3.4
UK (1979)	60.8	42.0	32.6	5.7
Canada (1981)	59.0	36.3	35.9	7.5
Australia (1981)	60.7	27.4	46.0	7.2
Australia (1985)	59.3	32.6	39.6	7.8
Germany (1984)	62.9	27.0	49.2	6.2
Norway (1979)	55.7	41.5	NA	NA
Switzerland 1982)	77.0	51.4	52.9	2.6

Note: The results in Table 1 are based upon data from the Luxembourg Income Study. 'No dependency' represents those couples in economically egalitarian marriages, where the dependency range is between – 9 and 9 and 'Total dependency' refers to couples where the wife has no contribution.
Source: Hobson, 1990

of the estimates ($A384,000) from an Australian study which computed different amounts according to education-level and number of children. What is perhaps most significant is that the major loss is associated with the birth of the first child. This accounts for almost half of a women's potential lifetime earnings. Subsequent children account for only between 5 and 10 per cent of additional loss. The loss is somewhat higher for women with higher education, because of their capacity to command a higher level of income when they are employed (see Table 2). There is a great deal of variation in the proportion lost according to education-level. Beggs and Chapman (1988) also report research from the USA which has estimated far lower rates of loss, around $US43,000 ($A75,000) in 1981. This difference is partly accounted for by assuming higher future working-rates for today's younger mothers. While Beggs and Chapman acknowledge this as a possibility, they point out that they themselves actually underestimated income losses for older women by assuming employment at current rates. Although there can be much debate about the precise assumptions underlying such projections it certainly cannot be disputed that having children seriously reduces women's lifetime earning capacity.

This loss of income makes the significance of women's caring role very clear. Because it remains women who take prime responsibility for caring within the society, it is not possible to consider women's welfare state without taking into account the availability of forms of care for family members, and child care is obviously central.

Table 2 Forgone total earnings at age 60 from different education and child-bearing scenarios (*$000*)

Number of children	Investment rate of interest		
	0%	5%	7%
	High education		
0	0	0	0
1	439	1316	2100
2	537	1576	2499
3	615	1776	2762
	Average education		
0	0	0	0
1	336	929	1455
2	384	1059	1656
3	419	1145	1782
	Low education		
0	0	0	0
1	282	738	1141
2	310	817	1264
3	330	868	1340

Source: Beggs and Chapman, 1988

Daytime care of children of school age is effectively provided for under the guise of compulsory education, though even this leaves the time between the start and finish of school and the normal hours of paid employment to be catered for. At school, supervision is inevitably, though incidentally, provided as students are educated to take up their roles as workers and citizens. Governments in capitalist countries have, however, been more reluctant providers of care for children of pre-school age, something which cannot be divorced from a noted historical reluctance to facilitate women's employment. With the exception of the period of the Second World War, when in Britain, the USA, Australia and Sweden, for example, governments provided for the care of children of women workers who were required to fill the labour shortage, child care has not, until very recently, been a priority service in the advanced capitalist nations. There remains great variation in the degree of particular governments' commitment even today.

In many countries, day care for children is still not a priority of government. In Britain, problematic attitudes have a long history, reflecting not only reluctance on the part of the authorities but also on the part of mothers. The first nursery was opened by a voluntary organization in Marylebone in 1850. This was inspired by the French example, where between 1840 and 1867 over 400 crèches were established throughout the country. Despite initial support by influential charity workers, early British nurseries were not very successful. Nor were they popular with poor mothers who preferred to maintain informal arrangements. Sweden opened its first crèche in 1854, to cater for the children of poor mothers. The Swedish authorities were not keen on crèches, seeing them as only appropriate in cases of dire necessity, though nursery schools were greeted with enthusiasm.

Concern with high infant mortality-rates led to other attempts by the British state to intervene in child care. In 1891, a regulation was enacted making it illegal for a woman to return to work within four weeks of childbirth. The onus was, however, on employers to enforce the regulations, which meant that the law was more honoured in the breach than the observance. It was criticized by some feminists at the time as another example of the attempts of male trade unionists to eject women from the workforce. A more realistic solution emerged in 1911, with the introduction of the **National Insurance** scheme which allowed workers to insure for maternity leave.

Underlying much of the British debate on child care and infant mortality last century was the liberal view of the home as a private haven which should not be invaded by government. In 1874, a speaker to the National Association for the Promotion of Social Science claimed to be prepared to 'see even a higher rate of infant mortality' rather than see intrusion 'one iota further on the sanctity of the domestic hearth and the decent seclusion of private life'. This liberal philosophy still affected government attitudes in Britain in the eighties, casting child care as largely a private, domestic responsibility. Where public day care has been provided, it has been mainly of a custodial kind, provided largely for the poor to alleviate problem circumstances. The interests of 'non-welfare working mothers' were excluded. Day care that is utilized by working parents has been largely sought through informal, kin or friendship networks or on a private commercial basis. While commercial care facilities are, in theory, subject to regulation by local authorities, the policing of the regulations is haphazard. Educational programmes are available for children of pre-school age, but the hours that these are available are unlikely to be suited to the hours a mother works.

Child care is not extensively provided on a collective basis in the USA either and must largely be purchased on the commercial market. Vicki Smith (1987) contends that child care in the USA remains 'one of the most formidable issues influencing women's labour market status'. She suggests that it needs to be given priority as an issue by trade unions and working women's organizations. In Japan most child care is provided by relatives, though private centres are springing up to meet the new demand as more and more mothers join the labour market.

In Denmark, Norway and Sweden, child care has been afforded much more central importance. In Sweden and Denmark it is provided as a universal service, aimed both at serving the needs of working parents and the educational needs of children. Denmark was the first of the Scandinavian countries to provide extensive day care on a 'mass consumption' basis, as the rate of dual-income families rose. Norway has not provided the same volume of day care as Sweden and Denmark, but the amount still outstrips that which is commonly found in Western Europe. The Scandinavian countries do not have services provided on a commercial basis; they are supported by central and **municipal governments**. Consumer contributions to costs vary, with rates around 22 per cent for Denmark, 21 per cent in Norway and 10 per cent in Sweden in 1984. From the mid-eighties, services in Denmark were under some financial pressure, along with state social expenditure generally, and some cost-saving measures were instituted. The Swedish government, on the other hand, has been extending services, having committed itself, through legislation in 1985, to the provision of municipal day-care for all children aged 18 months to 6 years by 1991.

Australian policies in the late eighties fell somewhere between Britain and Sweden, though the number of places falls far short of the Scandinavian countries. In Australia up to 1972, the very small amount of care that was available was provided by local government and charitable organizations and, as in Britain, this was largely reserved for families where there were severe social problems. Non-welfare working mothers, also as in Britain, relied on informal arrangements or commercial centres, something which many still do. However, since 1972, there has been a gradual but significant increase in available services, under pressure partly from the women's movement but, probably more decisively, under pressure of the demands of the labour market for women workers. The federal government funds non-profit organizations to provide services, and subsidizes the fees of parents on a means-tested basis. Despite this commitment, in 1988 the care funded by government was only sufficient to cater for 9.5 per cent of pre-school children, though this represents a marked increase from the 1982 figure of 5.8 per cent. The vast difference in national provision is illustrated by the fact that the Swedish commitment to provide full coverage of day care was triggered by dissatisfaction with a coverage of 42 per cent of all pre-school children, when the full demand in 1984 was estimated to be 64 per cent.

References

Barrett, M. and McIntosh, M. (1982) *The Anti-Social Family*, London: Verso.

Beggs, J. and Chapman, B. (1988) *The Forgone Earnings from Child-Rearing in Australia*, Canberra: Centre for Policy Research, Research School of Social Sciences, Australian National University.

Graham, H. (1987) 'Being poor: perceptions and coping strategies of lone mothers', in Brannen, J. and Wilson, G. (eds) *Give and Take in Families: Studies in resource distribution*, London: Allen & Unwin.

Hobson, B. (1990) 'No exit, no voice: women's economic dependency and the welfare state', *Acta Sociologica, 33* (3), September.

Kamerman, S. (1984) 'Women, children and poverty: public policies and female-headed families in industrialised countries', *Signs, 10* (2).

Rose, H. (1983) 'Women, work and welfare in the world economy', in Baldock, C. and Goodrick, D. (eds) *Women's Participation in the Development Process*, proceedings of the Women's Section of ANZASS Congress, Perth.

Smith, V. (1987) 'The circular trap: women and part-time work', in Sassoon, A. S. (ed.) *Women and the State*, London: Hutchinson.

Key terms

The following key terms appear in the text above. They have been defined below to aid with the reading of this item.

non-custodial parents parents who do not have legal custody of a child

OECD Organization for Economic Co-operation and Development – an organization whose members are the advanced industrial nations

National Insurance a system set up to pay for welfare benefits through contributions to the National Insurance Fund

municipal governments local or regional government – as distinct from national government

Questions

1 What are the limitations of the term 'the feminization of poverty'?

2 Why might concerns about the 'breakdown of the family' be seen as an example of 'familism'?

3 Summarize the degree of dependence women in the UK suffer as compared to other OECD nations.

4 What is the estimate given for the lifetime loss of earnings of a woman in the UK bearing and raising two children?

5 To what extent does sociological evidence concerning contemporary trends support the notion that child care is still not a priority service in advanced capitalist nations?

Reading 15.5 **Poverty and racism**

Pete Alcock (from) *Understanding Poverty* (1993) London: Macmillan, pp. 147–56.

Editorial comments

In his survey of poverty, Pete Alcock provides sections that focus on the way social divisions impact upon the distribution and experience of poverty in the UK. In this extract the focus is on racism and poverty and in particular how the operation of the benefit system impacts on the lives of ethnic minorities in this country, leaving them much more likely to suffer poverty and deprivation.

Racism in benefits

BECAUSE OF THEIR relative exclusion from the labour market black people in Britain experience disproportionate levels of dependency upon the benefits system; and, because of low levels of benefit, dependency is closely related with poverty and deprivation. Direct evidence of the numbers of black people dependant upon benefits is difficult to obtain, however, because within the social security system records are not kept of the ethnic origin of claimants. Thus conclusions have to be drawn from other sources about black people's experience of benefits. ...

Within the state benefit system itself black claimants are likely to be disproportionately dependent upon less generous and lower status **means-tested benefits**. This is because, as with much of the post-welfare state in Britain, the **Beveridge** social security system failed to recognize the ways in which its structures could operate to exclude certain groups of people. This is particularly true of NI benefits which are paid in return for contributions made during employment. Black people's relative exclusion from employment is also likely to exclude them from NI benefits. And in the case of pensions, especially earnings-related pensions which are based on contributions made throughout a working life, immigration to Britain as adults or periods of absence abroad can effectively disqualify black people from full entitlement.

Other apparently neutral qualifications for benefit entitlement may also operate against black people because of their immigrant status. This applies in particular to the residence tests applied to some benefits. For instance the major disability benefits, Disability Living Allowance (DLA), Severe Disablement Allowance (SDA) and Invalid Care Allowance (ICA), have a requirement of 26 weeks residence in Britain in the preceding 12 months, and in the past some of these periods were much longer. Recent immigrants may be likely to be excluded by these tests, potentially resulting in severe poverty for black people with disabilities.

The effect of their exclusion from NI and noncontributory benefits is likely to force black claimants into greater dependence upon means-tested benefits. However here too exclusionary practices may operate to cause hardship. Means-tested benefits are only available to those ordinarily resident in Britain, and claimants are thus technically required to establish this when they make a claim. Normally speaking this is a formality, but as we shall see, some recent immigrants are excluded from such entitlement and evidence of resident status may be required.

This has resulted in past practices of 'passport checking' for all suspicious black claimants in social security offices. Passport checking operates as an invidious disincentive to any black claimants to seek benefit support, whatever their residence status, and can lead to problems if passports are not readily obtainable. Social security officers are instructed not to request passports routinely as proof of entitlement, but, as Gordon and Newnham (1985) discuss, the practice has become so widespread that 'many black claimants volunteer their passports believing it is only a matter of time before they are asked to produce them'. They quote one case where

> L, a 22 year old student, born in Britain, was asked for his passport four times in twelve months when he was claiming benefit in Manchester and Huddersfield.

And even where passports are produced social security staff may misunderstand or misinterpret their status and thus refuse benefit or remove passports, causing further hardship.

The requirement to produce passports as evidence of entitlement acts as a particular disincentive for many black claimants because of its apparent link with immigration control. Immigrants who do not have a right to remain in the country may expose their status if they claim benefits in order to relieve poverty, for information provided to social security offices may well be passed on to Home Office immigration control. Much more seriously, however, fear of the Home Office connection may be likely to dissuade many perfectly legitimate black claimants from ever approaching the DSS because of misplaced uncertainty about their status in the country (see Gordon and Newnham, 1985).

Even for some of those who do have residence rights in Britain, however, immigration status may affect potential benefit entitlement for a number of reasons. Most important here is the so-called 'no recourse to public funds rule'. Under this provision within the Immigration Rules, all dependants coming to join their families in Britain are excluded from claiming support from public funds. Public funds includes all the major means-tested benefits, including IS, and housing for homeless families under the Housing Act 1985. The intention of the rule is to prevent immigrants from coming to Britain in order to claim state support; its effect is to exclude from even minimum benefit protection significant numbers of new entrants who may have no other practical source of support if the arrangements made on their entry fall through. ...

In addition to the formal exclusions of black

claimants from full benefit entitlement as a result of rules with discriminatory impact there are a number of informal means by which racist practices may exclude them from receipt of support. A survey of black clients using Citizens' Advice Bureaux revealed many such practices, described by NACAB (1991) as 'barriers to benefit'. These include delays in processing benefit claims while – unnecessary – checks are carried out to determine entitlement, and intrusive questioning to establish certain personal details such as marital status where marriages have been contracted abroad. They can also include direct racist discrimination against black claimants, however, as was revealed in a PSI study of the administration of SB in 1982. Part of the PSI study involved observation of officers in social security offices, and it revealed disturbing examples of racism amongst some officers, one of whom is quoted as saying, 'We get quite a few Pakis like that wandering in like lost sheep' (Cooper, 1985). The DSS was initially sufficiently alarmed by this part of the report to prevent its publication along with the other findings (Berthoud, 1984), and it was only released a year later.

Even where treatment is formally equal, however, black people may in practice be denied equal access to support because of the failure of the benefits system to address more generally the particular problems they may experience. Most important here is the language barrier. ...

Thus although the problem of take-up of benefits is a significant one throughout the social security system, culture and language problems may make it a more serious one for black (non)claimants. For instance a survey in Batley in 1973 revealed that 39 per cent of 'immigrant' households were not claiming benefits to which they were entitled, compared with 23 per cent of indigenous households (Gordon and Newnham, 1985), and a more recent survey of FC claimants by National Opinion Polls for the National Audit Office revealed lower levels of take-up of means-tested education and health benefits amongst non-British/Irish respondents (Amin and Oppenheim, 1992). These differences are likely to represent a significant accentuation of benefit-related poverty for Britain's black population.

Disadvantage and deprivation

The problem of poverty is not just a problem of insecure or inadequate cash incomes. Poverty as deprivation includes a broader range of disadvantages, exclusions and powerlessness resulting in a quality of life which is poorer and more restricted. For black people in Britain the existence of racism at all levels within the social structure means that most of these broader features of deprivation are also likely to affect them disproportionately. And in addition racism itself

adds a further burden to the problems with which they have to cope.

Housing, as we know, is a significant source of inequality and deprivation; and housing conditions differ widely. ...

The PSI survey found that West Indians were more likely to live in low-quality rented accommodation such as high-rise flats, and Asians were more likely to live in old houses with few amenities (Brown, 1984). Asians are more likely to own their homes, but they may have experienced difficulty obtaining mortgages. ...

Inequalities in health can also be associated with severe deprivation, and as recognized in the Black Report on health inequalities racial differences can be detected here too (Townsend et al., 1988). As Grimsley and Bhat (1988) discuss, there is evidence of higher rates of mortality, and perinatal and infant mortality, amongst sections of the black community, and these are generally associated with poorer health. Black people also suffer from some debilitating diseases which do not affect the indigenous population, such as sickle cell anaemia amongst West Indians. And because of a different, poorer diet other diseases may be more prevalent, for instance rickets (caused by a deficiency of vitamin D) amongst Asians. ...

Another state service within which black people do not in practice receive equal treatment is education. As well as being a form of deprivation in itself, failure or under-achievement in education is also closely linked with poverty and inequality later in life. ...

The Swann Report on the education of children from ethnic minority groups (Swann, 1985) laid much of the blame for inequalities within education on racism within the wider community. But there is much further evidence to suggest that black people's experience of education is structured by racism within the service and not just outside it. Given the importance that education plays in shaping the attitudes and expectations of future generations, this provides depressing evidence of likely future inequalities.

Deprivation in housing, health and education add significantly to the financial inequality of black people in Britain, and they have remained important despite the introduction in the 1960s of race relations legislation designed to prevent direct and indirect discrimination and promote equality of opportunity. However these indirect consequences may be compounded by some of the more direct scars of racism in ways which may severely deplete the quality of life enjoyed, or endured, by those who suffer under them. Racial harassment is part of a daily burden borne by most, it not all, black people in Britain. It is a burden which white people can never fully understand, and which many do not even recognize, although they may be contributing to it. Harassment ranges from an experience of difference, and distance, to suffering as the victim of violence and disturbance.

All forms of harassment constitute deprivation, but for many black people harassment is a serious problem. The PSI survey found that West Indians were thirty-six times more likely than whites to experience racially motivated offences, and Asians fifty times more likely to. These include abuse and assaults in public, which can discourage black people from sharing public spaces, and threats and attacks in their homes, which can produce enduring fear and insecurity at the heart of black people's daily lives.

The experience of racial harassment is not confined either to the poor inner city areas where large numbers of black people live. Indeed the support and strength of black neighbours and friends in such areas may in part make such deprivation a little easier to bear. But the concentration of disadvantage found in such areas, especially when compounded by the fear and isolation produced by harassment, may contribute to an experience of poverty for black people which is overlain by feelings of exclusion and entrapment.

This has led some commentators, particularly in the US (see Wilson, 1987), to suggest that this separates out sections of the black population as a ghetto-dwelling 'underclass' experiencing a different quality of life from the rest of the population, and increasingly therefore experiencing different expectations and aspirations too. Without the negative, exclusionary overtones this notion has also been raised in some British discussions of the experience of black people (see Rex and Tomlinson, 1979).

Certainly the geographical concentration of disadvantage, overlain with the discrimination of racism, provides a peculiarly acute form of poverty for many black people in Britain, as in the US and many other advanced industrial countries. However, there are serious theoretical and political problems associated with the use of the 'underclass' concept to describe or explain localized or racialized deprivation, in particular the implication it can readily carry that poor black inner city residents are in some ways the cause, rather than the victims, of their exclusion from the standards of life enjoyed by the majority of the rest of society. This is a similar tendency to that which identifies 'race' as being linked to poverty or inequality; and the focus on supposed racial or ethnic differences obscures the racism which is still the real source of black people's greater experience of deprivation and disadvantage.

References

Amin, K. and Oppenheim, C. (1992) *Poverty in Black and White*, London: CPAG.

Berthoud, R. (1984) *The PSI Study: The reform of Social Security*, London: PSI.

Brown, C. (1984) *Black and White in Britain*, London: Heinemann.

Cooper, S. (1985) *Observations in Supplementary Offices*, London: PSI.

Gordon, P. and Newnham, A. (1985) *Passport to Benefits: Racism in Social Security*, London: CPAG/Runnymede Trust.

Grimsley, M. and Bhat, A. (1988) 'Health', in Bhat, A., Carr-Hill, R. and Ohri, S. (eds) *Britain's Black Population: a new perspective*, 2nd edn, Aldershot: Gower.

NACAB (1991) *Barriers to Benefit*, London: NACAB.

Rex, J. and Tomlinson, S. (1979) *Colonial Immigrants in a British City*, London: Routledge & Kegan Paul.

Swann Report (1985) *Education for All*, London: HMSO.

Townsend, P., Davidson, N. and Whitehead, M. (eds) (1988) *Inequalities in Health*, Harmondsworth: Penguin.

Wilson, W. J. (1987) *The Truly Disadvantaged*, Chicago: University of Chicago Press.

Key terms

The following key terms appear in the text above. They have been defined below to aid with the reading of this item.

means-tested benefits benefits that are only available to those who prove they are entitled to them, usually through some consideration of the private means available to them

Beveridge the author of the 1942 Beveridge Report, which laid the foundations for the construction of the modern welfare state

Questions

1 Explain in your own words how the structures of the benefit system effectively exclude certain groups.

2 Summarize the differences between the various ethnic groups mentioned in the extract, in relation to their likelihood of suffering racial harassment

3 Why does the author feel that the use of the term 'underclass' to describe racialized deprivation is problematic.

4 Suggest three examples of how a person may suffer poverty as deprivation.

5 Assess the relative importance of the various factors discussed in the extract which lead ethnic minorities to suffer from poverty and deprivation.

Reading 15.6 **Power, privilege and income inequality**

John Westergaard (from) *Who Gets What?* (1995)
Cambridge: Polity, pp. 131–6.

Editorial comments

Westergaard's book argues that class remains a key determinant of a person's social conditions and opportunities in life and is therefore a counter-blast to the various 'end-of-class'-type analyses that seemed to predominate in the late 1980s. In this extract he looks at the way trends in income in the 1980s served to maintain class inequalities.

Income trends from around 1980

THE MOST OBVIOUS information with which to start to test fashionable conjecture about the erosion of class as a significant influence on most people's experiences in life concerns trends in the distribution of **real income**. In fact the evidence on this score points incontrovertibly to widening class fissures since the end of the 1970s: not just between top and bottom, but across the entire range.

Growth of the gap between rich and poor is now so well known that it needs little underlining. Signals accumulated steadily over the 1980s that, while levels of living improved 'on average' and people already well off became very much better off, material circumstances for the poor at best stayed much as before and at worst actually deteriorated. Estimates for the full decade 1979–89 confirmed the trend by showing real increases in disposable income to the order of nearly 40 per cent on balance for the wealthiest one-fifth of households, but a mean fall of some $4\frac{1}{2}$ per cent for the poorest one-fifth. So much for '**trickle down**' of new wealth to the bottom. True, figures of this sort are open to revision at their edges; and they cannot, by the nature of their compilation, show changes in the situation of individual people or households over time. They leave the polarization of incomes since around 1980 beyond dispute, however; and they run plainly counter to the notion that class as a force for unequal life experience is on its way out. They do so, at least, unless class concomitantly has come to play much less part than before in shaping income inequalities. Counter-intuitive though that suggestion may be, it still needs checking as we go along. But it finds little support from the estimates just summarized which show, for example, that the fall in real levels of living recorded for many households in the poorest-quintile category – concentrated especially on families with children – was not an artefact of shifts in household composition during the period.

Yet if class by these signs is still very much a force to keep the poor poor, selective reading of the same signs has been taken often to support one version of

revisionist conjecture: the thesis of emergently overriding division between new underclass and affluent classless majority. Yes, the poor have lost out, and their numbers have grown. But, so the argument goes, most households have gained; and the prodigious rate of their gains is evident from the growth of 'average' real incomes: by about a quarter from 1979 to 1989; by upwards of a third perhaps to 1991, according to a recent if somewhat overstated figure (Department of Social Security, 1993).

The inference, however, proves feeble once the 'average' is picked apart. Averages mislead when the variations around them are very wide and skew; and just this is the case here. Take the latest available official estimates of household incomes 'below average' just mentioned (DSS, 1993). They show that, *after* deduction of housing costs, disposable post-tax incomes fell by fully 14 per cent in real terms for the poorest one-in-ten of all households over the years 1979–90/1; stayed level without gain for the next-poorest tenth; but rose by well over 30 per cent 'on average' across the population as a whole. Yet no decile-category in the entire lower half of the population gained anything like that notional-average improvement of material living standards. Even the fifth decile up the scale – households up to mid-point – saw their real incomes rise over the twelve years by only a little more than a fifth; and for the third and fourth decile-groups, below them, real incomes after housing costs grew on balance by no more than about 7 and 16 per cent respectively, very much less than the average on which revisionists have pinned their postulate of phenomenally growing mass prosperity. Alternative calculations of real-income changes *before* deduction of housing costs show less actual loss for the very poorest; some little gain for the next-poorest one-in-ten; smaller differences in outcome, overall, among the five lower-half deciles. But the point remains, all the firmer, that for at least 50 per cent of the population, household incomes in real terms grew at best far less than the artefactual average; and at rates only modest by the standards of the fairly even-spread growth that had prevailed in the much-maligned 1960s.

The average so exceeded even mid-level experience, of course, because there were formidable gains for people in the higher reaches of the income scale. Just how formidable is not visible from the official report cited above; for this is, ingeniously, confined to losses and gains among households 'below average income'. But as noted already, parallel analysis for the 1980s alone – when gains 'on average' came to nearly 25 per cent over eight years but to less than half of that, by generous measure, even for the fifth decile-category up the scale (Department of Social Security, 1990) – indicates an almost 40 per cent growth of real incomes for the best-off one-fifth of households from 1979 to 1989. Taken up to 1991, a ministerial answer to a parliamentary question gives a corresponding figure of well over 50 per cent, and of more than 60 per cent for just the richest one-in-ten. Concentration of enhanced advantage within this upper cluster has been still more marked, and appears to have continued despite renewed recession. Directors of the top 100 companies in Britain thus, on balance, more than doubled their own pay in real terms from 1983 to 1992, the rise proceeding apace even after business profits went into decline again at the end of the 1980s.

To summarize, it is not just the poor who have drawn short straws, if any, from economic growth since 1989. Even people up to mid-point incomes, and a number some way above that level, have gained quite little either by comparison with the rich or by past standards of rising prosperity. The poor are much less a minority by virtue of exclusion from benefit of radical-right market boom than are the wealthy by virtue of high-boosted privilege from it. What then explains the drastic widening of income inequalities over the past fifteen years or so, right across the board as this process has worked?

Two main sets of factors were involved: changes in public policy, and market changes which in turn received extra boost from policy changes. To sum up, the successive governments under new-right leadership in Britain have not (at least yet) dismantled 'the welfare state' in the radical fashion to which their most vocal ideologues aspire. But if what they have done is more like tinkering, it is tinkering on a large scale as the results have accumulated. The details on either side of the ledger – benefits and taxes – need not hold us up here. It is enough to look at the net impact of changes under the two headings together. An estimate is available of the consolidated effects on disposable household incomes of these changes over the ten years 1979–89, so calculated as to exclude the effects both from other sources and of differences in composition between households at different levels

of income (Johnson and Stark, 1989). This points to some real-term gain of money-in-hand for most households in consequence of shifts in direct-tax-cum-benefit provision during the decade – to an average tune of about £7 a week per household. But single people living on their own sustained a mean loss; there was, on balance, neither gain nor loss for pensioners relying mainly or exclusively on state support, or for unemployed couples without children; and while a majority of other households did gain something, this was little except for those high up the income ladder. In fact, of the total net addition to privately disposable incomes that came from the decade's changes in direct-taxes-cum-benefits, little short of half (some 46 per cent) went to just the richest one-in-ten of all households; and another third (34 per cent) to the next three decile-groups down the scale. This then left only one-fifth of the bounty to be shared out among the entire 60 per cent of households with incomes from 'good middling' down to the poorest; and among these, indeed, the 40 per cent with incomes from below middle and downwards got barely 8 per cent of the total. On this score again, near-exclusion from financial gain in the 1980s was *not* confined to a minority in poverty. It extended well up the ladder, and the very poorest, in fact, drew just a little more than those a step or two above them.

So the cumulative package of changes in taxation and benefit provision during the period gave overwhelming weight to favouring those already well favoured. That bias must indeed have been rather greater than even these figures show since, concerned with money-in-hand before personal spending, they leave aside the effects of indirect taxes that fall on money only when it is spent. Such taxes generally have a regressive edge, and have been stepped up as income tax has fallen. Running to 1989, moreover, the estimate used here stops just short of the extension, in 1990, of local poll tax from Scotland to England and Wales: a measure which added yet another, and very visible, twist to regression. But then this record also stops short of 1990's replacement of Mrs Thatcher by Mr Major, and of the tortuous unwinding of poll tax which followed. Save for the coming of council tax instead, however, the change in cabinet leadership involved no government retreat from the line of regressive redistribution, pursued in social policy during the 1980s. It would in any case take far more than some moderate softening to erase the stark imprint which that decade's shifts of tax-benefit provision left on class structure in Britain. Moreover market changes then – and since, during the second deep recession of the new era – have left at least as stark an imprint.

Take the pattern of earnings in paid employment as offering the simplest sign – high unemployment apart

– of these changes in the labour market. Polarization was here again to the fore in the 1980s. Over the ten years from 1980 to 1990, pre-tax salaries for full-time non-manual work thus rose by about 40 per cent in real terms for the highest-paid decile among both men and women in such work, even disregarding non-cash perks which also boomed at the top. But wages at the bottom increased only little in purchasing power during the same period: by barely 8 per cent over ten years for the lowest-paid decile among women in full-time manual employment; and indeed by under 2 per cent for their male counterparts, in this case a near-standstill of real wages for a decade. (Calculated from data in the *New Earnings Survey 1990*, by application of the Retail Price Index, All Items.)

Yet, once more, polarization cannot be taken as evidence for increased segregation of an impoverished underclass from a well-set 'middling mass'. As in respect of income distribution at large, so too in respect of earnings from employment many people 'in the middle' experienced only modest gains from the 1980s' growth of pay packets. Median earnings from full-time work rose, it is true, by one-fifth in real terms for men; and by well over one-quarter for women. (Women's pay disadvantages *vis-à-vis* men in fact diminished in respect of full-time employment. This was the only trend contrary to the polarization otherwise at work, though – with men's earnings from full-time work generally still half as high again as women's in 1990 – gender differentials by no means vanished.) But even the best-paid manual workers – fashionably seen as hyper-prototypical of a new middling mass – found their real wage increases from 1980 to 1990 short of the notional median rise. Here again, gross averages are a misleading statistic when, as during this decade, a great deal of the total gain went to the already well-paid. Among men, upper-quartile salaries from full-time *non-manual* employment thus rose in real terms by fully 33 per cent over the period: a rate of gain nearly twice that even for the best-paid decile of manual workers; well over twice that for the best-paid quartile among the latter, and some three times that for the 'average' male manual worker, whose real wages rose only by 10½ per cent during the decade. Among women the ratios of differential gain were much the same, if in a pattern a little sharper still in its contrasts between high boom towards the top, modest rises in the middle and only slow growth further down the range.

The point that needs emphasis about those con-

trasts is, to repeat, that they applied up and down the whole range: they set no distinct line of division between excluded minority and commonly thriving mass majority. Certainly the lowest-paid lagged furthest behind in real-term rise of earnings. But many others' shares in growth – while bigger for each step up the scale – were still quite small by earlier postwar standards. Those of almost all manual workers, and of low-grade office workers too, fell well short of the 'average' rises on which commentators tend to fasten. It was the higher and highest echelons of salary-earners who drew the long straws in the pay growth of the decade: a minority at the top rather than at the bottom. As pointed to by such data from summary national statistics these constituted a sizeable minority, it is true. They ranged over business managers, administrators, professionals and entertainers of diverse kinds – much of the 'service class'. But leading the way among them were very much smaller numbers of high executives in private enterprise. Their privileged salaries, typically swollen well into the six-figure range, in turn prompted pressure for competitive part-emulation at the peaks of the public sector and among top management of newly privatized public facilities.

In short, pay stratification simply grew sharper across the board, except as between women and men in full-time employment. And while limited in impact both by continuing gender discrimination at large and by many women's dependence on part-time work, the exception itself underlines the pattern of class stratification associated with accentuated pay stratification. When inequalities of pay widened so much in the 1980s, it was in main part because differentials grew between different types and levels of employment: between the broad and crude categories of manual and non-manual work distinguished in the summary official statistics; between wage-earners of different skills, trades, sectors or corners of the labour markets, salaried people on career paths of greater though varying dependability, and top-flight professionals and executives or dealers in business and finance especially. And when the latter gained so much more than others overall, it was because they could add to their golden pay rises also good chunks of property income – including spin-off from the share-option schemes that proliferated on corporation boards – and, not least, the benefits of large cuts in top-rate taxation: all privileges distinctly of a class character.

References

Department of Social Security (DSS) (1990) *Households Below Average Income*, London: HMSO.

Department of Social Security (DSS) (1993) *Households Below Average Income: a statistical analysis 1979–1990/91*, London: HMSO.

Johnson, P. and Stark, G. (1989) *Taxation and Social Security 1979–1989*, London: Institute for Fiscal Studies.

Key terms

The following key terms appear in the text above. They have been defined below to aid with the reading of this item.

real income this compares changes in income levels over time, with the effect of inflation removed. It therefore measures changes in real purchasing power

'trickle down' a phrase used by New Right thinkers to suggest that the best way to make the poor richer was to encourage enterprise and thus make the rich richer – then wealth would trickle down the social scale

Questions

1 Identify the change in real living standards, after direct tax and cash benefits, between 1979 and 1988 for both the top and bottom twenty per cent of households.

2 According to the author, which groups have gained and which have lost, in terms of the distribution of income, over the last 20 years in the UK?

3 What does the author see as the main factors affecting the distribution of income over the last 20 years?

4 How far do sociological arguments support the notion that changes in the 1980s and 1990s have led to a great increase in privileges of a class character?

Reading 15.7 **Poverty and wealth**

John Scott (from) *Poverty and Wealth: Citizenship deprivation and privilege* (1994) London: Longman, pp. 110–20.

Editorial comments

John Scott argues that it is important to consider poverty along with wealth since, he believes, there is a link between the two. The link is that both conditions can be measured in terms of notions of citizenship and deprivation, and in this sense poverty is about experiencing social deprivation relative to the standard of life of the majority of the population of a country, while being wealthy is to have advantages as compared to other groups in society. Privilege, which is what wealth provides, is therefore a parallel term to poverty, since both are related to notions of citizenship. In this reading, we look at the evidence he provides on the wealthy in the UK today.

Poverty and wealth: today

TO FALL WITHIN the top 1 per cent of personal asset holders in 1986 a person needed to hold assets valued at £190,000 or more, while those in the bottom 50 per cent would have held only an average of £2,500 each. Twenty thousand people – the top 0.05 per cent – were estimated to have been millionaires in 1986. These very wealthy people had a distinctive pattern of asset holding. Where the assets of the less well off were embodied mainly in their home, those of the very wealthy were likely also to include substantial financial assets, such as company shares. Despite the spread of shareholdings that has taken place with the **privatization** of companies that were previously publicly owned, the vast majority of privately owned shares are highly concentrated. In 1981, for instance, the top 1 per cent of the adult population held three quarters of all privately owned company shares.

The principal cause of the extreme degree of economic inequality that existed in Britain for the first half of the twentieth century, according to Josiah Wedgwood (1929) and other pioneer researchers, was the inheritance of land and financial assets by the wealthy. Through inheritance, Wedgwood argued, the wealthy were able to maintain and even to enhance their position at the top of the economic hierarchy. A study by Harbury and Hitchens published in 1979 used an extension of Wedgwood's own methods in order to test the validity of his claims and to try to assess whether the argument was still valid for the second part of the century.

Harbury and Hitchens went directly to the probate

records in order to investigate the assets of the wealthy and to compare them with those of their parents and their children. Their intention was to investigate the 'top wealth leavers', who, they believed, comprised the top 0.1 per cent of property holders. In order to take account of the changing value of money with inflation, they used a variable cut-off threshold to identify this group. In 1957, they argued, the threshold level would be property valued at £100,000, while for 1973 the threshold level had to be raised to £200,000. Evidence from Chiozza-Money (1905) and other early studies suggests that the corresponding figure for the beginning of the century would have been around £5,000. Samples were drawn for the years 1902, 1925, 1957, 1965, and 1973, the samples for the earlier years being drawn so as to include the top wealth leavers and certain others who fell just below this threshold. Using biographical reference books, General Register Office records, and, in many cases, direct approaches to the families concerned, they traced the deaths of the parents of the top wealth leavers and, for earlier years, of the children of those in their samples. The total database, then, allowed Harbury and Hitchens to investigate the profile of the top wealth leavers at each period and also to investigate the sources and the destinations of their wealth.

Harbury and Hitchens (1979) defined the 'inheritors' as those whose wealth was equal to or greater than that of their parents, *and* whose parents had themselves been wealthy. Their re-analysis of Wedgwood's data for the 1920s suggested that there had been little change in the significance of inheritance between the 1920s and the 1950s. After 1957, however, they detected some signs of a declining trend in the significance of inheritance among top wealth leavers. Their initial analysis was limited to the inheritance of men from their fathers. Taking as the yardstick of 'wealth' the level of £100,000 (at 1957 prices) that was used to identify top wealth leavers, it can be seen from Table 1 that the proportion of 'inheritors' was 51 per cent in 1957, 45 per cent in 1965, and 36 per cent in 1973. There was, therefore, a constant decline in the significance of inheritance from 1957 to 1973. Within this overall trend, however, the decline over the period of almost twenty years was far less marked among the extremely wealthy than it was for other categories. They found, for example, that 7 per cent of top wealth leavers in 1973 had millionaire fathers, compared with 9 per cent in 1957.

Harbury and Hitchens considered a number of factors that suggested this declining significance of inheritance in the postwar period might be more apparent than real. Their first point was that increases in taxation might be expected to have led to higher levels of

Table 1 Inheritance by top wealth leavers, 1957–73

Amount left by father (£)	Top wealth leavers (%)			
	1957	1965	1973 Men	1973 Women
More than 1m	9	4	7	4
500,000–1m	10	8	6	12
250,000–499,999	14	12	8	14
100,000–249,999	18	21	15	25
50,000–99,999	12	10	11	10
25,000–49,999	5	13	11	7
10,000–24,999	5	9	13	8
5,000–9,999	3	3	3	1
1,000–4,999	7	3	5	7
Less than 1,000	15	17	21	12

Note: Figures are calculated at constant prices (1957 levels)
Source: Calculated from Harbury and Hitchens (1979)

tax avoidance among the wealthy. To the extent that the wealthy passed on their wealth to their sons and daughters during their own lifetimes, figures that were based on estate duty statistics would underestimate the true extent of inheritance. The general level of the figures would also be influenced by any tendency for parents to distribute their wealth among all their children rather than simply to an eldest son. The death of a man with, say, £200,000 would result in a single top wealth holder if his wealth passed intact to his eldest son; while an equal distribution of his wealth among three children would produce no top wealth holders. Figures based on *individuals*, then, may underestimate the significance of inheritance within *families*. While this might be expected to have a constant influence at each of the periods investigated, any long-term trend away from **primogeniture** and towards more equal distribution within families would produce an apparent trend away from inheritance.

While the bulk of their research concerned male wealth, Harbury and Hitchens did undertake some analyses of women's wealth. It can be seen from Table 1 that 55 per cent of female top wealth leavers in 1973 were the daughters of men who were themselves top wealth leavers. This figure is far higher than that for men. Indeed, the proportion of female top wealth leavers whose fathers left a substantial amount of money was generally higher than that for men. Inheritance seems to play a greater role in the wealth of women than it does in that of men.

The true significance of inheritance must take account of wealth inherited from all sources, and not simply from a person's father. Harbury and Hitchens went on to examine the wealth that was inherited from mothers and from fathers-in-law as well as that which came from fathers. Looking at those male top wealth leavers who were not the sons of top wealth leavers, they discovered that many of these men had, in fact, still inherited substantial sums from their fathers (see Table 1). Fifty-eight per cent of male top wealth leavers dying in 1973 had fathers who left £25,000 or more (at 1957 prices). Of those who did not inherit this much from their fathers, one in seven had fathers-in-law who had left more than this. Taking account of the 'independent' wealth of mothers, rather than simply that which they had inherited from their husbands before passing it on to their sons, had a similar effect on the total level of inheritance. ...

A regular, annual survey of the rich undertaken for the *Sunday Times* newspaper provides some useful insights into the nature of the very wealthy in Britain today. The survey was first published in 1989, and the 1990 survey appeared in book form (Beresford, 1990). The book lists the 'top 400' wealthy individuals and families, and claims to be virtually complete for this very top level of wealth. The definition of wealth that was used was constrained by the criteria of visibility and measurability. Thus, land, shares, and houses were included, but cash in bank accounts was not. ...

With these reservations in mind, what conclusions can be drawn from the study? There were 20,000 British millionaires in 1990. The *Sunday Times* list covered the 400 wealthiest of these people, their wealth ranging from £20 million up to £6,700 million. The overall size distribution of these fortunes is shown in Table 2. Collectively, the 400 super-rich individuals and families held £543 thousand million in assets, with more than 40 per cent of this being held by the top ten alone. Almost half of the super rich had fortunes valued at over £100 million. Around 40 per cent of the total wealth of the top 400 was held as financial assets, mainly company shares. These financial assets were frequently held through trusts and, for the wealthiest, they were managed through a family office. ...

Table 3 shows the sources of wealth among the top 400. Just under a quarter of the fortunes, accounting for a third of the total wealth that was held by the super rich, could be regarded as landed fortunes, these increasingly involving urban property as well as agricultural holdings. The greater significance of urban property for personal wealth is also apparent from the fact that 18.5 per cent of the super rich derived their wealth from the ownership of companies that were engaged in property development, construction, or hotels. Just under one third of the super-rich fortunes derived from manufacturing industry, which accounted for a quarter of the total wealth. ...

Table 2 The top 400 super rich, 1990

Wealth (£m)	No.
Over 1,000	12
500–1,000	5
300–499	14
200–299	12
100–199	47
90–99	6
80–89	10
70–79	27
60–69	23
50–59	52
40–49	45
30–39	66
20–29	81
Total	400

Source: Calculated from Beresford (1990)

Table 3 Sources of wealth, 1990

Source of wealth	People and families No.	People and families %	% of wealth
Land	85	21.25	33.0
Property	43	10.75	5.7
Building	20	5.00	2.0
Hotels	11	2.75	2.2
Retailing	32	8.00	14.2
Food production	16	4.00	2.5
Brewing	6	1.25	0.7
Shoes	2	0.50	0.5
Other industry	104	26.00	19.7
Publishing	24	6.00	4.7
Entertainment	20	5.00	2.0
Trading	2	0.50	0.1
Shipping	1	0.25	1.6
Finance	27	6.75	6.0
Other	7	1.75	3.1

Source: Calculated from Beresford (1990)

The landowners, predominantly drawn from the old peerage, were among the wealthiest of the super rich. About a quarter of the top 400 were peers, mainly dukes, earls, and viscounts, but not all of the peers were landowners. To these can be added the Queen and the Prince of Wales, the two wealthiest people in the country. The position of the royal family is, of course, unique: the sheer size of their wealth reflects their identification with the structure of the state and, not unimportant, their exemption for many years from the payment of income tax and estate duty. They do, however, follow a similar approach to that of other major landowners towards the management of their land. Typical of the traditional landowners was the Duke of Westminster (Gerald Grosvenor), the inheritor of land and other property worth £4,200 million. The core of the family estate was acquired 300 years ago, and includes much of Mayfair and Belgravia, together with parts of Oxford Street and Bond Street. An acre of land in Mayfair had an estimated value of £23.5 million: the Duke had 300 acres in Mayfair. During the last 100 years the Grosvenor family acquired additional rural property in England, especially in Cheshire, as well as land in Scotland and Ireland. ...

Retailing and property development were particularly important and interlinked areas of wealth generation, forming part of a narrow range of service industries that produced a large number of 'first-generation' super rich. Among the older-established members of this group, however, were Garfield Weston (a third-generation member of the family that owned Associated British Foods), fourth-generation members of the Sainsbury family, third- and fourth-generation members of the Vestey shipping and food family, Gerald Ronson (second-generation property management), Sighismund Berger (second-generation urban property), and Lord Forte and Rocco Forte (first- and second-generation hotel chain). ...

In assessing inheritance it is, as Harbury and Hitchens pointed out, difficult to date the first generation of true wealth, and it is therefore difficult to separate the 'inheritors' from the 'self-made'. The compilers of the *Sunday Times* survey claimed that only 162 of the top 400 were 'inheritors', these being defined as those who were in an obvious and direct line of inheritance of family wealth. Yet there are other less obvious cases and examples of smaller-scale inheritance, often of an indirect nature. Clearly the number of true inheritors was underestimated, as suggested by the Harbury and Hitchens study. Viscount Hambleden, of the family that owns the firm of W. H. Smith, shows the problems that are involved in dating wealth accumulation. The family firm as an important source of wealth is now in its fourth generation, having expanded after acquiring the licence to supply newspapers on railway stations in the Victorian heyday of the railway. But the family had been involved in the newspaper business in a smaller way for a generation before this time. Indeed, most of the established business fortunes had started in a fairly small way and accumulated substantial wealth within one generation. A related model is that of Sir James Goldsmith, who built up a massive retailing and financial services group, but who inherited considerable capital from both his father and his father-in-law. It was this accumulation of wealth on the basis of 'seed corn' assets that has, in general, been maintained and increased over subsequent generations.

Those among the super rich who showed a fairly clear self-made pattern at an early stage included Sir John Moores (Littlewoods supermarkets and football pools), Robert Maxwell (publishing), Harry Hyams (urban property), Tiny Rowland (trading and publishing), and Alan Sugar (Amstrad electronics). Paul McCartney was, perhaps, the best example of a 'self-made' businessman in the super-rich league. Beginning in the music business in a small rock group, he became, as a member of the Beatles, a multimillionaire through the astute plough-back of his massive earnings at the time of the group's success. In 1987 he was reported to be receiving £3,750 per hour simply from composer royalties. Music, in fact, was one of the most striking routes of entry to the super rich for the genuinely self-made: the top 400 included Elton John, Mick Jagger, George Harrison, Phil Collins, and Rod Stewart. Also included was Richard Branson, who made his fortune through the Virgin music and airline businesses.

In only 23 of the top 400 cases was a woman named as the principal wealth holder. While this may, in part, reflect a lack of knowledge or sexist assumptions on the part of the researchers, it undoubtedly represents the very real exclusion of most women from active participation in the control of their family wealth. Most prominent of the female wealth holders was the Queen, though she was not, of course, typical. One of the very few women shown as a wealth holder in her own right was Anita Roddick of the Body Shop, who was worth £152 million.

There are, analytically, two sections within the wealthy: those with substantial *property* and those who are high *income* earners. There will, of course, be a considerable degree of overlap between these two sections. While land ownership and small businesses remain of considerable importance, the main source of income and assets for the propertied and the high earners is increasingly to be found within the corporate sector of big business. Company shares and other financial assets are the fundamental forms of property, and it is from salaried appointments at the highest level of the corporate system that the high earners receive their incomes. The propertied will, in general, be the more established, as they have accumulated or inherited income-generating assets that can be passed on to the next generation of their families. The high earners will tend to be rather more peripheral and less secure, as they cannot easily ensure the privileges of their family inter-generationally. This can be achieved only if they are able to use their income to accumulate substantial wealth – which is very difficult – or can convert their income into social and cultural assets such as private schooling for their children. This strategy would enhance the opportunities of their children to enter high-earning occupations, but it is a precarious basis for inter-generational social reproduction and passes on to the next generation the problem of the perpetuating of advantages.

There are two primary sources of propertied wealth within the corporate sector of big business: *entrepreneurial capital* and impersonal *institutional capital* (see Scott, 1986). Entrepreneurial capital is based in the direct family ownership or control of a business undertaking by an individual or a family. The operations of the enterprises that they own and control determine their personal advantages. The largest of the entrepreneurial firms include those owned by the Vestey, Rothschild, Moores, Cayzer, Sainsbury, and Pearson families, though the bulk of entrepreneurial capital is to be found in medium- and small-sized enterprises that may still generate high levels of personal wealth. It is for this reason that the wealthy include the capitalist class of property owners and income recipients together with substantial numbers of the entrepreneurial middle class (Scase and Goffee, 1982).

Many of the wealthiest entrepreneurial families are the descendants of the nineteenth century capitalist entrepreneurs, which suggests the relevance of an inter-generational model of wealth for business families. A small enterprise may grow in size through the ploughing back of profits or through the successful mobilization of small 'seed corn' inheritances from the wider family. The enterprise or the wealth derived from it will normally be passed on to the next generation of the family. Such an enterprise may eventually reach the stage where it generates sufficient liquid wealth to sustain a large family group of inheritors. This is particularly likely to occur if the enterprise can be formed into a joint stock company and all or part of the family holding can be sold on the stock exchange. In these circumstances, the family wealth can be diversified through investment in a range of assets rather than being tied up in one enterprise. The individuals at an early stage in this generational process will appear to be 'self-made' accumulators of their assets, while those in later generations will appear to be 'inheritors'. At any particular point of time, then, a study of wealth will find some 'self-made' wealth holders, but these people will, in all likelihood, pass on their wealth to the next generation of their family. Today's 'self-made' person is tomorrow's 'inheritor'.

The sector of impersonal, institutional capital comprises those companies that are owned and controlled by financial institutions – banks, insurance companies, pensions funds – and that are themselves controlled in exactly the same way. There is a depersonalized system of ownership and control (Scott, 1985) that operates in the interests of the beneficiaries of the institutions. It is often held that the main beneficiaries of the institutional system of investment are the pensioners and ordinary insured persons, but this is not the case. The top income and asset holders are the major beneficiaries of the institutional system of ownership: they are well placed in terms of occupational earnings as directors and executives, they have large private bank trust accounts, substantial unit trust and life assurance savings schemes, and, naturally, generous pension schemes. These people also have direct shareholdings in the companies with which they are involved, and this further boosts their incomes. Many of the propertied rich hold blocks of shares in a large number of the companies in the sector of institutional capital, giving them a *rentier* orientation towards their wealth. Through a strategy of diversifying their wealth, they come to own significant non-controlling stakes in a large number of companies. Where such holdings are substantial, but below the level required for control, they may still be able to influence company affairs or to gain a seat on the company board of directors and so can enter directly into ensuring that the system continues to operate to their advantage.

References

Beresford, P. (ed.) (1990) *The Sunday Times Book of the Rich*, London: Weidenfeld & Nicolson.

Chiozza-Money, L. G. (1905) *Riches and Poverty*, London: Macmillan.

Harbury, C. and Hitchens, D. M. W. N. (1979) *Inheritance and Wealth Inequality in Britain*, London: Allen & Unwin.

Scase, R. and Goffee, R. (1982) *The Entrepreneurial Middle Class*, London: Croom Helm.

Scott, J. (1985) *Corporations, Classes and Capitalism*, 2nd edn, London: Hutchinson.

Scott, J. (1986) *Capitalist Property and Financial Power*, Hassocks: Wheatsheaf.

Wedgwood, J. (1929) *The Economics of Inheritance*, Harmondsworth: Penguin.

Key terms

The following key terms appear in the text above. They have been defined below to aid with the reading of this item.

privatization the selling off of state assets to private individuals and organizations. This was a central policy of the Conservative governments of the 1980s and early 1990s

primogeniture the situation where the first born male

inherits all the assets left by deceased relatives, along with any titles they held

Questions

1 What factor was seen as the principal cause of economic inequality in Britain in the first half of the twentieth century?

2 Identify the proportion of the top 400 wealthiest people who were:
a landowners
b musicians
c women.

3 Scott argues that, analytically, the rich can be divided into two sections. Identify these and explain the difference between them.

4 Explain the difference between entrepreneurial capital and institutional capital.

5 Assess the relative importance of inheritance and enterprise in creating the wealthy upper class in contemporary Britain.

Reading 15.8 **The class analysis of poverty**

Erik Olin Wright (from) 'The class analysis of poverty', in *Interrogating Inequality* (1994) London: Verso, pp. 32–41, 43 and 45–50.

Editorial comments

In this paper, first outlined at a conference on health inequalities in 1993, Erik Olin Wright provides an analytical distinction between four very different approaches to the explanation of poverty. He goes on to discuss the importance of the distinction between oppression and exploitation. In this way, his arguments feed into more general issues about class analysis and Marxist theory, while presenting a clear Marxist explanation of the way capitalism causes poverty.

The four general approaches to explaining poverty

TO UNDERSTAND THE distinctiveness of the ['class analysis'] approach, it will be useful to contrast four general ways of explaining poverty found in both the scholarly literature and popular consciousness. These four approaches differ along two dimensions: first, whether they see the *individual* or *society* as the central unit of analysis for the most salient causes of poverty, and second, whether they see poverty as an unfortunate *by-product* of certain causes or as an *inherent feature* of the system in question. As illustrated in Table 1, I will refer to these four kinds of explanations of poverty as the genetic inferiority approach (individual/inherent), the culture of poverty approach (individual/by-product), the ravages of social change approach (societal/by-product), and the class exploitation approach (societal/inherent).

Poverty as the result of inherent individual attributes

This form of explanation constitutes a special kind of 'blaming the victim': the poor are poor because they individually suffer from some inherent flaw, generally linked to genetic inferiority affecting their intelligence. These days, relatively few scholars lay much importance on genetic factors in explaining poverty, except for arguments that attempt to link racial differentials in poverty to alleged racial differences in IQ. Still, even

Table 1 General types of explanations of poverty

Site of the explanation	Nature of the explanation	
	Unfortunate by-product	*Inherent feature*
Individual attributes	Culture of poverty	Genetic/racial inferiority
Social systems	Ravages of social change (liberal reformist)	Class exploitation (Marxist class analysis)

though genetics-based explanations of poverty do not find favour in the academy, they remain relatively popular with the public at large. ...

Poverty as the by-product of contingent individual characteristics

A more common approach to explaining poverty among social scientists sees the central cause of poverty as various *contingent* attributes of individuals which render them incapable of effectively functioning in contemporary society. These attributes are not inherent in the individual; they are by-products of various social and cultural processes. Nevertheless, the most salient explanation for why the poor are poor is that they lack the right values, they are lazy or in other ways have flawed motivation, they are too present-oriented and unable to delay gratification, they have low self-esteem, etc.

Because of its emphasis on values and norms, this approach to poverty is generally referred to as the 'culture of poverty thesis'. In its strongest versions, the explanation of poverty centres on cultural socialization, the intergenerational transmission of a set of values that perpetuate endless cycles of poverty (Lewis, 1959 and 1966). Somewhat more moderate versions place more stress on current conditions of life and how these may generate certain kinds of preferences, habits, and values. Long-term deprivations, for example, may explain short time horizons. Or, as William Julius Wilson (1987) has emphasized, the lack of role models of success through hard work for inner city black youth may explain low self-esteem, fatalism, low motivation for work, and other traits which reproduce poverty. In any event, for either the strong or moderate version of the culture of poverty thesis, once generated, these values and personality traits are seen as embedded in the individual, not simply as superficial correlates of poverty. ...

Poverty as a by-product of social causes

This is undoubtedly the most popular kind of explanation of poverty found among liberal social scientists. While individual attributes may play some role in explaining poverty, the main explanation is sought in the nature of the opportunity structure that disadvantaged people face. ... The decline of manufacturing, and in particular the decline of job structures containing the diverse mix of skilled, semi-skilled and unskilled jobs available to previous generations of unskilled immigrants, has virtually destroyed the possibility of routes out of poverty for significant segments of the black population. This general tendency in the American economy has been exacerbated by the massive evacuation of jobs from the inner city and the flight of the black middle class from the ghetto, so the general decline in opportunity has been compounded by severe social isolation. No one intended this calamity and no one really benefits from it, but it has the consequence of significantly deepening the problem of poverty.

With this diagnosis of the causes of poverty, the solution is generally seen as twofold. First, a massive effort needs to be devoted to the problem of skill formation and education so that disadvantaged children are equipped to participate actively in the labor market. Secondly, serious jobs programs, generally assumed to require considerable expansion of public works, need to be created to employ people with marginal skills. Both of these solutions require an expansion of the 'affirmative state'.

While social by-product views of poverty tend to be associated with liberal reformists, there are conservatives who adopt a version of this approach. Charles Murray (1984), for example, sees the problem of the underclass in the United States as an unfortunate by-product of well-meaning welfare policies instituted in the 1960s and expanded in the 1970s. He argues that **AFDC** programmes have the effect of creating incentives for people to act irresponsibly and to engage in strategies which perpetuate their poverty. He does not believe that this creates deep-seated personality flaws, but simply that poor people are acting rationally when they exploit the generosity of the welfare system. The solution, he argues, is to eliminate virtually all welfare programmes and thus radically change the incentive structure facing poor people. With these altered incentives they will begin to work hard, act responsibly and thus 'raise themselves out of poverty'. ...

Poverty as a result of the inherent properties of the social system

The least familiar approach to explaining poverty among Americans is the view that poverty should be seen as an inherent attribute of the functioning of certain kinds of social systems. The most prominent version of this view is identified with the Marxist tradition, and sees poverty in contemporary capitalism as generated by the core dynamics of class exploitation. Poverty is not an accident; it is not a by-product. It is an inherent, and crucial, feature of a society whose economic structure is grounded in class and exploitation. The pivotal idea is that there are powerful and privileged actors who have an active interest in maintaining poverty. It is not just that poverty is an unfortunate consequence of their pursuit of material interests; it is an essential *condition* for the *realization* of their interests. To put it bluntly, capitalists and other exploiting classes benefit from poverty. ...

There are two principle variants of this general view of poverty. The first, identified with revolutionary Marxism, argues that the only way to reduce poverty significantly is to eliminate capitalism altogether. It is not just that poverty is *good* for capitalism; it is *essential* for its very survival. Thus, there is no real prospect for significantly reducing poverty inside of capitalism. The second variant, generally associated with social democracy, argues that capitalism can be significantly tamed, that while capitalists have real, material interests in sustaining poverty, significant redistribution of income is compatible with the survival of capitalist institutions. As a result, if the power of capitalists and their allies can be effectively challenged *inside of capitalism*, significant inroads against poverty can be achieved. In these terms, Sweden is often held up as an exemplary case where bourgeois forces were politically defeated or forced to compromise with powerful defenders of the underprivileged. Swedish capitalists did not want to help the poor; they were forced to help the poor by the combined forces of the Swedish labour movement and the Social Democratic Party. As a result, wealthy people live less well in Sweden than in the United States. This means that there are losers – that there is a **zero-sum** aspect to meaningful solutions to poverty. And, because there are real losers, it is unlikely that serious solutions will be politically based purely on consensus across social classes. ...

So far, I have only gestured at the substantive arguments of a class analysis of poverty. In this section I will fill out the argument. To do this it is necessary to define carefully three key concepts: economic oppression, economic exploitation, and class. Once these concepts are defined, I will explain how they generate a social system in which poverty plays a crucial functional role.

Oppression and exploitation

Economic oppression can be defined as a situation in which three conditions are satisfied:

a The material welfare of one group of people is causally related to the material deprivations of another.
b The causal relation in (a) involves coercively enforced exclusion from access to productive resources.
c This exclusion in (b) is morally indictable.

This is a fairly complex definition. Without (c), a fair competition between two people for a prize in which the ownership of the prize is backed by property rights (and thus by coercion) would count as a form of economic oppression. Without (b), simple cheating would be considered a form of oppression (assuming that the cheating in question was viewed as morally indictable). Without (a), we have economically gratuitous exclusion – exclusion from resources from which no one derives material benefit. 'Economic oppression' is thus a situation in which the material benefits of one group are acquired at the expense of another, and in which morally indictable coercive exclusion from resources is an essential part of the process by which this occurs. The introduction of (c), of course, renders judgments of the oppressive nature of a particular inequality highly contentious, since there will generally be disputes about the moral standing of the exclusions that back up the inequalities in question.

Economic oppression defined in this way can take many forms. Of particular salience to class analysis is the distinction between exploitative and non-exploitative economic oppression. Economic exploitation is a specific form of economic oppression defined by a particular kind of mechanism through which the welfare of exploiters is causally related to the deprivations of the exploited. In exploitation, *the material well-being of exploiters causally depends upon their ability to appropriate the fruits of labour of the exploited*. The welfare of the exploiter therefore depends on the *effort* of the exploited, not merely on the deprivations of the exploited. In non-exploitative economic oppression there is no transfer of the fruits of labour from the oppressed to the oppressor; the welfare of the oppressor depends on the exclusion of the oppressed from access to certain resources, but not on their effort. In both instances, the inequalities in question are rooted in ownership of and control over productive resources.

The crucial difference between exploitation and non-exploitative oppression is that in an exploitative relation, the exploiter *needs* the exploited since the exploiter depends upon the effort of the exploited. In the case of non-exploitative oppression, the oppressors would be happy if the oppressed simply disappeared. Life would have been much easier for the European settlers in North America if the continent had been unihabited by people. Genocide is thus always a potential strategy for non-exploitative oppressors. It is not an option in a situation of economic exploitation because exploiters require the labour of the exploited for their material well-being. It is no accident that culturally we have the saying, 'the only good Indian is a dead Indian', but not the saying 'the only good worker is a dead worker'. The contrast between South Africa and North America in their treatment of indigenous peoples reflects this difference poignantly: in North America, where the indigenous people were oppressed (by virtue of being coercively displaced from the land) but not exploited, genocide was the basic policy of social control in the face of resistance; in South Africa, where the European settler population heavily depended upon African labour for its own prosperity, this was not an option.

Exploitation, therefore, does not merely define a set of *statuses* of social actors, but a pattern of on-going interactions structured by a set of social relations, relations which mutually bind the exploiter and the exploited together. This dependency of the exploiter on the exploited gives the exploited a certain form of power, since human beings always retain at least some minimal control over their own expenditure of effort. Social control which relies exclusively on repression is costly and, except under special circumstances, often fails to generate the required levels of diligence and effort on the part of the exploited. As a result, there is generally systematic pressure on exploiters to moderate their domination and in one way or another to try to elicit some degree of consent from the exploited, at least in the sense of gaining some level of minimal co-operation from them. Paradoxically perhaps, exploitation is thus a constraining force on the practices of the exploiter. This constraint constitutes a basis of power for the exploited.

The non-exploited oppressed may also have some power, but it is generally more precarious. At a minimum oppressed people have the power that comes from the human capacity for physical resistance. However, since their oppressors are not economically constrained to seek any kind of cooperation from them, this resistance is likely very quickly to escalate into quite bloody and violent confrontations. It is for this reason that the resistance of Native Americans to displacement from the land led to massacres of Native Americans by white settlers. The pressure on oppressors to seek accommodation is very weak; the outcomes therefore tend to become simply a matter of the balance of brute force between enemies. ...

Class

Underlying both the concept of simple material oppression and the concept of exploitation is the idea that there are various kinds of productive resources which are important for material welfare and which have the property that one's welfare is enhanced by excluding others from access to the resource. Oppression occurs when one group illegitimately excludes another from access to those resources. Exploitation occurs when such exclusion from resources also gives the owners of the resource the capacity to appropriate the fruits of labour of others. If I kick the peasants off the land and let them fend for themselves in the bush, then I have merely oppressed them materially; if I use my ownership of the land as a basis for hiring them back to work the fields, then I exploit them.

The concept of class, within the Marxist tradition, is closely tied to this understanding of exploitation. Classes are categories of social actors defined by the property relations which generate exploitation. In the above example, the landowner and the peasant are in different classes because (a) they are bound together through a specific set of social property relations (or, as they are often called, social relations of production) and (b) the landowner exploits the peasant. Homeowners and the homeless, on the other hand, would generally not constitute two classes.

More generally, one can define a range of different kinds of class relations in terms of the pivotal form of productive resources that provides the basis for exploitation. Marxists have traditionally focused on two such resources: capital and labour. Slavery is based on a form of class relations in which the slave-master owns the slave and by virtue of that ownership exploits the slave. Capitalism is based on a form of class relations in which the capitalist owns the means of production, the worker owns labour-power, and by virtue of these property rights in capital and labour, the capitalist is able to exploit the worker through the employment relation. ...

Class, exploitation and poverty

The concepts we have been exploring suggest that the general problem of poverty needs to be broken down into two sub-problems: poverty generated inside exploitative relations, and poverty generated by non-exploitative oppression. The former corresponds to what in contemporary policy discourse is called 'the working poor'; the latter corresponds to the 'under-class'.

The working poor

If one takes a static view of the economy, then it is easy to attribute the existence of the working poor to the intersection of two facts: (1) many firms have low levels of productivity and in order to compete they can only offer low wages; and (2) many workers have low levels of skills or limited possibility of geographical mobility and thus are constrained to accept such poor-paying jobs. Within a class analysis framework, however, the existence of a sizeable population of working poor in an otherwise affluent society can be viewed, to a significant extent, as one of the many dynamic consequences of a weak, fragmented, and relatively conservative labour movement. A strong, solidaristic labour movement is likely to be committed to reducing wage inequalities within the working class. When such a movement is closely linked to a political party capable of using the power of the state to back up such egalitarian commitments, then one would predict a long-term disappearance of impoverished employed workers.

The 'solidarity wage' policy in Sweden, for example, was a deliberate policy of the labour movement to raise the wages of the most poorly paid sectors of the working class as a way of reinforcing the long-term solidarity of the labour movement. This strategy was complemented by the well-known 'active labour market policy' of the social democratic state, which was committed to retraining workers when firms became uncompetitive by virtue of rising wages. The distribution of income among workers, and in particular the extent to which a stratum of impoverished employed workers exists, therefore, should not be viewed simply as a spontaneous result of 'natural' market forces, but as the result of the exercise of power by social forces with different interests.

The concept of the 'working poor', in this context, should not be seen as only referring to the stratum of poor employed workers within a rich country. The employment of poor Mexican workers in US automakers' factories in northern Mexico also follows the same logic. In this case the issue of class power is the absence of a solidaristic international labour movement capable of constraining the capacity of multinational firms to pay Third World workers miserable wages. The existence of the working poor employed by multinational firms in Third World countries thus, in part, reflects power relations, not simply impersonal market forces.

The underclass

The term 'underclass' is used in a variety of ways in contemporary policy discussions. Sometimes it is meant to be a pejorative term rather like the old Marxist concept of 'lumpenproletariat'; other times it is used more descriptively to designate a segment of the poor whose conditions of life are especially desperate and whose prospects for improvement are particularly dismal. One way of giving this concept a more precise theoretical status is to link it to the concepts of exploitation and oppression: and 'underclass' can be defined as a category of social agents who are economically oppressed but not consistently exploited within a given class system.

Different kinds of class structures will tend to have different forms of an 'underclass'. In many parts of the world today and throughout much of human history, the pivotal resource which defines the underclass is land. Landlords, agrarian capitalists, peasants, and exploited agrarian producers all have access to land; people who are excluded from such access constitute the underclass of agrarian societies. In these terms, Native Americans were transformed into an underclass in the nineteenth century when they were pushed off the land into the reservations.

In contemporary advanced capitalism, the key resource that defines the predicament of the underclass is labour-power itself. This might seem like an odd statement since in capitalism, at least since the abolition of slavery, everyone supposedly owns one 'unit' of labour-power, him or herself. The point is that some people do not in fact own productively usable labour-power. The situation is similar to that of a capitalist owning outmoded machines. While the capitalist physically controls these pieces of machinery, they cease to be 'capital' – a productive resource – if they cannot be deployed within a capitalist production process profitably. In the case of labour-power, a person can physically control his or her own labouring capacity, but that capacity can cease to have economic value in capitalism if it cannot be deployed productively. This is the essential condition of the 'underclass'. They are oppressed because they are denied access to various kinds of productive resources, above all the necessary means to acquire the skills needed to make their labour-power saleable. As a result, they are not consistently exploited. ...

Understood in this way, the underclass consists of human beings who are largely expendable *from the point of view of the rationality of capitalism*. As in the case of native Americans, who became a landless underclass in the nineteenth century, repression rather than incorporation is the central mode of social control directed towards them. Capitalism does not need the labour-power of unemployed inner-city youth. The material interests of the wealthy and privileged segments of American society would be better served if these people simply disappeared. However, unlike in the nineteenth century, the moral and political forces are such that direct genocide is no longer a viable strategy. The alternative, then, is to build prisons, to cordon off the zones of cities in which the underclass live. In such a situation the main potential power of the underclass against their oppressors comes from their capacity to disrupt the sphere of consumption, especially through crime and other forms of violence, not their capacity to disrupt production through their control over labour. ...

Adding a class analysis perspective to the analysis of poverty is not just adding another variable to a laundry list of factors in a multivariate model. It changes the way we think about the political dynamics at stake in attempts to do something about the problem. Specifically, since a class analysis of poverty argues that there are significant numbers of privileged people with a strong, positive material interest in maintaining poverty, significant advances towards reducing poverty in the United States must place the problem of power and struggles over power at the centre of the political agenda.

References

Lewis, O. (1959) *Five Families*, New York: Basic Books.

Lewis, O. (1966) *La Vida*, New York: Basic Books.

Murray, C. (1984) *Losing Ground*, New York: Basic Books.

Wilson, W. J. (1987) *The Truly Disadvantaged*, Chicago: University of Chicago Press.

Key terms

The following key terms appear in the text above. They have been defined below to aid with the reading of this item.

AFDC Aid to Families with Dependent Children (AFDC) is part of the American welfare system

zero-sum a term used to describe a situation where one group can gain only by taking from another and therefore the gains to one and the losses to the other cancel each other out – resulting in a zero sum

Questions

1 Explain in your own words what is meant by the 'culture of poverty thesis'.

2 Identify the key elements of the distinction the author draws between oppression and exploitation.

3 Explain how exploitation places a limit on the actions of exploiters.

4 Why does the author argue that the underclass consists of people who, from the point of view of the rationality of capitalism, are expendable?

5 To what extent do sociological arguments support the notion that poverty is the result of inherent features of capitalism?

Further reading

The following texts may represent a useful starting point for further investigation of the ideas contained within this chapter.

George, V. and Wilding, P. (1994) *Welfare and Ideology*, London: Harvester Wheatsheaf.

Hills, J. (1995) *Inquiry into Income and Wealth*, York: Joseph Rowntree Foundation

Hutton, W. (1996) *The State We're In*, London: Vintage.

Le Grand, J. (1990) 'The state of welfare', in Hills, J. (ed.) *The State of Welfare: The welfare state in Britain since 1974*, Oxford: Oxford University Press

Lowe, R. (1993) *The Welfare State in Britain Since 1945*, Basingstoke: Macmillan.

Oppenheim, C. and Harker, L. (1996) *Poverty: The facts*, 3rd edn, London: CPAG.

Williams, F. (1989) *Social Policy: A critical introduction*, Cambridge: Polity.

Coursework suggestions

1 **Conduct a study considering the validity of the notion of welfare regimes and its applicability to the recent welfare history of the UK.**

2 **Conduct a case-study of the effect of the government's 'welfare-to-work' programme in your local area, or in relation to specific groups such as lone parents or the disabled.**

3 **Use secondary sources to investigate the structure of the very wealthy in your local area.**

16

The mass media

Chapter summary

Reading 16.1 **Traditional Marxism and dominant ideology** *page 468*

Marx and Engels suggest that ruling class domination is secured through ideological measures. This represents a classic Marxist statement on the nature of ruling class ideology in society and the development of a 'dominant ideology'.

Reading 16.2 **Deviancy amplification and the media** *page 469*

Jock Young explores the relationships between the subjective judgements and labels of the media concerning social definitions of 'the criminal' and the role the media can play in the amplification of criminal images in the audience.

Reading 16.3 **The effects of the media** *page 473*

Greg Philo, a leading member of the Glasgow University Media Group, argues that although for some media audiences 'seeing is believing', many can resist and fight media images.

Reading 16.4 **How and why do women 'read' magazines?** *page 477*

Ballaster *et al.* explore the ideological content of women's magazines. They seek to explore how and why women's magazines are pleasurable to female audiences.

Reading 16.5 **War reporting** *page 482*

Philip M. Taylor attempts to critically analyse the reporting of the Gulf War of 1991. He claims that the so-called 'as-it-happens', 'round-the-clock' media coverage of the war was not as neutral and as 'instant' as perhaps claimed at the time.

Reading 16.6 **Investigating media bias** *page 487*

John Eldridge – a member of the Glasgow University Media Group – reflects, in this reading, on the intellectual and theoretical influences upon contemporary media research. In doing so he takes a critical view of Baudrillard's post-modern ideas.

Reading 16.7 **The reporting of 'disasters' in the media** *page 491*

Jonathan Benthall takes an empirical approach to the study of the media, where he investigates the ways in which the media report issues of famine, relief aid and natural disaster in the undeveloped and developing worlds.

Reading 16.8 **Patriarchal ideology and femininity in the media** *page 495*

Joan Smith focuses upon the ways in which women as mothers are portrayed in the media – and especially in newspapers – from a critical feminist perspective.

Introduction: Reading the sociology of the mass media

Most contemporary analyses of the mass media start from the observation that most, if not all, households in the UK are exposed in some form to the media – be it print, audio and/or visual. In this respect, the contemporary media is an important aspect of social reality for the majority of social actors. Given this, it is no surprise to find that the analysis of the media – of its effects, content and uses – is a major preoccupation of many academic sociologists.

For some, the media is a powerful source or agent of socialization – it shapes, moulds and dictates what is presented to us as 'reality'. Some go even fur-

ther still and argue that the media is such an all-encompassing force in the contemporary world that audiences are little more than victims of media ideology – puppets of social control. Others have argued that even if the media contains deliberate ideological bias – and this is by no means certain – audiences are active social agents, who can fight, reject, resist and subvert media messages.

The eight readings contained within this chapter can be located within the various sociological positions above. Whereas most of the readings suggest that bias is present in the media, many disagree on the possible consequences of this bias – if any.

The bias observed by these readings covers a large range, including political bias, bias at times of war and 'natural disasters', and stereotypical representations of femininity. Perhaps it is important here to recognize and reflect upon the observation that the media will always be biased in some senses, since it is impossible to represent the whole of the world's events all the time. By its very nature the phenomenon of the 'news' is based upon selection – it is a manufactured product behind which many decisions have been made and many pieces of 'news' actively sought, rejected or even ignored. Although it could not be anything other than a partial picture of reality, the important question is how do audiences respond to such a picture? Is there such a thing as an audience – or are there audiences? Are audiences active and creative or passive and manipulated? Does the audience give meaning to the media or take meaning from the media?

The traditional Marxist account of the ideological role of the mass media is often referred to as a hypodermic syringe model of media effects. Ideological bias is seen to benefit the ruling class who both own and control the media. Media effect is both deliberate and direct – the audience passively 'soaks up' pro-establishment thinking which supports the status-quo in society. This argument is represented in **reading 16.1**, by Marx and Engels (originally published in 1846), who argue that the masses are victims of the massive agency of socialization and social control that is the media – a starting point for most contemporary left-of-centre sociological analyses.

In contrast, many thinkers associated with a more action theory approach would take issue with the above view of the audience as passive, manipulated by media messages. Interpretative or interactionist sociologies would adopt one of two approaches. Firstly, the media may be crucial in the construction of a dominant definition of social reality. Media images and messages provide the social actor with scripts to follow – we can learn cultural values and definitions of how to behave. This argument is reflected in the work of Jock Young (1973), in **reading 16.2**, who argues that the media is able to perpetuate dominant definitions of criminal stereotypes in society. Interestingly enough, on a much more macro and structural level, this argument might also be voiced by functionalist thinkers and even some members of the New Right.

Secondly, many interpretative sociologists, from the point of view of their phenomenological methodology, may suggest that, since social actors are creative and reflective creatures able to manipulate the symbolic universe within which they act and interact, media messages may be used in the construction of social reality but not in a totally passive fashion.

This phenomenological argument has been adopted by many more recent thinkers in conjunction with a left-of-centre Marxist analysis. These modern Marxists or neo-Marxists argue that whereas bias that supports an exploitative capitalist society does exist it is not necessarily deliberate and not necessarily passively accepted. For example Greg Philo (1990), in **reading 16.3**, argues that the cultural background and personal experiences of the audience group may dictate the likelihood of the effect taking place. As relatively unique social actors, our personal biography of actions, interactions, meanings and life experiences form a framework or context through which we critically view media messages – we may believe messages regarding situations we have no direct experience of, but equally we can reject messages that contradict our direct lived and meaningful experience.

Like Philo, Philip M. Taylor (1992), in **reading 16.5**, is concerned to identify the powerful manufacturing processes which shape what we, as the audience, come to know as 'news'. Taylor argues that rather than the reporting of the 1991 Gulf War being 'as-it-happens' – a claim made by Cable News Network (CNN) at the time – instead, the reporting of the Gulf War was moulded by agenda setting, gate-keeping and non decision making. The media 'reality' of the event was mediated to the audience through censorship and reporting guidelines.

The ideas of post-modern thinker Jean Baudrillard, cited in **reading 16.6** by John Eldridge (1993), takes the argument of media effect even further. He argues that the contemporary media, in a post-modern society where ultimate truth has been dismantled, have become 'simulations' of reality. Because we turn to the media's flickering TV screens for knowledge and personal experience, the media's distorted and partial images become more real than our actual 'real' experience. The media becomes 'hyper-real' – the key shaper of meaning in an otherwise distorted, chaotic and meaningless social existence.

Finally, the offerings by Joan Smith (1997), in **reading 16.8**, Ballaster *et al.* (1991), in **reading 16.4** and Jonathan Benthall (1993), in **reading 16.7**, deal – respectively – with the representation of femininity and the representation of so-called 'natural disasters' in the media. Both Smith and Benthall argue that the media is biased and conveys false impressions to its audience – impressions that may shape social reality.

Reading 16.1 **Traditional Marxism and dominant ideology**

Karl Marx and Frederich Engels (from) *The German Ideology* (1970, originally published in 1846) London: Lawrence & Wishart, pp. 64–6.

Editorial comments

This is a frequently cited, classic Marxist interpretation of culture in a capitalist society and as such is often the starting point of many modern media analyses. Marx and Engels argue that the ideas in any age which rule come from the rulers themselves. Thus, laws, cultural values, religious customs and in our contemporary technological age, dominant media messages, serve the interests of capitalism.

The ruling class and ruling ideas

THE IDEAS OF the ruling class are in every **epoch** the ruling ideas, i.e. the class which is the ruling *material* force of society, is at the same time its ruling *intellectual* force. The class which has the means of material production at its disposal, has control at the same time over the means of mental production, so that thereby, generally speaking, the ideas of those who lack the means of mental production are subject to it. The ruling ideas are nothing more than the ideal expression of the dominant material relationships, the dominant material relationships grasped as ideas; hence of the relationships which make the one class the ruling one, therefore, the ideas of its dominance. The individuals composing the ruling class possess among other things consciousness, and therefore think. Insofar, therefore, as they rule as a class and determine the extent and compass of an epoch, it is self-evident that they do this in its whole range, hence among other things rule also as thinkers, as producers of ideas, and regulate the production and distribution of the ideas of their age: thus their ideas are the ruling ideas of the epoch. For instance, in an age and in a country where royal power, aristocracy, and bourgeoisie are contending for mastery and where, therefore, mastery is shared, the doctrine of the separation of powers proves to be the dominant idea and is expressed as an 'eternal law'.

The **division of labour**, which we already saw above as one of the chief forces of history up till now, manifests itself also in the ruling class as the division of mental and material labour, so that inside this class one part appears as the thinkers of the class (its active, conceptive ideologists, who make the perfecting of the illusion of the class about itself their chief source of livelihood), while the others' attitude to these ideas and illusions is more passive and receptive, because they are in reality the active members of this class and have less time to make up illusions and ideas about themselves. Within this class this cleavage can even develop into a certain opposition and hostility between the two parts, which, however, in the case of a practical collision, in which the class itself is endangered, automatically comes to nothing, in which case there also vanishes the semblance that the ruling ideas were not the ideas of the ruling class and had a power distinct from the power of this class. The existence of revolutionary ideas in a particular period presupposes the existence of a revolutionary class; about the premises for the latter sufficient has already been said.

If now in considering the course of history we detach the ideas of the ruling class from the ruling class itself and attribute to them an independent existence, if we confine ourselves to saying that these or those ideas were dominant at a given time, without bothering ourselves about the conditions of production and the producers of these ideas, if we thus ignore the individuals and world conditions which are the source of the ideas, we can say, for instance, that during the time that the aristocracy was dominant, the concepts honour, loyalty, etc. were dominant, during the dominance of the bourgeoisie the concepts freedom, equality, etc. The ruling class itself on the whole imagines this to be so. This conception of history, which is common to all historians, particularly since the eighteenth century, will necessarily come up against the phenomenon that increasingly abstract ideas hold sway, i.e. ideas which increasingly take on the form of universality. For each new class which puts itself in the place of one ruling before it, is compelled, merely in order to carry through its aim, to represent its interest as the common interest of all the members of society, that is, expressed in ideal form: it has to give its ideas the form of universality, and represent them as the only rational, universally valid ones. The class making a revolution appears from the very start, if only because it is opposed to a *class*, not as a class but as the representative of the whole of society; it appears as the whole mass of society confronting the one ruling class. It can do this because, to start with, its interest really is more connected with the common interest of all other non-ruling classes, because under the pressure of hitherto existing conditions its interest has not yet been able to develop as the particular interest of a particular class. Its victory, therefore, benefits also many individuals of the other classes which are not winning a dominant position, but only insofar as it now puts these individuals in a position to raise themselves into the ruling class. When the French bourgeoisie overthrew the power of the aristocracy, it thereby made it possible for many proletarians to raise themselves above the proletariat, but only insofar as they become bourgeois. Every new class, therefore, achieves its **hegemony** only on a broader basis than that of the class ruling previously, whereas the opposition of the non-ruling class against the new ruling class later develops all the more sharply and profoundly. Both these things determine the fact that the struggle to be waged against this new ruling class, in its turn, aims at a more decided and radical negation of the previous conditions of society than could all previous classes which sought to rule.

Key terms

The following key terms appear in the text above. They have been defined below to aid with the reading of this item.

epoch a stage/period in history

division of labour the separation of the labour/manufacturing process into stages or independent tasks and jobs

hegemony dominance of one class by another through a 'war of ideas'

Questions

1 What implications does the argument of Marx and Engels in the above passage have for the socialization process in society?

2 What aspects of society would contain these 'ruling ideas'?

3 Why do you think it is more important for the ruling class to rule over the masses through ideology rather than just by physical force?

Reading 16.2 **Deviancy amplification and the media**

Jock Young (from) 'The myth of the drug taker in the mass media', in S. Cohen and J. Young (eds) *The Manufacture of News: Deviance, social problems and the mass media* (1973) London: Constable, pp. 314–22.

Editorial comments

In adopting a Marxist-interactionist theoretical stance, Young has argued elsewhere that the media can play a key role in the production, reproduction and transmission of deviant labels in society. He also suggests that an interplay exists between police definitions of criminality, public definitions, a criminal's own deviant labels and media reporting. The process whereby deviant activities are both exaggerated through the media and actual criminal behaviour is increased by media labelling is referred to as a process of amplification. In this reading Young suggests that the images of drug taking in the media are largely 'mythical'.

The myth of the drug taker in the mass media

THE MOST AMAZING quality of mass media reporting of the drug problem is their ability to get the wrong end of the stick. Indeed in *The drugtakers* I formulated, with tongue in cheek, Young's Law of Information on Drugs. Namely, that the *greater* the public health risk (measured in number of mortalities) of a psychotropic substance, the *less* the amount of information (including advertising) critical of its effects. Tobacco, alcohol, the barbiturates, amphetamines, heroin, LSD and marihuana (listed in declining public health risk) would all seem to fit this proposition – apart from those exceptional and short-lived occasions when lung cancer scares occur. It is the explanation of the social basis of this 'Law' with which this article is concerned.

We live in a world which is extremely socially segregated: direct experience of individuals with behaviour different from our own conventions and values is rare. It is in just such a world that we come to rely on the mass media for a sizeable proportion of our information as to the goings on of outsiders to our small discrete social worlds. Criticism of the mass media has centred round the notion that journalists are biased, misinformed or just plain deceitful. The impression is given that if the profession were to revamp its ethics and remove its bias, the body of responsible journalism would be uncovered and the population receive from then on the simple facts of the matter, to interpret as they please. Minor adjustments have to be made to the set after which the picture will focus and the facts be held objectively. I wish to suggest, to the contrary, that 'facts' do not speak for themselves, that they are only given meaning in terms of the **frame of reference** provided. Further, that the mass media offer an amazingly systematic frame of reference. It is not random bias but a consistent world view which is purveyed. The model of society held by the mass media, and implicit in their reporting of both deviant and normal, I will term consensualist. Its constitution is simplicity itself: namely, that the vast majority of people in society share a common definition of reality – agree as to what activities are praiseworthy and what are condemnable. That this consensus is functional to an organic system which they envisage as society. That behaviour outside this reality is a product of irrationality or sickness, that it is in itself meaningless activity which leads nowhere and is, most importantly, behaviour which has direct and unpleasant consequences for the small minority who are impelled to act this way. The model carries with it a notion of merited rewards and just punishments. It argues for the equitable nature of the *status quo* and draws the parameters of happiness and experience. Specifically, it defines material rewards as the payment for hard work, sexual pleasure as the concomitant of supporting the nuclear family, and religious or mystical experience as not an alternative interpretation of reality but as an activity acceptable only in a disenchanted form which solemnizes (their word) the family and bulwarks the *status quo*. The illicit drug taker is, I want to suggest, the deviant *par excellence*. For his culture disdains work and revels in **hedonism**, his sexual relations are reputedly licentious and promiscuous, and the psychdelics promise a re-enchantment of the world – a subversive take-on reality.

It is not drugs *per se* which are denigrated – for our culture is historically normal in that drug use is ubiquitous. Rather it is drugs taken for hedonistic reasons. The social drinker who is relaxing between his work bouts, the middle-aged barbiturate addict who needs drugs in order to sleep, the tranquillizer habitué who takes drugs in order to ease his work or marital tensions – or even the physician morphine addict who uses the drug to keep him working under pain or stress: all of these individuals are ignored or treated lightly. It is when drug use is seen as unrelated to productivity, when it leads to 'undeserved' pleasures, when it gives rise to experiences which question the taken-for-granted 'reality', that the forces of condemnation are bought into play.

The mass media carries a mythology of the average man and the deviant – within which Mr Average is seen to prosper and be content in his universe of hard work and industrious consumption and the deviant is portrayed as being beset by forces which lead to ineluctable misfortune. But the real world outside this spectacle differs radically from this. For often the worker doubts the fairness of his rewards, the middle-class housewife surveys her Ideal Home with ambivalence, the husband eyes his secretary and then goes back to his wife, the adolescent Seeker looks at the Established Church and cannot for the life of him see how it refers to the same reality as that of the Christian mystics. For popular consciousness is a collage of contradictions: it is both sceptical and complacent, satisfied and discontented, rational and superstitious, conservative and downright subversive. It is on this base that the mass media acts. For there exists widespread suspicion that the sacrifices made are not worth the rewards received. This is the basis for what Albert Cohen calls moral indignation. Thus he writes:

> … the dedicated pursuit of culturally approved goals, the adherence to normatively sanctioned means – these imply a certain self restraint, effort, discipline, inhibition. What is the effect of others who, though their activities do not manifestly damage our own interests are morally undisciplined, who give themselves up to idleness, self indulgence, or forbidden vices? What effect does the propinquity of the wicked have upon the peace of mind of the virtuous?
> *(Cohen, 1965)*

What Cohen is arguing is that deviant activities, even although they may have no direct effect on the interests of those who observe them, may be condemned because they represent concrete examples of individuals who are, so to speak, dodging the rules. For if a person lives by a code of conduct which forbids certain pleasures, which involves the deferring of gratification in certain areas, it is hardly surprising that he will react strongly against those whom he sees to be taking short cuts. This is a partial explanation of the vigorous repression against what Edwin Schur calls 'crimes without victims': homosexuality, prostitution, abortion and drug taking.

The mass media have discovered that people read avidly news which titillates their sensibilities and confirms their prejudices. The ethos of 'give the public what it wants' involves a constant play on the normative worries of large segments of the population; it utilizes outgroups as living Rorschach blots on to which collective fears and doubts are projected. Moral indignation, if first galvanized by the newspapers and then resolved in a *just* fashion, makes a fine basis for newspaper readership. To this extent then newspaper men are accurate when they suggest that they are just giving the public what it wants, only what this represents is reinforcing the consensual part of the popular consciousness and denigrating any subversive notions.

The widespread appeal of the mass media rests, therefore, on its ability to fascinate and titillate its audience and then reassure by finally condemning. This is a propaganda of a very sophisticated sort, playing on widespread discontent and insecurities and little resembling the crude manipulative model of the mass media commonly held in liberal and left circles.

Illicit drug use is custom built for this sort of treatment. A characteristic reaction to drug use is that of ambivalence for, as with so many social relationships between 'normal' and 'deviant', the normal person simultaneously both covets and castigates the deviant action. This after all is the basis of moral indignation, namely that the wicked are undeservedly realizing the covert desires of the virtuous. Richard Blum captured well this fascination–repulsion relationship to drug use when he wrote:

> Pharmaceutical materials do not dispense themselves and the illicit drugs are rarely given away, let alone forced on people. Consequently, the menace lies within the person, for there would be no drug threat without a drug attraction. The amount of public interest in stories about druggies suggests the same drug attraction and repulsion in ordinary citizens. 'Fascination' is the better term since it implies witchcraft and enchantment. People are fascinated with drugs – because they are attracted by the states and conditions drugs are said to produce. That is another side to the fear of being disrupted; it is the desire for release, for escape, for magic, and for ecstatic joys. That is the derivation of the menace in drugs – their representation as keys to forbidden kingdoms inside ourselves. The *dreadful* in the drug is the *dreadful* in ourselves.
> *(Blum, 1969)*

This is an explanation of the hostility and attraction which drugs evoke. It makes understandable the findings in opinion polls on both sides of the Atlantic which show the drug pusher to be evaluated a higher community menace than the property criminal. It is rooted in moral indignation. Alasdair MacIntyre captured the attitude well when he wrote:

> Most of the hostility that I have met with comes from people who have never examined the facts at all. I suspect that what makes them dislike cannabis is not the belief that the effects of taking it are harmful but rather a horrifying suspicion that here is a source of pure pleasure which is available to those who have not earned it, who do not deserve it.
> *(MacIntyre, 1968)*

I want to suggest that the media unwittingly have set themselves up as the guardians of consensus; that as major providers of information about actions, events, groups and ideas they forge this information in a closed consensual image. Further I want to suggest that the myths generated and carried by the media although based on ignorance are not of a random nature. The myths are grounded in a particular view of society which throws up certain contradictions which they attempt to solve. They contain certain simple structures irrespective of whether one considers the myth of the prostitute, the criminal, the striker, the pornographer, the delinquent, or the drug taker.

The mass media is committed, on one hand, to reporting that which is newsworthy and, on the other, to interpreting it within a consensual frame of reference. This leads to the first major contradiction that the media must face: for it is precisely alternative deviant realities such as the world of the illicit drug user which are simultaneously highly newsworthy and, because they are alternative realities, violations of the consensual image of society. For if different realms of meaning exist, and illicit pleasure is in fact pleasurable, then the mass media world of the happy worker and joyful consumer is threatened. The contradiction is resolved by a skilful defusing of deviant action. Namely, that much drug taking is a product of personality disorders and is, moreover, unpleasurable. Illicit pleasure, the tinder of moral indignation, is accentuated in reporting in order to maximize its news value. The forbidden is thus potentially all the more tempting. To circumvent this the myth contains the notion of in-built justice mechanisms. Atypical pleasure leads to atypical pain. Thus premarital sexual intercourse gives rise to VD, LSD to madness and marihuana to pitiful degeneracy. Whatever the outcome the message is the same: *deviancy is unpleasurable*. No one would voluntarily choose to be a drug user of this sort, because of the sticky fate that awaits him. Only the sick person, impelled by forces beyond his control, would find himself involved in such an activity. Thus initially there is a **bifurcation** of the world and human nature into:

a the normal rational average citizen who lives in well normed communities, shares common values, and displays a well-deserved happiness – he is the vast majority

b the tiny minority of psychologically sick whose actions are determined by their affliction and are probably a product of social disorganization. Moreover, their deviancy has an in-built punishment. They are unhappy because of their deviancy. Normality is seen to be rewarded and deviance punished. The underlying message is simple: the rational is the pleasurable is the handsomely rewarded is the freely chosen is the meaningful is the non-deviant; the irrational is the painful is the punished is the determined is the meaningless is the deviant.

The overtypical 'man in the street' makes free choices to work hard, marry and consume regularly. He relaxes at the right time and place with beer and cigarettes which give him 'luxury' and 'deep pleasure' but do not threaten either the ethos of productivity or the mundane world of taken for granted experience. ...

But the mass media sometimes find themselves in a position where a growing body of opinion insists that certain illicit activities are both pleasurable and harmless. As in the case of marihuana, a crisis of confidence occurs. This is solved by what I shall term the nemesis effect. Namely that those individuals who violate the natural law of happiness and productivity ineluctably suffer in the *long run*. Thus in the long run deviancy must be seen to be unpleasurable. In this mould the stereotype of marihuana has changed. Initially it reflected the exaggerated ambivalence of the mass media towards drugs. Thus, it held promise of uninhibited pleasure, yet plummeted the taker into unmitigated misery. So we had a distorted spectrum ranging from extreme sexuality, through aggressive criminality, to wildly psychotic episodes. The informed journalist, more recently, however, found this model difficult to affix to marihuana usage. He, therefore, switched gear and indicated how the innocuous pleasures of smoking are paid for by the sacrificial few who mysteriously escalate to the nightmares of heroin addiction. ...

Every now and then an initially legitimate body of experts will come up with evidence which grossly violates the stereotype. The reception the mass media gave the Wootton Report is fascinating in that we have a government setting up an Advisory Committee to try and elucidate the 'objective' facts about the drug problem which came up with results which violated the political canons that implicitly circumscribed the possible answers that could be accepted as 'objective'! This violation of the consensual myth was dealt with by a flood of invective from the mass media. It:

a reaffirmed that corruption was the reason for marihuana smoking – that innocent youngsters had been corrupted by evil pushers

b (most remarkable) suggested that an innocent (ivory-towered) Wootton Committee had been corrupted by a pro-pot lobby.

The corrupter–corrupted imagery was thus used against both the marihuana smoker *and* the Committee that suggested amelioration of their suggestion. As Lady Wootton noted later in the House of Lords:

The causes of the [hysteria] are familiar to students of social psychology. They occur in other connections as well particularly in relation to sexual crimes, and they are always liable to recur when the public senses that some 'critical and objective study threatens to block an outlet for indulgence in the pleasures of moral indignation.

To conclude, the mass media portrayal of the drug taker is not a function of random ignorance but a coherent part of a consensual mythology. The mass media are a double-coated pill, for if on the outside they titillate a taste for illicit delights, on the inside, they contain a palliative. They stimulate interest and bromide desire. The myth of the drug user is rooted in moral indignation; it bulwarks the hypothetical world of the normal citizen, it blinkers its audience to deviant realities outside the consensus, it spells out justice for the righteous and punishment for the wicked. Although much of its world view is fantasy, its effects are real enough. For by fanning up moral panics over drug use, it contributes enormously to public hostility to the drug taker and precludes any rational approach to the problem. It also provides a bevy of convenient **scapegoats** on to which real material and moral discontent can be directed and significant structural changes averted.

References

Blum, R. (1969) *Society and Drugs*, San Francisco: Jossey-Bass Inc., p. 335.

Cohen, A. K. (1965) 'The sociology of the deviant act', *American Sociological Review 30*, pp. 5–14.

MacIntyre, A. (1968) 'The cannabis taboo', *New Society*, 5 December, p. 848.

Key terms

The following key terms appear in the text above. They have been defined below to aid with the reading of this item.

frame of reference a set of ideas through which we can understand the world around us

hedonism pleasure-seeking

bifurcation dividing into two; forking into two branches

scapegoat blaming social problems on an often innocent social group (real or imaginary) and suggesting that they should be a target for reprisal

Questions

1 What does Young say about our experience of the world as an individual and how we use the media?

2 Young argues that the media does not have random bias but a systematic world view. What does he suggest about the content of this world view?

3 What is the appeal to the audience of the way in which the media portrays drug taking?

4 Young describes the media as the 'guardians of consensus'. What does he mean by this?

Reading 16.3 **The effects of the media**

Greg Philo (from) *Seeing and Believing: The influence of television* (1990) London: Routledge, pp. 1–8.

Editorial comments

For Philo, the effects of the media might be dependent upon the nature of the audience. Whereas some are victims of the media, others have the power to resist and to reject media messages. Our lived experience may enable us to read the media critically and sometimes to expose bias for what it is. That bias exists, Philo is in no doubt, but he wishes to push the 'media effects' debate further than simplistic and crude 'hypodermic syringe' models.

Seeing and believing

TELEVISION IS THE main source of information on national and world events for most of us. But do we believe what we see and what we are told? It has always been difficult to show how media *content* relates to public *belief*.

It is possible sometimes to make broad assertions about the 'effects' of the media. One way of doing this is to compare the results of opinion polls with media content. For example, research into media coverage of the disease AIDS has shown correlations between themes developed in the media and changes in public knowledge. In 1987 the Media Group at Glasgow University analysed television and press coverage of AIDS for the DHSS and the Central Office of Information, as part of a wider study of public belief in this area. Table 1 shows the number of references in the media to various ways of catching AIDS. Table 2 shows the percentage of a population sample who showed an awareness of these without being prompted.

These tables show how trends in public awareness can relate to media content. For example, there is a constant flow of references in the media to sexual contact as a way of catching AIDS. Public awareness of this is high and steady at 86%. But in the media, blood and saliva/kissing are both low at 27 and 20 references. The BMRB opinion study shows that these are both falling in people's awareness (relative to earlier studies). The dominant theme in media reports on ways of catching AIDS at this time was injections/injecting drugs, with a total of 172 references. This is the only category of public awareness that is shown to be rising.

Such studies can indicate general trends, but they are still couched at a very broad level. They show little of how any specific section of the public relates to information from the media or the processes by which beliefs develop.

There is a long history in communication research of attempting to explain these key relationships.

From 'mass society' to 'reinforcement'

Some of the earliest attempts to explain the relation between the media and public belief used the concept of the **mass society**. This offered a view of the contemporary world as composed of fragmented individuals, increasingly subject to powerful propaganda messages. Its influence on media theory grew in part from the historical experience of the rise of fascism in Europe and from how totalitarian political systems were understood to have used the control of communications. The theory of the mass society has its roots in nineteenth-century sociology with its focus on the breakdown of organic traditional societies and the emergence of large scale urban society. Leon Bramson (1961), in a study of the influence of the theory, traces its view of the isolated individual through the work of theorists such as H. Marcuse and T. Adorno of the Frankfurt school. C. Wright Mills also utilizes the concept, although he did not believe that contemporary public opinion in the USA was wholly controlled by the media. He does, however, write of a growing problem in which:

> in the mass society of media markets, competition goes on between the crowd of manipulators with

Table 1 Ways AIDS 'can be caught' (Number of references press and television March/April 1986)

Sexual contact	85
Blood	27
Saliva/kissing	20
Injections/injecting drugs	172

Table 2 Main ways of catching AIDS (spontaneous responses) (British Market Research Bureau)

Sexual contact	86%
Blood	63% falling
Saliva/kissing	24% falling
Injections/injecting drugs	22% rising

their mass media on the one hand, and the people receiving their communications on the other. 'Answering back' by the people is systematically unavailable.
(Quoted in Eldridge, 1987)

The theoretical arguments on the mass society had some features in common with **behaviourist** trends in social science which saw the individual as 'responding' to direct stimuli.

Beliefs about the impact of media had also been strengthened by key instances of its effects. These included the notorious rendering of *War of the Worlds* by Orson Welles in 1938, which panicked New Yorkers. ... The search for such direct media effects on individual behaviour was extended in the post-war period to the study of areas such as television violence and the effect of exposure to election coverage on voting behaviour. But the relation between media messages, belief and behaviour was found to be more complex than a simple stimulus followed by a response. In practice it was very difficult to show that exposure to a set of violent images produced measurable effects on children's behaviour. The reliability of the experimental methods used in this area was questioned and the results were inconclusive.

Dennis McQuail (1977) writes of a second phase in mass communications research in which the general conclusion was that the media were unlikely to be major contributors to the direct change of individual opinions, attitudes or behaviour. As summarized by Klapper (1960) this view was that:

1 Mass communication ordinarily does not serve as a necessary and sufficient cause of audience effects, but rather functions among and through a nexus of mediating factors and influences.

2 These mediating factors are such that they typically render mass communication a contributory agent, but not the sole cause, in a process of reinforcing the existing conditions. (Regardless of the condition in question – be it the vote intentions of audience members, their tendency toward or away from delinquent behaviour, or their general orientation toward life and its problems – and regardless of whether the effect in question be social or individual, the media are more likely to reinforce than to change).
(Klapper, 1960)

This signalled a major transformation from seeing the media as an all-powerful force on the individual. The new focus was on how messages were received and used by people in the audience either as individuals or in the context of small social groups. The 'uses and gratifications' approach assumed that the individuals' values and interests led to a selective perception and shaping of what was seen and heard. What was taken from the media might depend upon individual preferences and psychology. For example, a programme might be attractive to one person for its dramatic or exciting qualities while someone else might be interested in it for the information which it contains. The early research in the USA used survey techniques to ask people about the 'gratifications' which they took from programmes such as quiz shows.

The attempts which had been made to gauge media effects had largely focused on possible changes in attitude following exposure to campaigns on issues such as health, voting or buying goods. The general conclusion was that they had no or very little effect. But, as McQuail argues, the results were in part conditioned by the limited nature of the studies:

These were mainly experiments or surveys designed to measure short-term changes occurring in individuals, and concentrating especially on the key concept of attitude. Alternative research approaches might take a longer time span, pay more attention to people in their social context, look at what people know (in the widest sense) rather than at their attitudes and opinions, take account of the uses and motives of the audience member as mediating any effect, look at structures of belief and opinion and social behaviour rather than individual cases, take more notice of the *content* whose effects are being studied.
(McQuail, 1977)

As he notes, there was often a failure to examine the specific content of messages and their meaning to the audience in terms of how they related to wider systems of social values and beliefs. The media are part of a process of cultural reproduction and their content consists of much more than isolated pieces of information or opinion. Thus a campaign message during an election does not simply tell us how to vote. It also implicitly assumes the legitimacy of a certain type of political system. Similarly, an advertisement for a product may contain implicit assumptions about 'acceptable' or desirable lifestyles. McQuail's point is that the search for instant, measurable effects on the individual has led to a neglect of the role of the media in developing political and social cultures over long periods of time:

the media work most directly on consciousness by providing the constructed images of the world and of social life and the definitions of social reality. In effect, the audience member learns about his or her social world and about himself from the media presentation of society (given that most of the time, most of this is not directly accessible). The media provide the materials for responding to experience and these accumulate over time in a long-term process of socialisation. The effects of the media on the individual are not only indirect, they may have happened long ago, certainly in the past.
(McQuail, 1977)

The media are conveying much more than a single message on who to vote for, or which brand of product to buy. Messages are situated within political and cultural assumptions about what is normal and acceptable within the society. In news production, these include beliefs about hierarchies of access, about who has the right to speak, what are the key political institutions, and what is 'acceptable' behaviour. On an everyday level, the television, press, and radio also provide information about specific events, which tacitly relate to these unspoken assumptions. For example, news journalists might assume a consensus amongst their audience that violence should not be used in resolving political/industrial disputes. News reports might then give specific instances of violent behaviour (as in the miners' strike), and allocate blame to one 'side' in the conflict. In doing so the reports assume a consensus on the value that violence is 'wrong'. The reports are thus situated within, and contribute to, political and social cultures which are constantly developing.

In this way the news may offer a 'preferred' view of events, but we cannot assume that its audience will all accept this interpretation. The consensus that violence is wrong is not likely to be matched by a common agreement on who should be blamed. For example, attitudes on whether police or pickets are more likely to start trouble may vary between different groups in the society (as between groups of working-class trade unionists and middle-class professionals). Such differences within the audience may affect the way in which information from the media is received. This acceptance or rejection of the television message is conditioned partly by differences in political culture. Such cultures are not static and cannot be seen as simply determining how individuals respond. The cultures themselves are clearly subject to change from a variety of influences, one of which could be new information which is received from the media. One of the findings of this study is that political cultures do not always insulate those within them from the preferred media view. Trade unionists and others who were sympathetic to the striking miners were more likely to reject the news account of the origins of violence, but they did not always do so.

Some new approaches

The uses and gratifications perspective offered a relatively static model, in which individuals were seen as using specific messages according to their own interests and purposes. If there was an effect on belief it was largely construed as being one of reinforcement. But as we have seen, this model does not come to terms with the complexity either of what is being transmitted by the media or of the cultures within which the messages are being received.

A contemporary variant on this perspective is the argument that what people see and understand in media messages depends upon their pre-existing beliefs or political 'bias'. This theory has appeared most recently in work by Michael Tracey and Guy Cumberbatch who pursued the general theme that 'bias lies in the eye of the beholder'.

There are difficulties with this perspective. We can accept that what people understand and believe is not simply a result of what they are told by the media. But there are problems with the assertion that our understanding of new information is determined by pre-existing cultural and political assumptions. The most obvious questions are: where do frameworks of belief come from?, how do they develop over time?, and how may they alter in relation to new information and new experiences? We cannot write off the effect of the media simply because a small number of stimuli are not seen to have much effect on developed systems of belief.

If we are to understand the role of the media in the reproduction or development of these systems, then a detailed analysis of media content is an initial priority. In pursuing this, a number of theorists have recently examined the processes by which news reporting can establish both the priorities of discussion and the ways in which controversial issues are to be understood. These 'ways of understanding' or interpretative frameworks were seen as being related to class perspectives in the society as a whole. It was also assumed that if the content of news was produced from within such perspectives then it might be interpreted differently according to the class position and cultural assumptions of different groups within the audience.

The communication process does not, therefore, consist of the media providing stimuli to isolated individuals who interpret them according to fixed preconceptions. Rather, the cultures of any given moment are part of a social *process* in which beliefs are produced and contested in the conflict between groups and classes. The media are one site of this struggle to establish the dominance of some ways of understanding. This is so whether the arguments relate to economic or political policy, such as on the role of strikes in the decline of the economy, or whether they are about definitions of political action such as whether a 'terrorist' is to be called a 'guerilla' or a 'freedom fighter'. No one claims that exposure to a preferred media view will necessarily and instantly transform political allegiance. But it is crucial to study the manner in which such arguments are developed in media accounts and in audience beliefs to form strands of political cultures, and to analyse the processes by which they are overlaid by new information and different forms of experience.

To examine these processes requires a methodology which focuses on groups rather than individuals and which can reveal how what is understood from the media relates to existing systems of belief. In pursuing this it did not seem very useful to show audiences a particular programme and then attempt to gauge possible 'effects'. Instead it seemed more fruitful to ask groups to write their own programmes. This would show what they thought the content of the news to be on a given issue. It might then be possible to compare this with what they actually believed to be true and to examine why they either accepted or rejected the media account. This approach made members of the public temporarily into journalists and became the basis for this study.

The current work

As a whole, this book has been organized such that the introduction deals broadly with the main problems in studying communications and audiences as they were understood up until the 1970s. At this point there were major new developments in critical theory and specifically in the analysis of media content and its reception. In Europe and the USA there was an intensification of interest in the ability of the media to influence public consciousness. The concept of 'agenda setting' was used to indicate the ability of the media to establish the priorities for public discussion. In other words, the media could tell the public what to think *about* if not exactly what to think. Rogers and Dearing (1988) describe the rise of this new paradigm in the United States:

> The new communication scholars typically had pre-doctoral experience in journalism or broadcasting, followed by social science training emphasizing the work of Lewin, Hovland, Lasswell, and Lazarsfeld, plus courses in statistical methods and quantitative research methods. The new breed 'knew' from their personal backgrounds that the mass media had effects, even though the scientific findings of the field's four founders generally indicated only minimal effects of the media. This paradox between past professional beliefs versus scientific results sent the new communication scholars off in search of evidence of strong media effects.
> *(Rogers and Dearing, 1988)*

In Britain, there were attempts to go beyond this paradigm by analysing the 'preferred meaning' of news accounts and the manner in which television and press reporting was organized around specific ways of understanding.

References

Bramson, L. (1961) *The Political Context of Sociology*, Princeton: Princeton University Press.

Eldridge, J. (1987) 'Mass media, public opinion and democracy', Presidential address at Belfast: British Association for the Advancement of Science.

Klapper, J. (1960) *The Effects of Mass Communications*, New York: Free Press.

McQuail, D. (1977) 'The influence and effects of mass media', in Curran, J. *et al.* (eds) *Mass Communication and Society*, London: Edward Arnold.

Rogers, E. and Dearing, J. (1988) 'Agenda-setting research: Where has it been, where is it going?', *Communication Yearbook*.

Key terms
The following key terms appear in the text above. They have been defined below to aid with the reading of this item.

mass society the argument that society is a mass of isolated individuals – victims of the many media messages they are exposed to, unable to reflect on their own direct lived experience for themselves

behaviourist coming from the psychological theory which argues that like animals, humans simply go through life responding to external stimuli in their environment

Questions

1 What did mass society arguments say about the effects of the media?

2 What is the 'uses and gratifications' approach? What does Philo think of this way of understanding media influence?

3 What does Philo say about the role of the media audience?

4 What does Philo say about bias in the media?

Reading 16.4 **How and why do women 'read' magazines?**

R. Ballaster, M. Beetham, E. Frazer and S. Hebron (from) *Women's Worlds: Ideology, femininity and the woman's magazine* (1991) London: Macmillan, pp. 1–3, 8–15 and 173–6.

Editorial comments

A great deal of feminist analysis starts from the observation that 'the personal is political' or, in other words, that experiences from one's own life can be the site of political struggle. This is the starting point for the analysis of women's magazines attempted by Ballaster and her colleagues in this extract: this almost every-day cultural product which gives its female audience pleasure is seen to be a site for the construction of gender identity. However, as Ballaster *et al.* note, even if such magazines do portray an ideological image of femininity, can we assume that their audience read these cultural products in an uncritical fashion?

Feminism and women's magazines

WHEN WE BEGAN work for this book we realized that our enthusiasm stemmed from our mutual pleasure in reading women's magazines, tempered by the knowledge that this pleasure is by no means pure, unambiguous or unproblematic. The magazine is for us both an object of academic interest and an object of consumption. Reading women's magazines can have exactly the same kind of effect as eating two or more bars of chocolate – the original craving was real but seems in the end to have been for the wrong thing. For all of us, of course, women's magazines have been a continuing presence in our lives but as feminists they have become an obvious subject for analysis and criticism, a staple topic for consciousness raising groups.

The seminar series which prompted this book raised several interesting issues. First, the discussion revolved precisely around the question raised above of why women's magazines are or are not pleasurable for women (and men) readers, and, more particularly, feminist readers. Why, when their contents fill us with outrage, do we nevertheless enjoy reading them? Second, it turned to the vexed question of the **ideological** function of women's magazines. Most participants felt strongly that the magazines discussed (including the eighteenth- and nineteenth-century ones) offer representations of women which are either downright reactionary or, at least, subtly maintain sexual difference and women's subordination. On the other hand, of course, most of the participants in the seminar, including the authors, identified themselves as feminists who *resisted* the models of **femininity** in the magazines, although many felt that they had been partly responsible for past 'false consciousness', unfulfillable desire, discontent and disappointment.

Third, and at a more theoretical level, the seminar raised the issue of the relation between literary and social theory in analysis of popular culture. Critical 'literary' readings of magazines have focused on the construction of an implied reader who is simultaneously 'produced' and 'subjected' by the text. These reading techniques have been adopted and adapted in sociological interpretation of the role of popular culture in the reproduction of capitalist and patriarchal social order. However, in both cases the implied reader seems to have been taken as exhaustive for the purposes of analysis and little attention paid to 'her' relation to the historical reader.

We focus, in this book, on the conflict between two 'dominant' analyses of women's magazines common to both these disciplines. Broadly, the first represents the magazine as a bearer of pleasure, the second sees it as a purveyor of oppressive ideologies of sex, class and race difference. In academic criticism – literary, cultural, and sociological – these are two alternative approaches, expounded by different theorists from different conceptual traditions, but, of course, for the actual reader of the magazine at the point of consumption, they can and do exist simultaneously. This conflict suggests another duality at the heart of the woman's magazine. It is at the same time a medium for the sale of commodities to an identifiable market group, women, and itself a commodity, a product sold in the capitalist market place for profit. It is also, of course, a text, a set of images and representations which construct an imaginary world and an imaginary reader. What is the relation *between* the different levels and functions, social and textual, of the women's magazine? …

Critical analysis of women's magazines

The cover of *Cosmopolitan* for January 1988 advertises one of its leading features with the caption 'Men who hate women and the women who love them'. The world of the magazine is one in which men and women are eternally in opposition, always in struggle, but always in pursuit of each other; relations between them are beset by difficulty, frustration and failure.

Yet, possible solutions like the dissolution of two exclusive and opposed gender categories, or the separation of women from men, or the dismantling of the power structures which now legitimate gender difference, have no place in the women's magazine. The **heterogeneity** of the magazine form, then, has its limits. Certain solutions and conclusions that might result from its representation of heterosexual relations are clearly not meant to be drawn. How does the women's magazine demarcate and delimit its own 'reading' of femininity?

Critical analysts of the women's magazine attend to two kinds of issue. First, there are those which come under the heading of 'theme' proper, or subject-matter, such as gender opposition, domesticity, royalty, and so on. Second, issues come under the heading of 'formal textual features' to do with layout, the 'tone' of address to the reader, distribution of advertising, fiction, features, and so forth. Of course, formal and substantive features of magazines in practice affect and even positively shape one another.

Many analysts have been struck by the intimate tone employed to address the reader, the cosy invocation of a known commonality between 'we women'. Despite status, wealth, class and race distinctions, the magazine assumes a shared experience between women: 'It wouldn't matter if Jacqueline Onassis had a billion or a trillion dollars … she is in exactly the same boat as you are when it comes to raising teenagers'. It is not only the editors and publishers who use this inclusive voice. A crucial feature of women's magazines is the readers' contributions in the form of letters, true life stories, the 'make-over'. The voice of the readers in all these contexts resonates with exactly the same register of intimacy as that of the professional producers of the magazine. It matters not at all whether this is because, as readers frequently suspect, all such contributions may be written by the professionals themselves. The *effect* is to make of producers and reader one group.

Such inclusivity is patently false. The 'ideal' or 'implied' reader of most women's magazines is self-evidently middle-class, white, and heterosexual. This inclusivity of address effectively marginalizes or makes deviant black, working-class or lesbian women. Here, then, is an example of a formal, textual feature of the women's magazine – the intimacy of the editorial or journalistic 'we' – which works to define its content or theme, woman.

The construction of women as a homogeneous group, or even a group at all, is primarily achieved by the invocation of its supposedly 'natural' opposite – men. From the girl's magazine to the most popular women's magazines, such as *Woman*, there is an evident tension between the need to confirm the centrality and desirability of men in all women's lives and the equally insistent recognition of men as a problem for and threat to women. They are lazy, untidy, sometimes violent, require constant maintenance and upkeep both physically and psychically, are prone to faithlessness and heart attacks and, in recent years and registering the currency of a 'popular feminism', sexist and oppressive. This analysis of men as problematic is congruent, up to a point, with a feminist analysis of relations between men and women as quasiclass conflictual relations, relations of domination and oppression. But only up to a point. For, after all, magazines are part of an economic system as well as part of an ideological system by which gender difference is given meaning. They exist primarily as commodities and as the vehicle for advertisements of other commodities. If women are to continue to buy and consume commodities, not only for themselves, but for their families, they cannot also be sold feminist analyses of gender relations. …

As well as the contradiction within magazines different magazines continually stress the qualities which distinguish them from their rivals. It is in this light that we must read their own protestations of *exclusivity*, their stress on the *difference* between 'Cosmo girls' or 'Company readers' and the rest of the vast undifferentiated mass of (by implication) boring and conventional women. The *Cosmo* girl and the *Company* reader is, in reality, distinguished from her sisters by her consumption patterns or, as the industry terms it, 'lifestyle'. Publishers and editors of British magazines can always identify their readers in terms of the Registrar General's socio-economic classes which are demarcated by the criterion of occupation (frequently, in the case of women, by husband's or father's occupation). They are only, however, interested in occupation in so far as it is a determinant of 'lifestyle'. The differentiation of the female reader is then bound up with the exigencies of capitalist markets; collective character is determined by what we (are able to) buy.

Notwithstanding the contradictions, tensions and difficulties involved in sustaining it as a coherent project, magazines which co-exist at any given historical moment do share a notion of femininity. Looking at the magazines of the late twentieth century, we can identify certain features which recur. A glance at almost any sample of magazines will suggest that whatever else femininity (and especially female sexuality) might be, it is certainly punishable. This is most evident in the fiction of 'True Romance' magazines, in which women who succumb to their sexual desires more often than not also succumb to severe psychological torment, illness, and even death, but it is also discernible in features such as the celebrity profile, the 'triumph over tragedy' true life experience, and that perennial favourite, the 'problem page'. The heroines of magazines suffer, appallingly and all the time. If they have positively sinned against the conformist sexual ideology of the magazine, their suffering may be brought to an end by repentance; if their only sin is that of being female then stoical resignation, passivity and 'goodness' will finally bring its reward.

Valerie Walkerdine, in analysing the fiction offered by the British girls' magazine *Bunty*, has pointed out the pattern of suffering at the hands of wicked step-parents, cruel teachers, or nasty bullying enemies inflicted on the magazine's heroines. In these stories the heroine's goodness through adversity is finally rewarded with the restoration of family and love (Walkerdine, 1984). Tania Modleski puts forward a strikingly similar analysis of the heroine's fate in Harlequin or Mills & Boon romances. Here the hero's cruelty and seeming contempt is finally transformed despite himself through the sheer passive virtue of the heroine (Modleski, 1984). We might conclude, then, that in the romance structures shared by both popular fiction and the women's magazine femaleness is in itself punishable, but can only be transcended or transformed through the acquisition and display of an excessive femininity. Interestingly, Barbara Phillips argues that this theme is continued in the self-consciously feminist magazine *Ms*. Biographical articles in *Ms* feature a range of women in public life (trades-union organizers, campaigners against rape, etc.) who all 'succeed' because they put other people first and enjoy the intrinsic rewards of selfless devotion to duty and community (Phillips, 1978).

Women's magazines almost without exception situate women (all women) either firmly *in* the domestic sphere or in close proximity to it. Magazines vary between those that encourage women to work the double shift (run a home, raise children, reproduce husband and family on a daily basis, dress and groom spectacularly, climb a career ladder and maintain professional and emotional relationships outside the family circle) and those which encourage them to resist any pressure to leave the home. The latter 'reassert' the value of the domestic sphere, particularly that of maternity, and harp on the high cost to women of pursuing paid work. ...

Conspicuous by its absence and in contrast to the pervasiveness of the **motif** of domesticity is the theme of public and civic life, political progress or political institutions. This is not to say that subjects of a 'political' nature never feature in the magazines – they appear in three ways. First, discussion of 'issues' such as ecology, rape, incest, and homelessness invariably speaks to readers' 'personal' concerns about the quality of their family life or their children's future. Second, fairly frequent interviews with politicians, their wives, or leading public figures attend to their domestic setting and environment. Passions and convictions are discussed only in the context of an enquiry into the conflicting demands of job and family, a revelation of 'personality' through a discussion of taste in clothes, nightlife, friends. *Reality* is clearly the world of the family; that of civic virtue, the production of a collective life outside the family, political struggle, is quite unreal. To learn the truth about a politician is to learn the details of his or her domestic existence. Third, many of the weeklies now carry information about legal and political rights, more often than not presented as political goods for consumption. Policy, according to the magazine, is subject to the same laws of supply and demand as fashion. Laws on women and taxation are evaluated in the same manner as the respective merits of different kinds of washing-machine. Once again the forging of community cannot be understood as a public and civic process.

At the heart of the women's magazine lies the paradox that 'natural' femininity can be achieved only through hard labour. Most recently, this discourse of gender acquisition has had to negotiate with the problem of *feminism*. Ours and others' readings of magazines crucially shows the discourse of gender that structures the genre to be intertwined with those of race, class, nation and age. Magazines acknowledge or construct social class differences in terms of 'lifestyle' or consumption, but consistently deny the existence of structured class or race conflict, offering only personal or moral resolutions to problems proceeding from these stratifications. Racial difference in particular is barely acknowledged in the contemporary British women's magazine. We are, to a woman, assumed to be white; when addressed at all, blackness is not understood as a political but an aesthetic category, taken on a par with the 'divisions' between women of dry and greasy hair, large and small breasts.

The feminine virtues of passive goodness, personal service to others and devotion to the domestic sphere by definition preclude women from productive activity in the public sphere. In the eighteenth century men read and circulated journals in the coffee-houses of London which also served as a distribution outlet for publishers. With the advent of magazines addressed to women, publishers developed means of distributing their product to the family home, to be read and circulated in the drawing-room. Women came to be conceived of as that phenomenon much beloved of the contemporary marketing man, the *final* consumer. The complete separation of coffee house from tea table, the public from the private is, of course, a myth. The writing of this myth continues throughout the nineteenth and twentieth centuries. Advertisers now conceive of women as primary consumers; their recycling of images of domestic bliss and eschewal of any civic or public values serves to maintain the continual circulation of that myth.

And consumption is, undeniably, pleasurable. We must take care not to overdraw the picture of a population sated on pure consumption, the distopian nightmare of the theorist of mass culture of the post-war era. The pleasure of consumption and that of the fantasy of possibilities of infinite consumption is central to the success of the magazine form and we cannot afford simply to reject it as cultural brain-washing. ...

From their inception, women's magazines have posited female subjectivity as a problem, and themselves as the answer, offering themselves to female readers as a 'guide to living', a means of organizing, responding to, and transforming their experience as women. However, they also, as a result of their claim to 'represent' rather than direct or influence the female social body, find themselves reproducing those very contradictions and paradoxes they ostensibly promise to resolve. Women's magazines have been and remain structured by this significant tension between their self-representation as a 'voice' for women and as a 'leader' of them. This tension is echoed in that between the magazine's function as a disseminator of fantasy and aspirational 'ideals' for women and as a means of representing the reality of women's lives in all their diversity, difficulty and confusion. On the micro level we can see this conflict acted out in the material on 'royalty' which occupies so large a space in modern weeklies: the women of the Royal Family are presented as 'just like us', facing the same problems of juggling priorities – children and 'work', retaining their husbands' attentions, expressing their creative impulses as well as their nurturing abilities – but they also appear as models and patrons of the most expensive fashions, as international travellers, 'superconsumers' on a scale unobtainable, if not unimaginable, for any reader of the magazine.

This confusion between the women's magazine as fantasy machine and as social realist text continues to bedevil any attempt to assess the ideological effects on its readers. Put simply, is it possible to ascertain whether readers consider the representations of femininity offered in the magazine 'true'? And, if they do, should we be seeking to do away with the form altogether, rather than writing a book about it, sensitive to its pleasures? As we have noted, most experienced readers of women's magazines are well acquainted with their codes and conventions and are inclined, particularly those readers who consider themselves 'educated' or 'intellectual', to seek to explain away or excuse their continued loyalty to a conservative form by insisting that they read it only as fantasy or escape.

We obviously cannot lay the blame for women's oppression at the door of women's magazines. This would be tantamount to confirming their own understanding of female liberation as a matter of 'personal' transformation rather than political action. There are many more influential economic, social and cultural causes for women's low pay and low status throughout the world. However, we would argue that the form's conservatism lies precisely in the fact that it cannot conceive of economic, social, cultural or political change as means of resolving the gender contradictions and inequities it addresses. Despite the fact that women's magazines are produced collectively and offer diverse perspectives on the condition of 'women', they are remarkably consistent in the resolutions they offer to the 'problem' of being female. Women are repeatedly told that their problems can only be dealt with through individual, rather than collective, responsibility. Agony columns, readers' letters, single articles, do, of course, insist on the commonality of women's experience. For every reader with a problem, there is another to tell her that she has 'been through the same thing'. Ultimately, however, women are informed that they must 'help themselves' and thus, implicitly, that their problems are their responsibility and may be of their own making. In other words, women's magazines are so structured, ideologically and formally, that they cannot offer political resolutions to what they consistently define as 'personal' problems.

It could be argued that it is this 'personalized' politics that differentiates women's magazines from other magazines and from the newspaper as periodical literature. 'Serious' and 'news' features have become more common in the major women's weeklies. Such articles attempt to offer a 'woman's' perspective on world politics by focusing on humanitarian issues and, in particular, on individual women's experiences of war, famine, and political oppression. As a result, the magazine, as elsewhere, rarely connects the disparate issues it addresses, presenting its 'news' coverage as single problems with single solutions, and seeking to stimulate its readers to sentimental identification and moral outrage, rather than political resistance. Fundamentally, then, women's magazines cannot recognize the collective noun 'woman' as a political category, since the interests of 'woman' are always already conceived of as 'personal'.

There are, of course, positive aspects to the women's magazines' insistent identification of femininity with the 'personal', the 'individual' and the 'private'. Evidently, the women's magazine, in privileging what it defines as emotional, sexual and personal issues and in specifying that these areas are women's priority and primary concern, puts women at the centre of all experience. Men exist only at the margins of this world, most strikingly in the fashion-plate where they usually appear only in the background or at the side of the picture admiring the self-confident woman who strides toward the camera. Men are, of course, a constant reference point; much of women's activity, as defined by the magazine, is directed toward 'humanizing', modifying, responding suitably to men's anti-social behaviour. But, in so doing, the magazine reverses the conventional hierarchy of gendered subjects in cultural representations – masculinity functions as the 'not-feminine', the 'other' of woman, whether it is represented as dangerous or familiar. The women's magazine, like the romantic fiction so central to its formation, converts the public/private divide, habitually used to repress women, into an asset: 'Marking the boundaries between public and private spheres is a key part of the process of securing female subordination. But in romance this female, domestic space, this very powerlessness and dependence, are promoted to the foreground as a form of power and value and self-fulfilment' (Batsleer et al., 1985).

Would it be possible, then, to produce a popular magazine for women that identifies and analyses the subject 'woman' as a political category? The feminist monthly, Spare Rib, has maintained its own relatively small corner of the market on precisely this basis. Spare Rib interestingly shares many of the conventions and difficulties we have identified in its more conventional counterparts, but frequently addresses them directly rather than glossing over them. Its 'news' articles, like those in Woman although with a different emphasis, seek to identify a 'woman's angle' on political conflict; its reviews of contemporary books, plays, films and television, like those in Cosmopolitan, seek out positive images of femininity. Most significantly, in recent years Spare Rib's letter pages have been largely taken up with the problem of the magazine's capacity to represent and express diversity amongst women (in particular ethnic and racial difference, differences of sexual orientation, and 'party' political difference). Unsurprisingly perhaps, of all the women's magazines, Spare Rib comes closest to admitting that such 'diversity' may in fact be con-

flict, that the homogenizing category 'woman' can serve in some contexts to repress, rather than promote, political resistance.

The argument of this book would suggest that we cannot look at the women's magazine in isolation from the other cultural phenomena that women consume in order to 'make sense' of their experience as women, or through which they acquire gender identity and gender difference. Nor, even if it were possible, could we expect that a wholesale conversion of the women's magazine into a feminist medium would transform social structures on its own. **Ideological apparatuses** are, after all, only 'relatively autonomous'. The magazines we have looked at in this study do render under analysis what we might term a 'resisting reading', exposing the ideological and social contradictions that problematize the business of 'becoming female' for women. However, it is clear that women readers do not consume the women's magazine in order to be intellectually or politically challenged. Indeed, most women's magazines foster the idea that they are an 'easy' read. Their heterogenous form exposes the paradoxical nature of constructions of female identity (women should be thin but their first love is the chocolate cake, they should have 'careers' but childcare is their individual responsibility), but the 'preferred' reading does not call women readers' attention to such paradoxes. Rather, they are encouraged to consume each element of the magazine as a separate entity. Few women, as we have noted, read their magazines from cover to cover, beginning to end. Nor, it is clear, does the exposure of ideological contradiction necessarily result in revolutionary activity.

Despite these reservations, we would stress that the women's magazine must be understood as a cultural form in which, since its inception, definitions and understandings of gender difference have been negotiated and contested rather than taken for granted or imposed. Women's magazines are in the main produced and published for profit, not spiritual or feminist gain, but their form does offer a unique opportunity for debate and exchange.

References

Batsleer, J. et al. (1985) *Rewriting English: Cultural politics of gender and class*, London: Methuen.

Modleski, T. (1984) *Loving with a Vengeance: Mass-produced fantasies for women*, New York and London: Methuen.

Phillips, E. B. (1978) 'Magazine heroines: Is Ms. just another member of the Family Circle?', in Tuchman, Kaplan Daniels and Benet (eds) *Hearth and Home*.

Walkerdine, V. (1984) 'Some day my prince will come: Young girls and the preparation for adolescent sexu-

ality', in McRobbie and Nava (eds), *Gender and Generation*, pp. 162–84.

Key terms

The following key terms appear in the text above. They have been defined below to aid with the reading of this item.

ideological a set of ideas or a world view (often false) which for feminists and Marxists constrain and limit the truth of exploitation

femininity what it is to be female in society

false consciousness seeing the world through ideology, hidden from the truth of social reality

heterogeneity different, wide-spread and unrelated

motif theme

ideological apparatuses social institutions which produce and reproduce ideology and false consciousness and in doing so act as forms of social control

Questions

1 What three reasons prompted Ballaster *et al.* to study women's magazines in the very first place?

2 Ballaster *et al.* suggest that there are two dominant interpretations of women's magazines. What are they?

3 What is suggested in the extract about the audience of women's magazines?

4 What are the key themes of 'femininity' as identified in the content of young girls' and women's magazines?

5 What do Ballaster *et al.* conclude about how women 'read' these magazines?

Reading 16.5 **War reporting**

Philip M. Taylor (from) *War and the Media: Propaganda and persuasion in the Gulf War* (1992) Manchester: Manchester University Press, pp. vii–viii, x, 8–10, 14–19.

Editorial comments

For Taylor the television reporting of the Gulf War was unlike anything seen before by a media audience. In many respects the war was fought through the medium of television, both sides manipulated media messages – taking advantage of the new media technology of global satellite coverage. For the audience such coverage was 'instant'. We, as the audience, saw the 'direct truth', the media was truly a 'mirror on the world'. However, it is this view that Taylor takes issue with.

War and the media

THIS IS A book about how the allied coalition and the government of Iraq attempted to influence, utilize and manipulate the ways in which the Gulf War was presented by the media to the outside world between mid January and early March 1991. It is only in part about the media coverage of the conflict *per se* since the book concentrates on the point at which the policy and the presentation, the war and the media, came together on both sides to form **propaganda**. It also embraces, as far as it is yet possible to do so, a preliminary examination of psychological warfare methods employed during the war. Most of the information contained in these pages, however, is gleaned from the media coverage itself – from the press, television and radio. This should immediately place one on the alert in so far as any study of war propaganda is concerned given that the output of the media managers has provided the main sources of information for this book. An analysis of Gulf War propaganda is thus in danger of becoming an extension of that propaganda, merely reiterating uncritically the themes churned out by both sides during the conflict itself.

How to be on guard against this? Well, of course, not everything is propaganda. On the other hand, the point at which information and propaganda merge in wartime is frequently obscured. The degree, for example, to which the flow of information in a war zone is controlled by military and political authorities who wish to see the media adopt a particular perspective on what is actually happening needs to be at the forefront of our minds. The type of questions that need to be asked therefore are: what arrangements were made for the release of information, and why? How much censorship was taking place? What alternative sources of information were open to the news gatherers, and were they used? To what extent did the media coverage simply echo or reflect official sources of information? And how far back did journalists stand from what was being told to them, or were they merely drawn into the media management system?

With these questions in mind, the media coverage has been used as a source both of information and of propaganda. The focus is Anglo-American, reflecting the leading contributions made by those two countries to the multinational coalition operating under United Nations' auspices, although it does need to be remembered that Britain's military involvement totalled only about 5 per cent of the whole. It might therefore be argued that the British were allocated a role in the media arrangements that was favourably disproportionate to their actual military contribution. Nonetheless, because the coalition was unequivocally American-led and the arrangements made for the media were largely dictated by the United States, this book cannot help but recognize and reflect that.

Although the Gulf War really began on 2 August 1990 when Iraq invaded Kuwait, this book deals exclusively with the period of January and February 1991 when Iraq was faced with armed confrontation by the multinational coalition. Every effort has been made to consider all branches of the media representatively, although in the three principal case studies around which the story of the propaganda war is told – the battle of Khafji, the Amiriya bunker/shelter bombing, and the battle of Mutlah Gap – particular attention has been devoted to the television coverage. The inadequacy of describing a visual medium without the images is a problem that remains to be overcome in book form. ...

The seductive nature of television's capacity for immediacy gives the impression of 'instant history'. The arrival of the video cassette recorder has added a further dimension. Instead of television being an ethereal medium, gone with the wind at the moment it is transmitted, it can now be played back, scrutinized, evaluated, verified and criticized. It has become, provided the VCR's *record* button has been pressed, a record like any other. As such, therefore, it has to be treated with considerable caution. Apart from being an important source for what has been transmitted at a particular moment in time, what is it a record of? How reliable is it as a source of information? How and under what conditions was it made? What was the purpose of making it? What impact did it have? Historians dealing with this brave new world of television as evidence are already familiar with these types of questions. But before they and others can deal with television's particular characteristics as an audio-visual record, they must first understand the medium itself.

It is now possible for audiences to scrutinize television, as a source of information and opinions, in the same way that it has long been possible to do with the press. This is also true of radio, of course, but the sheer social penetration of television in the Western world* gives it a significance that may have been fully appreciated by wartime media managers but has yet to be fully taken on board outside of a few academic departments. In fact the ramifications of the video-recorder for political systems which entertain notions of accountability have yet to be discussed widely in democracies, although the role of smuggled video-tapes in the undermining of totalitarian systems in Eastern Europe has been mooted for some time as a contributory factor in the political transformation of that part of the world. Equally, direct broadcasting by satellite or trans-frontier broadcasting provide television with a significance in international relations which has yet to be widely appreciated in terms of its global implications for diplomacy as we approach the 21st century. The Gulf War, then, was the first major international conflict fought against the background of accessible global telecommunications and domestic video-recorders, and might thus prove to be a watershed in the way states publicly conduct their relations with one another. ...

The degree to which television featured so prominently at the outset of this major international conflict provided an indication of the central role which the media generally were to play throughout the war. But it is important to stress right at the outset that there were essentially two wars going on: the war itself, fought by the coalition's combined military forces against the regime of Saddam Hussein, and the war as portrayed by the media. The latter did not necessarily reflect the reality of the former. It will take some time for an authoritative history of the 'real war' to be written, a task which will be possible only when the official records are opened to public scrutiny, just as it will require the benefit of a broader timespan than that allowed here to evaluate the wider international significance and consequences of the conflict. But, in the meantime, there is already a good deal of information, and especially about the media's war record, to be able to draw some preliminary conclusions about the manner in which the conflict was allowed to be portrayed by both the Allied and the Iraqi authorities.

Television is often regarded as a window on the world and in some respects it is. But, in wartime, its potential to become a window onto the actual battle front is limited, not just by the nature of the medium itself but also by the curtain of darkness which military censorship attempts to draw over it. The window thus becomes a mirror for the images generated by those controlling the information. The existence of this censorship caused considerable friction between the coalition and the media and much debate within the latter (and presumably the former) both during and since the war. We can as yet, however, measure only that part of the media debate which is conducted within the public domain, and it will be some time before the results of even routine secret official enquiries concerning the effectiveness of coalition media policy will become more widely available. Moreover, although an examination of the wartime media record might lead one to conclude that the coalition's media managers were sometimes more at odds with the journalists than they were with the enemy forces, this would be somewhat misleading because in fact military–media relations were in most respects more harmonious than they have been at

---

* In Britain, for example, more than 20 million viewers were regularly tuning in to evening television news broadcasts, as compared with some 15 million newspaper readers. During the first week of the war, 12 out of the top 30 BBC programmes were news broadcasts.

any time since the Korean War back in the early 1950s. There were on the other hand considerable squabbles within the media themselves, with some journalists who felt that they had managed to keep their distance from the coalition's propaganda line arguing that the majority of their colleagues had not. It was this minority who invariably felt that the media had merely become a mouthpiece for the coalition; it was they who generally welcomed the presence of Western journalists in Baghdad to serve as a counterweight to Allied propaganda; and it was they who, in turn, were criticized for helping Iraqi propaganda, let alone for being self-righteous. But, like all interpretations – journalistic, political, creative or moral – it depends what side you are on. And, in wartime, sides have a tendency towards polarization. The fact remains that, at the time, there was comparatively little friction about the media's role in reporting the war. There was admittedly some (assiduously chronicled in this book), but it was not really a major issue. It all happened too quickly for military–media relations to become so soured that they became a *cause célèbre*; it is only since the war that serious recriminations have followed. Furthermore, as this book will attempt to demonstrate, the emerging post-war feeling that the Americans stopped the fighting too soon, before the job of removing Saddam Hussein from power had been achieved *inter alia* by the complete destruction of his armed forces, belies the wartime propaganda record concerning limited and clearly identifiable coalition war aims that was so central to sustaining public support for its actions. ...

The ability of journalists from coalition countries to transmit live instantaneous reports from an enemy capital under fire had never occurred before in the history of warfare. Yet the journalists, it must be remembered, were in Baghdad because the Iraqis permitted them to be. There were no Iraqi journalists in Riyadh, although in a sense there was no need for them to be because the coalition permitted Western journalists there comparatively more open access to what it was doing than Baghdad was ever likely to allow. Besides, the Iraqi government (as distinct from its people) could see and hear what the rest of the world's media were reporting, which, in itself, should immediately raise all sorts of question marks about what the coalition was – or even should have been – allowing those media to relate and portray. The suspicion remains that the coalition used global television for disinformation purposes and for sending signals as well as propaganda to Saddam. ...

Here is revealed one of the dangers of assuming that television provided us with a live insight into the realities of modern warfare. While subscribers to CNN increased and indeed television viewing figures around the world rose considerably, creating in the process

a new species of 24-hour television war 'couch potato' suffering from 'Scudavision', what audiences were seeing or hearing was not necessarily what was actually happening or that which was most significant. Television war addicts were in a sense mesmerized by the live coverage, reducing their capacity to stand back from the images objectively or critically. The expectational level which this aroused was extraordinary: 'usually nothing happens, but nobody can ever be certain. For this is real-time, the unexpected, the brink of the future, not a repeat or a recording or an edited version of reality'. Yet it has to be remembered that the television war was a major event partly because television made it so. Contrast, for example, the six weeks of coverage with the virtual total absence of footage from the eight-year war between Iraq and Iran. Even Vietnam, which lasted a little longer, was denied the kind of 24-hour saturation coverage which the Gulf War received. This sheer quantity of coverage must not be allowed to detract from the quality of what was being shown, although it often did. Perhaps he exaggerated the point, but David Halberstam was not far wide of the mark when he suggested in the *New York Times*:

> Contemporary technology is dazzling, offering rare, almost addictive immediacy. 'We should make our motto "We are the world, we are wired"', a TV executive said recently talking about his network's capacity for instantaneous coverage. What he meant was this: If we are there, the event if important; if we are not the event is not.
> *(Halberstam, 1991)*

But while simply 'being there' may have given the conflict an importance which really only history will be able to contextualize, the media event does nonetheless beg understanding. For, in a sense, the media were the story of this war, not just because they themselves made it so but also because they were allowed to make it so by political and military authorities which needed the media for particular purposes of their own. As I have already pointed out, the full and real story will eventually be told once the archives are opened. But in the meantime, we do have access to the media version of that story, and this can tell us something about the role of the media in modern society, about their growing global significance as we stand at the dawn of a new world telecommunications order, and possibly it can even tell us something about ourselves, the audience. Alas, the media record can tell us only a very limited amount about the war itself.

In another sense, however, the broad outlines of the war are already known, albeit in the most general of terms. Since the conflict, as various details begin to emerge, altering slightly here and fine tuning there the media record of the time, we do not as yet have a vastly different picture from that which was being portrayed while the war was going on. No major event that went unreported during or immediately after the war has since emerged to alter our overall view, and nor perhaps will it until we learn the details of the Iraqi version of events. Conversely, as Channel 4's Nik Gowing has pointed out, once the war ended and the news management systems broke down, enabling correspondents to cover the plight of the Kurds in stark contrast to what had been seen of the Iraqi occupation of Kuwait, 'politicians no longer set the agenda. Television images dictated it for them'. Yet he also reminded us that 'journalists did not emerge from military restrictions in the desert bursting to reveal information which had been suppressed' and felt that, despite a handful of exceptions, the 'information aplenty' filtering out at the time meant that 'the mosaic of war could, by and large, be assembled with an acceptable degree of accuracy within the obvious controls of information flow in a continuous military operation'. It was, of course, the question of what constituted 'an acceptable degree of accuracy' which will continue to exercise media critics and scholars for some time to come.

Conceptually speaking, the medium is *not* the message. It may have become the message for audiences who view it uncritically but, for genuine understanding, it is vital to appreciate the context in which the text, the audio-visual message, is delivered. Television, particularly in the United States, is a consumer industry and, especially today, a highly competitive one. It is rooted in certain technologies, the creative and cost-effective utilization of which is vital to its appeal and thus to its success. Moreover, television cameras 'see' only what they are pointed at; what goes on behind the camera operator's back can be reported only by words and is not part of the visual record. The angle of vision is in turn determined by either what that operator can point at or which he decrees or hopes will be of interest to his editors. The result is to amplify what is before the camera lens and to minimize the significance of what is behind it.

Live television is another aspect of this phenomenon but with different rules of operation; there is always the risk that the direct point-to-multipoint communicative process of live TV, by-passing the editors, will contain images which require explanation now denied by the instantaneous nature of the transmission. This can be both exciting for audiences and dangerous to authorities wishing to control the context in which the images are presented and perceived, as in wartime. During the Gulf War, the race to get a story first often meant that television companies became victims of their own technology in so far as the normal editorial processes, which involve a cumulative application of judgement and context, were

being by-passed owing to the excitement of the event taking place before the camera's angle of vision. With the print media, for example, news passes through a series of editorial processes that takes considerably longer to reach the audience, with the result that the non-visual, what goes on behind the camera if you like, is also incorporated to a greater extent than on live television. The medium of live television as a vehicle for relating news instantaneously thus assumes the potential equally for relating uncontextualized or even false information immediately. As well as conveying, uniquely, a sense of involvement and immediacy, it can thus also amplify and distort. It might indeed be both a window and a mirror, but television is also a flawed microscope.

In some respects, it is possible to draw a wartime analogy between the information front and the battle front. On the battlefield itself, of course, communications are vital to the overall command and direction of a battle, and modern technology is capable of providing vast amounts of information from each of the individual fighting units. Disrupting this communication is essential to defeating the enemy militarily. The trick from an intelligence point of view is how to assess and evaluate correctly these various micro levels of information and come up with a macro perspective. The same is in fact true for journalists. In wartime, however, the simple fact of the matter is that, like the overall strategic battle plan, the desired macrocosmic view has invariably already been worked out in advance by propagandists who want to ensure that a particular perspective is taken of the conflagration by pointing journalists to this microscopic or that particular point. One trick from a propaganda point of view, therefore, is how to expose or counter the perceptions being created by the other side. But the essential point is that, although there appears to be more news and information publicly available in modern warfare, it is subject to a whole host of political and military, not to mention technical, limitations with the result that, in the end, what is allowed to reach the public does not necessarily say very much about what is actually going on but certainly says a great deal about the concerns of those controlling the instruments of communications and the images they wish to see predominate. Thus, when the military are able to set the media agenda, it is then that the medium and the message tend to merge into one. This was the major philosophy behind the controversial news pool system employed by the coalition during the Gulf War. We need I. F. Stone to remind us of the dangers created by the reliance of reporters on official information sources when he said: 'They know a lot of things I don't know, but a lot of what they know isn't true.'

Because television is primarily a picture-led

medium, it is at its best when depicting, for example, generalized details of military hardware and action rather than when explaining preparations. As a result, it is again often criticized for its inability to present the wider context of any given issue, especially a war. The Gulf conflict was fought on a wide variety of fronts – economic, diplomatic, psychological, political – as well as military. But it was the military aspects which television most favoured and its coverage thus tended to create a somewhat simplistic impression of the multifarious aspects of warfare as well as an illusion of open coverage that basically lacked hard information beyond the most general of details. When so many processes of selection and omission are taking place – by the media themselves, by the military, by the enemy – it became virtually impossible to distinguish between what was simply information and what was in fact propaganda.

Here, we immediately face another conceptual problem concerning the use of the word 'propaganda'. Propaganda, to most people, means lies or at best half-truths. In wartime, 'they' – the enemy – conduct propaganda, whereas 'we' deal with honest news and information. This assumption lay behind the description of coalition pool reports being 'cleared' whereas reports emanating from Baghdad were 'censored'. If 'we' have to engage in such activity, it is only because 'they' are doing it; because they are telling lies about us, we have to correct false impressions with the truth – which is in itself a convenient way of distinguishing 'our' propaganda from 'theirs' and implies that 'our' propaganda is not really propaganda at all. Yet as it was pointed out in *Newsweek* just before the end of the war:

Propaganda is a broad approach to persuasion that encompasses several disciplines ... the most persuasive propaganda is that which is both graphic and demonstrably true. In theory, reporters in democratic societies work independent of propaganda. In practice they are treated during war as simply more pieces of military hardware to be deployed. While the allies play it straighter than Iraq, much of the information they release has propaganda value, too.
(Newsweek, 1991)

Notions that propaganda is somehow a sinister or evil activity designed to subvert human reason and exploit irrational emotion unfortunately remain firmly entrenched in popular consciousness and greatly hinder our understanding of it as a particular form of the processes of persuasion. In fact propaganda has only become a dirty word since the First World War. Before 1914, it meant simply the means by which the proponent of a particular doctrine (principally a religious one) propagated his beliefs among his audience. But, to reiterate, propaganda is simply a *process of persuasion*. As a concept, it is neutral and should be devoid of value judgements. Propaganda is one of the means by which the adherents of a particular cause seek to engender such views in an audience which would induce a desired perception of what is actually going on, and lead to them acting in a desired way, involving amongst other methods the deliberate selection and omission of accurate information as well as falsehoods – the more effective propaganda being that which is unlikely to be identified as such at the time.

References

Halberstam, D. (1991) *New York Times*, 21 February.

Newsweek (1991), 25 February.

Key term

The following key term appears in the text above. It has been defined below to aid with the reading of this item.

propaganda biased information manipulated to help a particular political interest

Questions

1 What are the theoretical and research questions Taylor attempts to investigate?

2 What technological changes does Taylor suggest made the coverage of the Gulf War different from other, previous war reporting?

3 How was the Gulf War presented to the audience?

4 What does Taylor say about propaganda in the reporting of the Gulf War?

Reading 16.6 **Investigating media bias**

John Eldridge (from) 'Whose illusion? Whose reality? Some problems of theory and method in mass media research', in *Getting the Message: News, truth and power* (1993) by the Glasgow University Media Group, J. Eldridge (ed.), London: Routledge, pp. 331–2 and 342–9.

Editorial comments

In this reading Eldridge attempts to give an overview of some of the key theoretical positions and themes in the contemporary analysis of media bias and media effects. Eldridge argues that the contemporary media offers its many varied audiences a whole variety of images, signs and symbols – so much so, that the media is 'saturated' into society. This often overwhelming variety of media images and experiences, he argues, raises new problems and new interests for the study of the media.

Whose illusion? whose reality?

Some problems of theory and method in mass media research

IF PEOPLE DEFINE a situation as real it will be real in its consequences. When W. I. Thomas coined the **aphorism** he was pointing to the power that beliefs could exercise over the actions of individuals and groups. Sociological and anthropological research contains many illustrations of the dictum, from the protestant ethic to cargo cults. We can recall the events at Jonesville (named after the religious leader Jim Jones) in Guyana, when a whole community defined a situation in a way that led them to participate in a mass suicide. Yet to define a situation as real is to say nothing of the truth or falsity of what is being stated, believed in or acted upon.

It happens that in the history of the mass media a notable instance exists of a situation being defined as real by large numbers of people and which indeed had real consequences for them and yet it was not true but fictional. This was in October 1938 when CBS broadcast a version of H. G. Wells's *War of the Worlds* in its radio play slot, Mercury Theatre of the Air. The effect on many listeners, particularly those who tuned in after the Orson Welles programme had begun, was to create panic and distress. According to Hadley Cantril and his colleagues at least 1 million out of the 6 million listeners were severely frightened or panicked, believing that the United States really had been invaded by the Martians. In this drama, delivered in the format of an actuality news programme, many of the audience came to accept the reality of a large number of events, which would have taken much longer than the short time span of the programme to have occurred in fact.

We may say that this section of the radio audience was suffering under an illusion. Yet the episode intervened in their everyday lives and was real in its consequences. For them fiction became fact and the

illusion shaped their experience and so they proceeded to define their reality. In trying to account for this we might want to refer to the skill of the producer and the actors, the news format, which as a source of public information people had come to trust, and so on. But it remains that the people who panicked based their action on a mistaken belief.

As social scientists we are not too surprised that such a thing could happen, although we do well to note that 5 of the 6 million were not so persuaded. Things are not always as they seem. ...

We live today not only in a media saturated society but in a media saturated world. It is difficult to analyse the significance of mass media which have multiplied in forms (books, radio, television, press, records, cinema, video), have developed in technologies to the most sophisticated kinds of electronics, have increased the speed of production and distribution of their products, and within each medium have diversified in the genres available. These products are commodities and as such become part of the everyday life of those who buy and consume them. The research agenda which is entailed in explaining and interpreting these developments is formidable and intimidating. And the activity of disseminating such work can scarcely be done today without employing the mass media, which become, in consequence, both a topic and a resource for the researcher. So, in their time Marcuse's *One Dimensional Man* (1964) and McLuhan's *Understanding Media* (1964) became paperback best sellers.

The difficulty and importance of the task is shown if we reflect on Lucien Febvre and Henri-Jean Martin's brilliant study, *The Coming of the Book* (1984). This is an account of the impact of printing between 1450 and 1800. It is enough for present purposes to mention that the study encompasses material factors relating to the growth of paper-making in Europe; technical considerations concerning the nature of the printing process; economic and commercial questions affecting costs, finance and distribution (the book as a commodity); the social organization of book production and the geographical locations; and a discussion of the book as a force for change, with notable reference to the Reformation, and its impact on the use of national languages at the expense of Latin. As the authors point out, this was a fateful development with incalculable and certainly not wholly intended consequences. They also make clear that whatever the advantages of mass circulation might be for propagandizing and social control from above, this was far from the whole story since this medium was also a vehicle for subversion – with challenges to existing political and religious authorities – and booksellers and printers could come under surveillance and harassment as a result of their pivotal activities. Yet this study relates to one medium only.

When we come to consider the multi-media world we now inhabit, with its multi-messages, **multi-signifying** systems and modes of discourse, the size, the scope and the velocity of it all, with its spiralling interconnections and its fragmentary discontinuities, the classical enlightenment task of understanding, explaining, interpreting and evaluating is difficult to accomplish. Let us acknowledge the difficulties but also suggest that the denial in principle of the enlightenment project (farewell to reason) may itself be a product of intellectual vertigo (all that is solid melts into air) and perhaps, if understandably, a failure of nerve. Let us take Jean Baudrillard as an instructive case in point. In particular, consider what he has to say about **hyper-reality** – a term which in his usage would displace and make superfluous the questions of this essay: whose illusion?; whose reality? This is most evident in his essay '**Simulacra** and simulations': 'Of the same order as the impossibility of rediscovering an absolute level of the real, is the impossibility of staging an illusion. Illusion is no longer possible, because the real is no longer possible' (Baudrillard, 1988). What can this mean? Baudrillard starts with a discussion on the possible relationships between representations (signs) and reality and goes on to distinguish three of these modes from simulation, where there is no relationship to reality. The first three define a position on the distinction between appearance and reality. Thus appearances in the form of representations may be regarded as reflecting a basic reality so there is no illusion: they are therefore reliable *good* appearances. Or they may be seen as masking and perverting a basic reality and are unreliable *evil* appearances. Or representations mask the absence of a basic reality and have the character of manipulation and sorcery. The theological and metaphysical resonances of this are commented upon by Baudrillard. Having pointed out that in western the-

ology there is the assumption that a sign could refer to a depth of meaning, and that something could guarantee this meaning, namely God, he asks:

> But what if God himself can be simulated, that is to say, reduced to the signs which attest his existence? Then the whole system becomes weightless; it is no longer anything but a gigantic simulacrum: not unreal, but a simulacrum, never again exchanging for what is real, but exchanging in itself, in an uninterrupted circuit without reference or circumstance.
> (Baudrillard, 1988)

This indeed is the fourth category. This death of God is the death of all metaphysics so that the notion of a mirror – whether true, distorting or inverted – linking appearances with reality, is also dead. By extension this is the death of the critical project of Marxism because the age of simulation results in the liquidation of all referentials, so it is pointless to suppose that enlightened thought can seek to control capital by imposing rules on it. For the left, therefore, to hold out 'the mirror of equivalence, hoping that capital will fall for this phantasmagoria of the social contract and fulfill its obligations to the whole of society' is useless because 'capital is a monstrous, unprincipled undertaking, nothing more' (Baudrillard, 1988). But in saying this Baudrillard actually reverts to the third category since he defines capital as a sorcery of the social relations – a challenge to society which should be responded to as such. How can this be if, in his own terms, the category of the social itself is, like God before it, reduced to the signs which attest to its existence? Carried to its conclusion this is to abandon the possibility of critique since such activity only multiplies the signs and accelerates the play of simulation. So categories like production and power can no longer be subject to critical appraisal – it is always, in his view, a false problem to want to restore the truth beneath the simulacrum. And yet, in its place, we have mysticism and melancholy reflection. Societies without power are societies without the social, and according to Baudrillard we do not know how to handle the mourning process. In my view he resorts to paradox and metaphysics in the name of anti-metaphysics, which I think is well enough illustrated in the following quotation:

> Power ... for some time now produces nothing but signs of its own resemblance. And at the same time, another figure of power comes into play: that of a collective demand for *signs* of power – a holy union which forms around the disappearance of power. Everybody belongs to it more or less in fear of the collapse of the political. And in the end the game of power comes down to nothing more than the *critical* obsession with power: an obsession with its death; an obsession with its survival which becomes

the greater the more it disappears. When it has totally disappeared, logically we will be under the total spell of power – a haunting memory already foreshadowed everywhere, manifesting at one and the same time the satisfaction of having got rid of it … and grieving its loss.
(Daudrillard, 1988)

We can note the rhetorical devices here: the use of terms like nothing but and nothing more than, the reference to logic and the metaphor of sorcery – the total spell of power. But it is one thing to recognize that sign systems can multiply and feed on each other and can indeed serve to 'hype' reality through public relations, collusion in the staging of media events and so on, but quite another to postulate that power is disappearing in its own simulations. However adequately or imperfectly the mass media may define, interpret or narrate the existence of torture, starvation and forms of oppression in the world, they are pointing to an experienced reality. It is because we have the capacity to protest this and claim that things could be other – a capacity that finds expression in the media events of Band Aid and the like, in Mandela concerts and music tours for Amnesty International and a response from millions of people across the world – that we do not find it logically or empirically necessary to follow Baudrillard in his cult of death – mourning for a post-modernist society that owes more to his own fevered imagination and obsessions than to an analysis that has any evidential weight or substance.

A more interesting and instructive case is that of Umberto Eco. I refer specifically to the collection of essays, *Travels in Hyper-Reality* (1987). As with Baudrillard the site for discussion is the USA. For Eco the reason for his journey into hyper-reality is to search for instances:

> where the American imagination demands the real thing and, to attain it, must fabricate the absolute fake; where the boundaries between game and illusion are blurred, the art museum is contaminated by the freak show, and falsehood is enjoyed in a situation of 'fullness', of *horror vacui*.
> *(Eco, 1987)*

So we visit, among other places, the Lyndon Johnson centre in Austin, Texas, with its full-scale reproduction of the Oval Office; the Museum of the City of New York, where a portrait of Peter Stuyvesant is 'reproduced' as a three dimensional statue; and the Movieland Waxwork Museum in California. Of this we read:

> As a rule there are mirrors, so on your right you see Dracula raising the lid of a tomb, and on the left your own face reflected next to Dracula's, while at times there is the glimmering figure of Jack the Ripper or of Jesus, duplicated by an astute play of corners, curves, and perspective, until it is hard to decide which side is reality and which illusion.
> *(Eco, 1987)*

So:

> When you see Tom Sawyer immediately after Mozart or you enter the case of The Planet of the Apes after having witnessed the Sermon on the Mount with Jesus and the Apostles, the logical distinction between the Real World and Possible Worlds is definitively undermined.
> *(Eco, 1987)*

And there is Disneyland (which is also discussed by Baudrillard). For Eco it is at once absolutely realistic and absolutely fantastic. The Main Street reconstruction of the nineteenth-century frontier street calls to mind an imaginative past – yet in that street you can enter shops and buy obsessively within the play fantasy mode. 'What is falsified is our will to buy, which we take as real, and in this sense Disneyland is really the quintessence of consumer ideology' (Eco, 1987). Yet this mixture of fake and truth, fantasy and reality, fact and fiction is used by Eco not to say, as Baudrillard does, that Disneyland is America, but to offer it as an allegory of the consumer society, where choice is regulated and truth reconstructed and the individual controlled and made passive by the system. However, the real world of the multinationals, the conglomerates, the world of advertising – with its fact and fiction intermingled – remains open for critique. Whereas Baudrillard becomes a participant in the cultural pessimism he identifies, Eco retains an ironic, critical detachment, while being sceptical with existing critical positions within Marxism. Why is this?

Here we must recall that Eco is the author of the highly formal, systematically presented *A Theory of Semiotics* (1977). This is based on models that indicate senders and receivers of messages and the channels through which messages come. From this flows a discussion of codes – their varieties and contexts – which itself is necessarily associated with the ways in which sources encode their messages and receivers decode them. Hence we can learn about and identify the nature of communicative power. Yet in the real world Eco found difficulty in identifying power and intentions. In 'The multiplication of the media' (Eco, 1987) he takes as an example the production and advertisement of polo shirts with a brand logo, which can then be found on a TV programme with young people wearing the shirt, which then becomes an encouragement for viewers to buy the shirt with 'the young look'. So the media act and interact – they are media of media. Who then is sending the message and producing the ideology? Eco does not deny the role of ideology but 'according to the channel under consideration, in a certain sense the meaning of the message changes, and perhaps also its ideological weight. There is no longer Authority, all on its own (and how consoling it was!)' (Eco, 1987). That is to say, from the shirt designer through to the manufacturer, the advertisers, the TV personnel all are in but also outside of authority: 'Power is elusive, and there is no longer any telling where the "plan" comes from. Because there is, of course, a plan, but it is no longer intentional, and therefore it cannot be criticized with the traditional criticism of intentions' (Eco, 1987). So the simple solutions are no longer credible. But this is a challenge: 'We shall have to start again from the beginning, asking one another what's going on?' (Eco, 1987).

I was reminded of the way in which the various media can interrelate, reinforcing or passing opinions on one another, during the miners' strike. The inter-relationship becomes part of the reality we seek to comprehend. The Edinburgh Television Festival was itself a media event in 1984, when a debate took place on media coverage of the miners' strike with Arthur Scargill and Alastair Hetherington as the main protagonists and with other contributions from journalists, a miner and the wife of the general secretary of the National Union of Mineworkers. The debate itself made use of video which had either been shown on television or film, or was from amateur video material. So there were arguments, references back to material and evidence and differences of interpretation. The following day on BBC *Newsnight* the debate was covered as a journalistic item. If one had been present at the debate, as I had, it was possible to see what kind of selecting and editing had taken place between the original event and its treatment in this new context. It is possible for a researcher to indicate the differences by careful accounts. What also interested me, however, was that the debate about the 'fairness' of the coverage became an occasion to suggest that there was additional evidence to show that television coverage was fair. So we had reference to some British Film Institute (BFI) research which had received coverage in yet another medium – the *Sunday Times*. Upon comparison of the two accounts it was possible to indicate some crucial differences, namely the reference in the *Sunday Times* to the finding that 6 per cent of questions to Mr MacGregor, then Chairman of the National Coal Board (NCB), were recorded as hostile by the researchers as against 39 per cent of questions to Mr Scargill. And then, yet another medium, the opinion poll, was cited to show that the majority of viewers thought television coverage of the miners' strike was 'fair'. The opinion poll did not relate to either the experience or knowledge of the strike of the people sampled, but it was in any event used as evidence. Now I do not think it possible to give a final account of all these and subsequent inter-

relations, but I do think it possible to analyse the processes that were going on. But there is a reality – experienced reality – which the media both comment on and are part of. It is the reality of broken bones and bruised bodies, of lost jobs, of protracted court cases, of dying communities. The explanations and contextualizing of these things will remain in some measure matters of controversy, but there are recalcitrant facts which cannot be relativized out of existence.

If power is elusive that does not mean it is disappearing, but rather that it is difficult to locate precisely. I think this is why, in another essay, 'Towards a semiological guerilla warfare', Eco (1987) emphasizes the importance of developing strategies that will enable audiences to control the message and its interpretative possibilities. For him the battle for the survival of people as responsible beings in the communications era is to be won not where the communication originates but where it arrives. The concern here is to restore a critical dimension to passive reception. This educational task can sound formidable, even utopian, but for Eco it is an emancipatory project:

> The methods of this cultural guerilla have to be worked out. Probably in the inter-relation of the various communications media, one medium can be employed to communicate a series of opinions on another medium. To some extent this is what a newspaper does when it criticizes a TV programme. But who can assure us that the newspaper article will be read in the way we wish? Will we have to have recourse to another medium to teach people how to read the newspaper in a critical fashion?
> *(Eco, 1987)*

But it is the educational task to seek for ways of doing this work – displaying to viewers and readers and listeners the possibilities for highlighting perspectives, checking codes and interpreting messages. This practice would be a response to the technological imperatives of the mass media and a form of resistance to the elusive, sometimes anonymous power which produces and suffuses the media.

I have considerable sympathy with this view with its emphasis on a coping strategy of resistance to the power of the mass media, which also serves as a stimulus for the development of reception theory. At the same time the strategies of control are not always so opaque and diffuse as to make scrutiny and critique possible. There is much that can be done in the area of news management and information control and the role of public relations. Agendas are not simply set within the media but as a product of on-going relationships with specific interest groups. Thus Karin Newman (1986) has shown how the British government's privatization policy was accompanied by policies of media manipulation and information management. There is no deep mystery about this. The marketing of British Telecom involved a campaign in which audiences were segmented and targeted to receive appropriate messages in different parts of the media. This kind of research calls for tenacity and staying power rather than deep analytical insight. It is still possible to identify interest groups even in a multi-media world. Some interests are more visibly evident than others – sometimes they are expressed directly, at other times there is deception. We can as researchers make more visible the nature and activities of multinational conglomerates in the field of communications and draw attention to matters of value-relevance. We can articulate the relationships between government and the media and the tactics and strategies of control and resistance in that sphere. Such work can be seen as complementary to that which Eco advocates. That is why I choose to conclude with a quotation from Raymond Williams which is found in *Towards 2000*:

> there are very strong reasons why we should challenge what now most controls and constrains us: the idea of such a world as an inevitable future. It is not some unavoidable real world, with its laws of economy and laws of war, that is now blocking us. It is a set of identifiable processes of *realpolitik* and *force majeure*, of nameable agencies of power and capital, distractions and disinformation, and all these interlocking with embedded short-term pressures and the interwoven subordinations of an adaptive common sense. It is not in staring at these blocks that there is any chance of movement past them. They have been named so often that they are not even, for most people, news. The dynamic moment is elsewhere, in the difficult business of gaining confidence in *our own* energies and capacities.
> *(Williams, 1985)*

References

Baudrillard, J. (1988) 'Simulacra and simulations', in Poster, M. (ed.) *Selected Writings*, Cambridge: Polity Press, pp. 166–84.

Eco, U. (1977) *A Theory of Semiotics*, London: Macmillan.

Eco, U. (1987) *Travels in Hyper-Reality*, London: Jonathan Cape.

Febvre, L. and Martin, H. J. (1984) *The Coming of the Book*, London: Verso.

McLuhan, M. (1964) *Understanding Media*, London: Routledge & Kegan Paul.

Marcuse, H. (1964) *One Dimensional Man*, London: Routledge & Kegan Paul.

Newman, K. (1986) *The Selling of British Telecom*, New York: St Martin's Press.

Willams, R. (1985) *Towards 2000*, Harmondsworth: Penguin.

Key terms

The following key terms appear in the text above. They have been defined below to aid with the reading of this item.

aphorism a short saying or general rule which is considered to contain some sort of deep meaning

multi-signifying indicating, suggesting, standing for something on a number of levels

hyper-reality the term used by post-modernists to mean 'that which is more real than real', which comes from the media

simulacra a term used by post-modernist thinker Baudrillard to refer to a media based hyper-reality where media 'simulations' define audience experience

semiotics the academic study of signs and symbols

Questions

1 What does Eldridge suggest about the ability of the media to define 'reality' for its audience?

2 What does Eldridge say about the changing nature of the media in contemporary times?

3 In the extract what do Eco and Baudrillard say about the 'hyper-reality' of the media in society?

4 What does Eldridge suggest is the purpose of the sociological analysis of the media?

Reading 16.7 **The reporting of 'disasters' in the media**

Johathan Benthall (from) *Disasters, Relief and the Media* (1993) London: I. B. Tauris, pp. 10–13, 26–9 and 36–40.

Editorial comments

Taking the related examples of 'natural disasters' and 'relief aid', in this empirical piece, Benthall argues that the media representations of these events is highly ideological – and at times frequently racist. He suggests that the media are involved in agenda-setting and gate-keeping processes which often shape and mould the information the Western world has about these issues – and thus shapes the audience's ideas about, and responses to, these situations.

Disasters, relief and the media

When is a disaster?

THE BIBLE RECORDS numerous plagues, floods, famines and destructions of cities. In 79 BC, the city of Pompeii in southern Italy was buried in volcanic ash. The most damaging earthquakes have killed hundreds of thousands of people at a time and destroyed whole cities. Millions of people have died at various times as a result of flooding of one river in China, the Hoang Ho; 21 million from the worldwide influenza epidemic of 1918–19; 1.5 million from the Irish famines of the 1840s. These estimates take no account of the sufferings and privations of survivors, or of the economic impact. The impact of extreme physical events is invariably more devastating when it occurs among poor, vulnerable populations.

Large numbers of people live in areas prone to the risk of natural disasters such as flood plains or geological fault zones. 'Natural' disasters in ordinary usage are those which do not result primarily from human actions, yet their effects can be greatly mitigated with proper foresight and preparedness. Many disasters which appear to be 'natural' are in fact symptoms of the incompetence or irrationality with which we manage resources. ...

Fortunately a large proportion of the world's populations live out their lives in relative freedom from disaster. But we cannot be sure that it will not strike us, however secure we may feel, and we can no longer ignore disasters which are far away, if only because television and photo-journalism bring them ever closer to us. Yet it will be argued in this book that the coverage of disasters by the press and the media is so selective and arbitrary that, in an important sense, they 'create' a disaster when they decide to recognize it. To be more precise, they give institutional endorsement or attestation to bad events which otherwise have a reality restricted to a local circle of victims. Such endorsement is a prerequisite for the marshalling of external relief and reconstructive effort. The endorsement is not decided by some mysterious Moloch but by quite small numbers of professional editors and reporters, whose decisions on whether or not to apply the 'hallmark' of recognition can have far-reaching chains of consequences, both positive and negative.

The vast majority of natural disasters such as floods and earthquakes are not reported at all in the international media. Some cases of warfare and civil strife might be happening on the dark side of the moon for all we read or hear about them. The media in each country understandably record their own disasters, and in Western countries a priority is accorded to disasters afflicting citizens of the wealthier countries. The media tend to be specially concerned by high death counts, as opposed to the longer-term effects of disasters on economic and social life; yet even high death counts do not guarantee that a particular disaster gets onto the front pages and the television screens.

Disasters may be roughly classified as follows:

1 The *sudden elemental*, prompted by climatic and geological forces (though often aggravated by man-made errors). As in the case of earthquakes, these are often to a great extent unpredictable. Some elemental events can be tracked in advance by a few weeks (for instance, river floods) or a few days (for instance, tropical hurricanes).
2 The *foreseeable*, such as most famines and epidemics.
3 The *deliberate*, resulting from wars and civil strife.
4 The *accidental*, resulting from some kind of technological mishap.

Some disasters include elements of all four types.

It is now generally recognized that even the 'sudden elemental' disasters nearly always include a human element. Many occur in vulnerable populated areas, that is, places where human beings have created conditions of vulnerability. Buildings are the principal cause of death from earthquakes. According to the USA's Overseas Development Council, agricultural modernization and **demographic** pressure push six out of ten poor people to live on land which is specially vulnerable to disasters. At least one whole sovereign state, the Republic of the Maldives, is at serious risk from a rise in the sea level, and much of Bangladesh is endemically prone to tidal waves and flooding. This is one category of disaster which may actually be increasing in incidence and gravity, because of land degradation and population pressures.

A more useful distinction, cutting across that between natural and man-made disasters, can be drawn between sudden and chronic. The sudden disasters are generally easier to cope with. When on a large scale they frequently attract considerable media interest which stimulates compassion and an urgent response. Chronic disasters pose more complex problems. Among chronic disasters we must include environmental emergencies such as deforestation and the pollution of air and water, and epidemic or endemic diseases such as cholera and AIDS, which are so closely linked in the Third World with poverty. The relief of such chronic disasters merges conceptually with long-term development aid. ...

Disasters as media constructs

Before we review the sequence of major disasters covered by the media during 1991, consider those which do *not* get into the media. To start with, Communist countries pre-*perestroika* did not encourage publicity for their disasters, natural or man-made. The mere fact that journalists now have access to areas where there have been floods or earthquakes, or industrial accidents like Chernobyl, has greatly broadened the geographical range of news about disasters.

In the late 1950s a nuclear waste accident in the eastern Soviet Union resulted in many small communities being removed from Soviet maps (the area is now known as the Eastern Urals Radioactive Trace). The Tangshan earthquake in eastern China in 1976, which struck an industrial city of a million people at night without warning, is said to have claimed 240,000 lives and obliterated some 7,000 families; though it was reported in the world media, the Chinese government of the day relied entirely on its own resources for relief and reconstruction.

Planned violations of human rights such as the Chinese destruction of the Tibetan monasteries, and the slaughter of hundreds of thousands of Tibetans by Chinese security forces, caused minimal protest in the Western world, largely because journalists had no access to Tibet and were therefore unable to report the atrocities. In East Timor people have lost their lives at the hands of the Indonesian government over many years while attracting hardly any journalistic interest until recently, even though the UN Security Council resolutions in 1975 and 1976 called on the Indonesian government to withdraw. A few human rights organizations, helped by dedicated journalists and campaigners, have sustained some degree of public concern in the West for Tibet and East Timor, but not enough to convince Western governments to put any substantial pressures on China or Indonesia respectively.

It can be said, therefore, that disasters do not exist – except for their unfortunate victims and those who suffer in their aftermaths – unless publicized by the media. In this sense the media actually *construct* disasters. The disasters which are assured of ample coverage are the more unusual ones, such as the extraordinary explosion of Lake Nyos in Cameroon in August 1986, which released a cloud of carbon dioxide that killed 1,746 people as well as nearly all other living things that it touched. A well-publicized disaster or civil war in one part of the world takes the media heat off other countries, enabling leaders to choose their moment to do things which they do not want to be widely known.

Governments and national relief agencies come under intense pressure to respond to those emergencies which are in the public eye. A great responsibility therefore rests on those who control and filter the news. The news system appears to aspire to having one disaster at a time to wrack the public's conscience. This has been described by a French television journalist as the 'funnel effect' (*phénomène de l'entonnoir*): 'There is only room for one overwhelming emotion a day or week. ... There'll always be forgotten countries.' This may be a function of the way the human brain works; more likely, it is a professional assumption of journalists.

Paul-Henri Morard of the ICRC says that after many years of experience he cannot understand the reasons for which the media will pick up one disaster story rather than another, and then just as suddenly drop it. For instance, in July 1991 when I interviewed him he was trying to get the media interested in filming 350,000 exhausted Ethiopian soldiers walking down from the Aswan Dam to Addis Ababa, since their plight had hardly been reported and there was thus no interest from governments in supporting ICRC efforts to assist them. This was as visually dramatic and emotionally poignant an event as the retreat of Napoleon's army from Russia. Yet no one was interested in filming it: the television companies' money had been spent covering the Gulf war, and their attention was currently all on Yugoslavia. Sometimes, he says, a well-known person or a TV crew will light on a trouble-spot somewhere and there will be a snowball effect. (Another experienced journalist has adduced the parable of the Gadarene swine.) Morard thinks it is pointless to try to change the direction of the media unless you have a huge network of influence, and probably not even then. ...

Crucial role of the media

The importance of the media is clear. Perceived **humanitarian** needs are increasing. There is no reason to assume that Africa is doomed to famine, but it is virtually certain that AIDS in Africa will be a major scourge leaving millions of orphans and a 'demographic hour-glass' with the loss of productive adults; in many other countries, too, HIV-related sickness and death will escalate. There is no decline in the incidence of civil strife, with some 13 civil wars in progress in Africa alone in 1991 (a few of them fortunately now more or less resolved), and atrocities in former Yugoslavia which have shocked even hardened observers. Fewer countries remain closed to the media than during the 1970s and 80s, so that journalists have more opportunities to cover emergencies. Enterprising reporters are becoming adept at gaining access to closed countries through contact with guerrilla forces, for instance in Afghanistan and Burma.

In countries prone to food shortages, the agencies' early warning systems are improving, so that there is no excuse for lack of preparedness. Poverty and poor public health are clearly seen to be factors which aggravate all kinds of emergency. WHO statistics show that the mortality rate for disasters in rich countries is far less than that in poor countries (48 times higher per square kilometre, 27 times higher per each disaster, 3.5 times higher per 1,000 inhabitants). This brings the problem back to long-term economic and health-planning.

Is the generosity of donor nations – the public purse and private charity taken together – increasing to meet these needs? Apparently not. Most of the major Western nations have endured a serious recession for the last two to three years. Many other demands for public and private spending pile up. In Britain, we are asked to dip into our pockets to support domestic institutions which were formerly the undisputed financial responsibility of the State, such as the Royal Botanic Gardens at Kew, or the universities. Countless new and genuine needs for charitable giving arise: from child psychotherapy to saving the chimpanzee. Civil unrest in the inner cities of some industrial nations alerts their politicians to the need for investment in the social fabric at home. The liberation of the Soviet Union and Eastern Europe has resulted in many urgent demands for development funding, in countries whose rulers used to make a virtue of not asking for charity. ...

The British public is generous to charities in general and relief and development in particular. All the major agencies' annual incomes rose considerably in 1991, but British Government aid to the Third World is not keeping up in real terms with inflation. The British Government's aid spending has fallen to about 0.3 per cent of Gross National Product (GNP), far short of the UN's aid target of 0.7 per cent and well behind Norway, Netherlands, Denmark, Sweden, France and Finland, where the proportion is over 0.6 per cent. Aid spending by British NGOs increased in 1990 from £150 million in the previous year to £184 million, an increase of 13 per cent after inflation. However, this figure is dwarfed by the net flow of money from developing countries to Britain, which was about £25 billion. Third World aid is at best an insignificant election issue between the political parties.

The only way to reverse the downward spiral is to find new ways of using the media to generate a more informed public knowledge of disasters and emergencies, including chronic disasters. This knowledge should in turn generate both a higher degree of pressure on national politicians to support UN agencies and others such as ICRC which depend on government donations, and also a higher revenue for the NGOs from individuals. (It is, incidentally, by no means unknown for substantial individual donations to go to government bodies. For instance, readers of the *Independent* in London donated £500,000 for reconstruction after the Iranian earthquake in 1990. WHO acted as intermediary between the newspaper and the Iranian government, and the money was spent on building more secure structures.)

There are two possible approaches to adopt in pursuit of this objective. One is to ride with the media's own way of doing things. The other is to try to discover how the media function, and to devise alternative routes. Both approaches must be tried. The first is the more realistic, the second the more radical.

'Compassion fatigue', 'donor fatigue' and 'appeal fatigue' are expressions frequently heard in the aid agencies. Some of them, pointing to their expansion of revenue and expenditure from year to year, deny that such fatigue exists. There is some opinion-poll evidence that the British public, especially the 18–24 age group, is increasingly supportive of constructive aid to the Third World and sceptical about government policies. But the expansion of tangible revenue is only achieved by means of marketing campaigns whose persistence *Time* magazine or the *Reader's Digest* would not be ashamed of. £30 million raised from the public for British agencies to relieve famine in Africa in six months may seem a large sum, but it is a small figure both in relation to governmental budgets for, say, military spending, and in relation to the need, which is to avert the risk of an avoidable holocaust. There is increasing evidence that repeated or long-lasting emergencies do sap donors' goodwill. We are all as individuals able to think of good reasons for *not* responding to needs; and the same is true of governments. When the media, too, get the impression that a chronic disaster has become a normal way of life, it thereby ceases to be news.

Public disasters are like the private disasters affecting our individual lives. Even the gravest of sudden accidents or misfortunes are made a little less difficult to bear because of the atmosphere of high drama that surrounds them, rallying support from relatives, friends and neighbours. It is the chronic, gnawing affliction which is most difficult to manage and assuage, and which too often fails to hold friends' attention. This is true on the domestic scale, where we communicate as individuals one-to-one; it is no different on the public scale, when communication is through the mass media.

Key terms

The following key terms appear in the text above. They have been defined below to aid with the reading of this item.

demographic relating to the population make-up

humanitarian offering compassion; having the interests of humanity at heart; ending human suffering

Questions

1 What does Benthall suggest about how disasters are classified? What is the media's role in this process?

2 Why is the role of the media in aid and charity work seen as 'crucial'?

3 How might the media attention of some issues of relief actually inhibit real help taking place?

Reading 16.8 **Patriarchal ideology and femininity in the media**

Joan Smith (from) 'Single, white, fertile', in *Different For Girls: How culture creates woman* (1997) London: Chatto & Windus, pp. 103–8 and 112–17.

Editorial comments

Smith argues that newspapers present an ideological image of the family which controls and regulates women's position in society. She suggests that 'deviant' women in families – and especially single female parents – are used as scapegoats.

Single, white, fertile

IT MUST HAVE been one of the most unflattering pictures ever taken of a normally glamorous woman: Paula Yates arriving at Heathrow Airport from Australia, weary lines creasing her eyes and mouth, dark roots visible in her dyed blonde hair, lips smeared with salmon-pink lipstick as though she'd hastily applied it on the plane. 'Paula: I'll fight to keep my children' was the accompanying headline in the *Evening Standard*, above a story announcing that drugs – allegedly a small quantity of opium – had been found at Yates's Chelsea home during her absence on the other side of the world. It didn't help that she was wearing a wildly inappropriate black cocktail dress with a plunging neckline, giving her the appearance of someone emerging bleary-eyed from a nightclub at dawn rather than a defiant mother battling for custody of her children. Nor did the fact that, as the *Evening Standard* revealed, she had flown to London without her sick two-month-old daughter Heavenly Hiraani Tiger Lily, who was being cared for by her father, the rock star Michael Hutchence, in Australia. The **subtext** was blatant: Yates's predicament was hardly surprising when she looked such a mess *and* had abandoned her baby in order to make her hasty trip to London. Just to make things worse, an unfortunate coincidence of timing meant that Yates made her appearance on the front page of the *Standard* on the same day as Mandy Allwood, whose doctors were desperately trying to prevent her multiple pregnancy from miscarrying. The contest was straightforward, good mother versus bad, with no prizes for guessing who was the winner.

Ever since her divorce from Bob Geldof, Yates has been a figure of fun, ridiculed for giving her children silly names, for having her breasts enlarged, and for dashing off a self-serving autobiography in an indecently short time. Ian Hislop, editor of *Private Eye*, mauled her mercilessly when she was ill-advised enough to appear on the satirical TV programme *Have I Got News For You*, mocking her writing, her vocabulary and her breasts with equal ferocity. The stories which appeared after the alleged drugs find, however, broke new ground. Yates was portrayed as a careless mother, a divorcee with a younger lover who had exposed her daughters to drugs – thus pushing one of the late twentieth century's most effective panic buttons – and then compounded the offence by leaving her tiny baby on another continent while she flew home to face the music. And what was the sequel to these dramatic events? Yates's recently appointed PR woman resigned in a fit of righteous indignation – a loss most of us could bear with equanimity – but that was all. No charges were brought against Yates, Hutchence or anyone else who lived in her house, while her childcare arrangements continued much as before.

Paula Yates may be a silly, vain woman, but there is no evidence that she neglects or in any other way mistreats her daughters. On the contrary, she has written two books about childcare which irritated many readers with their noisy advocacy of a very traditional model of motherhood, including an insistence that women with small children should stay at home – advice she herself ignored when she was a presenter on *The Big Breakfast*. And while some of the most mawkish paragraphs in her autobiography are about her daughters, there is a transparent sincerity to her protestations that 'I've always tried to do my best for all of my ... children and they, in turn, have given my life a real focus. They were, and still are, absolutely central to my existence.' It was simply Yates's bad luck that, for a moment at least, she appeared to embody everything that's considered bad about mothering at a time when the collapse of the nuclear family, and the consequent rise in the number of single-parent families, has produced a fevered debate about the way children are brought up. Single mothers, a category so elastic that it can be stretched to accommodate any woman who isn't living with her husband and two perfect children in a state of familial bliss, are currently being blamed for everything from truancy to exam failure to murder ...

Leading psychologists say that the breakdown of the family has created a new generation of 'latchkey children' – many of whom suffer neglect and abuse.

Who is responsible for creating 'latchkey children'? Since fathers have never been expected to be at home when their children return from school, the answer is obvious. The story marked a return to a favourite theme for the *Sunday Telegraph*, which had run a leader page piece entreating 'Spare the job, mother, and save the child' only four weeks earlier. The article was uncompromising, as even the byline announced: 'The chief cause of juvenile delinquency is the working mother, says Lynette Burrows'. Writing about the campaign to 'remoralize our youth' in the wake of 'several horrible murders' – presumably she was thinking about, among others, the killing of two-year-old James Bulger in Liverpool by two ten-year-old boys and the murder by a teenage boy of the London head teacher Philip Lawrence – Burrows wrote despairingly about 'young tearaways' who observe only 'the law of the jungle'. She savaged laws which supposedly outlaw smacking and fiscal policies which discriminate against women who stay at home with their children, but reserved her strongest criticism for the effect which jobs have on mothers:

> Capitalism is devouring the family and the effect is pernicious. One reason why today's unrealistic approach to childrearing has taken hold is that women have been collectivized and demoralized. Millions of women who were once mistresses in their own homes have become mere paid servants in the businesses of others. Even though they were only the boss in something as small as a family, it was the most important thing in their lives, and it gave them confidence and authority. They knew about bringing up children and would have been affronted by today's suggestion that they needed lessons in doing it.

(Lynette Burrows, Sunday Telegraph, *27 October 1996)*

Referring to the widely publicized campaign on moral issues launched by Philip Lawrence's widow, Frances, Burrows argued that such initiatives could not succeed unless 'mothers take them up in their own homes and neighbourhoods. And they cannot do that unless they are there in more than a part-time capacity.' Women, she insisted, 'are largely responsible for how young people turn out. Men traditionally have rightly [*sic*] deferred to women in training the young, but today's women are ill-equipped to do it.' These are breath-taking arguments from a stridently right-wing newspaper whose editorial line would normally offer uncritical support to a free market in labour, as well as insisting on the pivotal role of a male-dominated organization – the Church of England – in setting moral standards. An atmosphere of moral panic is not, however, conducive to consistency, and it is no accident that the anguished and emotional debate about the behaviour of children and adolescents is taking place at a moment when many people are suffering from not just **fin de siècle** but millennarian anxiety. Yet the oddest thing about Burrows's article is not its quasi-Marxist denunciation of the alienation of women in the contemporary workforce. It is the complete absence of the word 'father' from her analysis – a feature her article shares with many others on this theme, even in newspapers with a more liberal agenda, such as the *Guardian*. It is a strange fact that when the collapse of the nuclear family is under discussion, the spotlight falls not on the *couples* who are supposed to be its bedrock but exclusively on the female partner.

Think for a moment: have you ever seen a headline announcing that 'working dads are blamed for children's failures'? That headline appeared, with one significant difference, on the front page of the *Guardian* in February 1997; it was of course working *mums*, not dads, whose influence on children was under attack. The *Guardian* story was a trail for a *Panorama* programme on BBC television the same evening which claimed to have discovered 'middle-class deprivation' among families where *both* parents chose to work full-time. The entire programme was devoted to the findings of a single academic study of 600 families in Barking and Dagenham, which suggested that children whose mothers worked full-time were twice as likely to fail their GCSEs as those with mothers working part-time. The media got so excited about this one limited study that the *Sunday Times* reported it on its front page the day before the programme was transmitted under the uncompromising headline 'Children of working mothers face exam failure'. Alternative explanations of the findings, such as the question of whether the parents in the study were able to afford decent childcare, were not canvassed in any of the frankly sensational front-page coverage. ...

Absent fathers: that, in a nutshell, is the problem John Major's government was trying to address when it set up the much-maligned Child Support Agency. The organization's aim, as stated in its annual report, is 'to replace a child maintenance system which was failing large numbers of children, the parents with whom they lived and the general taxpayer'; its principal task, laid down in the Child Support Acts of 1991 and 1995, is 'to ensure that parents who live apart meet their financial responsibility to their children whenever they can afford to do so'. The scale of this task is indicated by a single statistic, the CSA's live caseload in 1997, which was 1.8 million cases.

The CSA's inefficiency when it was first set up, and a few well-publicized instances in which men received huge bills which turned out to be inaccurate, have tended to overshadow its achievements. Yet, now that all the fuss has died down and teething problems have been ironed out, it is possible to examine its statistics and get a sense of the extraordinary state of affairs it was set up to deal with. Since 1995, no absent parent has been required to pay more than 30 per cent of net income in child support; indeed, far from facing bills running into hundreds of pounds, the *average* amount due under a CSA assessment is around £25 per week. Even so, the CSA has had to cope not only with the problem of separated couples where one partner is reluctant to co-operate with its financial investigations but with parents who have vanished altogether. In 1995–6 alone it undertook more than 55,000 specialist traces in order to track down missing parents, bringing the total since its inception to nearly 133,000. We are talking here, not to put too fine a point on it, about parents who have disappeared without a forwarding address, leaving their partners and offspring to get by as best they can – either by working, existing on handouts from their families or claiming state benefits. And what kind of people might these be? Here is the only clue we get from the CSA annual report:

In many of these cases our staff have to establish *paternity* [my emphasis], which can be a difficult and sensitive process, requiring interviewing of alleged absent parents, DNA testing and court proceedings. We have introduced improved guidelines to support staff involved in tracing absent parents.

In other words, CSA staff are having to confront *fathers* who have not only abandoned their families but deny all responsibility for them. In fact, according to the agency's press office, 95.2 per cent of the people who have to make regular payments are absent fathers, and only 4.8 per cent absent mothers. Here is another fascinating statistic from the agency's annual report: since the introduction of a DNA Paternity Testing Scheme in 1995, 85 per cent

of those tested have 'proved to be the parent'. Once again, if we put this into plain English, it means that of those men who protest, when confronted by a CSA official, that they never met the woman in question or merely bought her a drink at a disco, seventeen out of twenty are lying. And what they are trying to avoid is paying around £25 a week for the upkeep of the children they have fathered.

In a rational world, these figures might well indicate some sort of crisis about how we as a society bring up and support children. But is it really a crisis, as everyone from newspaper columnists and documentary-makers to politicians keep telling us, of *motherhood?* It would not to be difficult to mount an alternative case in which it is *mothers*, whether they stay at home or work part-time or have full-time jobs, who are struggling to maintain some semblance of family life in the face of a wholesale flight by *men* from their responsibilities. Organizations like the lobbying group Families Need Fathers counter this charge by claiming that many men are unwillingly ejected from their families by women who find new partners or simply prefer to be on their own, an argument which fails to address the crucial question of what kind of fathering they were providing before the relationship broke down; choosing to be a single mother is such a momentous decision for most women that they are unlikely to make it without good reasons, which might include a partner's violence, infidelity or a disinclination to accept his share of parental responsibility. Are we really to believe that of those hundred thousand or so fathers whose whereabouts were unknown, until the CSA tracked them down at the taxpayer's expense, every single one of them was unreasonably thrown out by his wife or partner?

There is a well-known psychological mechanism, called displacement, which transfers anxiety from one subject which is too painful to contemplate on to another, easier target. The most obvious explanation for the sometimes daily attacks on mothers in the British press, whether they appear in a newspaper such as the *Telegraph* or the supposedly more liberal *Guardian*, is that we live in a moral climate which would rather scapegoat women than face unpalatable truths about men. Perhaps it is *men* who should be spending more time with their children, and be more involved in their day-to-day care, and more realistic about the cost of bringing up a child from the day it is born to the moment it leaves school or university – but that would involve a wholesale reappraisal of the way we approach the different demands of work and of being a parent. It would also require a recognition of the extent to which we like the *idea* of children without being anything like so keen on the reality. Everyone loves imaginary babies, as evidenced by the speed with which an anti-abortion group raised tens of thousands of pounds in 1996 in the hope of persuading an anonymous pregnant woman in London not to abort one of the twins she was carrying. Yet the truth is that millions of real live children in Britain live below the poverty line – a fact which could just as easily be responsible for their failure to thrive educationally, morally or physically as the style of mothering they are receiving.

'One in three British babies born in poverty' was the headline above a front-page story in the *Independent on Sunday* as recently as November 1996; according to the accompanying text, the British government's own figures revealed that, in 1995–6, 215,000 babies were born into families which were receiving state benefits because they were on the breadline – 30 per cent of all the children born in that period. The figures, compiled by the House of Commons library from social security statistics, showed that more than 200,000 mothers received maternity payments from the social fund, and that 30,000 of these went to low-income families rather than people entirely dependent on state benefits. Using an entitlement to welfare benefits as an index of poverty, the paper also reported that the number of children living in families dependent on supplementary benefit had increased from one million in 1979, when the Conservatives returned to power, to 2.8 million on the roughly equivalent benefit, income support, in 1992.

Poverty, the growing inequality between rich and poor families, absent fathers, a state education system which fails thousands of poorer pupils: any or all of these could lie behind the crisis of unruly youth, if indeed there is one in Britain today rather than an unhealthy and sensational concentration on some high-profile cases. Why look for complex explanations, however, when that old standby, female **altruism** or its absence, is so easily to hand? What women have yet to learn is that as soon as they have a baby, they are unwittingly signing up to take part in a contest they can never win. In previous centuries mothers used to die for their offspring, either in childbirth or from complications afterwards, and those apparently self-immolating examples are still lodged, subliminally, in our brains. I say 'apparently' because puerperal fever and the other infections which carried women off were hardly a matter of choice, yet the pairing of motherhood and self-sacrifice is so firmly established that many people have never tried – wouldn't even want – to unpick it. In that sense, a mother can never be altruistic enough, for any decision which even has the appearance of putting her interests before those of her children – from taking a job or setting up with a new partner – merely emphasizes how far she is from the ideal. ...

No one has ever written like this about *fathers*. The irony is that, while everything a woman does for her children is taken for granted, fathers are idealized and forgiven for their absences. Indeed, anyone who reads newspapers might come away with the impression that children who turn out well are a credit to their fathers, while those who go wrong, whether we are talking about teenagers failing their GCSEs or knifing their schoolmates, are the sole responsibility of their mothers. So deeply ingrained is this view that detectives hunting some particularly vicious rapist or serial killer more often than not announce that they are looking for a loner 'who lives with his mother' – and we all know what *that* means. Fathers are off the hook in this culture. Women, beware: never forget that all our hearts belong to Daddy.

Key terms

The following key terms appear in the text above. They have been defined below to aid with the reading of this item.

subtext hidden meaning, reading 'between the lines'

fin de siècle concerned with the end of the century

altruism unselfish concern for others

Questions

1 According to Smith how are single female mothers represented in the media?

2 What differences are there between the portrayal of mothers and fathers in the media?

3 What other causes might there be for contemporary 'social problems', which are ignored when women are used as scapegoats instead?

Further reading

The following texts may represent a useful starting point for further investigation of the ideas contained within this chapter.

Primary texts

For a classic illustration of media bias from a neo-Marxist perspective, see:

Glasgow University Media Group (1976) *Bad News*, London: Routledge.

Glasgow University Media Group (1980) *More Bad News*, London: Routledge.

Glasgow University Media Group (1982) *Really Bad News*, London: Writers' and Readers' Cooperative.

For a good, general, contemporary 'reader' on the media see:

Curran, J. and Gurevtich, M. (eds) (1991) *Mass Media and Society*, New York: Edward Arnold.

Finally, for an empirical study on the representation of ethnicity see:

Van Dijk, T. A. (1991) *Racism and the Press: Critical studies in racism and migration*, London: Routledge.

Secondary texts

Dutton, B. (1986) *The Media*, London: Longman.

Kirby, M. *et al.* (1997) 'The mass media', in *Sociology in Perspective*, Oxford: Heinemann Educational.

Trowler, P. (1996) *Investigating the Media*, 2nd edn, London: Collins Educational.

Coursework suggestions

1 The nature of the media audience

Using the more qualitative methods of semi-structured or unstructured interviews, you could investigate the audiences' motivations for television viewing of some of the topics dealt with in the readings in this chapter – for example viewing of warfare or famine issues. This coursework could be based upon a theoretical interpretation of the audience as active rather than passive, another idea presented in the readings.

2 Construction of femininity in the media

Taking a theoretical orientation based upon feminist ideas – as presented in readings 16.4 and 16.8 – you could undertake the content analysis of television news, newspapers or women's magazines in order to investigate the contemporary themes or characteristics of the modern 'ideology of femininity'. The research question to address could be: 'to what extent has the representation of women changed since the publication of some of the ideas presented in this chapter?' This investigation could draw upon the complementary methods of content analysis and semiology.

17

Community, locality and nation

Chapter summary

Reading 17.1 *Gemeinschaft* and *Gesellschaft* *page 502*

Ferdinand Tönnies summarizes his consensus-based theory of community development and change. In the first stage, relationships are based on likeness; in the second they are based on difference, but co-operation is equally evident.

Reading 17.2 **Cornerville: an early ethnographic study** *page 503*

William Foote Whyte establishes his ethnographic credentials by explaining that an understanding of a community comes from personal involvement with it. This takes time and may require 'insiders' to give the sociologist a 'foot in the door'. For Foote Whyte, explicit hypotheses represent the end of research rather than starting points.

Reading 17.3 **Postwar romanticism** *page 506*

Much of the immediate postwar community sociology is accused of being too consensual; of emphasizing harmonious relationships over ones based on conflict. The beginning of this reading shows evidence of some 'romanticism', but later Brian Jackson also shows awareness of conflict, although he doesn't bring this to the fore.

Reading 17.4 **Postwar conflict theory** *page 508*

John Rex and Robert Moore's study of the Sparkbrook area of Birmingham is often seen as the first major step forward in empirical community sociology. Its Weberian approach emphasizes different market positions and conflict developing out of competition for housing.

Reading 17.5 **Community as cultural symbolism rather than structure** *page 511*

For traditional functionalist and Marxist sociologists, community is often seen as an imposed structure which can then be seen to break down with modernization. Anthony Cohen's view is that a community is more a matter of symbols which are subjective and inconsistent. They evolve rather than break down.

Reading 17.6 **A critique of 'communitarian utopianism'** *page 515*

David Harvey has long written about the evolution of urban areas. In this reading he argues that inability to see urbanization as an on-going process based on heterogeneity leads to simplistic policy decisions which are doomed to failure.

Reading 17.7 **The Californian School** *page 518*

The post-modernists of the Californian School have placed urban development firmly at the centre of contemporary sociological debates about the nature of society in general. Edward Soja is one of the key players, and in this reading he explains six 'geographies' of urban change, using Los Angeles as the premier example.

Reading 17.8 **National identity: in the mind of the beholder** *page 524*

As Cohen sees community existing in the subjective interpretations of individuals, Benedict Anderson sees national identity as imagined, rather than an objective reality. He feels that such developments can be traced to the spread of global capitalism and the printed word.

Introduction: Reading the sociology of community, locality and nation

The structure and function of community was a central issue in the sociology of several classical sociologists, such as Emile Durkheim and Ferdinand Tönnies. They attempted to examine the causes and consequences of industrialization and urbanization on the people of what they regarded as a 'modern society'. These processes were seen to have rendered obsolete traditional social networks based on kinship and locality, creating a new social era based on the industrial division of labour, where social ties were still interdependent but based on functional differences/needs rather than similarities of lifestyle. Given that we are all members of communities, localities and nations, it is surprising that community sociology has only returned to sociological prominence in more recent times. Contemporary sociologies of the family, education, politics, religion, the economy and such like are likely to place notions of community (be they local, national or global) in a prominent position.

Perhaps one of the reasons why the sociology of community fell from prominence was due to the seemingly circular discussions about the exact definition of the term 'community'. All sociologists felt that they alone had the right definition, but without agreement over the definition, they could not agree on the topic of study and there could be little effective comparison of their findings and conclusions.

Several of the readings in this chapter consider what makes a community. Tönnies (1887) (**reading 17.1**) did so by juxtaposing what he called *Gemeinschaft*, the community of pre-industrial societies, with *Gesellschaft*, based on association rather than communal ties. Community, he claimed, existed when all the people of a locality had similar beliefs, culture and lifestyles. William Foote Whyte (1981) (**reading 17.2**) writing in the 1940s, although not bound up in the debate over the concept of community, was one of the first to show that *Gemeinschaft*-type relationships could exist in localized urban settings. These might have been seen as closer to *Gemeinschaft* due to extended kinship and other homogenizing factors such as religion, poverty, cultural roots and racism. These urban localities were later dubbed 'urban villages' by Herbert Gans (1962). The classic works of Tönnies and Foote Whyte also show the differences between macro/structural- and micro/action-focused sociology, indicating that philosophical starting points can affect the findings and conclusions drawn in research.

Brian Jackson (1972), in his postwar study of Huddersfield (**reading 17.3**), felt able to suggest that similarities of lifestyle – due to factors such as type of work, income, poverty, kinship and leisure networks – created a working-class community clearly different from that of the middle class. Again, this is evidence that community could exist in an urban setting. Yet other sociological commentators might suggest that Jackson's lack of emphasis on conflict within the locality resulted in an over-romanticized view of working-class community (a criticism he didn't accept). Such commentators would view Rex and Moore's (1974) Weberian study of a locality within Birmingham (**reading 17.4**) as more realistic, because they argued that conflict existed due to competition for housing. Where Marx saw ownership and control of the means of production as indicative of economic power, Weber thought ownership of domestic property, like housing, equally important. Rex and Moore used this hypothesis to develop a criteria for social structure based on 'housing classes', which they believed were determined by ownership and allocation of an area's housing stock. The resulting conflict created a community divided by racial origin.

Anthony Cohen (1995) (**reading 17.5**), influencd by symbolic Interactionist ideas, and Benedict Anderson (1983) (**reading 17.8**), a neo-Marxist, veer away from the sociological debate which suggests that an objective, measurable definition of community is required. Both suggest that community is imagined and subjective, with Cohen feeling that it is not scientifically measurable. What is more important is the impact that personal definitions of community have on individuals, their interactions and the structures around them. However, their differing perspectives lead them to distinct conclusions: Cohen, who argues that there can be no generalizations, concludes that identities are as various as the number of people holding them, while Anderson concludes that a generalized super-structure could exist.

The processes that form and result from urban areas and urban living are related to the idea of what community is. If Tönnies was right in his conclusion that urbanization led to a loss of community, then a century of continued development and enlargement of urban forms creates for some a nightmare scenario – the potential breakdown of communal society prophesied by films such as *Escape from New York* and *Blade Runner*. Many sociologists, however, are not prepared to accept such a 'dystopian' (anti-ideal) vision. David Harvey (1996), in **reading 17.6**, draws on Marxist and post-modern urban sociology to acknowledge that urban areas are continually changing and have negative facets. However, these should be seen as exciting challenges to be solved by drawing together different people and developing discussion based on the diversity of viewpoints. An over-arching singular community, advocated by policy commentators as the only possible solution to urban problems, is – according to Harvey – neither true nor desirable. The future lies in the acceptance of difference.

Another important contemporary sociologist, Edward Soja (1996), offers a complementary analysis in **reading 17.7**. His post-modern perspective leads him to emphasize heterogeneity and lack of consistency in urban forms. Using Los Angeles as a primary example of a post-modern city he notes how six key changes are evident in urban forms. He feels that it is too early to suggest whether the outcome will be positive or negative, but he is excited by the challenge of monitoring the changes as they take place and developing conclusions based on his observations.

Reference

Gans, H. (1962) *The Urban Villagers*, New York: Free Press.

Reading 17.1 *Gemeinschaft and Gesellschaft*

Ferdinand Tönnies (from) *Community and Association* (1974, originally published in 1887) London: Routledge & Kegan Paul, pp. 270–2.

Editorial comments

This work is seen alongside the mechanical/organic schema of Durkheim (1938, orig. pub. 1893) as the starting point of the debate about whether rural and urban communities are essentially different. It is a good example of the structural functionalist argument of evolutionary change based on adaptation to environments, with *Gemeinschaft* (community) and *Gesellschaft* (association) existing as pure ends of a continuum. Most of the later work on community can be seen as an attempt to prove Tönnies right or wrong.

Reference

Durkheim, E. (1938) *The Division of Labour in Society*, Glencoe: Free Press (orig. pub. 1893).

Gemeinschaft and Gesellschaft

The periods

TO CONCLUDE OUR theory, two periods stand thus contrasted with each other in the history of the great systems of culture: a period of Gesellschaft follows a period of Gemeinschaft. The Gemeinschaft is characterized by the social will as concord, **folkways**, **mores**, and religion; the Gesellschaft by the social will as convention, legislation, and public opinion. The concepts correspond to the types of external social organization, which may be classed as follows:

A. Gemeinschaft

1. Family life = concord. Man participates in this with all his sentiments. Its real controlling agent is the people (*Volk*).
2. Rural village life = folkways and mores. Into this man enters with all his mind and heart. Its real controlling agent is the commonwealth.
3. Town life = religion. In this the human being takes part with his entire conscience. Its real controlling agent is the church.

B. Gesellschaft

1. City life = convention. This is determined by man's intentions. Its real controlling agent is Gesellschaft *per se*.
2. National life = legislation. This is determined by man's calculations. Its real controlling agent is the state.
3. Cosmopolitan life = public opinion. This is evolved by man's consciousness. Its real controlling agent is the republic of scholars.

With each of these categories a predominant occupation and a dominating tendency in intellectual life are related in the following manner:

(A)
1. Home (or household) economy, based upon liking or preference, *viz*., the joy and delight of creating and conserving. Understanding develops the norms for such an economy.
2. Agriculture, based upon habits, i.e., regularly repeated tasks. Co-operation is guided by custom.
3. Art, based upon memories, i.e. of instruction, of rules followed, and of ideas conceived in one's own mind. Belief in the work and the task unites the artistic wills.

(B)
1. Trade based upon deliberation; namely, attention, comparison, calculation are the basis of all business. Commerce is deliberate action *per se*. Contracts are the custom and creed of business.
2. Industry based upon decisions; namely, of intelligent productive use of capital and sale of labour. Regulations rule the factory.
3. Science, based upon concepts, as is self-evident. Its truths and opinions then pass into literature and the press and thus become part of public opinion.

Epochs of the periods

In the earlier period family life and home (or household) economy strike the keynote; in the later period commerce and city life. If, however, we investigate the period of Gemeinschaft more closely, several **epochs** can be distinguished. Its whole development tends toward an approach to Gesellschaft in which, on the other hand, the force of Gemeinschaft persists, although with diminishing strength, even in the period of Gesellschaft, and remains the reality of social life.

The first period is formed by the influence of the new basis of social organization which results from the cultivation of the soil: neighbourhood relation is added to the old and persisting kinship relations, village to the clan. The other epoch comes into existence when villages develop into towns. The village and town have in common the principle of social organization in space, instead of the principle of time which predominates through the generations of the family, the tribe, and the people. Because it descends from common ancestors, the family has invisible **meta-physical** roots, as if they were hidden in the earth. The living individuals in the family are connected with each other by the sequence of past and future generations. But in village and town it is the physical, real soil, the permanent location, the visible land, which create the strongest ties and relations. During the period of Gemeinschaft this younger principle of space remains bound to the older principle of time. In the period of Gesellschaft they become disconnected, and from this disconnection results the city. It is the exaggeration of the principle of space in its urban form. In this exaggeration, the urban form becomes sharply contrasted with the rural form of the same principle, for the village remains essentially and almost necessarily bound to both principles. In this sense, the whole continual development may be considered as a process of increasing urbanization. 'It may be said that the whole economic history of Gesellschaft, i.e., of the modern nations, is in essence summarized in the change in the relationship between town and country' (Karl Marx, 1954; orig. pub. 1867). That is, from a certain point on, the towns by their influence and importance achieve, in the nation, predominance over the rural organization. In consequence, country and village must use more of their own productive forces for the support and furtherance of the urban areas than they can spare for purposes of reproduction. Therefore the rural organization is doomed to dissolution, which in consequence leads later on to the decay of its organs and functions.

Reference

Marx, K. (1954) *Capital*, vol. 1, London: Lawrence & Wishart (orig. pub. 1867).

Key terms

The following key terms appear in the text above. They have been defined below to aid with the reading of this item.

folkways the norms of the group

mores customs and conventions

epochs stages/periods in history

metaphysical beyond what is natural

Questions

1 What are the main differences between *Gemeinschaft* and *Gesellschaft*?

2 How does *Gemeinschaft* change into *Gesellschaft*?

3 Does this basic schema accurately describe the differences between pre-modern and modern society? Give reasons for your answer.

Reading 17.2 **Cornerville: an early ethnographic study**

William Foote Whyte (from) *Street Corner Society: The social structure of an Italian slum* (1981, originally published in 1943) Chicago and London: University of Chicago Press, pp. 291–6.

Editorial comments

This was one of the first, certainly one of the most well-known, applications of ethnography to the study of modern society/community. As ethnography, it broke with the structural/positivistic tradition of the likes of Tönnies by aiming to gain understanding of the day-to-day reality of communal interaction in a micro setting, through personal involvement rather than detached science. It may also be seen to stand opposed to Tönnies by finding community (*Gemeinschaft*) in an urban setting. In this reading, Foote Whyte explains how he became involved in the community of 'Cornerville' by making contact with 'Doc' and the Martini family.

Street corner society

IN A SENSE, my study began on the evening of February 4, 1937, when the social worker called me in to meet Doc. She showed us into her office and then left so that we could talk. Doc waited quietly for me to begin, as he sank down into a chair. I found him a man of medium height and spare build. His hair was a light brown, quite a contrast to the more typical black Italian hair. It was thinning around the temples. His cheeks were sunken. His eyes were a light blue and seemed to have a penetrating gaze.

I began by asking him if the social worker had told him about what I was trying to do.

'No, she just told me that you wanted to meet me and that I should like to meet you'.

Then I went into a long explanation which, unfortunately, I omitted from my notes. As I remember it, I said that I had been interested in congested city districts in my college study but had felt very remote from them. I hoped to study the problems in such a district. I felt I could do very little as an outsider. Only if I could get to know the people and learn their problems first hand would I be able to gain the understanding I needed.

Doc heard me out without any change of expression, so that I had no way of predicting his reaction. When I was finished, he asked: 'Do you want to see the high life or the low life'?

'I want to see all that I can. I want to get as complete a picture of the community as possible'.

'Well, any nights you want to see anything, I'll take you around. I can take you to the joints – **gambling joints** – I can take you around to the street corners. Just remember that you're my friend. That's all they need to know. I know these places, and, if I tell them that you're my friend, nobody will bother you. You just tell me what you want to see, and we'll arrange it'.

The proposal was so perfect that I was at a loss for a moment as to how to respond to it. We talked a while longer, as I sought to get some pointers as to how I should behave in his company. He warned me that I might have to take the risk of getting arrested in a raid on a gambling joint but added that this was not serious. I only had to give a false name and then would get bailed out by the man that ran the place, paying only a five-dollar fine. I agreed to take this chance. I asked him whether I should gamble with the others in the gambling joints. He said it was unnecessary and, for a greenhorn like myself, very inadvisable.

At last I was able to express my appreciation. 'You know, the first steps of getting to know a community are the hardest. I could see things going with you that I wouldn't see for years otherwise'.

'That's right. You tell me what you want to see, and we'll arrange it. When you want some information, I'll ask for it, and you listen. When you want to find out their philosophy of life, I'll start an argument and get it for you. If there's something else you want to get, I'll stage an act for you. Not a scrap, you know, but just tell me what you want, and I'll get it for you'.

'That's swell. I couldn't ask for anything better. Now I'm going to try to fit in all right, but, if at any time you see I'm getting off on the wrong foot, I want you to tell me about it'.

'Now we're being too dramatic. You won't have any trouble. You come in as my friend. When you come in like that, at first everybody will treat you with respect. You can take a lot of liberties, and nobody will kick. After a while when they get to know you they will treat you like anybody else – you know, they say familiarity breeds contempt. But you'll never have any trouble. There's just one thing to watch out for. Don't spring [treat] people. Don't be too free with your money'.

'You mean they'll think I'm a sucker'?

'Yes, and you don't want to buy your way in'.

We talked a little about how and when we might get together. Then he asked me a question. 'You want to write something about this'?

'Yes, eventually'.

'Do you want to change things'?

'Well – yes. I don't see how anybody could come down here where it is so crowded, people haven't got any money or any work to do, and not want to have some things changed. But I think a fellow should do the thing he is best fitted for. I don't want to be a reformer, and I'm not cut out to be a politician. I just want to understand these things as best I can and write them up, and if that has any influence. ...'

'I think you can change things that way. Mostly that is the way things are changed, by writing about them'.

That was our beginning. At the time I found it hard to believe that I could move in as easily as Doc had said with his sponsorship. But that indeed was the way it turned out.

While I was taking my first steps with Doc, I was also finding a place to live in Cornerville. My fellowship provided a very comfortable bedroom, living-room, and bath at Harvard. I had been attempting to commute from these quarters to my Cornerville study. Technically that was possible, but socially I became more and more convinced that it was impossible. I realized that I would always be a stranger to the community if I did not live there. Then, also, I found myself having difficulty putting in the time that I knew was required to establish close relations in Cornerville. Life in Cornerville did not proceed on the basis of formal appointments. To meet people, to get to know them, to fit into their activities, required spending time with them – a lot of time day after day. Commuting to Cornerville, you might come in on a particular afternoon and evening only to discover that the people you intended to see did not happen to be around at the time. Or, even if you did see them, you might find the time passing entirely uneventfully. You might just be standing around with people whose only occupation was talking or walking about to try to keep themselves from being bored.

On several afternoons and evenings at Harvard, I found myself considering a trip to Cornerville and then rationalizing my way out of it. How did I know I would find the people whom I meant to see? Even if I did so, how could I be sure that I would learn anything today? Instead of going off on a wild-goose chase to Cornerville, I could profitably spend my time reading books and articles to fill in my woeful ignorance of sociology and **social anthropology**. Then, too, I had to admit that I felt more comfortable among these familiar surroundings than I did wandering around Cornerville and spending time with people in whose presence I felt distinctly uncomfortable at first.

When I found myself rationalizing in this way, I realized that I would have to make the break. Only if I lived in Cornerville would I ever be able to understand it and be accepted by it. Finding a place, however, was not easy. In such an overcrowded district a spare room was practically nonexistent. I might have been able to take a room in the **Norton Street Settlement House**, but I realized that I must do better than this if possible.

I got my best lead from the editor of a weekly English-language newspaper published for the Italian-American colony. I had talked to him before about my study and had found him sympathetic. Now I came to ask him for help in finding a room. He directed me to the Martinis, a family which operated a small restaurant. I went there for lunch and later consulted the son of the family. He was sympathetic but said that they had no place for any additional person. Still, I liked the place and enjoyed the food. I came back several times just to eat. On one occasion I met the editor, and he invited me to his table. At first he asked me some searching questions about my study· what I was after, what my connection with Harvard was, what they had expected to get out of this, and so on. After I had answered him in a manner that I unfortunately failed to record in my notes, he told me that he was satisfied and, in fact, had already spoken in my behalf to people who were suspicious that I might be coming in to 'criticize our people'.

We discussed my rooming problem again. I mentioned the possibility of living at the Norton Street House. He nodded but added: 'It would be much better if you could be in a family. You would pick up the language much quicker, and you would get to know the people. But you want a nice family, an educated family. You don't want to get in with any low types. You want a real good family'.

At this he turned to the son of the family with whom I had spoken and asked: 'Can't you make some place for Mr Whyte in the house here'?

Al Martini paused a moment and then said: 'Maybe we can fix it up. I'll talk to Mama again'.

So he did talk to Mama again, and they did find a place. ...

At first I communicated with Mama and Papa primarily in smiles and gestures. Papa knew no English at all, and Mama's knowledge was limited to one sentence which she would use when some of the young boys on the street were making noise below her window when she was trying to get her afternoon nap. She would then poke her head out of the window and shout: 'Goddam-sonumabitcha! Geroutahere'!

Some weeks earlier, in anticipation of moving into the district, I had begun working on the Italian language myself with the aid of a Linguaphone. One morning now Papa Martini came by when I was talking to the phonograph record. He listened for a few moments in the hall trying to make sense out of this peculiar conversation. Then he burst in upon me with fascinated exclamations. We sat down together while I demonstrated the machine and the method to him. After that he delighted in working with me, and I called him my language professor. In a short time we reached a stage where I could carry on simple conversations, and, thanks to the Linguaphone and Papa Martini, the Italian that came out apparently sounded authentic. He liked to try to pass me off to his friends as *paesano mio* – a man from his own home town in Italy. When I was careful to keep my remarks within the limits of my vocabulary, I could sometimes pass as an immigrant from the village of Viareggio in the province of Tuscany.

Since my research developed so that I was concentrating almost exclusively upon the younger, English-speaking generation, my knowledge of Italian proved unnecessary for research purposes. Nevertheless, I feel certain that it was important in establishing my social position in Cornerville – even with that younger generation. There were schoolteachers and social workers who had worked in Cornerville for as much as twenty years and yet had made no effort to learn Italian. My effort to learn the language probably did more to establish the sincerity of my interest in the people than anything I could have told them of myself and my work. How could a researcher be planning to 'criticize our people' if he went to the lengths of learning the language? With language comes understanding, and surely it is easier to criticize people if you do not understand them.

Key terms

The following key terms appear in the text above. They have been defined below to aid with the reading of this item.

gambling joints unlicensed, and therefore illegal, places where gambling took place

social anthropology the study of the culture and social organization of human groups, usually in non-industrial societies and usually adopting ethnography as the research method

Norton Street Settlement House a recreation and lodging centre, with teachers and social workers. Its aim was to help new arrivals in the city adapt to city ways of life

Questions

1 Why was Doc so important?

2 What difficulties did Foote Whyte face in becoming a participant observer and how were they overcome?

3 Foote Whyte talks of 'changing things'. Is this the role of the sociologist?

4 Is it acceptable to break the law, as Foote Whyte did by visiting illegal 'gambling joints', in order to get relevant sociological evidence?

Reading 17.3 **Postwar romanticism**

Brian Jackson (from) *Working Class Community: Some general notions raised by a series of studies in northern England* (1972, originally published in 1968) London: Routledge and Kegan Paul, pp. 72–8.

Editorial comments

Jackson began his study of Huddersfield in 1958, with the help of Dennis Marsden. Both were particularly influenced by Young and Willmotts' *Family and Kinship in East London* (1957) but also other studies in the developing genre of community studies. It aimed to illustrate the causes and consequences of working-class communities and to consider whether the perceived affluence of the immediate postwar period had changed them. Although divided by a variety of specific interests, a generalized working-class community was identified, drawn together by manual labour, poverty, kinship and neighbourhood social networks.

Reference

Young, P. and Willmott, M. (1957) *Family and Kinship in East London*, London: Routledge & Kegan Paul.

In the mill

Focusing in

ON A FOGGY day, the district of Aggbridge, lying in the bottom of the valley, is blotted out by the smoke from its thirty mill chimneys. The black buildings can look dreary enough. But on a fine summer day the yellow and brown stone shows through its soot covering. In the dinner hour mill-workers flock out into the streets, so that anyone not wearing a dark blue overall is out of place. Here and there in the millyards there are quick games of football; men and women sit on walls by the river, or squat on their heels in the sun talking and watching.

Tea-time is not so leisurely. There is a rush for buses. Some men can spare a few minutes for a pint before they go home. Under their dirty fawn raincoats they still wear dark blue overalls with trousers perhaps a bit too short, showing the turn-ups of a brown or grey striped suit made of that indestructible worsted which was a staple product of local mills between the wars. About half the men wear cloth caps, but these are not popular with the young. Indoors, men can be seen through the windows sitting in shirt sleeves at their tea. Women bring their babies out on the steps to look at the workmen passing, and to watch for their husbands. In a small corner shop the daughter just home from grammar school serves on, still dressed in the shirt and tie and red skirt of her school uniform.

By the bus-stop a crowd of people sit inside a fish and chip shop, not buying anything, passing the time of day with the old man there. Half-a-dozen West Indian girls come running, with a gangling motion, laughing and jostling each other for a seat on the stone slabs of a low wall; their clothes are the same dusty colours that the local women wear. Men in the queue look on, not saying anything, but when the bus comes they are alert to prevent queue-jumping. The bus conductor has been on this route at this time for many years and knows his 'customers' intimately: 'There y're y'old bugger. Ah've been waiting for thee. Hurry up: Ah've gett'n thee a job as a neet-watchman'.

Mill

Gradually smaller mills have had to close down, or they have been bought out by larger combines. Cartwrights, the mill of this chapter, is the biggest in this part of Huddersfield, employing over 2,000 people in good times. They once made a suit from wool, freshly sheared from a sheep, in two and a half hours: a 'world record' for twenty years. The mill is an aggregate of five smaller companies, each of which specialized in a single textile process. It still retains the character of these separate sections, and the office building carries brass plates with engraved names of the original companies.

The canal cuts through the centre of the mill, with a lock next to the warehouse, but the lockgates have gone and canal water now spills over concrete weirs. In the canal, there is filmy blue-green water, the bottom visible at the edges, ripples from fish rising to catch small white flies, rocks and debris, rusting iron bars, the upward curve of two springs from a pram carriage, and just visible below the surface, an old skep basket, crushed and disintegrating. A side road comes across the valley at right angles, twisting through between the different buildings of the mill. Here and there, lanes lead off into a dye-house, or a large yard: but some buildings are sited awkwardly and men have to climb down from loading bays six feet above the ground if they want to fetch tea from the canteen by the shortest route. There are pleasanter roads into the mill, stony cart-tracks leading down from the main road past small mill-ponds set among trees, and some people come to work this way; but the main flow is down the hill and over the canal bridge, where at dinner-time a woman from the local shop brings a basket of fish and chips to sell.

Each mill has a striking square watch-tower, Victorian, on the lines of a medieval castle turret. One mill-building is very much like another, with rectangular rows of windows, seldom cleaned, and little architectural decoration. But more important to the work-people are the irregular nooks and crannies and the lavatories. These are the meeting-places on which much of the mill's informal social life depended. ...

Lavatories

Because they were the only places where a man could reasonably expect to be free from the surveillance of authority, the lavatories occupied a unique place in the mill's social life. Smoking was officially prohibited and there was no provision for men to meet for a five-minute break, so that lavatories became the unofficial smoking room. They were labelled 'MALES', and within range of the finishing shed there were two. Once inside the shed was a nub and centre of social life, with up to twenty men there at unofficially 'recognized' break-times. It was a long, high narrow room with a row of ten WCs down one side, each in its own wooden cubicle, and a urinal at one end. Those WCs not actually in use formed seats for some men who propped the doors open so that they could talk to friends squatting against tiled walls opposite or leaning against the wooden partitions. Floor and guttering were always littered with cigarette butts and matchstalks. The once-white tiles were thickly stained with dark brown nicotine from tobacco smoke.

In summer men felt the need of a 'breath of fresh air' and a look at the weather outside. Then they went to a lavatory in the mill yard, where they could meet men from the weaving and spinning sections of the mill. By chance, just outside this lavatory was a small patch of ground in an angle between two buildings. It was screened from the yard and the view of passing officials by a large buttress. It was a draughty, smelly, dusty corner at the best of times, where large black smuts often fell from a nearby chimney. Here someone had made a crude seat with a plank across two irregular knobs of concrete.

There were two other meeting-places. The canteen was used by about half the work-people, and it was the occasion for friends to sit together rather than for meeting newcomers. Every area of this canteen had its own intimate groups, apparently quite haphazardly seated, but really strictly defined. A new man, early in for dinner at an empty table, was warned, 'You don't want to sit there; you'll be among t'women'. After dinner in the large mill yard other steady groups sat on window ledges or bales of shoddy, or they squatted on their heels against walls of buildings, eyeing the men and girls as they walked back to work, some of them eating ice-cream. 'Look at yond feller wi' t' black coat' (a West Indian with very long hair). 'See that on a dark night and you wouldn't half run'! 'We've gett'n a new flapper. That's a short skirt in't it. If It were any shorter she'd be showing all she's got'. There were always one or two men, like the man who stands at the public bar, who preferred to harangue rows of seated men from a standing position, never quite joining any group.

Community

Cartwrights as a whole was not a 'community' in any simple sense. The urge towards a closer life together flickered and spurted up here and there, sometimes strongly. But this group of one hundred or so men and women who worked in and around the finishing shed was shot through by divisions which were deep, although they seldom appeared on the surface.

Outwardly all was friendly and intensely physical in an uninhibited way. Men touched each other very readily: all over there were mock fights and practical jokes, with wrestling, men putting up fists and patting bald heads, offers to buffet, jostle or trip anyone who came within reach. In quiet conversation the urge was to touch, draw aside by an elbow, rest a hand on a shoulder, or simply to lean close. There was an absent-minded quality in the way men worked, waiting for distractions, eager to seize any excuse for a laugh and a joke. Work became second nature and the mill's bustling life proceeded, with work as the reason for men's presence but not their main concern. Some simple jobs were performed by men described as 'simple'. But this equation of intellectual capacity with work did not hold in the majority of jobs, where the only satisfaction offered by work was a task such as rolling a piece of cloth neatly so that the end of the roll should be flat.

Noise was a severe handicap on some machines, which rendered conversation difficult at normal distances until men had learned to lip-read a little and to give to their voices a penetrating tone so that they could speak without strain. There was a knack, too, in avoiding fatigue from gazing too long at cloth streaming over rollers or along waving arms before it fell into natural folds. Watching this was a sure way to induce sleep. Jobs were ostensibly tied down to one machine, but new work brought in from other departments was dumped with no particular system on the scrays, so that there was a constant circulation of men looking for pieces. These pieces had to

be piled on stout wooden carts searched out from all parts of the finishing shed, as they were emptied by other men. There was the trip to find the foreman, to the stores, to the water-tap. Tea was brought round twice a day, and there was a queue at the urn. And above all there were the lavatories which were full of talking men two or three times each morning, and perhaps twice in the afternoon. Everybody might get to know, casually or intimately as he chose, almost all the men and women, boys and girls working in and around the finishing shed. 'It's like coming back home. I know three quarters of this lot', said a man who had been away at another mill for five years. Anyone coming through on 'business' was hailed from each machine and passing girls ran a gauntlet of friendly inquiries and embraces.

Questions

1 Do the districts of Aggbridge and Cartwright's Mill appear to be communities in consensus or conflict?

2 What contribution did the lavatories make to the mill community?

3 What is the value of a small study like Jackson and Marsden's to sociology in general?

4 Could we expect life in Huddersfield to be similar today? What reasons or evidence could be used to support your answer?

Reading 17.4 **Postwar conflict theory**

John Rex and Robert Moore (from) *Race, Community and Conflict: a study of Sparkbrook* (1974) London: Oxford University Press, pp. 3–7, 36–9. Reprinted by permission of Oxford University Press.

Editorial comments

This study was one of the first postwar community studies to consider widespread conflicts. It adopted

the Weberian view that the market situation – the position from which a group of individuals competed for scarce resources (in this case housing) – created inequalities and conflict. In the reading, Rex and Moore explain why they feel the dominant perspective of the time – functionalism – provided an inadequate explanation of urban life, especially the operation of the housing market. They then provide evidence to back up their critique of functionalism and their use of the Weberian perspective.

Race, community, and conflict

THE THEORETICAL APPROACH of the sociologist to the explanation of human behaviour which enjoys widespread popularity is what is called 'functionalism'. The functionalist approach consists in explaining any recurrent aspect of human behaviour in terms of the contribution which it makes to the maintenance of a social system. So widespread, indeed, has this approach become that Kingsley Davis in his presidential address to the American Sociological Association in 1959 suggested that all sociology was functionalist (Kingsley Davis, 1959).

The criticism to which functionalism has been subject, however, is that, in emphasizing **sociological**

determinism it allows too little scope for human agency and appears to affirm that what is, must necessarily be. This would seem to be particularly true of the formulation of functionalist methodology by Radcliffe-Brown (1965), who draws on the analogy between social and organic systems and argues that a sociological explanation must show the contribution which a recurrent activity makes to satisfying the needs of the social structure, just as a biological explanation shows the contribution made by an organic activity to maintaining the organic structure.

Yet even Radcliffe-Brown realizes that this analogy is imperfect in one crucial respect. For whereas organic systems cease to exist when crucial functions are not performed (i.e., organisms die), social systems may continue to exist but change their type. Thus any adequate formulation of the functionalist methodology must take account of this fact. Robert Merton (1957) has suggested that this more adequate formulation can be attained by revising certain of the basic functionalist assumptions. These are: the postulate that everything has a function; the postulate of functional integration (i.e., of some sort of natural harmony of human activities); and the postulate of functional indispensability. Instead of these assumptions Merton proposes that it should be recognized that some activities occur which have no function or are even 'dysfunctional', that what is functional from the point of view of maintaining one partial structure may be dysfunctional from the point of view of maintaining another, and that, for any particular social function, there may be more than one feasible activity.

Merton, however, implicitly takes over the language of the **organic analogy** and it is not always clear what the partial structures are in terms of whose maintenance activities are being explained. The real problems involved in functionalist explanation only become apparent when they are set out not in terms of an analogical language, but in a language appropriate to the study of social action and interaction.

What we have assumed is that the determinants of an ongoing social system are to be found in the varied and sometimes conflicting interests of the typical actors in that system. For the achievement of their goals each of these actors ideally requires certain forms of behaviour of those around him, that is to say he requires the existence of certain structures of social relations. It is in this context that we can see clearly that what is functional from the one point of view is dysfunctional from the point of view of another. Thus, to take the central problem of our text as an example, in a situation of housing shortage it will be functional from the point of view of the established residents that they should enjoy privileges in the allocation of housing. But this is highly dysfunctional from the point of view of new immigrants. ...

... we begin by considering the goals of typical actors representing the various host and immigrant groups, the various politico-economic classes and more specifically what we have called '**housing classes**'. We also refer to groups distinguished by more subtle criteria. It is out of the clash of interests, the conflicts and the truces between these groups that Birmingham society emerges.

It is important to emphasize, however, that the existence of conflicting group interests does not mean that there is a perpetual war of all against all, or of class against class, in Birmingham. If there were, Birmingham society would indeed cease to exist. What

happens in such a situation is that the various groups mobilize what power they can to enforce compliance with their wishes, but that a point is reached in the power struggle where a realistic adjustment of interests is arrived at, at least temporarily, or organizational means are established for peaceful bargaining about which aims of which group shall be realized. Thus it is possible ... to recognize the existence of some overall social system, consisting of those 'institutions of the truce' or those organizational means through which conflicts and tensions are managed. While we reject the conservative **teleology** of old-fashioned functionalism, we do not feel that there is any necessity to go to the other extreme and to posit limitless conflict.

There is another kind of integrative mechanism which serves to blur and modify conflict, of which we were profoundly aware in our study. This is that while various groups did have conflicting interests, they were also to some extent recognized as forming a status hierarchy, so that members of 'lower' groups aspired to membership of the higher. Moreover, it was the case, and usually is the case, that the associations and organizations through which the struggle of interests was fought out had historically inherited forms which modified the purposes of those who sought to use them to attain their own goals. Thus associational and communal life was organized in such a way as to blunt some of the conflicts inherent in the situation.

Our sociological perspective, then, does draw upon some of the insights of functionalism. Even though we do recognize and, indeed, emphasize conflict we recognize some kind of overall system within which behaviour has to be explained. Thus we reject the utopianism which assumes that any desired course of action can be pursued, because we recognize that actions have unintended consequences of a systematic kind, and because we recognize the existence of conflicting social pressures. And we also reject the **empiricism** of those who, having abandoned the perspective of the interconnectedness of social structure, concentrate on the analysis of single and isolated links in the causal chain. ...

On the most general level we accept the hypothesis that in modern urban industrial societies the structure of social relations is determined by a pattern of conflicting interests set up by the differential control by different groups of men of material facilities. That much is agreed by two great traditions of sociological theory, those of Marx and of Max Weber. But we agree with Max Weber when, in his analysis of the formation of classes, he gives equal consideration to ownership of domestic property and ownership of the means of industrial production (Bendix and Lipset, 1953). We do not believe that an adequate sociology of the city could be written without making this assumption. What then is the social structure which is set up by the ownership and control of housing in Birmingham?

In so far as the figures [given earlier in Rex and Moore's book] may be applied to Birmingham, there are clearly three classes of people to be found in the city. Slightly less than one-third will be owner-occupiers. Rather more than two-fifths will be tenants of private landlords. The remainder, rather less than a quarter, will be tenants of the Council. The owner-occupiers, however, will include a small proportion who share their houses with tenants and the tenants of private landlords a proportion who do not rent a whole house. Thus we may say that there are five classes produced by the system of house-ownership and allocation: (1) the outright owner-occupiers; (2) the council house tenants; (3) the tenants of whole private houses; (4) the lodging-house proprietors; and (5) the tenants of lodging-houses. Being a member of one or other of these classes is of first importance in determining a man's associations, his interests, his lifestyle, and his position in the urban social structure; moreover, each class has its own qualifications for entry.

Owner-occupiers must have certain qualifications as regards capital, amount of income and type of income. They must also qualify in advance in terms of their style of life. They must have at least enough capital for a deposit to obtain a mortgage. Their income has to be sufficiently large to convince a building society that they can make their repayments and their employment has to be sufficiently secure and regular, for the same reason. They must be capable of convincing the building society that they will keep the property which is mortgaged in reasonable condition and they must not sub-let any part of the property.

A number of categories of people are excluded from the owner-occupier class by these criteria. Many casual and unskilled workers, for example, are either unable to produce a deposit or have incomes which are too low or too irregular to make them good risks. So far as immigrants are concerned, access to the mutual aid system which operates in their own primary communities, together with their willingness to work overtime, makes it possible for some of them at least to obtain a deposit. But they are more than likely to be excluded on other grounds. The possibility of their return to their homelands and their greater vulnerability to redundancy mean that they cannot be counted as having stability of employment. And their style of life, which may involve low standards of furnishing and an obligation to house kinsmen, will exclude many others. As a consequence the number of immigrants who succeed in entering the class of owner-occupiers is small.

A council house tenancy is obtained as we have seen on grounds of need and on grounds of long residence. It also depends upon having a certain style of life and upon not having an obligation to take lodgers. Most immigrants are excluded on grounds of residence alone, but those who do qualify on these grounds are likely to be admitted only to the inferior council houses. The upper sub-class of council tenants in council-built flats and houses will include very few immigrants.

These two classes enjoy a considerable *de facto* security of tenure, even though the council tenants are in theory subject to eviction at short notice. This is not true of the remaining classes. Tenancies of whole houses owned by private landlords are increasingly difficult to obtain because of the demolition of old rented property. But even where such tenancies are available they are rarely advertised and friendship or kinship with the landlord or with neighbours may be an important criterion in the selection of these tenants. Moreover, unlike the council, private landlords do not choose their tenants on the basis of formally defined standards. The private landlord has the power to discriminate according to his own whims. Since nearly all landlords who let whole-houses are English, the overwhelming likelihood is that these tenancies will not be given to coloured immigrants.

The fourth housing possibility is that of living in and owning a lodging-house. To join this class the one requirement is that an individual should control a relatively large amount of capital and have a good prospect of a large income for a relatively short period. It is easier for an immigrant to obtain these qualifications than to acquire those which are essential for any of the three classes mentioned above. He can, by borrowing from relatives and friends, accumulate fairly large amounts of capital. He can usually give a character reference to the bank or moneylender and he can point to the prospect of a large income from rents. But these qualifications are sufficient only if the house concerned is one in which no one has a long-term interest and if it has sufficient rooms to guarantee a good rent income.

Finally, we have the housing class who need have no qualifications at all apart from their willingness to pay a high rent in relation to housing space offered during an insecure tenancy. This will include all those in employment who for one reason or another cannot obtain accommodation elsewhere, and who cannot obtain the capital to put down the deposit on a house. It will include the immigrants, many people with irregular forms of family life, and social deviants. Their relationship with their landlord is likely to be simply a market relationship. This has both advantages and disadvantages. The advantages lie in the fact that he does offer accommodation and offers it 'with no questions asked' – that is, without considering any other criteria such as colour, style of life, and even security of income. The disadvantages lie in over-crowding, high rent, lack of privacy, and an absence of any choice as to who one's neighbours shall be.

This housing class is more diverse than any other and lacks the capacity and perhaps the desire to orga-nize itself as an interest group. The discharged pris-oner, the deserted wife, the coloured immigrant, and the prostitute have little in common except their hous-ing conditions, and such groupings of tenants as emerge are more likely to be ethnic or kin-groupings than groups of tenants as such. One should perhaps add that they are also joined by fellow-residents who are not simply tenants like themselves but friends and kin of the landlord, paying only a nominal rent.

References

Bendix, R. and Lipset, S. M. (1953) *Class, Status and Power*, Glencoe: Free Press.

Kingsley Davis (1959) 'Presidential address to the American Sociological Association, 1959', *American Sociological Review*, vol. 24, no. 6, December, pp. 757–72.

Merton, R. (1957) *Social Theory and Social Structure*, Glencoe: Free Press.

Radcliffe-Brown, A. (1965) *Structure and Function in Primitive Society*, London: Cohen & West.

Key terms

The following key terms appear in the text above. They have been defined below to aid with the reading of this item.

social determinism a structural idea that social behaviour is caused (determined) by institutions rather than by free will

organic analogy a functionalist example, which likens the interdependence of society's structures to that of the organs of the human body

housing classes divisions of groups of people accord-ing to the type of house they lived in and/or were competing for

teleology another way of saying that social behaviour is pre-determined

empiricism the sociological tradition that argued for scientific measurement of social life

Questions

1 According to Rex and Moore, what are the failings of functionalist theory?

2 Why is their Weberian-influenced account thought to be more useful?

3 'What ... is the social structure which is set up by the ownership and control of housing in Birmingham?' (p. 510, column one)

4 What is the market situation of the immigrant?

Reading 17.5 **Community as cultural symbolism rather than structure**

Anthony Cohen (from) *The Symbolic Construction of Community* (1995, originally published in 1985) London: Routledge, pp. 11–16.

Editorial comments

Traditionally sociologists saw a community as all of the people within a given geographical location. It was thought that this fact alone was enough to give people a shared consciousness or way of thinking. This con-sciousness determined their actions. Cohen criticizes this view because it takes no account of the individ-ual. He argues that boundaries between communities are not simply a matter of geography but a matter of symbols or 'mental constructs'. We may not see them as factually accurate but if they are 'real' for the peo-ple who hold them they become 'reality', creating boundaries for social action. For Cohen there can be no factual reality, so we need to gain understanding of the varieties of interpretations of community.

The symbolic construction of community

Symbolism and boundary

'COMMUNITY' IS ONE of those words – like 'culture', 'myth', 'ritual', 'symbol' – bandied around in ordi-nary, everyday speech, apparently readily intelligible to speaker and listener, which, when imported into the discourse of social science, however, causes immense difficulty. Over the years it has proved to be highly resistant to satisfactory definition in **anthro-pology** and sociology, perhaps for the simple reason that all definitions contain or imply theories, and the theory of community has been very contentious. At its most extreme, the debate has thrown up **ideologically** opposed propositions which are equally untenable. For example, it used to be claimed that modernity and community are irreconcilable, that the characteristic features of community cannot survive industrialization and urbanization. It is a spurious argument for its opposition of 'community' and 'modernity' rests only upon ascribing stipulatively to community those features of social life which are supposed, by definition, to be lacking from modernity! Moreover, it is an argument which unjustifiably claims the authority of such seminal scholars as Durkheim, Weber, Tönnies and Simmel – unjustifiably because, as I shall argue, it perpetrates a misinterpretation, or highly selective reading, of these earlier writers. Others have suggested that the domination of modern social life by the state, and the essential confrontation of classes in capitalist society, have made 'community' a nostalgic, bourgeois and anachronistic concept. Once again, the argument is based entirely upon a highly particularistic and sectarian definition. However, its redundancy can be claimed not only on philosophical grounds, but also as being evident in the massive upsurge of community consciousness – in such terms as ethnicity, localism, religion, and class itself – which has swept the 'modern' world in recent years.

There is no attempt made in this book to formulate yet another definition. Rather, it is proposed to follow Wittgenstein's advice and seek not lexical meaning, but *use*. A reasonable interpretation of the word's use would seem to imply two related suggestions: that the members of a group of people (a) have something in common with each other, which (b) distinguishes them in a significant way from the members of other **putative** groups. 'Community' thus seems to imply simultaneously both similarity and difference. The word thus expresses a *relational* idea: the opposition of one community to others or to other social entities. Indeed, it will be argued that the use of the word is only occasioned by the desire or need to express such a distinction. It seems appropriate, therefore, to focus our examination of the nature of community on the element which embodies this sense of discrimination, namely, the *boundary*.

By definition, the boundary marks the beginning and end of a community. But why is such marking necessary? The simple answer is that the boundary encapsulates the identity of the community and, like the identity of an individual, is called into being by the exigencies of social interaction. Boundaries are marked because communities interact in some way or other with entities from which they are, or wish to be, distinguished (see Barth, 1969). The manner in which

they are marked depends entirely upon the specific community in question. Some, like national or administrative boundaries, may be statutory and enshrined in law. Some may be physical, expressed, perhaps, by a mountain range or a sea. Some may be racial or linguistic or religious. But not all boundaries, and not *all* the components of *any* boundary, are so objectively apparent. They may be thought of, rather, as existing in the minds of their beholders. This being so, the boundary may be perceived in rather different terms, not only by people on opposite sides of it, but also by people on the same side.

We are talking here about what the boundary means to people, or, more precisely, about the meanings they give to it. This is the *symbolic* aspect of community boundary and, in so far as we aspire to understand the importance of the community in people's experience, it is the most crucial. To say that community boundaries are largely symbolic in character is, though, not merely to suggest that they imply different meanings for different people. It also suggests that boundaries perceived by some may be utterly imperceptible to others. For example, when the 1974–79 Labour Government formulated proposals for governmental devolution to Wales and Scotland, it did so on the apparent premise that there was sufficient unanimity of attitude within each of these entities to give particular legal expression to their boundaries. But such an assumption proved to be quite unjustified. The argument went very much further than whether devolution was, or was not a good thing, or whether this power or that discretion should or should not be devolved to the new authorities. Rather, it caused people *within* these entities to question whether the boundaries as envisaged by Whitehall were those most salient to them. The question became not simply, 'Are the Scots different from the English'?, but, 'How different am I, as a particular Scot, from him, another particular Scot'? In other words, is the boundary dividing Scotland from England more meaningful to the highlander than those which distinguish him from the lowlander, the Glaswegian from the Edinburghian; the Shetlander from the Orcadian; the inhabitants of one Shetland island from those of another; the members of one township of a Shetland island from the members of another. As one goes 'down' the scale so the 'objective' referents of the boundary become less and less clear, until they may be quite invisible to those outside. But also as you go 'down' this scale, they become more important to their members for they relate to increasingly intimate areas of their lives or refer to more substantial areas of their identities.

Moreover, it is as one descends the scale that one approaches 'community' as something more than a rhetorical figment. When government leaders refer to the Common Market as a 'community', they may be regarded as indulging in rhetoric: stating an aspiration to common interest which is all too obviously missing in reality. But when the inhabitants of a Shetland island talk of 'their community', they refer to an entity, a reality, invested with all the sentiment attached to kinship, friendship, neighbouring, rivalry, familiarity, jealousy, as they inform the social process of everyday life. At this level, community is more than oratorical abstraction: it hinges crucially on consciousness.

This consciousness of community is, then, encapsulated in perception of its boundaries, boundaries which are themselves largely constituted by people in interaction. It is in part this process, the symbolic constitution of boundaries, that is referred to in the title of this book. But, in addition to recognizing the symbolic constituents of community consciousness, we have also to reveal the essentially symbolic nature of the idea of community itself, again essentially enshrined in the concept of boundary.

Boundaries enclose elements which may, for certain purposes and in certain respects, be considered to be more like each other than they are different. But they also mark off these elements from those which differ. In this regard, the boundaries of communities perform the same function as do the boundaries of all categories of knowledge. If we extract from this total cognitive stock a sub-genus, categories of *social* knowledge, we find that all such categories are marked by symbolism (see Needham, 1979). The symbolism may be explicit as, for example, in rituals which discriminate among roles, between life and death, between stages and statuses in the life cycle, between gender, between generations, between the pure and the polluted. It may be explicit in the arcane fantasy of myth and totem. But much of our symbolism does not have a special vocabulary or idiomatic behaviour: it is, rather, part of the meaning which we intuitively ascribe to more instrumental and pragmatic things in ordinary use – such as words. Philosophers have long since drawn our attention to the capacity of language to express attitude as well as to denote object. In Cranston's examples, words such as 'freedom' and 'democracy' do not merely describe forms of government and legal status. They also tell us how to regard these forms. They are 'hurrah' words, as opposed to 'boo' words (Cranston, 1954). The anthropologist, Mary Douglas, similarly shows that the use of the word 'dirt' does rather more than signify the particles which lie under the finger nail: it also expresses an attitude, 'ugh'!, and prescribes a remedy, 'scrub'! (Douglas, 1966).

Symbols, then, do more than merely stand for or represent something else. Indeed, if that was all they did, they would be redundant. They also allow those who employ them to supply part of their meaning. If we refer again to the examples of categories mentioned above, age, life, father, purity, gender, death, doctor, are all symbols shared by those who use the same language, or participate in the same symbolic behaviour through which these categories are expressed and marked. But their meanings are *not* shared in the same way. Each is mediated by the idiosyncratic experience of the individual. When I think about 'fatherhood', my reflections on paternity in general are informed by *my* experience of *my* father and of *my* children. Were I, a Scot, voting in the devolution referendum, I should not merely have measured myself against the English, but would refract 'Scottishness' through my personal experience – as Shetland fisherman, Kincardine farmer, Fife miner or Clydeside shipbuilder, father, son, brother, agnostic, music lover, socialist, and so forth. Symbols do not so much express meaning as give us the capacity to make meaning.

Not *all* social categories are so variable in meaning. But those whose meanings are the most elusive, the hardest to pin down, tend to be those also hedged around by the most ambiguous symbolism. In these cases the content of the categories is so unclear that they exist largely or only in terms of their symbolic boundaries. Such categories as justice, goodness, patriotism, duty, love, peace, are almost impossible to spell out with precision. The attempt to do so invariably generates argument, sometimes worse. But their *range* of meanings can be glossed over in a commonly accepted symbol precisely because it allows its adherents to attach their own meanings to it. They share the symbol, but do not necessarily share its meanings. Community is just such a boundary-expressing symbol. As a symbol, it is held in common by its members; but its meaning varies with its members' unique orientations to it. In the face of this variability of meaning, the consciousness of community has to be kept alive through manipulation of its symbols. The reality and efficacy of the community's boundary – and, therefore, of the community itself – depends upon its symbolic construction and embellishment. ...

Symbolism and meaning

'If you live in Shinohata', wrote Ronald Dore, 'the "outside world" begins three hundred yards down the road ...' (Dore, 1978). We do not have to construe community just in terms of locality, but more properly, in the sense which Dore expresses so lucidly and describes with such affectionate evocation of the Japanese village he studied at intervals for twenty-five years: the sense of a primacy of belonging. Community is that entity to which one belongs, greater than kinship but more immediately than the abstraction we call 'society'. It is the arena in which people acquire their most fundamental and most substantial experience of social life outside the confines of the home. In it they learn the meaning of kinship through being able to perceive *its* boundaries – that is, by juxtaposing it to non-kinship; they learn 'friendship'; they acquire the sentiments of close social association and the capacity to express or otherwise manage these in their social relationships. Community, therefore, is where one learns and continues to practice how to 'be social'. At the risk of substituting one indefinable category for another, we could say it is where one acquires 'culture'.

Learning to be social is not like learning grammar or the Highway Code. It is not reducible to a body of rules. Of course, one can identify rule-like principles in culture. Thus, for example, we can say that the Temne of Sierra Leone reserve the right hand to upper bodily behaviour; the left, to cope with the lower body (Littlejohn, 1972). We could make a similarly generalized statement in suggesting that the Whalsay Islanders of Shetland avoid open dispute or the public assertion of opinion (Cohen, 1977). These 'principles' are sufficiently observed in practice that their contravention would identify the perpetrator as outsider or as deviant. They differ from more objective rules, however, in that they are not associated unambiguously, nor even obviously, with a fixed and shared rationale. The Temne might well discriminate between left- and right-handedness, but this is not to say that they all do so for the same reason, nor

for any 'conscious' reason, nor that they would accept the interpretations of their behaviour offered by Littlejohn's supposedly authoritative informant. People attach their own meanings to such prescriptions and proscriptions. In this respect, they are less *rules* of society than its symbols. Thus, when we speak of people acquiring culture, or learning to be social, we mean that they acquire the symbols which will equip them to be social.

This symbolic equipment might be compared to vocabulary. Learning words, acquiring the components of language, gives you the capacity to communicate with other people, but does not tell you *what* to communicate. Similarly with symbols: they do not tell us *what* to mean, but give us the capacity to make meaning. Culture, constituted by symbols, does not impose itself in such a way as to determine that all its adherents should make the same sense of the world. Rather, it merely gives them the capacity to make sense and, if they tend to make a similar kind of sense it is not because of any deterministic influence but because they are doing so with the same symbols. The quintessential referent of community is that its members make, or believe they make, a similar sense of things either generally or with respect to specific and significant interests, and, further, that they think that that sense may differ from one made elsewhere. The reality of community in people's experience thus inheres in their attachment or commitment to a common body of symbols.

References

Barth, F. (1969) *Ethnic Groups and Boundaries*, London: Allen & Unwin.

Cohen, A. (1977) 'For a political ethnography of everyday life', *Ethnos*, 3–4.

Cranston, M. (1954) *Freedom: a new analysis*, London: Longman.

Dore, R. (1978) *Shinohota: Portrait of a Japanese village*, New York: Pantheon.

Douglas, M. (1966) *Purity and Danger*, London: Routledge & Kegan Paul.

Littlejohn, J. (1972) *Right and Left*, London: University of Chicago Press.

Needham, R. (1979) *Symbolic Classification*, Santa Monica: Goodyear Publishing.

Key terms

The following key terms appear in the text above. They have been defined below to aid with the reading of this item.

anthropology the study of the culture and social organization of human groups, usually in non-industrial societies and usually adopting ethnography as the research method

ideologically relating to ideas based on theoretical or philosophical standpoints rather than objective reality

putative supposed or 'defined' groups

Questions

1 Why study 'community'?

2 Why does Cohen concentrate on *using* the word community rather than *defining* it?

3 Why should *boundaries* between people be seen as symbolic, subjective and perceived, rather than objective and scientifically clear?

4 What is the purpose of *boundaries*?

Reading 17.6 **A critique of 'communitarian utopianism'**

David Harvey (from) 'Cities or urbanisation', in *City* journal (1996) issue 1/2, January, London: City Editorial, pp. 38–41 and 54–6.

Editorial comments

David Harvey is one of the most important urban sociologists of the last twenty years. Influenced by Marxist theories of ownership and control in capitalist society and post-modern theories of flexible post-Fordist production processes, he has aimed to explain how urban areas change. In this reading he acknowledges the claims of many, that urban processes create challenges of numerous kinds, but argues that they can't be solved by the application of idealistic manifestos such as those advocated by communitarians. Communitarians argue that urban problems result from a loss of community, but Harvey feels that communities can be part of the problem. The answer lies in accepting difference and providing a public voice for all groups inhabiting the city.

Cities or urbanization?

AT THE BEGINNING of this century, there were no more than a dozen or so cities in the world with more than a million people. They were all in the advanced capitalist countries and London, by far the largest of them all, had just under seven million. At the beginning of this century, too, no more than seven per cent of the world's population could reasonably be classified as 'urban'. By the year 2000 there may well be as many as 500 cities with more than a million inhabitants while the largest of them, Tokyo, São Paulo, Bombay and possibly Shanghai, will boast populations of more than twenty million, trailed by a score of cities, mostly in the so-called developing countries, with upwards of ten million. Some time early next century, if present trends continue, more than half of the world's population will be classified as urban rather than rural.

The twentieth century has been, then, *the* century of urbanization. Before 1800 the size and numbers of urban concentrations in all social formations seem to have been strictly limited. The nineteenth century saw the breach of those barriers in a few advanced capitalist countries, but the latter half of the twentieth century has seen that localized breach turned into a universal flood of massive urbanization. The future of most of humanity now lies, for the first time in history, fundamentally in urbanizing areas. The qualities of urban living in the twenty-first century will define the qualities of civilization itself.

But judging superficially by the present state of the world's cities, future generations will not find that civilization particularly congenial. Every city has its share (often increasing and in some instances predominant) of concentrated impoverishment and human hopelessness, of malnourishment and chronic diseases, of crumbling or stressed out infrastructures, of senseless and wasteful consumerism, of ecological degradation and excessive pollution, of congestion, of seemingly stymied economic and human development, and of sometimes bitter social strife, varying from individualized violence on the streets to organized crime (often an alternative form of urban governance), through police state exercises in social control to massive civic protest movements (sometimes spontaneous) demanding political-economic change. For many, then, to talk of the city of the twenty-first century is to conjure up a **dystopian** nightmare in which all that is judged worst in the fatally flawed character of humanity collects together in some hell-hole of despair.

In some of the advanced capitalist countries, that dystopian vision has been strongly associated with the long-cultivated habit on the part of those with power and privilege of running as far from the city centres as possible. Fuelled by a permissive car culture, the urge to get some money and get out has taken command. Liverpool's population fell by 40 per cent between 1961 and 1991, for example, and Baltimore City's fell from close to a million to under 700,000 in the same three decades. But the upshot has been not only to create endless suburbanization, so-called 'edge cities', and sprawling megalopoli, but also to make every village and every rural retreat in the advanced capitalist world part of a complex web of urbanization that defies any simple categorization of populations into 'urban' and 'rural' in that sense which once upon a time could reasonably be accorded to those terms.

The haemorrhaging of wealth, population and power from central cities has left many of them languishing in limbo. Needy populations have been left behind as the rich and influential have moved out. Add to this the devastating loss of jobs (particularly in manufacturing) in recent years and the parlous state of the older cities becomes all too clear. Nearly 250,000 manufacturing jobs have been lost in Manchester in two decades while 40,000 disappeared from Sheffield's steel industry alone in just three short catastrophic years in the mid 1980s. Baltimore likewise lost nearly 200,000 manufacturing jobs from the late 1960s onwards and there is hardly a single city in the United States that has not been the scene of similar devastation through deindustrialization.

The subsequent train of events has been tragic for many. Communities built to service now defunct manufacturing industries have been left high and dry, wracked with long-term structural unemployment. Disenchantment, dropping out, and quasi-legal means to make ends meet follow. Those in power rush to blame the victims, the police powers move in (often insensitively) and the politician-media complex has a field day stigmatizing and stereotyping an underclass of idle wrongdoers, irresponsible single parents and feckless fathers, debasement of family values, welfare junkies, and much worse. If those marginalized happen to be an ethnic or racially marked minority, as is all too often the case, then the stigmatization amounts to barely concealed racial bigotry. The only rational response on the part of those left marginalized is urban rage, making the actual state of social and, even more emphatically, race relations (for all the campus rhetoric on political correctness) far worse now than it has been for several decades.

But is this a universal tale of urban woe I tell? Or is it something rather more confined to the specific legacies of old-style capitalist industrialization and the cultural predilections of the anti-urban Anglo-Saxon way of life? Central cities throughout continental Europe are, for example, undergoing a singular revival. And such a trend is not merely confined to a few centres, like Paris with its longstanding process of embourgeoisement accelerated by all the *grands projets* for which the French are justly famous. From Barcelona to Hamburg to Turin to Lille, the flow of population and affluence back into the city centres is marked. But, on inspection, all this really signifies is that the same problematic divisions get geographically reversed. It is the periphery that is hurting and the soulless *banlieu* of Paris and Lyon that have become the centres of riot and disaffection, of racial discrimination and harassment, of deindustrialization and social decay. And if we look more closely at what has been happening in the Anglo-Saxon world, the evidence suggests a dissolution of that simple 'doughnut' urban form of inner city decay surrounded by suburban affluence (made so much of in the late 1960s), and its replacement by a complex checkerboard of segregated and protected wealth in an urban soup of equally segregated impoverishment and decay. The unjustly infamous 'outer estates' of Glasgow are interspersed with affluent commuter suburbs and the now emerging socio-economic problems

of the inner suburbs in many US cities have forced the wealthy seeking security either further out (the urbanization of the remotest countryside then follows) or into segregated and often highly protected zones wherever they can best be set up. ...

The corporate enemy has largely moved out of town and corporations don't seem to need cities or particular communities any more. The upshot is to leave the fate of the cities almost entirely at the mercy of real estate developers and speculators, office builders and finance capital. And the bourgeoisie, though still mortally afraid of crime, drugs, and all the other ills that plague the cities, is now seemingly content to seal itself off from all of that in urban or (more likely) suburban and exurban gated communities suitably immunized (or so it believes) from any long-term threats, secure in the knowledge that urban protests can be repressed by main force and so never become real revolutions. Having lost the fear of imminent revolution that so preoccupied the nineteenth-century bourgeois, all that is left is an occasional shiver of media-instilled fear as the riots taking place on the other side of town play live on television screens in terrifyingly comfortable living rooms. ...

Faced, for example, with the innumerable problems and threats that urban life today poses, many analysts have reached for some simple solution – to try and turn large and teeming cities, so seemingly out of control, into **urban villages** where, it is believed, everyone can relate in a civil fashion to everyone else in an urbane and gentle environment. ...

Many contemporary analysts, post Herbert Gans's study on *The Urban Villagers* (1962), believe that cities are mainly constituted as collections of urban villages anyway. Jencks (1993) thinks that even Los Angeles can be dissolved into twenty-eight townships and Peter Hall, while admitting the whole idea sounds a bit banal, can cheerfully assert the fundamental truth that London is indeed a collection of villages. In Britain, Prince Charles leads the way on this emotional charger with his emphasis upon the urban village as the locus of urban regeneration. And he is followed in this by a whole host of people across the political and social spectrum, attracting support from marginalized ethnic populations and impoverished and embattled working-class populations as well as from the upper-class nostalgics who think of it all as a civilized form of real estate development encompassing sidewalk cafés, pedestrian precincts and Laura Ashley shops. It is never clear, of course, where the big and dirty industries might go (or, for that matter, where the great 'unwashed and unwanted' might reside). And all those things that make cities so exciting – the unexpected, the conflicts and the adrenaline surge that comes with exploring the urban unknown – will be tightly controlled and screened out with the big signs that say 'no deviant behaviour accepted here'.

No matter; the idea of the urban village or of some kind of communitarian solution to urban problems is both attractive and powerful (judging by the innumerable books and articles devoted to the subject). And it is so not only because of nostalgia for some long-lost mythical world of intimate village life, ignoring the fact that most of the populist migration out of villages arose precisely because they were so oppressive to the human spirit and so otiose as a form of socio-political organization. It also appeals because some mythical social entity called 'community' can perhaps be re-created in an urban village and 'community spirit' and 'community solidarity' is, we are again and again urged to believe, what will rescue us from the deadening world of social dissolution, grab-it-yourself materialism and individualized selfish market-oriented greed that lies at the root of all urban ills. The Christian base community concept, for example, vital brainchild of the now vastly constrained theology of liberation, is even brought into Baltimore as the solution to urban problems (McDougall, 1993).

This ideal would not have the purchase it does were there no truth at all to it. My own guess is that the only things stopping riots or total social breakdown in many cities are the intricate networks of social solidarities, the power and dedication of community organizations, and the hundreds of voluntary groups working round the clock to restore some sense of decency and pride in an urbanizing world shell-shocked by rapid change, unemployment, massive migrations and all of the radical travails inflicted by capitalist modernity passing into the nihilistic downside of postmodernity.

But community has always meant different things to different people and, even when something that looks like it can be found, it often turns out to be as much a part of the problem as a panacea. Well-founded communities can exclude, define themselves against others, erect all sorts of keep-out signs (if not tangible walls). As Young (1990) has uncompromisingly pointed out:

> Racism, ethnic chauvinism, and class devaluation, I suggest, grow partly from the desire for community, that is from the desire to understand others as they understand themselves and from the desire to be understood as I understand myself. Practically speaking, such mutual understanding can be approximated only within a homogeneous group that defines itself by common attributes. Such common identification, however, entails reference also to those excluded. In the dynamics of racism and ethnic chauvinism in the United States today,

the positive identification of some groups is often achieved by first defining other groups as the other, the devalued semihuman.

What is at work here is (a) a mythic belief that a 'thing' called community can be created as some free-standing and autonomous entity endowed with causative and salving powers (b) the belief that the qualities of this 'thing' can be internally defined in a manner that can be isolated from 'others' and 'outsiders', and (c) a belief that external relations are contingent and occasional rather than integral and continuous.

A more **dialectical view** would have it that entities like communities, while not without significance, cannot be understood independently of the social processes that generate, sustain and also dissolve them and that it is those social processes that are fundamental to social change. By this I do not mean to assert that the construction of a certain kind of spatio-temporal form designated as 'community' can have no relevance or interest (for it often is, as Young asserts, a way to advance racist, classist and ethnico-religious exclusionism as well as, on occasion, a source of comfort and sustenance in the face of adversity and a zone of political empowerment). But by abstracting from the dialectic of thing-process relations, our vision of the possibilities for social action becomes so restricted as frequently to be self-nullifying if not self-destructive to the initial aims, however well intentioned (as, for example, in the case of trying to import the ideal of Christian base communities as panacea for the conditions of deprivation and marginalization experienced by the African American population in Baltimore). There are, it seems to me, far better ways to understand the relations between 'community' and social processes by translating the whole issue into one of the dialectics of space-place relations as one aspect of the overall production of spatio-temporality integral to social processes. The idea that the Greek 'communitas' or the medieval village can somehow be rebuilt in Bombay or São Paulo from that standpoint appears little less than absurd. This is, I would submit, no way to substitute for the much more tricky problem of creating a politics of heterogeneity and a domain of publicness that stretches across the diverse spatio-temporalities of contemporary urbanized living. As Young (1990) puts it: 'If city politics is to be democratic and not dominated by the point of view of one group, it must be a politics that takes account of and provides voice for the different groups that dwell together in the city without forming a community'.

References

Gans, H. (1962) *The Urban Village*, New York: Free Press.

Jencks, C. (1993) *Heteropolis*, London: Academy Editions.

McDougall, H. (1993) *Black Baltimore*, Philadelphia: Temple University Press.

Young, I. M. (1990) *Justice and the Politics of Difference*, Princeton: Princeton University Press.

Key terms

The following key terms appear in the text above. They have been defined below to aid with the reading of this item.

dystopian relating to a 'nightmare' vision of the future

urban villages the idea that community, which Tönnies and others saw decline with urbanization, can exist in sub-areas of the city. This was an idea first put forward by Herbert Gans in the book *The Urban Villagers* (1962)

dialectical view the idea that new things arise from the clash of opposites

Questions

1 Why call the twentieth century the 'century of urbanization'?

2 How have urban areas changed in the latter half of the century?

3 Why describe urban areas as a 'checker-board' or 'urban soup'?

4 What are the strengths and weaknesses of communitarian analyses of urban life?

Reading 17.7 **The Californian School**

Edward W. Soja (from) 'Los Angeles 1965–1992: from crisis-generated restructuring to restructuring-generated crisis', in Scott, A. J. and Soja, E. W., *The City: Los Angeles and urban theory at the end of the twentieth century* (1996) Berkley, Los Angeles and London: University of California Press, pp. 432–6, 438–46 and 448–54.

Editorial comments

As a city undergoing post-modernity, Los Angeles has been singled out for special attention in recent urban sociology, particularly by the Californian School. Soja, one of the leading lights of the School, argues that Los Angeles has continually re-structured itself to meet the challenge of global economic, demographic, and social re-structuring. He identifies six key changes to the city. Although they have happened to other major cities he argues that they are more obvious in Los Angeles, making it worthy of special study.

Los Angeles, 1965–1992

AS ANOTHER SEVERE recession hit urban America (1979–1982) and Reaganomics began to take hold, Los Angeles was 'discovered' by a group of local urban analysts who sought to construct in their studies not only a deeper understanding of what was happening in Los Angeles but also a picture of how these local developments might provide insight into the changes taking place in the regional, national, and global economies. *Urban restructuring* was the central theme of this new literature on the greater Los Angeles region. In the decade from 1982 to 1992, it would generate more significant scholarly writings on Los Angeles than had been produced in the preceding two centuries.

The most influential discovery shaping this new literature came from the realization that the urban region of Los Angeles had developed from the 1920s as one of the world's largest industrial growth poles, that those distracting dream factories of Hollywood stood amid what was becoming the largest manufacturing city in North America. That this industrial expansion was continuing apace during a period of extensive deindustrialization elsewhere intensified the challenge of making practical and theoretical sense of the apparently anomalous Los Angeles experience. Between 1970 and 1980, the entire country experienced a net addition of less than a million manufacturing jobs and New York lost well over 300,000, triggering descriptions of wholesale industrial decline and the rise of '**postindustrial**' society. In the same decade, however, the far from *post*-industrial Los Angeles region added 225,000 new manufacturing jobs, as well as 1,300,000 people and an even larger number of total jobs in all categories of employment. How could this extraordinary countercurrent be explained? Why had it been so invisible for so long?

What impact was it having on the local economy? Was this industrialization in Los Angeles merely a continuation of postwar trends, or was it taking new forms and directions? How could this aggregate picture of a booming regional economy be reconciled with increasing local indications of intensifying poverty, unemployment, and homelessness?

These and other questions initiated an empirical and theoretical exploration of the dynamics of urban restructuring in Los Angeles that was attuned to the particularities of the regional context and, at the same time, connected to more general debates on the changing organization of the national and global political economies. Reflecting the spatial perspective that has informed much of this urban restructuring research, its findings can be summarized around six 'geographies', each representing an important dimension of accelerated urban change as well as a particular approach to interpreting the 'new' Los Angeles that took shape in the period between 1965 and 1992. As will become evident here ... the study of urban restructuring has expanded well beyond the initial focus on industrial change to raise issues of much broader local and global significance.

Exopolis: the restructuring of urban form

Los Angeles has been participating in the redefinition of urban form throughout the twentieth century. The classic model of urban form, built primarily around the nineteenth-century industrial capitalist city, presented a monocentric picture of increasing geographic regularity patterned by the dynamics of employment and residential agglomeration. Everything revolved around the singular city centre. From its peak densities of population, jobs, and fixed capital investment rippled concentric zonations of residential land use, household composition, and family life. Stretching these concentricities outward were radial sectors that developed particular cross-cutting specializations: zones of industry and commerce, usually one high-income residential area extending from the centre to the suburban fringe, and one or more working-class zones, typically associated with tightly segregated communities of racial and ethnic minorities. Cities that had grown large before the nineteenth-century surge in urban industrialization displayed much less regularity, but even in these cases regularities could be found by those who assiduously searched for them.

From its first major urban boom in the late nineteenth century, Los Angeles seemed to have a **morphological** mind of its own. The classic urban forms were never entirely absent, and glimmerings of them are discoverable even today, but from the beginning the Los Angeles urban fabric took on a very different texture. Although the centrality of downtown Los Angeles has been recognizable for more than two hundred years, the surrounding urban region grew as a fragmented and decentred metropolis, a patchwork quilt of low-density suburban communities stretching over an extraordinarily irregular terrain of mountains, valleys, beaches, and deserts. Both tying the fabric together and giving it its unusual elasticity was first a remarkable network of interurban electric railways and then an even more remarkable freeway system, each visibly focused on the downtown node but spinally tapping a multiplicity of increasingly outlying centres and peripheries. ...

By 1992, the sprawling regional metropolis had filled in most of a sixty-mile circle drawn around the downtown Civic Center, encompassing the builtup area of five counties and a constellation of more than 160 cities and municipalities. With a population approaching 15 million, Los Angeles today has become one of the world's largest 'megacities' (another of the many new terms devised to capture contemporary urbanization trends) and was rapidly catching up to the three other megacities of the so-called First World: Tokyo, New York, and London.

This growth was marked by continued *decentralization* of residential population, industrial establishments, corporate offices, and retail activities into the outer reaches of the sixty-mile circle, following trends established in nearly all North American cities since the end of the nineteenth century. But between 1965 and 1992, this decentralization seemed to break out from its conventional metropolitan boundaries. As before, manufacturing and office development in particular moved outward through the concentric rings and along sectoral zones into satellite cities and suburban green spaces. But increasingly, they burst out even further to fuel what, after the 1980 census, was called (somewhat prematurely, it now seems) the 'great non-metropolitan turnaround', when for the first time in US history, small towns and nonmetropolitan counties grew more rapidly than either the central cities or the suburban rings. The suburbs at least were able to rebound in the 1980s (more on this in a moment), but what became clearer was that the scale and scope of decentralization was becoming increasingly *globalized*, that American manufacturing was not only leaving its metropolitan concentrations, it was leaving the country entirely. This meant that the dynamics shaping urban form could no longer be seen as confined within the metropolitan space, even when expanded to include the larger national system of cities. The local was becoming global more than ever before, and this was demanding new ways of understanding the 'specificity' of the urban.

The restructuring of Los Angeles exemplified all of these decentralization trends. At the same time as decentralization was occurring, however, there was another major development that was reshaping urban form in Los Angeles and many other metropolitan regions even more dramatically, a *recentralization* process that would place much greater stress on the traditional conceptual frameworks of urban analysis. The primary form of this recentralization can be described most simply as peripheral urbanization or the urbanization of suburbia ...

At the simplest descriptive level, peripheral urbanization refers to the growth of cities in suburbia, the increasing concentration of jobs, factories, offices, shopping centres, entertainment and cultural activities, heterogeneous populations, new immigrants, gangs, crime, and a host of other attributes once thought to be specifically urban in areas that never before had experienced such intensive agglomeration. In recent years, this urbanization of suburbia has triggered a burst of descriptive invention to provide a vocabulary commensurate with the new forms taking shape, with what some have described as 'the city turned inside out'. Counterurbanization and the growth of Outer Cities are perhaps now the most widely used terms, but the list of alternatives is expanding: postsuburbia, edge cities, urban villages, metroplex, technopoles, technoburbs, technopolis.

Drawing particularly on the Los Angeles experience, I have added another summative term, 'Exopolis', literally the 'city without' in the double sense of the expanding Outer (vs. the Inner) City as well as the city that no longer is, the ex-city. This double meaning signals an explicit attack on our conventional usage of the terms urban, suburban, exurban, and nonurban to describe divisions within contemporary metropolitan areas. As geographic restructuring works increasingly to blur these distinctions, we must not only revamp our vocabulary but also reconceptualize the very nature of urban studies, to see urban form more as a complex and polycentric regional mosaic of geographically uneven development affecting and affected by local, national, and global forces and influences. ...

Flexcities: the changing geography of production

Accompanying the changing **urban morphology** of Los Angeles have been substantial shifts in the urban social division of labour and in the corporate organization and technology of industrial production. This important link between industrial restructuring and the restructuring of urban form has been a key focus for much of the new literature on Los Angeles. It has also contributed to a changing emphasis within urban studies more generally and in the practices of urban and regional planning. For most of this century, urban analysis and urban planning have given primary attention to matters of collective consumption: housing, the

provision of social services, public welfare policies and anti-poverty programmes, the development of mass transit systems, land use regulation, and the emergence of urban social movements around these issues. Today, more and more attention (in money, time, and effort) is being given to the production side of the urban economy and to such questions as how to attract new businesses to stem economic decline and contend with the larger forces of global economic restructuring.

Academic analyses of this powerful relation between industrial and urban restructuring have hinged around a pronounced shift in industrial organization and technology from the Fordist-Keynesian practices of mass production and mass consumption that dominated the postwar economic boom in the United States to what is increasingly described today as a post-Fordist system of flexible production and corporate development that has been at the forefront of urban economic restructuring since at least 1965. Fordist mass production was rooted in dedicated assembly lines and vertically integrated production systems feeding off increasing internal economies of scale that were sustainable only by huge oligopolistic corporations engaged in a relatively stable social contract with the largest trade unions and a federal government dedicated to priming the consumption pump of the national economy through Keynesian practices of demand stimulation and social welfare provision. ...

[The] new regime is characterized by more flexible (vs. hierarchical) production systems located in transactions-intensive clusterings of predominantly small and middle-sized firms intertwined to achieve increasing 'external' economies of scope through complex subcontracting arrangements, improved inventory control, the use of numerically controlled (i.e., computerized) machinery, and other techniques that allow for easier responses to market signals, especially in times of economic recession and intensified global competition. With the increasing disintegration of the postwar social contract through union-busting, wage give-backs, corporate restructuring, government withdrawal from most sectors of the economy (with the major exception of the defence industry), and the weakening of the federally sustained welfare safety net (signaling what some have described as a shift from the welfare state to the warfare state), traditional Fordism was no longer sustainable at its former level.

The result of all this was a complex process of unprecedented *deindustrialization* linked to an initially experimental but increasingly focused *reindustrialization* that has had significant repercussions on the regional economic geography of America. Sunrise industries and the growing Sun Belt contrasted with the setting sun of heavy industrial Fordism in the Frost

Belt signalled one of the most dramatic regional role reversals in US history ...

For most of the period between 1965 and 1992 ... a process of post-Fordist industrial development ... was rapidly reconstituting the regional economy in at least three different ways. Receiving the most analytical and popular attention was the development of the 'technopoles' of Southern California, the high-technology-based complexes of industrial estates, research and development offices, and supportive business services that propelled the growth of the Outer Cities and clustered around them what is reputed to be the world's largest urban concentration of engineers, physical scientists, mathematicians, computer technicians, and military weapons specialists. It is no surprise that Los Angeles became one of the 'textbook' cases for studying the new pathways of post-Fordist industrialization and regional development.

While the technopoles have spun their eddies of industrial growth primarily in the Outer (Flex) Cities, two other forms of flexible specialization have sustained the redevelopment of the Inner City and especially downtown Los Angeles. The first revolves around craft-based production networks and the dense clustering of many small and middle-sized firms highly adaptive to national and global market signals and changes in style and consumer preferences; while the second is built primarily on the provision of specialized financial services and technologically advanced communications and information processing. For each, the Inner City of Los Angeles has been particularly receptive.

Cosmopolis: globalization and world city formation

Central to the transformation of Los Angeles has been an expansive internationalization process that accelerated after the major changes in federal immigration policy that took place in that turning point year of 1965. It has compressed within the region the most culturally heterogeneous population of investors, entrepreneurs, workers, and families any city has ever seen. Perhaps as many as 5 million migrants have moved to Los Angeles since 1965, with the vast majority coming from the Latin American and Asian countries of the Pacific Rim. Accompanying this immigration has been an equally global and heterogeneous inflow of capital investment, especially from Japan, Canada, the European Economic Community, the East Asian NICs (newly industrialized countries), and the oil-rich states of the Middle East. Together these flows of labour and capital have probably been more responsible than any other restructuring process for the continued economic growth of the region and the radical changes that have taken place in the regional built environment and the character of everyday urban life.

If the industrially restructured Exopolis has turned the city inside out, the new Cosmopolis has turned it outside in again in a far-reaching **globalization** of the local, a process that has given birth to a new term: '**glocalization**'. After years of relatively unsuccessful local promotion, the development of downtown Los Angeles accelerated dramatically in the 1970s with the influx of foreign capital and the availability of a cheap, unorganized, and seemingly limitless supply of immigrant workers. For the first time, a high-profile central city appeared that was almost commensurable with the size and complexity of the regional economy. Although still far from the heights and densities of Manhattan or Chicago's Loop, downtown development in Los Angeles more directly reflected the effects of economic and cultural glocalization. Its specific geography was split in two, with a half-city of First World skyscrapers and financial power standing starkly above a half-city of Third World cultures and street scenes. ...

[A] corona of diverse ethnic communities ... surrounds and sustains the downtown financial, commercial, and government complex. This inner ring is the heartland of the Los Angeles Cosmopolis, a special type of **world city** where the very nature of urban cosmopolitanism, glocalization, and modern world cityness is currently being redefined.

In this ring of ethni-cities is a dazzling constellation of global cultures that simultaneously reaches out to every corner of the world and draws into Los Angeles an amazing array of 'foreign' influences. It also provides an unusually rich testing ground for urban multiculturalism and what can be described as the new cultural politics of identity and difference, far removed from the imagic melting pot of Anglofying Americanization. ...

The list of separate cultural worlds microcosmed in what Charles Jencks has called the 'heteropolis' of Los Angeles seems endless, but there is still another dimension to this complex panorama of urban multiculturalism, a growing cultural syncretism that may prove to be the most important new development arising from the contemporary Cosmopolis. ... Multiform 'composite' cultures are slowly taking shape and expressing their admixture on the local landscape and daily life: in the creation of new cuisines, designs, clothing, and styles of popular art and music; and in the development of new cultural and political identities. Los Angeles, for example, has been a major centre for the assertion of Latino identity (vs. such imposed categories as Hispanic or Spanish-speaking) as a means of uniting the diverse populations whose homelands stretch from Cape Horn to the Rio Grande. Even greater heterogeneity is being synthesized in the growth of Asian-American identity, with Los Angeles again taking a leading role. Many other forms of cross-cultural fusion and coalition building are taking place in the schools and neighbourhoods, in community organizations and housing projects, in local government and cultural festivals, in ways that we are only beginning to recognize and understand. ...

Splintered labyrinth: the repolarized metropolis

Paralleling the spatial structure of the globalized post-Fordist Exopolis is a social and economic structure that has become increasingly fluid, fragmented, decentred, and rearranged in ways that differ significantly from the old class-divided city of the bourgeoisie and proletariat; the neatly apportioned hierarchical city of the wealthy, the middle class, and the poor; and the 'two Americas' city of black versus white that was described in the aftermath of the 1960s urban insurrections. This polychotomous segmentation and repolarization has begun to reconstitute the extremes of wealth and poverty and derigidify the social boundaries of class, race, and income grouping, challenging our old ways of understanding the sociology of urbanism.

There are now, for example, more millionaires than ever before in Los Angeles, many constituting a reserve army of the wealthy that includes rock stars and baseball players, computer software specialists and real estate agents, hairdressers and employment headhunters, drug dealers and dentists, as well as thousands of home owners who were lucky enough to buy at the right time in the right place. Never before has the top 10 per cent of the income ladder been so heterogeneous, so segmented, and so politically unpredictable. And in many ways, the same can be said for the bottom 20 per cent, which now contains representatives from the same occupations and backgrounds as the millionaires and displays much the same political unpredictability.

As is by now clear, urban restructuring in Los Angeles deepened poverty even under conditions of rapid regional economic growth and job generation. As many as 80,000 people are now homeless on any given night in the region, and perhaps three times as many are homeless at some point in the average year. But this is only the most visible tip of an iceberg of extreme poverty that broadens into a population of well more than half a million living precariously in housing conditions little better than those of the worst Third World squatter settlements and shantytowns, a situation that has created what is arguably the most severe urban housing crisis in America. Many of the more than 1.3 million living below the poverty line in LA County in 1989 (the numbers have increased dramatically since then) are unemployed and welfare dependent, an unquestionable core of what urban sociologists and policy makers have recently begun to call the 'permanent urban underclass'. But just as many, perhaps more, are part of the rapidly growing and primarily Latino contingent of the working poor, often labouring for well more than forty hours a week at more than one job for wages that are insufficient to feed and clothe a family.

A perverse symbiosis has developed between the extremes of wealth and poverty in Los Angeles, each feeding the growth of the other. Occasionally, the perversity is exposed in startling ways, as in several clear cases of what can only be called slavery. Immigrants from Indonesia, China, and Central America have been imported (in one case as 'entertainers' with cultural visas) and sold to wealthy households as live-in domestic servants. Their passports are kept by their 'owners' who provide limited room and board for their services. This new slavery, however, is just one step below what is present in the sweatshops and many other businesses (and households), where undocumented workers are paid subliminal wages at often hazardous worksites and under the constant threat of deportation. The bottom of the poverty iceberg and the new urban social division of labour is indeed broad and deep.

The great Los Angeles job machine has had a 'missing middle', bifurcating instead into a small stream of high-paying jobs feeding the new technocracy and a raging torrent of low-wage work (much also involved in feeding the new technocracy) that barely deserves the adjective *subsistence*. This multivalent polarization is no longer easily definable by simple racial, ethnic, occupational, class, or immigrant status categories and binary oppositions. ...

Unending eyes: revamping the Carceral City

The new topography of race, class, gender, age, income, and ethnicity has produced an incendiary urban geography in Los Angeles, a landscape filled with violent edges, colliding turfs, unstable boundaries, peculiarly juxtaposed lifespaces, and enclaves of outrageous wealth and despair. How this immanently conflagratory metropolis was kept from socially exploding until 1992 is wound up in the development of the Carceral City, a geography of warlike fortification and enclosure, of ever-watchful surveillance and creative means of social and spatial control, a place where *police* has become an insistent substitute for *polis*. Provocative descriptions of the Carceral City feature prominently in Mike Davis's *City of Quartz*, probably the best and most widely read of all the books to have been written about contemporary Los Angeles. Merely listing some of the chapter headings and topic outlines of *City of Quartz* provides a telling synopsis of the history and geography of the Carceral City.

Most direct is chapter 4, 'Fortress LA', a *tour de*

force through the built environment of security-obsessed urbanism. Its headings include 'The Destruction of Public Space' (described as a 'security offensive' to meet 'the middle-class demand for increased spatial and social insulation'); 'The Forbidden City' ('taking the form of a brutal architectural edge or glacis that defines the new Downtown as a citadel'); 'Sadistic Street Environments' ('hardening the city surface against the poor', with bum-proof bus benches, absent public lavatories, razor-wire protected trash bins, and overhead sprinkler systems that work randomly through the night to discourage sidewalk sleepers); 'Frank Gehry as Dirty Harry' (on the fortresslike 'stealth houses' of this leading LA architect); 'The Panopticon Mall' (from the 'mall-as-panopticon-prison' to the 'housing-project-as-strategic-hamlet'); 'From Rentacop to Robocop' (the 'frenetic effort' of affluent neighbourhoods to 'insulate home values and lifestyles' in **gated communities**, 'high-tech castles', 'belligerent lawns', and the 'voracious consumption of private security services'); 'The LAPD as Space Police' (the LAPD's Star Wars-like 'metamorphosis into a techno-police'); 'The Carceral City' (honing in on the prisons around downtown that contain 'the largest incarcerated population in the nation'), and finally, 'The Fear of Crowds' (on the increasing attempts to control or prevent all public gatherings and to erase the last vestiges of public space). ...

The policed metropolis is augmented by the quieter presence of what may be the most extensive network of military installations around any major city, a global strike force allegedly prepared to take on any challenge anywhere in the universe. Several military enclosures are scheduled to close down in the 1990s, but their abundance and versatility guarantees a continued impact even if converted to peacetime functions. To illustrate, troops were able to prepare for the Persian Gulf War in the deserts of Southern California, replicating conditions so faithfully that there were special manoeuvres around the desert hamlet of Bagdad. At a more intimate scale, lethal weapons are also kept in most households and in many automobiles, creating a heterogeneous, fragmented, and highly mobile militia that also patrols the turfs and edges of the Carceral City, attempting with violence to keep everyone in their place and, increasingly along the freeways, in their proper lane and going at appropriate speeds. In restructured Los Angeles, the potential for violence has been raised to new heights, triggering often-fatal attractions to a disciplinary technology of security and surveillance that patrols the region with endless eyes. ...

Simcities: restructuring the urban imaginary

A sixth restructuring helps to complete the picture of urban transformation. In many ways, it is a deeper behavioural, cultural, and ideological restructuring and is accordingly more difficult to capture in quick descriptions. What it represents is a radical change in the urban imaginary, in the ways we relate our images of the real to empirical reality itself. It is thus at its roots an inherently epistemological restructuring, one that affects our everyday life and how we make practical sense of the contemporary world, what it means to be alive here and now, in a particular place and at a particular time. Rooted in this changing collective and individual consciousness of the contemporary, its new perils and possibilities, the sixth restructuring more directly than any other links the urban transformations of Los Angeles to the broader current debates on modernity and postmodernity. ...

In the late modern world of Los Angeles, specialized entertainment centres such as Disneyland and Hollywood actively provided consumers with technologically more advanced **hypersimulations** and fantasy worlds. Over the past thirty years, however, these 'real fakes' have escaped from their formerly circumscribed territories and manufactories to infiltrate more deeply than ever before into the intimate everyday life of postmodern urban society, economy, polity, and culture. In these new secular sites and situations, the hypersimulations of urban reality have been blurring, more than ever before, the older distinctions between our images of the real and the reality itself, inserting into the confusion a **hyperreality** that is increasingly affecting where we choose to live and work, what we wear and eat, how we relate to others, who we vote for, how we shape our built environment, how we fill our leisure time – in other words, all the activities that together constitute the social construction of urban life. ...

The new American city can be seen as increasingly recomposed into 'variations on a theme park', divertingly organized as a hyperreal world of simulated cultures, lifestyles, and consumer preferences. In the theme-parked city, one chooses to live not only according to old standards of affordability, proximity to work, or access to good public facilities. One also chooses, if such choice is available, a symbolic site that simulates a particular lifestyle theme, that re-creates one's own fantasyland or frontierland or experimental community of tomorrow. The patchwork of specialized residential communities this produces is much more fine-grained in its territoriality than the race- and class-segregated cities of the past, for it contains not only the older segregations but many more new ones as well.

Today in Los Angeles there are specialized Leisure Worlds and Sun Cities for different groupings of the elderly, apartment-blocked marinas for the swinging singles set, gay and lesbian cities such as West Hollywood, an engineers ghetto in the beach cities south of the international airport, and special places and spaces for families committing their children to Olympic competition (Mission Viejo youth won more gold medals in 1984 than all but six or seven countries), or an ecotopian environment, or the California Promise. There are residential developments and urban villages for those who may wish to live in replicas of Cervantes' Spain or a Greek island ('Welcome to Mykonos'! one advertisement proclaims), of Nashville or New Orleans, Little Tokyo or Little Saigon, old-time white suburbia or old New England. These very real and compulsively attractive Simcities, to borrow the name of a popular video game, are available nearly everywhere in Los Angeles ...

Just as one can visit Thailand or Germany in Disney World without having to travel long distances, so too can one taste the food, observe the people, hear the language, and sense the traditions of nearly every nation on earth without leaving Los Angeles County. It takes only a little flight of fancy to imagine the day when visitors to the LA Cosmopolis-cum-Carceral City of the future will be able to purchase books of tickets to visit Korealand, Blackworld, Little Tijuana, Olympic Village, Redneck Country, Funky Venice, Off-Earth suburbia, and a technopole or two, tearing off stubs for a restaurant meal, a cultural encounter, or an entertaining night on the town.

Key terms

The following key terms appear in the text above. They have been defined below to aid with the reading of this item.

postindustrial post-modernists argue that some cities have moved beyond a mass industrial manufacturing phase to one based on small-batch production and service provision. The latter society is often referred to as post-Fordist

morphological, urban morphology the shape/spread of the city

globalization the increasing connectedness of social, political and economic life across the globe

glocalization global influences are adapted and adopted by local interpretations

world city a globalized city, reliant on 'foreign' influences

gated communities residential areas protected by high walls, CCTV and gates monitored by security guards

hypersimulations these might be exact replicas of another object or imagined 'replicas' of objects that never existed at all!

Questions

1 Why are words such as 'urban', 'suburban' and 'nonurban' no longer useful?

2 What effects has post-Fordist production had on the city?

3 How is Los Angeles' population global and local at the same time?

4 How has the distribution of wealth in Los Angeles changed?

5 Why does Los Angeles appear to be a city at war with itself?

6 How can Los Angeles be likened to a theme park?

Reading 17.8 **National identity: in the mind of the beholder**

Benedict Anderson (from) *Imagined Communities* (1983) London: Verso, pp. 5–7, 36, 139–43.

Editorial comments

Ethnic identity has become a major issue in recent times. In some areas, such as the former Yugoslavia and Rwanda, civil war has resulted from a failure to share a national identity. For many sociologists like the neo-Marxist Benedict Anderson, there is no objective reason why one person should be of a particular nationality and another a mile down the road should be of another. Instead, the distinction should come down to imagination; the two must think they are different and then behave accordingly. These ideas are similar to those adopted by Anthony Cohen (**reading 17.5**) for explaining community.

Imagined communities

I PROPOSE THE following definition of the nation: it is an imagined political community – and imagined as both inherently limited and sovereign.

It is *imagined* because the members of even the smallest nation will never know most of their fellow-members, meet them, or even hear of them, yet in the minds of each lives the image of their communion. (Cf. Seton-Watson, *Nations and States*: 'All that I can find to say is that a nation exists when a significant number of people in a community consider themselves to form a nation, or behave as if they formed one'. We may translate 'consider themselves' as 'imagine themselves'.) Renan referred to this imagining in his suavely back-handed way when he wrote that 'Or l'essence d'une nation est que tous les individus aient beaucoup de choses en commun, et aussi que tous aient oublié bien des choses' [But the essence of a nation is that every individual has lots of things in common, and also that they have all forgotten many things]. With a certain ferocity Gellner (1964) makes a comparable point when he rules that 'Nationalism is not the awakening of nations to self-consciousness: it *invents* nations where they do not exist'. The drawback to this formulation, however, is that Gellner is so anxious to show that nationalism masquerades under false pretences that he assimilates 'invention' to 'fabrication' and 'falsity', rather than to 'imagining' and 'creation'. In this way he implies that 'true' communities exist which can be advantageously juxtaposed to nations. In fact, all communities larger than primordial villages of face-to-face contact (and perhaps even these) are imagined. Communities are to be distinguished, not by their falsity/genuineness, but by the style in which they are imagined. Javanese villagers have always known that they are connected to people they have never seen, but these ties were once imagined particularistically – as indefinitely stretchable nets of kinship and clientship. Until quite recently, the Javanese language had no word meaning the abstraction 'society'. We may today think of the French aristocracy of the *ancien régime* as a class; but surely it was imagined this way only very late. To the question 'Who is the Comte de X'? the normal answer would have been, not 'a member of the aristocracy', but 'the lord of X', 'the uncle of the Baronne de Y', or 'a client of the Duc de Z'.

The nation is imagined as *limited* because even the largest of them, encompassing perhaps a billion living human beings, has finite, if elastic, boundaries, beyond which lie other nations. No nation imagines itself coterminous with mankind. The most messianic nationalists do not dream of a day when all the members of the human race will join their nation in the way that it was possible, in certain epochs, for, say, Christians to dream of a wholly Christian planet.

It is imagined as **sovereign** because the concept was born in an age in which Enlightenment and Revolution were destroying the legitimacy of the divinely-ordained, hierarchical dynastic realm. Coming to maturity at a stage of human history when even the most devout adherents of any universal religion were inescapably confronted with the living *pluralism* of such religions, and the allomorphism between each faith's **ontological** claims and territorial stretch, nations dream of being free, and, if under God, directly so. The gage and emblem of this freedom is the sovereign state.

Finally, it is imagined as a *community*, because, regardless of the actual inequality and exploitation that may prevail in each, the nation is always conceived as a deep, horizontal comradeship. Ultimately it is this fraternity that makes it possible, over the past two centuries, for so many millions of people, not so much to kill, as willingly to die for such limited imaginings.

These deaths bring us abruptly face to face with the central problem posed by nationalism: what makes the shrunken imaginings of recent history (scarcely more than two centuries) generate such colossal sacrifices? I believe that the beginnings of an answer lie in the cultural roots of nationalism.

Essentially, I have been arguing that the very possibility of imagining the nation only arose historically when, and where, three fundamental cultural conceptions, all of great antiquity, lost their axiomatic grip on men's minds. The first of these was the idea that a particular script-language offered privileged access to ontological truth, precisely because it was an inseparable part of that truth. It was this idea that called into being the great transcontinental **sodalities** of Christendom, the Islamic Ummah, and the rest. Second was the belief that society was naturally organized around and under high centres – monarchs who were persons apart from other human beings and who ruled by some form of cosmological (divine) dispensation. Human loyalties were necessarily hierarchical and centripetal because the ruler, like the sacred script, was a node of access to being and inherent in it. Third was a conception of temporality in which cosmology and history were indistinguishable, the origins of the world and of men essentially identical. Combined, these ideas rooted human lives firmly in the very nature of things, giving certain meaning to the everyday fatalities of existence (above all death, loss, and servitude) and offering, in various ways, redemption from them.

The slow, uneven decline of these interlinked certainties, first in Western Europe, later elsewhere, under the impact of economic change, 'discoveries' (social and scientific), and the development of increasingly rapid communications, drove a harsh wedge between cosmology and history. No surprise then that the search was on, so to speak, for a new way of linking fraternity, power and time meaningfully together. Nothing perhaps more precipitated this search, nor made it more fruitful, than print-capitalism, which made it possible for rapidly growing numbers of people to think about themselves, and to relate themselves to others, in profoundly new ways.

The 'last wave' of nationalisms, most of them in the colonial territories of Asia and Africa, was in its origins a response to the newstyle global imperialism made possible by the achievements of industrial capitalism. As Marx put it in his inimitable way: 'The need of a constantly expanding market for its products chases the bourgeoisie over the whole face of the globe' (Marx and Engels, 1956; orig. pub. 1848). But capitalism had also, not least by its dissemination of print, helped to create popular, vernacular-based nationalisms in Europe, which to different degrees undermined the age-old dynastic principle, and egged into self naturalization every dynasty positioned to do so. Official nationalism – weld of the new national and old dynastic principles (the *British Empire*) – led in turn to what, for convenience, one can call 'Russification' in the extra-European colonies. This ideological tendency meshed neatly with practical exigencies. The late-nineteenth-century empires were too large and too far-flung to be ruled by a handful of nationals. Moreover, in tandem with capitalism the state was rapidly multiplying its functions, in both the metropoles and the colonies. Combined, these forces generated 'Russifying' school-systems intended in part to produce the required subordinate cadres for state and corporate bureaucracies. These school-systems, centralized and standardized, created quite new pilgrimages which typically had their Romes in the various colonial capitals, for the nations hidden at the core of the empires would permit no more inward ascension. Usually, but by no means always, these educational pilgrimages were paralleled, or replicated, in the administrative sphere. The interlock between particular educational and administrative pilgrimages provided the territorial base for new 'imagined communities' in which natives could come to see themselves as 'nationals'. The expansion of the colonial state which, so to speak, invited 'natives' into schools and offices, and of colonial capitalism which,

as it were, excluded them from boardrooms, meant that to an unprecedented extent the key early spokesmen for colonial nationalism were lonely, bilingual intelligentsias unattached to sturdy local bourgeoisies.

As bilingual intelligentsias, however, and above all as early-twentieth-century intelligentsias, they had access, inside the classroom and outside, to models of nation, nation-ness, and nationalism distilled from the turbulent, chaotic experiences of more than a century of American and European history. These models, in turn, helped to give shape to a thousand inchoate dreams. In varying combinations, the lessons of creole, vernacular and official nationalism were copied, adapted, and improved upon. Finally, as with increasing speed capitalism transformed the means of physical and intellectual communication, the intelligentsias found ways to bypass print in propagating the imagined community, not merely to illiterate masses, but even to literate masses *reading* different languages.

Patriotism and racism

I have tried to delineate the processes by which the nation came to be imagined, and, once imagined, modelled, adapted and transformed. Such an analysis has necessarily been concerned primarily with social change and different forms of consciousness. But it is doubtful whether either social change or transformed consciousnesses, in themselves, do much to explain the *attachment* that peoples feel for the inventions of their imaginations – or why people are ready to die for these inventions.

In an age when it is so common for progressive, cosmopolitan intellectuals (particularly in Europe?) to insist on the near-pathological character of nationalism, its roots in fear and hatred of the Other, and its affinities with racism, it is useful to remind ourselves that nations inspire love, and often profoundly self-sacrificing love. The cultural products of nationalism – poetry, prose fiction, music, plastic arts – show this love very clearly in thousands of different forms and styles. On the other hand, how truly rare it is to find *analogous* nationalist products expressing fear and loathing.* Even in the case of colonized peoples, who have every reason to feel hatred for their imperialist rulers, it is astonishing how insignificant the element of hatred is in these expression of national feeling. Here, for example, are the first and last stanzas of *Ultimo Adiós*, the famous poem writ-

---

* Can the reader think immediately of even three Hymns of Hate? The second stanza of God Save the Queen/King is worded instructively: 'O Lord our God, arise/Scatter her/his enemies,/And make them fall;/Confound their politics,/Frustrate their knavish tricks;/On Thee our hopes we fix;/God save us all'. Notice that these enemies have no identity and could as well be Englishmen as anyone else since they are 'her/his' enemies *not* 'ours'. The entire anthem is a paean to monarchy, not to the/a nation – which is not once mentioned.

ten by Rizal as he awaited execution at the hands of Spanish imperialism:

1. Farewell, dear Land, beloved of the sun,
Pearl of the Orient seas, lost Paradise!
Gladly, I will to you this life undone;
Were it a fairer, fresher, fuller one,
I'd cede it still, your weal to realize ...

12. What matters then that you forget me, when
I might explore your ev'ry dear retreat?
Be as a note, pulsing and pure; and then,
Be scent, light, tone; be song or sign, again;
And through it all, my theme of faith, repeat.

13. Land I enshrine, list to my last farewell!
Philippines, Love, of pains my pain extreme,
I leave you all, all whom I love so well,
To go where neither slaves nor tyrants dwell,
Where Faith kills not, and where God reigns supreme.

14. Farewell to all my soul does comprehend –
O kith and kin in my home dispossessed;

Give thanks my day oppressive is at end;
Farewell, sweet stranger, my delight and friend;
Farewell, dear ones. To die is but to rest.

Notice not only that the nationality of the 'tyrants' goes unmentioned, but that Rizal's passionate patriotism is expressed superbly in 'their' language.

Something of the nature of this political love can be deciphered from the ways in which languages describe its object: either in the vocabulary of kinship (motherland, *Vaterland*, *patria*) or that of home (*heimat* or *tanah air* – earth and water, the phrase for the Indonesians' native archipelago). Both idioms denote something to which one is naturally tied. In everything 'natural' there is always something unchosen. In this way, nation-ness is assimilated to skin-colour, gender, parentage and birth-era – all those things one can not help. And in these 'natural ties' one senses what one might call 'the beauty of *gemeinschaft*'. To put it another way, precisely because such ties are not chosen, they have about them a halo of disinterestedness.

References

Gellner, E. (1964) *Thought and Change*, London: Weidenfeld & Nicholson.

Marx, K. and Engels, F. (1956) *The Communist Manifesto*, Moscow: Foreign Language Publishing House.

Seton-Wallace, H. (1977) *Nations and States*, Boulder Colorado: West View Press.

Veyra, J. (1946) *El Ultimo Adiós de Rizal: Estudio critico-expositivo*, Manila, Bureau of Printing.

Key terms

The following key terms appear in the text above. They have been defined below to aid with the reading of this item.

sovereign independent and supreme

ontological relating to philosophy, or beliefs, about the nature of existence

sodalities social associations or organizations

Questions

1 How should communities – local to national – be distinguished?

2 In what ways is the nation imagined?

3 The loss of which previous certainties led to the rise of nationalism as a new reliable bond?

4 What is the relationship between language and nationalism?

Further reading

The following texts may represent a useful starting point for further investigation of the ideas contained within this chapter.

Primary text

Pryce, K. (1986) *Endless Pressure: a study of West Indian lifestyles in Bristol*, Bristol: Bristol Classical Press.

This is a modern British study in the style of Foote Whyte's Street Corner Society. *It uses the ethnographic method to study the West Indian community in St Paul's, Bristol.*

Secondary texts

For an excellent summary of the key debates in the study of community with lots of references to contemporary material, see:

Crow, G. and Allan, G. (1994) *Community Life: an introduction to local social relations*, London: Unwin Hyman.

For a collection of extracts and commentary, in a similar style to this book but based purely on community and urban issues, see:

Kasinitz, P. (1995) *Metropolis: Centre and symbol of our times*, Basingstoke: Macmillan.

Coursework suggestions

1 **The study of social life in a limited locality**
You could research social behaviour in a geographically limited area like a common room or café using observation or participant observation, as Jackson did when researching the social uses of the toilets at Cartwright's Mill. You could adopt the theoretical position of a symbolic interactionist. Remember that there will be ethical issues that you will need to think through.

2 **Do people see themselves belonging to a community?**
You could use interviews or questionnaires (or both) to test:

a Cohen's ideas of a symbolic community. Do people feel that they belong to a particular community? If yes, why, and what definitions do they use? Are their definitions seen as subjective, imaginative categories or something objective and 'real'? If no, why? In both cases you might want to know how people thought things would change in the future.

b Anderson's ideas of an imagined community or nation. Use interviews or questionnaires to find out whether people see themselves as holding the same nationality as that stated in their passport. What does their official or perceived nationality mean to them? How is this represented? Do they take pride in their official nationality? Why/why not? What do they think is the future for their nation, and nations in general? You could adopt a variety of theoretical positions for this project.

18

Power and politics

Chapter summary

Reading 18.1 **The power élite** *page 531*
A long established debate in political sociology is based upon the question: 'is there a ruling class or ruling élite in capitalist society?' In this reading, C. Wright Mills argues for the existence of a 'power élite' in the Western world.

Reading 18.2 **The state in 'modernity'** *page 534*
Claus Offe discusses the contemporary nature of democratic societies. He notes that contemporary political legitimation of the state comes from the legitimacy given by 'the will of the people', but he questions just how much say 'we' as 'the people' ultimately have in a 'democracy'.

Reading 18.3 **A new world order?** *page 538*
For Francis Fukuyama, from a New Right perspective, the Marxist political project is at an end. Contemporary global social life happens in the context of a 'new world order' where East and West have converged and old class-based politics have given way to a new era of Western-style global democratic capitalism.

Reading 18.4 **Knowledge and power in the post-modern condition** *page 541*
Lyotard, from a post-modern perspective, argues that contemporary power struggles are based upon the ownership and manipulation of knowledge in society.

Reading 18.5 **Power, discipline and discourse** *page 545*
For Michel Foucault – using a post-structural analysis – power is seen to exist in the spread of various discourses in society. These are specialized languages which define, label and control the identity of those objects or actors 'under their gaze'.

Reading 18.6 **The end of the political?** *page 548*
Jean Baudrillard suggests that in a post-modern society, politics – as we used to understand this term – has come to an end. Politics has lost its claims to truth and is seen as yet another 'game', no longer rooted in the reality of those in society.

Reading 18.7 **The reinvention of politics in a 'risk society'** *page 551*
Arguing against post-modern definitions of the nature of politics, Ulrich Beck suggests, instead, that contemporary social life is characterized by the creation of a 'risk society' in which politics is slowly being reinvented in a different image.

Reading 18.8 **Beyond left and right** *page 555*
Continuing Beck's theme of the problems with post-modern ideas about politics, in this reading Anthony Giddens argues that we need to go beyond our previous ideas of 'left wing' and 'right wing' class politics.

Introduction: Reading the sociology of power and politics

The starting point of political sociology, in general, is to draw a distinction between the interrelated concepts of 'power' and 'politics'. Whereas 'politics' is seen as the struggle for power, the concept of 'power' itself is based upon the idea of the 'battle of wills'. Or, expressed a different way, to hold 'power' as an individual or group involves an ability to get your own way at the expense of the will of others.

We can draw another distinction between the lev-els at which politics – the struggle for power – operates. Areas in social life where political struggles take place (known as 'sites of power') are not just limited to the actions of those in government, or violent armed struggles between revolutionary groups, but instead politics is a wide category existing at both a macro and a micro level. Sites of power in contemporary life can be anything from power in interpersonal communication, gender relations in a family, the ability of a professional group to have their 'professional' status recognized in law, up to and including the actions in the House of Commons of those elected to run the country. Sociological ideas on both power and politics are thus fundamental to the subject as a whole. Indeed, every sociological theory can be seen as a theory of how power operates in society – from the ideas of functionalism on the 'conscience collective'; feminist analyses of the power of men over women (i.e. 'patriarchy'); through to the analysis of the class struggle by Marxist sociologists. The phenomena of the distribution of power across social life is vital to the understanding of social life in general.

Since the introduction of a systematic Marxist-orientated body of knowledge in the discipline of sociology, 'class' has been seen as a – if not *the* – major source of social division and political struggle in capitalism (a situation often criticized by feminist thinkers as being 'malestream': ignoring the consequences of gender in society). Since the work of Weber – and after the various manifestations of neo-Weberianism that sociology has witnessed – the nature of class power has been under much debate. For Marxists, class power comes from the ownership of the means of production. Conversely, a relationship of non-ownership results in the selling of one's labour power to the capitalist class in an exploitative social relationship hidden by the use of ideological control.

For those sociologists influenced more by Weber than Marx, power is held not by a ruling class but by a ruling élite: a group that is different from the ruling capitalist class in Marxist literature since this élite does rule, but not necessarily through the ownership of the means of production. Instead, this élite may manipulate knowledge, the law, a professional status, etc. **Reading 18.1**, from the classic work *The Power Elite* by C. Wright Mills (1956), suggests that a ruling élite group does exist in Western society – a group made up of élites from business, party politics and the military.

The traditional sociological analysis of issues of power and politics has not just focused upon class as a major source of power, but also upon the existence of the state as a tool of power. In **reading 18.2** by Claus Offe (1996) from *Modernity and the State* we see a contemporary discussion of the nature of the democratic state.

Contemporary social theorizing starts with the observation made above – that the sites for political struggle are many and varied in social life. However, for many contemporary sociologists the starting point for discussions of power still lies with the ideas of Marx himself. Much of the contemporary discussion within political sociology is 'a debate with the ghost of Marx'. In **reading 18.3**, New Right thinker Francis Fukuyama (1992) argues that the Marxist idea of the 'end of history' can no longer be seen as possible. There will no longer be the possibility for a class revolution to create a classless society, communism. Instead, history *has* ended – no more dramatic political change is possible. But this 'end' envisaged by Fukuyama is very different to that predicted by Marx. For Fukuyama, contemporary life has resulted in the 'end of ideology' where Western-style capitalism is seen to have become a model for the global organization of social life. The ideas of Fukuyama can be identified as an 'end of class analysis'. Class struggle is no longer a dynamic that moves society onwards.

Many contemporary thinkers claim that we live in a 'post-political age'. By this they mean that the traditional class-based politics of the past have given way to a dismantled political culture where individuals either give up on politics totally, or turn to micro levels of political struggle in a 'DIY culture' where there is no such thing as dominant political meaning or legitimacy. These post-political analyses come mainly from those involved in the post-modern movement in social theory. For Jean-François Lyotard (1984) we live under a *Postmodern Condition* where knowledge has become relative; there are no longer any dominant guidelines to follow in order to assess the truth of a given claim – there are simply many truths. For Lyotard, all previous legitimation claims – which contain power – from traditional and modern forms of social organization have become 'big stories' or rather, 'meta-narratives' – religion, science, democratic politics are all as true as each other.

In **reading 18.4**, Lyotard claims that a major feature of the post-modern condition is the fact that due to increased relativity, knowledge itself has become a site of power.

Taking the idea of knowledge as power further still, in **reading 18.5** post-structuralist thinker Michel Foucault (1984) argues that specialized knowledge or specialized language, in the form of 'discourse', operates to control the body in society. He suggests that discourses often operate in 'specialized spaces' or sites of discipline and surveillance. For example, the discourse of pedagogy operates in the site of the school; the discourse of psychology operates in the site of the asylum; medicine in the hospital, etc.

Borrowing a methodology of historical analysis from German philosopher Friedrich Nietzsche (1956, originally published 1887) Foucault adopts a 'genealogy' of power and discipline in society. The genealogical method of historical study looks not for continuities and evolutions but for the opposite: discontinuity and historical ruptures. For Foucault, history is about the 'birth of difference'. He argues that the concept of 'insanity', the discourse which provides the 'gaze' under which individuals are controlled as being 'insane', and the site of this discourse (the asylum) were all born at the same time as the concept of 'sanity' – one can not exist without the other. Foucault seeks to uncover the hidden history of marginalized, oppressed and controlled groups and individuals, who are controlled through the surveillance of a discourse.

For Jean Baudrillard (1993), in the interview which makes up **reading 18.6**, contemporary life is characterized by the rise of a post-modern society. In such a society, as claimed by Lyotard above, truth and reality become relative. The consequences of this for politics are that Baudrillard claims we now live in a 'post-political age' where politics is empty of meaning. Baudrillard writes of the rise of 'silent majorities' and the 'end of the social' (1983) where social actors are apathetic towards, and disillusioned with, politics.

The final two readings in this chapter take issue with the idea of the post-modernization of political life and culture. Both Ulrich Beck (1994) in **reading 18.7**, and Anthony Giddens (1994) in **reading 18.8** argue that contemporary social life is still essentially 'modernist' in nature – but the precise form of such modernity has moved on slightly from that envisaged by the founders. Today, we are seen to live in a period of *Reflective Modernization*, characterized by the development of what Beck has termed a '*Risk Society*' (1992), and what Giddens refers to as 'manufactured uncertainty'.

In a 'risk society' social life becomes characterized by the calculation and avoidance of risks, or harms. Lifestyles are developed that are 'reflective' in nature: individuals are able to reflect upon, or think about, their identity and roles in society while assessing the risks of any actions they may make. Politics in a risk society also becomes a question of the avoidance of risks, rather than based upon previous class identities. Giddens has noted that these risks are 'manufactured' by humans in the very first place – especially by science and technology.

Rather than a post-modern 'end of the political', both Beck and Giddens suggest that the epoch of 'reflective modernization' is characterized by the continuation of the political – but in a reinvented character rather than the simple modernization that came before it.

References

Baudrillard, J. (1983) *In the Shadow of the Silent Majorities: Or, the end of the social*, New York: Semiotext.

Beck, U. (1992, orig. pub. 1986) *Risk Society: Towards a new modernity*, London: Sage.

Nietzsche, F. (1956, orig. pub. 1887) *On the Genealogy of Morals*, New York: Doubleday.

Reading 18.1 **The power élite**

C. Wright Mills (from) *The Power Elite* (1956) Oxford: Oxford University Press, pp. 274–9.

Editorial comments

Although written about the United States of America, Mills' idea of the 'power élite' can be seen as a criticism of the Marxist idea of a ruling class who own the means of production – a point noted by Mills himself in this reading. Instead of a ruling class, Mills argues for the long-term existence of a threefold élite group made up of economic, political and military leaders. Mills suggests that this élite group is in its fifth historical stage of development and he attempts to describe the nature of this élite group's character and rule.

The power élite

WE STUDY HISTORY, it has been said, to rid ourselves of it, and the history of the power élite is a clear case for which this maxim is correct. Like the tempo of American life in general, the longterm trends of the power structure have been greatly speeded up since World War II, and certain newer trends within and between the dominant institutions have also set the shape of the power élite and given historically specific meaning to its fifth **epoch**:

I. In so far as the structural clue to the power élite today lies in the political order, that clue is to decline of politics as genuine and public debate of alternative decisions – with nationally responsible and policy-coherent parties and with autonomous organizations connecting the lower and middle levels of power with the top levels of decision. America is now in considerable part more a formal political democracy than a democratic social structure, and even the formal political mechanics are weak.

The long-time tendency of business and government to become more intricately and deeply involved with each other has, in the fifth epoch, reached a new point of explicitness. The two cannot now be seen clearly as two distinct works. It is in terms of the executive agencies of the state that the rapprochement has proceeded most decisively. The growth of the executive branch of the government, with its agencies that patrol the complex economy, does not mean merely the 'enlargement of government' as some sort of autonomous bureaucracy: it has meant the ascendancy of the corporation's man as a political eminence. ...

II. In so far as the structural clue to the power élite today lies in the enlarged and military state, that clue becomes evident in the military ascendancy. The warlords have gained decisive political relevance, and the military structure of America is now in considerable part a political structure. The seemingly permanent military threat places a premium on the military and upon their control of men, material, money, and power; virtually all political and economic actions are now judged in terms of military definitions of reality: the higher warlords have ascended to a firm position within the power élite of the fifth epoch. ...

III. In so far as the structural clue to the power élite today lies in the economic order, that clue is the fact that the economy is at once a permanent-war economy and a private-corporation economy. American capitalism is now in considerable part a military capitalism, and the most important relation of the big corporation to the state rests on the coincidence of interests between military and corporate needs, as defined by warlords and corporate rich. Within the élite as a whole, this coincidence of interest between the high military and the corporate chieftains strengthens both of them and further subordinates the role of the merely political men. Not politicians, but corporate executives, sit with the military and plan the organization of war effort.

The shape and meaning of the power élite today can be understood only when these three sets of structural trends are seen at their point of coincidence: the military capitalism of private corporations exists in a weakened and formal democratic system containing a military order already quite political in outlook and demeanour. Accordingly, at the top of this structure, the power élite has been shaped by the coincidence of interest between those who control the major means of production and those who control the newly enlarged means of violence; from the decline of the professional politician and the rise to explicit political command of the corporate chieftains and the professional warlords; from the absence of any genuine civil service of skill and integrity, independent of vested interests.

The power élite is composed of political, economic, and military men, but this instituted élite is frequently in some tension: it comes together only on certain coinciding points and only on certain occasions of 'crisis'. In the long peace of the nineteenth century, the military were not in the high councils of state, not

of the political directorate, and neither were the economic men – they made raids upon the state but they did not join its directorate. During the thirties, the political man was ascendant. Now the military and the corporate men are in top positions.

Of the three types of circle that compose the power élite today, it is the military that has benefited the most in its enhanced power, although the corporate circles have also become more explicitly intrenched in the more public decision-making circles. It is the professional politician that has lost the most, so much that in examining the events and decisions, one is tempted to speak of a political vacuum in which the corporate rich and the high warlord, in their coinciding interests, rule.

It should not be said that the three 'take turns' in carrying the initiative, for the mechanics of the power élite are not often as deliberate as that would imply. At times, of course, it is – as when political men, thinking they can borrow the prestige of generals, find that they must pay for it, or, as when during big slumps, economic men feel the need of a politician at once safe and possessing vote appeal. Today all three are involved in virtually all widely ramifying decisions. Which of the three types seems to lead depends upon 'the tasks of the period' as they, the élite, define them. Just now, these tasks centre upon 'defence' and international affairs. Accordingly, as we have seen, the military are ascendant in two senses: as personnel and as justifying **ideology**. That is why, just now, we can most easily specify the unity and the shape of the power élite in terms of the military ascendancy.

But we must always be historically specific and open to complexities. The simple Marxian view makes the big economic man the *real* holder of power; the simple liberal view makes the big political man the chief of the power system; and there are some who would view the warlords as virtual dictators. Each of these is an oversimplified view. It is to avoid them that we use the term 'power élite' rather than, for example, 'ruling class'.

'Ruling class' is a badly loaded phrase. 'Class' is an economic term; 'rule' a political one. The phrase, 'ruling class', thus contains the theory that an economic class rules politically. That short-cut theory may or may not at times be true, but we do not want to carry that one rather simple theory about in the terms that we use to define our problems; we wish to state the theories explicitly, using terms of more precise and unilateral meaning. Specifically, the phrase 'ruling class', in its common political connotations, does not allow enough autonomy to the political order and its agents, and it says nothing about the military as such. It should be clear to the reader by now that we do not accept as adequate the simple view that high economic men unilaterally make all decisions of national consequence. We hold that such a simple view of 'economic **determinism**' must be elaborated by 'political determinism' and 'military determinism'; that the higher agents of each of these three domains now often have a noticeable degree of autonomy; and that only in the often intricate ways of coalition do they make up and carry through the most important decisions. Those are the major reasons we prefer 'power élite' to 'ruling class' as a characterizing phrase for the higher circles when we consider them in terms of power.

In so far as the power élite has come to wide public attention, it has done so in terms of the 'military clique'. The power élite does, in fact, take its current shape from the decisive entrance into it of the military. Their presence and their ideology are its major legitimations, whenever the power élite feels the need to provide any. But what is called the 'Washington military clique' is not composed merely of military men, and it does not prevail merely in Washington. Its members exist all over the country, and it is a coalition of generals in the roles of corporation executives, of politicians masquerading as admirals, of corporation executives acting like politicians, of civil servants who become majors, of vice-admirals who are also the assistants to a cabinet officer, who is himself, by the way, really a member of the managerial élite.

Neither the idea of a 'ruling class' nor of a simple monolithic rise of 'bureaucratic politicians' nor of a 'military clique' is adequate. The power élite today involves the often uneasy coincidence of economic, military, and political power.

Even if our understanding were limited to these structural trends, we should have grounds for believing the power élite a useful, indeed indispensable, concept for the interpretation of what is going on at the top-side of modern American society. But we are not, of course, so limited: our conception of the power élite does not need to rest only upon the correspondence of the institutional hierarchies involved, or upon the many points at which their shifting interests coincide. The power élite, as we conceive it, also rests upon the similarity of its personnel, and their personal and official relations with one another, upon their social and psychological affinities. In order to grasp the personal and social basis of the power élite's unity, we have first to remind ourselves of the facts of origin, career, and style of life of each of the types of circle whose members compose the power élite.

The power élite is *not* an aristocracy, which is to say that it is not a political ruling group based upon a nobility of hereditary origin. It has no compact basis in a small circle of great families whose members can and do consistently occupy the top positions in the several higher circles which overlap as the power élite. But such nobility is only one possible basis of common origin. That it does not exist for the American élite does not mean that members of this élite derive socially from the full range of strata composing American society. They derive in substantial proportions from the upper classes, both new and old, of local society and the metropolitan 400. The bulk of the very rich, the corporate executives, the political outsiders, the high military, derive from, at most, the upper third of the income and occupational pyramids. Their fathers were at least of the professional and business strata, and very frequently higher than that. They are native-born Americans of native parents, primarily from urban areas, and, with the exceptions of the politicians among them, overwhelmingly from the East. They are mainly Protestants, especially Episcopalian or Presbyterian. In general, the higher the position, the greater the proportion of men within it who have derived from and who maintain connections with the upper classes. The generally similar origins of the members of the power élite are underlined and carried further by the fact of their increasingly common educational routine. Overwhelmingly college graduates, substantial proportions have attended Ivy League colleges, although the education of the higher military, of course, differs from that of other members of the power élite.

Key terms

The following key terms appear in the text above. They have been defined below to aid with the reading of this item.

epoch a stage in history; in this case, a distinctive phase in the development of Mills' power élite group

ideology a set of ideas that justify and legitimate a position of power for an individual or group; usually associated with a misleading set of beliefs as to the precise nature of social reality

determinism the belief that one variable determines or causes another. In this use, Mills notes that Marxist ideas are often seen as 'economically determinist' since Marx believes that class formation and relationships determine all else in a society

Questions

1 According to Mills, how has the structure and nature of the power élite changed over time to its present-day form, in the 'fifth epoch' identified in the reading?

2 How do Mills' ideas differ to those of Marx?

3 What does Mills say about the relationships between the three groups of élites when making decisions?

4 To what extent do you agree with Mills? Can you think of other sources of power in society other than the economic, political and military, as identified by Mills himself?

Reading 18.2 **The state in 'modernity'**

Claus Offe (from) *Modernity and the State: East, West* (1996) Cambridge: Polity Press, pp. 89–97: it first appeared in G. Hofmann and W. A. Perger (eds) *Die Kontroverse. Weizsäckers Parteienkritik in der Diskussion* (1992) Frankfurt: Eichborn Verlag, pp. 126–42.

Editorial comments

Over the past decade or so, a number of thinkers including Offe have made the observation that democracy ('rule of the people') appears to be the most legitimate of all political systems in the West. Even though the nature of how such democracy is achieved often differs, and in some cases critics of a given system may take issue with exactly how much say 'the people' actually have, nonetheless, the claim to 'democracy' is used over and over again to justify rule. Being democratic (or, at least, being *seen* to be democratic) is something that 'the people' who live under the territory of control of a contemporary nation-state have come to expect.

However, the observation that democracy is a principle form of legitimacy in the world, has in turn led many to question just what democracy means and to ask exactly how it is achieved. This critical stance on all things so-called 'democratic' is the tone taken by Offe in the reading below. If the rule of the modern state is based upon the will of the people, he asks, who then are 'the people' and how exactly can we go about identifying their 'will'?

In search of the 'will of the people'

IN A QUITE specific sense, there is no alternative to liberal democracy today: there are no theoretical alternatives worthy of attention that would serve to justify collectively binding decisions made via the agency of the empirical will of the citizens. Needless to say, this does not exclude practices by states and political associations that endeavour to survive without a theoretical form of justification that can be taken seriously and, in extreme cases, rely on mobilizing ethnic and chauvinist support or the tactics of gang warfare. As soon as we start talking about **legitimating justifications**, however, then there is indeed no alternative to the 'will people' as the final agency justifying political rule. The law admittedly defines at any given point in time the scope of democratic decision-making. But such law is itself 'positive', that is, it is in turn subject to democratic legislative decisions. The economy also places limitations on democratic decisions. It is impossible in the long term to decide politically to spend more than the tax base created by economic activity yields. And, of course, physical laws cannot be decided or simply annulled democratically. Yet, within these broad limits, politics is generated by democratic sovereignty and can only expect to be obeyed if it refers to this origin.

There is, in other words, 'no alternative' to liberal democracy. I do not mean this in the sense that there are alternatives still in existence but which have been rejected as less worthy of being considered valid when compared with liberal democracy, as based on universal, free, and equal adult suffrage. Instead, the opposite is the case: such an alternative *no longer* exists in modern societies. Democracy, therefore, does not resemble an elected **constitutional** form (that could consequently be changed by election), but rather an ineluctable fact. Alternatives to liberal democracy, irrespective of whether they have their foundations in a dynasty, a theocracy, a particular philosophy of history, or in natural law, simply no longer come into consideration factually, especially after the events of 1989 and the breakdown of state socialism. No one would be prepared to take them seriously. Modern societies are condemned to rely solely on the 'will of the people' as it ensues from equal and free rights of participation when it comes to the basis for justifying themselves, that is, to the final agency of and impetus for collectively binding decisions.

Democracy has changed from being a virtue we should adhere to and has become a fact that we have to get by with. This does not preclude, above all in the process of European integration, that the 'final agency' for justification, namely the 'will of the people', is filtered through so many interim stages that the people themselves are hardly able to recognize the results of their will in the double sense of the word. It is, I believe, above all the prospect of a fore-seeably deficient democracy in an integrated Europe that has prompted the political élites in Germany today to start thinking of compensatory aids. ...

(1) The will of the people is initially *fictitious* because it cannot be conceived of as an entity which can be consulted at any moment, as can the holy book of religions of revelation. Nor is it something from which we can glean, if necessary with the assistance of authorized scholars (or pollsters?), binding instructions as to the right path to pursue with political decisions. Instead, we must assume that no 'will of the people' exists on most themes at most times. What exist are the factual, temporal, and socially differentiated preferences of citizens. In other words, some citizens want this or that decision, so opt for one thing, others opt for another, and, moreover, they want one thing today, another tomorrow. Furthermore, most people are undecided anyway whether they actually want something with regard to most matters at most times, because the *attentive energy* which the normal citizen can devote to political matters is far too limited, and citizens, rationally enough, do not have a great deal of *confidence* that it is worthwhile investing more energy in the first place. It would be thus by pure chance if the confusion of voices expressing individual opinions and preferences, even those coloured and predefined by associations and party politics, were to meet even the most modest of criteria for *objective logical consistency, intrinsic concurrence*, and *temporal constancy*. And these are precisely the features which we impute to someone when we believe that he or she has a 'will', and a well-considered, stabilized, informed will at that, and therefore one that is worthy of consideration and recognition. ...

To impute a political 'will' to 'the' people in the first place, of the sort that occurs in the usual talk of 'popular will' or 'the will of the voters', is thus a turn of phrase which amounts to using a metaphor that is as sublime as it is risky. In this context we should bear in mind the essentially uncontroversial fact that the 'will' of the people is an *artefact* of those institutional procedures which we ostensibly only use to *measure* precisely that will. The will of the people *does not exist* prior to these procedures and independent of them, but instead *arises* in them. The will of the people has the character of an answer, and what is important, then, is the question which is put in order to come up with the answer, and the procedure used to arrive at it.

(2) What arises in these procedures and what is then represented by the people and by the political élites as the 'will of the people' is decidedly *fallible*, just as,

of course, the will of those in political office or invested with political authority is fallible. The question is thus whether, given irreversible *democratic* conditions, fallibility or erroneousness are even meaningful criteria, because, and this is by definition the case in liberal democracies, where there is no truth and correctness that serves as the basis of political decisions, there can also be no errors or false decisions. Or at least not as long as the political decisions do not go against *constitutional law* with regard to the procedures by which they must be reached, that is, are recognized to be impermissible and therefore without effect. ...

(3) The fact that the will of the people can be seduced has, essentially, only to do with a subordinate case of its fallibility. Let us assume that, as stated above, the popular will is first formed in the process by which it is measured, and outside that process at best dons the shadowy form of unconnected and fluctuating elements of will. This being the case, with regard to the **social construction** *of the will of the people* by the media, the political parties, associations, and educational institutions, great effort must be made to ensure that the dissemination of information and attention is 'undistorted' and 'balanced' in a sense that is hard to define and even harder to create norms for. The interested manner in which such institutions and collective actors appeal to fears, prejudices, passions, interests, and hopes may, on the one hand, improve the ability of citizens to make rational decisions. It may, on the other, mislead them, by which I mean that decisions result which, in the sense explained above, are retrospectively to be considered 'false'. To the extent that the latter is the case, we can speak of the will of the people having been 'seduced' or 'mislead'. The corresponding dangers clearly grow to the degree that citizens depend in the process of will formation on premade decisions for their orientation. This is the case to an exceptional degree in all areas of politics today. The sheer complexity of things renders us veritable illiterates on most public matters, because all of us, whether mere citizens or holders of offices or authority, will never get far with our own experiences and ability to judge. We are correspondingly dependent on the questions for which decisions are to be made being prepared in advance in a manner we can trust, and on the alternatives, including the foreseeable consequences, being fairly and sincerely presented to us. The enormous amount of help we need before being able to judge creates correspondingly great opportunities for abuse on the part of those (regularly interested) parties on whom we rely for help.

In this context we must in particular warn against the

widespread and false assumption that procedures which focus less on electing representatives and more on a direct democratic poll of opinion, such as popular initiatives, petitions for referendums, and the referendums themselves, *ipso facto inevitably* generate more *authentic* results than do the usual procedures of a representative democracy, specifically periodic elections to legislative bodies. This assumption is usually based on the notion that such a result is forthcoming because such popular procedures are *not* mediated via the institutionalised competition of the political parties. And it is false not only because of the limited ability we all have to judge matters, but also because popular initiatives and petitions for referendums can, certainly at the federal level, clearly only be organised by the political parties. To this extent, what would be involved would merely be twofold competition between the parties under the simple pretext of suspending or correcting them. Thanks to the pollsters who are constantly monitoring the political opinions of the population, government policy is consistently to a great extent in line with the population's preferences on important matters. Given that the political élites are already acquainted with these opinions, where they are conveyed through the referendum-like functions of political opinion polling, and given that they have cause to heed them, it is not exactly obvious why an additional channel of communication, namely referendums etc., should lead to the government being made aware of additional contents. Oppositional political preferences which have even the remotest chance of achieving a quorum have turned up on the pollsters' x-ray screens long before they have had a chance to crystallize into suggestions or proposed bills. To this extent the political élites again have the upper hand when it comes to the preemptive dispersal and pacification of popular initiatives.

Against the background of these deliberations we can now go on to take rough stock of the relative capacity of representative procedures as opposed to procedures involving direct democratic votes on issues where it comes to measuring and concomitantly creating the will of the people. …

Forms of the legislature based on **plebiscites** are characterized by advantages and disadvantages that offset each other. The underlying totality of citizens can only answer given questions with yes or no, and when answering (or at least we cannot preclude this happening) are subject to moods and emotions specific to that moment in time. The latter can, moreover, be controlled by a third party directing their attention. The 'nascent need for regulation in the people', which a typical petition speaks of with moving sensitivity, might just as easily have been *teased into birth* by strategic parties. Conversely, to their

credit, citizens directly involved in legislation are clearly relatively free of an innate desire to maintain power – if not necessarily free of an interest in acquiring power. Thus, in the case of potential forms of legislation by the people, we should exclude all such matters (such as fiscal laws) where we can reasonably expect that worries about the size of their disposable income may tempt many citizens to attribute less importance to the state provision of infrastructure and collective goods than they otherwise would, or would want to.

On the other hand, a broad consensus among international scholars in the areas of theories of democracy and political sociology expressly confirms the assumption that the democratic political system has failings. These could lead to lower acceptance of its institutions and to the latter ceasing to be able to function in an integrative, binding, and legitimizing manner. This could perhaps be alleviated by involving citizens to a greater degree in various ways. But we must warn here against innovations that adhere to the logic of *exchange* and are introduced with great haste and little reason. For example, those made with the gesture: We, the politicians, are granting you, the citizens, great rights to participate and take the initiative. We expect in return that in future you show greater respect toward the agencies of politics and the administrators thereof. For it is neither certain that the 'political caste' does indeed forfeit overall control with the introduction of such innovations, nor can we assume that, should it do so, the citizens would really honour the concessions granted it in the manner expected. To oversimplify, the problem at hand can be portrayed in terms of two points.

1 Large political organizations, above all, political parties, but also trade unions and other associations, have lost much of their function as a point of orientation for their members and for the public as a whole. In view of the complexity of the decisions they have to make and the plurality of values and interests that have to be taken into account in the process, the actors shaping our political life are themselves dwindling in stature. They leave behind them a vacuum of moral and political leadership and are therefore suspected of essentially acting as an opportunistic cartel exercising patronage and endeavouring to stay in power.

2 The ongoing process of individualization and differentiation within society is drying out the ground which was once fertile for major political communities that functioned as points of orientation and as the seedbed of solidarity. Instead, it promotes the confined and oscillating formation of political preferences. Each trend fosters the other: the talk is of the 'gradual death of a steady political clientele',

of increasing **apathy** and cynicism on the one hand, and of a dearth of ideas and a lack of clear profile among the political parties, on the other. The latter have substantially lost the ability to mobilize their clientele behind them and therefore cling to state and, above all, financial guarantees for their survival, pursuing a strategy of cartel formation to the detriment of potential third parties.

Now one could bemoan these trends or 'realistically' accept them. What is probably not a bone of contention is the fact that taken together the effect of the two trends leads to a decay in society's *political resources*, that is, to a devaluation of the institutional means with which society can purposively influence its own development and subject this to control. At the same time, the overall trend improves the chances of those on the political market who use populist 'direct sales' to callously sell anything on the political market which is likely to find a ready buyer. And they do so by appealing to innate resentment or an individual instinct for greater wealth.

The introduction of citizens' initiatives, petitions for referendums, referendums themselves, and consultational and definitive polling of or votes by citizens is by no means the only way of enhancing the opportunities for citizens to help shape politics. Two other levels of reinvigorating institutions may possibly serve the same goal far more effectively. The first is to open up the system of political institutions to a far greater

extent to the *discursive processes of the political public sphere*, processes that establish the norms in the first place; and the second is the internal *democratization of political parties* and possibly also of associations. After all, democratization can be effected not only from 'below' through forms of participation involving plebiscites, but also 'internally' (participatory rights in political parties) and 'externally' (via public opinion). It appears conceivable that if clear successes can be scored at these two levels, the option being debated of augmenting the representative system by means of elements of direct democratic involvement of the electorate could probably be dispensed with altogether. Furthermore, in this light, the possibility of augmenting political will formation by means of direct democratic participation is in reality a relatively meagre basis for improvement. And it is a basis that political élites currently enjoy chiselling away at, in part because thus they can seem to offer decisive concessions without actually doing so. It allows them in the main still to exercise the right to formulate the issues and only then ask the people to take a decision on them. In fact, under certain conditions they would also gain the welcome opportunity to shirk their responsibility for tricky issues where decisions have to be made, particularly international issues, by leaving the task of decision-making in these cases to the purported original agency of the 'will of the people' as expressed by plebiscite.

Key terms

The following key terms appear in the text above. They have been defined below to aid with the reading of this item.

legitimating justifications a set of ideas which make something seem correct – for example, in the reading, Offe argues that being seen to be democratic legitimates the ideas and decisions of the government

constitutional set down in the law of a given society, explaining how the political system of such a society should operate

social construction created by cultural forces in society

plebiscites direct expressions of public political opinion – usually through a vote

apathy not wishing to be bothered, or to get involved. Offe argues that many people are apathetic about political issues in today's society

Questions

1 What does Offe mean by his observation that there is 'no alternative' to democracy in today's world?

2 How can the will of the people be 'seduced'? What possible consequences does this have in society?

3 Do you think Offe feels that the Western world is as democratic as it claims to be? Explain your answer.

4 What does Offe say about the 'death of the political'?

5 Given the ideas and observations in this reading, do you think it is ever possible for a society to be truly 'run by the people'?

Reading 18.3 **A new world order?**

Francis Fukuyama (from) *The End of History and the Last Man* (1992) New York: The Free Press, pp. xi–xxiii.

Editorial comments

This reading comes from the introduction to Fukuyama's book, where he comments upon the reaction amongst the academic community to an article he wrote claiming that we have reached the 'end of history' – and the end of class dynamics in society. Fukuyama argues, from a New Right perspective, that we live in a new era of history – one where the nature of politics is changing and that the global model for all political futures will be the liberal democracy of Western capitalism.

'The end of history' and the 'last man'

THE DISTANT ORIGINS of the present volume lie in an article entitled 'The End of History'? which I wrote for the journal *The National Interest* in the summer of 1989. In it, I argued that a remarkable consensus concerning the legitimacy of **liberal democracy** as a system of government had emerged throughout the world over the past few years, as it conquered rival **ideologies** like hereditary monarchy, fascism, and most recently communism. More than that, however, I argued that liberal democracy may constitute the 'end point of mankind's ideological evolution' and the 'final form of human government', and as such constituted the '**end of history**'. That is, while earlier forms of government were characterized by grave defects and irrationalities that led to their eventual collapse, liberal democracy was arguably free from such fundamental internal contradictions. This was not to say that today's stable democracies, like the United States, France, or Switzerland, were not without injustice or serious social problems. But these problems were ones of incomplete implementation of the twin principles of liberty and equality on which modern democracy is founded, rather than of flaws in the principles themselves. While some present-day countries might fail to achieve stable liberal democracy, and others might lapse back into other, more primitive forms of rule like **theocracy** or military dictatorship, the *ideal* of liberal democracy could not be improved on.

The original article excited an extraordinary amount of commentary and controversy, first in the United States, and then in a series of countries as different as England, France, Italy, the Soviet Union, Brazil, South Africa, Japan, and South Korea. Criticism took every conceivable form, some of it based on simple misunderstanding of my original intent, and others penetrating more perceptively to the core of my argument. Many people were confused in the first instance by my use of the word 'history'. Understanding history in a conventional sense as the occurrence of events, people pointed to the fall of the Berlin Wall, the Chinese communist crackdown in Tiananmen Square, and the Iraqi invasion of Kuwait as evidence that 'history was continuing', and that I was *ipso facto* proven wrong.

And yet what I suggested had come to an end was not the occurrence of events, even large and grave events, but History: that is, history understood as a single, coherent, evolutionary process, when taking into account the experience of all peoples in all times. This understanding of History was most closely associated with the great German philosopher G. W. F. Hegel. It was made part of our daily intellectual atmosphere by Karl Marx, who borrowed this concept of History from Hegel, and is implicit in our use of words like 'primitive' or 'advanced', 'traditional' or 'modern', when referring to different types of human societies. For both of these thinkers, there was a coherent development of human societies from simple tribal ones based on slavery and subsistence agriculture, through various theocracies, monarchies, and feudal aristocracies, up through modern liberal democracy and technologically driven capitalism. This evolutionary process was neither random nor unintelligible, even if it did not proceed in a straight line, and even if it was possible to question whether man was happier or better off as a result of historical 'progress'.

Both Hegel and Marx believed that the evolution of human societies was not open-ended, but would end when mankind had achieved a form of society that satisfied its deepest and most fundamental longings. Both thinkers thus posited an 'end of history': for Hegel this was the liberal state, while for Marx it was a communist society. This did not mean that the natural cycle of birth, life, and death would end, that important events would no longer happen, or that newspapers reporting them would cease to be published. It meant, rather, that there would be no further progress in the development of underlying principles and institutions, because all of the really big questions had been settled. ...

... good news has come. The most remarkable development of the last quarter of the twentieth century has been the revelation of enormous weaknesses at the core of the world's seemingly strong dictatorships, whether they be of the military-authoritarian Right, or the communist-totalitarian Left. From Latin America to Eastern Europe, from the Soviet Union to the Middle East and Asia, strong governments have been failing over the last two decades. And while they have not given way in all cases to stable liberal democracies, liberal democracy remains the only coherent political aspiration that spans different regions and cultures around the globe. In addition, liberal principles in economics – the '**free market**' – have spread, and have succeeded in producing unprecedented levels of material prosperity, both in industrially developed countries and in countries that had been, at the close of World War II, part of the impoverished Third World. A liberal revolution in economic thinking has sometimes preceded, sometimes followed, the move toward political freedom around the globe.

All of these developments, so much at odds with the terrible history of the first half of the century when **totalitarian** governments of the Right and Left were on the march, suggest the need to look again at the question of whether there is some deeper connecting thread underlying them, or whether they are merely accidental instances of good luck. By raising once again the question of whether there is such a thing as a Universal History of mankind, I am resuming a discussion that was begun in the early nineteenth century, but more or less abandoned in our time because of the enormity of events that mankind has experienced since then. ...

Economic interpretations of history are incomplete and unsatisfying, because man is not simply an economic animal. In particular, such interpretations cannot really explain why we are democrats, that is, proponents of the principle of popular sovereignty and the guarantee of basic rights under a rule of law. ...

The struggle for recognition provides us with insight into the nature of international politics. The desire for recognition that led to the original bloody battle for prestige between two individual combatants leads logically to imperialism and world empire. The relationship of lordship and bondage on a domestic level is naturally replicated on the level of states, where nations as a whole seek recognition and enter into bloody battles for supremacy. Nationalism, a modern yet not-fully-rational form of recognition, has been the vehicle for the struggle for recognition over the pilot hundred years, and the source of this century's most intense conflicts. This is the world of 'power politics', described by such foreign policy 'realists' as Henry Kissinger.

But if war is fundamentally driven by the desire for recognition, it stands to reason that the liberal revolution which abolishes the relationship of lordship and bondage by making former slaves their own masters should have a similar effect on the relationship between states. Liberal democracy replaces the irrational desire to be recognized as greater than others with a rational desire to be recognized as equal. A world made up of liberal democracies, then, should have much less incentive for war, since all nations would reciprocally recognize one another's legitimacy. And indeed, there is substantial empirical evidence from the past couple of hundred years that liberal democracies do not behave imperialistically toward one another, even if they are perfectly capable of going to war with states that are not democracies and do not share their fundamental values. Nationalism is currently on the rise in regions like Eastern Europe and the Soviet Union where peoples have long been denied their national identities, and yet within the world's oldest and most secure nationalities, nationalism is undergoing a process of change. The demand for national recognition in Western Europe has been domesticated and made compatible with universal recognition, much like religion three or four centuries before.

This book addresses the question of the 'end of history', and the creature who emerges at the end, '**last man**' In the course of the original debate over the *National Interest* article, many people assumed that the possibility of the end of history revolved around the question of whether there were viable alternatives to liberal democracy visible in the world today. There was a great deal of controversy over such questions as whether communism was truly dead, whether religion or ultranationalism might make a comeback, and the like. But the deeper and more profound question concerns the goodness of liberal democracy itself, and not only whether it will succeed against its present-day rivals. Assuming that liberal democracy is, for the moment, safe from external enemies, could we assume that successful democratic societies could remain that way indefinitely? Or is liberal democracy prey to serious internal contradictions, contradictions so serious that they will eventually undermine it as a political system? There is no doubt that contemporary democracies face any number of serious problems, from drugs, homelessness, and crime to environmental damage and the frivolity of consumerism. But these problems are not obviously insoluble on the basis of liberal principles, nor so serious that they would necessarily lead to the collapse of society as a whole, as communism collapsed in the 1980s.

Writing in the twentieth century, Hegel's great interpreter, Alexandre Kojève, asserted intransigently that history had ended because what he called the 'universal and homogeneous state' – what we can understand as liberal democracy – definitely solved the question of recognition by replacing the relationship of lordship and bondage with universal and equal recognition. What man had been seeking throughout the course of history – what had driven the prior 'stages of history' – was recognition. In the modern world, he finally found it, and was 'completely satisfied'. This claim was made seriously by Kojève, and it deserves to be taken seriously by us. For it is possible to understand *the* problem of politics over the millennia of human history as the effort to solve the problem of recognition. Recognition is the central problem of politics because it is the origin of tyranny, imperialism, and the desire to dominate. But while it has a dark side, it cannot simply be abolished from political life, because it is simultaneously the psychological ground for political virtues like courage, public spiritedness, and justice. All political communities must make use of the desire for recognition, while at the same time protecting themselves from its destructive effects. If contemporary constitutional government has indeed found a formula whereby all are recognized in a way that nonetheless avoids the emergence of tyranny, then it would indeed have a special claim to stability and longevity among the regimes that have emerged on earth.

But is the recognition available to citizens of contemporary liberal democracies 'completely satisfying'? The long-term future of liberal democracy, and the alternatives to it that may one day arise, depend above all on the answer to this question. The Left would say that universal recognition in liberal democracy is necessarily incomplete because capitalism creates economic inequality and requires a division of labour that *ipso facto* implies unequal recognition. In this respect, a nation's absolute level of prosperity provides no solution, because there will continue to be those who are relatively poor and therefore invisible as human beings to their fellow citizens. Liberal democracy, in other words, continues to recognize equal people unequally.

The second, and in my view more powerful, criticism of universal recognition comes from the Right that was profoundly concerned with the leveling effects of the French Revolution's commitment to human equality. This Right found its most brilliant spokesman in the philosopher Friedrich Nietzsche, whose views were in some respects anticipated by that great observer of democratic societies, Alexis de Tocqueville. Nietzsche believed that modern democracy represented not the self-mastery of former slaves, but the unconditional victory of the slave and a kind of slavish morality. The typical citizen of a liberal democracy was a 'last man' who, schooled by the founders of modern liberalism, gave up prideful belief in his or her own superior worth in favour of comfortable self-preservation. Liberal democracy produced 'men without chests', composed of desire and reason but lacking *thymos*, clever at finding new ways to satisfy a host of petty wants through the calculation of long-term self-interest. The last man had no desire to be recognized as greater than others, and without such desire no excellence or achievement was possible. Content with his happiness and unable to feel any sense of shame for being unable to rise above those wants, the last man ceased to be human.

Following Nietzsche's line of thought, we are compelled to ask the following questions: Is not the man who is completely satisfied by nothing more than universal and equal recognition something less than a full human being, indeed, an object of contempt, a 'last man' with neither striving nor aspiration? Is there not a side of the human personality that deliberately seeks out struggle, danger, risk, and daring, and will this side not remain unfulfilled by the 'peace and prosperity' of contemporary liberal democracy? Does not the satisfaction of certain human beings depend on recognition that is inherently unequal? Indeed, does not the desire for unequal recognition constitute the basis of a liveable life, not just for bygone aristocratic societies, but also in modern liberal democracies? Will not their future survival depend, to some extent, on the degree to which their citizens seek to be recognized not just as equal, but as superior to others? And might not the fear of becoming contemptible 'last men' not lead men to assert themselves in new and unforeseen ways, even to the point of becoming once again bestial 'first men' engaged in bloody prestige battles, this time with modern weapons?

This books seeks to address these questions. They arise naturally once we ask whether there is such a thing as progress, and whether we can construct a coherent and directional Universal History of mankind. Totalitarianisms of the Right and Left have kept us too busy to consider the latter question seriously for the better part of this century. But the fading of these totalitarianisms, as the century comes to an end, invites us to raise this old question one more time.

Key terms

The following key terms appear in the text above. They have been defined below to aid with the reading of this item.

liberal democracy a system of political organization where voting takes place to decide on the ruling party – who are supposed to be answerable to those they represent

ideologies sets of ideas which justify positions of power

'end of history' originally a Marxist idea – influenced by the writing of German philosopher Hegel – which claims that the pattern of development to be experienced by society is based upon a linear path of evolution which, one day, will stop changing

theocracy government by religious leaders

free market a form of economic organization based upon the belief that economics can be left to run itself rather than having state involvement or intervention

totalitarian(ism) a type of political organization based on violence and control, where freedom of speech is usually limited and free elections do not take place

'(the) last man' a social actor who lives through and experiences the final stages in the end of history

Questions

1 How does Fukuyama borrow from Marx and Hegel the idea of a logic of history which leads to the 'end of history'?

2 What is the future of society according to the reading above?

3 Using your knowledge of Marxism from elsewhere, how would Marxist sociologists criticize the ideas of Fukuyama? To what extent does he provide an ideological justification for capitalist expansion?

Reading 18.4 **Knowledge and power in the post-modern condition**

Jean-François Lyotard (from) *The Postmodern Condition: A report on knowledge* (1984, originally published in France in 1979) Manchester: Manchester University Press, pp. xxiii–xxv, 3–5 and 14–17.

Editorial comments

For Lyotard, both knowledge and language are seen as sites of power in the post-modern age. In these extracts, firstly, he argues that the nature of knowledge in general – and scientific knowledge in particular – has changed in contemporary social life. Knowledge is now a commodity of power: it is a 'thing', an object to be bought and sold, and those who collect the most have power over others who have less.

Secondly, Lyotard goes on to argue that communication between individuals involves the use of 'language-games' which are themselves sites of power – language acts (i.e. speech) being action involving the manipulation of definitions of power.

The postmodern condition

THE OBJECT OF this study is the condition of knowledge in the most highly developed societies. I have decided to use the word *postmodern* to describe that condition. The word is in current use on the American continent among sociologists and critics; it designates the state of our culture following the transformations which, since the end of the nineteenth century, have altered the game rules for science, literature, and the arts. The present study will place these transformations in the context of the crisis of narratives.

Science has always been in conflict with narratives. Judged by the yardstick of science, the majority of them prove to be fables. But to the extent that science does not restrict itself to stating useful regularities and seeks the truth, it is obliged to legitimate the rules of its own game. It then produces a **discourse** of legitimation with respect to its own status, a discourse called philosophy. I will use the term *modern* to designate any science that legitimates itself with reference to a **metadiscourse** of this kind making an explicit appeal to some grand narrative, such as the **dialectics** of Spirit, the **hermeneutics** of meaning, the emancipation of the rational or working subject, or the creation of wealth. For example, the rule of consensus between the sender and addressee of a statement with truth-value is deemed acceptable if it is cast in terms of a possible unanimity between rational minds: this is the **Enlightenment narrative**, in which the hero of knowledge works toward a good ethico-political end – universal peace. As can be seen from this example, if a metanarrative implying a philosophy of history is used to legitimate knowledge, questions are raised concerning the validity of the institutions governing the social bond: these must be legitimated as well. Thus justice is consigned to the grand narrative in the same way as truth.

Simplifying to the extreme, I define *postmodern* as incredulity toward metanarratives. This incredulity is undoubtedly a product of progress in the sciences: but that progress in turn presupposes it. To the obsolescence of the metanarrative apparatus of legitimation corresponds, most notably, the crisis of metaphysical philosophy and of the university institution which in the past relied on it. The narrative function is losing its functors, its great hero, its great dangers, its great voyages, its great goal. It is being dispersed in clouds of narrative language elements – narrative, but also denotative, prescriptive, descriptive, and so on. Conveyed within each cloud are pragmatic valencies specific to its kind. Each of us lives at the intersection of many of these. However, we do not necessarily establish stable language combinations, and the properties of the ones we do establish are not necessarily communicable. ...

Postmodern knowledge is not simply a tool of the authorities; it refines our sensitivity to differences and reinforces our ability to tolerate the incommensurable. ...

Our working hypothesis is that the status of knowledge is altered as societies enter what is known as the postindustrial age and cultures enter what is known as the postmodern age. This transition has been under way since at least the end of the 1950s, which for Europe marks the completion of reconstruction. The pace is faster or slower depending on the country, and within countries it varies according to the sector of activity: the general situation is one of temporal disjunction which makes sketching an overview difficult. A portion of the description would necessarily be conjectural. At any rate, we know that it is unwise to put too much faith in futurology.

Rather than painting a picture that would inevitably remain incomplete, I will take as my point of departure a single feature, one that immediately defines our object of study. Scientific knowledge is a kind of discourse. And it is fair to say that for the last forty years the 'leading' sciences and technologies have had to do with language: phonology and theories of linguistics, problems of communication and **cybernetics**, modern theories of algebra and informatics, computers and their languages, problems of translation and the search for areas of compatibility among computer languages, problems of information storage and data banks, telematics and the perfection of intelligent terminals, paradoxology. The facts speak for themselves (and this list is not exhaustive).

These technological transformations can be expected to have a considerable impact on knowledge. Its two principal functions – research and the transmission of acquired learning – are already feeling the effect, or will in the future. With respect to the first function, genetics provides an example that is accessible to the layman: it owes its theoretical paradigm to cybernetics. Many other examples could be cited. As for the second function, it is common knowledge that the miniaturization and commercialization of machines is already changing the way in which learning is acquired, classified, made available, and exploited. It is reasonable to suppose that the proliferation of information-processing machines is having, and will continue to have, as much of an effect on the circulation of learning as did advancements in human circulation (transportation systems) and later, in the circulation of sounds and visual images (the media).

The nature of knowledge cannot survive unchanged within this context of general transformation. It can fit into the new channels, and become operational, only if learning is translated into quantities of information. We can predict that anything in the constituted body of knowledge that is not translatable in this way will be abandoned and that the direction of new research will be dictated by the possibility of its eventual results being translatable into computer language. The 'producers' and users of knowledge must now, and will have to, possess the means of translating into these languages whatever they want to invent or learn. Research on translating machines is already well advanced. Along with the hegemony of computers comes a certain logic, and therefore a certain set of prescriptions determining which statements are accepted as 'knowledge' statements.

We may thus expect a thorough exteriorization of knowledge with respect to the 'knower', at whatever point he or she may occupy in the knowledge process. The old principle that the acquisition of knowledge is indissociable from the training (*Bildung*) of minds, or even of individuals, is becoming obsolete and will become ever more so. The relationship of the suppliers and users of knowledge to the knowledge they supply and use is now tending, and will increasingly tend, to assume the form already taken by the relationship of commodity producers and consumers to the commodities they produce and consume – that is, the form of value. Knowledge is and will be produced in order to be sold, it is and will be consumed in order to be valorized in a new production: in both cases, the goal is exchange. Knowledge ceases to be an end in itself, it loses its 'use-value'.

It is widely accepted that knowledge has become

the principal force of production over the last few decades; this has already had a noticeable effect on the composition of the work force of the most highly developed countries and constitutes the major bottleneck for the developing countries. In the postindustrial and postmodern age, science will maintain and no doubt strengthen its preeminence in the arsenal of productive capacities of the nation-states. Indeed, this situation is one of the reasons leading to the conclusion that the gap between developed and developing countries will grow ever wider in the future.

But this aspect of the problem should not be allowed to over-shadow the other, which is complementary to it. Knowledge in the form of an informational commodity indispensable to productive power is already, and will continue to be, a major – perhaps *the* major – stake in the worldwide competition for power. It is conceivable that the nation-states will one day fight for control of information, just as they battled in the past for control over territory, and afterwards for control of access to and exploitation of raw materials and cheap labour. A new field is opened for industrial and commercial strategies on the one hand, and political and military strategies on the other.

However, the perspective I have outlined above is not as simple as I have made it appear. For the **mercantilization** of knowledge is bound to affect the privilege the nation-states have enjoyed, and still enjoy, with respect to the production and distribution of learning. The notion that learning falls within the purview of the State, as the brain or mind of society, will become more and more outdated with the increasing strength of the opposing principle, according to which society exists and progresses only if the messages circulating within it are rich in information and easy to decode. The ideology of communicational 'transparency', which goes hand in hand with the commercialization of knowledge, will begin to perceive the State as a factor of opacity and 'noise'. It is from this point of view that the problem of the relationship between economic and State powers threatens to arise with a new urgency. ...

As I have already said, economic 'redeployment' in the current phase of capitalism, aided by a shift in techniques and technology, goes hand in hand with a change in the function of the State: the image of society this syndrome suggests necessitates a serious revision of the alternate approaches considered. For brevity's sake, suffice it to say that functions of regulation, and therefore of reproduction, are being and will be further withdrawn from administrators and entrusted to machines. Increasingly, the central question is becoming who will have access to the information these machines must have in storage to guarantee that the right decisions are made. Access to data is, and will continue to be, the prerogative of

experts of all stripes. The ruling class is and will continue to be the class of decision makers. Even now it is no longer composed of the traditional political class, but of a composite layer of corporate leaders, high-level administrators, and the heads of the major professional, labour, political, and religious organizations.

What is new in all of this is that the old poles of attraction represented by nation-states, parties, professions, institutions, and historical traditions are losing their attraction. And it does not look as though they will be replaced, at least not on their former scale. ...

This breaking up of the grand Narratives leads to what some authors analyse in terms of the dissolution of the social bond and the disintegration of social aggregates into a mass of individual atoms thrown into the absurdity of Brownian motion. Nothing of the kind is happening: this point of view, it seems to me, is haunted by the paradisaic representation of a lost 'organic' society.

A *self* does not amount to much, but no self is an island; each exists in a fabric of relations that is now more complex and mobile than ever before. Young or old, man or woman, rich or poor, a person is always located at '**nodal points**' of specific communication circuits, however tiny these may be. Or better: one is always located at a post through which various kinds of messages pass. No one, not even the least privileged among us, is ever entirely powerless over the messages that traverse and position him at the post of sender, addressee, or referent. One's mobility in relation to these language game effects (language games, of course, are what this is all about) is tolerable, at least within certain limits (and the limits are vague); it is even solicited by regulatory mechanisms, and in particular by the self-adjustments the system undertakes in order to improve its performance. It may even be said that the system can and must encourage such movement to the extent that it combats its own entropy; the novelty of an unexpected 'move', with its correlative displacement of a partner or group of partners, can supply the system with that increased performativity it forever demands and consumes. ...

The trivial cybernetic version of information theory misses something of decisive importance, to which I have already called attention: the agonistic aspect of society. The 'atoms' [which form the matter of the social system] are placed at the crossroads of pragmatic relationships, but they are also displaced by the messages that traverse them, in perpetual motion. Each language partner, when a 'move' pertaining to him is made, undergoes a 'displacement', an alteration of some kind that not only affects him in his capacity as addressee and referent, but also as sender. These 'moves' necessarily provoke 'countermoves' – and everyone knows that a countermove that is merely reactional is not a 'good' move. Reactional countermoves are no more than programmed effects in the opponent's strategy; they play into his hands and thus have no effect on the balance of power. That is why it is important to increase displacement in the games, and even to disorient it, in such a way as to make an unexpected 'move' (a new statement).

What is needed if we are to understand social relations in this manner, on whatever scale we choose, is not only a theory of communication, but a theory of games which accepts agonistics as a founding principle. In this context, it is easy to see that the essential element of newness is not simply 'innovation'. Support for this approach can be found in the work of a number of contemporary sociologists, in addition to linguists and philosophers of language.

This 'atomization' of the social into flexible networks of language games may seem far removed from the modern reality, which is depicted, on the contrary, as afflicted with bureaucratic paralysis. The objection will be made, at least, that the weight of certain institutions imposes limits on the games, and thus restricts the inventiveness of the players in making their moves. But I think this can be taken into account without causing any particular difficulty.

In the ordinary use of discourse – for example, in a discussion between two friends – the interlocutors use any available ammunition, changing games from one utterance to the next: questions, requests, assertions, and narratives are launched pell-mell into battle. The war is not without rules, but the rules allow and encourage the greatest possible flexibility of utterance.

From this point of view, an institution differs from a conversation in that it always requires supplementary constraints for statements to be declared admissible within its bounds. The constraints function to filter discursive potentials, interrupting possible connections in the communication networks: there are things that should not be said. They also privilege certain classes of statements (sometimes only one) whose predominance characterizes the discourse of the particular institution: there are things that should be said, and there are ways of saying them. Thus: orders in the army, prayer in church, denotation in the schools, narration in families, questions in philosophy, performativity in businesses. Bureaucratization is the outer limit of this tendency.

However, this hypothesis about the institution is still too 'unwieldy': its point of departure is an overly 'reifying' view of what is institutionalized. We know today that the limits the institution imposes on potential language 'moves' are never established once and for all (even if they have been formally defined). Rather, the limits are themselves the stakes and provisional results of language strategies, within the institution and without. Examples: Does the university have a place for language experiments (poetics)? Can you tell stories in a cabinet meeting? Advocate a cause in the barracks? The answers are clear: yes, if the university opens creative workshops; yes, if the cabinet works with prospective scenarios; yes, if the limits of the old institution are displaced. Reciprocally, it can be said that the boundaries only stabilize when they cease to be stakes in the game.

This, I think, is the appropriate approach to contemporary institutions of knowledge.

Key terms

The following key terms appear in the text above. They have been defined below to aid with the reading of this item.

post-modern relating to the period of social history after the 'modernity' of the founders – a period characterized by a decline in absolute truth

discourse a set of specialized languages which have the power to define the object 'under their gaze'

metadiscourse a set of languages and ways of thinking about discourses; a discourse about discourse

dialectics a way of thinking that uses the conflict between two opposites to produce something new. For example, Marxism is a theory that uses dialectical thinking, since class conflict produces revolutionary struggle towards a new social order

hermeneutics the study of interpreting how action is meaningful to individuals

Enlightenment the period of western European history after the Renaissance when science rose to the fore as a principle form of knowledge. Enlightenment thinkers believed that, through rationality, humans could master the world of nature completely

narrative 'story'. Used by Lyotard to refer to any important knowledge claim in a post-modern age, where – since all knowledge is relative – all claims to the truth are as true as each other, thus they are all 'big stories', or 'metanarratives'

cybernetics the study of structures and systems as machines; comparing human-made systems and their functioning to biological systems

mercantilization the process of mercantilism, meaning the economic idea from the 1800s that wealth depends upon the ownership of precious metals. This became a political justification for colonialism by the Western world

nodal points in mathematics, a 'node' is a point on a web or a map; a specific point in a system where two branches of the system intersect

atomization becoming 'atom-like'; society becoming reduced to separate parts. Also known as a 'mass society' theory – where social living experiences a 'decline of community' and life becomes privatized and isolated

Questions

1 According to Lyotard, what are the characteristics of a 'post-modern condition' in social life?

2 According to the reading, what changes to scientific knowledge have taken place?

3 According to Lyotard, how is knowledge a commodity of power?

4 To what extent do you agree with Lyotard that knowledge and language are forms of power in society?

Reading 18.5 **Power, discipline and discourse**

Michel Foucault (from) 'The means of correct training', in P. Rabinow (ed.) *The Foucault Reader* (1984, originally published in *Discipline and Punish* by Foucault, in France in 1975) Harmondsworth: Penguin, pp. 188–93 and 204–5.

Editorial comments

In this extract – originally published in Foucault's work *Discipline and Punish* – Foucault writes of a very special sort of power, that is contained within a total institution. These sites of power, such as the hospital, the mental asylum, the army barracks, the prison, the factory and the school are all seen by Foucault to operate a very similar form of control on the individual as an object of surveillance. Through the manipulation of timetables, examinations and routines, the individual becomes an 'object' under the 'gaze' of a discourse: a specialized language which disciplines the body.

Foucault has an image of contemporary social life as based on a web of discourses – all of which contribute to the creation, and therefore the control or 'discipline', of our self-image. Society is based on the surveillance of the body: limiting action and controlling the space and time we act in.

The Means of Correct Training

AT THE BEGINNING of the seventeenth century, Walhausen spoke of 'strict **discipline**' as an art of correct training. The chief function of the disciplinary power is to 'train', rather than to select and to levy; or, no doubt, to train in order to levy and select all the more. It does not link forces together in order to reduce them; it seeks to bind them together in such a way as to multiply and use them. Instead of bending all its subjects into a single, uniform mass, it separates, analyses, differentiates, carries its procedures of decomposition to the point of necessary and sufficient single units. It 'trains' the moving, confused, useless multitudes of bodies and forces into a multiplicity of individual elements – small, separate cells; organic autonomies; genetic identities and continuities; combinatory segments. Discipline 'makes' individuals; it is the specific technique of a power that regards individuals both as objects and as instruments of its exercise. It is not a triumphant power, which because of its own excess can pride itself on its omnipotence; it is a modest, suspicious power, which functions as a calculated but permanent economy. These are humble modalities, minor procedures, compared with the majestic rituals of sovereignty or the great apparatuses of the state. And it is precisely they that were gradually to invade the major forms, altering their mechanisms and imposing their procedures. The legal apparatus was not to escape this scarcely secret invasion. The success of disciplinary power derives no doubt from the use of simple instruments: hierarchical observation, normalizing judgment, and their combination in a procedure that is specific to it – the examination.

Hierarchical observation

The exercise of discipline presupposes a mechanism that coerces by means of observation; an apparatus in which the techniques that make it possible to see induce effects of power and in which, conversely, the means of coercion make those on whom they are applied clearly visible. Slowly, in the course of the classical age, we see the construction of those 'observatories' of human multiplicity for which the history of the sciences has so little good to say. Side by side with the major technology of the telescope, the lens, and the light beam, which were an integral part of the new physics and cosmology, there were the minor techniques of multiple and intersecting observations, of eyes that must see without being seen; using techniques of subjection and methods of exploitation, an obscure art of light and the visible was secretly preparing a new knowledge of man.

These 'observatories' had an almost ideal model: the military camp – the short-lived, artificial city, built and reshaped almost at will; the seat of a power that must be all the stronger, but also all the more discreet, all the more effective and on the alert in that it is exercised over armed men. In the perfect camp, all power would be exercised solely through exact observation; each gaze would form a part of the overall functioning of power. The old, traditional square plan was considerably refined in innumerable new projects. The geometry of the paths, the number and distribution of the tents, the orientation of their entrances, the disposition of files and ranks were exactly defined; the network of gazes that supervised one another was laid down …

For a long time this model of the camp, or at least its underlying principle, was found in urban development, in the construction of working-class housing estates, hospitals, asylums, prisons, schools: the spatial 'nesting' of hierarchized surveillance. The principle was one of 'embedding' (*encastrement*). The camp was to the rather shameful art of surveillance what the dark room was to the great science of optics.

A whole problematic then develops: that of an architecture that is no longer built simply to be seen (as with the ostentation of palaces), or to observe the external space (cf. the geometry of fortresses), but to permit an internal, articulated and detailed control – to render visible those who are inside it; in more general terms, an architecture that would operate to transform individuals: to act on those it shelters, to provide a hold on their conduct, to carry the effects of power right to them, to make it possible to know them, to alter them. Stones can make people docile and knowable. The old simple schema of confinement and enclosure – thick walls, a heavy gate that prevents entering or leaving – began to be replaced by the calculation of openings, of filled and empty spaces, passages and transparencies. In this way the hospital building was gradually organized as an instrument of medical action: it was to allow a better observation of patients, and therefore a better calibration of their treatment; the form of the buildings, by the careful separation of the patients, was to prevent contagions; lastly, the ventilation and the air that circulated around each bed were to prevent the deleterious vapours from stagnating around the patient, breaking down his humours and spreading the disease by their immediate effects. The hospital – which was to be built in the second half of the century and for which so many plans were drawn up after the Hôtel-Dieu burnt down for the second time – was no longer simply the roof under which penury and imminent death took shelter; it was, in its very materiality, a therapeutic operator.

Similarly, the school building was to be a mechanism for training. It was as a pedagogical machine that Pâris-Duverney conceived the École Militaire, right down to the minute details that he had imposed on the architect, Gabriel. Train vigorous bodies, the imperative of health; obtain competent officers, the imperative of qualification; create obedient soldiers, the imperative of politics; prevent debauchery and homosexuality, the imperative of morality. A fourfold reason for establishing sealed compartments between individuals, but also apertures for continuous surveillance. The very building of the École was to be an apparatus for observation; the rooms were distributed along a corridor like a series of small cells; at regular intervals, an officer's quarters was situated, so that 'every ten pupils had an officer on each side'; the pupils were confined to their cells throughout the night; and Pâris had insisted that 'a window be placed on the corridor wall of each room from chest level to within one or two feet of the ceiling. Not only is it pleasant to have such windows, but one would venture to say that it is useful, in several respects, not to mention the disciplinary reasons that may determine this arrangement'. In the dining rooms was 'a slightly raised platform for the tables of the inspectors of studies, so that they may see all the tables of the pupils of their divisions during meals'; latrines had been installed with half-doors, so that the supervisor on duty could see the head and legs of the pupils, and also with side walls sufficiently high 'that those inside cannot see one another'. This infinitely scrupulous concern with surveillance is expressed in the architecture by innumerable petty mechanisms. These mechanisms can only be seen as unimportant if one forgets the role of this instrumentation, minor but flawless, in the progressive objectification and the ever more subtle partitioning of individual behavior. The disciplinary institutions secreted a machinery of control that functioned like a microscope of conduct; the fine, analytical divisions that they created formed around men an apparatus of observation, recording, and training. How was one to subdivide the gaze in these observation machines? How was one to establish a network of communications between them? How was one so to arrange things that a homogeneous, continuous power would result from their calculated multiplicity?

The perfect disciplinary apparatus would make it possible for a single gaze to see everything constantly.

A central point would be both the source of light illuminating everything and a locus of convergence for everything that must be known: a perfect eye that nothing would escape and a centre toward which all gazes would be turned. This is what Ledoux had imagined when he built Arc-et-Senans; all the buildings were to be arranged in a circle, opening on the inside, at the centre of which a high construction was to house the administrative functions of management, the policing functions of surveillance, the economic functions of control and checking, the religious functions of encouraging obedience and work; from here all orders would come, all activities would be recorded, all offences perceived and judged; and this would be done immediately with no other aid than an exact geometry. Among all the reasons for the prestige that was accorded, in the second half of the eighteenth century, to circular architecture, one must no doubt include the fact that it expressed a certain political utopia. ...

Hierarchized, continuous, and functional surveillance may not be one of the great technical 'inventions' of the eighteenth century, but its insidious extension owed its importance to the mechanisms of power that it brought with it. By means of such surveillance, disciplinary power became an 'integrated' system, linked from the inside to the economy and to the aims of the mechanism in which it was practiced. It was also organized as a multiple, automatic, and anonymous power; for although surveillance rests on individuals, its functioning is that of a network of relations from top to bottom, but also to a certain extent from bottom to top and laterally; this network 'holds' the whole together and traverses it in its entirety with effects of power that derive from one another: supervisors, perpetually supervised. The power in the hierarchized surveillance of the disciplines is not possessed as a thing, or transferred as a property; it functions like a piece of machinery. And, although it is true that its pyramidal organization gives it a 'head', it is the apparatus as a whole that produces 'power' and distributes individuals in this permanent and continuous field. This enables the disciplinary power to be both absolutely indiscreet, since it is everywhere and always alert, since by its very principle it leaves no zone of shade and constantly supervises the very individuals who are entrusted with the task of supervising; and absolutely 'discreet', for it functions permanently and largely in silence. Discipline makes possible the operation of a relational power that sustains itself by its own mechanism and which, for the spectacle of public events, substitutes the uninterrupted play of calculated gazes. Thanks to the techniques of surveillance, the 'physics' of power, the hold over the body, operates according to the laws of optics and mechanics, according to a whole play of spaces, lines, screens, beams, degrees, and without recourse, in principle at least, to excess, force, or violence. It is a power that seems all the less 'corporal' in that it is more subtly 'physical'.

... It is often said that the model of a society that has individuals as its constituent elements is borrowed from the abstract juridical forms of contract and exchange. Mercantile society, according to this view, is represented as a contractual association of isolated juridical subjects. Perhaps. Indeed, the political theory of the seventeenth and eighteenth centuries often seems to follow this schema. But it should not be forgotten that there existed at the same period a technique for constituting individuals as correlative elements of power and knowledge. The individual is no doubt the fictitious atom of an 'ideological' representation of society; but he is also a reality fabricated by this specific technology of power that I have called 'discipline'. We must cease once and for all to describe the effects of power in negative terms: it 'excludes', it 'represses', it 'censors', it 'abstracts', it 'masks', it 'conceals'. In fact, power produces; it produces reality; it produces domains of objects and rituals of truth. The individual and the knowledge that may be gained of him belong to this production.

Is it not somewhat excessive to derive such power from the petty machinations of discipline? How could *they* achieve effects of such scope?

Key term

The following key term appears in the text above. It has been defined below to aid with the reading of this item.

discipline a formalized practice which controls the physical body by legitimating some actions and condemning and limiting others. Discipline usually occurs in particular times and in particular spaces – such as on a school timetable

Questions

1 For Foucault the hospital, army barracks, school, etc. are all based on similar mechanisms of discipline. Describe these disciplinary practices.

2 What does Foucault suggest about self-identity under the 'gaze' of disciplinary practices?

3 At the end of the reading Foucault notes that we shouldn't think of power in 'negative terms' only. What do you think he means by this? How might the effects of disciplinary discourses be liberating?

Reading 18.6 The end of the political?

Jean Baudrillard (from) 'Forget Baudrillard: Interview with Sylvere Lotringer', in M. Gane (ed.) *Baudrillard Live: Selected interviews* (1993) London: Routledge, pp. 99–100, 112–15 and 117–19.

Editorial comments

In these extracts, presented in the form of an interview, Jean Baudrillard suggests that in a 'post-modern' society we witness the 'end of politics'. By this he means that linear or evolutionary images of social development (as held by the founders of sociology) need to be rejected: there is no pattern, there is no ultimate goal of truth towards which human societies progress. Instead, all there is are the 'pieces of meaning' left behind by the political. We have no means by which to judge the truth claims made by politicians and their competing ideologies so the only course left for the majority of the population is to give up on politics.

Forget Baudrillard

Interview with Sylvere Lotringer

SL: *LET'S BEGIN AT the end or, rather at the ends: the end of production, the end of history, the end of the political. Your reflections begin with a series of liquidations. Has the time come to put Western civilization in the wax museum? Is everything now for sale?*

I don't know if it's a question of an 'end'. The word is probably meaningless in any case, because we're no longer so sure that there is such a thing as linearity. I would prefer to begin, even if it sounds a little like science fiction, with a quotation from *Die Provinz des Menschen* (The Human Province), a recent book by Elias Canetti. It is possible, he says – and he finds the idea rather painful – that starting from a precise moment in time the human race has dropped out of history. Without even being conscious of the change, we suddenly left reality behind. What we have to do now, continues Canetti, would be to find that critical point, that blind spot in time. Otherwise, we just continue on with our self-destructive ways. This hypothesis appeals to me because Canetti doesn't envisage an end, but rather what I would call an '**ecstasy**', in the primal sense of that word – a passage at the same time into the dissolution and the transcendence of a form.

SL: *History survives its disappearance, but somewhere its spirit got snatched away. ...*

History isn't over, it is in a state of **simulation**, like a body that's kept in a state of hibernation. In this irreversible comma everything continues to function all the same, and eventually can even seem to amount to history. And then, surreptitiously (as Canetti has it), it's possible that everything is no longer real or true. In any case we would no longer be in a position to decide on that.

SL: *The 'end' you're talking about would be the end of all finalities – together with an exacerbated, empty parody of their resurgence.*

There is no end in the sense that God is dead, or history is dead. I would prefer not to play the role of the lugubrious, thoroughly useless prophet. It is not a tragic event, something highly charged with emotion, something that you could mourn – for there would still be something to be done about it. Suddenly, there is a curve in the road, a turning point. Somewhere, the real scene has been lost, the scene where you had rules for the game and some solid stakes that everybody could rely on.

SL: *How did that happen? Has this really happened?*

That's fiction. History has stopped meaning, referring to anything – whether you call it social space or the real. We have passed into a kind of **hyper-real** where things are being replayed *ad infinitum*. ...

SL: *Can you still invoke a strategy to account for situations in which the subject has no place?*

Only an 'objective' strategy that no one could recognize. What I foresee is a transposition of all forms and the impossibility of any politics. There is something like a threshold of inertia. Beyond that, forms snowball, terror is unleashed as an empty form. ...

SL: *Must all political rituals necessarily be programmed?*

Politics functioned in terms of distinctive oppositions: the left or the right. As in other areas you have the true or the false, the beautiful or the ugly, etc. Now, at a given point the energy of a situation stopped depending on this kind of dissociation. It is no longer the dialectic of the two terms that organizes things, but the fact that the forms each go their separate ways, meaninglessly, senselessly. It is the truer than true, or the falser than false. A form shoots off in a kind of relentless logic, uncalculated, without any history, without any memory, the way cancer cells go off in an organic direction. That logic seems to me more interesting because it does after all correspond more to the way things are evolving nowadays.

SL: *Where do you see that logic at work in the political field right now? In the media?*

The media are supposed to be a fabulous distortion. But behind that analysis still lurks a symbolic demand for truth. Where does that distortion come from? Placing the media in the system of will–choice–liberty is really hopeless. All you can do is invoke a total alienation of the political subject, accuse the power structure of manipulating, etc. The power structure doesn't manipulate TV, it functions exactly the way it does. It relies on representations, it also secretes them with the scant political relief of a TV image, without accuracy or energy, to the point of merging with the civil society in the indistinction of the political scene. Meaning manages to disappear in the horizon of communication. The media are simply the locus of this disappearance, which is always a challenge to the powers that be. It's becoming urgent to reformulate a theory of the media as '*agents provocateurs*' of information overload, turning political debate into a gigantic abyss. Let's get rid of the notion that the media mystify and alienate. We've had enough of that.

SL: *The theory of alienation has become the echo necessary to the media for their existence. It amounts indirectly to giving them the benefit of an intention. They don't deserve that.*

You're right. In the **transpolitical**, there is no more who. Then if it isn't the power structure, which seems pretty clear, if there is no longer a subject, is there a strategy of the object, objective irony?

SL: *The media industry never does anything but reproduce its own necessity. As William Burroughs said: all things considered, the public could get along very well without the news.*

There you have it. All that is done now is to display a range of choices which are all equally potential or fulfilled. Have you heard this story about Beau Brummell? He travelled a great deal, always in the company of his manservant. One day he was in Scotland, in a region where there are many lakes, each one more beautiful than the last. Brummell turned to his servant and asked him, 'Which lake do I prefer'? Having to choose is really a bore. That's what servants are for. In any case, that's not what counts. Power – Knowledge – Will – let the inventors of those ideas take responsibility for them. It makes perfect sense to me that the great masses, very snobbishly, delegate to the class of intellectuals, of politicans, this business of managing, of choosing, of knowing what one wants. They are joyously dumping all those burdensome categories that no one, deep down inside, really wants any part of. That people want to be told what they want is certainly not true; it is not clear either that they really want to know what they want, or that they desire to want at all. The whole edifice of socialism is based on that assumption. They start from the fact that this is what people ought to want, that they are social in the sense that they are supposed to know themselves, know what they want. I think we have pressed beyond that point, beyond truth, beyond reality.

SL: *Objective irony, that would be the masses' offhand way of getting rid of their responsibilities turning power back to its fantasies, knowledge to its obsessions, will to its illusions. The silent majority, as you see it then, is not the accomplice of law and order, but rather its silence is a dead silence. The masses are playing dead. And this stubborn silence, this insolent reserve, would sanction the disappearance of the social.*

Exactly. The large systems of information relieve the masses of the responsibility of having to know, to understand, to be informed, to be up on things. Advertising relieves people of the responsibility of having to choose, which is perfectly human and perfectly horrible. As for power, it has always seemed ironic to me to delegate it to someone. That's like catching him in a trap, and that trap closes on the political class itself. I see all of this as a profound reversal of strategy on the part of the masses. They are no longer involved in a process of subversion or revolution, but in some gigantic devolution from an unwanted liberty – with some evil genius lurking behind it all. I think we are beginning to realize how much terror lies at the heart of the paradise of communication. Beyond that, events are inconsequential, and that is even more true for theories.

SL: *But there is power in the fact of being inconsequential.*

That was what interested me about May '68. Behind the political, revolutionary and historical scene, and also behind the failure, there was the power of an event which managed to absorb its own continuity. It makes it implode, succeeds in swallowing its own energy and disappearing.

SL: *May '68 swept down on France like an avalanche, and no sooner had it appeared than it disappeared, mysteriously, practically without a trace.*

Then where has all that energy gone? Nowhere – certainly not into socialism, in any case. It must have been reabsorbed somewhere – without necessarily remaining underground so as to emerge later. For me May '68 was the first event that corresponded to this inertial point of the political scene. Continuity disappears. Only such things are fascinating. ...

SL: *You once tried, along with Virilio, to theorize the concept of the 'transpolitical'. Is the transpolitical situated on the other side of the political logic of consequences? Can that be a way of saving the political?*

The efforts to save it, that is what we are witnessing all around us. Those efforts are occupying the scene. The present, or recent, form of socialism in France – I call it 'ecstatic' – in that sense it is transpolitical. It proceeds from a model. Socialism realizes, hyperrealizes, a model which no longer has any veracity or original passion.

SL: *The transpolitical would be a negative notion then? It's the same scene but emptied out from within.*

In that sense, yes. That is part of the exterminating analysis. I'm not crazy about the term itself. It's almost too 'figurative'. It signifies that there could still be a beyond, and that we ought to go and take a look at what's going on there. I prefer the formulation in terms of that point Canetti describes. We don't know what happened after that. The traditional points of reference are no longer usable, but we don't know what we are in. To demand a degree of truth is always problematical. Fascism was already something like that. It was a kind of potentialization. That is why it remains relatively inexplicable in political terms, such as capitalism or class struggle.

SL: *There is a secret to fascism.*

Yes. It derives its overwhelming necessity precisely from its being isolated and disconnected, as in the case of the catastrophe, but this necessity is far beyond any rational finality. The secret lies in that total autonomy of a narrative, of a form, a myth, that can no longer be described in a logical, coherent and acceptable manner, but runs amok. Past a certain threshold of inertia, forms start snowballing, stampeding, and terror is unleashed as an empty form. There comes about a swept-away effect, an effect that feeds on itself and can become the source of immense energies, as fascism did, unfortunately. When effects go faster than causes, they devour them. I could easily see the 'speed-up' analysed by Virilio from this angle, as an attempt to accelerate faster than linearity can. Movement goes somewhere, speed goes nowhere. May '68 was an illogical event, irreducible to simulation, one which had no status other than that of coming from some place else – a kind of pure object or event. Its strangeness derives from a logic of our own system, but not from its history. It is a

prodigious effect, and it is situated on the other side of that crucial point Canetti describes and that I mentioned earlier.

SL: *The cause of an event is always imagined after the fact. After that jolly May, we were treated to the curious spectacle of causes racing after effects.*

May '68 is an event which it has been impossible to rationalize or exploit, from which nothing has been concluded. It remains indecipherable. It was the forerunner of nothing.

SL: *There are no children of May.*

Perhaps a kind of 'secret' is involved here too.

SL: *Tell me about secrets.*

There are fundamentally two kinds of secrets. The obscene form of the secret involves a saturation of the event with explanations. The other kind involves something which is not hidden and therefore cannot be expressed directly in words. It is this second kind of secret which makes the event somehow innocent. Now what can you do with that? Ordinarily, when things happen, you pick them up as best you can as a subject. In the case of May '68, we have been forced to give all our subjective energy to the object.

SL: *The event becomes a kind of slippery object that refers each subject back to his/her own fantasies without ever allowing itself to be touched. There are no children of May.*

That event disappeared without leaving a trace other than this secondary and parodic effect, this second or thirdhand product manufactured to occupy a political scene that has been utterly absorbed and destroyed: French socialism.

SL: *The socialists' error is to have occupied the vacuum and to have allowed themselves to be sucked into the black hole of politics.*

There are two ways of seeing this. You can say there used to be a political sphere and there isn't any more, following a Foucauldian genealogy. That was how Foucault talked about man. There is no longer a scene of politics the way it was organized around the history of power relations, production, classes. Power is no longer an objective, locatable process. This is what I say is lost, if we can speak of an end of something. We are elsewhere. If, on the contrary, the political sphere consists in knowing how to play on an event or a thing on the basis of its objective or conscious end – but in order to ward it off – then power, in political terms, becomes a kind of challenge.

SL: *A challenge from the powers that be not to exercise power?*

I wonder, in fact, if true power, the power that deepens the meaning of politics, is not the one that pulls back from itself, that plays out its own death, without even willing it consciously. The secret of power is that it can no longer be occupied, no longer be taken. When 'power' is confused with the 'power structure', you know it is no longer power. It becomes extremely vulnerable.

SL: *Could we not conceive this phenomenon in a more active fashion? The political as the art of not occupying a position yourself, but creating a void for others to rush into it.*

The political sphere must keep secret the rule of the game that, in reality, power doesn't exist. Its strategy is, in fact, always creating a space of optical illusion, maintaining itself in total ambiguity, total duplicity, in order to throw the others into this space.

Key terms

The following key terms appear in the text above. They have been defined below to aid with the reading of this item.

ecstasy the situation where there is so much information, so many pieces of meaning in 'reality', that all sense – all understanding – disappears

simulation when all the population of a society has to turn to are (obscured) media representations of 'truth'. There is no such thing as *the* truth – only media simulations of reality

hyper-real more real than real! Where media representations (simulations) are seen as truth, since there is no other source of meaning for the audience to turn to

transpolitical that which comes after, and goes beyond, the political – where meaning is lost

Questions

1 Baudrillard is a controversial figure in contemporary social thought due both to his ideas and the playfully and deliberately obscure way in which he presents them. Since he is an academic, do you think it is right for Baudrillard to play with meaning in this way?

2 What does Baudrillard have to say about the 'end of the political'? Why does he describe our current social situation as the 'impossibility of politics'?

3 Do you think Baudrillard is correct to suggest that the political has 'ended'? Has politics become unimportant in social life?

Reading 18.7 **The reinvention of politics in a 'risk society'**

Ulrich Beck (from) 'The Reinvention of Politics: Towards a theory of reflective modernization', in U. Beck, A. Giddens and S. Lash *Reflective Modernization: Politics, traditions and aesthetics in the modern social order* (1994) Cambridge: Polity Press, pp. 1–12.

Editorial comments

In this reading, Ulrich Beck explains the shape of politics in a period of 'reflective modernization' in a 'risk society'. He argues that rather than the rise of post-modernity and the end of politics, the political is slowly changing, but not ending.

THE YEAR 1989 will go down in history, it seems fair to predict, as the symbolic date of the end of an **epoch**. As we are very aware today, 1989 was the year in which the communist world, quite unexpectedly, fell apart. But is this what will be remembered in fifty years' time? Or will the collapse of the communist nation-states of Eastern and Central Europe then be interpreted akin to Prinzip's shot at Sarajevo?

Despite its apparent stability and its self-indulgent stand, it is already clear that the West was not left unaffected by the collapse of the East. 'Institutions founder on their own success', Montesquieu argued. An enigmatic yet exceptionally topical contention. The West is confronted by questions that challenge the fundamental premises of its own social and political system. The key question we are now confronting is whether the historical symbiosis between capitalism and democracy that characterized the West can be generalized on a global scale without exhausting its physical, cultural and social foundations. Should we not see the return of nationalism and racism in Europe precisely as a reaction to the processes of global unification? And should we not, after the end of the cold war and the rediscovery of the bitter realities of 'conventional' warfare, come to the conclusion that we have to rethink, indeed reinvent, our industrial civilization, now the old system of industrialized society is breaking down in the course of its own success? Are not new social contracts waiting to be born?

'Reflexive modernization' means the possibility of a creative (self-)destruction for an entire epoch: that of industrial society. The 'subject' of this creative destruction is not the revolution, not the crisis, but the victory of Western modernization.

> The bourgeoisie cannot exist without continually revolutionizing the instruments of production, that is, the relations of production, hence all social relationships. Unchanged maintenance of the old mode of production, by contrast, was the primary condition for the existence of all previous industrial classes. Constant revolutionizing of production, uninterrupted disturbance of all social relations, everlasting uncertainty and agitation, distinguish the bourgeois epoch from all earlier times. All fixed, fast-frozen relationships, with their train of venerable ideas and views, are swept away, all new ones become obsolete before they can ossify. All that is solid melts into Air, all that is holy is profaned, and the people are at last forced to face with sober senses the real conditions of their lives and their relations with their fellows.
>
> *(Marx and Engels, 1972)*

If simple (or orthodox) modernization means, at bottom, first the disembedding and second the re-embedding of traditional social forms by industrial social forms, then reflexive modernization means first the disembedding and second the re-embedding of industrial social forms by another modernity.

Thus, by virtue of its inherent **dynamism**, modern society is undercutting its formations of class, stratum, occupation, sex roles, nuclear family, plant, business sectors and of course also the prerequisites and continuing forms of natural techno-economic progress. This new stage, in which progress can turn into self-destruction, in which one kind of modernization undercuts and changes another, is what I call the stage of reflexive modernization.

The idea that the dynamism of industrial society undercuts its own foundations recalls the message of Karl Marx that capitalism is its own gravedigger, but it means something quite different. First, it is not the crises, but, I repeat, the victories of capitalism which produce the new social form. This means, second, that it is not the class struggle but rather normal modernization and further modernization which are dissolving the contours of industrial society. The constellation that is coming into being as a result of this also has nothing in common with the by now failed utopias of a socialistic society. What is asserted instead is that high-speed industrial dynamism is sliding into a new society without the primeval explosion of a revolution, bypassing political debates and decisions in parliaments and governments.

Reflexive modernization, then, is supposed to mean that a change of industrial society which occurs surreptitiously and unplanned in the wake of normal, autonomized modernization and with an unchanged, intact political and economic order implies the following: a **radicalization** of modernity, which breaks up the premises and contours of industrial society and opens paths to another modernity. ...

Reflexive modernization, as a broad-scale, loose-knit and structure changing modernization, deserves more than philanthropic curiosity as a kind of 'new creature'. Politically as well, this modernization of modernization is a major phenomenon which requires the greatest attentiveness. For one thing, it implies difficult-to-delimit deep insecurities of an entire society, with factional struggles on all levels that are equally difficult to delimit. At the same time, reflexive modernization encompasses only one developmental dynamism, which by itself, although against a different background, can have precisely opposite consequences. In various cultural groups and continents this is joined by nationalism, mass poverty, religious fundamentalism of various factions and faiths, economic crises, ecological crises, possibly wars and revolutions, not forgetting the states of emergency produced by great catastrophic accidents – that is, the conflict dynamism of risk society in the narrower sense.

Reflexive modernization must of course be analytically distinguished from the conventional categories of social change – crisis, social transformation and revolutions – but it can also coincide with these traditional conceptualizations, favouring, overlapping and intensifying them. Thus one would have to ask:

First, under what conditions does reflexive modernization turn into what kind of social crises?

Second, what political challenges are connected to reflexive challenges, and what answers to them are conceivable in principle?

Third, what is the meaning and the implication of superpositions of reflexive modernization with antagonistic developments – prosperity and social security, crisis and mass unemployment, nationalism, world poverty, wars or new migratory movements? How then should reflexive modernizations be decoded in contradictory constellations in an international and intercultural comparison?

Does modernity, when applied to itself, contain a key to its self-control and self-limitation? Or does that approach simply set loose one more whirl in a whirl of events where there is no longer any control?

Self-criticism of risk society

Anyone who conceives of modernization as a process of autonomized innovation must count on even industrial society becoming obsolete. The other side of the obsolescence of the industrial society is the emergence of the risk society. This concept designates a developmental phase of modern society in which the social, political, economic and individual risks increasingly tend to escape the institutions for monitoring and protection in industrial society.

Two phases can be distinguished here: first, a stage in which the effects and self-threats are systematically produced but do not become public issues or the centre of political conflicts. Here the self-concept of industrial society still predominates, both multiplying and 'legitimating' the threats produced by decision-making as 'residual risks' (the 'residual risk society').

Second, a completely different situation arises when the dangers of industrial society begin to dominate public, political and private debates and conflicts. Here the institutions of industrial society become the producers and legitimators of threats they cannot control. What happens here is that certain features of industrial society become *socially* and *politically* problematic. On the one hand, society still makes decisions and takes actions according to the pattern of the old industrial society, but, on the other, the interest organizations, the judicial system and politics are clouded over by debates and conflicts that stem from the dynamism of risk society.

Reflection and reflexivity

In light of these two stages, the concept of 'reflexive modernization' can be differentiated against a fundamental misunderstanding. This concept does not imply (as the adjective 'reflexive' might suggest) *reflection*, but (first) *self-confrontation*. The transition from the industrial to the risk period of modernity occurs undesired, unseen and compulsively in the wake of the autonomized dynamism of modernization, following the pattern of latent side effects. One can virtually say that the constellations of risk society are produced because the certitudes of industrial society (the consensus for progress or the abstraction of ecological effects and hazards) dominate the thought and action of people and institutions in industrial society. Risk society is not an option that one can choose or reject in the course of political disputes. It arises in the continuity of autonomized modernization processes which

are blind and deaf to their own effects and threats. Cumulatively and latently, the latter produce threats which call into question and eventually destroy the foundations of industrial society.

This type of confrontation of the bases of modernization with the consequences of modernization should be clearly distinguished from the increase of knowledge and scientization in the sense of self-reflection on modernization. Let us call the autonomous, undesired and unseen, transition from industrial to risk society *reflexivity* (to differentiate it from and contrast it with *reflection*). Then 'reflexive modernization' means self-confrontation with the effects of risk society that cannot be dealt with and assimilated in the system of industrial society – as measured by the latter's institutionalized standards. The fact that this very constellation may later, in a second stage, in turn become the object of (public, political and scientific) reflection must not obscure the unreflected, quasi-autonomous mechanism of the transition: it is precisely abstraction which produces and gives reality to risk society.

With the advent of risk society, the distributional conflicts over 'goods' (income, jobs, social security), which constituted the basic conflict of classical industrial society and led to attempted solutions in the relevant institutions, are covered over by the distributional conflicts over 'bads'. These can be decoded as conflicts of distributive responsibility. They erupt over how the risks accompanying goods production (nuclear and chemical mega-technology, genetic research, the threat to the environment, overmilitarization and the increasing emiseration outside of Western industrial society) can be distributed, prevented, controlled and legitimized. ...

The concept of risk society brings up the epochal and systemic transformation in three areas of reference.

First, there is the relationship of modern industrial society to the resources of nature and culture, on the existence of which it is constructed but which are being dissipated in the wake of a fully established modernization. This applies to nonhuman nature and general human culture, as well as to specific cultural ways of life (for example the nuclear family and the gender order), and social labour resources (for example housework, which has conventionally not been recognized as labour at all, even though it was what made the husband's wage labour possible in the first place).

Second, there is the relationship of society to the threats and problems produced by it, which for their part exceed the foundations of social ideas of safety. For that reason, they are apt to shake the fundamental assumptions of the conventional social order as soon as people become conscious of them. This applies to components of society, such as business, law or science, but it becomes a particular problem in the area of political action and decision-making.

Third, collective and group-specific sources of meaning (for instance, class consciousness or faith in progress) in industrial society culture are suffering from exhaustion, break-up and disenchantment. These had supported Western democracies and economic societies well into the twentieth century and their loss leads to the imposition of all definition effort upon the individuals; that is what the concept of the 'individualization process' means. Yet individualization now has a rather different meaning. The difference, to Georg Simmel, Emile Durkheim and Max Weber, who theoretically shaped this process and illuminated it in various stages early in the twentieth century, lies in the fact that today people are not being 'released' from feudal and religious-transcendental certainties into the world of industrial society, but rather from industrial society into the turbulence of the global risk society. They are being expected to live with a broad variety of different, mutually contradictory, global and personal risks. ...

The return of uncertainty

In this context we should also reconsider the essence of today's 'ecological crisis'. The metamorphosis of unseen side-effects of industrial production into foci of global ecological crises no longer appears as a problem of the world surrounding us – a so-called 'environmental problem' – but a profound institutional crisis of industrial society itself. As long as these developments are seen against the conceptual horizon of industrial society, then, as negative effects of apparently responsible and calculable action, their system-destroying effects go unrecognized. Their systemic consequences appear only within the concepts and in the perspective of risk society, and only then do they make us aware of the necessity of a new reflexive self-determination. In the risk society, the recognition of the unpredictability of the threats provoked by techno-industrial development necessitates self-reflection on the foundations of social cohesion and the examination of prevailing conventions and foundations of '**rationality**'. In the self-concept of risk society, society becomes reflexive (in the narrower sense of the word), which is to say it becomes a theme and a problem for itself.

> The core of these irritations is what could be characterized as the 'return of uncertainty to society'. 'Return of uncertainty to society' means here first of all that more and more social conflicts are no longer treated as problems of order but as problems of risk. Such risk problems are characterized by having no unambiguous solutions; rather, they are distinguished by a fundamental ambivalence, which can usually be grasped by calculations of probability, but not removed that way. Their fundamental ambivalence is what distinguishes risk problems from problems of order, which by definition are oriented towards clarity and decidability. In the face of growing lack of clarity – and this is an intensifying development – the faith in the technical feasibility of society disappears almost by necessity.
> (Bonss, 1993)

... In his review of *Risk Society*, Bauman (1991) criticized the 'optimism' – some would say the illusion – which is also a basis of my diagnosis. This critique is based, as can be said from my perspective, on the widespread misunderstanding that risk issues are issues of order, or can at least be treated as such. That is what they are, but that is also precisely what they are not. Instead they are the form in which the instrumentally rational logic of control and order leads itself by virtue of its own dynamism *ad absurdum* (understood in the sense of 'reflexivity', that is, unseen and undesired, not necessarily in the sense of 'reflection'; see above). This implies that a breach is beginning here, a conflict inside modernity over the foundations of rationality and the self-concept of industrial society, and this is occurring in the very centre of industrial modernization itself (and not in its marginal zones or those which overlap with private life-worlds).

Industrial society, the civil social order and, particularly, the welfare state and the insurance state are subject to the demand to make human living situations controllable by instrumental rationality, manufacturable, available and (individually and legally) accountable. On the other hand, in risk society the unforeseeable side and after-effects of this demand for control, in turn, lead to what had been considered overcome, the realm of the uncertain, of ambivalence, in short, of alienation. Now, however, this is also the basis of a multiple-voiced self-criticism of society. ...

In a political and existential sense, the fundamental question and decision that opens up here is, will the new manufactured incalculability and disorder be opposed according to the pattern of instrumental rational control, that is by recourse to the old offerings of industrial society (more technology, market, government and so on)? Or is a rethinking and a new way of acting beginning here, which accepts and affirms the ambivalence – but then with far-reaching consequences for all areas of social action? Corresponding to the theoretical axis, one could call the former *linear* and the latter *reflexive*. Alongside the analytical and empirical interpretation of this distinction, the 'politically empirical' and 'normative philosophical' interpretation of these twin terms is becoming possible and necessary (but that goes beyond the purpose of this essay).

References

Bauman, Z. (1991) *Modernity and Ambivalence*, Cambridge: Polity.

Bonss, W. (1993) 'Ungewissheit als soziologisches problem', *Mittelweg*, vol. 36, no. 1, pp. 20f.

Marx, K. and Engels, F. (1972; orig. pub. 1848) 'Communist Manifesto', *Werke*, vol. v, Berlin, pp. 465.

Key terms

The following key terms appear in the text above. They have been defined below to aid with the reading of this item.

epoch a stage in social history

dynamism a process that moves society onward, into new directions

radicalization becoming politically motivated in one's action; political action which questions 'the way things are'

rationality reflective thinking which involves the breaking down of a given object of study into its component parts to increase understanding

Questions

1 What social changes does Beck highlight as being 'evidence' of great political change in a period of 'reflective modernization'?

2 What is 'reflective modernization'?

3 What is the nature of politics in a 'risk society'?

4 How realistic do you find this idea of a 'risk society'?

Reading 18.8 **Beyond left and right**

Anthony Giddens (from) *Beyond Left and Right: The future of radical politics* (1994) Cambridge: Polity Press, pp. 1–7.

Editorial comments

In this reading, Giddens can be seen to continue the themes contained within reading 18.7 by Beck. Giddens suggests that developments in social life have led to the emergence of a post-traditional society in which politics needs to be redefined.

Beyond left and right

WHAT CAN IT mean to be politically radical today? For the spectre which disturbed the slumbers of bourgeois Europe, and which for more than seventy years took on solid flesh, has been returned to its nether world. The hopes of radicals for a society in which, as Marx said, human beings could be 'truly free' seem to have turned out to be empty reveries.

The idea of political radicalism has long been bound up primarily with socialist thought. To be a 'radical' was to have a certain view of the possibilities inherent in history – radicalism meant breaking away from the hold of the past. Some radicals were revolutionaries: according to them revolution, and perhaps only revolution, could produce that sharp separation which they sought from what went before. Yet the notion of revolution was never the defining feature of political radicalism; this feature consisted in its progressivism. History was there to be seized hold of, to be moulded to human purposes, such that the advantages which in previous eras seemed given by God, and the prerogative of the few, could be developed and organized for the benefit of all.

Radicalism, taking things by the roots, meant not just bringing about change but controlling such change so as to drive history onwards. And it is that project which now seems to have lapsed. How should one react to such a situation? Some say that the possibilities of radical change have been foreclosed. History, as it were, has come to an end and socialism was a bridge too far. Yet couldn't it be claimed that, far from the possibilities of change having been closed off, we are suffering from a surfeit of them? For surely there comes a point at which endless change is not only unsettling but positively destructive – and in many areas of social life, it could be argued, this point has certainly been reached.

Such a train of thought appears to lead well away from what are usually thought of as radical political philosophies, towards, in fact, conservatism. The main thrust of conservative thought from the days of Edmund Burke has been a suspicion of radical change in most or all of its forms. Yet here we find something very surprising, which demands explanation. Conservatism, in certain of its currently most influential guises in Europe, and to some extent elsewhere in the world, has come to embrace more or less exactly what it once set out to repudiate: competitive capitalism and the processes of dramatic and far-reaching change that capitalism tends to provoke. Many conservatives are now active radicals in respect of that very phenomenon which previously they held most dear – tradition. 'Away with the fossils we have inherited from the past': where is such a sentiment most commonly to be heard? Not on the left, but on the right.

Conservatism become radical here confronts socialism become conservative. With the fall of the Soviet Union, many socialists have come to concentrate their energies on protecting the welfare state in the face of the strains to which it has become subject. Some socialists, it is true, continue to say that authentic socialism has never been tried, arguing that the disappearance of Communism is a windfall rather than a disaster. Communism, in this view, was a form of **authoritarian dogmatism**, deriving from a revolution betrayed, while reformist socialism of the sort found in Western Europe was dragged down by trying to accommodate to capitalism rather than surpassing it. However, this thesis is threadbare indeed and socialists have mostly been thrown back on to the defensive, their position in the '**vanguard of history**' reduced to the more modest task of protecting welfare institutions.

Of course, radicals on the left do have another direction towards which to turn their eyes: to the new social movements, such as those concerned with feminism, ecology, peace or human rights. The 'universal proletarian' cannot bear the weight of the left's historical aspirations; perhaps these other agencies will take over? For not only do such groups seem 'progressive', their chosen mode of political organization, the social movement, is the same as that which was supposed to convey the proletariat to its ultimate victory.

But it is plain enough that the new social movements cannot readily be claimed for socialism. While the aspirations of some such movements stand close to socialist ideals, their objectives are disparate and sometimes actively opposed to one another. With the possible exception of some sections of the green movement, the new social movements are not 'totalizing' in the way socialism is (or was), promising a new 'stage' of social development beyond the existing order. Some versions of feminist thought, for example, are as radical as anything that went under the name of socialism. Yet they don't envisage seizing control of the future in the way the more ambitious versions of socialism have done.

The world of the late twentieth century, one must conclude, has not turned out as the founders of socialism anticipated when they sought to give direction to history by overcoming tradition and dogma. They believed, reasonably enough, that the more we, as collective humanity, get to know about social and material reality, the more we shall be able to control them in our own interests. In the case of social life in particular, human beings can become not just the authors but the masters of their own destiny.

Events have not borne out these ideas. The world we live in today is not one subject to tight human mastery – the stuff of the ambitions of the left and, one could say, the nightmares of the right. Almost to the contrary, it is one of dislocation and uncertainty, a 'runaway world'. And, disturbingly, what was supposed to create greater and greater certainty – the advance of human knowledge and 'controlled intervention' into society and nature – is actually deeply involved with this unpredictability. Examples abound. Consider, for instance, the debate about global warming, which concerns the possible effects of human activities on climatic change. Is global warming happening, or is it not? Probably the majority of scientists agree that it is; but there are others who question either the very existence of the phenomenon or the theory advanced to account for it. If global warming is indeed taking place, its consequences are difficult to assess and problematic – for it is something which has no real precedents.

The uncertainties thus created I shall refer to generically as *manufactured uncertainty*. Life has always been a risky business. The intrusion of manufactured uncertainty into our lives doesn't mean that our existence, on an individual or collective level, is more risky than it used to be. Rather, the sources, and the scope, of risk have altered. Manufactured risk is a result *of* human intervention into the conditions of social life and into nature. The uncertainties (and opportunities) it creates are largely new. They cannot be dealt with by age-old remedies; but neither do they respond to the **Enlightenment** prescription of more knowledge, more control. Put more accurately, the sorts of reactions they might evoke today are often as much about *damage control* and *repair* as about an endless process of increasing mastery.

The advance of manufactured uncertainty is the outcome of the long-term maturation of modern institutions; but it has also accelerated as the result of a series of developments that have transformed society (and nature) over no more than the past four or five decades. Pinpointing these is essential if we are to grasp the altered context of political life. Three sets of developments are particularly important; they affect especially the industrialized countries, but are also to an increasing degree worldwide in their impact.

Globalization, tradition, uncertainty

First, there is the influence of intensifying *globalization* – a notion much bandied about but as yet only poorly understood. Globalization is not only, or even primarily, an economic phenomenon; and it should not be equated with the emergence of a 'world system'. Globalization is really about the transformation of space and time. I define it as *action at distance*, and relate its intensifying over recent years to the emergence of means of instantaneous global communication and mass transportation.

Globalization does not only concern the creation of large-scale systems, but also the transformation of local, and even personal, contexts of social experience. Our day-to-day activities are increasingly influenced by events happening on the other side of the world. Conversely, local lifestyle habits have become globally consequential. Thus my decision to buy a certain item of clothing has implications not only for the international division of labour but for the earth's ecosystems.

Globalization is not a single process but a complex mixture of processes, which often act in contradictory ways, producing conflicts, disjunctures and new forms of stratification. Thus, for instance, the revival of local nationalisms, and an accentuating of local identities, are directly bound up with globalizing influences, to which they stand in opposition.

Second, and partly as a direct result of globalization, we can speak today of the emergence of a *post-traditional social order*. A post-traditional order is not one in which tradition disappears – far from it. It is one in which tradition changes its status. Traditions have to explain themselves, to become open to interrogation or discourse. At first sight, such a statement might seem odd. For haven't modernity and traditions always been in collision? Wasn't overcoming tradition the main impetus of Enlightenment thought in the first place?

As expressed in the expansion of modernity, Enlightenment thought did destabilize traditions of all sorts. Yet the influence of tradition remained strong: more than this, in earlier phases of the development of modern societies a refocusing of tradition played a major part in consolidating the social order. Grand traditions were invented or reinvented, such as those of nationalism or of religion. No less important were reconstructed traditions of a more down-to-earth kind, to do with, among other areas of social life, the family, gender and sexuality. Rather than being dissolved, these became reformed in such a way as to plant women firmly in the home, reinforce divisions between the sexes and stabilize certain 'normal' canons of sexual behaviour. Even science itself, seemingly so wholly opposed to traditional modes of thought, became a sort of tradition. Science, that is, became an 'authority' which could be turned to in a relatively unquestioning way to confront dilemmas or cope with problems. In a globalizing, culturally cosmopolitan society, however, traditions are forced into open view: reasons or justifications have to be offered for them.

The rise of *fundamentalism* has to be seen against the backdrop of the emergence of the post-traditional society. The term 'fundamentalism' has only come into wide currency quite recently – as late as 1950 there was no entry for the word in the *Oxford English Dictionary*. In this case, as elsewhere, the appearance of a new concept signals the emergence of new social forces. What is fundamentalism? It is, so I shall argue, nothing other than tradition defended in the traditional way – but where that mode of defence has become widely called into question. The point about traditions is that you don't really have to justify them: they contain their own truth, a ritual truth, asserted as correct by the believer. In a globally cosmopolitan order, however, such a stance becomes dangerous, because essentially it is a refusal of dialogue. Fundamentalism tends to accentuate the purity of a given set of doctrines, not only because it wishes to set them off from other traditions, but because it is a rejection of a model of truth linked to the dialogic engagement of ideas in a public space. It is dangerous because it is edged with a potential for violence. Fundamentalisms can arise in all domains of social life where tradition becomes something which has to be *decided about* rather than just taken for granted. There arise not only fundamentalisms of religion but of ethnicity, the family and gender, among other forms.

The transformation of tradition in the present day is closely linked to the transformation of nature. Tradition and nature used to be relatively fixed 'landscapes', as it were, structuring social activity. The dissolution of tradition (understood in the traditional way) interlaces with the disappearance of nature, where 'nature' refers to environments and events given independently of human action. Manufactured uncertainty intrudes into all the arenas of life thus opened up to decision-making.

The third basic change affecting contemporary societies is the expansion of *social reflexivity*. In a detraditionalizing society individuals must become used to filtering all sorts of information relevant to their life situations and routinely act on the basis of that filtering process. Take the decision to get married. Such a decision has to be made in relation to an awareness that marriage has changed in basic ways over the past few decades, that sexual habits and identities have altered too, and that people demand more autonomy in their lives than ever before. Moreover, this is not just knowledge about an independent social reality; as applied in action it influences what that reality actually *is*. The growth of social reflexivity is a major factor introducing a dislocation between knowledge and control – a prime source of manufactured uncertainty.

A world of intensified reflexivity is a world of *clever*

people. I don't mean by this that people are more intelligent than they used to be. In a post-traditional order, individuals more or less have to engage with the wider world if they are to survive in it. Information produced by specialists (including scientific knowledge) can no longer be wholly confined to specific groups, but becomes routinely interpreted and acted on by lay individuals in the course of their everyday actions.

The development of social reflexivity is the key influence on a diversity of changes that otherwise seem to have little in common. Thus the emergence of 'post-Fordism' in industrial enterprises is usually analysed in terms of technological change – particularly the influence of information technology. But the underlying reason for the growth of 'flexible production' and 'bottom-up decision-making' is that a universe of high reflexivity leads to greater autonomy of action, which the enterprise must recognize and draw on.

The same applies to bureaucracy and to the sphere of politics. Bureaucratic authority, as Max Weber made clear, used to be a condition for organizational effectiveness. In a more reflexively ordered society, operating in the context of manufactured uncertainty, this is no longer the case. The old bureaucratic systems start to disappear, the dinosaurs of the post-traditional age. In the domain of politics, states can no longer so readily treat their citizens as 'subjects'. Demands for political reconstruction, for the eliminating of corruption, as well as widespread disaffection with orthodox political mechanisms, are all in some part expressions of increased social reflexivity.

Key terms

The following key terms appear in the text above. They have been defined below to aid with the reading of this item.

authoritarian the belief (and practice) that strong law and order is needed in society to stop disorganization and chaos

dogmatism a biased belief, unquestioned and held without looking at the evidence

vanguard of history those who cause historical change. For Marx, the working class were a vanguard since they caused the change to communism from capitalism

Enlightenment the period of western European history after the Renaissance when science rose to the fore as a principle form of knowledge. Enlightenment thinkers believed that, through rationality, humans could master the world of nature completely

Questions

1 How are contemporary 'risks' different to those of the past?

2 What three developments are seen by Giddens as being fundamental to contemporary life? Explain each in detail.

3 What does Giddens mean by a 'post-traditional social order'?

4 What problems does Giddens identify with traditional radical politics in the present age?

Further reading

The following texts may represent a useful starting point for further investigation of the ideas contained within this chapter.

Primary texts

For a classic Marxist introduction to issues of political sociology, see:

Bottomore, T. (1993) *Political Sociology,* 2nd edn, London: Pluto Press.

For two books, important for the theoretical ideas they raise, see:

Beck, U. (1992) *Risk Society,* London: Sage.

Habermas, J. (1988) *Legitimation Crisis,* Cambridge: Polity Press.

Secondary texts

Accessible general texts on the sociology of power and politics include:

Kirby, M. (1995) *Investigating Political Sociology,* London: Collins Educational.

Riley, M. (1988) *Power, Politics and Voting,* London: Harvester-Wheatsheaf.

For a good introduction to the ideas of globalization (becoming increasingly important in this topic area) see:

Waters, M. (1995) *Globalization,* London: Routledge.

For a feminist review of the sociology of politics (amongst other areas) see:

Abbott, P. and Wallace, C. (1997) *An Introduction to Sociology: Feminist perspectives,* 2nd edn, London: Routledge.

Coursework suggestions

1 An analysis of political lifestyles in a 'risk society'

This piece of research could test the ideas of Beck and Giddens contained within readings 18.7 and 18.8. Questionnaires and/or in-depth interviews could be used to try to assess whether class or uncertainty is the basis for lifestyle choices, social action and political action.

2 An assessment of the sociological significance of eco-politics

This piece of research could examine the question: 'Does a rise in a commitment to environmentalism prove that politics has not "ended" but changed shape?'

This research could test the ideas of post-modernists versus the ideas of Beck and Giddens. Are eco-politics an example of the breaking down of politics and class identity, or are they more to do with the rise of a risk society and therefore the continuation of modernity rather than 'post'-modernity? Questionnaires and interviews could be used in this study.

19
Religion and belief systems

Chapter summary

Reading 19.1 **An introduction to theories of religion**   *page 561*

A great deal of the sociological study of religion – like a great deal of sociology in general – rests upon the ideas of the classical sociologists themselves: the founders. Bocock and Thompson review the ideas of the founders and relate them to more contemporary concerns.

Reading 19.2 **Marxist interpretations of the role of religion in society**   *page 566*

Perhaps Marx's most famous statement on religion is the claim that he regards it as an 'opium of the people'. This extract considers this classic statement in more detail.

Reading 19.3 **Durkheimian interpretations of the role of religion in society**   *page 568*

For Durkheim, the importance of collective religious ritual around a common sacred belief system is vital for social stability.

Reading 19.4 **Religion, ideology and utopia**   *page 570*

Due to the influence of a Marxist perspective, when considering the role of religion in society, many commentators talk of the ideas of 'ideology' and 'false consciousness'. Karl Mannheim defines the latter concept here.

Reading 19.5 **Religion, world-building and reality**   *page 572*

Adopting a phenomenological perspective, Peter Berger argues that religious ideas can help social actors to 'world-build' – to impose onto the chaos of nature the order needed for meaningful human action to take place.

Reading 19.6 **An overview of the secularization debate**   *page 575*

A vital question in the contemporary sociology of religion is 'to what extent has religion declined in society?' Malcolm Hamilton extract considers various responses to this question.

Reading 19.7 **Moving the sociology of religion forward: the body and religion**   *page 582*

For Bryan Turner, sociological theorizing on the nature and role of religion in society is part of a much wider theoretical theme: the sociological discussion of the body in society.

Reading 19.8 **Foucault, sexuality and religious discourse**   *page 587*

Michel Foucault sees religion as an example of a discourse which controls, regulates and disciplines the human body – in this case, the social and cultural expression of sexuality.

Introduction: Reading the sociology of religion and belief systems

The ideas, themes, issues and theories that come together in the sociology of religion, ideology and belief systems have their origin in the birth of the subject in the very first place. For the founders – especially Comte, Durkheim and Weber – sociology was a rational scientific study of human social life. This evolution of rationality in 'modernity' was both the object of the sociological gaze, and equally, a histori-

cal and cultural development which lead to the development of sociology itself. For Comte, scientific thought (of which sociology was a part) would take over from religion as the principle form of knowledge.

This classical legacy in the sociology of religion is well documented by Bocock and Thompson (1985) in **reading 19.1**. They illustrate how the key concepts of the founders can be investigated by looking at their ideas on the role of religion in society: the Marxist idea of ideology; Durkheimian ideas of social solidarity; and Weberian ideas of the role of cultural values in society, in opposition to the Marxist materialist conception of historical development.

For Marx, religion is seen as a form of ideological control. As he states in **reading 19.2**, religion is 'the opium of the people' (1984, originally written in 1844) – it is a set of values that legitimate unequal power relationships in society by justifying poverty. For Marxists, religion – and other forms of ideology such as education and the media – create a false consciousness amongst the masses. This idea is defined by Karl Mannheim in **reading 19.4** from his book *Ideology and Utopia* (1936).

From the classical tradition offered sociology by Emile Durkheim in *The Elementary Forms of the Religious Life* (1915), we see a different interpretation of the role played by religion in society. In this case religion is a form of social cement. It bonds individuals together into a value consensus. It allows the development of a conscience collective which is internalized through collective ritual. As Durkheim suggests in **reading 19.3**, religion – or, in his terms 'the sacred' – is a human universal: it exists in every society because of its vital functions. This leads Durkheim to argue that religion will survive the process of industrialization, although its symbols will be in a transformed form. This is a different image to the inevitable secularization (the decline of religion) predicted by Comte

A third interpretation on the role of religion in society is offered by Peter L. Berger (1967) in **reading 19.5**. Adopting a phenomenological approach – influenced by the Weberian emphasis on the study of meaning and motives which dictate social action – Berger argues that religious ideas create a 'sacred cosmos'. Religion helps in the process of 'world-building' to give meaning to the otherwise chaotic existence of nature. Religion gives us a sense of stability by providing answers which allow action to take place.

Given these three interpretations of religion – religion as ideology, as social cement and as a source of meaning – many contemporary sociologists are concerned with the future existence of religion. Has religion declined in contemporary social life? This issue – the idea of secularization – is surveyed by Malcolm B. Hamilton (1995) in **reading 19.6**.

Views on secularization can be roughly divided into two broad approaches: firstly, the idea that religion can be seen to have declined in society. This is usually seen to be a consequence of the rise of a scientific and rational society. Secondly, secularization can be understood as a process not of decline but of transformation. Therefore, in contemporary social life, we are witnessing not the decline but the change, the revival, of sacred symbols. Once again, these ideas can be seen as a product of the influence of the founders – especially Comte and Durkheim.

The sociology of religion, as well as reflecting classical concerns such as those outlined above, has also been developed recently by the very contemporary concern of a sociology of the body. For theorists such as Bryan S. Turner (1991) the sociologies of health and religion are but a smaller part of a wider theoretical project: the development of an overall sociology of the body, both in the sense of the individual body and the group (as the body of society).

In **reading 19.7** Turner outlines what he considers to be the main weaknesses of previous sociologies of religion. Rather than see religion exclusively as either ideology, cement or meaning, Turner attempts to unite some of these concerns into what he calls a 'materialist explanation' of religion. Turner argues that we should unite the ideas of Marx, Engels and Weber along with more contemporary ideas from post-structural thinkers such as Michel Foucault. Religion should be seen as an instrument for the discipline and control of the human body.

Michel Foucault (1981) in **reading 19.8** continues the theme of the discipline and surveillance of the body due to religious constraint. Taking the issue of the historical development of sexual liberation, Foucault argues that we need to make more open the previously hidden history of so-called sexual deviance. He suggests that the contemporary concern with liberation hides the fact that the body and its sexuality is still constrained, labelled and disciplined. This so-called process of liberation in fact hides a far more problematic series of power relations.

What is interesting to note is that this contemporary sociological concern with the body takes us back in many ways to the classical debate we began with – the idea that religion is a source of social control.

Reading 19.1 **An introduction to theories of religion**

Robert Bocock and Kenneth Thompson (eds) (from) *Religion and Ideology* (1985) Manchester: Manchester University Press, pp. 1–8.

Editorial comments

Bocock and Thompson give a review of classical interpretations of the role of religion in society – focusing principally on the ideas of Marx, Durkheim and Weber. They then go on to discuss the importance of the idea of ideology to the sociology of religion, and apply this idea to some more contemporary concerns.

Religion and ideology

IT IS WIDELY appreciated that the study of cultural forms and processes has been greatly stimulated in recent years by a more sophisticated and flexible Marxism than that which existed in the decades of Stalinist orthodoxy. Whereas the older, economistic Marxism relegated religion and other cultural phenomena to the category of mere epiphenomena – part of a superstructure determined by the economic base – recent Marxist-inspired debates about ideology and culture have allowed a higher degree of relative autonomy to such phenomena. The sociology of religion has much to gain from a careful consideration of developments in the analysis of ideology, and in return it has much to offer, particularly by a reappraisal of the light thrown on ideology by the classical sociologists of religion and by some social anthropologists' work on symbolic structures and processes.

Classical statements and their development

Durkheim's special contribution to the study of religion as ideology was to show how its symbolic representation corresponds to something socially real (leaving aside any supernatural reference, which cannot be studied sociologically) and yet in an imaginary way. As he puts it, 'if in the midst of these mythologies and theologies we see reality clearly appearing, it is none the less true that it is found there only in an enlarged, transformed and idealized form' (Durkheim, 1915). Like Marx, Durkheim made clear that religion and ideology have a social basis, particularly in patterns of social relations and organization, but they also have a degree of autonomy, following certain rules peculiar to culture. In rejecting the crude Marxist **historical materialism** of his own day, Durkheim had something in common with those present day Marxists who would agree with his statement of the need to avoid producing a theory of religion that was 'a simple restatement of historical materialism' (Durkheim, 1915).

It was Max Weber, above all, who produced the most sensitive and complex account of the 'elective affinities' between social groups (classes, status groups, occupations, sexes) and sets of beliefs or ideologies (meaning systems, legitimations, theodicies). The contrasts he drew between religious messages that contain theodicies of good fortune for the privileged, and those which contain theodicies that offered compensation to the underprivileged, are still instructive for the sociology of religion. Similarly, his perceptive discussions of the different ideological inclinations of various intellectual strata, provide a link with Marxist insights, such as those of Gramsci on 'organic intellectuals' (the leaders of thought in each class). Like Durkheim, and no doubt Gramsci also, Weber rejected a crudely reductionist explanation of the relation between beliefs/ideologies and material-base/interests. Beliefs and ideologies could not be reduced to a mere function or reflection of material circumstances and interests:

> It is not our thesis that the specific nature of a religion is simply a 'function' of the social situation of the stratum which appears as its characteristic bearer, or that it represents the stratum's 'ideology' or that it is a 'reflection' of the stratum's material or ideal interest situation.
> *(Weber, 1969)*

Nevertheless, Weber was far from falling over into the opposite, idealist, extreme, which would have led to the unsociological conclusion that social relations and social circumstances do not affect beliefs and values. He wanted to arrive at a formulation which would do justice to material circumstances and interests and also to the channelling effects of ideas in determining people's actions:

> Not ideas, but material and ideal interests, directly govern men's conduct. Yet very frequently the 'world images' that have been created by 'ideas' have, like switchmen, determined the tracks along which action has been pushed by the dynamic of interest. 'From what' and 'for what' one wished to be redeemed and, let us not forget, 'could be' redeemed, depended upon one's image of the world.
> *(Weber, 1969)*

The Marxist tradition for a long time reflected the rather ambiguous and sometimes contradictory accounts of ideology to be found in the various writings of Marx and Engels. In the early writings of the young Marx, which were of a philosophical nature, he considered religion in the context of alienation, a condition giving rise to false consciousness and a systematized pattern of beliefs that he called ideology. In their later historical and political writings, Marx and Engels (especially the latter), tended to explain religious phenomena as directly motivated by class interests. Thus, English religiosity was contrasted, by Engels, with working-class radicalism and bourgeois free-thinking on the Continent, and explained in terms of the greater cunning of the English bourgeoisie in safeguarding their class interests by spreading religion among the workers and pretending to be religious themselves. This reductionist explanation of ideology as a simple function of class situation and interests is inadequate ...

Marx's analysis of ideology was potentially much more subtle and suggestive when he avoided the pitfalls of a reductionist class interest theory and focused instead on homologies or parallels between the principles of symbolization in different ideological spheres (e.g. religion and economics) and related these to principles of structuration in the relevant social formation. However, Marx did not pursue the analysis of symbolisation very far and tended to fall back on the notion of ideas simply being a 'reflection' of the 'real' world. As in the statement in *Capital* that:

The religious world is but the reflex of the real world. And for a society based upon the production of commodities, in which the producers in general enter into social relations with one another by treating their products as commodities and values, whereby they reduce their individual private labour to the standard of homogeneous human labour – for such a society, Christianity with its *cultus* of abstract man, more especially in its bourgeois developments, Protestantism, Deism, etc., is the most fitting form of religion.
(Marx and Engels, 1957)

Recent developments in the analysis of ideology have been concerned with improving explanation of how and why ideology takes a particular form and of how it works. Two important developments are discernible: Firstly, more attention has been given to what Geertz has called 'autonomous process of symbolic formulation', which entails examining ideologies as systems of interacting symbols and the ways in which they provide plausible interpretations of problematic social reality for particular groups (Geertz, 1966). This has led to a greater appreciation of the complexity and variability of symbolic processes, which cannot be differentiated simply in terms of false consciousness versus true consciousness. Secondly, there is now an awareness of the field of ideology in relation to classes and groups as being one of contestation and a 'lived relationship', not a mechanical process.

Culture, ideology and rationality

Although this book acknowledges that many of the developments in the analysis of ideology have derived from debates within Marxism, it also recognizes that many of the classical works on the sociology of religion were implicitly concerned with religion's ideological character and effects. A bridge between these classical studies and recent developments, including the Marxist-inspired debates, is provided by Clifford Geertz's discussions of religion and ideology as cultural systems. Geertz defines culture as 'an historically transmitted pattern of meanings embodied in symbols, a system of inherited conceptions expressed in symbolic forms by means of which men communi-

cate, perpetuate, and develop their knowledge about and attitudes towards life' (Geertz, 1966).
Geertz defines religion as:

... (1) a system of symbols which acts to (2) establish powerful, pervasive, and long-lasting moods and motivations in men by (3) formulating conceptions of a general order of existence and (4) clothing these conceptions with such an aura of factuality that (5) the moods and motivations seem uniquely realistic.
(Geertz, 1966)

Ideology, for its part, refers 'to that part of culture which is actively concerned with the establishment and defence of patterns of belief and value', whilst bearing in mind that 'the patterns of belief and value defended may be, of course, those of a socially subordinate group, as well as those of a socially dominant one, and the "apology" therefore for reform or revolution' (Geertz 1966). The difference between science and ideology as cultural systems is to be sought in the types of symbolic strategy for encompassing situations that they respectively represent. 'Where science is the diagnostic, the critical, dimension of culture, ideology is the justificatory, apologetic, one' (Geertz, 1966).

Science can itself, however, become part of an ideological system of beliefs and values, as in Comtean positivism, and Stalinist dialectical materialism. In these kinds of belief system science is seen as an alternative set of beliefs and values which can replace those of traditional religions. The notion of 'science' comes to form a central component of such ideologies – that is, science is the measure of all things. On the other hand, some belief systems claim to be sciences, such as astrology, scientology and some forms of meditation. These systems of belief, however, do not welcome critical appraisal of their predictions or techniques, and might be better seen as ideologies rather than sciences. Only complete relativists try to maintain that there is no difference between education into some form of critical rational thinking, and indoctrination, or socialization into an ideology, such that the notion of an educated public, open to reasoned argument, is virtually meaningless. **Relativists**, however, cannot use reasoned arguments to support their view that there is no such thing as science, for they do not accept that rational criteria for assessing such arguments exist.

The problem of whether or not there are thought to be any universal standards of **rationality** arises in acute form whenever people from the modern West try to understand and explain cultures in which modern forms of 'rationality', as found in sciences and technologies, are absent. An earlier generation of anthropologists, working in the first few decades of the twentieth century, produced mainly descriptive studies of the way of life, including the beliefs and ritual practices, of people living in pre-literate societies. These belief systems, often termed 'primitive religions', 'witchcraft' and 'magic', were explicitly or implicitly compared with modern science. For example, studies were made of the attempts by pre-literate peoples to cure illnesses using magic, or to explain why someone fell ill as the result of the work of witchcraft. ...

The work of empirical, field research orientated anthropologists led to many social scientists adopting a relativistic position about other cultures; that is to say, some of them adopted an approach which refused to make judgements, on the basis of modern scientific assumption, about other cultures' values, beliefs and ritual practices, such as those involved in magic and witchcraft. All beliefs, values, rituals and symbols were seen as having some plausibility in their own social settings, and should not be judged by western standards of rationality. Such relativism seemed to be consistent with a broadly liberal, tolerant approach, which many western social scientists accepted. It was challenged by events in Europe, especially with the rise of fascism and Nazism during the economic crises of the early part of the twentieth century. It was all very well to be tolerant of other cultures which were made known to Europeans and Americans by anthropologists; it was quite another matter to be tolerant of the new ideologies which emerged in Europe. The belief systems of tribal groups could be invested with a degree of plausibility by westerners, but not those of fascists, Nazis and racists, by such groups of liberal-minded social scientists. Relativism was found to have its limitations in this period of European and American history.

The effects of these developments are still operating in recent debates about nationality and cultural relativism. For instance, some writers, such as Steven Lukes (1970) argue that there are some universal rational criteria which must be used in understanding what members of any society are trying to assert, criteria which include the concept of negation, the laws of identity and non-contradiction, within logic. Lukes holds a position which is influenced by those who thought that social scientists cannot be complete relativists, and he can be seen as an example of someone inclined towards a non-relativist position, but who avoids the simple error of cultural ethnocentrism. Others have taken a less universalistic position about the existence of some basic logical laws and concepts which operate in all cultures, and are more inclined to raise questions about the supposed rational, scientific, ethical and technological superiority of the west at the end of the twentieth century compared with some other cultures. In part, this is held on the grounds that western culture is not a unity, and is full of contradictions which can produce a sense of futility and aimlessness among some groups.

Religion, conflict and legitimation

Some of these cultural contradictions within western capitalist societies have been the subject matter of debates about the role that religion has played in ideological contestation, particularly with regard to the Industrial Revolution in England. This was a subject that attracted the attentions of Weber, Marx and Engels, and also of some French historians who contrasted the revolutionary enthusiasm of their own country with the religious enthusiasm of the English. It was suggested that the channelling of ideological enthusiasm in a religious direction, particularly by Methodism, Evangelicalism and the Sunday school movement, was a crucial distraction in the formation of the English working class. ...

Another major area where the contradictions and lack of unity to be found in contemporary western culture appears in sharp focus is in the variations which exist in relationship to religion. Christianity has been the major religion historically in the west, but it is no longer so dominant as perhaps it once was. Sociologists have contributed to the analysis and understanding of the role of religion in modern societies, especially in the emphasis they have given to the social and psychological functions of religion, as distinct from its cognitive beliefs. (Here the work of Durkheim, Marx, Weber and Freud, has been especially significant.) As a cognitive explanatory system, Christianity has appeared weak when compared with the sciences of physics, astronomy, biology and even the social sciences. However, as a symbolic system offering values backed by sacred authority, **legitimation** to a variety of political views and positions and emotional, therapeutic compensations throughout the life-cycle to those who can find comfort in religious symbolism and rituals, it remains largely unrivalled. Even modern political ideologies such as communism, fascism and national socialism have not achieved the hold over both the collective and the personal lives of people in the ways in which traditional religions, and the more recent forms of religious sectarianism, have achieved in the past and the present. ...

In Britain, there is a particular ideological use of some of the symbols of Christianity which is found in the 'civil religion', as it might be called, of the rituals surrounding the monarch and the other members of the Royal Family. It is here that some sociologists and social theorists perceive an ideological role for Britain's civil religion in the creation and legitimation of major cultural and political values, especially in the area of gender roles and sexual morality. These cultural values come to appear to be backed up by the sacred authority of the Church, in part because the monarch is Head of the Church of England and of the Church of Scotland, as well as being Head of State. Other sociologists and social theorists do not attach much, if any, weight to the civil religion of Britain in the maintenance of its economic and political structures, seeing the cultus of royalty as not much more than a popular diversion, created and sustained by the mass media, and of no major political or socio-cultural significance. The economic and political structures are seen by these sociologists as being maintained and reproduced by more direct material interests and pressures operating upon different classes. It is possible to argue that both of these positions have some plausibility if a distinction is made between the role of civil religion in reproducing patriarchal cultural definitions of gender and sexuality, and the legitimation of capitalism as a mode of production on the one hand, and the actual social and economic processes involved in the reproduction of capitalist social relations in the spheres of production and consumption on the other. ...

Conclusion

We are suggesting that, on the one hand, a purely materialistic social theory, which perceives only material interests lying behind ideologies and religions, cannot do justice to the relative autonomy of religious symbolism and values in many societies both in the past and in the world since the end of the Second World War. On the other hand, social theories, in sociology or elsewhere, which treat religious symbolism in isolation from the social formation in which such symbolism is located, fail to acknowledge that religion is part of a wider cultural, economic and political set of relations. In so doing such approaches ignore the 'elective affinity' between a status group or class and a particular road to salvation, and the influence this had on the development of religious symbolism – an influence which whilst it is not fully determining is often important in giving a particular stamp to a religious belief system. In this way, it is possible to see ideological elements in a particular religion, that is, aspects of its belief and value systems which bear the imprint of the classes and status groups which have been its main bearers, or carriers, and in whose interests it may have been modified. But this is a two-way process – the carriers, themselves, are constituted in part by ideology and bear its imprint.

References

Durkheim, E. (1915) *The Elementary Forms of the Religious Life*, London: Allen & Unwin.

Geertz, C. (1966) in Banton, M. (ed.) *Anthropological Approaches to Religion*, London: Tavistock Publications.

Lukes, S. (1970) 'Some problems about rationality', in Wilson, B. R. (ed.) *Rationality*, Oxford: Basil Blackwell.

Marx, K. and Engels, F. (1957) *On Religion*, Moscow: Foreign Languages Publishing House.

Weber, M. (1969) *The Sociology of Religion*, Beacon Press.

Key terms

The following key terms appear in the text above. They have been defined below to aid with the reading of this item.

historical materialism the term given to the Marxist theory of history: the belief that the pattern of history moves forward due to the dynamics of class conflict

relativists relativism is the belief that moral judgements cannot be made between cultures – we must accept all values as equally true

rationality the process of breaking something down in order to analyse it in a systematic fashion. Weber believed that rationality was an essential characteristic of the modern world

legitimation giving power to rule; backing up with justifications

Questions

1 Describe the contributions to the sociology of religion made by:
 a Marx
 b Durkheim
 c Weber.

2 How is religion like an 'ideology' according to the reading?

3 What does the passage say about the contribution religion makes to culture?

4 How does religion give legitimacy to power-relations?

Reading 19.2 **Marxist interpretations of the role of religion in society**

Karl Marx (from) 'Toward the critique of Hegel's philosophy of right' (originally published in Germany in 1844), in K. Marx and F. Engels, *Basic Writings on Politics and Philosophy* (1984) edited by L. S. Feuer, Aylesbury: Fontana/Collins, pp. 303–7.

Editorial comments

In Marxist sociology, capitalist social control is secured by both ideological and repressive means. Religion was seen by Marx as a major contributor to capitalist ideology. He felt that religion justified exploitation and inequality – giving hope for freedom in another life, after death. This reading – a classic Marxist statement – demonstrates the ideological qualities of religion.

Toward the critique of Hegel's philosophy of right

THIS ESSAY WAS printed in 1844, in the *Deutsch-Französiche Jahrbücher*, of which Marx was one of the editors. Here, for the first time, Marx avowed his faith in the proletariat as the class that would dissolve the 'hereto existing world' with all its forms of 'self-alienation'. – L. S. Feuer (ed.)

For Germany the *criticism of religion* is in the main complete, and criticism of religion is the premise of all criticism.

The *profane* existence of error is discredited after its *heavenly oratio pro aris et focis* [speech for the altars and hearth] has been rejected. Man, who looked for a superman in the fantastic reality of heaven and found nothing there but the *reflection* of himself, will no longer be disposed to find but the *semblance* of himself, the non-human [*Unmensch*], where he seeks and must seek his true reality.

The basis of irreligious criticism is: *Man makes religion*, religion does not make man. In other words, religion is the self-consciousness and self-feeling of man, who either has not yet found himself or has already lost himself again. But *man* is no abstract being, squatting outside the world. Man is *the world of man*, the state, society. This state, this society produce religion, *a perverted world consciousness*, because they are *a perverted world*. Religion is the general theory of that world, its encyclopedic compendium, its logic in a popular form, its spiritualistic *point d'honneur*, its enthusiasm, its moral sanction, its solemn completion, its universal ground for consolation and justification. It is *the fantastic realization* of the human essence because the *human essence* has no true reality. The struggle against religion is therefore mediately the fight against *the other world*, of which religion is the spiritual *aroma*.

Religious distress is at the same time the *expression* of real distress and the *protest* against real distress. Religion is the sigh of the oppressed creature, the heart of a heartless world, just as it is the spirit

of an unspiritual situation. It is the *opium* of the people.

The abolition of religion as the *illusory* happiness of the people is required for their *real* happiness. The demand to give up the illusions about its condition is the *demand* to *give up a condition which needs illusions*. The criticism of religion is therefore in embryo *the criticism of the vale of woe*, the *halo* of which is religion.

Criticism has plucked the imaginary flowers from the chain not so that man will wear the chain without any fantasy or consolation, but so that he will shake off the chain and cull the living flower. The criticism of religion disillusions man, to make him think and act and shape his reality like a man who has been disillusioned and has come to reason, so that he will revolve round himself and therefore round his true sun. Religion is only the illusory sun, which revolves round man as long as he does not revolve round himself.

The task of history, therefore, once the *world beyond the truth* has disappeared, is to establish the *truth of this world*. The immediate *task of philosophy*, which is at the service of history, once the *saintly form* of human self-alienation has been unmasked, is to unmask self-alienation in its *unholy forms*. Thus the criticism of heaven turns into the criticism of the earth, the *criticism of religion* into the *criticism of right*, and the *criticism of theology* into the *criticism of politics*. …

But no particular class in Germany has the consistency, the penetration, the courage, or the ruthlessness that could mark it out as the negative representative of society. No more has any estate the breadth of soul that identifies itself, even for a moment, with the soul of the nation, the geniality that inspires material might to political violence, or that revolutionary daring which flings at the adversary the defiant words: *I am nothing, but I must be everything*. The main stem of German morals and honesty, of the classes as well as of individuals, is rather that *modest egoism* which asserts its limited-ness and allows it to be asserted against itself. The relation of the various sections of German society is therefore not dramatic but epic. Each of them begins to be aware of itself and begins to camp beside the others with all its particular claims not as soon as it is oppressed, but as soon as the circumstances of the time relations, without the section's own participation, create a social substratum on which it can in turn exert pressure. Even the *moral self-feeling of the German middle class* rests only on the consciousness that it is the common representative of the Philistine mediocrity of all the other classes. It is therefore not only the German kings who accede to the throne mala-propos, it is every section of civil society which goes through a defeat before it celebrates victory and develops its own limitations before it overcomes the limitations facing it, asserts its narrow-hearted essence; thus the very opportunity of a great role has passed away before it is at hand, and every class, once it begins the struggle against the class opposed to it, is involved in the struggle against the class below it. Hence the higher nobility is struggling against the monarchy, the bureaucrat against the nobility, and the bourgeois against them all, while the proletariat is already beginning to find itself struggling against the bourgeoisie. The middle class hardly dares to grasp the thought of emancipation from its own standpoint when the development of the social con-ditions and the progress of political theory already declare that standpoint antiquated, or at least problematic. ...

Where, then, is the *positive* possibility of a German emancipation?

Answer: In the formation of a class with *radical chains*, a class of civil society which is not a class of civil society, an estate which is the dissolution of all estates, a sphere which has a universal character by its universal suffering and claims no *particular right* because no *particular wrong* but *wrong generally* is perpetrated against it; which can invoke no *historical* but only its *human* title, which does not stand in any one-sided opposition to the consequences but in all-round opposition to the presuppositions of the German political system; a sphere, finally, which cannot eman-cipate itself without emancipating itself from all other spheres of society, and thereby emancipating all other spheres of society, which, in a word, is the *complete loss* of man, and hence can win itself only through the *complete re-winning of man*. This dissolution of society as a particular estate is the *proletariat*.

The proletariat is beginning to appear in Germany as a result of the rising *industrial* movement. For it is not the *naturally arising* poor but the *artificially impoverished*, not the human masses mechanically oppressed by the gravity of society but the masses resulting from the *drastic dissolution* of society, mainly of the middle estate, that form the proletariat, although, as is easily understood, the naturally aris-ing poor and the Christian Germanic serfs gradually join its ranks.

By heralding the *dissolution of the hereto existing world order* the proletariat merely proclaims *the secret of its own existence*, for it is the *actual* disso-lution of that world order. By demanding the *nega-tion of private property* the proletariat merely raises to the rank of a *principle of society* what society has raised to the rank of *its* principle, what is already incorporated in *it* as the negative result of society without its own participation. The proletarian then finds himself possessing the same right in regard to the world which is coming into being as the *German king* in regard to the world which has come into being when he calls the people *his* people as he calls the horse *his* horse. By declaring the people his pri-vate property the king merely proclaims that the private owner is king.

As philosophy finds its *material* weapon in the proletariat, so the proletariat finds its *spiritual* weapon in philosophy. And once the lightning of thought has squarely struck this ingenuous soil of the people, the emancipation of the Germans into *men* will be accomplished.

Let us sum up the result:

The only *practically* possible liberation of Germany is liberation from the standpoint of *the* theory which proclaims man to be the highest essence of man. In Germany emancipation from the *Middle Ages* is pos-sible only as emancipation from the *partial* victories over the Middle Ages as well. In Germany *no* kind of bondage can be shattered without *every* kind of bondage being shattered. The *fundamental* Germany cannot revolutionize without revolutionizing *from the foundation*. *The emancipation of the German is the emancipation of man*. The *head* of this emancipation is *philosophy*, its *heart* is the *proletariat*. Philosophy cannot be made a reality without the abolition of the proletariat, the proletariat cannot be abolished with-out philosophy being made a reality.

When all inner requisites are fulfilled, the *day of German resurrection* will be proclaimed by the *crow-ing of the Gallic cock*.

Questions

1 What does Marx say about the origins of religious beliefs – and what consequences does this have for his view on religion?

2 According to Marx, what does religion do for those who follow it?

3 According to Marx, how are the functions of religion ideological?

4 Using the passage and your knowledge of Marxism from elsewhere, how might religious ideas benefit the capitalist class?

Reading 19.3 **Durkheimian interpretations of the role of religion in society**

Emile Durkheim (from) *The Elementary Forms of the Religious Life* (1915) (originally published in France in 1912) London: Allen and Unwin, pp. 427–9.

Editorial comments

For Durkheim, like Marx (see reading 19.2), religion is a source of social control. Unlike Marx, however, Durkheim believes that this control is vital for the continuation of social solidarity. He makes the point that religion – in his terms, the 'sacred' – is a human universal and as such will continue to evolve, through different expressions and symbols, over time.

Elementary forms of religious life

THERE IS SOMETHING eternal in religion which is destined to survive all the particular **symbols** in which religious thought has successively enveloped itself. There can be no society which does not feel the need of upholding and reaffirming at regular intervals the collective sentiments and the collective ideas which make its unity and its personality. Now this moral remaking cannot be achieved except by the means of reunions, assemblies and meetings where the individuals, being closely united to one another, reaffirm in common their common sentiments; hence come ceremonies which do not differ from regular religious ceremonies, either in their object, the results which they produce, or the processes employed to attain these results. What essential difference is there between an assembly of Christians celebrating the principal dates of the life of Christ, or of Jews remembering the exodus from Egypt or the promulgation of the decalogue, and a reunion of citizens commemorating the promulgation of a new moral or legal system or some great event in the national life?

If we find a little difficulty today in imagining what these feasts and ceremonies of the future could consist in, it is because we are going through a stage of transition and moral mediocrity. The great things of the past which filled our fathers with enthusiasm do not excite the same ardour in us, either because they have come into common usage to such an extent that we are unconscious of them, or else because they no longer answer to our actual aspirations; but as yet there is nothing to replace them. We can no longer impassionate ourselves for the principles in the name

of which Christianity recommended to masters that they treat their slaves humanely, and, on the other hand, the idea which it has formed of human equality and fraternity seems to us today to leave too large a place for unjust inequalities. Its pity for the outcast seems to us too Platonic; we desire another which would be more practicable; but as yet we cannot clearly see what it should be nor how it could be realized in facts. In a word, the old gods are growing old or already dead, and others are not yet born. This is what rendered vain the attempt of Comte with the old historic souvenirs artificially revived: it is life itself, and not a dead past which can produce a living cult. But this state of incertitude and confused agitation cannot last for ever. A day will come when our societies will know again those hours of creative effervescence, in the course of which new ideas arise and new formulæ are found which serve for a while as a guide to humanity; and when these hours shall have been passed through once, men will spontaneously feel the need of reliving them from time to time in thought, that is to say, of keeping alive their memory by means of celebrations which regularly reproduce their fruits. We have already seen how the French Revolution established a whole cycle of holidays to keep the principles with which it was inspired in a state of perpetual youth. If this institution quickly fell away, it was because the revolutionary faith lasted but a moment, and deceptions and discouragements rapidly succeeded the first moments of enthusiasm. But though the work may have miscarried, it enables us to imagine what might have happened in other conditions; and everything leads us to believe that it will be taken up again sooner or later. There are no gospels which are immortal, but neither is there any reason for believing that humanity is incapable of inventing new ones. As to the question of what symbols this new faith will express itself with, whether they will resemble those of the past or not, and whether or not they will be more adequate for the reality which they seek to translate, that is something which surpasses the human faculty of foresight and which does not appertain to the principal question.

But feasts and rites, in a word, the cult, are not the whole religion. This is not merely a system of practices, but also a system of ideas whose object is to explain the world; we have seen that even the humblest have their **cosmology**. Whatever connection there may be between these two elements of the religious life, they are still quite different. The one is turned towards action, which it demands and regulates; the other is turned towards thought, which it enriches and organizes. Then they do not depend upon the same conditions, and consequently it may be asked if the second answers to necessities as universal and as permanent as the first.

When specific characteristics are attributed to religious thought, and when it is believed that its function is to express, by means peculiar to itself, an aspect of reality which evades ordinary knowledge as well as science, one naturally refuses to admit that religion can ever abandon its speculative rôle. But our analysis of the facts does not seem to have shown this specific quality of religion. The religion which we have just studied is one of those whose symbols are the most disconcerting for the reason. There all appears mysterious. These beings which belong to the most **heterogeneous** groups at the same time, who multiply without ceasing to be one, who divide without diminishing, all seem, at first view, to belong to

an entirely different world from the one where we live; some have even gone so far as to say that the mind which constructed them ignored the laws of logic completely. Perhaps the contrast between reason and faith has never been more thorough. Then if there has ever been a moment in history when their heterogeneousness should have stood out clearly, it is here. But contrary to all appearances, as we have pointed out, the realities to which religious speculation is then applied are the same as those which later serve as the subject of reflection for philosophers: they are nature, man, society. The mystery which appears to surround them is wholly superficial and disappears before a more painstaking observation: it is enough merely to set aside the veil with which mythological imagination has covered them for them to appear such as they really are. Religion sets itself to translate these realities into an intelligible language which does not differ in nature from that employed by science; the attempt is made by both to connect things with each other, to establish internal relations between them, to classify them and to systematize them. We have even seen that the essential ideas of scientific logic are of religious origin. It is true that in order to utilize them, science gives them a new elaboration; it purges them of all accidental elements; in a general way, it brings a spirit of criticism into all its doings, which religion ignores; it surrounds itself with precautions to 'escape precipitation and bias', and to hold aside the passions, prejudices and all subjective influences. But these perfectionings of method are not enough to differentiate it from religion. In this regard, both pursue the same end; scientific thought is only a more perfect form of religious thought. Thus it seems natural that the second should progressively retire before the first, as this becomes better fitted to perform the task.

Key terms

The following key terms appear in the text above. They have been defined below to aid with the reading of this item.

symbols things that stands for something else. For Durkheim, religion was a source of scared symbols which stood for group membership and which therefore bonded a society together

cosmology beliefs about the nature and origins of the universe

heterogeneous unrelated, not in a state of solidarity

Questions

1 According to Durkheim, how does religion bind us together in society?

2 How does Durkheim's ideas on religion differ from those of Marx in reading 19.2?

3 What does Durkheim have to say about the future of religion? Explain why he believes this.

Reading 19.4 **Religion, ideology and utopia**

Karl Mannheim (from) *Ideology and Utopia: an introduction to the sociology of knowledge* (1936) London: Routledge & Kegan Paul, pp. 84–7.

Editorial comments

Moving on from the classical sociological traditions represented by readings 19.2 and 19.3, Karl Mannheim has further developed Marxist ideas on religion. It is believed by many who take a Marxist-orientated approach, that revolution will not happen until the masses are aware of their exploitation. However, cultural ideas – given by education, the media and in this case religion – may hamper the development of revolutionary consciousness, instead leading to a 'false consciousness' where the existing state of society is seen as normal and beyond question. This is referred to as the ideological role of religion.

The problem of false consciousness

THROUGH THE **DIALECTICAL** process of history there inevitably proceeds the gradual transition from the non-evaluative, total, and general conception of **ideology** to the evaluative conception. The evaluation to which we now refer, however, is quite different from that previously known and described. We are no longer accepting the values of a given period as absolute, and the realization that norms and values are historically and socially determined can henceforth never escape us. The ontological emphasis is now transferred to another set of problems. Its purpose will be to distinguish the true from the untrue, the genuine from the spurious among the norms, modes of thought, and patterns of behaviour that exist alongside of one another in a given historical period. The danger of '**false consciousness**' nowadays is not that it cannot grasp an absolute unchanging reality, but rather that it obstructs comprehension of a reality which is the outcome of constant reorganization of the mental processes which make up our worlds. Hence it becomes intelligible why, compelled by the dialectical processes of thought, it is necessary to concentrate our attention with greater intensity upon the task of determining which of all the ideas current are really valid in a given situation. In the light of the problems we face in the present crisis of thought, the question of 'false consciousness' is encountered in a new setting. The notion of 'false consciousness' already appeared in one of its most modern forms when, having given up its concern with transcendental-religious factors, it transferred its search for the criterion of reality to the realm of practice and particularly political practice in a manner reminiscent of pragmatism. But contrasted with its modern formulation, it still lacked a sense of the historical. Thought and existence were still regarded as fixed and separate poles, bearing a static relationship to one another in an unchanging universe. It is only now that the new historical sense is beginning to penetrate and a dynamic concept of ideology and reality can be conceived of.

Accordingly, from our point of view, an ethical attitude is invalid if it is oriented with reference to norms, with which action in a given historical setting, even with the best of intentions, cannot comply. It is invalid then when the unethical action of the individual can no longer be conceived as due to his own personal transgression, but must be attributed rather to the compulsion of an erroneously founded set of moral axioms. The moral interpretation of one's own action is invalid, when, through the force of traditional modes of thought and conceptions of life, it does not allow for the accommodation of action and thought to a new and changed situation and in the end actually obscures and prevents this adjustment and transformation of man. A theory then is wrong if in a given practical situation it uses concepts and categories which, if taken seriously, would prevent man from adjusting himself at that historical stage. Antiquated and inapplicable norms, modes of thought, and theories are likely to degenerate into ideologies whose function it is to conceal the actual meaning of conduct rather than to reveal it. In the following paragraphs we cite a few characteristic examples of the most important types of the ideological thinking that has just been described.

The history of the taboo against taking interest on loans may serve as an example of the development of an antiquated ethical norm into an ideology. The rule that lending be carried on without interest could be put into practice only in a society which economically and socially was based upon intimate and neighbourly relations. In such a social world 'lending without interest' is a usage that commands observance without difficulty, because it is a form of behaviour corresponding fundamentally to the social structure. Arising in a world of intimate and neighbourly relations this precept was assimilated and formalized by the Church in its ethical system. The more the real structure of society changed, the more this ethical precept took on an ideological character, and became virtually incapable of practical acceptance. Its arbitrariness and its unworldliness became even more evident in the period of rising capitalism when, having changed its function, it could be used as a weapon in the hands of the Church against the emergent economic force of capitalism. In the course of the complete emergence of capitalism, the ideological nature of this norm, which expressed itself in the fact that it could be only circumvented but not obeyed, became so patent that even the Church discarded it.

As examples of 'false consciousness' taking the form of an incorrect interpretation of one's own self and one's role, we may cite those cases in which persons try to cover up their 'real' relations to themselves and to the world, and falsify to themselves the elementary facts of human existence by deifying, romanticizing, or idealizing them, in short, by resorting to the device of escape from themselves and the world, and thereby conjuring up false interpretations of experience. We have a case of ideological distortion, therefore, when we try to resolve conflicts and anxieties by having recourse to absolutes, according to which it is no longer possible to live. This is the case when we create 'myths', worship 'greatness in itself', avow allegiance to 'ideals', while in our actual conduct we are following other interests which we try to mask by simulating an unconscious righteousness, which is only too easily transparent.

Finally an example of the third type of ideological distortion may be seen when this ideology as a form of knowledge is no longer adequate for comprehending the actual world. This may be exemplified by a landed proprietor, whose estate has already become a capitalistic undertaking, but who still attempts to explain his relations to his labourers and his own function in the undertaking by means of categories reminiscent of the patriarchal order. If we take a total view of all these individual cases, we see the idea of 'false consciousness' taking on a new meaning. Viewed from this standpoint, knowledge is distorted and ideological when it fails to take account of the new realities applying to a situation, and when it attempts to conceal them by thinking of them in categories which are inappropriate.

This conception of ideology may be characterized as evaluative and dynamic. It is evaluative because it presupposes certain judgments concerning the reality of ideas and structures of consciousness, and it is dynamic because these judgments are always measured by a reality which is in constant flux.

Complicated as these distinctions may appear to be at first glance, we believe that they are not in the least artificial, because they are merely a precise formulation of and an explicit attempt to pursue logically implications already contained in the everyday language of our modern world.

This conception of ideology (and utopia) maintains that beyond the commonly recognized sources of error we must also reckon with the effects of a distorted mental structure. It takes cognizance of the fact that the 'reality' which we fail to comprehend may be a dynamic one; and that in the same historical epoch and in the same society there may be several distorted types of inner mental structure, some because they have not yet grown up to the present, and others because they are already beyond the present. In either case, however, the reality to be comprehended is distorted and concealed, for this conception of ideology and utopia deals with a reality that discloses itself only in actual practice. At any rate all the assumptions which are contained in the dynamic, evaluative conception of ideology rest upon experiences which at best might conceivably be understood in a manner different from the one here set forth, but which can under no conditions be left out of account.

Key terms

The following key terms appear in the text above. They have been defined below to aid with the reading of this item.

dialectical moving forward based upon a conflict of opposite parts. For example, Marxism is a study of dialectical forces since history is the product of class conflict which results in revolutionary change. This idea is based on the philosophy of Hegel – a great influence on Marx

ideology a set of ideas that justify positions of power and in doing so oppress the masses in society, thereby not allowing them to think for themselves or to question society

false consciousness accepting oppression without question – not seeing the reality of your 'true' situation. Marxists believe that false consciousness is the barrier to revolution

Questions

1 According to Marxist ideas in general, how is religion an ideology that produces a 'false consciousness'?

2 Give examples from the text of the ideological role played by religion in justifying power in society.

3 What does Mannheim have to say about the 'dynamic' qualities of ideologies?

Reading 19.5 **Religion, world-building and reality**

Peter L. Berger (from) *The Sacred Canopy: Elements of a sociological theory of religion* (1967) New York: Anchor Books, pp. 3–6 and 24–8.

Editorial comments

For Berger, adopting a phenomenological approach, religion – as part of culture – helps to 'world-build'. In other words, it provides meanings and motives which allow social actors to make sense of reality and to build a cultural stability onto the chaos of nature. Berger suggests that religion helps develop what he calls 'nomos' – the opposite to Durkheim's idea of anomie, not normlessness but meaningfulness. It is interesting to note that although performing sociological analysis on a micro level – concerned with the development of social symbols and knowledge – there is a certain similarity with the more macro ideas of Durkheim here. Both suggest that the function of the 'sacred' is to allow humans to make sense of the world around them.

Religion and world-construction

EVERY HUMAN SOCIETY is an enterprise of **world-building**. Religion occupies a distinctive place in this enterprise. Our main purpose here is to make some general statements about the relationship between human religion and human world-building. Before this can be done intelligibly, however, the above statement about the world-building efficacy of society must be explicated. For this explication it will be important to understand society in **dialectic** terms.

Society is a dialectic phenomenon in that it is a human product, and nothing but a human product, that yet continuously acts back upon its producer. Society is a product of man. It has no other being except that which is bestowed upon it by human activity and consciousness. There can be no social reality apart from man. Yet it may also be stated that man is a product of society. Every individual biography is an episode within the history of society, which both precedes and survives it. Society was there before the individual was born and it will be there after he has died. What is more, it is within society, and as a result of social processes, that the individual becomes a person, that he attains and holds onto an identity, and that he carries out the various projects that constitute his life. Man cannot exist apart from society. The two statements, that society is the product of man and that man is the product of society, are not contradictory. They rather reflect the inherently dialectic character of the societal phenomenon. Only if this character is recognized will society be understood in terms that are adequate to its empirical reality.

The fundamental dialectic process of society consists of three moments, or steps. These are externalization, objectivation, and internalization. Only if these three moments are understood together can an empirically adequate view of society be maintained. Externalization is the ongoing outpouring of human being into the world, both in the physical and the mental activity of men. Objectivation is the attainment by the products of this activity (again both physical and mental) of a reality that confronts its original producers as a facticity external to and other than themselves. Internalization is the reappropriation by men of this same reality, transforming it once again from structures of the objective world into structures of the subjective consciousness. It is through externalization that society is a human product. It is through objectivation that society becomes a reality *sui generis*. It is through internalization that man is a product of society.

Externalization is an anthropological necessity. Man, as we know him empirically, cannot be conceived of apart from the continuous outpouring of himself into the world in which he finds himself. Human being cannot be understood as somehow resting within itself, in some closed sphere of interiority, and *then* setting out to express itself in the surrounding world. Human being is externalizing in its essence and from the beginning. This anthropological root fact is very probably grounded in the biological constitution of man. *Homo sapiens* occupies a peculiar position in the animal kingdom. This peculiarity manifests itself in man's relationship both to his own body and to the world. Unlike the other higher mammals, who are born with an essentially completed organism, man is curiously 'unfinished' at birth. Essential steps in the process of 'finishing' man's development, which have already taken place in the foetal period for the other higher mammals, occur in the first year after birth in the case of man. That is, the biological process of 'becoming man' occurs at a time when the human infant is in interaction with an extra-organismic environment, which includes both the physical and the human world of the infant. There is thus a biological foundation to the process of 'becoming man' in the sense of developing personality and appropriating culture. The latter developments are not somehow superimposed as alien mutations upon the biological development of man, but they are grounded in it.

The 'unfinished' character of the human organism at birth is closely related to the relatively unspecialized character of its instinctual structure. The non-human animal enters the world with highly specialized and firmly directed drives. As a result, it lives in a world that is more or less completely determined by its instinctual structure. This world is closed in terms of its possibilities, programmed, as it were, by the animal's own constitution. Consequently, each animal lives in an environment that is specific to its particular species. There is a mouse-world, a dog-world, a horse-world, and so forth.

By contrast, man's instinctual structure at birth is both underspecialized and undirected toward a species-specific environment. There is no man-world in the above sense. Man's world is imperfectly programmed by his own constitution. It is an open world. That is, it is a world that must be fashioned by man's own activity. Compared with the other higher mammals, man thus has a double relationship to the world. Like the other mammals, man is *in* a world that antedates his appearance. But unlike the other mammals, this world is not simply given, prefabricated for him. Man must *make* a world for himself. The world-building activity of man, therefore, is not a biologically extraneous phenomenon, but the direct consequence of man's biological constitution.

The condition of the human organism in the world is thus characterized by a built-in instability. Man does not have a given relationship to the world. He must **ongoingly** establish a relationship with it. The same instability marks man's relationship to his own body. In a curious way, man is 'out of balance' with himself. He cannot rest within himself, but must continuously come to terms with himself by expressing himself in activity. Human existence is an ongoing 'balancing act' between man and his body, man and his world. One may put this differently by saying that man is constantly in the process of 'catching up with himself'. It is in this process that man produces a world. Only in such a world produced by himself can he locate himself and realize his life. But the same process that builds his world also 'finishes' his own being. In other words, man not only produces a world, but he also produces himself. More precisely, he produces himself in a world.

In the process of world-building, man, by his own activity, specializes his drives and provides stability for himself. Biologically deprived of a man-world, he constructs a human world. This world, of course, is culture. Its fundamental purpose is to provide the firm structures for human life that are lacking biologically.

It follows that these humanly produced structures can never have the stability that marks the structures of the animal world. Culture, although it becomes for man a 'second nature', remains something quite different from nature precisely because it is the product of man's own activity. Culture must be continuously produced and reproduced by man. Its structures are, therefore, inherently precarious and predestined to change. The culture imperative of stability and the inherent character of culture as *un*stable together posit the fundamental problem of man's world-building activity ... while it is necessary that worlds be built, it is quite difficult to keep them going.

Culture consists of the totality of man's products. Some of these are material, others are not. Man produces tools of every conceivable kind, by means of which he modifies his physical environment and bends nature to his will. Man also produces language and, on its foundation and by means of it, a towering edifice of symbols that permeate every aspect of his life. There is good reason for thinking that the production of non-material culture has always gone hand in hand with man's activity of physically modifying his environment. Be this as it may, society is, of course, nothing but part and parcel of non-material culture. Society is that aspect of the latter that structures man's ongoing relations with his fellowmen. As but an element of culture, society fully shares in the latter's character as a human product. Society is constituted and maintained by acting human beings. It has no being, no reality, apart from this activity. Its patterns, always relative in time and space, are not given in nature, nor can they be deduced in any specific manner from the 'nature of man'. If one wants to use such a term as designating more than certain biological constants, one can only say that it is the 'nature of man' to produce a world. What appears at any particular historical moment as 'human nature' is itself a product of man's world-building activity. ...

The social world intends, as far as possible, to be taken for granted. Socialization achieves success to the degree that this taken-for-granted quality is internalized. It is not enough that the individual look upon the key meanings of the social order as useful, desirable, or right. It is much better (better, that is, in terms of social stability) if he looks upon them as inevitable, as part and parcel of the universal 'nature of things'. If that can be achieved, the individual who strays seriously from the socially defined programmes can be considered not only a fool or a knave, but a madman. Subjectively, then, serious deviance provokes not only moral guilt but the terror of madness. For example, the sexual programme of a society is taken for granted not simply as a utilitarian or morally correct arrangement, but as an inevitable expression of 'human nature'. The so-called 'homosexual panic' may serve as an excellent illustration of the terror unleashed by the denial of the programme. This is not to deny that this terror is also fed by practical apprehensions and qualms of conscience, but its fundamental motorics is the terror of being thrust into an outer darkness that separates one from the 'normal' order of men. In other words, institutional programmes are endowed with an ontological status to the point where to deny them is to deny being itself – the being of the universal order of things and, consequently, one's own being in this order.

Whenever the socially established nomos attains the quality of being taken for granted, there occurs a merging of its meanings with what are considered to be the fundamental meanings inherent in the universe. Nomos and cosmos appear to be co-extensive. In archaic societies, nomos appears as a microcosmic reflection, the world of men as expressing meanings inherent in the universe as such. In contemporary society, this archaic cosmization of the social world is likely to take the form of 'scientific' propositions about the nature of men rather than the nature of the universe. Whatever the historical variations, the tendency is for the meanings of the humanly constructed order to be projected into the universe as such. It may readily be seen how this projection tends to stabilize the tenuous nomic constructions, though the mode of this stabilization will have to be investigated further. In any case, when the nomos is taken for granted as appertaining to the 'nature of things', understood cosmologically *or* anthropologically, it is endowed with a stability deriving from more powerful sources than the historical efforts of human beings. It is at this point that religion enters significantly into our argument.

Religion is the human enterprise by which a sacred cosmos is established. Put differently, religion is cosmization in a sacred mode. By sacred is meant here a quality of mysterious and awesome power, other than man and yet related to him, which is believed to reside in certain objects of experience. This quality may be attributed to natural or artificial objects, to animals, or to men, or to the objectivations of human culture. There are sacred rocks, sacred tools, sacred cows. The chieftain may be sacred, as may be a particular custom or institution. Space and time may be assigned the same quality, as in sacred localities and sacred seasons. The quality may finally be embodied in sacred beings, from highly localized spirits to the great cosmic divinities. The latter, in turn, may be transformed into ultimate forces or principles ruling the cosmos, no longer conceived of in personal terms but still endowed with the status of sacredness. The historical manifestations of the sacred vary widely, though there are certain uniformities to be observed cross-culturally (no matter here whether these are to be interpreted as resulting from cultural diffusion or

from an inner logic of man's religious imagination). The sacred is apprehended as 'sticking out' from the normal routines of everyday life, as something extraordinary and potentially dangerous, though its dangers can be domesticated and its potency harnessed to the needs of everyday life. Although the sacred is apprehended as other than man, yet it refers to man, relating to him in a way in which other non-human phenomena (specifically, the phenomena of non-sacred nature) do not. The cosmos posited by religion thus both transcends and includes man. The sacred cosmos is confronted by man as an immensely powerful reality other than himself. Yet this reality addresses itself to him and locates his life in an ultimately meaningful order.

On one level, the antonym to the sacred is the profane, to be defined simply as the absence of sacred status. All phenomena are profane that do not 'stick out' as sacred. The routines of everyday life are profane unless, so to speak, proven otherwise, in which latter case they are conceived of as being infused in one way or another with sacred power (as in sacred work, for instance). Even in such cases, however, the sacred quality attributed to the ordinary events of life *itself* retains its extraordinary character, a character that is typically reaffirmed through a variety of rituals and the loss of which is tantamount to secularization, that is, to a conception of the events in question as *nothing but* profane. The dichotomization of reality into sacred and profane spheres, however related, is intrinsic to the religious enterprise. As such, it is obviously important for any analysis of the religious phenomenon.

On a deeper level, however, the sacred has another opposed category, that of chaos. The sacred cosmos emerges out of chaos and continues to confront the latter as its terrible contrary. This opposition of cosmos and chaos is frequently expressed in a variety of cosmogonic myths. The sacred cosmos, which transcends and includes man in its ordering of reality, thus provides man's ultimate shield against the terror of anomy. To be in a 'right' relationship with the sacred cosmos is to be protected against the nightmare threats of chaos. To fall out of such a 'right' relationship is to be abandoned on the edge of the abyss of meaninglessness. It is not irrelevant to observe here that the English 'chaos' derives from a Greek word meaning 'yawning' and 'religion' from a Latin one meaning 'to be careful'. To be sure, what the religious man is 'careful' about is above all the dangerous power inherent in the manifestations of the sacred themselves. But behind this danger is the other, much more horrible one, namely that one may lose all connection with the sacred and be swallowed up by chaos. All the nomic constructions, as we have seen, are designed to keep this terror at bay. In the sacred cosmos, however, these constructions achieve their ultimate culmination – literally, their apotheosis.

Human existence is essentially and inevitably externalizing activity. In the course of externalization men pour out meaning into reality. Every human society is an edifice of externalized and objectivated meanings, always intending a meaningful totality. Every society is engaged in the never completed enterprise of building a humanly meaningful world. Cosmization implies the identification of this humanly meaningful world with the world as such, the former now being grounded in the latter, reflecting it or being derived from it in its fundamental structures. Such a cosmos, as the ultimate ground and validation of human nomoi, need not necessarily be sacred. Particularly in modern times there have been thoroughly secular attempts at cosmization, among which modern sci-

ence is by far the most important. It is safe to say, however, that originally *all* cosmization had a sacred character. This remained true through most of human history, and not only through the millennia of human existence on earth preceding what we now call civilization. Viewed historically, most of man's worlds have been sacred worlds. Indeed, it appears likely that only by way of the sacred was it possible for man to conceive of a cosmos in the first place.

It can thus be said that religion has played a strategic part in the human enterprise of world-building. Religion implies the farthest reach of man's self-externalization, of his infusion of reality with his own meanings. Religion implies that human order is projected into the totality of being. Put differently, religion is the audacious attempt to conceive of the entire universe as being humanly significant.

Key terms

The following key terms appear in the text above. They have been defined below to aid with the reading of this item.

world-building creating a meaningful reality in which social actors can make sense of the world around them: the purpose of all culture

dialectic based on a relationship between two opposites

sui generis (Latin) meaning above and beyond the individual

ongoingly a reality that is created by others before our birth and continued by us as we go about our daily lives. This is a key concept in phenomenological sociology

Questions

1 Why does Berger describe social life as a 'dialectic phenomenon'?

2 How might religion contribute to an 'ongoingly' created reality, or to use other words, how does it help to 'world-build'?

3 How is society *sui generis*?

4 According to Berger, what is a 'sacred cosmos'?

5 What functions does the establishment of a sacred cosmos perform?

Reading 19.6 **An overview of the secularization debate**

Malcolm B. Hamilton (from) *The Sociology of Religion: Theoretical and comparative perspectives* (1995) London: Routledge, pp. 166–9 and 174–81.

Editorial comments

The issue of secularization – 'the decline of religion' – is an important debate within the sociology of

religion, and one which, once more, has its legacy in classical thought, since Comte, Marx and Weber believed that religion would decline, whereas Durkheim believed that sacred symbols themselves would transform into different forms (see reading 19.3). The contemporary secularization debate is based on these two interpretations: decline and transformation – as this overview illustrates.

Secularization

WHETHER MODERN SOCIETY is secularized or undergoing a process of secularization depends very much on what one means by religion. Much of the dispute

on the question of secularization stems from the fact that there are radically different conceptions of what religion is among theorists. Wilson (1982) points out that those who use functionalist definitions tend to reject the secularization thesis while those using substantive definitions are more likely to support it. Some have defined religion in such inclusive terms that there would always be something which would count as religion. For such writers secularization is an impossibility. It is ruled out almost by definition. Such inclusive definitions, however, are, as we have seen, highly problematic.

Even when one defines religion in a more restrictive way, disagreement remains on the question of secularization. Much of it stems from the question (which is closely related to that of the definition of religion) of what one means by secularization. The term has been used in a number of different ways. A useful survey is provided by Shiner (1966). Shiner distinguishes six meanings or uses of the term. The first refers to the decline of religion whereby previously accepted religious symbols, doctrines and institutions lose their prestige and significance culminating in a society without religion. The second refers to greater conformity with 'this world' in which attention is turned away from the supernatural and towards the exigencies of this life and its problems. Religious concerns and groups become indistinguishable from social concerns and non-religious groups. Third, secularization may mean the disengagement of society from religion. Here religion withdraws to its own separate sphere and becomes a matter for private life, acquires a wholly inward character and ceases to influence any aspect of social life outside of religion itself. Fourth, religion may undergo a transposition of religious beliefs and institutions into non-religious forms. This involves the transformation of knowledge, behaviour and institutions that were once thought to be grounded in divine power into phenomena of purely human creation and responsibility – a kind of anthropologized religion. The fifth meaning is that of desacralization of the world. The world loses its sacred character as man and nature become the object of rational–causal explanation and manipulation in which the supernatural plays no part. Finally, secularization may mean simply movement from a 'sacred' to a 'secular' society in the sense of an abandonment of any commitment to traditional values and practices, the acceptance of change and the founding of all decisions and actions on a rational and utilitarian basis. Clearly this usage is far wider than any which refer only to an altered position of religion in society.

Clearly, these meanings are by no means mutually exclusive. The diversity, however, is linked to the diversity of meanings of religion and leads Shiner, echoing Martin (1965), to say that the appropriate conclusion to come to is that the term should be dropped entirely. This seems somewhat premature. The core meaning of the term would seem to be the

decline, and perhaps ultimate disappearance, of specifically religious beliefs and institutions which seems to encompass Shiner's first, second, fourth and fifth meanings. The processes involved might be different, and would each require empirical investigation, but the end result would seem to be much the same. Secularization in this sense may or may not be occurring and may or may not be a permanent process. If it is not, what may be occurring is something like Shiner's second meaning – privatization of religion. Or this may simply be an aspect or a phase of the first set of processes.

In any case, there seems no need to abandon the term or the concept. Much confusion has been caused by those who have sought to define secularization out of consideration (Martin, 1965) sometimes on the grounds that the term is a weapon used by those opposed to religion to undermine it. ...

Disagreement on the question of secularization is not, however, only a matter of terms and concepts. There is much dispute about whether contemporary society is less religious than past societies, whatever one understands by religion. It is sometimes argued that we have a false view of the religious nature of past societies and that there was as much irreligion in the past as there is today. The notion of an 'age of faith' is an illusion created partly as a result of concentrating on the religious beliefs and attitudes of the élite, of which we have more abundant information, and failing to look at those of the ordinary people. Against this, writers like Wilson (1982) have rejoindered that such a view tends to be founded on the assumption that secularization is the same thing as dechristianization. The claim that the past was just as secular as the present, and therefore the present just as religious as the past, actually amounts to the claim that the past was no more Christian than the present and the present, therefore, no less religious than the past. But the survival of paganism and 'folk religion' in ostensibly Christian societies testifies to their more religious character than contemporary society. It will hardly do, either, to dismiss the paganism, folk religion and magical beliefs and practices of the past as not being true religion as Turner (1991) does. To do so would, by implication, exclude the belief systems of most tribal societies from the category of 'religion' and restrict it unduly solely to the world religions such as Christianity, Buddhism and Islam. Even then there would be serious problems in dealing with folk and popular interpretations of these.

Turner, however, does not take a straightforward anti-secularization stance. Both the secularization and anti-secularization theorists are right up to a point, he argues. In the feudal era Catholic Christianity was very much the ethos of the upper class or nobility but remained weak among the peasants. There was and was not a golden age of religiosity against which one can contrast the present situation. This was the golden age of élite religiosity which functioned largely to provide an ideological prop for the system of property rights and inheritance. It aided the land-owning class in controlling sexuality, especially of women, in such a way as to bolster the property distribution system based upon primogeniture which was designed to maintain the concentration of land ownership in the hands of the nobility. The landless peasantry found little to attract them in Catholicism and remained often indifferent or even hostile to it and wedded to pagan or folk practices of a superstitious or magical kind.

While acknowledging very probable differences between élite and peasant belief and practice one can hardly consider this a very strong argument against the secularization thesis for the reason already stated. It is, in any case, somewhat dubious to argue that the influence of Catholic Christianity in the feudal era was based primarily on considerations of property transference. While it may have been put to this use by the land-owning class and while this may have entailed a certain interpretation of Christian teaching, it is misleading and a one-sided analysis to claim that this is the essential role of medieval Christianity. We have only to think of the cult of the Virgin Mary and of the saints to see that it had great significance as a popular form of belief and practice which addressed the concerns of ordinary peasants as it continues to do in many rural peasant communities today, especially in the Third World and developing countries. And just as it may often flourish alongside indigenous pagan and folk beliefs and practices in these regions so it probably coexisted similarly with pagan and folk religion in the feudal era in Europe.

Another argument that those opposed to the secularization thesis tend to stress is the alleged prevalence of many private and individual practices in modern society outside the context of organized religion – from private prayer to superstition, from listening to religious broadcasts on the radio to an interest in astrology and reading one's stars in magazines. Again the question of the definition of religion arises here. There is a tendency to favour extremely inclusive definitions on the part of some of those who deny that secularization is a particular feature of contemporary society.

A second problem with this argument, as Wilson (1976) has pointed out, is that if the alleged religiosity underlying such private activities does not find expression in any institutionalized or collective form that in itself testifies to the precarious position of religion in contemporary society. Wilson acknowledges that many individuals may, in fact, retain some form of private religious belief or practice in a largely sec-

ularized society. For him secularization is the 'process by which religious institutions, actions and consciousness lose their social significance' (1966). Loss of social significance, however, may be a stage on the way to the demise even of private religiosity. ...

It is certainly true that the spread of science has helped to undermine religion. Once science came to have the prestige that it won and to form the basis of so many aspects of life it could not but help call religious views of the world into question. But this is so not so much because of anything inherently contradictory in a scientific outlook and a religious one. Religion does not necessarily, at least in any fundamental sense, address itself to the same kind of question or problem that science does. Religion does not necessarily ask how things in the natural world are connected or related empirically. It may be solely concerned with the question why things are the way they are, given that they are that way. Science may reveal to us the way the world is constructed but the questions about the meaning of the world and of human existence remain. It has sometimes been said that science does not tell us anything that we *really* want to know. It depends of course on what we do really want to know or think knowable and it does not follow that religion can tell us this either but the point is that they need not necessarily come into conflict with one another (Stark and Bainbridge, 1985).)

They need not but in fact they generally have in the Western tradition because religious doctrine has sought to pronounce on empirical matters and on the basis of scripture rather than on the basis of empirical evidence. It was bound to lose in these struggles; that over the position of the earth in the solar system and over evolution being notable examples. And it was bound to be somewhat discredited as a result.

Wilson is well aware of these points but does not draw the appropriate conclusions from them. For him it is simply that religion suffered a loss of prestige. The crucial point, however, is that while this is true, it is not the fundamental process. It is not an inevitable consequence that religion or even Christianity need be undermined by the growth of science. Specific doctrines may indeed be so undermined but not necessarily the religious view of the world if it can adjust and modify its doctrines. Evolution, for example, may still present a mystery which for some requires a religious interpretation as to its meaning. The essential point is that science does not just appear from nowhere. The critical, open, sceptical attitude which characterizes science is a recent phenomenon which seems to have arisen in specific social and historical conditions – the same social and historical conditions that initiated the long road towards secularization. It was not simply the result of a slow accumulation of knowledge and evidence about the natural world. For hundreds of years little scientific progress was made in Europe which under the domination of medieval Catholicism remained less open to new ideas, less innovative and less original in thought than the ancient Greeks had been. Science quite suddenly burst forth in the early modern era. ...

The process of secularization has not, however, been a smooth and continuous one. Social developments rarely are. There have been religious revivals and declines and the graph of religiosity has its peaks and troughs. Some have detected an overall decline. Others have seen longer-range cycles and regard the secularizing trend as having reached its peak and can see signs of the re-emergence of religion. The rise of the New Religious Movements and of Christian fundamentalism are the developments most often pointed to as evidence of this. Nor has the pattern of secularization been an even or homogeneous one across different societies. The process of secularization is greatly affected by the surrounding social context, or the religious history of the country.

The author who has paid most attention to the different patterns of secularization, David Martin (1978), bases his analysis primarily upon the degree of religious pluralism or of religious monopoly present in the society but incorporates, also, a wide range of variables in his account including the strength of religious minorities and their geographical dispersion, the relationship between religious groupings and the dominant élites and the inherent character of the various religious traditions. The main types of situation distinguished by Martin are: first, that of total monopoly where the tradition is Catholic; second, the duopolistic type where a Protestant Church is the major organization but with a large Catholic minority; third, the still more pluralistic situation exemplified by England with a large state Church and a wide range of dissenting and other groups; fourth, the fully pluralist but Protestant-dominated case such as the United States; and finally those countries that have no Catholic presence, including Scandinavia and the Orthodox countries. Martin traces the complex implications of the changing role of religion in society in each of these types and the diverse consequences of this changing role for many aspects of public and private life.

Turning to the question of the permanence of secularization and alleged religious revival, Stark and Bainbridge (1980, 1985) have argued that secularization is a self-limiting process. Neither is it anything new in their view. It is part of the normal cycle of religious development. The process of denominationalization by which sects progressively lose their sectarian character and move in the direction of becoming Churches is part of the process of secular-

ization. Ultimately, Churches decline as a result of their tendency to develop ever more extreme worldliness, engendering the emergence of revived religious groups (sects) or new innovative developments (cults). While acknowledging that the rise of science stimulated an unprecedented, rapid and extreme degree of secularization in contemporary society, Stark and Bainbridge argue that science cannot fulfil many central human needs and desires. It cannot remove all suffering and injustice in this life, it cannot offer an escape from individual extinction, it cannot make human existence meaningful. Only God can do these things in peoples' eyes. Religion, then, will not only survive and rise to prominence again, it will be transcendental or supernaturalist in form. It is more likely to be, further, the innovative cult movements rather than the sectarian revivals of established traditions that will flourish since the latter can only come up against, in their turn, the same forces which have brought about a degree of secularization in the first place. The new cult movements, however, are generally free of the deficiencies of the older traditions which have made them inappropriate to the needs of an altered social situation.

Signs of the continued central importance of religion and its potential reinvigoration are found by Stark and Bainbridge in the fact that those who report no religious affiliation or belief in their surveys are more likely to accept or show interest in some form of unorthodox or fringe supernaturalism such as astrology, yoga and Transcendental Meditation. Americans who have grown up in non-religious homes are more likely to belong to a religious denomination than not to. And although the more secularized American denominations are in decline, the least secularized are not. Finally, recent decades have witnessed the emergence of hundreds of new religious movements.

Stark and Bainbridge reject the charge of Wilson (1976) and Fenn (1978) that the new sects and cults are marginal, insignificant 'consumer items' in the religious supermarket. Such a view fails to see the potential importance of new religions and is rooted in Christian-Judaic parochialism. It also stems from a failure to distinguish between different types of cult. Stark and Bainbridge consider that it is what they call the cult movement that is significant not what they term the audience cult and the client cult. The audience cult has no formal organization and is a form of consumer activity. Its doctrines and ideas are disseminated and consumed through magazines, books, and the media. An example might be UFO enthusiasts. The client cult is rather more organized but only to the extent that the typical services offered – teachings, therapies, and so on – are offered on the basis of a practitioner–client relationship requiring some degree of organization on the practitioner's side but none among the clientele. Both of these differ from the fully organized cult movement which differs from the sect only in that it is a new group standing quite outside older and more established religious traditions. Stark and Bainbridge's theories apply only to cult movements. The tendency to conflate cult movements, audience and client cults has led others, Stark and Bainbridge claim, to mistakenly assess all cults, including cult movements, as trivial and marginal phenomena.

Stark and Bainbridge offer empirical verification of their theory in the form of two derivative hypotheses which can be tested using data they have gathered. The first hypothesis holds that cults will abound where conventional Churches are weakest because in these areas a greater proportion of the population, free from attachment to established Churches, perhaps as a result of geographical mobility, will be able to experiment with new ideas. The second hypothesis holds that there will be a greater incidence of sectarian revival than new cultic experiments where the traditional Churches are relatively strong. Stark and Bainbridge find their hypotheses confirmed by their data and conclude that cult and sect formation are not functional alternatives to secularization but different responses. Secularization has greatly undermined the traditional Churches but it has not produced an irreligious population, only an unchurched one. Even in areas of low Church membership belief in the supernatural remains high.

Stark and Bainbridge may be criticized on the ground that whatever the strength of the correlations they find the numbers involved in new cults and sects remains extremely low and insignificant. Against this Melton (1993) shows that new sects, cults and movements have been founded at an accelerating rate in the United States and, while a few do disappear, most of them continue to survive and to flourish. Melton's argument is based entirely upon the number of new sects and cults. The crucial statistic, however, is the ratio of recruits to the new movements to the loss of membership of the older mainstream denominations and sects. This loss is far greater than the increase in numbers involved in the new movements at least as far as Europe is concerned. Stark and Bainbridge's analysis, even if it applies to the United States, would seem to be somewhat ethnocentric.

Anticipating such a point, Stark and Bainbridge are careful to point out that they do not think that the new sects and cults are filling the gap left by the Churches, only that to the degree that a population is unchurched there will be efforts to fill the void. This still leaves them rather open to the criticism that such efforts will remain precisely that rather than achievements. They also fail to address the question of why

it is that audience and client cults have mushroomed in recent decades. It is these, perhaps, rather than cult movements that are coming to typify the modern spiritual scene, leading us to question their rejection of Wilson's claim that it is the very marginality of these phenomena which testifies to the degree to which religion finds difficulty retaining any hold in the contemporary situation. Stark and Bainbridge take refuge in the claim that we do not know whether some, or perhaps only one, of these new movements will take off in the future just as new movements have in the past. This is, however, to enter into speculation and cannot in itself support their theory. Also, as Dobbelaere (1987) points out, we should not forget that most of the world religions only took root among the masses with the help of rulers. Since then the structures of society have changed in such a way that it is extremely unlikely that the historical processes that led to state promotion and dissemination of particular religious systems will ever be repeated. And if many efforts continue to be made by individuals and groups to promote new religions none may succeed to any great extent. It may be, to use an analogy from Berger (1971), that the supernatural cannot rise above the status of a rumour. It may be that the contemporary predicament is that people do need and desire the kind of promises that religion has traditionally offered but find all the alternatives, old and new, no longer credible.

Rather similar to Stark and Bainbridge's emphasis on the potential significance of the new cult movements is Campbell's view of the role of the cultic milieu (1972, 1982). Whereas specific cults generally are transitory, the cultic milieu is, he claims, a constant feature of society. It is characterized by seekership and there has been a major shift in contemporary society away from commitment to specific doctrines and dogmas and towards seekership, or in other words a valuation of individual intellectual and spiritual growth. This is reminiscent of Wallis's 'epistemological individualism' (Wallis, 1984). Rationalization, then, does not, in Campbell's view, promote permanent secularization but may actually strengthen the superstitious, esoteric, spiritual and mystical tendencies in modern culture. Even those who acknowledge the superiority of science are not usually in a position to judge between orthodox and heterodox claims and are likely to accept beliefs in flying saucers, extrasensory perception and a whole host of other quasi-scientific beliefs. Sharot (1989) points out that since what characterizes science is its acknowledgement that it does not have all the answers and probably never will, it leaves much territory for magical ideas to occupy since these can claim to explain what science cannot. In so far as people may not come to wholly endorse the scientific world view, and it is unlikely that they will, they will be susceptible to all manner of magical and mystical beliefs. Such beliefs are likely to be highly individualistic and fragmentary. This is because ... in contemporary industrialized societies individuals play a variety of specialized roles which are not amenable to legitimation by overarching meaning systems.

Luckmann (1967) has also characterized contemporary societies as having no need for such overarching systems of values because they do not need religious legitimation. Religion becomes an aspect of private life, of individual choice from a variety of alternatives which can be constructed into a personally satisfying system. This leads Luckmann to argue that modern societies are witnessing a profound change not in the location of the religious away from the 'great transcendences' concerned with other-worldly matters, life and death, [but] towards the 'little transcendences' of life which concern self-realization, self-expression and personal freedoms. ...

Fenn (1972, 1978) discerns five stages in the process of secularization. The first is the differentiation of religious roles and institutions which begins very early and of which the emergence of a distinct priesthood is a part but which continues throughout the history of religion. The second stage consists in the demand for clarification of the boundary between religious and secular issues. Secular structures are generally differentiated from religious ones well before the spheres of jurisdiction of these religious and secular institutions have become clear. They may never, in fact, become wholly distinct but remain blurred. This blurring of the distinction between the sacred and profane is itself something that may be promoted by the very process of secularization itself. The third stage involves the development of generalized religious symbols which transcend the interests of the various components of society. In the American context, Fenn is referring here to the development of what has been called the 'civil religion'. In stage four, minority and idiosyncratic 'definitions of the situation' emerge. Political authority is secularized but there is a dispersion of the sacred as many groups seek legitimacy on religious grounds. Finally, in stage five there is a separation of individual from corporate life.

At several stages the contradictory nature of the process can be seen. The emergence of a civil religion is a stage of the process and yet also a form of desecularization. In attempting to determine definitions of situations the state may seek to curb religious autonomy and restrict the scope of religion, especially sectarian forms, and yet at the same time seek to borrow the authority of sacred themes and principles in order to legitimate itself.

Fenn suggests that the form of religious culture which is perhaps most compatible with modernity is that which grants a limited scope to the sacred and which promotes a low degree of integration between corporate and individual value systems. It is occult and esoteric religion which best exemplifies this type of religious culture. It can be practised without coming into conflict with everyday occupational roles since it confines itself to very particular times, places, objects, and issues. It provides an ecstatic and magical form of activity and an opportunity to indulge in the irrational against the enforced rationality of formal and bureaucratically structured organizations and roles of everyday life. Clearly Fenn is close to Campbell in this view and Wallis's 'epistemological individualism' would fit well here. A recent study ... shows how followers of witchcraft and magic in the London and surrounding areas of South Eastern England are for the most part well-educated, well-qualified professionals many of whom are scientifically trained and employed in such industries as computers and as research chemists. ...

For Fenn, then, religion may persist in modern society but with a very different role and character. Secularization actually produces a distinctive religious style appropriate to modern circumstances.

> Secularization does not drive religion from modern society but rather fosters a type of religion which has no major functions for the *entire* society. ... The affinity between secular societies and certain types of sectarian religiosity, then, derives from the tendency of both to foster the disengagements of the individual's deepest motivations and highest values from the areas of political and economic action.
> *(Fenn, 1972)*

There are many advantages in Fenn's approach, particularly his emphasis on secularization as the boundary between sacred and secular being a matter of social contest and the complex and often contradictory nature of the process. There is a worrying aspect to his work, however, which stems from his very deliberate eschewal of any attempt to define his terms and concepts clearly or to directly address central debates. He considers that any attempt to define too precisely what religion or secularization mean would fail to reflect the ambiguous and highly contested meanings these terms have in everyday life. He abdicates any responsibility to state as precisely as he can what he means by religion and secularization by declaring his intention to put such difficulties themselves at the core of his analysis since they provide critical information as to the nature of secularization which is 'lost by analysts who use only satisfyingly clear concepts with adequate boundaries' (1978). A technically adequate vocabulary is of little use, he claims, in interpreting the contradictory aspects of secularization. There is much confusion in such claims. It may be true that critical information might be overlooked in the desire to fix concepts precisely but it does not follow that one's own vocabulary can be vague, loose and contradictory in confronting the issues. Fenn confuses the contradictory nature of the *process* of secularization with the contradictory nature of the concepts that have been used to describe it and with the contradictions that exist within and between discussions, debates and theories about it. How could Fenn know that the contradictions and disagreements about the meaning of secularization can provide useful information about the nature of the process unless he knows what the process in essence is? His conception is, in fact, left to a large extent implicit apart from the characterization of it as the separation of the sacred from the secular. Such a conception is clearly related to the more inclusive definitions of religion which are associated with Durkheimian and functionalist approaches in which Fenn's roots clearly lie and with which he has not entirely broken despite his criticisms of the functionalist account of religion.

References

Berger, P. (1971) *A Rumour of Angels*, Harmondsworth: Penguin.

Campbell, C. (1972) 'The cult, the cultic milieu and secularization', in Hill, M. (ed.) *A Sociological Yearbook on Religion*, London: SCM Press.

Campbell, C. (1982) 'The new religious movements, the new spirituality and post-industrial society', in Barker, E. (ed.) *New Religious Movements: a perspective for understanding society*, New York: Edwin Mellen.

Dobbelaere, K. (1987) 'Secularization: a multi-dimensional concept', *Current Sociology, 29* (2).

Fenn, R. K. (1972) 'Towards a new sociology of religion', *Journal for the Scientific Study of Religion, 11* (1).

Fenn, R. K. (1978) *Toward a Theory of Secularization*, Stoors, Conn.: Society for the Scientific Study of Religion.

Luckmann, T. (1967) *The Invisible Religion*, New York: Macmillan.

Martin, D. A. (1965) 'Towards eliminating the concept of secularization', in Gould, J. (ed.) *Penguin Survey of the Social Sciences*, Harmondsworth: Penguin.

Martin, D. A. (1978) *A General Theory of Secularization*, Oxford: Blackwell.

Melton, J. G. (1993) 'Another look at new religions', *Annals*, AAPSS, 527.

Sharot (1989) 'Magic, religion, science and secularization', in Neusner, J. *et al.* (eds) *Religion, Science and Magic*, New York: Oxford University Press.

Shiner, L. (1966) 'The concept of secularization in empirical research', *Journal for the Scientific Study of Religion, 6*.

Stark, W. and Bainbridge, W. S. (1980) 'Secularization, revival and cult formation', *Annual Review of the Social Sciences of Religion, 4*.

Stark, W. and Bainbridge, W. S. (1985) *The Future of Religion*, Berkeley: University of California Press.

Turner, B. (1991) *Religion and Social Theory*, 2nd edn, London: Sage.

Wallis, R. (1984) *The Elementary Forms of the New Religious Life*, London: Routledge.

Wilson, B. (1966) *Religion in Secular Society*, London: C. A. Watts & Co.

Wilson, B. (1976) *Contemporary Transformations of Religion*, London: Oxford University Press.

Wilson, B. (1982) *Religion in Sociological Perspective*, Oxford: Oxford University Press.

Questions

1 In what way is the secularization debate based on a question of definition?

2 What six meanings of the term secularization are highlighted by Shiner?

3 What problems for the sociology of religion might there be in this question of definition?

4 Describe the beliefs of those sociologists who suggest that secularization is taking place.

5 What alternative model to the idea of 'religious decline' is presented? Describe this model and its theorists in some detail.

Reading 19.7 **Moving the sociology of religion forward: the body and religion**

Bryan S. Turner (from) *Religion and Social Theory,* 2nd edn (1991) London: Sage, pp. 1–5 and 7–13.

Editorial comments

For Turner, the existing sociology of religion needs up-dating. He suggests that the sociologies of religion and health can both be seen as but smaller versions of the wider 'sociology of the body'. In *Religion and Social Theory* he adopts what he calls a 'materialist' approach to the sociology of the body – using religion as an example of his ideas. Turner sees religion as an example of the control, discipline and surveillance of the body.

Religion and social theory

A materialist interpretation of religion

RELIGIOUS DISCOURSES ON evil, justice and human freedom are not abstract speculations of a remote, metaphysical nature; they enter into the basic rhythm of mundane life – birth, procreation, ageing and death. Questions about religion cannot, in my view, ever be divorced from questions of the body. The finitude of our corporality is part of the 'mistake' and the reproduction of bodies, confirmation of the parody. Hence, sexuality sooner or later challenges any rational interpretation we may attempt to foist on the labyrinth of reality. As Borges drily notes, religious practices tend to divide around either ascetic control or orgiastic release. The debate over the social roles of Dionysian and Apollinian forces provides a major linking theme from Nietzsche (1967) to Gouldner's study of classical Greece and the origins of sociology (1967).

The study of religion is thus a **materialist** enterprise, since our corporality is constitutive of our experience of the parody of existence. In religious systems, the body is a vehicle for the transmission of holiness and a major symbol of evil as 'flesh'; it is the means by which the soul is educated and the obstacle to our salvation; our health and our salvation are necessarily conjoined, but our sickness may be either a sign of religious election or a mark of damnation. Tradition has it that Jesus and Muhammad were respectively physically handicapped and epileptic.

A materialist interpretation of religion normally implies **reductionism**. It suggests that religion can be 'explained away' by demonstrating that religion is merely a reflection of more basic social processes or simply the expression of economic interests or a rationalization of psychological needs. In this study, I argue that the historical and sociological importance of religion as fundamental to human life can only be grasped by an analysis of the relationship between religion, the body, family and property. My notion of 'mate-rialist' starts, therefore, with Foucault's observation that we must pose 'first the question of the body' rather than ideology. By implication, I am critical of the whole trend in the sociology of religion to treat 'the question of meaning' as a theoretical rather than material issue. Sociologists have treated the Borgesian 'parody' as simply cognitive rather than corporeal.

In this study, I follow Weber's introductory statement in *The Sociology of Religion* that the 'elementary forms of behaviour motivated by religious or magical factors are oriented to *this* world' (1966). The two features of this world which are crucial for the social functions of religion are the control of property through the family and the organization of bodies in social space. In theoretical terms, these two features bring together the traditional concerns of Marxism and the more recent perspective of structuralism. A materialist interpretation of religion does not, therefore, regard religious data as mere epiphenomena of more fundamental social processes; on the contrary, it locates religion at the centre of social production and reproduction.

Most textbooks in the sociology of religion are themselves highly ritualistic. The routine rehearsal of traditional themes has the function of integrating a community of scholars around a common set of beliefs. Like the Arunta tribe in Durkheim's classic study of aboriginal religion (1961), sociologists are also bound by *religio*, in the form of sacred texts and professional rituals. The contents page of any major textbook on the sociology of religion over the last fifteen years has a predictable range of topics: the origins of the discipline, the Protestant Ethic thesis, the church–sect typology, secularization and modern cults. Although some of the major collections of essays in the discipline show a wider range of empirical and analytical interests, the sociology of religion has followed a remarkably narrow range of theoretical interest. The central analytical question has been: 'What is religion'? and the difficulty of providing a satisfactory answer to that question has consequently dominated the debate about secularization in industrial societies. The question is, without doubt, significant in both the philosophy and sociology of religion, but it has had the effect of inducing a certain theoretical sterility and repetitiveness within the discipline. The endless pursuit of that issue has produced an analytical cul-de-sac. It seems appropriate to attempt to raise new questions and topics of a wider theoretical interest and therefore definitions of religion may, at least for the time being, be relegated to an appendix. Although this is heretical, the device has a certain economic utility.

Weaknesses of contemporary sociology of religion

The contemporary state of sociology of religion can be said to exhibit three major weaknesses. First, it has not played a role in or constituted a part of any major theoretical debate in modern sociology. The sociology of religion is a theoretical side-show in relation to, for example, neo-Marxist debates about modes of production and ideology, French structuralist discussions of subjectivity and power, and critical theory's discussion of knowledge, the state and legitimacy. The sociology of religion has tended to regard the crude metaphor of base/superstructure in classical Marxism as the only possible Marxist account of ideology in which religion is simply a reflection of economic relations of production.

... It is difficult to see how the sociology of religion could be taken to be a serious subject in the light of its absence from contemporary debates in sociology. This absence is, in my view, at least partly explained by the fact that sociology of religion has remained deeply embedded in a conventional frame of knowledge and focused on a narrow range of topics.

The second characteristic of much modern sociology of religion is its primary concern with the subjectivity of the social actor, manifested in the analysis of religious beliefs, world-views, definitions of alternative realities, commitments to the sacred cosmos and so forth. There are clearly good credentials for such a position in the interpretative sociology of Max Weber, in Talcott Parsons's critique of rational positivism (1937), in G. H. Mead's social philosophy of action (1934) and generally in the phenomenological tradition of writers like Alfred Schutz (1972).

This concentration on individual subjectivity has, however, a number of limiting consequences within the sociology of religion. It draws attention to the cognitive dimension of religious activity, so that rituals and practices take second place. Attempts to spell out a number of dimensions of religiosity in the work of Charles Glock and Rodney Stark (1965) have left religious beliefs in a central location to theory and

research. The preference for hermeneutical and **phenomenological** perspectives has meant that much sociology of religion remains content with detailed descriptions of the nature and content of religious belief and subjective experience, whereas explanations of the origins, functions and effects of religious practices and institutions are neglected. Dissatisfaction with both the structural-functionalism of an earlier tradition and Marxism has meant that the question 'What is religion, from the subjective perspective of the social actor'? has replaced the question 'What are the social effects of religious phenomena in society'?

This study of religion is, by contrast, mainly concerned with a range of theories which are engaged with the problem of the social consequences of religion for class relationships, family organization, state legitimacy and the control of individuals and populations. By examining these problems, the book looks backwards to the tradition of Nietzsche, Weber, Engels and Freud, but forwards to the modern contributions of Lévi-Strauss, Foucault, Elias, Sennett and Ladurie. Traditional analyses of religion and secularization can thus be set in the context of debates about ideology, modes of production, power and knowledge.

Such an approach takes sociology away from the approach of Peter Berger, whose *The Social Reality of Religion* (1969) dominated sociology of religion in the 1970s. By defining religion as a process of constructing symbolic worlds (the sacred canopy), Berger was able to forge an interesting and important alliance between the sociology of religion and the sociology of knowledge. However, Berger took sociology back to Feuerbachian anthropology by claiming that, in essence, man is a religious animal, forced to construct a meaningful world. The approach ignored the Marxist argument that 'the person' is an effect of an ensemble of social relations which, in turn, reflect the complex structure of class positions. The *prevalence* of religious beliefs in human groups cannot be equated with the *effectivity* of religious beliefs in the coherence of classes, the operation of the legal system, the distribution of property and the transformation of relations of production.

It is difficult to move from Berger's highly general statements about the subjective reality of sacred worlds and the religious essence of the human enterprise to specific analyses of the role of religion, for example, in class societies. This study of religion largely follows, therefore, a theoretical position developed in *The Dominant Ideology Thesis* (Abercrombie, Hill and Turner, 1980) which criticized sociologists for assuming that the social presence of beliefs was evidence that such beliefs have direct and specific societal consequences. A second argument of that study was that sociologists too frequently examine the articulate and literary beliefs of a dominant class as evidence of the existence of a general, dominant ideology. Sociologists of religion are far too ready to take theological beliefs as their data and recent attempts to analyse 'common religion' do not radically avoid this problem.

The third limitation of contemporary sociology of religion is its narrow empirical focus on Western forms of religion. In practice, the sociology of religion is very largely the sociology of Christianity. This narrow empirical range was especially characteristic of British sociology in the 1960s and 1970s; *A Sociological Yearbook of Religion in Britain* was illustrative of the competent work done in this genre. This tradition has been supplemented by good ethnographic studies of cults and sects in America and Britain, alongside a rich crop of publications on Hare Krishna, Divine Light Mission, the Unified Family and, more exotically, Yaqui spirit-possession. The trend towards the sociology of cults has now gone so far that mainstream Christianity has to some extent been neglected. The principal exception to this picture is provided by the social history of Catholicism. ...

Religion, individuals and populations

This study is materialist, therefore, in two senses. To follow a distinction made by Michel Foucault, my aim is to trace the relationships between religion and the body of individuals, and between religion and the body of populations. The term 'religion' is derived from *religio*, the bond of social relations between individuals; the term 'sociology' is derived from *socius*, the bond of companionship that constitutes societies. Following Durkheim (1961), we may define religion as a set of beliefs and practices, relating to the sacred, which create social bonds between individuals. We may define sociology, naively, as the 'science of community'. Sociology in general and the sociology of religion in particular are thus concerned with the processes which unite and disunite, bind and unbind social relationships in space and time.

The body of individuals
The theme of this study is that religion has the function of controlling the sexuality of the body in order to secure the regular transmission of property via the family. Because property transmission through primogeniture within the patriarchal family is crucial in securing the economic and political unity of the dominant class, any general theory of the social effects of religion has to concern itself with the question of social class. The importance of religion for subordinate social groups is very different from its importance in the dominant class. Among subordinate groups, I follow the tradition of Engels (1965), Weber (1966) and

Mannheim (1960) in arguing that religion can express opposition through millenarianism, sectarianism and chiliasm in the form of resentment. Alternatively, religion offers hope, compensation and accommodation. In general, however, I take a critical view of any argument that suggests that religion is a social cement which binds social classes together within a common world-view.

... This treatment of religion presupposes that society is organized in terms of family units, laws of inheritance and private property. More precisely, it assumes that wealth is transmitted from one generation to the next through the family and that the family unit is the major source of wealth. In feudalism, religious control of sexuality, especially the sexuality of wives and sons, was crucial to the control of private feudal rights to land; the confessional, penance and other sacraments were important in the social control of women and the production of legitimate offspring. In competitive capitalism, religious control of sexuality was again important in the distribution of property; where the capitalist family was the primary source of future investment for accumulation.

The body of populations
In societies where the state and public ownership are more prominent than private ownership, religion has a different role in relationship to individuals. In late capitalism, where there is a degree of separation of ownership and control (Hill, 1981), the importance of the family for economic accumulation declines and there is less emphasis on the importance of legitimacy and monogamy. There is no longer an economic requirement for sexual restraint among property-owners, since the public corporation rather than the family firm dominates the economy. There is, however, a strong social requirement for the regulation of urban populations in order to achieve public order and to secure taxation.

Traditional religious controls over the body are now transferred to public disciplines which are exercised within the school, factory, prison and other 'total institutions'. Religion may continue within the private space of the body of individuals, but the public space of the body of populations is now subordinated, not to the **conscience collective**, the sacred canopy or the civil religion, but to secular disciplines, economic constraint and political coercion. The public realm is desacralized in Western industrial societies. In global political terms, for a variety of contingent reasons, militant Islam and orthodox Judaism assume a significant political role in the context of post-colonial struggles. In Western societies, the disappearance of religion from the political arena undermines the legitimacy of the state, which is forced to depend on constraint as the principal basis of stability. ...

Religion, society and economics

This analysis of religion is sharply differentiated from those approaches which either treat religion as simply a matter of individual subjectivity or satisfy themselves with descriptive accounts of the organizational forms of sects, cults and denominations. Following Weber, this study of religion is primarily concerned with the institutional linkage between religion, society and economics. This concern involves two separate arguments.

First, it rejects the sociological importance of the subjective orientation of social actors in the explication of social regularities. This position follows from theoretical arguments first elaborated in *The Dominant Ideology Thesis* (Abercrombie *et al.*, 1980), in which social actors and social classes were treated as primarily carriers of structural arrangements. In turn, this position depends on the notion that the relations of production in society impose a certain logic on the behaviour of individuals: human agency always operates within the constraints established by the dominant mode of production.

Second, it does not follow from this argument that my interpretation of religion entails *vulgar* reductionism. There is never a mechanistic fit between base and superstructure, because, at the level of the social formation, numerous contingent relations between classes, groups and institutions 'deflect' the logic of economic reproduction. The requirements of the dominant mode of production are never entirely satisfied or provided at the level of the social formation. The economy is dominant only in 'the last analysis'; many features of the culture of a society – aesthetics, doctrines concerning Christ's messianic status, theories of scriptural authority, hymnology, ecclesiology and so forth – may have little or no bearing on the operation of economic forms and thus enjoy a relative autonomy from the economic base. Sociologists who wish to devote their academic lives to belletrist analyses of these cultural forms are at liberty to do so, but they do not seriously advance sociology as a systematic science of society.

As a materialist perspective on religion, this text is written against the grain of conventional accounts within the sociology of religion. In order to defend the autonomy and importance of the study of religion within sociology, sociologists of religion have laboured the point that religion is an autonomous cultural phenomenon which cannot be reduced to economic interest or political requirements, that religion significantly influences individual behaviour and that religion is a crucial human interpretation of the existential condition of individuals. The sociology of Max Weber figures large in this interpretation of religion as an independent symbolic activity, because Weber gave special emphasis to religious theodicies and to religion as pre-eminently 'meaningful behaviour'.

This approach to Weber's study of religion tends, however, to minimize Weber's crucial concern for the linkages between religion, economics and politics; in these areas, Weber often wrote in a reductionist fashion in treating the 'ethics' of the world religions as fundamentally shaped by the social location of their carriers. For example, Weber saw the theological content of Islam as determined by the worldly interests of warriors. Furthermore, in Weber's view, religion as such grew out of specifically this-worldly concerns for health and wealth.

The theological systematization of **theodicy** is the product of a stratum of religious intellectuals. Theodicy is not the outcome of purely metaphysical speculations about the 'meaning of life' in general, but is rooted in the immediate issues of our corporeal finitude. A materialist perspective on religion can, therefore, be seen as a play upon the terms *corporalis* and *corporate*. This study is primarily concerned with the corporality of the individual and the corporation of society, with the place of religion in the production of societies and the reproduction of individuals or, in Foucault's terms, with 'the body of individuals and the body of populations':

> The discipline of the body and the regulations of the population constituted the two poles around which the organization of power over life was deployed.
> *(Foucault, 1981)*

A materialist sociology has to be concerned with the production of wealth and the production of bodies, with the relationship between the social distribution of bodies and commodities, and with the social institutions (the family, religion and the state) which mediate these basic processes of production and reproduction.

A historical-materialist perspective

A materialist perspective on religion does not treat religious beliefs and practices as inconsequential and trivial. On the contrary, it situates religion in our experience of physical and physiological reality. As such, materialism is perfectly in tune with the physicality of the Christian tradition and by extension with the Abrahamic roots of Islam and Judaism. The theological and symbolic core of traditional Christianity is focused on the fatherhood of God, the incarnation of Christ, the suffering on the Cross, the glorious resurrection of the body and the life of the world to come. It is difficult to escape the materialism of the eucharistic feast of Christ's blood and body or the materialistic metaphors of Christ's body and the body of the Church.

This perspective is not, furthermore, merely characteristic of Catholic cosmology, since it is, for example, prominent in Protestant worship and hymnology. The rapture of Charles Wesley's hymns, for example:

> O let me kiss Thy bleeding feet,
> And bathe and wash them with my tears!

is typical of the Methodist response to Christ's physical suffering. This is not to deny that, at various points in the history of Christianity, there has been a profound spiritualization of religion, breaking the connection between body and spirit, and presenting Christianity as a superior manifestation of the religious quest by virtue of its negation of the equation of sin and sickness, of flesh and evil. The Holy Family thus becomes a denial of the earthly family, or at least a perfected simile. But this very process of spiritualization continues to rely on 'primitive' analogies, metaphors and duplications of matter and spirit, body and soul, the subjectivity of conscience and the objectivity of society:

In the hallway there is a mirror which faithfully duplicates all appearances. Men usually infer from this mirror that the library is not infinite (if it really were, why this illusory duplication?); I prefer to dream that its polished surfaces represent and promise the infinite.
(Borges, 1970)

A materialist interpretation reduces religion to its elementary forms in the production and duplication of material existence – the corporality of individuals and the corpus of society. Religion thus lies at the crucial interchange between nature and culture in the formation of societies and the creation of human attributes. This interchange cannot, however, be understood in general, but only in the context of the material mode of production of individuals and societies. The materialist theory of religion is, by definition, a historical-materialist perspective; it is, as Engels noted in *The Origin of the Family, Private Property and the State*, the study of the production of the means of subsistence and of the production of human beings.

References

Abercrombie, N. *et al.* (1980) *The Dominant Ideology Thesis*, London.

Berger, P. L. (1969) *The Social Reality of Religion*, London.

Borges, J. L. (1970) *Labyrinths*, Harmondsworth.

Durkheim, E. (1961) *The Elementary Forms of Religious Life*, New York.

Engels, F. (1965) *The Peasant War in Germany*, London.

Foucault, M. (1981) *The History of Sexuality: Vol. 1: an introduction*, Harmondsworth.

Glock, C. Y. and Stark, R. (1965) *Religion and Society in Tension*, Chicago.

Gouldner, A. W. (1967) *Enter Plato: Classical Greece and the origins of social theory*, London.

Hill, S (1981) *Competition and Control at Work: the new industrial sociology*, London.

Mannheim, K. (1960) *Ideology and Utopia*, London.

Mead, G. H. (1934) *Mind, Self and Society*, Chicago.

Nietzsche, F. (1967) *Twilight of the Idols and the Anti-Christ*, Harmondsworth.

Parsons, T. (1937) *The Structure of Social Action*, Glencoe, Ill.

Schutz, A. (1972) *The Phenomenology of the Social World*, London.

Weber, M. (1966) *The Sociology of Religion*, London.

Key terms

The following key terms appear in the text above. They have been defined below to aid with the reading of this item.

materialist concerned with measurements of production and labour; to do with the sociological study of the body and its production

reductionism when a theory or explanation reduces a complex aspect of social life to a simple observation – often seen as a criticism

phenomenological based on the ideas of Edmund Husserl, which suggest that reality exists as a subjective set of symbolic meanings and motives

conscience collective a Durkheimian term meaning a shared set of norms, values and moral sentiments

theodicy a set of ideas that explain – within a religious context – ideas of God and evil

Questions

1 How and why is the sociology of religion a 'materialist enterprise' for Turner?

2 How does Turner combine the ideas of both Marx and Weber?

3 What three limitations does Turner identify in the sociology of religion? Why are these a particular problem?

4 How can the sociology of religion be used to study the sociology of 'the body'?

5 What recommendations does Turner make for future avenues for development in the sociology of religion?

Reading 19.8 **Foucault, sexuality and religious discourse**

Michel Foucault (from) *The History of Sexuality: Vol. 1: an introduction* (1981) (originally published in France in 1976) Harmondsworth: Penguin, 3–13.

Editorial comments

As seen in reading 19.7 by Bryan Turner, a great deal of contemporary social theory is concerned to develop a sociology of the body: to investigate the ways in which power controls the body in society. A great deal of this contemporary concern can be seen to have developed from the historical work by Michel Foucault, who is interested to chart the rise of relations of power and control. In this reading, Foucault suggests that we should make problematic our common-sense historical understanding of the process of so-called modern sexual liberation – an aspect of the body often controlled by religious beliefs.

The history of sexuality

FOR A LONG time, the story goes, we supported a Victorian regime, and we continue to be dominated by it even today. Thus the image of the imperial prude is emblazoned on our restrained, mute, and hypocritical sexuality.

At the beginning of the seventeenth century a certain frankness was still common, it would seem. Sexual practices had little need of secrecy; words were said without undue reticence, and things were done without too much concealment; one had a tolerant familiarity with the illicit. Codes regulating the coarse, the obscene, and the indecent were quite lax compared to those of the nineteenth century. It was a time of direct gestures, shameless **discourse**, and open transgressions, when anatomies were shown and intermingled at will, and knowing children hung about amid the laughter of adults: it was a period when bodies 'made a display of themselves'.

But twilight soon fell upon this bright day, followed by the monotonous nights of the Victorian bourgeoisie. Sexuality was carefully confined; it moved into the home. The conjugal family took custody of it and absorbed it into the serious function of reproduction. On the subject of sex, silence became the rule. The legitimate and procreative couple laid down the law. The couple imposed itself as model, enforced the norm, safeguarded the truth, and reserved the right to speak while retaining the principle of secrecy. A single locus of sexuality was acknowledged in social space as well as at the heart of every household, but it was a utilitarian and fertile one: the parents' bedroom. The rest had only to remain vague; proper demeanour avoided contact with other bodies, and verbal decency sanitized one's speech. And sterile behaviour carried the taint of abnormality; if it insisted on making itself too visible, it would be designated accordingly and would have to pay the penalty.

Nothing that was not ordered in terms of generation or transfigured by it could expect sanction or protection. Nor did it merit a hearing. It would be driven out, denied, and reduced to silence. Not only did it not exist, it had no right to exist and would be made to disappear upon its least manifestation – whether in acts or in words. Everyone knew, for example, that children had no sex, which was why they were forbidden to talk about it, why one closed one's eyes and stopped one's ears whenever they came to show evidence to the contrary, and why a general and studied silence was imposed. These are the characteristic features attributed to repression, which serve to distinguish it from the prohibitions maintained by penal law: repression operated as a sentence to disappear, but also as an injunction to silence, an affirmation of nonexistence, and, by implication an admission that there was nothing to say about such things, nothing to see, and nothing to know. Such was the hypocrisy of our bourgeois societies with its halting logic. It was forced to make a few concessions, however. If it was truly necessary to make room for illegitimate sexualities, it was reasoned, let them take their infernal mischief elsewhere: to a place where they could be reintegrated, if not in the circuits of production, at least in those of profit. The brothel and the mental hospital would be those places of tolerance: the prostitute, the client, and the pimp, together with the psychiatrist and his hysteric – those 'other Victorians', as Steven Marcus would say – seem to have surreptitiously transferred the pleasures that are unspoken into the order of things that are counted. Words and gestures, quietly authorized, could be exchanged there at the going rate. Only in those places would untrammelled sex have a right to (safely insularized) forms of reality, and only to clandestine, circumscribed, and coded types of discourse. Everywhere else, modern puritanism imposed its triple edict of taboo, nonexistence, and silence.

But have we not liberated ourselves from those two long centuries in which the history of sexuality must be seen first of all as the chronicle of an increasing repression? Only to a slight extent, we are told. Perhaps some progress was made by Freud; but with such circumspection, such medical prudence, a scientific guarantee of innocuousness, and so many precautions in order to contain everything, with no fear of 'overflow', in that safest and most discrete of spaces, between the couch and discourse: yet another round of whispering on a bed. And could things have been otherwise? We are informed that if repression has indeed been the fundamental link between power, knowledge, and sexuality since the classical age, it stands to reason that we will not be able to free ourselves from it except at a considerable cost: nothing less than a transgression of laws, a lifting of prohibitions, an irruption of speech, a reinstating of pleasure within reality, and a whole new economy in the mechanisms of power will be required. For the least glimmer of truth is conditioned by politics. Hence, one cannot hope to obtain the desired results simply from a medical practice, nor from a theoretical discourse, however rigorously pursued. Thus, one denounces Freud's conformism, the **normalizing** functions of psychoanalysis, the obvious timidity underlying Reich's vehemence, and all the effects of integration ensured by the 'science' of sex and the barely equivocal practices of sexology.

This discourse on modern sexual repression holds up well, owing no doubt to how easy it is to uphold. A solemn historical and political guarantee protects it. By placing the advent of the age of repression in the seventeenth century, after hundreds of years of open spaces and free expression, one adjusts it to coincide with the development of capitalism: it becomes an integral part of the bourgeois order. The minor chronicle of sex and its trials is transposed into the ceremonious history of the modes of production; its trifling aspect fades from view. A principle of explanation emerges after the fact: if sex is so rigorously repressed, this is because it is incompatible with a general and intensive work imperative. At a time when labor capacity was being systematically exploited, how could this capacity be allowed to dissipate itself in pleasurable pursuits, except in those – reduced to a minimum – that enabled it to reproduce itself? Sex and its effects are perhaps not so easily deciphered; on the other hand, their repression, thus reconstructed, is easily analysed. And the sexual cause – the demand for sexual freedom, but also for the knowledge to be gained from sex and the right to speak about it – becomes legitimately associated with the honour of a political cause: sex too is placed on the agenda for the future. A suspicious mind might wonder if taking so many precautions in order to give the history of sex such an impressive filiation does not bear traces of the same old prudishness: as if

those valorizing correlations were necessary before such a discourse could be formulated or accepted.

But there may be another reason that makes it so gratifying for us to define the relationship between sex and power in terms of repression: something that one might call the speaker's benefit. If sex is repressed, that is, condemned to prohibition, nonexistence, and silence, then the mere fact that one is speaking about it has the appearance of a deliberate transgression. A person who holds forth in such language places himself to a certain extent outside the reach of power; he upsets established law; he somehow anticipates the coming freedom. This explains the solemnity with which one speaks of sex nowadays. When they had to allude to it, the first demographers and psychiatrists of the nineteenth century thought it advisable to excuse themselves for asking their readers to dwell on matters so trivial and base. But for decades now, we have found it difficult to speak on the subject without striking a different pose: we are conscious of defying established power, our tone of voice shows that we know we are being subversive, and we ardently conjure away the present and appeal to the future, whose day will be hastened by the contribution we believe we are making. Something that smacks of revolt, of promised freedom, of the coming age of a different law, slips easily into this discourse on sexual oppression. Some of the ancient functions of prophecy are reactivated therein. Tomorrow sex will be good again. Because this repression is affirmed, one can discreetly bring into coexistence concepts which the fear of ridicule or the bitterness of history prevents most of us from putting side by side: revolution and happiness; or revolution and a different body, one that is newer and more beautiful; or indeed, revolution and pleasure. What sustains our eagerness to speak of sex in terms of repression is doubtless this opportunity to speak out against the powers that be, to utter truths and promise bliss, to link together enlightenment, liberation, and manifold pleasures; to pronounce a discourse that combines the fervour of knowledge, the determination to change the laws, and the longing for the garden of earthly delights. This is perhaps what also explains the market value attributed not only to what is said about sexual repression, but also to the mere fact of lending an ear to those who would eliminate the effects of repression. Ours is, after all, the only civilization in which officials are paid to listen to all and sundry impart the secrets of their sex: as if the urge to talk about it, and the interest one hopes to arouse by doing so, have far surpassed the possibilities of being heard, so that some individuals have even offered their ears for hire.

But it appears to me that the essential thing is not this economic factor, but rather the existence in our era of a discourse in which sex, the revelation of truth, the overturning of global laws, the proclamation of a new day to come, and the promise of a certain felicity are linked together. Today it is sex that serves as a support for the ancient form – so familiar and important in the West – of preaching. A great sexual sermon – which has had its subtle theologians and its popular voices – has swept through our societies over the last decades; it has chastised the old order, denounced hypocrisy, and praised the rights of the immediate and the real; it has made people dream of a New City. The Franciscans are called to mind. And we might wonder how it is possible that the lyricism and religiosity that long accompanied the revolutionary project have, in Western industrial societies, been largely carried over to sex.

The notion of repressed sex is not, therefore, only a theoretical matter. The affirmation of a sexuality that has never been more rigorously subjugated than during the age of the hypocritical, bustling, and responsible bourgeoisie is coupled with the grandiloquence of a discourse purporting to reveal the truth about sex, modify its economy within reality, subvert the law that governs it, and change its future. The statement of oppression and the form of the sermon refer back to one another; they are mutually reinforcing. To say that sex is not repressed, or rather that the relationship between sex and power is not characterized by repression, is to risk falling into a sterile paradox. It not only runs counter to a well-accepted argument, it goes against the whole economy and all the discursive 'interests' that underlie this argument.

... Briefly, my aim is to examine the case of a society which has been loudly castigating itself for its hypocrisy for more than a century, which speaks verbosely of its own silence, takes great pains to relate in detail the things it does not say, denounces the powers it exercises, and promises to liberate itself from the very laws that have made it function. I would like to explore not only these discourses but also the will that sustains them and the strategic intention that supports them. The question I would like to pose is not, Why are we repressed? but rather, Why do we say, with so much passion and so much resentment against our most recent past, against our present, and against ourselves, that we are repressed? By what spiral did we come to affirm that sex is negated? What led us to show, ostentatiously, that sex is something we hide, to say it is something we silence? And we do all this by formulating the matter in the most explicit terms, by trying to reveal it in its most naked reality, by affirming it in the positivity of its power and its effects. It is certainly legitimate to ask why sex was associated with sin for such a long time – although it would remain to be discovered how this

association was formed, and one would have to be careful not to state in a summary and hasty fashion that sex was 'condemned' – but we must also ask why we burden ourselves today with so much guilt for having once made sex a sin. What paths have brought us to the point where we are 'at fault' with respect to our own sex? And how have we come to be a civilization so peculiar as to tell itself that, through an abuse of power which has not ended, it has long 'sinned' against sex? How does one account for the displacement which, while claiming to free us from the sinful nature of sex, taxes us with a great historical wrong which consists precisely in imagining that nature to be blameworthy and in drawing disastrous consequences from that belief?

It will be said that if so many people today affirm this repression, the reason is that it is historically evident. And if they speak of it so abundantly, as they have for such a long time now, this is because repression is so firmly anchored, having solid roots and reasons, and weighs so heavily on sex that more than one denunciation will be required in order to free ourselves from it; the job will be a long one. All the longer, no doubt, as it is in the nature of power – particularly the kind of power that operates in our society – to be repressive, and to be especially careful in repressing useless energies, the intensity of pleasures, and irregular modes of behaviour. We must not be surprised, then, if the effects of liberation vis-à-vis this repressive power are so slow to manifest themselves; the effort to speak freely about sex and accept it in its reality is so alien to a historical sequence that has gone unbroken for a thousand years now, and so inimical to the intrinsic mechanisms of power, that it is bound to make little headway for a long time before succeeding in its mission.

One can raise three serious doubts concerning what I shall term the 'repressive hypothesis'. First doubt: Is sexual repression truly an established historical fact? Is what first comes into view – and consequently permits one to advance an initial hypothesis – really the accentuation or even the establishment of a regime of sexual repression beginning in the seventeenth century? This is a properly historical question. Second doubt: Do the workings of power, and in particular those mechanisms that are brought into play in societies such as ours, really belong primarily to the category of repression? Are prohibition, censorship, and denial truly the forms through which power is exercised in a general way, if not in every society, most certainly in our own? This is a historico-theoretical question. A third and final doubt: Did the critical discourse that addresses itself to repression come to act as a roadblock to a power mechanism that had operated unchallenged up to that point, or is it not in fact part of the same historical network as the thing it denounces (and doubtless misrepresents) by calling it 'repression'? Was there really an historical rupture between the age of repression and the critical analysis of repression? This is a historico-political question. My purpose in introducing these three doubts is not merely to construct counter-arguments that are symmetrical and contrary to those outlined above; it is not a matter of saying that sexuality, far from being repressed in capitalist and bourgeois societies, has on the contrary benefited from a regime of unchanging liberty; nor is it a matter of saying that power in societies such as ours is more tolerant than repressive, and that the critique of repression, while it may give itself airs of a rupture with the past, actually forms part of a much older process and, depending on how one chooses to understand this process, will appear either as a new episode in the lessening of prohibitions, or as a more devious and discreet form of power.

The doubts I would like to oppose to the repressive hypothesis are aimed less at showing it to be mistaken than at putting it back within a general economy of discourses on sex in modern societies since the seventeenth century. Why has sexuality been so widely discussed, and what has been said about it? What were the effects of power generated by what was said? What are the links between these discourses, these effects of power, and the pleasures that were invested by them? What knowledge (*savoir*) was formed as a result of this linkage? The object, in short, is to define the regime of power-knowledge-pleasure that sustains the discourse on human sexuality in our part of the world. The central issue, then (at least in the first instance), is not to determine whether one says yes or no to sex, whether one formulates prohibitions or permissions, whether one asserts its importance or denies its effects, or whether one refines the words one uses to designate it; but to account for the fact that it is spoken about, to discover who does the speaking, the positions and viewpoints from which they speak, the institutions which prompt people to speak about it and which store and distribute the things that are said. What is at issue, briefly, is the over-all 'discursive fact', the way in which sex is 'put into discourse'. Hence, too, my main concern will be to locate the forms of power, the channels it takes, and the discourses it permeates in order to reach the most tenuous and individual modes of behaviour, the paths that give it access to the rare or scarcely perceivable forms of desire, how it penetrates and controls everyday pleasure – all this entailing effects that may be those of refusal, blockage, and invalidation, but also incitement and intensification:

in short, the 'polymorphous techniques of power'. And finally, the essential aim will not be to determine whether these discursive productions and these effects of power lead one to formulate the truth about sex, or on the contrary falsehoods designed to conceal that truth, but rather to bring out the 'will to knowledge' that serves as both their support and their instrument.

Let there be no misunderstanding: I do not claim that sex has not been prohibited or barred or masked or misapprehended since the classical age; nor do I even assert that it has suffered these things any less from that period on than before. I do not maintain that the prohibition of sex is a ruse; but it is a ruse to make prohibition into the basic and constitutive element from which one would be able to write the history of what has been said concerning sex starting from the modern epoch. All these negative elements – defences, censorships, denials – which the repressive hypothesis groups together in one great central mechanism destined to say no, are doubtless only component parts that have a local and tactical role to play in a transformation into discourse, a technology of power, and a will to knowledge that are far from being reducible to the former.

In short, I would like to disengage my analysis from the privileges generally accorded the economy of scarcity and the principles of rarefaction, to search instead for instances of discursive production (which also administer silences, to be sure), of the production of power (which sometimes have the function of prohibiting), of the propagation of knowledge (which often cause mistaken beliefs or systematic misconceptions to circulate); I would like to write the history of these instances and their transformations. A first survey made from this viewpoint seems to indicate that since the end of the sixteenth century, the 'putting into discourse of sex', far from undergoing a process of restriction, on the contrary has been subjected to a mechanism of increasing incitement; that the techniques of power exercised over sex have not obeyed a principle of rigorous selection, but rather one of dissemination and implantation of polymorphous sexualities; and that the will to knowledge has not come to a halt in the face of a taboo that must not be lifted, but has persisted in constituting – despite many mistakes, of course – a science of sexuality. It is these movements that I will now attempt to bring into focus in a schematic way, bypassing as it were the repressive hypothesis and the facts of interdiction or exclusion it invokes, and starting from certain historical facts that serve as guidelines for research.

Key terms

The following key terms appear in the text above. They have been defined below to aid with the reading of this item.

discourse a set of languages that control and constrain individual identity; a form of power that shapes and moulds those under its gaze

normalizing becoming seen as 'normal', i.e. being labelled and controlled – giving a legitimate right to be under surveillance in society

Questions

1 What does Foucault have to say about our common-sense understanding of the history of sexuality?

2 How might religion – as a discourse – limit the expression of sexuality?

3 Why does Foucault wish to make problematic a history of sexuality?

4 How can sexuality be seen as an exercise in power?

Further reading

The following texts may represent a useful starting point for further investigation of the ideas contained within this chapter.

Primary texts

Although not represented here for thematic reasons, the ideas of classical sociologist Max Weber have also been influential on the sociology of religion. In particular see:

Weber, M. (1930) *The Protestant Ethic and the Spirit of Capitalism* (orig. pub. 1905) London: Allen & Unwin.

For a discussion of the ideas of secularization, see:

Luckmann, T. (1967) *The Invisible Religion,* Basingstoke: Macmillan.

Stark, R. and Bainbridge, W. S. (1985) *The Future of Religion,* Berkeley: University of California Press.

Wilson, B. R. (1966) *Religion in a Secular Society,* London: C. A. Watts & Co.

An interesting empirical study of religious movements, which also raises some very important methodological issues, is:

Barker, E. (1984) *The Making of a Moonie,* Oxford: Blackwell.

Secondary texts

Accessible texts for the student new to this topic include:

Bruce, S. (1995) *Religion in Modern Britain,* Oxford: Oxford University Press.

Thompson, I. (1986) *Religion,* London: Longman.

Thompson, K. (1986) *Beliefs and Ideology,* London: Tavistock.

Coursework suggestion

An understanding of religious commitment

Using more phenomenological ideas – as represented by Peter Berger in reading 19.5 – a series of in-depth interviews could be conducted with people who consider themselves to be 'religious'. This study could investigate the nature of religious commitment: how does one behave if one is 'religious'? A comparative study may provide some interesting results.

Exploring themes in sociology

The following table indicates some of the main inter-relationships between the readings in this volume. This is not an exhaustive list, and should be used in conjunction with the indexes that follow in order to help you read around the topic in question.

If you are interested in the family, for example, then you might also like to see **readings 6.2, 6.6, 6.8, 16.8** and **19.8**. These may help you develop a wider understanding of issues relevant to family sociology and to identify links with themes from other topic areas.

Chapter	Other relevant readings
Chapter 3 Sociological theory	2.2, 2.3, 2.6, 2.8; 5.1, 5.3, 5.8; 7.3; 8.1, 8.2; 12.1, 12.6; 16.1; 18.4, 18.5; 19.2, 19.3, 19.5
Chapter 4 Research methods	2.2, 2.3; 9.6, 9.7; 17.2
Chapter 5 Stratification: class	3.1; 14.4; 15.6, 15.7, 15.8; 17.3; 18.1, 18.8
Chapter 6 Stratification: sex and gender	2.8; 3.8; 7.8; 8.1, 8.3, 8.4; 12.6; 14.5; 15.4; 16.8
Chapter 7 Stratification: 'race' and ethnicity	5.6; 6.5; 9.4, 9.8; 14.6; 15.5; 17.4
Chapter 8 The family	6.2, 6.6, 6.8; 16.8; 19.8
Chapter 9 Education and training	4.6; 7.6; 18.5
Chapter 10 Work, organizations and leisure	3.3; 5.4; 11.6; 18.5
Chapter 11 Culture and identity	3.6; 5.3, 5.8; 7.3, 7.4, 7.7; 10.4, 10.7; 16.3, 16.4, 16.6, 16.8; 17.5, 17.7, 17.8
Chapter 12 Deviance	8.6; 14.2; 16.2
Chapter 13 World development	16.5, 16.7
Chapter 14 Health	15.1, 15.2; 19.7, 19.8
Chapter 15 Wealth, welfare and Poverty	5.1, 5.4, 5.6; 10.1; 13.4; 18.1
Chapter 16 The mass media	11.2, 11.3, 11.4, 11.6, 11.8
Chapter 17 Community, locality and nation	7.3, 7.4, 7.7; 10.4, 10.7; 11.5, 11.8; 13.6, 13.8
Chapter 18 Power and politics	3.5; 5.2, 5.5, 5.7; 12.4, 12.7; 13.2, 13.8; 16.1, 16.5
Chapter 19 Religion and belief Systems	3.2; 14.1, 14.8

Author index

A

Abbott, Pamela 4, 5, 27–30
Abercrombie, N. 132, 583, 585
Adriaansens, H. P. M. 48
Agger, B. 288
Ahmad, W. I. U. 402, 403, 420–3
Alcock, Pete 431, 432, 448–51
Alexander, Jeffrey 31, 32, 46–50
Alibhai-Brown, Yasmin 175
Althusser, Louis 32, 47, 233, 435
Anderson, Benedict 500, 501,
    524–7
Anthony, Andrew 166–7
Archer, Margaret 69, 70, 81–5
Atkinson, D. 48

B

Bagguley, Paul 105, 107, 128–34
Bainbridge, W. S. 578–9
Bales, R. F. 206
Ball, S. 233, 234
Ballaster, R. 466, 467, 477–82
Barker, M. 253
Barrett, Michèle 26–7, 196, 197, 444
Bart, B. 422
Batsleer, J. 481
Baudrillard, Jean 57, 230, 308, 310,
    321–23, 467, 488–9, 529, 531,
    548 51
Bauman, Zygmunt 4, 5, 18–20,
    110, 551
Beauvoir, Simone de 145, 146,
    147–51
Beck, Ulrich 26, 116, 140, 327, 329,
    360, 366, 383, 529, 531, 551–5
Beetham, M. 477–82
Beggs, J. 446
Bell, Daniel 115, 116, 121
Beneria, L. 64
Benthall, Jonathan 466, 467, 491–5
Bentham, Jeremy 345
Berger, Peter L. 4, 5, 14–17, 560,
    561, 572–5, 579, 583
Berle, A. A. 114
Bern, Sandra 168
Bernstein, Basil 232, 233, 235–7
Bernstein, Eduard 114
Bhaskar, Roy 78, 79, 80
Bhat, A. 450
Bird, Lise 260
Blaikie, P. 385
Blinder, Alan 272
Blum, Richard 471
Blumer, Herbert 179–81
Bly, Robert 147, 166–7
Bocock, Robert 560, 561–5
de Bonald, Louis, Vicomte 8
Bonss, W. 554
Boorse, Christopher 424, 425
Borges, J. L. 582, 586
Bosanquet, N. 187
Boserup, E. 64
Bottomore, T. 139
Bourdieu, Pierre 26, 140, 234, 257,
    258, 259, 310, 319

Bourne 198
Bowe, R. 233
Bowles, Samuel 232, 233, 237–41
Box, S. 354
Boyne, R. 242
Bradley, Harriet 105, 107–8, 139–43
Bradshaw, J. 438
Bragg, Valerie 242–3
Bramson, Leon 473
Braverman, Harry 267, 269, 294,
    295–6, 297
Brittan, Arthur 180
Brodie, Bernard 397
Brown, Carol 65
Bryant, Christopher 69, 70, 71–4
Brym, R. 139
Bryson, Lois 431, 432, 444–8
Bullough, B. 168
Bullough, V. 168
Bundred, Steve 350
Burawoy, Michael 267, 269, 294–8
Burgess, E. 228–9
Burrows, Lynette 496
Bury, J. B. 6
Butler, Josephine 209
Buttel, F. 383

C

Callinicos, Alex 31, 32, 54–8
Campbell, B. 434
Campbell, C. 579
Canetti, Elias 548
Carby, H. 196, 197, 198, 199
Carlstein, T. 59, 60
Casey, K. 263
Castells, M. 288
Castles, Stephen 183
Chapman, B. 446
Charles, Prince of Wales 516
Cheale, D. 201, 227–30
Chiozza-Money, L. G. 456
Chodorow, Nancy 291
Cicourel, A. V. 258
Clark, T. 116
Clarke, John 267, 269, 303–6,
    324–8
Clarke, Simon 284
Clausen 375
Cohen, Albert 470
Cohen, Anthony 500, 501, 511–14
Cohen, I. R. 82, 85
Cohen, Stanley 327, 328, 329,
    332–7, 346, 356–60
Cole, Tony 431, 432, 433–436
Collins, Patricia Hill 263, 264
Comte, Auguste 4, 5, 6, 8–9,
    10–12, 71, 560
Condorcet, Marquis de 6–8, 9
Coote, A. 434
Coser, L. A. 46
Craib, Ian 4, 5, 21–4
Cranston, M. 513
Critcher, Chas 267, 269, 303–6,
    342–8
Crook, Stephen 140, 142

D

Dahrendorf, Ralf 25, 129, 130–1,
    140
Darwin, Charles 51, 153, 154
Davidson, N. 103, 402, 412–15
Davis, Kingsley 508
Davis, Mike 55, 522–3
Dearing, J. 476
Denzin, Norman 229, 230
Devine, F. 141
Doane, Mary Ann 315
Dobbelaere, K. 579
Doeringer, Peter B. 187
Dore, Ronald 273, 513
Douglas, Mary 513
Doyal, Lesley 402, 403, 415–19,
    422
Doyle, Bertram 178
Durkheim, Émile 4, 5, 12–14, 25,
    31, 32, 42–5, 59–61, 62, 69, 70,
    75, 76, 82, 232, 233, 327, 328,
    329–32, 341, 560–2, 568–9,
    572, 575, 582, 584
Duster, Troy 179–81
Dworkin, A. 65

E

Easy, Walter 351
Eco, Umberto 489–90
Edgar, D. 255
Edwards, R. 91
Edwards, T. 233–4, 241–4, 255
Egerton, M. 233
Eldridge, John 466, 467, 487–91
Elliot, Faith Robertson 201, 202,
    217–22
Engels, Friedrich 32, 33–7, 201,
    202, 203–6, 466, 467, 468–9,
    552, 562
Engermann, Stanley 181
Epstein, Debbie 232, 234, 249–52
Ericson, Richard V. 329, 360–3
Esping-Andersen, Gøsta 431, 432,
    441–4

F

Fanon, Franz 421
Farrington, D. P. 352
Febvre, Lucien 487–8
Fenn, R. K. 580–1
Feyerabend, Paul 73
Fiske, John 308, 309, 316–17, 326
Fitz, J. 233
Foote Whyte, William 500, 501,
    503–6
Ford, Henry 268, 279, 280
Foucault, Michel 31, 32, 50–3, 132,
    232, 234, 249–51, 310, 319,
    328, 329, 359, 360, 403, 425,
    529, 530, 545–7, 560, 561, 582,
    585, 587–91
Fowler, Norman 439–40
Fraser, D. 433
Frazer, E. 477–82
Frazer, Gordon 402, 403, 404–6

Freud, Sigmund 202, 206, 207, 407, 588
Fröbel, F. 365, 366, 368–72
Fukuyama, Francis 269, 529, 530, 538–41

G
Gallie, D. 130
Gans, Herbert 501
Garber, J. 89
Garfinkel, Harold 69, 70, 85–9
Gates, Bill 271
Geertz, Clifford 563
Gellner, E. 525
Genovese, Eugene D. 48
George, Susan 365, 366, 376–9
Gerstein, D. R. 48
Gerwitz, S. 233–4, 241–4
Giddens, Anthony 4, 5, 24–7, 31, 33, 59–63, 81, 82, 83, 69, 70, 71, 72, 73–4, 75–8, 84, 116, 129, 132, 529, 555–8
Gill, S. 390–1
Gillespie, Marie 308, 309, 312–14
Gilroy, Paul 261, 262–3
Gintis, Herbert 48, 232, 233, 237–41
Gittins, D. 201, 202, 214–17
Glaser, Barry 181
Glock, Charles 583
Goffman, Erving 25, 432
Gold, A. 233
Golding, Peter 308, 310, 323–6, 433, 435
Goldthorpe, John H. 26, 54, 122, 141
Goode, W. J. 46
Gordon, B. 421
Gordon, P. 449
Gorer, Geoffrey 209
Gorz, André 116
Gouldner, A. W. 46, 48, 582
Gowing, Nik 485
Graham, H. 444
Gramsci, Antonio 32, 267, 268, 276–80, 281, 298, 316, 342, 345, 348, 562
Grimsley, M. 450
Guillaumin, C. 64H

H
Habermas, Jurgen 48, 72, 80
Haggerty, Kevin D. 329, 360–3
Halberstam, David 484
Hale, C. 354
Hall, Peter 516
Hall, Stuart 26, 282, 327, 328, 342–8
Halpin, D. 233
Halsey, A. H. 232, 233
Hamilton, Malcolm 560, 561, 575–81
Hammersley, Martyn 89
Hanmer, Jalna 28
Haraszti, Miklós 296
Harbury, C. 455–7, 458
Harman, Chris 55
Harrigan, J. 394
Harris, C. 176
Harris, Nigel 365, 366–7, 386–90, 391
Hartmann, Heidi 267, 269, 289–93

Harvey, David 139, 500, 501, 515–18
Hawkins, Peter 236–7
Hayter, Teresa 365, 366, 372–6
Hebron, S. 477–82
Hegel, G. W. F. 538
Heidegger, Martin 50
Heidensohn, Frances 327, 329, 352–6
Heinrichs, J. 368–72
Henderson, J. 288
Henderson, L. J. 46
Henry, J. 89
Henry, J. S. 377, 378
Hernes, H. M. 65
Herrnstein, Richard 171, 172, 189–91
Hesse, Mary 80
Hey, Valerie 69, 70, 89–93
Hill, S. 583
Hirst, Paul 365, 367, 396–400
Hislop, Ian 495
Hitchens, D. M. W. N. 455–7, 458
Hobsbawm, Eric 48
Hobson, B. 445
Hodges, Tony 315
Hoggart, Richard 308, 309, 311–12
Holmwood, J. 117
Homans, George C. 46
hooks, bell 217, 253, 264
Horowitz, Irving Louis 25
Howard, Michael 159
Huberman, A. M. 98
Hudson, Mark 142
Hughes, Angela 165–6
Hughes, Everett 181
Humphrey, C. R. 383
Hutton, Will 267, 268, 270–6

I
Illich, Ivan 402, 403, 408–11

J
Jackson, Ben 365, 366, 379–82
Jackson, Brian 500, 501, 506–8
Jacques, M. 282
Jameson, F. 139
Jefferson, Tony 342–8
Jencks, Charles 516, 521
Jenkin, Patrick 439
Johnson 91
Jones, Steve 145, 146, 153–6, 170
Joseph, Keith 131
Joshua, H. 177
Juteau, D. 64

K
Kamerman, S. 445
Karabel, J. 232
Keat, R. 72
Kellner, Douglas 308, 310, 321–23
Kenway, Jane 241
Kermode, Frank 57
Keynes, John Maynard 47, 119, 138
King, L. S. 425
Kinnock, Neil 120
Kissinger, Henry 539
Klapper, J. 474
Knowles, Caroline 171, 172–3, 195–9

Kojève, Alexandre 539–40
Kolakowski, L. 71–3, 294
Kosack, Godula 183
Kowinski, William S. 299
Kreye, O. 368–72
Kroker, Arthur 57
Kuhn, Manfred 180
Kuhn, Thomas 23, 75–76
Kumar, Krishan 4, 5, 6–9, 267, 268, 280–5

L
Lal, Barbara 171, 172, 178–81
Lamont, M. 259
Laquer, Thomas 168
Lareau, A. 259
Lash, S. 141, 267, 268–9, 285–9
Laurin, N. 64
Law, D. 390–1
Layder, D. 84
Lea, John 327, 328–9, 348–51
Lee, David 105, 106–7, 114–19
Lenin, Vladimir Illyich 7
Lévi-Strauss, Claude 290–1, 343
Lewis, Oscar 414
Lilley, M. 253
Lipset, S. 116
Llewellyn, Mandy 89
Locke, H. 228, 229
Lockwood, D. 117
Lofland, John 181
Lorenz, Konrad 153
Lotringer, Sylvere 548–51
Lucey, H. 260
Luckmann, T. 580
Luhmann, Nikolas 26
Luke, T. 287
Lukes, Steven 26, 564
Luxemburg, Rosa 385
Lyndon, Deirdre 166
Lyndon, Neil 147, 166
Lyon, D. 140
Lyotard, J. F. 54, 116, 242, 529, 530, 541–5

M
Mac an Ghaill, Mairtin 232, 234, 252–7
McGuigan, J. 310
McIntosh, M. 196, 197, 444
MacIntyre, Alasdair 71, 471
McKinnon, Catherine 251
McLaren, P. 265
McNamara, Robert 372
Macnicol, J. 130, 131
McQuail, Dennis 474
McRobbie, Angela 89, 233
Madge, N. 131
Major, John 120, 123, 453
Malthus, Thomas 8
Mann, Kirk 105, 107, 128–34
Mann, Michael 27
Mannheim, Karl 560, 561, 570–1
Manuel, Frank 6, 7
Marcos, Ferdinand 377
Marcos, Imelda 377
Marshall, G. 107, 122, 141, 142
Marshall, T. H. 115
Martin, David 576, 578
Martin, Emily 426–7

Martin, Henri-Jean 487–8
Marx, Karl 7, 32, 33–7, 48, 62, 105, 106, 108–10, 114–15, 117, 135–6, 141, 288, 295, 339, 343, 345, 385, 466, 467, 468–9, 503, 526, 538, 560, 561, 562–3, 566–8
Mead, G. H. 583
Means, G. C. 114
Meier, August 180
Melton, J. G. 579
Melzer, Bernard 180
Menzies, K. 48
Mercer, K. 142
Mercer, Sharmila 171, 172–3, 195–9
Merton, R. K. 25, 46, 509
Meyrowitz, J. 288
Michels, Robert 25
Middleton, S. 433, 435
Miles, M. B. 98
Miles, Robert 171, 172, 185–8
Miliband, Ray 127
Mill, John Stuart 209
Miller, H. 244
Millet, Kate 64
Mills, C. Wright 473–4, 529, 530, 531–4
Mirza, Heidi Safia 232, 234, 261–6
Modleski, Tanya 479
Modood, Tariq 171, 172, 191–5, 232, 233, 245–9
Montesquieu, Charles Louis de Secondat, Baron de 7, 551
Moore, Robert 500, 501, 508–11
Moore, Suzanne 308, 309, 314–16
Morard, Paul-Henri 493
Morgan, D. H. 201, 223–7
Mort, Frank 308, 310, 315, 319–21
Mosley, P. 394
Mullard, C. 250
Mulvey, Laura 314
Murdock, Graham 308, 310, 323–6
Murray, Charles 129, 171, 172, 189–91, 461
Myrdal, G. 129

N
Nettleton, Sarah 402, 403, 426–9
Newman, Karin 490–1
Newnham, A. 449
Nietzsche, F. W. 50, 530, 540, 582
Nisbet, R. 347–8

O
Oakley, Ann 27–8, 145, 146, 147, 151–2, 167–9, 201, 202, 211–14, 428
Offe, Claus 529, 530, 534–7
Ogza, J. 233
Ohmac, K. 398
Olin Wright, Eric 431, 432, 460–5
Ortner, Sherry 168, 290
Oudshoom, Nellie 168
Outhwaite, William 69, 70, 78–80

P
Pahl, R. E. 27, 117–18, 131
Pareto, Vilfredo 25, 46

Park, Robert 172, 178–9, 181
Parker, Dorothy 148, 150
Parmar, P. 142, 199
Parsons, Talcott 23, 24, 25, 31, 32, 46–9, 75, 201, 202, 206–8, 402, 403, 406–8, 421, 424, 583
Patel, Pragna 145, 147, 158–60
Payne, Geoff 105, 107, 120–3
Pearson, G. 346
Perkins, T. E. 253
Petras, James 180
Phillips, Barabara 479
Philo, Greg 466, 467, 473–6
Phizacklea, Annie 188
Piore, Michael 281
Plummer, K. 253
Pollak, O. 353, 355
Popper, Karl 72, 74
Porpora, D. V. 83
Power, S. 233
Pratt, M. 354–5

R
Radcliffe-Brown, A. 46, 508
Rattansi, A. 242
Reagan, Ronald 55, 366, 374
Reay, Diane 232, 234, 257–61, 262
Redclift, Michael 365, 366, 382–6
Renan 525
Rex, John 129, 171, 172, 182–5, 500, 501, 508–11
Rhind, David 101
Ribbens, J. 91
Richardson, Diana 28
Ritzer, George 267, 269, 298–303
Rizal, José 526–7
Roberts, Brian 342–8
Robinson, Victoria 28
Rocher, G. 48
Rogers, E. 476
Rorty 56
Rosaldo, M. Z. 64, 290
Rose, H. 122, 444
Rothman 359
Roy, Donald 296
Rustin, Michael 282
Rutherford, Jonathan 142, 145, 147, 165–7
Rutter, M. 131

S
Sabel, Charles 280–1
Saint-Simon, Henri, Comte de 6, 7, 71
Samuel, Raphael 54
Sarantakos, Sotirios 69, 70, 93–9
Saunders, P. 107, 122
Savage, M. 140–1
Saville, John 435
Scase, R. 141
Schur, Edwin 470
Schutz, Alfred 76, 77, 86, 583
Sciulli, D. 48
Scott, Joan 321
Scott, John 105, 107, 123–8, 431, 432, 455–60
Scull, Andrew 359
Scully, D. 422
Seddon, J. 365, 367, 390–5

Segal, Lynne 320
Seidler, V. J. 28
Sen, Amartya 379
Sen, G. 64
Seton-Wallace, H. 525
Sharot, S. 579–80
Shiner, L. 576
Shorter, E. 217
Shover, N. 357–8
Shusterman, Richard 56
Sivanandan, A. 140
Skeggs, Beverley 91
Skellington, Richard 171, 172, 173–5
Sklair, Leslie 365
Slattery, Martin 69, 70, 99–104
Smith, Adam 433
Smith, Dorothy 29
Smith, Joan 466, 467, 495–8
Smith, J. W. 81
Smith, N. 385
Smith, Vicki 447
Soja, Edward 500, 501, 518–24
Solomos, John 171, 172, 176–8
Sontag, Susan 57
Spear, Allan 180
Spivak, G. C. 264
Stanley, Liz 145, 147, 156–7
Stanworth, M. 428
Stark, Rodney 583
Stark, W. 578–9
Stewart, A. 117
Stone, I. F. 485
Stones, Rob 32
Strauss, Anselm 181
Streeck, Wolfgang 272

T
Taylor, F. W. 277, 280
Taylor, Ian 327, 328, 337–41
Taylor, J. G. 48
Taylor, Philip M. 466, 467, 482–6
Taylor, Steve 103
Thatcher, Margaret 55, 366, 374, 453
Thomas, David 147, 165
Thomas, W. I. 487
Thompson, E. P. 434
Thompson, Graham 365, 367, 396–400
Thompson, J. B. 81, 84, 132
Thompson, Kenneth 242, 560, 561–5
Thorne, Barry 168
Tomlinson, Sally 171, 172, 182–5
Tönnies, Ferdinand 500, 501, 502–3
Townsend, P. 103, 402, 412–15
Toye, J. 394
Trotsky, Leon 150
Turgot 6, 7–8
Turner, Bryan S. 81, 105, 106–7, 114–19, 140, 141, 402, 403, 406–8, 423–6, 560, 561, 576, 582–6

U
Urry, J. 72, 132, 267, 268–9, 285–9
Useem, M. 128

W

Walby, Sylvia 31, 33, 63–7, 145, 147, 161–4, 269
Walfod, G. 244
Walker, Alan 130, 431, 432, 437–40
Walker, J. 254
Walkerdine, Valerie 250, 259, 260, 479
Wallace, Claire 4, 5, 27–30
Wallace, T. 177
Wallis, R. 579, 580
Walters, Margaret 315
Walton, J. 365, 367, 390–5
Walton, Paul 327, 328, 337–41
Watson, Catherine 365, 366, 372–6
Weber, Max 25, 31, 32, 38–41, 72, 73, 74, 105, 106, 110–14, 117, 118, 124, 135, 141, 267, 269,

298, 303, 509, 562, 582, 583, 585, 558
Wedgwood, Josiah 455
Westergaard, John 105, 107, 134–9, 431, 432, 452–5
Whitty, G. 232, 233–4, 241–4
Wilby, Peter 242
Williams, Raymond 491
Williams, Shirley 129
Willis, Paul 233, 308, 309–10, 318–19
Willmott, P. 201, 202, 208–11
Wilson, B. 575–6, 577
Wilson, Roy 184
Wilson, William Julius 25, 26, 27, 461
Winch, Peter 76
Wise, Sue 145, 146–7, 156–7

Wolff, Janet 27
Wood, J. 254
Woolf, Virginia 156
Wootton, Lady 472
Wright, Erik Olin 54
Wright Mills, C. 27
Wriston, W. 287

Y

Yates, Paula 495–6
Young, I. M. 517
Young, Jock 327, 328–9, 337–41, 348–51, 466, 467, 469–72
Young, M. F. D. 201, 202, 208–11, 233

Z

Zola, I. K. 420

Subject index

A

abuse 201, 202, 217–22, 438
action, structure relationship 59–62, 70, 75, 77, 78–9, 81–5
action theory 46
Aestheticism 56–7, 58
Africa 378, 380–1
Afro-Caribbeans
   see also black feminism
   higher education 232, 245–6, 247, 248, 249, 262
   identity 192–3
   immigration 176–7, 182, 183
   race surveys 173–5
   single parent families 445
   welfare 450
   women 158–60, 163
agency 60, 77, 78, 81–5
aid, international 365, 366, 372–6, 494
AIDS 417, 473, 493
Americanism 267, 268, 277–80
anthropology 18, 26, 46, 152
   belief systems 563–4
   evolutionary 153, 154–5
   methodology 69, 70
   sex/gender distinction 151
   sexual division of labour 289, 290–1
Asia 272–3
Asians
   see also black feminism
   cultural change 309, 312–14
   higher education 245–6, 247, 248, 249, 262
   identity 192–5
   immigration 176–7, 182, 183
   race surveys 173–5
   welfare 450
   women 158–60, 163
assimilation, social 178, 179, 181

B

background expectancies 85–8, 89
bias, media 466, 467, 475, 487–91
biological determinism 146, 153
biological essentialism 168, 169
biology 30, 149, 151–2, 427, 572–3
   see also evolution
black feminism 145, 147, 158–60, 171, 172–3, 196–9
   domestic violence 222
   education 232, 234, 261–6
body
   female 426–9
   health 402, 403, 423–6
   religion 561, 582, 584, 585, 587
bourgeoisie 33–7, 40, 149, 205, 587, 588
   see also embourgeoisement; middle classes
British Social Attitudes survey 103, 141, 173, 175

C

California School 500, 518
capitalism
   see also production
   class 105, 106–7, 109, 123–8, 136, 139, 143
   classlessness 105, 107, 114–18, 120–3
   conservatism 555–6
   crime 328, 342, 345, 347
   disorganized 285–8
   dominant ideology 468
   economic locations 123–6, 127
   education 232, 233, 237–41
   environmental issues 383–4, 385
   ethnicity 172, 185–8, 198

family structure 203, 204, 205
   gender relations 63
   globalization 267, 268–9, 285–9, 390–1, 394–5, 396
   labour 62, 267, 269, 294–7
   Marxist critique of 31, 34–7
   military relationship 532
   New Right 267, 268, 270–5, 529, 530, 538–41
   overconsumptionism 31, 32, 54, 55, 57, 58
   patriarchy 66, 267, 269, 289–94
   poverty 461–2, 463, 464
   religion relationship 584
   Third World 386, 388, 389
   urbanization 515, 516
care in the community 431, 432, 437–40
caste 112–13
census 100, 101–3, 121
children
   see also education
   abuse 201, 202, 217–22
   discourse 250
   family 201, 202, 206–7, 226, 229
   parenting 213, 496, 497
Christianity 38, 564–5, 576–7, 578, 584, 585–6
citizenship 63–4, 67, 115, 116, 176
class 105–44
   see also élites; middle classes; status; upper classes; working classes
   capitalism 105, 106–7, 109, 123–8, 136, 287
   class consciousness 107, 108–10, 139, 141, 238–9, 269
   classlessness 105, 107, 114–18, 120–3, 134–5, 140

cultural hegemony 316
division of labour 42, 44
dominant ideology 466, 467, 468–9
education 237–40, 247–8, 257, 258–60
ethnicity 108, 181, 182–5, 186–7
gender 66, 108, 142
health 402, 403, 412–15
homosexuality 255
housing 501, 509–11
income 431, 432, 452–5
inequality 105, 107–8, 115, 117, 134–9, 140
labour process theory 294–7
Marx 105, 106, 108–10, 114–15, 117, 135–6, 141
Marxism 33–7, 107, 530, 567
    capitalism 120, 139, 140
    ideology 562
post-modernism 105, 106, 107–8, 116, 139–43
poverty 431, 432, 460–5
reflexivity 285–6
social mobility 105, 107, 117, 120, 121–3
underclass 105, 107, 128–34, 135, 464, 522
urban restructuring 522
welfare regimes 441, 442
collective action 111, 263
colonialism 386, 390, 421, 526
    immigration 171, 172, 176–7, 182–5
common sense 18, 19–20, 25–6, 85, 88, 337, 348
    crime 328, 332, 342, 345
communication, risk 360–1, 362–3
communism 33–7, 203, 479–80, 539, 551, 556
communitarianism, critique of 500, 501, 515–18
community 500–28
    conflict theory 500, 501, 508–11
    crime 349, 350–1, 361
    cultural symbolism 500, 511–14
    ethnic 112–13
    ethnography 500, 501, 503–6
    national identity 500, 501, 524–7
    symbolic 140, 142, 143
    urbanization 500, 501, 503, 515–24
    working class 501, 506–8
compensatory education 232, 233, 235–7
competition 35, 272, 273, 400
conflict theory 32, 46, 500, 501, 508–11
consensus 43, 470, 471
conservatism 343–4, 441, 442, 443, 461, 555–6
consumerism 140–1, 213, 310, 312, 523
    'McDonaldization' 267, 269, 298–303
    political economy 324–5

contraception 197, 208, 209, 402, 417–18, 429
corporatism 124–8, 137, 282, 284–6, 289, 441
covering-law model of explanation 79, 80
crime 327–64
    see also punishment
    explanations of 327, 328, 342–8
    feminism 327, 329, 352–6
    functionalism 327, 328, 329–32
    Marxism 339
    New Left Realism 327, 328–9, 348–51
    penal system 52
    policing 327, 329, 350–1, 360–3
    scepticism 327, 328, 332–7
    social control 327, 329, 336, 337, 338, 342, 356–60
    underclass 129, 130
criminology 327, 328–9, 332–6, 337–41, 346, 348–51
critical theory 80
cults 578–9
culture 308–26
    consumerism 140–1
    culturalism 308, 309, 310, 316–17
    ethnicity 308, 309, 312–14
    gender issues 158, 168
    health 423–5
    masculinity 308, 309, 310, 314–16, 319–21
    media effect on 474–5
    multiculturalism 521–2
    political economy 308, 310, 323–6
    post-modernism 116, 308, 310, 321–23
    post-structuralism 308, 310, 319–21
    relativism 308, 309, 311–12, 564
    world-building 573
    youth subcultures 308, 309–10, 318–19
culture of poverty 130, 131, 134, 414–15, 460–1
cybernetics 46, 49, 322, 542, 544

D
debt crisis, Third World 365, 366, 373, 376–9, 391, 392–3
democracy 412, 529, 530, 534–7, 538–40, 541
    class relationship 115
    relativism 311
dependency theory 366
determinism 146, 153, 345, 346, 508, 511, 533
deviance 327–64
    see also crime
    functionalism 327, 328, 329–32
    labelling 424–5, 466, 467, 469–72
    'sceptical sociology' 332–6

sexual 573–4
sickness 407
social control 356–7, 358, 359
social reaction to 339–40
diaspora 112–13, 313, 314
discipline 545–7
discourse 51, 53
    education 232, 234, 249–52
    masculinist 263
    power 529, 530, 541, 544, 545–7
discrimination, educational 84, 248
discursive practices 250, 252
disorganized capitalism 285–8
division of labour 34, 36, 42–5
    dominant ideology 468
    Durkheim 31, 32, 42–5
    education relationship 237, 238, 239–40
    new international 365, 366, 368–72
    sexual 64, 65, 201–2, 223–4, 289–91, 305–6
divorce 162, 165, 202, 216, 227
domestic violence 158–60, 162, 202, 217–22, 227, 352
domesticity 211, 212, 214, 479
dominant ideology 132, 134, 466, 467, 468–9
dual labour market 183, 187

E
East Asia 272–3
economics
    see also capitalism; labour; production
    adjustment policies 365, 367, 374, 381–2, 387, 390–5
    competition 35, 272, 273, 400
    environment relationship 383–4
    free market 31, 32, 34, 270–5, 539, 541
        Third World 365, 366, 381–2
    globalization 165, 167, 267, 268–9, 285–9, 396–400
    Keynesian 116, 119, 136, 138, 268
    'McDonaldization' 267, 269, 298–303
    Marxism 34–7
    New Right 267, 268, 270
    patriarchy 267, 269, 289–94
education 232–66
    see also schools
    black feminism 232, 234, 261–6
    compensatory 232, 233, 235–7
    discrimination 84, 248
    Durkheim 232
    ethnicity 190, 232, 233, 245–9, 250–1, 450
    gender issues 161, 162
    habitus 232, 234, 257–61
    homosexuality 232, 234, 252–7

education– cont.
  Marxism 232, 233, 237–41
  politicization of 51
  post-modernism 232, 233–4,
    241–5
  power/knowledge discourse
    232, 234, 249–52
  sociological 4, 16–17
elderly people 437, 438, 440
elision 81–3, 84, 85
élites 107, 127–8, 137–8, 529, 530,
  531–4
embourgeoisement 135, 138, 142,
  143
empiricism 14, 17, 71, 80
employment
  see also labour
  class 121
  education 237, 238, 239–40
  ethnicity 200
  immigrants 182–8
  leisure distinction 305–6
  poverty 442, 454, 461
  women 66, 132, 161–2, 164,
    223–6, 434
Enlightenment 7, 9, 32, 150, 544,
  558
  knowledge 5, 541, 556
  women 148
entrepreneurs 39, 110, 113, 125,
  126, 127, 459
environment 365, 366, 382–6, 554
epiphenomenalism 81, 85, 168, 169
Ethiopia 380
ethnicity 29, 171–200
  see also black feminism;
    racism
  activism 263–4
  Chicago School 171, 172,
    178–81
  class relationship 108
  culture 308, 309, 312–14
  economic inequality 137
  education 232, 233, 245–9,
    261, 262–5, 450
  feminism 29
  health 402, 403, 420–3, 450
  homosexuality 255
  immigrants 171–2, 176–8,
    180, 182–8, 196
  Marxist analysis 171, 172,
    185–8
  New Right 171, 172, 189–91
  police 362
  post-modern identity 171,
    172, 191–5
  power/knowledge relation-
    ship 250–1
  segregation 112–13
  welfare 431, 432, 448–51
ethnography 69, 70, 89–93, 141,
  143, 233
  community 500, 501, 503–6
  ethnic culture 313–14
ethnomethodology 69, 70, 85–9,
  341
evolutionary theory 8–9, 46, 49,
  51–3, 145, 146, 153–6
explanation 23, 24, 62, 79, 80,
  342–3

exploitation, economic 462–3
export-orientated industrialization
  369, 370, 372

F
Fabianism 125, 128
false consciousness 477, 481, 560,
  561, 570–1
family 201–31
  abuse 201, 202, 217–22
  black feminism 196–7, 217
  feminism 201, 202, 208,
    211–19, 221–2, 226, 227
  functionalism 201, 202,
    206–8, 217
  gender roles 201, 202, 206–8,
    210, 211–13, 223–7
  ideology 201, 202, 214–17
  Marxism 201, 202, 203–6
  post-modernism 201, 202–3,
    227–30
  single parent 131–2, 213, 214,
    444–5, 496–8
  symmetrical 201, 202, 208–11
  systems theory 219
famine 365, 366, 379–82
fashion 309–10, 318–19, 320
femininity 146, 148, 149, 152, 321
  media 467, 477, 478, 479, 480
  sexuality 226
feminism
  see also black feminism;
    gender; patriarchy
  activism 145, 147, 158–60,
    263–4
  capitalism 267, 269, 289–94
  crime 327, 329, 352–6
  ethnicity 171, 172–3, 195–9
  family 201, 202, 208, 211–19,
    221–2, 226, 227
  field relations 89–90, 91
  health 402, 403, 415–19,
    426–9
  male perspective 145, 147,
    165–7
  male sexuality 309, 315
  malestream research bias 5,
    27–30, 145, 146–7, 156–7
  media 466, 467, 477–82,
    495–8
  post-modernism 242
  sex/gender distinction 145,
    147, 151, 167–9
  sexual inequality 145, 146,
    147–51, 161–4
feudalism 34, 35, 37, 291, 576–7,
  584
field relations 89–91, 93
Fordism 55, 58, 276–84, 520
  see also neo-Fordism; post-
    Fordism
  Gramsci 267, 268, 276–80,
    281
free market economics 31, 32, 34,
  270–5, 539, 541
  world development 365, 366,
    381–2
functionalism 31, 32, 75
  critique of 508–9
  demise of 46–9

deviance 327, 328, 329–32
family 201, 202, 206–8, 217
health 402, 403, 406–8, 421,
  424

G
gaze 90, 91
  female 309, 314, 315–16
  medical 426
  power 530, 545, 546
Gemeinschaft/Gesellschaft 500, 501,
  502–3
gender 145–70
  capitalism 267, 269, 289–94
  class 66, 108, 142
  domestic abuse 218, 221–2
  ethnicity relationship 197–8
  family 201, 202, 206–8, 210,
    211–13, 223–7
  genetics 145, 146, 153–6
  identity 192
  inequality 136–7, 147–51,
    161–4, 267, 269, 289–94
  malestream research bias
    145, 146–7, 156–7
  masculinity 145, 147, 149,
    165–7
  patriarchy 63–7, 145, 147,
    161–4
  roles 145, 146, 151–2
  schools 260
  sex distinction 145, 147, 151,
    167–9
  social mobility 122
genetics 145, 146, 153–6, 460
globalization 365, 367, 388–9,
  396–400, 556–7
  capitalism 139, 143, 267,
    268–9, 285–9
  cultural 314
  employment 165, 167
  Marxism 288
  urban development 519,
    521
'grand narratives' 118, 119, 141,
  143
'Green Revolution' 374, 384, 386
Gulf War 466, 467, 482–6

H
habitus 140, 232, 257–61, 319, 321
  Bourdieu 234, 257, 258, 259
health 402–430
  body perceptions 402, 403,
    423–6
  class inequalities 402, 403,
    412–15
  critique of medical profes-
    sion 402, 403, 408–11
  ethnicity 402, 403, 420–3, 450
  feminism 402, 403, 415–19,
    426–9
  functionalism 402, 403,
    406–8, 421, 424
  science/religion relationship
    402, 403, 404–6
  women's movements 402,
    403, 415–19
hegemony 138, 188, 265, 316–17,
  397–8

class 269, 294, 296, 298, 469
  ideology 328, 347, 348
hermeneutics 75, 76, 77, 80
heterosexuality, schools 233, 234,
  252, 253, 254, 255
hierarchy 239–40, 545–6, 547
higher education 232, 233, 245–9,
  261, 262–5
historical materialism 560, 562,
  565
history 8, 31, 32, 33–7, 38–41
homeostasis 46, 49, 219, 222
homosexuality 232, 234, 252–7,
  422
    deviance 573–4
    male culture 310, 315–16,
    320
housing classes 501, 509–11
humanism 4, 14–17
hyper-reality 467, 488–9, 491, 523,
  548, 551

I
iatrogenesis 402, 403, 410–11
idealism
    left 349, 350, 351
    Weberian 32, 38–41
identity 191–2, 212, 223–7, 230,
  313
    collective 196, 199
    ethnic 171, 172, 191–5
    fragmentation of 105, 106,
    107–8, 116, 139–43
    national 500, 501, 524–7
ideology
    crime/deviance 339, 342–4,
    348
    dominant 132, 134, 466, 467,
    468–9
    false consciousness 570–1
    family 201, 202, 214–17
    media 489–90
    political 16
    racism 185–7, 421
    religion 560, 561–5
    underclass 132–3, 134
immigrants 171–2, 176–8, 180,
  182–8
    black feminism 196
    conflict theory 509, 510
    urban restructuring 521, 522
    welfare 449
in vitro fertilization (IVF) 416, 428
income
    inequality 136, 137, 324,
    413–14, 432, 452–5
    upper classes 457–9
    women 445, 446
individualism 82, 83, 229
Industrial Revolution 291–3, 433,
  434, 564
industrialization 5, 34–7, 368–72,
  377, 518–19, 520–1
inequality
    see also discrimination;
    racism; sexism
    class 105, 107–8, 115, 117,
    134–9, 140
    educational 244
    family 216, 220

gender 136–7, 147–51, 161–4,
  267, 269, 289–94
    health 402, 403, 412–15
    of income 324, 413–14, 431,
    432, 452–5
    liberal democracy 540
    racial 171–5, 176–7, 182–5,
    188, 196–9
    sexual 145, 146, 147–51,
    161–4, 432, 434
    social 42, 43, 44, 45
    structural 247, 249
    of wealth 55, 136, 137
intellectuals 50–3, 115
intelligence, ethnicity relationship
  171, 172, 189–91
interactionism 328
internalization 357, 358, 360, 572
International Monetary Fund
      (IMF) 365, 367, 376, 382,
      395
    adjustment policies 365, 367,
    381, 390–5
    aid 374, 375
    debt crisis 378
interpretative sociology 75–8, 467

J
Japan 272–3, 274, 285, 286
Jews 112–13
joint stockholdings 114, 119, 124,
  125, 459
just-in-time 272, 276

K
Keynesian economics 116, 119,
      136, 138, 268
knowledge 8–9, 71–3, 74, 75, 77
    post-industrialism 115
    power relationship 31, 32,
    50–3, 249–52, 529, 530,
    541–5
    risk communication 360, 361,
    362–3

L
labelling theory 424–5, 426
labour
    capitalism 39–40, 464
    class 54, 109
    contract 62
    dual labour market 183, 187
    European capitalism 271
    Fordism 277–9
    Japan 273
    labour process theory 267,
    269, 294–8
    patriarchy 291–3
    post-Fordism 280–4
    Third World 369, 371, 387,
    388–9
language 59–60, 233, 235, 236–7
Latin America 376, 377–8, 402,
  416, 417, 418–19
law 19, 38, 40–1, 159–60, 345–6,
  350
the Left 122, 242, 282, 311, 396,
  540
left idealism 349, 350, 351
leisure 267, 269, 303–6

liberal democracy 534–7, 538–40,
  541
liberal pluralism 324, 326
liberalism 47, 115, 343, 344–7, 441,
  442
lifestyle 112, 113, 140, 478, 479
linguistics, structural 322, 323
Los Angeles 500, 501, 518–24

M
'McDonaldization' 267, 269,
  298–303
magazines, women's 466, 467,
  477–82
magic 402, 404–6, 564
malestream 4, 5, 27, 145, 146–7,
  156–7
    crime research 327, 329,
    352–6
market liberalization see free
      market economics
marriage 163, 216, 221, 223,
  224–5, 254
    Marxism 203, 204–5
    women 152, 199, 208–9
    working classes 212
Marxism
    see also communism; neo-
    Marxism; socialism
    class 107, 108–10, 117, 530,
    567
      capitalism 114–15, 120,
      139, 140
      ideology 562
    Communist Manifesto 31, 32,
    33–7
    crime 359
    criticism of sociology 25
    culture 321, 322, 323
    domestic violence 222
    education 232, 233, 237–41
    ethnicity 171, 172, 185–8
    family 201, 202, 203–6
    labour process theory 267,
    269, 294–7
    media 466, 467, 468–9
    Parsonianism comparison 48
    patriarchy 63, 67, 269
    post-Fordism 281
    poverty 431, 432, 460–5
    radicalism 55–6
    religion 560, 561, 562–3,
    566–8, 570–1, 583
    underclass 130
masculinity 145, 147, 149, 152,
  165–7
    cultural definitions of 308,
    309, 310, 314–16, 319–21
    domestic violence/abuse
    218, 220, 221–2
    in schools 252, 254–5
mass society 473–4, 476
materialism
    historical 31, 32, 33–7
    religion 561, 582–6
media 466–99
    see also television
    bias 466, 467, 475, 487–91
    class 144
    crime 343, 349

media – cont.
 deviancy 466, 467, 468–72
 disaster reporting 466, 467,
  491–5
 effects of 466, 467, 473–6
 male culture 319
 Marxism 466, 467, 468–9
 politics 549
 post-modern families 227,
  229, 230
 racism 342
 war reporting 466, 467,
  482–6
 women 466, 467, 477–82,
  495–8
medical profession 402, 403,
  408–11, 420
mental illness 408, 421, 424–5,
  438–9
methodological individualism 82,
  83
methodology 13, 14, 17, 23,
  69–104
 malestream 145, 146–7, 156–7
middle classes
 family 208, 209, 225
 homosexuality 255
 identity 142
 linguistic codes 236–7
 new 54–5, 56, 57, 58, 141
 welfare 443
 women's health 427
migrants see immigrants
misogyny 166, 167, 255
mobility, social 105, 107, 117, 120,
  121–3
modernism 56, 57, 228, 229
modernity 25, 228, 229, 531
 community relationship 512
 post-traditionalism 557
 reflexive modernization 531,
  551–5
modernization theory 366
monogamy 203–4
moral panics 129, 134, 342, 348,
  349, 350, 354
multiculturalism 521–2
multinational companies see
  transnational corpora-
  tions

N
'nanny state' 130, 134
national identity 500, 501, 524–7
nationalism 365, 367, 386, 525–7,
  539
nationality 192, 193, 195
naturalism 60, 73, 78, 79, 80
nature-nurture debate 145, 146,
  202
neo-Fordism 243, 244, 267, 268,
  283
neo-functionalism 31, 32, 46–50
neo-liberalism 115, 118, 242, 244,
  286, 289
neo-Marxism 47–8, 106, 328, 337
 leisure 267, 269, 303–6
 Marx 48
 national identity 500, 501,
  524–7

neo-Weberianism 106, 118
New Left Realism 327, 328–9,
  348–51
'New Man' 166, 315, 319
'new middle class' 54–5, 56, 57,
  58, 141
New Right 55, 115, 116, 282, 366,
  453
 education 4, 242
 ethnicity 171, 172, 189–91
 free market economics 31, 32
 political economy 267, 268,
  270–6
 politics 529, 530, 538–41
 social mobility 120, 122
 welfare 134, 432
new social movements 294, 298,
  556
'New Times' school 281–2
Newly Industrializing Countries
  (NICs) 365, 366–7,
  386–90, 391
news 466, 467, 475, 482–6, 491–4
nominalism 72, 148, 150
non-probability sampling 93,
  96–7, 99
normativism, health 424, 425
norms 570–1

O
objectivity 20, 22, 156
observation 77, 86–8, 89–93
Office of Population Censuses
  and Surveys (OPCS) 100,
  101, 103
official statistics 69, 70, 99–104
oppression
 black women 198–9
 economic 462–3
 women 157
other
 ethnic minorities as 402, 420
 women as 29–30, 148, 149,
  150
overconsumptionism 31, 32, 54,
  55, 57, 58
ownership 114–15, 124–6, 137

P
paradigms 23, 24, 75–76, 343,
  348
parenting 213, 225, 235–6
patriarchy 23, 24, 145, 147, 161–4
 black feminism 196, 197–8,
  199
 capitalism 31, 33, 63–7, 267,
  269, 289–94
 domestic violence 221, 222
 family 202, 212, 225, 226
pedagogy, racial 263, 264, 266
petty bourgeoisie 124, 128
phenomenalism 71, 72
phenomenology 341, 560, 561,
  572, 583, 586
pluralism 106, 107, 243, 324, 326,
  578
police 327, 329, 350–1, 360–3
 gender-based violence 160,
  162
 racism 173

policy
 care in the community 431,
  432, 437–40
 research aims 25, 26, 27
 underclass 132
political economy 308, 310, 323–6,
  338, 340, 341
politics 529–59
 see also power
 black feminism 198, 199
 class 115, 134, 135, 138
 democracy 529, 530, 534–7
 élites 529, 530, 531–4, 536,
  537
 globalization 398
 ideologies 16
 left/right divide 529, 555–8
 New Right 529, 530, 538–41
 police relationship 350–1
 postmodernism 529, 530,
  531, 541–5, 548–51
 racism 179, 186
 risk society 529, 531, 551–5
 sociologists' orientations 25
 women's movements 162
 working class struggles 56,
  58
 world development 372–3,
  374, 375
polygamy 154, 155, 199, 203, 206
Poor Laws 431, 432, 433–436
popular opinion 534–5
populism 311, 312
positivism 4, 5, 10–12, 69, 70, 71–4
 Comte 4, 5, 10–12, 71
 crime/deviance 340, 345
 realism contrast 78, 79, 80
post-Fordism 242–3, 244, 267, 268,
  280–5, 520–1, 558
 class 115–16, 119
post-industrialism 115, 121, 518,
  524
post-modernism
 class 105, 106, 107–8, 116,
  135, 139–43
 community 500, 501, 511–14,
  518–24
 critique of 31, 32, 54–8
 culture 308, 310, 321–23
 education 232, 233–4, 241–5
 ethnic identity 171, 172,
  191–5
 family 201, 202–3, 227–30
 knowledge/power relationship 529, 530, 541–5
 media 467
 politics 529, 531, 548–51
post-structuralism 32, 56, 529
 crime 328, 329
 culture 308, 310, 319–21
poverty 431–65
 see also aid; wealth; welfare
 care in the community 431,
  432, 437–40
 class 105, 107, 128–34, 431,
  432, 460–5
 culture of 130, 131, 134,
  414–15, 460–1
 cycle of 84, 130, 461
 famine 365, 366, 379–82

health relationship 412,
    413–15
income inequality 431, 432,
    452–5
racism 431, 432, 448–51
urban restructuring 522
power
    class stratification 105, 106,
        110–14, 137
    élites 529, 530, 531–4
    gender roles 224
    knowledge relationship 31,
        32, 50–3, 249–52, 529,
        530, 541–5
    media 488–9, 490
    politics relationship 529–30,
        549, 550–1
    sexual repression 588, 589,
        590
    surveillance 530, 545–7
    zero-sum theories of 62, 63
praxis 60, 83–4, 263, 266
pregnancy 152, 418–19, 422, 428
probability sampling 93–6, 99
production
    Fordism 55, 58, 267, 268,
        276–84, 520
    Industrial Revolution 291–3
    international division of
        labour 365, 366, 368–71
    just-in-time 272, 276
    labour process theory 295–7
    means of 34, 35, 39, 120,
        204
    neo-Fordism 243, 244, 267,
        268, 283
    post-Fordism 242–3, 244, 267,
        268, 280–5, 558
        class 115–16, 119
        urbanization 520–1
proletariat 33–7, 40, 50, 111, 117,
    150, 567
    labour process theory 294–5
    women 149
propaganda 471, 482–6
property 110, 111–12, 124–5,
    457–8
prostitution 203, 204
protectionism 387, 390
psychoanalysis 219, 407, 408
psychology 82–3, 218–19
public/private distinction 63,
    64–6, 162–4, 226, 290,
    293, 481
punishment 327, 328, 329–32, 343,
    350, 357–8

Q
quangos 137, 138, 162, 164

R
race see ethnicity; racism
racism
    see also black feminism;
        ethnicity
    British attitudes 171, 172,
        173–5, 200
    capitalist exploitation 185–8
    community 516, 517
    crime 348–9

education 92, 262, 263
health issues 420, 421, 422
homosexuality 255
immigration 171–2, 176–7,
    184
media 342, 491
nationalism relationship 526
New Right 189–91
poverty 431, 432, 448–51
symbolic interactionism
    178–81
radicalism 25, 55–6, 57, 555
random sampling 93–6, 99
rape 160, 162, 163, 221, 227, 352
rationalism 9, 38, 41, 148, 150
rationalization, Weberian 267,
    269, 298–303
realism 69, 70, 72, 73, 78–80, 83
    New Left 327, 328–9, 348–51
reductionism 23, 24, 78, 79, 82,
    586
    religion 562, 582, 585
reflexivity 32–3, 75, 76, 77, 285–6,
    289
    see also self-reflexivity
    reflexive modernization 531,
        551–5
'Regulation School' 282–3
relativism 251, 252, 565
    cultural 308, 309, 311–12
    religion 563, 564
religion 560–91
    see also theodicy
    ideology 560, 561 5
    Marxism 560, 561, 562–3,
        566–8, 570–1, 583
    materialist explanation of
        560, 561, 582–6
    patriarchy 215
    rationalism conflict 41
    science relationship 402, 403,
        404–6, 569, 577–8, 579 80
    secularization 560, 561,
        575–81
    self-identity 192, 193
    sexuality 560, 561, 587–91
    Weber 562, 582, 583, 585
    world-building 560, 561,
        572–5
Renaissance 15, 17, 38, 41
rentiers 110, 113, 125, 126, 127,
    459
repatriation 175, 176, 177, 188
repression, sexual 587–91
reproduction
    capitalist 105, 107, 123–8
    new reproductive technolo-
        gies 416, 419, 427–9
    social 233, 234, 237–41, 458–9
    women 152, 154, 155, 197,
        402, 415–19
research 25–7, 69–104, 116–17,
    142, 333, 336
retro style 308, 309–10, 318–19
revolution 7, 36, 37, 295, 555
the Right 128, 129, 311, 396, 540
rights 160, 362, 402, 416–19, 493
risk society 327, 329, 360–3
    Ulrich Beck 529, 531, 551–5
ritual 112, 423

roles
    family 201, 202, 206–8, 210,
        211–13, 223–7
    gender 145, 146, 151–2
romanticism, post-war 500, 501,
    506–8

S
the sacred 568, 572, 574–5, 576,
    580, 584
sampling techniques 69, 70, 93–9
schools
    see also education
    black supplementary 232,
        262, 263, 264
    compensatory education
        235–6
    ethnicity 190
    girls' friendships 90–3
    habitus 257–60
    homosexuality in 232, 234,
        252–6
    public 84, 127
    social reproduction 233, 237,
        239–40
    surveillance 546
science
    capitalism relationship 40
    common sense distinction
        19–20
    ideology 563
    knowledge 541, 542
    method 69, 73
    naturalism 78, 80
    paradigms 23
    patriarchy 146–7, 215
    religion relationship 402,
        403, 404–6, 569, 577–8,
        579–80
sociology as 5, 8–9, 14, 71
secularization 8, 9, 343, 560, 561,
    575–81
self-reflexivity 90, 91, 93
semiotics 322, 323, 489, 491
service class 121–2, 124, 128, 140,
    287
sex
    gender distinction 145, 147,
        151, 167–9
    genetics 145, 146, 153–6
    marriage 204
sexism 196, 198–9, 219, 255
sexual abuse 218–22
sexual harassment 162
sexuality 65, 66, 203, 215, 422
    see also heterosexuality;
        homosexuality; repro-
        duction
    autonomy 416, 417, 419
    femininity 226
    gender roles 224
    male 221, 222
    religion 560, 561, 582, 584,
        587–91
    in schools 252–6
'sick role' 402, 403, 406–8, 421,
    424
signs 322–3, 488–9
single parent families 131–2, 213,
    214, 444–5, 496–7

social class *see* class
social control 327, 329, 336, 337, 338, 342, 356–60
Social Darwinism 132, 134, 420, 435
social democratic welfare state 441–3
social facts 5, 12, 13, 60, 61
social market 271, 276
social mobility 105, 107, 117, 120, 121–3
social movements 162, 164, 179, 263, 282
social security *see* welfare
socialism 40, 442, 550, 555, 556
    see also communism; Fabianism
    decline of 55–6, 57
    science relationship 51–2
    state 297, 298
socialization 47, 85, 240, 258, 344, 573
    family 201, 202, 206–8
    gender 145, 146, 148–50, 223–4
solidarity 31, 42, 43–4, 45, 149, 330, 332
'specific intellectual' 50–3
state 34, 38, 198, 288, 296–7, 396–8
status 105, 106, 110–13, 117, 141, 178, 181
stereotyping 248, 253, 467, 472
stratification
    class 105–44, 239
    ethnicity 171–200
    sex and gender 145–70
structural linguistics 322, 323
structuration 31, 33, 59–63, 75, 77, 81, 82
structure
    action relationship 59–62, 69, 70, 75, 77, 78–9, 81–5
    deviance 338
    domestic violence/abuse 218, 219, 220–1
    health relationship 412, 413–14
    inequality 247, 249
    patriarchal 65, 66
style 57, 309–10, 318–19, 320
subcultures 220, 308, 309–10, 318–19
suburbanization 515, 516, 519–20
suicide (Durkheim) 4, 5, 12–14
supplementary schools, black 232, 262, 263, 264
surveillance 361–2, 530, 545–7
surveys 100–3
sustainable development 384, 385, 386
'symbolic communities' 140, 142, 143
symbolic interactionism 172, 178–81
symbolism 500, 511–14, 563, 564, 565, 568–9
symmetrical family 201, 202, 208–11
systems 46, 47, 49, 206, 207, 219

T
Taylorism 278, 280, 283, 284
technology 287, 288, 302, 542
    education 241, 243
    media 483, 485, 487
    medical 409
    police use of 363
television 467, 473–6, 489–90
    consumption 324–5
    ethnicity 308, 309, 312–14
    post-modern families 229–30
    war reporting 482–6
Thatcherism 267, 268, 270, 282
theodicy 8, 9, 585, 586
Third World
    aid 365, 366, 372–6, 494
    debt crisis 365, 366, 373, 376–9, 391, 392–3
    division of labour 365, 366, 368–72
    economic adjustment policies 365, 367, 374, 381–2, 387, 390–5
    famine 365, 366, 379–82
    national reformism 365, 366–7, 386–90
trade unions 36, 111, 183–4, 271, 388–9, 442
transnational corporations 281, 284, 373, 376, 398, 399

U
underclass 105, 107, 128–34, 135, 464, 522
    ethnicity 451
    race issues 172, 182, 183, 185
underdevelopment 366, 369, 370
unemployment 133, 184, 368, 369, 515–16
    capitalism 270, 274, 285, 286
    global superiority of 397–8, 400
    McDonaldization 298–303
    underclass 129, 130
universities *see* higher education
upper classes 10, 107, 123–8, 132, 533
    wealth 136, 137, 138, 431, 432, 455–60
urbanization 500, 501, 503, 515–24

V
values 15, 44, 72, 74, 80
violence
    domestic 158–60, 162, 202, 217–22, 224, 227, 352
    urban 523

W
war 397, 400, 466, 467, 482–6, 539
wealth 55, 127–8, 136, 431, 432, 455–60
Weberianism 114, 117–18, 141, 172, 501, 508, 530

welfare 431–51
    capitalist systems 270, 271–2, 274, 275
    care in the community 431, 432, 437–40
    conservative model 441, 442, 443, 461
    liberal model 441, 442
    'nanny state' 130, 134
    Poor Laws 431, 432, 433–436
    post-modernism 116
    racism 431, 432, 448–51
    social democratic model 441–3
    women 65, 431, 432, 434, 444–8
West Indians *see* Afro-Caribbeans
women 27–30, 36, 122, 132, 142, 222
    see also feminism; gender; patriarchy
    crime 327, 329, 352–6
    family 201, 203–5, 208–10, 214, 215, 216
    health 402, 403, 415–19, 422, 426–9
    media 466, 467, 477–82, 495–8
    political movements 162
    positivism 10, 11
    sexualization of male body 309, 314–16
    violence against 158–60, 162, 218–21, 224, 227, 348, 352
    wealth 456, 458
    welfare 431, 432, 434, 444–8
work *see* employment; labour; production
working classes
    see also proletariat; underclass
    community 501, 506–8
    crime 328–9, 346–7, 349, 350, 351
    culture 309, 311
    decline of 116
    education 232–3, 235–7, 240
    family 201, 202, 208–11, 212
    gender identification 142
    political struggles 56, 58
    reflexivity 285–6
    youth subcultures 318
World Bank 365, 367, 382, 395
    adjustment policies 381, 392, 393–4
    aid 372, 374, 375
    famine 380
    international trade 391
world development 365–401
    see also Third World
    environmental issues 365, 366, 382–6
    globalization 365, 367, 388–9, 396–400
world systems theory 367, 368

Y
youth 144, 308, 309–10, 318–19, 362